American Women Writers

*A Critical Reference Guide
from Colonial Times to the Present*

A Critical
Reference Guide
from Colonial Times
to the Present

ABRIDGED EDITION

AMERICAN WOMEN WRITERS

Edited by Langdon Lynne Faust

UNGAR · NEW YORK

1988

The Ungar Publishing Company
370 Lexington Avenue
New York, NY 10017

Printed in the United States of America

Library of Congress Cataloging-in-Publication Data

American women writers.

   Includes index.
   1. American literature—Women authors—History and
criticism.   2. American literature—Women authors—
Bio-bibliography.   3. Women authors, American—
Biography—Dictionaries.   I. Faust, Langdon Lynne.
II. Title.
PS147.A42   1988   810'.9'9287   87-19204
ISBN 0-8044-3157-4

Preface

This one-volume edition of *American Women Writers* is an abridgment of the pioneering four-volume set that owes its publication to the growing interest in women's studies. The positive response of readers and critics to the original work (edited by Lina Mainiero and myself and published from 1979 to 1982) has been most gratifying. As the voluminous original is largely a reference work for libraries, however, there is a need for an edition more readily within the reach of the individual while still serving the interests of both scholar and general reader.

An important purpose of *American Women Writers* has been to present neglected authors of merit and assess them in the light of modern interest in women's position in American society. Many articles herein reflect the difficulties of practicing the craft of writing in a society that puts special obstacles in the path of women's literary ambition. Very few books by women appeared in the eighteenth century. Of these, most were devotional, many were published posthumously, and almost all carried an apology for the impropriety of presenting a woman's views to the public. But by the mid-nineteenth century women not only made up a majority of the reading public but, in spite of all obstacles, were responsible for a significant number of the nation's best sellers. With the rapid expansion of the periodical market, women became contributors and editors. They produced a wide range of fiction and nonfiction, children's stories, inspirational literature, scholarly works, journalism, and temperance and suffrage propaganda.

Of the more than one thousand biographical-critical articles in the original edition of *American Women Writers*, some four hundred have been selected for this abridgment. They include the more important writers and those whose works have some particular historical significance. Coverage of a range of writers with the greatest variety of style, subject, and genre has been maintained. Here are novelists, short-story writers, and poets, women who wrote for Broadway and the little-theater movement, for movies (silent and talking), for radio and television. It is altogether a record of a very considerable achievement.

Authors are listed under the names used by the Library of Congress. Although this is not the perfect solution to the vexing problem of what names to use for women who changed them when they married—there is probably no perfect solution—it does mean that usage here is coordinated with that of most libraries. The index includes cross-references for other names the women used. Each article is headed by data on birth, ancestry, and marriage. There is a brief summary of the writer's life and a description and evaluation of her major works, followed by a list of published books and a secondary bibliography.

The contributors—all trained scholars—have updated and revised articles wherever necessary. Some few articles have also been added. The continuing commitment of the contributors to the project has made this abridged edition much more than simply a shorter version of the earlier work.

LLF

Contributors to the Abridged Edition

Allen, Suzanne
  Caroline Gordon
  Laura Keane Zametkin
    Hobson
  Lillian Smith

Anderson, Celia Catlett
  Cornelia Lynde Meigs

Anderson, Nancy G.
  Dorothy Scarborough

Armeny, Susan
  Lavinia Lloyd Dock

Armitage, Shelley
  Ina Donna Coolbrith
  Anne Ellis

Bach, Peggy
  Evelyn Scott

Bakerman, Jane S.
  Dorothea Frances Canfield
    Fisher
  Margaret Millar
  May Sarton
  Gene Stratton-Porter
  Mary Alsop Sture-Vasa
  Dorothy Uhnak
  Jessamyn West

Bannan, Helen M.
  Elizabeth Bacon Custer
  Elaine Goodale Eastman
  Helen Maria Fiske Hunt
    Jackson
  Elizabeth Gertrude Levin
    Stern

Barbour, Paula L.
  Jane Auer Bowles

Baruch, Elaine Hoffman
  Susan Sontag

Baytop, Adrianne
  Margaret Walker
  Phillis Wheatley

Beasley, Maurine
  Mary E. Clemmer Ames
  Kate Field

Benardete, Jane
  Abby Morton Diaz
  Mary Abigail Dodge
  Lydia Howard Huntley
    Sigourney

Ben-Merre, Diana
  Helen McCloy

Berke, Jacqueline
Harriet Stratemeyer Adams
Eleanor Hodgman Porter

Berry, Linda S.
Georgia Douglas Camp Johnson

Bienstock, Beverly Gray
Anita Loos
Cornelia Otis Skinner

Bird, Christiane
Harriet Mulford Stone Lothrop

Bittker, Anne S.
Mary Margaret McBride

Bixler, Phyllis
Frances Eliza Hodgson Burnett

Blair, Karen J.
Jane Cunningham Croly

Bordin, Ruth
Elizabeth Margaret Chandler

Breitsprecher, Nancy
Zona Gale

Bremer, Sidney H.
Elia Wilkinson Peattie
Edith Franklin Wyatt

Brett, Sally
Bernice Kelly Harris
Edith Summers Kelley
Ida Minerva Tarbell

Brown, Lynda W.
Caroline Lee Whiting Hentz
Anne Newport Royall

Buchanan, Harriette Cuttino
Josephine Lyons Scott Pinckney
Lizette Woodworth Reese

Bucknall, Barbara J.
Pearl Sydenstricker Buck
Ursula K. LeGuin
Phyllis McGinley
Hannah Whitall Smith

Burns, Lois
Shirley Jackson

Byers, Inzer
Annie Heloise Abel
Catherine Drinker Bowen
Carrie Lane Chapman Catt
Frances Manwaring Caulkins
Angelina Emily Grimké
Sarah Moore Grimké
Martha Joanna Reade Nash Lamb
Alma Lutz
Margaret Bayard Smith

Carnes, Valerie
Janet Flanner

Carr, Pat
Flannery O'Connor

Carroll, Linda A.
Jean Craighead George

Clark, Susan L.
Mignon Good Eberhart

Cleveland, Carol
Patricia Highsmith

Cohn, Jan
Mary Roberts Rinehart

Cook, Martha E.
Annie Fellows Johnston
Katherine Sherwood Bonner
    McDowell
Mary Noailles Murfree

Cook, Sylvia
Olive Tilford Dargan
Grace Lumpkin

Coultrap-McQuin, Susan
Catharine Read Arnold
    Williams

Cowell, Pattie
Bathsheba Bowers
Annis Boudinot Stockton

Crabbe, Katharyn F.
Jane Andrews

Cutler, Evelyn S.
Rose Cecil O'Neill

Dame, Enid
Edna St. Vincent Millay

Davidson, Cathy N.
Laura Jean Libbey
Tabitha Gilman Tenney

Davis, Thadious M.
Anna Julia Haywood Cooper
Mary Evelyn Moore Davis
Shirley Graham
Rhoda Elizabeth Waterman
    White

Deegan, Mary Jo
Sophonisba Preston
    Breckinridge
Helen Merrell Lynd

DeMarr, Mary Jean
Charlotte Armstrong
Doris Miles Disney
Janet Ayer Fairbank
Rachel Lyman Field
Agnes Newton Keith
Alice Caldwell Hegan Rice
Mari Sandoz
Anya Seton
Ruth Suckow
Agnes Sligh Turnbull
Carolyn Wells

Deming, Caren J.
Elaine Sterne Carrington

Denniston, Dorothy L.
Paule Marshall

Donovan, Josephine
Louise Imogen Guiney
Sarah Orne Jewett
Lucy Larcom
Celia Laighton Thaxter

Eliasberg, Ann Pringle
Dorothy Thompson

Estess, Sybil
Elizabeth Bishop

Etheridge, Billie W.
Abigail Smith Adams
Mercy Otis Warren

Evans, Elizabeth
Helen MacInnes Highet
Anne Tyler
Eudora Welty

Ewell, Barbara C.
Eliza Jane Poitevent
Nicholson

Faust, Langdon
Frances Elizabeth Caroline
Willard

Ferguson, Mary Anne
Sally Benson
Doris Betts
Tess Slesinger

Fleenor, Juliann E.
Catharine Esther Beecher
Emily Chubbuck Judson
Margaret Sanger

Fowler, Lois
Frances Dana Barker Gage
Ida Husted Harper

Franklin, Phyllis
Judith Sargent Murray
Elsie Worthington Clews
Parsons

Frazer, Winifred
Dorothy Day

Freibert, Lucy M.
Jessica Nelson North
MacDonald

Friedman, Ellen G.
Anna Hempstead Branch
Joyce Carol Oates

Gabbard, Lucina P.
Clare Boothe Luce

Gartner, Carol B.
Rachel Louise Carson
Mary Putnam Jacobi
Myra Kelly

Gaskill, Gayle
Jean Collins Kerr

Giles, Jane
Catharine Maria Sedgwick

Ginsberg, Elaine K.
Amelia Jenks Bloomer
Maria Susanna Cummins
Hannah Webster Foster
Betty Wehner Smith
Emma Dorothy Eliza Nevitte
Southworth

Gladstein, Mimi R.
Ayn Rand

Goldman, Maureen
Esther Edwards Burr

Gorsky, Susan R.
Djuna Barnes

Gowing, S. Julia
Rebecca Harding Davis

Graham, Theodora R.
Louise Bogan
Josephine Miles
Harriet Monroe

Grant, Mary H.
Julia Ward Howe

Greene, Dana
Sophia Hume
Lucretia Coffin Mott

Greyson, Laura
Hannah Arendt

Groben, Anne R.
Ella Wheeler Wilcox

Guin, Sandra Carlin
Louella Oettinger Parsons

Hamblen, Abigail Ann
Margaret Wade Campbell Deland
Mary Eleanor Wilkins Freeman

Hardesty, Nancy A.
Phoebe Worrall Palmer
Elizabeth Cady Stanton
Emma Hart Willard

Hardy, Willene S.
Mary Therese McCarthy

Healey, Claire
Hilda Doolittle
Amy Lowell

Helbig, Alethea K.
Lucretia Peabody Hale
Madeleine L'Engle

Henderson, Katherine
Joan Didion

Hill, Vicki Lynn
Bessie Breuer
Helen Hamilton Gardener
Theresa Serber Malkiel
Dorothy Myra Page
Marie Van Vorst
Mary Heaton Vorse
Helen Maria Winslow

Hobbs, Glenda
Harriette Louisa Simpson Arnow

Hoeveler, Diane Long
Babette Deutsch
Jessica Mitford
Frances Jane Crosby Van Alstyne

Holdstein, Deborah H.
Mae West

Hornstein, Jacqueline
Sarah Symmes Fiske
Sarah Parsons Moorhead
Sarah Wentworth Apthorp Morton
Sarah Osborn

Jane Turell
Elizabeth White

Howard, Lillie
Fannie Cook

Hughson, Lois
Mary Ritter Beard
Barbara Tuchman

Johnson, Claudia D.
Olive Logan

Johnson, Lee Ann
Mary Hallock Foote

Johnson, Robin
Marianne Craig Moore

Jones, Judith P.
Eleanor Clark

Kahn, Miriam
Ruth Fulton Benedict
Margaret Mead

Karp, Sheema Hamdani
Adrienne Cecile Rich

Kaufman, Janet E.
Eliza Frances Andrews
Elizabeth Avery Meriwether
Katharine Prescott Wormeley

Keeshen, Kathleen Kearney
Marguerite Higgins

Kern, Donna Casella
Frances Fuller Victor

Kessler, Carol Farley
Elizabeth Stuart Phelps
Elizabeth Stuart Phelps Ward

Kimball, Gayle
Harriet Elizabeth Beecher
Stowe

King, Margaret J.
Emily Price Post
Mary Elizabeth Wilson
Sherwood

Knapp, Bettina L.
Anaïs Nin

Koengeter, L. W.
Maria Gowen Brooks
Hannah Mather Crocker
Margaretta V. Bleeker
Faugeres
Rose Wilder Lane

Kohlstedt, Sally Gregory
Anna Botsford Comstock
Almira Hart Lincoln Phelps

Koon, Helene
Anna Cora Mowatt Ritchie
Sally Sayward Barrell Wood

Kouidis, Virginia M.
Mina Loy

Krieg, Joann Peck
Mary Baker Glover Eddy

Kuznets, Lois R.
Esther Forbes

Lamping, Marilyn
Ida B. Wells Barnett
Pauline Elizabeth Hopkins

Loeb, Helen
Inez Haynes Irwin

Londré, Felicia Hardison
Agnes De Mille
Anne Crawford Flexner
Rose Franken
Marguerite Merington
Lillian Mortimer
Martha Morton
Josephina Niggli

McCarthy, Joanne
Kay Boyle
Betty Bard MacDonald
Kathleen Thompson Norris

McClure, Charlotte S.
Gertrude Franklin Horn
Atherton

McDannell, M. Colleen
Ellen Gould Harmon White

McFadden-Gerber, Margaret
Sally Carrighar
Wilma Dykeman
Josephine Winslow Johnson

McGovern, Edythe M.
Susan Glaspell
Lorraine Hansberry
Charlotte Shapiro Zolotow

MacPike, Loralee
Elizabeth Hardwick
Emily Kimbrough

Madsen, Carol Cornwall
Emmeline Blanche Woodward
Wells

Maida, Patricia D.
Lillian O'Donnell

Mainiero, Lina
Willa Sibert Cather

Maio, Kathleen L.
Anna Katharine Green Rohlfs
Metta Victoria Fuller Victor

Margolis, Tina
Rochelle Owens

Masel-Walters, Lynne
Inez Haynes Irwin
Miriam Florence Folline
Leslie

Masteller, Jean Carwile
Annie Nathan Meyer

Matherne, Beverly M.
Alice Gerstenberg

Mayer, Elsie F.
Anne Morrow Lindbergh

Menger, Lucy
Jane Roberts

Mitchell, Sally
Cora Miranda Baggerly Older
Rose Porter

Moe, Phyllis
Helen Stuart Campbell
Eliza Lee Cabot Follen
Sarah Chauncey Woolsey

Mollenkott, Virginia Ramey
  Grace Livingston Hill Lutz
  Marjorie Hope Nicolson

Morris, Linda A.
  Marietta Holley
  Frances Miriam Berry
    Whitcher

Mortimer, Gail
  Katherine Anne Porter

Mossberg, Barbara Antonina
  Clarke
  Sylvia Plath
  Genevieve Taggard

Moynihan, Ruth Barnes
  Abigail Scott Duniway

Mussell, Kay
  Phyllis Ayame Whitney

Nance, Guin A.
  Elizabeth Spencer

Neils, Patricia Langhals
  Emily Hahn

Newman, Anne
  Julia Mood Peterkin
  Amélie Rives Troubetzkoy

Nichols, Kathleen L.
  Miriam Coles Harris
  Susanna Haswell Rowson
  Anne Sexton

Norman, Marion
  Lucretia Maria Davidson
  Margaret Miller Davidson

Orsagh, Jacqueline E.
  Martha Gellhorn

Payne, Alma J.
  Louisa May Alcott

Petersen, Margaret
  Emily Dickinson
  Janet Lewis

Pettis, Joyce
  Zora Neale Hurston

Phillips, Elizabeth
  Elizabeth Fries Lummis Ellet
  Jean Garrigue
  Estelle Anna Robinson Lewis
  Frances Sargent Locke Osgood
  Mabel Loomis Todd
  Sarah Helen Power Whitman

Piercy, Josephine K.
  Anne Dudley Bradstreet

Pogel, Nancy
  Constance Mayfield Rourke

Poland, Helene Dwyer
  Susanne Katherina Knauth
    Langer

Pringle, Mary Beth
  Charlotte Perkins Stetson
    Gilman

Puk, Francine Shapiro
  Dorothy Rothschild Parker

Rayson, Ann
  Ann Lane Petry

Richmond, Velma Bourgeois
Frances Parkinson Wheeler
Keyes
Agnes Repplier

Roberts, Audrey
Caroline Matilda Stansbury
Kirkland

Roberts, Bette B.
Lydia Maria Francis Child

Roberts, Elizabeth
Eliza Ann Youmans

Rogers, Katharine M.
Lillian Hellman

Rowe, Anne
Elizabeth Madox Roberts
Constance Fenimore Woolson

Rudnick, Lois P.
Mabel Ganson Dodge Luhan

Ryan, Rosalie Tutela
Jane Erminia Starkweather
Locke

Schleuning, Neala Yount
Meridel Le Sueur

Schoen, Carol B.
Hannah Adams
Emma Lazarus
Penina Moise

Schull, Elinor
Adela Rogers St. Johns

Schwartz, Helen J.
Elizabeth Meriwether Gilmer

Seaton, Beverly
Mary Hartwell Catherwood
Gladys Bagg Taber
Susan Bogert Warner
Kate Douglas Smith Wiggin
Laura Ingalls Wilder
Mabel Osgood Wright

Shakir, Evelyn
Ednah Dow Littlehale Cheney

Sharistanian, Janet
Elizabeth Janeway
Helen Waite Papashvily

Sherman, Sarah Way
Sarah Knowles Bolton
Alice Brown
Rose Terry Cooke
Louise Chandler Moulton
Mary Alicia Owen

Shinn, Thelma J.
Margaret Ayer Barnes
Kate O'Flaherty Chopin
Martha Finley
Shirley Ann Grau
Harriet Elizabeth Prescott
Spofford

Shortreed, Vivian H.
Elizabeth Oakes Prince Smith
Jane Grey Cannon Swisshelm

Skaggs, Peggy
Helen Adams Keller
Catherine Marshall

Slaughter, Jane
Elizabeth Gurley Flynn

Smelstor, Marjorie
Frances Anne Kemble

Smith, Susan Sutton
Adelaide Crapsey
Caroline Wells Healey Dall
Harriet Farley
Eliza Ware Rotch Farrar
Caroline Howard Gilman
Sarah Jane Clarke Lippincott
Sarah Margaret Fuller Ossoli
Harriet Jane Hanson Robinson
Phoebe Atwood Taylor
Mary Virginia Hawes Terhune
Jean Webster

Snipes, Katherine
Laura Riding Jackson
Carson Smith McCullers

Sprague, Rosemary
Sara Teasdale

Springer, Marlene
Edith Newbold Jones Wharton

Sproat, Elaine
Lola Ridge

Stanford, Ann
Sarah Kemble Knight
May Swenson

Staples, Katherine
Alma Sioux Scarberry

Stauffer, Helen
Bess Streeter Aldrich
Bertha Muzzy Sinclair

Steele, Karen B.
Elizabeth Wormeley Latimer
Mary Traill Spence Lowell
Putnam

Stein, Karen F.
Alice Ruth Moore Dunbar
Nelson
Elinor Hoyt Wylie

Stinson, Peggy
Jane Addams
Agnes Smedley
Anzia Yezierska

Swidler, Arlene Anderson
Aline Murray Kilmer
Sister Madeleva

Sylvander, Carolyn Wedin
Jesse Redmon Fauset
Mary White Ovington

Szymanski, Karen
Eliza Woodson Burhans
Farnham

Tebbe, Jennifer L.
Elizabeth Cochrane
Rheta Childe Dorr
Anne O'Hare McCormick
Anna Louise Strong

Terris, Virginia R.
Lilian Whiting

Thiébaux, Marcelle
Faith Baldwin Cuthrell
Julia Caroline Ripley Dorr
Ellen Anderson Gholson
Glasgow
Marjorie Kinnan Rawlings

Thomas, Gwendolyn
Pauli Murray

Thompson, Dorothea Mosley
Mary Simmerson Cunningham
Logan

Townsend, Janis
Mildred Aldrich
Gertrude Stein

Treckel, Paula A.
Alice Morse Earle
Lucy Maynard Salmon
Eliza Roxy Snow Smith

Turner, Alberta
Barbara Howes
Denise Levertov
Muriel Rukeyser

Uffen, Ellen Serlen
Fannie Hurst

Wahlstrom, Billie J.
Alice Cary
Betty Friedan

Walker, Cynthia L.
Edna Ferber

Wall, Cheryl A.
Gwendolyn Brooks
Frances Ellen Watkins
Harper

Ward, Jean M.
Ella Rhodes Higginson

Werden, Frieda L.
Kate Millett

White, Barbara A.
Lillie Devereux Blake
Sarah Josepha Buell Hale
Sara Payson Willis Parton

Wright, Catherine Morris
Mary Mapes Dodge

Yee, Carole Zonis
Leane Zugsmith

Yongue, Patricia Lee
Zoë Akins

Zilboorg, Caroline
Charlotte Ann Fillebrown
Jerauld

Abbreviations of Reference Works

AA   American Authors, 1600–1900: A Biographical Dictionary of American Literature (Eds. S. J. Kunitz and H. Haycraft, 1938).

AW   American Women: Fifteen-Hundred Biographies with Over 1,400 Portraits (2 vols., Eds. F. E. Willard and M. A. Livermore, 1897).

CA   Contemporary Authors: A Bio-Bibliographical Guide to Current Authors and Their Works (various editors, 1962–present).

CAL   Cyclopaedia of American Literature, Embracing Personal and Critical Notices of Authors and Selections from Their Writings (2 vols., Eds. E. A. Duyckinck and G. L. Duyckinck, 1866).

CB   Current Biography: Who's News and Why (Eds. M. Block, 1940–1943; A. Rothe, 1944–1953; M. D. Candee, 1954–1958; C. Moritz, 1959–present).

DAB   Dictionary of American Biography (10 vols., Eds. A. Johnson and D. Malone; 5 suppls., Eds. E. T. James and J. A. Garraty; 1927–1977).

FPA   The Female Poets of America (Ed. R. W. Griswold, 1849).

HWS   History of Woman Suffrage (Vols. 1–3, Eds. E. C. Stanton, S. B. Anthony, and M. J. Gage; Vol. 4, Eds. S. B. Anthony and I. H. Harper; Vols. 5 and 6, Ed. I. H. Harper; 1881–1922).

LSL   Library of Southern Literature, Compiled under the Direct Supervision of Southern Men of Letters (16 vols., Eds. E. A. Alderman and J. C. Harris; Suppl., Eds. E. A. Alderman, C. A. Smith, and J. C. Metcalf, reprinted 1970).

NAW   Notable American Women, 1607–1950: A Biographical Dictionary (3 vols., Eds. E. T. James, J. W. James, and P. S. Boyer, 1971).

NCAB   National Cyclopedia of American Biography: Being the History of the United States As Illustrated in the Lives of the Founders, Builders, and Defenders of the Republic, and of the Men and Women Who Are Doing the Work and Moulding the Thought of the Present Time (various editors, Vols. 1–57, 1892–1976; Vols. A–M, Permanent Series, 1930–1978).

20thCA   Twentieth Century Authors: A Biographical Dictionary of Modern Literature (Eds. S. J. Kunitz and H. Haycraft, 1942).

20thCAS   Twentieth Century Authors, First Supplement: A Biographical Dictionary of Modern Literature (Eds. S. J. Kunitz and V. Colby, 1955).

WA   World Authors, 1950–1970: A Companion Volume to Twentieth Century Authors (Ed. J. Wakeman, 1975).

Abbreviations of Periodicals

In the bibliographies, periodicals have been abbreviated in conformity with the Modern Language Association master list of abbreviations. Newspapers and magazines not in that list are abbreviated as follows:

AHR   American Historical Review
CathW   Catholic World
CSM   Christian Science Monitor
EngElemR   English Elementary Review
JSocHis   Journal of Social History
KR   Kirkus Review
NewR   New Republic
NYHT   New York Herald Tribune
NYHTB   New York Herald Tribune Books
NYT   New York Times
NYTMag   New York Times Magazine
NYTBR   New York Times Book Review
PW   Publisher's Weekly
SatEvePost   Saturday Evening Post
ScribM   Scribner's Magazine
VV   Village Voice
WallStJ   Wall Street Journal
WLB   Wilson Library Bulletin
WrD   Writer's Digest
WSCL   Wisconsin Studies in Contemporary Literature

American Women Writers

A Critical Reference Guide
from Colonial Times to the Present

Annie Heloise Abel

B. *18 Feb. 1873, Fernhurst, Sussex, England; d. 14 March 1947, Aberdeen, Washington*
D. *of George and Amelia Anne Hogben Abel; m. George Cockburn Henderson, 1922*

A.'s family emigrated to Salina, Kansas, in 1884. She attained her literary prominence as an authority on American Indian history. Her master's thesis was "Indian Reservations in Kansas and the Extinguishment of Their Title" (1902). Her doctoral dissertation, "The History of Events Resulting in Indian Consolidation West of the Mississippi," won the American Historical Association's Justin Winsor Prize in 1906 and was published in the *Annual Report* of that year.

A.'s major work was the three-volume study, *The Slaveholding Indians*. The first volume was *The American Indian as Slaveholder and Secessionist: An Omitted Chapter in the Diplomatic History of the Confederacy* (1915). In A.'s view, though there was slaveholding among Indian tribes, only the Choctaw and Chickasaw were drawn to the Confederacy because of concern about slavery. The South, out of its own needs, notably strategic concern for territorial solidarity, offered a number of concessions. Most significant perhaps were Confederate guarantees of criminal and civil rights. The South also offered to give Indians control of their own trade, but that offer was later rescinded. Through General Albert Pike, the Confederacy made its approaches to the western tribes, and his wartime disaffection with the Confederacy over its betrayal of promises to the Indians would prove costly to the South.

Despite Southern concessions, A. noted, the Indians "actually fought on both sides and for the same motives and impulses as whites." In her view, it was the failure of the U.S. government to provide the promised protection for the Southern Indians which led them to ally with the Confederacy. From first to last, she maintained, military conditions and events determined political ones.

In the next two volumes, *The American Indian as Participant in the*

Civil War (1919) and *The American Indian under Reconstruction* (1925), A. traced the tragic consequences of Indian involvement in the sectional strife.

Throughout her work A. proves to be both an effective researcher and a perceptive scholar who wrote with sympathy about problems the Indians encountered. Although occasionally she wrote in a paternalistic or romantic tone, she is a sympathetic but essentially objective historian. Her English background, she noted, freed her from sectional attachments in dealing with Civil War issues. And she could likewise appraise with detachment the conflict between Indian claims and American expansionist urges. Her work is marked with a sense of the tragedy which befell the Indians, but that sense did not obscure her judgment. If, in her final view, the fate of the Indians was determined by white greed and power, she recognized also the part which the Indians' "inability to learn from experience" played in the final outcome. The breadth of her research and her capacity for informed, detached judgment gave her work its strength and power.

WORKS: *Brief Guide to Points of Historical Interest in Baltimore City* (1908). *Proposals for an Indian State, 1778–1878* (1909). *The Official Correspondence of James S. Calhoun* (edited by Abel, 1915). *The American Indian as Slaveholder and Secessionist* (1915). *A New Lewis and Clark Map* (1916). *The American Indian as Participant in the Civil War* (1919). *The American Indian under Reconstruction* (1925). *A Sidelight on Anglo-American Relations, 1839–1858* (edited by Abel, with F. J. Klingsberg, 1927). *Chardon's Journal at Fort Clark, 1834–39* (edited by Abel, 1932). *Tabeau's Narrative of Loisel's Expedition to the Upper Missouri* (edited by Abel, 1939).

BIBLIOGRAPHY: For articles in reference works, see: *NAW* (article by F. Prucha).

Other references: *AHR* (July 1947). *Mississippi Valley Historical Review* (March 1916; March 1920). *Yale University Obituary Record of Graduates* (1946–47).

INZER BYERS

Abigail Smith Adams

B. *11 Nov. 1744, Weymouth, Massachusetts; d. 28 Oct. 1818, Quincy,*
   Massachusetts
D. *of William and Elizabeth Quincy Smith; m. John Adams, 1764*

Due to her poor health, A.'s formal education was virtually non-existent. Fortunately, however, she was surrounded by literate adults who guided her studies, which ranged from Plato, Locke, and Burke to the Bible. A. bore five children in the first eight years of her marriage to John Adams, who became the second U.S. president in 1797. Her son John Quincy was the sixth president.

A.'s claim to literary fame rests upon the hundreds of letters picturing her times in warmly human terms. John was her favorite correspondent, but she wrote extensively to her large family and to a wide circle beyond, including such intellectuals as Mercy Otis Warren and Thomas Jefferson.

In *New Letters of Abigail Adams* (1947), editor Stewart Mitchell printed her correspondence to her older sister, Mary Cranch. To Mary more than anyone else, A. wrote of "women's concerns"—smallpox and fevers, incompetent servants, inflation, poor food, bad weather, and the deplorable state the White House was in when she arrived to become its first mistress.

Mitchell's publication corrects the bowdlerized portrait of A. rendered by her Victorian grandson, Charles Francis Adams. His *Letters of Mrs. Adams* (2 vols., 1840–41) and *Familiar Letters of John Adams and His Wife Abigail Adams during the Revolution* (1876) not only censor her passionate declarations of love to John, but also delete much from her personal accounts of pregnancies and childbirth, the dysentery epidemic of 1775, and smallpox inoculations.

The Book of Abigail and John is limited to what its editors consider the best letters of A. and her husband. In them, A.'s affectionate nature is expressed freely. Her loneliness and pride in herself and in her husband is described, too: "I miss my partner, and find myself uneaquuil [*sic*] to the cares which fall upon me; . . . I hope in time to have the Reputation of being as good a Farmeress as my partner has of being a good Statesman."

A. never hesitated to address herself to political matters. Two issues which drew strong reaction from her were slavery and women's rights. Writing to John in 1774, she wished "most sincerely there was not a slave in the province." Concerning women's rights, A. wrote early in 1776 the letter for which she is most famous: "[A]nd by the way in the new Code of Laws which I suppose it will be necessary for you to make I desire you would Remember the Ladies, and be more generous to them than your ancestors." Undaunted by John's reply denying her petition and charging her with being "saucy," she retorted, "I can not say that I think you very generous to the Ladies, for whilst you are proclaiming peace and good will to Men, Emancipating all Nations, you insist upon retaining absolute power over Wives."

Never dull, always animated, A.'s letters are more like conversations than compositions. For the most part, her style is easy and natural. Her spelling is phonetic, underscoring the verbal nature of her writing, and her punctuation follows natural pauses rather than written conventions. Her letters tell us how it felt to live through the American Revolution and what it was like to be a New England Puritan in Europe in the late eighteenth century. More than that, however, they help us understand the creative force we call the "Puritan ethic."

WORKS: *Letters of Mrs. Adams, the Wife of John Adams* (Ed. C. F. Adams, 2 vols., 1840–41). *Familiar Letters of John Adams and His Wife Abigail Adams during the Revolution* (Ed. C. F. Adams, 1876). *New Letters of Abigail Adams, 1788–1801* (Ed. S. Mitchell, 1947). *Adams Family Correspondence* (Eds. L. H. Butterfield et al., 4 vols., 1963–73). *The Book of Abigail and John* (Eds. L. H. Butterfield et al., 1975).

BIBLIOGRAPHY: Bobbe, D., *Abigail Adams, the Second First Lady* (1929). Bradford, G., *Portraits of American Women* (1919). Gordon, L., *From Lady Washington to Mrs. Cleveland* (1889). Ketcham, R. L., in *"Remember the Ladies": New Perspectives on Women in American History*, Ed. C. V. R. George (1975). Minningerode, M., *Some American Ladies: Seven Informal Biographies* (1926). Richards, L. E., *Abigail Adams and Her Times* (1936). Shepherd, J., *The Adams Chronicles: Four Generations of Greatness* (1975). Stone, I., *Those Who Love* (1965). Whitney, J., *Abigail Adams* (1949).

Other references: *ScribM* (Jan. 1930).

BILLIE W. ETHERIDGE

Hannah Adams

B. 2 Oct. 1755, Medfield, Massachusetts; d. 15 Dec. 1831, Brookline, Massachusetts
D. of Thomas and Eleanor Clark Adams

The second of five children, A. was considered too frail to attend public school and was educated at home. Discovering that she was unable to support herself at needlework, A. undertook a literary career. Although excessively modest and timid, she was the first and for many years the only woman permitted to use the Boston Atheneum. Her learning was prodigious. While her books were successful, poor business arrangements limited the income she derived from them.

The research into religious sects that A. had begun for her own edification became, in 1784, her first published volume, *Alphabetical Compendium of the Various Sects Which Have Appeared from the Beginning of the Christian Era to the Present Day*. In its objectivity, it represented a major improvement over existing works on the subject, and although it contains some misinformation due to inaccurate sources, the scope of its coverage is impressive. Edited and retitled for later editions, it includes a dictionary listing of the separate Christian sects, a survey of the beliefs of non-Christian groups, and a geographical breakdown of world religions.

For her *Summary History of New England* (1799), A. undertook serious primary research, delving into state archives and old newspapers, causing serious injury to her eyesight. The material, which covers events from the sailing of the *Mayflower* through the adoption of the federal Constitution, is presented in a clear, straightforward manner with occasional attempts to recreate particularly affecting scenes such as the farewell of the Pilgrims from Holland.

The *Abridgement of the History of New England for the Use of Young People* (1807) involved a protracted controversy with Dr. Jedidiah Morse over unfair competition, eventually resolved in A.'s favor. In revising her *History*, A. edited it for greater smoothness and clarity, but simplified neither the language nor the thought. She added a paragraph at the end of each chapter to point up the moral lesson to be learned from the event.

While working on the *Abridgement*, A. published *The Truth and Ex-*

cellence of the Christian Religion Exhibited (1804), surveying the support which laymen had given to their religion since the 17th c. Divided into two parts, it first presents brief biographies of sixty men, showing how their lives exemplified the Christian spirit. The second part provides excerpts listed under various kinds of "Evidence in Favor of Revealed Religion." Most of the material was drawn from the writings of those covered in the first section, but it also includes selections by the Marchioness de Dillery, Hannah More, and a Mrs. West.

The History of the Jews from the Destruction of Jerusalem to the Present Time (1812) represented one of the first attempts to relate their story sympathetically, a story which A. described as a "tedious succession of oppression and persecution." Written to encourage efforts to convert the Jews, her discussion of the early period stresses its substantiation of "our Savior's prediction" of their fate. Not completely free from bias, A. nevertheless carefully recorded the confiscatory taxes, the mass murders, and the expulsions suffered by the Jews.

A. was probably the first professional woman writer in America, pursuing her career despite the knowledge that the "penalties and discouragements attending authors in general fall upon women with double weight." Although most discussions of A. adopt her own designation of herself as a "compiler," she was, in fact, a fine historian whose meticulous research included examination of primary materials when available, extraordinarily wide reading of secondary sources, and a remarkable objectivity. Her histories are no longer relevant, but her contributions to historiography deserve attention.

WORKS: *Alphabetical Compendium of the Various Sects Which Have Appeared from the Beginning of the Christian Era to the Present Day* (1784). *Summary History of New England* (1799). *The Truth and Excellence of the Christian Religion Exhibited* (1804). *Abridgement of the History of New England for the Use of Young People* (1807). *The History of the Jews from the Destruction of Jerusalem to the Present Time* (1812). *A Narrative of the Controversy between the Rev. Jedidiah Morse, D.D., and the Author* (1814). *A Concise Account of the London Society for Promoting Christianity Amongst the Jews* (1816). *Letters on the Gospels* (1824). *Memoir of Hannah Adams* (Ed. J. Tuckerman, 1832).

BIBLIOGRAPHY: Brooks, V. W., *The Flowering of New England* (1936).
Other references: *The Dedham Historical Register* (July 1896). *The New England Galaxy* (Spring 1971). *New England Magazine* (May 1894).

CAROL B. SCHOEN

Harriet Stratemeyer Adams

B. 3 Dec. 1892, Newark, New Jersey; d. 27 March 1982, Pottersville,
   New Jersey
Writes under: Victor Appleton II, May Hollis Barton, Franklin W. Dixon,
   Laura Lee Hope, Carolyn Keene, Ann Sheldon, Helen Louise Thorndyke
D. of Edward and Magdalene Van Camp Stratemeyer; m. Russell Vroom
   Adams, 1915

Better known under a variety of pen names, A. may well be the most prolific woman writer of all time. Author of the perennially popular Nancy Drew mysteries for young girls and the equally popular Hardy Boys and Tom Swift, Jr., series for young boys, she has also written numerous volumes in the Bobbsey Twins, Honey Bunch, and Dana Girls series. All of these, along with the famous Rover boys, were originated by her father who founded the Stratemeyer Syndicate in 1901. A "writing factory" located in Maplewood, New Jersey, it still turns out the most successful series books ever written for American youngsters roughly eight to fourteen years of age. The Hardy Boys and Nancy Drew series alone sell sixteen million copies a year.

When he died in 1930, Stratemeyer left to his daughters, Harriet and Edna, the job of keeping up the seventeen sets of series then in print. Edna remained in the business for twelve years; Harriet still remains a senior partner, working with three junior partners to update earlier titles to create new volumes. A. herself has written 179 volumes and shows no signs of slowing down. She has written all fifty-five titles in the Nancy Drew series, including rewrites of the first three originated by her father: the young sleuth's blue roadster with running boards had to be replaced, along with outdated hair styles and various dialects which the modern reader would find offensive.

Characters produced by the Stratemeyer Factory are either good or bad because, A. maintains, mixed characters don't interest children. Plots are spun according to a strict formula guaranteed to satisfy adolescent fantasy: action and suspense packed into twenty cliff-hanging chapters. Only eighteen years of age, Nancy Drew is omniscient and omnipotent, solving mysteries that baffle adults, professional detectives, and the well-intentioned police who, however hard they try, are never as quick-thinking and fast-acting as Nancy.

A 1914 graduate of Wellesley College, an English major with deep interests in religion, music, science, and archeology (her favorite Nancy Drew book, *The Clue in the Crossword Cipher*, 1967, is based on "astounding" archeological discoveries among the Inca ruins), A. is an active alumna and a 1978 winner of the Alumnae Achievement Award. Wellesley's motto, "Non Ministrari Sed Ministrare" (not to be ministered unto but to minister), has been A.'s own guiding principle and the lesson she hopes to teach young readers who gather in schools and libraries all over the country to hear her speak. "Don't be a gimme, gimme kind of person," she tells them in an amusingly loose translation of the Latin. A. has endowed a chair at Wellesley to be known as the Harriet Stratemeyer Adams Professor in Juvenile Literature.

A. travels widely (South America, Hawaii, Africa, the Orient), using the foreign settings to provide "authentic backgrounds" for her stories, especially for the Nancy Drews. Indeed, Nancy—whom she regards as "a third lovely daughter" (in addition to her two real-life daughters)—is rarely out of A.'s thoughts when she takes a trip.

A.'s books have been translated into more than a dozen languages and, although considered nonliterary, they are now staples in most children's libraries.

WORKS: The Nancy Drew Mystery Series (as Carolyn Keene; 56 books, 1930–78). The Barton Books for Girls Series (as May Hollis Barton; 15 books, 1931–50). The Dana Girls Series (as Carolyn Keene; 32 books, 1934–78). The Hardy Boys Series (as Franklin W. Dixon; 20 books, 1934–73). The Tom Swift Series (as Victor Appleton II; 21 books, 1935–72). The Bobbsey Twin Series (as Laura Lee Hope; 15 books, 1940–67). The Honey Bunch Series (as Helen Louise Thorndyke; 7 books, 1945–55). The Linda Craig Series (as Ann Sheldon; 4 books, 1960–66).

BIBLIOGRAPHY: Keene, C., in *The Great Detectives*, Ed. O. Penzler (1978). Prager, A., *Rascals at Large; or, The Clue in the Old Nostalgia* (1971).
For articles in reference works, see: *CA* (1968).

JACQUELINE BERKE

Jane Addams

B. 6 Sept. 1860, Cedarville, Illinois; d. 21 May 1935, Chicago, Illinois
D. of John and Sarah Weber Addams

A. was born into a prominent northwestern Illinois family headed by a father who had served with Abraham Lincoln in the state legislature. Her mother died when A. was two, and A. tried to model herself after her highly-respected father. She attended the Rockford Female Seminary and, for one year, Woman's Medical College in Philadelphia. She never married; the closest emotional ties over her lifetime were to her father and to a few women friends.

A.'s name is most often associated with Hull House, the renowned settlement she founded in 1889 in the immigrant slums of Chicago. Her experiences there formed the basis for her efforts, carried out on a local, national, and international scale, for social reform. She devoted herself to such causes as child-labor legislation, woman suffrage, educational reform, and world peace. She helped found the Women's International League for Peace and Freedom (WILPF) and served as its president until her death. In 1931, she was corecipient of the Nobel Peace Prize. A. wrote ten books, countless articles, and lectured extensively, presenting to a wide audience her conviction that citizens of the new urban-industrial age must move beyond individualism toward a new social ethic.

Her first book, *Democracy and Social Ethics* (1902), is a perceptive analysis of the new industrial American society peopled by masses of immigrants and urban poor. In six essays adapted from earlier articles and lectures, A. suggests that changes in industrial and household relations, in politics and education and organized charity, and in ways of understanding the role of women will be necessary if true democracy is to be extended successfully into the new age. Her view that women's political and social role should be expanded so that women could become caretakers of the well-being and morality not just of their families but of society at large is typical of the viewpoint known as social feminism.

Newer Ideals of Peace (1907) continues and expands A.'s analysis, suggesting that as a social ethic of morality is put into practice, the need for war will disappear. *The Spirit of Youth and the City Streets* (1909),

A.'s own favorite among her books, and *A New Conscience and an Ancient Evil* (1912), a study of prostitution, are pioneering contributions to the field of urban sociology.

A.'s best-known work is *Twenty Years at Hull-House* (1910), the classic autobiography she published at age fifty. The book describes Hull House and its cultural, educational, political, and humanitarian activities, but its broader focus is the education of A. herself. She was indebted to the thought or moral example of such diverse figures as John Ruskin, Abraham Lincoln, Leo Tolstoy, her friend John Dewey, and to the founders of the settlement house in London known as Toynbee Hall. But she also learned from the ideas and problems of her immigrant neighbors, for she viewed Hull House not as a charitable mission to the downtrodden but as a forum where diverse nationalities and social classes could interact for the betterment of all.

Like all autobiography, *Twenty Years at Hull-House* is selective and stylized in its presentation of events. A. writes lucidly and sometimes movingly, enlivening her narrative with anecdotal accounts of the people and situations she met in her Hull House work. She adopts the persona of a seeker, rather than a dispenser, of enlightenment, but she writes with moral earnestness and with a naive optimism that justice and peace will be made to prevail.

During the next two decades, A. passed for a time beyond liberal social reform to positions which many regarded as radical and even seditious. She was a pacifist during World War I, an internationalist in the isolationist 1920s, a supporter of civil liberties when the prevailing mood was suppressive of dissent. A. discusses her peace efforts, and the condemnation and self-doubt she suffered because of her unpopular views, in *Peace and Bread in Time of War* (1922), and in *The Second Twenty Years at Hull-House* (1930) . The latter book is a disjointed but still interesting account of A.'s continuing reform activities and of her view of the postwar years. It includes one of A.'s favorite pieces: an analysis of the appeal to women of the rumor, spread widely in 1913, that a devil baby resided at Hull House.

Even before her death, A. had become a legendary figure. Unfortunately, the image of her which survives is that of the do-gooder—of Saint Jane, the lady in long skirts who helped the poor. But A. was a social reformer of far-ranging breadth and influence, a gifted writer, and a first-rate intellect. She was not so much an original thinker as a perceptive observer of the society around her, and an able synthesizer and popularizer of the ideas of the leading social theorists of her time. A.'s work and writing helped make possible the liberal reforms of the Progressive Era and of the New Deal and helped arouse the social conscience of two generations of Americans.

WORKS: *Democracy and Social Ethics* (1902). *Newer Ideals of Peace* (1907). *The Spirit of Youth and the City Streets* (1909). *Twenty Years at Hull-House, with Autobiographical Notes* (1910). *A New Conscience and an Ancient Evil* (1912). *The Women at The Hague* (with E. Balch and A. Hamilton, 1915). *The Long Road of Woman's Memory* (1916). *Peace and Bread in Time of War* (1922). *The Second Twenty Years at Hull-House, September 1909 to September 1929, with a Record of a Growing World Consciousness* (1930). *The Excellent Becomes the Permanent* (1932). *My Friend, Julia Lathrop* (1935). *Jane Addams: A Centennial Reader* (Ed. E. C. Johnson, 1960). *The Social Thought of Jane Addams* (Ed. C. Lasch, 1965).

BIBLIOGRAPHY: Commager, H. S., Foreword to *Twenty Years at Hull-House* by Jane Addams (1961). Davis, A. F., *American Heroine: The Life and Legend of Jane Addams* (1973). Farrell, J. C., *Beloved Lady: A History of Jane Addams's Ideas on Reform and Peace* (1967). Lasch, C., *The New Radicalism in America (1899–1963): The Intellectual as a Social Type* (1965). Lasch, C., Introduction to *The Social Thought of Jane Addams* (1965). Levine, D., *Jane Addams and the Liberal Tradition* (1971). Linn, J. W., *Jane Addams: A Biography* (1935). Scott, A. F., Introduction to *Democracy and Social Ethics* by Jane Addams (1964).

For articles in reference works, see: *DAB. NAW* (article by A. F. Scott). *NCAB.*

Other references: *Commentary* (July 1961). *Daedalus* 93 (Spring 1964). *JSocHis* 5 (Winter 1971–72). *JHI* 22 April–June 1961).

PEGGY STINSON

Zoë Akins

B. 30 Oct. 1886, Humansville, Illinois; d. 29 Oct. 1958, Los Angeles, California
D. of Thomas J. and Elizabeth Green Akins; m. Hugo C. Rumbold, 1932

A. grew up and went to school in Illinois and Missouri. She expressed an early interest in the theater and acting. When she left St. Louis for New York in 1909—with romantic dreams of going on stage and with the determination and pluck for which she was always admired—she encountered her first defeat: she was told she had no acting talent. A. decided, however, to stay in New York and write plays. When she submitted poetry to *McClure's* magazine, the managing editor, Willa Cather, who was to become a lifelong friend and correspondent, rejected the poetry but told her, prophetically, that she should write for the stage.

Although A.'s first published book was a volume of poetry, *Interpretations* (1911), and although she eventually wrote a novel, *Forever Young* (1941), she is best known for her original dramas, comedies, screenplays, and adaptations. She began to generate attention in 1916 with her vers libre drama, *The Magical City*. She went on to write *Déclassée* (1919), perhaps the best original play of that year. A.'s high comedies, like *Papa* (1913) and *Greatness: A Comedy* (1921) demonstrate continued sophistication and even greatness. She later turned her art, however, to the more popular situation comedies, which, on the whole, do not possess the dramatic quality of her early original work. Her sharp wit and sense of irony, especially, were quite lost in the shift from high to situation comedy. A. won the 1935 Pulitzer Prize for drama for *The Old Maid*, an adaptation of a novella by another of her literary friends, Edith Wharton.

While it is true that A.'s writing is uneven and occasionally suffers from what Mielech calls "romantic excesses" associated with postwar American drama, and while many of her otherwise attractive protagonists periodically engage in a rhetoric that is uncharacteristic or platitudinous, much of her excellence has gone unappreciated. Some of her efforts at characterization have been misconstrued as overindulgence or a lapse in realism. A.'s significance, it seems, lies in her extremely sharp and sympathetic understanding of human foibles in general and of female folly and frustration in particular.

In a play like *Daddy's Gone A-Hunting* (1921), for example, A. insightfully portrays the all-too-common situation of a woman blindly committed to fidelity to a confused husband who psychologically abuses her and who manipulates and keeps her with him largely through the guilt he—as well as society—stirs up in her. When she finally rejects his "open marriage" ideas and leaves him, she flees to another, kinder man who "keeps" her sexually and financially, but whom she refuses to marry because she will not get a divorce. Although the play is recognized for its unorthodox focus on the troubled quest for personal freedom, it is more powerful for its quiet repudiation of woman's considerable dependence on man and for its unhappy admission that women like Edith—most women for that matter—find the world "unsafe" when their traditional sources of security are taken from them. Neither Edith's initial decision to remain true to her adulterous husband nor her later decision to live with Greenough in the face of society's censure is completely admirable according to A. Her keen irony underscores Edith's appalling lack of personal identity and purposiveness, and the reader experiences her horror when she realizes that she cannot expect men or children to provide meaning and identity for her.

In general, A.'s plays—whether serious dramas or high comedies—emphasize the distortions in values, attitudes, and manners which society promulgates. She is simultaneously both amused and disturbed by the often pathetic efforts of her dramatic characters to extricate themselves from the web of social behavior patterns and thinking that they cannot really understand.

A. is probably not a great playwright, but she is surely worthy of more notice and exposure than she has been receiving.

WORKS: (Most of A.'s plays were never published as books.) *Interpretations* (1911). *Papa: An Amorality in Three Acts* (1913). *Cake upon the Waters* (1919). *The Old Maid* by E. Wharton (dramatization by Akins, 1935). *The Little Miracle* (1936). *The Hills Grow Smaller* (1937). *Mrs. January and Mr. Ex* (1944; alternate title, *Plans for Tomorrow*).

BIBLIOGRAPHY: Meilech, R. A., "The Plays of Zoë Akins Rumbold" (Diss., Ohio State Univ., 1974).

Other references: *American Mercury* (May 1928). *SatR* (11 May 1935). *WLB* (June 1935).

PATRICIA LEE YONGUE

Louisa May Alcott

B. 29 Nov. 1832, Germantown, Pennsylvania; d. 6 March 1888, Boston, Massachusetts
Wrote under: L.M.A., Louisa May Alcott, A. M. Barnard, Flora Fairfield, A.M. D. of Amos Bronson and Abba May Alcott

A. was the daughter of Bronson Alcott, the high priest of Transcendentalism, friend and admirer of Emerson and Thoreau. Although the early years of her life were marked by poverty and uncertainty, as her father sought to establish his "perfect school," they were rewarding years. She had little institutionalized education, but her father taught her under his advanced educational theories. Her love of drama gave her an awareness of the melodramatic and sensational in everyday life. Her attempts to augment the family income by teaching, sewing, working as a servant, and acting as a companion provided the raw material for her own creative works.

Flower Fables (1855), a collection of imaginative fantasies for children, was the first book published under A.'s own name. Earlier, her poems had been published under the pseudonym Flora Fairfield, and scattered throughout her career were "necessity tales," sometimes lurid and sensational, also published pseudonymously. With *Hospital Sketches* (1863) and *Little Women* (1868), A. became an institution, a center of public attention. She wrote on contemporary issues such as suffrage, temperance, prison reform, and child labor.

The positive critical reception of *Hospital Sketches*, which is based on A.'s brief career as a Civil War nurse, convinced its author that success lay in portraying real life rather than flights of fancy. The experiences of "Tribulation Periwinkle" rank with Whitman's poetic record in the pictures of suffering gallantly borne and the compassion of those who served as nurses.

Throughout her career, A. produced autobiographical poems, essays, and stories. "Thoreau's Flute" (1863) reflects her hours spent at Walden Pond; "Transcendental Wild Oats" (1873) provides a frank, humorous-pathetic account of her family's abortive Utopia (Fruitlands); and "Ralph Waldo Emerson" (1882) pays tribute to the guardian angel of the Alcott family.

Little Women was an instant success, with multiple editions and translations in more than thirty languages. The simple everyday events and small crises of Jo, Meg, Beth, and Amy, and the warmth of the family life provided by "Marmee" and Mr. March, along with the friendship of Laurie, Mr. Laurence, and the sharp-tongued Aunt March have influenced every generation since 1868. Although Jo's marriage to Professor Bhaer disappointed many readers who hoped she would marry Laurie and disapproved of his eventual marriage to Amy, the Bhaer family soon developed its own personality.

In *Little Men* (1871) and *Jo's Boys* (1886), A. not only gave Jo two boys of her own but provided a whole school of boys and girls of all ages, races, and levels of wealth, who were loved and educated on the estate bequeathed by Aunt March. The freedom of the learning environment is reminiscent of Amos Bronson Alcott's avant-garde philosophy; the lessons of love and duty taught to the March girls are transmitted to all. The readers' interest in the destinies of the twelve boys who lived at Plumfield led A. to write *Jo's Boys*, set ten years later than *Little Men*.

Although the destinies of all the characters who peopled *Little Men* are traced in *Jo's Boys*, the changes which fifteen years brought in the author herself are evident in the ending of the book. Despite the pleas of young readers, Dan's imprisonment as the result of killing a man, even by accident, shuts him off from marrying Bess, the exquisite daughter of Amy and Laurie. Nan, Meg's daughter, defends her position as a new woman and pursues her career as a doctor, while Bess becomes an artist and Josie an actress, before they become wives.

Lesser known but equally delightful are *Eight Cousins* (1875) and *Rose in Bloom* (1876), which trace the adventures of Rose and her seven cousins, adding more memorable portraits to A.'s gallery and providing the author with many opportunities to comment upon the silliness of values and customs of Victorian society.

The critical reception of A.'s works during her lifetime varied greatly but was generally favorable. Throughout much of the 20th-c. she has been widely known only as the author of *Little Women*, but her honesty, realism, and reluctance to overmoralize continue to win her new readers and critical attention.

WORKS: *Flower Fables* (1855). *Hospital Sketches* (1863). *Moods* (1865). *Morning-Glories, and Other Stories* (1868). *Kitty's Class Day* (1868). *Aunt Kipp* (1868). *Psyche's Art* (1868). *Three Proverb Stories* (1868). *Little Women, or Meg, Jo, Beth and Amy* (1868). *Little Women*, Part Second (1869). *An Old-Fashioned Girl* (1870). *Little Men: Life at Plumfield with Jo's Boys* (1871). *My Boys: Aunt Jo's Scrap-Bag, I* (1872). *Shawl-Straps: Aunt Jo's Scrap-Bag, II* (1872). *Work: A Story of Experience* (1873). *Cupid and Chow-Chow: Aunt Jo's Scrap-Bag, III* (1874). *Eight Cousins; or, The Aunt-Hill* (1875). *Silver Pitchers; and Independence, a Centennial Love Story* (1876). *Rose in Bloom: A Sequel to Eight Cousins* (1876). *A Modern Mephistopheles* (1877). *Under the Lilacs* (1878). *My Girls: Aunt Jo's Scrap-Bag, IV* (1878). *Jack and Jill: A Village Story* (1880). *Proverb Stories* (1882). *An Old-Fashioned Thanksgiving: Aunt Jo's Scrap-Bag, V* (1882). *Lulu's Library, I* (1886). *Jo's Boys and How They Turned Out: A Sequel to Little Men* (1886). *Lulu's Library, II* (1887). *A Garland for Girls* (1888). *Lulu's Library, III* (1889). *Recollections of My Childhood's Days* (1890). *Comic Tragedies Written by Jo and Meg and Acted by the Little Women* (1893). *Behind a Mask: The Unknown Thrillers of Louisa May Alcott* (ed. M. Stern, 1975).

BIBLIOGRAPHY: Anthony, K. S., *Louisa May Alcott* (1936). Bonstelle J., and M. DeForest, eds., *Little Women Letters from the House of Alcott* (1914). Cheney, E., *Louisa May Alcott: Her Life, Letters, and Journals* (1889). Gulliver, L., *Louisa May Alcott: A Bibliography* (1932). Meigs, C. L., *The Story of the Author of Little Women: Invincible Louisa* (1933). Moses, B., *Louisa*

May Alcott, Dreamer and Worker: A Story of Achievement (1909). Papashvily, H. W., *Louisa May Alcott* (1965). Peare, C. O., *Louisa May Alcott: Her Life* (1954). Stern, M. B., *Louisa May Alcott* (1950). Ullom, J. C., *Louisa May Alcott: A Centennial for 'Little Women'* (1969).

For articles in reference works, see: *Bibliography of American Literature*, Ed. J. N. Blanck (1955).

Other references: *ALR* 1 (Winter 1973). *Bibliographical Society of America Papers* 37 (1943). *NEQ* (June 1943; Dec. 1949). *NYTMag* (Dec. 1964).

ALMA J. PAYNE

Bess Streeter Aldrich

B. 17 Feb. 1881, Cedar Falls, Iowa; d. 3 Aug. 1954, Lincoln, Nebraska
Wrote under: Bess Streeter Aldrich, Margaret Dean Stephens
D. of James Wareham and Mary Anderson Streeter; m. Charles Aldrich, 1907

A.'s grandparents immigrated to frontier Iowa in the 1890s. The families' experiences there became the basis for A.'s most successful novels. After graduating from Iowa State Teachers' College in Cedar Falls in 1901, A. taught for six years. She wrote articles for teachers' magazines and stories for primary-school children. Shortly after her marriage she moved to Elmwood, Nebraska. When her husband, a banker and lawyer, died suddenly in 1925, A. became the sole support of her four children. Writing now became her profession.

In 1930, she became book editor of the *Christian Herald*. She was awarded an Honorary Doctorate of Literature in 1935 from the University of Nebraska, and she was elected to the Nebraska Hall of Fame in 1973.

The Rim of the Prairie (1925), A.'s first novel, is a contemporary story of Nancy, a farm girl living near a small town remarkably similar to Elmwood, Nebraska. Through the recollections of the old people, Aunt Biney and Uncle Jud Moore, A. recounts details of the settling of this part of the country, as civilization and modern farming overtake the wild prairie. The author's knowledge and love of nature, her descriptions of the rolling hills and the flowers of the prairie, are well expressed here, as in all her books.

A Lantern in Her Hand (1928) is a much better work, perhaps because actual events form its basis, several from her family history. The character of Abbie Deal, who moves from Illinois to Iowa in 1854, then marries and homesteads with her husband in Nebraska, is based on her mother. In spite of sorrow, hardship, and lack of opportunity to develop her talents, Abbie has a happy life. The "lantern in her hand" has lighted her children's way. The novel was immensely popular, a bestseller for years. It is probably A.' s best book. Later works sometimes are variations of its theme, setting, and events.

A.'s work is romantic, optimistic, and "wholesome." Her stories usually end happily, her romances join those who should be joined. Some of them are sentimental. Nevertheless, they display certain strengths. Characterization is often excellent, as are her descriptions of nature. The background is always the Midwest, and she describes it precisely and accurately. Although A. is most noted for her stories of the settling of the Midwest, her short stories give fine details of middle-class family life in the midwestern small town of the 1920s and 1930s. Her stories and articles were published in many of the leading periodicals.

A.'s style is not mannered or dated; neither is it remarkably original. The careful attention A. gives to details—dates, clothing styles, food, customs—are strong points, creating a realistic background. The hardships of settling the frontier and of country living, such as the back-breaking labor, particularly for the women, the lack of refinements, the inconvenient kitchens, the bare and ugly houses, are details such as Hamlin Garland often gives. But whereas Garland points out the hopelessness of the unremitting hard labor in fighting poverty, dirt, and squalor, A. affirms life, and her characters find, usually, some reason for happiness, be it through love or belief in honor and duty.

WORKS: *Mother Mason* (1924). *The Rim of the Prairie* (1925). *The Cutters* (1926). *A Lantern in Her Hand* (1928). *A White Bird Flying* (1931). *Miss Bishop* (1933). *Spring Came on Forever* (1935). *The Man Who Caught the Weather* (1936). *Song of Years* (1939). *The Drum Goes Dead* (1941). *The Lieutenant's Lady* (1942). *Journey into Christmas, and Other Stories* (1949). *The Bess Streeter Aldrich Reader* (1950). *A Bess Streeter Aldrich Treasury* (ed. R. S. Aldrich, 1959).

BIBLIOGRAPHY: Aldrich, R., *A Bess Streeter Aldrich Treasury* (1959). Marble, A. R., *A Daughter of Pioneers: Bess Streeter Aldrich and Her Books* (n.d.). Meier, A. M., "Bess Streeter Aldrich: Her Life and Works" (Master's thesis, Kearney State College, 1968). Williams, B. C., *Bess Streeter Aldrich, Novelist* (n.d.).

Other references: *Appleton's Book Chat* (1 Feb. 1930; 21 Nov. 1931). WLB (April 1929).

HELEN STAUFFER

Mildred Aldrich

B. 16 Nov. 1853, Providence, Rhode Island; d. 19 Feb. 1928, Huiry, France
Wrote under: Mildred Aldrich, H. Quinn
D. of Edwin and Lucy Ayers Baker Aldrich

A. grew up in Boston. She attended the Hancock School, Girls High School, and trained in the natural sciences at the Lowell Scientific Institute.

A.'s professional career was consistently in the field of journalism. For twelve years, A. was secretary to the manager of the Boston *Home Journal* and a contributor under the pseudonym H. Quinn. She edited *The Mahogany Tree*, a journal of ideas. During 1892 and 1893, A. submitted three substantial pieces on theater to *Arena*. She joined the *Boston Journal* in 1894, and moved the following year to the *Boston Herald*. There she strengthened further her already strong reputation for astute dramatic criticism. Sometime around the turn of the century, but before 1904, A. moved to Paris, where she represented several American theatrical producers and wrote for American magazines. She retired to the French countryside in 1914, when she was sixty-one. Her hilltop home, La Creste, afforded a view of the site of the Battle of the Marne.

A. wrote four firsthand accounts of life in wartime France from La Creste. *A Hilltop on the Marne* (1915), her most successful book, first appeared in the *Atlantic Monthly*. It treats the progress of the battle, the spirit and commitment of both soldiers and villagers. The work's strength derives from the compression of events and A.'s expanding understanding, which the reader shares. *On the Edge of the War Zone* (1917) covers the period September 16, 1914–March 28, 1917, and is more diffuse in its approach. Of special interest are A.'s reports on gas warfare and descriptions of soldiers' wartime entertainments. *The Peak of the Load* (1918) deals with "the waiting months on the hilltop from the entrance of the stars and stripes to the second victory on the Marne." In *When Johnny Comes Marching Home* (1919), A. describes how "the countryside settled down" after the armistice.

Told in a French Garden, August, 1914 (1916) is A.'s sole work of fiction. By a "strange irony of Fate," nine people find themselves in provincial France in the darkest days of the war. To raise their spirits, they follow Boccaccio's example in *The Decameron*, and each relates a story following the day's dinner. Prologues and epilogues frame the stories and reveal the conflicts in values the participants display.

A. also wrote the foreword to *The Letters of Thomasina Atkins (W.A.A.C.) on Active Service* (1918). This volume recounts Atkins's experiences in the British Women's Auxiliary Army Corps stationed "somewhere in France." For her help in swaying American opinion towards entrance into World War I and her assistance to soldiers and refugees, A. was awarded the Legion of Honor by the French government in 1922.

WORKS: *A Hilltop on the Marne* (1915). *Told in a French Garden, August, 1914* (1916). *On the Edge of the War Zone* (1917). *The Peak of the Load* (1918). *When Johnny Comes Marching Home* (1919).

BIBLIOGRAPHY: Stein, G., *The Autobiography of Alice B. Toklas* (1932). Mellow, J. R., *Charmed Circle: Gertrude Stein and Company* (1973).

JANIS TOWNSEND

Mary E. Clemmer Ames

B. 6 May 1831, Utica, New York; d. 18 Aug. 1884, Washington, D.C.
Wrote under: Mary Clemmer Ames, M.C.A., Mary Clemmer
D. of Abraham and Margaret Kneale Clemmer; m. Daniel Ames, 1851;
m. Edmund Hudson, 1883

The oldest of seven children, A. moved with her family to Westfield, Massachusetts, where she attended the Westfield Academy. Her career began in 1859, when she sent letters from New York City, where she was living temporarily with the poets Alice and Phoebe Cary, to the Utica *Morning Herald* and the Springfield (Massachusetts) *Republican*.

After her marriage to a minister ended, A. began a "Woman's Letter from Washington," for the New York *Independent*. The column continued from 1866 until her death. She also wrote for the Brooklyn *Daily Union* and for the Cincinnati *Commercial*.

A.'s literary significance stems mainly from her column in the influential weekly, the *Independent*. It made her one of the best known of a group of post-Civil War women Washington correspondents, known as "literary ladies." Avoiding social news, she concentrated on political issues, defending the freed Negro and civil rights, and sharply criticizing the excesses of Gilded-Age politics. She moved in the same social circles as leading politicians and used them as news sources.

In spite of her participation in the masculine worlds of both politics and journalism, A. repeatedly told her readers that she modestly shrank from public notice and preferred the domestic scene to the political arena. Asserting her career had been the product of financial necessity, she justified it morally on the grounds that women journalists had a spiritual duty to purify politics, even if their efforts brought them unwelcome personal attention. She did not appear publicly to support woman suffrage, although she did advocate it. Considering suffrage less important than economic gains, she wrote: "Women can live nobly without voting; but they cannot live without bread."

A.'s weekly columns bore the hallmark of popular Victorian literature—excessive sentiment, self-conscious moralizing, and verbosity. Still, they provided an intriguing picture of a woman standing apart from the seamy side of politics and pinpointing politicians guilty of drunkenness and corruption. The books based on her columns—*Outlines of Men, Women and Things* (1873) and *Ten Years in Washington* (1873)—emphasized people and places rather than politics. Part guidebook to the capital, *Ten Years in Washington*, a subscription book reprinted three times, was crammed with historical lore. *Outlines* included descriptions of scenic spots, biographical sketches of literary and theatrical figures, and, more importantly, several essays dealing with relations between the sexes. A. urged men to subscribe to the "pure" moral standards of women and exhorted women to educate themselves. Her most successful work of nonfiction, *A Memorial to Alice and Phoebe Cary*, a gushing tribute to the women who had befriended her, drew critical acclaim in that sentimental era.

Making a virtue of what was obviously a handicap to a Washington correspondent—her sex—she contended that her womanhood gave her the right to comment on political issues to promote reform. Trading on the Victorian myth that women possessed a higher moral sense than do men, she showed that a facile woman writer could make a place for herself by pointing a finger of righteous scorn and indignation at the men who ran the country.

WORKS: *Victoire* (1864). *Eirene, or, A Woman's Right* (1871). *A Memorial to Alice and Phoebe Cary* (1873). *Outlines of Men, Women and Things* (1873). *Ten Years in Washington* (1873). *His Two Wives* (1875). *Memorial Sketch of Elizabeth Emerson Atwater* (1879). *Poems of Life and Nature* (1883).

BIBLIOGRAPHY: Beasley, M. H., *The First Women Washington Correspondents* (George Washington University Studies No. 4, 1976). Beasley, M. H., and S. Silver, *Women in Media: A Documentary Source Book* (1977). Hudson, E., *An American Woman's Life and Work: A Memorial of Mary Clemmer* (1886). Whiting, L., *Our Famous Women* (1884).

For articles in reference works, see: *NAW* (article by J. Cutler Andrews).

Other references: *Arthur's Home Magazine* (Dec. 1884). *The Cottage Hearth* (Feb. 1875). *The Independent* (28 Aug. 1884).

MAURINE BEASLEY

Eliza Frances Andrews

B. 10 Aug. 1840, Washington, Georgia; d. 21 Jan. 1931, Rome, Georgia
Wrote under: Elzey Hay
D. of Garnett and Annulet Ball Andrews

A. was born at Haywood, the plantation home of her parents. The family was moderately wealthy by southern standards, owning about two hundred slaves. A. attended the Washington Seminary for Girls and graduated in the first class from the LaGrange Female College in 1857.

When Georgia seceded from the Union in January 1861, A.'s father achieved notoriety for his uncompromising opposition to secession and his subsequent refusal to support the new Confederacy. Although he permitted three of his sons to join the Confederate army, he did not tolerate the secessionist views of his daughters, which led to many family arguments.

In December 1864, A. began her diary, published as *The War-time Journal of a Georgia Girl* (1908), with an account of a trip to visit her sister near Albany, Georgia. A. and a younger sister had to travel over rough, partially destroyed roads, with the ever-present fear of ambush by Sherman's men. Once at their sister's, however, the two girls enjoyed a round of visits and parties, strangely gay for a time of political and military disintegration. A.'s fine eye for detail gives the reader a fascinating portrait of social life in the rural Confederacy. Occasionally she lapses into girlish concerns, reporting all the compliments she received on her appearance, but her natural skepticism always rescues her and the diary from silliness. In March 1865, A. returned to Washington, Georgia, to witness the fall of the Confederacy. There she met Jefferson Davis on his flight from his pursuers.

After her father's death in 1873, A. began teaching school. She served as principal of the Girl's High School in Yazoo City, Mississippi, later became principal of a girl's seminary in Washington, Georgia, and from 1885 to 1896 taught French and literature at the Wesleyan Female College in Macon, Georgia. A. then returned home to Washington to teach botany in the public high school. After her retirement from teaching, she published two textbooks on botany.

A.'s literary career began in 1865 with an article on Reconstruction in Georgia published in the New York *World*. A second article on women's life and fashions appeared in *Godey's Lady's Book* the following year.

Her first novel, *A Family Secret* (1876), quickly became a bestseller. This mystery, set in the immediate postwar South, revolves around the romance between Audley Malvern and Ruth Hartleur and their attempts to discover the secret of Ruth's parents and the unusual ring she wears. It is filled with such typical 19th-c. literary conventions as a ghost in a graveyard and mistaken identities. The last chapter is called "Everybody Gets Married and Lives Happy Forever After." Two other novels were equally popular.

WORKS: *A Family Secret* (1876). *A Mere Adventurer* (1879). *Prince Hal; or, the Romance of a Rich Young Man* (1882). *Botany All the Year Round; a Practical Textbook for Schools* (1903). *Seven Great Battles of the Army of Northern Virginia: A Program of Study and Entertainment* (1906). *The Wartime Journal of a Georgia Girl* (1908). *A Practical Course in Botany, With Especial Reference to Its Bearings on Agriculture, Economics, and Sanitation* (1911).

The papers of Eliza Frances Andrews are in the Garnett Andrews Papers, Southern Historical Collection, University of North Carolina Library, Chapel Hill, North Carolina.

BIBLIOGRAPHY: Coulter, E. M., *Travels in the Confederate States* (1948). Hart, B. S., *Georgia Writers* (1929). King, S. B., Jr., ed., *The Wartime Journal of a Georgia Girl* (1960).

For articles in reference works, see: *AW. Living Writers of the South*, Ed. M. T. Tardy (1872). *NAW* (article by J. Patton).

JANET E. KAUFMAN

Jane Andrews

B. 1 Dec. 1833, Newburyport, Massachusetts; d. 15 July 1887, Newburyport, Massachusetts
D. of John and Margaret Demmon Rand Andrews

A. was born and raised in the midst of the vigorous nationalism of mid-19th-c. New England. She inherited from her family a spirit of intellectual concern and benevolence which, taken together with a broad outlook, led her to become one of the earliest proponents of internationalism in education. A.'s school friends at the Putnam Free School at Newburyport and the State Normal School at West Newton, Massachusetts, included a sister-in-law of education reformer Horace Mann. Mann persuaded A. that she would find the kind of education she wanted at his new college, Antioch, where, subsequently, she was the first student to register. However, the onset of a neurological disorder described as "spinal affection" cut short her education in the middle of the first year and left her an invalid for the next six years. Nonetheless, Mann's influence reinforced her commitment to belief in one's responsibility to society, a commitment that influenced the direction of the teaching and writing she practiced during the remainder of her life.

In 1860, sufficiently recovered from her illness to work, A. founded a primary school in her home. This school, characterized by advanced educational methods including experiments, plays, games, and stories, was extremely successful and continued to be A.'s life for the next twenty-five years. In her school she cultivated observation, individual responsibility, and creative expression in the hope of molding responsible citizens for life in a society where all people were equal.

A.'s first book, *Seven Little Sisters Who Live on the Round Ball That Floats in the Air* (1861), grew out of stories she created to supplement the geography lessons in her school. Each story focuses on a little girl in a different culture and emphasizes that although the external circumstances of life are very different for each child, each is happy and is one of God's family. The same motive held for the sequel, *Each and All: Seven Little Sisters Prove Their Sisterhood* (1877) and for a historical counterpart, *Ten Boys Who Lived on the Road From Long Ago to Now* (1886), which traces "our race from its Aryan sources to the present." Through these books, all of which emphasize the kinship of children throughout the world, A. hoped to offset the effect of books like Peter Parley's, in which children from other lands were characteristically made to look strange and unlike the children for whom the books were intended. The books also provided an alternative morality to that of the McGuffey readers which depicted virtue as being of personal rather than of social concern.

WORKS: *The Seven Little Sisters Who Live on the Round Ball That Floats in the Air* (1861). *Each and All: Seven Little Sisters Prove Their Sisterhood* (1877). *Geographical Plays for Young Folks at Home and School* (1880). *The Child's Health Primer* (1885). *Ten Boys Who Lived on the Road from Long Ago to Now* (1886). *Only A Year and What It Brought* (1888). *The Stories Mother Nature Told Her Children* (1889). *The Stories of My Four Friends* (1900).

BIBLIOGRAPHY: Green, N. K., *A Forgotten Chapter in American Education: Jane Andrews of Newburyport* (1961). Hopkins, L. P., Foreword to *Seven Little Sisters Who Live on the Round Ball That Floates in the Air* by J. Andrews (1897). Spofford, H. P., *A Little Book of Friends* (1916).
    Other references: *EngElemR* (May 1936).

KATHARYN F. CRABBE

Hannah Arendt

B. *14 Oct. 1906, Hanover, Germany; d. 4 Dec. 1975, New York City*
D. *of Paul and Martha Cohn Arendt; m. Heinrich Bleucher, 1940*

The only child of nonreligious, German-Jewish parents, A. received her formal education in Germany. She studied philosophy under Karl Jaspers at Heidelberg and took her doctorate in 1928, after completing a dissertation on St. Augustine. When the Nazis came to power in 1933, she fled to France, and then emigrated to the United States. A. made her greatest mark on the American academic community. An innovative and forceful political theorist, she taught at various universities across the country.

A.'s best-known work, *The Origins of Totalitarianism* (1951, 1958), deals with the rise of totalitarianism in Germany and Russia. It offers a description of the fundamental structure of a totalitarian regime and presents an account of social and political conditions—such as the growth of imperialism and anti-Semitism—on which they were built. Above all, A.

attributed the success of totalitarian movements to what she called "organized loneliness." Loneliness, for A., is not merely solitude; it is a condition in which individuals have lost contact with the world as well as with one another. Worldless people do not understand themselves as belonging to the world because they no longer have the ability to add anything of their own to that world. Without a world shared between them, such people lack a "common sense"; they cannot differentiate between reality and fiction—and are easily manipulated by the logic of totalitarian ideology.

In *The Human Condition* (1958), A. considers the meaning of free political action in terms of a distinction between private and public realms. In *On Revolution* (1963), she analyzes the character of revolutionary movements in the modern age.

In 1961, A. went to Jerusalem for *The New Yorker* magazine to cover the trial of Adolf Eichmann. Her report, which appeared first as a series of articles and then as *Eichmann in Jerusalem* (1963), aroused considerable and bitter controversy. A. shocked her readers by asserting that while Eichmann's behavior had been monstrous, his character was not. What struck A. most about the Nazi war criminal was his banality. *The Life of the Mind* (1977), suggests that Eichmann's ability to commit monstrous crimes was related to his lack of thought. The capacity to judge between good and evil, in other words, is related to thought. In *Thinking*, the first volume of this two-part posthumously published work, A. maintained a distinction between reason and intellect, thinking and knowing. It is through thinking that human beings attempt to satisfy their quest for meaning.

To some, A. was an elitist who cared little about the suffering masses around the world. To others, her sensitive writings on political action and the public arena, authority, tradition, violence, and truth provide insight into some of the most perplexing dilemmas of the modern era. It is in the nature of political theory to challenge old ways of thinking and to force its audience to think about political things from a new perspective. In the spirit of this tradition, A. may be controversial and frustrating, but she is never dull.

WORKS: *Der Liebesbegriff bei Augustin* (1930). *Rahel Varnhagen: The Life of a Jewess* (1947). *The Origins of Totalitarianism* (1951; rev. ed., 1958). *Between Past and Future* (1954; rev. ed., 1968). *The Human Condition* (1958). *On Revolution* (1963). *Eichmann in Jerusalem* (1963; rev. ed., 1965). *Men in Dark Times* (1968). *On Violence* (1969). *Crises of the Republic* (1969). *Rahel Varnhagen: The Life of a Jewish Woman* (1974). *The Life of the Mind* (2 vols., 1977).

BIBLIOGRAPHY: Canovan, M., *The Political Thought of Hannah Arendt* (1974).

Other references: *NewR* (15 June 1963; 21 Oct. 1978; 12 April 1980). *NYRB* (26 Oct. 1978). *NYTRB* (19 May 1963; 28 May 1978). *Political Theory* (May 1977; Nov. 1979; Aug. 1980). *Review of Politics* 15 (Jan. 1953). *SocR* 44 (Spring 1977).

LAURA GREYSON

Charlotte Armstrong

B. 2 May 1905, Vulcan, Michigan; d. 18 July 1969, Glendale, California
Wrote under: Charlotte Armstrong, Jo Valentine
D. of Frank Hall and Clara Pascoe Armstrong; m. Jack Lewi, 1928

Having begun as poet (several poems appeared in *The New Yorker*) and playwright (two plays ran briefly on Broadway), A. soon turned to writing suspense novels, her first three being conventional detective stories. The detective, MacDougal ("Mac") Duff is a former history professor who has discovered he prefers real-life puzzles to academic ones. In *Lay On, Mac Duff!* (1942), and in *The Case of the Weird Sisters* (1943), he is the conventional outsider who solves other people's mysteries and then moves on. In *The Innocent Flower* (1945), however, he becomes involved with a divorcee and her six children; with his commitment to them, A.'s use of him ends.

A number of A.'s stories are inverted mysteries in which the identity of the criminal is revealed early. In other novels, suspense is created by a race against time. Sometimes, terror is evoked when an innocent person is trapped in an enclosed space with several people, at least one of whom poses a threat. *The Case of the Weird Sisters*, a Mac Duff mystery, falls into this group, as does *The Albatross* (1957), in which, ironically, the threatening characters are invited into the home of the victims. Variants are *The Girl with a Secret* (1959), *The Witch's House* (1963), and *The Turret Room* (1965).

Another novel of particular interest is *A Little Less Than Kind* (1963), the Hamlet story reset in contemporary California. Using the Shakespearean situation, A. examines motivations and relationships, and although her denouement is quite different from Shakespeare's, it develops logically from the situation and characters. *A Dram of Poison* (1956), despite its serious central situation, is a comic novel, with an unlikely set of characters uniting in a common purpose and discovering in the process much that is admirable in each other.

Along with family relationships, A. was especially interested in children and old people. A recurring motif in her work is that of an innocent child thought responsible for a death. Concern over the impact of the accusation on the child leads others to seek out the truth, and an adult murderer is unmasked (*The Innocent Flower*, 1945, and *The Mark of the Hand*, 1963).

A recurrent theme in A.'s novels is that of our responsibility toward one another. Characters are shown involving themselves in others' problems because they know that if they do not help, no one else will. The title character in *The One-Faced Girl* (1963) defines "good guys" as those who "don't want other people hurt. They feel it, themselves. So if any one is in pain or trouble, then they not only *want* to help, they are obliged. They just about *have* to." This concept underlies much of A.'s fiction; combined with her skill in handling complex plots and her interest in motivation and character, it helps to account for the consistent popularity her work has had.

WORKS: *Ring Around Elizabeth, a Comedy in Three Acts* (1942). *Lay On, Mac Duff!* (1942). *The Case of the Weird Sisters* (1943). *The Innocent Flower: A MacDougal Duff Mystery* (1945). *The Unsuspected* (1946). *The Chocolate Cobweb* (1948). *Mischief* (1950). *The Black-Eyed Stranger* (1951). *Catch-As-Catch-Can* (1952). *The Trouble in Thor* (1953). *The Better to Eat You* (1954). *Walk out on Death* (1954). *The Dream Walker* (1955). *Murder's Nest* (1955). *Alibi for Murder* (1956). *A Dram of Poison* (1956). *The Albatross* (1957). *Duo: The Girl with a Secret and Incident at a Corner* (1959). *The Seventeen Widows of Sans Souci* (1959). *Something Blue* (1959). *The Mark of the Hand and Then Came Two Women* (1963). *A Little Less Than Kind* (1963). *The One-Faced Girl* (1963). *The Witch's House* (1963). *The Turret Room* (1965). *Dream of Fair Woman* (1966). *The Gift Shop* (1966). *I See You* (1966). *Lemon in the Basket* (1967). *The Balloon Man* (1968). *Seven Seats to the Moon* (1969). *The Protege* (1970).

BIBLIOGRAPHY: Cromie, A., Prefaces to *The Charlotte Armstrong Reader* (1970), *The Charlotte Armstrong Treasury* (1972), and *The Charlotte Armstrong Festival* (1975).

Other references: *NYHTB* (13 Sept. 1959). *NYTBR* (25 June 1950; 15 July 1951; 28 March 1954; 16 Jan. 1955; 5 Aug. 1956; 10 Nov. 1957; 12 April 1959; 10 Nov. 1963; 11 April 1965; 7 May 1967; 29 Oct. 1967).

MARY JEAN DeMARR

Harriette Louisa Simpson Arnow

B. 7 July 1908, Wayne County, Kentucky
Writes under: H. Arnow, Harriette Arnow, Harriette Simpson Arnow,
  Harriette Simpson, H. L. Simpson
D. of Elias and Mollie Jane Denney Simpson; m. Harold Arnow, 1939

A.'s best fiction is rooted in Kentucky, her native ground. With both parents descendants of original Kentucky settlers, A. grew up hearing family stories dating from the American Revolution. These kindled the child's desire to write fiction and tell stories herself. She attended Berea College for two years, taught school for a year, then studied at the University of Louisville, where she received a B.S. degree in 1930. In an act her family viewed as scandalous, A. quit her job in 1934 and moved to a furnished room in downtown Cincinnati near the city library, resolving to read "the great novels" and to write. She supported herself with odd jobs and worked for the Federal Writers' Project. After her marriage to newspaperman Arnow, A. moved with him to a farm in southern Kentucky. They settled in their current Ann Arbor home in 1950.

A. received national attention in 1935 with two short stories published in little magazines. Both demonstrate her skill at characterization and at depicting shocking violence. In 1936, she published the novel *Mountain Path*. It is based on A.'s experience of boarding with a hill family in a remote Kentucky hollow and teaching in a one-room schoolhouse; her year there was her first prolonged stay with the people who were to become the primary subjects of her fiction.

"The Washerwoman's Day," published in *Southern Review* (Winter, 1936), is A.'s best and most anthologized short story. She movingly depicts the self-righteousness and the arrogance church members feel toward the "poor white trash" who violate their notions of decency. This story anticipates A.'s fuller treatment of narrow piousness in *Hunter's Horn* (1949) and *The Dollmaker* (1954).

Hunter's Horn, A.'s second novel, was a critically acclaimed bestseller. The story of a hill farmer's obsessive chase after an elusive red fox, *Hunter's Horn* dramatizes the cost of a compulsion as maniacal and as mythic as Ahab's stalking of Moby Dick.

A.'s third novel, *The Dollmaker* (1954) is a masterwork and another bestseller. Gertie Nevels, the hulking heroine who tries to preserve her integrity and her family's unity after their migration from the Kentucky mills to a wartime housing project in Detroit, is A.'s most arresting character. The novel won A. the Friends of American Literature Award and was voted best novel of the year in the *Saturday Review*'s national critics' poll.

Two social histories are the result of twenty years of research on the settlers of southern Kentucky and northern Tennesee from 1780 to 1803. *Seedtime on the Cumberland* (1960) and *Flowering of the Cumberland* (1963), containing vivid reenactments of the settlers' everyday crises, are often as gripping as A.'s best fiction.

A. most recent novels lack the full-bodied characters and narrative drive that propel her earlier work.

Although A.'s work is now enjoying a reassessment, it has still not achieved the stature her talent merits. Too often writers whose work is firmly rooted in one locale are relegated to a minor status by the term "regional," which can suggest a limited appeal.

Far outdistancing other writers treating hill people from the southern Appalachian region, A. is the first and only American novelist to describe them with fidelity and justice and to place them in a setting that is authentic to the last detail. But A. does more than evoke an area no other writer has captured. Like Twain and Faulkner, she creates a private world whose inhabitants face dilemmas reaching beyond geographical boundaries. Her best fiction depicts the conflict between an individual conscience and society—whether it be family, community, or the wider world. If A.'s novels at times need streamlining, they contain worlds as palpable and as real as the reader's own. If her hardy combatants fail to achieve their goals, they nonetheless take responsibility for the outcome of their lives, and endure.

WORKS: *Mountain Path* (1936). *Hunter's Horn* (1949). *The Dollmaker* (1954). *Seedtime on the Cumberland* (1960). *Flowering of the Cumberland* (1963). *The Weedkiller's Daughter* (1970). *The Kentucky Trace: A Novel of the American Revolution* (1974). *Old Burnside* (1977).

BIBLIOGRAPHY: Eckley, W., *Harriette Arnow* (1974). Hobbs, G., "Harriette Arnow's Literary Journey: From the Parish to the World" (Ph.D. diss., Harvard Univ., 1975). Hobbs, G., in *GR* 4 (Winter 1979). Oates, J. C., Afterword to *The Dollmaker* by Harriette Arnow (1972).

Other references: *KCN* 2 (Fall 1976). *Nation* (31 Jan. 1976). *NYHTB* (6 Sept. 1936).

GLENDA HOBBS

Gertrude Franklin Horn Atherton

B. *30 Oct. 1857, San Francisco, California; d. 15 June 1948, San Francisco*
Wrote under: Asmodeus, Gertrude Atherton, Frank Lin
D. of Thomas and Gertrude Franklin Horn; m. George H. Bowen Atherton,
1876

The daughter of a Yankee businessman from California and of a southern belle, A. spent the first thirty years of her life in and around San Francisco, a city whose history and destiny she utilized as subject and background for her favorite character, a new western woman. She sporadically attended private schools, eloped at seventeen with a suitor of her mother's, bore two children, and rebelled against the conventions of domestic life. Only after the death of her husband did she begin her serious writing career in New York in 1888.

Her first significant novel was *Patience Sparhawk and Her Times* (1897), published in London where her novels at first attracted more critical attention than in the U.S. This novel introduces the new western woman, who in three subsequent novels symbolizes the evolution of Western civilization at the turn of the century. In *Patience Sparhawk and Her Times*, A. offers, from the point of view of an aspiring western woman an ironic appraisal of American self-reliance and society in the 1890s. Through her characterization of the heroine as an idealistic, self-reliant, but passionate woman, born into lowly, isolated circumstances in California, A. narrates a romantic-realistic and psychological version of the 19th-c. argument over the effect of heredity and environment on the development of the individual.

In *American Wives and English Husbands* (1898), A.'s independent-spirited heroine, Lee Tarleton, proud of her Creole heritage and aristocratic California upbringing, is confronted with the "solid fact" of English tradition and convention, personified by Cecil Maundrell, scion of a landed English family, whom she marries and who expects her to become his second self. Their marriage tests the past and present values of the two civilizations in regard to the relationship between man and woman and to the perpetuation of the race. In this novel and also in *The Doomswoman* (1893), *The Californians* (1898), and *Ancestors* (1907),

A. penetrates the facade of civilization that organizes the basic relationship between man and woman and between individuals and nature. She displayed a continually ironic stance toward the argument on heredity and environment by labeling as a "fool's paradise" an individual's excessive and illusory dependence on either inherited characteristics or a given environment as a path to happiness. Her independent and self-conflicted heroine challenges the assumption that a woman unthinkingly accepts a passive, procreative function as a definition of herself and of the relationship between herself and nature and between herself and civilization.

A. enacted her criticism of Howells's "dull" realism by a call for originality and imagination in American literature. From Hippolyte Taine, she borrowed the technique of lifting a type of character out of the commonplace conditions to which he or she was apparently doomed and transferring him or her to an environment, replete with change and opportunity, where latent potentialities could be developed.

From her first novel to her last, A.'s genius lies in her ability to tell exciting stories about worthy characters, even though her style and form do not always succeed by current critical standards.

WORKS: *What Dreams May Come* (1888). *Hermia Suydam* (1889). *Los Cerritos, A Romance of the Modern Time* (1890). *A Question of Time* (1891). *The Doomswoman* (1893). *Before the Gringo Came* (1894, enlarged in *The Splendid Idle Forties*, 1902). *A Whirl Asunder* (1895). *Patience Sparhawk and Her Times* (1897). *His Fortunate Grace* (1897). *The Californians* (1898). *American Wives and English Husbands* (1898). *A Daughter of the Vine* (1899). *Senator North* (1900). *The Aristocrats* (1901). *The Conqueror* (1902). *A Few of Hamilton's Letters* (1903). *Mrs. Pendleton's Four-in-Hand* (1903). *Rulers of Kings* (1904). *The Bell in the Fog, and Other Stories* (1905). *The Traveling Thirds* (1905). *Rezánov* (1906). *Ancestors* (1907). *The Gorgeous Isle* (1908). *Tower of Ivory* (1910). *Julia France and Her Times* (1912). *Perch of the Devil* (1914). *California, an Intimate History* (1914). *Mrs. Balfame* (1916). *Life in the War Zone* (1916). *The Living Present* (1917). *The White Morning* (1918). *The Avalanche* (1919). *Transplanted* (1919). *The Sisters-in-Law* (1921). *Sleeping Fires* (1922). *Black Oxen* (1923). *The Crystal Cup* (1925). *The Immortal Marriage* (1927). *The Jealous Gods* (1928). *Dido, Queen of Hearts* (1929). *The Sophisticates* (1931). *Adventures of a Novelist* (1932). *The Foghorn* (1934). *Golden Peacock* (1936). *Rezánov and Doña Concha* (1937). *Can Women Be Gentlemen?* (1938). *The House of Lee* (1940). *The Horn of Life* (1942). *Golden Gate Country* (1945). *My San Francisco* (1946).

BIBLIOGRAPHY: Courtney, W. L., *The Feminine Note in Fiction* (1904). Jackson, J. H., *Gertrude Atherton* (1940). Knight, G. C., *The Strenuous Age in American Literature* (1954). McClure, C. S., *Gertrude Atherton* (Boise State Univ. Western Writers Series, 1976). Parker, G. T., *William Dean*

Howells: Realism and Feminism (Harvard English Studies, 1973). Starr, K., *Americans and the California Dream, 1850–1915* (1973). Underwood, J. C., *Literature and Insurgency* (1914).

Other references: *ALR* 9 (Spring 1976). *The American West* (July 1974). *The Bookman* (July 1929). *CHSQ* 55 (Fall 1976). *SJS* 1 (1975).

CHARLOTTE S. McCLURE

Djuna Barnes

B. *12 June 1892, Cornwall-on-Hudson, New York; d. 18 June 1982, New York City*
D. *of Wald and Elizabeth Chappell Barnes*

B. began her career as a journalist. A longtime resident of Europe, her stories, poems, and plays reflect the life and attitudes of the post-World War I Paris expatriates.

B. is best known for *Nightwood* (1936). Using symbolism and a surrealistic atmosphere B. presents a group of American expatriates, living in fashionable 1890s-style decadence, who reveal the abnormality of their world and their individual psychological natures through their words and their interactions. In his introduction to the novel, T. S. Eliot highly praises its gothic qualities, its insistence on horror and doom. He compares B.'s work to Elizabethan tragedy, not only for its themes and motifs but also for its technical brilliance in wit, characterization, and language. Eliot is not wrong in his assessment of the mood of the novel, but his exaggerated praise for *Nightwood* has led to a questionable evaluation of B.'s work.

B.'s stories are peopled by characters whose thoughts and behavior reveal the strange workings of twisted, obsessed minds. The characters with whom the reader is led to sympathize embrace life in all its ambiguities and possibilities. Such a character is Madame von Bartmann in "Aller et Retour," a woman whose advice to the daughter she has not seen for seven years might be B.'s advice to her characters: "think everything" and "do everything," not just for the sake of experience but to gain self-knowledge. The mother is sufficiently selfish to feel relief when her daughter responds by announcing her engagement. Since her daughter will be sheltered by a traditional, protective husband, Madame von Bartmann is saved from responsibility. The reader is led to scorn such characters as the daughter, while feeling sorry for them. They function as foils for the mysterious, even macabre characters in whom B.'s interest lies.

Imagery and word choice intensify the ambiguous horror which marks most of B.'s stories. Dark nights, evenings at dusk, dust, decay, and illness are prevalent. Death, whether from old age, illness, or from sudden unexplained violence, is a repeated symbol. The prevailing atmosphere of decay and quiet brutality makes death seem inevitable.

These motifs and devices are typified in "Spillway," the title story in the 1962 collection. Julie Anspacher returns home to her husband with a child he knew nothing about. Years earlier she had been told she would die from tuberculosis: for five years she lived on in a sanitorium, and had a child, daughter of a fellow patient. Julie's lover is dead, her child has weak lungs, and Julie's own death is near. The child is clearly symbolic of what Julie terms "death perpetuating itself." Julie explains her affair by saying that she and her lover knew they would endanger anyone who was not already dying from tuberculosis. But the child's existence causes Julie's husband to shoot himself, so that Julie's prophecy is ironically fulfilled. This story is typical of B.'s work, in its nearly humorless presentation of sickness and death, frustrated lives filled with tension, and strained sexuality tinged with the grotesque or the violent.

B.'s work is limited in scope, with a few motifs and themes used repeatedly. It is difficult to identify with her characters because of the hyperbolic presentation. Yet there is power in B.'s language and images, and in her ability to evoke an atmosphere of tension and psychological unease. Her work has influenced writers ranging from Isak Dinesen and John Hawkes to Anaïs Nin, who, in her diary, praises B.'s poetic insight and language.

WORKS: *The Book of Repulsive Women* (1915). *A Book* (1923). *Ryder* (1928). *A Night Among the Horses* (rev. and enlarged ed. of *A Book*, 1929). *Nightwood* (1936). *The Antiphon* (1958). *Selected Works* (1962).

BIBLIOGRAPHY: Baxter, C., "A Self-Consuming Light: Nightwood and the Crisis of Modernism," *JML* 3. Johnsen, W. A., "Modern Women Novelists: Nightwood and the Novel of Sensibility," *BuR* 21. Moers, E., *Literary Women* (1976).

SUSAN R. GORSKY

Margaret Ayer Barnes

B. 8 April 1886, Chicago, Illinois; d. 26 Oct. 1967, Cambridge, Massachusetts
D. of Benjamin F. and Janet Hopkins Ayer; m. Cecil Barnes, 1910

Descended on both sides from colonial English families who settled in America in the middle 1600s, B. attended the University School for Girls in Chicago and majored in English and philosophy at Bryn Mawr College, where she was influenced by the feminist president, M. Carey Thomas. While raising three sons, she appeared in performances of the Aldis Players in Lake Forest, Illinois, and of the North Shore Theater in Winnetka, Illinois. Her stories, published by the *Pictorial Review,* were later collected and published in book form as *Prevailing Winds* (1928). B. wrote three plays (two in collaboration with Edward Sheldon, a dramatist and personal friend) and five novels, winning the Pulitzer Prize in 1931 for *Years of Grace* (1930). After the publication of her last novel, *Wisdom's Gate* (1938), B. returned to writing occasional short stories and lecturing.

Prevailing Winds shows evidence of the skills that would bring her critical acclaim, but the narrow focus that would cause her ultimate neglect by most literary critics can also be seen. From her theatrical experience she had learned to define character through conversations. Her careful observations of character, however, were limited to the upper-middle-class society of Chicago in the first third of the 20th c.

Distracted by the element of social history in B.'s fiction, many critics overlooked important underlying themes. Feminism, a major theme which grew out of her education at Bryn Mawr, appeared in early short stories through the portrayals of Martha Cavendish in "The Dinner Party" and of Kate Dalton in "Perpetual Care." Both are women prominent in Chicago society who have chosen marriage and socially conventional lives, but each is confronted with a situation that leads her to question those choices and seek an opportunity to break with convention. Each resolves that the choice has come too late: Martha has learned to live in her thoughts and let the world go as it will; Kate in the end settles for memories to avoid upsetting her children by changing her life.

Most of the women in B.'s novels follow the examples of these two women, but in each succeeding novel they seem less satisfied with the choice. In *Years of Grace*, which traces the life of Jane Ward Carver to the eve of the Great Depression, Jane abandons early adherence to the feminist principles instilled in her at Bryn Mawr and elects to fill the traditional roles of wife and mother. Already before her marriage, she had admitted she lacked the courage of her convictions: "She who thinks and runs away, lives to think another day. . . . I don't act at all. . . . I just drift." When she is offered an opportunity to defy convention and marry Jimmy Trent, she chooses to remain with her responsibilities. Only when her daughter Cicily breaks the pattern by divorcing her husband to marry Albert Lancaster, does Jane wonder if her "struggle to live with dignity and decency and decorum" had been a worthy goal.

Olivia Van Tyne Ottendorf in *Westward Passage* (1931) temporarily accepts her second chance at an artistic life with Nick Allen, but soon returns gratefully to her husband and the limited society she had known. She has been educated only for such a role, and the reader recognizes her, as the critic Lloyd C. Taylor, Jr., points out, as "a victim of an intricately structured social system that securely, if deceptively, deprives the woman of any training that does not contribute to the creation of the lady and the socialite."

B. resolves her interest in feminist themes in her final novel, *Wisdom's Gate*. She returns to the Carver family of *Years of Grace* and chronicles Cicily's life after her marriage to Albert Lancaster. Cicily has broken the pattern of her past, and although she does not achieve greater fulfillment, she gains uncompromising clarity. The topics of divorce and adultery are examined objectively and honestly. While lacking the unity and scope of B.'s earlier novels, *Wisdom's Gate* portrays a marriage based on the honesty of a woman who has the courage of her convictions.

WORKS: *Prevailing Winds* (1928). *Age of Innocence* (1928). *Jenny* (with E. Shelton, 1929). *Dishonored Lady* (with E. Shelton, 1930). *Years of Grace* (1930). *Westward Passage* (1931). *Within This Present* (1933). *Edna His Wife* (1935). *Wisdom's Gate* (1938).

BIBLIOGRAPHY: Barnes, E. W., *The Man Who Lived Twice: The Biography of Edward Sheldon* (1956). Lawrence, M., *The School of Femininity* (1936). Stuckey, W. J., *The Pulitzer Prize Novels: A Critical Backward Look* (1966). Taylor, L. C., Jr., *Margaret Ayer Barnes* (1974). Wagenknecht, E. C., *Chicago* (1964).

Other references: *North American Review* (Jan. 1934).

THELMA J. SHINN

Ida B. Wells Barnett

B. 16 July 1862, Holly Springs, Mississippi; d. 25 March 1931, Chicago, Illinois
Wrote under: Ida B. Wells Barnett, Ida B. Wells, Iola
D. of Jim and Elizabeth Warrenton Wells; m. Ferdinand L. Barnett, 1895

Born six months before the Emancipation Proclamation to parents who were slaves, B. was the oldest of eight children. In 1878, when a yellow-fever epidemic raged, she was left an orphan and became the head of her family. She attended Shaw University and became a teacher in a nearby county school at an early age.

B.'s first public denunciation of discrimination came when she sued the Chesapeake and Ohio Railroad Company over its refusal to allow her to ride in a first-class coach. She won her case in 1884, but her elation was short-lived when the Supreme Court of Tennessee overturned the verdict in 1887.

B. taught for seven years in the public schools in Memphis while also writing articles for local religious weeklies. Eventually she became the editor and part-owner of the *Free Speech and Headlight*. When her articles protesting the conditions in the black schools led to her dismissal from her teaching position, she became a full-time journalist.

On 9 March 1892, three young black men were lynched in Memphis, and B.'s vehement editorial outcry led to the destruction of her offices by the irate white citizens of Memphis. Her absence from the city at the time of the incident probably saved her from bodily harm.

Writing in New York for the *New York Age*, B. continued her polemics against lynchings. Her articles were compiled in pamphlet form and published in October 1892 as *Southern Horrors*.

Finding little support for her antilynching crusade in America, B. journeyed to England in 1893. Here she found the English audience and press more attentive and sympathetic to her pleas.

A Red Record: Tabulated Statistics and Alleged Causes of Lynchings in the United States, 1892–1893–1894, based on figures printed in the *Chicago Tribune*, was published in 1895 when B. arrived back in America. In 1909, she was a featured speaker at the National Negro Conference. From this group emerged the National Association for the Advancement of Colored People, of which she is listed as a founder, though she was never an active member. B. established the Negro Fellowship

League in 1910 to aid needy blacks in finding shelter, food, and employment. She became the first woman probation officer in Chicago, and also organized the Alpha Suffrage Club in 1914 to encourage black women to use their new voting rights.

Intolerant, impudent, impatient, indomitable, and indefatigable are all words that come to mind when reading *Crusade for Justice*, B.'s autobiography, begun in 1928 and edited and published by her daughter, Alfreda M. Duster, in 1970. Intolerant she was—of both whites and blacks who refused to support her crusade, and of those in the ministry, in journalism, and in public office who spoke and acted in a less than honest way. Impudent—for daring to challenge a railroad company in the courts, for daring to rebuke in print black ministers whose private lives were not impeccable, for daring to approach two presidents of the United States, McKinley and Wilson, with the problems of black people.

Crusade for Justice reveals B. as devoted almost equally to her crusade against lynching and to her role as a mother to her children. In her children's early childhood days she withdrew from her most active participation in public affairs, though she had at one time taken her first-born infant with her on a lecture tour so that she might still nurse him. Her interest in children was evidenced by her agitation for a kindergarten for black children similar to Jane Addams's Hull House, which led to a friendship with Miss Addams.

Born a slave, yet an outspoken advocate of human rights, B. has earned her place as one of the foremost early black feminists.

WORKS: *Southern Horrors: Lynch Law in All Its Phases* (1892). *The Reason Why the Colored American Is Not in the World's Columbian Exposition—The Afro-American's Contribution to Columbian Literature* (1893). *A Red Record: Tabulated Statistics and Alleged Causes of Lynchings in the United States, 1892–1893–1894* (1895). *Mob Rule in New Orleans: Robert Charles and His Fight to the Death* (1900). *On Lynchings; Southern Horrors; A Red Record; Mob Rule in New Orleans* (1969). *Crusade for Justice: The Autobiography of Ida B. Wells* (Ed. A. M. Duster, 1970).

Ida B. Wells Barnett's unpublished diary and letters are in the possession of her daughter, Alfreda M. Duster.

BIBLIOGRAPHY: Aptheker, H., ed., *A Documentary History of the Negro People in the United States* (1969). Bontemps, A., and J. Conroy, *They Seek a City* (1945). Dann, M. E., ed., *The Black Press, 1827–1890: The Quest for National Identity* (1971). Lerner, G., ed., *Black Women in White America: A Documentary History* (1972). Loewenberg, B. J., and R. Bogin, eds., *Black Women in Nineteenth-Century American Life: Their Words, Their Thoughts, Their Feelings* (1976).

MARILYN LAMPING

Mary Ritter Beard

B. 5 Aug. 1876, Indianapolis, Indiana; d. 14 Aug. 1958, Phoenix, Arizona
D. of Eli Foster and Marassa Lockwood Ritter; m. Charles Austin Beard, 1900

Educated at De Pauw University, then a rather conservative Methodist institution, B. received her Ph.D. in 1897. She spent her early married years in England in the circle around Ruskin Hall, a center for new economic thought, then moved to New York City and studied at Columbia University, where her husband, the most vital intellectual influence in her life, was to join the faculty.

B.'s earliest books, *American Citizenship* (1914, in collaboration with her husband), *Woman's Work in Municipalities* (1915), and *A Short History of the American Labor Movement* (1920), reflect her lifelong interests: labor, sociology, and women's studies.

The books she wrote with her husband in the 1920s and 1930s, both the school texts and the enormously successful four-volume *The Rise of American Civilization* (1927–1942), were highly influential. The first two volumes of *The Rise of American Civilization* were the product of two decades of Progressive intellectual attack on the formalism of 19th-c. American historical writing, which tended to see American institutions in an ideal, abstract way. The particular economic interpretation of the Revolution which pitted agrarian democrats against capitalist aristocrats, and the view of the Civil War as a second revolution, were widely accepted until after World War II, when Charles A. Beard came under attack for viewing earlier American history from the perspective of the Progressive fight for reform against an entrenched capitalism. Indeed, the Beards modified their economic determinism in the 1940s and gave greater play to the force of ideas and ideals than they had before. But their most significant contribution was their salutory reminder that ideals do not exist outside of social contexts.

While the great collaborative effort with her husband has now largely entered the realm of intellectual history, B.'s pioneering work in women's studies, notably in *On Understanding Women* (1931) and *Woman as Force in History* (1946), remains generative today. Encouraged by the nascent field of anthropology, which was producing work showing woman as the originator of agriculture and the domestic arts, B. studied social realities as disparate as woman's legal status in England and woman's contribution to Pythagorean philosophy in ancient Greece, in order to discover her true status and achievement. Such a vision was obscured, she argued, not only by male bias and social mythology, but by feminists who themselves promulgated a false view of women as a subject sex. The fullest and most important treatment of these views appears in *Woman as Force in History*.

The questions she raises there remain with us, but her answers are sometimes problematic. While her argument against the idea of "equality" as the touchstone for woman's relation to man points out the difficulties it engenders, the argument remains inconclusive. Nor does the book resolve a contradiction in her view of women's contribution. While B. sometimes seems to be saying that women are a peculiarly civilizing force, at other times she seems to be saying only that they have been more of a force both for good and for bad than we have realized. Still, the book leaves us two important lines of thought: one is the definition of woman's just role. B. believed that the early imitation of men by feminists was in part a function of the individualism of 19th-c. America, and that as society moved toward more collectivist forms, alternatives for women would emerge. The other line of thought is that history is not simply the account of the politician, the banker, and the general. Until history describes events on the level of domestic economy and family relationship as well, woman's true force, B. believes, will not be understood, nor will the true causes and effects of history.

WORKS: *American Citizenship* (with C. A. Beard, 1914). *Woman's Work in Municipalities* (1915). *A Short History of the American Labor Movement* (1920). *A History of the United States* (with C. A. Beard, 1921). *The Rise of American Civilization* (Vols. 1 and 2, with C. A. Beard, 1927). *The American Labor Movement: A Short History* (1931). *On Understanding Women* (1931). *America Through Women's Eyes* (ed. by Beard, 1933). *A Changing Political Economy As It Affects Women* (1934). *Laughing Their Way* (ed. by Beard with M. B. Bruere, 1934). *The Making of American Civilization* (with C. A. Beard, 1937). *America in Mid Passage* (Vol. 3, *The Rise of American Civilization*, with C. A. Beard, 1939). *The American Spirit: A Study of the Idea of Civilization in the United States* (Vol. 4, *The Rise of American Civilization*, with C. A. Beard, 1942). *A Basic History of the United States* (with C. A. Beard, 1944). *Woman as Force in History: A Study in Traditions and Realities* (1946). *The Force of Women in Japanese History* (1953). *The Making of Charles A. Beard* (1955).

BIBLIOGRAPHY: Carroll, B. A., *Liberating Women's History: Theoretical and Critical Essays* (1976). Hofstadter, R., *The Progressive Historians* (1968).
Other references: *NewR* (1946). *NYT* (27 Dec. 1931). *PolSciQ* (Sept. 1927).

LOIS HUGHSON

Catharine Esther Beecher

B. 6 Sept. 1800, East Hampton, New York; d. 12 May 1878, Elvira, New York
D. of Lyman and Roxanne Foote Beecher

Sister of Harriet Beecher Stowe, B. was an educator and writer who attempted to expand the domestic power of women. Following the death of her mother, B., age sixteen and the eldest of thirteen children, assumed the family and household responsibilities.

After the death of her fiancé, Alexander Metcalf Fisher, B. established the Hartford Female Seminary in May 1823 with the money inherited from him. She also organized the Western Female Institute in Cincinnati (1832–1837) and the Ladies' Society for Promoting Education in the West, and helped to establish three female colleges (in Burlington, Iowa, in Quincy, Illinois, and in Milwaukee, Wisconsin).

Although B. left the Hartford Female Seminary in 1831, it was considered one of the most significant advances made in early-19th-c. education for women. It marked B.'s first attempt to redefine a new relationship with American culture for herself and for other women.

The author of over thirty books, B. expanded the sentimental view of women as saintly and moral creatures, complements of their immoral and competitive mates. She maintained that the American woman had difficult and peculiar duties which derived mainly from the crudeness and disorder of an expanding nation. She asserted in *Letters to the People on Health and Happiness* (1855) that "it is obvious that Providence designed that the chief responsibility of *sustaining the family state*, in all its sacred and varied relations and duties should rest mainly on the female sex."

B.'s most popular volumes were *A Treatise on Domestic Economy* (1841) and *Domestic Receipts* (1846), written for the use of young wives. *The American Woman's Home* (1869), written with her sister, provides a wide range of advice for home management.

In *The Elements of Mental and Moral Philosophy* (1831), B. asserted that woman was the moral guardian of her culture. Common sense must be used to determine morality, and personal conscience must dominate over doctrine. This position moved theology to social grounds and placed B. in direct conflict with her father, the Reverend Lyman Beecher, a Calvinist.

The major characteristic of B.'s Christianity, however, was passivity, not social activity. She spoke against active abolitionism, asserting in *An Essay on Slavery* (1837) that "Christianity is a system of *persuasion*, tending, by kind and gentle influence, to make men *willing* to leave their sins." B. maintained that women had a proper place, a proper sphere, and that place was out of politics and within the home, influencing men through quiet, proper petition and through the education of their children.

As might be expected, B. was an avid opponent of woman's suffrage, attempting instead to expand the woman's base of power in the home. Although she advocated democracy, she did not feel that it led to women's active participation in politics and to furthering social change. Instead she asserted that there was a social order based on age, health, and the most important distinction, gender.

B. is a transitional figure whose writings influenced women to move from a state of subordination to one in which they attempted to secure a greater role in their changing, shifting society. She was confronted by a competitive society in which men aggressively sought wealth and position, and she perceived this activity as unworthy of women. Women, unlike men, could effect change only by influence and passivity. Aggression and force were male prerogatives.

B.'s solution was to create a quiet eye of the storm and to call it the American Home. There women could rule supreme and men could return for moral refreshment and rest. In this quiet haven, the American Home, B. placed her sentimentalized version of the American woman. She herself never married.

WORKS: *Suggestions Respecting Improvements in Education* (1829). *The Elements of Mental and Moral Philosophy* (1831). *Arithmetic Simplified* (1832). *Primary Geography* (1833). *The Lyceum Arithmetic* (1835). *An Essay on the Education of Female Teachers* (1835). *Lectures on the Difficulty of Religion* (1836). *An Essay on Slavery* (1837). *The Moral Instructor* (1838). *A Treatise on Domestic Economy* (1841). *Letters to Persons Who Are Engaged in Domestic Service* (1842). *The Duty of American Women to Their Country* (1845). *Domestic Receipts* (1846). *Truths Stranger Than Fiction* (1850). *The True Remedy for the Wrongs of Women* (1852). *Letters to the People on Health and Happiness* (1855). *Physiology and Calisthenics* (1856). *Common Sense Applied to Religion* (1857). *Calisthenic Exercises* (1860). *An Appeal to the People* (1860). *Religious Training of Children in the School* (1864). *The American Woman's Home* (with H. B. Stowe; 1869). *Principles of Domestic Science* (with H. B. Stowe; 1870). *Woman Suffrage and Woman's Profession* (1871). *Work for All, and Other Tales* (1871). *Woman's Profession as Mother and Educator* (1872). *Miss B.'s Housekeeper and Healthkeeper* (1873). *The New Housekeeper's Manual* (1873). *Educational Reminiscences and Suggestions* (1874).

BIBLIOGRAPHY: Cross, B. M., *The Educated Woman in America* (1965). Douglas, A., *The Feminization of American Culture* (1977). Harveson, E. M., *Catharine Esther Beecher* (1932). Sklar, K. K., *Catharine Beecher: A Study in American Domesticity* (1973). Woody, T., *A History of Women's Education in the United States* (1966).

Other references: *AQ* 18 (Summer 1966). *Civil War History* 17 (June 1971).

JULIANN E. FLEENOR

Ruth Fulton Benedict

B. 5 June 1887, New York City; d. 17 Sept. 1948, New York City
Wrote under: Ruth Benedict, Anne Singleton
D. of Frederick Samuel and Beatrice Joanna Shattuck Fulton; m. Stanley
Rossiter Benedict, 1914

B.'s father, a surgeon and cancer researcher, died before she was two, leaving her mother to bring up B. and her younger sister on their maternal grandparents' farm in central New York. An attack of measles when she was a child left B. partially deaf, an infirmity from which she suffered personally and professionally throughout her life.

An outstanding student, B. won a scholarship to Vassar College, where she graduated Phi Beta Kappa in 1909. She became disillusioned with her marriage early, especially when the longed-for children never came. When her desire for a job of her own met with her husband's discouragement, she slowly withdrew from him. In 1919, B. enrolled in the New School for Social Research, where she studied anthropology under Elsie Clews Parsons and Alexander Goldenweiser. From there she went to Columbia and received her doctorate under Franz Boas in 1923. She started teaching there that year. Her dissertation, *The Concept of the Guardian Spirit in North America*, about American Indian religion, was published in 1923. Her early fieldwork was done among several American Indian tribes.

Throughout these early years of anthropological apprenticeship, B. remained a sensitive and solitary person, expressing her inner battles with loneliness and the painful relationship with her husband in verse, some of which she published in *Poetry* and *Nation* under the pseudonym of Anne Singleton. In 1930, she and Stanley separated, and at that time

Boas appointed her assistant professor at Columbia. Soon thereafter, her depressions lifted, the need for Anne Singleton faded, and slowly the separate lives she led became fused together in her work.

In 1934, *Patterns of Culture,* her most famous book, was published. It has since been translated into fourteen languages and is still regarded as one of the best introductions to anthropology. Combining problems of psychology and the individual with those of anthropology and culture, she evolved a theory which stated that culture was not only the condition within which personality developed, but was itself a "personality writ large." All culture, she postulated, is structured into patterns which impose a harmony upon the disparate components of life; for any one culture there is a dominant pattern, an overriding cultural temperament.

During the war years, B. became more interested in humanism and published several books about racism.

From 1943 to 1945, B. worked in Washington in the Office of War Information, concentrating on Rumania, Thailand, and Japan. This led to her pioneering work with literate informants from urban centers and a new shift in anthropology to the analysis of complex modern societies. B.'s most gracefully and cogently written book is *The Chrysanthemum and the Sword* (1946). Using an intensive analysis of interviews and literary material, it concerns itself with themes in Japanese culture, stressing primarily those that have to do with reciprocal relations between people. She deals with the hierarchical organization of Japanese life, portrays the structure of obligations to emperor, family, and self, and examines the strong sense of shame so dominant in the culture. The underlying humanist message of the book is that the only way Japan could be reintegrated into the world is by using the favorable Japanese patterns of culture as the building blocks rather than by imposing European values from without. The book had a tremendous impact in the U.S. In 1947, following its great success, the Office of Naval Research gave Columbia University an extensive grant to establish under B.'s direction a program of "Research in Contemporary Cultures," the most ambitious program of anthropological research the U.S. had yet seen.

After Boas's death in 1942, B. was the leading American anthropologist as well as the first American woman to become a prominent social scientist and leader in her profession. Her great contribution was her integration of the idea of patterns, which she slowly pieced together in her own life and applied to her work. In so doing, she gave her profession a theoretical orientation at a time when science for the first time was trying to deal with total cultures. B.'s critics accuse her of never having written a full ethnography and of having done fieldwork either among people living in disintegrating cultures or among literate informants from cultures far away. Some have criticized her patterns as overly simplistic. However, her deafness, shyness, and childhood traumas that cut her personal life off from others were probably not only responsible for her anthropological weaknesses, but are possibly what gave her both the ability to view cultures at a distance and the tolerance for deviance that led to her very great contributions.

WORKS: *The Concept of the Guardian Spirit in North America* (1923). *Tales of the Cochiti Indians* (1931). *Patterns of Culture* (1934). *Zuni Mythology* (2 vols., 1935). *Race: Science and Politics* (1940). *The Races of Mankind* (with G. Weltfish, 1943). *The Chrysanthemum and the Sword: Patterns of Japanese Culture* (1946). *Rumanian Culture and Behavior* (1946). *Thai Culture and Behavior* (1946). *An Anthropologist at Work: Writings of Ruth Benedict* (Ed. M. Mead, 1959).

BIBLIOGRAPHY: Mead, M., ed., *An Anthropologist at Work* (1949). Mead, M., *Ruth Benedict* (1974).
    For articles in reference works, see: *NAW* (article by D. Fleming). *NCAB*.
    Other references: *AA* (51, 1949; 59, 1957). *Minzokugaku Kenkyu* 14 (Japanese Journal of Ethnology, 1949). *Ruth Fulton Benedict: A Memorial* (Viking Fund, 1949). *UTQ* 18 (1949).

MIRIAM KAHN

Sally Benson

B. 3 Sept. 1900, St. Louis, Missouri; d. 21 July 1972, Woodland Hills, California
D. of Alonzo Redway and Anna Prophater Smith; m. Reynolds Benson, 1919

After B.'s family moved to New York City, she attended the Horace Mann School, started working at seventeen, married at nineteen, had a daughter, and later divorced her husband. She wrote newspaper interviews and movie reviews and in 1929 contributed the first of her 108 stories to *The New Yorker*. B. also edited a volume of myths and wrote mystery reviews for *The New Yorker* and more than twenty screenplays.

People Are Fascinating (1936) includes almost all the stories B. had published in *The New Yorker* and four from the *American Mercury*.

"The Overcoat" and "Suite 2049" were O. Henry prize stories for 1935 and 1936. The title story offers an ironic perspective on the volume: a woman dramatist reads drama into mundane lives. B. reveals the mediocrity of self-deluded and self-indulgent characters but is compassionate about their attempts to deal with their own mediocrity, with poverty and aging, with meaningless lives.

In *Emily* (1938), B. writes somewhat longer stories that allow for character development and elicit compassion for those caught in dilemmas, particularly those of growing up. "Professional Housewife" scathingly reveals the emptiness of that role, as well as that of a door-to-door salesman. When scattered in *The New Yorker* these stories seem witty; in this collection they seem depressing.

Despite libraries' classification, *Junior Miss* (1941) is not a children's book. Each story humorously shows a young girl's attempt to learn about herself and the world; collectively, the stories reveal the human condition. B.'s light touch does not hide the seriousness of Judy's problems and the inadequacies of most adult strategies for coping with them. The dramatization by Jerome Chodorov and Joseph Fields (1942) achieved success by hardening the delicacy gained by B.'s stream-of-consciousness technique; it has the "rounded ends" and "climaxes" B. disliked, and creates a popular stereotype. Readers of the stories will perceive *Junior Miss* as a rare account of female rites of passage.

Meet Me in St. Louis (1942) is a collection of twelve stories, dealing with family life, based on B.'s sister's diary of their family at the time of the World's Fair in St. Louis at the turn of the century. It was made into a popular movie starring Judy Garland.

B.'s stories are "slices of life" in which characters, through stream-of-consciousness or dialogue, reveal foolish pretenses; swift narration and irony preclude sentimentality but sometimes result in cruel revelations. Cumulatively her women are stereotypes of frivolous, stupid, and wasteful upper-middle-class New Yorkers. But B. also described the male self-deception and use of power that compel women to utilize manipulative strategies. Her portraits of young girls reveal the anguish of their socialization.

WORKS: *People Are Fascinating* (1936). *Emily* (1938). *Stories of the Gods and Heroes* (1940). *Junior Miss* (1941). *Meet Me in St. Louis* (1942). *Women and Children FIRST* (1943).

BIBLIOGRAPHY: *Writers and Writing* (22 July 1972). *NYT* (22 July 1972).

MARY ANNE FERGUSON

Doris Betts

B. 4 June 1932, Statesville, North Carolina
D. of William Elmore and Mary Ellen Freeze Waugh; m. Lowry Matthews
  Betts, 1952

Since winning a *Mademoiselle* award in 1953, B. has published seven volumes of fiction. She has been a journalist, a college teacher (at the University of North Carolina, Chapel Hill, and elsewhere), and an active citizen of her town and state (Sanford, North Carolina) on whose history two of her novels focus. She has won several awards and a Guggenheim Fellowship (1958–59).

The Gentle Insurrection, and Other Stories (1954), though published when the author was twenty-two, shows mature understanding of human powers and limitations. In the title story, the daughter of a sharecropper, out of both fear and family loyalty, rejects her chance to escape with a lover; other stories show characters coping with handicaps, poverty, aging, and racial discrimination. There is no sentimentality; a chain-gang, murder, maternal rejection, patriarchal ruthlessness, bitter sexual frustration are dispassionately presented. B.'s characteristic use of interior monologue for ironic self-revelation, her concern for morality and religion, her use of animal symbols, and her humor are all already apparent.

In *The Astronomer, and Other Stories* (1966), the title story is a novella whose central character, a working-class widower, tries to fill his life by pursuing astronomy but finds he cannot fill the emptiness without involvement with other people. B.'s increased control of her medium is evident in the economy with which several lives are simultaneously revealed. In the other stories in this collection, B. succinctly portrays people who deal with life the best they can but not always effectively.

Though excellent in characterization, B.'s first three novels lack the deftness and sure ironic voice of the short stories. *Tall Houses in Winter* (1957), B.'s first novel, is overplotted and melodramatic, and only somewhat redeemed by convincing character portrayal. *The Scarlet Thread* (1964), a historical novel, is noteworthy primarily for its vivid scenes and biblical symbolism. *The River to Pickle Beach* (1972) skillfully uses symbols of nature to make this novel a powerful affirmation of life.

With *Beasts of the Southern Wild, and Other Stories* (1973) and

Heading West (1981), B. moves from the category of Southern regionalist into the mainstream of American literature. An assured ironic voice convincingly tells fantastic, comic adventures as characters leave home on journies of self-discovery and female heroes become paradigms of modern psychological and religious search for ultimate meanings.

B.'s characters, often grotesque, gain dignity from confronting loneliness, family and racial tensions, aging, and death. She achieves rare authenticity about women through detailing graphically the birth process, the emotional effects of abortion, hysterectomy, and childlessness. B.'s discussions of the aesthetics of writing reflect her award-winning teaching.

WORKS: *The Gentle Insurrection, and Other Stories* (1954). *Tall Houses in Winter* (1957). *The Scarlet Thread* (1964). *The Astronomer, and Other Stories* (1966). *The River to Pickle Beach* (1972). *Beasts of the Southern Wild, and Other Stories* (1966). *Heading West* (1981).

BIBLIOGRAPHY: Wolf, G., in *Kite-flying and Other Irrational Acts: Conversations with Twelve Southern Writers*, Ed. J. Carr (1972).
Other references: Chapel Hill *Weekly* (3 May 1972). *Red Clay Reader* (1970). *The Sanford* (5 Dec. 1974).

MARY ANNE FERGUSON

Elizabeth Bishop

B. 8 Feb. 1911, Worcester, Massachusetts; d. 6 Oct. 1979, Boston, Massachusetts
D. of William Thomas and Gertrude Bulmer Bishop

When B. was eight-months old, her father died suddenly, and her mother subsequently suffered a nervous collapse from which she never recovered. B. was taken first to live with her maternal grandparents in Nova Scotia, where her grandfather owned a tannery and farmed, and at age six to live with her paternal grandparents in Worcester, Massachusetts, so that she could be educated in the U.S.

At Vassar College, she and several other young women, among them Mary McCarthy, began a magazine, the *Conspirito*, which rivaled the more traditional *Vassar Review*. After the two publications were amalgamated, however, B. was a regular contributor to the review. The best of her pieces written during these years was a short story, "In Prison," which appeared in the *Partisan Review* in 1938. The year before she graduated (1934), B. met Marianne Moore, who encouraged her to write rather than attend medical school, as she had intended. Moore became a lifelong friend.

B.'s adult life was nearly nomadic, and travel became a central metaphor in her work. She lived and traveled in England, Europe, North Africa, and South America. She lived in Brazil for fifteen years.

B.'s first book of poetry, *North and South* (1946), includes the well-known poems "Florida," "The Map," "The Fish," "The Man-Moth," "The Unbeliever," and "A Miracle for Breakfast." The book was widely acclaimed by critics, who especially praised B.'s descriptive acumen, her reticence, and her subtle ability to metamorphose her encounters with simple objects or scenes into extraordinarily profound imaginative experiences.

North and South; A Cold Spring (1955) won the Pulitzer Prize for poetry in 1956. It was not as widely acclaimed as her first, but it contains several fine new poems. Among them are "Cape Breton," "Over 2000 Illustrations and a Complete Concordance," and "The Bight." In "At the Fishhouses," her characteristic process of "looking once more" and her tendency toward total immersion enable her to reach a final understanding of the meaning of the primordial element—the sea—which supports the fishhouses. The epistemology that she reveals in the last six lines in this poem (and in "Cape Breton," as well) is intriguing. For B. the nature of reality is always to be imagined, it can never be known. Nor would an encounter with the "real," were it possible, necessarily be a desirable experience.

Many critics consider *Questions of Travel* (1965) B.'s best book. It contains many poems, such as "Arrival at Santos," "Manuelzinho," "Brazil, January 1, 1502," "The Burglar of Babylon," and the title poem, about Brazilian people and B.'s experiences in Brazil. In "Questions of Travel," she finds her initial experience of the interior of Brazil so demanding that she begins to wonder if she should ever have come to this place, or if it would not have been better merely to stay at home where the scenery is familiar, comfortable, and safe. By the end of the poem, however, B. appears to discover her own resolution to her questions. She must witness all of the strangeness that she can. Indeed, the corpus of B.'s work seems to imply that if one is to be a perceptive tourist, a sensitive person, or an imaginative artist, one must be constantly vulnerable to every new and strange horizon to which one is exposed.

The Complete Poems (published in 1969) won the National Book Award that year. In 1976, Bishop was awarded the Neustadt International

Prize for Literature from *World Literature Today*.

Since her first book, B. has been hailed as a virtuoso of descriptive poetry, one who has learned from Marianne Moore and from the imagists. Yet her work differs significantly from those who may have influenced her. For B. an image, a phenomenon, is never merely "remarkable." She does not merely record or describe; she is not simply a descriptive poet. Many critics have neglected to realize that for B., re-presentation is a process by which the artist may discover subjectively. B. is mimetic in the sense of giving accurate perceptions of particular realities. She appears to know, however, that to represent is never simply to copy. Any abstract knowledge for B. comes by way of some concrete acknowledgment of the given world. Yet she combines acknowledgment with imaginative leaps, and the knowledge which results changes constantly. Everything in B.'s world is always open to question, revision, and reinterpretation.

WORKS: *North and South* (1946). *North and South; A Cold Spring* (1955). *The Diary of Helen Morley* (translated by Bishop, 1957). *Brazil* (*Life* World Library Series, 1962). *Questions of Travel* (1965). *The Burglar of Babylon* (1968). *The Complete Poems* (1969). *An Anthology of Twentieth-Century Brazilian Poetry* (edited and translated by Bishop, with E. Brasil, 1972). *Geography III* (1976).

BIBLIOGRAPHY: Jarrell, R., *Poetry and the Age* (1972). Jarrell, R., *Third Book of Criticism* (1963). Kalstone, D., *Five Temperaments* (1977). Moore, M., "Archaically New," *Trial Balances* (1935); and "Senhora Helena," *A Marianne Moore Reader* (1961).

Other references: *Nation* (28 Sept. 1946). *NewR* (5 Feb. 1977). *NYTBR* (1 June 1969). *Ploughshares* (2, 1975; 3, 1976). *PR* (Spring 1970). *Salmagundi* (Summer–Fall 1974). *SoR* (Autumn 1977). *SR* (Summer 1947). *WLT* (Winter 1977).

SYBIL ESTESS

Lillie Devereux Blake

B. 12 Aug. 1833, Raleigh, North Carolina; d. 30 Dec. 1913, Englewood,
New Jersey
Wrote under: Lillie Devereux Blake, Lillie Devereux Umsted
D. of George and Sarah Johnson Devereux; m. Frank Umsted, 1855;
m. Grenfill Blake, 1866

B. was born into a distinguished southern family. When her father died in 1837, her mother moved to New Haven, Connecticut, where B. attended a girls' school and received private tutoring in the Yale undergraduate course. Mother and daughter were very close and remained so throughout their lives.

When B. "came out" at age seventeen, she became renowned for her beauty and led a strenuous social life. In her writings she often refers to this period of her life, noting that she was taught to regard social success as the only worthwhile goal for a woman. "I was always a belle, flattered and fêted. I only wonder that I was not entirely ruined by an ordeal that would be pretty certain to turn the head of a fairly well-balanced man." She portrays in her fiction, which includes several novels and novellas and hundreds of short stories, many young women enfeebled by flattery, enforced idleness, and what she calls "false education."

In 1869, B. became involved in the women's rights movement, to which she devoted the rest of her life and most of her subsequent writings. From 1879 to 1890 she was president of the New York State Woman Suffrage Association and from 1886 to 1900 president of the New York City Woman Suffrage League. She was an excellent speaker, and her writings on women's rights are remarkable for their wit and humor; they are often in the form of satire or parable.

B. ran for president of the National American Woman Suffrage Association (NAWSA) in 1900, but was forced to withdraw in favor of Susan B. Anthony's choice, Carrie Chapman Catt. B.'s philosophy and approach differed from Anthony's in several respects. She was often true to her aristocratic background, expressing concern that suffrage workers be well-dressed, well-behaved "ladies," and she inaugurated such events as the Pilgrim Mothers' Dinners, held annually at the Waldorf-Astoria. More importantly, she believed that suffrage was only one means of improving women's status. As chair of NAWSA's Committee on Legislative Advice, she advocated campaigning to secure legislation favorable to women and agitating for the appointment of women to new positions (e.g., school trustees, factory inspectors, physicians in mental hospitals, and police matrons). She was instrumental in achieving many of these gains in New York State.

Although she avoids the worst excesses of the sentimental fiction of the times, B. writes much to the general pattern. Spirited young women develop fatal fascinations for evil Lovelace types in her stories and may or may not be saved by their honorable suitors; young lovers are separated, reunited, and then part forever when they discover they are siblings.

In B.'s early writings, characters who espouse feminist sentiments are punished. For instance, in *Southwold* (1859), the protagonist, when rejected by a man she loves, becomes embittered and "bold and even unfeminine" in her opinions. She shocks other characters by not taking every word of the Bible literally and by claiming that Christianity has harmed women's status. The book ends with her suicide. Interestingly enough, B. later was to espouse the opinions her protagonist had expressed. "Dogmatic theology, founded on masculine interpretation of the Bible," was the subject of attack in her *Woman's Place To-Day* (1883), a series of lectures delivered in response to a misogynist theologian. B. was also one of the contributors to Elizabeth Cady Stanton's controversial *Woman's Bible* (1895).

B.'s last novel, *Fettered for Life; or, Lord and Master* (1874), is a feminist work in which wife abuse, unjust marriage laws, discrimination in employment, and lack of educational opportunities for women are illustrated and discussed by the characters. Female friendships are strong in the novel, and the "hero," a successful reporter who frequently rescues the female characters, turns out to be a woman in disguise. When she adopted male attire, she found that "my limbs were free; I could move untrammelled, and my actions were free; I could go about unquestioned. No man insulted me, and when I asked for work, I was not offered outrage."

WORKS: *Southwold* (1859). *Rockford; or, Sunshine and Storm* (1863). *Forced Vows; or, A Revengeful Woman's Fate* (1870). *Fettered for Life; or, Lord and Master* (1874). *Woman's Place To-Day* (1883). *A Daring Experiment and Other Stories* (1892).

BIBLIOGRAPHY: Blake, K. D., and M. L. Wallace, *Champion of Women: The Life of Lillie Devereux Blake* (1943).
For articles in reference works, see *HWS. NAW* (article by W. R. Taylor).

BARBARA A. WHITE

Amelia Jenks Bloomer

B. 27 May 1818, Homer, New York; d. 30 Dec. 1894, Council Bluffs, Iowa
D. of Ananias and Lucy Webb Jenks; m. Dexter C. Bloomer, 1840

B.'s parents were natives of Rhode Island. She received only a few years' schooling at the district school in Courtland County, New York, but was evidently well enough educated to teach in another school when she was seventeen years old.

Her husband, a lawyer and editor of the *Seneca County Courier*, encouraged her to contribute articles on social, political, and moral subjects to his paper. She also began to take an active part in the temperance movement, writing frequently for the *Water Bucket*, an organ of the temperance society of Seneca Falls, New York. She attended the first meeting on women's rights held in Seneca Falls in 1848 but did not actively participate. In 1849 she began the publication of a periodical called the *Lily*, writing on such subjects as temperance, education, unjust marriage laws, and woman suffrage. By 1853, the *Lily* had a circulation of four thousand subscribers. It was the first newspaper owned, edited, and controlled by a woman and devoted solely to the interests of women.

Through the *Lily* B. met Elizabeth Cady Stanton and Susan B. Anthony. She also met Elizabeth Smith Miller, a cousin of Mrs. Stanton, who was the first to wear the short skirt and full Turkish trousers that came to be known as "bloomers." Several of the women adopted the costume, finding it more comfortable, more sanitary, and better adapted to the active life they were leading than the corsets and voluminous skirts that were the fashion. They ceased wearing the costume only when they discovered that their attire was distracting from the message of women's rights.

In 1852 B. began lecturing on temperance and women's rights, never speaking extemporaneously but always carefully writing out and delivering her speeches from manuscript. The following year her husband purchased an interest in the *Western Home Visitor* and the Bloomers moved to Mount Vernon, Ohio. She continued publishing the *Lily*, served as assistant editor of the *Western Home Visitor*, a literary weekly with a fairly large circulation, and lectured occasionally. Early in 1855, when her husband decided to relocate in Council Bluffs, Iowa, it was necessary to cease publication of the *Lily*, but she did not discontinue writing and speaking on behalf of temperance and women's rights. She was instrumental in organizing the Iowa Woman's State Suffrage Society and worked zealously for her church and community.

As a writer B. produced prose that was graceful, clear, and often infused with passion. Her early writings were devoted to temperance, imploring women to unite in that cause. Warning all those who supported it not to relax their vigilance, she wrote in one early essay: "Those who feel most secure will find to their dismay that the viper has only been crushed for a time, and will rise again upon his victim with a firmer and more deadly grasp than before." In starting her journal she made it clear in her first editorial that "it is woman that speaks through the *Lily*. . . . Like the beautiful flower from which it derives its name, we shall strive to make the *Lily* the emblem of 'sweetness and purity'; and may heaven smile upon our attempt to advocate the great cause of Temperance reform!"

Always a woman of strong opinions on almost every subject, she introduced herself to the readers of the *Western Home Visitor* by saying: "What I have been in the past, I expect to be in the future,—an uncompromising opponent of wrong and oppression in every form, and a sustainer of the right and the true, with whatever it may be connected." The causes B. advocated included employment and education for women. The failure to educate women for meaningful occupations she considered a serious wrong and insisted that "parents do a great injustice to their daughters when they doom them to a life of idleness or, what is worse, to a life of frivolity and fashionable dissipation."

B.'s lecture on suffrage, written originally in 1852 and delivered and revised many times through the years, is perhaps one of the finest examples of the clear, forceful, and logical arguments presented in that cause. She ends this stirring speech by calling woman's admission to the ballot box "the crowning right to which she is justly entitled" and states that "when woman shall be thus recognized as an equal partner with man in the universe of God—equal in rights and duties—then will she for the first time, in truth, become what her Creator designed her to be, a helpmeet for man. With her mind and body fully developed, imbued with a full sense of her responsibilities, and living in the conscientious discharge of each and all of them, she will be fitted to share with her brother in all of the duties of life; to aid and counsel him in his hours of trial; and to rejoice with him in the triumph of every good word and work."

It is indeed unfortunate that B.'s skill as a writer is overshadowed by the association of her name with a short-lived and ridiculed experiment in female attire.

WORKS: *Life and Writings of Amelia Bloomer* (Ed. D. C. Bloomer, 1895).

BIBLIOGRAPHY: For articles in reference works, see: *Appleton's Cyclopedia of American Biography*, Eds. J. G. Wilson and J. Fiske (1888). *AW. DAB.*

ELAINE K. GINSBERG

Louise Bogan

B. 11 Aug. 1897, Livermore Falls, Maine; d. 4 Feb. 1970, New York City
D. of Daniel Joseph and Mary Helen Shields Bogan; m. Curt Alexander, 1916;
m. Raymond Holden, 1925

B. was educated at Mount St. Mary's Academy, Manchester, New Hampshire, the Boston Girls' Latin School, and for a year at Boston University. Her first husband, an army officer, died in 1920, shortly after the birth of their daughter, B.'s only child. Her second husband was a poet and, from 1929 to 1932, managing editor of *The New Yorker*; the couple was divorced in 1937. For most of B.'s adult life her home was New York City.

Reluctant to offer details about her personal life, B. valued privacy and close friendships. Published letters to Edmund Wilson, Rolfe Humphries, Morton Zabel, Theodore Roethke, May Sarton, and others reveal a warm, witty, spontaneous side of B., not often evident in her poetry. They also refer to recoveries from nervous breakdowns in 1931 and 1933, as well as to the severe difficulties she experienced in the mid-1930s supporting herself by writing.

Besides poetry, B. wrote some fiction and collaborated in translations from German and French. Two volumes of her criticism consist mainly of articles and reviews from *Nation*, *Poetry*, *Scribner's*, *Atlantic Monthly*, and *The New Yorker*, for which she was a regular reviewer of poetry from March 1931 to December 1968.

While B. advocated primarily formal poetry—in Eliot's words, "verse as speech" and "verse as song"—her critical judgment was far from orthodox. She opposed women's attempts to imitate "a man's rougher conduct" in life and art, observing that there were no authentic women Surrealists, since Surrealism's "frequent harsh eroticism, its shock tactics, and its coarse way with language, comes hard to women writers, whose basic creative impulses usually involve tenderness and affection." The younger women poets she praised were, in following Marianne Moore, "close but detached observers of the facts of nature," able to "display a woman's talent for dealing intensely and imaginatively with the concrete."

B. received many awards for her poetry, among them the Bollinger Prize. The qualities most frequently cited in her poetry are those her friend Leonie Adams notes in a 1954 review of the *Collected Poems*: firmness diction and tone, concision of phrase, and concentrated singleness of effect. Allen Tate, Ford Madox Ford, and Theodore Roethke compared her lyrics to those of the Elizabethan metaphysical mode. Abjuring free verse and experimental forms, B. worked in consciously controlled lyric form with a restraint and precision which contained passionate feeling. "Minor art," she wrote, "needs to be hard, condensed and durable." A few critics of her work have found that control scrupulous to the point of limitation and perhaps the result of unwillingness to reveal herself entirely. There is a clear distancing of poet from subject in the early works of *Dark Summer* (1929); and in all but a few poems B. objectifies responses to experience and ideas through the use of third person or of a persona.

B.'s greatest skill lies in metric variation and in rendering descriptions in taut language whose sound values are brilliant yet seemingly effortless as in "Night," "Song for the Last Act," "Animal, Vegetable, and Mineral," "Roman Fountain," "After the Persian." The subject matter of B.'s poetry includes love, loss, grief, mutability, the struggle of the free mind, marriage, and dream. There is no mention of the city or society; settings and imagery are drawn from nature—the country or sea, seasons and storms.

There is also a recurrent interest in women: struggling to maintain a free mind and independent being ("Sonnet," "The Romantic," "For a Marriage," "Betrothed"); failing to imagine and risk ("Women"); breaking into fury and madness ("The Sleeping Fury," "Evening in the Sanitarium"); experiencing love and surviving its endings ("Men Loved Wholly Beyond Wisdom," "Fifteenth Farewell," "My Voice Not being Proud," "Portrait"). Adrienne Rich has justly called attention to "the sense of mask, of code, of body-mind division, of the 'sleeping fury' beneath the praised, severe, lyrical mode."

WORKS: *Body of this Death* (1923). *Dark Summer* (1929). *The Sleeping Fury* (1937). *Poems and New Poems* (1941). *Achievement in American Poetry, 1900–1950* (1951). *Collected Poems, 1923–1952* (1954). *Selected Criticism* (1955). *The Glass Bees* by Ernst Juenger (translated by Bogan, 1961).

Elective Affinities by Goethe (translated by Bogan, 1963). *The Journal of Jules Renard* (translated by Bogan, with E. Roget, 1964). *The Golden Journey: Poems for Young People* (edited by Bogan, with W. J. Smith, 1965). *The Blue Estuaries: Poems, 1923–1968* (1968). *A Poet's Alphabet: Reflections on the Literary Art and Vocation* (Eds. R. Phelps and R. Limmer, 1970). *The Sorrows of Young Werther* by Goethe (translated by Bogan, 1971). *Novella* by Goethe (translated by Bogan, 1971). *What the Woman Lived: Selected Letters of Louise Bogan, 1920–70* (Ed. R. Limmer, 1973).

BIBLIOGRAPHY: Bowles, G. L., "Suppression and Expression in Poetry by American Women: Louise Bogan, Denise Levertov, and Adrienne Rich" (Ph. D. diss., Univ. of California at Berkeley, 1976). Smith, W. J., *Louise Bogan: A Woman's Words* (1971).

Other references: *BB* 33 (1976). *ChiR* 8 (Fall 1954). *IowaR* 1 (1970). *MAQR* 67 (Aug. 1960). *TCL* 23 (May 1977).

THEODORA R. GRAHAM

Sarah Knowles Bolton

B. 15 Sept. 1841, Farmington, Connecticut; d. 21 Feb. 1916, Cleveland, Ohio
Wrote under: Sarah Knowles Bolton, Sarah Knowles
D. of John Segar and Elizabeth Miller Knowles; m. Charles Edward Bolton, 1866

B. traced her ancestry to the New England colonists. After her father's death in 1852, she moved with her mother to an uncle's house in Hartford, Connecticut. There B. met Harriet Beecher Stowe and Lydia Sigourney, both lasting influences.

B.'s poetry appeared in the *Waverly Magazine* when she was fifteen. Following her graduation from the Hartford Female Seminary in 1860, she taught in Natchez, Mississippi. However, the outbreak of the Civil War sent her home to keep school in Meriden, Connecticut. Her first book, *Orlean Lamar, and Other Poems* (1864), published when she was twenty-three, received mixed reviews. *Wellesley* (1865), a novel about the Hungarian patriot Kossuth, was serialized in the *Literary Recorder* a year later. She published several other books of didactic and sentimental poetry and fiction. In 1866, B. and her husband settled in Cleveland, Ohio, where they became deeply involved in the temperance movement. In her writings, she supported temperance, woman suffrage, and higher education.

Charles Bolton lost his real estate business in the financial panic of 1873. Their struggle to repay his debts spurred B.'s developing career as a journalist and author. From 1878 to 1881, she served as an editor of the Boston paper, the *Congregationalist*. While accompanying her husband on business trips to England in 1878 and 1881, she investigated women's higher education and factory working conditions. In 1883, she presented her findings on British labor relations in an influential paper delivered before the American Social Science Foundation.

While B.'s books shed light on 19th-c. reform movements and the rise of popular education, they are perhaps most valuable to students of women's history. In *Some Successful Women* (1888), *Famous Leaders among Women* (1895), and other collections, B. demonstrates that a woman can win self-respect and worldly fame through intelligence and hard work. Like the fictional Horatio Alger stories, these biographies stress the importance of education, discipline, and self-reliance. According to them, the rapidly changing modern world offers many opportunities for the self-made woman, and stands to benefit from her humanizing influence.

Yet, B.'s work reveals the strain of reconciling traditional female roles with ambition and leadership. In presenting individual women as models, she carefully balances their "masculine" achievements with "feminine" qualities: self-sacrifice, piety, sympathy. Mary Livermore's career, for example, "illustrates the work a woman may do in the world, and still retain the truest womanliness." Helen Hunt Jackson will be remembered because "she forgot self and devoted her strength to the cause of others."

However, B.'s championship of intellectual training, economic independence, and assertive roles for women is much more vigorous than her dutiful nods to the "cult of true womanhood." Her deeper feelings about woman's proper role appear in her portrayal of male/female relations. While convention requires her repudiation of George Eliot's unmarried living arrangement with George Henry Lewes, B. goes on to present a laudatory portrait of their relationship, noting especially Lewes's support of George Eliot's career. Her study of the Brownings also stresses their equality and mutual respect: "Their marriage was an ideal one. Both had a grand purpose in life. Neither individual was merged in the other." B.'s treatment of women who preferred to remain single is equally sympathetic.

B. encouraged young women to take themselves—their minds and their ambitions—seriously. While she showed that women could achieve success in fields such as medicine, literature, education, art, and politics, she also reassured her audience that "true" womanliness and professionalism were compatible. Men, she argued, preferred educated, independent women—it was a "libel" on the sex to think otherwise. Although B.'s skills as a publicist may have gained the upper hand, her optimistic vision bolstered feminine resolve. Her biographies of strong, fully realized women gave American girls crucial models on which to pattern their lives.

WORKS: *Orlean Lamar, and Other Poems* (1864). *Wellesley* (1865). *The Present Problem* (1874). *Facts and Songs for the People. Prepared Specially for Use in the Blaine and Logan Campaign* (1884). *How Success Is Won* (1885). *Lives of Poor Boys Who Became Famous* (1885). *Lives of Girls Who Became Famous* (1886). *Social Studies in England* (1886). *Stories from Life* (1886). *Famous American Authors* (1887). *From Heart and Nature* (with C. K. Bolton, (1887). *Famous American Statesmen* (1888). *Some Successful Women* (1888). *Famous Men of Science* (1889). *Ralph Waldo Emerson* (1889). *Famous English Authors of the Nineteenth-Century* (1890). *Famous European Artists* (1890). *Famous English Statesmen of Queen Victoria's Reign* (1891). *Famous Types of Womanhood* (1892). *Famous Voyagers and Explorers* (1893). *Famous Leaders among Men* (1894). *Famous Leader among Women* (1895). *The Inevitable, and Other Poems* (1895). *Nuggets; or, Secrets of Great Success* (with F. T. Wallace, 1895). *Famous Givers and Their Gifts* (1896). *The Story of Douglas* (1898). *Every-day Living* (1900). *Our Devoted Friend the Dog* (1902). *Charles E. Bolton: A Memorial Sketch* (1907). *Sarah K. Bolton: Pages from an Intimate Autobiography* (Ed. C. K. Bolton, 1923). *What to Read and How to Write* (n.d.).

BIBLIOGRAPHY: Bolton, C. K., *The Boltons in Old and New England* (1890).
    For articles in reference works, see: *AW. NCAB.*
SARAH WAY SHERMAN

Catherine Drinker Bowen

B. *1 Jan. 1897, Haverford, Pennsylvania; d. 1 Nov. 1973, Haverford, Pennsylvania*
D. *of Henry Sturgis and Aimee Beaux Drinker; m. Ezra Bowen, 1919*

Although B. began her career as a writer of fiction, including a novel, *Rufus Starbuck's Wife* (1932), she early chose the role of biographer.

Music gave a central focus for B.'s early biographical works, *Beloved Friend: The Story of Tchaikowsky and Nadejda von Meck* (1937) and *Free Artist: The Story of Anton and Nicholas Rubinstein* (1939). The first work involves interweaving letters by the composer and his patron into a biographical narrative, the second portrays the Rubinsteins' interaction with the musical and political world of late tsarist Russia. In these works, B. early revealed her skill in characterization.

In the 1940s, B. found a new biographical focus: men of law and their role in the development of free government. From this concern came three biographies. *Yankee from Olympus: Justice Holmes and His Family* (1944), is a three-generational study, reaching back for the "roots that permitted so splendid a flowering" in Holmes's own life. In her portrait of Holmes as legal pioneer, judicial dissenter, and man of ideas and passion, B. impressively achieves her aim "to bring Justice Holmes out of legal terms into human terms."

In *John Adams and the American Revolution* (1950), B. concentrates on the lawyer as political leader. She stresses Adam's commitment to British constitutional principles and his growing disillusionment with British practices, and she depicts with force and clarity his role in the colonies' developing independence.

With *The Lion and the Throne: The Life and Times of Sir Edward Coke, 1552–1634* (1957), B. turned to the English roots of American constitutionalism. Her account centers on Coke's transformation from chief prosecutor for the Crown to ardent champion of the House of Commons and the Petition of Right. Her portrait of this "difficult but impressive man" gives full due to the complexity of his nature and his role as jurist and legal authority.

Her last work was *The Most Dangerous Man in America: Scenes from the Life of Benjamin Franklin* (1974). In this account of five periods of Franklin's life, B. traces his change from adherent to critic of Great Britain and explored the complexities of his personality and roles. The book is also a personal document, including reflective essays that indicate her own affirmative response to this Englightenment man.

B. wrote several works on biographical writing itself, including *Adventures of a Biographer* (1959), a series of informal essays, and *Biography: The Craft and the Calling* (1969), a study of biographical problems and techniques. B. also wrote *Friends and Fiddlers* (1935), informal, anecdotal essays on chamber music by amateurs, and *Family Portraits* (1970), a history of the Drinker family.

B. took the narrative approach to biography, focusing both on the individual personality and the age itself. The intricacies of personal development concerned her most, rather than the critical exploration of historical issues. In her early work, B. often utilized fictional devices, such as transposing letters and diary entries into conversation. With the Coke biography, however, she abandoned such techniques, relying henceforth on a skilled use of documents and mastery of detail to convey the sense of reality.

WORKS: *The Story of an Oak Tree* (1924). *A History of Lehigh University* (1924). *Rufus Starbuck's Wife* (1932). *Friends and Fiddlers* (with B. von Meck, 1935). *Beloved Friend: The Story of Tchaikowsky and Nadejda von Meck* (1937). *Free Artist: The Story of Anton and Nicholas Rubinstein* (1939). *Yankee from Olympus: Justice Holmes and His Family* (1944). *John Adams and the American Revolution* (1950). *The Writing of Biography* (1951). *The Lion and the Throne: The Life and Times of Sir Edward Coke, 1552–1634* (1957). *The Biographer Looks for News* (1958). *Adventures of a Biographer* (1959). *The Nature of the Artist* (1961). *The Historian* (1963). *Francis Bacon: The Temper of a Man* (1963). *Miracle at Philadelphia: The Story of the Constitutional Convention, May to September, 1787* (1966). *Biography: The Craft and the Calling* (1969). *Family Portrait* (1970). *The Most Dangerous Man in America: Scenes from the Life of Benjamin Franklin* (1974).

BIBLIOGRAPHY: *AHR* (Oct. 1957). *Atlantic* (July 1957). *NewR* (29 May 1944; 2 Nov. 1974). *NYT* (18 June 1950; 23 June 1963; 20 Nov. 1966). *SatR* (11 June 1950).

INZER BYERS

Bathsheba Bowers

B. ca. 1672, Massachusetts; d. 1718, South Carolina
D. of Benanuel and Elizabeth Dunster Bowers

Noted for its eccentricity, B.'s life has attracted more attention than her writing. She was born to English Quakers who settled in Charlestown. Though they endured the Puritan persecution of Quakers themselves, the Bowers sent their daughters to Philadelphia to escape it.

B. remained single all her life, building a small house, which became known as "Bathsheba's Bower," at the corner of Little Dock and Second Streets. Furnishing her home with books, a table, and little else, she became a gardener, a vegetarian, and, according to her niece Ann Bolton, as much of a recluse "as if she had lived in a Cave under Ground or on the top of a high mountain." Although B. was a Quaker by profession, Bolton's diary reports that she was "so Wild in her Notions it was hard to find out of what religion she really was of. She read her Bible much but I think sometimes to no better purpose than to afford matter for dispute in w[hich] she was always positive." B. eventually became a Quaker preacher, taking her ministry to South Carolina.

Though records exist today for only a single volume, B. is said to have written a number of books: B., in fact, spoke of her "Works" in the plural. B.'s extant volume, *An Alarm Sounded to Prepare the Inhabitants of the World to Meet the Lord in the Way of His Judgments* (1709), used the conventions of spiritual autobiography to trace her life as a seemingly endless series of fears to be overcome. Making an analogy between herself and Job, B. outlined a progression of divinely ordained tests which served to place her in a special relationship with God. One by one, B. conquered her terrors of death, of hell, of her own strong pride, of writing and publishing, of preaching, even of nudity. Her spiritual progress toward a kind of self-control dictated by God is presented in *An Alarm* as an example that others may follow.

Interestingly, B. perceived her most difficult task to be the struggle against her own ambition, her "chief evil" and "very potent Enemy." Paradoxically, she viewed the publication of *An Alarm* as a triumph over that personal ambition. Though presenting her life to the public as an example for emulation may seem an act of pride, B. emphasized the "Scorn and Ridicule" her audacity would bring: "'tis best known to my self how long I labored under a reluctancy, and how very unwilling I was to appear in print at all; for it was, indeed, a secret terror to me to think of making a contemptible appearance in the world. . . ." Response to *An Alarm* went unrecorded, but readers today may be interested in B.'s use of a conventional spiritual autobiography for her unconventional activities in writing, publishing, and preaching.

WORKS: *An Alarm Sounded to Prepare the Inhabitants of the World to Meet the Lord in the Way of His Judgments* (1709).

BIBLIOGRAPHY: Cowell, P., *Women Poets in Pre-Revolutionary America, 1650–1775* (1981). Paige, L. R., *History of Cambridge, Massachusetts, 1630–1877* (1877). Watson, J. F., *Annals of Philadelphia, and Pennsylvania, in the Olden Times . . .* (1905).

Other references: *PMHB* 3 (1978).

PATTIE COWELL

Jane Auer Bowles

B. 22 Feb. 1917, New York City; d. 4 May 1973, Malaga, Spain
D. of Sydney and Clair Stajer Auer; m. Paul Bowles, 1938

After attending public schools in Long Island, B. was tutored by a French professor in Switzerland. In 1935 she finished *Le Phaeton hypocrite*, a novel in French which was never published and which has disappeared. After 1938 she and her husband lived in Central America, Europe, Mexico, and New York City. From 1947 they spent most of their time in Tangier, Morocco.

B. finished her only novel, *Two Serious Ladies*, in 1941, and from 1944 to 1953 was engaged in writing and revising her only full-length play, *In the Summer House*, ultimately produced in New York City in 1953 by the Playwrights' Company.

Most of the short stories which constitute the remainder of B.'s works were written during the 1940s. According to Paul Bowles, B. became hypercritical of her writing in the 1950s. In 1957 she suffered a cerebral hemorrhage which deprived her of her ability to read and write. Her health worsened slowly, and she died in 1973, in Malaga, Spain.

All of B.'s stories are about women and their attempts at independence; male characters are seldom important, even as blocking characters. When B.'s women characters cannot find themselves, it is other women who are holding them back. The essential B. plot presents a woman who seeks to break away from tradition and find new adventures in the outside world, and a second woman—sister, companion, lover—who tries to keep her at home within the old habits of dependence.

In *Two Serious Ladies*, (1943), Christina Goering tries to earn salvation by leaving her home and her female companion to challenge the hated outside world. There she takes up with a series of increasingly menacing male strangers, the last of whom abandons her. The second serious lady is Frieda Copperfield, who leaves her husband for a prostitute named Pacifica, who ultimately forces Frieda to share her with a young man. The promiscuity, bisexuality, and sadomasochism in this novel are seldom erotic, but tend instead to illustrate the hidden horror in human relationships, most of which consist of greedy individual truth-seekers bouncing their needs off each other.

It is the relationship between sisters that B. examines in her best short story, "Camp Cataract," part of the collection *Plain Pleasures* (1966). Harriet leaves her sisters every year to stay at Camp Cataract, in hopes that she can get used to the outside world and ultimately leave home permanently. Her sister Sadie tries to convince her that "you don't grow rich in spirit by widening your circle but by tending your own." When Sadie panics and comes after Harriet, Sadie realizes that it is she who is going on that journey from home, not Harriet. Sadie is perhaps the only Bowles character who gets to the end of her search for herself, but that quest ends in her death. Rather than emerging free from her clinging sister, Harriet appears to exchange her for an aggressively dependent friend.

B. introduced almost the same plot in overtly lesbian form in her unfinished story "Going to Massachusetts," which appears with other fragments from B.'s notebooks in a posthumous collection called *Feminine Wiles* (1976).

Through her constant resetting of these pairs of warring women, B. presents a full picture of the female psyche and the extremes to which the personality is driven by the pressures of modern society. Her representative woman tries to realize her potential within a world that tells her to be chaste, experienced, loyal to her family, supportive of her man, and independent. B. describes this fragmented world and its absurd expectations in a style which is eccentric, and sometimes almost surrealistic. Characters form attachments and abandon each other rapidly and unreasonably; they speak their minds to each other with a frankness which the reader does not expect in the middle- to upper-class world that B. portrays. These sudden twists force the reader to share in the sense of menace and confusion that the freedom-seeking Bowles heroine feels in her relationship to the world.

WORKS: *Two Serious Ladies* (1943). *Plain Pleasures* (1966). *Collected Works of Jane Bowles* (1966). *Feminine Wiles* (1976).

BIBLIOGRAPHY: For articles in reference works, see: *WA*.

Other references: *Life* (16 Dec. 1966). *Mlle* (Dec. 1966). *Novel* (1968). *SatR* (14 Jan. 1967).

PAULA L. BARBOUR

Kay Boyle

B. 19 Feb. 1902, St. Paul, Minnesota
D. of Howard P. and Katharine Evans Boyle; m. Richard Brault, 1922;
m. Laurence Vail, 1931; m. Joseph von Franckenstein, 1943

B. studied music and architecture before marrying a French engineering student and moving to his home in Brittany. The marriage had crumbled by 1926, but B. remained in Europe until after the fall of France in 1941.

In 1946, B. returned to Europe as a foreign correspondent for *The New Yorker*, while her third husband served with the War Department in occupied Germany. She later taught at various American universities and has been professor of English at San Francisco State since 1963. She received Guggenheim Fellowships in 1934 and 1961, and the O. Henry Prize for best short story in 1935 ("The White Horses of Vienna") and 1941 ("Defeat").

B.'s settings are frequently European. Her novel, *Plagued by the Nightingale* (1931), is loosely based upon a summer with her Breton relatives. At first, the novel was praised as a sensitive treatment of an American abroad, but today it has taken on new interest as the story of a young couple who decide not to have children (because of hereditary disease) and are bitterly opposed by their rigid, provincial family.

B.'s acute awareness of European social and political conditions is revealed in "The White Horses of Horses of Vienna," where swastika fires bloom at night on the Austrian mountains, prefiguring Nazi domination; the Lippizaners (the famed white stallions) symbolize a lost nobility; and a tamed fox foreshadows the savage future.

Two of B.'s finest novellas are "The Crazy Hunter" (1940) and "The Bridegroom's Body" (1940). "The Crazy Hunter" is a horse that is suddenly struck blind, but its young owner refuses to allow it to be destroyed. B. carefully works through the blindness-sight motif, interweaving it with complex relationships between a weak father, a strong-willed mother, and a budding daughter. "The Bridegroom's Body" dwells on the fatal attraction and isolation of love.

Fascinated by "the subtlety in human relations," B. is often concerned with political issues, which she has always met fearlessly; for B., "silence is not a position." Her book, *The Smoking Mountain: Stories of Germany during the Occupation* (1951), has been called "the finest interpretation of that place and time . . . written in English." Though B. clearly does not sympathize with the Nazis, she exhibits compassion for a proud and defeated people. Perhaps her best-known novel is *Generation without Farewell* (1960), written from the viewpoint of a German journalist who identifies with the Americans and rejects his own countrymen, only to discover that he really belongs to neither world.

Although B. began as a poet, her prose is far more skillful than her verse. Her novels, always technically well-constructed, often contain brilliant passages. Her strongest prose form is the novella. Here she can create a single, sustained theme, and embroider and enrich upon it.

B. is at her best when writing about highly complex human beings caught in political, social or psychological turmoil, struggling to maintain identity and balance. Her outrage at the violation of human dignity is carefully muted, revealed rather than preached. She writes with consummate skill and passionate sincerity, and is recognized as a major novella writer in American fiction.

WORKS: *Wedding Day, and Other Stories* (1929). *Plagued by the Nightingale* (1931). *Year before Last* (1932). *The First Lover, and Other Stories* (1933). *Gentlemen, I Address You Privately* (1933). *My Next Bride* (1934). *Death of a Man* (1936). *The White Horses of Vienna, and Other Stories* (1936). *Monday Night* (1938). *A Glad Day* (1938). *The Youngest Camel* (1939). *The Crazy Hunter* (1940). *Primer for Combat* (1942). *Avalanche* (1944). *American Citizen* (1944). *A Frenchman Must Die* (1946). *Thirty Stories* (1946). *1939* (1948). *His Human Majesty* (1949). *The Smoking Mountain: Stories of Germany during the Occupation* (1951). *The Seagull on the Step* (1955). *Three Short Novels* (1958). *Generation without Farewell* (1960). *Breaking the Silence: Why a Mother Tells Her Son about the Nazi Era* (1962). *Collected Poems* (1962). *Nothing Ever Breaks Except the Heart* (1966). *Pinky, the Cat Who Liked to Sleep* (1966). *The Autobiography of Emanuel Carnevali* (1967). *Being Geniuses Together: 1920–1930* (with R. McAlmon, 1968). *Pinky in Persia* (1968). *The Long Walk at San Francisco State, and Other Essays* (1970). *Testament for My Students, and Other Poems* (1970). *The Underground Woman* (1975). *Fifty Stories* (1980).

BIBLIOGRAPHY: Gado, F., "Kay Boyle: From the Aesthetics of Exile to the Polemics of Return" (Ph.D. diss., Duke Univ., 1968). Jackson, B. K., "The Achievement of Kay Boyle" (Ph.D. diss., Univ. of Florida, 1968). Madden, C. F., ed., *Talks with Authors* (1968). Moore, H. T., *Age of the Modern, and Other Literary Essays* (1971). Tooker, D., and R. Hofheins, *Fiction: Interviews with Northern California Novelists* (1976).

Other references: *CE* 15 (Nov. 1953). *Crit* 7 (1965). *KenR* 22 (Spring 1960). *NYT* (10 July 1966).

JOANNE McCARTHY

Anne Dudley Bradstreet

B. 1612, Northampton, England; d. 16 Sept. 1672, Andover, Massachusetts
Wrote under: A Gentlewoman in those parts; A Gentlewoman in New-England
D. of Thomas and Dorothy Yorke Dudley; m. Simon Bradstreet, 1628

B.'s youth was spent in England. She had the advantage of living in the household of the Earl of Lincoln, where her father was trusted steward and friend of the earl. Dudley, called by B. "A magazine of history," believed in the education of his daughter. She had complete access to the excellent library of the earl. Here, too, she learned to know and love another protégé of the earl, Simon Bradstreet, whom she married two years before the Dudleys and the Bradstreets sailed on the *Arbella* for Massachusetts Bay in 1630. B.'s father was governor of Massachusetts, and her husband succeeded him when B. was no longer alive.

B. was the first British-American to have a volume of poetry published, and at a time when the Puritan woman's place was in the home. Governor Winthrop, in 1645, was certain that the wife of the Governor of Hartford had lost her wits because she "gave herself wholly to reading and writing . . . if she had attended her household affairs and such as belong to women and not gone out of her way and calling to meddle in such things as are proper for men, whose minds are stronger, etc., she had kept her wits and might have improved them usefully and honorably in the place God had set her."

But B. did write poems which would not have seen the light of day had not an admiring brother-in-law, with family connivance, carried them off to England and had them published under the astonishing title of *The Tenth Muse Lately Sprung up in America* (1650).

As was becoming to a Puritan woman, B.'s first poetry was about biblical themes. Her models were Du Bartas's *Divine Weeks and Works* (1605), a widely read account of the creation, and Sir Walter Raleigh's *History of the World* (1614), a popular book that began with the creation and continued the history of mankind to show God's divine purpose in human events. The first 174 pages of *The Tenth Muse* consist of quaternions—"The Foure Elements," "The Foure Humors of Man's Constitution," "The Foure Ages of Man," "The Foure Monarchies"—all written in closed couplets, all slavishly imitative of Du Bartas. Following the "four times four poems" is "A Dialogue between Old England and New, concerning the present troubles, Anno 1642," which is original in content and bold in her political concern.

B. was not pleased with her poems in print. She set about revising her first poetry, and she continued writing anew, this time with freedom and originality in thought and structure. The second (American) edition, with these changes and additions, appeared in 1678, six years after her death. It is upon these new poems—religious meditations, domestic poems, love poems, and elegies upon lost members of her family—that her reputation as a poet of excellence rests.

The most highly regarded poem of all is "Contemplations," composed of thirty-three stanzas, skillfully wrought, each stanza an entity, yet all interrelated and all expressing the poet's recognition of God in nature, a subject so rare that it did not find its fruition until the Romantic period. An equally remarkable poem in the second edition is "The Flesh and the Spirit," which S. E. Morison called "One of the best expressions in English literature of the conflict described by St. Paul in the eighth chapter of his Epistle to the Romans."

In 1867, John Harvard Ellis edited a complete edition of B.'s work. There is a brief but moving autobiography, revealing the spiritual doubts of a good Puritan woman. Her "Meditations" were short prose pieces showing the influence of the aphoristic essays of Bacon, emblems similar to those of Quarles, and spiritual commentaries like the Psalms, Proverbs, and Ecclesiastes.

The estimate of B.'s later poetry has grown with the years. Moses Coit Tyler and John Harvard Ellis were two scholars who recognized her worth (in the 19th c.). Conrad Aiken was the first to include her in his anthology of American literature; Samuel Eliot Morison, the distinguished historian, pronounced her the best American woman poet before Emily Dickinson.

WORKS: *The Tenth Muse Lately Sprung up in America* (1650; 2nd ed., 1678). *The Works of Anne Bradstreet, in Prose and Verse* (Ed. J. H. Ellis, 1867). *The Tenth Muse* (Ed. J. K. Piercy, 1965). *The Works of Anne Bradstreet* (Ed. J. Hensley, 1967).

The papers of Anne Bradstreet are at Houghton Library, Harvard University.

BIBLIOGRAPHY: Berryman, J., *Homage to Mistress B.* (1956). Fuess, C. M., *Andover, Symbol of New England* (1959). Morison, S. E., *Builders of the Bay Colony* (1930). Phillips, E., "Women among the Moderns Eminent for Poetry," *Theatrum Poetarum* (1675). Piercy, J. K., *Anne Bradstreet* (1965). Tyler, M. C., *A History of American Literature during the Colonial Period* (1897). White, M. W., *Anne Bradstreet, the Tenth Muse* (1971).

JOSEPHINE K. PIERCY

Anna Hempstead Branch

B. 18 March 1875, New London, Connecticut; d. 8 Sept. 1937, New London,
  Connecticut
D. of John Locke and Mary Lydia Bolles Branch

B., the younger of two children, was born in Hempstead House at New London, Connecticut, where her mother's family, the Hempsteads, had lived since 1640. Her father was a New York lawyer; her mother wrote popular children's stories and poems. Following B.'s graduation from Smith College in 1897, she studied dramaturgy at the American Academy of Dramatic Arts in New York, training which is reflected in her numerous verse plays and dramatic monologues.

B. was connected with a number of philanthropic, social work, and art organizations, but most of her time was divided between the Christodora House, a Lower-East-Side settlement house, and Hempstead House, where she lived with her mother. At Christodora, B. established and directed the activities of the Poet's Guild, an association organized to bring poetry to the neighborhood, especially the children, but which also provided occasions for such poets as Edwin Arlington Robinson, Vachel Lindsay, Robert Frost, Carl Sandburg, Sara Teasdale, Ridgely Torrence, Margaret Widdemer, and B. herself to read and discuss poetry.

B.'s poems have a variety of subjects and settings, but even those poems with apparently secular subjects are tinged with a religious and mystical apprehension. In B.'s eclectic first volume, *Heart of the Road* (1901), many of the poems are "road" poems in which the road symbolizes transience. The dramatic monologue "The Keeper of the Halfway House," for instance, depicts an ironically dependent relationship between the transient and the permanent. An innkeeper, a priestly figure who points "the way" to travelers, sits beside a vacant chair, knowing someone will come and fill it and then move on. In this volume, the reader is struck by a haunting precision of some of B.'s lines and by her ability to sustain a mood.

B.'s second volume, *The Shoes That Danced* (1905), contains a strange mixture of settings (e.g., fairyland, New York City, a monastery) and of characters (e.g., Watteau, shop girls, a Puritan minister). Although in sections of the volume B. indulges in greeting-card sentiments, the title verse drama is intriguing and suggestive.

Along with some masterful poems expressing metaphysical doubt and some unexceptional reworkings of great Romantic poems ("Selene" of Keats's "Endymion" and "The Wedding Feast" of Coleridge's "The Rime of the Ancient Mariner"), *Rose of the Wind* (1910) contains B.'s longest and most famous work, "Nimrod," a Miltonic epic named after the Babylonian king. Although it was highly regarded by B.'s contemporaries, the diction now seems strained and the imagery imitative.

B.'s most satisfying volume is *Sonnets from a Lock Box* (1929). In the title sequence of thirty-eight sonnets, B. sheds her personae and speaks in the first person. The sequence is distinguished from some of B.'s earlier work by its directness of expression and originality. It moves from a portrayal of various types of entrapment and enslavement to a search for a means of escape. B. seeks liberation in mystical systems, invoking alchemy, astrology, cabalistic symbolism, numerology, and "Holy Logic." Yet B. intimates that the problem and the solution are secondary to the poetry, the "music," that they inspire.

Although B.'s poetry is at times derivative and contains a large population of fairies, kings, clouds, shepherds, along with the archaic diction appropriate to such a poetic population. B. had a genuine gift and an authentic voice. Her deepest subjects are language and what is to her its truest expression, poetry—"the changeless reflection of the changing dream." For B., words are divine manifestations that not only create, order and give meaning to reality, but that are the very stuff of life: "I say that words are men and when we spell/ In alphabets we deal with living things."

In her time, B. was compared to Robert Browning, Christina Rossetti, and the metaphysical poets. E. A. Robinson and other contemporaries regarded B. as a major figure, repeatedly including her name in discussions of poets of the day. Although she was not as successful as were Blake and Yeats in universalizing a private mystical system, she holds a secure place among the minor poets of the United States.

WORKS: *Heart of the Road* (1901). *The Shoes That Danced* (1905). *Rose of the Wind* (1910). *A Christmas Miracle and God Bless this House* (1925). *Bubble Blower's House* (1926). *Sonnets from a Lock Box* (1929). *Last Poems of Anna Hempstead Branch* (Ed. R. Torrence, 1944).

BIBLIOGRAPHY: Bolles, J. D., *Father Was an Editor* (1940). Cary, R., *The Early Reception of E. A. Robinson: The First Twenty Years* (1974). Widdemer, M., *Golden Friends I Had* (1964).

For articles in reference works, see *NAW* (article by J. T. Baird, Jr.). *20th CA.*

Other references: *NYT* (9 Sept. 1937).

ELLEN G. FRIEDMAN

Sophonisba Preston Breckinridge

B. 1 April 1866, Lexington, Kentucky; d. 30 July 1948, Chicago, Illinois
D. of William Campbell Preston and Issa Desha Breckinridge

Born of a respected, intellectual family, B. graduated from Wellesley College in 1888 but experienced a period of uncertainty characteristic of educated women at this time, who were seen as anomalies with few career opportunities available to them. B. taught high school in Washington, D.C., until 1894, when she returned to her father's home and law office. By 1895, being the first woman successfully to pass Kentucky's bar exams, B. decided to return to school because she could not obtain legal clients. Thus began a lifelong career at the University of Chicago. In 1901 B. earned a Ph.D. in political science and in 1904 a J.D. Simultaneously she worked as an assistant dean of women, and as a faculty member, first in the household administration and later in the social services administration departments.

In 1907, B. moved into Hull House, the social settlement, together with a graduate-school friend, Edith Abbott, and lived there intermittently until 1920. At age forty-one, she turned her life and career fully to the study of social welfare and change.

Women's rights soon emerged as a central concern in her writing and everyday life. She became vice-president of the National American Woman Suffrage Association in 1911, and as a lawyer she helped draft bills regulating women's wages and hours of employment. She was also an active member of the National Trade Women's League, the Women's League, the Women's City Club of Chicago, the American Association of University Women, and the Women's International League for Peace and Freedom.

New Homes for Old (1921) is a fascinating account of difficulties encountered by immigrant women in American society. Chapters on altered family relationships, housecleaning, saving and spending money, and child care provide information on the dramatic changes in everyday life facing the foreign-born housewife. Organizations established to help mitigate the stress created by these situations are discussed, presenting a historical view of social services in this area.

B. and Abbott, as pioneers in social work education, wrote a remarkable series of six books—they each wrote three—which contain selected documents and case records on a variety of social problems. These "texts" helped establish the case-work method of study and reporting in social work and provided a vivid account of individual lives as they were affected by social change, legislation, and public agencies.

Public Welfare Administration in the United States (1927), B.'s first contribution to this series, notes early (1601) origins of legislation and institutions concerning the destitute and mentally ill. Subsequent changes and the resulting hodge-podge of control and disorder, a legacy to today's welfare state, are noted in legal precedents and in statements made by leading authorities of the day in agency management and administration. In the revised edition (1938), the expanding but still chaotic role of the federal government is noted.

Marriage and the Civic Rights of Women (1932) discusses the relationship between marital status and citizenship. A key legislation reviewed is the Cable Act of 1922: for the first time American women could retain their citizenship when marrying an alien. This book is an astute combination of law, social relations, and women's rights. The terseness and clarity of the text, the comprehensive work done by women internationally, the case studies of foreign-born women in America, make this an early classic on the legal status of women and the social barriers they encountered in obtaining citizenship rights.

Any student and scholar of women's role in society from 1890–1933 will find *Women in the Twentieth Century: A Study of their Political, Social and Economic Activities* (1933) a must on their reading lists. The growth of women's participation in life outside the home emerged from women's clubs, increased access to institutions for higher education, the suffrage movement, and concern with the political arena. Data is given on income and the distribution of women in various occupations, with a number of tables providing an invaluable baseline for assessing changes or stability in income, and distribution in occupations over time. Since this historical period is remarkable for its relatively high proportion of women professionals, the chapters discussing professional and near-professional women, women's earnings, and women in business offer factual information that gives a uniquely comparative, historical base to issues still vital to women today.

As a woman completely dedicated to social equality, B.'s life was deeply enmeshed with those of other women who were associated with Hull House: Jane Addams, Julia Lathrop, Grace Abbott, and Edith Abbott. Reading and evaluating B.'s writings, one must consider them as products of her contacts with this group, with other intellectuals, such as

Marion Talbot, and with her students. Her contributions to education and social reform attest to her success as a dedicated and intelligent scholar and educator.

WORKS: *Administration of Justice in Kentucky* (1901). *Legal Tender* (1903). *The Modern Household* (with M. Talbot, 1912). *The Child in the City* (1912). *The Delinquent Child and the Home* (with E. Abbott, 1912). *Truancy and Non-attendance in the Chicago Schools: A Study of the Social Aspects of the Compulsory Education and Child Labor Legislation of Illinois* (with E. Abbot, 1917). *New Homes for Old* (1921). *Madeline McDowell Breckinridge* (1921). *Family Welfare Work* (1924). *Public Welfare Administration in the United States* (1927; rev. ed. 1938). *Marriage and the Civic Rights of Women* (1932). *Women in the Twentieth Century: A Study of Their Political, Social, and Economic Activities* (1933). *Social Work and the Courts* (1934). *The Tenements of Chicago, 1908–1935* (with E. Abbott, 1936). *The Illinois Poor Law and Its Administration* (1939).

BIBLIOGRAPHY: For articles in reference works, see: *DAB. NAW* (article by C. Lasch). *NCAB.*

Other references: *SSR* (Dec. 48; March 1949; Sept. 1949).

MARY JO DEEGAN

Bessie Breuer

B. *19 Oct. 1893, Cleveland, Ohio*
D. *of Samuel Aaron and Julia Bindley Freedman; m. Mr. Breuer; m. Carl Kahler; m. Henry Varnum Poor, 1925*

After graduating from the Missouri State University School of Journalism. B. worked for several years as a newspaper reporter, first for the St. Louis *Times* and subsequently for the New York *Tribune*, where she was editor of the women's department and, briefly, Sunday editor. After staff work for the American Red Cross publicity department, *Ladies' Home Journal*, and *Harper's*, she went to France where her friendships with Kay Boyle and Laurence Vail encouraged her to turn her attention toward fiction writing. She wrote for such periodicals as *World's Work*, *Pictorial Review* (often in collaboration with Henry Ford), *House Beautiful, The New Yorker*, and *Mademoiselle* until the 1960s.

B.'s early publications often centered on the significance and implications of post-suffrage feminism. One of these articles, "Feminism's Awkward Age" (*Harper's*, April 1925), a discussion of the difficulty the modern woman faces in attempting to integrate personal and sexual needs with vocational and political goals, provides an excellent introduction to concerns which were crucial in B.'s later fiction. She often concentrates on the fate of women who flounder in endless introspection, unsatisfying jobs, and painful relationships; women who lack either the consolations of a conventional identity or a mass movement in which to submerge themselves. B.'s fiction is sexually explicit and unsparing in its delineation of her heroine's confusion. These tendencies, as well as her experimental style, caused the critical reception of her novel to be frequently negative.

B.'s first novel, *Memory of Love* (1934), is written in the voice of a married man as he remembers an affair he had years before with a woman separated from her husband. For the narrator, a man who prides himself on his sexual exploits, this woman is unexpectedly captivating. Alternating between equally intense moments of attraction and repulsion, the narrative recounts their passionate, tempestuous affair. Finally, the protagonist is forced to abandon this woman when his wealthy parents threaten to cut off his income unless he returns to his socially more prestigious wife. The novel seems to stand as B.'s commentary on the extreme vulnerability of the sexually active "new" woman.

B.'s most successful novel, *The Daughter* (1938), is the story of a young woman, Katy, and her divorced mother. Living on an income provided by Katy's prominent father (with the stipulation that no acknowledgment of the connection be made public), the two women drift from one second-rate resort to another. The mother enjoys a series of casual affairs while the daughter retreats more deeply into a carefully constructed aesthetic artifice of classical music and contemporary poetry. Most of the action takes place in a west coast of Florida hotel where the daughter has her first affair. Lacking her mother's resiliency, this purely physical involvement almost destroys the girl. She attempts suicide.

In addition to its remarkable characterization of Katy, *The Daughter* is memorable because of B.'s repeated juxtaposition of the aimless resort world of her characters and the wider panorama of world events. If her characters do not care, B. seems to, and insistently reminds her readers of the sociopolitical background against which her novel is set. Only Katy has any sense of the significance of this wider world. The best that she can do, however, is to fantasize that in a different place, with a different personality, she too could have been a Jane Addams or a La Pasionaria.

Joanna Trask, the heroine of B.'s *The Actress* (1955), seems at first to be a continuation of the passive, introspective, and excessively vulnerable heroines typical of B.'s early fiction. But the novel traces Joanna's gradual development, a process characterized by B. as a movement toward assuming responsibility for her own actions and control over her own fate. She becomes more active than acted upon and, for the first time in B.'s fiction, sexual experience is viewed as necessary and healthy. The novel ends with the optimistic assertion that Joanna will not only combine a career and a family, but do it well.

B.'s fiction will strike the modern reader as unexpectedly contemporary, in part because of B.'s innovative narrative techniques and her interest in the relationship between woman's sexual and social identities. B. is an often fascinating writer who deserves more serious attention than she has yet received.

WORKS: *Memory of Love* (1934). *The Daughter* (1938). *The Bracelet of Wavia Lea, and Other Stories* (1947). *Sundown Beach* (1948; produced by E. Kazan, 1948). *The Actress* (1955). *Take Care of My Roses* (1961).

BIBLIOGRAPHY: Blake, F., *The Strike in the American Novel* (1972). Hill, V., "Strategy and Breadth: The Socialist-Feminist in American Fiction" (Ph.D. diss., State Univ. of New York at Buffalo, 1979).

For articles in reference works, see: *American Women*, Ed. D. Howes (1939). *20thCA*.

Other references: *CW* (24 Sept. 1948). *NewR* (20 Sept. 1948). *NY* (18 Sept. 1948). *Newsweek* (20 Sept. 1948). *SatR* (16 April 1938; 28 Dec. 1946; 17 Jan. 1949). *Theatre Arts* (Jan. 1949). *WLB* (Oct. 1938).

VICKI LYNN HILL

Gwendolyn Brooks

B. 7 June 1917, Topeka, Kansas
D. of David and Keziah Wims Brooks; m. Henry Blakely, 1939

B. attended public schools in Chicago and was graduated from Wilson Junior College in 1936. A poetry workshop at Chicago's South Side Community Art Center in the early 1940s introduced B. to the rigors of poetic technique; her extraordinary talent was soon recognized. In 1945 her first volume, *A Street in Bronzeville*, appeared. A plethora of prizes quickly followed: grants from the American Academy of Arts and Letters and the National Academy of Arts and Letters, two Guggenheim Fellowships, and, in 1950, the Pulitzer Prize for poetry. She was the first black poet so honored. A similar kind of recognition was hers when in 1968 she was named poet-laureate of Illinois.

In addition to numerous honorary degrees, B. achieved an unusual distinction when in 1971 black poets of all ages contributed to a volume, *To Gwen with Love*. The presence of so many young writers was, in part, a response to a shift in B.'s political stance. From a rather apolitical integrationist in the 1940s, she became in the 1960s a strong advocate of black consciousness. This process of change is described in B.'s autobiography, *Report from Part One* (1972).

In *A Street in Bronzeville* B. penned memorable vignettes of the residents of "Bronzeville," the black neighborhood of Chicago. Significantly, although the characters in these poems are poor, the emphasis is not on their material poverty but on their struggle to sustain their spiritual and aesthetic well-being. In "The Sundays of Satin-Legs Smith," a narrative poem which is a marvel of technical proficiency, the protagonist draws on his considerable imaginative powers to create a world on Sundays which contrasts sharply to the drudgery of his workdays. The poem celebrates Smith's resourcefulness, his sensuality, and his keen aesthetic sense; yet it reveals the lack of substance underneath the style.

Annie Allen (1949), awarded the Pulitzer Prize, is her most experimental work. Its subject is akin to her earlier poems: a young black girl comes of age, hoping to live out the drama and romance she fantasies. But the poverty and powerlessness which she kept at bay in her girlhood threaten her womanhood.

B.'s only novel, *Maud Martha* (1953), illumines the life of a young black woman who must ward off continual, often petty, assaults to her human dignity. *Maud Martha* was one of the first novels to portray a black girl's coming of age.

Written at the height of the civil-rights struggle, *The Bean Eaters* (1960) contains more topical poems than B.'s earlier books; her subjects include lynching and Emmett Till, school integration and Little Rock, and the violence accompanying the arrival of a black family in an all-white neighborhood.

The epic title poem of *In the Mecca* (1968) brilliantly captures the mood of disillusionment and defiance of urban America in the 1960s. It is B.'s most richly textured poem. In her typical fashion, she combines formal eloquence and ordinary speech, and they are perfectly fused. B. employs various forms, but free verse and blank verse predominate. Visually rich as well, the poem projects razor-sharp images and a gallery of memorable and diverse characters. It is a tour de force.

B. was the first black American woman to achieve critical recognition as a poet. Observers have noted influences on her work as diverse as T. S. Eliot and Robert Frost, Langston Hughes and Wallace Stevens. Stylistically, she often remolds traditional verse forms such as the ballad and the sonnet to suit her poetic purposes; she also employs modern forms brilliantly. Philosophically, she is a humanist, particularly concerned with exploring the strengths and travails of black women in her work. By any reckoning, hers is one of the major voices of 20th-c. American poetry.

WORKS: *A Street in Bronzeville* (1945). *Annie Allen* (1949). *Maud Martha* (1953). *Bronzeville Boys and Girls* (1956). *The Bean Eaters* (1960). *Selected Poems* (1963). *In the Mecca* (1968). *Riot* (1968). *Family Pictures* (1970). *The World of Gwendolyn Brooks* (1971). *A Broadside Treasury, 1965–1970* (edited by Brooks, 1971). *Jump Bad: A Chicago Anthology* (edited by Brooks, 1971). *Aloneness* (1971). *Report from Part One* (1972). *The Tiger Who Wore White Gloves* (1974). *Beckonings* (1975).

BIBLIOGRAPHY: Jaffe, D., in *The Black American Writer*, Ed. C. W. E. Bigsby (1969). Juhasz, S., *Naked and Fiery Forms: Modern American Poetry by Women—A New Tradition* (1976). Kent, G., *Blackness and the Adventure of Western Culture* (1972). Miller, R. B., *Langston Hughes and Gwendolyn Brooks: A Reference Guide* (1978). Spillers, H., in *Shakespeare's Sisters: Feminist Essays on Women Poets*, Eds. S. Gilbert and S. Gubar (1979).

Other references: *Black Scholar* 3 (Summer 1972). *Black World* (June 1973). *CLAJ* (Dec. 1962; Dec. 1963; Sept. 1972; Sept. 1973). *ConL* 12 (Winter 1970). *SBL* 4 (Autumn 1973).

CHERYL A. WALL

Maria Gowen Brooks

B. c. 1794, Medford, Massachusetts; d. 11 Nov. 1845, Mantanzas, Cuba
Wrote under: Maria del Occidente
D. of William and Eleanor Cutter Gowen; m. John Brooks, 1810

When Maria was orphaned in her childhood, she came under the protection of John Brooks, a Boston merchant. In 1810, the fifty-year-old merchant married his fifteen-year-old ward. The marriage was evidently an unhappy one, and she threw herself into her studies. Maria's dissatisfaction with her marriage was exacerbated when John suffered financial losses and moved the family to backwater Portland, Maine. There she met the Canadian officer who became her romantic fixation. John died in 1823, and Maria moved to Cuba where relatives owned coffee plantations. On a subsequent visit to Canada, she became engaged to the Canadian officer, but they were estranged through a series of misunderstandings. Maria attempted suicide twice. In 1826 she began a correspondence with the British poet laureate Robert Southey. After trips to England and Europe, Maria returned to Cuba, where she died of a tropical fever.

In 1820 some of B.'s poetry was published in a volume titled *Judith, Esther, and Other Poems, by a Lover of the Fine Arts*. The personae in these poems are all female. In "Judith" and "Esther," B. deals with the psychological aspects of the trials of these biblical heroines. "The Butterfly" presents an analogue to relationships between the sexes: a poet is too wrapped up in his own concerns to save an exquisite butterfly from the flame. The frank but almost naive "Written after passing an evening with E. W. R. A******, Esq., who has the finest person I ever saw" warmly describes the physical charms of the Canadian officer with whom B. had fallen in love.

In 1833, Robert Southey supervised publication of *Zophiel; or, The Bride of Seven*, which tells the story of a fallen angel's love for a mortal woman. In it, B. was not afraid to include many passionate and "forbidden" scenes, or to describe vividly human physical beauty. *Zophiel* is "dense" in the manner of Milton and contains full and learned notes on Middle-Eastern history, sorcery, and biblical tradition, with many literary, botanical, cultural, and geographical references, as in the work of Yeats and Eliot. Deeply scholarly in one sense, its actual expression is similar to the sensuality of Keats's *Eve of St. Agnes* and Coleridge's symbolistic uncanniness in *Christabel*.

In 1838, B.'s *Idomen; or, The Vale of Yumuri* was published serially in the Boston *Saturday Evening Gazette*. Several publishers refused the fictionalized autobiography as "too elevated to sell," so B. published it privately in New York in 1843. Idomen, the heroine, is "formed in every nerve for the refinements of pleasure," although her real life is a round of "duties" and "wearisome employments." For B., virtuous passion is a sign of intellectual and emotional consciousness.

The almost hallucinatory clarity of *Idomen*'s imagery heightens the impression that many of its images and scenes must be interpreted symbolically, even as archetypes. The Edenic myth is everywhere apparent—in the idyllic Cuban scenes, but also in the celestially majestic frozen glory of the rivers and mountains of Canada. Idomen herself seems a pattern of the human soul. Caught in a dull marriage as the soul is caught in the mortal body, she yearns for the Ideal Absolute as personified by Ethelwald, a character based on B.'s Canadian officer. Yet Idomen cannot have Ethelwald in this world, for some mysterious inability to communicate with him intervenes even after she is freed by the death of her husband. This is one manifestation of a continuing theme of psychic or supernatural fates or impulses which leads to an exploration of suicidal tendencies and the hypersensitive imagination. Idomen acts out the Christ-like cycle of death, resurrection, and ascension, although such an allegory may have been unconscious on B.'s part. It is as a psychological novel of considerable subtlety that *Idomen* will capture the modern imagination.

It can hardly be explained why B. is not better known and studied. Her work is good, at times great, but she was too large for her assigned role in the social and intellectual world of her time. In this and in the continued lack of recognition of her worth, she is an archetype of the early American woman writer.

WORKS: *Judith, Esther, and Other Poems, by a Lover of the Fine Arts* (1820). *Zophiel; or, The Bride of Seven* (1833). *Idomen; or, The Vale of Yumuri* (1843).

The papers of Maria Gowen Brooks are in the Boston Public Library, Yale University Library, and the Library of Congress.

BIBLIOGRAPHY: Grannis, R., *An American Friend of Southey* (1913). Griswold, R., *Southern Literary Messenger* (1913). Gustafson, Z., Introduction to *Zophiel* by M. G. Brooks (1978). Southey, R., *The Doctor* (1834).

For articles in reference works, see: *Appleton's Cyclopedia of American Biography* (1888). *CAL. DAB. NAW* (article by T. G. Varner).

Other references: *American Collector* (Aug. 1926). *Graham's Magazine* (Aug. 1848). Medford *Historical Register* (Oct. 1899).

L. W. KOENGETER

Alice Brown

B. 5 Dec. 1857, Hampton Falls, New Hampshire; d. 21 June 1948, Boston, Massachusetts
Wrote under: Alice Brown, Martin Redfield
D. of Levi and Elizabeth Lucas Brown

After graduating from Robinson Female Seminary, B. taught school in New England, but soon decided on a literary career. She wrote for the *Christian Register*, then joined the staff of *The Youth's Companion* in 1885.

In Boston, B. belonged to a group of young Bohemian artists led by the poet Louise Imogen Guiney. The collaborations of the two close friends included a biography of Robert Louis Stevenson (1896) and the founding of the Women's Rest Tour Association. During these years B. wrote in support of women's rights and prison-reform movements.

An advocate of American involvement in World War I, she often commented on politics, criticizing the direction of modern life. In her later years, her passion for privacy and religious mysticism carried her further from the mainstream. Highly praised as late as the 1920s, B.'s work was virtually forgotten by the time of her death.

During a career that spanned seven decades, B. wrote in almost every genre, including criticism, biography, and sketches. She considered herself primarily a poet, but the Victorian idealism and strained diction of her verse has not aged well.

B.'s greatest public recognition came to her as a dramatist. In 1914, amid much publicity, she won the $10,000 Winthrop Ames prize for the best play submitted by an American author. Her entry, *Children of Earth* (1915), later opened on Broadway to mixed reviews and a short run. B.'s one-act plays, often adapted from her stories, were more successful.

B.'s fiction is now considered her best work, particularly her early local-color stories. *Meadow-Grass* made her literary reputation in 1895; *Tiverton Tales* confirmed it in 1899. Both consist of loosely connected sketches portraying the fictional village of Tiverton, a farming community close to the sea and modeled after Hampton Falls. These and subsequent stories were compared favorably to the work of Sarah Orne Jewett and Mary Wilkins Freeman. Although B.'s portraits of spinsters and rebellious wives (especially in "A Day Off" and "The Other Mrs. Dill") are as fine in their way as Freeman's, her good-natured humor, idealism, and careful craftsmanship bring her closer to Jewett's more pastoral regionalism.

However, B.'s work can stand easily without such comparisons. Described as a "little masterpiece," "Farmer Eli's Vacation" demonstrates B.'s gentle irony, control of plot, and psychological acuity. Having dreamed all his life of seeing the ocean, only six miles from his pastures, Eli makes the journey at last. The vision is more than he can bear; "He faced [the sea] as a soul might face Almighty Greatness, only to be stricken blind thereafter." Leaving his family camping by the shore, Eli hurries home gratefully to his cows and barns, the world he knows and loves best. "Local color" is too narrow a category for this fine story.

As public interest in regional writing waned at the turn of the century, B. experimented with other genres. Unlike many local colorists, she made the transition successfully. Between 1900 and 1920, she published over 130 stories in prominent magazines. In these short pieces and her many novels, B. attempts more urban settings and sophisticated characters. Her themes concern the strain of reconciling city and country, the industrial future with the values of the agrarian past.

Critical opinion of this later work is mixed. B.'s growing skill as a storyteller and firmer control of structure have been noted by one critic, who observed, however, that she mistakenly adopted an elaborate figurative style beyond her powers. Only when she returned to her New England characters, with their earthy straightforward dialect, did she regain the grace and authenticity of her early work. Although such novels as *Old Crow* (1922) and *John Winterbourne's Family* (1910) achieve a greater philosophical and psychological depth than the more charming local-color stories, B.'s artistry could not keep pace with her ambition; her characters, puppetlike, mouth lofty ideas instead of embodying them.

A devoted artist, B.'s local-color stories hold their own against the more famous work of Jewett and Freeman and represent a distinctive contribution to the genre. Through a synthesis of symbolic and realistic representation, her work conveys an essentially romantic pastoralism. B.'s sentimentality is, however, offset by knowing humor; her idealism is expressed with subtlety. Fresh, evocative, and lovingly detailed, her sketches of country life show a disciplined literary craft. Her New Englanders speak and act with authenticity; their dilemmas are universal, their resolutions sometimes wise and always human.

WORKS: *Stratford-by-the-Sea* (1884). *The Fools of Nature* (1887). *Three Heroines of New England Romance* (with L. I. Guiney and H. P. Spofford, 1894). *Meadow-Grass: Tales of New England Life* (1895). *Robert Louis Stevenson* (with L. I. Guiney, 1896). *The Rose of Hope* (1896). *By Oak and Thorn* (1896). *Women of Colonial and Revolutionary Times—Mercy Otis Warren* (1896). *The Road to Castalay* (1896). *The Day of His Youth* (1897). *Tiverton Tales* (1899). *King's End* (1901). *Margaret Warrener* (1901). *Judgement* (1903). *The Mannerings* (1903). *The Merrylinks* (1903). *High Noon* (1904). *The County Road* (1906). *The Court of Love* (1906). Chap. XI of *The Whole Family* (a novel by twelve authors, 1908). *Rose MacLeod* (1908). *The Story of Thryza* (1909). *Country Neighbors* (1910). *John Winterbourne's Family* (1910). *The One-Footed Fairy* (1911). *My Love and I* (1912). *The Secret of the Clan: A Story for Girls* (1912). *Robin Hood's Barn* (1913). *Vanishing Points* (1913). *Joint Owners in Spain: A Comedy in One Act* (1914). *Children of Earth: A Play of New England* (1915). *The Prisoner* (1916). *Bromley Neighborhood* (1917). *The Flying Teuton, and Other Stories* (1918). *The*

Loving Cup: A Play in One Act (1918). *The Black Drop* (1919). *Homespun and Gold* (1920). *The Wind between the Worlds* (1920). *Louise Imogen Guiney* (1921). *One-Act Plays* (1921). *Old Crow* (1922). *Ellen Prior* (1923). *Charles Lamb: A Play* (1924). *The Mysteries of Ann* (1925). *Dear Old Templeton* (1927). *The Golden Ball* (1929). *The Marriage Feast: A Fantasy* (1931). *The Diary of a Dryad* (1932). *The Kingdom in the Sky* (1932). *Jeremy Hamblin* (1934). *The Willoughbys* (1935). *Fable and Song* (1939). *Pilgrim's Progress* (1944).

BIBLIOGRAPHY: Langill, E. D., "Alice Brown: A Critical Study" (Ph.D. diss., Univ. of Wisconsin, 1975). Overton, G., *The Women Who Make Our Novels* (1922). Pattee, F. L., *The New American Literature, 1890–1930* (1930). Toth, S. A., "More than Local Color: A Reappraisal of Rose Terry Cooke, Mary Wilkins Freeman, and Alice Brown" (Ph.D. diss., Univ. of Minnesota, 1969). Walker, D., *Alice Brown* (1974). Westbrook, P., *Acres of Flint: Writers of Rural New England* (1951). Williams, B., *Our Short Story Writers* (1920). Williams, Sister M., "The Pastoral in New England Local Color: Celia Thaxter, Sarah Orne Jewett, and Alice Brown" (Ph.D. diss., Stanford Univ., 1972).

Other references: *ALR* 2 (Spring 1972). *Atlantic* (July 1906). *Book Buyer* (Nov. 1896). *WS* 1 (1972).

SARAH WAY SHERMAN

Pearl Sydenstricker Buck

B. *26 June 1892, Hillsboro, West Virginia; d. 6 March 1973, Danby, Vermont*
Wrote under: Pearl S. Buck, John Sedges
D. *of Absalom and Caroline Stulting Sydenstricker; m. John Lossing Buck, 1917;*
m. Richard J. Walsh, 1935

The daughter of American missionaries who took her to China at the age of three months, B. grew up in close contact with the Chinese and had no intention of ever leaving China except for periods of study, at Randolph-Macon Women's College and Cornell University. Twentieth-century struggles, however, destroyed traditional China and made it impossible for her to continue living there. In 1932, she returned to the U.S. She divorced her husband and, in 1935, married her publisher, Richard J. Walsh. B.'s original incentive to earn money by writing had been her realization, in 1928, that her daughter was retarded. She also raised nine adopted Asian children and supported many philanthropic organizations.

Throughout her career, beginning with her first book, *East Wind: West Wind* (1930), B. wrote to explain China to the West, although she also wrote about other Asian countries and the U.S.

The Good Earth (1931), acknowledged as B.'s best work, is the story of Chinese peasants—Wang Lung, a farmer, and O-Lan, the slave girl he marries. It became a worldwide bestseller and won B. the Pulitzer Prize in 1931 and the Howells Medal of the American Academy of Arts and Letters in 1935. *Sons* (1932) and *A House Divided* (1935) carry the saga of Wang Lung's family through two more generations. The novel on which B. was working at her death, "Red Earth," was to have told the story of the modern descendents of Wang Lung.

Among B.'s lesser-known novels are several of particular interest. *Pavilion of Women* (1946) tells how a Chinese lady finds fulfillment in a spiritual love for an Italian priest. *Peony* (1948) presents the assimilation of the Chinese Jews. *Imperial Woman* (1956) tells the story of Tzu Hsi, who was dowager empress of China when B. was a child.

B. wrote biographies of her mother, *The Exile*, and of her father, *Fighting Angel* (both published in 1936). Her portraits of her parents are fresh, vivid, and true. She describes her father and his evangelical fervor with tenderness, understanding, and an admiration that is not lessened by a touch of humor. The same qualities appear in her portrait of her mother, along with a fellow feeling of sympathy for the trials her mother had to endure. B.'s mother deeply felt the loss of a child who succumbed to tropical disease—and felt almost as deeply her husband's refusal to treat her as an equal. *The Child Who Never Grew* (1950) tells the story of B.'s own retarded daughter.

B.'s obituary in the *New York Times* said that by 1972 she had published more than eighty-five novels and collections of short stories and essays and that more than twenty-five volumes still awaited publication. She has always been popular with the general public. Her simple style, her feeling for traditional values, and her skill in writing on universal themes account for her appeal. Her Confucian tutor had taught her to consider the novel a form of popular entertainment, unworthy of the scholar, and she wished to be popular because she liked ordinary people. In 1938, B. received the Nobel Prize "for rich and genuine portrayals of Chinese life and for masterpieces of biography."

SELECTED WORKS: *East Wind: West Wind* (1930). *The Good Earth* (1931). *Sons* (1932). *The Young Revolutionist* (1932). *The First Wife, and Other Stories* (1933). *Far and Near* (1934; pub. as *Twenty-seven Stories*, 1943). *The Mother* (1934). *A House Divided* (1935). *The Exile* (1936). *Fight-*

ing Angel (1936). *This Proud Heart* (1938). *Of Men and Women* (1941). *American Unity and Asia* (1942). *Dragon Seed* (1942). *The Promise* (1943). *What America Means to Me* (1943). *Portrait of a Marriage* (1945). *Pavilion of Women* (1946). *The Big Wave* (1947). *Peony* (alternative title, *The Bond Maid*, 1948). *Kinfolk* (1949). *The Child Who Never Grew* (1950). *God's Men* (1951). *The Hidden Flower* (1952). *Come, My Beloved* (1953). *Imperial Woman* (1956). *Command the Morning* (1959). *A Bridge for Passing* (1962). *The Time Is Noon* (1966). *Pearl Buck's America* (1971). *The Goddess Abides* (1972). *Words of Love* (1974). *Secrets of the Heart* (1976).

BIBLIOGRAPHY: Doyle, P. A., *Pearl S. Buck* (1965). Harris, T. E., *Pearl S. Buck: A Biography* (2 vols., 1969–71). Spencer, C., *The Exile's Daughter: A Biography of Pearl S. Buck* (1944). Van Gelder, R., *Writers and Writing* (1946).

BARBARA J. BUCKNALL

Frances Eliza Hodgson Burnett

B. 24 Nov. 1849, Manchester, England; d. 29 Oct. 1924, Plandome, New York
D. of Edwin and Eliza Boond Hodgson; m. Swan Moses Burnett, 1875;
m. Stephen Townsend, 1900

B., the middle of five children, lived until she was sixteen in Manchester, England. A dame school she attended there provided her only formal education. In 1865, after her businessman father died, the family joined a relative in Knoxville, Tennessee, where financial need prompted B. to sell her first story, published when she was nineteen. In 1873, she married an eye specialist, with whom she had two sons. B.'s writing proved a major means of the young family's support. Her success as a writer of popular fiction made her a celebrity and allowed her family to enjoy an expensive international life-style. In 1898, B. and her husband were divorced. From 1900 to 1907 she was married to Stephen Townsend, whose theatrical aspirations she had been championing since 1889 in London, while she was overseeing the stage production of her stories.

B.'s career was productive as well as long. Her fifty-five titles include five bestsellers, and thirteen of her stories and novels were adapted for the stage in England or America. After her first story was published in *Godey's Lady's Book* in 1868, B. wrote formulaic love stories for fashionable magazines before graduating to novels. Several of these, novels of working-class and political life such as *That Lass o' Lowries* (1877), *Louisiana* (1880), and *Through One Administration* (1883), gained her critical recognition as a serious artist. American reviewers compared her work favorably with that of George Eliot and placed her in the front rank of young American fiction writers.

Little Lord Fauntleroy (1886), based on her son Vivian, established B.'s reputation as a popular writer. Intended primarily for children, the book became a bestseller and was soon translated into more than a dozen languages. B.'s stage version was popular in England and France as well as in America. In 1921, Mary Pickford starred in a film version.

After this success, B. wrote more books for children, two of which continue to find an appreciative audience: *A Little Princess* (1905), which was made into a 1939 film starring Shirley Temple, and *The Secret Garden* (1911), a pastoral novel considered a juvenile classic.

The books that found their way onto annual lists of bestsellers, however, were novels of fashionable social life written for adults: *A Lady of Quality* (1896), the story of a strong-willed woman in early 18th-c. England; *The Shuttle* (1907), a novel about an Anglo-American marriage; *T. Tembarom* (1913), a Horatio-Alger type sequel to *The Shuttle*; and *The Head of the House of Coombe* (1922), a portrayal of social life in London before World War I.

B.'s life and writing were characterized by tensions between the serious artist and the popular writer, the independent woman and the self-sacrificing wife and mother. While she was laboring over a 512-page portrayal of Anglo-American relationships (*The Shuttle*), she would shock her readers with a heroine who has been reared as a boy and later kills her lover with a riding whip (*A Lady of Quality*), then dash off a novella about a woman who, through self-abasing humility, wins the hand of a wealthy nobleman (*The Making of a Marchioness*, 1901).

B.'s recent biographer, Ann Thwaite, suggests that B.'s first bestseller changed her from a talented realist comparable to Elizabeth Gaskell into a pen-driving machine turning out inferior romances. But it can also be argued that B. excelled when she stayed close to the fairy tale, as in her best-known children's works, or when her tensions as artist and woman were allowed to inform and discipline her work, as in *The Making of a Marchioness*, which contains within the literary context of a romantic Cinderella tale a scathing portrayal of women's plight in the Edwardian marriage market.

WORKS: *Dolly* (1877, reprinted as *Vagabondia*, 1883). *Pretty Polly Pemberton* (1877). *Surly Tim* (1877). *That Lass o'Lowries* (1877; dramatization, 1878).

Theo (1877). *Earlier Stories, First and Second Series* (1878). *Kathleen* (1878). *Miss Crespigny* (1878). *Our Neighbor Opposite* (1878). *A Quiet Life* (1878). *The Tide on the Moaning Bar* (1878). *Haworth's* (1879). *Jarl's Daughter* (1879). *Natalie* (1879). *Louisiana* (1880). *Esmeralda* (1881). *A Fair Barbarian* (1881). *Through One Administration* (1883). *Little Lord Fauntleroy* (1886). *Editha's Burglar* (1888; dramatization, *Nixie*, 1890). *The Fortunes of Philippa Fairfax* (1888; dramatization, *Phyllis*, 1889). *The Real Little Lord Fauntleroy* (1888). *Sara Crewe* (1888). *A Woman's Will; or, Miss Defarge* (1888). *The Pretty Sister of José* (1889; dramatization, 1903). *Little Saint Elizabeth* (1890). *The Drury Lane Boys' Club* (1892). *Giovanni and the Other* (1892). *The Showman's Daughter* (1892). *The One I Knew the Best of All* (1893). *Piccino, and Other Child Stories* (1894). *The Two Little Pilgrims' Progress* (1895). *A Lady of Quality* (1896; dramatization, 1897). *The First Gentleman of Europe* (1897). *His Grace of Osmonde* (1897). *In Connection with the De Willoughby Claim* (1899; dramatization, *That Man and I*, 1904). *The Making of a Marchioness* (1901). *The Methods of Lady Walderhurst* (1901). *In the Closed Room* (1905). *A Little Princess* (1905; produced 1902). *The Dawn of a To-morrow* (1906; produced 1909). *Racketty Packetty House* (1906; produced 1912). *The Troubles of Queen Silver-Bell* (1906). *The Cozy Lion* (1907). *The Shuttle* (1907). *The Good Wolf* (1908). *The Spring Cleaning* (1908). *Barty Crusoe and His Man Saturday* (1909). *The Land of the Blue Flower* (1909). *The Secret Garden* (1911). *My Robin* (1912). *T. Tembarom* (1913). *The Lost Prince* (1915). *Little Hunchback Zia* (1916). *The White Peope* (1917). *The Head of the House of Coombe* (1922). *Robin* (1922). *In the Garden* (1925).

BIBLIOGRAPHY: Burnett, C. B., *Happily Ever After* (1969). Burnett, V., *The Romantick Lady* (1927). Laski, M., *Mrs. Ewing, Mrs. Molesworth, and Mrs. Hodgson Burnett* (1950). Thwaite, A., *Waiting for the Party: The Life of Frances Hodgson Burnett* (1974).

Other references: *American Literary Realism* 8 (Winter 1975). *ChildL* 7 (1978). *CE* 41 (April 1980).

PHYLLIS BIXLER

Esther Edwards Burr

B. 1732, Northampton, Massachusetts; d. April 1758, Princeton, New Jersey
D. of Jonathan and Sarah Pierrepont Edwards; m. Aaron Burr, 1752

B. was the third of eleven children of Sarah Pierrepont and the prominent minister, Jonathan Edwards. At the age of twenty she married Aaron Burr, pastor of the Presbyterian church at Newark, New Jersey, and later a founder and second president of Princeton College. At twenty-six years of age, B., having been widowed a year, died from the results of an innoculation against the small pox.

In 1754, B. began a journal of her daily life and exchanged it periodically with one kept by her friend, Sarah Prince, of Boston. B.'s journal is valuable for the views it gives of the Puritan woman's life in the mid-18th c. and for the insights it contains into how Puritan values and habits of mind helped a woman to understand and evaluate the world that she lived in.

The dominant themes of the journal are the loneliness and hardship of everyday existence which are only made endurable by the knowledge of God's providential guidance of human affairs. For example, when her second child was born, B. was entirely alone, but her faith in God helped her to meet the ordeal: "I felt very gloomy when I found I was actually in labour to think that I was, as it were, destitute of earthly friends—no mother, no husband, and none of my particular friends that belong to the town . . . only my dear God was all of these relations to me." On another occasion she was visiting her father in Stockbridge, Massachusetts, where the community was expecting an Indian attack. She had a momentary crisis of faith: "I want to be made willing to die in any way God pleases, but I am not willing to be butchered by a barbarous enemy nor can't make myself willing." Ultimately she trusted in Providence and prayed for survival: the Indians never attacked.

In the Puritan manner the journal records events large and small— for God's will was manifest in every activity of life. Thus, the journal tells of visitations to the sick, attendance at sermons, entertainment of the governor's wife with "cakes" on militia day, the depradations of the French and the Indians, the political maneuverings of the Newark community, the circumstances of the religious revival of the mid-1750s, and the problems of moving to Princeton and of establishing the college —all given with frank, moral assessments of what B. thinks of the behavior of her contemporaries. Her commentary on the protestations of the local government as it prepared to meet the threatened advance of the French and the Indians is typical: "I am perplexed about our publick affairs, the Men say (tho not Mr. Burr, he is not of that sort) that women have no business to concern themselves about 'em but to trust to those that know better and be content to be destroyed—because they did all for the best—Indeed, if I was convinced that our great men did as they really thought was for the Glory of God and the good of the country, it would go a great ways to make me easy."

As a result of this personal evaluation of the events and interests of her time, B.'s journal has a warm, emotional quality which makes the incidents of the past come alive. She is frank and explicit, never falsely sentimental or literary. Like the preachers she heard regularly, B. kept to the plain style, proudly asserting that the "busy housewife" had no time to be "literary." The journal is, then, a moving story of a woman's growth to maturity within the Puritan tradition of provincial America.

WORKS: *Esther Burr's Journal* (Ed. J. Rankin, 1902), an untrustworthy edition containing many pages that appear to be fabrications.

The papers of Esther Edwards Burr are at Yale University, Andover-Newton Theological School (Newton, Massachusetts), and Princeton College.

BIBLIOGRAPHY: Axtell, J., *A School Upon a Hill* (1974). Cott, N., *The Bonds of Womanhood: Woman's Sphere in New England, 1780–1835* (1977). Other references: *NEQ* 3 (1930).

MAUREEN GOLDMAN

Helen Stuart Campbell

B. 4 July 1839, Lockport, New York; d. 22 July 1918, Dedham, Massachusetts
Wrote under: Helen C. Weeks, Campbell Wheaton
D. of Homer H. and Jane E. Campbell Stuart; m. Grenville Mellen Weeks, 1860

Under her married name, C. wrote five children's books as well as many stories in *Riverside Magazine* and *Our Young Folks*. After 1877, C. adopted her mother's maiden name (Campbell) and she wrote works mainly for an adult audience: novels, magazine articles, cookbooks, studies of poverty and women workers. Experience as a teacher in cooking schools qualified C. to become household editor of *Our Continent* (1882–84).

From 1894 to 1912 C. was closely associated with Charlotte Perkins Gilman. They coedited *Impress* in San Francisco and worked in Unity Settlement in Chicago. Eventually C. lived with the Gilmans in New York. During this period she lectured on home economics at the University of Wisconsin in 1895, and at Kansas State Agricultural College in 1897 and 1898. Her final years were spent in Massachusetts.

The Ainslee Series, consisting of *Grandpa's House* (1868), *The Ains-*

lee Stories (1868), *White and Red* (1869), and *Four and What They Did* (1871) reveal C.'s ability to create troublesome, lively children who tumble from one misadventure to another as they explore their New England or midwestern surroundings. The liveliest and most amusing are Ainslee, five-year-old hero of the second book, and Sinny, his black friend. Although no more than a collection of stories, this book is unified by its temporal frame and by the background of New England village life. While Harry in *White and Red* is hardly an interesting hero, the account of his journey and the description of Indian characters and customs in Red Lake capture the imagination and make the tale a valuable portrait of the American past. *Six Sinners* (1877), a boarding-school story written under the name Campbell Wheaton, lacks the freshness of C.'s earlier work, but maintains her characteristic flashes of humor.

His Grandmothers (1877), which marks C.'s transition from juveniles to the adult novel, is a light-hearted sketch of a household turned upside down by a flint-hearted New England grandmother. It stands in lively contrast to C.'s subsequent novels, which often (to the detriment of the fiction) attempt to treat such social themes as the role of heredity, the economic plight of women, the relation of diet to disease, the greed and corruption of postwar America.

Mrs. Herndon's Income (1886), C.'s most important novel, has too many characters and a poorly constructed plot, manipulated to suit the author's moral vision. It is partially redeemed, however, by the comic presence of Amanda Briggs and by the realistic description of New York slums. *Miss Melinda's Opportunity* (1886) uses a smaller canvas and a simpler plot, but is equally didactic. For the modern reader the interest lies less in the scheme for cooperative housekeeping than in the characterization of Miss Melinda and the evocation of New York in the Gilded Age.

C.'s reform writing, as Robert Bremner points out, places her in the company of propagandists "who hoped to alter conditions by rousing the conscience of the nation." *The Problem of the Poor* (1882) and *Darkness and Daylight* (1891) describe life in New York's slums and McAuley's Water Street Mission. *Prisoners of Poverty* (1887) attacks the exploitation of women in New York sweatshops and department stores, employing case histories to illustrate the effects of starvation wages. *Prisoners of Poverty Abroad* (1889) feebly echoes its predecessor in a superficial survey of women workers in Europe. Less emotional than the earlier studies and buttressed by statistics, *Women Wage-Earners* (1893), which received an award from the American Economic Association, treats the plight of women factory workers across America, condemning low wages, long hours, and poor sanitation. C. concludes by recommending the organization of women's labor clubs and the appointment of women inspectors, as well as higher wages and a shorter working week.

As a fiction writer, C. was a minor figure, memorable only for the local color and abundant humor of her children's stories. Her role as reformer, however, was more significant. C.'s studies of women wage-earners stirred the conscience of her age and led to the formation of consumers' leagues in the 1890s, which monitored retail stores to assure fair labor practices.

WORKS: *Grandpa's House* (1868). *The Ainslee Stories* (1868). *An American Family in Paris* (1869). *White and Red: A Narrative of Life among the Northwest Indians* (1869). *Four and What They Did* (1871). *Six Sinners or School Days in Bantam Valley* (1877). *His Grandmothers* (1877). *Unto the Third and Fourth Generation* (1880). *The Easiest Way in Housekeeping and Cooking* (1881). *Patty Pearson's Boy: A Tale of Two Generations* (1881). *The Housekeeper's Year Book* (1882). *The Problem of the Poor* (1882). *Under Green Apple Boughs* (1882). *A Sylvan City or Quaint Corners in Philadelphia* (with others, 1883). *The American Girl's Home Book of Work and Play* (1883). *The What-To-Do Club: A Story for Girls* (1885). *Good Dinners for Every Day in the Year* (1886). *Mrs. Herndon's Income* (1886). *Miss Melinda's Opportunity* (1886). *Prisoners of Poverty* (1887). *Roger Berkeley's Probation* (1888). *Prisoners of Poverty Abroad* (1889). *Darkness and Daylight* (with T. Knox and T. Byrnes, 1891). *Anne Bradstreet and Her Time* (1891). *Some Passages in the Practice of Dr. Martha Scarborough* (1893). *Women Wage-Earners* (1893). *In Foreign Kitchens* (1893). *Household Economics* (1896). *The Heart of It: A Series of Extracts from the Power of Silence and The Perfect Whole* (edited by H. Campbell, with K. Westendorf, 1897).

BIBLIOGRAPHY: Bremner, R. H., *From the Depths: The Discovery of Poverty in the U.S.* (1956). Darling, F. L., *The Rise of Children's Book Reviewing in America, 1865–1881* (1968). Gilman, C. P., *The Living of Charlotte Perkins Gilman* (1935). Taylor, W. F., *The Economic Novel in America* (1942). Wright, Lyle H., *American Fiction, 1876–1900* (1966).

For articles in reference works, see: *Literary Writings in America: A Bibliography* (1977). *NAW* (article by R. Paulson).

PHYLLIS MOE

Sally Carrighar

B. ca. 1905, Cleveland, Ohio
D. of George Thomas Beard and Perle Avis Harden Wagner

In *Home to the Wilderness* (1973), C. tells a sad story. Partially disfigured at birth by a high-forceps delivery, she was abhorrent to her mother, who once attempted to strangle her. The psychotic woman, loathing even her daughter's touch, sought to deprive C. of all love and openly urged her to commit suicide. C. was rescued from utter wretchedness by her father's devotion, her own remarkable determination, and the supportive atmosphere of Wellesley College. She tried various artistic careers: pianist, dancer, and film production assistant, only to have her mother repeatedly snatch success from her. While undergoing psychoanalysis, C. attempted to establish herself as a fictionalist, failed, and "abandoned words." Convalescing in San Francisco from depression and heart disease, she began feeding the birds outside her window. The birds became fellow-creatures; a mouse nesting inside her radio actually sang to her, and in a revelation she understood her vocation: nature writing. Words need not be abandoned, only the bizarre human world of madness, violence, greed.

After seven years of study, C. published *One Day on Beetle Rock* (1944), a narrative treating the interaction of various species in a Sierra Nevada habitat. C. discovered that she could portray this interaction effectively by adopting in successive chapters the point of view of specific organisms and describing how a dramatic natural event (e.g., a flash flood) affects them. To present the "consciousness" of a female mosquito is of course risky, for the writer appears to be anthropomorphizing nature. But the literary strategy of *Beetle Rock* proved itself in *One Day at Teton Marsh* (1947), about the Grand Tetons; *Icebound Summer* (1953), about the north coast of Alaska; and *The Twilight Seas* (1975), about the blue whales.

These objective narratives, in which the narrator never speaks in her own voice, are only a portion of C.'s corpus. Her personal writings give a good introduction to the land and people of northern Alaska. *Moonlight at Midday* (1958) narrates her adventures researching *Icebound Summer* in the tiny village of Unalakleet; it examines Eskimo life, both the traditional ways and the changes wrought by the white man. *Wild Voice of the North* (1959) is the story of her husky, Bobo, whom she rescued and cared for while living and writing in Nome. C. has worked in other genres as well: a play, *As Far as They Go* (1956), celebrates Alaskan history and pioneer life. An historical novel, *The Glass Dove* (1962), portrays a young girl whose farm home in southern Ohio becomes a station on the Underground Railroad.

Wild Heritage (1965) is C.'s most ambitious work. It synthesizes much of the pioneering work in the field of ethology and includes many of C.'s own observations from her years in various wildernesses. The work treats life experiences which humans share with animals: parenthood, sex, aggressiveness, and play. She is especially concerned with what tendencies of animals are learned. In reporting her observations, she uses the technique of her nature narratives, dramatizing the behavior of a single individual of the species.

But one finally returns to C.'s autobiography, *Home to the Wilderness* (1973), for her most deeply felt writing, for her observations that man's morality originates in nature, for her comments about females as naturalists. Nature was C.'s healer and vocation; she could approach it with naive joy, reverence, and awe. But she also knew it as a scientist who relies only on objective observation. That C. successfully combined these two modes of cognition is perhaps her greatest achievement.

WORKS: *Exploring Marin* (1941). *One Day on Beetle Rock* (1944). *One Day at Teton Marsh* (1947). *Prey of the Arctic* (1951). *Icebound Summer* (1953). *As Far as They Go* (1956). *Moonlight at Midday* (1958). *Wild Voice of the North* (1959). *The Glass Dove* (1962). *Wild Heritage* (1965). *Home to the Wilderness* (1973). *The Twilight Seas* (1975).

BIBLIOGRAPHY: NYHTBR (28 Sept. 1947; 19 July 1953). NYT (10 Dec. 1944). NYTBR (28 March 1965). *San Francisco Chronicle* (25 Sept. 1947). SatR (20 March 1965). SatRL (24 Feb. 1945). *Weekly Book Review* (26 Nov. 1944).

MARGARET McFADDEN-GERBER

Elaine Sterne Carrington

B. 1892, New York City; d. 4 May 1958, New York City
Wrote under: Elaine Sterne Carrington, John Ray, Elaine Sterne
D. of Theodore and Mary Louise Henriques Sterne; m. George Dart
  Carrington, 1920

While growing up in New York City, C.'s earliest ambition was to become a musical comedy star. Instead, she became the most prolific writer of radio serials. She also wrote short stories, plays, and songs.

At eighteen, C. sold her first story, "King of the Christmas Feast," to *St. Nicholas* magazine. At nineteen, she won the first prize in a scenario-writing contest sponsored by the New York *Evening Sun* in cooperation with Vitagraph for a script entitled *Sins of the Mothers*. Two more prizes that year—one in a New York *Morning Telegraph* scenario contest and another in a *Collier's* magazine short story contest —launched C.'s professional career. *Nightstick*, a play written under the name of John Ray, was lengthened and produced as a film under the title *Alibi* (1929).

Like the plays, C.'s stories concern courtship, marriage, and child rearing. Plots based on secret engagements, elopements, hopeless love between people of different classes, and friction between child and stepparent are common. The central characters generally are of the middle class—wives who "like to gossip," storekeepers whose shops are "clean as a whistle," young women with "milk-white skin" and "ash-blond hair," and steady young men who like to do "the deciding."

Ten of C.'s short stories are collected in a volume entitled *All Things Considered* (1939). The sentimentality of the stories is redeemed by some incisive and devastating portraits in situations critics have deemed worthy of Evelyn Waugh or John Collier. C.'s fondness for ambiguity caused some reviewers to find "a streak of sharp satire running under the gloss." A cool, sparse style allows the characters occasionally to break free of humdrum plots.

C. moved to radio scriptwriting with her first series, *Red Adams* (1932), later renamed *Red Davis*. The series starred Burgess Meredith as Davis, a "supposedly typical, happy-go-lucky, middle-class teen-ager, who lived in the supposedly typical small town of Oak Park." C. drew the plots from her own experiences as a wife and mother, incorporating (in her words) "all the pangs of adolescence from both the children's and parents' points of view."

Under the sponsorship of Proctor & Gamble, the program was renamed *Forever Young*, and then *Pepper Young's Family* (1936–1956). The setting became the town of Elmwood, and Red Davis became Pepper. What began as a comedy had emerged as a thoroughgoing soap opera. In 1938 it was on the air at three different hours every day and was carried by both the NBC and CBS networks.

Rosemary (1944–1955) was, as the show's opening announcement proclaimed, "dedicated to all the women of today." Each episode began with "This is *your* story—this is *you*." The serial told the story of the Dawson family and centered upon Rosemary Dawson's marriage to Bill Roberts. A young working woman at the begining, Rosemary quickly became the woman of domestic experience, the wife and mother endowed with the goodness and kindness required of soap opera heroines. C.'s intense patriotism (she also wrote scripts for the U.S. Treasury Department) manifested itself in appeals to listeners to buy war bonds. In addition, C.'s characters urged each other to buy Easter Seals, to help returning prisoners of war, or to support some other worthy cause.

Acknowledged as the originator of the radio soap opera, C. established a simple principle for plots that often were complex: "the life of a middle-class family and the bringing up of children in an understanding way." This principle led C. to focus on youthful characters, complete with current slang, a focus which television soap operas of the 1970s have reestablished. The "understanding way" of bringing up children involved humor, which was often present in C.'s scripts. Plots—in which illogic was not uncommon—were always subordinate to characters. In C.'s words, "The story must be written about people you come to know and like and believe in. What happens to them is of secondary importance. Once characters are firmly established and entrenched in the hearts of listeners, the latter will have to tune in to find out what becomes of the characters because of what they feel for them." For over twenty years C. succeeded in creating characters that evoked such loyalty from listeners. Without question, the "Queen of the Soapers," as C. was known, had earned her title.

WORKS: *Alibi* (film, released 1929). *Five Minutes from the Station: A Comedy of Life that Comes Close to Being a Tragedy* (1930). *All Things Considered* (1939). *Red Adams* (radio drama, 1932; later entitled *Red Davis;* later entitled *Forever Young;* later entitled *Pepper Young's Family*, 1936–1956). *When a Girl Marries* (radio drama, 1939–1956). *Rosemary* (radio drama, 1944–1955). *Follow Your Heart* (TV drama, 1953).

BIBLIOGRAPHY: Edmondson, M., and D. Rounds, *From Mary Noble to Mary Hartman: The Complete Soap Opera Book* (1976).

For articles in reference works, see: *CB* (1940).

Other references: *NYHT* (19 Nov. 1939). *New York Post* (25 Jan. 1940). *NYT* (12 Nov. 1939; 11 Feb. 1940; 5 May 1958). *Newsweek* (20 Oct. 1941; 3 May 1954). *The Parents' Magazine* (June 1942). *Time* (26 Aug. 1946). *Variety* (8 May 1940; 16 June 1943).

CAREN J. DEMING

Rachel Louise Carson

B. 27 May 1907, Springdale, Pennsylvania; d. 14 April 1964, Silver Spring, Maryland

D. of Robert Warden and Maria McLean Carson

C. shared her mother's love of nature and books. Publication of stories in *St. Nicholas* magazine when she was ten enhanced C.'s determination to be a writer. She discovered biology at college and zoology at Johns Hopkins University (M.S. 1932).

In 1936, C. took a civil service job with the Fisheries Bureau, where by 1947 she was editor-in-chief for the U.S. Fish and Wildlife Service. In 1937, *Atlantic Monthly* published "Undersea," based on a rejected radio script C. had written for the bureau. *Under the Sea-Wind* (1941) was published just before Pearl Harbor. Reviews were excellent but sales poor, until it was reissued in 1952 and joined her huge success, *The Sea Around Us* (1951), on the bestseller list.

In *The Sea Around Us*, C. provides an intensive look at the secrets beneath the sea's deceptive surface, employing history and geology as well as marine biology. "Mother Sea" covers the development of the sea and its islands; "The Restless Sea" deals with wind, water, and tides; and "Man and the Sea about Him" completes the global picture by interweaving human relationships. While utilizing the major wartime advances made in oceanography, C. never lost sight of the deeper significance of such strides, nor of the normal limitations of nontechnical readers. Her thorough detail and precise work reflect consultation with no less than one thousand printed sources, voluminous correspondence, and frequent discussions with oceanographers around the world.

The Sea Around Us received the National Book Award and the John Burroughs Medal. It remained on the bestseller list for eighty-six weeks and was translated into thirty-two languages.

The Edge of the Sea (1955) began as "a popular guide" to the seashore to make people realize the beach is "more than a place to get sunburned," but evolved into an ambitious study of ecological relationships. She saw it as a biological counterpart to the physical descriptions of *The Sea Around Us*, an exploration of the transition zone between land and sea where evolution can actually be seen taking place.

C. completed *Silent Spring* (1962) as she endured the combined effects of cancer, sinus problems, heart disease, and arthritis, and while caring for the young great-nephew she adopted when his mother died in 1957. The death of C.'s mother, always her close companion, in 1958 caused her great suffering. Her mother, C. wrote to a friend, "more than anyone else I know, embodied Albert Schweitzer's 'reverence for life.' "

A book about death which exalts life, *Silent Spring* sparked international controversy when it proved to the public how much harm resulted from thoughtless and uncontrolled use of pesticides. Although the chemical industry fomented personal attacks on her as an "hysterical woman" and issued propaganda to undercut her facts, C.'s work was vindicated by the 1963 report of the President's Science Advisory Committee.

Silent Spring opens with a stark, shocking fable of one composite town's "silent spring" after pesticides have poisoned the environment, destroying not only insects, but the birds which feed on them. She then marshalls massive documentation of the effects organic pesticides have already produced, not only on birds, but on human beings as well. The book closes with a temperate consideration of the future use of pesticides, and of all man's tamperings with his surroundings. She was careful to search out and include feasible alternatives, such as using biological controls as a partial replacement for chemical spraying.

C. was a scientist, perceptive, meticulous, accurate; an artistic writer, concerned with cadences, images, the need to enlighten yet delight; a philosopher, always seeking the lucid pattern beneath seemingly complex and unmanageable details; and a mystic, aware of the spirit that she felt animated all life.

WORKS: *Under the Sea-Wind: A Naturalist's Picture of Ocean Life* (1941). *The Sea Around Us* (1951). *The Edge of the Sea* (1955). *Silent Spring* (1962). *The Sea* (1964). *The Sense of Wonder* (1965). *The Rocky Coast* (1971).

BIBLIOGRAPHY: Brooks, P., *The House of Life: Rachel Carson at Work* (1972). Brooks, P., *Speaking for Nature: How Literary Naturalists from Henry Thoreau to Rachel Carson Have Stamped America* (1980). Gartner, C. B., *Rachel Carson* (1982). Graham, F., Jr., *Since Silent Spring* (1979). Sterling, P., *Sea and Earth: The Life of Rachel Carson* (1970). Whorton, J., et al., *Before Silent Spring: Pesticides and Public Health in Pre-DDT America* (1974).

For articles in reference works, see: *Current Biography* (1951; 1964).
Other references: *American Forests* (July 1970). *SatR* (16 May 1964).

CAROL B. GARTNER

Alice Cary

B. 26 April 1820, Mount Healthy, Ohio; d. 12 Feb. 1871, New York City
Wrote under: Alice Carey, Alice Cary, Patty Lee
D. of Robert and Elizabeth Jessup Cary

Growing up in what was then considered the Far West—around Cincinnati, Ohio—C. found educational opportunities limited to those offered by a small country school, from which she was removed altogether quite early. Remarkably, with neither education, books, literary friends, nor encouragement, C. and her sister Phoebe developed and sustained their literary talents. Both sisters began to publish first in western and then in eastern newspapers and journals.

In 1850, C. moved to New York, where Rufus W. Griswold praised her work in his *Female Poets of America*. It was also admired by other writers, including Edgar Allan Poe and Whittier, whose poem "The Singer" is about her. Phoebe joined C. in 1851, and by 1856 both women had well-established literary reputations. Their home in New York City became the center of a literary salon that for fifteen years met each Sunday.

C. was a firm believer in abolition and women's rights, although many of her poems show woman's noblest role to be that of wife and mother. Despite her illness—C. suffered for years with tuberculosis, the disease that had killed her mother and two sisters by the time she was fifteen and would eventually kill her—and her self-imposed rigorous writing schedule, she served as the first president of the first women's club in America, which is now known as Sorosis.

A prolific writer, C. authored five volumes of poetry, several novels, and several books of sketches and short stories. Although generally too didactic for modern sensibilities, her poetry was better than that of most of her contemporaries.

The most interesting personae of C.'s poetry are the women. A recurring figure is that of the unmarried but pregnant woman. This figure in "Morna" and later in "No Ring" is "not mother, wife, nor bride." Seduced and abandoned, she dies of a broken heart. Consistently, C. urges understanding, offers poverty as both explanation and excuse, and stands quietly on the woman's side. A second figure is the strong woman, who although she looks happily upon marriage, retains her own identity. Such a woman is found in "The Bridal Veil," in *Ballads, Lyrics, and Hymns* (1866).

It is in C.'s prose, however, that the modern reader would be most interested. *Clovernook* (1852, later appearing in five pirated editions printed in England), *Clovernook Children* (1855), and *Pictures of Country Life* (1859) taken together make a significant contribution to our understanding of early western community life. The sketches are not romantic; they depict lives that were deprived, hard, and marked by early deaths.

There is ample material for study in C.'s prose, especially for those interested in the folklore of women. Material incidental to the story lines gives fascinating glimpses into a world in which, as Aunt Caty in *Clovernook Children* tells us, "widders [are] sometimes better off than wives," and in which an unmarried woman of twenty-five is a local tragedy. These stories are simple but satisfying, and especially remarkable for their vivid portrayal of life in the West.

WORKS: *Poems of Alice and Phoebe Cary* (1950). *Clovernook; or, Recollections of Our Neighborhood in the West* (1st series, 1852; 2nd series, 1853). *Hagar: A Story for Today* (1852). *Lyra, and Other Poems* (1852). *Clovernook Children* (1855). *Poems* (1855). *Married, Not Mated; or, How They Lived at Woodside and Throckmorton Hall* (1856). *Adopted Daughter, and Other Tales* (1859). *The Josephine Gallery* (edited by Cary, with P. Cary, 1859). *Pictures of Country Life* (1859). *Ballads, Lyrics, and Hymns* (1866). *The Bishop's Son* (1867). *Snow-Berries: A Book for Young Folks* (1867). *A Lover's Diary* (1868). *The Born Thrall* (1871). *The Last Poems of Alice and Phoebe Cary* (Ed. M. C. Ames, 1873). *Ballads for Little Folks* (Ed. M. C. Ames, 1874). *The Poetical Works of Alice and Phoebe Cary; with a Memorial of Their Lives* (Ed. M. C. Ames, 1877).

BIBLIOGRAPHY: Ames, M. C., *A Memorial to Alice and Phoebe Cary, with Some of Their Later Poems* (1873). Derby, J., *Fifty Years among Authors, Books, and Publishers* (1884). Venable, W. H., *Beginnings of Literary Culture in the Ohio Valley* (1891).

For articles in reference works, see: *AW. CAL. FPA. NAW* (article by M. W. Langworthy). *NCAB*.

BILLIE J. WAHLSTROM

Willa Sibert Cather

B. 7 Dec. 1873, Gore, Virginia; d. 24 April 1947, New York City
Wrote under: Willa Cather, Willa Sibert Cather
D. of Charles Fectigue and Virginia Boak Cather

C., the first of seven children, was raised on a farm in the hills of northern Virginia. In 1883, her family moved to the Nebraska frontier and, in 1884, to Red Cloud, a "bitter, dead little western town," where C. lived for the next six years. She began publishing short stories while attending the University of Nebraska in Lincoln (B.A. 1895).

From 1896 to 1906, C. lived in Pittsburgh, Pennsylvania, working first at the *Home Magazine* and the *Daily Leader* and then as a high-school teacher. She published a volume of poetry and one of short stories while she was in Pittsburgh.

In 1906, C. joined the staff of *McClure's* magazine in New York City; she became managing editor in 1909. In 1911, after finishing her first novel, *Alexander's Bridge* (1912), she left *McClure's* to concentrate on her writing. In the following years, she began to write about the people of the Nebraska frontier of her childhood.

O Pioneers! (1913) and *My Ántonia* (1918) are lyric novels of the land and of the lives of strong women on the Nebraska frontier. *My Ántonia*, C.'s most widely read novel, is told by Jim Burden, Antonia's childhood friend, who looks back on their past from the perspective of a successful but unhappy eastern lawyer. He sees Antonia as the apotheosis of the pioneer woman who conquered the land and as a personification of eternal values.

The novels written after WWI reflect C.'s increasing concern about the materialism and spiritual aridity of the technological 20th c.

The least distinguished of these—*One of Ours* (1922)—was awarded a Pulitzer Prize. A novel of World War I, it tells the story of Claude Wheeler, a young man who has spent a dreary life on a Nebraska farm and has a brief experience of beauty and fulfillment in France before he is killed in action.

A Lost Lady (1923), set at the end of the era of transcontinental railroad expansion, is the story of Marian Forrester, the beautiful, young wife of a man who had been a dynamic railroad builder in the days of the conquest of the West. As her husband's health and fortunes fail, Mrs. Forrester's world is restricted to Sweet Water, a small railway-junction town.

The novel describes the disillusionment of the narrator, an idealistic young man and a devoted family friend, with Mrs. Forrester's accommodation to materialistic society.

This slender book is surely one of the high points of American fiction. C.'s unaffected, powerful, and lucid style is the result of her untiring struggle for, as she formulated it herself, the correct and appropriate word, which makes possible "the gift of inner empathy."

The Professor's House (1925) also contrasts the contemporary materialistic world with a more ideal world in harmonious relation with nature. Professor St. Peter does, in the end, reach some understanding of how he can survive in his family's world of money and status, but the center of the novel is "Tom Outland's Story," an account of the discovery of the ruins of cliff dwellings in the Southwest.

My Mortal Enemy (1926), a short novel that has not been well-received by all critics, is about the mystery of character. Myra Henshawe, marrying against the wishes of her rich uncle, has given up wealth and the Roman Catholicism in which she was raised for love, which has proved distinctly unsatisfying. She experiences deep conflict not only with her husband but with her own sharply divided character. Myra has many bad qualities—she is arrogant, jealous, and greedy—but she strongly desires immortality and wholeness.

C.'s most mysterious work derives its impact from what remains unsaid, from the depths that seem constantly to be assaulting the cool surface. Religion, Myra comes to believe, "is different from everything else; *because in religion seeking is finding.*" Through a variety of images, C. suggests that Myra's sin was to have sought and found false gods, the most deceitful of which is romantic love. By rejecting the Roman Catholicism of her childhood and the position she was born to, she has lost herself. C. does full justice to the compelling lure of eros, which continues to exert its power over Myra and Nellie Birdseye, the narrator of the story.

Death Comes for the Archbishop (1927), based on the lives of Jean Baptiste Lamy and Joseph Machebeuf, is the chronicle of two 19th-c. French priests assigned to set up an apostolic vicariate in New Mexico Territory. Within a framework similar to a picaresque novel, C. includes biographical sketches, stories of miracles and legends of saints, and description of the Southwestern landscape. *Shadows on the Rock* (1931), set in 17th-c. Quebec, is another novel about the Catholic faith in the New World.

In her last years, C. published two novels—not among her best—two volumes of short stories—one of them, *Obscure Destinies* (1932), contains two excellent stories—and a collection of critical essays—*Not under Forty*

(1936). The last title reflects C.'s claim that she was not writing for the younger generation who, she believed, could not share or understand her values.

The more closely one looks at C.'s works in the context of her life, the more clearly one sees that C. was always writing about herself. "Life began for me when I ceased to admire and began to remember," she said. This reserved woman, who went to unusual lengths to maintain privacy, was driven by an inexorable need to give form to and reveal, albeit indirectly, her inner self. Some of the power in her works surely comes from this tension—the romantic confessional temperament writing in the classical restrained mode.

It is C.'s lot to be America's least comprehended major novelist. Wallace Stevens said about her that "we have nothing better than she is." But the particularity of her genius is elusive, and comments about C.'s work often focus on its less central aspects.

On C.'s style, there is little dissent—her prose is of the highest quality, variously described as classical, restrained, wonderfully transparent. C. wrote language of a kind that is not indigenous to American letters, yet the nature of her genius was such that the prose sounds impeccably American.

C.'s lyrical and profound evocations of nature in its many forms are not surpassed in American letters, and she is one of the few American writers who can take her place among the great European writers who have gloriously pictured the natural world.

C. has, as could not be otherwise, been recognized as a religious writer. It was Henry Steele Commager who wrote: "And all her novels and stories . . . were animated by a single great theme, as they were graced by a single felicitous style. The theme was that of the supremacy of moral and spiritual over material values, the ever recurrent but inexhaustible theme of gaining the whole world and losing one's soul." C. may have been a mystic who saw this world as a prism of God.

Many critics of the 1920s considered her to be the best American writer of her day. C.'s rank is more qualified today, but the tide has started to turn, and C.'s work is apparently to be revived with vigor and enthusiasm.

WORKS: *April Twilights* (1903; enlarged ed., 1923). *The Troll Garden* (1905). *Alexander's Bridge* (1912). *O Pioneers!* (1913). *The Song of the Lark* (1915). *My Ántonia* (1918). *Youth and the Bright Medusa* (1920). *One of Ours* (1922). *A Lost Lady* (1923). *The Professor's House* (1925). *My Mortal Enemy* (1926). *Death Comes for the Archbishop* (1927). *Shadows on the Rock* (1931). *Obscure Destinies* (1932). *Lucy Gayheart* (1935). *Not under Forty*

(1936). *Sapphira and the Slave Girl* (1940). *The Old Beauty, and Others* (1948). *On Writing* (1949). *Writings from Willa Cather's Campus Years* (Ed. J. R. Shively, 1950). *Willa Cather in Europe: Her Own Story of the First Journey* (Ed. G. N. Kates, 1956). *Early Stories* (Ed. M. R. Bennett, 1957). *Willa Cather's Collected Short Fiction, 1892–1912* (Ed. M. R. Bennett, 1965). *The Kingdom of Art: Willa Cather's First Principles and Critical Statements, 1893 to 1896* (Ed. B. Slote, 1966). *The World and the Parish: Willa Cather's Articles and Reviews, 1893–1902* (Ed. W. M. Curtin, 1970). *Uncle Valentine, and Other Stories* (Ed. B. Slote, 1973).

BIBLIOGRAPHY: Auchincloss, L., *Pioneers and Caretakers: A Study of Nine American Women Writers* (1965). Bennett, M., *The World of Willa Cather* (1961). Bloom, E. A., and L. D. Bloom, *Willa Cather's Gift of Sympathy* (1964). Brown, E. K., and L. Edel, *Willa Cather: A Critical Biography* (1953). Commager, H. S., *The American Mind* (1950). Daiches, D., *Willa Cather: A Critical Introduction* (1951). Edel, L., *Willa Cather: The Paradox of Success* (1960). Lewis, E., *Willa Cather Living* (1953). McFarland, D. T., *Willa Cather* (1972). Murphy, J. J., ed., *Five Essays on Willa Cather* (1974). Randall, J. H., III, *The Landscape and the Looking Glass: Willa Cather's Search for Value* (1960). Rapin, R., *Willa Cather* (1930). Schroeter, J., ed., *Willa Cather and Her Critics* (1967). Sergeant, E. S., *Willa Cather: A Memoir* (1963). Slote, B., and V. Faulkner, eds., *The Art of Willa Cather* (1974). Stouck, D., *Willa Cather's Imagination* (1975). Trilling, L., *After the Genteel Tradition* (1964). Van Ghent, D., *Willa Cather* (Univ. of Minnesota Pamphlets on American Writers, No. 36, 1964). Woodress, J., *Willa Cather: Her Life and Art* (1970).

LINA MAINIERO

Mary Hartwell Catherwood

B. *16 Dec. 1847, Luray, Ohio; d. 26 Dec. 1902, Chicago, Illinois*
Wrote under: Mary Hartwell Catherwood, Mary Hartwell
D. of Marcus and Phoebe Thompson Hartwell; m. James Catherwood, 1877

After graduation in 1868 from Granville Female College, Granville, Ohio, C. taught in Ohio and Illinois before she was able to support herself by writing. Her early work combines strands of critical realism and melodrama. She published many short stories and long serials in magazines such as the *Atlantic* and *Lippincott's*.

Historians of American fiction suggest that C.'s importance lies in her having been the first novelist to write popular romantic historical novels, forecasting the best-selling genre at the turn of the century. C. was the first woman novelist born west of the Alleghenies and the first woman novelist to be a college graduate. As a writer, however, she is much more important today because of her works of critical realism and her pioneering regional material. Her two early novels, *A Woman in Armor* (1857) and *Craque-o-Doom* (1881), contain tantilizing hints of the social realist she might have become. *A Woman in Armor*, despite its melodramatic plot, has a detailed if satiric description of the town in which the action is set, Little Boston, and a faintly feminist theme.

C.'s major literary achievement as a regional realist can be found in her short stories, three volumes of which are still in print. Her relentless portrayal of various Midwest towns, from Ohio to Indiana and Illinois, attests to her craftsmanship. Surrounded by the beauty of nature and the seasons, her towns are dreary cultural wastelands peopled with squalid characters who, however, often illustrate such basic qualities of human nature as parental love. Except for "The Spirit of an Illinois Town," her most realistic stories are not collected and can only be found in periodicals. When C. abandoned realism, however, she did not leave the short story behind. In fact, she was one of the few writers who tried to use the materials of historical romance in the short-story form.

In 1889, with the publication of *The Romance of Dollard*, an historical romance based on the work of Francis Parkman, C. took a new direction. From then until her death, she wrote romantic historical fiction, using the French settlement of the West and Canada as background. While remaining in the Midwest (in 1886 she helped found the Western Association of Writers), she turned her back on realistic treatment of midwestern material. At her famous confrontation with Hamlin Garland at the Chicago World's Fair of 1893, she argued for "the aristocratic in literature."

C.'s most popular novel, *Lazarre* (1901), is based on the claims of Eleazar Williams (1789–1858) that he was the lost dauphin of France. The novel is well written and exciting, with violence, dramatic scenes such as a visit to Napoleon, traditional American characters such as Johnny Appleseed, and a romantic ending in which Lazarre gives up the throne of France for the woman he loves and the freedom of the western plains. Otis Skinner dramatized *Lazarre* in 1902 and the play had a successful if not spectacular run.

C. has a remarkable record of "firsts" to her name, and her early work is worth reading. It is ironic that perhaps her career as a serious writer was betrayed by her disdain for those prairie villages that she so realistically portrayed. "The aristocratic in literature" has lost its charms for the modern reader, who eagerly looks for evidence of just such provincial experience as C. (and her characters) longed to escape.

WORKS: A Woman in Armor (1875). *The Dogberry Bunch* (1879). *Craque-o-Doom* (1881). *Rocky Fork* (1882). *Old Caravan Days* (1884). *The Secrets at Roseladies* (1888). *The Romance of Dollard* (1889). *The Story of Tonty* (1890). *The Lady of Fort St. John* (1891). *Old Kaskaskia* (1893). *The White Islander* (1893). *The Chase of St. Castin, and Other Stories* (1894). *The Days of Jeanne d'Arc* (1897). *The Spirit of an Illinois Town* (1897). *Bony and Ban: The Story of a Printing Venture* (1898). *Heroes of the Middle West: French* (1898). *Mackinac, and Other Lake Stories* (1899). *The Queen of the Swamp, and Other Plain Americans* (1899). *Spanish Peggy* (1899). *Lazarre* (1901; dramatization by O. Skinner, 1902).

BIBLIOGRAPHY: Dondore, D. A., *The Prairie and the Making of America* (1926). Garland, H., *Roadside Meetings* (1931). Price, R., "A Critical Biography of Mary Hartwell Catherwood" (Ph.D. diss., Ohio State Univ., 1943). Wilson, M. E., *Biography of Mary Hartwell Catherwood* (1904).

For articles in reference works, see: *DAB. NAW* (article by R. Price).

Other references: *AL* 17 (1945). *Bulletin of Cincinnati Historical Society* (1964). *Michigan Historical Magazine* 30 (1946).

BEVERLY SEATON

Carrie Lane Chapman Catt

B. 9 Jan. 1859, Ripon, Wisconsin; d. 9 March 1947, New Rochelle, New York
D. of Lucius and Maria Clinton Lane; m. Leo Chapman, 1885; m. George William Catt, 1890

A key architect of the woman-suffrage victory in 1920, C. was essentially an activist-lecturer rather than a writer. In 1917, she edited her first book, *Woman Suffrage by Federal Constitutional Amendment*, a series of six essays, four of which C. wrote herself. Here she analyzes briefly the political obstacles women face and focuses on the practical reasons why the federal amendment route seemed the only truly feasible one. She discussed the problems of fraud women encountered in seeking state suffrage amendments and the causes of failure of the three 1916 referenda. She concluded with a chapter countering objections to the federal amendment.

Woman Suffrage and Politics (1923), which C. wrote with Nettie Rogers Shuler immediately after the 1920 victory, is her major work. She gives primary attention not to the history of the woman-suffrage drive itself, nor even to her own role in devising the final winning strategy. Rather, she deals with the question of why that victory had been so long delayed. C. contends that the delay was not caused by hostile or indifferent public opinion; instead, it was the result of political maneuvering, the "buying and selling of American politics."

Apart from these two books, C.'s other publications were generally speeches later issued as pamphlets. Prior to 1920, woman suffrage dominated her concern; later, her major cause became world peace. One of the most significant suffrage pamphlets was *The Winning Strategy*, a 1916 speech in which C. presented her blueprint for the final victory campaign: a double effort for state enfranchisement and the federal amendment.

The thrust of her concern as proponent of world peace is seen in *The Status Today of War vs. Peace* (1928). She defined two great causes of war as being first, the dependence on "war preparedness as the way to peace" and second, economic colonialism with its underlying racism. The hope for peace she found in antiwar treaties between civilized nations and in an educated public opinion in which women must play a key part.

C.'s writings generally reflect the cool, logical style that hallmarked her political action. She avoids rhetorical flashes, relying instead on perceptive analysis and the weight of historical evidence. She saw suffrage as an evolutionary step, the logical outcome of an earlier commitment to democracy.

Though generally objective in her writings, C. in *Woman Suffrage and Politics* often spoke as a partisan deeply wounded in the political struggle. The cost of the long-delayed victory for many women, she argued, was disillusionment with political parties. It is perhaps a mark of the cost of that struggle to herself that after 1920 her major cause was the nonpartisan one, world peace.

WORKS: *Woman Suffrage and Its Basic Argument* (Interurban Woman Suffrage Series, no. 2, 1907). *Woman Suffrage and the Home* (Interurban Woman Suffrage Series, no. 4, 1907). *A Bit of History* (Interurban Woman Suffrage Series, no. 5, 1908). *Perhaps* (ca. 1910). *Do You Know?* (1912). *Woman Suffrage* (1913). *Feminism and Suffrage* (1914). *The Winning Strategy* (1916). *Address to the Congress of the United States* (1917). *Woman Suffrage by Federal Constitutional Amendment* (ed. by Catt, 1917). *Objections to the Federal Amendment* (1919). *Woman Suffrage and Politics* (with N. R. Shuler,

1923). *The Status Today of War vs. Peace* (1928). *Then and Now* (1939). *Who Can Answer?* (1939).

BIBLIOGRAPHY: Peck, M. G., *Carrie Chapman Catt* (1944). *HWS.*
 Other references: *American Political Science Review* (Aug. 1923). *NYT* (13 May 1923).

INZER BYERS

Frances Manwaring Caulkins

B. *26 April 1795, New London, Connecticut; d. 3 Feb. 1869, New London, Connecticut*
D. *of Joshua and Fanny Manwaring Caulkins*

C. centered her literary attention on two radically different areas of concern: the religious education of young people and local history. She began her work in the 1830s writing for the American Tract Society, which published a wide range of her work over the next thirty years, including religious and educational books for children.

C.'s major achievements as a writer, however, came in the area of local history. She wrote first *The History of Norwich, Connecticut, from Its Settlement in 1660 to January, 1845*. A second, revised edition carried the history to 1866. She also wrote *The History of New London, Connecticut* (1852), with a second edition continuing to 1860.

In the early sections of both works, C. deals with the local Indian tribes, their leadership conflicts, and their relationships with the new English settlers. In her view, "the providence of God" had prepared the way for peaceable settlement, for the tribes, weakened by conflict, eagerly sought new allies. Her perspective on the Indians is sympathetic, although at times condescending, and she stresses their dependent qualities. She underscores what she sees as the paternalistic concern of Norwich leaders for the Indians.

C. stresses the early religious focus of town life, the decline of fervor in the late 17th c., and the impact of the 18th-c. Great Awakening. She stresses the work of Tennent, Davenport, and Whitefield, citing the positive impact of revivalism as well as the problems of church division and separatism. She also notes the role in New London of the Rogerene sect, typical of religious extremists in their "determination to be persecuted."

While her primary focus is on political and religious history, C. also has a sound grasp of local, social, and economic history. She notes the close hold on town leadership by descendants of the early town fathers; not until the end of the 18th c. was there substantial expansion in the Norwich leadership ranks.

Of the two histories, that of New London has the more localized view, stressing personalities and incidents often of purely local concern. In both histories, C. takes the view that events of local history "illustrate classes of men and ages of time." She writes with ease; her tone is at times romantic. While she does not escape totally the self-congratulatory notes of the native, she does attempt to evaluate events within a broader historical perspective.

Though the material differs sharply, there is a common denominator in her two types of writing. Both in her writing for the American Tract Society and in her histories, C. has in mind young people and their concerns. A sense of God's providence informs both types of works and she seeks to arouse through history "a more affectionate sympathy for your ancestors."

WORKS: The Child's Hymn Book (1835). Children of the Bible: As Examples and as Warnings (1842). The History of Norwich, Connecticut, from Its Settlement in 1660 to January, 1845 (1845; rev. ed. 1866). The Tract Primer (ca. 1848). Memoir of the Rev. William Adams, of Dedham, Mass., and of the Rev. Eliphalet Adams, of New London, Conn., and Their Descendants, with the Journal of William Adams, 1666–1682 (1849). Bride Brook: A Legend of New London, Connecticut (1852). The History of New London, Connecticut (1852; rev. ed. 1860). Eve and Her Daughters of Holy Writ; or, Women of the Bible (1861). Ye Antient Buriall Place of New London, Connecticut (1899). The Stone Records of Groton (Ed. E. S. Gilman, 1903).

BIBLIOGRAPHY: Haven, H. P., "Memoir," in History of Norwich (1874). Trumbull, H. C., A Model Superintendent: A Sketch of the Life . . . of Henry P. Haven (1880). Wilcox, G. B., In Memoriam, Miss Frances Manwaring Caulkins (1869).

For articles in reference works, see: NAW (article by M. Freiberg).

Other references: New London County Historical Society Records (1890–94).

INZER BYERS

Elizabeth Margaret Chandler

B. 24 Dec. 1807, Wilmington, Delaware; d. 2 Nov. 1834, Tecumseh, Michigan
D. of Thomas and Margaret Evans Chandler

The youngest child and only daughter of a prosperous Quaker farmer of English stock, C. lost her mother in infancy, was orphaned at nine, and was raised by her grandmother and three Quaker aunts in Philadelphia. She attended Quaker schools until only twelve or thirteen and was an avid reader all her life. At an early age she showed her talents as a poet: at nine she produced a poem called "Reflections on a Thunder Gust," at sixteen she began to publish a few poems in the public press. At eighteen "The Slave Ship" brought her a prize from the editors of Casket, in which it was published.

Benjamin Lundy, the antislavery publisher, noticed "The Slave Ship" and reprinted it in the Genius of Universal Emancipation. Lundy recruited C. as a regular contributor, and two years later she became the editor of "The Female Repository," the women's department of his paper. C. moved with her brother to the Michigan frontier in 1830, but continued as editor of the Genius's women's department until her death, despite Lundy's complaints about the difficulties of regular communication with a forest outpost.

C. was the first American woman author to make slavery the principal theme of her writing. Half of her published poems and essays dealt with slavery, African life, the emancipation movement, or the American Indian. "The Slave Ship" employed a poignant theme which she used repeatedly: the wrenching despair and horror experienced by proud and independent Africans snatched from their native shores and transported in chains to the Americas and lifelong slavery.

In "The Afric's Dream" she shows the fettered slave remembering his former home where he lay under his own banana tree: "My own bright stream was at my feet, / And how I laughed to lave, / My burning lip and cheek and brow, / In that delicious wave!" C. showed amazing empathy with the black slave of whom she could have had no direct knowledge.

Most of her poems have strong rhythms as well as vivid imagery. Frequently they were sung as hymns at antislavery meetings, or recited as dramatic presentations.

In her essays C. emphasized the contradiction between slavery and the Declaration of Independence, the degrading effect of slavery on master as well as slave, and the need to destroy the economic base of slavery by refusing to use products which were produced by slave labor. In a series of lively pieces, "Letters to Isabel," published in the *Genius*, C. berates an imaginary friend for hesitating to forego the pound cakes and ice creams made with slave-produced sugar, for "devotion to the cause of justice and mercy."

C. was also an early believer in the need for women to champion humane causes. In her essay "To the Ladies of the United States," which appeared in *Genius*, she chided women for deceiving themselves when they protested that they had no power to ameliorate the horrors of slavery: "American women! Your power is sufficient for its extinction! And, oh! by every sympathy most holy to the breast of women, are ye called upon for exertion of that potency."

WORKS: *Essays, Philanthropic and Moral* (1836). *The Poetical Works of Elizabeth Margaret Chandler* (1836).

BIBLIOGRAPHY: Clark, G., *The Liberty Minstrel* (1844). Lundy, B., in *The Poetical Works of Elizabeth Chandler* (1836).

For articles in reference works, see: *DAB. FPA. NAW* (article by S. Lintner). *Woman's Record*, S. J. Hale (1853).

Other references: *MichH* (Dec. 1955).

RUTH BORDIN

Ednah Dow Littlehale Cheney

B. 27 June 1824, Boston, Massachusetts; d. 19 Nov. 1904, Boston, Massachusetts
D. of Sargent Smith and Ednah Parker Dow Littlehale; m. Seth Wells Cheney, 1853

Writer, activist, and self-proclaimed jack-of-all-trades, C. was the third daughter of a New England family of comfortable means and liberal sentiments. The independent spirit she displayed as a child found a home when, as a very young woman, C. came under the influence of transcendentalists Theodore Parker, Bronson Alcott, and, above all, Margaret Fuller.

As ardent an abolitionist as her mentors, C. led the way after the Civil War in recruiting Boston teachers for freedmen's schools in the South. But for most of her eighty years, her energies as a reformer were devoted primarily to improving the educational, occupational, and political opportunities available to women.

In 1853, C. married portrait artist Seth Wells Cheney. His death five years later left her with an infant daughter who herself died at the age of twenty-six.

For all her reform activities, C. thought of herself first as a writer. Three of her early books, *Faithful to the Light* (1871), *Sally Williams* (1874), and *Child of the Tide* (1874), are better-than-average children's fiction. Though marred by the besetting sins of the period and the genre—sentimentality, didacticism, and unlikely coincidence—they are absorbing stories which often correct conventional sexist stereotypes.

In 1875, C. published the "Memoir of [surgeon] Susan Dimock," first of several elegies written in tribute to family, friends, and colleagues. The finest, clearly a labor of love, is the sketch of her idol, Margaret Fuller, included in the 1902 volume, *Reminiscences*. Rich in anecdote and personal reminiscence, it shows C. at her sensible, insightful, generous best.

C.'s skills as a biographer again show to advantage in the *Journals of Louisa May Alcott* (1889), which she edited and extensively annotated. Later biographers are indebted to this fine work not only because it includes some journal entries now lost in the original, but because C. does not shrink from presenting the author of *Little Women* "without disguise." Alcott's passionate dissatisfactions are laid bare, as is the compulsive self-denial that embittered her life. Feminist interpretation, however appropriate it might seem, enters only indirectly, perhaps because of C.'s desire to lay no blame, especially on Bronson Alcott.

But *Nora's Return* (1890), a nondramatic sequel to Ibsen's *Doll's House*, is avowedly feminist. It is also outrageously simplistic, contrived, and, inadvertently, very funny.

The delightful opening of C.'s last major work, *Reminiscences* (1902), recalls a time when Boston was all but an island, town criers called out descriptions of lost children, and Election Day was celebrated with oysters, lobster, and baked beans on the Common. Personally revealing detail abounds—C. staying awake in church by pricking her finger and writing in blood in her prayer book, C. being asked to leave a Beacon Hill school because of her "bad influence on the other girls." Later sections of the autobiography, however, are flat and strangely impersonal.

Colleagues like Julia Ward Howe attributed much of C.'s success as a reformer to her judiciousness, calm disposition, and broad-mindedness. The same qualities illuminate her writing, which is consistently lucid, unpretentious, and humane. Much of it deserves notice today only as social history, but her children's fiction still entertains, and her biographies of Alcott, Fuller, and parts of *Reminiscences* hold their own as literature. At moments, C. achieved the kind of originality that sometimes blossoms out of diligent research and honest, compassionate reporting.

WORKS: *Handbook for American Citizens* (1866). *Patience* (1870). *Faithful to the Light* (1871). *Social Games* (1871). *Sally Williams* (1874). *Child of the Tide* (1874). *Memoir of Susan Dimock* (1875). *Memoir of Seth Wells Cheney* (1881). *Gleanings in the Field of Art* (1881). *Memoir of John Cheney, Engraver* (1888). *Memoir of Margaret Swan Cheney* (1889). *Journals of Louisa May Alcott* (1889). *Nora's Return* (1890). *Stories of Olden Times* (1890). *Memoirs of Lucretia Crocker and Abby W. May* (1893). *Life of Christian Daniel Rauch* (1893). *Reminiscences* (1902).

The letters of Ednah Cheney are at the Boston Public Library, the Massachusetts Historical Society, Smith College, and the Schlesinger Library, Radcliffe College.

BIBLIOGRAPHY: For articles in reference works, see *AW*. *NAW* (article by S. Ingerbritsen). *Representative Women of New England*, Ed. Howe, J. W. (1904).

Other references: *Memorial Meeting of the New England Women's Club* (1905). *Women's Journal* (26 Nov. 1904).

EVELYN SHAKIR

Lydia Maria Francis Child

B. *11 Feb. 1802, Medford, Massachusetts; d. 20 Oct. 1880, Wayland, Massachusetts*
Wrote under : L. Maria Child, Mrs. Child
D. of David Convers and Susanna Rand Francis; m. David Lee Child, 1828

C. was the youngest of six children born to a prosperous baker and real-estate broker and his wife. At twelve C. lost her mother and lived with her sister Mary and her husband. On her eighteenth birthday, announcing her independence, she moved to Watertown, Massachusetts, to stay with her brother Convers Francis, a Unitarian minister. She opened a girls' school and startled parents by encouraging her pupils' independent spirit. C.'s literary work included light romances, domestic books for women and children, and historical tracts advocating the rights of black slaves, Indians, and women.

Hobomok (1824), C.'s early attempt to write an American romance, presents the Indian as a noble savage, and makes a plea for tolerance. *The Rebels* (1825) portrays the tensions leading up to the Revolution. In 1826 C. began the *Juvenile Miscellany*, the first periodical for children in the U.S., which ran successfully for eight years. With the wide reception of her practical guide, *The Frugal Housewife* (1829), C. became well known and respected as a literary figure in New England.

This reputation was dashed almost overnight with the publication of *An Appeal in Favor of That Class of Americans Called Africans* in 1833. In her preface to this historical antislavery document, C. wrote: "I am fully aware of the unpopularity of the task I have undertaken; but though I *expect* ridicule and censure, it is not in my nature to *fear* them." C. not only suffered financial ruin and social ostracism, but was forced to end her *Juvenile Miscellany*.

C.'s constant and selfless devotion to abolitionism was supported by her husband David Lee Child, a founder of the New England Anti-Slavery Society in 1832. In addition to writing many pamphlets in support of the cause, financing slave biographies, such as *Incidents in the Life of a Slave Girl* (1861), and editing the *National Anti-Slavery Standard* from 1841 to 1849, C., along with her husband, sheltered fugitive slaves at their residence in Wayland, Massachusetts. Her courageous zeal persisted late into her career when she published the *Freedmen's Book* (1865), the profits of which she donated to the Freedmen's Aid Association. Used as a text in schools for freed slaves, the book stressed the importance of moral principles, good health, neatness, thrift, and politeness, citing black heroes as inspiring examples.

C.'s approach to reform was well thought out and literary. Her documents combined strong argument, carefully researched analysis, and sincere compassion. These faculties are also evident in her feminist works. For a Ladies Library series she wrote biographies of exemplary women and a *History of the Condition of Women in Various Ages and Nations* (1835), in which she argued for female equality.

Best acknowledged as an abolitionist writer, C.'s versatility with feminist tracts, historical romances, and domestic books for women and children points to the principal motive behind all of her work: that of educating her readers and helping them to adopt a moral and humane way of life. She appealed to the young in her *Flowers to Children* (1844, 1846, 1855), which contains the famous "Boy's Thanksgiving" poem beginning with "Over the river and through the woods/ To grandfather's house we go." She addressed the elderly in *Looking toward Sunset* (1864), a miscellaneous collection designed to give "some words of consolation and cheer to my companions on the way," which was applauded by Whittier and Bryant. Even in her romances, she incorporated her ideas on social reform: feminism in *Philothea* (1836) and antislavery in *The Romance of the Republic* (1837). Hers was a lifelong commitment to humanitarian values.

WORKS: *Hobomok: A Tale of Early Times* (1824). *The Rebels; or, Boston before the Revolution* (1825). *The Juvenile Souvenir* (1828). *The First Settlers of New England; or, Conquest of the Pequods, Naragansets, and Pokanokets. As Related by a Mother to Her Children* (1829). *The Frugal Housewife* (1829; later editions, *The American Frugal Housewife*). *The Colonel: A Collection of Miscellaneous Pieces, Written at Various Times* (1831). *The Girl's Own Book* (1831). *The Mother's Book* (1831). *Biographies of Lady Russel and Madam Guion* (1832). *Biographies of Madame de Stael and Madame Roland* (1832). *An Appeal in Behalf of that Class of Americans Called Africans* (1833). *Biographies of Good Wives* (1833). *The Oasis* (edited by Child, with contributions by Child et al., 1834). *History of the Condition of Women in Various Ages and Nations* (2 vols., 1835). *The Anti-Slavery Catechism* (1836). *The Evils of Slavery and the Curse of Slavery* (1836). *Philothea: A Romance* (1836). *The Family Nurse* (1837). *Authentic Narratives of American Slavery* (edited by Child, 1838). *The Anti-Slavery Almanac* (1843). *Letters from New York* (2 vols., 1843–45). *Flowers for Children* (3 vols., 1844–46). *Fact and Fiction* (1846). *Isaac T. Hopper: A True Life* (1853). *New Flowers for Children* (1855). *The Progress of Religious Ideas through Successive Ages* (3 vols., 1855). *Autumnal Leaves: Tales and Sketches in Prose and Rhyme* (1856). *Correspondence between L. M. Child and Gov. Wise and Mrs. Wise (of Virginia)* (1860). *The Duty of Disobedience to the Fugitive Slave Act: An Appeal to the Legislators of Massachusetts* (1860). *The Patriarchal Institution, Described by Members of its Own Family* (1860). *The Right Way the Safe Way, Proved by Emancipation in the West Indies and Elsewhere* (1860). *Incidents in the Life of a Slave Girl* by H. Jacobs (edited by Child, 1861). *The Freedmen's Book* (1865). *A Romance of the Republic* (1867). *Looking towards Sunset: From Sources New and Old, Original and Selected* (1868). *An Appeal for the Indians* (1868).

BIBLIOGRAPHY: Baer, H. G., *The Heart Is Like Heaven: The Life of Lydia Maria Child* (1964).
For articles in reference works, see: *CAL. DAB. Female Prose Writers of*

America, J. S. Hart (1852). *NAW* (article by L. Filler). *NCAB. Woman's Record*, S. J. Hale (1853).

BETTE B. ROBERTS

Kate O'Flaherty Chopin

B. 8 Feb. 1851, St. Louis, Missouri; d. 22 Aug. 1904, St. Louis, Missouri
D. of Thomas and Eliza Faris O'Flaherty; m. Oscar Chopin, 1870

Descended on her mother's side from the French and Creole elite of St. Louis and on her father's side from Irish newcomers, C., after her father's death in 1855, was raised in a household dominated by three generations of widowed women. She moved with her husband to New Orleans, where she bore five sons in ten years. The family then settled in Cloutiersville in the Natchitoches Parish, the setting of many of her best stories. C's husband died in 1882, and she then returned to her mother's home in St. Louis to begin a new life as a writer.

Despite its pedestrian style, C.'s first novel, *At Fault* (1890), is notable for antiromantic characters and an absence of moralizing. The first American novel to treat divorce amorally, it tells of a young widow's attempts to apply the morality she has been taught to life itself. When she learns that her suitor had divorced a weak, alcoholic wife in the past, she insists that he return to mend the damage he had done. The subsequent remarriage proves destructive to everyone involved, ultimately leading to the wife's death. Our heroine must admit that it was she who was "at fault," learning that "there is rottenness and evil in the world, masquerading as right and morality."

Allowing her characters to live "in the world" produced the bold realism of the short stories collected in Chopin's next two books, *Bayou Folk* (1894) and *A Night in Acadie* (1897). These stories, many of them published earlier in magazines, established her reputation as a local colorist because of her vivid recreations of the lives and language of Creoles and Acadians in Louisiana. Both collections further explore the theme of nature versus civilization, and they also show an increasing concern with women's quest for self-fulfillment.

C.'s exploration of this women's quest began with her first published stories. In "Wiser Than a God" Paula Van Stolz chooses a career over a marriage which could have provided love and economic security, but then succeeds both in becoming a famous pianist and in gaining the love of her music professor.

C.'s women, however, are not biologically free. In her highly praised masterpiece, "Desiree's Baby," C. tells of a woman who drowns herself and her baby when her husband inaccurately suspects her of having the black blood that manifested itself in their child.

Biology is also the key to understanding Edna's fate in *The Awakening* (1899). Edna, strongest and most controversial of C.'s heroines, has immersed herself in an empty marriage and a confusing maternity. Awakening to a sense of herself through her exposure to the more natural Creole society and through the attentions of Robert LeBrun, she chooses to express herself artistically and sensually despite social and personal repercussions. But although Edna walks away from her marriage and from her children, she cannot escape the biological reality of motherhood. Neither can she achieve her artistic goals, because the artist in C.'s novel can only gain her career at the expense of both her social and her sensual self. Edna chooses to save the self she has discovered, but she must do so at the cost of the life she owes her children. As she walks to the beach to join herself with the eternal flux of Nature symbolized by the sea, "the children appeared before her like antagonists who had overcome her; who had overpowered and sought to drag her into the soul's slavery for the rest of her days. But she knew a way to elude them." The hostile reception of this novel seems to have silenced its author, who thereafter wrote only ten more stories, mostly for young people.

C.'s superb psychological insight, especially into the lives of her women, her vivid descriptions of Creole and Acadian life, and her deep-felt concern with human relationships and social institutions will preserve her reputation long after the initial excitement of her rediscovery by contemporary critics has passed.

WORKS: At Fault (1890). *Bayou Folk* (1894). *A Night in Acadie* (1897). *The Awakening* (1899). *The Complete Works of Kate Chopin* (Ed. P. Seyersted, 2 vols, 1969).

BIBLIOGRAPHY: Leary, L., *Southern Excursions: Essays on Mark Twain and Others* (1971). Seyersted, P., *Kate Chopin: A Critical Biography* (1969). Springer, M., *Edith Wharton and Kate Chopin: A Reference Guide* (1976).

For articles in reference works, see: *DAB. NAW* (article by S. Nissenbaum). *NCAB.*

Other references: *ALR 8* (1975). *AQ* 25 (1973). *BB* 32 (1975). *DAI* 36 (1975). *Kate Chopin Newsletter*. *LaS* 14 (1975). *MarkhamR* 3 (1968). *SoR* 11 (1975).

THELMA J. SHINN

Eleanor Clark

B. 6 July 1913, Los Angeles, California
D. of Frederick Huntington and Eleanor Phelps Clark; m. Robert Penn
Warren, 1952

Although born in California, C. grew up in Roxbury, Connecticut, and describes herself as an "unregenerate Yankee." She attended a one-room country school in Roxbury, convent schools in Europe, and then Rosemary Hall. After her graduation from Vassar in 1934, she wrote essays and reviews for a number of periodicals including the *Partisan Review*, the *Kenyon Review*, the *New Republic*, and the *Nation.* Her writing has continued to show the control and conciseness which the essay demands. From 1936 to 1939, C. was a member of the editorial staff of W. W. Norton; in 1937, she edited with Horace Gregory a collection of works by young writers called *New Letters in America*. It included her first published short story.

After the publication of her first novel, *The Bitter Box* (1946), C. received grants from the Guggenheim Foundation and an award from the National Institute of Arts and Letters. *The Bitter Box*, a heavily symbolic novel, deals with the acceptance of life as it is and the possibility of redemption through love and suffering. C. carefully manipulates point of view, balancing surrealism and stream of consciousness with a commentary by an objective narrator who is more interested in ideas than events.

In 1952, C. finished the first of her unusual "travel" books produced during long periods abroad, *Rome and a Villa*. Although it is concerned with setting, the book's effect is meditative rather than descriptive. It reveals a keen awareness of atmosphere and the passing of time. C.'s observations are not limited to place but encompass the political, literary, and personal as well. Katherine Anne Porter has said that *Rome and a Villa* is "autobiographical in the best sense" because it reflects the impact of the outer world upon the inner.

For her next book, *The Oysters of Locmariaquer* (1964), C. was awarded the National Book Award for nonfiction. *Oysters*, too, is a book about a place, and it too belongs to a unique genre. It combines the techniques of the essay and the novel to portray life in a little town on the northwest coast of France which nurtures and produces most of the world's oysters.

Eyes, Etc. A Memoir (1977), like so much that C. has written, belongs in a class of its own. It is a moving but never sentimental account of a brief period in her life, shortly after she learned that she was rapidly going blind. *Eyes* tells of the author's angry and always realistic response to "the event," her "affliction." But the book is also an opinionated and wry commentary on contemporary life, especially on our melodramatic and simplistic methods of coping with frustration and disaster. Against this background are woven the events of the *Iliad* and the *Odyssey*. C. constantly contrasts Homer's tough-minded portrayal of suffering and heroism with feeble modern attempts to cope with life. The book contains the familiar themes of past and present, renewal, suffering, and survival. Her style is even more cryptic than usual, due, perhaps, to the circumstances under which she now writes.

WORKS: *New Letters in America* (edited by Clark, with H. Gregory, 1937). *Dark Wedding* by Ramón José Sender (translated by Clark, 1943). *The Bitter Box* (1946). *Rome and a Villa* (1952). *Song of Roland* (adaptation by Clark, 1960). *The Oysters of Locmariaquer* (1964). *Baldur's Gate* (1970). *Dr. Heart: A Novella, and Other Stories* (1974). *Eyes, Etc.: A Memoir* (1977).

BIBLIOGRAPHY: CW (13 June 1952). Ms. (Nov. 1977). *The Nation* (27 April 1946). NYRB (30 July 1964). SatR (29 Oct. 1977).

JUDITH P. JONES

Elizabeth Cochrane

B. 5 May 1865, Cochran's Mills, Pennsylvania; d. 27 Jan. 1922, New York City
Wrote under: Nellie Bly
D. of Michael and Mary Jane Cochran; m. Robert L. Seaman, 1895

C. spent her youth in a small milltown; her education, except for one year in a local boarding school, was directed by her father, a lawyer and mill owner. After his death, C. moved to Pittsburgh with her mother and sought work for their support. She worked for the Pittsburgh *Dispatch* before moving to New York at twenty where she won a job with Joseph Pulitzer's New York *World*. She worked there until 1895. C.'s husband was an industrialist and a New York socialite. After his death in 1910, she controlled his failing business interests through 1919, and then, returning to journalism, she worked on the New York *Journal* until her death in 1922.

Ten Days in a Mad-house (1887) contains stories written for the *World*, an article about Blackwell's Island Insane Asylum, sketches on servant girls' experiences at employment agencies, and a piece on shop girls working in a paper box factory.

The story of Blackwell's Island, pronounced by the *World* to be "an immense sensation everywhere," established C. as a journalist in New York. She pretended insanity in order to "chronicle" the "simple tale of life in an asylum." She illustrates conditions and treatment of patients by describing her own experiences and the experiences of women she met. Her narrative, written in unadorned prose, is a dramatic and realistic account. Although this and other stories appeared under sensational headlines—"Behind Asylum Bars" or "Nellie Bly as a White Slave"—her exposé journalism, in both content and style, is an early manifestation of the Progressive era's muckraking journalism.

Six Months in Mexico (1888), C.'s most thoughtful and stylistically pleasing (although often repetitive) book, is an examination of national character and an exposé of corruption and exploitative social conditions. C. went to Mexico in late 1886, at a time when few other American journalists were providing the public with first-hand information about their neighboring country. While the book indicates C.'s sensitivity to unjust social conditions, especially for women and the native Indian population, and provides a record of the responses of an American middle-class woman toward a culture both alien and "beautiful" to her, it is occasionally condescending in tone.

C. received the widest attention for a stunt: she broke the record of Jules Verne's fictional hero Phineas Fogg by traveling around the world in seventy-two days. Chronicling her journey in *Nellie Bly's Book: Around the World in Seventy-two Days* (1890), C. presents herself as a "free American girl" encountering diverse cultures, all exciting and exotic, but none measuring up to the American way of life. She provides colorful descriptions of peoples and customs while maintaining the suspense of her race against time. From San Francisco to New York, C. was met with extraordinary public adulation; her journey was celebrated in song and dance; toys, clothing, and games carried her name. C.'s story of "Nellie Bly's stunt" and the public response to it are material for a case study of the rapidly changing relationship between the press and the popular mind in the late 19th c.

WORKS: *Ten Days in a Mad-House; or, Nellie Bly's Experience on Blackwell's Island* (1887). *Six Months in Mexico* (1888). *Nellie Bly's Book: Around the World in Seventy-two Days* (1890).

BIBLIOGRAPHY: Marzolf, M., *Up From the Footnote: A History of Women Journalists* (1977). Noble, I., *Nellie Bly: First Woman Reporter* (1956). Quillan, J., *Nellie Bly* (produced 1946). Rittenhouse, M., *The Amazing Nellie Bly* (1956). Ross, I., *Ladies of the Press* (1936).

For articles in reference works, see *AW. NAW* (article by B. Weisberger). Other references: *The Pittsburgh Press* (8 Jan. 1967; 15 Jan. 1967).

JENNIFER L. TEBBE

Anna Botsford Comstock

B. 1 Sept. 1854, Otto, Cattaraugus County, New York; d. 24 Aug. 1930, Ithaca, New York
Wrote under: Anna Botsford Comstock, Marion Lee
D. of Marvin and Phebe Irish Botsford; m. John Henry Comstock, 1878

While attending Cornell University from 1874 to 1876 C. studied zoology under John Comstock, whom she later married. In 1885 she completed a B.S. degree in natural history and about that time began systematic study of wood engraving with John P. Davis of Cooper Union in New York City. Childless, C. had several overlapping careers which were unplanned, the apparent result of her patient application to tasks which provided income or personal potential. Both her autobiographical account, *The Comstocks of Cornell* (posthumously published in 1953), and reminiscences of Cornell students reflect a determinedly cheerful woman who once observed, "our usual way has ever been to pretend that we like whatever happens."

C. illustrated her husband's college textbooks, *An Introduction to Entomology* (1888) and *A Manual for the Study of Insects* (1894); in the latter she was also credited as "junior author." Her contribution was even more evident in *Insect Life* (1897), a simplified textbook on entomology.

In the 1890s C. became involved in the nature study movement, lecturing and writing leaflets on special natural history topics for classroom use. State support for the Cornell extension programs permitted her unprecedented appointment as assistant professor for the summer session in 1898. After protest by some trustees her rank was changed to lecturer, but in 1913 she was again named assistant professor, and in 1920, professor.

Like other leaders in the nature-study movement, C. insisted that her goal was not to teach scaled-down species hunting or microscopical work but rather "to give pupils an outlook regarding all forms of life and their relationship one to another." Nonetheless, her work is accurate, unlike much natural-history writing of the period, and C. often includes taxonomic terms. *How to Know the Butterflies* (1904), for example, begins with an elementary account of butterfly characteristics, outlines methods for collecting, and then discusses twelve families in detail. Such manuals as *How to Keep Bees* (1905), *The Pet Book* (1914), and *Trees at Leisure* (1916) contain anecdotal and literary materials as well as practical advice.

Much of C.'s own energy was channeled into popular lectures and essays which are romantic without being sentimental and suggest her belief in moral education. *Ways of the Six-footed* (1903) contains ten stories illustrating the social organization of insects, their communication by sound, their use of mimicry as a defense strategy, and other adaptive features. The chapter on ants, bees, and wasps is entitled "The Perfect Socialism." C. did not belabor the analogy here nor ascribe human characteristics to the insects; she did, however, use human experience to describe animal behavior as an educational device.

Many of C.'s essays appeared in *The Chautauquan* and *Country Life in America*. She briefly edited *Boys and Girls* (1903–7), a nature-study magazine, before turning it over to her Cornell colleague Martha Van Rensselaer. For years she contributed to the educational *Nature Study Review* (1906–23), serving as its editor from 1917 until its merger with *Nature Magazine*. Typically, her contributions underscored the value of all life, the importance of understanding nature, and the interrelationship among creatures. Personal anecdote was a prominent feature.

C.'s single most important volume was a compendium of her earlier work consolidated into the 900-page *Handbook of Nature Study* (1911). Not discouraged by the skepticism of her husband and her coworker Liberty Hyde Bailey about the need for such a text, C. provided a teaching guide for elementary teachers dealing with animal life, plant life, and the "earth and sky." The *Handbook* outlined programs for nature study in the classroom and outside, provided review questions, and suggested additional references. Vindication of her initiative came in twenty-four editions and translation into eight languages of the *Handbook.* C.'s text became known as the "nature Bible" because of her sensitive counselling on such topics as children's attitude toward death when dealing with predatory behavior, and because of her concern that living creatures be returned to their natural habitat after study.

Only once did C. attempt to write fiction. *Confessions to a Heathen Idol* (1906), written under the pseudonym Marion Lee, is a romantic fantasy without any reference to C.'s daily work of science.

In 1923 the League of Women Voters named C. one of the twelve greatest women in the United States. Popular yet scholarly in her science writing, she was a key figure in the nature-study movement, and a moving force on the Cornell campus.

WORKS: *Ways of the Six-footed* (1903). *How to Know the Butterflies* (with J. H. Comstock, 1904). *How to Keep Bees* (1905). *Confessions to a Heathen Idol* (1906). *Handbook of Nature Study* (1911). *The Pet Book* (1914). *Trees at Leisure* (1916). *Nature Notebook Series* (1920). *The Comstocks of Cornell* (Eds. G. W. Herriar and R. G. Smith, 1953).

The papers of Anna Botsford Comstock are at the Cornell Collection of Regional History and University Archives, Cornell University.

BIBLIOGRAPHY: For articles in reference works, see: *NAW* (article by K. Jacklin). *NCAB.*

Other references: *Annual Review of Entomology* 21 (1975). *ScM* 62 (1946).

SALLY GREGORY KOHLSTEDT

Fannie Cook

B. 4 Oct. 1893, St. Charles, Missouri; d. 25 Aug. 1949, St. Louis, Missouri
D. of Julius and Jennie Frank; m. Jerome E. Cook, 1915

C. grew up and attended school in St. Louis. She received her B.A. from the University of Missouri in 1914, and her M.A. from Washington University in 1916. Though C. published widely and was a painter of some distinction, she is largely remembered for her novel, *Mrs. Palmer's Honey* (1946), which was judged the most important literary contribution "to the importance of the Negro's place in American life." C. was dedicated to defining and improving the Negro's "place" and that of other oppressed groups. She was a member of the Mayor's Committee on Race Relations, an adviser to the National Association for the Advancement of Colored People, and the 1940 chairperson of the Missouri Committee for Rehabilitation of Sharecroppers.

In 1935, C. won first prize in a *Reader's Digest* contest for new writers. Her short works published between 1940 and 1946 reflect her conviction that unions are the only solution for the ailments of struggling people. In "Killer's Knife Ain't Holy," Ambor, the preacher-protagonist, is asked to choose between the church and the union. He chooses both, aiming to serve his people in every way possible. Whereas he had once preached that black men would achieve their kingdom after death, now that he has joined the union and understood what unionization made possible, he preaches the possibility of kingdom on earth. One must *"organize fer Jesus."* C.'s theme in all her novels is basically the same: the coming of age of the individual and, often by extension, of the group to which he or she belongs. *Boot-Heel Doctor* (1941) and *Mrs. Palmer's Honey* best illustrate this point.

The latter novel was criticized for its labor propaganda. One reviewer for *The New Yorker* said that what started as a "quietly perceptive study of a very lovable Negro girl" abruptly shifts to "a sort of labor tract with characters are not so important as people as they are as espousers of the cause for democracy, unionization, justice for all."

Though the master-servant relationship is clearly upheld and therefore seemingly sanctioned in C.'s works, it should be pointed out that the black maids, or their male counterparts working in the factories and the fields, somehow appear to be more capable than their white "charges." They are always "looking after" their white employers as though they needed "tending to" as much as the cooking and cleaning. In fact, it is to C.'s credit that she endows her maids, whether they are serving blacks or whites, with so much dignity that, like them, we too pity those who must be cared for and we become convinced that the white world would be in dire straits without the input of blacks.

C. always renders reality as she sees it, but always manages to suggest that reality can be changed, that it must be improved upon. She writes simply, lovingly, using regional dialects and regional prejudices and shortcomings to convey verisimilitude. Her main characters are "big people spiritually who are lesser people in society." They are always neighborly, always engaging, gently nudging themselves, even when not fully developed as characters, into the reader's life for keeps.

WORKS: *The Hill Grows Steeper* (1938). *Boot-Heel Doctor* (1941). *Mrs.*

Palmer's Honey (1946). *Storm Against the Wall* (1948). *The Long Bridge* (1949).

BIBLIOGRAPHY: For articles in reference works, see: *American Novelists of Today*, Ed. H. R. Warfel (1951). *CB* (1946; 1949).

Other references: *NYT* (26 Aug. 1949). *PW* (23 Feb. 1946; 17 Sept. 1949). *WLB* (10 Oct. 1949).

LILLIE HOWARD

Rose Terry Cooke

B. *17 Feb. 1827, Hartford, Connecticut; d. 18 July 1892, Pittsfield, Massachusetts*
Wrote under: Rose Terry Cooke, Rose Terry
D. of Henry Wadsworth and Anne Wright Hurlburt Terry; m. Rollin H. Cooke, 1873

Born into an old New England family, C. at sixteen graduated from the Hartford Female Seminary. Following her conversion that year, she became a lifelong member of the Congregational church. To support herself, she taught school. In 1848, a legacy gave C. leisure to write. Although she considered herself primarily a poet, she is remembered mainly as a local colorist and short-story writer.

C.'s published works include two volumes of poetry, a novel, children's stories, religious sketches, and more than a hundred short stories. Her verse now seems conventional and spiritless. Only her short stories endure.

For almost forty years C.'s fiction appeared in prominent magazines, where it had a decisive impact on the development of regional or local-color writing. Although the local colorists she influenced soon overshadowed her, Van Wyck Brooks felt that some of C.'s tales were never surpassed by later authors.

Rich in realistic detail and shrewd social observation, C.'s stories re-create rural New England before and during the 19th-c. migration to cities and prairies. C. knew the regional mind as it was shaped by Calvinism and hard work, bleak landscapes, and scanty resources. Although she could treat her characters with broad Yankee humor, she took their "controversies with Providence" seriously and reviewed their eccentric behavior with the sympathetic but critical eye of the insider.

Domestic scenes, rendered lovingly, dominate C.'s fiction. Critical of women's rights activists, she often reminds readers that a woman's place is in her home, under the "headship" of a good husband. However, in "Mrs. Flint's Married Experience," a miserly deacon works his wife nearly to death, grudging her even food and clothing; C.'s repudiation of the patriarchy which supports him is compelling. In "How Celia Changed Her Mind" and "Polly Mariner, Tailoress," C. characterizes outspoken and self-determined spinsters with evident sympathy. Although many of C.'s stories are too didactic, the best probe the Puritan psyche with considerable sophistication.

C.'s respect for Calvinism's moral seriousness is reflected in her careful analysis of character and motivation. Nevertheless, she criticizes the Puritan tradition's legalism and emotional repression and argues that its "sour sublimity" should be sweetened with mercy and human love, the Christian nurture of social bonds.

C.'s importance as an innovator is increasingly clear. A major influence on local-color writing, C. turned the dialect story to serious themes and gained it a place in respectable literary magaznies. Her portrayal of spinsters, deacons, handymen, and farm women opened new possibilities for the representation of everyday life. C. smoothed the transition from the sentimental romances of the 1850s to the realism of William Dean Howells—a role evidenced by C.'s style, which swings from florid romantic rhetoric to vernacular dialect and concrete historical detail. Although her tales are loosely structured and occasionally plotless, their focus on character is a hallmark of the modern short story. Read primarily for her impact on later writers, and for her depiction of a lost time and place, C. offers a significant handful of stories valuable in their own right.

WORKS: *Poems* (1861). *Groton Massacre Centennial Poem* (1881). *Somebody's Neighbors* (1881). *A Lay Preacher* (1884). *Root-Bound, and Other Sketches* (1885). *No* (1886). *The Sphinx's Children* (1886). *The Deacon's Week* (1887). *The Deacon's Week. And What Deacon Baxter Said* (1887). *Happy Dodd* (1887). *The Old Garden* (1888). *Poems* (1888). *Steadfast, the Story of a Saint and a Sinner* (1889). *Polly and Dolly, and Other Stories* (1890). *Huckleberries Gathered from New England Hills* (1891). *Little Foxes* (1904).

BIBLIOGRAPHY: Brooks, V. W., *New England: Indian Summer* (1940). Downey, J., "A Biographical and Critical Study of Rose Terry Cooke" (Ph.D. diss., Univ. of Ottawa, 1956). Jobes, K. T., "The Resolution of Solitude: A Study of Four Writers of the New England Decline" (Ph.D. diss., Yale Univ.,

1961). Martin, J., *Harvests of Change: American Literature 1865–1914* (1967). Patee, F. L., *The Development of the American Short Story* (1923). Spofford, H. P., *A Little Book of Friends* (1916). Toth, S. A., "More Than Local Color: A Reappraisal of Rose Terry Cooke, Mary Wilkins Freeman, and Alice Brown" (Ph.D. diss., Univ. of Minnesota, 1969).

Other references: *BB* 21 (1955). *KCN* 2 (1976). *WS* 1 (1972).

SARAH WAY SHERMAN

Ina Donna Coolbrith

B. 10 March 1842, Nauvoo, Illinois; d. 29 Feb. 1928, San Francisco, California
Given name: Josephine D. Smith
D. of Don Carlos and Agnes Coolbrith Smith; m. Robert B. Carsley, 1859

C. was four months old when her father died and with his death, C.'s mother moved the family to St. Louis, Missouri, where she married printer William Pickett. In 1849, two years after the gold rush began, Pickett took his wife and children to California. They settled in Los Angeles where C. spent her early teens and twenties. At eleven, she began writing verses and publishing in the local paper, the Los Angeles *Star*. *The California Home Journal* also printed many of her early poems.

After a disappointing marriage to Robert Carsley, a partner in the Salamander Iron Works, C. divorced her husband and moved to San Francisco. Here she broke all associations with her unpleasant past and adopted her pseudonym, Ina Donna Coolbrith. Soon her writings attained a local reputation, and when, in 1868, Bret Harte founded the *Overland Monthly*, he named her as one of the co-editors. Primarily a poet, she did write reviews on occasion. C. wrote for the *Californian*, *Harper's Weekly*, *Century*, *Scribner's* and other magazines and became a close associate and friend of Mark Twain, Ambrose Bierce, and Joaquin Miller. With George Stoddard and Bret Harte, she was said to complete the "Golden Gate Trinity" of authors. In 1915, C. was named poet laureate of California by a World Congress of Authors.

Despite C.'s rich personal history, she wrote little of her poetry from autobiographical or topical experiences. An early poem about the ambush of Sheriff Barton, written when she was sixteen and published in the Los Angeles *Star*, is a rare exception to her later sentimental lyrics. Of C.'s mature work, done primarily for the *Overland Monthly* and her books, only four poems refer to her personal past: "Retrospect," "Fragment of an Unfinished Poem," "Unrest," and "A Mother's Grief."

"Fragment of an Unfinished Poem" (*Poetry of the Pacific*, 1867) illustrates the unfortunately brief retrospective period when C. molded a sensuous perception of her disillusioning past: "The soft star closes to the golden days/ I dreamed away, in that far, tropic clime,/ Wherein Love's blossom budded, bloomed and died." In "Unrest" C.'s topic is her failed marriage; the poet "cannot sleep" for the "mourning memory/ Her dream domains." She searches for hopes that have perished on "ruined footpaths" and "by the grave of Love" kneels and "sheds no tear." No doubt C. could make such resolves by forging a new identity in San Francisco where she kept her past a secret, even from close friends. Yet a poem like "A Mother's Grief" (*Outcroppings*, 1866), which mourns the loss of an infant, perhaps Robert Carsley's child, hint that the wounds were permanent.

Because of her reticence on subjects of her past, C.'s "Blossom Time," her second published poem in the *Overland Monthly*, is viewed as typical of the majority of her work in theme and style. It celebrates the coming of spring. What was a personal passion in the autobiographical poems becomes a wistful sadness mixed with love of nature.

When evaluating the writing of C., one must remember the established literary tastes that influenced the poetry of the period and the attitudes that conditioned women writers. There is a strength in C.'s imagery which takes her beyond the sentimental lyricists of her day. As G. Stoddard said of her work: "She has no superior among the female poets of her own land, and scarcely an equal. Her poems are singularly sympathetic; I know of none more palpably spontaneous. The minor key predominates; but, there are a few lark-like carols suffused with the 'unpremeditated art' of heavenly inspiration."

WORKS: *A Perfect Day, and Other Poems* (1881). *The Singer by the Sea* (1894). *Songs from the Golden Gate* (1896).

BIBLIOGRAPHY: Rhodehamel, J., and R. Wood, *Ina Coolbrith, Librarian and Laureate of California* (1973). Walker, F., *San Francisco's Literary Frontier* (1939). Walker, F., *A Literary History of Southern California* (1950).

Other references: *Pacific Historian*, 17 (1973). *Westward* Vol. 1, No. 4 (1928).

SHELLEY ARMITAGE

Anna Julia Haywood Cooper

B. *10 Aug. 1858, Raleigh, North Carolina; d. 27 Feb. 1964, Washington, D.C.*
D. of George Washington and Hanna Stanley Haywood; m. George A. C.
Cooper, 1877

Born a slave in Wake County, North Carolina, C. began her remarkable career at the age of six when she entered St. Augustine's Normal and Collegiate Institute (an Episcopalian school) in Raleigh. There she became a "Pupil Teacher" when only nine years old. From that time until her death at age 105, C. dedicated her life to teaching. The education of others and herself defined the pattern of C.'s career. In 1881, C. enrolled at Oberlin College in Ohio, where she received both a B.A. (1884) and an M.A. (1887). During her matriculation, she continued to teach, holding a position at the college preparatory, Oberlin Academy. In 1884, she returned to the South and to her alma mater, St. Augustine's, as an instructor of Latin, Greek, and mathematics. St. Augustine's became the springboard for C.'s career as a writer.

From 1901 to 1906, C. was principal of the "M" Street (later Dunbar) High School in Washington, D.C. She received a doctorate from the Sorbonne University in Paris in 1925, at a time when few women, especially black women, held a doctorate. C. was sixty-seven. Two books in French are the result of her graduate research at the Sorbonne.

Her first book, *A Voice from the South by a Black Woman of the South* (1892), is a collection of essays, treatises, and reflections, based upon keen feminist insights and heightened racial awareness, which resulted from C.'s own experiences. Her literary reputation rests primarily upon this pioneering volume.

The preface, "Our Raison d'Etre," announces that C. has raised her voice as a black woman who "can more sensibly realize and more accurately tell the weight and the fret" of black life in the South. Her objective is to present the woman's point of view, the "other side" by one who "lives there," and who is "sensitive . . . to social atmospheric conditions." C.'s emphasis emerges out of an awareness that just as whites "were not to blame if they cannot *quite* put themselves in the dark man's place, neither should the dark man be wholly expected fully and adequately to reproduce the exact Voice of the Black Woman." Her vision is clear, intelligent, and forceful.

C.'s essays are not merely impassioned pleas by a woman for the equitable treatment of her race. Thoughtful and scholarly, her work evidences a comprehensive understanding of the position of women in America. Written in an energetic yet graceful prose, her essays are as engaging as they are persuasive. They constitute a significant contribution to the cultural and intellectual history of women and blacks in the U.S. It is fortunate that her collection, reprinted in 1969, is available to contemporary readers.

C. had a lengthy career that she depicted as a conscious attempt to rectify the "one muffled strain in the Silent South," the voice of blacks. She believed that the black woman, in particular, had been "mute." C.'s life and work provided a voice for the "hitherto voiceless black woman of America."

WORKS: *A Voice from the South by a Black Woman of the South* (1892). *L'Attitude de la France à l'égard de l'esclavage pendant la révolution* (1925). *Le Pèlerinage de Charlemagne: Voyage à Jérusalem et à Constantinople* (1925). *Legislative Measures Concerning Slavery in the United States* (1942). *Equality of Races and the Democratic Movement* (1945). *The Life and Writings of the Grimké Family* (1951). *The Third Step* (n.d.).

The papers of Anna Julia Cooper are at the Moorland–Spingarn Research Center, Howard University.

BIBLIOGRAPHY: Bogin, R., and B. J. Lowenberg, *Black Women in Nineteenth-Century American Life* (1976). Harley, S., in *The Afro-American Woman: Struggles and Images*, Eds. S. Harley and R. Terborg-Penn (1978). Lerner, G., ed., *Black Women in White America: A Documentary History* (1972). Majors, M. A., *Noted Negro Women: Their Triumphs and Activities* (1893).

For articles in reference works, see: *Afro-American Encyclopedia*, Ed. J. T. Haley (1976).

Other references: *Baltimore Afro-American* (14 March 1964). *The Parent-Teacher Journal* (May 1930).

THADIOUS M. DAVIS

Adelaide Crapsey

B. 9 Sept. 1878, Brooklyn, New York; d. 8 Oct. 1914, Rochester, New York
D. of Algernon Sidney and Adelaide Trowbridge Crapsey

C. was taken to Rochester in 1879 when her father became rector of St. Andrew's Church. In 1893 C. and her sister Emily were sent to Kemper Hall, an Episcopal boarding school in Kenosha, Wisconsin. After graduation from Vassar in 1901, C. spent one year at home in Rochester and then returned to Kemper Hall to teach history and literature. Around 1903 C. first began to suffer from the fatigue that was a symptom of her fatal disease. From 1906 to 1908 she served as instructor of literature and history at a preparatory school in Stamford, Connecticut. Failing health caused C. to give up teaching, however, and in December 1908 she went to Europe, living in Rome, London, and Kent. In London C. continued her work on the "application of phonetics to metrical problems." In 1911 C. returned to America and began work immediately as an instructor in poetics at Smith College. From September 1913 to August 1914 C. underwent treatment for her tuberculosis in a private nursing home at Saranac Lake, New York. After returning to her family's home in Rochester she suddenly grew worse and died.

C. had long been experimenting with poetic forms. She filled her commonplace book with poems by W. S. Landor, T. L. Beddoes, Oscar Wilde, and Lionel Johnson. Many of her poems show the influence of these and earlier poets, even as they exhibit her own reticence, humor, and interest in experiments in sound and form. Although her consciousness of contemporary poetic and artistic developments is important, it is also essential to recognize the role of C.'s own informed craftsmanship and studies in metrics in shaping her poetry, which shows affinities with the Georgian and Imagist movements.

The cinquain, a five-line poetic form invented and named by C., is "built on stresses, one for the first line, two for the second, three for the third, four for the fourth, with a drop back to one for the fifth line. In the poet's opinion this made the most condensed metrical form in English that would hold together as a complete unit." Although the cinquain is built of stresses rather than syllables, it resembles such Japanese forms as the *haiku* and *tanka* in its brevity and in its juxtaposition of images. C.'s finest cinquains, including "Amaze," "Niagara," "Roma Aeterna," and "Snow," involve a superposition of ideas or intersection between the eternal and the momentary, the motionless and the moving. These qualities, and the distinctive compression of C.'s best work, have led Louis Untermeyer to describe C. as an "unconscious Imagist" and Yvor Winters to state that C. "achieves more effectively than did most of the Imagists the aims of Imagism."

C.'s unfinished work on prosody, on which she worked so hard while in England and at Smith, was published after her death with a preface by Esther Lowenthal. *A Study in English Metrics* (1918) divides English poets into three classes according to the proportions of monosyllabic, dissyllabic, and polysyllabic words used.

The reticence and firm control characteristic of her finest poems marked C.'s own conduct. Her letters to her family and friends provide a rare opportunity to study a person always private and elusive, although never reclusive or withdrawn until her health had been seriously impaired. Her letters from Saranac Lake show her fighting bravely and humorously what she herself knew to be a losing battle; "vital, vivid, and detailed," they "seldom fail to convey an extremely alert intelligence and a sensitivity to what she perceived was going on in the intellectual world."

WORKS: *Verse* (1915). *A Study in English Metrics* (1918). *The Complete Poems and Collected Letters of Adelaide Crapsey* (Ed. S. S. Smith, 1977).

BIBLIOGRAPHY: Bragdon, C., *Merely Players* (1929). Bragdon, C., *More Lives Than One* (1938). Crapsey, A. S., *The Last of the Heretics* (1924). O'Connor, M. E., "Adelaide Crapsey: A Biographical Study" (M.A. thesis, Notre Dame Univ., 1931). Osborn, M. E., *Adelaide Crapsey* (1933). Smith, S. S., *The Complete Poems and Collected Letters of Adelaide Crapsey* (1977). Winters, Y., *Forms of Discovery* (1967). Winters, Y., *In Defense of Reason* (1947).

Other references: *Adam: International Review* (1970). *TLS* (5 May 1978). *Univ. of Osaka College of Commerce Festschrift* (n.d.). *Vassar Miscellany* (1915).

SUSAN SUTTON SMITH

Hannah Mather Crocker

B. 27 June 1752, Boston, Massachusetts; d. 11 July 1829, Roxbury,
  Massachusetts
Wrote under: A Lady of Boston
D. of Samuel and Hannah Hutchinson Mather; m. Joseph Crocker, 1779

With Cotton and Increase Mather her great-grandfather and grandfather, C. has claims to a particular sort of American blue blood. Her husband was a captain in the Continental army and a Harvard graduate. It was not until after her children were grown that C. turned to writing and more public concerns. "When child-rearing duties are past," she said, "this is a fully ripe season" for older women to deliver their "well-digested thoughts for the improvement of the rising generation." C.'s initial publication, *A Series of Letters on Free Masonry* (1815), was written to support her old friends, the Society of Free Masons, when they came under attack in 1810 for carousing in Boston lodges. In the year before her marriage, C. had organized a number of her friends into a female Mason society. C. not only defended the Masons in her treatise, but took the revolutionary position of encouraging women to "promote science and literature" in formal societies, as more suitable to their dignity than those frivolous activities ordinarily thought appropriate for female leisure.

The next year, in *The School of Reform; or, The Seaman's Safe Pilot to the Cape of Good Hope* (1816), C. extends an enthusiastic but occasionally graceless exhortation to seamen against drinking. C.'s *Observations on the Real Rights of Women, with their appropriate duties, agreeable to Scripture, reason and common sense* was published by subscription in 1818. C. is clearly familiar with the foremost feminist thinking of her day and she dedicates her *Real Rights of Women* to Hannah More, an eminent English evangelical writer. C. even praises Mary Wollstonecraft as "a woman of great energy and a very independent mind," although she does "not coincide with her opinion respecting the total independence of the female sex."

Using Christian justice as her basis, C. uncompromisingly insists that men and women have equal powers and faculties. Women's minds are equal to the tasks of the statesman, lawyer, or minister, and only "local circumstances and domestic cares" have prevented them from being as productive as men. But C. makes concessions to what she considers social reality and political necessity: "For the interest of their country, or in the cause of humanity, we shall strictly adhere to the principle and the impropriety of females ever trespassing on masculine ground: as it is morally incorrect, and physically improper."

Women's roles lie in the training of men, and in the teaching of peace and virtue. They must be the psychological counselors who "convince by reason and persuasion," who are "calm and serene" under all crises, and who "soothe and alleviate the anxious cares of men." "Right" takes on the meaning of duty and obligation. "Every female" has the "right" to cover the faults of those around her with the "mantle of meek charity." Women have "rights" to be virtuous, loving, religious, and sympathetic, and thus support and improve human society.

Harmonious relations between the sexes are the basis not only of family life, but the greatness of the nation as well. C. maintains that it was the "mutual virtue, energy, and fortitude of the sexes" that accomplished the American Revolution, and insists that their proper union will preserve it.

The title *Observations on the Real Rights of Women* (1818) is a misnomer. It is, rather, a commonplace book generally imparting advice on the sensible and Christian conduct of life. As a consistent discussion of women's particular issues, it is certainly a failure.

C. was a natural patriot and reformer, and her sincere convictions of the efficacy of human will and energy in solving problems is in the best American tradition. It is her great energy and force of character that appears through the occasionally clumsy form of her writing to convince us of her essential genius as a person, if not as a writer.

WORKS: *A Series of Letters on Free Masonry* (1815). *The School of Reform; or, The Seaman's Safe Pilot to the Cape of Good Hope* (1816). *Observations on the Real Rights of Women, with their appropriate duties, agreeable to Scripture, reason and common sense* (1818).

The papers of Hannah Mather Crocker are at the Massachusetts Historic and Genealogical Society.

BIBLIOGRAPHY: Hill, B., ed., *The Diary of Isaiah Thomas, 1805–1828* (1909).

For articles in reference works, see: *DAB. NAW* (article by J. James).

Other references: *New York Historical Magazine* (March 1965; May 1865).

L. W. KOENGETER

Jane Cunningham Croly

B. 19 Dec. 1829, Market Harborough, Leicestershire, England; d. 23 Dec. 1901,
 New York City
Wrote under: Jennie June, Mrs. J. C. Croly
D. of Joseph and Jane Cunningham; m. David Goodman Croly, 1856

C.'s father's Unitarianism was ill-received by his English neighbors and in 1841 the family moved to Poughkeepsie and then to Wappinger's Falls, New York. C. studied at home, taught district school, kept house for her older brother, a Congregationalist minister, and wrote a popular semimonthly newspaper for his congregation. In 1855, she moved to New York City and began her career as a professional journalist. Unable to win employment as a regular staff member of a city newspaper because she was a woman, C. was assigned to write a regular column on fashion for ladies. In 1857, she became one of the earliest syndicated woman columnists, and was carried in newspapers in New York, New Orleans, Richmond, Baltimore, and Louisville.

In 1856, C. married an Irish immigrant on the staff of the New York *Herald*. In 1859, he bought, edited, and published the Rockford *Daily News* in Illinois, where C.'s official duty was to write a column entitled "Gossip with and for Ladies." C.'s first child, Minnie, was born before the Crolys moved back to New York in 1860 to work on the *World*, where C. wrote the woman's column from 1862 to 1872. In addition to newspaper work, C. contributed to *Graham's Magazine*, *Frank Leslie's Weekly*, and *Demorest's Monthly Magazine*, coediting the latter for many years. She produced a popular cookbook, several sewing manuals, and three collections of her newspaper columns. She supported the family with her writing and by teaching journalism when her husband, due to illness, left newspaper work in 1875.

C. developed an interest in the woman's club movement of her day. She became an influential member of many clubs, including the Woman's Endowment Cattle Company, the Association for the Advancement of Women, the Women's Press Club of New York, the Association for the Advancement of Medical Education for Women, and, most important, a founder of the literary club, Sorosis. Later in life, C. edited clubwomen's magazines and wrote organizational histories.

C.'s collected articles, like *Jennie Juneiana* (1864), provide vignettes of the domestic world, some as harmless as descriptions of Christmas day and patchwork quilts, but others filled with anger at male arrogance and thoughtlessness. Husbands who opened their wives' mail, fussed about meals, and demanded pristine households when they themselves were shamefully careless, won her scorn. C. also found fault with women, describing them as "hidden under clouds of dyspepsia, nervousness, overeating, personal neglect, personal abuse, vanity, deceit, treachery, fibbing, equivocation, and a hundred other signs of equal magnitude." For all her criticism, however, C. felt women had a special potential to become loving, loyal, morally superior, sensitive, perfect beings.

C.'s observations enabled her to define the sources of women's shortcomings. She considered education for girls in the ornamental arts to be useless, a restriction keeping them from the path of perfection. C. also faulted woman's behavior, clothing, and ambitions. Instead, she advocated devotion to home duties, declaring that they prepared women to extend their superior influence beyond family life to identify and rectify injustice. Use of domestic handbooks like her own would minimize household duties and allow women to enter the clubs where they would broaden their education, confidence, friendships, and abilities to analyze and solve social problems.

C.'s brand of women's rights, less shocking than the radical and militant woman suffrage movement, won greater numbers of supporters. The club magazines C. edited won adherents for her movement, and in speech as Sorosis' presiding officer, she alluded to the success of her writing and club activity: "We shall live . . . to see the Woman's Club the conservator of public morals, the uprooter of social evils, the defender of women against women as well as against men, the preserver of the sanctities of domestic life, the synonym of the brave, true, and noble in women."

C.'s *History of the Woman's Club Movement in America* (1898) is further testimony to the appeal of her analysis and solution to women's oppression in the nineteenth century. The work is a staggering 1190-page reference work, with entries describing one thousand clubs—a careful compendium of their programs, leaders, and histories, C.'s introduction is an ambitious and early work in women's history, looking back as far as 5th-c. monasticism for precedents to women's organizations. C.'s modesty, however, caused her to minimize her own contribution to the movement of women's club development.

SELECTED WORKS: *Jennie Juneiana: Talks on Women's Topics* (1864). *Jennie June's American Cookery Book* (1866). *For Better or Worse* (1875). *Knitting and Crochet* (1885). *Needle Work* (1885). *Sorosis: Its Origin and*

History (1886). *Thrown on Her Own Resources* (1891). *The History of the Woman's Club Movement in America* (1898). *Memories of Jane Cunningham Croly* (1904).

The papers of Jane Cunningham Croly are at the Arthur and Elizabeth B. Schlesinger Library, Radcliffe College; in the Sorosis Papers, Sophia Smith Collection, Smith College Library; and in the Caroline M. Severance Papers, Huntington Library, San Marino, California.

BIBLIOGRAPHY: Blair, Karen J., "The Clubwoman as Feminist: The Woman's Culture Club Movement in the U.S., 1868–1914" (Ph.D. diss., State Univ. of New York at Buffalo, 1976). Forcey, C., *The Crossroads of Liberalism* (1961). Wells, M., *Unity in Diversity: The History of the General Federation of Women's Clubs* (1953). Winant, M. D., *A Century of Sorosis, 1868–1968* (1968). Wingate, C. F., *Views and Interviews on Journalism* (1875). Wood, M. I., *The History of the General Federation of Women's Clubs* (1912).

For articles in reference works, see: *AW. DAB. Daughters of America*, P. A. Hanaford (1883). *NAW* (article by E. Schlesinger). *NCAB.*

Other references: *Demorest's Monthly Magazine* (Jan. 1871). *Journalism Quarterly* (Spring 1963). *New York History* (Oct. 1961). *NYT* (24 Dec. 1901). *Woman's Journal* (4 Jan. 1902; 11 Jan. 1902).

KAREN J. BLAIR

Maria Susanna Cummins

B. 9 April 1827, Salem, Massachusetts; d. 1 Oct. 1866, Dorchester, Massachusetts
D. of David and Mehitable Cave Cummins

Both of C.'s parents were descendants of prominent New England families. The Cummins family (the name was originally spelled with a "g") can trace their roots to Isaac Cummings, a Scottish immigrant who settled in Ipswich shortly before 1638.

C.'s father, a man of cultivated taste, made certain that she received a classical education, and he encouraged his daughter's writing talents. After her father's death she lived quietly in Dorchester, devoting the rest of her life to her writing and to church work.

C.'s first novel, *The Lamplighter*, was published in Boston in 1854 and shortly afterward in London. It was the most talked about novel of the year and an immediate best seller. The average sale during the first two months after publication was five thousand copies a week; by the end of the first year it had sold seventy thousand. Her second novel, *Mabel Vaughan* (1857), was not so popular, but in 1858 both novels were selected for publication by the Leipzig-based Tauchnitz Library of British and American Authors, an indication of her international fame.

C.'s novels are filled with pious sentiments and moral formulae, typical of the genre, called "folk fiction" by some, which led to Hawthorne's comment in 1855 that "America is now wholly given over to a d——d mob of scribbling women. . . ." Specifically he asked, "What is the mystery of these innumerable editions of *The Lamplighter?*"

The success of *Lamplighter* is no mystery at all. Relying liberally on Dickens and the Brontë sisters, it tells the story of an abandoned and mistreated orphan, Gerty, befriended by a kindly old lamplighter (aptly named Trueman Flint) and then by a wealthy young blind woman, Emily Graham, who becomes her patron and teacher. The story recounts Gerty's transformation from a ragged, ignorant orphan into a self-reliant and virtuous young woman, "the image of female goodness and purity." By the novel's end Gerty has found her long-lost father (who turns out to be Emily Graham's stepbrother and former lover) and will marry her childhood sweetheart, now a successful businessman.

C.'s second novel, *Mabel Vaughan* (1857), features a heroine who is not a poor orphan waif but who is nevertheless the victim of a series of calamities. Once a pampered child of fashion, she finds herself left nearly penniless and charged with the care of two incorrigible nephews, a melancholic father, and an alcoholic brother. A great part of this novel is set in the West and the reader is introduced to some interesting pioneer characters as well as, in the city scenes, such stock characters as a dying orphan who exemplifies piety and submissiveness to God's will.

Both of these novels relied upon the best-selling formula of the sentimental-domestic novel for their appeal: the plots feature calamities, sudden reversals of fortune, long-lost relatives, and the reform of profligates; the central characters are young women who grow in strength and piety throughout the novel, enabling them to accomplish the gentle subjugation and reform of rogues, alcoholics, and conscienceless men.

El Fureidis (1860), C.'s third novel, is a story of Palestine and Syria, and her fourth, *Haunted Hearts* (1864), is a rather pedestrian sentimental tale. Neither of these approached *Lamplighter* in popular appeal.

WORKS: *The Lamplighter* (1854). *Mabel Vaughan* (1857). *El Fureidis* (1860). *Haunted Hearts* (1864).

BIBLIOGRAPHY: Hart, J. D., *The Popular Book* (1950). Koch, D. A., Introduction to *The Lamplighter* by M. S. Cummins (1968). Mott, F. L., *Golden Multitudes* (1947).

For articles in reference works, see: *AA. DAB. NAW* (article by O. E. Winslow).

ELAINE K. GINSBERG

Elizabeth Bacon Custer

B. 8 April 1842, Monroe, Michigan; d. 4 April 1933, New York City
Wrote under: Elizabeth B. Custer, Elizabeth Bacon Custer
D. of Daniel S. and Sophia Page Bacon; m. George Armstrong Custer, 1864

The only surviving child of a prominent Michigan judge, C. spent the five years between her mother's death in 1854 and her father's remarriage in boarding schools and with relatives. Returning to Monroe, C. became close to her stepmother, and graduated as valedictorian from Boyd's Seminary in 1862. The following winter C. met Captain George Armstrong Custer, then visiting Monroe on leave from Civil War duty. Overcoming parental opposition to C.'s involvement with a soldier, they courted by mail and married in 1864.

C. accompanied her husband to the Virginia front, where he became a major general. His postwar military career took C. to posts in Texas, Kansas, Kentucky, and Dakota Territory, where she learned of his fatal "last stand."

Although C.'s life extended fifty-seven years beyond her husband's, she kept her marriage vows, fulfilling what she believed were her "responsibilities" as "the widow of a national hero" by writing and lecturing.

C. wrote to perpetuate her husband's memory, scrupulously avoiding army political disputes by focusing on the domestic aspects of frontier cavalry life. Her first book, *Boots and Saddles* (1885), describes C.'s life in Dakota with General Custer from 1873 to 1876. C. emphasizes the closeness within and among army couples as both result of and defense against wilderness isolation. Although she tried to appear "plucky," C. expresses her overwhelming fear of Indians and often gives thanks that, as a woman, she was not required to be brave. Women were, however, required to wait; C. compellingly presents the shared anxiety of wives left at Fort Lincoln while husbands fought and died at Little Big Horn.

The enthusiastic reception of her first book led C. to write her reminiscences of earlier campaigns. In *Tenting on the Plains* (1887), C. describes her experiences following General Custer in Kansas and Texas from 1865 to 1867. Insects, illness, and scorpions dominate C.'s recollections of the march to Texas, and her Kansas memories include prairie fire, flood, and cholera. Racism pervades her accounts of blacks in Reconstruction Texas, Mexican mule drivers, and American Indians; class bias colors her portraits of those who attained officers' positions through war service rather than West Point. She alludes to postwar dissension in the ranks, but ends her book before the court-martial and suspension that interrupted her husband's career.

In *Following the Guidon* (1890), C. picks up the story when her husband returned to duty in Kansas in 1868 to join the campaign that culminated in the Battle of Washita. C. vividly recalls her fearful visits with captured Indians and tribal peace council delegates, while glorifying her husband's honest treatment of those he helped defeat. She also explains how constantly menacing rattlesnakes and Indians impair enjoyment of recreational hunting, riding, and horse and mule racing. Her posthumously published letters to husband and family reveal the pampered, pious, and principled aspects of her personality.

C.'s works provide important insights into one woman's attempt to redefine "lady" to fit the regimen of cavalry life. The closeness she depicts among army wives balances the traditional emphasis on military male bonding. While marred by prejudice, self-deprecation, and repetition, and intentionally incomplete by avoidance of controversy, C.'s writings are lively and lucid accounts of an unusual female life style.

WORKS: *Boots and Saddles, or Life in Dakota with General Custer* (1885). *Tenting on the Plains, or General Custer in Kansas and Texas* (1887). *Following the Guidon* (1890). *General Custer at the Battle of Little Big Horn, June 25, 1876* (1897). *The Boy General: Story of the Life of Major-General George A. Custer* (ed. by M. E. Burt, 1901). *The Custer Story: The Life and Intimate Letters of General George A. Custer and His Wife Elizabeth* (ed. M. Merington, 1950).

BIBLIOGRAPHY: Frost, L. A., *General Custer's Libbie* (1976). Stewart, J. R., introduction to E.B.C.'s *Boots and Saddles* (1961 ed.).

For articles in reference works, see: *American Women*, F. E. Willard and M. A. Livermore, eds. (1897).

Other references: *Collier's* (29 Jan. 1927). *Harper's* (Jan. 1891). *Nation* (30 April 1885). *NYT* (11 May 1888; 5 April 1933). *Psychohistory Review* (Fall 1980). *Winner's* (30 June 1935).

HELEN M. BANNAN

Faith Baldwin Cuthrell

B. 1 Oct. 1893, New Rochelle, New York; d. 18 March 1978, Norwalk,
  Connecticut
Wrote under: Faith Baldwin, Faith B. Cuthrell
D. of Stephen C. and Edith Hervey Finch Baldwin; m. Hugh H. Cuthrell, 1920

C. spent a fashionable girlhood in Manhattan and Brooklyn Heights. She could read at three and at six was writing a drama, "The Deserted Wife." She first published verse in her teens, prose in her twenties. C.'s books, stories, poems, and articles appeared steadily from 1921 to 1977, bringing her enormous popular and financial success. Many of her novels were made into films. She was a founder and faculty member of the Famous Writers School in Westport, Connecticut.

C.'s family history emerges in *The American Family* (1935), based on her grandfather's diaries. Tobias Condit takes his wife to China in the 1860s to work as a missionary. Their son is sent to America to be educated, returning to China as a doctor. The sequel, *The Puritan Strain* (1935), centers on Dr. Condit's daughter Elizabeth.

Courtship and marriage with their attendant joys and crises are C.'s favored themes. Her first novel, *Mavis of Green Hill* (1921), shows the maturing of a childlike bride, once an invalid, into a passionate wife. *Something Special* (1940) explores the threats to a union of fourteen years. Satisfactory resolutions are always brought about. C.'s novels are usually told from the woman's viewpoint and reveal an intimate group of women's problems.

Salient problems are the work women do and its relation to love and marriage. C.'s heroines are secretaries, hostesses, nurses, actresses, real estate brokers. They sell bonds and securities, design dresses, and run beauty salons. *White Collar Girl* (1933) speaks of the wasted talent of girls from affluent families who stay in their hometowns to wrap up fudge in the Goodie Shoppe. *Private Duty* (1935) describes the working girl's lot, the long days, the social life crammed into after-hours, the little sleep. Rich girls might work for pleasure: "To be a working girl and socially secure gave one a certain cachet. Working without the social security made all the difference." *Career by Proxy* (1939) queries whether a wealthy girl ought to work, thus taking employment from one who needs it. In *Hotel Hostess* (1938), an unsympathetic male supposes women usually work for frivolous reasons, or because they are "exhibitionists."

Conflict between career and marriage is a frequent theme. C.'s suitors and husbands generally regard the woman's work as unnecessary, or inimical to their mutual happiness. C. writes searchingly of the emotion on both sides. Most often C.'s heroines vainly strive to keep both marriage and career going, finally abandoning the career. In *Self-Made Woman* (1939) the clash is acute, the resolution uneasy. The wife capitulates to her dominant, sexually magnetic husband with "an awareness of defeat."

C.'s nonfiction, following her husband's death, includes the inspirational, semiautobiographical *Face Toward the Spring* (1956) and *Many Windows: Seasons of the Heart* (1958). From July 1958 to December 1965 she wrote the monthly feature "The Open Door" for *Woman's Day* magazine, which she expanded to produce *Testament of Trust* (1960), *Harvest of Hope* (1962), *Living by Faith* (1964), and *Evening Star* (1966). Reflective and discursive, these "almanac books" follow the year's cycle. C. shares her thoughts on the seasonal activities and weather, on gardens and rooms, on love, sorrow, books, travel, memories, prayer, and people.

Among C.'s last works are the six Little Oxford novels: *Any Village* (1971), *No Bed of Roses* (1973), *Time and the Hour* (1974), *New Girl in Town* (1975), *Thursday's Child* (1976), and *Adam's Eden* (1977). Seasons are breathtakingly beautiful in this suburban town, a "collage" of Westchester, Connecticut, and Long Island. Life is friendly and comfortable. A cast of characters reappears; new people pass through or settle, usually the heirs, relatives, or friends of the inhabitants. The principal action is the forming of a marriage, or an adjustment to marriage of a sympathetic young pair (maturer lovers marry or remarry offstage), who will in subsequent novels have already started a family and become part of the backdrop for the next set of lovers.

C. produced highly professional popular fiction, skillfully plotted, swift-paced, and entertaining. She captures the accents of daily speech, from plain talk to breezy dialogue. Her characters are middle- and upper-class Americans, living in Manhattan penthouses, luxurious country estates, and suburban communities. C. explores matters of concern to women—work, money, love, marriage, motherhood, divorce, dignified age. Her heroines are self-possessed women of mettle, some quietly independent, others spitfires. Individuals, couples, families, and neighbors resolve their difficulties. C.'s inspirational works praise the seasons, the pleasures of books, dwellings, and precious objects, and the importance of solitude and friendship alike.

WORKS: *Mavis of Green Hill* (1921). *Laurel of Stonystream* (1923). *Magic and Mary Rose* (1924). *Sign Posts* (1924). *Thresholds* (1925). *Those Difficult Years* (1925). *Three Women* (1926). *Departing Wings* (1927). *Rosalie's Career* (1928). *Betty* (1928). *Alimony* (1928). *The Incredible Year* (1929). *Garden Oats* (1929). *Broadway Interlude* (1929, with Achmed Adullah). *Judy: A Story of Divine Corners* (1930). *Make-Believe* (1930). *The Office Wife* (1930). *Babs: A Story of Divine Corners* (1931). *Skyscraper* (1931; film version, 1932). *Today's Virtue* (1931). *Mary Lou: A Story of Divine Corners* (1931). *Self-Made Woman* (1932). *Week-End Marriage* (1932, with Achmed Adullah; film version, 1933). *Girl on the Make* (1932). *District Nurse* (1932). *Myra: A Story of Divine Corners* (1932). *White Collar Girl* (1933). *Beauty* (1933; film version, 1933). *Love's a Puzzle* (1933). *Innocent Bystander* (1934). *Within a Year* (1934). *Wife vs. Secretary* (1934). *Honor Bound* (1934). *American Family* (1935). *The Puritan Strain* (1935). *The Moon's Our Home* (1936; film version, 1936). *Men are Such Fools!* (1936; film version, 1938). *Private Duty* (1936). *Girls of Divine Corners* (1936). *Omnibus: Alimony; The Office Wife; Skyscraper* (1936). *The Heart Has Wings* (1937). *That Man Is Mine* (1937). *Twenty-Four Hours a Day* (1937). *Manhattan Nights* (1937). *Hotel Hostess* (1938). *Enchanted Oasis* (1938). *Rich Girl, Poor Girl* (1938). *White Magic* (1939). *Station Wagon Set* (1939). *The High Road* (1939). *Career by Proxy* (1939). *Letty and the Law* (1940). *Medical Center* (1940). *Picnic Adventures* (1940). *Rehearsal for Love* (1940). *Something Special* (1940). *Temporary Address: Reno* (1941). *And New Stars Burn* (1941). *The Heart Remembers* (1941). *Blue Horizons* (1942). *Breath of Life* (1942). *Five Women in Three Novels* (1942). *. . . The Rest of My Life With You* (1942). *You Can't Escape* (1943). *Washington, USA* (1943). *Change of Heart* (1944). *He Married a Doctor* (1944). *Romance Book* (1944). *A Job for Jenny* (1945). *Second Romance Book* (1945). *Arizona Star* (1945). *No Private Heaven* (1946). *Woman on Her Way* (1946). *Give Love the Air* (1947). *Sleeping Beauty* (1947). *They Who Love* (1948). *Marry for Money* (1948). *The Golden Shoestring* (1949). *Look Out for Liza* (1950). *The Whole Armor* (1951). *The Juniper Tree* (1952). *Widow's Walk* (1954). *Face Toward the Spring* (1956). *Three Faces of Love* (1957). *Many Windows* (1958). *Blaze of Sunlight* (1959). *Testament of Trust* (1960). *Harvest of Hope* (1962). *The West Wind* (1962). *The Lonely Man* (1964). *Living by Faith* (1964). *There Is a Season* (1966). *Evening Star* (1966). *The Velvet Hammer* (1969). *Take What You Want* (1970). *Any Village* (1971). *One More Time* (1972). *No Bed of Roses* (1973). *Time and the Hour* (1974). *New Girl in Town* (1975). *Thursday's Child* (1976). *Adam's Eden* (1977).

BIBLIOGRAPHY: Cooper, P., *Faith Baldwin's American Family* (1938). Van Gelder, R., *Writers and Writing* (1946).

For articles in reference works, see: *CA* (1969). *20thCA. 20th CAS.*

Other references: *CSMMag* (11 Jan. 1947). *Colliers* (27 May 1944). *Cosmopolitan* (Aug. 1959). *Good Housekeeping* (Oct. 1943). *NRTA Journal* (Sept.–Oct. 1975). *NY Post* (2 Sept. 1972). *NYT* (25 Oct. 1973; 20 March 1978). *Pictorial Review* (Dec. 1935). *SatEvePost* (14 March 1936). *SatRL* (11 April 1936; 29 April 1939). *Time* (8 July 1935). *Writer* (May 1940).

MARCELLE THIÉBAUX

Caroline Wells Healey Dall

B. 22 June 1822, Boston, Massachusetts; d. 17 Dec. 1912, Washington, D.C.
D. of Mark and Caroline Foster Healey; m. Charles Henry Appleton Dall, 1844

Daughter of a prosperous Boston merchant who had "desired a son" and was "determined I should supply the place of one," D. received a thorough education and was devoted to her father until her desire to spend her life in charitable and religious work conflicted with her father's desire that she pursue a literary career. Her marriage to Reverend Dall produced a son and a daughter but the union was not happy. In 1855 he went as a Unitarian missionary to India, where he remained, except for occasional visits, until his death in 1886.

D. helped Pauline Wright Davis organize the woman's rights convention in Boston in 1855, and she organized and delivered one of the principal addresses at the 1859 New England woman's rights convention, also in Boston. She was one of the founders of the American Social Science Association.

Essays and Sketches (1849) collects D.'s early essays on moral and religious subjects, which had been published in newspapers and periodicals since she was thirteen. In *The Liberty Bell* (1847), another collection of her writings, she holds, in contrast to her later writings and actions, that political activity for women is "utterly incompatible with the more previous and positive duties of the nursery and the fireside." A series of nine lectures, delivered between 1859 and 1862, was described in the New York *Evening Post* as "the most eloquent and forcible statement of the Woman's Question which has been made."

D. calls for the removal of educational and legal barriers so that each human being can fully develop, and insists on woman's right to work and her right to receive equal pay for equal work. D.'s convincing historical analysis, well supplied with examples, shows that women have "since the beginning of civilization" shared the hardest and most unwholesome work, that they have always been the worst paid, and that their efforts to find "new avenues of labor" (e.g., efforts to train women as watchmakers) have often been met "by the selfish opposition of man." She feels that such opposition will be overcome and that all the work woman asks for "will inevitably be given."

A consistent advocate of coeducation and higher education for women, D. responded to Dr. Edward H. Clarke's book *Sex in Education* (1873), in which he claimed that women's health could not withstand the strain of a college education. Her review affirms her belief that no "greater difference of capacity, whether physical or psychical, *will be* found between man and woman than *is* found between man and man," that a proper coeducational system will make possible the fullest development of both sexes, and that "whatever danger menaces the health of America, it cannot, thus far, have sprung from the overeducation of her women." She calls upon women, "contented in ignominious dependence, restless even to insanity from the need of healthy employment and the perversion of their instincts, and confessedly looking to marriage for salvation," to "make thorough preparation for trades or professions" and to abide by the consequences of their resolutions.

D. was, in later years, a prolific writer of obituary tributes, devotional pamphlets, genealogical studies, and quasihistorical works.

SELECTED WORKS: *Essays and Sketches* (1849). *What We Really Know about Shakespeare* (1855). *Woman's Right to Labor; or, Low Wages and Hard Work* (1860). *A Practical Illustration of "Woman's Right to Labor"; or, A Letter from Marie E. Zakrzewska* (edited by Dall, 1860). *Historical Pictures Retouched* (1860). *Woman's Rights under the Law* (1861). *The College, the Market, and the Court* (1867). *Patty Gray's Journey: From Boston to Baltimore* (1869). *Patty Gray's Journey: From Baltimore to Washington* (1870). *On the Way; or, Patty at Mount Vernon* (1870). *Sex and Education* (1874). *The Romance of the Association* (1875). *My First Holiday* (1881). *The Life of Dr. Anandabai Joshee* (1888). *Margaret and Her Friends* (1895). *Alongside* (1902).

BIBLIOGRAPHY: Buell, L., *Literary Transcendentalism* (1973). Riegel, R. E., *American Feminists* (1963).

For articles in reference works, see: *HWS. NAW* (article by S. Nissenbaum).

Other references: *HLB* 22 (Oct. 1974). *NEQ* (March 1969).

SUSAN SUTTON SMITH

Olive Tilford Dargan

B. 1869, Grayson County, Kentucky; d. 22 Jan. 1968, Asheville, North Carolina
Wrote under: Fielding Burke, Olive Tilford Dargan
D. of Elisha Francis and Rebecca Day Tilford; m. Pegram Dargan

Raised in Kentucky and Missouri in an academic family, D. was educated at George Peabody College for Teachers in Nashville, and later at Radcliffe College, where she met her future husband, Pegram Dargan. She began her writing career as a poet and lyrical dramatist living in New York, but, following her husband's death by drowning in 1915, she returned to Kentucky and wrote about the southern mountain people. Her literary approach ranged from bemused local-color anecdotes written during the 1920s to angry Marxist novels written during the Depression. Throughout her long life, D. published social fiction under the pseudonym Fielding Burke while using her real name for poetry and local-color stories.

D.'s early lyrical dramas give some clues to the intensely political nature of her mature fiction. *The Mortal Gods* (1912), though archaic in form and remote in setting, is nevertheless a powerful study of the oppression of the working class in modern industrial society. In her collection of plays, *The Flutter of the Gold Leaf* (1922), D. explores conflicting emotional and intellectual loyalties, and the different impulses created by personal and public roles. The plays were not well received by critics.

D.'s more conventional poetry was treated admiringly. The sonnet collection, *The Cycle's Rim* (1916) was described by one reviewer as "in a class with Elizabeth Barrett Browning's *Sonnets from the Portuguese*."

The extent of D.'s left-wing intellectual leanings becomes apparent in *Highland Annals* (1925), a collection of short stories about the poor-white inhabitants of the southern mountains. Although these sketches exhibit many of the traditional features of southern local-color writing—tall tales, extravagant humor, rhapsodic appreciation of nature, quaintness of language and custom—they also note the ominous threat of the exploitative cotton-mill and the vulnerability of the poor-white woman who suffers both for her class and for her sex.

A bloody strike among hitherto docile workers in a textile mill in Gastonia, North Carolina, in 1929 gave D. the ideal setting for her first novel. *Call Home the Heart* (1932) is about the predicament of Ishma, a southern poor white woman who is torn between her love for her husband, family, and mountain life, and an overwhelming desire to seek freedom from the obligations they heap upon her. But when Ishma deserts her family for an urban, industrial life with a lover, she only finds a new set of duties. She discovers the poor worker trapped by the cruel paternalism of the textile factories, and she slowly educates herself in the intricacies of Marxist socialism until she is ready to participate fully in strike organization. However, just when Ishma's intellectual principles appear to have triumphed, she flees back to her husband and family, driven by ancient prejudices against the black workers who embrace her, and drawn by her yearning for a husband's love and the tranquil beauty of the mountains. Many critics applauded what they called the novel's final "retreat into art" after Marxist and feminist "propaganda." However, D. leaves no doubt that Ishma's retreat, though passionate and consoling, is a failure of principle—a step backward from the new consciousness she seemed to be approaching. The novel implies that there can be no reconciliation of pleasure and principle, that one must always be subordinate to the other.

D. returned to the predicament of Ishma in her second proletarian novel, *A Stone Came Rolling* (1935). Here the heroine achieves the triumph of principle, but only at the cost of the death of her beloved husband. She returns to dedicate her energy to revolutionary activities with a new sense of the danger of a wasted life. Though D.'s novels show a clear Marxist emphasis, their power lies in their sensitivity to the circumstances of an intellectual and passionate woman who discovers that personal happiness is the price demanded by both the traditional feminine role and the revolutionary feminist one.

After the 1930s, D., like most other leftward-leaning American writers, retreated from extreme ideological concerns. She returned to anecdotal fiction of the mountain people in *From My Highest Hill* (1941) and to a liberal treatment of labor warfare among organizing mine workers in *Sons of the Stranger* (1947). However, it is in the earlier novels of political engagement that D. produced her finest and most original work.

WORKS: *Path Flower, and Other Verses* (1904). *Semiramis, and Other Plays* (1904). *Lords and Lovers, and Other Dramas* (1906). *The Mortal Gods, and Other Plays* (1912). *The Cycle's Rim* (1916). *The Flutter of the Gold Leaf, and Other Plays* (with F. Peterson, 1922). *Lute and Furrow* (1922). *Highland*

Annals (1925). *Call Home the Heart* (1932). *A Stone Came Rolling* (1935). *From My Highest Hill: Carolina Mountain Folks* (1941). *Sons of the Stranger* (1947). *The Spotted Hawk* (1958). *Innocent Bigamy, and Other Stories* (1962).

BIBLIOGRAPHY: Polsky, T., *North Carolina Authors: A Selective Hand-book* (1952). Rideout, W. B., *The Radical Novel in the U.S. 1900–1954: Some Interrelations of Literature and Society* (1956).

Other references: *Nation* (8 Jan. 1936). *NewR* (29 Jan. 1936). *NYTBR* (15 Dec. 1935). *North Carolina Librarian* (Spring 1960). *SatRL* (16 April 1932).

SYLVIA COOK

Lucretia Maria Davidson

B. 27 Sept. 1808, Plattsburg, New York; d. 27 Aug. 1825, Plattsburg, New York
D. of Oliver and Margaret Miller Davidson

D. received her early schooling at home and later was sent to Troy Female Academy. Her health, already delicate, was further undermined by the school's excessively ambitious curriculum and the virtual absence of outdoor exercise. After three months at another school, Miss Gilbert's Albany Academy, D. returned home to die, not quite seventeen years old.

Restricted by her inexperience, D. sensibly drew her writing subject matter either from her daily life or from her studies. From history, biblical and national, came "David and Jonathon," "Ruth's Answer to Naomi," the prose "Columbus," and the spirited "Vermont Cadets"; from the classroom, the humorous "Week before Examination" which was deservedly popular with her schoolmates; from her brief but poignant personal encounters with suffering, mental and physical, poems like "Headache" and "Fears of Death." These latter, especially, have the ring of sincerity, transcending her usual level of stock images and poetic diction.

Amir Khan, and Other Poems, selected by her mother and with a biographical introduction by the artist and inventor Samuel Morse, was published in 1829. Copies were sent by Morse to a number of leading writers. In his covering letter to Robert Southey, the poet laureate of England, Morse invited comparison with other youthful prodigies such as Chatterton and White, of "this new genuis which sprang up and bloomed in the wilderness, assumed the female form and wore the features of exquisite beauty and perished in the bloom." Southey's response was an eleven-page review in the prestigious *London Quarterly* (1829), the conclusion of which, Poe protested, was "twice as strong as was necessary to establish her fame in England-fearing America." Within thirty years, no less than fifteen editions appeared on both sides of the Atlantic, all but the first preceded by the biographical sketch by Catharine Sedgwick. A German translation was published in 1844, and an Italian edition in 1906.

Edgar Allan Poe, in a review challenging Southey's encomium, argues that we must "distinguish that which, in our heart is love of [her] worth, from that which, in our intellect, is appreciation of [her] poetic ability; with the former, as critic, we have nothing to do." "This distinction," he adds, "would have spared us much twaddle on the part of commentators." This distinction is one very difficult to make, however, in the case of D. She wrote before there was enough American poetry to form a standard and died before her own poetic skills and critical powers could be properly developed.

WORKS: *Amir Khan, and Other Poems* (Ed. M. Davidson, 1829). *Poetical Remains of the Late Lucretia Maria Davidson* (Ed. M. Davidson, 1846; rev. eds., 1857 and 1860). *Poems by Lucretia Maria Davidson* (Ed. M. O. Davidson, 1871).

BIBLIOGRAPHY: Brooks, V. W., *The World of Washington Irving* (1944). Curry, K., ed., *New Letters of Robert Southey* (1965). Dewey, M. E., *Life and Letters of Catharine Sedgwick* (1871). Mabee, C., *Samuel Morse: The American Leonard* (1944).

MARION NORMAN

Margaret Miller Davidson

B. 26 March 1823, Plattsburg, New York; d. 25 Nov. 1838, Saratoga, New York
D. of Oliver and Margaret Miller Davidson

D. received the best education at home from her chronically ill mother. Anxious to assume the family poetic mantle bequeathed her by her dying sister Lucretia, she eagerly absorbed the ideas, tastes, and moral and religious standards of her mother toward whom she formed an exceptionally close attachment. Frequent extended vacations and changes of residence proved unable to arrest D.'s fatal tuberculosis. She died at fifteen.

Mrs. Davidson who, three years earlier when negotiating for a new edition of Lucretia's poetry, had introduced her younger daughter to Washington Irving, now provided him with all that remained of Margaret's poems. She also gave him copious memoranda which he used, often verbatim, for his biographical introduction to D.'s *Poetical Remains* (1841). A second edition was called for in the same year, one each in London and Philadelphia the following year, and by 1864, there were twenty editions in all.

D.'s poems, as is hardly surprising, reflect two main influences: Lucretia, whom she idolized and emulated as far as she could, and her mother, whom she reflected so completely that it is difficult to determine if there was anything of her own. D.'s poems are, on the whole, longer than most of her sister's, written in quatrains rather than rhyming couplets and express stronger religious faith and devotion. Many deal with her various homes and the flowers, trees, rivers, and mountains surrounding them. Despite her mother's disapproval of extensive memorizations, echoes (perhaps unconscious) of Cowper, Thomson, and Scott constantly recur. Among D.'s better efforts are the paraphrases of the twenty-third and forty-second psalms, the "Hymn of the Fire-Worshippers," and "The Destruction of Sodom and Gomorrah"; but these are clearly inferior to Lucretia's handling of similar biblical material.

D.'s mother inadvertently did her a disservice in exposing to the public juvenile verse that should have been reserved for the uncritical eyes of family and close friends. D. was surprisingly popular for the quarter century after her death, but today one is apt to dismiss her as a faint echo of her more promising older sister.

WORKS: *Biographical and Poetical Remains of the Late Margaret Miller Davidson* (Ed. W. Irving, 1841).

BIBLIOGRAPHY: Griswold, R., *Female Poets of America* (1848). May, C., *The American Female Poets* (1848). Poe, E. A., *Complete Works*, Harrison, J., ed. (1902).

MARION NORMAN

Mary Evelyn Moore Davis

B. 12 April 1852, Talladage, Alabama; d. 1 Jan. 1909, New Orleans, Louisiana
Wrote under: Mrs. M. E. M. Davis, Mollie Moore Davis, Mollie Evelyn Moore
  Davis, Mollie E. Moore
D. of John and Marian Lucy Crutchfield Moore; m. Thomas Edward Davis,
  1874

An only daughter in a family of nine children, D. grew up in rural Alabama and on a plantation near San Marcos, Texas, which later provided rich material for her poetry and fiction. In 1860 her first poems appeared in the local newspaper, the *Tyler* (Texas) *Reporter*. Between 1861 and 1865, her poetry, inspired by the Civil War, was printed in the *Reporter* and a number of southern newspapers. During the 1880s, D. turned increasingly to the writing of fiction for publication in national literary magazines.

D.'s more popular poems typify her musical, energetic versification and skillful handling of rhyme. A number of poems after 1869 suggests a shift in D.'s interests from short lyrics to narratives and monologues, such as "The Golden Rose," "The Ball (A True Incident)," and "Eleanor to Arthur," which is possibly autobiographical.

In War Times at La Rose Blanche (1888), her first book of prose and her best-known work, is a semiautobiographical story sequence, which now, however, appears superficial. *Under the Man-Fig* (1895), D.'s first and most fully realized novel, is a southwestern tale of mystery and romance that reveals her fascination with the past. The intricate plot, characteristic of all her novels, involves a wide spectrum of characters spanning several generations and every social class in a small Texas town. The work is most effective in its deft use of regional dialect, historical detail, and humorous characters.

An Elephant's Track, and Other Stories (1897) serves as a sampler of D.'s work in short fiction, in which she is technically at her best. This volume contains fifteen stories depicting rural Texas folk, Louisiana Creoles, and plantation blacks. Among the more memorable are "A Bamboula" and "The Love Stranche," which delve into the mysterious world of voodoo, and "At La Glorieuse" and "The Soul of Rose Dédé," which treat ghosts as an everyday reality. D.'s achievement in the stories lies in her subtle handling of regional settings, faithful rendering of rural mores, and vivid delineation of the different socioeconomic levels of southern society.

The Wire Cutters (1899), a novel set primarily in a rural Texas community, is reminiscent of the work of Charles Dickens in its ingenious plot complications and numerous secret identities. This work contains D.'s most controversial subjects—divorce and physical abuse in marriage—and her most complex characterizations, particularly of women who, though entangled in some stock situations, emerge convincingly as strong individuals. Concerned with the struggle against the fencing in of pasture lands and water sources, *The Wire Cutters* reflects D.'s interest in Texas history.

New Orleans Creole society inspired two of D.'s major works, *The Little Chevalier* (1903), a historical novel regarded as her best, and *The Price of Silence* (1907), her most popular novel. Set in the French Louisiana territory of the mid-18th c., *The Little Chevalier* is an adventure story of intrigue and love on a grand scale. It realistically depicts the manners and milieu of the early Creoles. *The Price of Silence* focuses on a Creole family in contemporary New Orleans whose surviving matriarch guards a family secret. D. effectively portrays the attitudes, activities, and speech of the upper-class French Creoles, but her treatment of the theme of miscegenation is weak in conception and execution.

Equally adept at portraying Texas or Louisiana, plantation or city, D. is exact in locating her work in time, and faithful to contemporary conditions of dress, travel, worship, and entertainment. She has a discerning eye for visual details and paints accurate pictures of background scenes, natural landscapes, and physical appearance of characters, though her tendency is toward the more appealing details. Although her painstaking attention to exteriors does not compensate for her avoidance of much that is beneath the surface in human beings and in personal interactions, D. is an engaging storyteller whose romances and adventures consistently hold the reader's attention.

WORKS: *Minding the Gap, and Other Poems* (1867). *Poems by Mollie E. Moore* (1869). *In War Times at La Rose Blanche* (1888). *Under the Man-Fig* (1895). *A Christmas Masque of Saint Roch, Père Dagobert, and Throwing the Wanga* (1896). *An Elephant's Track, and Other Stories* (1897). *Under Six Flags: The Story of Texas* (1897). *The Wire Cutters* (1899). *The Queen's Garden* (1900). *Jaconetta: Her Love* (1901). *The Mistress of Odd Corner* (1902). *The Yellow Apples* (with P. Stapleton, 1902). *A Bunch of Roses, and Other Parlor Plays* (1903). *The Little Chevalier* (1903). *A Bunch of Roses* (1907). *Christmas Boxes* (1907). *A Dress Rehearsal* (1907). *The New System* (1907). *The Price of Silence* (1907). *Queen Anne Cottages* (1907). *The Moons of Balcanca* (1908). *Selected Poems* (Ed. G. King, 1927).

BIBLIOGRAPHY: Wilkenson, C., "The Broadening Stream: The Life and Literary Career of Mary Evelyn Moore Davis" (Ph.D. diss., Univ. of Illinois, 1947).

For articles in reference works, see: *DAB. The Living Writers of the South*, Ed. J. W. Davidson (1896). *LSL. NAW* (article by C. Wilkenson).

Other references: *LaS* (Summer 1962).

THADIOUS M. DAVIS

Rebecca Harding Davis

B. 24 June, 1831, Washington, Pennsylvania; d. 29 Sept. 1910, Mt. Kisco, New York
D. of Richard W. and Rachel Leet Wilson Harding; m. Lemuel Clarke Davis, 1863

D.'s uneventful and comfortable childhood was spent first in Big Spring, Alabama, and later in Wheeling, Virginia, (now West Virginia) where she lived until her marriage. The eldest of five children, she was tutored privately at home, but her education was, for the most part, acquired by means of her own extensive reading. She relates in *Bits of Gossip* (1904) that at the age of twelve she was profoundly moved by Nathanial Hawthorne's *Twice-Told Tales* in which "the commonplace folk and things which I saw every day took on a sudden mystery and charm." Encouraged by her parents, she began to write at an early age, although it was not until the publication of "Life in the Iron Mills" (*Atlantic Monthly*, April, 1861) that she gained any real recognition.

In 1862, D. visited her publisher in Boston, Massachusetts, and became acquainted with the intellectual coterie in Concord which included Bronson Alcott, Louisa May Alcott, George Ticknor, Nathanial Hawthorne, Ralph Waldo Emerson, and their disciples. D.'s charming portrayal in *Bits of Gossip* of this famous group reveals a great deal of sensitivity and insight.

After her marrige D. settled with her husband in Philadelphia and, in keeping with her beliefs concerning the true vocation of women, devoted herself to her home and family. Her feelings are expressed most strongly in *Pro Aris et Focis—A Plea for Our Altars and Hearths* (1870), where she earnestly asserts that "the highest female intellect finds its greatest delight, in contemplating and admiring the representative men of genius." By way of further explanation she maintains that the female brain "is not capable of such sustained and continuous mental exertion as man's."

Her convictions did not, however, entirely inhibit her own career, and in 1869 she became a contributing editor to the New York *Herald Tribune*. She also continued to publish; essays, articles, and stories appeared in major adult and juvenile periodicals. After her husband's death in 1904, D. applied herself almost entirely to the career of her well-known son, the novelist and journalist Richard Harding Davis.

It is D.'s early work which is most worthy of attention, especially the remarkable "Life in the Iron Mills," a portrayal of Wheeling mill workers as she observed them. It is harsh and unflinching in its realism. Eschewing the romanticism of many of her contemporaries, D. presents a bleak picture of the degrading existence imposed by poverty and hard labor. So powerful is the depiction that at the time many believed it to have been written by a man. Later the same year, *Atlantic* published "A Story for To-day" (published in book form as *Margret Howth*, 1862), followed in the next year by "John Lamar" and "David Gaunt," both of which present the grim horrors of the Civil War. D. never acceded to the popular glorification of war as a patriotic deity but warned, in Bits of Gossip, that "the garments of the deity are filthy and that some of her influences debase and befoul a people."

In what is by far her finest novel, *Waiting for the Verdict* (1868), D. deals with the tragic aftermath of the Civil War, particularly the race problems it engendered. Despite the fact that the work is marred by melodrama, it displays an extraordinary sensitivity to its subject.

It is regrettable that D.'s later work does not fulfill its early promise. Her style increasingly lapses into the sentimental and melodramatic tendencies of the time, becoming more appropriate for the romantic potboilers she often contributed to *Peterson's* magazine. Nevertheless, the significance of D.'s early work to the development of American realism cannot be overestimated. "Life in the Iron Mills," in particular, deserves recognition as a landmark in the history of American literature.

WORKS: *Margret Howth* (1862). *Dallas Galbraith* (1868). *Waiting for the Verdict* (1868). *Pro Aris et Focis—A Plea for Our Altars and Hearths* (1870). *Berrytown* (1872). *John Andross* (1874). *Kitty's Choice* (1874). *A Law Unto Herself* (1878). *Natasqua* (1886). *Kent Hampden* (1892). *Silhouettes of American Life* (1892). *Doctor Warrick's Daughters* (1896). *Frances Waldeaux* (1897). *Bits of Gossip* (1904).

BIBLIOGRAPHY: Downey, F., *Richard Harding Davis: His Day* (1933). Langford, G., *The Richard Harding Davis Years* (1961). *Quinn, A. H., American Fiction* (1936). Sheaffer, H. W., "Rebecca Harding Davis, Pioneer Realist" (Ph.D. diss., Univ. of Pennsylvania, 1947). Wann, L., *The Rise of Realism* (1942). Wyman, M., "Women in the American Realistic Novel" (Ph.D. diss., Radcliffe College, 1950).

For articles in reference works, see: *AA. DAB. NAW* (article by M. Wyman Langworthy). *NCAB.*

Other references: *American* 3 (4 March 1882). *NYT* (30 Sept. 1910).

S. JULIA GOWING

Dorothy Day

B. 8 Nov. 1897, Bath Beach, New York; d. 29 Nov. 1980, New York City
D. of John and Grace Satterlee Day; common-law husband Forster Battingham

As an eight-year-old, D. first experienced that "sweetness of faith" in a Methodist Sunday school that later caused her to become a devout Roman Catholic. After the San Francisco earthquake, which destroyed the newspaper plant for which D.'s father worked, the family moved to Chicago, where D. spent her girlhood years. She studied for two years at the University of Illinois at Urbana, where she further developed her interest in socialism, begun in high school.

At age eighteen, D. began a serious journalistic career as a reporter for the socialist *New York Call*. Later she wrote for Max Eastman's revolutionary publication, *The Masses*. After the suppression of *The Masses* by the government, D. went to Washington with a group of militant suffragists, who were arrested and sentenced to thirty days in prison. This was the first of a number of imprisonments which D. underwent throughout the years for her activism in the causes of peace and justice.

During 1918, D. came to know the Provincetown Players and talked long hours with Eugene O'Neill about religion and death as they walked the streets or "sat out the nights in taverns, in waterfront back rooms."

With five thousand dollars for the movie-rights to her novel, *The Eleventh Virgin* (1924), D. bought a small bungalow on Raritan Bay, Staten Island. There she had a daughter by her common-law husband, Forster Battingham, an anarchist, who parted with her when she later had the child baptised in the Catholic Church. In *From Union Square to Rome* (1938) she tells the story of her conversion, and in her autobiography, *The Long Loneliness* (1952), of her struggle against Catholic priests whose vision did not extend beyond their parish.

Like many other writers in the 1920s, D. spent some fruitless months on a screen-writing assignment in Hollywood, thereafter going with her daughter, Tamar, to Mexico City, where she supported herself by writing articles about the life of the people for *Commonweal*. Back in New York, she met Peter Maurin, whose ideas dominated the rest of her life. He encouraged her to start a paper for the workingman, extolling "personalist action" and using love as a means of changing institutions to enable each individual to lead a full life. In Union Square on May 1, 1933, a day of massive celebration of Russian and world-wide communism, D. heroically hawked the first issue of *The Catholic Worker*, a four-page tabloid-size paper, which urged social Christian action in place of the Marxist communism of *The Daily Worker*. For almost half a century, she continued to publish every month this liberal voice of the Catholic church.

Among the many charitable farms and houses of refuge for the poor and homeless which she helped found are the Maryfarm Retreat House, Newburgh, New York; St. Joseph's House of Hospitality, New York City; Peter Maurin Farm, Pleasant Plains, Staten Island; Maryfarm, Easton, Pennsylvania; Chrystie Street House, New York City; and the Tivoli Farm Retreat on the Hudson. *The Catholic Worker* offices on Mott Street have also served as soup kitchen for the hungry. This tough-minded but gentle-hearted woman, who seemed a saint to wanderers lacking food and shelter, has been the inspiration for numerous Worker Groups, where friendship as well as food is shared.

WORKS: *The Eleventh Virgin* (1924). *From Union Square to Rome* (1938). *House of Hospitality* (1939). *On Pilgrimage* (1948). *The Long Loneliness* (1952). *I Remember Peter Maurin* (1958). *Thérèse* (1960). *Loaves and Fishes* (1963). *On Pilgrimage: The Sixties* (1972).

BIBLIOGRAPHY: Coles, R., *A Spectacle unto the World: The Catholic Worker Movement* (1973). Hennacy, A., *Autobiography of a Catholic Anarchist* (1945). Hennacy, A., *The Book of Ammon* (1970). Maurin, P., *Catholic Radicalism: Phrased Essays for the Green Revolution* (1949). Miller, W. D., *A Harsh and Dreadful Love: Dorothy Day and the Catholic Worker Movement* (1973). O'Brien, D. J., *American Catholics and Social Reform: The New Deal Years* (1968). Sheehan, A., *Peter Maurin: Gay Believer* (1959).

Other references: *The Catholic Worker* (1933 to present). *NY* (4 Oct. 1952; 11 Oct. 1952). *NYRB* (28 Jan. 1971).

WINIFRED FRAZER

Margaret Wade Campbell Deland

B. 28 Feb. 1857, Allegheny, Pennsylvania; d. 13 Jan. 1945, Boston, Massachusetts
Given name: Margaretta Campbell
D. of Sample and Margaretta Wade Campbell; m. Lorin F. Deland, 1880

D. was educated in private schools before entering Cooper Union, in New York City, for a course in drawing and design. After graduation, she was appointed assistant instructor at Girls' Normal School (now Hunter College.)

D.'s first novel, *John Ward, Preacher* (1888), is a story of religious doubt and adamant orthodoxy. D. had been brought up a strict Presbyterian, but in the years following her marriage she found herself painfully questioning her earlier religious attitudes. She finally left her family's denomination and, with her husband, was confirmed in the Episcopal church. It was many years, however, before she was at peace with her convictions, and *John Ward, Preacher* was the result of her own soul-searching. It made her suddenly famous, for it was much discussed, and often angrily denounced as wicked and immoral.

D. followed this first novel with a steady output of fiction so popular that she became one of the best-known writers of her day. Four honorary doctorates were awarded her, and, in 1926, she was one of the first women elected to membership in the National Institute of Arts and Letters.

"Essentially a novelist of character," as one writer calls her, D. created a group of likable men, women, and children who appear time after time in her various novels and short stories. These are inhabitants of a small town, "Old Chester," which was modelled on Manchester, where she grew up. Dominating the Old Chester scene is the all-wise, all-compassionate Dr. Lavendar, Rector of St. Michael's Church. The plots are concerned with sin and its expiation, self-sacrifice, maternal love, pride, and oddly assorted marriages. Through them all runs a strong current of religion, for D.'s people conceive of a deity who is intensely personal. Also apparent is a delightful appreciation of nature—the shifting seasons, flowers, hills, rivers.

Though D.'s fiction is definitely dated, it is extremely useful to any student seeking to understand the values and mores of a bygone era. Further, while its faint gloss of sentimentality, its assertions regarding extramarital relations, and its firm insistence on the need for renouncing "sin" may seem quaint and unreal to the modern reader, D.'s work does portray the timeless qualities of personal integrity, devotion, and courage.

WORKS: *The Old Garden* (1886). *John Ward, Preacher* (1888). *A Summer Day* (1889). *Philip and His Wife* (1890). *Sidney: The Story of a Child* (1892). *The Wisdom of Fools* (1894). *Mr. Tommy Dove and Other Stories* (1897). *Old Chester Tales* (1899). *Dr. Lavendar's People* (1903). *The Common Way* (1904). *The Awakening of Helena Richie* (1906). *An Encore* (1907). *The Iron Woman* (1911). *The Voice* (1912). *Partners* (1913). *The Hands of Esau* (1914). *Around Old Chester* (1915). *The Rising Tide* (1916). *The Vehement Flame* (1922). *New Friends in Old Chester* (1924). *The Kays* (1926). *Captain Archer's Daughter* (1932). *Old Chester Days* (1935). *If This Be I* (1935). *Golden Yesterdays* (1941).

BIBLIOGRAPHY: Dodd, L. H., *Celebrities at Our Hearthside* (1959). Overton, G., *The Women Who Make Our Novels* (1928). Williams, B. C., *Our Short Story Writers* (1920).

For articles in reference works, see: *NAW* (article by J. Levenson). *NCAB*. *20th CA*.

Other references: *NYT* (14 Jan. 1945).

ABIGAIL ANN HAMBLEN

Agnes De Mille

B. *1905, New York City*
D. *of William C. and Anna George De Mille; m. Walter Prude, 1943*

D.'s mother was the daughter of political economist Henry George. Her father was a successful playwright, but after an unexpected flop on Broadway he went west to join his younger brother, Cecil B. De Mille, and became a movie director.

D.'s first book, *Dance to the Piper* (1951), begins with her family's move from New York City to Hollywood in 1914, covers her difficult

years of struggle to become a dancer and to launch a career, and culminates with her first two solid choreographic successes, *Rodeo* (1942)
and *Oklahoma!* (1943). The book ranges from child's-eye sketches of
personalities who frequented the De Mille household, such as Geraldine Farrar, Ruth St. Denis, Elinor Glyn, and Charlie Chaplin, to more
detailed portraits of those who affected D.'s dance career—Martha Graham, Argentina, Marie Rambert, Antony Tudor, Lucia Chase.

Enthusiasm and honesty are the keynotes of D.'s literary style. Her
greatest enthusiasm is for other accomplished artists, and her most brutal
honesty concerns her own limitations. At fifteen, she says, "I considered
my body a shame, a trap and a betrayal. But I could break it. I was a
dancer." She is absolutely forthright in her advice on careers in dance,
with constructive suggestions for dance teachers and critics, in *To a
Young Dancer* (1962). In several of her books, she discusses how the
development of professional dance, like the development of female consciousness, has been retarded by social, religious, and economic restraints.

Lizzie Borden: A Dance of Death (1968) is a book-length study of
the creation of her 1948 folk ballet, *Fall River Legend*. D.'s historical
research was meticulous, as it was for her earlier, illustrated *Book of the
Dance* (1963). After a careful exploration of the scene of Lizzie Borden's
crime, D. conducts the reader through her own transformation of historical fact into dance-drama. Accidents, personality clashes, and economic obstacles make of the creative process itself a taut, suspenseful
narrative. In her *Russian Journals* (1970), D. recalls the stunned appreciation of Soviet audiences for this ballet when it was performed by American Ballet Theater on its USSR tour.

Where the Wings Grow (1978) covers the earliest period in D.'s life,
before she had any serious thought of becoming a dancer. In this childhood memoir of summers at Merriewold, in Sullivan County, New York,
D. evokes a turn-of-the-century way of life innocent of indoor plumbing
and refrigeration, with home remedies, Irish-Catholic house servants,
lemonade, and embroidery on the verandah, and ladies—like her mother—
who prided themselves on their sheltered, genteel public image, even
though it masked a great deal of anguished drudgery. This book is a
landmark in D.'s literary career, because its lyricism and passion and the
interest it sustains depend not at all upon the author's reputation as a
dancer and choreographer.

Long recognized for her energetic contributions to American dance
theater, D. is now respected as a serious and prolific writer as well. Five
of her ten books are autobiographical; the others, like most of her

magazine articles and speaking engagements, deal more specifically with dance as an artistic and social form of expression. D. is much in demand as a speaker, for she displays in person, as in her writing, a very engaging zeal and wit.

WORKS: *Dance to the Piper* (1951). *And Promenade Home* (1956). *To a Young Dancer* (1962). *The Book of the Dance* (1963). *Lizzie Borden: A Dance of Death* (1968). *Russian Journals* (1970). *Speak to Me, Dance with Me* (1973). *American Ballet Theatre, 35th Anniversary Gala* (with L. Chase, 1975). *Where the Wings Grow* (1978). *America Dances* (1980). *Reprieve: A Memoir* (1981).

BIBLIOGRAPHY: For articles in reference works, see: *CB* (1943). *Notable Names in the American Theatre*, Eds. J. T. White et al. (1976).
Other references: *Dance Magazine* (Oct. 1971; Sept. 1973; Nov. 1974; June 1974). *NYTBR* (13 Jan. 1952; 12 Oct. 1968).

FELICIA HARDISON LONDRÉ

Babette Deutsch

B. 22 Sept. 1895, New York City; d. 13 Nov. 1982, New York City
D. of Michael and Melanie Fisher Deutsch; m. Avrahm Yarmolinsky, 1921

Of German descent, D. grew up in New York City, where she received her B.A. from Barnard College in 1917. Although best known as a poet, D. has published novels, translations, literary criticism, and children's books.

In 1919, D. published her first volume of poems, *Banners*, whose title piece celebrates the Russian Revolution as "new freedoms, and new slavery." *Honey out of the Rock* (1925), D.'s second book, contains a number of short imagistic poems, biblically inspired ballads, and poems to her son. Both volumes display the influence of imagism, Japanese haiku, and Greek and Jewish culture.

Considered by some critics to be D.'s best work, *Epistle to Prometheus* (1930), is a letter written by a contemporary to the Greek god. It is a survey of man's history, beginning with his creation and tracing the Promethean spirit as it has inspired humanity in 5th-c. Greece, 18th-c. France, and 20th-c. Russia.

D.'s final three volumes of poetry, *One Part Love* (1939), *Take Them,*

Stranger (1944), and *Animal, Vegetable, and Mineral* (1954), all reveal her rage at the destruction of World War II. In "To Napoleon" she asks, "But who will cut the growth/ That gnaws at Europe now?" D.'s poetry has been collected in two volumes: *Collected Poems, 1919–62* (1963) and *Coming of Age: New and Selected Poems* (1959).

As a novelist, D. began her career with *A Brittle Heaven* (1926), a thinly veiled autobiography about a young woman's youth, education, and marriage. The novel reveals the major conflicts facing a woman struggling to define herself both as a professional writer, and a wife and mother. D.'s second novel, *In Such a Night* (1927), is essentially a series of character sketches showing the influence of Virginia Woolf's stream-of-consciousness technique in *Mrs. Dalloway*. D.'s other novels are *Mask of Silenus* (1933), a historical novel based on Socrates' life, and *Rogue's Legacy* (1942), a tale patterned after the life of the French poet, François Villon.

D.'s critical writings are concerned with the correlation between modern poetry and modern society. *Potable Gold: Some Notes on Poetry and This Age* (1929) discusses the influence of technology on poetry and the poet's relationship to his public. *This Modern Poetry* (1935) and *Poetry in Our Time* (1952) both analyze major poetic figures and study the interrelationship between poet and politics. According to D., the modern poet must "create a myth beyond the power of man" and therefore be a "true revolutionary."

WORKS: *Banners* (1919). *Honey out of the Rock* (1925). *A Brittle Heaven* (1926). *In Such a Night* (1927). *Potable Gold: Some Notes on Poetry and This Age* (1929). *Fire for the Night* (1930). *Epistle to Prometheus* (1930). *Mask of Silenus* (1933). *This Modern Poetry* (1935). *One Part Love* (1939). *Rogue's Legacy* (1942). *Take Them, Stranger* (1944). *Poetry in Our Time* (1952). *Animal, Vegetable, Mineral* (1954). *Poetry Handbook: A Dictionary of Terms* (1956). *Coming of Age: New and Selected Poems* (1959). *Collected Poems, 1919–62* (1963).

BIBLIOGRAPHY: For articles in reference works, see *CA* (1977).

Other references: *NYHTB* (12 July 1959). *Poetry* (1964). *SatR* (25 July 1959). *TLS* (18 June 1964). *VQR* (1964).

DIANE LONG HOEVELER

Abby Morton Diaz

B. 22 Nov. 1821, Plymouth, Massachusetts; d. 1 April 1904, Belmont,
Massachusetts
Given name: Abigail Morton
D. of Ichabod and Patty Weston Morton; m. Manuel Diaz, 1845

Christened Abigail, known as Abby, D. was the only daughter of
Ichabod Morton, a shipbuilder, liberal Unitarian, and social reformer.
In 1842 he took his family to the Transcendental utopian community, Brook Farm, where D. remained until 1847, teaching in the Association's infant school. She later taught school in Plymouth and began
writing. In May 1861, her first story appeared in the *Atlantic Monthly*,
and she eventually published in many leading juvenile and domestic
magazines of the day. D. was a founder and, from 1881 to 1892, president
of the Women's Educational and Industrial Union of Boston which she
saw as a "sisterhood" allying urban women of means with country girls
seeking work in the city. In the 1880s and 1890s D. traveled widely, organizing women's unions and lecturing at women's clubs. She was active
in the woman-suffrage movement which she saw as an outgrowth of
the abolition of slavery. In her later years she became interested in
Christian Science and published articles on religious subjects.

D.'s best, and most successful, juvenile fiction is *The William Henry
Letters* (1870), first published in 1867 in the magazine *Our Young Folks*.
Epistolary in form, it recounts the adventures of a mischievous red-
headed boy raised by his loving grandmother. Overall the *Letters* sentimentally evoke family life and simple fun in an idealized New England
village. Theodore Roosevelt in his *Autobiography* (1913) described this
book, one of his favorites, as a "good healthy" story, "teaching manli-
ness, decency and good conduct."

Two sequels were popular: *William Henry and His Friends* (1871)
and *Lucy Maria* (1874). The latter, apparently loosely autobiographical,
concerns a girl who took up "school-keeping with too much self-
confidence" and soon concluded that it is a "very solemn thing" to give
"even one life its first direction." Lucy Maria wants to do "heart-
teaching," rather than head-teaching; like D. at Brook Farm, she takes
her students into the woods to interest them in "flowers, trees, insects

—all natural objects." On woman suffrage, Lucy Maria, again like D. at this time, disclaims personal interest in the vote (except on "some neighborhood affair" such as the "location of a schoolhouse") but feels that other women should have the vote if they want it, as suffrage is a natural right.

D.'s interest in improving home life and the instruction of young children is evinced in several of her most effective books: *The Schoolmaster's Trunk* (1874), *A Domestic Problem* (1875), *Bybury to Beacon Street* (1887), *Only a Flock of Women* (1893). These novels are set in small towns that have little social life. Isolated and repressive, they are half-way stations between the old-fashioned village and the modern city. Families struggle to maintain "decent" standards and parents wear themselves out with work. To reform these conditions, D. proposes various domestic economies, simplifying women's chores so that they may devote more time to their children and to self-improvement. Men, she feels, should share household tasks, so that they may appreciate the difficulty of women's work. The community should meet convivially to discuss its problems.

Through more than twenty years, D. was a prolific author of juvenile stories and essays. These consistently reflect her affection for children and a charming delight in games and pastimes. The volumes of domestic advice are pleasantly stated, chatty, down-to-earth. Many of the household reforms D. suggests have since been accomplished by labor-saving machinery, but her comments testify to the physical difficulty of farm and village life for women a century ago. D.'s early exposure to Transcendental or Emersonian idealism is evident to the end of her life in her views of children, education, and the prospect of moral improvement.

WORKS: *The Entertaining Story of King Bronde, His Lily and His Rosebud* (1869). *The William Henry Letters* (1870). *William Henry and His Friends* (1871). *Lucy Maria* (1874). *The Schoolmaster's Trunk* (1874). *A Domestic Problem* (1875). *A Storybook for the Children* (1875). *Neighborhood Talks, As Reported By Mr. Codding* (1876). *Birds of Prey* (with N. A. Calkins, 1878). *Cat Family* (with N. A. Calkins, 1878). *The Jimmyjohns, and Other Stories* (1878). *Scratching Birds* (with N. A. Calkins, 1878). *Swimming Birds* (with N. A. Calkins, 1878). *Wading Birds* (with N. A. Calkins, 1878). *Brave Little Goose-girl: Little Stories for Little Folks* (1880). *Christmas Morning* (1880). *Merry Christmas* (1880). *Molasses Candy* (1880). *Simple Traveller* (1880). *The Story of Boxberry* (1880). *King Grimalkin and Pussyanna* (1881). *Polly Cologne* (1881). *Chronicles of the Stimpcett Family and Others* (1882). *Spirit As Power* (1886). *The Law of Perfection* (1886). *Bybury to Beacon Street* (1887). *The John Spicer Lectures* (1887). *Leaves of Healing* (1887). *Conventions during the Anti-Slavery Agitation* (1889). *In the Strength of the Lord* (1889). *Mother*

Goose's Christmas Party (1891). *Only a Flock of Women* (1893). *The Law of Perfection* (1895). *The Religious Training of Children* (1895). *The Flatiron and the Red Cloak* (1901). *"Those People from Skyton,"* and *Nine Other Stories* (1906).

BIBLIOGRAPHY: Codman, J. T., *Brook Farm* (1884). Croly, J. C., *History of the Women's Club Movement in America* (1898). Donham, S. A., "History of the Women's Educational and Industrial Union" (Diss., Radcliffe College, 1955). Swift, L., *Brook Farm* (1900).

For articles in reference works, see: *AW. NAW* (article by J. Benardete). Other references: *Women's Journal* (14 April 1904).

JANE BENARDETE

Emily Dickinson

B. 10 Dec. 1830, Amherst, Massachusetts; d. 15 May 1886, Amherst, Massachusetts
D. of Edward and Emily Norcross Dickinson

D. was one of three children. Her older brother and younger sister were always her closest companions. Her father—a Massachusetts judge, member of the state legislature, a U.S. congressman, and an exemplar of the Puritan ethic of industry and public service—was "too busy with his briefs" to notice his children. Her mother appears to have been an equally remote parent, a semi-invalid for much of her children's lives, and, in D.'s view, a failure as a mother. D. once wrote a friend, "I never had a mother."

D. attended Amherst Academy and was sent for a year to Mount Holyoke Female Seminary. Except for occasional visits to neighboring cities and a trip with her father to Washington, D.C., she did not leave her birthplace again. By her thirtieth year she had withdrawn even from the life of Amherst. To the townspeople she became a legendary figure, an eccentric spinster who dressed always in white, rarely received a visitor, and refused to venture beyond the family house and garden.

Found in her room after her death was a manuscript, in the style of homemade pamphlets, of almost nine hundred poems, only seven of which she had published. All were short lyrics, often no more than a quatrain or two; almost all were untitled and undated; some were unfinished; some appeared in variant versions. The labor of collecting additional manuscripts and of publishing selections of her verse was undertaken first by family and friends, none of whom suspected their actual value. The first *Poems by Emily Dickinson* appeared four years after her death, to mainly hostile reviews. Periodically, as new poems, originally sent to friends, were discovered, new collections followed. In this century the number of poems has continued to increase; more than 650 were published for the first time as late as 1945. The authoritative text of all known poems, numbering almost 1800, is the three-volume edition by Thomas H. Johnson, which appeared in 1955. (The poems cited below are identified by their numbers in the Johnson edition.)

The subjects of D.'s poetry are, broadly, the subjects of lyric tradition: love, nature, death, and God. Her religious attitudes, in all their bewildering variety, permeate the bulk of her verse. In some of these religious poems she is seemingly the orthodox believer, "Given in marriage unto Thee" (317). More often she acknowledges herself the disbeliever whom "Christ omitted," observing of her exclusion that "The abdication of belief/ Makes the behavior small" (1551). Characteristically, she is both doubter and quester, probing the mysteries of death, immortality, and eternity, appropriating biblical sources of Calvinist theology, but preferring to question on her own terms—"Infinitude, hadst thou no face/ That I might look on Thee?" (564).

Death was a common theme in D.'s poetry. In one of her most famous poems, "Because I could not stop for Death" (712), death appears personified, and with the eerie "civility" of a gentleman caller, escorts her to her grave: "The carriage held but just ourselves/ And Immortality."

D.'s love poems are also usually about parting, separation, and loss. They support the biographical evidence that she suffered from a secret and hopeless love that explains her years of seclusion. The identity of the man has not been established. Circumstantial evidence suggests Charles Wadsworth, a married minister with whom she corresponded for many years. Other candidates have been suggested.

The most impassioned poems are the "renunciation" and "bridal" poems of the 1860s, in which earthly separation is a prelude to spiritual reunion in heaven. In these, the theological doctrines of Divine Election and the Marriage Covenant are applied to a spiritual "contract" with a temporal groom. The subject is sometimes handled with an ingenuity reminiscent of John Donne, as in "I cannot live with you" (640).

Many of D.'s nature poems are slight, whimsical exercises describing the particulars available in her own garden—a caterpillar, a garden snake, a robin, or butterfly. Their charm is in their metaphorical exactitude. A snake becomes a "whip-lash,/ Unbraiding in the sun" (986). In its larger aspects, nature may be responsive to her moods, but it never becomes the surrogate divinity of Emersonian transcendentalism. It remains remote, a "haunted house" from which man is excluded, an ominous reminder of transiency and human isolation.

The strengths, as well as the strangeness, of D.'s poetry derive in large measure from her Puritan heritage. She saw, as she said, "New Englandly." In the waning years of Puritanism, life remained for her a spiritual drama. She lived the drama, and she recorded it with the terseness of her native idiom. She did not translate the terms of the conflict simplistically into those of good and evil—evil did not interest her—but into the shifting oppositions of doubt and belief, of the known and the unknowable. Even her major themes—denial and renunciation—were the themes of the Puritan pulpit, enacted in the rigorous lives and other-worldliness of her ancestors. Her favorite verse forms were the short lines and stanza patterns of the hymnal.

D. is noted for the technical irregularities that aroused the scorn of some of her 19th-c. reviewers—and caused drastic revisions by early editors: off-rhymes, broken meters, curious punctuation, and ungrammatical phrasing. These are given less importance by the less conventional-minded critics of today. The flaws rarely obtrude on her better poetry, and when they do, they hardly outweigh its virtues. At her best, she is a skillful prosodist, who adapted rhyme and meter to her purposes, achieving emotional shadings unobtainable by conventional means. Her elliptical grammar remains troublesome. It adds to an already highly abbreviated style the mark of mannerism, of private note-taking. Ivor Winters's assessment that she is "one of the greatest poets of our language" has stood.

WORKS: *Poems of Emily Dickinson* (Eds. M. L. Todd and T. W. Higginson, 1890; second series, 1891; third series, Ed. M. L. Todd., 1896). *The Single Hound* (Ed. M. D. Bianchi, 1914). *The Complete Poems of Emily Dickinson* (Eds. M. D. Bianchi and A. L. Hampson, 1924). *Further Poems of Emily Dickinson* (Eds. M. Bianchi and A. L. Hampson, 1929). *The Poems of Emily Dickinson* (Eds. M. D. Bianchi and A. L. Hampson, 1930). *Unpublished Poems of Emily Dickinson* (Eds. M. D. Bianchi and A. L. Hampson, 1935). *Poems by Emily Dickinson* (Eds. M. D. Bianchi and A. L. Hampson, 1937). *Ancestors' Brocades: The Literary Debut of Emily Dickinson* (Ed. M. T. Bingham, 1945). *Bolts of Melody: New Poems of Emily Dickinson* (Eds. M. L. Todd and M. T. Bingham, 1945). *The Poems of Emily Dickinson* (Ed. T. H. Johnson, 3 vols., 1955). *The Letters of Emily Dickinson* (Eds. T. H. Johnson and T. Ward, 3 vols., 1958). *The Years and Hours of Emily Dickinson* (Ed. J. Leyda, 2 vols., 1960). *Final Harvest: Emily Dickinson's Poems* (Ed. T. H. Johnson, 1961).

BIBLIOGRAPHY: Anderson, C. F., *Emily Dickinson's Poetry: Stairway of Surprise* (1960). Blackmur, R. P., *Language as Gesture* (1952). Cambon, G., in *Transcendentalism and Its Legacy*, Eds. M. Simon and T. H. Parsons (1966). Chase, R., *Emily Dickinson* (1951). Cunningham, J. V., *Collected Essays* (1976). Donoghue, D., *Emily Dickinson* (Univ. of Minnesota Pamphlets on American Writers No. 81, 1969). Frye, N., *Fables of Identity* (1963). Gelpi, J., *Emily Dickinson: The Mind of the Poet* (1965). Griffith, C., *The Long Shadow: Emily Dickinson's Tragic Poetry* (1964). Higgins, D., *Portrait of Emily Dickinson: The Poet and Her Prose* (1967). Pearce, R. H., *The Continuity of American Poetry* (1961). Sewall, R. B., *The Life of Emily Dickinson* (1974). Tate, A., *Collected Essays* (1959). Ward, T., *The Capsule of the Mind: Chapters in the Life of Emily Dickinson* (1961). Winters, Y., *Maule's Curse* (1938).

Other references: *Perspectives USA* (Spring 1956).

MARGARET PETERSON

Joan Didion

B. 5 Dec. 1934, Sacramento, California
D. of Frank Reese and Eduene Jerrett Didion; m. John Gregory Dunne, 1964

D. was graduated from the University of California at Berkeley with a B.A. in English in 1956, and in that same year became an associate feature editor with *Vogue* magazine in New York City. She remained at *Vogue* until 1963, the year in which she published her first novel, *Run River*, set in Sacramento in the 1940s. Between 1963 and 1969 D. wrote essays and feature articles for *Vogue*, the *National Review*, *Harper's*, *Holiday*, and, most regularly, the *Saturday Evening Post*. D. has written several screenplays with her husband.

Slouching towards Bethlehem (1968) is a collection of essays which had been published previously, the majority in the *Saturday Evening Post*. In reading them together, however, one sees that they make a powerful statement about American society in the 1960s. The title essay describes the variety of young people D. met in 1967 when she spent some time in Haight-Ashbury. It is a vivid narrative, a recording of actual dialogue which conveys the pathetic naiveté of the "flower children," drifting through drug-filled days, their lives circumscribed by a few vague ideas rendered only in pale and repetitious platitudes. The other essays which comprise the first section of the collection, entitled "Life Styles in the Golden Land," are companion pieces to the title essay in that they either dramatize a desperation for immediate gratification or recall with nostalgia the old American values of courage, self-sufficiency, and privacy. In all of these essays California emerges as the last frontier of American idealism, the place where people act out their largely vain hopes for peace, for community, for eternal romance.

D. has all the qualities of a brilliant essayist. Her themes are clear, her anecdotes dramatic, her style swift and crisp. In addition to their merit as models of prose style, her essays increase our understanding of her fiction. "Notes from a Native Daughter" narrates the history of the Sacramento Valley, and "Los Angeles Notebook" depicts that city as one of impersonal tensions, while providing sketches of the barren relationships that we find in *Play It as It Lays* (1970).

In 1972 D. alienated many feminists with an essay in the *New York Times Book Review* that attacked feminists for their tendency to become obsessed with trivia. The essay makes explicit a view of women that is pervasive in her fiction; women share, she believes, a "sense of living one's deepest life underwater, that dark involvement with blood and birth and death." In the same essay D. attacked narrow feminist interpretations of literature, expressing the view that, since the writer is committed to the "exploration of moral distinctions and ambiguities," all political interpretations of literature must of necessity represent a distortion.

Ironically, there is much in D.'s fiction to appeal to the true feminist. All three of her novels concern the experience of women—their relationships with men, with their parents and children, and with each other.

D.'s deepest concern, however, is with the illusions on which people build their lives, illusions made necessary by the death of old values and the absence of viable new ones. Her novels dramatize the consequences of social, economic, and political change that occurs so rapidly as to produce disorder in individual lives, in families, and, ultimately, in whole societies.

The novel *Play It as It Lays* is a biting portrayal of a world in which people use each other to gain success, recognition, or sensual pleasure. Because men possess most of the power, women are especially likely to be victims. As narrator of the novel, D. is unobtrusive, completely neutral; she simply presents Maria's thoughts and actions. As a consequence of her technique, the reader is not sure of her attitude towards her central character. Some reviewers of the novel considered Maria the victim of a brutal society; others considered her malevolent. The truth lies somewhere between these extreme interpretations. As a child-woman, Maria was far too fragile for the society in which she lived; however, through her passivity she participated in her own exploitation, so that her breakdown became, in effect, a self-confirming prophecy.

In her recent novel, *A Book of Common Prayer* (1977), D. employs as narrator the strongest female character found in her fiction. This is D.'s most ambitious novel in several respects. It has the most complex narrative structure: since the narrator met Charlotte Douglas late in both their lives, she must convincingly reconstruct all of the previous action involving her. It also has the most complex cast of characters, four of whom—Charlotte, Grace, and Charlotte's two husbands—are fully developed, and the most complex setting, with scenes in San Francisco, New York City, and several southern cities, all interlaced with scenes in Boca Grande, a fictitious Central American country which D. renders as convincing as any of the other locales.

In these last two novels D. has refined a style which is tight and colloquial, stripped of any expansive descriptions or explanations. The strength of her fiction resides in this dramatic style, which she uses to bring the reader close to the events and characters and to render complex, often ironic, relationships through pure dialogue. Writing now at the height of her powers, D. can be looked to for significant future contributions to American fiction.

WORKS: *Run River* (1963). *Slouching towards Bethlehem* (1968). *Play It as It Lays* (1970). *A Book of Common Prayer* (1977). *The White Album* (1979).

BIBLIOGRAPHY: Commentary (July 1977). *Harper's* (Dec. 1971). *Ms.* (Jan. 1973). *NYTBR* (3 April 1977).

KATHERINE HENDERSON

Doris Miles Disney

B. 22 Dec. 1907, Glastonbury, Connecticut; d. 8 March 1976, Fredericksburg, Virginia
D. of Edward Lucas Hart and Elizabeth Anne Malone Miles; m. George J. Disney, 1936

D. was a prolific, versatile writer of mystery and suspense; she has been praised for never repeating herself and skillfully varying her approaches. She created three detectives; each is a fully realized and distinct character. Jim O'Neill, a county detective; Jefferson DiMarco, an insurance claim adjuster, the most famous; and David Madden, a U.S. postal inspector.

In D.'s fiction, suspense evolves from both plot and character. Her characters are rounded and consistently portrayed, their relationships and motivations often creating complex plots. She was particularly adept at characterizing children. For example, Jenny, an eight-year-old girl in *Don't Go into the Woods Today* (1974), and Sandy, a seven-year-old boy recuperating from rheumatic fever in *Heavy, Heavy Hangs* (1952), are sometimes cranky, frequently confused by the grown-up world, occasionally disobedient, but often charming and always believable.

D. began with true mysteries, in which the criminal's identity is withheld until the climax (see, for example, *A Compound for Death*, 1943, and *Murder on a Tangent*, 1945, both Jim O'Neill mysteries). *Dark Road* (1946), a Jeff DiMarco story, is an inverted mystery, in which the murderer's identity and motivation are revealed early. Hazel Clements causes her husband's death because of her desire to be reunited with an old lover. Her greed and ambition are clearly shown, but so is the awful background which helps explain her. At the end, the question of responsibility is paramount, her lover recognizing that he has been her unwitting accomplice.

For several novels D. turned to the past. *At Some Forgotten Door* (1966), a variation on gothic romance, has a partly predictable plot but builds suspense gradually, as the heroine fits together clues which help her understand both her origins and her present danger. Both mysteries are clarified in a powerful climactic scene. *Dark Lady* (1960) blends past and present. A young professor rents a cottage in which the wife of a gifted young writer had been murdered seventy-five years earlier. Becoming obsessed with the writer's beautiful sister-in-law, he solves the old mystery and learns to see his own present more clearly.

D.'s novels are consistently interesting and readable. The originality of her plots, the effectiveness of her characterizations, and her skill in controlling tone make her a leader among mystery writers. In addition, her ability to show how victims sometimes precipitate their fates and how the commission of a crime affects the criminal gives her work a depth often lacking in this genre.

WORKS: *A Compound for Death* (1943). *Murder on a Tangent* (1945). *Dark Road* (1946). *Who Rides a Tiger* (1946). *Appointment at Nine* (1947). *Enduring Old Charms* (1947). *Testimony by Silence* (1948). *That Which Is Crooked*

(1948). *Count the Ways* (1949). *Family Skeleton* (1949). *Fire at Will* (1950). *Look Back on Murder* (1951). *Straw Man* (1951). *Heavy, Heavy Hangs* (1952). *Do unto Others* (1953). *Prescription: Murder* (1953). *The Last Straw* (1954). *Room for Murder* (1955). *Trick or Treat* (1955). *Unappointed Rounds* (1956). *Method in Madness* (1957). *My Neighbor's Wife* (1957). *Black Mail* (1958). *Did She Fall or Was She Pushed?* (1959). *No Next of Kin* (1959). *Dark Lady* (1960). *Mrs. Meeker's Money* (1961). *Find the Woman* (1962). *Should Auld Acquaintance* (1962). *Here Lies . . .* (1963). *The Departure of Mr. Gaudette* (1964). *The Hospitality of the House* (1964). *Shadow of a Man* (1965). *At Some Forgotten Door* (1966). *The Magic Grandfather* (1966). *Night of Clear Choice* (1967). *Money for the Taking* (1968). *Voice from the Grave* (1968). *Two Little Children and How They Grew* (1969). *Do Not Fold, Spindle, or Mutilate* (1970). *The Chandler Policy* (1971). *Three's a Crowd* (1971). *The Day Miss Bessie Lewis Disappeared* (1972). *Only Couples Need Apply* (1973). *Don't Go into the Woods Today* (1974). *Cry for Help* (1975). *Winifred* (1976).

BIBLIOGRAPHY: LJ (15 May 1966). NYHTB (31 Oct. 1948; 21 Oct. 1951). NYTBR (13 Jan. 1946; 22 May 1949; 15 Dec. 1968). WLB (June 1954).

MARY JEAN DeMARR

Lavinia Lloyd Dock

B. 26 Feb. 1858, Harrisburg, Pennsylvania; d. 17 April 1956, Chambersburg, Pennsylvania
D. of Gilliard and Lavinia Bombaugh Dock

D. was one of six children of a well-to-do family long settled in central Pennsylvania. Nurtured on a sense of elite responsibility, D., her botanist sister Mira, and physician brother George all had careers in which they tried to harness trained expertise to civic purposes, from conservation to sex education.

D. attended private schools and in 1886 graduated from the training school for nurses at Bellevue Hospital in New York. In the late 1880s, after working as a visiting nurse, she began to pursue an administrative and teaching career. A decade later she became a member of the all-female "family" at the Henry Street Settlement in New York and a devoted friend of its founder, Lillian D. Wald. D. recalled that at Henry Street, her home for nearly twenty years, she "began to think." Already a feminist, she became a supporter of the labor movement and a socialist.

D. was an activist who wrote to encourage the professionalization of nursing, the emancipation of women, and the reform of American industrial society. From 1900 to 1923, she edited departments in the *American Journal of Nursing* (which she helped to found) and, from 1905 to 1908, in *Charities and the Commons*. Her career as a nurse, reformer, and writer ended soon after 1922 when she retired to care for an invalid sister.

In the 1890s, as the first successful attempts to unite nurses nationally began, D. advocated organization in speeches and magazine articles. *Short Papers on Nursing Subjects* (1900) shows that at Henry Street D. had learned to hope organization would awaken nurses' social consciences as well as their aspirations to professional status. The book's most important essay, "Ethics—or a Code of Ethics?," influenced by the pragmatism of Henry Street–supporter John Dewey, argues that neither a written code nor the self-interested advice physicians gave nurses could nourish a living ethical sense. This could develop only as nurses participated in self-governing associations and learned democratic social responsibility (as members of women's club did) and solidarity (as members of trade unions did).

In *Hygiene and Morality* (1910), D.'s contribution to the movement against prostitution and for sex education, the themes of women's autonomy and social mission temporarily eclipse the theme of organization. D. argues that the "discoveries and teachings of science" confirm "personal and civic morality." Vice is not only a moral evil which enslaves women but a menace to public health. Like tuberculosis, then the target of a lively campaign, it must be vanquished by teaching individuals to shun contagion and by rooting out social conditions where disease flourished. Prostitution, which "fosters" venereal disease, results from the economic vulnerability and, ultimately, the "political and legal inferiority" of women. The book culminates in the argument that enfranchising women would prevent prostitution and disease by helping women earn honest livings and creating a voting bloc in favor of laws protecting women and children.

In her most ambitious work D. fuses the themes which had preoccupied her since the 1890s. Mary Adelaide Nutting, the coauthor of the four-volume *History of Nursing* (1907–12), had conceived and mapped out the project. But it was D. who did most of the writing and interpreted nursing history as a record of women's efforts to govern themselves and serve society. Because training-school courses used a shortened version (published by D. and Isabel Stewart in 1920) and the authors of other nursing history textbooks appropriated its arrangement, ideas, omissions, and distortions, the *History* helped shape the professional self-image of many 20th-c. American nurses.

Like *Hygiene and Morality*, the *History of Nursing* argues that freeing women necessarily benefits society. D.'s hopes for the emancipation of women and the remaking of American society rest on the belief shared by Wald, Jane Addams, an other feminists that women's special nature destines them for redeeming social roles. D. believes that motherliness defines women, but insists that women can and must express that motherliness actively and outside the home. Her vocabulary displays her assumption that women are by nature active and beneficent.

D.'s writings are propaganda. Although scrupulous about specific facts, she evades topics she dislikes and feels no obligation to understand or present adversaries' viewpoints. Her books and articles are therefore not always dependable guides to the events they describe. But, although they emphasize feminist goals which other nurses left implicit in their programs, they offer insight into the minds of the founders of modern American nursing. The verve, the conviction, and even the lack of balance in D.'s writings also place them among the most vivid and personal expressions of American feminism.

WORKS: *Text-book of Materia Medica for Nurses* (1890). *Short Papers on Nursing Subjects* (1900). *A History of Nursing* (4 vols., with M. Nutting, 1907–12). *Hygiene and Morality: A Manual for Nurses and Others* (1910). *A Short History of Nursing* (with I. Stewart, 1920). *History of American Red Cross Nursing* (with S. Pickett, C. Noyes, et al., 1922).

There is material by and about D. in the papers of Lillian D. Wald at the New York Public Library and Butler Library, Columbia University; in the papers of M. Adelaide Nutting at Teachers College, Columbia University; and in the Dock family papers at the Pennsylvania Historical and Museum Commission, Harrisburg, Pennsylvania.

BIBLIOGRAPHY: Dock, L. L., "Self-Portrait," *Nursing Outlook* 25 (Jan. 1977).

Other references: *American Journal of Nursing* (July 1907; Sept. 1910; Feb. 1956; June 1956). *Nursing Outlook* 17 (June 1969). *NYT* (18 April 1956). *Survey* 24 (20 Aug. 1910).

SUSAN ARMENY

Mary Abigail Dodge

B. 31 March 1833, Hamilton, Massachusetts; d. 17 Aug. 1896, Hamilton,
  Massachusetts
Wrote under: Gail Hamilton
D. of James Brown and Hannah Stanwood Dodge

D. spent her early adult years teaching and, in 1858, she became governess to the children of Gamaliel Bailey, editor of the antislavery *National Era* in Washington, D.C. With his help she established herself as a writer. From 1865 to 1867 she was an editor of *Our Young Folks*. After 1871 she spent much of each year in Washington in the home of Congressman James G. Blaine, whose wife was D.'s first cousin. Blaine was Speaker of the House and a frequent presidential hopeful. In his household D. met politicians, writers, and numerous famous persons of the day. In these years she wrote on political issues, especially civil service reform.

The literary style of Gail Hamilton is characteristically lively, opinionated, and often argumentative. Several of her books are feminist in tone. D. often proclaims her personal and professional independence and encourages a similar spirit in others. *Country Living and Country Thinking* (1861), based upon D.'s experience as a woman running her family's farm, urges women to consider careers other than marriage, and especially to consider writing, despite the "fine, subtle, impalpable, but real" prejudice against "female writers." The economic argument for independence appears again in *Woman's Worth and Worthlessness* (1872), in which D. notes that a woman is not "supported" by a man "when she works as hard in the house as he does out of it."

For many years D. was closely associated with Blaine: she worked with him on his *Twenty Years of Congress* (1884–86) and many believed that she also drafted his speeches. Her biography of Blaine, undertaken as a tribute, is eulogistic and nonanalytical. Her verse, collected and published posthumously by her sister H. Augusta Dodge, in *Chips, Fragments, and Vestiges* (1902), is derivative.

D.'s most characteristic theme, derived from her own experience as a writer, is the need to train woman for spiritual and economic independence. Given her insistence on the need for independence, it seems ironic that D.'s own career, as well as her social contacts, depended to a great degree upon her association with Blaine, and that much of her work for him cannot be recognized as independent from that framework.

WORKS: *Country Living and Country Thinking* (1861). *Courage!* (1862). *Gala Days* (1863). *A Call to My Countrywomen* (1863). *Stumbling-Blocks* (1864). *A New Atmosphere* (1865). *Scientific Farming* (1865). *Skirmishes and Sketches* (1865). *Red Letter Days in Applethorpe* (1866). *Summer Rest* (1866). *Wool Gathering* (1868). *Woman's Wrong* (1868). *Memorial to Mrs. Hannah Stanwood Dodge* (1869). *A Battle of the Books* (1870). *Little Folk Life* (1872). *Woman's Worth and Worthlessness* (1872). *Child World* (1873). *Twelve Miles from a Lemon* (1874). *Nursery Noonings* (1875). *Sermons to the Clergy* (1876). *First Love Is Best* (1877). *What Think Ye of Christ* (1877). *Our Common School System* (1880). *Divine Guidance* (1881). *The Spent Bullet* (1882). *The Insuppressible Book* (1885). *A Washington Bible Class* (1891). *English Kings in a Nutshell* (1893). *Biography of James G. Blaine* (1893). *X-Rays* (1896). *Gail Hamilton's Life in Letters* (Ed. H. A. Dodge, 1901). *Chips, Fragments, and Vestiges* (Ed. H. A. Dodge, 1902).

BIBLIOGRAPHY: Beale, H. S., ed., *Letters of Mrs. James G. Blaine* (1908). Dodge, M. A., *Memorial to Mrs. Hannah Stanwood Dodge* (1869). Spofford, H. R., *A Little Book of Friends* (1916). Tryon, W. S., *Parnassus Corner: A Life of James T. Fields* (1963).

For articles in reference works, see: *AW. NAW* (article by M. W. Langworthy).

JANE BENARDETE

Mary Mapes Dodge

B. 26 Jan. 1830, New York City; d. 21 Aug. 1905, Onteora Park, New York
D. of James Jay and Sophia Furman Mapes; m. William Dodge, 1851

D.'s family moved often, finally settling in Irvington, New Jersey, where, on a large farm, overlooking Staten Island and Manhattan, her father conducted horticultural experiments and edited a magazine called *The Working Farmer*. When D. rejoined her family at the farm after the death of her husband, her father started her writing for his magazine in order to occupy her time and assuage her grief. D. also began telling stories to her two young sons.

As a result of her boys' interest in the Dutch sport of skating, which was just becoming popular in the U.S., and her frequent visits with a Dutch family who told her stories of Holland, D. wrote *Hans Brinker; or, The Silver Skates,* which has been translated into many languages is still a bestseller after more than a hundred years.

From 1865 on, D. helped to edit a magazine called *Hearth and Home,* until asked by Roswell Smith of the Century Company to start a children's magazine for them. So in 1873, D. became the editor of *St. Nicholas,* the greatest children's magazine of all time. *Hans Brinker* and *St. Nicholas* established D.'s top-notch reputation, but she also produced a number of other books.

St. Nicholas set a new and lasting pattern for children's literature: Kipling wrote *The Jungle Books* and Frances Hodgson Burnett *Little Lord Fauntleroy* (1886) for the magazine. Other top authors, among them Robert Louis Stevenson, Samuel Clemens, Alfred Tennyson, eager to be published in this vital periodical, also sent D. their work. Many reputations were made in these pages. *St. Nicholas* was still thriving when, at age seventy-five, D. died at her summer residence in Onteora Park, New York.

WORKS: *Irvington Stories* (1864). *Hans Brinker: or, The Silver Skates* (1865). *A Few Friends and How They Amused Themselves* (1869). *Rhymes and Jingles* (1874). *Theophilus and Others* (1876). *Along the Way* (1879). *Donald and Dorothy* (1883). *Baby World* (1884). *The Land of Pluck* (1894). *When Life Is Young* (1894).

BIBLIOGRAPHY: For articles in reference works, see: *AW. DAB. NAW* (article by H. S. Commager). *NCAB.*

Other references: *Century* (Nov. 1905). *Critic* (Oct. 1905). *Current Literature* (Oct. 1905). *NYT* (22 Aug. 1905). *St. Nicholas* (Oct. 1905).

CATHERINE MORRIS WRIGHT

Hilda Doolittle

B. 10 Sept. 1886, Bethlehem, Pennsylvania; d. 27 Sept. 1961, Zurich, Switzerland
Wrote under: H. D.
D. of Charles L. and Helen Wolle Doolittle; m. Richard Aldington, 1915

D. was the daughter of a professor of astronomy and the granddaughter of the principal of a local Moravian seminary, who was a descendant of a member of the original 18th-c. mystical order knows as the Unitas Fratrum, or Moravian Brotherhood. Since the founding of the order, the concept of *Unitas Fratrum* has been identified with "the Mystery which lay at the center of the world." Young D. participated in Moravian religious exercises and rituals, all of which had a profound effect upon her. In *Tribute to Angels* (1945), more than forty years after her childhood experiences, she returned to the enigmatic "Mystery," the essence of Moravian belief, describing it as "the point in the spectrum/where all light becomes one/ . . . as we were told as children."

Educated chiefly in private schools, D. spent a year and a half at Bryn Mawr, withdrawing in 1906 due to a "slight breakdown." She became engaged briefly to Ezra Pound, who encouraged her to pursue her classical studies and to continue to write serious poetry. Soon after, D. left for London to begin the life of an expatriate, and rarely returned to America.

In 1913, D. married the British poet Richard Aldington. Later (1917) she assumed the editorship of *The Egoist*, while she earnestly pursued her career as a poet. The period between 1915 and 1920 was filled with personal crisis: a miscarriage in 1915, the death of her older brother in combat in 1918, separation from Aldington (final divorce in 1938), and the death of her father in 1919. In 1919, D. found herself essentially alone, seriously ill, and pregnant. She wrote from her flat in war-torn London: "Death! Death is all around us!" The foregoing events precipitated a severe breakdown, and D. eventually sought the help of Sigmund Freud, whom she refers to as the "blameless physician" in her brilliant psychobiography, *Tribute to Freud*, published in 1956.

Following World War I, D. wrote thirteen volumes of poetry, along with translations, essays, dramas, film criticism, and novels. When her *Collected Poems*, the volume that established her reputation, was published in 1925, many of the vital experiences that tempered her writing had occurred.

The early tightly honed, discrete Imagist poems are familiar to most readers. In them with clarity, precision, and control, D. described pear trees with "flower-tufts/thick on the branch"; sea poppies "spilled near the shrub pines/to bleach on the boulders"; or grapes "red-purple/their berries dripping/with wine." D.'s final, major modern poetic sequences, *Helen in Egypt* (1961), is less well known. Throughout her work, however, from the slender Imagist verse to the final monumental poetic sequence, D. was in search of what she dimly defined as "a myth, the one reality." This would permit her not only to articulate her emotions but would also allow her the freedom to create an "organizing structure" in which she could function as both a woman and an artist.

D. ingeniously shaped the classical world to her own temperament, weaving and reweaving the legends of the past into modern form, emulating myth in order to gain a sense of the spiritual, the timeless. For D., events, emotions, experiences, became continuations of a simpler, more structured mythic past, which she found more manageable than the immediate, chaotic contemporary scene. As she developed her skills, D. was able to transfer mythic patterns from one culture to another, as reflected in her wide-ranging vision of Woman throughout the ages, which is included in *Tribute to Angels*. More notably, however, in *The Walls Do Not Fall* (1944), she comfortably mingles classical allusions with observations of the shell-shocked, bombed-out, devastation of London: "there as here, ruin opens/the tomb, the temple . . . /the shrine lies open to the sky/the rain falls . . . /sand drifts, eternity endures." Typically D. emphasizes once again her concept of identity and self-possession in the lines: ". . . living within/you beget, self-out-of-self/ . . . that pearl-of-great-price."

The search for "a myth, the one reality" was successfully achieved by means of the pervasive, legendary figure of Helen in D.'s last major work. In the earlier Imagist poem, "Helen," the heroine, a wan maiden with "still eyes in (a) white face" is clouded with subtle ambiguities—she is the Helen Greece could love "only if she were laid/white ash amid funereal cypresses." In *Helen in Egypt*, the mature, intelligent, confident Helen struggles for self-definition following the cataclysmic Trojan War. With "things remembered forgotten/remembered again," Helen assembles and reassembles her thoughts and emotions and resolves: "I *must* fight for Helena." In this long poem D. artfully weaves and reweaves the mythic pattern until the legendary figure of Helen (the

Woman who will not now be denied) achieves her identity: "I am awake/ . . . I *see* things clearly at last,/ the old pictures are really there."

With *Helen in Egypt*, D. herself achieves self-definition, and brings to a close her search for an identity, "the one reality," for which she had been striving all her life.

D.'s work transcends the limitations of the Imagist movement, for which she allegedly was not only the inspiration but, together with Ezra Pound and Richard Aldington, also a formulator of its principles. Currently she is, and justifiably so, identified as a modern. Norman Holmes Pearson, D.'s literary executor, contends that D. is in "the very center of the modern poetic movement . . . and will increasingly be recognized" when her audience not only learns how to read her poetry but becomes familiar with classical mythology.

WORKS: *Sea Garden* (1916). *Hymen* (1921). *Heliodora, and Other Poems* (1924). *Collected Poems* (1925). *Palimpsest* (1926). *Hippolytos Temporizes: A Play in Three Acts* (1927). *Hedylus* (1928). *Red Roses for Bronze* (1931). *The Walls Do Not Fall* (1944). *Tribute to Angels* (1945). *The Flowering of the Rod* (1946). *By Avon River* (1949). *Tribute to Freud* (1956). *Selected Poems of H. D.* (1957). *Hermetic Definition* (1958). *Bid Me to Live* (1960). *Helen in Egypt* (1961). *End to Torment: A Memoir of Ezra Pound* (Eds. N. H. Pearson and M. King, 1979).

BIBLIOGRAPHY: Coffman, S. K., *Imagism: A Chapter for the History of Modern Poetry* (1951). Hughes, G., *Imagism and the Imagists* (1931). Mearns, H., *Hilda Doolittle* (The Pamphlet Poets, 1926). Monroe, H., *Poets and Their Art* (1932). Quinn, V., *Hilda Doolittle* (1968). Swann, T. B., *The Classical World of Hilda Doolittle* (1962). Waggoner, H. H., *American Poets: From the Puritans to the Present* (1968).

Other references: *ConL* 10 (Autumn 1969). *Poetry* (June 1962).

CLAIRE HEALEY

Julia Caroline Ripley Dorr

B. 13 Feb. 1825, Charleston, South Carolina; d. 18 Jan. 1913, Rutland, Vermont
Wrote under: Julia C. R. Dorr, Caroline Thomas
D. of William Y. and Zulma De Lacy Thomas Ripley; m. Seneca M. Dorr, 1847

D.'s mother's family fled from Santo Domingo to the U.S. during a slave uprising. Her father was a bank president, and she spent most of her formative years in Vermont receiving her education there at Middlebury seminary. D. enjoyed the friendship of R. W. Emerson, Edmund Clarence Stedman, and Oliver Wendell Holmes, among others. She was a founder of the Rutland Library, and received a Litt.D. from Middlebury College in Vermont.

D.'s first novels, *Farmingdale* (1854), *Lanmere* (1856), and *Sibyl Huntington* (1869), deal with young women living in New England villages who are subject to a grinding routine of home chores. These novels are noteworthy for their realistic depiction of family bitterness and the round of household activities: tubs filled with laundry, milk pans to be scalded, rag rugs to be pieced, work baskets piled with mending. Each novel contains pointed discussions on books, learning, literature, and libraries, offered as the heroines' reprieve from woman's toil.

Expiation (1873) views domestic tragedy from the stance of a neighborly female narrator who is middle-aged, tranquil, unmarried. The plot involves hereditary insanity, its concealment by a young wife, an adolescent son's attempt to kill his mother, a coffin that yields up its supposed corpse. Gothic horrors come to light amidst the beauties of the Vermont countryside, descriptions of which D. excells in: the riot of green, the meadows and uplands, brawling trout streams, the barefoot boy and the singing thrush, wild roses and honeysuckles under a sapphire sky.

D.'s poetry appeared in newspapers and magazines such as *Scribner's*, *Harper's*, *Atlantic Monthly*, and *Sartain's Union Magazine of Literature and Art*. Her poems were anthologized in Emerson's *Parnassus* (1874), and Stedman's *An American Anthology* (1900). D. experimented with a variety of forms—narratives, dramatic monologues, patriotic and war verses, historic celebrations, sonnets, hymns, and ballads.

D.'s travel books are companionable, anecdotal, and historically informative. *Bermuda* appeared in 1884. *The Flower of England's Face; sketches of English Travel* (1895) takes the reader from Wales to Scotland with a long stop at Haworth to collect firsthand reminiscences about the Brontës. *A Cathedral Pilgrimage* (1896) revels in rustic gardens, chapels, spires, "ruined arches, forsaken courts open to all the sky, and columns ivy-grown and lichen clad." It imaginatively recreates medieval life and recounts legends of martyrs and warriors.

Despite D.'s dislike of suffering women poets as expressed in *Farmingdale*, she was unable to keep the lachrymose strain out of her own last works. Her poetic diction includes the formalized lyrical utterance of her shorter poems, as well as the colloquial forthrightness of her dramatic monologues. The same chatty directness is evident in her books of travel and advice, and recalls the vigor of her early domestic novels. Her interest in family problems arising from cruelty, pride, or error enters into her narrative poems. Like many women poets of her time, she tended to give them exotic, medieval, Germanic, or oriental settings; however, the regional locales of her New England fiction bestow a more enduring value on her portrayals of family life.

WORKS: *Farmingdale* (1854). *Lanmere* (1856). *Sibyl Huntington* (1869). *Poems* (1872). *Bride and Bridegroom* (1873). *Expiation* (1873). *Friar Anselmo and Other Poems* (1875). *Bermuda. An Idyl of the Summer Islands* (1884). *Afternoon Songs* (1885). *Poems* (1892). *The Fallow Field* (1893). *"The Flower of England's Face": Sketches of English Travel* (1895). *A Cathedral Pilgrimage* (1896). *In Kings' Houses: A Romance of the Days of Queen Anne* (1898). *Afterglow* (1900). *Poems, Complete* (1901). *Beyond the Sunset, Latest Poems* (1909). *Last Poems* (1913). *W. Y. R. A Book of Remembrance* (n.d.).

BIBLIOGRAPHY: Baym, N., *Woman's Fiction: A Guide to Novels by and about Women in America, 1820–1870* (1978). Carleton, H., *Genealogy and Family History of Vermont* (1903). Crockett, W. H., *Vermont the Green Mountain State* (1921). Morse, J. J., ed., *Life and Letters of Oliver Wendell Holmes* (1896). Ripley, H. W., *Genealogy of a Part of the Ripley Family* (1867). Stedman, L., and G. M. Gould, eds., *Life and Letters of E. C. Stedman* (1910). Thiébaux, M., in *Theory and Practice of Feminist Literary Criticism*, Eds. G. Mora and K. S. Van Hooft (1982).
For articles in reference works, see: *AA. AW. DAB.*

MARCELLE THIÉBAUX

Rheta Childe Dorr

B. 2 Nov. 1866, Omaha, Nebraska; d. 8 Aug. 1948, New Britain, Pennsylvania
Given name: Reta Louise Childe
D. of Edward and Lucie Childe; m. John Pixley Dorr, 1892

The daughter of Episcopalian parents, D. joined the National Woman Suffrage Association at twelve, attended the University of Nebraska for one year, and enrolled at the Art Students' League in New York City in 1890. She took her first reporting job on the New York *Evening Post* and was a muckraker at *Everybody's Magazine* and *Hampton's* from 1907 to 1912. Briefly a member of the Socialist Party, she became active in the Republican Party in 1916. A militant suffragist, she edited the *Suffragist*, and from 1913 to 1916 was a member of the Heterodoxy, an early feminist discussion group. As a foreign correspondent she covered the Pankhursts' suffrage struggle in England, the Russian Revolution, World War I, and Mussolini's march into Rome.

D. was the author of several books, most of which (aside from her autobiography) consist of materials she previously published in newspapers and magazines. As an autobiography, *A Woman of Fifty* (1924) represents both a highly successful creative act and a "self-revelation." Illustrating the traditional effort of an American intellectual to relate personal experience to the pattern of cultural change, D. sketched a political journey—one which led from a progressive vision of cooperative millenialism to a conservative faith in a "sane, practical democracy," with the "Great War" acting as the important transforming experience. However, D. was firm in her commitment to feminism; the chronological narrative revolves around her own early awakening to feminism, and her struggle as a journalist to support herself and her son. Throughout her lifetime, D. worked to bring others from a perception of women as a "ladies' aid society to the human race" to an affirmation of their "breaking into the human race" with "full freedom."

In *What Eight Million Woman Want* (1910), D. dealt with "woman's invasion of industry" as a permanent factor in the American economy, carefully employing data obtained from reporting on all social classes of women in Europe and America. Having investigated various employments by working as a laundress, seamstress, department store clerk, and assembly-line worker, D. sympathetically revealed the "intimate lives of the factory workers in order to tell their story as they would tell it themselves if they had a chance." She also emphasized the social-reform activities of educated middle-class women's organizations, concluding that the fulfillment of their demands for women's economic, social, and political freedom was in the best interest of a democratic society. D. reiterated these beliefs in *Susan B. Anthony* (1928), a witty and sympathetic biography and history of women's life in America which dramatically situated Anthony within the social context of the post-Civil War era.

D. was a war correspondent from 1917 to 1918. *Inside the Russian Revolution* (1917) condemned Bolshevik politics and marked her break with New York socialist friends. Interpreting events in terms of "excesses" of an "unruly, unreasoning, sanguinary mob" intent on disengaging from the "Great war," D. recommended a large dose of American economic aid and the "help and guidance" of strong leaders with pragmatic republican values. D. ably captured the feeling of a country at war in her description of the July Revolution and the "women's batallion of death"; but *Inside the Russian Revolution* was marred by its strong ethnocentric bias.

D. was among the first journalists to report "hard news" about all classes of women, and she was among the best of the muckracking journalists. While her war correspondence was not consistently outstanding, she was among only a few women who obtained western-front reporting assignments during World War I. Her autobiography must be considered not only an "extraordinarily revealing" document but also a provocative commentary on American culture.

WORKS: *What Eight Million Women Want* (1910). *Inside the Russian Revolution* (1917). *A Soldier's Mother in France* (1918). *A Woman of Fifty* (1924). *Susan B. Anthony: The Woman Who Changed the Mind of a Nation* (1928). *Drink: Coercion or Control?* (1929).

BIBLIOGRAPHY: Banner, L. W., *Woman in Modern America: A Brief History* (1974). Filler, L., *Crusaders for American Liberalism* (1939). Marzolf, M., *Up from the Footnote: A History of Women Journalists* (1977). Ross, I., *Ladies of the Press* (1936).

For articles in reference works, see: *NAW* (article by L. Filler).

Other references: *Bookman* (11 March 1911). *Books* (21 Oct. 1928).

JENNIFER L. TEBBE

Abigail Scott Duniway

B. 22 Oct. 1834, Groveland, Illinois; d. 11 Oct. 1915, Portland, Oregon
D. of John Tucker and Ann Roelofson Scott; m. Benjamin C. Duniway, 1853

The second daughter among twelve children, D. grew up on the Illinois frontier. At seventeen, she accompanied her family on the overland trail to Oregon, keeping a journal of their 1852 crossing which is one of the best of the genre. Her mother and baby brother died of cholera on the way, and the family arrived virtually destitute in Oregon.

D.'s first novel, *Captain Gray's Company* (1859), is a fictionalized account of her wagon trail journey to Oregon and her early life in an Oregon town. It reveals as much about its author and her attitudes as about her milieu. Agrarian as well as feminist in principle, D. was writing for "the world's workers, the stay and strength of our land," and hoped her book would "be instrumental in causing the sterner to look more to the welfare of the weakest of the . . . weaker sex." More realistic than many other women's novels of the time, the book was nevertheless criticized by D.'s political and religious opponents for being too romantic. It remains of interest for its pervasive wit and its historical detail.

Between May 1871 and January 1887, D. published and edited a weekly newspaper called the *New Northwest*. It advocated both women's rights and human rights and circulated throughout the Pacific Northwest and to women in other parts of the country. Its lively style, strong opinions, revelations of political and social scandals, and fervent advocacy of legal reforms and woman suffrage made it a particularly influential and controversial publication. In it D. also serialized sixteen more of her own novels. These were essentially polemical, featuring strong, mistreated female heroines who suffer numerous adversities and finally triumph over refined ladies and antisuffragist enemies. Though flawed as literature, the stories include extraordinary details of frontier family life and social relationships. Many passages show a fine gift for writing dialogue and humor.

D. also lectured extensively, bringing her message to isolated women and men with fervor and courage. Each year she averaged two hundred lectures, and traveled three thousand miles by steamboat, mud-wagon, stagecoach, horseback, and railroad. She lectured her way across the country six times and became vice-president of the National Woman Suffrage Association in 1884. D.'s "editorial correspondence" now constitutes a unique historical record of the people and places she saw.

Though D. almost succeeded in winning woman suffrage in Oregon and Washington during the 1880s, the closing of the frontier led to changes which delayed it for another generation. From 1887 until her death, D. continued to write and lecture, publishing in the *Portland Oregonian*, the *Pacific Empire* (which she edited), and the *Coming Century*. When woman suffrage was declared in 1912, she wrote the official proclamation of victory and became the first woman voter in Oregon.

D.'s ambition and achievement as a writer was undoubtedly affected by her lack of formal education. Her historical role is more significant than her literary achievements because she never had the leisure, economic means, or intention to write for art's sake. Nevertheless, the quality of D.'s vigorously amusing polemics is worthy evidence of her strong convictions and forceful, talented personality.

WORKS: *Captain Gray's Company; or, Crossing the Plains and Living in Oregon* (1859). *My Musing* (1875). *David and Anna Matson* (1876). *From the West to the West: Across the Plains to Oregon* (1905). *Path Breaking* (1914).

BIBLIOGRAPHY: Bandow, G. R., "In Pursuit of a Purpose: Abigail Scott Duniway and the *New Northwest*" (M.A. thesis, Univ. of Oregon, 1973). Capell, L., "Biography of Abigail Scott Duniway" (M.A. thesis, Univ. of Oregon, 1934). Morrison, D. N., *Ladies Were Not Expected: Abigail Scott Duniway and Women's Rights* (1977). Moynihan, R. B., *Circuit Rider for Women: Abigail Scott Duniway of Oregon* (forthcoming, 1983). Roberts, L. M., "Suffragist of the New West: Abigail Scott Duniway and the Development of the Oregon Woman Suffrage Movement" (B.A. thesis, Reed College, 1969). Richey, E., *Eminent Women of the West* (1975). Ross, N. W., *Westward the Women* (1944). Smith, H. K., *The Presumptuous Dreamers* (1974).

RUTH BARNES MOYNIHAN

Wilma Dykeman

B. 20 May 1920, Asheville, North Carolina
Wrote under: Wilma Dykeman, Wilma Dykeman Stokely
D. of Willard Jerome and Bonnie Cushman Cole Dykeman; m. James R.
  Stokely, Jr., 1940

D.'s works betray a twofold love of southern Appalachia: the fervid love of an immigrant for the new land, and the comfortable, well-rooted love of one whose forebearers have shaped a region's history. Her father came from New York state but married into a long-established Asheville family, thus partially removing the "newcomer" stigma. After graduating from Northwestern University, D. returned home to marry poetwriter James Stokely. They remained in Appalachia, writing, teaching, raising a family, and lecturing. Stokely died in 1977. D. continues her work, living now in the village of Newport, Tennessee.

The South—but most especially the Appalachian South—is D.'s subject. Her novels, biographies, histories, and regional landscapes explore such themes as the mountain woman's unique social role, technology and "progress" as threats to mountain environments, the interconnectedness of blacks and whites, the crucial impact of Protestantism. D.'s first work, *The French Broad* (1955), nicely showcases her talent for social history. The French Broad River rises in the mountains of Transylvania County, North Carolina, changes directions through the region several times, and finally joins the Holston to form the Tennessee River at Knoxville. A river study, says D., is the best kind of travel book, for it enables one to get the feel of the region. *The French Broad* is structured both chronologically and thematically; central figures of the region's past and present are detailed, as anecdotes illuminate such topics as the divisiveness of the Civil War, Appalachian religiosity, the fashionable watering places of the 19th c., or the prototypical mountain midwife.

D.'s other social histories combine the same informality and personal engagement. The 1957 book, *Neither Black nor White*, written with James Stokely, responded to the Brown school desegregation decision of 1954. It tried to understand "the many Souths" and "discover, record and interpret a republic of the human mind." For its contribution to race relations, the book received the Hillman award. D. and Stokely later produced *The Border States* (1968), and in 1975 D.'s bicentennial history of Tennessee appeared. The book depicts that state's three geographical regions and shows how Tennessee remains in many ways a frontier area.

D.'s storytelling knack is apparent in her three novels, all of which explore regional themes. Centering on the character of Lydia McQueen, *The Tall Woman* (1962) portrays the special functions that mountain women performed during the Civil War and Reconstruction. *The Far Family* (1966) delineates the mountain woman's importance in preserving tradition and family; sociologically, her role resembles both that of the heroically strong black woman and the southern plantation wife. *Return the Innocent Earth* (1973) explores the impact of industrial development on the region.

D.'s three biographies manifest her talent for social history and strong characterization. *Seeds of Southern Change* (1962), also written with Stokely, traces the life of Will Alexander (1884–1956), a southern white liberal who, as director of the "Commission on Interracial Cooperation," and later as chief of Roosevelt's Farm Security Administration, did as much as any one person to direct the South toward economic and racial justice. *Prophet of Plenty* (1966) explores the life and work of W. D. Weatherford (1875–1970), a champion of Appalachia whose fund-raising work at Berea College gave it national renown.

Edna Rankin McKinnon is the subject of D.'s third biography, *Too Many People, Too Little Love* (1974). The younger sister of Jeannette Rankin, the first woman elected to Congress, Edna began lobbying in Washington in 1936 for birth control and then worked in Appalachia and around the world, establishing birth control and family planning clinics. D. says that Edna's story interested her because it combined the three most important issues of the 20th c.—the population explosion, the changing status of women, and the necessity for world peace.

D., not often given a careful reading because of her "regionalism," deserves a wider critical audience. She uses an easy and flowing style, perfectly suited to the anecdotal character of much of her work. She excels in describing folkways and vividly captures mountain speech. Her themes—though regional at base—are in the best sense universal human concerns.

WORKS: *The French Broad* (1955). *Neither Black nor White* (with J. Stokely, 1957). *Seeds of Southern Change: The Life of Will Alexander* (with J. Stokely, 1962). *The Tall Woman* (1962). *The Far Family* (1966). *Prophet of Plenty: the First Ninety Years of W. D. Weatherford* (1966). *The Border States: Kentucky, North Carolina, Tennessee, Virginia, West Virginia* (with J. Stokely, 1968). *Look to This Day* (1968). *Return the Innocent Earth* (1973). *Southern Appalachian Books: An Annotated Selected Bibliography* (1973). *Too Many People, Too Little Love—Edna Rankin McKinnon: Pioneer for Birth Control* (1974). *Tennessee, a Bicentennial History* (1975).

BIBLIOGRAPHY: *Chicago Sunday Tribune* (29 July 1962). *CSM* (5 May 1955). *NYHTB* (1 May 1955). *NYTBR* (1 July 1962; 3 June 1973; 8 Sept. 1974). *SatEvePost* (April 1974).

MARGARET McFADDEN-GERBER

Alice Morse Earle

B. 27 April 1851, Worcester, Massachusetts; d. 16 Feb. 1911, Hempstead, Long Island, New York
Given name: Mary Alice Morse
D. of Edwin and Abigail Mason Clary Morse; m. Henry Earle, 1874

E., antiquarian and social historian, was a descendant of men important in the history of New England and Massachusetts. She was educated at Worcester High School and at Dr. Gannett's boarding school in Boston. After her marriage E. moved to Brooklyn Heights and remained there her entire life. Her early life was devoted to her husband and the care of her four children, with little thought to a career in writing or history. After the death of her husband E. traveled extensively through Europe with her sister. It was about this time that family members, particularly her father, began urging her to write professionally.

The publication of *The Sabbath in Puritan New England* (1891) marked the beginning of E.'s writing career, and during the next twelve years she wrote, edited, and contributed to the publication of seventeen books and over thirty articles describing various aspects of early American history. All of E.'s works deal with the human, domestic side of American history. Utilizing primary source materials—wills, letters, journals, newspapers, court records—E. pieced together an accurate picture of what everyday life was like in colonial America.

E. had a particular interest in the role played by women in early America. All of her books contain a great deal of information on the economic and social activities of women in families and their respective communities. In *The Diary of Anna Green Winslow, a Boston School Girl of 1771* (1894) and *Margaret Winthrop* (1895) E. views her subjects as representative women of their times, and utilizes them as focal points for discussing the everyday lives, duties, and responsibilities of women in the colonial era.

Colonial Dames and Good Wives (1895) deals with the roles played by women in America from first settlement to the American Revolution. Primarily devoted to investigation of the women of New England, E. also makes reference to notable women who lived in the middle and southern colonies. As a general work on the history of women in America, it is a valuable and informative book even today.

The most widely read and referred to book written by E., *Home Life in Colonial Days* (1898) is an informative and entertaining account of daily life. Starting with an account of the kinds of homes lived in by the early settlers and how they were constructed, E. devotes chapters to the histories of such subjects as the lighting, food, drink, clothing, and gardens of the first settlers of America.

E. considered *Two Centuries of Costume in America, 1620–1820* (two volumes, 1902) her finest work. In the many years since its publication, no other work of its accuracy and detail has appeared. With her extensive knowledge of the life-styles and activities of early Americans, E. offers a stimulating discussion of the significance of the costumes worn by the colonists with respect to their lives.

E.'s articles and books were widely read and appreciated by her contemporaries. Celebration of the Revolutionary centennial in 1876 had reawakened popular interest in early American history. This popular interest demanded a new kind of historical literature devoted to the life of American society and E.'s books and articles found a welcoming audience. She never sacrificed her scholarship and historical integrity to meet the demands of her public, however. Her research was always of the highest quality, and she shared an interest in unearthing historical truths with professionally trained historians. Although her books are sometimes repetitive (possibly because she was so prolific), they are, with few exceptions, valuable and still enjoy popularity today.

WORKS: *The Sabbath in Puritan New England* (1891). *China Collecting in America* (1892). *Customs and Fashions of Old New England* (1893). *Costume of Colonial Times* (1894). *Diary of Anna Green Winslow, a Boston School Girl of 1771* (edited by Earle, 1904). *Colonial Dames and Good Wives* (1895). *Margaret Winthrop* (1895). *Colonial Days in Old New York* (1896). *Curious Punishments of Bygone Days* (1896). *Historic New York* (1897). *Chap Book Essays* (1897). *Home Life in Colonial Days* (1898). *In Old Narragansett: Romances and Realities* (1898). *Child Life in Colonial Days* (1899). *Stage Coach and Tavern Days* (1900). *Old Time Gardens* (1901). *Sun Dials and Roses of Yesterday* (1902). *Two Centuries of Costume in America, 1620–1820* (2 vols., 1903).

The papers of Alice Morse Earle are in the Sophia Smith Collection, Smith College, Massachusetts.

BIBLIOGRAPHY: For articles in reference works, see: *DAB. NAW* (article by W. Garrett).

Other references: *NYT* (18 Feb. 1911). *NYHT* (18 Feb. 1911). *Old Time New England* (Jan. 1947). Worcester (Mass.) *Telegram* (18 Feb. 1911).

PAULA A. TRECKEL

Elaine Goodale Eastman

B. *9 Oct. 1863, Mount Washington, Massachusetts; d. 22 Dec. 1953, Hadley, Massachusetts*
Wrote under: Elaine Goodale Eastman, Elaine Goodale
D. *of Henry Sterling and Dora Hill Read Goodale; m. Charles A. Eastman, 1891*

For her first eighteen years, E.'s world was Sky Farm, the Goodales' Berkshire homestead. There she learned about literature from her mother, about nature from her father, and started combining these lessons in poetry at the age of seven. In 1883, after the single year of boarding school that family finances allowed, E. began teaching Indian students at Hampton Institute in Virginia. Visiting Dakota convinced E. that reservation schools would accelerate Indian assimilation, and she established a government day school among the Sioux in 1886. Her teaching success earned her appointment in 1890 as Supervisor of Education in the

Dakotas. In 1891 E. married Santee Sioux Dr. Charles A. Eastman (Ohiyesa), and resigned her position, dedicating herself to her husband and his people.

Thirty years of marriage brought E. six children, and frequent relocations due to her husband's fluctuating career. E. attempted to augment her family income by writing, editing Carlisle Indian School's newspaper and her husband's works, arranging his lectures, and running a summer camp. Financial tension, editorial resentment, and her husband's rumored infidelity ended E.'s marriage in 1921, although both kept their separation secret. E. returned to the Berkshires, continuing to write until shortly before her death at ninety.

E.'s literary career began early, when three volumes of poetry she and her younger sister Dora had written for family gatherings were published and enthusiastically received. E.'s development of death and rejuvenation themes, her love imagery, and her deft use of language and rhyme belie her youth. In *Journal of a Farmer's Daughter* (1881), she romantically celebrates in prose and poetry and annual cycle of rural life. Nearly fifty years later, E. collected her subsequently published verse in *The Voice at Eve* (1930), which reflects the broadened interests and insight of her maturity. Her dominant themes include woman as giver, the painful joy of loving, the noble vanishing Indian, and intercultural understanding.

When E. embraced the cause of Indian education, she moved from poetry to polemics, writing many articles and pamphlets urging establishment of reservation day schools and Protestant missions. Although she admitted that all could learn "Some Lessons from Barbarism" (1890) regarding women's dress, equality, and generosity, she constantly emphasized the goal of assimilating the Indians into American culture. *Pratt: The Red Man's Moses* (1935) is a biography of the founder of Carlisle Indian School, the federal government's first boarding school for Indians. E. praises General Richard Henry Pratt's efforts (although she voices her preference for day schools) and condemns policies contrary to the assimilationist philosophy that she and Pratt shared.

Consistent with this emphasis, E. appraised the value of Native American oral traditions narrowly, as stories for children. With her husband, she published two collections of Sioux tales, and she simplified folklore selected from various anthropological collections in *Indian Legends Retold* (1919). She also wrote several works of sentimental prose fiction for children.

E.'s only adult novel, *Hundred Maples* (1935), focuses upon Ellen

Strong who, regretting her early marriage, wanders in search of herself. She eventually accepts her complicated ties to family, and to the Vermont landscape hallowed by her foremothers. *Sister to the Sioux* (1978) is a posthumously published autobiography.

E.'s writings provide much insight into the ambiguities of intercultural relations and of the female sacrifice of career for motherhood. E.'s inability to reconcile both her sincere regard for the Sioux with her ethnocentrism and her need for self-expression within her marriage describes one woman's experience of the eternal conflict between ideals and reality.

WORKS: *Apple Blossoms: Verses of Two Children* (with D. R. Goodale, 1878). *In Berkshire with the Wild Flowers* (with D. R. Goodale, 1879). *All Round the Year: Verses from Sky Farm* (with D. R. Goodale, 1881). *Journal of a Farmer's Daughter* (1881). *The Coming of the Birds* (1883). *Wigwam Evenings: Sioux Folktales Retold* (with C. A. Eastman, 1909). *Smoky Day's Wigwam Evenings: Indian Stories Retold* (with C. A. Eastman, 1910). *Little Brother o' Dreams* (1910). *Yellow Star: A Story of East and West* (1911). *The Eagle and the Star: American Indian Pageant Play in Three Acts* (ca. 1916). *Indian Legends Retold* (1919). *The Luck of Oldacres* (1928). *The Voice at Eve* (1930). *Hundred Maples* (1935). *Pratt: The Red Man's Moses* (1935). *Sister to the Sioux: The Memoirs of Elaine Goodale Eastman, 1885–91* (Ed. K. Graber, 1978).

BIBLIOGRAPHY: Wilson, R., "Dr. Charles Alexander Eastman (Ohiyesa), Santee Sioux" (Ph.D. diss., Univ. of New Mexico, 1977).

For articles in reference works, see: *NCAB. The Twentieth Century Biographical Dictionary of Notable Americans*, Ed. R. Johnson (1904).

Other references: *Atlantic* (Aug. 1928). *Mississippi Valley Historical Review* (March 1936). *NYT* (23 Dec. 1953). *NYTBR* (26 May 1935).

HELEN M. BANNAN

Mignon Good Eberhart

B. 6 June 1899, Lincoln, Nebraska
D. of William Thomas and Margaret Hill Good; m. Alanson C. Eberhart, 1923; m. John Hazen Perry, 1946; m. Alanson C. Eberhart, 1948

E. attended Nebraska Wesleyan University and received a Litt. D. from that same institution in 1935. Although she published plays (*Eight*

O'Clock Tuesday, 1941, with Robert Wallsten; *320 College Avenue*, 1938, with Frederick Ballard) and short stories during the first half of her career, E. later wrote only novels of suspense, for which the Mystery Writers of America awarded her their Grand Master Award in 1971.

Several of E.'s novels, such as *The Cup, the Blade, or the Gun* (1961) and *Family Fortune* (1976), both set during the Civil War, and *Enemy in the House* (1962), set during the American Revolution, are historical. The majority of her novels, however, are contemporary in setting. Most are set in the U.S. or the West Indies and, particularly during WWII, display considerable patriotism. Often her novels feature some sort of inclement weather as a commentary to the human conflicts. E.'s style is leisurely, with dialogue that serves to reiterate rather than advance the plot; these techniques not only increase the atmosphere of suspense that is her trademark, but also buy time for character development.

E.'s main characters are women, who find antagonists in jealous female rivals or relatives and show respect to older women. With only one exception (*Another Man's Murder*, 1957), E.'s novels are told from a female character's point of view and the murderers are usually male. Her heroines are primarily cast in the roles of marriageable young women suddenly confronted with love triangles. They may work for a living (*The White Dress*, 1945; *Danger Money*, 1974) but they rarely hold positions of power.

E.'s heroines are not always virginal but they are always passive. They are often married to older men who physically abuse them (*Speak No Evil*, 1941; *Woman on the Roof*, 1963) or to men who practice a type of psychic torture (*Fair Warning*, 1936). Sometimes the husband exercises crippling control even in his absence (*Message from Hong Kong*, 1969; *The Unknown Quantity*, 1953; *Never Look Back*, 1950). Invariably, these husbands become the victims of murder, and the progress to their various deaths goes hand in hand with awakening on the part of their wives. The path to a newfound consciousness in a married E. heroine is twofold: the woman initially learns to understand and reject her present subordinate position to her husband, but in the second stage of the process she voluntarily begins to rely upon another man —generally younger and always more physically attractive than her spouse. This man usually becomes her husband at the conclusion of the novel.

In the characters of Susan Dare in *The Cases of Susan Dare* (1934) and Nurse Sarah Keate in *The Patient in Room 18* (1929), however, E.

develops a different type of female protagonist, a woman who relies more on her brains than on her ability to be attractive to a man. Moreover, Dare and Keate are not humorless creatures; unlike their confused counterparts in the other novels, they have a feel for the good joke, for the lucidrous situation, and for comedy in tragedy.

While E.'s novels lack the compassion of those of Charlotte Armstrong, the plotting of those of Agatha Christie, or the lively literacy and profundity of those of Dorothy L. Sayers, Margery Allingham, or Ngaio Marsh, they offer a blend of mystery, suspense, and romance not found in the works of those other authors, and they appeal to a different audience.

WORKS: *The Patient in Room 18* (1929). *While the Patient Slept* (1930). *The Mystery of Hunting's End* (1930). *From This Dark Stairway* (1931). *Murder by an Aristocrat* (1932). *The Dark Garden* (1933). *The White Cockatoo* (1933). *Murder of My Patient* (1934). *The Cases of Susan Dare* (1934). *The House on the Roof* (1935). *Fair Warning* (1936). *Danger in the Dark* (1936). *The Pattern* (1937). *320 College Avenue* (with F. Ballard, 1938). *The Glass Slipper* (1938). *Hasty Wedding* (1938). *The Chiffon Scarf* (1939). *The Hangman's Whip* (1940). *Eight O'Clock Tuesday* (with R. Wallsten, 1941). *With This Ring* (1941). *Speak No Evil* (1941). *Wolf in Man's Clothing* (1942). *Unidentified Woman* (1943). *The Man Next Door* (1943). *Sisters* (1943). *Escape the Night* (1944). *The White Dress* (1945). *Wings of Fear* (1945). *Five Passengers from Lisbon* (1946). *Another Woman's House* (1947). *House of Storm* (1949). *Hunt with the Hounds* (1950). *Never Look Back* (1950). *Dead Men's Plans* (1952). *The Unknown Quantity* (1953). *Man Missing* (1954). *Post Mark Murder* (1956). *Another Man's Murder* (1957). *Melora* (1959). *Jury of One* (1960). *The Cup, the Blade, or the Gun* (1961). *Enemy in the House* (1962). *Run Scared* (1963). *Call after Midnight* (1964). *R.S.V.P. Murder* (1965). *Witness at Large* (1966). *Woman on the Roof* (1968). *Message from Hong Kong* (1969). *El Rancho Rio* (1970). *Two Little Rich Girls* (1971). *Murder in Waiting* (1973). *Danger Money* (1974). *Family Fortune* (1976).

BIBLIOGRAPHY: Haycraft, H., *Murder for Pleasure: The Life and Times of the Detective Story* (1941).

For articles in reference works, see: *20thCA*.

Other references: *PW* (16 Sept. 1974).

SUSAN L. CLARK

Mary Baker Glover Eddy

B. *16 July 1821, Bow, New Hampshire; d. 3 Dec. 1910, Chestnut Hill,*
Massachusetts
D. *of Mark and Abigail Ambrose Baker; m. George Washington Glover, 1843;*
m. Daniel Patterson, 1853; m. Asa Gilbert Eddy, 1877

Founder of the Christian Science movement and of the Church of Christ, Scientist, E. was originally a member of the Congregational church. In 1862 she received treatment for a nervous ailment from Phineas P. Quimby, noted Massachusetts practitioner of "animal magnetism," and became interested in mind cure. In 1866 E. sustained a serious spinal injury from which she recovered through what she later described as the total conviction that her life was in God and God was Life.

In the same year her husband deserted E. and for the next three years she lived with various friends and relatives. In 1870 she wrote a textbook, *The Science of Man*, and began teaching in Lynn, Massachusetts. In 1875 she published the first edition of *Science and Health*, and organized the Christian Science Association in 1876. The year 1879 saw the establishment of the Church of Christ, Scientist, and 1881 the chartering of the Massachusetts Metaphysical College. Both were dissolved in 1889 in preparation for the founding in Boston of the Mother Church in September 1892. By 1900 a network of six hundred churches existed, and Christian Science was no longer a sect but an organized religion.

Known chiefly for its emphasis on psychical healing, Christian Science embraces a full theology. Though E. firmly professed herself and her religion to be Christian, orthodox Christianity rejected both. Basic to Christian Science is the doctrine that God is All, Life, and Mind. Since God is Spirit, the only manifestation of life is in Spirit, not in matter. Matter, sin, pain, and death are all erroneous concepts, part of the great error, the belief in evil. Healing, then, is an important part of overcoming the error involved in the belief in the ills of the flesh.

Christian Science rejects all anthropomorphic and personal ideas associated with God. E.'s identification of Christian Science as the Holy Comforter linked it to that aspect of God which she saw as feminine. At one point in the evolution of *Science and Health* she went so far as to speak of God as "She," but the reference was dropped from succeeding editions.

E. recognized the power of the written word in disseminating doctrine. In her life there were close to four hundred editions of *Science and Health* published. The monthly *Christian Science Journal* began in 1883, in 1898 the weekly *Christian Science Sentinel* appeared, and in 1908 the daily newspaper, the *Christian Science Monitor*, was established. The *Monitor* is one of the most respected among international newspapers.

At one time the object of severe criticism and ridicule (see Mark Twain's *Christian Science*, 1907), Christian Science is now a recognized part of the religious institution in America, a denomination whose members maintain more than twenty-five hundred churches. E. served as pastor of the Mother Church in Boston for many years, and never relinquished leadership of the movement until her death. Her *Manual of the Mother Church* (1895) still provides the framework of government for the churches, and *Science and Health* remains the religion's basic text. Thus E.'s imprint on Christian Science is as strong now as it was when she founded it.

WORKS: *The Science of Man* (1870). *Science and Health* (1875). *Christian Healing* (1880). *The People's God* (1883). *Historical Sketch of Metaphysical Healing* (1885). *Defence of Christian Science* (1885). *Christian Science: No and Yes* (1887). *Rudiments and Rules of Divine Science* (1887). *Unity of Good and Unreality of Evil* (1888). *Retrospection and Introspection* (1891). *The Manual of the Mother Church* (1895). *Miscellaneous Writings* (1896). *The First Church of Christ, Scientist, and Miscellany* (1913). *Science and Health with Key to the Scriptures* (1910).

BIBLIOGRAPHY: Gottschalk, S., *The Emergence of Christian Science in American Religious Life* (1973). Milmine, G., *The Life of Mary Baker Glover Eddy and the History of Christian Science* (1909). Orcutt, W. D., *Mary Baker Eddy and Her Books* (1913). Peel, R., *Mary Baker Eddy: The Years of Discovery* (1966), *Mary Baker Eddy: The Years of Trial* (1971), *Mary Baker Eddy: The Years of Authority*.

JOANN PECK KRIEG

Elizabeth Fries Lummis Ellet

B. Oct. 1812 (?), Sodus Point, New York; d. 3 June 1877, New York City
D. of William Nixon and Sarah Maxwell Lummis; m. William Henry Ellet,
  ca. 1835

Overlooked in traditional chronicles of military and political events, E. is the first historian of American women. She is important also as an early social historian. E.'s first significant work was *The Women of the American Revolution* in two volumes (1848), supplemented by a third volume (1850) and by the *Domestic History of the American Revolution* (1850). (The two original volumes were reprinted in 1974 as *The Eminent and Heroic Women in America*.)

Noting a dearth of sources, fragmentary anecdotes, meager correspondence and documents, the distortions of reminiscences, and other scholarly handicaps, E. also observed that "women's sphere is secluded" and "in very few instances does her personal history, even though she may fill a conspicuous position, afford sufficient incident . . . and salient points for description," in contrast to the actions of men. Her work, then, is primarily episodic; and the methodology of it a result of the limitations she recognized.

Scrupulous in the use of reliable accounts, E. provides contexts and settings for the remarkably varied activities of women in the "heroic age of the republic." While she concentrates on the wives, sisters, mothers, and daughters whose existence was devoted to the men fighting the War of American Independence and forming a new nation, E. also presents many remarkable instances of the independent exploits of women.

Achieving success with the histories, E. further explored the lives of American women by writing three books that obviously reflect the range and vigor of a developing country: *Pioneer Women of the West* (1852), *The Queens of American Society* (1867), and *The Court Circles of the Republic* (1869). Having grown up on the Lake Ontario frontier and having lived in both the South and the North, E. took a broad, liberal view of regional and human diversities.

The thesis of *Court Circles* is that "a fair idea" of a political administration can be gained from the fashionable life and everyday habits of a president and those who surround him. Consequently, E. describes the attitudes, practices, and influence of successive social circles from Washington to Grant. Antics and the ambience of entertainments, conversations and orations, balls, teas, weddings, funerals, and inaugurals suggest differences in the character and spirit of the nation's leaders. Perhaps the best written of E.'s books, *Court Circles* is based on letters, journals, and gossip. The style is bold and easy. There are good moments: one president has his butcher to dinner, another a country merchant; the black servant of an American foreign minister speaks French or German or Russian so that guests will feel at home; a president's wife reports that Charles Dickens looked bored when he visited her, and she preferred the company of Washington Irving; two suffragists argue on the street about whether women should wear pantaloons. It is ironic that E. is often remembered as a gossip; she was expert at putting together true stories for the historical record.

WORKS: Euphemio of Messina by S. Pellico (trans. by Ellet, 1834). *Poems, Translated and Original* (1835). *Rambles about the Country* (1847). *The Women of the American Revolution* (3 vols., 1848–50). *Family Pictures from the Bible* (1849). *Domestic History of the American Revolution* (1850). *Pioneer Women of the West* (1852). *Summer Rambles in the West* (1853). *The Practical Housekeeper* (1857). *Women Artists in All Ages* (1859). *The Queens of American Society* (1867). *The Court Circles of the Republic* (1869).

BIBLIOGRAPHY: Bayless, J., *Rufus Wilmot Griswold* (1943). Beard, C. and M., *The Rise of American Civilization* (1927). Moss, S. P., *Poe's Literary Battles* (1963). Poe, E. A., "Autography," in *The Complete Works of Poe*, (Vol. 15, Virginia ed., 1902).

For articles in reference works, see: *CAL. NAW* (article by A. Lutz).

ELIZABETH PHILLIPS

Anne Ellis

B. *1875, Missouri; d. Aug. 1938, Denver, Colorado*
D. *of Albert Laurence and Rachel Sweareangen Heister; m. G. Fleming, 1895; m. Herbert Ellis, 1901*

When still a child, E. traveled with her family behind an oxen team to Silver Cliff, Colorado. As E. remembers: "I went up the gulch at the age of six and came down at the age of sixteen." When she came down, a seasoned veteran of life in Colorado's mining towns, it was with the first batch of experience that would make her a writer.

Soon after the family's move from Missouri, E.'s father left his wife for a job in Buffalo and never came back. One of E.'s earliest memories is of the abject poverty which drove her mother to take one of her pieced quilts door to door trying to trade it for food. In 1882, her mother married a miner, and the family moved to Bonanza. Here, though never free of want, they survived the ups and downs of the mining business chiefly through her mother's ingenuity as a cook and seamstress. Miners (with names like "Si Dore" and "Picnic Jim"), fancy women, cliff-climbing, first love, a first milk cow, dances, tales of women's rights, and dresses made of cabin curtains—all these filled E.'s life and later her writings. Though school consisted primarily of home mastery of a fifth-grade reader, E. remarked that "when one cannot read, one thinks a lot."

Shortly after her mother's death in 1893, E. married and moved to a new mine, the Only Chance, to stake a claim. Living from hand to mouth most of these years, E. spent much of her spare time writing. In 1938, her friends rallied to pay for the necessary clothes and travelling expenses when she received a telegram invitation to appear at the University of Colorado to receive an honorary Master of Letters degree. At that time she had published her three autobiographical works—*The Life of an Ordinary Woman* (1929), *Plain Anne Ellis* (1931), and *Sunshine Preferred* (1934).

The Life of An Ordinary Woman gives valuable first-hand description and analysis of the mining West. It focuses on the variety of characters and activities characteristic to a mining town: "A New Mine," "The Baby's First Bed," "Theatricals," "Seeing a Prize Fight," "Cripple Creek Troubles," "The First Telephone." In *Plain Anne Ellis*, E. details house-building, contracting with the government to travel with and cook for a telephone gang, sheep shearing, race relations, Indian maneuvers, county politics, and equal-rights conventions. *Sunshine Preferred*, though not as interesting as E.'s earlier works, nevertheless offers a rare insight into sanitariums of the 1920s and 1930s and a few glimpses of life in Albuquerque and Santa Fe, New Mexico.

One of the most refreshing rewards of reading E.'s books is the abundant humor that characterizes her style. She also has a talent for putting herself in perspective, which greatly enhances the psychological insight that her works provide. E.'s observations are often straightfor-ward accounts of an active mind and a vibrant body for whom the

Victorian mores of her era fell by the wayside. Of her political experiences, she writes: "These men, who were supposed to be my friends, tried to make it hell for me; but I, who recognize no hell, was neither worried, frightened nor disturbed; in fact, I rather enjoyed it; holding the whip hand was for me a new experience." It's no surprise that this is the same woman of whom Irene McKeehan, professor of English at the University of Colorado, said: "Out of hardships and limitations she had made comedy and tragedy, touching the commonplace with the magic of interest, transmuting ordinary life into literaature."

WORKS: *The Life of An Ordinary Woman* (1929). *Plain Anne Ellis* (1931). *Sunshine Preferred* (1934).

BIBLIOGRAPHY: *NYT* (30 Aug. 1931; 19 Aug. 1934). *NYTBR* (29 Sept. 1929). *The Colorado Quarterly* (Summer 1955).

SHELLEY ARMITAGE

Janet Ayer Fairbank

B. 7 June 1878, Chicago, Illinois; d. 28 Dec. 1951, Wauwautosa, Wisconsin
D. of Benjamin F. and Janet Hopkins Ayer; m. Kellogg Fairbank, 1900

The older sister of novelist Margaret Ayer Barnes, F. was educated in private schools and attended the University of Chicago.

A dedicated worker for woman suffrage, F. was a member of the executive committee of the Democratic National Committee (1919–20), served as Illinois Democratic national committeewoman (1924–28), and was a delegate to the Democratic national convention (1932). During World War I she was a member of the Woman's National Liberty Loan Committee and of the Illinois Committee of the Woman's Division of the Council for National Defense. Before World War II, she was a national officer of the America First Committee, and in 1940 she campaigned for Willkie. F.'s most notable philanthropic activity was her twenty-four years on the board of the Chicago Lying-in Hospital, including service as its president.

Three of F.'s novels form a trilogy. *The Cortlandts of Washington Square* (1922) introduces Ann Byrne, ten-year-old ward of a wealthy New Yorker, and follows her growing up in the years prior to and during the Civil War. The novel concludes with her marriage to Peter Smith, a young worker from Chicago who promises they will be "partners." *The Smiths* (1925), set in Chicago, stretches from the Civil War almost to World War I. It is the story of a marriage: Ann's shattering discovery that to Peter being "partners" does not mean involving her in his business; the birth and rearing of children; and Peter's growth in wealth and status. Throughout, Ann's increasing strength and wisdom parallel the rise of the city. *Rich Man, Poor Man* (1936) centers on Ann's grandson, Hendricks Smith, and his wife, Barbara, tracing their involvement in Roosevelt's Progressive Party, World War I, and the suffragist movement. Though sometimes described as a "suffrage novel," the book does not depict that movement very fully, and the portrayal of Barbara, the suffragist, is not completely sympathetic. F.'s interest was in character delineation, not in propaganda.

Her two other novels of note both bear thematic relationships with the trilogy. *The Lions' Den* (1930), a political novel, has as its protagonist an idealistic young Wisconsin congressman. His disillusionment, partial corruption, and eventual courageous behavior when tested make up the substance of the novel. *The Bright Land* (1932), perhaps F.'s finest novel, tells the life story of Abby-Delight Flagg, child of New England Puritans, brought up in a world where women face hard work and, all too often, early death in childbirth. Partly to escape her dour father, she elopes, and the second half of the novel tells of her married life in Galena, Illinois, during its years first as a boom town and then in decline. Like Ann Smith, Abby-Delight grows in strength and wisdom, but she has more humor and is less idealized than Ann.

Once popular, F.'s fiction is neglected now. Her favored Illinois settings during the 19th and 20th centuries are objectively presented, and her characters, particularly her women, are sharply and believably delineated. The novels move at a leisurely pace, sometimes with little action, although F. occasionally attempted even battle scenes. In *The Cortlandts of Washington Square*, her impressionistic presentation, from the point of view of a young woman caught up in it, of the Battle of Gettysburg is gripping. Her studies of historical trends and political issues are serious and perceptive. Although the quantity is not great, the quality of her work is high; her claim upon our attention is greater than has been recognized in recent times.

WORKS: *At Home* (1910). *In Town, & Other Conversations* (1910). *Three Days More* (1910). *Report of National Woman's Liberty Loan Committee for the Victory Loan Campaign, April 21st to May 10th, 1919* (compiled by Fairbank, 1920). *The Cortlandts of Washington Square* (1922). *The Smiths* (1925).

Idle Hands (1927). *The Lions' Den* (1930). *The Bright Land* (1932). *The Alleged Great-Aunt* by H. K. Webster (completed by Fairbank, with M. A. Barnes, 1935). *Rich Man, Poor Man* (1936).

BIBLIOGRAPHY: For articles in reference works, see: *NCAB*, 39. *20thCA*. *20thCAS*.

Other references: *Literary Digest International Book Review* (Sept. 1925). *NYTBR* (15 Oct. 1922; 28 June 1925; 7 Dec. 1930). *SatR* (7 Jan. 1933; 12 Dec. 1936).

MARY JEAN DeMARR

Harriet Farley

B. ca. 18 Feb. 1813, Claremont, New Hampshire; d. 12 Nov. 1907, New York City
D. of Stephen and Lucy Saunders Farley; m. John Intaglio Donlevy, 1854

The sixth of ten children of a Congregational minister and his wife, who became "harmlessly insane" after bearing the ten children, F. began contributing to her family's support when she was fourteen. After plaiting straw for hats, binding shoes, and engaging in other home manufactures, she made a brief and unrewarding attempt to teach and then went to work in the Lowell textile mills in 1837. In Lowell, as the autobiographical "Letters from Susan" show, she felt free to attend lectures, sample different churches, and join an improvement circle. In spite of the thirteen-hour working day and the crowded corporation boardinghouse, she felt that the work offered the best economic rewards for women and didn't require "very violent exertion, as much of our farm work does."

When the two products of the improvement circles, the *Lowell Offering* and the *Operatives Magazine*, were bought by a local Whig newspaper in 1842 and combined under the name of the *Lowell Offering*, F. and Harriott Curtis, assisted by Harriet Lees, became editors and, later, owners.

Under attack from Sarah G. Bagley and others, F. denied that her magazine was supported by the corporations, but F.'s father and brother both received help from mill-owner Amos Lawrence, and the Hamilton

Company bought up $1,000 worth of back numbers during the *Lowell Offering*'s last year.

Determinedly genteel and noncontroversial, the *Lowell Offering* lost its audience as the ten-hour movement gained in strength, and its appeal waned even further when the well-written labor paper, the *Voice of Industry*, appeared in Lowell in October 1845. The *Offering* ceased publication in December, but after the failure of the ten-hour movement in 1847, it was revived as the *New England Offering*, with F. as both editor and publisher. Her efforts, however, again proved unsuccessful with the operatives. After the failure of the *Offering* in 1850, F. moved to New York City, where she became a contributor to *Godey's Lady's Book*. After her marriage, F. gave up her writing, of which her husband did not approve.

F.'s avowed intention in the publications she edited was to bring a little "cheer" into the lives of female operatives, and the literary nature of the magazines was, she thought, above sordid issues. Her first signed editorial said of the operatives: "We should like to influence them as moral and rational beings. . . . Our field is a wide one. . . . With wages, board, etc., we have nothing to do—these depend on circumstances over which we have no control." F. assumed that her readers were too lady-like to press for reforms by surrounding "City Hall in a mob, but, if wronged, would seek redress in some less exceptionable manner."

F.'s essays and stories, though sometimes self-consciously literary and "tiresomely inspirational," often provide insights into the lives and aspirations of the female factory workers. Her most interesting sketches, because most realistic and closely based on her own experience, are the "Letters from Susan," which appeared in the 1844 numbers of the *Lowell Offering*. "Susan" gives her first impressions of Lowell, of the crowding and noise as well as the economic and intellectual independence. Such stories as "The Sister" and "Evening before Pay-Day" use factory and boardinghouse backgrounds for sentimental homilies of self-sacrificing sisters or daughters.

F.'s poetry, like most of the poetry in her magazines, is undistinguished: Lacking true details, it is more removed than her other writing from the real experience of the workers' lives.

WORKS: *Shells from the Strand of the Sea of Genius* (1847). *Operatives Reply to . . . Jere. Clemens* (1850). *Happy Nights at Hazel Nook; or, Cottage Stories* (1854). *Fancy's Frolics; or, Christmas Stories Told in a Happy Home in New England* (1880).

BIBLIOGRAPHY: Eisler, B., *The Lowell Offering: Writings by New England Mill Women* (1977). Foner, P. S., *The Factory Girls* (1977). Josephson, H., *The Golden Threads: New England's Mill Girls and Magnates* (1949). Robinson, H. H., *Loom and Spindle; or, Life among the Early Mill Girls* (1898).

For articles in reference works, see: *AA. CAL. DAB*, III, 2. *NAW* (article by G. R. Taylor). *NCAB*, 11.

SUSAN SUTTON SMITH

Eliza Woodson Burhans Farnham

B. *17 Nov. 1815, Rensselaerville, New York; d. 15 Dec. 1864, New York City*
Wrote under: Eliza W. Farnham
D. *of Cornelius and Mary Wood Burhans; m. Thomas Jefferson Farnham, 1836; m. William Fitzpatrick, 1852*

While her first husband was away on exploring expeditions in the Far West, F. developed her interests in reform. Her most controversial work was at Sing Sing prison where, as matron from 1844 to 1848, she revolutionized the treatment of female prisoners through her phrenological approach to the problem of rehabilitation. She resigned after frequent conflicts with conservative staff members who denounced her environmentalism and determinism. In California, where she went in 1849 to settle her first husband's estate, she visited and criticized San Quentin prison and lectured on various subjects. In 1858, she addressed the New York Women's Rights Convention on her theory of female biological and moral superiority. During the Civil War, she became involved in the Women's Loyal National League, which sought a constitutional amendment abolishing slavery. She also nursed the wounded at Gettysburg.

F.'s writing shows the independence of mind, the curiosity, and the strength that she exhibited in her life. *Life in Prairie Land* (1846) is a vivid account of her experiences in Illinois. The account of her life in the West, *California, In-Doors and Out* (1856), is colorful and compelling. The reader is drawn into the world of California after the Gold Rush, when a woman's appearance brought crowds of gaping men to the street. In this very fluid, primitive society, F. bought her own ranch, built her own house, and traveled on horseback unchaperoned. The last part of the book, which describes and evaluates California society and culture, tends to be moralistic, although F.'s analysis of the particular problems of women in frontier society is penetrating.

Eliza Woodson (1864) is an autobiographical novel treating F.'s life as a foster child in a home where she was treated as a household drudge and denied the benefits of a formal education. The fictional heroine reflects F.'s own character as a tough, determined individual who works hard to achieve her goals, overcoming all obstacles. Clearly, F.'s independence of thought and her interest in biological evolution originated in her childhood.

Woman and Her Era (1864), F.'s major work, argues that women are not only morally superior to men but biologically superior as well. Her position is based on the following syllogism: "Life is exalted in proportion to its Organic and Functional complexity; Woman's Organism is more complex and her totality of Function larger than those of any other being inhabiting our earth; Therefore her position in the scale of Life is the most exalted, the Sovereign One." Reproductive functions, commonly cited to demonstrate female inferiority, are used in F.'s philosophy to place woman far above the male.

The same idea dominates *The Ideal Attained* (1865). This novel's heroine, Eleanora Bromfield, is an ideal, superior woman who tests and transforms the hero, Colonel Anderson, until he is a worthy mate who combines masculine strength with the nobility of womanhood and is ever ready to sacrifice himself to the needs of the feminine, maternal principle.

In a society that defined the true woman as submissive, pure, and weak, F. forged her own definitions of female selfhood and lived by her own standards. Both her theory and practice (sometimes contradictory) provided alternatives for women unsatisfied with the narrow lives laid out for them by their culture.

WORKS: *Life in Prairie Land* (1846). *Rationale of Crime* by M. Sampson (introduction by Farnham, 1846). *California, In-Doors and Out; or, How We Farm, Mine, and Live Generally in the Golden State* (1856). *My Early Days* (1859; rev. ed., *Eliza Woodson; or, The Early Days of One of the World's Workers*, 1864). *Woman and Her Era* (1864). *The Ideal Attained; Being the Story of Two Steadfast Souls, and How They Won Their Happiness and Lost It Not* (1865).

BIBLIOGRAPHY: Davies, J. D., *Phrenology, Fad and Science* (1955). Kirby, G. B., *Years of Experience* (1887). Lewis, W., *From Newgate to Dannemora: The Rise of the Penitentiary in New York, 1796–1848* (1965). Mount Pleasant State Prison, *Annual Report of the Inspectors* (1846). Prison Association of

New York, *First, Second,* and *Third Reports* (1845, 1846, 1847) and *First Report of the Female Department* (1845). Woodward, H. B., *The Bold Women* (1953).

For articles in reference works, see: *AA. CAL. DAB,* III, 2. *HWS,* I. *NAW* (article by W. D. Lewis). *NCAB,* 4.

Other references: *Atlantic* (Sept. 1864). New York *Tribune* (16 Dec. 1864). *NYT* (18 Dec. 1864).

KAREN SZYMANSKI

Eliza Ware Rotch Farrar

B. 12 July 1791, Dunkirk, France; d. 22 April 1870, Springfield, Massachusetts
Wrote under: Eliza Farrar
D. of Benjamin and Elizabeth Barker Rotch; m. John Farrar, 1828

Daughter and granddaughter of Nantucket Quakers who had emigrated to France to establish a tax-free whaling port, F. went with her family to England during the Reign of Terror. At her father's estate near Milford Haven she received an excellent education and grew up among eminent European and American visitors. When her father lost his fortune in 1819, she went to live with her grandparents in New Bedford, Massachusetts. Disowned as too liberal by the Quaker meeting there, she became a Unitarian. Except for trips to England to visit her parents, she spent the rest of her life in Massachusetts.

In her "Address to Parents" at the beginning of *The Children's Robinson Crusoe* (1830), F. praises Defoe's work for its "spirit" and "naturalness": "It seems to be exactly what it purports to be, the narrative of a profane, ill-educated, runaway apprentice of the 17th c." F. then asks, "Can such a tale, though perfect in itself, be suited to children who have been carefully guarded from all profaneness, vulgarity, and superstition?" Her version of Crusoe is accordingly cleansed of such faults as his "disobedience to his parents, and his inordinate love of adventure" and endowed with qualities parents would wish their children to admire and cultivate: "industry, perseverance, resignation to the will of God." To increase the utility of her hero's adventures, F. adds "as much information about domestic arts as could well be interwoven with the story" and makes Friday into a native "of a mild, affectionate, and tractable nature."

F. presented another proper hero to be emulated by children in *The Story of the Life of Lafayette as Told by a Father to His Children* (1831). Henry Moreton tells his father that he wishes he lived in the days of Alexander or Caesar and could see these great men; his father takes issue with Henry's idea of these men as great, and reminds him that he has seen on Boston Common "one of the most extraordinary men that ever lived!" Again, the hero's life acquires value as an example and lesson, but his actions are generally left to speak for themselves without intrusive moralizing. The tale takes seventeen evenings. Stirring events are briskly and clearly related, the moral intent doesn't interfere with the often exciting story and interesting anecdotes, and many vignettes of Moreton family life provide humor.

A manual of advice, *The Young Lady's Friend* (1836), was F.'s most important work, widely popular in England and America and reprinted as late as 1880. F. addresses her work to middle-class girls who have finished school. It opens with a brisk chapter of warning to those who assume that their intellectual life ends when they leave the schoolroom and a second chapter "On the Improvement of Time." It closes with a chapter on "Mental Culture" and impressive lists of books for a "course of reading" on history, biography, and travel. In between, she holds to an essentially conservative view of "woman's peculiar calling," but emphasizes practical details of behavior and treats these with gentle amusement and, above all, common sense.

The Young Lady's Friend provides valuable insight into the activities and preoccupations of the 19th-c. American middle class. *Recollections of Seventy Years* (1865), F.'s last book, furnishes fascinating glimpses of life in England and France between 1783 and 1819. Her method is anecdotal, and many of her lively anecdotes seem, in themselves, to furnish enough material for entire novels. F. cared for her invalid husband for fourteen years before his death in 1853. These are the tales she told to enliven his sickroom. They remain beguiling entertainment today.

WORKS: *The Children's Robinson Crusoe* (1830). *The Story of the Life of Lafayette as Told by a Father to His Children* (1831). *John Howard* (1833). *The Youth's Letter-Writer* (1834). *The Young Lady's Friend* (1836). *Recollections of Seventy Years* (1865).

BIBLIOGRAPHY: Carson, G., *The Polite Americans* (1966). Hopkins, V. C., *Prodigal Puritan: A Life of Delia Bacon* (1959). Lynes, R. J., *The Domesticated Americans* (1963). Schlesinger, E. B., "Two Early Harvard Wives: E. F. and Eliza Follen," *NEQ* (June 1965).

For articles in reference works, see: *The Female Prose Writers of America, with Portraits, Biographical Notices, and Specimens of Their Writing*, J. S. Hart (1852). *NAW* (article by E. B. Schlesinger). *NCAB*, 13.

SUSAN SUTTON SMITH

Margaretta V. Bleecker Faugeres

B. *11 Oct. 1771, Tomanick, New York; d. 14 Jan. 1801, Brooklyn, New York*
Wrote under: Margaretta V. Faugeres
D. *of John J. and Ann Eliza Schuyler Bleecker; m. Peter Faugeres, 1792*

F. was an heiress to both the wealth and the intellectual traditions of two of the most respected families in New York. Against her father's wishes, she married a French physician, Peter Faugeres. Called an "infidel," Faugeres was actually a member of the popular Jacobin circles. F. was an enthusiastic supporter of what she took to be the new millenium of human freedom; her choice of Bastille Day as marriage day shows the whole bent of her alliance. She was marrying a movement rather than a man. Unfortunately, her husband abused her and quickly ran through the fortune left to her by her father. F. and her infant daughter were reduced to living in a granary for some time in 1796. Faugeres died of yellow fever in 1798, and F. thereafter supported herself by teaching school in New Brunswick, New Jersey, and Brooklyn, New York. Broken in health and spirit, she was only twenty-nine years old when she died.

The majority of F.'s work was produced before she was twenty. In 1793, F. prepared *The Posthumous Works of Ann Eliza Bleecker*, a collection of her mother's work supplemented with F.'s own poetry and prose, including an affecting "Memoir." After 1795, she wrote some pieces for the *New York Monthly Magazine* and the *American Museum* and, in 1797, published "The Ghost of John Young," but her literary output was hampered by her family problems.

Her tendency towards sentimental melancholy, the sadness sincere, is expressed in highly artificial language in the early poems included in *The Posthumous Works*. Although rendered fairly obscure by an abundance of private references, her poetic language is very formal, with few naturalist touches. There is an excessive use of the infelicitous neoclassical poetical devices: "fleecy tribe" is substituted for sheep, birds are the "feather'd choir," personifications are overabundant. The unhappy and short life of her mother, acting upon an immature imagination, to which the pose of melancholy seemed the height of human delicacy, contributed to the themes that would now seem morbid for an eighteen-year-old girl.

Supplementing these sad strains are several lively patriotic poems. F. was genuinely convinced of the noble renewal of human liberty embodied by the American and French revolutions. In her long topographical poem, "The Hudson" (1793), one of the few pieces in which she employs natural description, F.'s primary purpose is to give an account of the political history of the Hudson River during the American Revolution.

In 1795 she offered *Belisarius: A Tragedy* to the John Street Theatre. It was refused, but published by subscription that same year. Written simply and tastefully in blank verse, the message of pacifism, antimaterialism, and the vanity of power is extraordinary for the times. In a clear analogy with French politics, Belisarius is the just man caught between corrupt courtiers on the one hand, and heartless and cruel revolutionists on the other. Belisarius represents uncompromising human values. The play quietly exposes the vanity of fame and pomp and maintains the sacredness of ordinary human life.

The further development of F.'s maturity of mind and political opinion can be seen in "The Ghost of John Young," a monody opposing capital punishment, "shewing how inconsistent sanguinary Laws are, in a Country which boasts of her Freedom and Happiness."

F. appears to have been an extraordinarily fair and good woman, "a favorite among her literary acquaintances" whose life of early genius and promise so quickly disintegrated into ruin. Her political idealism is typical of many talented women of this era; so is the personal tragedy that prevented many of them, F. included, from living long enough to develop maturity of literary judgment and production.

WORKS: *The Posthumous Works of Ann Eliza Bleecker in Prose and Verse. To Which Is Added, a Collection of Essays, Prose and Poetical, by Margaretta V. Faugeres* (1793). *Belisarius: A Tragedy* (1795).

BIBLIOGRAPHY: For articles in reference works, see: *Biographie Universelle*, M. Michaud (1855). *CAL* (article on Ann Eliza Bleecker, 1877). *FPA. NAW* (article on Ann Eliza Bleecker by L. Leary). *Nouvelle Biographie Generale*, J. C. F. Hoefer (1958).

L. W. KOENGETER

Jessie Redmon Fauset

B. 27 April 1882, Camden County, New Jersey; d. 30 April 1961, Philadelphia, Pennsylvania
D. of Redmon and Annie Seamon Fauset; m. Herbert Harris, 1929

F. was the youngest of seven children born to an African Methodist Episcopal minister in Philadelphia. F.'s family was poor, but her father's black church position and interest in books and art kept the family "working, aspiring, and discussing." The children were educated as much as biases would permit. With opportunities nearer to home shut off because of her race, F., the first black woman at Cornell University, graduated Phi Beta Kappa and spent many years teaching French at an all-black high school in Washington, D.C.

Correspondence from 1903 with W. E. B. DuBois, the black sociologist, led F. to early involvement with the National Association for the Advancement of Colored People. In 1919, DuBois persuaded her to move to New York City to work with *The Crisis*, of which he was the editor. As its literary editor from 1919 to 1926, F. discovered and published Langston Hughes, Countee Cullen, Jean Toomer, Claude McKay, and other "Harlem Renaissance" writers. She also published her own work, held and attended innumerable literary soirees with black and white writers, and traveled abroad with DuBois's Pan-African conferences. F. edited and did most of the writing for the *Brownies' Book*, a delightful monthly magazine for black children.

F. also contributed to black American literature a large body of her own creative writing. Her poetry, frequently anthologized, her short stories, and her essays—which show sensitivity to racism and sexism worldwide—were published primarily in *The Crisis*, 1912–29, and in the *Brownies' Book*, 1920–21. It is for her four novels, however, that F. is primarily remembered.

There Is Confusion (1924) was written in response to the picture drawn of black life by a white writer, T. S. Stribling, in *Birthright*. F. believed that she could more accurately and honestly depict characters of her own race. Through the story of Joanna Marshall and Peter Bye, from childhood to marriage, she makes clear her themes and concerns.

History, heredity, and environment impinge on the free will of F.'s characters, and their roles as women and black Americans come close to limiting and defining them.

F.'s second novel, *Plum Bun* (1929), deals with a topic frequent in black literature: Angela Murray, the lighter of two sisters, "passes" for white. Attention by critics to the subject matter of the book has led to their ignoring its formal strengths, which represent a distinct improvement over the writing in F.'s first novel and which make *Plum Bun* the best of her four novels.

The Chinaberry Tree (1931) concentrates in a rather nostalgic way on black home and community life in a small New Jersey village. Formally, it takes Greek mythology and drama as its most immediately recognizable analogue. The comparison with Greek drama is evident, from a tragically inescapable family curse with overtones of incest, to the seasonal pattern of death and rebirth.

F.'s last published novel zeroed in on the ironies of American black life with more directness and less sentimentality than any of her work. In *Comedy: American Style* (1933), race discrimination is internalized in the black characters, particularly in the destructive power of Olivia Carey. Themes have not changed much from F.'s 1924 novel, but what has changed is her willingness to unstintingly depict those who are destroyed by their environments, as well as those who overcome them.

F.'s literary strengths are those of her own character. Intelligence and curiosity are supplemented by kindness, generosity, graciousness, and tolerance. She had no dominating passion, no driving opinions which scattered all else before them. Her books are more exploratory than dogmatic, more searching than protesting. The facts of her life and her time make clear the struggle and hard work which gave her strength.

WORKS: *There Is Confusion* (1924). *Plum Bun* (1929). *The Chinaberry Tree* (1931). *Comedy: American Style* (1933).

BIBLIOGRAPHY: Aptheker, H., ed., *The Correspondence of W. E. B. DuBois* (1973). Bone, R., *The Negro Novel in America* (1966). Bontemps, A., *The Harlem Renaissance Remembered* (1972). Braithwaite, W., in *The Black Novelist*, Ed. R. Hemenway (1970). Davis, A., *From the Dark Tower: Afro-American Writers, 1900–1960* (1974). Gayle, A., *The Way of the New World: The Black Novel in America* (1976). Huggins, N., *Harlem Renaissance* (1971). Hughes, L., *The Big Sea* (1940). Sylvander, C. W., *J. R. F., Black American Writer* (1980).

For articles in reference works, see: *Black American Writers Past and Present: A Biographical and Bibliographical Dictionary*, T. Rush and A. Myers (1975). *Profiles of Negro Womanhood*, S. Dannett (1966). *20thCA*. *20thCAS*.

Other references: *CLAJ* 14 (1971); 17 (1974). *Freedomways* (Winter 1975). *Phylon* (June 1978). *Southern Workman* (May 1932).

CAROLYN WEDIN SYLVANDER

Edna Ferber

B. 15 Aug. 1887, Kalamazoo, Michigan; d. 16 April 1968, New York City
D. of Jacob Charles and Julia Neuman Ferber

F. began her writing career as a newspaper reporter in Appleton, Wisconsin, Milwaukee, and Chicago, but wrote her first novel, *Dawn O'Hara* (1911), during a prolonged illness. She earned sudden success and great popularity with her stories of Emma McChesney, a traveling saleswoman (1913, 1914, 1915).

In 1925, F. won the Pulitzer Prize for *So Big* (1924), her best novel, and a few years later saw her novel *Show Boat* (1926) transformed into a classic American musical. Her love of the theater was further indulged through her successful collaboration with George S. Kaufman, with whom she wrote such popular plays as *Royal Family* (1928), *Dinner at Eight* (1932), and *Stage Door* (1936). *Royal Family* was successfully revived in 1975. F. was seriously disillusioned by World War II; her postwar novels were more idea-laden and contrived, although she remained a popular novelist to her death.

In *So Big*, Selina Peake, the properly raised daughter of a gambler, is forced to make her own way in the world after her father is accidentally killed. She takes a teaching position in High Prairie, a Dutch farming community outside Chicago, and spends the rest of her life there. After the death of her husband, Selina struggles by herself to run their truck farm and to raise her son, Dirk, nicknamed "So Big." Dirk's youth is the counterpoint in every respect of Selina's. Where she cherishes life, he cherishes success; where she reveres beauty, he reveres money. By the novel's end, Dirk is an immensely wealthy, successful, miserable young man.

Show Boat deals with three generations of women—Parthenia Ann Hawks, Magnolia Hawks Ravenal, and Kim Ravenal—but the novel centers on Magnolia, her bizarre childhood on her father's showboat, her idyllic love affair with Gaylord Ravenal, her marital difficulties as she learns that her husband is a confirmed gambler, and her determination to provide for her daughter after Gaylord's desertion. As in many F. novels, the heroine's daughter is not nearly her mother's equal. Also as in most F. novels, there is a subplot concerned with racist attitudes, here about the mulatto showboat actress Julie, whose role was expanded in the musical.

Cimarron (1929) is F.'s most overtly feminist novel. Sabra Venable Cravat moves with her husband Yancey to the recently opened territory of Oklahoma. Despite his many talents, Yancey is impractical and irresponsible and seems unable to stay in one place longer than five years at a time. Thus, in addition to the housework and the raising of her children, Sabra finds herself helping with Yancey's newspaper—the first in Oklahoma—and, on those occasions when Yancey abandons her, running it herself. Yancey is the dreamer; Sabra the doer. She becomes Oklahoma's first U.S. congresswoman.

Clio Dulaine Maroon, the protagonist of *Saratoga Trunk* (1941), is as close as F. ever came to creating an antiheroine. Clio, illegitimate daughter of an established Creole family (the Dulaines) on her father's side and a series of "loose" women (including a free woman of color) on her mother's, returns from France to New Orleans to avenge herself on the Dulaines and to make her fortune by marrying a millionaire. Clio realizes at the last minute that love is more important than money, but luckily Clint Maroon, a Texan adventurer who has been making his fortune among the detested railroad men while Clio tries to marry one of them, can now provide both love and money.

F.'s writing remained untouched by the innovations of her contemporaries. She was neither responsible for any innovations of her own, nor did her own work appreciably evolve in terms of style, content, or structure. Still, her work deserves serious consideration for her treatment of the land, her feminism, and her egalitarianism.

Even when F. writes about the land, her novels are first and foremost about women—strong women, pioneer women, women determined to hold on to the land and to keep their families together. The women always triumph and often survive their men; the visionaries see their dreams come true, and the practical ones see the present inexorably improving toward the future. Although F. is not in the tradition of the great American literary experimenters, she is a solid member of another tradition, that of the celebrators of America.

WORKS: Dawn O'Hara: The Girl Who Laughed (1911). *Buttered Side Down*

(1912). *Roast Beef, Medium: The Business Adventures of Emma McChesney* (1913). *Personality Plus: Some Experiences of Emma McChesney and Her Son, Jock* (1914). *Emma McChesney and Co.* (1915). *Fanny Herself* (1917). *Cheerful by Request* (1918). *Half Portions* (1920). *$1200 a Year* (with N. Levy, 1920). *The Girls* (1921). *Gigolo* (1922; film version, 1926). *So Big* (1924; film versions, 1925, 1953). *Eldest* (1925). *Minick* (with G. S. Kaufman, 1925; film versions, 1925, 1932). *Show Boat* (1926; film versions, 1929, 1936, 1951). *Mother Knows Best: A Fiction Book* (1927; film version, 1928). *Royal Family* (with G. S. Kaufman, 1928; film version, 1930). *Cimarron* (1929; film versions, 1931, 1961). *American Beauty* (1931). *Dinner at Eight* (with G. S. Kaufman, 1931; film version, 1933). *They Brought Their Women: A Book of Short Stories* (1933). *Come and Get It* (1935; film version, 1936). *Stage Door* (with G. S. Kaufman, 1936; film version, 1937). *Nobody's in Town* (1938). *A Peculiar Treasure* (1939). *The Land Is Bright* (with G. S. Kaufman, 1941). *Saratoga Trunk* (1941; film version, 1945). *Great Son* (1945). *One Basket: Thirty-One Short Stories* (1947). *Bravo* (with G. S. Kaufman, 1949). *Giant* (1952; film version, 1956). *Ice Palace* (1958; film version, 1960). *A Kind of Magic* (1963).

BIBLIOGRAPHY: Shaughnessy, M. R., *Women and Success in American Society in the Works of E. F.* (1976).

For articles in reference works, see: *CA*, 5–8 (1969); 25–28 (1971). *20thCA. 20thCAS. Wisconsin Writers: Sketches and Studies*, W. A. Titus (1974).

Other references: *BB* 22 (1958). *Chicago Jewish Forum* 13. *MTJ* 13. *NYTBR* (5 Oct. 1952).

CYNTHIA L. WALKER

Kate Field

B. 1 Oct. 1838, St. Louis, Missouri; d. 19 May 1896, Honolulu, Hawaii
Given name: Mary Katherine Keemle Field
D. of Joseph M. and Eliza Riddle Field

The daughter of an actor and newspaper publisher and an actress, F. became the ward of a millionaire uncle, Milton L. Sanford, following her father's death when she was eighteen. The Sanfords financed her education at Lasell Seminary, Auburndale, Massachusetts, and took her to Italy, where she was the darling of Anthony Trollope and other members of the writers' colony in Florence. Her support for the Union in the Civil War caused Sanford, a Southern sympathizer, to change his mind about making her his heir.

To support herself she turned to journalism, writing travel letters for the Springfield (Massachusetts) *Republican* and other newspapers. She lectured on the lyceum circuit, wrote humorous accounts of various journeys to Europe, and undertook a mildly successful theatrical career. She also did commercial publicity. *The Drama of Glass* (n.d.) was a slick advertisement for the Libby Glass Company disguised as a brief "history" of glass-making. Although she received valuable stock for publicizing the newly invented telephone, she lost the proceeds in an unsuccessful dressmaking venture to promote simpler styles.

Desiring a platform for her views, she founded a weekly newspaper, *Kate Field's Washington*, which lasted from 1890 to 1895. She died a year later in Hawaii, where she had gone to regain her health after the newspaper failed.

Genuine gifts of humor and social satire characterize *Hap-Hazard* (1873), a collection of letters from the New York *Tribune* that feature the trials of a lady lecturer and poke fun at both the British monarchy and the nouveau riche American tourists. *Ten Days in Spain* (1875) bristles with her American middle-class prejudices displayed on travels through Spain during a political upheaval.

Kate Field's Washington focused on her own personality and special interests. It featured book reviews, theatrical news, novelettes, and drawing-room comedies, often written by F. herself. Although slight in content, several of her plays were produced. Her kaleidoscopic opinions championed numerous causes: temperance (not abstinence); the right of the rich to conspicuous consumption; cremation; prohibition of Mormon polygamy; international copyrights; the arts; and tariff and civil service reform. She weakly endorsed woman suffrage.

Although F. demonstrated considerable literary talent, her importance lies less in what she wrote than in what she represented—the accomplishments of an intelligent and independent American woman in the late Victorian era. Her significance as a journalist stems from her views on the news, including reform efforts and politics, in an era when it was unusual for a woman to found and run a newspaper.

WORKS: *Adelaide Ristori* (1867). *Pen Photographs of Charles Dickens's Readings* (1868). *Planchette's Diary* (1868). *Mad on Purpose: A Comedy* (1868). *Hap-Hazard* (1873). *Ten Days in Spain* (1875). *Charles Albert Fechter* (1882). *The Drama of Glass* (n.d.).

BIBLIOGRAPHY: Beasley, M. H., *The First Women Washington Correspondents* (George Washington Univ. Studies #4, 1976). Sadlier, M., *Anthony Trollope* (1927). Trollope, A., *An Autobiography* (1883). Whiting, L., *K. F.: A Record* (1899). Woodward, H., *The Bold Women* (1953).

For articles in reference works, see: *DAB*, III, 2. *NAW* (article by David Baldwin). *NCAB*, 6.

Other references: *NYT* (31 May 1896). *Records of the Columbia Historical Society* (1973–74).

MAURINE BEASLEY

Rachel Lyman Field

B. *19 Sept. 1894, New York City; d. 15 March 1942, Beverly Hills, California*
Wrote under: Rachel Field
D. of Matthew D. and Lucy Atwater Field; m. Arthur S. Pederson, 1935

Descended from a distinguished family, F. was educated in public schools. She attended Radcliffe College and later wrote synopses for a silent film company.

For about the first two-thirds of F.'s writing career, she was primarily a writer of juvenile literature for children of varying ages. Her one-act plays (many separately published in acting versions) include farces, comedies, serious and poetic dramas, modern reinterpretations of old stories, and nostalgic period pieces. Lacking literary pretension, they are nevertheless stageworthy. F.'s juvenile poems also show her versatility, for she worked in a number of forms and types, but tendencies toward sentimentality and rhythmic monotony lessen their effectiveness.

The best of F.'s work for young people is to be found in three juvenile novels. *Hitty: Her First Hundred Years* (1929) was awarded the Newbery Medal for children's literature. Set in the 19th c., it is the history of a wooden doll, narrated by herself. The parts depicting the Maine F. loved are especially vivid and evocative. *Calico Bush* (1931) covers one year (1743–44) in the life of a French girl indentured to an English family who settle in Maine. Her sense of isolation, both as a foreigner and as a pioneer, is well conveyed, as are the terrors and delights of frontier life.

Hepatica Hawks (1932) has as its protagonist a fifteen-year-old girl who is 6′4″ tall and a member of a freak show. The novel takes her from an early acceptance of her differentness through a period of desperate yearning for friends of her own age and participation in normal society. Eventually she finds a place (as a Wagnerian soprano) where her size is not a hindrance. Told with restraint, the novel movingly conveys its message, that it is all right to be different.

In her last years, F. turned to writing novels for adults. *To See Ourselves* (1937), written with her husband, is a comic Hollywood novel of little significance. More ambitious are two historical novels. *Time out of Mind* (1935), set in Maine, shows the decline of a shipbuilding family as seen by a young woman intimately connected with it. It is a story of family conflict, pitting young against old and artistic against materialistic values. *All This, and Heaven Too* (1938) is F.'s imaginative and sympathetic reconstruction of the experiences of a young Frenchwoman who was involved in a celebrated 19th-c. murder trial and later came to the U.S. and married F.'s great-uncle.

Less substantial is *And Now Tomorrow* (1942), the story of a wealthy young woman temporarily afflicted with deafness; it is played out against the contemporary background of the Depression and labor strife. The female protagonists of the three latter novels are all forced by circumstances to find in themselves strength, endurance, and breadth of sympathy and understanding. They learn, in an image F. uses several times, to become trees and not vines.

F.'s work, in many genres, shows her concern for craftsmanship and her broad sympathies. The single most frequently occurring image in her work, the patchwork quilt, is indicative: peculiarly a woman's image, it suggests women's creativity, nostalgia for the past, and the creation of something new, beautiful, and useful from old and heterogeneous materials. F. tended toward sentimentality, and her three major works are all old-fashioned "romantic" novels. Nevertheless, they are mature studies of human relationships and of suffering and growth. These novels, with the best of her work for young people, should secure for her a lasting, if modest, literary reputation.

WORKS: *Six Plays* (1922). *The Pointed People: Verses & Silhouettes* (1924). *An Alphabet for Boys and Girls* (1926). *Eliza and the Elves* (1926). *Taxis and Toadstools: Verses and Decorations* (1926). *A Little Book of Days* (1927). *The Magic Pawnshop: A New Year's Eve Fantasy* (1927). *The Cross-Stitch Heart, and Other One-Act Plays* (1928). *Little Dog Toby* (1928). *Polly Patchwork* (1928). *The White Cat and Other Old French Fairy Tales* by Mme. d'Aulnoy (arranged by Field, 1928). *American Folk and Fairy Tales* (edited by Field, 1929). *Hitty: Her First Hundred Years* (1929). *Pocket-Handkerchief Park* (1929). *A Circus Garland* (1930). *Patchwork Plays* (1930). *Points East: Narratives of New England* (1930). *Calico Bush* (1931). *The Yellow Shop* (1931). *The Bird Began to Sing* (1932). *Hepatica Hawks* (1932). *Fortune's Caravan* by L. Jean-Javal (adapted by Field, 1933). *Just across the Street* (1933). *Branches Green* (1934). *God's Pocket: The Story of Captain Samuel Hadlock, Junior, of Cranberry Isles, Maine* (1934). *Susanna B. and William C.* (1934). *People from Dickens: A Presentation of Leading Characters from the*

Books of Charles Dickens (1935). *Time out of Mind* (1935; film version, 1947). *Fear Is the Thorn* (1936). *To See Ourselves* (with A. Pederson, 1937). *All This, and Heaven Too* (1938; film version, 1940). *All through the Night* (1940). *Ave Maria: An Interpretation from Walt Disney's "Fantasia," Inspired by the Music of Franz Schubert* (1940). *Christmas Time* (1941). *And Now Tomorrow* (1942; film version, 1944). *Prayer for a Child* (1944). *Christmas in London* (1946). *Poems* (1957). *The Rachel Field Story Book* (1958).

BIBLIOGRAPHY: For articles in reference works, see: *CB* (May 1942). *Junior Book of Authors*, Eds. S. J. Kunitz and H. Haycraft (1951). *NAW* (article by C. Meigs). *Newbery Medal Books, 1922–1955*, Eds. B. M. Miller and E. W. Field (1955). *20thCA. 20thCAS.*

Other references: *NYHTB* (31 May 1942). *NYTBR* (13 Nov. 1932; 7 April 1935; 30 Oct. 1938; 31 May 1942). *SatR* (15 Nov. 1930; 22 Oct. 1938).

MARY JEAN DeMARR

Martha Finley

B. 26 April 1821, Chillicothe, Ohio; d. 30 Jan. 1909, Elkton, Maryland
Wrote under: Martha Farquharson, Martha Finley
D. of James Brown and Maria Theresa Brown Finley

Both of F.'s parents, first cousins of Scotch-Irish descent, died before she was twenty-five. F. supported herself by teaching and writing. Beginning in 1856, F. published more than twenty Sunday-school books under the name of Martha Farquharson for the Presbyterian Board of Publication in Philadelphia. (Farquharson is Gaelic for Finley.)

Popular success and financial security came with *Elsie Dinsmore* (1867). The tremendous popularity of this book, both in America and in England, led F. to write a series of juvenile novels exploring the life of her heroine from childhood to old age. In twenty-eight volumes, Elsie captured the religious and feminine devotion of the 19th-c. reading public. By 1876, F. was able to buy her own home in Elkton, Maryland, where she lived out her eighty years comfortably. The Elsie books alone earned her a quarter of a million dollars.

None of F.'s other works can compare in importance with the Elsie Dinsmore series, which has challenged psychologists and literary historians to define its formula of success. Despite what critics have seen as F.'s "amateurish craftsmanship, superficial moralizing, and lame scholarship," despite even the character of the heroine who, in the eyes of one critic, is "a nauseous little prig," Elsie Dinsmore captured the attention of more than twenty-five million readers.

Some of the elements that attracted young readers to the Elsie books are easy to explain: This fairy-tale heroine is a blonde heiress, unjustly mistreated by the relatives who take her in while her father is in Europe and after her beautiful mother has died. Uncompromisingly moral, unfailingly sweet, Elsie reminds us of Cinderella and Snow White. The fundamentalist religious values that emerge in her meditations and the Biblical quotations render the fairy tale acceptable to the Christian society of 19th-c. America.

With Elsie's southern heritage, F. also provided a topical attraction. What could be more glamorous to her predominantly northern audience immediately after the Civil War than the echo of a lost world—the world of plantations and delicate southern ladies such as Elsie's mother had been, the world of black mammies such as "poor old Aunt Chloe," with her heavy dialect and unswerving devotion to young Elsie? In fact, Ruth Suckow goes so far as to suggest that when Elsie saves her southern father, she is really saving the whole South and committing the rebels to the fundamentalist religious values of her creator, F. herself.

The father-daughter theme which permeates the Elsie books has been seen as psychologically excessive. Elsie worships her father, and even though she does marry (a friend of her father's who is himself much older than she), after her husband's death she is once again with her devoted parent. Some have seen this theme as reinforcing the "father knows best" attitude prevalent in Victorian society, but in fact, Elsie gains power over the most powerful person in her life, her own father, by her religious devotion.

One might argue, as Suckow does, that Elsie represents the truth that "a woman craves a master," yet within the religious framework Elsie Dinsmore controls the lives of all around her. The 19th-c. woman could hardly hope to achieve more than Elsie held out to her: beauty, riches, the love of her father, a husband, and children. Best of all, she exemplified victory after victory over the oppressors of the world, even over that all powerful demigod, her father. Only God was more powerful than Elsie Dinsmore—and He was on her side.

WORKS: *Cassella; or, The Children of the Valleys* (1867). *Elsie Dinsmore* (1868). *Elsie's Holidays* (1869). *An Old Fashioned Boy* (1870). *Wanted: A Pedigree* (1870). *Elsie's Girlhood* (1872). *Our Fred; or, Seminary Life at Thurston* (1874). *Elsie's Womanhood* (1875). *Elsie's Motherhood* (1876). *Elsie's Children* (1877). *Mildred Keith* (1878). *Signing the Contract and What it Cost* (1878). *Mildred at Roselands* (1879). *Elsie's Widowhood* (1880). *The Thorn in the Nest* (1880). *Mildred and Elsie* (1881). *Grandmother Elsie* (1882). *Mildred's Married Life* (1882). *Elsie's New Relations* (1883). *Elsie at Nantucket* (1884). *Mildred at Home* (1884). *The Two Elsies* (1885). *Elsie's Kith and Kin* (1886). *Mildred's Boys and Girls* (1886). *Elsie's Friends at Woodburn* (1887). *Christmas with Grandma Elsie* (1888). *Elsie and the Raymonds* (1889). *Elsie Yachting with the Raymonds* (1890). *Elsie's Vacation* (1891). *Elsie at Viamede* (1892). *Elsie at Ion* (1893). *The Tragedy of Wild River Valley* (1893). *Elsie at the World's Fair* (1894). *Elsie's Journey on Inland Waters* (1894). *Mildred's New Daughter* (1894). *Elsie at Home* (1897). *Elsie on the Hudson* (1898). *Twiddledetwit: A Fairy Tale* (1898). *Elsie in the South* (1899). *Elsie's Young Folks* (1900). *Elsie's Winter Trip* (1902). *Elsie and Her Loved Ones* (1903). *Elsie and Her Namesakes* (1905).

BIBLIOGRAPHY: Brown, J. E., "The Saga of Elsie Dinsmore," *University of Buffalo Studies* (1945). Ely, W. A., *The Finleys of Bucks* (1902). Suckow, R., "Elsie Dinsmore: A Study of Perfection, or How Fundamentalism Came to Dixie," *Bookman* (Oct. 1927).

For articles in reference works, see: *AA. American Authors*, M. L. Rutherford (1894). *AW. DAB*, III, 2. *Indiana Authors and Their Books, 1816–1916*, Ed. R. E. Banta (1949). *NAW* (article by C. T. Kindilien). *NCAB*, 11. *Ohio Authors and Their Books*, Ed. W. Coyle (article by J. Blanck, 1962).

Other references: Baltimore *Sun* (31 Jan. 1909). *NY* (14 March 1936).

THELMA J. SHINN

Dorothea Frances Canfield Fisher

B. *17 Feb. 1879, Lawrence, Kansas; d. 9 Nov. 1958, Arlington, Vermont*
Wrote under: Dorothy Canfield, Dorothy Canfield Fisher
D. of James Hulme and Flavia Camp Canfield; m. James Redwood Fisher, 1907

After extensive formal education (Ph.B., Ohio State; Ph.D., Columbia; graduate work, Sorbonne), F. and her husband traveled widely, eventually settling in Vermont, home of F.'s ancestors. During World War I, F. did relief work in France, and she remained active in public life throughout her career, serving as secretary of New York's Horace Mann School, as the first woman on the Vermont Board of Education, and on the editorial board of the Book-of-the-Month Club (1926–51).

F.'s interest in education and her love of the U.S. and of Vermont are steadily reflected in her works, which include textbooks, commentaries on education (*A Montessori Mother*, 1912; *The Montessori Manual*, 1913), patriotic reflections (*American Portraits*, 1946; *Our Independence and the Constitution*, 1950), translations (Papini's *Life of Christ*, 1923; Tilgher's *Work*, 1930), Vermont, poetry (*Another Night for America*, 1942), and fiction.

Perhaps F.'s most lastingly popular work, *Understood Betsy* (1917), is the story of a fearful, sickly little girl who, through a change of guardians and environments, becomes an independent, capable child. Written in a pleasant, conversational tone, the book codifies some of F.'s major ideas: the importance of early training, the value of work, the necessity for self-confidence, and the virtues—as she perceived them—of the American heritage.

These ideas, as well as attacks on big business and materialism, are central to *The Bent Twig* (1915), the story of Sylvia and Judith Marshall. Tested sorely, the sisters grow from their experiences, primarily through an awareness of their mother's dictum that if life is to be good, both joys and sorrows must be accepted. In an episode about a mulatto family passing for white, F. makes a plea for racial understanding without glossing over the biases and limitations of the period.

Seasoned Timber (1939) sets F.'s attack on anti-Semitism within the narrative frame of Timothy Hulme's romance in middle age. The relationship between Timothy and his Aunt Lavinia illustrates F.'s realism. Both characters are as capable of self-delusion as they are of self-sacrifice. Flashbacks based upon oral tradition vivify the Vermont setting.

Marriages in transition are a frequent plot device. *The Brimming Cup* (1921) compares and contrasts the marital relationships of Neale and Marise Crittenden and of Gene and Nelly Powers. Both women are mothers, both are clearly at the hub of their families, and both are tempted by attractive, sensual, single men. While the resolution of the Powers' difficulty is melodramatic, Marise's decision that sexual union is valid only when it nourishes personal growth is a convincing presentation of a basic F. theme. Another theme, the importance of woodland reclamation, appears here also, and regional customs are well drawn.

A woman of extraordinary energy, F. was one of the most popular writers of her day and is considered particularly adroit at exploring the drama of everyday life, portraying the inner growth of thoughtful, sensitive characters, and employing skillful variations of the interior monologue.

WORKS: Emile Augier, Playwright-Moralist-Poet (1899). *Corneille and Racine in England* (1904). *Elementary Composition* (with G. B. Carpenter, 1906). *Gunhild: A Norwegian American Episode* (1907). *The Secret of Serenity* (1908). *A Montessori Mother* (1912). *The Squirrel Cage* (1912). *The Montessori Manual* (1913). *Mothers and Children* (1914). *The Bent Twig* (1915). *Hillsboro People* (1915). *A Peep into the Educational Future* (1915). *Fellow Captains* (with S. N. Cleghorn, 1916). *The Real Motive* (1916). *Self-Reliance* (1916). *Understood Betsy* (1917; dramatized by S. N. Cleghorn, 1934). *Home Fires in France* (1918). *The Day of Glory* (1919). *The Brimming Cup* (1921). *Rough-Hewn* (1922). *What Grandmother Did Not Know* (1922). *The French School at Middlebury* (1923). *Life of Christ* by G. Papini (translated by Fisher, 1923). *Raw Material* (1923). *The Home-Maker* (1924; film version, 1925). *Made-to-Order Stories* (1925). *Her Son's Wife* (1926). *Why Stop Learning?* (1927). *The Deepening Stream* (1930). *Learn or Perish* (1930). *Work* by A. Tilgher (translated by Fisher, 1930). *Basque People* (1931). *Our Children: A Handbook for Parents* (edited by Fisher, with S. M. Gruenberg, 1932). *Vermont Summer Homes* (1932). *Bonfire* (1933). *Moral Pushing and Pulling* (1933). *Tourists Accommodated* (1934). *Fables for Parents* (1937). *On a Rainy Day* (with S. F. Scott, 1938). *The Election on Academy Hill* (1939). *Seasoned Timber* (1939). *A Family Talks about War* (1940). *Liberty and Union* (with S. N. Cleghorn, 1940). *Nothing Ever Happens and How It Does* (with S. N. Cleghorn, 1940). *In the City, and In the City and on the Farm* (with E. K. Crabtree and L. C. Walker, 1940). *My First Book* (with E. K. Crabtree and L. C. Walker, 1940). *Runaway Toys* (with E. K. Crabtree and L. C. Walker, 1940). *Tell Me a Story* (1940). *To School and Home Again* (with E. K. Crabtree and L. C. Walker, 1940). *Under the Roof* (with E. K. Crabtree and L. C. Walker, 1941). *Under the Sea* (with E. K. Crabtree and L. C. Walker, 1941). *Another Night for America* (1942). *Our Young Folks* (1943). *American Portraits* (1946). *Book-Clubs* (1947). *Highroads and Byroads* (with E. K. Crabtree and L. C. Walker, 1948). *Four-Square* (1949). *Something Old, Something New* (1949). *Our Independence and the Constitution* (1950). *Paul Revere and the Minute Men* (1950). *A Fair World for All* (1952). *Vermont Tradition* (1953). *Dorothy Canfield Fisher on Vermont* (1955). *A Harvest of Stories* (1956). *Memories of Arlington, Vermont* (1957). *And Long Remember* (1959). *Report on Old Age* (n.d.).

BIBLIOGRAPHY: McCallister, L., "D. C. F.: A Critical Study" (Diss., Case Western Reserve Univ., 1969). Yates, E., *Pebble in a Pool* (1958).

For articles in reference works, see: *NCAB*, 44. *20thCA*. *20thCAS*.

Other references: *Educational Forum* (Nov. 1950). *SatR* (11 Oct. 1930; 29 Nov. 1958).

JANE S. BAKERMAN

Sarah Symmes Fiske

B. 1652, Charleston, Massachusetts; d. 2 Dec. 1692, Braintree, Massachusetts
D. of William Symmes; m. Moses Fiske, 1671

F. was the granddaughter of the noted minister Zachariah Symmes and the daughter of a justice of the peace for the county of Middlesex. Her mother, whose name is unknown, died when she was very young. Her husband was ordained minister of the Braintree (now Quincy), Massachusetts, congregation. He had a profitable ministry, which included a house and six acres, as well as a substantial yearly income. F. and her husband had fourteen children, which probably contributed to her early death.

F.'s only published work is her spiritual autobiography, a document which she prepared for admission to church membership. *A Confession of Faith; or, A Summary of Divinity* (1704) was written in 1677, when F. was twenty-five years old. The manuscript circulated among her acquaintances for many years after her death, until it was printed. Such posthumous publication was common for works by early American women writers.

Whereas most spiritual autobiographies of the 17th c. express the inner turmoil of the writer in the struggle for salvation, F.'s confession is notable for its impersonal tone and religious erudition. Its highly structured form evidences her familiarity with Ramist logic, the system of reasoning used by the New England Puritans in their theological discourses.

The form and content which F. chose for her confession reflect intense religious study. Each topic she discusses is broken into subtopics or subsets for definition and analysis; then each subset is further analyzed. F.'s topics include the truth of the Bible, God's creation of the natural world, the Fall and its consequences, sin and death, grace and predestination, and the nature of Christ. She also discusses the organization of the church and the significance of the sacraments. She concludes with a brief but striking apocalyptic vision. Puritan historiography—that is, history viewed as God's redemptive scheme—provides the organizing principle for her beliefs, as she discusses events from the beginning of time to the end of the world.

F.'s work is not outstanding for its originality of thought or style.

But the purpose of the document—admission to church membership—precluded creativity. The posthumous publication of her theological discussion and review is important because it indicates an early recognition of women's ability to contribute to religious subjects in an intellectual and educative manner.

WORKS: *A Confession of Faith; or, A Summary of Divinity, Drawn Up, By a Young Gentlewoman* (1704).

BIBLIOGRAPHY: Pierce, F. C., *Fiske and Fisk Family* (1896). Vinton, J. A., *The Symmes Memorial* (1873).

JACQUELINE HORNSTEIN

Janet Flanner

B. 13 March 1892, Indianapolis, Indiana; d. 7 Nov. 1978, New York City
Wrote under: Janet Flanner, Genêt
D. of Francis and Mary-Ellen Hockett Flanner

Born to Quaker parents, F. attended preparatory school in Tudor Hall, Indianapolis, spent a year in Germany with her parents, then entered the University of Chicago in 1912. After being expelled from the university as a "rebellious influence" in the dormitory, she returned to Indianapolis (1916–17) and then went on to New York City, becoming, in her own words, "the first cinema critic ever invented."

A trip to Greece, Crete, Constantinople, and Vienna ended with her settling down in Paris in 1922. Harold Ross, a former New York acquaintance, asked her to write a small "Paris Letter" for a newly conceived magazine called *The New Yorker*. For fourteen years F. wrote all of *The New Yorker*'s Paris letters, and in the 1930s, all of its London letters, under the pseudonym of "Genêt."

When F. returned to the U.S. in 1939, she continued writing her profiles and sketches for *The New Yorker*. After the fall of France, her articles became more overtly political; she also began speaking and writing extensively on France and French culture and politics. She now wrote for *The New Yorker* a more ambitious series (under her own name) on conditions in unoccupied France, on the "bitter civil war of words" between the generations of the two world wars, and on the revival of the Church in the wake of the poverty and deprivation suffered by postwar France.

F.'s books include a novel, *The Cubical City* (1926), which she describes as "really a character sketch and not a novel at all." Three volumes—*An American in Paris* (1940), *Paris Journal, 1944–65* (1966), *Paris Journal, 1965–71* (1971)—comprise the collected *New Yorker* "Paris Letters" and represent, in many ways, the best of F.'s achievement. She invented the formula for her Paris letters: a mixture of incisive epigram, personal and political profiles, and news, mixed with critical reviews of cinema, theater, opera, and gallery openings.

Always it is the characteristic blend of the personal and the political, the temper of the times and the mood of the streets, that marks her writing. The ripening of the mushrooms called *les trompettes de la mort* is detailed no less meticulously than the rise and decline of General de Gaulle's political fortunes. Details become significant in a way that mere reportage is not. Current fashions in the streets and shops, vegetables in the market, holiday celebrations, and even a run of good weather signal, as stock-market reports could not do, France's economic recovery from the war. And the death of Colette, a nationally loved figure, is in F.'s hands more than the occasion for reporting the funeral of a noted author; it is, quite literally, the end of an era in literary and social history. *Paris Journal* exemplifies, at its best, the blend of memoir and reportage, as well as the keen sense of irony, that F. had by then perfected.

WORKS: *The Cubical City* (1926). *Chéri* by Collete (translated by Flanner, 1929). *Maeterlinck and I* by G. Leblanc (translated by Flanner, 1932). *Souvenirs; My Life with Maeterlinck* by G. Leblanc (translated by Flanner, 1932). *An American in Paris: Profile of an Interlude between Two Wars* (1940). *Petain: The Old Man of France* (1944). *Men and Monuments* (1957). *Paris Journal, 1944–65* (Ed. W. Shawn, 1966). *Paris Journal, 1965–71* (Ed. W. Shawn, 1971). *Paris Was Yesterday, 1925–1939* (Ed. I. Drutman, 1972). *London Was Yesterday, 1934–1939* (Ed. I. Drutman, 1975). *Janet Flanner's World: Uncollected Writings, 1932–1975* (Ed. I. Drutman, 1979).

BIBLIOGRAPHY: For articles in reference works, see: *CB* (May 1943). *Indiana Authors and Their Books, 1816–1916,* Ed. R. E. Banta (1949). *WA.*

Other references: *Lost Generation Journal* (Winter 1976). New York *Post* (3 Oct. 1941). New York *World Telegram* (21 Jan. 1941). *Time* (22 April 1940; 9 Nov. 1942).

VALERIE CARNES

Anne Crawford Flexner

B. 27 June 1874, Georgetown, Kentucky; d. 11 Jan. 1955, New York City
D. of Louis G. and Susan Farnum Crawford; m. Abraham Flexner, 1898

After her graduation from Vassar College in 1895, F. supported herself by tutoring for two years in Louisville, Kentucky, until she had saved enough money to go to New York City. There, she attended the theater regulary and began writing plays. After a two-year engagement, she married Flexner, a prominent educator. In his 1940 autobiography, he wrote of their union: "We agreed at the outset of our married life that her interest and work were as sacred as mine; and for over forty years we have tried to respect each other's individuality and that of our two daughters." Encouraged by F., her younger daughter Eleanor Flexner also became a writer and published books on American drama and the woman-suffrage movement in America.

In 1901, Harrison Grey Fiske opened his Manhattan Theater with F.'s first professionally produced play, *Miranda of the Balcony*, which featured Minnie Maddern Fiske in the title role. The *New York Times* review stated that "Mrs. Flexner has written a strong emotional drama of modern style and the audience of last night was quick to recognize its value."

That success enabled F. to obtain the rights to dramatize Alice Hegan Rice's *Mrs. Wiggs of the Cabbage Patch* in 1904. F. took a number of liberties with the original plot in order to sustain a narrative line throughout the three-act play structure, but she preserved all the flavor of the novel in her sprightly, humorous dialogue and characterizations. It became F.'s most frequently performed play.

Aged 26, F.'s last play, was produced in 1936. In the seventeen years since her latest produced play, F. had traveled extensively in Europe with her husband. Her abiding interest in British literature is reflected in this interpretation of the romance of John Keats and Fanny Brawne. The action spans the year between the publication of Keats's *Endymion* and his departure for Italy, where he was to die six months later at age twenty-six. There is an artificial quality to the opening scene in which Keats, Byron, Shelley, Gifford, Lockhart, and Fanny's mother are all brought into the reception room of Keats's publisher. The audience is won over in subsequent scenes, however, by F.'s deft characterization, and by dialogue in which even the incorporation of familiar lines from Keats's poetry is made to sound natural. F. departed from the traditional view of Fanny Brawne by treating her as sensitive and sincere in her love for Keats, even to the point that she spends the night with him on the eve of their separation. The sympathetic interpretation of her character was vindicated by the publication a few months later of Fanny Brawne's letters to Keats's sister.

F.'s plays were audience-pleasers and might be summed up, in the words of one reviewer, as "crisp, clean, wholesome, and refreshing fun." Seven of F.'s plays were produced in New York over a thirty-five-year period. They reveal a variety of interests and a better-than-average talent as a dramatist for the pre-World War I period.

WORKS: *A Man's Woman* (1899). *Miranda of the Balcony* (1901). *Mrs. Wiggs of the Cabbage Patch* (dramatization of the novel by A. H. Rice, 1903). *A Lucky Star* (dramatization of the novel, *The Motor Chaperone*, by C. N. and A. N. Williams, 1909). *The Marriage Game* (1913). *Wanted—An Alibi* (1917). *The Blue Pearl* (1918). *All Soul's Eve* (1920). *Aged 26* (1936).

BIBLIOGRAPHY: Flexner, A., *I Remember: An Autobiography* (1940).
Other references: *Nation* (2 Jan. 1937). *Theatre Arts Monthly* (Feb. 1937; June 1937).

FELICIA HARDISON LONDRÉ

Elizabeth Gurley Flynn

B. 7 Aug. 1890, Concord, New Hampshire; d. 5 Sept. 1964, Moscow, USSR
D. of Thomas and Elizabeth Gurley Flynn; m. Jack Archibald Jones, 1908

The daughter of first-generation Irish immigrants, F. was raised in an atmosphere of concern for social and political issues. Her parents were both members of the Socialist Party, and her mother was a strong women's rights advocate. When the family moved to the South Bronx, New York, in 1900, F. was introduced to city poverty and to radical political activity. At twelve she won the prize in a Socialist Party debate, and at sixteen gave her first public speech, "What Socialism Will Do for Women," at the Harlem Socialist Club. Later that year she was arrested in New York City (the first of many arrests) for speaking without a public permit.

In 1906, F. joined the Industrial Workers of the World (I.W.W.) and a year later quit school to travel throughout the U.S. as one of the I.W.W.'s most effective speakers and organizers. F. had a son in 1910, and in that same year she separated from her husband (with formal divorce notice in 1920) because she was not prepared to give up her political activity to settle into a more limited domestic life. Both her mother and her sister Kathie provided an important home base for F. and her son after the separation.

During World War I and in the postwar years, as government arrests of radical political leadership increased, F. was the moving force in several labor defense leagues. She became seriously ill in 1927 and for about ten years lived in semiretirement with a friend in Portland, Oregon. Against the advice of her doctor, she returned to the East Coast in 1936, joined the Communist Party of the U.S., became a columnist for the *Daily Worker* in 1937, and in 1938 was elected to the party's national committee. In 1952, she was arrested for subversive activities under the Smith Act and served from January 1955 to May 1957 at the women's prison in Alderson, West Virginia. Upon her release she returned to party activity and was elected national chair in 1959, a post she held until her death while on a visit to the USSR.

All of F.'s writing relates directly to her political activism and focuses on the rights and problems of workers, on the status and corresponding activities of working women, and on civil liberties in general. Underlying all these works is the attempt to acquaint future generations with the historical legacy of the workers' struggle in the U.S. and with the role of working-class leadership in this struggle. Referring to a speech made to the party in 1945, F. noted that it had been "partly biographical, partly confessional, and partly an evaluation of our weaknesses." The perspective expressed in this statement—combined with a continued advocacy of working-class rights and a belief in socialism as the solution to economic, social, and political problems—characterizes all of her writing. F.'s strength as a writer rested on her ability to present ideas with clarity, simplicity, and personal fervor.

In addition to numerous pamphlets, journal and newspaper articles (in *Political Affairs* and *Solidarity*, for example), and regular columns in the *Daily Worker* and *Sunday Worker* from 1937 to 1964, F. also wrote two major works that are primarily autobiographical. *I Speak My Own Piece* (1955, reprinted in 1973 as *The Rebel Girl*, incorporating F.'s own editorial comments) describes her life, her contemporaries, and the events of radical working-class history from 1906 to 1926, using amusing and pertinent anecdotal material. At times the events and people are idealized, in keeping with her purpose to insure that the heroic struggle of those early days would not be lost to history. At the time of her death F. had completed only the notes and outlines for the sequel to this volume, to cover what she called her "second life."

The Alderson Story (1963) details the experiences of F.'s 1952 trial and the following period of imprisonment. It is of more than autobiographical significance because F. tries to record, in a series of prison poems, the voices and emotions of other women with whom she associated in the prison. The book thus becomes a document on women's prison experience in addition to a chapter in her life.

F.'s associates and friends considered her a "great political leader and a great human being." Her ability to express complex issues in simple, unassuming, yet convincing language made her one of the most effective popular leaders of her time. Her autobiographical and political writings are among the best sources available for the history of women's involvement in radical U.S. politics.

WORKS: *Women in the War* (1942). *Women Have a Date with Destiny* (1944). *Women's Place in the Fight for a Better World* (1947). *The Twelve and You* (1948). *The Plot to Gag America* (1950). *Communists and the People* (1953). *I Speak My Own Piece: Autobiography of "The Rebel Girl"* (1955; reprinted as *The Rebel Girl*, 1973). *Horizons of the Future for a Socialist America* (1959). *Freedom Begins at Home* (1961). *The Alderson Story: My Life As a Political Prisoner* (1963). *The McCarran Act: Fact and Fancy* (1963).

The largest collection of Elizabeth Gurley Flynn's writings and personal records is located at the American Institute for Marxist Studies, New York City.

BIBLIOGRAPHY: Dixler, E. J., "The Woman Question: Women and the American Communist Party, 1929–41" (Ph.D. diss., Yale Univ., 1974). Maupin, J., *Labor Heroines: Ten Women Who Led the Struggle* (1974). Wertheimer, B. M., *We Were There: The Story of Working Women in America* (1977).

Other references: *Nation* (17 Feb. 1926). *Political Affairs* (Oct. 1964; Nov. 1964). *Radical America* (Jan.-Feb. 1975).

JANE SLAUGHTER

Eliza Lee Cabot Follen

B. 15 Aug. 1787, Boston, Massachusetts; d. 26 Jan. 1860, Brookline, Massachusetts
Wrote under: Eliza Lee Follen, Mrs. Follen, Mrs. C. T. C. Follen
D. of Samuel and Sally Barrett Cabot; m. Charles Theodore Christian
Follen, 1828

One of thirteen children, and assured by her family's prominence of a stimulating social and intellectual environment, F. early became a friend and follower of William E. Channing and taught in his Unitarian Sunday school. She married a German political refugee who, from 1830 to 1835, was professor of German literature at Harvard. A son was born in 1830. During the Harvard years the couple became friends of Harriet Martineau and worked actively in the antislavery cause.

Because F. had previously written two works of fiction, edited the *Christian Teachers' Manual*, and composed poems and stories for children, it was natural for her after her husband's death in 1840 to turn to her pen for a livelihood. She edited *Gammer Grethel* (1840), the first American edition of Grimm's fairy tales, and the *Child's Friend*, a juvenile periodical, from 1843 to 1850. In addition to writing a biography of her husband, she composed poetry, plays, and stories for children. Until her death she remained active in the abolition movement, working on committees and writing numerous tracts.

The first and most popular of F.'s stories for children was *The Well-Spent Hour* (1827–28), in which nine-year-old Catherine Nelson learns through benevolence and self-control the meaning of a sermon text: "Let them show their piety at home." Although this didactic tale, suitable for the Sunday-school library, substitutes conversations for action and episodes for plot, its kindly tone and benign view of childhood are winning. *The Birthday* (1832) takes up the history of Catherine just before her fourteenth year, when her father's financial losses force the mother and children to move to a country cottage. The ensuing idyll of family life, which includes stories told during a party, suffers from a contrived plot and the heavy-handed contrast of good and evil so typical of early 19th-c. children's literature.

Simpler in content and more graceful in execution are F.'s short tales, such as *True Stories about Dogs and Cats* (1855), *The Old Garret*

(1855), and *The Pedler of Dust Sticks* (1855), later collected with other tales in the twelve-volume *Twilight Stories* (1858). In *The Old Garret*, where discarded objects—a wig, a musket, a broadsword, a tea kettle—give their biographies, F. adopts the technique, associated with Hans Christian Andersen, of having inanimate objects assume a narrator's role.

Although her children's poetry is now almost forgotten, F. was a pioneer who turned from the harsh, morbid verse characteristic of early 19th-c. American children's poetry to rhymes frankly meant to give more pleasure than instruction. *Little Songs* (1833), reprinted as the final volume of *Twilight Stories*, was intended, she tells us, "to catch something of that good-natured pleasantry and musical nonsense which makes Mother Goose so attractive to children of all ages." Even though the verse in this volume lacks the vigor of traditional nursery rhymes, it is remarkable both for its response to children's tastes and for its gentle vision of childhood.

F.'s adult fiction, *The Skeptic* (1835) and *Sketches of Married Life* (1838), deals ostensibly with marriage. The first work, however, resembles a religious tract both in the account of Alice Grey's efforts to save her husband from the influence of his free-thinking cousin and in F.'s recommendations of Dr. Channing's Unitarian writings. In the second work, a domestic novel, F. creates a heroine who demonstrates, as Helen Papashvily points out, "the marked ability of women in the practical concerns of everyday life."

F.'s *Life of Charles Follen* (1840), for which she traveled to Germany to obtain additional material, is a sympathetic but unsentimental treatment of her husband's life.

A woman of conviction, both in her support of religion and in her opposition to slavery, F. is notable for bringing to American children's literature of the pre-Civil War period a sensitive concern for the feelings and tastes of her young readers.

WORKS: *The Well-Spent Hour* (1827–28). *Selections from the Writings of Fénelon* (edited by Follen, 1829). *Hymns, Songs, and Fables for Children* (1831). *Sequel to "The Well-Spent Hour"; or, The Birthday* (1832). *Words of Truth* (1832). *Little Songs for Little Boys and Girls* (1833). *The Skeptic* (1835). *Sketches of Married Life* (1838). *Hymns and Exercises for the Federal Street Sunday School* (1839). *Nursery Songs* (1839). *Poems* (1839). *Sacred Songs for Sunday Schools, Original and Selected* (1839). *Gammer Grethel; or, German Fairy Tales and Popular Stories* (edited by Follen, 1840). *The Liberty Cap* (1840). *Life of Charles Follen* (1840). *The Works of Charles Follen with a Memoir of His Life* (1841–42). *Made-up Stories* (1855). *The Old Garret* (3 vols., 1855). *The Pedler of Dust Sticks* (1855). *Poems* (1855). *To Mothers in the Free States* (1855). *True Stories about Dogs and Cats* (1855). *Conscience* (1858). *May Morning and New Year's Eve* (1858). *Piccolissima* by A. Montgolfier (translated by Follen, 1858). *Travellers' Stories* (1858). *Twilight Stories* (12 vols., 1858). *What Animals Do and Say* (1858). *Home Dramas for Young People* (compiled by Follen, 1859). *Our Home in the Marsh Land; or, Days of Auld Lang Syne* (1877).

BIBLIOGRAPHY: Meigs, C., *A Critical History of Children's Literature* (1969). Papashvily, H. W., *All the Happy Endings* (1956). Wright, L. H., *American Fiction, 1774–1850* (1969).

For articles in reference works, see: *AA. DAB*, III, 2. *FPA. NAW* (article by E. B. Schlesinger). *NCAB*, 7.

Other references: *ElemEngR* 8 (1931). *NEQ* 38 (1965).

PHYLLIS MOE

Mary Hallock Foote

B. 19 Nov. 1847, Milton, New York; d. 25 June 1938, Hingham, Massachusetts
D. of Nathaniel and Anne Burling Hallock; m. Arthur De Wint Foote, 1876

The youngest child of Quakers, F. was raised on the family farm in the Hudson River valley. After completing her schooling in 1864, she took the step, unusual for a young lady of her era, of enrolling at New York City's Cooper Union to study art. Over the course of three years at Cooper, she prepared herself for a career in black-and-white illustration. Her professional debut came in 1867 with the publication of four of her drawings in A. D. Richardson's *Beyond the Mississippi*.

During the following twenty-five years, F. enjoyed fame as one of the most accomplished of American illustrators. She executed drawings for many of the prominent giftbooks of the period, including Longfellow's *The Skeleton in Armor*, Whittier's *Mabel Martin*, and Hawthorne's *The Scarlet Letter*. Her illustrations were published regularly in *St. Nicholas* and *Century* magazines; "Pictures of the Far West," her most celebrated series, appeared in the latter during 1888–89. By the 1890s, F.'s position as "the dean of women illustrators" was secure, and she was elected to the National Academy of Women Painters and Sculptors.

F.'s success as an illustrator was ultimately eclipsed by her achievements as an author. After her marriage to a civil engineer, she spent much of her life in western mining camps whose picturesque aspects invited literary as well as visual interpretation. Her first attempt at serious prose, "A California Mining Camp," appeared in *Scribner's* in 1878 and highlighted her experiences in New Almaden, California; it was followed by descriptive sketches of other locales where her husband's profession took them. From a stay in Leadville, Colorado, came *The Led-Horse Claim* (1883), F.'s first novel and a modest bestseller.

Between 1883 and 1925, F. published eleven more novels and four volumes of short stories; she also wrote an excellent autobiography and numerous uncollected tales and sketches. Most of her fiction derived from material rooted deeply in her own experience: in particular, the tension between the urbane East and the boisterous West—between the genteel security of the East Coast and the pioneer existence beyond the Rockies—informed her writing. F., approaching her material more sympathetically as her appreciation for the West grew, made the frontier a subject of realistic interest and of romance. As Owen Wister observed, hers was the first voice "lifted to honor the cattle country and not to libel it."

F.'s finest writing came after 1895, once she had retired from professional illustration and had settled comfortably with her husband and three children in Grass Valley, California. Especially noteworthy is *The Desert and the Sown* (1902), a novel inspired in part from F.'s experiences in Idaho between 1884 and 1894. Although the plot covers only the three years between the arrival of Emily Bogardus in Idaho and the death of her estranged husband Adam in New York, the tale spans the family fortunes for three generations. A biblical framework reinforces the story's symbolic reconciliation of East and West, past and present. Two other significant works by F. are *Edith Bonham* (1917) and *The Ground-Swell* (1919). Both are poignant tributes to the past—the former dedicated to the memory of F.'s best friend, Helena Gilder, and the latter designed as a tribute to Agnes Foote, the author's youngest daughter, who died in 1904.

After 1919 F. ceased to publish, although during the 1920s she undertook a project that served as the capstone to her career. Written when she was nearing eighty and had not published for decades, F.'s *Reminiscences* (1972) is a truly distinguished autobiography of interest to historians as well as to literary scholars. From the quiet milldams of Milton to the noisy mining stamps of Leadville, from the frustration and disappointments of Idaho to the comforts and acclaim of the Grass Valley years, this personal account of a genteel Quaker "irretrievably married into the West" makes compelling reading. In 1932 F. returned with

Arthur to the East, living in Hingham, Massachusetts, until her death six years later.

To her 20th-c. successors F. bequeathed a legacy of western fiction which, at its best, provides fresh perspectives, substitutes sensitivity for sentimentality, and strives for fidelity. At a time when the West was still subject to humorous exploitation, F. was the first to achieve the stance of a discerning literary observer, while as a gifted illustrator she also contributed memorable interpretations of the frontier.

WORKS: *The Led-Horse Claim: A Romance of a Mining Camp* (1883). *John Bodewin's Testimony* (1886). *The Last Assembly Ball and The Fate of a Voice* (1889). *The Chosen Valley* (1892). *Coeur d'Alene* (1894). *In Exile, and Other Stories* (1894). *The Cup of Trembling, and Other Stories* (1895). *The Little Fig-Tree Stories* (1899). *The Prodigal* (1900). *The Desert and the Sown* (1902). *A Touch of Sun, and Other Stories* (1903). *The Royal Americans* (1910). *A Picked Company* (1912). *The Valley Road* (1915). *Edith Bonham* (1917). *The Ground-Swell* (1919). *A Victorian Gentlewoman in the Far West: The Reminiscences of Mary Hallock Foote* (Ed. R. W. Paul, 1972).

BIBLIOGRAPHY: Johnson, L. A., *M. H. F.* (1980). Maguire, J. H., *M. H. F.* (Boise State College Western Writers Series #2, 1972). Stegner, W., *Angle of Repose* (1971). Taft, R., *Artists and Illustrators of the Old West, 1850–1900* (1953).

For articles in reference works, see: *AW. DAB*, III, 2. *NAW* (article by T. Wilkens). *NCAB*, 6.

Other references: *Colorado Magazine* (April 1956). *Idaho Yesterdays* (Summer 1976). *Univ. of Wyoming Publications* (15 July 1956). *WAL* (May 1975).

LEE ANN JOHNSON

Esther Forbes

B. 28 June 1891, Westborough, Massachusetts; d. 12 Aug. 1967, Worcester, Massachusetts
D. of William Trowbridge and Harriette Merrifield Forbes; m. Albert Learned Hoskins, 1926

F. was the youngest of five children; her father was a judge, her mother a historian. She graduated from Bradford Academy in 1912 and studied at the University of Wisconsin (1916–18) before serving as a farmhand in Virginia in response to the war effort. Returning to New England, she became an editor from 1920 until her marriage.

During her marriage, F. traveled extensively abroad and continued to write. At the time of her divorce in 1933, she had already made a literary reputation as a historical novelist with *O Genteel Lady!* (1926) and *A Mirror for Witches* (1928). The height of her fame came in the 1940s when she won first the Pulitzer Prize in History for *Paul Revere and the World He Lived In* (1942) and then the Newbery Medal for *Johnny Tremain: A Novel for Young and Old* (1943). F. was the first woman member of the American Antiquarian Society and received seven honorary degrees.

F.'s earliest works are brief and focused upon the development of their heroines, who are of various types and fates. Several of these early novels explore the expression of female sexuality and its psychological connection with the attraction to the demonic in a repressive society that is part of, or heir to, the Puritan tradition. Lanice Bardeen in *O Genteel Lady!* is a sensual and intellectual Boston editor and writer of the late 19th c. who gives up both her passion for a Lawrence-of-Arabia type and for writing in order to marry a staid Harvard professor. In *A Mirror for Witches*, set in the late 17th c., Doll Bilby has a love affair with the "devil" and dies in childbirth, an accused witch, in a Salem prison. The novel is purportedly written by an 18th-c. apologist for the Salem witchcraft trials.

Johnny Tremain is the briefer, focused, and fictionalized outgrowth of *Paul Revere and the World He Lived In*, on which F. and her mother collaborated. Both the life of the real silversmith and the now-famous story of the silversmith's apprentice who adjusts to the handicap of a maimed hand and participates in the Boston revolutionary movement, display F.'s intense interest in the part that individuals, significant or insignificant, play in historical events. Both books clearly owe their immediate inspiration to F.'s concern with the meaning and nature of human freedom in the context of World War II.

Rainbow in the Road (1954), made into a musical in 1969, is F.'s last published work. It is a lyric lament for the unspoiled New England countryside before the coming of the railroad and for the ephemeral popular arts practiced by itinerant artists, "limners" (portrait painters), like its hero, Jude Rebough, and his ballad-making friend, Mr. Sharp. Although she was working on a study of witchcraft at the time of her death, *Rainbow in the Road* seems an appropriate swan song for F. herself, whose own choice of a rather popular art form, the historical novel, helped her to win immediate but perhaps transient recognition.

Even in her nonfiction, F.'s sole analytical thrust is psychological and somewhat Freudian. F. considers personalities and social relationships among personalities, rather than broader social, political, or economic issues. She saves her sharp sense of irony, expressed often in wry comments, for individual foibles and generally accepts learned but conventional interpretations of events. Perhaps only in *A Mirror for Witches*, with its craftily delineated narrator, and in *Johnny Tremain*, where the problems of an adolescent and of a new society reflect upon each other, do her talents as a novelist and a historian mesh artistically enough to transcend the limits of her genre. Here her efforts to depict the human universal in a particular period and place will probably earn her longer-lasting aesthetic esteem.

WORKS: *O Genteel Lady!* (1926). *A Mirror for Witches* (1928). *Miss Marvel* (1935). *Paradise* (1937). *The General's Lady* (1938). *Paul Revere and the World He Lived In* (with H. M. Forbes, 1942). *Johnny Tremain: A Novel for Young and Old* (1943). *The Boston Book* (with A. Griffin, 1947). *The Running of the Tide* (1948). *America's Paul Revere* (with L. Ward, 1948). *Rainbow in the Road* (1954; musical version, 1969).

BIBLIOGRAPHY: For articles in reference works, see: *CA*, 25–28 (1971); *Permanent Series* (1975). *Newbery Medal Books 1922-55*, Eds. B. M. Miller and E. W. Field (1955). *Something about the Author*, Ed. A. Commire (1971). *20thCA*. *20thCAS*.

Other references: *LJ* (15 May 1944). *NYT* (13 Aug. 1967).

LOIS R. KUZNETS

Hannah Webster Foster

B. *10 Sept. 1758, Salisbury, Massachusetts; d. 17 April 1840, Montreal, Canada*
Wrote under: A Lady of Massachusetts
D. of Grant and Hannah Wainwright Webster; m. John Foster, 1785

Little is known of either F.'s childhood or education, but the numerous historical and literary allusions in her books suggest that she was well-educated for her time and sex. F. is best known for her novel *The Coquette; or, The History of Eliza Wharton* (1797). After the publication of her second book, *The Boarding School; or, Lessons of a Preceptress to Her Pupils* (1798), F. wrote only short articles for newspapers. Upon her husband's death she moved to Montreal to live with two of her five children, two daughters who also wrote.

The Coquette, which is "founded on fact," was based on the life of Elizabeth Whitman of Hartford, Connecticut, a distant cousin of F.'s husband. It is a seduction novel in epistolary form (obviously much influenced by the novels of Samuel Richardson, such as the epistolary seduction novel, *Clarissa Harlowe*) with the typical strengths and weaknesses of this genre. Incidents are reported several times by different people, a technique that reveals character through a comparison of points of view. Many of the letters seem natural and spontaneous. Others, however, suffer from excessive length, didactic digressions, and an overemphasis on sentiment and sensibility.

From the novel's beginning Eliza emerges as a strong-willed young woman delighting in a newly found freedom from her parents and a dull fiancé. She is convincingly indecisive about her two new suitors, the admirable Mr. Boyer, a clergyman, and Major Sanford, who, she is warned, is " a second Lovelace" (the seducer in *Clarissa*).

Sanford, too, is a convincing and complex character. Seduction to Sanford is a game; he sees Eliza as a coquette and determines to "avenge [his] sex by retaliating the mischiefs she meditates." He writes: "If she will play with a lion, let her beware the paw, I say." Sanford is confident of his powers, but his pride is hurt by her friends' warnings against him and by her attraction to Boyer. These make him even more determined to win Eliza, which he does eventually, even though he has, in the meantime, married for money.

Justice appropriate to the seduction-novel genre is meted out to Eliza and Sanford, accompanied by lengthy confessions and moral lectures. The lessons are taught by the characters themselves, however, and their contrition seems real enough, a fact which makes *The Coquette* one of the better American examples of the genre.

The Coquette went through thirteen editions in its first forty years. *The Boarding School* was not so popular. It is dedicated to "the young ladies of America" and demonstrates how a clergyman's widow, Mrs. Williams, educates young girls to fulfill their future roles as well-bred ladies, wives, and mothers.

WORKS: *The Coquette; or, The History of Eliza Wharton* (1797). *The Boarding School; or, Lessons of a Preceptress to Her Pupils* (1798).

BIBLIOGRAPHY: Brown, H. R., *The Sentimental Novel in America, 1789–1860* (1940). Mott, F. L., *Golden Multitudes* (1947). Osborne, W. S., ed., *The Power of Sympathy and The Coquette* (1970). Petter, H., *The Early American Novel* (1971).

For articles in reference works, see: *AA. DAB*, III, 2. *NAW* (article by H. R. Brown).

Other references: *AL* (Nov. 1932).

ELAINE K. GINSBERG

Rose Franken

B. Dec. 1898, Gainesville, Texas
Wrote under: Rose Franken, Margaret Grant, Franken Meloney
D. of Michael and Hannah Younker Lewin; m. Sigmund Walter Anthony
   Franken, 1915; m. William Brown Meloney V, 1937

F.'s parents were separated when she was a few years old, and her mother took the four children to New York City to live with F.'s grandparents and several aunts, uncles, and cousins in a large house in Harlem. She attended the Ethical Culture School, but, having failed a sewing course, did not obtain a high-school diploma. At sixteen, she married a prominent oral surgeon ten years her senior. Two weeks later, they learned that he was tubercular. Their first year of marriage was spent in a sanitarium.

To take her mind off constant worrying about her husband's health, F. began writing short stories. After the publication of a novel, *Pattern* (1925), her husband suggested that she try playwrighting. Her first dramatic effort, *Fortnight*, was optioned but never produced or published. Her second play, first presented under the title *Hallam Wives* in a summer 1929 production in Greenwich, Connecticut, later became the very successful *Another Language* (1932).

After Sigmund Franken's death in 1933, F. moved with her three sons to California. She collaborated with her second husband on a number of screenplays. After their marriage, they moved to a Connecticut farm. Using the pen name Franken Meloney, they regularly published novels and magazine serials, to which he contributed the plots and she wrote the dialogue.

Another Language is a comedy-drama about the dangerously self-righteous attitudes of a middle-class family dominated by a possessive matriarch who encourages their tasteless and materialistic instincts. When F. brought the same family back to the stage in 1948 with her sixth and last professionally produced play, *The Hallams*, the characters had not changed.

Beginning with her dramatization of *Claudia* (1941), F. directed all of her own plays. Her second husband produced her third Broadway play, *Outrageous Fortune* (1943), and all subsequent ones. That play departed from her established style by raising questions about such social concerns as homosexuality, the treatment of black servants, marital difficulties in middle age, and anti-Semitism. Despite misgivings about F.'s attempt to handle so many themes in one play, some critics believed it to be her best work for the stage.

Her "Claudia" novels, begun in 1939 as a series of stories for *Redbook* magazine, became the basis for a play, a radio series, and two motion pictures, and they were widely published in translation abroad. It was *Claudia* that made F.'s name familiar to the public for two decades. Beginning with the first days of Claudia's marriage at eighteen to David Naughton, the series of novels chronicles, with humor and sentimental appeal, the gradual maturation of a child-wife. Eternally artless, impulsive, and charming, Claudia comes to grips with such problems as hiring servants, testing her sex appeal, becoming a mother, shopping in a posh dress salon, and coping with her own mother's death. Although the Claudia novels rely heavily upon illness, accidents, and death for the emotional upheavals that lead Claudia toward increasing self-awareness, they are essentially the saga of a blissful marriage.

Referring to her twenty-year involvement with Claudia, F. wrote in her autobiography, *When All Is Said and Done* (1963), that "the sheer technical task of remaining within her consciousness became increasingly onerous and demanding." F., however, was able to draw upon her own notably successful marriages. Her particular skill as a novelist and playwright is the ability to inject sparkle into trivial nuances of everyday life, and to unfold a narrative action largely through dialogue.

WORKS: *Pattern* (1925). *Another Language; a Comedy Drama in Three Acts* (1932). *Mr. Dooley, Jr.; a Comedy for Children* (with J. Lewin, 1932). *Twice Born* (1935). *Call Back Love* (with W. B. Meloney, 1937). *Of Great Riches* (1937). *Claudia* (1939; dramatization by Franken, 1941; screenplay by Franken, 1943). *Claudia and David* (1939; screenplay by Franken, 1946). *Strange Victory* (with W. B. Meloney, 1939). *When Doctors Disagree* (with W. B. Meloney, 1940; dramatization by Franken, 1943). *American Bred* (with W. B. Meloney, 1941). *The Book of Claudia* (containing *Claudia* and *Claudia and David*, 1941). *Another Claudia* (1943). *Outrageous Fortune; a Drama in Three Acts* (1943). *Beloved Stranger* (with W. B. Meloney, 1944). *Soldier's Wife; a Comedy in Three Acts* (1944). *Young Claudia* (1946). *The Hallams; a Play in Three Acts* (1947). *The Marriage of Claudia* (1948). *From Claudia to David* (1950). *The Fragile Years* (also published as *Those Fragile Years; a Claudia Novel*, 1952). *Rendezvous* (English title, *The Quiet Heart*, 1954). *Intimate Story* (1955). *The Antic Years* (1958). *The Complete Book of Claudia* (1958). *Return to Claudia* (1960). *When All Is Said and Done; an Autobiography* (1963). *You're Well Out of a Hospital* (1966).

BIBLIOGRAPHY: Mantle, B., *Contemporary American Playwrights* (1938). For articles in reference works, see: *American Novelists of Today*, H. R. Warfel (1951). *CB* (1947). *20thCA. 20thCAS.*
Other references: *NYT* (8 Jan. 1933). *NYTMag* (4 May 1941). *Players Magazine* (Spring 1974).

FELICIA HARDISON LONDRÉ

Mary Eleanor Wilkins Freeman

B. 31 Oct. 1852, Randolph, Massachusetts; d. 15 March 1930, Metuchen, New Jersey
Wrote under: Mary E. Wilkins Freeman, Mary E. Wilkins
D. of Warren E. and Eleanor Lothrop Wilkins; m. Charles Manning Freeman, 1902

F. was an attractive, rather introspective child. In 1867 her father, a builder, moved his family to Brattleboro, Vermont. F. attended the Brattleboro high school; she also attended Mt. Holyoke Seminary and Mrs. Hosford's Glenwood Seminary in West Brattleboro, for one year each. In 1883 she returned alone to Randolph, her mother, father, and only sister all having died. Here she lived with friends, the Wales family. She did not, however, confine herself to Randolph, but visited friends in the U.S. and traveled in Europe. After her marriage, F. settled in Metuchen, New Jersey. In 1921, F. obtained a legal separation from her husband, who had become an alcoholic requiring institutionalization. The year 1926 brought honors to F.: She was awarded the Howells medal for distinction in fiction by the American Academy of Letters, and she was elected to membership in the National Institute of Arts and Letters.

F. established herself as a children's author in the early 1880s. *Decorative Plaques* (1883) collected, in an ornamental format, twelve of her poems from the children's magazine, *Wide Awake*. In 1882, the first adult story she sold won a prize in a contest sponsored by the Boston *Sunday Budget*. "A Shadow Family" has been lost, but F. said later it was "quite passable as an imitation of Charles Dickens." Winning the contest caused her to concentrate on adult fiction, and her stories began to appear frequently in *Harper's Bazar* and *Harper's Weekly*. F.'s capacity for work was enormous, and in the years that followed she became an exceedingly popular author of both adult and juvenile short stories (including some eerie tales of the supernatural), novels, and poetry for children.

Her best stories and novels are about New England people and deal with several themes characteristic of them: stoical endurance in the face of hopeless poverty and adversity, unshakeable pride, and the fierce flame of Calvinistic religion.

A typical short story is "Calla-Lilies and Hannah," in which a girl, shielding her lover, courageously bears the villagers' reprobation for a theft she has not committed. Another is "A Taste of Honey," in which a young woman denies herself everything in the way of comfort and luxury to pay off a mortgage, even losing her fiancé because of the length of time involved.

Of the novels, *Pembroke* (1894) is F.'s greatest achievement, a novel that deserves to be recognized as an American classic. It is densely peopled, with every facet of the New England character in evidence: greed, parsimony, tenacity of purpose, industriousness, sexuality, fanaticism, unselfishness, even heroism. Symbolism is occasionally employed in a way that has reminded critics of Hawthorne's fiction.

An early play, *Giles Corey, Yeoman* (1893), is based on a true incident in the Salem witchcraft trials. Here F. skillfully tells the story of a farmer and his wife who are put to death; she does it so well that the drama, as she wrote it, may be effectively performed, though it has not often been produced on the stage.

As F. wrote more voluminously and her work appeared constantly in magazines, her style changed. Losing its distinctive New England flavor, it became increasingly elaborate, elegant, and, at times, unbearably precious. Although she continued to use New England locales and characters, she began to write also of prosperous suburban life in New Jersey. In addition, she tried to keep in step with fashions in fiction, writing a historical romance set in Virginia (*The Heart's Highway*, 1900), and a labor novel (*The Portion of Labor*, 1901). Both were embarrassing failures.

F.'s significance lies in those of her stories and novels that show New England life deglamorized. She never wrote anything one could call sordid, but her early work conveys the appalling poverty of remote New England farms and villages, the constriction of the lives there, the suffering, the meanness, and the occasional flashes of real nobility. Granville Hicks has said that "her stories made the record of New England more nearly complete."

WORKS: *Decorative Plaques* (1883). *The Adventures of Ann; Stories of Colonial Times* (1886). *A Humble Romance, and Other Stories* (1887). *A New*

England Nun, and Other Stories (1891). *The Pot of Gold, and Other Stories* (1892). *Young Lucretia, and Other Stories* (1892). *Giles Corey, Yeoman* (1893). *Jane Field* (1893). *Pembroke* (1894). *Comfort Pease and Her Gold Ring* (1895). *Madelon* (1896). *Jerome: A Poor Man* (1897). *Once upon a Time, and Other Child-Verses* (1897). *The People of Our Neighborhood* (1898). *Silence, and Other Stories* (1898). *In Colonial Times* (1899). *The Jamesons* (1899). *The Heart's Highway; a Romance of Virginia in the Seventeenth Century* (1900). *The Love of Parson Lord, and Other Stories* (1900). *The Portion of Labor* (1901). *Understudies; Short Stories* (1901). *Six Trees; Short Stories* (1903). *The Wind in the Rose-Bush, and Other Stories of the Supernatural* (1903). *The Givers; Short Stories* (1904). *The Debtor* (1905). *By the Light of the Soul* (1906). *"Doc" Gordon* (1906). *The Shoulders of Atlas* (1908). *The Fair Lavinia, and Others* (1909). *The Winning Lady, and Others* (1909). *The Green Door* (1910). *The Butterfly House* (1912). *The Yates Pride; a Romance* (1912). *The Copy Cat, and Other Stories* (1914). *An Alabaster Box* (with F. M. Kingsley, 1917). *Edgewater People* (1918).

BIBLIOGRAPHY: Foster, E., *M. E. W. F.* (1956). Hamblen, A. A., *The New England Art of M. E. W. F.* (1966). Hicks, G., *The Great Tradition* (1935). Pattee, F. L., *The New American Literature* (1930). Pattee, F. L., *Sidelights on American Literature* (1922). Quinn, A. H., *American Fiction* (1936).

For articles in reference works, see: *DAB*, IV, 1. *NAW* (article by E. Foster). *NCAB*, 9. *20thCA*.

Other references: *Atlantic* (May 1899).

ABIGAIL ANN HAMBLEN

Betty Friedan

B. 4 Feb. 1921, Peoria, Illinois
D. of Harry and Miriam Horowitz Goldstein; m. Carl Friedan, 1947

One of three children of parents who encouraged neither her reading nor her feminism, F. attributed her later awareness of oppression partly to being Jewish. In high school F. founded a literary magazine and graduated as class valedictorian. At Smith College she studied psychology with noted Gestalt psychologist Kurt Koffka and graduated in 1942 summa cum laude. After winning her second research fellowship at the University of California at Berkeley, she realized that to go on would commit her to a doctorate and a career as a psychologist. She gave in to what she called the pressure of the feminine mystique, gave up Berkeley for a nonprofessional job in New York City, and soon married and began raising her three children.

By the mid-1950s F. was deeply dissatisfied with her life. Approaching the resulting crisis thoughtfully, she began to wonder if other women shared her dissatisfaction. Through a questionnaire sent to her Smith College classmates, she discovered that her ailment was widespread and began several years of research which culminated in *The Feminine Mystique* (1963). She analyzed the post–World War II pressures that forced promising young women out of the colleges and into the suburbs to raise children. The book's impact has been widespread. It was excerpted in *McCall's, Saturday Review,* and elsewhere; it sold very well in the hardcover edition and has gone through many printings in paperback. Its central thesis is that those forces supposed to be "the chief enemies of prejudice"—that is, education, sociology, psychology, and the media—have, in effect, conned American women into believing that their entire identity and worth could be derived from being wives and mothers.

After publishing *The Feminine Mystique,* F. began actively to campaign against the feminine mystique in its variety of guises. She founded NOW, the National Organization for Women, in 1966. Attacked since its start by more radical women's groups who felt that it was too middle-class, too hierarchically structured, and too conservative in its aims, NOW became and has remained the largest and most visible feminist organization in the U.S. Since leaving the presidency of NOW in 1970, F. has continued her activism, interspersed with lecturing and teaching at various universities. She wrote a column for *McCall's,* "Betty Friedan's Notebook," and contributed to a wide range of magazines including *Saturday Review, Harper's, New York Times Magazine, Redbook, Ladies' Home Journal,* and *Working Women.*

In 1976, F. published *It Changed My Life: Writings on the Women's Movement.* In a series of essays and open letters, F. assesses the progress of the women's movement and her relationship with it. The book provides a personal as well as a movement history. It points, as well, to what F. sees as a necessary change in the women's liberation movement: it must transcend polarization and become "human liberation."

It is because so many women recognized in F.'s *Feminine Mystique* their own lack of fulfillment as human beings that she is credited with having begun the current women's movement, with having turned the nation's attention to the significance of women's problems. She has urged women to take a risk and attempt to improve the quality of their lives. Hers has been a loud, clear, and important voice, and she has earned her place in the history of the women's movement.

WORKS: *The Feminine Mystique* (1963). *Anatomy of Reading* (Eds. L. L. Hackett and R. Williamson, 1966). *Voices of the New Feminism* (Ed. M. L. Thompson, 1970). *It Changed My Life: Writings on the Women's Movement* (1976).

The papers of Betty Friedan are in the Schlesinger Library of Radcliffe College, Cambridge, Massachusetts.

BIBLIOGRAPHY: Janeway, E., *Man's World, Woman's Place* (1971). Lerner, G., *The Female Experience: An American Documentary* (1977). Ryan, M. P., *Womanhood in America from Colonial Times to the Present* (1975). Sochen, J., *Herstory: A Woman's View of American History* (1974). Sochen, J., *Movers and Shakers: American Women Thinkers and Activists, 1900–1970* (1973).

For articles in reference works, see: *CB* (Nov. 1970).

BILLIE J. WAHLSTROM

Frances Dana Barker Gage

B. *12 Oct. 1808, Marietta, Ohio; d. 10 Nov. 1880, Greenwich, Connecticut.*
Wrote under: Aunt Fanny, F. D. Gage, Frances Gage, Mrs. Frances Dana Gage
D. of Joseph and Elizabeth Dana Barker; m. James L. Gage, 1829

G., whose parents emigrated from New Hampshire to Ohio in 1788, was born on a farm, the fifth daughter and the ninth of ten children. Although her education was limited to that of most rural children in a large, hard-working family, she gained the habit of independence of thought and an interest in reform. Her mother, daughter of an educated New England family, encouraged her to learn as much as she could under the difficult circumstances of frontier life in Ohio; the parents' aid to fugitive slaves underscored their concern with social issues. G. drew from her background a toughness that served her well in life. After her marriage to a lawyer and businessman, she managed to rear eight healthy children while educating herself further, gaining respect as a prolific journalist and writer, and becoming increasingly active in reform.

G.'s concern over slavery extended to the problems of slaves freed during the Civil War. She spent some time during 1862 in a part of South Carolina controlled by the Union; here she worked with freed slaves who needed help in starting new lives. After the war, when she became better known as a journalist, she continued to urge northerners to give aid to the freedmen. Here, as in all her speaking and writing, she drew on her vigorous homely style to make telling points and to make the unfamiliar acceptable. Her impact on audiences was especially dramatic in her appeals for temperance, in which she used case histories to move women to tears and men to new resolutions. Her spontaneous, conversational manner helped her to win her audiences.

These gifts served her well in the women's rights movement. So eloquent was G. at the important Akron Convention (1851), that she unanimously won the election as president of the convention. G.'s reminiscences (in the *National Anti-Slavery Standard*, May 1866) provide the tone and feeling of the dramatic episode in which Sojourner Truth (a former slave, unable to read or write, but a moving speaker) rose to speak at the Akron convention, against the advice of some of the participants. G.'s own language does not lack color as she describes the importance of woman suffrage: she speaks of "war cries," the "advance-guarde," the "rebellion," and in a somewhat less militant tone, "most unwearied actors."

G. also wrote to support her large family. Under the pseudonym of Aunt Fanny (whose real identity was no secret) she wrote letters of advice to women in Amelia Bloomer's *The Lily*, Jane Grey Swisshelm's *The Saturday Visiter*, and other papers, especially feminist ones. Aunt Fanny's words about practical household matters often contained shrewd wit, especially in her reflections on the roles of men and women in daily life. As she counsels her readers on the making of soap, the use of practical clothing, the churning of butter, the efficient use of time, Aunt Fanny amuses herself and them with (often satiric) replies to anti-suffrage male correspondents about female frailty.

For a time G. also served as associate editor of both the Ohio *Cultivator* and *Field Notes*, farmers' weekly papers that disappeared after the Civil War. Later she published several temperance works and, in 1867, a volume of poems—sentimental verse to be sure, but they are accurate descriptions of farm life especially as that life reflects the position of women.

G. stands as one of those active, resourceful 19th-c. women, who—without the formal education of some of her contemporaries, such as Elizabeth Cady Stanton or Susan B. Anthony—succeeded in becoming an influential writer and a force in the women's rights movement. She exerted her influence through work in antislavery, temperance, and women's organizations, but even more through the homely, pithy writing with which she spread her ideas. Her work had perhaps its greatest impact on rural women, with whom she could easily establish rapport because of her similar background.

WORKS: *Christmas Stories* (1849). *The Man in the Well: A Temperance Tale* (1850). *Fanny's Journey* (1866). *Fanny at School* (ca. 1866). *Elsie Magoon; or, The Old Still-House in the Hollow* (1867). *Poems* (1867). *Gertie's Sacrifice; or, Glimpses at Two Lives* (1869). *Steps Upward* (1870).

BIBLIOGRAPHY: Brockett, L. P., and M. C. Vaughn, *Woman's Work in the Civil War* (1867). Hanson, E. R., *Our Woman Workers* (1882).

For articles in reference works, see: *AA. AW. DAB*, IV, 1. *Eminent Women of the Age*, Eds. J. Parton et al. (1869). *HWS*, I, II. *NAW* (article by E. H. Roseboom). *NCAB*, 2. *Ohio Authors and Their Books*, Ed. W. Coyle (1962).

Other references: New York *Tribune* (13 Nov. 1884).

LOIS FOWLER

Zona Gale

B. *26 Aug. 1874, Portage, Wisconsin; d. 27 Dec. 1938, Chicago, Illinois*
D. *of Charles Franklin and Eliza Beers Gale; m. W. L. Breese, 1928*

An only child, G. grew up in the sheltered small-town environment that became the setting for her fiction. She graduated from the University of Wisconsin at Madison in 1895. After working as a journalist in Milwaukee, G. went on to New York in 1900 and began selling stories and poems. She returned permanently to Wisconsin after winning the 1910 *Delineator* short-story prize of two thousand dollars.

A longtime friend of Jane Addams, G. was active with the Women's Peace Party, woman suffrage, La Follette Progressivism, the Wisconsin Dramatic Society, and the growing community-theater movement. Throughout the 1930s, she continued to write fiction and to work for social reform and peace. She saw to the publication and wrote the introduction to *The Living of Charlotte Perkins Gilman* in 1935.

The women in G.'s work are remarkable for the consistency of their development. Calliope Marsh, the leading personality of the Friendship Village stories, was based on G.'s mother and represents the wisdom that G. saw as basic to an ideal maternal model. *Heart's Kindred* (1915) and *A Daughter of the Morning* (1917) are declarations of G.'s own feminist awareness.

Her most successful novel is *Miss Lulu Bett* (1920), an unsentimental look at family and marriage customs. Lulu Bett, family "beast of burden," is shown in rebellion against the life her time and place have thrust upon her: It is a story of growth. There is no overt moralizing to interrupt the flow of the plot. G. adapted this novel herself for the stage, and, in 1921, won the Pulitzer Prize for drama. There was some controversy about the changes G. made in the ending of the play after a trial run, but in a letter to the editor of the New York *Tribune*, G. made it clear she understood the feelings that keep many Lulus locked in their shells for years until a dramatic emotional event sets them free.

G.'s short stories appeared in popular magazines and were then put out in book form; her novels were often serialized before appearing in complete form. She was a regular contributor to magazines, often on feminist topics. Besides adapting some of her other novels for the theater, she wrote a one-act play, *The Neighbors* (1914), which had great success with college and community groups across the country. G. published one book of poetry, *The Secret Way* (1921), which reveals her search for deeper-than-surface reality.

Working from life as she observed it, G. took ordinary occurrences and invested these events with power to affect the inner lives of her characters. G. expressed her own basic philosophy as "life is more than we can ever know it to be." Consequently, some of her work is flawed by too heavy a reliance on mysticism: the stories cannot always sustain the transcendent events within their framework. When G. is successful, however, she touches a response in the reader that rises above the sentimental.

WORKS: *Romance Island* (1906). *The Loves of Pelleas and Etarre* (1907). *Friendship Village* (1908). *Friendship Village Love Stories* (1909). *Mothers to Men* (1911). *Christmas* (1912). *Civic Improvement in the Little Towns* (1913). *When I Was a Little Girl* (1913). *Neighborhood Stories* (1914). *The Neighbors* (1914). *Heart's Kindred* (1915). *A Daughter of the Morning* (1917). *Birth* (1918; dramatization by Gale, *Mister Pitt*, 1915). *Peace in Friendship Village* (1919). *Miss Lulu Bett* (1920; dramatization by Gale, 1921). *The Secret Way* (1921). *Uncle Jimmy* (1922). *What Women Won in Wisconsin* (1922). *Faint Perfume* (1923; dramatization by Gale, 1934). *Preface to a Life* (1926). *Yellow Gentians and Blue* (1927). *Portage, Wisconsin, and Other Essays* (1928). *Borgia* (1929). *Bridal Pond* (1930). *The Clouds* (1932). *Evening Clothes* (1932). *Old Fashioned Tales* (1933). *Papa La Fleur* (1933). *Light Woman* (1937). *Frank Miller of Mission Inn* (1938). *Magna* (1939).

BIBLIOGRAPHY: Derleth, A., *Still Small Voice: The Biography of Z. G.* (1940). Gard, R., *Grassroots Theater: A Search for Regional Arts in America* (1955). Herron, I., *The Small Town in American Literature* (1939). MacDougall, P., *Some Will Be Apples* (film, 1974). Simonson, H. P., *Z. G.* (1962). Sochen, J., *Movers and Shakers: American Women Thinkers and Activists 1900–1970* (1974).

For articles in reference works, see: *DAB*, Suppl. 2. *NAW* (article by W. B. Rideout). *NCAB*, B. *20thCA*.

Other references: *American Magazine* (June 1921). Madison (Wisconsin) *Capital Times* (29–31 May 1974; 3, 4 June 1974).

NANCY BREITSPRECHER

Helen Hamilton Gardener

B. 21 Jan. 1853, Winchester, Virginia; d. 26 July 1925, Washington, D.C.
Given name: Alice Chenoweth
D. of Alfred Griffith and Katherine Peel Chenoweth; m. Charles Selden Smart,
1875; m. Selden Allen Day, 1902

The initial impetus to G.'s public career as an author, freethinker, suffragist, and political lobbyist came from her father, whose abolitionist activities and rejection of formal Episcopalian thought instilled in G. a strong commitment to independent scientific inquiry, sociological analysis, and concomitant activism. G. acknowledged this debt to her father in her last novel, *An Unofficial Patriot* (1894), a slightly fictionalized biography focusing on her father's conversion to the Methodist church and on his Civil War activities.

After an extensive education at various private schools in the Washington, D.C., area and two years of school teaching, G. moved with her husband to New York City, where she studied biology at Columbia University and lectured in sociology at the Brooklyn Institute of Arts and Sciences. In 1884, prompted by her friendship with the prominent agnostic and skeptic, Robert G. Ingersoll, G. gave a series of lectures devoted to the principles of free thought and a discussion of the relationship between heredity and environment.

Her first book-length publication, *Men, Women, and Gods* (1885), contains many of these lectures. It was published under the name Helen Hamilton Gardener, a name that she subsequently adopted in both her personal and professional life. It is not known whether she rejected her given name and her married name to further her assertion of individual independence, to shield her family from the uproar which accompanied many of her publications, or to underscore a growing dissatisfaction with her marriage.

From 1885 to 1890, G. published numerous essays and short stories in a wide variety of periodicals. Many of these pieces were collected in *Pushed by Unseen Hands* (1890) and *A Thoughtless Yes* (1890). In the former, G. describes the scope of her subject matter as "unanalyzed varieties of mental, moral, social, industrial, or other aberrations of what is by courtesy called civilized society." Here, as in all of her writings, G. insists that her readers formulate independent conclusions, conclusions invariably counterposed to their previous passivity.

G. continued this work in two essay collections, *Pulpit, Pew, and Cradle* (1892) and *Facts and Fictions of Life* (1893). Exploring such diverse topics as insurance fraud, penal reform, labor disputes, hypocrisy in religion and philanthropy, the subservient position of women, and tenement living conditions, these two books make G. one of the earliest of the American muckrakers. The most significant and widely discussed of these essays was "Sex in Brain," the result of a fourteen-month biological study conducted to refute the contention of Dr. W. A. Hammond, surgeon general of the U.S., that the brains of men and women are structurally different. G. originally presented the conclusions reached through this research to the International Council of Women in Washington, D.C., in 1888.

During the 1890s, when she served as contributor, associate editor, and, briefly, coeditor of B. F. Flower's reform-oriented magazine, *The Arena*, she was chiefly responsible for the journal's progressive stance on a wide variety of feminist issues.

G.'s two novels, *Is This Your Son, My Lord?* (1891) and *Pray You Sir, Whose Daughter?* (1892), explicitly confront and condemn the sexual double standard. The first of these attacks the hypocritical upbringing of young American men, especially with respect to the emphasis on external respectability rather than moral convictions and independent thought. G.'s condemnation of institutionalized Christianity as abettor of this false social system figures heavily in her argument.

The companion novel, *Pray You Sir, Whose Daughter?*, focuses on the lives of three young women. Here G. writes a strident, but effectively argued denunciation of an attempt by the New York state legislature to lower the age-of-consent law; she also condemns the low wages paid to working women, and attacks the inferior position of women in the marital relationship. The novel is especially significant for its memorable portrait of a "new-woman" heroine, Gertrude Foster.

Although Elizabeth Cady Stanton's prediction that G.'s writings would do for the women's rights movement what Harriet Beecher Stowe's

Uncle Tom's Cabin did for the abolitionist cause was not fulfilled, the two novels were frequently reprinted and were the subject of widespread controversy.

Throughout her long and varied career, G.'s commitment to feminism was a prominent aspect of her self-proclaimed separation from conventional thought and action. Possibly G.'s most significant contribution lay in her attack on the standards of propriety and respectability imposed upon the woman writer. In her essay, "The Immoral Influence of Women in Literature" (*Arena*, February 1890), for example, G. cites the need for an uncensored and distinctly female literary voice.

WORKS: *Men, Women, and Gods, and Other Lectures* (1885). *Pushed by Unseen Hands* (1890). *A Thoughtless Yes* (1890). *Is This Your Son, My Lord?* (1891). *Pray You Sir, Whose Daughter?* (1892). *Pulpit, Pew, and Cradle* (1892). *Facts and Fictions of Life* (1893). *An Unofficial Patriot* (1894; dramatized as *Rev. Griffith Davenport, Circuit Rider*, by J. Herne, 1899).

The papers of Helen Hamilton Chenoweth Gardener are in the Schlesinger Library, Radcliffe College, Cambridge, Massachusetts.

BIBLIOGRAPHY: Flexner, E., *Century of Struggle* (1959). Gordon, L., *Woman's Body, Woman's Right* (1976). *H. H. G. (Alice Chenoweth Day) 1853–1925* (privately printed memorial booklet, 1925). Hill, V. L., "Strategy and Breadth: The Socialist-Feminist in American Fiction" (Diss., SUNY at Buffalo, 1979). Park, M., *Front Door Lobby* (1960). Putnam, S., *400 Years of Freethought* (1894).

For articles in reference works, see: *AW. DAB*, IV, 1; Suppl. 4. *HWS*, IV, V. *NAW* (article by A. Washburn). *NCAB*, 9.

Other references: *American Journal of Physical Anthropology* (Oct.–Dec. 1927). *Arena* (Jan. 1891; June 1892; Dec. 1894). *Business Woman* (Jan. 1923). *Free Thought Magazine* (Jan. 1890; Jan. 1897; March 1901; July 1902). *Independent* (8 Sept. 1892). *Literary World* (13 Aug. 1892; 9 Sept. 1893). *Nation* (16 June 1892). *Woman Citizen* (2 May 1925).

VICKI LYNN HILL

Jean Garrigue

B. 8 Dec. 1914, Evansville, Indiana; d. 27 Dec. 1972, Boston, Massachusetts
D. of Allan Colfax and Gertrude Heath Garrigue

The youngest child of a postal inspector who published short fiction and a mother who was musical, G. spent her childhood in Indiana. She received a B.A. from the University of Chicago (1937) and an M.F.A.

from the University of Iowa (1943). She has taught in many American colleges and universities, and worked as an editor (serving as poetry editor of the *New Leader* from 1965 to 1971) and as a journalist. G. has received many awards.

For G., the Imagists made daring to write poetry possible. One of her earliest aims, she said, was to set to music what the eye brings forth. This disposition helped her to benefit from the examples of strict visual details, as well as to cope with the lack of structural necessity in the verse she first emulated.

In *Thirty-Six Poems, and a Few Songs* (1944), G. is both outside and inside the lucid scene: in the immediacy of the moment sight staggers and consciousness trembles ("With Glaze of Tears"), but the significance of the images balances the poems between an intimate and impersonal tone so that they are not as autobiographical as they are prototypical. The subjects are those of a young poet—the memory of the loss of brilliant innocence, the emptiness of a place in which a vision of a beautiful girl (a stranger) disappeared, questions about identity and love.

In *The Ego and the Centaur* (1947), the landscapes of youth are replaced by configurations for the "centre of the fury in which we live" and more elaborate structures. The poems are characterized by a tension between delicacy of feeling and suppressed rage for the fact that sensations are brutalized. Changes of style signal changes of subject from an exemplum on gaping at the handicapped animals and flightless birds in the false country of the zoo to the obvious satire of "There Is No Anti-Semitism in the Village."

The startling image of *The Monument Rose* (1953) suggests G.'s powerful modesty in relation to what T. S. Eliot calls "the ideal order" of literature's "existing monuments." Open to the full measure of the works of the past, G. says in effect: "Here's one flower." "The Maimed Grasshopper [with three simple eyes] Speaks Up" can be compared to the wit of the metaphysical poets, as she pleads warily for the particular against the universal view. Her virtuosity, neither imitative nor self-insistent, is proof of a mature woman's dedication to keeping language alive, and gives the book its stature.

G.'s work in prose, in the novella *The Animal Hotel* (1966) and in *Chartres and Prose Poems* (1970), although it has the aura of poetry, contributes to the irregular rhythms and colloquial lines that mark an almost radical anonymity of style in *Studies for an Actress, and Other Poems* (1973). The sense of an ending, the dominant death theme, accounts for the austere clarity of "Requiem," "Elegy," or "Movie

Actors Scribbling Letters Very Fast in Crucial Scenes." G. continues to write love poems, some of her best because they are as direct as prose heightened by bare metaphor: "To Speak of My Influences" ("Above all, your eyes") or "The Gift of Summer" ("Once more, my love, once more / I am where you were / When midsummered, you wrote / Outright on my heart").

Sensitive to literary tradition but audaciously independent in the search for new correspondences between the disconnections and discontinuities of the modern period, G. occupied the meeting place between knowledge and imagination, between reality and dream. Possessed of critical intelligence, she knew the truth "in the feeling that comes from seeing" as well as the power of the invisible in the visible. She was consequently both at home in the world and a stranger in it.

WORKS: *Thirty-Six Poems, and a Few Songs* (1944). *The Ego and the Centaur* (1947). *The Monument Rose* (1953). *A Water Walk by Villa d'Este* (1959). *Country Without Maps* (1964). *Marianne Moore* (1965). *The Animal Hotel: A Novella* (1966). *New and Selected Poems* (1967). *Chartres and Prose Poems* (1970). *Translations by American Poets* (edited by Garrigue, 1970). *Studies for an Actress, and Other Poems* (1973). *Love's Aspects: The World's Great Love Poems* (edited by Garrigue, 1975).

BIBLIOGRAPHY: For articles in reference works, see: *CA*, 37–40 (1973). *Indiana Authors and Their Books, 1917–1966*, Ed. D. E. Thompson (1974). *20thCAS*.

Other references: *New Leader* (29 Jan. 1968). *NewR* (2 Nov. 1953). *NYRB* (4 Oct. 1973). *Parnassus* (Winter 1975). *Poetry* (Dec. 1953; May 1960; June 1965; May 1968). *SatR* (19 June 1948). *SR* (Spring 1954). *YR* (Autumn 1973).

ELIZABETH PHILLIPS

Martha Gellhorn

B. *Nov. 1908, St. Louis, Missouri*
Writes under: *Martha Gellhorn, Martha Hemingway*
D. *of George and Edna Fischel Gellhorn; m. Ernest Hemingway, 1940; m. Thomas Matthews, 1953*

The only daughter of a distinguished physician and of a social reformer and suffragist, G. learned that one's purpose in life should consider the well-being of others. Her home environment fostered a profound respect for the individual and a confidence in her own ability to accomplish anything she was willing to work for.

G. left Bryn Mawr after her junior year to become a cub reporter for the Albany *Times Union*, quit after six months, and free-lanced for the St. Louis *Post-Dispatch*, publishing, before the age of twenty-one, an article in the *New Republic*. When *Collier's* published an unsolicited article on the life of Madrid during the Spanish Civil War, adding G.'s name to its masthead, G. knew that she had made herself a war correspondent, won a front-row seat to the history of her time, and wedged a place in a heretofore masculine world. In Spain, G. lived and worked with Ernest Hemingway. They were married in 1940 and divorced in 1945.

G. investigated Czechoslovakia before and after the Munich Pact, reported from Russian-bombed, subzero Finland, analyzed the British defenses in China, stowed away to see the Invasion of Normandy, flew in a Black Widow, and spent V-E Day in Dachau. After the war, she attended the Nuremberg and Eichmann trials, reported on the Six-Day and Vietnam wars. Scarcely returning to the U.S. for more than an extended visit, G. set up temporary residences in Spain, Cuba, Mexico, Italy, Kenya; today she lives and writes in her favored London.

Aiming to enlist support for those struggling to live their lives with decency—the poor in America's Depression, the republicans in Madrid, the refugees in Czechoslovakia, the Jews in Dachau—G. learned quickly to concentrate paragraphs into a few careful details. Rather than philosophize about the absurdity of war, G. utilized the power of image: a mother still walking her son across the street, unaware that the last shellburst had taken his life. G. made her pieces vivid by reordering what she saw into a natural unity, investing statistics with humanity.

Although her journalism appeared almost weekly in American magazines after 1940, G. never lost sight of her goal to write fiction. The autobiographical emphasis of her first novel, *What Mad Pursuit* (1934), continued to mar her fiction until the late 1940s. It was with the publication of *Liana* (1944), a novel about a powerless mulatto woman living on a Caribbean island, that G.'s fiction matured. Although she was still reporting in her black-and-white fashion on the Nazi atrocities, G. shifted in her fiction from a concern with political philosophies and external movements to an exploration of the individual and his or her inner needs.

In 1948, G. published her best work, a World War II novel called *The Wine of Astonishment*. Borrowing from her journalism the details needed to convince her readers of the external action which centers around the Battle of the Bulge, G. wrote about the isolation of the 20th-c. man and his power to break through the self-imposed imprisonment to a richer, more meaningful life. The lesson of responsible action, no longer sentimentalized in an autobiographical protagonist, was dramatically heightened by the encounter of a Jew, who had denied his heritage, with the atrocities of Dachau. The characters lose their hero or villain status and impress as human beings; the craft is careful and effective.

G.'s journalism was constantly applauded, and several of her war articles were collected into the much-praised *Face of War* (1959), but her fiction was received less enthusiastically. The three postwar volumes of short stories which G. chose to collect from many more surfacing in American magazines, however, reveal her fine craft and perception. *The Honeyed Peace* (1953), *Two by Two* (1958), and *Pretty Tales for Tired People* (1965) illustrate G.'s recurring themes of human liberation, the crush of poverty and war on the human psyche, the intensity of human relationships, and the way to invest meaning into otherwise meaningless lives.

G.'s journalism, at its best, functions for those who read it as a kind of conscience. Her fiction, at its peak, serves as a type of mirror, a compelling reflection of humanity and a penetrating glance at ourselves.

WORKS: *What Mad Pursuit* (1934). *The Trouble I've Seen* (1936). *A Stricken Field* (1940). *The Heart of Another* (1941). *Liana* (1944). *Love Goes to Press* (with V. Cowles, 1947). *The Wine of Astonishment* (1948). *The Honeyed Peace* (1953). *Two By Two* (1958). *The Face of War* (1959). *His Own Man* (1961). *Pretty Tales for Tired People* (1965). *Vietnam: A New Kind of War* (1966). *The Lowest Trees Have Tops* (1969). *Travels with Myself and Another* (1978). *The Weather in Africa* (1980).

BIBLIOGRAPHY: Baker, C., *Ernest Hemingway: A Life Story* (1969). Cowles, V., *Looking for Trouble* (1941). Matthews, T. S., *O My America! Notes on a Trip* (1962). Orsagh, J., "A Critical Biography of M. G." (Ph.D. diss., Michigan State Univ., 1978).

For articles in reference works, see: *20thCA. 20thCAS.*

Other references: *Guardian* (5 Oct. 1966). St. Louis *Post-Dispatch* (3 Oct. 1936). *Time* (18 March 1940).

JACQUELINE E. ORSAGH

Jean Craighead George

B. 2 July 1919, Washington, D.C.
Writes under: Jean Craighead, Jean George
D. of Frank and Carolyn Johnson Craighead; m. John L. George, 1944

G., writer, illustrator, and naturalist, attended Pennsylvania State University and edited its literary magazine. During World War II she worked as a reporter for the International News Service (1941–43) and the *Washington Post* and *Times-Herald* (1943–45). She worked as an artist for *Pageant* magazine (1945–46) and as reporter-artist for the Newspaper Enterprise Association (1946–47). G. married a conservationist and ecologist with whom she had three children; they were divorced in 1963.

In the 1960s and 1970s, G. wrote thirty-three books (and illustrated some of them), mostly for children. She also published many articles on nature subjects in *Reader's Digest*, for which she is a roving editor, and in other magazines. An unusual characteristic of G. is that, if at all possible, she lives with the animals she writes about; she reports having raised at least 173 wild pets.

My Side of the Mountain (1959) is the story of adolescent Sam Gribley, who is tired of living with his large family in a cramped city apartment and wants to go live in the Catskills on his great-grandfather's homestead. For thirteen months he does just that. He collects and cooks his own food, makes himself a home inside a tree trunk, and figures out a source of heat for protection against the cold mountain winters. He has a variety of animal friends, including Frightful, a young falcon he trains. The life is difficult and sometimes lonely, but Sam succeeds, and the story is told so realistically and with such detail that it all seems very credible.

The conflicts of adolescence are further explored in *The Summer of the Falcon* (1962), a story that seems to incorporate some of G.'s own biography. It is told through the cycle of a family's return, three summers in a row, to the grandfather's Victorian house in the mountains. The heroine struggles toward self-discipline. In one scene she is able to go ahead and use her wits to complete a cave rescue only after she has admitted her nearly overwhelming fear. Perhaps the ending is too pat, but this is more than outweighed by the book's basic strengths, including fascinating hawk lore.

Julie of the Wolves (1972) is the story of an adolescent Eskimo girl who is befriended by a wolf pack while searching for her lost father and a lost cultural tradition. G. captures the conflict of Eskimo life, the desire on the part of some to retain the old ways of living in harmony with the earth and the desire of others to enjoy some of the luxuries of "civilization"—such as radios, refined foods, alcohol, and high-powered rifles. *Julie of the Wolves*, with its sections of fine naturalistic writing, won the 1973 Newbery Medal and was voted among the ten best children's books of the last two hundred years by members of the Children's Literature Association.

Hook a Fish, Catch a Mountain (1975), like the earlier *Who Really Killed Cock Robin?* (1971), can be termed an ecological mystery, but like many other books by G., it is also a story of an adolescent trying to be accepted as an individual. Again, the protagonist is female, and again she is trying to shake off her lack of experience and her fears in order to become an able and independent outdoorsperson.

G.'s successful mixing of nature stories with novels centering on adolescents and their concerns works to the advantage of both genres. The adolescent concerns of learning to manage physical danger and fear, to take responsibility, to discipline oneself and to become a part of a group, as well as to develop independence, are set against the backdrop of the need for all humans to be aware of the interconnectedness of all the ecosystems of this earth. A deep understanding of nature's harmonies—beautiful and death-causing alike—pervades each of the books. G. is a fine writer who has chosen to write books that are primarily appropriate for young people, but at her best she is equally interesting to adults.

WORKS: *Vulpes, the Red Fox* (with J. L. George, 1948). *Vision, the Mink* (with J. L. George, 1949). *Masked Prowler: The Story of a Racoon* (with J. L. George, 1950). *Meph, the Pet Skunk* (with J. L. George, 1952). *Bubo, the Great Horned Owl* (with J. L. George, 1954). *Dipper of Copper Creek* (with J. L. George, 1956). *The Hole in the Tree* (1957). *Snow Tracks* (1958). *My Side of the Mountain* (1959; film version, 1969). *The Summer of the Falcon* (1962). *Red Robin, Fly Up* (1963). *Gull Number 737* (1964). *Hold Zero* (1966). *Spring Comes to the Ocean* (1966). *The Moon of the Bears* (1967). *The Moon of the Owls* (1967). *The Moon of the Salamanders* (1967). *Coyote in Manhattan* (1968). *The Moon of the Chickarees* (1968). *The Moon of the Fox Pups* (1968). *The Moon of the Monarch Butterflies* (1968). *The Moon of the Mountain Lions* (1968). *The Moon of the Wild Pigs* (1968). *The Moon of the Alligators* (1969). *The Moon of the Deer* (1969). *The Moon of the Gray Wolves* (1969). *The Moon of the Moles* (1969). *The Moon of the Winter Bird* (1969). *All upon a Stone* (1971). *Beastly Inventions* (1971). *Who Really Killed Cock Robin?* (1971). *Wildguide to the Everglades* (1971). *Julie of the Wolves* (1972). *All upon a Sidewalk* (1974). *Walking Wild Westchester* (1974). *Hook a Fish, Catch a Mountain* (1975). *Going to the Sun* (1976). *Dirty Work, Inc.* (1978). *Wentletrap Trap* (1978). *American Walk Book: An Illustrated Guide to the Country's Major Historical and Natural Walking Trails from the Northeast to the Pacific Coast* (1978). *River Rats, Inc.* (1979). *The Wounded Wolf* (1979). *The Cry of the Crow* (1980). *The Grizzley Bear with the Golden Ears* (1981). *Journey Inward* (1982). *The Wild, Wild Cookbook* (1982).

BIBLIOGRAPHY: Huck, C., and D. Kuhn, eds., *Children's Literature in the Elementary School* (1968). Sutherland, Z., and M. H. Arbuthnot, *Children and Books* (1977).

For articles in reference works, see: *Authors of Books for Young People*, Eds. M. E. Ward and D. A. Marquardt (1964). *CA*, 7-8 (1963). *More Junior Authors*, Ed. M. Fuller (1963). *Something About the Author*, Vol. 2, Ed. A. Commire (1971). *Who's Who in Children's Books: A Treasury of the Familiar Characters of Childhood*, M. Fisher (1975).

Other references: *Elementary English* (Oct. 1973). *Horn Book* (Aug. 1973). *WrD* (March 1974).

LINDA A. CARROLL

Alice Gerstenberg

B. 2 Aug. 1885, Chicago, Illinois; d. 28 July 1972, Chicago, Illinois
D. of Erich and Julia Wieschendorff Gerstenberg

G.'s grandparents on both sides of the family were Chicago pioneers. From her father she inherited endurance, and from her mother a love of theater. She attended the Kirkland School in Chicago and Bryn Mawr College.

Before writing plays, G. was interested in writing novels. Her first full-length play, a three-act version of Lewis Carroll's *Alice in Wonderland* and *Through the Looking Glass*, opened in 1915 at both the Fine Arts Theatre and the Booth Theatre in New York. G.'s next play, the one-act *Overtones*, her most original and best-known work, was produced in 1915 by the Washington Square Players at the Bandbox Theatre, New York, under the direction of Edward Goodman. It also played in

London, starring Lily Langtry. In 1922, G. wrote a three-act version of *Overtones* which she directed herself at Powers Theater in Chicago.

In *Overtones* G. created two lines of action to tell the story of Harriet and Margaret. Harriet has married for money and longs for the man she loves, while Margaret has married for love (the same man Harriet, too, had loved) and now longs for money. The surface action of the play, which reveals only the "civilized" selves of these women, is shown in conventional dramatic form, while the action below the surface reveals the subconscious selves of the two women in two characters named Hetty and Maggie. Harriet and Margaret exist in the present in a world as it appears to be; Hetty and Maggie speak of the past and life as they honestly feel them. The two actions placed side by side create not just a conventional conflict between two women, but a compelling irony and a conflict wthin each character, Harriet-Hetty and Margaret-Maggie.

Overtones was heralded as representing a new formula in theater. Today it is still seen as a forerunner of later psychological drama by major playwrights, including Eugene O'Neill, who acknowledged its influence on his work. This same concern for the dramatic "representation" of the subconscious is obvious in *Strange Interlude* (1928) and in *Days Without End* (1932), both of which use masks to draw the conflict between the false outer self and the painfully honest subconscious self.

The Pot Boiler (later titled *Dress Rehearsal*), a comedy about the pretensions of conventional theater, and *Fourteen*, a light satire on the pettiness of high-society dinner parties, along with *Overtones*—all appearing in G.'s second collection, *Ten One-Act Plays* (1921)—are G.'s most popular plays. They have appeared in numerous anthologies of one-act plays and have been produced by little theaters all over the U.S., England, and Australia.

G. was one of the original members of the Chicago Little Theatre, the first little theater in the U.S., which was founded by Maurice Browne in 1912. In 1921, she and Annette Washburne founded the Chicago Junior League Theatre for children. For two years, G. was this theater's director. Using her early model for children's theater, junior leagues have developed in communities all over the country.

G.'s most significant contribution to the little-theater movement is her founding of The Playwright's Theatre of Chicago (1922–45), which was designed to offer the local playwright an opportunity to produce plays. For her work as playwright and producer, G. won the Chicago Foundation for Literature Award in 1938. Her articles on little theater appear in *Townsfolk Magazine*, *The Little Theatre Monthly*, and *The Drama*. G. has also enjoyed a modest career as an actress.

G.'s characters, mostly women, inhibited by outworn institutions and by their own fears, make choices that lead to honest self-expression. Needing new dramatic forms to express the daring of her unconventional characters, G. took the comic form and gave it not only a variety of structures but a modern psychological dimension as well. G.'s dramaturgy reflects her own vitality as a woman and as a playwright dedicated to a new theater which placed artistic integrity as its highest goal.

WORKS: *A Little World* (1908). *Unquenched Fire* (1912). *Alice in Wonderland* (dramatization of *Alice in Wonderland* and *Through the Looking Glass* by L. Carroll, 1915). *The Conscience of Sarah Platt* (1915). *Ten One-Act Plays* (1921). *Four Plays for Four Women* (1924). *The Land of Don't Want To* by L. Bell (dramatization by Gerstenberg, 1928). *Overtones* (1929). *Comedies All* (1930). *Water Babies* by C. Kingsley (dramatization by Gerstenberg, 1930). *Star Dust* (1931). *When Chicago Was Young* (with H. Clark, 1932). *Glee Plays the Game* (1934). *Within the Hour* (1934). *Find It* (1937). *London Town* (dramatization by Gerstenberg, 1937). *The Queen's Christmas* (1939). *Time for Romance* (with M. Fealy, 1942). *Victory Belles* (with H. Adrian, 1943). *The Hourglass* (1955). *Our Calla* (1956). *On the Beam* (1957). *The Magic of Living* (1969).

BIBLIOGRAPHY: Dean, A., *Comedies All* (1930). Sievers, D., *Freud on Broadway* (1955).
Other references: *NewR* (20 Nov. 1915).

BEVERLY M. MATHERNE

Caroline Howard Gilman

B. 8 Oct. 1794, Boston, Massachusetts; d. 15 Sept. 1888, Washington, D.C.
Wrote under: Caroline Gilman, Caroline Howard, Clarissa Packard
D. of Samuel and Anna Lillie Howard; m. Samuel Gilman, 1819

G.'s father died when she was two, her mother when she was ten. She had an irregular education, as the family moved from one Boston suburb to another. After her marriage to a Unitarian minister she moved to Charleston, South Carolina. Three of her seven children died in infancy.

In 1832, G. began publication of the *Rose Bud; or, Youth's Gazette*, one of the earliest American magazines for children. Renamed the *Southern Rose-Bud* in 1833 and the *Southern Rose* in 1835, it gradually became a general family magazine before ceasing publication in 1839. Many of G.'s writings appeared first in its pages.

In *Recollections of a Housekeeper* (1834), "Clarissa Packard" gives a brief account of her education and then describes her first years of marriage. Because its first-person narrator is solidly middle-class (Mr. Packard is an attorney), Clarissa Packard's chronicle presents a "case history" of the "disestablishment" of the American woman as described by Ann Douglas in *The Feminization of American Culture*. Her duties as a housekeeper seem to consist largely of training cooks, hired girls, or nursemaids; and the domestic crises of her early marriage usually involve the unexpected departure of one or more of these servants. She emphasizes throughout that she can roast and boil, make puddings and pies, sweep and dust, and she is pleased that her mother has educated her for usefulness: "My mother was proud to say that I could manufacture a frilled shirt in two days, with stitches that required a microscope to detect them." She is busy, however, teaching others to do her cooking, sweeping, and washing. No sooner does she train women than they tire of devoting themselves to her and her family and want to get married and have lives of their own.

Much of the humor in the *Recollections of a Housekeeper* is afforded by the vocabulary and accents of the rustic New Englanders who come to serve and by their inability to grasp the forms (and perhaps the spirit) of such service.

When G. wrote her chronicle of a New England housekeeper, she had already been living in Charleston for many years. The disestablishment of the middle-class housewife and the attitudes towards servants revealed in the first book reach a logical culmination in its companion-piece, *Recollections of a Southern Matron* (1838), which depicts all for the best in that best of all possible worlds, the southern plantation. The first-person narrator of this second book supplies more information on her background and early life, and a romantic plot with a subplot involving a secondary heroine, but the focus is again on scenes of domestic life. G. places great emphasis on the contentment of the slaves (they are always called "servants," but they stay around once they are trained), and she claims their lot is better than that of northern servants and mill-hands. G.'s letters to her children after the Civil War show her still unchanged in the opinion that slavery had benefited the slaves.

In *The Poetry of Travelling in the United States* (1838), G. sets out to "present something in the same volume which might prove attractive to both the Northern and Southern reader" and "to increase a good sympathy between different portions of the country."

G. also published collections of short stories, poetry (some with her daughter Caroline Howard Jervey), and novels. She prided herself most on her writings for children and young people, but these are now of interest mostly as indications of what Americans of the 1830s thought suitable reading for their children. Her position as a humorous chronicler of middle-class domesticity, North and South—a sort of early Erma Bombeck—became more and more difficult to sustain, as this New England-born Unitarian gave her sympathies to her adopted South.

WORKS: *Recollections of a Housekeeper* (1834). *The Lady's Annual Register and Housewife's Memorandum Book* (1838). *The Poetry of Travelling in the United States* (1838). *Recollections of a Southern Matron* (1838). *Letters of Eliza Wilkinson* (edited by Gilman, 1839). *Tales and Ballads* (1839). *Love's Progress* (1840). *The Rose-Bud Wreath* (1841). *Oracles from the Poets* (1844). *Stories and Poems for Children* (1844). *The Sibyl; or, New Oracles from the Poets* (1849). *Verses of a Life Time* (1849). *A Gift Book of Stories and Poems for Children* (1850). *Oracles for Youth* (1852). *Recollections of a New England Bride and a Southern Matron* (1852). *Record of Inscriptions in the Cemetery and Building of the Unitarian . . . Church . . . Charleston, S.C.* (1860). *Stories and Poems by Mother and Daughter* (with C. H. Jervey, 1872). *The Poetic Fate Book* (1874). *Recollections of the Private Centennial Celebration of the Overthrow of the Tea* (1874). *The Young Fortune Teller* (with C. H. Jervey, 1874).

BIBLIOGRAPHY: Saint-Amand, M. S., *A Balcony in Charleston* (1941).

For articles in reference works, see: *DAB*, Suppl. 1. *The Living Writers of the South*, Ed. J. W. Davidson (1869). *NAW* (article by S. Nissenbaum). *NCAB*, 13. *Women of the South Distinguished in Literature*, Ed. M. Forrest (1861).

Other references: *NCHR* (April 1934). *SAQ* (Jan. 1924).

SUSAN SUTTON SMITH

Charlotte Perkins Stetson Gilman

B. 3 July 1860, Hartford, Connecticut; d. 17 Aug. 1935, Pasadena, California
D. of Frederick Beecher and Mary A. Fritch Perkins; m. Charles Walter
Stetson, 1884; m. George Houghton Gilman, 1900

G.'s father left the family soon after G. was born. Although he made infrequent visits home and provided meager support for his family, he was largely responsible for G.'s early education, emphasizing reading in the sciences and history. Her only formal education consisted of brief attendance at the Rhode Island School of Design. Like her great-aunt, Harriet Beecher Stowe, G. was a reformer. At an early age, she recognized the plight (particularly the economic servitude) of her mother and many New England housewives. By age twenty-one, she was writing poetry that described the limitations of being female in late-19th-c. New England.

As a teenager, G. was a commercial artist, art teacher, and governess. Ten months after her marriage to Stetson, also an artist, their only daughter was born. G. suffered extreme depression after the birth and made a recuperative trip to California. She moved there in 1888 and divorced Stetson in 1894.

G. did not establish her reputation as a forceful writer and lecturer until the last decade of the century when she published a series of satiric poems in the *Nationalist*. She also began lecturing on a wide variety of topics. For a time she was a member of the National Movement, during which her writing and lectures reflected that group's nationalistic fervor.

In 1893, G. collected about seventy-five poems into a small volume entitled *In This Our World*. G. designed the cover, "based on Olive Screiner's *Three Dreams in a Desert*." The book was first published in England but enjoyed scanty success in the U.S., where, besides G.'s family and friends, William Dean Howells first recognized its greatness. He called G. "the only optimist reformer he ever met." The poems outline G.'s economic and social views and are considered by many to be a classic statement on the women's movement.

Women and Economics, originally titled *Economic Relation of the*

Sexes as a Factor in Social Development, appeared in 1898. This book's arguments in behalf of women's rights arise out of a firm and broad philosophical and historical base. G. calls American society "androcentric" and illustrates how traditionally male values have dominated almost every aspect of American life. It is considered one of the most important works on the women's movement.

Written in 1890 but not published as a separate work until 1899, *The Yellow Wall-Paper* is a fictional though partially autobiographical treatment of a woman artist's nervous breakdown. Having recently given birth, she is forced by her husband and physician to spend the summer in isolation in a Gothic-style country estate. She is forbidden to write, which is the one thing she truly wants to do. The result is the woman's madness, her delusion that another woman is trapped behind the wallpaper in her attic bedroom.

G.'s *Concerning Children* (1900) and *The Home* (1904) expand on arguments originally advanced in *Women and Economics.* Both suggest that children's lives can be stunted instead of enriched by a home in which the mother's sole occupation is housekeeping. G. argues instead for day-care centers where children are well cared for, and where they can continue to explore the "thrilling mystery of life." G. called *The Home* "the most heretical—and the most amusing—of anything I've done."

In 1900, G. married her first cousin, a lawyer from New York. During their honeymoon, G. read him the book she had been writing, *Human Work* (1904). It attempts to make the same claim for work that Cardinal Newman made for knowledge: that it is intrinsically valuable, its own end. According to G., work is both a responsibility and a pleasure. One does it because one is obligated to the human community.

In 1909, G. began a seven-year editorship of her own monthly periodical, the *Forerunner.* Written entirely by G. and containing twenty-one thousand words per issue, G. figured that the *Forerunner* equaled four books a year, of thirty-six thousand words apiece. The periodical contained articles on social and economic issues (invariably about women) and some poetry and fiction. It published two full-length novels by G.: *What Diantha Did* (1910) and *The Crux* (1911). *The Man-Made World* (1911) was also published in *Forerunner.* It juxtaposed male and female values. Women, G. wrote, are peace-loving and concerned with community. Contrarily, the prevailing values in our society are male: aggressiveness, competition, and destructiveness.

His Religion and Hers (1923) was published six years after G. had resigned from the *Forerunner.* In it, G. compares the male conception of the world (a postponement and preparation for the afterlife) with the female (heaven in the present time and place). She directs her argument toward current social considerations, suggesting that if women controlled society, they would place greater emphasis on practical issues: how to live comfortably and peacefully from day to day.

Her autobiography, *The Living of Charlotte Perkins Gilman* (1935), is an excellent source for understanding G.'s life, work, and death. Suffering from cancer and surviving her husband's unexpected death in 1934, G. lived quite peacefully for a time near her daughter in Pasadena, then committed suicide by chloroform. The conclusion of her autobiography is an appropriate epitaph and was part of a letter left to her survivors: "The one predominant duty is to find one's work and do it, and I have striven mightily at that. The religion, the philosophy, set up so early, have seen me through."

WORKS: *In This Our World* (1893). *Women and Economics* (1898). *The Yellow Wall-Paper* (1899). *Concerning Children* (1900). *The Home* (1904). *Human Work* (1904). *What Diantha Did* (1910). *The Crux* (1911). *The Man-Made World* (1911). *Moving the Mountain* (1911). *His Religion and Hers* (1923). *The Living of Charlotte Perkins Gilman: An Autobiography* (1935).

BIBLIOGRAPHY: Dell, F., *Women as World Builders* (1913). Wellington, A., *Women Have Told: Studies in the Feminist Tradition* (1930).

For articles in reference works, see: *DAB*, Suppl. 1. *HWS*, V, VI. *NAW* (article by C. N. Degler). *NCAB*, 13.

Other references: *AQ* (Spring 1956). *Canadian Magazine* (Aug. 1923). *Century Magazine* (Nov. 1923). *Poet-Lore* (Jan.-March 1899).

MARY BETH PRINGLE

Elizabeth Meriwether Gilmer

B. *18 Nov. 1870, Woodstock, Tennessee; d. 16 Dec. 1951, New Orleans, Louisiana*
Wrote under: Dorothy Dix
D. *of William and Maria Winston Meriwether; m. George Gilmer, 1888*

G.'s career as a newspaper columnist and reporter stemmed from her tragic marriage. The daughter of impoverished southern gentry, G. had little formal training and no work experience when, shortly after her marriage, she had to assume financial responsibility for herself and her husband, a victim of an incurable mental disease. Rejecting the idea of divorce, she began working as a woman's-page writer on the New Orleans *Picayune* in 1896. Successful as a columnist and reporter, G. moved to the New York *Evening Journal* in 1901, where she continued her column, "Dorothy Dix Talks," and covered sensational murder trials (usually involving women) and vice investigations. From 1917 until her death, she confined her newspaper writing to her advice column, first for the Wheeler syndicate and from 1923 for the Ledger syndicate.

Between 1912 and 1914, G., a supporter of woman suffrage, wrote three pamphlets on the subject. She also published a number of books of advice, some fictional in technique and southern in setting, like *Mirandy* (1914) and *Mirandy Exhorts* (1922), but mostly drawn from her columns, like *Fables of the Elite* (1902), *Hearts à la Mode* (1915), and *How to Win and Hold a Husband* (1939). In addition, she published travel books describing the customs and problems in the places she visited.

Best known for her column, reaching an estimated sixty-million readers worldwide with sympathy, humor, and common sense, G. dispensed sermonettes on courtship and marriage as well as answers to letters. She advised that women develop a positive self-image and know how to work at a job, but also retain femininity, good nature, and adaptability. Beginning many columns with "Men are a selfish lot," G. accepted the reality of a sexual double standard and advised her readers how to deal with that reality.

Convinced of the healthy and life-enriching power of love, G. nevertheless explained how to achieve that goal with imagery taken from games, hunting, and marketing, with what one reviewer has called "hard-boiled realism that would do credit to a brothel keeper." For example: "A young girl who lets any one boy monopolize her, simply shuts the door in the face of good times and her chances of making a better match." "Few grafts are more profitable than comforting a widower. But remember that fast work is required." And in a "recipe" book for marriage: "All wives should encourage their husbands in dough-making. It keeps them out of mischief and promotes domestic felicity."

Coexistent with the pragmatism, however, is the pride, independence, and self-worth G. advocates for all women. In *Woman's Lack of Pride* (ca. 1912), she writes that women lack sex pride "when they permit themselves to be classed politically with the offscourings of the earth [the criminal, the idiot, the insane].... All of woman's failures are due to her shame of her sex, and she will never succeed until she . . . realizes that . . . she is entitled to stand side by side with man, not to have to trail along in his wake like a humble slave."

Sociologists Robert and Helen Lynd in their sociological study of middle America, *Middletown* (1929), assess G.'s column as the best single available source to represent Middletown's views about marriage, and also as "perhaps the most potent single agency of diffusion from without shaping the habits of thought of Middletown in regard to marriage." G. defined the ideal of love and marriage, acknowledged the reality, and wrote pragmatic advice reflecting but also shaping the behavior and mores of her readers.

WORKS: *Fables of the Elite* (1902). *What's Sauce for the Gander Is Sauce for the Goose* (ca. 1912). *Woman's Lack of Pride* (ca. 1912). *Dorothy Dix on Woman's Ballot* (1914). *Mirandy* (1914). *Hearts à la Mode* (1915). *Mirandy Exhorts* (1922). *My Trip around the World* (1924). *Dorothy Dix, Her Book* (1926). *Mexico* (1934). *How to Win and Hold a Husband* (1939).

BIBLIOGRAPHY: Kane, H. T., *Dear Dorothy Dix* (1952). Lynd, R. S. and H. M. Lynd, *Middletown* (1929).
    For articles in reference works, see: *CB* (1940; Feb. 1952). *DAB*, Suppl. 1, 5. Other references: *NYT* (17 Dec. 1951). *Time* (14 Aug. 1939).

HELEN J. SCHWARTZ

Ellen Anderson Gholson Glasgow

B. 22 April 1873, Richmond, Virginia; d. 21 Nov. 1945, Richmond, Virginia
Wrote under: Ellen Glasgow
D. of Francis Thomas and Anne Jane Gholson Glasgow

G. was the eighth of her parents' ten children. Her father was director of the Tredegar Iron Works, chief armaments factory during the Civil War. His dour Scotch-Irish Calvinist background instilled in her qualities of strength G. was to sum up as a "vein of iron." This phrase and the staunch values it implied occur approvingly in over half her novels; yet she hated her father for his tyranny, his religious severity, his philandering. He was, she wrote, "more patriarchal than paternal." She adored her generous, long-suffering mother, a "perfect flower of the Tidewater" aristocracy. In her autobiography, *The Woman Within* (1954), G. described her own nature as deeply divided between this gentle mother and stern father.

G. acquired her learning at home. She was excused early from a formal education because of shyness and headaches at school. She lived most of her life in Richmond, although she traveled often to Europe, especially in her younger days, and lived in New York for years at a time.

G. held her work and literary reputation uppermost; these compensated for what she called "the long tragedy of my life." An especial burden was her deafness, which assailed her in adolescence and worsened. It isolated her, and plunged her into profound depressions. She consulted psychoanalysts and aurists. Eventually her hearing devices improved, but she never ceased to complain. Allusions in the novels to a "soundless tumult," a "rustling vacancy," apparently grow out of this affliction.

G.'s first two novels, *The Descendant* (1897) and *Phases of an Inferior Planet* (1898), together with *The Wheel of Life* (1906), wrestle with, among other things, the plight of the woman as artist. All are based in New York which, to G., meant intellectual Bohemia. The first two books show obvious signs of her deep reading of Darwin, Nietzsche, Henry George, Mill, Haeckel, Weismann, and other writers on heredity, milieu, class struggle, evolution, and survival. Gradually, the social concerns of these apprenticeship novels would be more skillfully integrated into her Virginia novels; and G.'s successes enabled her to drop the anxious woman artist theme.

With her Virginia novels, G. was breaking new ground. She wished to correct the sentimental picture of "Ole Virginia" perpetrated by romances of plantation life and the glorious defeat of the Civil War. The South suffered from what G. termed "evasive idealism." *The Battle-Ground* (1902) gently satirizes the prewar fable: honey-voiced belles, picturesque Negroes, a crusty old major and an enlightened governor disputing the virtues of slavery by a comfortable library fire. *The Deliverance* (1904) deals with tobacco farming and the moral struggles of a destroyed planter family in the post-Reconstruction period of 1878–90.

In writing about the New South, G. liked to show an underdog hero fighting his way to personal acceptance and public service. This pattern of action is found in several of G.'s novels of Virginia political life. *The Voice of the People* (1900), G.'s first Virginia novel, is one of the earliest fictional treatments of the southern poor white.

G. celebrates Virginia heroines in *Virginia* (1913), *Life and Gabriella* (1916), and *Barren Ground* (1925). One of her best works, *Virginia* traces the dawning self-knowledge—too late—and lifelong disillusionment of a southern woman bred conventionally and decorously to a romantic ideal of marriage.

Of *Barren Ground* and the novels that followed it, G. wrote that this was the work upon which "I like to imagine that I shall stand or fall as a novelist." The novel is among her best, and probably her most renowned. Seduced, pregnant, and abandoned, Dorinda Oakley leaves her Virginia farm home. Fortuitously she miscarries. Upon her return she adjusts her nature to the demands she establishes for her life: to remain aloof from love and all entanglements, to labor unremittingly to control the fertility of the worn and wasted land as it had controlled her parents' lives, and to prosper richly. At the last, as a strong, white-haired woman, Dorinda watches her erstwhile lover die. "For once in Southern fiction," wrote G., "the betrayed woman would become the victor instead of the victim."

Leaving the Virginia countryside, G. comes indoors with her Queenborough (i.e., Richmond) novels of manners: *The Romantic Comedians* (1926), *They Stooped to Folly* (1929), and the somberer *The Sheltered Life* (1932). *The Romantic Comedians* centers on the fatuous, aged, would-be lover, Judge Gamaliel Honeywell, whose "withered heart urgently craves to be green again." The word "happiness" recurs with ironic frequency. G's satiric vision is both classic and fresh in this work whose aphoristic dialogue is reminiscent of theater.

The comic possibilities of youth's encounters with age in a framework of sexual morality are also explored in *They Stooped to Folly*. G. introduces diverse women characters, focusing on the seduced and fallen women of three generations.

As in the other Queensborough novels, the themes of youth and age and the insufficiency of love are pervasive in *The Sheltered Life*, which observes the interaction of three generations of southerners before World War I. Courtly General Archbald reflects on the polite hypocrisies that warped lives in his youth. It is, however, the adherents of a newer morality, the new happiness seekers, who trample on those they love, but don't "mean anything."

Vein of Iron (1935) documents the lives of the Scotch-Irish "good people" of Ironside, a village of the Upper Valley of the James River in Virginia. The surrounding mountains loom as personal presences. G. takes her much-tried heroine Ada Fincastle from girlhood to middle age, from 1901 to 1933. The vision produced by the novel is one of nostalgia and of perpetual accommodation to necessity in the face of futility. In *Vein of Iron*, G. is best when extolling ancestral values, for she saw the future as a dying age.

Despite its being awarded a Pulitzer Prize, a belated consolation for the committee's having passed over *The Sheltered Life*, *In This Our Life* (1941) is a minor achievement. The portrayals of the elderly weary hero and his desperate daughters betray G.'s declining health and her difficulty in coming to grips with the modern world.

G.'s social perspectives and her thirst for realism made her a precursor of writers she failed to appreciate, notably a stylist like Faulkner. She was outspoken about newer writers, whom she characterized as amateurs and illiterates. As she grew older she found it difficult to cast aside the values she had once lightheartedly satirized. She saw the modern world as "distraught, chaotic, grotesque, . . . an age of cruelty without moral indignation, of catastrophe without courage." Her efforts to embrace the young within her artistic vision, even to deal with contemporary argot, turn out shrill and awry. Despite awards and honors during her lifetime, G.'s literary reputation suffered after her death.

G.'s best writing is in the comic spirit. There are fine humorous characterizations, many buried in the subplots of her novels. As an innovator, she rejected the South's codes and genteel fables to write about politics and industry rising up out of the Virginia soil. Race and stock are for her determinants of character in the battle for survival. Work, whether of the grower, the tycoon, or the artist, brings salvation. Manners are both valued and criticized. G. drew her chief inspirations from the land that bred the vein of iron and from the tremors of society. Past and present, the conflict of generations, the uneasy commerce between an older patriciate and the new working classes, mores and wars, ceremony and the fresh winds of change—these were the broad concerns of G.'s writing which she treated with the "blood and irony" she had prescribed for southern fiction.

WORKS: *The Descendant* (1897). *Phases of an Inferior Planet* (1898). *The Voice of the People* (1900). *The Battle-Ground* (1902). *The Freeman, and Other Poems* (1902). *The Deliverance* (1904). *The Wheel of Life* (1906). *The Ancient Law* (1908). *The Romance of a Plain Man* (1909). *The Miller of Old Church* (1911). *Virginia* (1913). *Life and Gabriella* (1916). *The Builders* (with H. W. Anderson, 1919). *One Man in His Time* (1922). *The Shadowy Third, and Other Stories* (1923). *Barren Ground* (1925). *The Romantic Comedians* (1926). *They Stooped to Folly* (1929). *The Old Dominion*

Edition of the Works of Ellen Glasgow (8 vols., 1929–1933). *The Sheltered Life* (1932). *Vein of Iron* (1935). *The Virginia Edition of the Works of Ellen Glasgow* (12 vols., 1938). *In This Our Life* (1941). *A Certain Measure: An Interpretation of Prose Fiction* (1943). *The Woman Within* (1954). *Letters of Ellen Glasgow* (Ed. B. Rouse, 1958). *The Collected Stories of Ellen Glasgow* (Ed. R. K. Meeker, 1963). *Beyond Defeat: An Epilogue to an Era* (Ed. L. Y. Gore, 1966).

BIBLIOGRAPHY: Auchincloss, L., *Pioneers and Caretakers* (1965). Ekman, B., *The End of a Legend: E. G.'s History of Southern Women* (1979). Godbold, E. S., Jr., *E. G. and the Woman Within* (1972). Holman, C. H., *Three Modes of Southern Fiction* (1966). Inge, M. T., ed., *E. G.: Centennial Essays* (1976). Jessup, J. L., *The Faith of Our Feminists: A Study in the Novels of Edith Wharton, E. G., Willa Cather* (1950). Kelly, W. W., *E. G.: A Bibliography* (1964). Kraft, S., *No Castles on Main Street: American Authors and Their Homes* (1979). McDowell, F. P. W., *E. G. and the Ironic Art of Fiction* (1960). Parent, M., *E. G.: Romancière* (1962). Raper, J. R., *Without Shelter: The Early Career of E. G.* (1971). Richards, M. K., *E. G.'s Development As a Novelist* (1971). Rouse, B., *E. G.* (1962). Santas, J. F., *E. G.'s American Dream* (1965). Thiébaux, M., *Ellen Glasgow* (1982).

For articles in reference works, see: *CB* (Jan. 1946). *DAB*, Suppl. 3. *LSL*. *NAW* (article by M. R. Kaufman). *NCAB*, C. *20thCA*. *20thCAS*.

Other references: *Ellen Glasgow Newsletter* (Ashland, Virginia).

MARCELLE THIÉBAUX

Susan Glaspell

B. 1 July 1876, Davenport, Iowa; d. 27 July 1948, Provincetown, Massachusetts
D. of Elmer S. and Alice Keating Glaspell; m. George Cram Cook, 1913;
m. Norman Matson, 1925

G. began her career writing numerous short stories—for popular magazines—in line with the sentimental and escapist mode popular at the time, and two conventional romantic novels. When she met and married her first husband, her life-style and the direction of her work changed radically. Her novel *Fidelity* (1915) is thematically connected to this love affair. With Eugene O'Neill, she and Cook became the founders of and prime contributors to the Provincetown Players, an experimental group begun on Cape Cod in 1915 to provide a place where native drama could develop freely outside the fetters of commercialism. The company, which moved to New York's Greenwich Village (as the Playwrights Theatre) in the fall of 1916, proved to be one of the most important and seminal forces in the history of American theater.

G.'s first one-act play, written with Cook, was part of the Province-town Players' initial season. Her second one-act play, *Trifles*, was produced in 1916 during the second summer season. (G.'s short-story adaptation of it, "A Jury of Her Peers," appeared in *Best American Short Stories* of 1916). On a bleak Iowa farm, a dour farmer, John Wright, has been found dead in his bed, his own rope around his neck. His wife, Minnie, who never appears onstage, is in custody pending investigation of the murder. The tacit agreement of two women onstage to conceal the telltale evidence of guilt implies that Wright was a man who deserved to die as he did, and their sympathy (with that of the audience) goes to the abused wife. After fifty years, this piece is still deservedly cited as an example of expert craftsmanship.

For the next two seasons G. continued to write, act in, and direct plays. Her first full-length play, *Bernice* (1920), in which again the heroine never appears onstage, was produced in 1919.

G. returned in *The Inheritors* (1921) to a favorite theme: the desirability of preserving the best values of pioneer character. The only character who represents the true spirit of her forefathers (the founders of a liberal college) and of America itself is the granddaughter Madeline Morton, who goes to jail for the rights of Hindu students protesting British domination of India.

In *The Verge* (1921), G. deals with a "new woman" again. However, Claire Archer is very different from Madeline. Claire is so intent on attaining her own freedom—an "otherness," she calls it—that she is driven over the edge of sanity when she rejects the past and present (ancestors, husband, and daughter) in hopes of a new future.

G. dramatizes the subject of the artist's life and connection to society in her final two plays, *The Comic Artist* (1928) and *Alison's House* (1930). The latter, dealing with the posthumous disposition of the poetry of a woman much like Emily Dickinson, was produced at the Civic Repertory Theatre, with Eva LeGallienne playing the role of the niece who favors publication. It won the Pulitzer Prize.

G. had only minor connections with the theater after 1931. She had returned to the novel in 1928 with *Brook Evans*. In *Ambrose Holt and Family* (1931), G. clearly connects the "free woman" of the 20th c. with the best qualities of the pioneer, as in her play *The Inheritors*. This novel and the one that followed, *The Morning Is Near Us* (1939), have philosophical depth, but little relevance to the time of the Great Depression. It was not until *Norma Ashe* (1942) and then *Judd Rankin's*

Daughter (1945) that G. took cognizance of failures inherent in midwestern isolationist attitudes, appropriate though they may have been for the original pioneers.

Because her work in the theater was of necessity much more experimental than her work in other genres, G.'s main significance stems from her Provincetown connection, not only as a playwright, but, more importantly, as an innovator instrumental in changing the course of American drama forever. The most striking hallmark of her best writing is her consistent emphasis on the need for human beings to fulfill their highest potential by utilizing what is desirable from the past and applying it with faith and courage to the future. Because she developed a broad humanistic viewpoint, she never became a typical midwestern regionalist in the narrow sense; she eschewed always the 20th-c. provincialism, superpatriotism, and fatuousness that evolved as Main Street, USA.

WORKS: *Glory of the Conquered* (1909). *The Visioning* (1911). *Fidelity* (1915). *Bernice* (with seven one-act plays, 1920). *The Inheritors* (1921). *The Verge* (1921). *The Road to the Temple* (1927). *Brook Evans* (1928). *The Comic Artist* (with N. Matson, 1928). *Fugitive's Return* (1929). *Alison's House* (1930). *Ambrose Holt and Family* (1931). *The Morning Is Near Us* (1939). *Cherished and Shared of Old* (1940). *Norma Ashe* (1942). *Judd Rankin's Daughter* (1945).

BIBLIOGRAPHY: Gelb, A., and B. Gelb, *O'Neill* (1960). Goldberg, I., *Drama of Transition* (1922). Hapgood, H., *A Victorian in a Modern World* (1939). Lewisohn, L., *Expression in America* (1932). Quinn, A. H., *History of American Drama from the Civil War to the Present Day* (1927). Vorse, M. H., *Time and the Town* (1942). Waterman, A. E., *S. G.* (1966).

For articles in reference works, see: *DAB*, Suppl. 4. *NAW* (article by A. E. Waterman). *NCAB*, 15. *20thCA*. *20thCAS*.

Other references: *Arts and Decoration* (June 1931). *Bookman* (Feb. 1918). *Commonweal* (20 May 1931). *Drama* (June 1931). *Independent Woman* (Jan. 1946). *Nation* (3 Nov. 1920; 6 April 1921; 4 April 1923). *NewR* (17 Jan. 1923). *NYT* (12 April 1931; 10 May 1931). *Palimpsest* (Dec. 1930). *Review of Reviews* (June 1909). *SatR* (30 July 1938). *WLB* (Dec. 1928). *Women's Journal* (Aug. 1928; June 1931).

EDYTHE M. McGOVERN

Caroline Gordon

B. 6 Oct. 1895, Merry Mount Farm, Kentucky; d. 11 April 1981, Chiapas, Mexico
Writes under: Caroline Gordon, Caroline Tate
D. of James Morris and Nancy Meriwether Gordon; m. Allen Tate, 1924

Born on her mother's ancestral farm in the Kentucky tobacco region near Tennessee, the setting for much of her fiction, G. was tutored by her father until she was ten. She then attended his all-boys classical school. In 1916, she received a B.A. from Bethany College in West Virginia. After teaching high school until 1920, she became a journalist for the *Chattanooga News*. While there she met many of the Agrarians, including Allen Tate.

G. readily identified with the Agrarians' traditional conservative values, favoring a stable, hierarchical society based on Christianity over an urban, technological society. G. became deeply involved in Tate's literary world; both spent much of the late 1920s in Europe on Guggenheim Fellowships. The Tates raised their daughter Nancy at Benfolly Farm, Tennessee, entertaining many artistic visitors.

Although G. and Tate were divorced in 1959, in 1960 they coedited a second edition of their successful and influential *The House of Fiction: An Anthology of the Short Story* (1950, 1960). Both this and G.'s *How to Read a Novel* (1957) adapt many New Critical poetic principles to fiction.

As Ford Madox Ford's literary secretary, G. finished her first novel, *Penhally* (1931), acclaimed by Ford as "the best novel that has been produced in modern America." It chronicles one hundred years of antebellum southern culture by tracing the decline of the Penhally estate and the Llewellyn family. The ancient virtues violently conflict with the inevitability of change.

In *Aleck Maury, Sportsman* (1934), her most popular novel, an old classics teacher, modeled on G.'s father, spends every spare moment hunting and fishing. Maury's ritualistic, almost sacramental devotion to sport allows him a dignity rarely possible in the chaos of the wasteland world which has replaced the Old South. Only the quest for love—apparent in many of G.'s women characters, like Maury's wife Molly—provides a similar dignity.

G.'s fiction of the late 1930s and the 1940s continued to develop her ancestral. regional material; it also reflected a growing emphasis on sophisticated knowledge in contrast to primitive innocence, while religion became a means of confronting the abyss, a terrifying image permeating her fiction.

The literary milieu at Benfolly Farm appears in several works, particularly *The Strange Children* (1951), G.'s first novel after her conversion to Catholicism in 1947. It traces the search for grace in a fallen world. The central intelligence of nine-year-old Lucy Lewis records the despair and materialism of the skeptical intellectual world and the need for an order only religious belief can provide.

The salvation that is possible in *The Strange Children* becomes real in *The Malefactors* (1956). Tom Claibourne, a nonproducing poet, must reevaluate the direction of his life after he leaves his wife Vera for the ambitious and intellectual poet, Cynthia Vail. Through the influence of Catherine Pollard, a symbol of Christian charity, Claibourne discovers that he is bound nowhere unless he can return to his wife. While in her earlier work the classical Greek world subtly patterned G.'s vision, in *The Malefactors* it is the archetypal world of Jungian psychology that prepares for Claibourne's religious conversion, reversing the pattern of action in G.'s fiction from death and destruction to grace.

G.'s worth as a novelist has been too often ignored by critics. She is more frequently identified as coeditor of *The House of Fiction* and as Allen Tate's former wife than as a creative artist in her own right. In addition, because her work is usually set in the South and because of her close association with the Agrarians, critics have tended to dismiss her too easily as a regionalist. Her talent for dealing with religious themes and with the themes of male/female relationships and the possibility of creativity in a wasteland world has been virtually overlooked by critics who miss the broader implications of the South in her fiction. Though G. is presently enjoying a renewal of interest, her novels, particularly *The Strange Children* and *The Malefactors*, have not received the attention they deserve. She is as fine a fiction writer as Robert Penn Warren and Allen Tate and should share equally in the acclaim so often accorded the Agrarians and New Critics as the generators of the Southern Renascence.

WORKS: *Penhally* (1931). *Aleck Maury, Sportsman* (1934). *None Shall Look Back* (1937). *The Garden of Adonis* (1937). *Green Centuries* (1941). *The Women on the Porch* (1944). *The Forest of the South* (1945). *The House of Fiction: An Anthology of the Short Story* (edited by Gordon, with A. Tate,

1950; rev. ed., 1960). *The Strange Children* (1951). *The Malefactors* (1956). *A Good Soldier: A Key to the Novels of Ford Madox Ford* (1957). *How to Read a Novel* (1957). *Old Red, and Other Stories* (1963). *The Glory of Hera* (1972). *The Collected Stories* (1981).

BIBLIOGRAPHY: Golden, R. E., and M. C. Sullivan, *Flannery O'Connor and Caroline Gordon: A Reference Guide* (1977). Landess, T. H., *The Short Fiction of Caroline Gordon: A Critical Symposium* (1972). McDowells, F. P., *Caroline Gordon* (Univ. of Minnesota Pamphlet, 1966). Stuckey, W. J., *Caroline Gordon* (1972).

For articles in reference works, see: *20thCA. 20thCAS.*

Other references: *Crit* (Winter 1956). *Renascence* (Fall 1963). *SR* (Summer 1946; Autumn 1949; Spring 1971).

SUZANNE ALLEN

Shirley Graham

B. 11 Nov. 1907, Evansville, Indiana; d. 27 March 1977, Peking, China
Wrote under: Shirley Graham DuBois, Shirley Graham
D. of David A. and Lizzie Etta Bell Graham; m. Shadrach T. McCanns, 1921;
m. William Edward Burghardt DuBois, 1951

G., a lifelong advocate of human rights, was born on the farm of her great-grandfather, a freed slave and blacksmith who used his home as an Underground Railroad station for runaway slaves. G. and her four brothers grew up in a variety of cities—New Orleans, Colorado Springs, and Spokane—in which their father, an African Episcopal minister, received pastoral assignments. G. married a year after completing high school, but within three years she became a widow with two sons to support.

G. studied music theory and composition at the Sorbonne. While there, she also learned about African music from West African students studying in France. In 1931, G. matriculated at Oberlin College, where she received both the B.A. and M.A. degrees. Her years there marked the beginning of her career as a dramatist and composer. G.'s one-act play, *Coal Dust*, and her three-act comedy, *Elijah's Ravens*, were performed during this period; both had been written in 1930. A music-drama, *Tom-Tom* (1932), was based upon G.'s knowledge of African rhythms; it was later revised into an opera for which G. wrote the libretto and music.

Although she was a successful dramatist, G.'s major literary contribution was made in the field of biography. Her decision to research and record the lives of significant black people was influenced indirectly by her cultural and political activities with the NAACP (National Association for the Advancement of Colored People), which appointed her a national field secretary in 1942, and directly by the death of her son Robert, who, because of his race, was mistreated in an army camp and denied proper hospital care.

G.'s biographies combine history and fiction in celebrating black life during a period of general neglect. They are primarily popular books that recognize the contributions made by blacks to American culture and preserve the history of black achievement for the world. Because G.'s biographies delineate heroic qualities for emulation and seem especially suited for young adults, they have become categorized as "juvenile" literature and have not received the critical attention they deserve.

G. wrote eleven biographies. Among the most successful is *Paul Robeson, Citizen of the World* (1946), which traces the life of the famous singer from his boyhood through his forty-sixth birthday. G. uses the musical patterns of a classical concerto and a modern blues to orchestrate the details of Robeson's life.

In *There Was Once a Slave: The Historic Story of Frederick Douglass* (1947), G. relies on an association between the North Star and liberty as the controlling metaphor for her poignant narrative. *Your Most Humble Servant* (1949), the first book-length treatment of Benjamin Banneker, a late 18th-c. astronomer, mathematician, and surveyor, is G.'s major work on a historical figure.

G. married the famous Harvard-trained social scientist, Dr. W. E. B. DuBois, four days after his eighty-third birthday and on the eve of his indictment as an "agent of a foreign principle." Their marriage culminated a thirty-year friendship during which G. was guided by DuBois's emphasis on "Beauty, Accomplishment, and Dignity" as the criteria of Negro art. Throughout the years of her marriage, G. devoted much of her attention to political work against oppression and to cultural activities for peace. She was also her husband's companion-helpmate on his final project, a massive *Encyclopedia Africana*, yet she did not live in his shadow; she helped to found *Freedomways*, a magazine on the African-American freedom movement, and was selected its first editor. Her last three books, *Gamal Abdel Nasser, Son of the Nile* (1972), *Zulu Heart* (1974), and *Julius K. Nyerere: Teacher of Africa* (1975), reflect G.'s international perspective after a decade of living on the African continent.

His Day Is Marching On: A Memoir of W. E. B. DuBois (1971) is essentially G.'s own biography. In it, she emerges as the exemplar of the values and virtues defining the heroic men and women of her biographies. The book is notable for its quiet celebration of love, loyalty, conviction, and courage. Sensitive and vivid in language, G.'s memoir documents a personal experience and outlines a cultural history.

WORKS: *Coal Dust* (1930). *Elijah's Ravens* (1930). *Tom-Tom* (1932). *Little Black Sambo* (1937). *The Swing Mikado* (1938). *I Gotta Home* (1939). *It's Morning* (1940). *Dust to Earth* (1941). *Track Thirteen* (1942). *Dr. George Washington Carver, Scientist* (with G. D. Lipscomb, 1944). *Paul Robeson, Citizen of the World* (1946). *There Was Once a Slave: The Heroic Story of Frederick Douglass* (1947). *The Story of Phillis Wheatley* (1949). *Your Most Humble Servant* (1949). *Jean Baptiste Pointe de Sable, Founder of Chicago* (1953). *The Story of Pocahontas* (1953). *Booker T. Washington: Educator of Hand, Head, and Heart* (1955). *His Day Is Marching On: A Memoir of W. E. B. DuBois* (1971). *Gamal Abdel Nasser, Son of the Nile: A Biography* (1972). *Zulu Heart: A Novel* (1974). *Julius K. Nyerere: Teacher of Africa* (1975).

BIBLIOGRAPHY: Bedini, S. A., *The Life of Benjamin Banneker* (1972). Miller, E., ed., *The Negro in America* (1970).

For articles in reference works, see: *Afro-American Encyclopedia*, Ed. J. T. Haley (1974). *Black American Writers: Bibliographical Essays*, Ed. M. T. Inge (1977). *Black Playwrights, 1823–1977: An Annotated Bibliography of Plays*, Eds. J. V. Hatch and O. Abdullah (1977). *CB* (Oct. 1946). *Negro Almanac*, Ed. H. A. Ploski (1976).

Other references: *Crisis* (Aug. 1932). *NYT* (5 June 1973; 5 April 1977).

THADIOUS M. DAVIS

Shirley Ann Grau

B. 8 July 1929, New Orleans, Louisiana
D. of Adolph Eugene and Katherine Onions Grau; m. James Kern
Feibleman, 1955

Daughter of a dentist, G. describes her family as "ordinary middle class. White. Protestant." However, she also admits that the family members were well enough set financially that they could choose not to work. Her mother was in her middle forties when G. was born, yet she had another daughter even later. G. attended the Booth Academy in Montgomery, Alabama, until she transferred to the Ursuline Academy in New Orleans as a senior. She attended Sophie Newcomb, the "girl's wing" of the all-male Tulane University, where she took many of her classes and met her future husband, a philosophy professor twenty-six years her senior.

They were married in New York City, where G. had moved to pursue her writing career, and live in New Orleans with their four children.

G.'s first collection of short stories, *The Black Prince* (1955), won immediate acclaim and was compared in its importance to J. D. Salinger's *Nine Stories* and to Eudora Welty's *A Curtain of Green*. These stories reveal concerns and characters that would dominate her later fiction. The first of these are her primitives, living—like young Joshua in the story of that name—in tune with nature, sharing its creative violence and hero-ically, if hopelessly, defying its destructive forces. They also introduce G.'s concern with city-bred southerners locked away from nature and with women trapped between stereotypes of the past and the confusion of the present.

These primitives burst forth in her first novel, *The Hard Blue Sky* (1958), a flawed work but with moments of great power. The Louisiana island fishermen of the novel take on mythic proportions, similar to the Aran Islanders in Synge's plays, owing to G.'s simple and realistic dia-logue, her vivid recreation of their daily struggles with nature, and her concentration on their awareness rather than on their innocence.

The modern woman steps forth again in G.'s next novel. Trapped in *The House on Coliseum Street* (1961) is Joan Caillet, who floats into an abortion only to be tossed and torn by its psychological aftermath. The emptiness within reflects the emptiness outside, and Joan's growing awareness of this emptiness, this lack of values within the surviving shell of southern society—perhaps of American society as a whole—leads her to destructive violence. G. seems to argue that unless individuals live in tune with nature, as do her primitives, their violence will destroy rather than recreate the world.

A similar violence is produced by Abigail Tolliver's discovery of hy-pocrisy in *The Keepers of the House* (1964). This Pulitzer Prize-winning novel combines G.'s primitives with her southern lady and blacks with whites, as she traces the heritage of a family that rises above the preju-dices of the stereotypes to assert the integrity of the individual. Abigail has been taught the role of the southern lady, but her grandfather, Wil-liam Howland, has given her an even more important legacy. The evi-dence of his love for his black housekeeper Margaret, a hardy primitive reminiscent of the folk-heroine Alberta in "The Black Prince," destroys Abigail's illusions of safety, thus exposing her to the violence of life it-self. But William Howland has also provided in his actions an example of humanity which keeps Abigail from being destroyed by her own rebellious violence, which enables her to be born again into a new aware-ness of life.

G.'s most recent novels, *The Condor Passes* (1971) and *Evidence of Love* (1977), as well as many of the stories from her most recent collection, *The Wind Shifting West* (1973), continue her interest in family and social heritage, but they concentrate more than ever on character studies. Each novel opens with an old man and ends with his death, in between examining the people and experiences of his life. Each also explores the interactions of love and money. The economic security of the central characters allows G. to touch only lightly on the social context except in flashbacks; the characters struggle instead with the complexity of human relationships and of personal identity.

G. displays throughout each novel her consummate skill at manipulating point of view, her unique ability to empathize with each character. Above all, she is a superb storyteller, creating her Louisiana world in rich detail and letting her characters live, speak, and argue for themselves. Although she has been criticized for her traditional style, her symbolic realism, with its roots in the Louisiana bayous of Kate Chopin, still rises far above imitation. Her originality is evident in her consistent philosophy of nature and in her uniquely female imagery, from the caverns of emptiness which haunt Joan in *The House on Coliseum Street* to the vivid description of his own birth offered by Edward Milton Henley as the first scene of *Evidence of Love*.

WORKS: *The Black Prince, and Other Stories* (1955). *The Hard Blue Sky* (1958). *The House on Coliseum Street* (1961). *The Keepers of the House* (1964). *The Condor Passes* (1971). *The Wind Shifting West* (1973). *Evidence of Love* (1977).

BIBLIOGRAPHY: Gossett, L. Y., *Violence in Recent Southern Fiction* (1965). For articles in reference works, see: *CA*, 1–4 (1967). *CB* (1959).

Other references: *Crit.* (6, 1963; 17, 1975). *Insula: Revista Bibliografica de Ciencias y Letras (Madrid)* (1966). *NewR* (18 April 1964; 24 Nov. 1973). *NYRB* (2 Dec. 1971). *NYTBR* (22 March 1964). *SatR* (21 March 1964). *SR* 70 (1962).

THELMA J. SHINN

Angelina Emily Grimké

B. 20 Feb. 1805, Charleston, South Carolina; d. 26 Oct. 1879, Hyde Park,
Massachusetts
Wrote under: A. E. Grimké, Angelina Grimké, Angelina Grimké Weld
D. of John Faucheraud and Mary Smith Grimké; m. Theodore Dwight
Weld, 1838

An abolitionist and women's rights pioneer, G. launched her meteoric
career in the abolitionist movement in a letter to William Lloyd Garrison
published in *The Liberator* (1835).

G.'s first pamphlet was *Appeal to Christian Women of the Southern
States* (1836). In the *Appeal* she attacked the traditional religious justi-
fications of slavery and focused instead on the God-given equality of
the slave as human being. The most powerful and original part of the
Appeal was her call to southern women to take action against slavery.
Though women lacked political power, they could free slaves who
were their own property, ameliorate the conditions for other slaves, and
petition legislatures for emancipation. Such actions might lead to fines
or imprisonment; nevertheless, she called women to civil disobedience.
She contended: "If a law commands me to sin, I will break it; if it calls
me to suffer, I will let it take its course unresistingly." G.'s *Appeal* was
the only abolitionist message by a southern woman addressed specifically
to southern women. As such it aroused violent opposition in the South.

G.'s second pamphlet, *An Appeal to the Women of the Nominally Free
States* (1837), stressed women's particular responsibility to their fellow
women in bondage. Female slaves are "our countrywomen . . . our sisters."

Letters to Catharine E. Beecher (1838) came in response to Beecher's
*Essay on Slavery and Abolitionism with Reference to the Duty of Ameri-
can Females* (1837). Beecher had attacked G. both for advocating abolition and for urging women's involvement therein. In the *Letters*, first
published serially in *The Liberator* and *The Emancipator* in 1837, G.
concentrated primarily on a detailed defense of the efficacy of immediate
abolition, but in two letters that deal specifically with the concept of
women's limited sphere, G. developed a strong feminist argument based
on a doctrine of human rights. According to G., "human beings have
rights because they are moral beings." As moral beings, women no less
than men must act publicly on moral issues. As human beings, women

should participate in making all laws concerning their own condition. She saw a new cause emerging out of the abolitionist controversy, a broad drive to reclaim the usurped rights of all disadvantaged persons, including women and slaves.

When she married Theodore Weld, her career as a writer came to an end. She collaborated with him and her sister, Sarah, in compiling *American Slavery As It Is: Testimony of a Thousand Witnesses* (1839). Some speeches and a letter on women's rights were later published. But it is on the three works written between 1836 and 1838 that her reputation rests.

As a writer, G. has a forceful and clean-cut style. Her arguments are lucid and cogent, and she writes with ease and directness. She utilizes 18th-c. reformist ideas to support her arguments, drawing heavily on environmentalist theories to explain the perversion of original equality. She also draws on 18th-c. republican ideology with its stress on the imperative necessity for moral virtue among citizens if the republic is to survive. Above all, however, as a 19th-c. evangelical reformer, she relies on religious arguments. The Bible offered the standard of judgment by which to determine the evils of slavery. It offered the religious-historical role models for women undertaking responsible moral action against slavery. In her religious convictions, G. found the basis for the formulation of the doctrine of human rights. In so doing, she finally fused the two causes with which her private life and her public career became identified, abolition and women's rights.

WORKS: *Slavery and the Boston Riot: A Letter to Wm. L. Garrison* (1835). *Appeal to Christian Women of the Southern States* (1836). *An Appeal to the Women of the Nominally Free States; Issued by an Anti-Slavery Convention of American Women & Held by Adjournment from the 9th to the 12th of May, 1837* (1837). *Letters to Catharine E. Beecher, in Reply to an Essay on Slavery and Abolitionism, Addressed to A. E. Grimké* (1838). *American Slavery As It Is: Testimony of a Thousand Witnesses* (edited by Grimké, with T. Weld and S. M. Grimké, 1839). *Letter from Angelina Grimké Weld to the Woman's Rights Convention, Held at Syracuse, September, 1852* (1852).

BIBLIOGRAPHY: Barnes, G. H., and D. L. Dumond, eds., *Letters of Theodore Dwight Weld, Angelina Emily Grimké, and Sarah Grimké,: 1822–1844* (2 vols., 1934). Birney, C., *The Grimké Sisters: Sarah and Angelina Grimké: The First Women Advocates of Abolition and Women's Rights* (1885). Lerner, G., *The Grimké Sisters from South Carolina: Rebels against Slavery* (1967). Lumpkin, K. Du P., *The Emancipation of Angelina Grimké* (1974). Weld, T. D., *In Memory: Angelina Grimké Weld* (1880).

For articles in reference works, see: *HWS*, I. *NAW* (article on Sarah Grimké, by B. L. Fladeland). *NCAB*, 2.

INZER BYERS

Sarah Moore Grimké

B. 26 Nov. 1792, Charleston, South Carolina; d. 23 Dec. 1873, Hyde Park, Massachusetts
D. of John Faucheraud and Mary Smith Grimké

G. made her impact upon American history and literature as an abolitionist and advocate of women's rights. Her first publication was a pamphlet, *An Epistle to the Clergy of the Southern States* (1836). In it, G. stresses the inherent conflict between slavery and Christianity, basing her argument against slavery on the premise that God had created all men equal. Referring to state laws and practices, she effectively demonstrates how the law kept ministers from meeting religious obligations to slaves, and she calls on the southern clergy to act as moral leaders against slavery.

G.'s second publication came out of an antislavery lecture tour of New England in 1837 and 1838. Because G. and her sister Angelina lectured publicly on abolition to both men and women, they were sharply criticized, especially by the Congregationalist Ministerial Association of Massachusetts. G. responded with fifteen letters, first published serially in 1837 in the New England *Spectator* and later collected as a book.

In the *Letters on the Equality of the Sexes* (1838), G. rejects indignantly the contention that women should not speak publicly on moral issues, asserting that as morally responsible individuals, they cannot do otherwise. She further argues that women should themselves become ministers. She went on to develop a full-fledged argument for women's equality. Again, she started with the religious premise. God had created man and woman with equal moral rights and duties. That original equality and responsibility remained unaltered by the Fall. Nor did Christ distinguish between male and female virtues. The biblical message is clear: "Whatever is right for man to do, is right for woman."

After the *Letters*, G. largely withdrew from writing. She collaborated with her sister and brother-in-law in compiling *American Slavery As It Is: Testimony of a Thousand Witnesses* (1839); she wrote occasionally for newspapers and did a translation of Alphonse de Lamartine's *Joan of Arc* (1867).

In explaining women's historical inequality, G. particularly stressed the environmentalist argument. She contrasted the role women in general were allowed to play with the role women in authority showed themselves capable of fulfilling. Especially she denounced the deliberate efforts to "debase and enslave" women's intellect. "All I ask of our brethren is that they take their feet from off our necks and permit us to stand upright." Only then can the validity of male assumptions about women's nature and abilities be tested.

Of the two publications of 1836–38, the *Epistle to the Clergy of the Southern States* is essentially a minor work. It added little to the antislavery argument, and the often turgid style of writing further limited its appeal. The *Letters on the Equality of the Sexes*, on the other hand, is a significant pioneering work written with power and originality. In it her style is forthright and lucid, the tone grave and dispassionate. Her arguments are lit with occasional flashes of ironic humor and anger.

WORKS: *An Epistle to the Clergy of the Southern States* (1836). *Letters on the Equality of the Sexes and the Condition of Woman; Addressed to Mary Parker, President of the Boston Female Anti-Slavery Society* (1838). *American Slavery As It Is: Testimony of a Thousand Witnesses* (edited by Grimké, with T. Weld and A. E. Grimké, 1839). *Joan of Arc: A Biography* by A. de Lamartine (translated by Grimké, 1867).

BIBLIOGRAPHY: See bibliography for Angelina Emily Grimké.

INZEL BYERS

Louise Imogen Guiney

B. 7 Jan. 1861, Boston, Massachusetts; d. 2 Nov. 1920, Chipping Camden, England
Wrote under: Louise Imogen Guiney, Roger Holden, P.O.L.
D. of Robert Patrick and Janet Margaret Doyle Guiney

An Irish Roman Catholic and daughter of a Civil War general, G. was something of a literary novelty in late 19th-c. Boston, yet she was warmly received into the by then well-established literary circle of Annie Adams Fields and Sarah Orne Jewett. Fields eventually bequeathed a large portion of her estate to G.

Her health was never excellent. She had a hearing impairment which grew steadily more severe. She collapsed twice from overwork, once in 1896 and again in 1897. These breakdowns were partially precipitated by the hostile reception she received after her appointment as post-mistress of Auburndale, Massachusetts, in 1894. A combination of anti-Irish, anti-Catholic, and antifemale sentiment led local citizens to organize a boycott to force her resignation. Later she was employed in the Catalogue Room of the Boston Public Library. G. emigrated to England in 1901 and devoted her later years to scholarly research at Oxford. At the same time, she moved toward a more reclusive life-style, as her religious dedication deepened. Her closest friends included Fred Holland Day, with whom she uncovered some important Keats material, Grace Denslow, and Alice Brown, with whom she traveled abroad. Brown dedicated her *The Road to Castaly* (1896) to G. and wrote her biography. They also collaborated on a book on Robert Louis Stevenson (1896).

G. published her first lyrics under pseudonyms ("P.O.L." and "Roger Holden") in 1880. Her first collection of poems, *Songs at the Start*, appeared in 1884; and her first collection of essays, *Goose-Quill Papers*, in 1885.

She considered *A Roadside Harp* (1893) her best poetical effort, while critics estimate *Patrins: A Collection of Essays* (1897) to include her most important critical work. Especially significant are the essays "On the Rapid versus the Harmless Scholar" and "Wilfull Sadness in Literature," in which she rejects Arnoldian "disinterestedness" as a proper critical attitude. Her collected lyrics, *Happy Endings*, were published in 1909.

G. was also a dedicated biographer and scholar. *Robert Emmet* (1904) is about an Irish nationalist, and *Blessed Edmund Campion* (1908) is about an English Jesuit martyr. She also put forth several important critical editions of relatively minor figures, such as *Katherine Philips*, *"The Matchless Orinda"* (1904). One volume of her magnum opus of scholarship, an anthology of Catholic poets from Thomas More to Alexander Pope, entitled *Recusant Poets*, was published posthumously in 1938.

G. favored the cavalier rather than the puritan spirit; her letters suggest a lively, engaged personality. In her works, she was attracted to flamboyant gypsy-like women such as Carmen. In 1896, she wrote a critical preface to Merimée's short story. "Martha Hilton," a vivacious Cinderella figure drawn from Portsmouth, New Hampshire, history, was G.'s contribution to *Three Heroines of New England Romance* (1894), which also included sketches by Harriett Prescott Spofford and Alice Brown.

Some consider that G.'s unpublished letters contain her finest writing. Two volumes of her letters were published in 1926. Yet even among her published works the consensus is that her religious lyrics are among the finest American contributions to the genre, and that her criticism contains much that is still of value.

WORKS: *Songs at the Start* (1884). *Goose-Quill Papers* (1885). *Brownies and Bogles* (1887). *Monsieur Henri: A Footnote to French History* (1892). *A Roadside Harp* (1893). *A Little English Gallery* (1894). *Lovers' Saint Ruth's, and Three Other Tales* (1895). *Robert Louis Stevenson* (with A. Brown, 1896). *Three Heroines of New England Romance* (with A. Brown and H. P. Spofford, 1894). *Patrins: A Collection of Essays* (1897). *England and Yesterday* (1898). *The Martyr's Idyl, and Shorter Poems* (1899). *Hurrell Fronde* (1904). *Katherine Philips, "The Matchless Orinda"* (edited by Guiney, 1904). *Robert Emmet* (1904). *Blessed Edmund Campion* (1908). *Happy Endings* (1909; rev. ed., 1927). *Letters* (2 vols., 1926). *Recusant Poets* (1938).

Many of Louise Imogen Guiney's unpublished letters are at the Dinand Library at Holy Cross College, Worcester, Massachusetts, and at the Library of Congress.

BIBLIOGRAPHY: Adorita, Sister M., *Soul Ordained to Fail: Louise Imogen Guiney, 1861–1920* (1962). Brown, A., *Louise Imogen Guiney* (1921). Fairbanks, H. G., *Louise Imogen Guiney: Laureate of the Lost* (1973). Guiney, G. C., *Letters of Louise Imogen Guiney* (1926). Tenison, E. M., *Louise Imogen Guiney: Her Life and Works* (1923).

For articles in reference works, see: *AW. DAB*, IV, 2. *NAW* (article by S. M. Parrish). *NCAB*, 9. *20thCA. 20thCAS.*

JOSEPHINE DONOVAN

Emily Hahn

B. *14 Jan. 1905, St. Louis, Missouri*
D. *of Isaac Newton and Hannah Hahn; m. Charles R. Boxer, 1945*

As a child, H. developed an adventurous spirit and an independent mind. Scorning custom and convention, she became the first woman to enroll in, and earn a degree from, the University of Wisconsin's College of Engineering. She also studied mineralogy at Columbia University, New

York City, and anthropology at Oxford, England. Later, many Americans would be scandalized when H. openly introduced her lovers to her readers.

Her first book, *Seductio ad Absurdum: The Principles and Practices of Seduction; a Beginner's Handbook* (1928), had a mixed reception. Some critics did not find her rules and regulations very interesting or very subtle and others were astonished by the gossipy episodes, but most readers found the book delightfully entertaining. Having begun her writing career, H. took on a wide variety of projects, including documentary reports, histories, novels, biographies, children's books, a guide book, a cookbook, and several autobiographical works.

In 1930, H. began a two-year stay, the first of several, in Africa. She lived with a tribe of Pygmies in the Ituri Forest of the Belgian Congo, where she worked with a doctor at a medical mission. *Congo Solo* (1933) was based on her diary. Although her vocabulary and expression often seem too rough, her informal and amusing style has proved appealing to many readers.

In 1935, H. set off on a world tour. She was to remain in China for nine years, settling in Hong Kong and beginning a career as *The New Yorker*'s China Coast correspondent. Her experiences amidst war and revolution had dramatic effects on her literary career, as well as on her personal life.

H.'s support of Chiang Kai-shek is unmistakable in *China to Me* (1944), a "partial autobiography" in which she recounts the dramatic political events as well as the trivial daily incidents that filled her days in Shanghai, Hong Kong, and Chungking. Although she undoubtedly tried to be objective in the biography *Chiang Kai-shek* (1955), her admiration for her subject resulted in a very defensive account of the corruption in his government and his lack of inspirational leadership.

H. continues to write on diverse topics. *Animal Gardens* (1967) is a history of zoos from the pre-Christian era in China and Egypt to the construction of the Milwaukee Zoo. *Breath of God* (1971) examines world folklore. *Once Upon a Pedestal* (1974) is an account of prominent women in art and literature from colonial times to the present. In *Lorenzo: D. H. Lawrence and the Women Who Loved Him* (1975), she depicts the writer as a neurotic, self-centered genius, to whom a great number of women were eager to dedicate themselves. Like so many of H.'s books, it is intriguing, gossipy, readable, and entertaining.

WORKS: *Seductio ad Absurdum: The Principles and Practices of Seduction;*

a Beginner's Handbook (1928). *Beginners' Luck* (1931). *Congo Solo: Misadventures Two Degrees North* (1933). *With Naked Foot* (1934). *Affair* (1935). *The Soong Sisters* (1941). *Mr. Pan* (1942). *China to Me: A Partial Autobiography* (1944). *Hong Kong Holiday* (1946). *Picture Story of China* (1946). *Raffles of Singapore: A Biography* (1946). *Miss Jill* (1947). *England to Me* (1949). *Purple Passage: A Novel about a Lady Both Famous and Fantastic* (1950). *A Degree of Prudery* (1950). *Francie* (1951). *Love Conquers Nothing: A Glandular History of Civilization* (1952). *Francie Again* (1953). *James Brooke of Sarawak: A Biography of Sir James Brooke* (1953). *Mary, Queen of Scots* (1953). *Meet the British* (1953). *Chiang Kai-shek: An Unauthorized Biography* (1955). *The First Book of India* (1955). *Diamond* (1956). *Francie Comes Home* (1956). *Leonardo da Vinci* (1956). *Kissing Cousins* (1958). *Aboab: First Rabbi of the Americas* (1960). *Around the World with Nelli Bly* (1960). *June Finds a Way* (1960). *Tiger House Party* (1960). *China Only Yesterday, 1850–1950: A Century of Change* (1963). *Indo* (1963). *Africa to Me: Person to Person* (1964). *Animal Gardens* (1967). *Romantic Rebels: An Informal History of Bohemianism in America* (1967). *The Cooking of China* (1968). *Zoos* (1968). *Time and Places* (1970). *Breath of God: A Book about Angels, Demons, Familiars, Elementals, and Spirits* (1971). *Fractured Emerald: Ireland* (1971). *On the Side of the Apes* (1971). *Once Upon a Pedestal* (1974). *Lorenzo: D. H. Lawrence and the Women Who Loved Him* (1975). *Mabel: A Biography of Mabel Dodge Luhan* (1977). *Look Who's Talking* (1978).

BIBLIOGRAPHY: For articles in reference works, see: *Authors of Books for Young People*, Eds. M. E. Ward and D. A. Marquardt (second ed., 1971). *CA*, 1–4 (1967). *CB* (July 1942). *NCAB*, H. *20thCAS*.

PATRICIA LANGHALS NEILS

Lucretia Peabody Hale

B. 2 Sept. 1820, Boston, Massachusetts; d. 12 June 1900, Boston, Massachusetts
D. of Nathan and Sarah Preston Everett Hale

H. came from a distinguished New England literary family. Her mother was a writer; her father, nephew of the famous revolutionary-war patriot, was owner-editor of the Boston *Daily Advertiser*. Among H.'s six brothers and sisters were Edward Everett, Unitarian clergyman, abolitionist, and writer, best known for his short story "A Man Without a Country"; Charles, consul general to Egypt at the time of the opening of the Suez Canal; and Susan, writer and traveler.

H. gained a reputation as a bright student at the highly regarded George B. Emerson School for Young Ladies, the graduates of which had the equivalent of a contemporary Bachelor of Arts degree. There she and four other girls comprised a group called the Pentad, maintaining their friendship for many years. When the Pentad visited one another, H. often made up stories for amusement when they were in bed at night. After her schooling, H. remained at home helping with the housework, sewing, attending cultural events, and writing. The only one of her immediate group never to marry, she became known as Aunt Lucretia to the children of her friends. She often visited their homes, telling stories to their children as she had to their mothers when she and they were children.

A prolific writer, H. began wielding a pen at a very early age, because the Hale children were often called upon to help out with editorials, book reviews, and translations. Although much of her work consisted of editorials and fillers for the journals her brothers published, she wrote texts and Sunday-school books, edited collections of games and needlework, and produced several novels and books of short stories, sometimes in conjunction with other writers. After the death of her father in 1863, H. supported herself by her writings.

Her first venture into fiction, *Margaret Percival in America* (1850), written in collaboration with Edward, was a religious novel that was well received and had modest sales. The first of her independent writings to attract attention was "The Queen of the Red Chessmen" (*Atlantic Monthly*, 1858), a short, fanciful tale in which a strong-willed red chess queen comes alive. A novel, *Six of One by Half a Dozen of the Other* (1872), a six-way collaboration with Harriet Beecher Stowe and Edward, among others, is an amusing comedy of manners.

H.'s claim to literary distinction, though she never knew it, came through her stories about the Peterkin family. The first one, "The Lady Who Put Salt in Her Coffee" (1868), was made up to amuse Meggie, the daughter of H.'s old school friend, Mrs. Lesley. One summer vacation, when Meggie was sick and forced to miss the family fun, H. sat down by her bedside and on the spot created the story about Mrs. Peterkin's problems with her cup of coffee. She later published it in the periodical *Our Young Folks*. Five more Peterkin stories were printed there, and still others followed in *St. Nicholas*, its successor. Some two-dozen stories were first put out in book form in 1880, and 1886 saw a sequel of eight more, *The Last of the Peterkins, with Others of Their Kin*. The stories were called after Mr. Lesley, whose first name was

Peter, his children forming the "kin," while Mrs. Lesley herself was the wise Lady from Philadelphia.

The first significant nonsense done for children in the U.S., the Peterkin stories became immensely popular throughout the nation, not only with children but with adults as well. Their gentle satire on American attitudes and ways tickled the national funny bone and helped people laugh at themselves. The lovable, foolish Peterkins of Boston consisted of Mr. and Mrs. Peterkin; Agamemnon, who had been to college; Elizabeth Eliza; Solomon John; and the three little boys, always nameless, but never without their india rubber boots.

Although the stories reflect the manners and attitudes of their period, in their revelation of character they ring true yet today, and it is upon the droll, whimsical adventures of this winning family of bumblers, still favorites with children, that H.'s reputation as a writer rests.

WORKS: *Margaret Percival in America* (with E. E. Hale, 1850). *Seven Stormy Sundays* (1859). *Struggle for Life* (1861). *The Lord's Supper and Its Observance* (1866). *The Service of Sorrow* (1867). *Six of One by Half a Dozen of the Other* (with E. E. Hale et al., 1872). *The Wolf at the Door* (1877). *Designs in Outline for Art-Needlework* (1879). *More Stitches for Decorative Embroidery* (1879). *Point-Lace: A Guide to Lace-Work* (1879). *The Peterkin Papers* (1880). *The Art of Knitting* (1881). *The Last of the Peterkins, with Others of Their Kin* (1886). *Fagots for the Fireside* (1888). *The New Harry and Lucy* (with E. E. Hale, 1892). *Stories for Children* (1892). *Sunday School Stories* (with B. Whitman, n.d.). *An Uncloseted Skeleton* (with E. L. Bynner, n.d.).

BIBLIOGRAPHY: Hale, E. E., *A New England Boyhood* (1893). Hale, N., Introduction to *The Complete Peterkin Papers* (1960).

For articles in reference works, see: *AA. DAB*, IV, 2. *The Junior Book of Authors*, Eds. S. J. Kunitz and H. Haycraft (1934). *NAW* (article by M. D. Wankmiller). *NCAB*, 5. *The Who's Who of Children's Literature*, Ed. B. Doyle (1968).

Other references: *Horn Book* (Sept.–Oct. 1940; April 1958). *PW* (28 Oct. 1957).

ALETHEA K. HELBIG

Sarah Josepha Buell Hale

B. 24 Oct. 1788, Newport, New Hampshire; d. 30 April 1879, Philadelphia, Pennsylvania
Wrote under: Cornelia, Sarah Josepha Hale, Mrs. Hale, A Lady of New Hampshire
D. of Gordon and Martha Whittlesey Buell; m. David Hale, 1813

H. was educated at home, in rural New Hampshire, by her mother, who, H. later said, encouraged her "predilection for literary pursuits," and by her older brother, who shared his college studies when on vacation from Dartmouth. H. conducted a private school for children from 1806 until 1813, when she married a lawyer. By her own account, H.'s married life was a model of domestic bliss. She admired her husband greatly and spent idyllic evenings with him in reading and study. In 1822, however, just before the birth of their fifth child, Hale died, leaving H. in financial distress. She soon turned to writing and, with the assistance of her husband's Masonic friends, published *The Genius of Oblivion* (1823), a thin volume of poetry.

Although the poems are undistinguished, they contain the seeds of themes H. was later to develop—the superiority of American character, the need for higher education for women, and the differing roles of the sexes (man "rides the wave" and "rules the flame," while woman is the "star of home"). In addition, the first line of the book, "No mercenary muse inspires my lay," is H.'s first pronouncement to the world of the self-image which, as skillful advertiser of herself and her magazines, she was to promote for the rest of her life: she became a writer only to raise funds to educate her children.

H.'s career was launched in 1827 with the publication of her first novel. *Northwood* is usually represented as one of the earliest novels to contrast American life in the North and South; however, the subtitle, *A Tale of New England*, more accurately describes H.'s intent. Southern scenes and characters are introduced, like British ones, to point up the characteristics of Yankee life.

Despite its flaws *Northwood* was original and became an instant popular success. Its renown brought H. an offer to edit a new magazine, and the year after the publication of her novel she found herself in Boston, the editor of *Ladies' Magazine*.

Although there had previously been female editors and periodicals for women, *Ladies' Magazine* was the first one of quality and the first to last more than five years. It attracted the attention of Louis Godey, an enterprising publisher who was editing an inferior magazine in Philadelphia. Godey offered to buy out the *Ladies' Magazine* and unite it with his *Lady's Book* under H.'s editorship. H. accepted and began an association which lasted from 1837 until 1877. She edited *Godey's Lady's Book* until she was in her ninetieth year.

Because Godey was able to finance the novel practice of paying contributors, H. could attract better writers, such as Edgar Allan Poe. She also expanded the number of domestic departments begun in *Ladies' Magazine*. In *Godey's* can be found the forerunners of most departments existing in today's home magazines.

Missing from *Godey's* were essays on the political, economic, and religious questions of the day. H.'s advocacy of education for women and other reforms was carried on principally in her editorial columns, for Godey, with an eye on circulation, forbade any controversial articles. Incredibly, the Civil War was never mentioned in *Godey's* pages. The magazine was successful, however, as circulation climbed from 10,000, in 1837, to 150,000, by 1860, an astounding figure for the time. *Godey's* was the arbiter of American taste and manners, and H.'s name became literally a household word.

During her career as editor, H. continued prolifically to produce her own work: fiction, collections of her sketches, recipe books, and household handbooks; she edited gift books, anthologies of verse and letters by women, and works for children. In her *Poems for Our Children* (1830) is "Mary Had a Little Lamb," the poem for which she is best known today, although her authorship of the first stanza has been disputed. H.'s major work is *Woman's Record; or, Sketches of All Distinguished Women from 'The Beginning' till A.D. 1850* (1853). This monumental biographical encyclopedia, still useful today, took her several years to write and contains some 2500 entries.

H. has been criticized for her views on slavery, but *Northwood* and *Liberia* (1853) have also been called antislavery novels. Interpretation of H. thus has varied widely. Some of her biographers claim she was a "militant feminist," others a "true conservative." Actually her philosophy, expressed repeatedly in her works, was internally consistent and explains many seeming contradictions. She believed that God created women morally superior to men. Eve's sin was less than Adam's, as she fell because of desire for spiritual truth and he from sensual appetite. Eve did sin, however, and woman's punishment is to be subordinate to her husband. She is required to work through him, elevating him and transforming his nature in order to save humanity. In America she is particularly to restrain his materialism and greed to save the nation. Woman's sphere is restricted—she must use her influence only in the domestic realm because if she entered public affairs she might be contaminated.

H.'s philosophy also explains the major contradiction in her life. She thought of herself as a reformer and indeed was an energetic and outspoken supporter of many causes. Yet, apart from her advocacy of education for women, the causes for which she labored were essentially trivial ones, such as eliminating the use of "female" as a noun, having Thanksgiving declared a national holiday, and raising money to complete the Bunker Hill Monument. H. wielded tremendous influence and could unite large numbers of women. She used her power to promote, in her words, women's "happiness and usefulness in their Divinely appointed sphere."

SELECTED WORKS: *The Genius of Oblivion* (1823). *Northwood: A Tale of New England* (1827; rev. ed., *Northwood; or, Life North and South: Showing the True Character of Both*, 1852). *Sketches of American Character* (1829). *Poems for Our Children* (1830). *Flora's Interpreter; or, The American Book of Flowers and Sentiments* (edited by Hale, 1832; rev. ed., 1849). *Traits of American Life* (1835). *The Ladies' Wreath* (compiled by Hale, 1837; rev. ed., 1839). *A Complete Dictionary of Poetical Quotations* (1850). *Liberia; or, Mr. Peyton's Experiments* (1853). *Woman's Record; or, Sketches of All Distinguished Women from 'The Beginning' till A.D. 1850* (1853; rev. eds., 1855, 1870). *Manners; or, Happy Homes and Good Society All the Year Round* (1868).

BIBLIOGRAPHY: Entrikin, I. W., *Sarah Josepha Hale and Godey's Lady's Book* (1946). Finley, R. E., *The Lady of Godey's* (1931). Fryatt, N. R., *Sarah Josepha Hale* (1975). *The Story of Mary and Her Little Lamb* (commissioned by H. Ford, 1928). Taylor, W. R., *Cavalier and Yankee* (1961). Wright, R., *Forgotten Ladies* (1928).

For articles in reference works, see: *AA. CAL. DAB*, IV, 2. *FPA. NAW* (article by P. S. Boyer). *NCAB*, 22.

Other references: *Historian* (Feb. 1970). *NEQ* (Jan. 1928).

BARBARA A. WHITE

Lorraine Hansberry

B. 19 May 1930, Chicago, Illinois; d. 12 Jan. 1965, New York City
D. of Carl Augustus and Nannie Perry Hansberry; m. Robert Nemiroff, 1953

Youngest of four children in a prosperous Republican, black family, H. spent two years at the University of Wisconsin, then went to New York City, where she studied African history under W. E. B. DuBois and worked on a radical monthly, *Freedom*, published by Paul Robeson. In her words, her editor there, Louis E. Burnham, taught her that "all racism is rotten, black or white, that everything is political, and that people tend to be indescribably beautiful and uproariously funny," tenets which are themes of her entire oeuvre.

By 1959, she had attained fame as the youngest American and the only black dramatist to win the Best Play of the Year award, for *A Raisin in the Sun* (1959). H. continued to write and work until her untimely death from cancer during the run of *The Sign in Sidney Brustein's Window* (1964). In addition to her dramatic works, essays, and journals, she made a significant contribution to the black movement by writing the text for a photographic journal, *The Movement: A Documentary of a Struggle for Equality* (1964), published shortly before she died.

A landmark in American theater, *A Raisin in the Sun* ran for 530 performances, toured extensively, and has been published and produced in over thirty countries. Its title and theme are based on a poem by Langston Hughes that questions, "What happens to a dream deferred?" The play derives its power from the inevitable conflicts which arise because each member of the Younger family has a different dream, an individual "plan" for escaping the dreary life of the Chicago ghetto in which they live.

H.'s second commercially produced play, *The Sign in Sidney Brustein's Window*, features a white protagonist, an engagé whose statements that he has always been "a fool who believes that death is waste and love is sweet . . ." and that "hurt is desperation and desperation is energy and energy can MOVE things" sound like the playwright's voice verbatim. Criticism by some reviewers on the basis that the characters are merely personifications of conflicting ways to view the world meant early closure, before giving the public a chance to estimate its value. Through herculean efforts—donations and advertisements sponsored by distinguished people in the American theater—it remained open until over eighty thousand people had seen the production. At H.'s death, the sign came down in New York, but the play was successful on tour and has had subsequent productions in a dozen countries, including a particularly distinguished one in Paris with Simone Signoret as translator and producer.

To H., her most important play was *Les Blancs* (1972), an accurate foretelling of what has happened in Africa in terms of black revolution. When produced posthumously (1970), there were cries of antiwhite bias, despite the fact that it deals as fairly with opportunistic blacks as with white capitalists.

In a similar vein, H.'s ninety-minute television drama, *The Drinking Gourd* (1960), commissioned by NBC for the Civil War centennial, was shelved as "too controversial," although many of its scenes are fore-runners of those done more recently on television in such plays as *Roots*.

Throughout her life, H. kept diaries, journals, and letters, and wrote many essays for newspapers and magazines. Bits and pieces of these, along with scenes from her plays, are well blended by Robert Nemiroff in *To Be Young, Gifted, and Black* (1969), a two-act drama. It was published as a book with extensive background notes and an introduction by James Baldwin.

This playwright's influence in the theater in terms of black performers, as well as black audiences—who saw themselves truthfully presented onstage for the first time in *A Raisin in the Sun*—was far greater than it might seem from the number of her works. Actually, since her death, there has been a growing interest in this woman whose philosophy was summed up in her address to young black writers. She said: "What I write is not based on the assumption of idyllic possibilities or innocent assessments of the true nature of life, but, rather, on my own personal view that, posing one against the other, I think that the human race does command its own destiny and that that destiny can eventually embrace the stars."

WORKS: *A Raisin in the Sun* (1959; film version, 1960; musical, *Raisin*, 1978). *The Drinking Gourd* (1960). *The Movement: A Documentary of a Struggle for Equality* (1964; English ed., *A Matter of Colour*, 1965). *The Sign in Sidney Brustein's Window* (1964). *To Be Young, Gifted, and Black* (Ed. R. Nemiroff, 1969). *Les Blancs: The Collected Last Plays of Lorraine Hansberry* (Ed. R. Nemiroff, 1972). *Raisin* (1973).

BIBLIOGRAPHY: For articles in reference works, see: *Black Theatre USA*, Ed. J. V. Hatch (1974). *CA*, 25–28 (1971). *CB* (Sept. 1959; Feb. 1965).

Other references: *Ebony* (18 Sept. 1963). *Freedomways* 19 (1979). New York *Amsterdam News* (29 Jan. 1972). *Newsweek* (20 April 1959). *NY* (9 May 1959). *NYT* (29 Nov. 1970). *SatR* (31 Dec. 1966). *Time* (10 Jan. 1969). *Vogue* (June 1959).

EDYTHE M. McGOVERN

Elizabeth Hardwick

B. 27 July 1916, Lexington, Kentucky
D. of Eugene Allen and Mary Ramsay Hardwick; m. Robert Lowell, 1949

H. holds a B.A. and M.A. from the University of Kentucky, Lexington, and did graduate work at Columbia University, New York City. A well-known figure in artistic, literary, and critical circles in New York and Boston, H. has published novels, short stories, critical and belletristic articles and reviews, and an edition of William James's letters. She is the editor of eighteen volumes of *Rediscovered Fiction by American Women* (1977). In 1948 she was awarded a Guggenheim Fellowship in fiction and in 1967 received the George Jean Nathan Award for outstanding drama criticism—the first woman ever to be so honored. Since 1964 H. has been adjunct professor of English literature at Barnard College, New York City. She has one daughter, Harriet, and is divorced from the poet Robert Lowell.

In March 1963, to fill the gap left by a printers' strike in New York City, H. became one of the founding editors of the *New York Review of Books*, for which she remains advisory editor and a frequent contributor. For many years she also wrote essays for the *Partisan Review* and other magazines.

H.'s short stories have appeared in *The New Yorker*, the *Partisan Review*, the *Sewanee Review*, and other magazines; four were chosen for reprinting in *Best American Short Stories*. In all her stories, H. reproduces the vagueness of human thought and motivation, the amorphousness of unexamined experience. Yet the stories demonstrate that the most ordinary human experience is the central core of life. In "The Mysteries of Eleusis" the delinquent girl embarking upon marriage with a soldier she barely knows, on the basis of a "love" she has only heard about, "dimly perceived that all this world was pitifully dependent upon the steady recurrence of the emotion into which she and the boy were drawn," an emotion neither of them can explicitly feel, let alone understand.

The theme of the unknowableness of human experience recurs in H.'s novels, which are less well known than her stories. *The Ghostly Lover* (1945) is a stream-of-consciousness *bildungsroman* of sorts. Marian Coleman is deprived of all emotional sustenance; her parents desert her, and her grandmother, with whom she lives, is virtually autistic. The novel deals with Marian's gradual realization that she alone can provide a connection between experience and emotion that will give meaning to her life.

H.'s second novel, *The Simple Truth* (1955), is somewhat more complex. In it a poor college youth is accused of murdering his rich girlfriend. His trial is presented through the minds of two casual observers —a middle-class, liberal graduate student who views the issue as one of class injustice, and a chemistry professor's wife who considers herself an aesthete. Both believe themselves more enlightened than the masses (i.e., the jury) and are therefore dismayed when the boy is acquitted. H. explores the need of liberals, of whatever persuasion, to consider themselves superior to the masses. Both novels focus on the formlessness of human experience and the difficulty of approaching another's mind. In the end, for H.'s characters, truth remains unknowable and feeling unsayable.

H.'s third novel, *Sleepless Nights* (1979), is a logical extension of her attempt to fix and focus the nature of human experience. Combining autobiography with fiction, the book presents the plotless musings of H. herself as a fictional old woman in a nursing home. The creation of self is explored mainly through the protagonist's perception of others, from the famous Billie Holiday to apparently insignificant maids and laundresses, made significant through naming and describing. Life—of the old woman in the nursing home, of H. in her New York apartment— becomes only what one chooses to remember and re-invent; "fact," says H., "is to me a hindrance to memory." In *Sleepless Nights* H.'s earlier overly diffuse style and her tendency toward reflection rather than action become, at last, explicit tools for defining the genesis and essence of the human individual.

H. is justly famed for her reviews and for her social criticism. It is not, however, always easy to differentiate the two. The attempt to capture the movement of thought which appears in her novels also informs the criticism with the brilliance of dialogue and encourages the reader to participate in the critical act. There is in all H.'s writing a gentility, an aristocracy, a respectful love affair with words and sentences that soothes as do the essays of Virginia Woolf. H.'s intimate concern with the English language is cause for quiet joy.

WORKS: *The Ghostly Lover* (1945). *The Simple Truth* (1955). *Selected Letters of William James* (edited by Hardwick, 1961). *A View of My Own* (1962). *Seduction and Betrayal* (1974). *Rediscovered Fiction by American Women: A Personal Selection* (18 vols., edited by Hardwick, 1977). *Sleepless Nights* (1979).

BIBLIOGRAPHY: For articles in reference works, see: *CA*, 5–8 (1969). *WA*.
Other references: *Nation* (5 May 1945). *NewR* (14 Feb. 1955). *NYTBR* (29 April 1979).

LORALEE MacPIKE

Frances Ellen Watkins Harper

B. 24 Sept. 1825, Baltimore, Maryland; d. 22 Feb. 1911, Philadelphia,
  Pennsylvania
Wrote under: Frances E. W. Harper, Frances Ellen Watkins
M. Fenton Harper, 1860

H., the author of the first novel published by an Afro-American woman, was the most popular black poet of her day. She was a sought-after lecturer, as well, speaking on behalf of abolitionism, temperance, and women's rights. Born to free parents, H. was orphaned at an early age, then reared and educated by an aunt and uncle active in the antislavery movement. She became self-supporting at age thirteen.

After working at various occupations—including nursemaid, seamstress, and teacher—H. found her true calling on the lecture platform. She gave her first speech in 1854 in New Bedford, Massachusetts; her subject was "The Education and the Elevation of the Colored Race." Few women in the abolitionist movement traveled so widely or spoke to so many audiences.

Apparently no copies of *Forest Leaves* (ca. 1845), an early book of poetry by H., are extant. *Poems on Miscellaneous Subjects* (1854), with an introduction by William Lloyd Garrison, went through some twenty editions by 1874. Her dramatic readings of her verse were highlights of her lectures, and according to William Still, with whom she worked on the Underground Railroad, more than fifty thousand copies of her books were sold.

H. married in 1860; she was the mother of one daughter. After her husband's death in 1864, H. resumed her career as a lecturer.

With the end of the Civil War, H. carried her message of education and moral uplift to the southern states. Here she took the greatest interest in meetings called exclusively for black women, whose needs she felt were more pressing than those of any other class.

H.'s poems are of a piece with her oratory, determinedly propagandistic and emotional. In poems such as "The Slave Auction" and "The Slave Mother," H. presents the horrors of slavery from a female point of view. These poems are unabashedly sentimental, but undeniably effective. Her frequently anthologized poem, "Bury Me in a Free Land," derives its considerable strength both from its powerful theme and its balladlike simplicity. H.'s is very much an oral poetry; it needs to be heard, not merely read. By all accounts, H. herself was an outstanding performer, rendering her lines with dramatic voice and gesture, with sighs and tears. Her stage presence reflected her oratorical skill, but it was clearly derived as well from her profound commitment to the freedom struggle.

The first novel by a black author to depict the Reconstruction, *Iola Leroy; or, Shadows Uplifted* (1892), drew heavily on H.'s experiences in the South after the Civil War. *Iola Leroy* also contains frequent flashbacks to earlier periods and thus embraces the whole of 19th-c. black experience.

The main characters, Iola Leroy and Robert Johnson, are mulattoes whose actions are motivated specifically by their desire to reunite their families after emancipation and generally by their desire to uplift the race. As mulattoes they enjoy certain privileges not shared by other blacks, notably access to education, but they are steadfast in their refusal to set themselves apart from their fellows.

Iola Leroy is not a well-written work; its weaknesses to a large degree are those of the sentimental novel, the literary genre to which it belongs. The plot is often confused and incredible, and the characters overly idealized. The novel is nevertheless valuable for its historical insights, especially its portrayal of the bravery of black soldiers during the war and of the sacrifices made by the black community during Reconstruction. In its Christian humanism and its dedication to the principle of equality, *Iola Leroy* dramatizes the ideals to which H. devoted her life.

WORKS: *Forest Leaves* (ca. 1845). *Poems on Miscellaneous Subjects* (1854). *Moses: A Story of the Nile* (1869). *Sketches of Southern Life* (1872). *Iola Leroy; or, Shadows Uplifted* (1892). *The Martyr of Alabama, and Other Poems* (ca. 1894).

BIBLIOGRAPHY: Lerner, G., *Black Women in White America: A Documentary History* (1973). Montgomery, J. W., *A Comparative Analysis of the Rhetoric of Two Negro Women Orators—Sojourner Truth and Frances Ellen Watkins Harper* (1968). Robinson, W. H., *Early Black American Poets* (1971). Sherman, J., *Invisible Poets: Afro-Americans of Nineteenth Century* (1974). Sillen, S., *Women against Slavery* (1955). Still, W. G., *The Underground Railroad* (1872).

For articles in reference works, see: *Black American Writers Past and Present*, T. G. Rush, C. F. Myers, and E. S. Arato (1975). *NAW* (article by L. Filler).

Other references: *Black World* (Dec. 1972).

CHERYL A. WALL

Ida Husted Harper

B. 18 Feb. 1851, Fairfield, Indiana; d. 14 March 1931, Washington, D.C.
D. of John Arthur and Cassandra Stoddard Husted; m. Thomas Winans
* Harper, 1871*

H. was a prolific writer and journalist and an active feminist. A suffragist of international reputation, H. traveled throughout the U.S. and Europe with Susan B. Anthony, who asked her to become her official biographer. She handled publicity for the National American Woman Suffrage Association when Carrie Chapman Catt served as president.

After leaving Indiana University to become principal of a high school in Indiana, H. began her writing career at twenty by sending articles under a male pseudonym to the Terre Haute *Saturday Evening Mail.* Under her own name she then wrote a column, "A Woman's Opinions," for that same newspaper for twelve years. She simultaneously edited weekly discussions of women's activities in the *Locomotive Fireman's Magazine,* the official organ of the union of which her husband was chief counsel. After her divorce in 1890, she joined the staff of the Indian-apolis *News*. From then on she devoted her life to her daughter, to writing, and to her activities in the woman suffrage movement.

Her career in journalism led her from Indiana to New York, where she wrote a column for the New York *Sun* (1899–1903) and, best-known, a woman's page in *Harper's Bazar* (1909–13). She devoted most of this writing to the suffrage movement; her interests, unlike those of Anthony, Elizabeth Cady Stanton, and Lucy Stone, centered on the primary importance of the vote for women. She offers detailed reports about the status of women and their right to vote in countries all over the world. Her insight into international politics gives to her work the standards of accurate social history. In *Harper's Bazar* she reported on working women demanding suffrage, on women as officeholders in states that had the vote, on the deaths of her friends who had "lived for the Movement," and on the joys of seeing her dreams become a reality: "Yes, woman suffrage is becoming fashionable and it is all very amusing to veterans of the cause. They understand fully that, underlying the fashion, are years of hard and persistent work yet ahead before a universal victory."

Her spirit is striking as she writes that "women of today who are not helping in the effort for the franchise do not know the joy they miss . . . so vital, so compelling, so full of the progressive spirit of the age." This same vigor appears in her two volumes of the *History of Woman Suffrage*, that monumental compilation begun by Anthony and Stanton. H. helped Anthony edit Volume Four, and herself edited Volumes Five and Six, dealing with state and national activities from 1900 to 1920. While the *History* contains records rather than interpretations of documents, speeches, and state and national activities, it nevertheless forms a coherent pattern of immense value for historians.

H. was Susan B. Anthony's Boswell: to her we owe a detailed study of Anthony's life and activities in two long volumes published in 1898. During later life she continued her work on the Anthony biography; Volume Three was published in 1908. The searcher for psychological insight will be disappointed by *The Life and Work of Susan B. Anthony*. Its deepest penetration in explaining Anthony's personality and motivation is through its astute description of Anthony's Quaker family background and of the encouragement in her education given by both parents.

Otherwise, the biography remains largely a chronicle, dull at times and burdened with detail. Stylistically, it belongs to the tradition of sentimental 19th-c. prose. Yet no historian concerned with Anthony's role in the 19th-c. women's movement can ignore the intimate details of social history in H.'s story: Anthony's role as teacher, her support of both temperance and Amelia Bloomer, her acceptance of hydropathic medicine, and her relationships and correspondence with leaders of social reform, such as Garrison, Stanton, Stone, and Antoinette Brown.

Though close to her daughter, who continued her mother's work in the women's movement, H. remained independent, spending her last years working in the headquarters of the American Association of University Women in Washington, D.C. Using her journalistic talent to good effect, H. served the suffrage movement well. The extent and variety of her writing is impressive; fourteen large indexed volumes of her writings stand in the Library of Congress.

WORKS: *The Life and Work of Susan B. Anthony* (Vols. 1 and 2, 1898; Vol. 3, 1908). *History of Woman Suffrage* (Vol. 4, edited by Harper, with S. B. Anthony, 1902; Vols. 5 and 6, edited by Harper, 1922).

BIBLIOGRAPHY: Lutz, A., *Susan B. Anthony* (1959).
For articles in reference works, see: *AW. DAB*, IV, 2. *Indiana Authors and Their Books, 1816–1916*, Ed. R. E. Banta (1949). *NAW* (article by C. J. Phillips). *NCAB*, 25.
Other references: Indianapolis *News* (16 March 1931). *NYT* (17 March 1931). Terre Haute *Star* (17 March 1931).

LOIS FOWLER

Bernice Kelly Harris

B. 8 Oct. 1893, Mt. Moriah, North Carolina; d. 13 Sept. 1973, Seaboard,
   North Carolina
Wrote under: Bernice Kelly Harris, Bernice Kelly
D. of William Haywood and Rosa Poole Kelly; m. Herbert Harris, 1926

Born the third of six children in an established farming family, H. spent her childhood and adult years in the coastal plains region that dominated her novels. Like other writers, including Carson McCullers, H.'s first writing efforts were childhood plays performed for family and friends. Her subsequent attempts at poetry and novel writing were short-lived. She attended Meredith College in Raleigh, North Carolina, expressly to train as a teacher of English. After graduation, H. taught for three years at an academy in the foothills of western North Carolina, instructing rural Baptist preachers in the rudiments of grammar. She then took a post with the Seaboard, North Carolina, public schools and remained in Seaboard the rest of her life.

In 1919, a summer-school class introduced H. to folk drama. Although she used her skills in drama primarily for pedagogical purposes, the years 1920 to 1926, when she encouraged students to write and to produce folk plays, provided an intense period of story collection and writing apprenticeship for herself. Her marriage and the obligatory retirement from teaching prompted her to write her own plays rather than to encourage others to write. From 1932 to 1938 she wrote folk drama, drawing from actual people and events in the North Carolina towns around her. Seven of the better plays were published collectively in 1940; almost all were produced at regional drama festivals.

H.'s novels grew out of her feature stories written on a free-lance basis for Raleigh and Norfolk newspapers. Encouraged by her editor, H. began in 1937 the work which became *Purslane*, published by the University of North Carolina Press in 1939. Also in 1939, H. interviewed tenant farmers for four pieces appearing in *These Are Our Lives*, the Federal Writers Project publication.

The nostalgic first novel impressed critics, but H.'s second novel, *Portulaca* (1941), a realistic portrait of the rural and small-town middle class, won even more support from the literary establishment on both sides of the Atlantic. It also necessitated the change to a commercial publisher, since the university press feared such blunt themes would offend southern readers.

All of H.'s novels have related characters and draw from real-life experiences of H. and those she knew. She is the narrator of a region, with a thorough understanding of its people and mores; as such she can be compared to Cather or Faulkner in her ability to evoke time and place—to produce social history in novel form. So skillful is she at delineating character from life that reviewers of her one novel dealing exclusively with black farmers (*Janey Jeems*, 1946) failed to understand that the characters were not white because the depiction did not follow accepted stereotypes. The characters of her seven novels encompass all classes, races, ages, and personalities of the region. The strength of her novels clearly lies in their vivid characterization, which evokes not only a sense of regional identity and folkways but also of dynamic humanity.

WORKS: *Purslane* (1939). *Folk Plays of Eastern Carolina* (1940). *Portulaca* (1941). *Sweet Beulah Land* (1943). *Sage Quarter* (1945). *Janey Jeems* (1946). *Hearthstones* (1948). *Wild Cherry Tree Road* (1951). *A Southern Savory* (1964).

BIBLIOGRAPHY: Walser, R., *B. K. H.: Storyteller of Eastern Carolina* (1955).

For articles in reference works, see: *American Novelists of Today*, Ed. H. Warfel (1951). *CA*, 5–8 (1969); 45–48 (1974). *CB* (1949).

Other references: *WLB* (Jan. 1949).

SALLY BRETT

Miriam Coles Harris

B. 7 July 1834, Glen Cove, New York; d. 23 Jan. 1925, Pau, France
Wrote under: Author of "Rutledge," Miriam Coles Harris, Mrs. Sidney S. Harris
D. of Butler and Julia Anne Weeks Coles; m. Sidney S. Harris, 1864

A descendant of Robert Coles of Suffolk, England, who accompanied John Winthrop to America in 1630, H. attended religious and exclusive private schools in New Jersey and New York City. After writing for periodicals and producing a bestseller at age twenty-six, H. married a New York lawyer, raised two children, and continued to produce popular novels, as well as travel and devotional books. Widowed in 1892, she spent most of her remaining years in Europe.

H.'s first novel, the bestseller *Rutledge* (1860), has been called the "first fully American example" of the gothic romance. It is narrated by the unnamed orphan heroine, a passionately resentful teenager who, in *Jane Eyre* fashion, falls in love with Rutledge, the older brooding hero—her temporary guardian—whose ancestral home hides a dark family secret. After being introduced to fashionable society by her worldly permanent guardian, the rebellious heroine becomes involved in a series of jealous misunderstandings, including a rash engagement to a handsome social climber who turns out to be a murderer and who commits suicide after the heroine hides him in the secret room at the Rutledge estate and he discovers he is Rutledge's illegitimate nephew. A period of penitence completes the education of the humbled heroine, who is finally reunited with the "masterful" Rutledge.

Like *Rutledge*, H.'s other fictions are characterized by psychological studies of negative feminine attitudes, religiously didactic themes, and sensational incidents. Anticipating in some ways the psychological realism of Henry James, H. probes, with surprising honesty, the degrees of hostility, powerlessness, and masochism experienced by an unusual variety of 19th-c. heroines: teenagers in *Rutledge* and in its juvenile counterpart, loosely based on H.'s schoolgirl days, *Louie's Last Term at St. Mary's* (1860); unhappily married heroines in *Frank Warrington* (1863) and *A Perfect Adonis* (1875); a young widowed mother in *Happy-Go-Lucky* (1881); and middle-aged mother-wives in *Phoebe* (1884) and *An Utter Failure* (1891).

H. frequently resolves her plots by transforming her rebellious heroines into self-abnegating women who exemplify the author's religious beliefs about renunciation of self and the world of vanity. Yet H.'s mixed feelings about her humbled heroines can be seen in the conclusion of *A Perfect Adonis:* The new bride asserts, "I can't see what I was created for," to which her bridegroom replies, "I can't either, except to make people want to possess you. To have and to hold you." Then he silences all further questions with an all-absorbing kiss, a romantic conclusion that is immediately undercut by the author's final remark: "It is a blessing that when you are a failure, you can forget it sometimes for a while. But the fact remains the same." Her last novel, *The Tents of Wickedness* (1907), interweaves a love story with a defense of the Roman Catholic Church.

Although melodramatic incident mars portions of her love plots, H.'s use of topical subjects also marks her as a forerunner of realism. *The Sutherlands* (1862) is a proslavery novel, while *Richard Vandermarck* (1871) contains one of the earliest literary portraits of the Wall Street businessman hero. A murder trial, realistically depicted, makes up a major segment of *Happy-Go-Lucky*, which also covers prejudice against Irish immigrants and lower-class poverty. Her last three novels treat daring sexual issues such as premarital sex, resentment of maternal duties, near-adultery, and divorce, as well as other topical subjects such as tenement conditions, racial violence, politics, and alcoholism.

H.'s minor place in literary history has depended solely on her most romantically sensational novel, the best-selling *Rutledge*, but all of her fictions contain perceptive, slightly ironic studies of a particular type of feminine psychology, portraits which, in their own limited ways, contributed to the development of the realistic tradition.

WORKS: *Rutledge* (1860). *Louie's Last Term at St. Mary's* (1860). *The Sutherlands* (1862). *Frank Warrington* (1863). *St. Philips* (1865). *A Rosary for Lent; or, Devotional Readings* (1867). *Roundhearts, and Other Stories* (1867). *Richard Vandermarck* (1871). *Dear Feast Lent: A Series of Devotional Readings* (1874). *A Perfect Adonis* (1875). *Missy* (1880). *Happy-Go-Lucky* (1881). *Phoebe* (1884). *An Utter Failure* (1891). *A Chit of Sixteen, and Other Stories* (1892). *A Corner of Spain* (1898). *The Tents of Wickedness* (1907).

BIBLIOGRAPHY: Baym, N., *Woman's Fiction: A Guide to Novels by and about Women in America* (1978). Cole, F. T., *The Early Genealogies of the Cole Families in America* (1887). Mott, F. L., *Golden Multitudes: The Story of Best Sellers in the United States* (1947).
For articles in reference works, see: *AA. DAB*, IV, 2. *NCAB*, 11.

KATHLEEN L. NICHOLS

Lillian Hellman

B. 20 June 1905, New Orleans, Louisiana
D. of Max and Julia Newhouse Hellman; m. Arthur Kober, 1925

H., an only child, spent her childhood in New York City and New Orleans. After two years at New York University, she took a job with a publisher, where she became acquainted with the literary world and met her future husband. After she and Kober got an amicable divorce, H. lived with Dashiell Hammett, the detective-fiction writer.

H. has published several volumes of distinguished memoirs. *An Unfinished Woman* (1969), which won a National Book Award, is H.'s vivid autobiography, running from her childhood in New Orleans to the death of Hammett in 1960. The whole book is characterized by painstaking honesty, as H. analyzes her rebellions and conflicts, her ambivalent attitudes toward money and the theater, and the tensions of her relationship with Hammett. Often she renders her experience in dramatic dialogues. *Pentimento* (1973) is H.'s reconsideration of certain themes in her life not developed in *An Unfinished Woman*. It consists mostly of portraits, of which the most memorable is that of her beloved girlhood friend "Julia," a passionate anti-Nazi who involved H. in the mission (especially perilous for a Jew) of carrying fifty thousand dollars into Berlin to ransom political prisoners. H.'s innocence, played against the elaborate subterfuges undertaken to safeguard her mission, makes for taut suspense. *Scoundrel Time* (1976) describes H.'s experience of political persecution in the 1950s.

Hammett guided her to the source for her first produced play, *The Children's Hour* (1934), an account of an actual libel suit in 19th-c. Scotland. It tells the story of Karen Wright and Martha Dobie, owners of a successful girls' school, who are ruined by a charge of lesbianism. Extremely successful, partly because of its then-shocking theme, the play ran for 691 performances on Broadway. *The Children's Hour* is a skillfully wrought melodrama deepened by psychological penetration and moral significance.

The Little Foxes (1939) is a gripping drama about the Hubbards of Alabama, who display the greed and driving egotism that H. saw in her mother's family. Ben and Oscar Hubbard and their sister, Regina Giddens, form a partnership with a northern industrialist to set up a profitable cotton factory in their town; but they cannot secure a controlling interest without obtaining money from Regina's husband, Horace, which he refuses to advance because he is disgusted by the Hubbards' ruthless greed. Throughout the play, mastery shifts between the brothers and their sister, depending upon who seems more likely to get control of Horace's money. In the end, Regina gains control by deliberately provoking him into a fatal heart attack.

Because the Hubbards are intended to be human beings as well as monsters of selfishness, H. decided to "look into their family background and find out what it was that made them the nasty people they were." In *Another Part of the Forest* (1947) she went back twenty years to show Ben, Oscar, and Regina as young people dominated by their father, Marcus. H. found humor as well as evil in people like the Hubbards, and made this more obvious in her second play about them.

The Autumn Garden (1951) is unlike H.'s earlier plays in emphasizing character over plot. In a handsome but shabby southern resort hotel, she gathers ten people who lack purpose, joy, and love. H.'s characterization here shows a notable advance in subtlety, as she views her people with more sympathy and less simple judgment.

Perhaps the most obvious characteristic of H.'s writing is her first-rate craftsmanship: the neat plotting of the Hubbard plays, where thrilling melodramatic climaxes are meticulously prepared for, as hints are dropped in the beginning, every one to be picked up by the end; the relief from this suspenseful melodrama through pathos or comedy; the sharp characterization and vividly authentic speeches, which at the same time economically move the plot along.

In her last two original plays—*The Autumn Garden* and *Toys in the Attic* (1960), which both present middle-aged people who come to recognize the bleakness of their lives, but find they cannot change them—

H.'s artistry appears more in character development. She relaxes her tight plotting to give her characters more room to develop, although she unfortunately retains some jarring melodramatic elements. H. is surely right in considering *The Autumn Garden* her finest play.

Well-made and popular as her plays have been, they are all redeemed from commercialism by their strong moral commitment. H. constantly makes the point, equally applicable to private and public affairs, that it is immoral to remain passive when evil is being done. She believes that a clear moral message "is only a mistake when it fails to achieve its purpose, and I would rather make the attempt, and fail, than fail to make the attempt." Only in a few cases, such as the anticlimactic discussion after Martha's death in *The Children's Hour* and the antifascist plays, does the moral message become obtrusive. Generally, it is organically part of her artistic structure and characterization. H.'s works, like her life, have consistently demonstrated responsibility, courage, and integrity.

WORKS: *The Children's Hour* (1934; film versions: *These Three*, 1936, *The Children's Hour*, 1962). *Days to Come* (1936). *The Little Foxes* (1939; film version, 1941; opera, *Regina*, 1949). *Watch on the Rhine* (1941; film version, 1943). *The North Star: A Motion Picture about Some Russian People* (1943). *The Searching Wind* (1944; film version, 1946). *Another Part of the Forest* (1947; film version, 1948). *Montserrat* by E. Roblès (adapted by Hellman, 1950). *The Autumn Garden* (1951). *The Selected Letters of Anton Chekhov* (edited by Hellman, 1955). *The Lark* by J. Anouilh (adapted by Hellman, 1955). *Candide* by Voltaire (dramatization by Hellman, with music by L. Bernstein and lyrics by R. Wilbur, J. LaTouche, and D. Parker, 1957). *Toys in the Attic* (1960; film version, 1963). *My Mother, My Father, and Me* (dramatization of the novel *How Much?* by B. Blechman, 1963). *The Big Knockover: Stories and Short Novels by Dashiell Hammett* (introduction by Hellman, 1966). *An Unfinished Woman: A Memoir* (1969). *Pentimento: A Book of Portraits* (1973; film version, *Julia*, 1977). *Scoundrel Time* (1976). *Maybe: A Story* (1980).

BIBLIOGRAPHY: Heilman, R. B., *The Iceman, the Arsonist, and the Troubled Agent* (1973). Heilman, R. B.. *Tragedy and Melodrama: Versions of Experience* (1968). Holmin, L. R., *The Dramatic Works of Lillian Hellman* (1973). Moody, R., *Lillian Hellman: Playwright* (1972). Triesch, M., *The Lillian Hellman Collection at the University of Texas* (1968).

For articles in reference works, see: *CB* (May 1941; June 1960). *NCAB*, G. *20thCA. 20thCAS.*

Other references: *Contact* III (1959). *Modern Drama* III (1960). *Paris Review* IX (1965).

KATHARINE M. ROGERS

Caroline Lee Whiting Hentz

B. 1 June 1800, Lancaster, Massachusetts; d. 11 Feb. 1856, Marianna, Florida
D. of John and Orpah Danforth Whiting; m. Nicolas Marcellus Hentz, 1824

H. was the eighth and youngest child of an old New England family directly descended from the Reverend Samuel Whiting, who settled in Massachusetts in 1636. Her father served as a colonel in the revolutionary war. Two years after H.'s marriage to a French entomologist, her husband became chairman of modern languages and belles-lettres at the University of North Carolina in Chapel Hill. This move was the first of many the family made following his erratic teaching career. H. bore five children; the oldest son died when he was two years old. In addition to rearing the children, running the household, supervising boarding students, and helping her husband with teaching and insect collecting, H. wrote verse, drama, tales, and novels. Reputedly, she could write easily in the midst of household distractions.

Her first novel, *Lovell's Folly* (1833), was suppressed by her family as "too personal." Some accounts say it was libelous. While in Kentucky, H. wrote a prize-winning play, *DeLara; or, The Moorish Bride* (1843). The five-act drama, set in a Spanish castle during the Moors' conquest of Spain, was produced in Philadelphia and Boston. Of her poems written for special occasions, perhaps the most important one was composed for the visit of Andrew Jackson to Florence, Alabama, in 1836. Her husband read the poem for President Jackson.

Although she began writing as a girl, H. did not become a well-known writer until the Philadelphia *Saturday Courier* serially published a domestic tale in 1844. It was later published in book form as *Aunt Patty's Scrap Bag* (1846). When her husband became chronically ill in the late 1840s, H., out of financial necessity, began the most prolific period of her writing at the age of fifty. Her novel, *Linda; or, The Young Pilot of the Belle Creole* (1850), became a bestseller. Seven more domestic novels and six collections of stories were published in rapid succession. Her books remained popular after her death until the end of the century. Two novels, *Eoline; or, Magnolia Vale* (1852) and *The Planter's Northern Bride* (1854), were reprinted in the 1970s.

While living in Cincinnati, H. knew Harriet Beecher Stowe. Both women belonged to a literary group, the Semi-Colons. Although they might have shared cultural interests, the issue of slavery separated them. H.'s novel, *The Planter's Northern Bride*, was written as an answer to *Uncle Tom's Cabin*. It is proslavery propaganda. In *Marcus Warland* (1852), probably composed before she had read Stowe's work, H. made only a partial defense of slavery, but the later novel is a full-blown counter-statement to abolition.

With other writers of antebellum novels, H. helped to create and perpetuate an image of ideal plantation life. This fictional world of pious belles, gallant gentlemen, and happy slaves appeals so strongly to the popular mind that the myth persists.

WORKS: *Lovell's Folly* (1833). *DeLara; or, The Moorish Bride* (1843). *Aunt Patty's Scrap Bag* (1846). *Mob Cap* (1848). *Linda; or, The Young Pilot of the Belle Creole* (1850). *Rena; or, The Snow Bird* (1851). *Eoline; or, Magnolia Vale* (1852). *Marcus Warland; or, The Long Moss Spring* (1852). *Helen and Arthur; or, Miss Thusa's Spinning Wheel* (1853). *Wild Jack; or, The Stolen Child, and Other Stories* (1853). *The Victim of Excitement* (1853). *The Planter's Northern Bride* (1854). *Robert Graham* (1855). *The Banished Son* (1856). *Courtship and Marriage* (1856). *Ernest Linwood* (1856). *The Lost Daughter* (1857). *Love after Marriage* (1857).

BIBLIOGRAPHY: Ellison, R. C., Introduction to *The Planter's Northern Bride* by C. L. W. Hentz (1970). Papashvily, H. W., *All the Happy Endings* (1956). Williams, B. B., *A Literary History of Alabama: The Nineteenth Century* (1979).

For articles in reference works, see: *AA. CAL. DAB*, IV, 2. *NAW* (article by H. W. Papashvily). *NCAB*, 6. *Ohio Authors and Their Books*, Ed. W. Coyle (1962).

Other references: *AL* 22 (1950). *AlaR* 4 (1951).

LYNDA W. BROWN

Marguerite Higgins

B. *3 Sept. 1920, Hong Kong; d. 3 Jan. 1966, Washington, D.C.*
D. *of Lawrence Daniel and Marguerite Godard Higgins; m. Stanley Moore, 1942; m. William E. Hall, 1952*

H. was born in the British Crown Colony of Hong Kong to a globe-trotting businessman and his French war bride. She was educated in France and later, when the Higgins family returned home to the U.S., she was enrolled in an exclusive private school in Oakland, California. After graduating from the University of California at Berkeley, with honors, in 1940, she went to work as a cub reporter for the local Vallejo *Times-Herald*. She was hired by the *New York Herald Tribune* after receiving her master's degree in New York from Columbia University's Graduate School of Journalism; she worked for the paper for the next twenty-one years.

After three routine years on the *Tribune*, reporting city visitors, suburban fires, and visiting royalty, H. won a coveted spot in the London bureau. Shortly thereafter, she transferred to the Paris bureau—largely because of her proficiency in French—and soon found herself reporting the wartime liberation of Europe. She made the front page regularly and built up a respected name for herself among the most experienced foreign correspondents in the world. She was twenty-five when the *Tribune* named her Berlin bureau chief. Tokyo bureau chief during the Korean War, H. was with the first reporters who made their way into Korea on returning evacuation planes, the only woman correspondent in Korea.

After her remarriage and the birth of two children, H. settled down to a less peripatetic schedule as a roving reporter for the *Tribune* and as a free-lance writer for many periodicals. In the mid-1950s, H. reopened the *Tribune*'s Moscow bureau, and in 1956 she returned to Washington to cover the diplomatic beat. From then on, her competition claimed H. could be counted on to show up wherever a crisis occurred, from the Congo to the Dominican Republic. In 1963, H. resigned to become a syndicated columnist for Long Island's *Newsday*.

H. became increasingly interested in Vietnam as that country opened up into one of the world's most controversial hot spots, and made ten trips to Vietnam. In late 1965, she was air ambulanced home, the victim of leishmaniasis, a disease brought on by the bite of a tropical sandfly, and within six weeks she was dead.

Out of her experiences covering the Korean conflict came *War in Korea: The Report of a Woman Combat Correspondent* (1951), which also appeared in a condensed form in *Woman's Home Companion* in 1951. The book was a bestseller, and H. became an overnight sensation, touring and lecturing throughout the country. In *Report of a Woman Combat Correspondent*, H. recounted her experiences on the front in Korea with a lively style and the sense of adventurous excitement she felt. Although the book tends to provide an unbalanced view of history, reviews were favorable, and it enjoyed a wide readership.

In 1954, she received a Guggenheim Fellowship, allowing her to make a ten-week tour of Russia. Her experiences and reactions to life in Cold

War Russia during the 13,500-mile trek are detailed in *Red Plush and Black Bread*, published in 1956.

H. and her long-time personal friend, the late newsman Peter Lisagor, together wrote and published *Overtime in Heaven: Adventures in the Foreign Service* (1964), a series of behind-the-scenes true stories of ten Foreign Service incidents. A highly entertaining set of adventure vignettes, the series won credits for its carefully researched and documented materials, although one critic noted they had created a "composite portrait of the Foreign Service man who looks suspiciously like a more moral James Bond."

Her Vietnam study, *Our Vietnam Nightmare* (1965), presented her research and conclusions on what was actually happening in Vietnam as a result of U.S. foreign policy and actions, covering the period from the Buddhist revolt and Diem's fall in 1963 to the changing political tactics of the Viet Cong in the summer of 1965. Herman Dinsmore, former *New York Times* international edition editor, called it "superb." He said, "she was not the most popular correspondent for one excellent reason: she was so brilliant she outshone every writer around her, men and women: and, of course, she was industrious, clever, and, of all things, patriotic."

WORKS: *War in Korea: The Report of a Woman Combat Correspondent* (1951). *News Is a Singular Thing* (1955). *Red Plush and Black Bread* (1956). *Jessie Benton Frémont* (1962). *Overtime in Heaven: Adventures in the Foreign Service* (with P. Lisagor, 1964). *Our Vietnam Nightmare* (1965).

BIBLIOGRAPHY: Editors of the Army Times, *American Heroes of Asian Wars* (1968). Fleming, A. M., *Reporters at War* (1970). Forese, A., *American Women Who Scored Firsts* (1958). Jakes, J., *Great War Correspondents* (1967). Kelly, F. K., *Reporters Around the World* (1957).

For articles in reference works, see: *CA*, 5–8 (1969); 25–28 (1971). *CB* (June 1951; Feb. 1966).

Other references: *Life* (2 Oct. 1950). *NYHT* (16 Feb. 1946; 19 Oct. 1950; 8 May 1951). *NYT* (8 May 1951). *Time* (25 Sept. 1950).

KATHLEEN KEARNEY KEESHEN

Ella Rhoads Higginson

B. ca. 1860, Council Grove, Kansas; d. 29 Dec. 1940, Bellingham, Washington
Wrote under: Ella Higginson, Ella Rhoads
D. of Charles and Mary Ann Rhoads; m. Russell Carden Higginson, ca. 1880

In the early 1860s, H.'s family crossed the plains from Kansas to the Grand Ronde Valley of Oregon. In 1870, they moved to Portland and then to a farm eight miles from town. Later they lived in Oregon City, where H. received her few years of education in a public school. The youngest of three children, H. enjoyed freedom from punishments and farm chores. Although the family was poor, their home was filled with good books, visitors, and conversation. Her father's ability as a storyteller and her mother's poetic sensitivity to the beauty of nature enriched H.'s childhood experiences.

At the age of eight, H. wrote her first poem and was encouraged to continue writing by her mother and sister, Carrie Blake Morgan, who later became known as a poet in her own right as the author of Path of Gold (1900). Her father and brother laughed at her early poetic attempts, but at fourteen H. published a love poem in the Oregon City paper. At sixteen she joined the newspaper staff to learn everything from typesetting to editorial writing. Early stories were contributed to the West Shore, a Portland literary magazine, and to the Salem Oregon Literary Vidette.

In 1888, H. moved to Whatcom (now Bellingham), Washington, with her husband. A druggist from New York, he possessed charming "Eastern" manners but, according to H., did not sufficiently encourage or appreciate her literary work. From Bellingham she edited a department entitled "Fact and Fancy for Women" for the weekly West Shore. Her first column, in 1890, presented advanced views on the controversial subject of divorce.

For twenty-five years after the demise of the West Shore in 1891, H. contributed fiction to national magazines such as Century, Harper's Weekly, Cosmopolitan, Short Stories, The New Peterson, McClure's, and Collier's. H.'s stories were collected in several volumes. Her stories of common people of the Far West were praised by the Overland Monthly as "unpretentious tales . . . told simply and naturally, yet so vivid and graphic are they, that they charm the reader from the first to the last." The *Outlook* described her as one of the best American short-story writers, while the Chicago *Tribune* noted: "Mrs. Higginson has shown a breadth of treatment and knowledge of the everlasting human verities that equals much of the best work of France."

H.'s poetry appeared in magazines such as *Atlantic*, *Harper's*, and *Scribner's*, and in the columns of many Pacific Coast and eastern newspapers. Two of her most popular poems were "God's Creed" and "Four Leaf Clover." Many of her poems were set to music and performed by singers such as Caruso, McCormack, and Calve. The vivid imagery and singing quality of her poetry were achieved through diligence—she often rewrote a dozen times—and keen observation of nature. Many poems deal with theme of the Pacific Northwest, and several, such as "The Grande Ronde Valley" and "The Evergreen Pine," are specifically about Oregon.

H.'s only published novel, *Mariella, of Out West* (1904), presents a young girl facing a hard frontier farming life, the economic boom of 1888–89, and the proposals of men who represent a variety of social backgrounds. The novel conveys a strong feeling for nature coupled with a sense of piety and spirituality. *Alaska, the Great Country* (1908), H.'s last book, is a combination of guide book, history, and romance.

As a writer of poetry, short stories, travel articles, songs, and one novel, H. achieved prominence in the ranks of Pacific Northwest authors and earned national and international recognition for several of her works. The states of Oregon and Washington both claimed her as a daughter, and she was honored in 1931 as Washington's poet laureate. H. realized her life's ambition based on what she termed "the consuming desire to write." As she explained, "It is the only thing I ever really wanted to do."

WORKS: *A Bunch of Western Clover* (1894). *The Flower That Grew in the Sand* (1896). *The Forest Orchid* (1897). *From the Land of the Snow Pearls* (1897). *When the Birds Go North Again* (1898). *The Voice of April-Land, and Other Poems* (1903). *Mariella, of Out West* (1904). *Alaska, the Great Country* (1908). *The Vanishing Race, and Other Poems* (1911).

The papers of Ella Rhoads Higginson are at the Oregon Historical Society, Portland, Oregon.

BIBLIOGRAPHY: Bright, V., in *With Her Own Wings*, Ed. H. K. Smith (1948). Horner, J. B., *Oregon Literature* (1902). Powers, A., *History of Oregon Literature* (1935). Turnbull, G. S., *History of Oregon Newspapers* (1939).
For articles in reference works, see: *AW*.

JEAN M. WARD

Helen MacInnes Highet

B. 7 Oct. 1907, Glasgow, Scotland
Writes under: Helen MacInnes
D. of Donald and Jessica Cecilia Sutherland McInnes; m. Gilbert Highet, 1932

H. earned an M.A. degree at Glasgow University in 1928 and received her diploma in librarianship from University College, London, in 1931. In 1939, she and her husband, a classics professor, left Oxford and settled in New York City. H. adopted a variant spelling of her family surname under which she has published. In addition to her eighteen novels, H. also has published a clever comic play on Ulysses's return, *Home Is the Hunter* (1964).

Ralph Harper in *The World of the Thriller* suggests that crime in detective stories threatens to destroy a portion of society and in spy stories the threat is that civilization will be undermined. The spy genre in America fully emerged with World War II, and H.'s *Above Suspicion* (1941) and *Assignment in Britanny* (1942)—still two of her best books—used contemporary events of the war and successfully established her reputation as a master of the thriller, as the queen of suspense, and as a popular writer of spy novels. Several of her novels have been made into films, and a new H. title predictably is a bestseller. Her audience extends into numerous countries where translations of her work have appeared.

In a MacInnes spy novel, professional agents abound, but interest usually centers on the amateur—an Oxford don, an architect, an artist, a lawyer, a playwright, a music critic—thrust into international intrigue to confront real dangers which are often serious enough to undermine the social structure. David Mennery in *Snare of the Hunter* (1974), Tom Kelso in *Agent in Place* (1976), and Colin Grant in *Prelude to Terror* (1978) illustrate her continued success in portraying the amateur agent effectively.

After World War II, H.'s subject matter involved data still vital and dangerous after the war; later she moved to complex political plots in which communist forces pose threats to individuals' safety and to the security of nations. Although H. has not moved into the elaborate gimmicks of the James Bond novels, readers nevertheless find sinister enemy agents, coded messages, kidnappings, elaborately planned secret meetings, narrow escapes, chases, betrayals, brutal murders, and love affairs—

devices that have made H.'s novels extremely popular over her writing career of nearly forty years. If the situations in her novels do not lead readers to serious self-examination and profound self-judgment, she does often present a character who is apolitical; who staunchly insists that good be recognized as good, evil as evil; and who acts relentlessly from strong beliefs.

Set throughout the world, H.'s novels reflect her extensive travel and careful research. Most reviewers have noted the convincing locales; others have complained that characters frequently are too good, too bad, or too idealistic. At times, multiple subplots and excessive literary and musical allusions weigh down the main story line. A more serious defect is occasional propaganda, which one reviewer of *Message from Málaga* (1971) saw as so marring her work that it is unreadable because "she seems now less concerned to tell a good story than to make an apologia for the United States, assailed by external enemies, riddled from within."

Nevertheless, H. combines adventure, a patriotic struggle against evil forces, individual heroism, and rewards by love in novels read by millions. *Friends and Lovers* (1947) and *Rest and Be Thankful* (1949), her two novels outside the spy genre, were not particularly successful. Her continued popularity has come from her spy novels, in which genre she is, as one reviewer has noted, "such a pro."

WORKS: *Sexual Life in Ancient Rome* by O. Kiefer (translated by Highet, with G. Highet, 1934). *Friederich Engels: A Biography* by G. Mayer (translated by Highet, with G. Highet, 1936). *Above Suspicion* (1941). *Assignment in Brittany* (1942). *While Still We Live* (1944). *Horizon* (1946). *Friends and Lovers* (1947). *Rest and Be Thankful* (1949). *Neither Five Nor Three* (1951). *I and My True Love* (1953). *Pray for a Brave Heart* (1955). *North from Rome* (1958). *Assignment: Suspense* (1961). *Decision at Delphi* (1961). *The Venetian Affair* (1963). *Home Is the Hunter* (1964). *The Double Image* (1966). *The Salzburg Connection* (1968). *Message from Málaga* (1971). *Snare of the Hunter* (1974). *Agent in Place* (1976). *Prelude to Terror* (1978).

BIBLIOGRAPHY: Breit, H., *The Writer Observed* (1956). Fadiman, C., *The Art of Helen MacInnes* (1971). MacInnes, H., Introduction to *Assignment: Suspense* (1961).
   For articles in reference works, see: *CB* (Nov. 1967). *20thCAS*.
   Other references: *Counterpoint* (1965). *Film Literature Quarterly*, V (1977).

ELIZABETH EVANS

Patricia Highsmith

B. 19 Jan. 1921, Fort Worth, Texas
Writes under: Patricia Highsmith, Claire Morgan
D. of Jay Bernard and Mary Coates Plangman

Both of H.'s natural parents were artists, as was her stepfather, Stanley Highsmith, whom her mother married when H. was three. By the time H. graduated from Barnard in 1942, she had decided to put her creative energy into writing rather than painting. But she still sees with a painter's eye; the landscapes and cityscapes of her crime novels are cleanly drawn and evocative. By 1949 she was able to travel to Europe, where she eventually settled, first in England, later in France.

It has been recognized for some time, especially in Europe, that H. writes crime novels of great psychological acuity. In 1964, Brigid Brophy ranked her with Georges Simenon, and critical opinion has increasingly confirmed Brophy's judgment. H.'s first novel, *Strangers on a Train* (1950), introduced a plot twist of considerable originality: an innocent, decent man meets a man who is evil, or mad, or both, and through this meeting and the collusion of events, the innocent becomes a murderer. *The Blunderer* (1954) repeats this configuration of main characters and lays heavy emphasis on the power of rumor and sensational publicity in modern society. The court of public opinion convicts Walter Stackhouse of a murder he has twice resisted the temptation to commit.

The Talented Mr. Ripley (1955) won the Mystery Writers of America Scroll and the Grand Prix de Littèrature Policière in 1957. It introduced a genuinely fascinating character, Tom Ripley, who also stars with chilling blandness in two later novels. Rarely has an amoral murderer been so likeable, had such good intentions, projected such pathos. Tom, having met Dickie Greenleaf, a man who has or is everything Tom wants, kills Dickie and then becomes him. Tom wears Dickie's clothes and personality until he has acquired sufficient confidence to reassume his own name. Tom's story is a sort of unholy rite-of-passage.

These three novels introduce the main themes which H.'s sixteen crime novels explore and the central plot device on which she rings a number of variations. Several of H.'s novels revolve around an increasingly compulsive relationship between a good and an evil man.

H. never exploits this device for the same thematic purposes twice. In

The Cry of the Owl (1962), the former mental patient and voyeur turns out to be the beleaguered innocent, and the clean-cut American boy is revealed as a natural killer, waiting for the right combination of circumstances to trigger his violence. In *The Two Faces of January* (1964), which was the Crime Writers of England's novel of the year, and *Those Who Walk Away* (1967), it is the innocent who attach themselves to the guilty and, for their own psychological purposes, haunt them. The main theme of *A Dog's Ransom* (1972) is the breakdown of the social institutions meant to protect the decent from predators.

In Tom Ripley, H. created the first of several characters who unite terrible innocence and terrible guilt in one personality. Vic Van Allen's well-earned reputation for being the most long-suffering of upright citizens protects him long enough to commit murder twice, in *Deep Water* (1957). In *This Sweet Sickness* (1960), when David Kelsey retreats into an imaginary life and personality in order to enjoy the success in love that reality has denied him, he begins a slow deterioration into dangerous madness.

One of H.'s major themes, then, is the ease with which a decent man can cross the line into criminality, or a sane one slip into insanity. In H.'s world, society can be counted on to accelerate these disasters in a variety of ways: by protecting the guilty, harassing the innocent, brutalizing prisoners, enjoying innuendo, wallowing in sensationalism, and tolerating terrorism.

H. should not be approached as a mystery or suspense novelist, since there are very few mysteries and little suspense in her books. In the service of plot, her police frequently behave like idiots and sometimes her protagonists' actions are incomprehensible. Anthony Boucher noted that two of her novels were too long, and it is a charge that could be leveled at many of them. At her best, however, she is a sensitive chronicler of psychological stress and deterioration, and a clear-eyed observer of social tragedy.

WORKS: *Strangers on a Train* (1950; film version, 1951). *The Price of Salt* (1952). *The Blunderer* (1954). *The Talented Mr. Ripley* (1955; film version, *Purple Noon*, 1961). *Deep Water* (1957). *A Game for the Living* (1958). *Miranda the Panda Is on the Veranda* (with D. Sanders, 1958). *This Sweet Sickness* (1960). *The Cry of the Owl* (1962). *The Glass Cell* (1964). *The Two Faces of January* (1964). *The Story-Teller* (English title, *A Suspension of Mercy*, 1965). *Plotting and Writing Suspense Fiction* (1966). *Those Who Walk Away* (1967). *The Tremor of Forgery* (1969). *Ripley Under Ground* (1970). *The Snail Watcher, and Other Stories* (English title, *Eleven*, 1970). *A Dog's Ransom* (1972). *Little Tales of Misogyny* (in German, 1974; in English, 1977). *Ripley's*

Game (1974). *The Animal Lover's Book of Beastly Murder* (1975). *Edith's Diary* (1977). *The Boy Who Followed Ripley* (1980).

BIBLIOGRAPHY: Brophy, B., *Don't Never Forget* (1966).
  For articles in reference works, see: *Contemporary Novelists*, Ed. J. Vinson (1976). *WA.*
  Other references: *London Magazine* (June 1969; June–July 1972). *TLS* (24 Sept. 1971).

CAROL CLEVELAND

Laura Keane Zametkin Hobson

B. 18 June 1900, New York City
Wrote under: Peter Field, Laura Z. Hobson
D. of Adella Kean and Michael Zametkin; m. Thayer Hobson, 1930

Most of H.'s childhood was spent on Long Island with her mother and father, a Russian émigré. Stefan Ivarin, the hero of her 1964 novel *First Papers*, closely resembles her father, who felt he must earn the right to his naturalization papers as a liberal editor of a Yiddish newspaper and an adamant labor leader. The warm portrait of the Ivarin family is simultaneously accurately detailed and sentimental in its evocation of the lower–East Side life as it moved from the relative calm at the turn of the century to the exciting, overcrowded pre–World War I period.

H.'s background in advertising and publishing greatly influenced her fiction. She worked as an advertising copywriter, as a reporter with the New York *Evening Post*, and, until 1940, as promotion director of *Time*, as well as writing short stories for popular magazines such as *Collier's*, the *Ladies' Home Journal*, *McCall's*, and *Cosmopolitan*. With her husband, H. wrote two westerns. Divorced in 1935, she lived with her adopted sons Michael and Christopher in New York City, where she has continued to contribute to popular magazines and newspapers as well as to publish short fiction throughout her career as a novelist.

H.'s first adult novel written on her own, *The Trespassers* (1943), establishes the liberal tone and controversial subject matter of all of her work. The double plot involves both a love story and a moral stand on the part of a strong, successful woman and a powerful radio tycoon. H. is quite adept at presenting the minutia of the well-to-do New York liberal, including the psychological intricacies of the male/female relationship as the lovers take opposing sides on the issue of the quota system that prevented refugees from immigrating to the U.S. One of the fascinating aspects of H.'s fiction is the consistent appearance of a strong-willed liberal female career woman who endangers her love relationship by supporting a cause—in this case the liberalization of the immigration laws.

Gentleman's Agreement (1947) analyzes the social and economic effects of anti-Semitism by tracing the experience of Phil Green, a Gentile magazine writer, as he pretends he is a Jew to gather material for a series on anti-Semitism. H. dramatizes so sharply the pain caused by anti-Semitism in the lives of Phil Green and those involved in his research that the reader identifies with and understands the subtle permeation of prejudice throughout the American culture, particularly in the liberal eastern establishment. The weakest element of the novel is the formulaic melodrama of the love relationship between Phil Green and Kathy Lacey, his editor's niece.

H.'s most successful novel, *Gentleman's Agreement* sold millions of copies and was translated into many languages. The film version received the New York Film Critics Award and the Academy Award for best picture of 1947. The effects of the notoriety surrounding the literary success, including the Hollywood ordeal, supplied much of the subject matter and insight for H.'s 1951 novel, *The Celebrity*.

H.'s fictional concerns reflect her personal zeal for tolerance and understanding. Her novels are for the most part propaganda novels and suffer artistically from the strength of the message overpowering the style. But H. is an effective storyteller and *Gentleman's Agreement*, though somewhat dated, can still succeed in creating a sharp awareness of the insidiousness and pain of bigotry.

WORKS: *Dry Gulch Adams* (with T. Hobson, 1934). *Outlaws Three* (with T. Hobson, 1934). *A Dog of His Own* (1941). *The Trespassers* (1943). *Gentleman's Agreement* (1947; film version, 1947). *The Other Father* (1950). *The Celebrity* (1951). *First Papers* (1964). *I'm Going to Have a Baby* (1967). *The Tenth Month* (1971). *Consenting Adult* (1975). *Over and Above* (1979).

BIBLIOGRAPHY: For articles in reference works, see: *CA*, 17–20 (1976). *CB* (Sept. 1947). *20thCAS*.

Other references: Chicago *Sun Book-Week* (2 March 1947). *Life* (27 Nov. 1964). *NYHTB* (9 March 1947; 8 Nov. 1964). *SatR* (27 Feb. 1965). *Time* (29 May 1950; 9 Nov. 1953).

SUZANNE ALLEN

Marietta Holley

B. 16 July 1836, Jefferson County, New York; d. 1 March 1926, Jefferson
    County, New York
Wrote under: Samantha Allen, Jemyma, Joshia Allen's Wife
D. of John Milton and Mary Taber Holley

The youngest of seven children, H. was born on the family farm where
she lived her entire life. Financial difficulties ended her formal education at fourteen, but she maintained a lifelong fondness for reading. In
the 1870s, she augmented her family's modest income by teaching piano
lessons. Always inordinately shy, she was fifty years old before she left
Jefferson County for the first time. Her shyness eventually prevented
her from accepting invitations to read her work in public or to address
the leading feminist reformers of the day. After the death of her parents, she lived alone with her unmarried sister, Sylphina, who died in
1915. Nothing about her private life reflects the fact that she was a celebrated humorist whose popularity rivaled Mark Twain's.

Although she initially wrote and published poetry under the pseudonym Jemyma, her contributions to the American vernacular-humor tradition began with *My Opinions and Betsey Bobbet's* (1873). H. created
in Samantha Allen, her commonsensical persona, an ideal spokesperson
for her primary theme: women's rights. H. made relatively unpopular
feminist ideas more acceptable by grounding them in the domestic perspective of a farm wife and stepmother. Even Samantha's nom de plume,
Josiah Allen's Wife, served as an ironic comment on women's subordinate social, political, and economic status.

Two antagonists to Samantha's feminism appear in the novel: Josiah
Allen and Betsey Bobbet. Josiah's views are suffused with sentimentality
and male egoism, while Betsey Bobbet, an aging spinster, holds that
woman's only sphere is marriage. Although Betsey soon disappeared
from H.'s work, Josiah continued as a comic foil to Samantha's feminism and common sense.

For her second novel, *Josiah Allen's Wife as a P. A.* [Promiscuous
Advisor] *and P. I.* [Private Investigator]: *Samantha at the Centennial*
(1877), H.'s publisher, Elisha Bliss, supplied her with extensive material
about the Centennial Exposition in Philadelphia. Thus began the practice
that became characteristic of H.'s humor; she wrote realistic descriptions

of places she never visited in person. The travel motif gave Samantha increased opportunity to expound upon a variety of feminist issues, in-including women's right to privacy, and to celebrate the wide range of talents displayed in the Woman's Pavillion at the Exposition.

In *My Wayward Pardner; or, My Trials with Josiah, America, the Widow Bump, and etcetery* (1880), inspired by an open letter from the women of Utah to the women of the U.S., H. responded to another contemporary issue, polygamy. She dramatized the abuses of polygamy by having Josiah, under the influence of a Mormon deacon, flirt with a widow. Although we never seriously believe Josiah will take a second wife, H. came perilously close to destroying the strong family unit that served as the basis for Samantha's domestic feminism.

H.'s fourth novel, *Sweet Cicely* (1885), dramatized the plight of women who married intemperate men. The novel was influenced by H.'s correspondence with Frances Willard, head of the Women's Christian Temperance Union, and it echoed the sentimental tone of temperance tracts. Because it dealt extensively with women's legal status, it was a great favorite of the feminist leaders; Susan B. Anthony wrote H. to tell her of the pleasure the novel gave her. It was not, however, a popular success.

In contrast, her next novel, *Samantha at Saratoga; or, Racin' after Fashion* (1887), was H.'s most popular work. It features Samantha and Josiah vacationing at the country's most fashionable resort, Saratoga. There H. attacks, through humor, society's preoccupation with the genteel values that were antithetical to her goals of full political and economic equality for women.

Between 1887 and 1914, H. wrote fourteen more humorous novels that addressed a variety of social issues, ranging from women's role in the Methodist church to American foreign policy. None of these, however, enjoyed the success of *Samantha at Saratoga*, and in many the quality of her humor declined. Nonetheless, H. made important contributions to the American vernacular-humor tradition and to the feminist movement. No other humorist made the opponents of feminism the targets of her humor, and no other feminist used humor as her primary weapon for furthering the women's rights movement. She gave to American literature one of its strongest and most eloquent heroines of the 19th c., and she was influential in making feminist principles acceptable to a wide audience of women.

WORKS: *My Opinions and Betsey Bobbet's: Designed As a Beacon Light, to Guide Women to Life, Liberty, and the Pursuit of Happiness, but Which May*

Be Read by Members of the Sterner Sect, without Injury to Themselves or the Book. (1873). *Joshia Allen's Wife as a P. A. and P. I.: Samantha at the Centennial. Designed As a Bright and Shining Light, to Pierce the Fogs of Error and Injustice That Surround Society and Josiah, and to Bring More Clearly to View the Path That Leads Straight on to Virtue and Happiness* (1877). *Betsey Bobbet: A Drama* (1880). *The Lament of the Mormon Wife: A Poem* (1880). *My Wayward Pardner; or, My Trials with Josiah, America, the Widow Bump, and etcetery* (1880). *Miss Richard's Boy, and Other Stories* (1883). *Sweet Cicely; or, Josiah Allen As a Politician* (1885). *Miss Jones' Quilting* (1887). *Poems* (1887). *Samantha at Saratoga; or, Racin' after Fashion* (1887). *Samantha Among the Brethren* (1890). *The Widder Doodle's Courtship, and Other Sketches* (1890). *Samantha on the Race Problem* (1892). *Tirzah Ann's Summer Trip, and Other Sketches* (1892). *Samantha at the World's Fair* (1893). *Samantha Among the Colored Folks* (1894). *Josiah's Alarm, and Abel Perry's Funeral* (1895). *Samantha in Europe* (1895). *Samantha at the St. Louis Exposition* (1904). *Around the World with Josiah Allen's Wife* (1905). *Samantha vs. Josiah: Being the Story of a Borrowed Automobile and What Came of It* (1906). *Samantha on Children's Rights* (1909). *Josiah's Secret: A Play* (1910). *Samantha at Coney Island and a Thousand Other Islands* (1911). *Samantha on the Woman Question* (1913). *Josiah Allen on the Woman Question* (1914).

BIBLIOGRAPHY: Blair, W., *Horse Sense in American Humor: From Benjamin Franklin to Ogden Nash* (1962). Blyley, K. G., "M. H." (Ph.D. diss., Univ. of Pittsburgh, 1936). Curry, J. A., "Women As Subjects and Writers of Nineteenth-Century American Humor" (Ph.D. diss., Univ. of Michigan, 1975). Morris, L. A. "Women Vernacular Humorists in Nineteenth-Century America: Ann Stephens, Frances Whitcher, and M. H." (Ph.D. diss., Univ. of California, Berkeley, 1978).

For articles in reference works, see: *AA. AW. DAB,* V, 1. *NAW* (article by M. Langworthy). *NCAB,* 9.

Other references: *Critic* (Jan. 1905).

LINDA A. MORRIS

Pauline Elizabeth Hopkins

B. 1895, Portland, Maine; d. 23 Aug. 1930, Cambridge, Massachusetts
Wrote under: Sarah A. Allen (?), Pauline Elizabeth Hopkins
D. of William A. and Sarah A. Allen Hopkins (?)

H. was educated in the public schools of Boston. Before she was graduated from the Girls' High School she had won a prize of ten dollars in gold, offered by the Congregational Publishing Society of Boston, for the best essay on "The Evils of Intemperance and Their Remedies." Initially she aspired to be a playwright and in 1879 wrote the musical drama *Slaves' Escape; or, The Underground Railroad*, also known as *Peculiar Sam*. Another play, *One Scene from the Drama of Early Days*, based on the biblical story of Daniel, was also written in this period.

From 1892 to 1895, she worked as a stenographer and eventually won a civil service appointment to the Bureau of Statistics on the Massachusetts Decennial Census, where she worked from 1895 to 1899. In May 1900, she resumed her literary career with a short story in the inaugural issue of *The Colored American Magazine*.

By May of 1903, she had become the literary editor of the magazine and contributed many short stories and essays, one series of twelve biographical articles on "Famous Men of the Negro Race," and another series on "Famous Women of the Negro Race." Two of her novels, *Winona: A Tale of Negro Life in the South and Southwest* and *Of One Blood; or, The Hidden Self*, were serialized in the magazine in 1902. Another serialized novel, *Hagar's Daughter*, was apparently also written by H., under the pen name Sarah A. Allen.

Because of ill health, H. left *The Colored American*, which had moved to New York, in 1904, and returned to the stenographic profession, this time at the Massachusetts Institute of Technology. Her only literary endeavor after this was a series of articles, "Dark Races of the Twentieth Century," which appeared in *The Voice of the Negro* from December 1904 through July 1905.

Contending Forces (1900), H.'s only novel published in book form, is a romance written in the typical genteel style common at the turn of the century. The plot centers on four young people in Boston who fall in love and, in spite of calamities, tragedies, and a complicated series of events, end up happily married and in possession of a lost family fortune. The "contending forces" in the novel are those problems and injustices which Afro-Americans encountered both in the North and in the South after the Civil War, such as the lack of political power, the difficulty in obtaining jobs, and, most serious, the lynchings which were such a common occurrence in the South. In her frequently didactic style she refers often to the inevitable, and desirable, mixing of the races through marriage. Mysticism and other psychic phenomena are important in the novel, existing concurrently with staunch, traditional Christianity. In the preface she speaks of herself as "one of the proscribed race" and frequently uses the terms "inferior" and "superior" when referring to the black race and the white race, respectively.

The serialized novels and numerous short stories share a similar style and subject matter; almost all have a strong mystical element, and many deal with interracial love and marriage. Many of her essays are biographical with an obvious didactic tone, and she invarably points out that perseverance and hard work have resulted in the various individuals' success. In an essay in *The Colored American* of June 1900, she advocates limited suffrage for women.

As one of the first black women writers H. has a secure niche among the "Talented Tenth" of the Negro race, as W. E. B. DuBois designates the Afro-American middle class of his day. Hers were not explicitly novels of protest, of which there were none at the turn of the century. She writes only of the black middle class and its problems. Her descriptive prose is often excessively florid, and when writing in dialect she falls short of authentic reproduction. Nonetheless, she occupies a unique place in the Afro-American literary heritage as a woman who did no less herself than what she expected of her readers.

WORKS: *Contending Forces: A Romance Illustrative of Negro Life North and South* (1900).

The papers of Pauline Elizabeth Hopkins are at Fisk University Library, Nashville, Tennessee.

BIBLIOGRAPHY: Bone, R., *The Negro Novel in America* (1965). Gloster, H., *Negro Voices in American Fiction* (1948). Loggins, V., *The Negro Author: His Development in America to 1900* (1964).

For articles in reference works, see: *Black American Writers Past and Present*, T. G. Rush, C. F. Myers, and E. S. Arata (1975).

Other references: *The Colored American Magazine* (Jan. 1901). *Phylon* (Spring 1972).

MARILYN LAMPING

Julia Ward Howe

B. 27 May 1819, New York City; d. 17 Oct. 1910, Newport, Rhode Island
D. of Samuel and Julia Rush Cutler Ward; m. Samuel Gridley Howe, 1843

H. was born into a wealthy New York City family. A combination of tutors and private schools provided H. with an excellent education in literature and the Romance languages. She later taught herself German and studied the German philosophers. During her sheltered childhood and youth, her only vent for her emotions was the writing of religious poetry. H.'s life of seclusion ended when she married Howe, the director of the Perkins Institute for the Blind. She bore six children in sixteen years.

Throughout the 1850s and 1860s, H. struggled to establish a literary career despite her husband's disapproval. She felt required to publish her first book of verse, *Passion Flowers* (1854), anonymously. The poems, regular in meter and rhyme, vary in theme and purpose. *Passion Flowers* contains a number of powerful emotional poems with themes of conflict, disappointment, and inadequacy. Although some of the poems in *Words for the Hour* (1857) continue to reflect H.'s inner turmoil and unhappiness, most of the verses are conventional in tone. *Words for the Hour* introduces what was to become H.'s primary poetic form: commemorative verses designed to celebrate a public event or notable personality. *Later Lyrics* (1866) contains a combination of sentimental, conventional, and public verse. H.'s final book of poetry, *From Sunset Ridge* (1898), reprints some of her early poems in addition to publishing new commemorative verse.

Other writing ventures included articles for the abolitionist newspaper *Commonwealth*, a brief stint as editor of *Northern Lights*, two travel books, travel letters to the New York *Tribune*, two wordy and unsuccessful plays, and a series of philosophical essays designed to be read as parlor lectures. H.'s one substantial literary success was the publication of her "Battle Hymn of the Republic," in the *Atlantic Monthly* (February 1862). The poem gained increasing popularity as the century progressed, but H.'s publishers forced her to recognize that the audience for her poetry was dwindling. By 1870, H. was casting around for other ways to express herself.

In 1868, H. embarked on two new projects which departed dramatically from the literary-salonière image which she had cherished for so long. She helped found the new American Woman Suffrage Association. She was an officer of the AWSA and its successor, the National American Woman Suffrage Association, for forty-one years. H. also helped found the New England Woman's Club and served as its president for thirty-eight years.

H.'s feminist theory pervaded her lectures, articles, and even her occasional sermons. It was an articulate blend of conventional notions about women's natural domesticity and moral superiority with more radical views concerning women's spiritual and intellectual equality with men. She saw traditional femininity as a power base which women should strengthen by broader education and work experience. As a means to these ends, she advocated a better distribution of power within the family and the state, opportunities for higher education for women, support for working women, and access to the professions. H. believed that America would achieve the glory to which she aspired during the 19th c. only when women had received the opportunities and respect they deserved.

As her sermons and lectures gained renown, H. came to see herself as a guardian of American virtue. Two of her published lectures—*Modern Society* (1881) and *Is Polite Society Polite?* (1895)—reflect her convictions concerning the manners and morals of the New England elite, combined with a new emphasis on woman's role in maintaining these values.

When, in the 1890s, old age limited H.'s mobility, she began a new career as an essayist for popular and religious magazines. She wrote about everything from "The Joys of Motherhood" to "Lynch Law in the South." The exposure which these publications provided built up a new, gratifying reputation for H. as "Queen of America" and "America's Grand Old Lady."

Although H.'s writings for public consumption were enormous, very few of them were published by a commercial establishment. The small fraction of her work which was published is not her best writing. The reams of articles and lectures which were never published, however, contain lively images and vigorous, convincing arguments. H.'s major contribution was her ability to galvanize thousands of women into cooperative action on behalf of their sex. Her flair for "finding the right word," as she put it, helped improve the status of women for generations, long after her poems and plays were forgotten.

WORKS: *Passion Flowers* (1854). *Words for the Hour* (1857). *The World's Own* (1857). *A Trip to Cuba* (1860). *Later Lyrics* (1866). *From the Oak to the Olive* (1868). *Sex and Education* (edited by Howe, 1874). *Memoir of Dr. Samuel Gridley Howe* (1876). *Modern Society* (1881). *Margaret Fuller, Marchessa Ossoli* (1883). *Is Polite Society Polite?; and Other Essays* (1895). *From Sunset Ridge; Poems, Old and New* (1898). *Reminiscences, 1819–1899* (1899). *Sketches of Representative Women of New England* (edited by Howe, 1904). *At Sunset* (1910).

The papers of Julia Ward Howe are at the Schlesinger Library, Radcliffe College; the Houghton Library, Harvard University; and the Library of Congress.

BIBLIOGRAPHY: Clifford, D., *Mine Eyes Have Seen the Glory: A Biography of Julia Ward Howe* (1979). Elliott, M., *The Eleventh Hour in the Life of Julia Ward Howe* (1911). Hall, F., *The Story of the "Battle Hymn of the*

Republic" (1916). Mead, E., *Julia Ward Howe's Peace Crusade* (1910). Richards L., and M. Elliott, *Julia Ward Howe, 1819–1910* (1915). Richards, L., *Two Noble Lives: Samuel Gridley Howe and Julia Ward Howe* (1911). Tharp, L., *Three Saints and a Sinner* (1956).

For articles in reference works, see: *AA. AW. CAL. DAB*, V, 1. *FPA. NAW* (article by P. S. Boyer). *NCAB*, 1.

MARY H. GRANT

Barbara Howes

B. 1 May 1914, New York City
D. of Osborne and Mildred Cox Howes; m. William Jay Smith, 1947

After graduating from Bennington College, Vermont, H. lived in Italy, England, France, and Haiti; she now lives in North Pownal, Vermont, and frequently visits the West Indies. She has two sons and is divorced. H. is the recipient of many fellowships and awards. Her professional activities have been literary rather than academic; she was editor of *Chimera* magazine from 1943 to 1947.

In her essay in *Poets on Poetry*, H. discusses the poets who have influenced her, her interest in translation and in adapting Old French and other literary forms to contemporary concerns, her purpose in writing, the importance in her work of domestic subject matter and of place, and her distrust of the "snarling little ego," her aversion to writers who "give in to violence and spite."

The constants in H.'s poetry are a detached, restrained tone which carries considerable tight-lipped intensity; an intellectual concern with physical and human nature and with the patterns and principles which underlie and relate their behavior; and a technique which is flexible, controlled, and relatively traditional. Unlike so many contemporary postmodernist poets, she does not write social protest about the women's movement or the Vietnam war, and she is neither confessional nor surrealistic. Also unlike them, she manipulates rather than abandons conventional prosody.

H. chooses many traditional subjects, such as still-life; mythological personages; *objets d'art;* specific persons ("To W. H. Auden on His Fiftieth Birthday"), places ("On a Bougainvillaea Vine at the Summer

Palace," "Views of Oxford Colleges"), and occasions; and nature interpreted by and for civilization: a deer in hunting season "dropped like a
monument," a dead toucan described as "a beak with a panache / chucked
like an old shell back to the Caribbean."

H.'s most insistent theme is that unrestricted emotion blinds and im-
prisons if allowed to dominate either life or art. In "The New Leda," H.
speaks of the woman dedicated to the god, whether Zeus or Christ:
"Her / limbo holds her like a fly in amber, / Beyond the reach of
life." In "For an Old Friend" she imagines the friend thinking, "This
hullabaloo about life / is not my forte"; in "Radar and Unmarked Cars,"
she writes ". . . our / Radar / Will hold us True: / We need / Love / At
a constant speed." Her aesthetic credo matches the personal one in
"Portrait of the Artist": "For dear life some do / Many a hard thing,
/ Train the meticulous mind / Upon meaning, seek / And find, and yet
discard / All that is not of reality's tough rind / . . . To be / Ascetic
for life's sake, / Honest and passionate."

The effect of this personal and aesthetic credo on her work is both
her poems' strength and their weakness. In a poem like "Still-life: New
England" the tone of restrained disgust and assumed indifference is deliberately and successfully used to create horror, the ironic opposite of
indifference. But when, in "Dream of a Good Day," H. puts all the
action of the poem into conventional romantic dreams of sailing and
discovering (i.e., making a poem), which are quite separate from reality,
and then uses only the last line to state but not to experience reality
("Then in the colloquial evening to come back to love"), the poem
suffers because the honesty is there without the passion.

Yet it is passion which makes her such a disciplined craftsperson. H.
speaks of the need to train the eye to notice and the ear to listen, to recognize the necessity of form ("language must have discipline to have
meaning"), and to distinguish between the forms of art and journalism.
It is this disciplined passion which enables her to make her poetry "a
way of life, not just an avocation," a way in which "one orders and
deepens one's experience, and learns to understand what is happening in
oneself and in others."

Overall, H.'s poetry strongly continues the "Apollonian" strain of
Eliot, Stevens, and Wilbur, rather than the "Dionysian" strain of Whitman and Williams. But though she has not quite Eliot's dramatic compression, nor Stevens's mercurial imagination, nor Wilbur's classical balance, her depth of perception, firm ironic tone, and technical control
make her a worthy member of their company.

WORKS: *The Undersea Farmer* (1948). *In the Cold Country: Poems* (1954). *Light and Dark: Poems* (1959). *23 Modern Stories* (edited by Howes, 1963). *From the Green Antilles: Writings of the Caribbean* (edited by Howes, 1966). *Looking Up at Leaves* (1966). *The Sea-Green Horse: Short Stories for Young People* (edited by Howes, with G. J. Smith, 1970). *The Blue Garden* (1972). *The Eye of the Heart: Stories from Latin America* (edited by Howes, 1973). *A Private Signal: Poems New and Selected* (1977).

The papers of Barbara Howes are at the Yale University Library, New Haven, Connecticut.

BIBLIOGRAPHY: Bogan, L., *Selected Criticism* (1955). Friedman, N., *Contemporary Poets* (1975). Nemerov, H., ed., *Poets on Poetry* (1966). Untermeyer, L., ed., *Modern American Poetry* (1962).

For articles in reference works, see: *CA*, 9–12 (1974). *Contemporary Poets*, Eds. J. Vinson and D. L. Kirkpatrick (1975). *WA*.

Other references: *Choice* (April 1978). *NYHTB* (15 Nov. 1959). *NYT* (4 April 1954). *SatR* (19 March 1949). *TLS* (10 Feb. 1978).

ALBERTA TURNER

Sophia Hume

B. 1702, Charleston, South Carolina; d. 26 Jan. 1774, London, England
D. of Henry and Susanna Bayley Wigington; m. Robert Hume, 1721

Born to a prosperous landowning family, H. was raised in the Anglican tradition of her father and educated for a life of elegance in high society. She married a lawyer and prominent citizen of Charleston; they had two children. After her husband's death in 1737 and a series of illnesses, she became increasingly preoccupied with religion and the necessity to convert to Quakerism, the religious tradition of her mother and maternal grandmother Mary Fisher (ca. 1623–1698). She subsequently moved to England and joined the Society of Friends.

In 1747, H. returned to Charleston, where in a series of public meetings she reproached the inhabitants for their sinful lives and called them to a life of simplicity as exemplified in Quakerism. In order to spread her concern for their salvation, she published, with the help of fellow Quakers in Philadelphia, *An Exhortation to the Inhabitants of the Province of South Carolina* (1748). This forcefully written but poorly organized appeal admonished Charlestonians to repent, to give up their diversionary, prideful, and ostentatious lives, and to seek good forms of recreation, live simply, and dress modestly. She made a special plea that females cease neglecting their children in their quest for diversion.

Returning to England, H. became a Quaker minister and wrote *A Caution to Such As Observe Days and Times* (1763). In this piece she warned formal Christians, those who "observe days and times," that God may bring them suffering as He did the Jews in order that they learn that His power was in the heart and not the world.

In an attempt to reform the Society of Friends and help stave off the decline in membership, H. published *Extracts from Divers, Antient Testimonies* (1766), a collection of early Quaker writings. In her introduction addressed to ministers, elders, and members of the Society, she urged them not to conform to the ways of the world but to become the "foundation for the church of Christ." In 1767, H. went back to Charleston in an attempt to revive Quakerism there. Unsuccessful, she returned to England, where she died in 1774.

The principal theme of H.'s writing is the call to repentance and nonworldliness which she found exemplified in Quaker life. Through rejection of worldly pleasures one came to enjoy the fruits of the spirit —joy, love, and peace—the highest of all pleasures. The rewards of simplicity, the universality of God's grace, and the indwelling of the Holy Spirit in each person are emphasized in her work. While she maintained a very traditional attitude toward woman's role, her Christian belief spurred her to write and speak publicly in defense of religion.

WORKS: *An Exhortation to the Inhabitants of the Province of South Carolina, to Bring Their Deeds to the Light of Christ, in Their Own Consciences* (1748). *A Caution to Such As Observe Days and Times. To Which Is Added, An Address to Magistrates, Parents, Mistresses of Families etc.* (1763). *Extracts from Divers, Antient Testimonies* (1766). *The Justly Celebrated Mrs. Sophia Hume's Advice* (1769).

BIBLIOGRAPHY: Bowden, J., *The History of the Society of Friends in America*, Vol. I (1850). Woolman, J., *The Journal and Essays of John Woolman*, Ed. A. M. Gummere (1922).

For articles in reference works, see: *NAW* (article by S. V. James).

DANA GREENE

Fannie Hurst

B. 18 Oct. 1889, Hamilton, Ohio; d. 23 Feb. 1968, New York City
D. of Samuel and Rose Koppel Hurst; m. Jacques S. Danielson, 1915

H., daughter of American-born Jews of German descent, was raised and educated in St. Louis, Missouri (B.A. 1909, Washington University). In 1910, eager to observe the working people of whom and for whom she wrote, H. moved to New York City. There she took assorted jobs as saleswoman, actress, and waitress, and started bombarding publications with her fiction. Her marriage to a Russian-born pianist, in which they both pursued separate careers, endured successfully until her husband's death in 1952.

H. became an established writer while still in her twenties. She began as a short-story writer, but she is best remembered for her best-selling novels, especially *Back Street* (1931) and *Imitation of Life* (1933). Her works have been widely translated, and many became successful films.

Back Street is about the beautiful Ray Schmidt, who is mistress to a married man and for over twenty years is confined to the "back streets" of his life. After her lover's death, Ray spends her last few years penniless at a European spa, surviving on the few francs winners at the casino throw to her; she dies alone in her room.

The novel's enormous popularity was due largely to two factors: It appeared during the Depression, when escapist entertainment was assured a large following, and it deals with the especially titillating subject of sex, which H. handles most cleverly. She avoids graphic description, knowing that the lack of it would afford greater excitement for her audience and, therefore, greater readership for her. Although we remain uncertain why the selfish and immature lover is even attractive to the lovely Ray, this is calculated; we are not meant to focus on the relationship, but on Ray, her feelings and responses. She is dominated, used, and ultimately destroyed, yet throughout the reader, perhaps recalling similar trials, identifies and empathizes profoundly.

In Imitation of Life, Beatrice Fay Chipley, widowed mother of a young daughter, sells maple syrup door-to-door with the help of Delilah, a black woman who also has an infant daughter. Beatrice becomes one of the most prominent businesswomen in America, but the novel ends with her realization that she must continue to live an "imitation of life" without a man to love.

Imitation of Life, in rough outline, is a woman's version of the timeless rags-to-riches American success story. But the specific type of irony evident at the conclusion, as well as its stereotyped characterization of the black "mammy" figure, places it solidly in its time. Feminists would be outraged at its underlying philosophy—that, regardless of professional achievements, life must be worthless without what Delilah terms "man-lovin'." H.'s audience, however, was attracted by the novel's sympathetic—today we would call it "sentimental"—depiction of the heroine; by its handling of the touchy matter of race relations; and by its "bittersweetness," still one of the recognizable marks of the popular novelist.

In her time, H. was very popular with readers and was scarcely taken seriously by critics. Today she retains our interest primarily because her works are accurate gauges of her contemporary audience's beliefs.

WORKS: *Just around the Corner* (1914). *Every Soul Hath Its Song* (1916). *Land of the Free* (1917). *Gaslight Sonatas* (1918). *Humoresque* (1919). *Back Pay* (1921). *Star Dust* (1921). *The Vertical City* (1922). *Lummox* (1923). *Appassionata* (1926). *Mannequin* (1926). *Song of Life* (1927). *A President Is Born* (1928). *Five and Ten* (1929). *Procession* (1929). *Back Street* (1931; film versions, 1932, 1941, 1961). *Imitation of Life* (1933; film versions, 1934, 1959). *Anitra's Dance* (1934). *No Food with My Meals* (1935). *Great Laughter* (1936). *Hands of Veronica* (1937). *We Are Ten* (1937). *Lonely Parade* (1942). *Hallelujah* (1944). *Any Woman* (1950). *The Man with One Head* (1953). *Anatomy of Me* (1958). *Family!* (1959). *God Must Be Sad* (1961). *Fool—Be Still* (1964).

BIBLIOGRAPHY: For articles in reference works, see: *CA*, 25–28 (1971). *NCAB*, E. *Ohio Authors and Their Books*, Ed. W. Coyle (1962). *20thCA*. *20thCAS*.

Other references: *Arts and Decoration* (Nov. 1935). *Bookman* (May 1929; Aug. 1931). *Mentor* (April 1928). *NYTBR* (25 Jan. 1942). *SatR* (Oct. 1937).
ELLEN SERLEN UFFEN

Zora Neale Hurston

B. 7 Jan. 1901, Eatonville, Florida; d. 28 Jan. 1960, Saint Lucie County, Florida
D. of John and Lucy Hurston

Born in the first incorporated black town in America, H. was the only writer in the 1920s and 1930s from a southern background who evaluated her southern exposure, realized the richness of her racial heritage, and built her fiction on it. At age nine, H. lost nearly all of her childhood security when her mother died, and she had to live from relative to relative, deprived of formal schooling, drifting through several domestic jobs.

Supporting herself, H. completed two years at Morgan College in Baltimore and enrolled at Howard University, where her first short fiction was published in a literary journal there. She moved to New York, became secretary to the popular novelist Fannie Hurst, and earned a scholarship to Barnard College, where she studied anthropology under Franz Boas. When she graduated in 1928, Dr. Boas had arranged a fellowship for H. to go south to collect folklore. The result of this southern expedition was *Mules and Men* (1935). Throughout the 1920s H. had continued to write short fiction which had been published in *Opportunity*. Her best efforts were "Spunk," "Sweat," and "The Gilded Six-Bits."

H.'s first novel, *Jonah's Gourd Vine* (1934), a narrative loosely based on the lives of her parents, chronicles the life of John Pearson, an itinerant preacher. Incorporating her knowledge of folklore into her fiction, H. depicts John's second wife as a character reliant on conjure to speed the first wife to an early death and to snare the protagonist quickly into marriage, a marriage which crumbles once he discovers the conjure tactics.

H. is lauded for her utilization of folklore, the ripeness and realism of black dialect, the poetic sermon, and the distinct racial flavor of *Jonah's Gourd Vine*. However, critics have faulted plot construction, characterization, and dialogue. Additionally, much of the criticism of H.'s fiction is the result of her choice of setting—Eatonville, Florida, a black town. H.'s critics accuse her of neglecting to confront the problems of racism which constituted a daily issue in the livelihood of blacks in the 1930s and 1940s. H. writes in her autobiography that what she wanted to write was a story about a man, but from what she had read and heard,

"Negroes were supposed to write about the Race problem. My interest lies in what makes a man or woman do such-and-so regardless of his color."

H.'s second novel, *Their Eyes Were Watching God* (1937), also set in Eatonville, is frequently acclaimed her best novel. It is the story of Janie, a young black woman who searches for happiness, self-realization, and love; she is a woman who refuses to settle for less than her own realistic appraisal of what love should be. After the death of her second husband, when Janie is forty years old, she marries a man much younger than she, who is unpretentiously one of the "folk," who loves and wants her without imposing restrictions on her. In the Florida Everglades where Janie and Teacake move after their marriage, they experience a few years of happiness working in the fields together, and Janie is serenely content being a part of the folk culture. Somewhat melodramatically, the novel ends, after a hurricane destroys the Everglades community and Teacake is bitten by a mad dog. Jane is forced to shoot and to kill Teacake because, mentally deranged by rabies, he tries to kill her. The characterization of Janie is excellent, and plot structure, depiction of the folk culture, and the use of black dialect are all equally fine.

H.'s last novel, *Seraph on the Suwanee* (1948), the only one in which a southern white woman is the protagonist, has received little critical attention. Nevertheless, Arvay Henson is the second of H.'s fully delineated protagonists. More than any other woman in H.'s fiction, Arvay offers a psychologically complete view of the complex entanglement of forces which impinge on the southern rural woman and make her life, both externally and internally, a continuous struggle.

From the early autobiographical story, "Drenched in Light" (1924), to her last novel, H. based her fiction on personal experience. The inclusion of folk elements gives a uniquely southern flavor to character and setting. As a writer who had grown up in the South, H. recognized the aesthetics of that particular setting and culture and utilized them as no other black writer of the 1920s or 1930s did.

WORKS: *Jonah's Gourd Vine* (1934). *Mules and Men* (1935). *Their Eyes Were Watching God* (1937). *Tell My Horse* (1938). *Moses, Man of the Mountain* (1939). *Dust Tracks on a Dirt Road* (1942). *Seraph on the Suwanee* (1948).

BIBLIOGRAPHY: Bone, R., *The Negro Novel in America* (1958). Hemenway, R., *Zora Neale Hurston: A Literary Biography* (1977). Huggins, N., *Harlem Renaissance* (1971). Hughes, L., *The Big Sea* (1940). Turner, D., *In a Minor Chord* (1971). Young, J., *Black Writers of the Thirties* (1973).

For articles in reference works, see: *CB* (May 1942; April 1960). *20thCA.* *20thCAS.*

Other references: *Black World* (Aug. 1972). *NYHTB* (22 Nov. 1943). *NYT* (2 Feb. 1960). *SBL* (Winter 1974).

JOYCE PETTIS

Inez Haynes Irwin

B. 2 March 1873, Rio de Janeiro, Brazil; d. 30 Sept. 1970
D. of Gideon and Emma Jane Hopkins Haynes; m. Rufus Hamilton Gillmore, 1897; m. William Henry Irwin, 1916

I. was educated in Boston schools and attended Radcliffe College from 1897 to 1900. At the turn of the century, Radcliffe was a center of suffragist sentiment. Determined to extend this feeling to college alumnae, I. and Maud Wood Park founded the Massachusetts College Equal Suffrage Association in 1900. This group expanded into the National College Equal Suffrage League, an active force in the enfranchisement campaign.

I.'s other feminist activities centered around the more radical wing of the suffrage movement, the National Woman's Party. Lead by Alice Paul and Lucy Burns, the party was patterned after the British suffrage movement in its militancy and political tactics. I. was a member of the party's advisory council; she wrote for the party's publications and was the party's biographer. *The Story of the Woman's Party* (1921) is flawed by its lack of objectivity and the failure to mention the other wing of the suffrage movement, but it is the only record of the party's activities, other than the stories repeated in I.'s more ambitious work on the history of American women, *Angels and Amazons* (1933).

I.'s first fictional work was published in *Everybody's* in 1904. She then became a regular contributor to British and American magazines and devoted herself to writing short stories and novels. Other than her feminist chronicles, I.'s only digressions from these genres occurred during World War I. Having become the wife of newspaperman Will Irwin after the death of Gillmore, I. visited the European fronts with her husband. Her accounts of these visits were printed in the magazines of three countries.

"The Spring Flight" was the O. Henry Memorial Award first-prize winner in 1924, a puzzling choice, for the story is a quasi-biographical sketch of William Shakespeare trying to overcome writer's block before composing *The Tempest*. It is ironic that I. received the highest acclaim for this story, so far removed from her field of expertise.

After a few ventures with highly sentimentalized and simplistic novels about orphaned children and an idealized brother and sister, I. began writing fiction that addressed the issues with which she is now most often associated—those underlying the suffrage movement. Of her feminist fiction, *The Lady of the Kingdoms* (1917) has been undeservedly forgotten. This long novel presents two young heroines, the beautiful and self-assured Southward and the plain and self-effacing Hester. I. uses both heroines to examine the conventional moralities women have been forced into, as well as the unconventional, even "immoral," ones women have chosen for themselves. Though I. may disapprove of the latter roles, she never condemns the women who choose them.

I. published two books dealing with divorce, *Gideon* (1927) and *Gertrude Haviland's Divorce* (1925). The heroine of the latter work is a fat, dull, sloppy woman who has further alienated her husband by being overly absorbed in her children. The book begins as Gertrude receives her husband's request for a divorce, follows her through mental illness, watches her recover as she realizes she is pregnant, and witnesses her transformation into a woman of resolution, intelligence, self-reliance, and new beauty. Her final triumph occurs when she rejects her husband's offer of remarriage; however, this victory is mitigated by the fact that Gertrude now realizes she loves and will marry another man. Also troubling is the assertion that having a baby is enough to end a woman's suffering, an attitude no doubt affected by I.'s failure to have children of her own.

In the 1930s and 1940s, I. returned to sentimental, descriptive novels and wrote upper-class murder mysteries and moralistic children's books. The strongest indictment that may be made against I. comes from these books, the last she wrote. She had run out of good ideas, and no longer had the ability to write strongly, to state issues clearly, and to imagine vital characters. I. apparently decided that those qualities of authorship she still possessed were good enough for children's books. She was a prolific writer whose finest works came early and whose mediocre later works have so thoroughly reduced her reputation as a writer of adult and children's fiction that she is virtually forgotten in these fields. Between 1917 and 1927, however, she wrote several impressively direct novels about divorce and women's roles.

WORKS: *June Jeopardy* (1908). *Maida's Little Shop* (1910). *Phoebe and Ernest* (1910). *Janey* (1911). *Phoebe, Ernest, and Cupid* (1912). *Angel Island*

(1914). *The Ollivant Orphans* (1915). *The Californians* (1916). *The Lady of the Kingdoms* (1917). *The Happy Years* (1919). *The Native Son* (1919). *Maida's Little House* (1921). *Out of the Air* (1921). *The Story of the Woman's Party* (1921). *Gertrude Haviland's Divorce* (1925). *Maida's Little School* (1926). *Gideon* (1927). *P. D. F. R.* (1928). *Confessions of a Businessman's Wife* (1931). *Family Circle* (1931). *Youth Must Laugh* (1932). *Angels and Amazons* (1933). *Strange Harvest* (1934). *Murder Masquerade* (1935). *The Poison Cross* (1936). *Good Manners for Girls* (1937). *A Body Rolled Downstairs* (1938). *Maida's Little Island* (1939). *Maida's Little Camp* (1940). *Many Murders* (1941). *Maida's Little Village* (1942). *Maida's Little Houseboat* (1943). *Maida's Little Theatre* (1946). *The Women Swore Revenge* (1946). *Maida's Little Cabins* (1947). *Maida's Little Zoo* (1949). *Maida's Little Lighthouse* (1951). *Maida's Little Hospital* (n.d.). *Maida's Little Farm* (n.d.). *Maida's Little House Party* (n.d.). *Maida's Little Treasure Hunt* (n.d.). *Maida's Little Tree House* (n.d.).

BIBLIOGRAPHY: For articles in reference works, see: *NCAB*, F. *20thCA. 20thCAS.*

LYNNE MASEL-WALTERS
HELEN LOEB

Helen Maria Fiske Hunt Jackson

B. *15 Oct. 1830, Amherst, Massachusetts; d. 12 Aug. 1885, San Francisco, California*
Wrote under: "*H. H.*," *Saxe Holm, Helen Hunt Jackson, Helen Jackson,* "*Marah*," "*No Name*," "*Rip Van Winkle*"
D. *of Nathan Welby and Deborah Vinal Fiske; m. Edward Bissell Hunt, 1852; m. William Sharpless Jackson, 1875*

The elder and more impetuous of two surviving children of a minister-turned-professor and his devout and educated wife, J. was raised in an atmosphere of learning, piety, and enforced propriety. Although her parents both succumbed to tuberculosis while J. was a teenager, she continued to attend private schools until 1850. J. married then-Lieutenant Hunt and began the restless life of an army wife and mother of two sons, one of whom survived infancy. In 1863 J.'s husband was killed testing his newly invented torpedo. When, two years later, J.'s son died, she turned to writing poetry as an outlet for her grief.

J.'s early poems won her recognition from the influential Thomas Wentworth Higginson; her subsequent prolific periodical publications gathered a wide popular audience and critical praise, even from Emerson. J. supported herself and traveled widely on the profits of her pen. Her generally pious and sentimental treatments of death, love, and nature themes date much of her poetry, but many of her *Verses* (1870) and *Sonnets and Lyrics* (1886) can still be appreciated for their skillful technique and use of language.

J.'s first prose efforts were travel pieces, enriched by her flair for observation of detail in interior decoration and natural scenery. Her descriptions of unconventional people encountered along her way reveal the lingering influence of J.'s narrowly proper upbringing.

While wintering in Colorado Springs in 1873, J. met Jackson, a Quaker banker and railroad promoter, whom she married two years later. J. continued writing and experimented in prose fiction. Her passion for anonymity continued; "Saxe Holm" aroused popular curiosity as the author of two series of J.'s short stories (1874 and 1876), and J. wrote two novels, *Mercy Philbrick's Choice* (1876) and *Hetty's Strange History* (1877), for her publisher's "No Name" series. These works, set in New England, focus upon strong women characters dealing with complications wrought by love, death, family responsibility, and illness. For example, Draxy Miller, a memorable "Saxe Holm" heroine, arranges her sick father's retirement, marries a minister, and takes over his pulpit after his death, all to the approval of the small-town community.

In 1879 J. heard Suzette "Bright Eyes" LaFlesche, an Omaha Indian, describe the wrongs suffered by Native Americans. Aroused by a righteous passion for justice for Indians comparable to abolitionist fervor, J. produced her most memorable works, and abandoned her pseudonyms to speak her mind. In *A Century of Dishonor* (1881), J. also abandoned fiction, writing impassioned history documenting several heinous examples of governmental perfidy practiced upon Indian tribes. J.'s strong indictment of the U.S. government and, by extension, its acquiescent populace, delighted reformers and enraged some critics who believed J.'s lack of objectivity damaged her case.

J. was most appalled by the wrongful treatment inflicted upon California's Mission Indians. She and Abbot Kinney served as official investigators, producing a *Report on the Conditions and Needs of the Mission Indians* (1883). J. was determined to publicize the situation of California's natives and, since government documents reach few, she wrote *Ramona* (1884), a romance involving a half-Indian girl raised on a

Spanish hacienda who elopes with an Indian, and subsequently shares his life as victim of land fraud and prejudice. *Ramona* has enjoyed continuing popularity in over three hundred reprintings, but unfortunately had little real impact upon Indian policy. Perhaps the outrage J. intended to arouse was lost in local color and drowned in tears, the very elements of *Ramona*'s story that have encouraged its frequent retelling in local pageants and national media productions.

Although most modern critics fault J.'s obvious sentimentality, her works are important, both as an index for the taste of her times as well as for their focus upon women who act to determine their destiny. Marriage is not the end of their stories; J. shows them coping with widowhood, poverty, infidelity, and work. The presentation of Native Americans in her works deserves some criticism for its "noble savage" inclination and implications of Indian passivity, but the aim of her writing, to reach and arouse a white audience susceptible to such stereotypes, must be considered in any evaluation. Readers may weep at Ramona's plight, but must still be subconsciously impressed by her strength of purpose.

WORKS: *Bathmendi: A Persian Tale* (1867). *Verses* (1870). *Bits of Travel* (1872). *Bits of Talk about Home Matters* (1873). *Saxe Holm's Stories* (Series 1, 1874). *The Story of Boon* (1874). *Bits of Talk in Verse and Prose for Young Folks* (1876). *Mercy Philbrick's Choice* (1876). *Hetty's Strange History* (1877). *Bits of Travel at Home* (1878). *Nellie's Silver Mine* (1878). *Saxe Holm's Stories* (Series 2, 1878). *Letters from a Cat* (1879). *A Century of Dishonor* (1881). *Mammy Tittleback and Her Family* (1881). *The Training of Children* (1882). *Report on the Conditions and Needs of the Mission Indians* (with A. Kinney, 1883). *Easter Bells* (1884). *Ramona* (1884). *Zeph* (1885). *Glimpses of Three Coasts* (1886). *The Procession of Flowers in Colorado* (1886). *Sonnets and Lyrics* (1886). *Between Whiles* (1887). *My Legacy* (1888). *A Calendar of Sonnets* (1891). *Poems* (1891). *Cat Stories* (1898). *Pansy Billings and Popsy* (1898). *Father Junipero and the Mission Indians* (1902). *Glimpses of California and the Missions* (1902).

Many of the papers of Helen Hunt Jackson are at the Huntington Library, San Marino, California.

BIBLIOGRAPHY: Higginson, T. W., *Contemporaries* (1899). Higginson, T. W., *Short Studies of American Authors* (1906). Odell, R., *H. H. J.* (1939).

For articles in reference works, see: *AA. AW. Appleton's Cyclopaedia of American Biography*, Vol. 3, Eds. J. G. Wilson and J. Fiske (1887). *Authors at Home*, Eds. J. L. and J. B. Gilder (1886). *CAL. DAB*, IX. *Herringshaw's National Library of American Biography*, Vol. 3 (1914). *NAW* (article by T. Wilkins). *Notable Women in History*, Ed. W. J. Abbott (1913). *Twentieth Century Biographical Dictionary of Notable Americans*, Vol. 6, Eds. R. Johnson and J. H. Brown (1904).

Other references: *American Literary Realism* (Summer 1969; Summer 1973). *AL* (Jan. 1931). *American Scholar* (Summer 1941). *Common Ground* (Winter 1946). *NYT* (6 April 1916; 15 May 1928; 7 Oct. 1936). *Southwest Review* (Spring 1959).

HELEN M. BANNAN

Laura Riding Jackson

B. 16 Jan. 1901, New York City
Writes under: Laura Riding Gottschalk, Laura Riding Jackson, Barbara Rich, Laura Riding
D. of Nathaniel S. and Sarah Edersheim Reichenthal; m. Louis Gottschalk, 1920; m. Schuyler Jackson, 1941

J., raised in a nonreligious Jewish household actively espousing socialism, is best known for her strikingly original poetry, although she has also written criticism, novels, and biographical sketches. She attended Cornell University, married Louis Gottschalk (divorced, 1925), then spent thirteen years abroad. She and Robert Graves were companions, establishing the Seizin Press in 1927 in Majorca. In 1939 they came to America, where Laura met and married Schuyler Jackson (poet, farmer, contributing editor of *Time*). For almost thirty years, she and her husband worked on a reference work called the *Dictionary of Exact Meaning*. Jackson died in 1970, however, and the work is still unfinished.

During the dozen years of J.'s association with Robert Graves, the two collaborated on literary criticism and on one odd, satirical novel, *No Decency Left* (1932). *A Survey of Modernist Poetry* (1927) is a perceptive discussion of innovative techniques in poetry, such as those practiced by E. E. Cummings, Ezra Pound, and T. S. Eliot. It analyzes the shortcomings of "temporary fads" such as Imagism and Georgianism and argues that modern experimental poetry, some of which they condemn to an early death, has been influenced by nonrepresentational art. Poets have too often simply abandoned coherent statement, creating abstract arrangements of emotionally laden phrases and sounds.

J. also shared with Graves an interest in the Greco-Roman world and the status of women in ancient times, as evidenced by her novel *A Trojan*

Ending (1937) and her biographical sketches of famous women, *Lives of Wives* (1939).

Most of J.'s poetry is free verse, with a sensitive use of assonance and repetition and relatively little concern for rhyme. Each poem is a different problem, and each seeks to match sound to sense. In this J. has been compared with Gertrude Stein.

Her poetry is often simultaneously playful and serious. Sometimes there is a trace of condescension toward nonpoetic thinking. In the first stanza of "Further Details," for example, the poet, who presumably arrives at the "higher" truth intuitively and holistically, speaks to the analytical, rational pursuer of knowledge: "The reward of curiosity / In such as you / (Statistician of doubt) / Is increased cause of curiosity. / And the punishment thereof, / To be not a cat."

J. is concerned with mental experience more than with sense experience. She favors philosophical subjects—the coexistence of multiplicity and sameness, the mysterious transformations of life and death, the ambiguous relationship between body and mind, the nature of love. Some readers find her poems obscure, but she implies that is the reader's fault, not hers: "Doom is where I am and I want to make this plain because I know there are people to whom it can be plain" (preface to *Poems: A Joking Word*, 1930). She sometimes combines humor with metaphysical fantasy, as in the delightful creation story, "The Quids." Other poems, like the enigmatic "Lucrece and Nara," convey some eerie insight quite beyond rational explanation. In 1943, Robert Graves referred to J. as writing in "the supreme female I, the original Triple Muse, who in her original Olympian mountain was mother of Apollo, *not* his chorus-girl troupe."

Her poetry has never achieved widespread popularity with general readers, but it is an important part of the modern flight from the conventions of 19th-c. romanticism. Her diction shows a deliberate avoidance of traditional sentiments, a bare minimum of imagery and metaphor, a tendency to abstraction. The vocabulary is often deceptively simple, yet the reader must intuit meaning from limited clues. At its worst, this may require sheer guesswork. At its best, it achieves a delicate precision and economy in the expression of complex meanings.

WORKS: *The Close Chaplet* (1926). *Voltaire: A Biographical Fantasy* (1927). *A Survey of Modernist Poetry* (with R. Graves, 1927). *Contemporaries and Snobs* (1928). *Love As Love, Death As Death* (1928). *Poems: A Joking Word* (1930). *Twenty Poems Less* (1930). *Laura and Francesco* (1931). *No Decency Left* (with R. Graves, 1932). *The Life of the Dead* (1933). *Poet: A Lying*

Word (1933). *Four Unposted Letters to Catherine* (1933). *Americans* (1934). *A Trojan Ending* (1937). *Collected Poems* (1938). *Lives of Wives* (1939).

BIBLIOGRAPHY: For articles in reference works, see: *Contemporary American Authors*, F. B. Millet (1944). *20thCA* (under "L. R."). *20thCAS.*
Other references: *CQ* (Spring 1971). *Poetry* (Aug. 1932, May 1939).

KATHERINE SNIPES

Shirley Jackson

B. *14 Dec. 1919, San Francisco, California; d. 8 Aug. 1965, North Bennington, Vermont*
D. *of Leslie H. and Geraldine Bugbee Jackson; m. Stanley Edgar Hyman, 1940*

Most of J.'s early life was spent in Burlingame, California, which she later used as the setting of her first novel, *The Road through the Wall* (1948). J. was interested in writing from childhood; she won a poetry prize at twelve, and while in high school began to keep a diary which recorded her writing progress.

J. was troubled early in life with a sense of inferiority. Her family moved to Rochester, New York, in 1933, and she attended the University of Rochester but left after a year because of depression. At home she practiced her craft, writing a consistent one thousand words a day. She entered Syracuse University in 1937, publishing in the student literary magazines and founding, with Stanley Hyman, the magazine *The Spectre*. With Hyman, who was to become a noted literary critic, J. had four children while both continued active literary careers.

"The Lottery" (1948) received mixed reactions when it appeared in *The New Yorker*, but many critics believed that this one short story would give J. lasting fame. She regarded her short stories as "tales" in the sense of Hawthorne's usage. J. writes about the hidden evil of the human mind, and her themes often concern evil disguised as good. "The Lottery" is a return to the concept of the Fisher King, the human who must be sacrificed for community good in order that the crops might prosper.

Hangsaman (1951), regarded as one of the best of J.'s early novels, is her first lengthy study of mental disturbance, in this case schizophrenia. The novel deals with the gradual breakdown of a brilliant seventeen-year-old girl, Natalie Waite, who, unable to cope with her first experience away from home at college, creates for herself a friend, Tony, with whom she can feel acceptance. The book comes to an optimistic conclusion, and Natalie will, supposedly, come to more reasonable terms with existence.

Life among the Savages (1953) and *Raising Demons* (1957), two collections of domestic chronicles, and J.'s uncollected articles, mainly from women's magazines, form the humorous side of J.'s work. She wrote realistically and with tongue in cheek of her own and her husband's eccentricities and of the problems of raising four children. Some of the incidents such as "The Night We All Had Grippe" and "Charles" have become classics of domestic humor. The Hymans tended to regard these works as "potboilers," but they give voice to the humorous side of J.'s character.

We Have Always Lived in the Castle (1962) was named one of the year's ten best novels by *Time* magazine. The play production, however, ran only four days on Broadway. The action takes place around the old Blackwood home, in which four people have died of arsenic poisoning. The survivors are Uncle Julian, an invalid, twelve-year-old Mary Katherine (Merricat), and her twenty-two-year-old sister Constance. Constance is tried and acquitted of the crime due to lack of evidence. The novel opens six years after the crime and follows mainly the characterization of Merricat, who turns out to be the murderer. Merricat is another of J.'s delineations of the psychologically unstable personality.

J. develops a broad topic range in her fiction, and her place as a competent and professional storyteller is well established. Her humor can be purely for fun or can run to black humor. She recognizes the existence of human evil with a blitheness that increases rather than decreases the sting. The psychological studies are completely plausible in the reasoning which they depict. J.'s style is sharp and clear; however, the clarity becomes a detriment to the development of a continuing philosophic statement. Her major works lack an essential depth or mystery, but J. will remain an important minor author for her quick, clear glimpses of the dark side of human nature.

WORKS: *The Road through the Wall* (1948). *The Lottery; or, The Adventures of James Harris* (1949). *Hangsaman* (1951). *Life among the Savages* (1953). *The Bird's Nest* (1954). *Witchcraft of Salem Village* (1956). *Raising Demons* (1957). *The Bad Children* (1958). *The Sundial* (1958). *The Haunting of Hill House* (1959). *Special Delivery* (1960). *We Have Always Lived in the Castle* (1962). *Nine Magic Wishes* (1963). *The Magic of Shirley Jackson* (Ed. S. E. Hyman, 1966). *Come Along with Me* (Ed. S. E. Hyman, 1968).

BIBLIOGRAPHY: Aldridge, J. W., *After the Lost Generation: A Critical Study of the Writers of Two Wars* (1958). Friedman, L., *S. J.* (1975). Lyons, J. O., *The College Novel in America* (1962).
  For articles in reference works, see: *20thCAS.*
  Other references: *Explicator* (March 1954).

LOIS BURNS

Mary Putnam Jacobi

B. 31 Aug. 1842, London, England; d. 10 June 1906, New York City
Wrote under: Mary Putnam Jacobi, Mary Putnam
D. of George Palmer and Victorine Haven Putnam; m. Abraham Jacobi, 1873

The descendant of American Puritan families and the eldest of eleven children, at fifteen J. traveled to the first public high school for girls in Manhattan, where her writing received critical attention. Her story "Found and Lost" was published in the *Atlantic Monthly* when she was seventeen, while another, "Hair Chains," appeared there in 1861. The family expected J. to be a writer, but she tended toward medicine.

In 1863, J. was the first woman to receive a degree from the College of Pharmacy in New York City. Since no male medical school would accept women, J. attended the Female Medical College of Pennsylvania. Believing that only in Paris, where no woman had ever studied medicine, could she find proper training, J. went there and fought to enter the École de Médicine. She supported herself by writing sketches, stories, and even a short novel for the New Orleans *Times*, the New York *Evening Post*, and both *Putnam's* and *Scribner's* magazines. Because she felt that fiction took more from her and left her poorer, she began her prolific medical writing (printed in medical journals and collections) with a series of charming, literate medical letters from Paris.

J. won a bronze medal for her thesis and graduated in 1871. Returning home one of the best-prepared physicians in America, she was ready to teach at the fledgling women's medical school of the New York Infirmary, to practice medicine, and to continue scientific research. J. wrote no more fiction.

J. married a prominent physician and had two children, but continued her profession. In 1896, came the onset of J.'s final illness. Brain tumors had been a subject of her medical writing, and she was the first to diagnose her own condition. Her description of her symptoms, published after her death, is a classic of medical literature.

All but one of J.'s magazine pieces were republished in *Stories and Sketches* (1907). All of the writing is graceful and lucid, with incident and character captured in concrete images. "Found and Lost" is a philosophical adventure story about a German who has found the source of the Nile, but loses it again when an American, seeking to commercialize it, goes with him. The best of this early writing, "Some of the French Leaders," presents incisive portraits of ineffectual politicians. A critic considered it "one of the ablest ever printed in an American magazine," with "intellectual grasp" and "grim and elucidating wit."

The remarkable *Question of Rest for Women during Menstruation* (1877), which won the prestigious Boyleston Prize from Harvard University, reflects classical background, research into medical literature, and questionnaires to women in all walks of life. Prepared with J.'s thorough, commonsense approach and literary flair, it should have forever retired the belief that women must inevitably withdraw from ordinary activity during menstruation. In the excellent historical overview, she points out that only in women have normal functions been considered pathological. Beliefs in temporary insanity, instability, or inability to make decisions during menstruation are demolished. Some of the medical theory is no longer valid, but the conclusions and recommendations are sensible, still pertinent, and thoroughly convincing.

J.'s writings about women's roles began with an article in the *North American Review* (1882), "Shall Women Practice Medicine?" In surveying the history of women in medicine, she notes that it is not an innovation at all. Women practiced freely when medicine was unpaid.

"Common Sense" Applied to Woman Suffrage (1894) combines history, clear dissection of the current situation, and incisive argument. "No one expected the vote to raise women's wages or drastically reform the social order," she wrote, "but what is . . . very seriously demanded, is that women be recognized as human beings." Her letter on "Modern Female Invalidism" (1895) comments: "Too much attention is paid to women as objects" while they remain "insufficiently prepared to act as independent subjects."

Despite her talent for imaginative literature, J. wrote little fiction and stopped entirely before she was thirty. She was a pioneer in medicine, both as a woman and simply as a physician, while successfully combining marriage and a profession and doing humanitarian social work. Commenting on her Paris thesis, a French medical journal noted her "poetic form, which does not detract from the value of the statement." She excelled in clear, incisive writing on controversial topics. The voluminous medical writings are characterized by wit, clarity, and literate style.

WORKS: *De la graisse neutre et de les acides gras* (1871). *Infant Diet* by A. Jacobi (revised, enlarged, and adapted to popular use by Jacobi, 1874). *The Question of Rest for Women during Menstruation* (1877). *The Value of Life: A Reply to Mr. Mallock's Essay, "Is Life Worth Living?"* (1879). *On the Use of the Cold Pack Followed by Massage in the Treatment of Anaemia* (with V. A. White, 1880). *Essays on Hysteria, Brain-Tumor, and Some Other Cases of Nervous Disease* (1888). *Physiological Notes on Primary Education and the Study of Language* (1889). *Uffelman's Manual of Dietetic Hygiene for Children* (edited by Jacobi, 1891). *"Common Sense" Applied to Woman Suffrage* (1894). *Found and Lost* (1894). *From Massachusetts to Turkey* (1896). *Stories and Sketches* (1907). *M. P. J., M.D.: A Pathfinder in Medicine* (1925).

The papers of Mary Putnam Jacobi are at the Schlesinger Library, Radcliffe College, Cambridge, Massachusetts.

BIBLIOGRAPHY: Hume, R. F., *Great Women of Medicine* (1964). Hurd-Mead, K. C., *Medical Women of America* (1933). Irwin, I. H., *Angels and Amazons: A Hundred Years of American Women* (1934). Marks, G., and W. K. Beatty, *Women in White* (1972). *In Memory of Mary Putnam Jacobi* (1907). Putnam, R., ed., *Life and Letters of Mary Putnam Jacobi* (1925). Truax, R., *The Doctors Jacobi* (1952).

For articles in reference works, see: *AW. DAB*, V, 1. *NAW* (article by R. Lubove).

Other references: *Jour. Hist. Med.* (Autumn 1949). *Med. Life* (July 1928).

CAROL B. GARTNER

Elizabeth Janeway

B. 7 Oct. 1913, Brooklyn, New York
D. of Charles H. and Jeanette F. Searle Hall; m. Eliot Janeway, 1938

The daughter of middle-class parents, J. attended Swarthmore College and graduated from Barnard College in 1935. She is married to a well-known economist and author and has two sons. The Janeways live in New York City.

J.'s first novel, *The Walsh Girls* (1943), is a psychological study of two sisters living in a New England town during the Depression. The younger, widow of a German intellectual killed at Dachau, experiences conflicting feelings about her new husband, a businessman, and about the institution of marriage. The elder, both prudish and independent, is committed to remaining single. *The Walsh Girls* is typical of J.'s novels in its focus on a small group, often a family, whose members are struggling with a crisis or through a period of transition, their personal dilemmas and relationships intersecting with events in a carefully delineated social and historical milieu.

For instance, *The Question of Gregory* (1949), set partly in Washington, D.C., and New England, studies the effects of a young man's death in wartime upon his parents and their marriage. *Leaving Home* (1953) follows two young sisters and a brother as they make their way into the world during the years 1933 to 1940. In *The Third Choice* (1959), an elderly and crippled woman, once a reigning beauty, and her niece, who is unable to substitute satisfaction in motherhood for satisfaction in marriage, struggle to salvage the past and come to terms with the present and future.

The strengths of J.'s best novels—*The Walsh Girls, The Question of Gregory*, and *The Third Choice*—are subtle and lucid handling of psychology, clean-cut writing, and precise depiction of milieu. Her treatment of relationships among women is particularly noteworthy. However, her works have sometimes been criticized for lacking a unifying theme or point of view.

Unable to deal with some of the large social issues of the 1960s in the kind of fiction she writes, "in which theme is carried by character," J. turned to nonfiction in her best-known work, *Man's World, Woman's Place: A Study in Social Mythology* (1971). The book, much praised for its clarity and undogmatic thoughtfulness, is based upon wide reading in history, philosophy, and the social sciences, as well as upon considerable personal experience. J.'s focus is the assertion that woman's place is in the home. She treats this from a contemporary perspective, showing that it no longer describes the experience of most women in the U.S., and from a historical one, showing its association with the development of the nuclear family. The book's most important contribution, however, is its scrupulous and well-developed treatment of the ways in which this concept functions as a myth, a complex of feeling, fact, and fantasy that satisfies emotional and social needs despite—and because of—its historical inaccuracy.

Between Myth and Morning: Women Awakening (1974) is a collection of thirteen essays, originally addressed to various audiences, on public and private aspects of women's lives. J. regards the women's movement as "irrevocable" because it is "rooted in reality, and reality has changed formidably." Partly because of this certitude, the book looks toward the future; it also suggests that the most significant aspect of women's past is the notions and limitations that have been applied to them, not the actions of women themselves. Individual essays are good, particularly on the difficulties that both sexes experience in dealing with changes in the relationship between private life and work, but the book as a whole does not represent a new stage in J.'s thinking.

Building on earlier ideas, in *Powers of the Weak* (1980) J. analyzes power as "a process of human interaction" shaped by both weak and strong rather than as "an attribute or possession" of the powerful. Drawing on child development, abnormal psychology, history, myth, and recent political events to show how the development of a sense of power over the practical universe is essential to creativity, how it can be interrupted or thwarted on both individual and group levels, and how it can be manipulated to benefit the few, J. argues that those who accept others' definitions of themselves as powerless instead of withholding legitimacy from their rulers acquiesce in their own subordination. Defining women as a paradigm of the historic condition of being weak, and drawing analogies between their status and those of groups such as children, subjects, slaves, and the physically handicapped, J. exhorts women to dissent, band together, and take risks in order to benefit themselves as individuals and as a group, and more importantly to help establish a regenerated social order.

WORKS: *The Walsh Girls* (1943). *Daisy Kenyon* (1945; film version, 1947). *The Question of Gregory* (1949). *The Vikings* (1951). *Leaving Home* (1953). *The Early Days of Automobiles* (1956). *The Third Choice* (1959). *Angry Kate* (1963). *Accident* (1964). *Ivanov Seven* (1967). *Man's World, Woman's Place: A Study in Social Mythology* (1971). *Between Myth and Morning: Women Awakening* (1974). *Powers of the Weak* (1980).

BIBLIOGRAPHY: For articles in reference works, see: *20thCAS.*
Other references: *Harper's* (Sept. 1971). *MR* 13 (1972). *Nation* (6 Nov. 1943; 2 Aug. 1975). *NewR* (12 Oct. 1974). *NYHTB* (21 Aug. 1941). *NYT* (29 Sept. 1974). *NYTBR* (17 Oct. 1943; 21 Aug. 1941; 3 May 1964; 20 June 1971). *SatR* (31 Oct. 1953). *TLS* (8 April 1960). *YR* 35 (1946).

JANET SHARISTANIAN

Charlotte Ann Fillebrown Jerauld

B. *20 April 1820, Old Cambridge, Massachusetts; d. 2 Aug. 1845, Boston, Massachusetts*
Wrote under: Charlotte A. Fillebrown, Mrs. Charlotte A. Jerauld
D. *of Richard and Charlotte Fillebrown; m. J. W. Jerauld, 1843*

The daughter of working-class parents, J. received her education in Boston's common schools. Although she left school at fourteen to work in a bookbindery, she read widely and was familiar with Shakespeare, Spenser, and Milton, while particular favorites were Byron, Scott, and Wordsworth. J. soon began to publish poetry in the Universalist magazine, the *Ladies Repository*, and later her work appeared in the annual *Rose of Sharon*. Not until 1841, however, did she start to publish her prose sketches—the real beginning of her literary life, as her editor Henry Bacon notes.

J. had suffered for most of her life from "a determination of blood to the brain," but it seems likely that complications after the birth of her son (born late in July 1845 and dying on August 1) as well as a severe postpartum depression (Bacon writes that within days of her child's birth she became "a raving maniac") contributed to her early death.

J.'s many letters to her close friend Sarah C. Edgarton Mayo reveal a sharp wit and sensitive eye for detail not often found in her poetry and abundant only in her later prose. This friendship produced dual poetic sequences and provided J. with a confidant for the more personal reflections that were frequently absent from her published writings.

J.'s poetry does not reveal the increasing facility and acuity of her prose, but some of her efforts are clearly tighter and fresher than those of many of her contemporaries. Her subjects, forms, and themes are conventional, but the poems rise above the conventional when she assumes a voice different from her own (as in "The Meccas of Memory"), when she experiments with form ("'No More'" and "Isabel" echo Poe's rhymes and rhythms), or when she adheres to the discipline of a strict form (her sonnets are generally better than her other poems, and those she writes with Mayo on alternate lines of "The Lord's Prayer" are good poems). Thematically, her verse tends to be dull: She stresses heaven as a peaceful home where life's problems are resolved; longs nostalgically for a happy childhood that will never return; and bewails sentimentally life's tragedies—ill-fated lovers, general loss, and the cycles of nature.

J.'s early prose is much like her poetry; however, her later prose, as she moves away from heroines who die young and plots based on series of disasters, reveals a talented writer beginning to find herself. Her final prose sketches comprise two groups of tales—"Lights and Shadows of Woman's Life" and "Chronicles and Sketches of Hazelhurst." In the first group, J. explores different women's lots. In each story the author uses a distinct tone—"Our Minister's Family" is essentially gay; "The Mother's Heart" is grim but relatively unsentimental; "The Irish Daughter-in-Law" is light and witty. J.'s concern with her characters' inner lives dominates these tales. In "The Mother's Heart" she examines the jealous and obsessive personality of Isabel Sommers, who is unable to have a child until her twelfth year of marriage. In "Caroline" the protagonist becomes insane when forced to give up her daughter. J.'s characters also grow more realistic in appearance: Hannah in "The Auld Wife" is rustically attractive if not beautiful by the standards of the 1840s; thus, J. notes her "well-developed figure, which gave ample evidence that it had never suffered from compression or whalebone, or any other bones, save those which Nature had given her."

The conversational and intimate relationship J.'s narrator creates with the reader pervades the tales of the first group and becomes a unifying element in "Chronicles and Sketches of Hazelhurst." These connected stories prefigure in delicacy and tone Sarah Orne Jewett's *Country of the Pointed Firs*, as J.'s unsentimentally nostalgic speaker invites the reader to join her on a walking tour of the village and "to gossip . . . about people and events, past and present." J.'s final prose suggests that she might have attained a high level of literary artistry.

WORKS: *Poetry and Prose by Mrs. Charlotte A. Jerauld, with a Memoir by Henry Bacon* (1850).

BIBLIOGRAPHY: Douglas, A., *The Feminization of American Culture* (1977). Mayo, S. C. E., *Selections from the Writings of Mrs. Sarah C. Edgarton Mayo, with a Memoir by Her Husband* (1849).

For articles in reference works, see: *Daughters of America*, P. A. Hanaford (1882).

CAROLINE ZILBOORG

Sarah Orne Jewett

B. 3 Sept. 1849, South Berwick, Maine; d. 24 June 1909, South Berwick, Maine
Wrote under: Caroline, A. C. Eliot, Alice Eliot, Sarah Orne Jewett,
  Sarah O. Sweet
D. of Theodore Herman and Frances Perry Jewett

J.'s life and works are rooted in the southern tier of Maine. Her own life was a favored one: Born into relative wealth, J. was educated at Miss Raynes's School and at Berwick Academy in South Berwick. She was, however, a somewhat listless student and later remarked that her real education came from her father, a country physician whom she often accompanied on house calls. He imparted to her his extensive knowledge of nature and of literature, and it was to some extent through these house visits that she came to know so intimately the people of her region.

J. earned success and modest fame as a writer at an early age. When she was eighteen years old, her story "Jenny Garrow's Lovers" was published in a weekly Boston periodical, *The Flag of Our Union.*

J. was sustained throughout her life by a group of intimate female friends. In her earliest diaries (1867–79) she describes her intense emotional attachment to several young women. Her most important liaison was with Annie Adams Fields of Boston. J. lived part of each year at Fields's Charles Street home, and the two traveled extensively together. Hundreds of letters remain to document the significance of this friendship to J. It seems likely that many of J.'s stories were written at least in part for Fields's amusement.

In her later years J.'s reputation was firmly established. Younger writers sought her advice, which she generously supplied. Her face was one of the few women writers on the "Authors" card deck of the time, which is supposedly where the young Willa Cather learned of J. Some of J.'s most perceptive and poignant advice may be found in her letters to Cather, who later acknowledged the influence of her mentor by dedicating *O Pioneers!* (1913) to J., noting that in J.'s "beautiful and delicate work there is the perfection that endures." Cather estimated J.'s *The Country of the Pointed Firs* (1896) as one of three American works guaranteed immortality.

Deephaven (1877), J.'s first book-length collection of stories, deals with a series of experiences and characters met by two young women during a summer vacation on the coast of Maine. The relationship between the two is handled somewhat sentimentally, but the character sketches display J.'s genius for the genre, although she later regarded this work as juvenilia. Contemporary reviews were slight and mixed. Reviews were increasingly favorable for three subsequent story collections.

J.'s first novel, *A Country Doctor* (1884), perhaps her most feminist work, is semiautobiographical. It is a classic *bildungsroman* concerning the growth to maturity of a young woman whose ambition is to become a doctor. The woman faces considerable prejudice and discrimination in her pursuit. Eventually she rejects a suitor and resolves to pursue her career.

A White Heron, and Other Stories (1886) marks the beginning of J.'s mature phase. Her mastery of style and a sophisticated sense of craft are quite evident in several of these stories, including the much-anthologized title story, "Marsh Rosemary," and "The Dulham Ladies."

In the decade following *A White Heron*, J. published several further collections, and J.'s best work is to be found among these. *The Country of the Pointed Firs*, generally considered J.'s masterpiece, is difficult to classify by genre. It is more unified than a collection of sketches but much looser than the traditional novel. Like *Deephaven* it uses the structural device of the relationship between two women, which anchors the character sketches to a continuing narrative event. The power of the work resides in the sense of mysterious personal depth many of the characters seem to possess. The protagonist, Mrs. Almiry Todd, one of J.'s enduring characters (prefiguring in many ways Willa Cather's Ántonia), is the town herbalist. She has a singular capacity for healing spiritual as well as physical ills, and is one of the prime sustainers of a sense of communication and of community among the scattered residents of the coastal settlement. J.'s own extensive knowledge of herbs is seen in this and other works.

The Country of the Pointed Firs includes several vignettes of characters who have lost touch with the mainstream of human relationship. J.'s tone is elegiac. The lament is for these failed lives, and perhaps ultimately, as many critics have suggested, for the general economic and social decline of New England in the latter half of the century. There is, moreover, a sense of the fragility and fleetingness of human bonds, seen in the poignant parting scene between Mrs. Todd and the narrator, a thinly disguised persona for J. But the work is not a tragedy, nor does it espouse the pessimism and fatalism of contemporary naturalistic novels. Rather, it conveys a sense of celebration, a sense of the triumph of the human community against the forces of spiritual destruction.

J.'s last major work, a historical novel, *The Tory Lover* (1901), was by far her most popular (it went into five printings in its first three months), but it has received the least critical approbation.

J. was writing in the heyday of realism (the critical principles of her editor at the *Atlantic Monthly*, William Dean Howells, were those of the realists), but she can be classified as a realist only with qualifications. In her own critical comments she rejected slice-of-life "objectivity" as an artistic ideal and insisted that personal point of view was an essential ingredient of competent fiction. J. wrote about ordinary people with gentle humor, respect, and compassion. Her mastery of style—her ability to fuse technique and content with her personality—has ensured that her work will survive.

WORKS: *Deephaven* (1877). *Play Days* (1878). *Old Friends and New* (1879). *Country By-Ways* (1881). *A Country Doctor* (1884). *The Mate of the Daylight, and Friends Ashore* (1884). *A Marsh Island* (1885). *A White Heron, and Other Stories* (1886). *The Story of the Normans* (1887). *The King of Folly Island, and Other People* (1888). *Betty Leicester: A Story for Girls* (1890). *Strangers and Wayfarers* (1890). *Tales of New England* (1890). *A Native of Winby, and Other Tales* (1893). *Betty Leicester's Xmas* (1894). *The Life of Nancy* (1895). *The Country of the Pointed Firs* (1896). *The Queen's Twin, and Other Stories* (1899). *The Tory Lover* (1901). *The Letters of Sarah Orne Jewett* (Ed. A. Fields, 1911). *Verses* (1916). *Sarah Orne Jewett Letters* (Ed. R. Cary, 1967). *The Uncollected Short Stories of Sarah Orne Jewett* (Ed. R. Cary, 1971).

BIBLIOGRAPHY: Auchincloss, L., *Pioneers and Caretakers: A Study of Nine American Women Novelists* (1965). Cary, R., ed., *Appreciation of Sarah Orne Jewett: Twenty-nine Interpretive Essays* (1973). Cary, R., *Sarah Orne Jewett* (1962). Frost, J. E., *Sarah Orne Jewett* (1960). Donovan, J., *New England and Local Color: A Study of Women's Literary Tradition* (1982). Donovan, J., *Sarah Orne Jewett* (1980). Harkins, E. F., and C. H. L. Johnston, *Little Pilgrimages among the Women Who Have Written Famous Books* (1902). Matthiessen, F. O., *Sarah Orne Jewett* (1929). Nagel, G. L., and J. Nagel, *Sarah Orne Jewett: A Reference Guide* (1978). Pickett, L. C., *Across My Path: Memories of People I Have Known* (1916). Richards, L., *Stepping Westward* (1931). Spofford, H. P., *A Little Book of Friends* (1916). Thorp, M. F., *Sarah Orne Jewett* (1966). Weber, C. C., and C. J. Weber, *A Bibliography of the Published Writings of Sarah Orne Jewett* (1949). Westbrook, P. D., *Acres of Flint: Writers of Rural New England, 1870–1900* (1951). Winslow, H. M., *Literary Boston of Today* (1902).

For articles in reference works, see: *AA. AW. DAB*, V, 2. *NAW* (article by W. Berthoff). *NCAB*, 1.

JOSEPHINE DONOVAN

Georgia Douglas Camp Johnson

B. 10 Sept. 1886, Atlanta, Georgia; d. May 1966, Washington, D.C.
Wrote Under: Georgia Douglas Johnson, Paul Tremaine
D. of George and Laura Jackson Camp; m. Henry Lincoln Johnson, 1903

Little is known about J.'s early childhood or her parents. She studied at Atlanta University (through the Normal program) and Oberlin College, Ohio. In 1909 she moved to Washington, D.C., with her lawyer husband. While living in the capital, J. wrote lyrics, poetry, short stories, and plays. She established the Literary Salon, a weekly Saturday-night meeting place for a burgeoning group of young poets, including many of the Harlem Renaissance writers. J. was active in several literary organizations, the Republican party, the pan-African movement, and human-rights groups connected with the Congregational church. Following her husband's death in 1925, she became a commissioner of conciliation with the Department of Labor (1925–34), held other government positions, remained active in racial and political organizations in New York and Washington, and continued to publish individual poems sporadically.

J. was the first black female to receive national recognition as a poet since Francis Harper, an abolitionist writer. Although her three major volumes were published within a ten-year span, each represents a distinctly different period in her life, flowing from the naive inquiry found in *The Heart of a Woman* (1918), through the pain and deprivation of being black recorded in *Bronze* (1922), to the mature acceptance of grief expressed in *Autumn Love Cycle* (1928). J. received many awards not only for her poetry but for her plays and short stories. Although J.'s literary strength is found in her poetry, her plays and short stories remain significant to the development of black American literature from a literary, as well as from a political and a historical, perspective.

The sixty-two poems in *The Heart of a Woman* are four-, eight-, and twelve-line queries regarding the nature of womanhood. While many of these poems are trite, J. expresses a haunting sensitivity toward women's unfulfilled aspirations in "The Dreams of the Dreamer" and

"Dead Leaves." Although sadness prevails in this volume, J. does not paint a bleak picture of womanhood. She finds solace in nature ("Peace" and "When I am Dead") and fulfillment in requited love ("Mate"). J. apparently believed that women were destined to the life of a voyeur—declaring that they lacked the freedom to express themselves openly, that they lacked the means of fulfilling their dreams, and that only through their lovers could they fully experience life.

Bronze is an energetic expression of the pain, humiliations, and fears of a 1920s black woman. The sixty-five poems in this volume are grouped under nine headings. J.'s greatest literary contribution to an understanding of womanhood and of her era is found in the ten poems in the "Motherhood" section. "Maternity" expresses a mixture of emotions as a child is awaited: pride is coupled with fear that, at worst, the child would be lynched and, at best, rejected by the world. "Black Woman" implies that it is cruel to bring black children into this world.

In *Autumn Love Cycle* an obvious stylistic and thematic maturity is displayed. J.'s dominant theme is the depth of mature love, as expressed in "I Want to Die While You Love Me," "Autumn," and "Afterglow," but there is the fear that lost youth can result in infidelity or in impotency. Many of these poems were probably written during the period when her husband suffered three strokes and eventually died. A dozen of the poems describe her adjustment to life without the physical presence of love.

J., together with other black writers after World War I, was responsible for bringing black poetry out of the bonds of dialect and into the realm of a high art form. The poets of her period eventually were overshadowed by the writers of the Harlem Renaissance, but their importance to the movement should not be underestimated. J.'s significance as both a black and a woman writer cannot be denied.

WORKS: *The Heart of a Woman, and Other Poems* (1918). *Bronze: A Book of Verse* (1922). *Blue Blood* (1927). *Plumes: Folk Tragedy* (1927). *Autumn Love Cycle* (1928).

BIBLIOGRAPHY: Bontemps, A., ed., *American Negro Poetry* (1974). Bontemps, A., *The Harlem Renaissance Remembered* (1972). Johnson, J. W., *The Book of American Negro Poetry* (1922). Locke, A., *The New Negro: An Interpretation* (1968). Mays, B., *The Negro's God As Reflected in His Literature* (1968). White, N., and W. Jackson, eds., *An Anthology of Verse by American Negroes* (1924).

For articles in reference works, see: *Black American Writers Past and Present*, T. G. Rush, C. F. Myers, and E. S. Arata (1975).

Other references: *Crisis* (Dec. 1952). *Journal of Negro History* (July 1972).

LINDA S. BERRY

Josephine Winslow Johnson

B. 20 June 1910, Kirkwood, Missouri
D. of Benjamin and Ethel Franklin Johnson; m. Thurlow Smoot, 1939;
  m. Grant G. Cannon, 1942

J. was reared on a one-hundred-acre farm in south-central Missouri. Reflecting on her mother's lineage, J. has noted the long dominance of franklins, i.e., Anglo-Saxon freeholders, untitled agrarians with a fervent attachment to specific pieces of land. The strength of this passion is intensified in J.

At the age of eight J. wrote a poem to mark the end of the war and glimpsed her vocation as a writer. Her first novel, *Now in November* (1934), brought her the Pulitzer Prize. Another novel—as well as poems and short stories—soon appeared, for in these years, J. says, she "wrote, if not endlessly, then enormously." Her first marriage, to a Labor Relations Board lawyer, only perpetuated her growing sense that (as she said in her autobiography, *Seven Houses: A Memoir of Time and Places*, 1973), "I seemed to be waiting to begin to live." Later, in Grant Cannon she found a partner whose hopeful nature temporarily dispelled her own profound pessimism. With Cannon, an editor of *Farm Quarterly*, she raised three children. His death in 1969 took from her one who, in her words, "made no lifelong truce with despair as I have made."

Although her work covers many decades and genres, the important themes almost all appear in the early fiction. *Now in November* celebrates the land and the self-sufficient farm family even while it deplores the Depression and the tyranny of weather. The work is lit by occasional set pieces of nature description, and by a clear attention to the limited point of view of the narrator, the middle daughter on a small Missouri farm, as she remembers her childhood and her growing understanding of her sister's mental illness.

J.'s second novel, *Jordanstown* (1937), about a small-town newspaperman and community organizer during the Depression, is less successful because the didactic ideology of socialist-realism is too little camouflaged. Still, *Jordanstown* has memorable elements. The later novels, *Wildwood* (1945) and *The Dark Traveler* (1963) are more disappointing; the anguish which is evident in the early fiction is here completely unrelieved.

J.'s short fiction, however, shows that more compact forms better display both her descriptive talents and her facility with surprise endings. "Gedacht," her first published short story, is the best of the *Winter Orchard* (1935) collection. It concerns a World War I veteran who, having lost his sight from poison gas, regains it briefly. J.'s early poetry incorporates the themes of her fiction: social protest, loss of religious faith, love of nature, and the struggle with cynicism.

A publishing hiatus of almost twenty years occurred in J.'s mid-career, and when she resumed publication, some very different genre preferences manifested themselves. She produced essays, memoirs, and diaries instead of fiction. J.'s vision is now quieter, more introspective, more ameliorated by the natural world, although social concerns and pessimism are still there.

Thus, *The Inland Island* (1969), a kind of nature journal in the style of Walden, laments the Vietnam War and promotes the environmental movement in the midst of solitary meditations and exquisite observations on the natural year. With *The Circle of Seasons* (1974), the text for a book of nature photographs, J. reiterates the themes begun in *Now in November*. It is both an ode and an elegy that celebrates and questions: "Will there be any rhythm and difference of season left, any feeling of the great circular flow of living things [for our children]?"

J. has contributed brilliantly to the "proletarian" tradition in American letters. Indeed, one is frequently tempted to rank her with the great shapers of that tradition, London, Sinclair, Norris, and Steinbeck. But J.'s activity displays other dimensions which make her difficult to categorize, for she is also a writer of naturalistic fiction, a didactic poet, a Thoreauvian essayist, and an anguished contemplative decrying militarism and the inhumanity of modern technology. In a time when the often-divided currents of agrarianism, radical trade unionism, conservationism, and militant pacifism seem about to form a curious new merger, J.'s lifelong nurturing of these concerns may prompt a rediscovery of her achievement.

WORKS: *Now in November* (1934). *The Winter Orchard, and Other Stories* (1935). *Unwilling Gypsy* (1936). *Jordanstown* (1937). *Year's End* (1937). *Paulina: The Story of an Apple-Butter Jar* (1939). *Wildwood* (1945). *The Dark Traveler* (1963). *The Sorcerer's Son, and Other Stories* (1965). *The Inland Island* (1969). *Seven Houses: A Memoir of Time and Places* (1973). *The Circle of Seasons* (1974).

The manuscripts and papers of Josephine Winslow Johnson are in the Rare Books Collection at Washington University, St. Louis, Missouri.

BIBLIOGRAPHY: For articles in reference works, see: *CA*, 25–28 (1971). *Contemporary Novelists*, Eds. J. Vinson and D. L. Kirkpatrick (1976). *NCAB*, H. *20thCA. 20thCAS.*

Other references: *Nation* (21 Aug. 1935). *NYHT* (13 Sept. 1934; 13 Aug. 1935). *NYT* (16 Sept. 1934; 11 April 1937). *NYTBR* (2 March 1969; 13 May 1973). *SatR* (3 April 1937; 15 Feb. 1969).

MARGARET McFADDEN-GERBER

Annie Fellows Johnston

B. 15 May 1863, Evansville, Indiana; d. 5 Oct. 1931, Pewee Valley, Kentucky
D. of Albion and Mary Erskine Fellows; m. William L. Johnston, 1888

J. grew up on a farm outside Evansville, Indiana. Although her father, a Methodist minister, died when she was only two, J. was influenced by him, through his theological books, and by her mother, who had strong ideas about the importance of education for women. J. attended public schools in Evansville and the University of Iowa (for a year). After teaching for several years and working for a time as a private secretary, she married her cousin, a widower. After his death in 1892, J. turned to writing as a career. Eventually, she and her three stepchildren settled in Pewee Valley, Kentucky, which J. fictionalized as Lloydsboro Valley in her popular "Little Colonel" series. In 1899, J.'s stepdaughter Rena died; two years later J. moved to Arizona for her stepson John's health, and then on to Texas, where they lived until his death in 1910.

As a children's author, J. was both prolific, with over forty volumes, and popular—reportedly, at her death her books had sold over a million copies. Some readers today are still familiar with J.'s thirteen-volume "Little Colonel" series, which began with the publication of *The Little Colonel* (1896). Unlike many authors of series books, J. allows her characters to mature. For example, we see Lloyd Sherman first as a five-year-old, impetuous and stubborn, and last as a young married woman, lovely and vivacious. Many people know J.'s most famous character only through David Butler's 1935 Fox film, "The Little Colonel," starring Shirley Temple as Lloyd and Lionel Barrymore as old Colonel Lloyd. The story of the conflict of pretty, spunky Lloyd with her crusty old grandfather, who severed relations with his only daughter, Elizabeth, when she eloped with a Yankee, was a perfect vehicle for Temple's talents.

J.'s work was commercially successful, and her publisher clearly took advantage of the popularity of the "Little Colonel" books. For example, in 1909 the Page Company issued *The Little Colonel's Good Times Book*, with blank pages for a child to record her "good times," as Betty Lewis did in *The Little Colonel's House Party* (1900). Many of the legends and tales in J.'s books were subsequently published as separate volumes, such as *The Legend of the Bleeding Heart* (1907) and *The Road of the Loving Heart* (1922), both of which first appeared in *The Little Colonel's House Party*.

J.'s works have the flaws of many children's books of the late 19th and early 20th centuries. The characters are idealized; the conflicts, resolved too easily; the themes, simplistic and naive. The typical world of J.'s fiction is one of wealth and aristocracy, in which separation of the races and the inferiority of blacks are assumed. But, interestingly, it is a world in which women are not automatically relegated to the life of wife and mother or to unfulfilled spinsterhood. Especially through the experiences of Lloyd Sherman and her friends, J. emphasizes the importance for women of education in academic subjects; likewise, she allows her young women the option of independence, through characters such as unmarried Joyce Ware, pursuing her career as a commercial artist in an apartment in New York.

A strong moral code underlies every work by J. Through legends and tales, some traditional and others original, J. cleverly makes points which her young characters are never allowed to miss. Readers of an earlier, simpler day took these lessons to heart and were inspired to model their lives after Lloyd, Betty, Joyce, and other characters; but contemporary readers in our complex age often find J.'s stories more didactic than inspiring or entertaining.

SELECTED WORKS: *Big Brother* (1894). *Joel: A Boy of Galilee* (1895). *The Little Colonel* (1896). *The Little Colonel's House Party* (1900). *The Little Colonel's Holiday* (1901). *The Little Colonel's Hero* (1902). *The Little Colonel at Boarding School* (1903). *The Little Colonel in Arizona* (1904). *The Little Colonel's Christmas Vacation* (1905). *The Little Colonel: Maid of Honor* (1906). *The Little Colonel's Knight Comes Riding* (1907). *The Little Colonel's Chum: Mary Ware* (1908). *Mary Ware in Texas* (1910). *Mary Ware's Promised Land* (1912). *Miss Santa Claus of the Pullman* (1913). *Georgina of the Rainbows* (1916). *It Was the Road to Jericho* (1919). *The Land of the Little Colonel: Reminiscence and Autobiography* (1929).

BIBLIOGRAPHY: Steele, E., "Mrs. Johnston's *Little Colonel*," in *Challenges in American Culture*, Eds. R. B. Browne, L. N. Landrum, and W. K. Bottoroff (1970).

For articles in reference works, see: *Arizona in Literature: A Collection of the Best Writings of Arizona Authors from Early Spanish Days to the Present Time*, M. G. Boyer (1971). *DAB*, V, 2. *Indiana Authors and Their Books, 1816–1916*, Ed. R. E. Banta (1949). *The Junior Book of Authors*, Eds. S. J. Kunitz and H. Haycraft (1934). *NAW* (article by A. W. Shumaker). *NCAB*, 13. *20thCA*.

Other references: *St. Nicholas* (Dec. 1913).

MARTHA E. COOK

Emily Chubbuck Judson

B. 22 Aug. 1817, Eaton, New York; d. 1 June 1854, Hamilton, New York
Wrote under: Emily Chubbuck, Fanny Forester, Mrs. Emily Judson
D. of Charles and Lavinia Richards Chubbuck; m. Adoniram Judson, 1846

J.'s self-taught skills enabled her to teach in local schools from 1832 to 1840. Enrolled at the Utica Female Seminary for one year, she remained there as a teacher of English composition from 1841 to 1846. She rose from poverty eventually to find fame and wealth with her early children's books. With the income from those books she was able to buy her family a home and to make their lives comfortable. J.'s short life-span of thirty-six years was a full and varied one. Her writing career divides into three clearly defined phases; in each she wrote under a different name.

Publishing under the name Emily Chubbuck, J. wrote several successful children's books between 1841 and 1844. Like other mid–19th-c. writers, J. writes consciously as an American and as a "republican." Her fiction is for young Americans, and all the stories are heavily moralistic and didactic. For example, the stories in *Charles Linn; or, How to Observe the Golden Rule* (1841) have the theme of self-sacrifice.

Publishing under the name of "Fanny Forester," J. wrote stories with a completely different tone, changing from the previously moral tone to one of irony and fancy. The sketches gathered into *Trippings in Author-Land* (1846) reveal a writer enjoying the world she was creating and perhaps enjoying the recreation of herself as Fanny Forester, a character in that world. Two more volumes continued to construct the village of Alderbrook, *Lilias Fane, and Other Tales* (1846) and *Alderbrook* (1846), which contained some of the same tales from *Lilias Fane*. Simplicity and unpretentiousness is praised; village life is uncomplicated and contains a community unknown to the larger, sprawling urban scene.

"Fanny Forester" returned several times to the character "Ida Ravelin," a genius, a poet, an angel (all synonyms in these stories), as she created her vision of the poet who is "not like them" but who can live completely in the ideal. By the time a revised edition (1847) of *Alderbrook* was published, J. wished to suppress "Ida Ravelin" and substitute "Angel's Pilgrimage," a very different story of human greed, murder, and cruelty, in which the angels try to change the world by continuing the holy mission begun by their prototype, Christ. The work published under "Fanny Forester" continued to bring J. money and fame. *Alderbrook* went through at least eleven editions.

The third phase of J.'s career began when she left the imaginary world of Alderbrook and entered into missionary life, marrying the Reverend Judson, who was nearly thirty years her senior, and going to Burma with him and three of his children from his second marriage. In this phase she published a *Memoir of Sarah B. Judson* (1849), her husband's second wife. This volume by its popularity furthered the cause of the missionaries. Printed in both London and New York, it was reprinted several times for a total of over thirty thousand copies. Less popular, *The Kathayan Slave* (1853) is a defense of missionary activity and maintains that the barbarism of the natives of Burma and India can only be alleviated through Christianity.

Her life and work indicate some of the tensions and contradictions inherent in mid–19th-c. America, its commercialism and also its idealism. Perhaps these tensions led her to frame her literary answer to them by assuming three different identities. These three different literary personalities, the didactic Emily Chubbuck, the frivolous and charming Fanny Forester, and the defensive Mrs. Emily Judson, need not coalesce into one personality, although the prevailing opinion is that identity is such a synthesis. In some writers the paradoxes of their cultures cause them to produce ambiguous and morally contradictory works. In others these same paradoxes produce moral absolutism in the writing and ambiguity in the identity of the writer herself. J. was such a writer.

WORKS: *Charles Linn; or, How to Observe the Golden Rule* (1841). *The Great Secret; or, How to Be Happy* (1842). *Allen Lucas: The Self-Made Man*

(1843). *John Frink; or, The Third Commandment Illustrated* (1844). *Alder-brook* (1846). *Lilias Fane, and Other Tales* (1846). *Trippings in Author-Land* (1846). *How to Be Great, Good, and Happy* (including *Allen Lucas; the Self-Made Man, Charles Linn; or, How to Observe the Golden Rule*, and *The Great Secret; or, How to Be Happy*, 1848). *Memoir of Sarah B. Judson* (1849). *A Mound Is in the Graveyard* (ca. 1851). *An Olio of Domestic Verses* (1852). *The Kathayan Slave* (1853). *My Two Sisters* (1854).

BIBLIOGRAPHY: Douglas, A., *The Feminization of American Culture* (1977). Kendrick, A. C., *The Life and Letters of Mrs. Emily Chubbuck Judson* (1860). Pattee, F., *The Feminine Fifties* (1940). Stuart, A. W., *The Lives of Mrs. Ann H. Judson and Mrs. Sarah B. Judson, with a Biographical Sketch of Mrs. Emily Chubbuck Judson* (1851).

For articles in reference works, see: *AA. CAL. DAB*, V, 2. *FPA. NAW* (article by E. E. Lewis). *NCAB*, 3.

JULIANN E. FLEENOR

Agnes Newton Keith

B. 6 July 1901, Oak Park, Illinois
D. of Joseph Gilbert and Grace Goodwillie Newton; m. Henry George
  Keith, 1934

Reared in California, K. graduated from the University of California at Berkeley in 1924. Her brief career with the San Francisco *Examiner* ended when she was brutally attacked by a frenzied drug addict. A prolonged incapacitation, including the loss of eyesight, followed. Surgery eventually restored her to health. Married to an English tropical-forestry expert, she found the materials for her sensitive and evocative books about Asia and Africa in their subsequent travels.

From 1934 to 1952 the Keiths lived in North Borneo. Four books are based on that experience. *Land Below the Wind* (1939), a bride's sunny report on her Eden, examines the life of westerners in an outpost of Empire, describes her experiences there, and characterizes her native friends. Like most of K.'s books, it is illustrated by her own sketches. *Three Came Home* (1947) is the story of imprisonment by the Japanese during World War II. K. and her young son were interned together, her husband in a neighboring camp. Despite its subject, the book is strangely affirmative: she shows brutality and humanity in both jailers and prisoners, stressing that war, not race, has dehumanized them all. Her depiction of the heroism of many prisoners and their Asian friends outside the camp is moving, and throughout she stresses the courage and endurance that enabled them to bring all thirty-four interned children through alive.

White Man Returns (1951) rounds off this series by showing the return to North Borneo after the war; the beginning of the process of rebuilding is central to this book. Similar to *Land Below the Wind* in approach and structure, it lacks the happy idealism of the first book; the war experience had destroyed K.'s Eden. Much later came yet another work based on the Borneo years, this time a novel, *Beloved Exiles* (1972). Only loosely autobiographical, it is less successful than the nonfiction works.

Having retired from his government's service, K.'s husband was, in 1953, prevailed upon to go to the Philippines for the Food and Agriculture Organization of the United Nations. *Bare Feet in the Palace* (1955) resulted. Like her first and third Borneo books, it is a mixture of personal experiences, sketches of people, and information about the society and its history. A central theme is the creation of democracy in Asia; the title refers to the coming of poor natives to the two-hundred-year-old former palace of Spanish governors, now the residence of a democratically elected president.

Children of Allah (1966), K.'s only non-Asian book, tells of their following assignment in Libya. K. used her previously successful formula here, and this work is particularly notable for its studies of Libyan Moslem women in various stages of subservience to and liberation from the veil and all that its wearing implies.

K.'s most recent book, *Before the Blossoms Fall* (1975), must be paired with *Three Came Home,* which had been widely admired in Japan. In 1973 she was sent by the Japan Foundation on a six-week visit to Japan, the goal being that she would write something that would increase understanding between Japan and the U.S. Important themes here are the young, the aged, and women's changing status and attitudes. Like her other books, it is a perceptive and sympathetic study, though K. admits she is unable completely to understand or trust these people, whom she nevertheless loves.

Throughout her career, and hinging on her imprisonment experience, K.'s attitude toward her Asian subjects altered subtly. While she was always sympathetic and even admiring, the earliest book also sometimes seems patronizing, and the idea of the white man's burden is not totally absent. The later books reveal a truer sense of equality and a surer stress on the values of alien cultures, along with a more open admission of inability thoroughly to understand them. All of the works, however, are both informative and absorbing.

WORKS: *Land Below the Wind* (1939). *Three Came Home* (1947; film version, 1949). *White Man Returns* (1951). *Bare Feet in the Palace* (1955). *Children of Allah* (1966). *Beloved Exiles* (1972). *Before the Blossoms Fall* (1975).

BIBLIOGRAPHY: For articles in reference works, see: *CA*, 17–18 (1967). *20thCAS*.

Other references: *Atlantic* (March 1966). *NYHTB* (6 April 1947; 5 Aug. 1951). *NYTBR* (12 Nov. 1939; 26 March 1972). *SatR* (5 April 1947; 13 Dec. 1955).

MARY JEAN DeMARR

Helen Adams Keller

B. 27 June 1880, Tuscumbia, Alabama; d. 1 June 1968, Westport, Connecticut
Wrote under: Helen Keller, Helen Adams Keller
D. of Arthur H. and Katherine Adams Keller

K. was nineteen months old when illness left her deaf and blind. She soon became wild and unmanageable, locked inside a dark, silent world that no humanizing influence seemed able to penetrate.

In the 1890s, almost no hope existed for educating people both deaf and blind, but K.'s parents turned to the Perkins Institution for the Blind in Boston for help. The institution sent Anne Sullivan, a new graduate who had recently had her own sight partially restored, to educate the child to whatever extent proved possible. Undreamed of success followed, and K. eventually, in 1904, earned a B.A. cum laude from Radcliffe College.

K. became friends with many of the world's greatest people, including Alexander Graham Bell, Mark Twain, William Dean Howells, Charlie Chaplin, and Andrew Carnegie. At least nine presidents received her, and a half-dozen of the most prestigious universities in the world bestowed honorary degrees upon her.

From 1924 until her death in 1968, K. was associated with the American Foundation for the Blind, traveling to every state in the U.S. and to every continent in the world, working to enlarge the possibilities for handicapped people.

K.'s first book was *The Story of My Life* (1902), first published serially by the *Ladies' Home Journal.* The book contains, in addition to her early autobiography, her letters from 1887 to 1901, passages from Anne Sullivan's reports about K.'s education, and comments by John Albert Macy.

K. describes the terrible isolation of the blind and deaf mute as a "twofold solitude" in which one can "know little of the . . . affections that grow out of endearing words and actions and companionship." She tells about an incident of unconscious plagiarism, which happened in 1892, and about the fear that grew from that "disgrace," saying that "even now I cannot be quite sure of the boundary line between my ideas and those I find in books. I suppose that is because so many of my impressions come to me through the medium of others' eyes and ears."

Midstream: My Later Life (1929) brings up to date the story of this remarkable woman and her teacher. It also gives the reader a lively picture of life in America during the first three decades of this century.

In *Midstream*, K. seems to delight in using images of sight and sound, perhaps because some critics had questioned the honesty of this aspect of her style. Surely she had experienced in some physical way the scene she describes thus: "Out of the big, red, gaping mouths of the furnaces leaped immense billows of fire." Such vivid sensory images enliven this entire book in a degree that would be noteworthy even in a writer without handicaps.

Teacher: Anne Sullivan Macy (1955) is certainly, as the title page proclaims, "a tribute by the foster-child of her mind." K. memorably describes the incredible difficulties faced by Sullivan in introducing K. to language. Once the child discovered that things have names, her education proceeded with astonishing rapidity. Sullivan is presented as a human being with more than her share of human problems and foibles, but when compared with K.'s earlier clean, concrete writing, the book seems somewhat repetitious and sentimental.

K.'s many other books include poetry (*Double Blossoms*, 1931) and social criticism (*Helen Keller, Her Socialist Years: Writings and Speeches*, 1967). But her best work is found in her autobiographical books.

WORKS: *The Story of My Life* (1902; film version, *Deliverance*, 1918). *Optimism, an Essay* (1903). *The World I Live In* (1908). *The Song of the*

Stone Wall (1910). *Out of the Dark: Essays, Letters, and Addresses on Physical and Social Vision* (1913). *My Religion* (1927). *Midstream: My Later Life* (1929). *We Bereaved* (1929). *Double Blossoms* (1931). *Peace at Eventide* (1932). *Helen Keller in Scotland* (Ed. J. K. Love, 1933). *American Foundation for the Blind, 1923–1938: A Report from Helen Keller to the Blind People of America* (1938). *Journal, 1936–1937* (1938). *Let Us Have Faith* (1940). *Teacher, Anne Sullivan Macy: a Tribute by the Foster-Child of Her Mind* (1955). *Open Door* (1957). *Helen Keller, Her Socialist Years: Writings and Speeches* (Ed. P. S. Foner, 1967).

BIBLIOGRAPHY: Braddy, N., *Anne Sullivan Macy: The Story behind Helen Keller* (1933). Brooks, V. W., *Helen Keller: Sketch for a Portrait* (1956). Gibson, W., *The Miracle Worker: A Play for Television* (1957). Graff, S., and P. A. Graff, *Helen Keller: Toward the Light* (1965). Harrity, R., and J. G. Martin, *The Three Lives of Helen Keller* (1962). Hickok, L. A., *The Touch of Magic* (1961). Peare, C. O., *The Helen Keller Story* (1959). Waite, H. E., *Valiant Companions: Helen Keller and Anne Sullivan Macy* (1959).

For articles in reference works, see: *CB* (Dec. 1942; July 1968). *LSL. NCAB*, 15.

PEGGY SKAGGS

Edith Summers Kelley

B. 1884, Ontario, Canada; d. 1956, Los Gatos, California
Wrote under: Edith Summers Kelley, Edith Summers
M. Allan Updegraff, 1908; m. Claude Fred Kelley, 1915

Like the protagonists of her two novels, K. struggled much of her adult life for financial security and for realization of her dream to be a writer. After taking an honors degree in languages from the University of Toronto, the nineteen-year-old Edith moved to New York and began working on Funk and Wagnall's *Standard Dictionary* project.

In 1906, K. became secretary to Upton Sinclair and part of the staff at Helicon Hall, Sinclair's socialist commune (inspired by Charlotte Perkins Gilman's plans for municipal housing, advanced in 1904). At the Hall she met two other aspiring writers cum janitors, Sinclair Lewis and Alan Updegraff. Both Lewis (to whom she was engaged) and Sinclair remained lifelong correspondents. The marriage to Updegraff produced two children; K. apparently was primary breadwinner as a teacher in the Hell's

Kitchen area of New York City. After her divorce she became the common-law wife of Claude Fred Kelley. The Kelleys pursued a series of mostly unprofitable jobs from 1914 to 1945: tenant tobacco farming in Kentucky; boardinghouse management in New Jersey; alfalfa and chicken ranching, and bootlegging in California. Thus, unlike Sinclair's journalistic fiction, K.'s novels reflect her own experiences and observations as an economically depressed rancher.

In *Weeds* (1923), Judith Pipinger is different from other members of her tenant tobacco-farming community in Kentucky because she is a throwback to purer pioneer stock, an exception to the usual results of inbreeding and poor nutrition. Her early repugnance to traditional female chores and her preference for "man's" (outdoors) work isolate her from the closely knit female subculture. This isolation is underlined by imagery linking Judith with natural (as opposed to societal) objects, and by a character "double," Jabez Moorhouse, an iconoclastic fiddler who shares Judith's intuitive grasp of beauty and meaning in life. With her marriage and subsequent motherhood, Judith is trapped in the very role she has despised; when Moorhouse dies, her death in spirit concludes the novel.

Encouraged by a monetary award from a civil-liberties group, K. began work in 1925 on a second novel, a study of the Imperial Valley in Southern California and "the life it harbors." From 1925 through 1929, K. wrote and revised as her knowledge of California development and the International Workers of the World increased, but *The Devil's Hand* was not published until 1974, eighteen years after her death.

Marriage proves to be a spiritual death for Rhoda Malone, an acknowledgment of defeat which closes *The Devil's Hand*. Tempted by her friend Kate Baxter to leave her passive and orderly life as an office clerk in Philadelphia, Rhoda takes on a partnership with Kate in a California alfalfa farm. Because Rhoda's is the central consciousness through which the story is told, focus is equally on what she sees and who she becomes. Her awareness of the exploitation of people like herself, and the Hindu, Mexican, and Oriental laborers, by rapacious realtors and big landowners gradually intensifies; two male friends serve (as did Moorhouse in *Weeds*) as examples of the individual freedom which Rhoda, as a woman, cannot achieve. Disheartened by the loss of these friends, the drudgery of profitless farming, and her realization that to challenge the economic system is to suffer social and material martyrdom, Rhoda marries the very realtor who initially took advantage of her ignorance.

K. is among several American women writers of the 1920s, such as Josephine Herbst, Frances Newman, Evelyn Scott, and Ruth Suckow, who have been "rediscovered" after being long forgotten or ignored. K. is also emerging as a master of fiction in the Dreiser, Garland, Howells vein. She does not limit her work to tedious cataloguing of realistic detail, but her work is firmly rooted in everyday experience. Although the imagery of her novels underlines the forgotten connection of men and women to nature, her fiction is oriented more toward sociological (even socialist) study; time and again she emphasizes the effect of social environment on individual fate. Thus, the feminist concerns grow naturally out of her realistic approach to life and fiction.

WORKS: *Weeds* (1923). *The Devil's Hand* (1974).

Selected papers of Edith Summers Kelley are in the Special Collections of the Morris Library, Southern Illinois University at Carbondale. Kelley's letters to Sinclair Lewis and to Upton Sinclair are in collections of the Lilly Library, Indiana University.

BIBLIOGRAPHY: Bruccoli, M., Afterword to *The Devil's Hand* (1974) and *Weeds* (1974). Irvin, H., *Women in Kentucky* (1979). Schorer, M., *Sinclair Lewis: An American Life* (1961).

Other references: *Michigan Papers in Women's Studies* (June 1975). *Regionalism and the Female Imagination* III (Spring 1977).

SALLY BRETT

Myra Kelly

B. 26 Aug. 1875, Dublin, Ireland; d. 30 March 1910, Torquay, England
D. of James and Annie Morrogh Kelly; m. Allan Macnaughton, 1905

K. came to New York City with her family when she was a child; they lived on the East Side, where her physician father developed a large practice. Educated first at convent schools, she attended Horace Mann High School and then Teachers College of Columbia University, receiving a diploma in 1899 as a teacher of manual training. Her experience at East-Side Public School 147, where she taught from 1899 to 1901, provided material for her popular stories about "Bailey's Babies."

K.'s long stream of published stories began with the sentimental "A Christmas Present for a Lady," which she had sent to two magazines, thinking both would reject it. When both accepted it, K. had complicated adjustments to make. She told friends later that no manuscript of hers was ever rejected. The story was included in her first book, *Little Citizens: The Humours of School Life* (1904).

Little Citizens caught the attention of Allan Macnaughton, president of Standard Coach Horse Company, who arranged to meet her. They were married in 1905; their one child, a boy, died in infancy. The Macnaughtons lived briefly at Oldchester Village, Orange Mountain, New Jersey, while working to establish a literary colony there.

In her scant thirty-five years, the prolific K. produced not only three books of East-Side stories but popular romantic tales as well. She also wrote essays about educational methods and effects, some of which appeared in collections with her stories. K. died from tuberculosis in England, where she had gone in hope of a cure. Her last books were published posthumously.

Little Citizens is a collection of K.'s earliest stories about the children in Constance Bailey's first-reader class, boys and girls primarily from poor Jewish immigrant families but including the son of the local Irish policeman for contrast and occasional conflict. K. wrote that she was not the model for Constance Bailey. " 'What I aspired to be and was not' Constance Bailey was. Only her mistakes are mine and her very earnest effort."

The stories were intended as educational, but have the charms of novelty and originality, although verisimilitude suffers in both incidents and dialogue. The humor that tempers the message is usually at the immigrant's expense and is often condescending, but it sometimes touches on the teacher's embarrassment as she realizes the limitations of her knowledge or experience.

Wards of Liberty (1907) contains more stories of Miss Bailey's fifty-eight students. There are disruptive influences like the nine-year-old "Boss" who is running his late father's cellar garment shop. K. believed the schools played a crucial role in helping immigrants get along in America, but the Boss's story shows that she recognized the system's limitations. The Boss has previously avoided all schooling and other Americanizing influences, but comes to school when he decides learning to read will bring better-paid work for his shop. Discouraged by the slow pace and unessential busy work, he disappears. His life has no room for childhood activities. He lives in a world the schools could not reach.

Although K. continues to emphasize the fun, under it rages revolt against conditions among the poor.

After several less critically successful novels, K. returned, as her critics hoped she would, to the world of her schoolchildren in *Little Aliens* (1910). There is still humor and pathos but with a deeper understanding of children and the nature of alienation. "Games in Gardens" shows how immigrants can misinterpret the bits of America that filter into their ghetto world, as the children try to don proper costume for track and field events. Miss Bailey takes her share of the satire for her inadequate communication. Whereas earlier K. had saved discussion for her essays, here she explains how natural these misunderstandings are with children "alien to every American custom, and prejudiced by religion and precept against most of them."

Although generally unknown now, K. achieved tremendous popular success, publishing frequently in mass-circulation magazines like *McClure's*. Even President Theodore Roosevelt sent her a letter of appreciation. She exaggerated both characters and incidents, looked for sentiment, and created wry humor always on the verge of pathos, but she was honest in her approach, often touching on serious issues such as the values of Americanization and the clash between immigrant and American traditions. Writing with warmth, sympathy, and as much understanding as she could muster, K. did much to acquaint the reading public with the harsh conditions of ghetto life and to suggest that Americans learn to know their immigrants before thoughtlessly attempting to Americanize them. When she left the narrow area of the East-Side schools, her stories were less well received and less significant.

WORKS: *Little Citizens: The Humours of School Life* (1904). *The Isle of Dreams* (1907). *Wards of Liberty* (1907). *Rosnah* (1908). *The Golden Season* (1909). *Little Aliens* (1910). *New Faces* (1910). *Her Little Young Ladyship* (1911).

BIBLIOGRAPHY: Fine, D. M., *The City, the Immigrant, and American Fiction* (1977). Friedman, L. M., *Pilgrims in a New Land* (1948). Lieberman, E., *The American Short Story: A Study of the Influence of Locality in Its Development* (1912).

For articles in reference works, see: *DAB*, V, 2. *NCAB*, 24.

Other references: *American Mercury* (Feb. 1926). *American Studies* (Spring 1978).

CAROL B. GARTNER

Frances Anne Kemble

B. 27 Nov. 1809, London, England; d. 15 Jan. 1893, London, England
Wrote under: Frances Anne Butler (Miss Fanny Kemble), Mrs. Butler,
 Frances Anne Kemble
D. of Charles and Maria Kemble; m. Pierce Butler, 1834

Born into London's leading theatrical family, K. was an actress who became one of the most articulate Victorian women of letters in both America and England. Daughter of an actor who was also manager of Covent Garden Theatre, K. received all her formal education at boarding schools in France. K.'s first stage performance, as Shakespeare's Juliet at Covent Garden in 1829, was a phenomenal success which transformed her life. K. became the pinup girl of the London stage, enjoying admiration from people in England and the provinces. In 1832 she toured America.

Her marriage to a wealthy Philadelphian initiated a period of emotional upheaval. K. gave up her acting career for marriage, but she never became the model 19th-c. woman. Instead of accepting the role of subservient wife, she demanded equality. Furthermore, instead of accepting and approving of her husband's homeland, she was quite critical of it. The record of her experiences, *Journal of a Residence in America* (1835), publicly announced her negative attitudes, much to the chagrin of her husband. A particularly crucial issue for him, as the owner of large Georgian plantations and hundreds of slaves, was K.'s passionate and outspoken opposition to the "peculiar institution." After the birth of her two daughters, two return visits to England, and numerous attempts to sever her relationship with Butler, K. left her husband and daughters in 1844.

K. returned to England, published a volume of poetry, and resumed her acting career. When Butler filed for divorce in 1848, she came back to America and spent her final years in public readings of Shakespeare, frequent visits to Europe, and, finally, in devoting herself to her lifelong ambition: writing. She wrote more memoirs, a critical work on Shakespeare, poetry, a comedy, and a novel (Henry James noted that not many people published a first novel at the age of 80). She developed friendships with a number of literary figures and died where she was born—in England.

Written twenty-two years before the outbreak of the Civil War and published in the same year that the slaves were emancipated, *Journal of a Residence on a Georgian Plantation, 1838–1839* (1863) describes the condition of the slaves in brutally realistic terms. Among many of the inhuman aspects which K. denounces, the painful life of women slaves is carefully detailed. Decrying their oppressed state of manual labor and continual childbearing, K. speaks of the females' "sorrow-laden existence" and their endurance of sufferings which appeared to be "all in the day's work." The book was well read during K.'s day, although its stark realism was disconcerting to the Victorian readership.

While posterity tends to remember K. as an actress, perhaps her place as a chronicler of the American experience should be reevaluated. Her autobiographical works, especially *Journal of a Residence in America* and *Journal of a Residence on a Georgian Plantation*, have a particular psychological and historical significance as documents that reveal the struggles and challenges facing a 19th-c. woman critical of national and regional narrowness.

The memoirs, bestsellers of their day, also contain keen insights into the enormous changes transforming the nation; K. recognized and evaluated the movement away from Victorian America toward the modern age. Criticized by some reviewers for her "racy" language and for her subjective judgments of particular individuals, K. nonetheless had the rare ability to write vivid and insightful observations of places, people, and historical changes she witnessed. Her journals are neither carefully crafted nor totally consistent pictures of life in early America, but they are rich psychological and cultural documents because of their author's complex personality, interests, and skills of observation. Perhaps Henry James's evaluation is the best assessment of K.: "There was no convenient or handy formula for Mrs. Kemble's genius, and one had to take her career, the juxtaposition of her interests, exactly as one took her disposition, for a remarkably fine cluster of inconsistencies."

WORKS: *Francis the First: A Tragedy in Five Acts* (1832). *Journal of a Residence in America* (1835). *The Star of Seville: A Drama in Five Acts* (1837). *A Year of Consolation* (1837). *Poems* (1844). *Poems* (1859). *Journal of a Residence on a Georgian Plantation, 1838–1839* (1863). *On the Stage* (1863). *Records of a Girlhood* (1878). *Notes upon Some of Shakespeare's Plays* (1882). *Records of a Later Life* (1882). *Poems* (1883). *Adventures of John Timothy Homespun in Switzerland* (1889). *Far Away and Long Ago* (1889).

BIBLIOGRAPHY: Armstrong, M., *Frances Kemble: The Passionate Victorian* (1938). Bobbe, D., *Frances Kemble* (1931). Driver, L., *Frances Kemble* (1933). Gibbs, H., *Yours Affectionately, Fanny* (1947). Marshall, D., *Frances Kemble* (1977). Wister, F. K., *Fanny: The American Kemble* (1972). Wright, C. C. *Frances Kemble and the Lovely Land* (1972).

For articles in reference works, see: *AA. British Authors of the Nineteenth Century*, Ed. S. J. Kunitz (1936). *DAB*, V, 2. *LSL. NAW* (article by H. L. Kleinfield).

MARJORIE SMELSTOR

Jean Collins Kerr

B. 10 July 1923, Scranton, Pennsylvania
Writes under: Jean Kerr
D. of Thomas J. and Kitty O'Neill Collins; m. Walter Kerr, 1943

K. earned an M.A. in theater from the Catholic University, where she met her husband, a dramatics professor who later became the *New York Times* theater critic. K. regards herself principally as a playwright and her essays as a diversion, but it is the latter that have gained vast popularity. The typical style of K.'s plays and essays is the carefully polished imitation of easy conversation.

K. wrote three plays for her husband's direction at the Catholic University. The third, *Jenny Kissed Me* (1948), opened on Broadway, starring the famous comic actor Leo G. Carroll. Collaborating with her husband and the musician Jay Gorney, K. won praise for energy and intelligence in the revue, *Touch and Go* (1949). In the successful Broadway production *John Murray Anderson's Almanac* (1953), K.'s sketch "Don Brown's Body" uses the violent, sexually suggestive style of Mickey Spillane's detective stories to lampoon orchestrated readings of Stephen Vincent Benet's Civil War poem.

In K.'s most successful play, *Mary, Mary* (1961), the title character discovers her true, timid nature through a new admirer's eyes but returns to her first love just before he can divorce her for a less disarming wife. K.'s urbane wit is not only richly decorative but integral to character: Mary antagonizes her husband not with her superior insight into his publishing business but with the hilarious sarcasm that masks her personal insecurity. Mary draws audience sympathy for her clever vulnerability, but she wins her man because she learns to demonstrate sophistication.

K.'s most successful book, *Please Don't Eat the Daisies* (1957), collects fifteen humorous sketches written for popular magazines. Intelligent literary allusion and stylish satire enliven the familiar essay form, making spirited fun of an alert woman's irritations with rambunctious sons, slick-magazine advice, and a celebrated husband. Phrasing motherly boasting as complaints, K. idealizes family affections. She burlesques the distressingly clichéd 1950s prescriptions for glamorous or maternal feminine behavior by opposing them with precise details. In 1965, K. adapted her sketches for a two-season NBC situation comedy about a suburban free-lance writer, a college dramatics professor, and their four sons.

The best pieces in *The Snake Has All the Lines* (1960) portray K. less as a homemaker than as an author revising a play in a rehearsal or growing cynical over mixed critical reviews. Tributes to her determined Irish mother and her awkward Catholic school days show K. learning the value of her generous verbal wit.

In the best essay of her collection *Penny Candy* (1970), K. combines her two personae of a mother and a student of literature to recall her success in bringing her sons to share her love of poetry. Unfortunately, the made-to-order sketches for *Family Circle* and the *Ladies' Home Journal*, which outnumber the more original work, force K. to act the housewife flustered by babytalk, wilting houseplants, cocktail parties, and her weight.

Humorously alert to absurd trivialities, the strong female character who dominates K.'s essays and plays saves herself from selfish insignificance by her own generous instinct. During the thirty years of her writing career, K.'s essays have grown loose and self-revealing while her stage comedies have faced increasingly difficult social issues within constricting dramatic unities. Wary of intimidating her readers, K. rarely mentions the strains her writing and successful marriage place on each other. With merry charm, in the early 1960s, she seemed to synthesize the careers of Larchmont homemaker and Broadway playwright and thus unexpectedly became an American ideal, without being forced to scrutinize the difference between the values she held and those she represented.

WORKS: *The Song of Bernadette* by F. Werfel (dramatization by Kerr, 1944). *Our Hearts Were Young and Gay* by C. O. Skinner and E. Kimbrough (dramatization by Kerr, 1946). *The Big Help* (1947). *Jenny Kissed Me* (1948). *Touch and Go* (with W. Kerr and J. Gorney, 1949). *King of Hearts* (with E. Brooke, 1954; film version, *That Certain Feeling*, 1956). *Please Don't Eat the Daisies* (1957; film version, 1960; television series, 1965–67). *Goldilocks* (with W. Kerr and L. Anderson, 1958). *The Snake Has All the Lines* (1960). *Mary, Mary* (1961; film version, 1963). *Poor Richard* (1964). *Penny Candy* (1970). *Finishing Touches* (1973). *How I Got to Be Perfect* (1978). *Lunch Hour* (1980).

BIBLIOGRAPHY: For articles in reference works, see: *CA*, 5–8 (1969). *CB* (July 1958). *WA*.

Other references: *New York Theatre Critics Reviews* (1946–73). *NYT* (18 Feb. 1973). *SatR* (30 Nov. 1957). *Theatre Arts* (March 1961). *Time* (14 April 1961).

GAYLE GASKILL

Frances Parkinson Wheeler Keyes

B. 21 July 1885, Charlottesville, Virginia; d. 3 July 1970, New Orleans, Louisiana
Wrote under: Frances Parkinson Keyes
D. of John Henry and Louise Fuller Johnson Wheeler; m. Henry Wilder Keyes, 1904

An only daughter, K. received but seven years of formal schooling—in Boston, Switzerland, Berlin—as was appropriate for a "gently born girl." Her husband, more than twenty years her senior, with whom she had three sons, was governor of New Hampshire and served three terms in the U.S. Senate. She describes her role as hostess in *Capital Kaleidoscope* (1937).

Always a rapid and omnivorous reader, K. wrote as a child but was not encouraged. She began publishing after her marriage because of desperate financial need. Soon a regular contributor to *Good Housekeeping*, K. was widely known for monthly "Letters from a Senator's Wife," which ran for fourteen years, and for other political analyses. A contributing editor from 1923 to 1936, K. wrote about her world trip in

1925–26 and another to South America in 1929–30. These formative years are described in *All Flags Flying* (1972), an incomplete autobiography published posthumously. K. contributed to other magazines, was editor of the Daughters of the American Revolution *National Historical Magazine* from 1937 to 1939, and was a frequent lecturer.

K.'s fame rests upon her extraordinary career as a best-selling novelist. Her first novel, *The Old Gray Homestead*, was published in 1919. Not until *Honor Bright* (1936) did she have a bestseller, but she was seldom without one throughout the next decades.

In spite of frequent and severe illness and a crippling back injury, K. was a person of great vitality and enthusiasm, many interests, extraordinary dedication to work, and an urgent need for fulfillment. She produced very long and fluent novels that reflected careful and diligent research to ensure correctness of setting and circumstance. She reveled in descriptions of rich foods, elegant clothes, gay parties, and exotic locales. Older civilizations fascinate, but also evidence decay; in her novels promise in the modern world lies in simplicity and hard work.

K. favored accounts of a family's fortunes through several generations. The first novels are set in New England, Washington, and Europe. Perhaps the most lavish is *Crescent Carnival* (1942), sumptuously detailing complex New Orleans traditions through three generations. After its enormous success K. spent her winters in Louisiana and developed a pattern in which she wrote Louisiana books alternatively with other novels. The highly successful *Dinner at Antoine's* (1948) added mystery to her customary romance.

The typical K. heroine is young, beautiful, naive, and in love with an older experienced man who is ennobled by passion for her. Temptations abound, but high principle triumphs, though the rule that a K. heroine is never seduced altered in the later novels. K.'s women are competent, loyal, and stoic in their acceptance of hardships. Some have personal careers, but usually their lives are shaped by marriage, and fulfillment comes in motherhood, woman's triumph for K.

Religion was important to K. Though her family was Congregational, she was attracted to formal ritual and was confirmed at fourteen in the Episcopal church. In *Along a Little Way* (1940) she describes her gradual growth to Catholicism and recent conversion. She wrote about a number of saints' lives and often described religious practice in her novels.

Her novels had a large audience in England and were also translated into several languages. K. received many awards and honorary degrees. Although resigned to not receiving critical acclaim, K. made a strong

case for her craft in *The Cost of a Best-Seller* (1950). Admittedly sentimental and often rhetorical, her high romance is strengthened by common sense and diversified incidents. K.'s exposition of political and social
circumstances and concern with international relations challenged American provincialism.

WORKS: *The Old Gray Homestead* (1919). *The Career of David Noble*
(1921). *Letters from a Senator's Wife* (1924). *Queen Anne's Lace* (1930).
Silver Seas and Golden Cities (1931). *Lady Blanche Farm: Senator Marlowe's
Daughter* (1933). *The Safe Bridge* (1934). *The Happy Wanderer* (1935).
Honor Bright (1936). *Capital Kaleidoscope* (1937). *Written in Heaven*
(1937). *Parts Unknown* (1938). *The Great Tradition* (1939). *Along a Little
Way* (1940). *Fielding's Folly* (1940). *The Sublime Shepherdess* (1940). *All
That Glitters* (1941). *The Grace of Guadalupe* (1941). *Crescent Carnival*
·(1942). *Also the Hills* (1943). *The River Road* (1945). *Came a Cavalier*
(1947). *Once on Esplanade* (1947). *Dinner at Antoine's* (1948). *All This Is
Louisiana* (1950). *The Cost of a Best-Seller* (1950). *Joy Street* (1950).
Therese: Saint of a Little Way (1950). *Steamboat Gothic* (1952). *Bernadette
of Lourdes* (1953). *The Royal Box* (1954). *Frances Parkinson Keyes Cook-
book* (1955). *Mother of Our Saviour* (1955). *The Blue Camellia* (1957). *Land
of Stones and Saints* (1957). *Victorine* (1958). *Frances Parkinson Keyes
Christmas Gift* (1959). *Mother Cabrini: Missionary to the World* (1959).
Station Wagon in Spain (1959). *The Chess Players* (1960). *Roses in December*
(1960). *The Third Mystic of Avila* (1960). *The Rose and the Lily* (1961).
Madame Castel's Lodger (1962). *The Restless Lady, and Other Stories* (1963).
Three Ways of Love (1963). *A Treasury of Favorite Poems* (1963). *The
Explorer* (1964). *I, the King* (1966). *Tongues of Fire* (1966). *The Heritage*
(1968). *All Flags Flying* (1972).

BIBLIOGRAPHY: For articles in reference works, see: *CA*, 5–8 (1969); 25–
28 (1971). *Catholic Authors: Contemporary Biographical Sketches, 1930–1947*,
Ed. M. Hoehn (1948). *20thCA. 20thCAS.*

Other references: *CathW* (Jan. 1943). *CSM* (28 Nov. 1950). *NYHTB* (19
Nov. 1939). *NYTBR* (8 Nov. 1936; 8 Nov. 1942; 9 Dec. 1945). *Time* (26 Dec.
1960).

VELMA BOURGEOIS RICHMOND

Aline Murray Kilmer

B. 1 Aug. 1888, Norfolk, Virginia; d. 1 Oct. 1941, Stillwater, New Jersey
Wrote under: Aline Kilmer, Aline Murray
D. of Kenton and Ada Foster Murray; m. Joyce Kilmer, 1908

Among the literary members of K.'s family were her father, an editor; her stepfather, Henry Mills Alden, the editor of *Harper's Magazine;* and her husband, one of the more famous poets of the day and the poetry editor of the *Literary Digest.* Two of her sons were published poets. K. was educated at Rutgers Prep and at the Vail-Deane School in Elizabeth, New Jersey. In 1913, both she and her husband entered the Roman Catholic Church. They were the parents of five children. In 1918, Sgt. Joyce Kilmer of the "Fighting 69th" was killed in action in France.

Although she had published a few poems before her marriage, selling her first poem to *St. Nicholas* magazine at age eleven, K. was always overshadowed by her husband, both professionally and socially. Most critics concede, however, that she was the better poet. After his death her reserve lessened, and she occasionally made lecture tours to help with expenses. She served as vice-president of the Catholic Poetry Society of America. The death of her husband had been preceded by the death of one child from polio and was followed in a few years by the death of another. Both the subject matter and the tone of her work were largely determined by these events and her task of bringing up a family alone.

In *Candles That Burn* (1919) K. presents intensely personal poems, most of them about children, and many of these dealing with the still-raw pain of personal bereavement or the fear of loss. In some of these she is unable to transcend the experience, yet already in this first volume one can occasionally see the note of gentle irony that pervades her best mature poetry.

Vigils (1921) continues K.'s emphasis on personal preoccupations. A mere two strings of her instrument suffice, she writes in "The Harp": "One is for love and one for death. . . . I play on the strings I know." Although the cry of pain reappears in many of these poems, the poet has learned to transmute her material and to choose more evocative imagery. The rhythms have become her own. Literary subjects—the Lady of Shalott and Sappho—appear.

In *The Poor King's Daughter* (1925), K. has perfected her distinctive tone of gentle but unrelieved disillusionment, of irony delicate but never bitter. The intimacy remains, but a reticence disciplines it. The poet has now learned to maintain distance and to detach the poetic process from the experience. In "Favete Linguis" the poet admires the plum tree heavy with blossom but warns: "You lift your lute to celebrate its beauty / And all its petals flutter to the ground." The theme of enforced silence emerges again in the fine poem "Against the Wall." Here the irony of the parent calmly mending armor for the sons' fights, while silently lamenting the emptiness of victory and glory, achieves tragic overtones by K.'s use of conversational language and rhythms.

K.'s prose works include two children's books and *Hunting a Hair Shirt* (1923), a collection of brief personal essays similar in theme and tone to her verse.

WORKS: *Candles That Burn* (1919). *Vigils* (1921). *Hunting a Hair Shirt* (1923). *The Poor King's Daughter, and Other Poems* (1925). *Emmy, Nicky, and Greg* (1927). *A Buttonwood Summer* (1929). *Selected Poems* (1929).

BIBLIOGRAPHY: For articles in reference works, see: *Catholic Authors: Contemporary Biographical Sketches, 1930–1947*, Ed. M. Hoehn (1948). *CB* (Dec. 1941).

Other references: *America* (18 Oct. 1941). *Bookman* (Dec. 1921; May 1925). *CathW* (June 1929). *Commonweal* (17 July 1929; 14 Aug. 1929).

ARLENE ANDERSON SWIDLER

Emily Kimbrough

B. 23 Oct. 1899, Muncie, Indiana
D. of Hal Curry and Charlotte Emily Wiles Kimbrough;
 m. John Wrench, 1926

K. graduated from Bryn Mawr College in 1921, studied at the Sorbonne in Paris, and in 1923 began a career in advertising copywriting for Marshall Field & Co. that was to lead, four years later, to the managing editorship of the *Ladies' Home Journal*, a position she held until 1929.

In 1929 she gave birth to twin daughters; she was divorced after only several years' marriage. By 1934 K.'s articles had begun to appear in various national magazines, including *Country Life, House and Garden, Travel, Readers' Digest,* and *Saturday Review of Literature.* Even a reader of *Parents' Magazine* would have come across her down-to-earth advice about raising twins. By 1968 she had devoted herself to accounts of her frequent travels to Europe and around America.

Emily Kimbrough used to be a household name. "Oh, I LOVED *Our Hearts Were Young and Gay,*" is the inevitable cry of almost anyone old enough to read in 1942. K.'s first and most famous work, written jointly with Cornelia Otis Skinner, was a chronicle of their nineteenth summer, spent in Europe contracting measles on an ocean liner, overnighting in an unsuspected brothel, lunching at the Ritz in Paris, and generally charming one continent with their exploits and another with the reminiscences of them. K.'s next volume, *We Followed Our Hearts to Hollywood* (1943), describes the summer she and Skinner spent writing a film script for *Our Hearts.*

And it is the amusement and satisfaction that remain with the reader of any of K.'s subsequent books, which followed *Our Hearts Were Young and Gay* in rapid succession. At one time, K.'s travel books were standard guides to England, Italy, Portugal, Greece, France, and Ireland; that they have fallen out of currency is our loss. Full of Michelin-type restaurant and hotel lore, news of vistas and sights far beyond the guidebooks, and chatty stories of the people behind the walls and doors forming the boundaries of most tourists' experiences, they were the guiding tour lights of an entire generation. K. does more than recount the sights seen or merely detail the humorous adventures of four middle-aged women who "no speaka da language"—she takes the reader into the atmosphere of the places she visits, and throughout she provides the reader with the most intimate historical details.

But it is not only for her travel books that K. deserves to be remembered. *Through Charley's Door* (1952) is an intimate biography of Marshall Field & Co. and takes the reader to the heart of Chicago's venerable department store. Equally good are her stories of her childhood. *How Dear to My Heart* (1944) introduces six-year-old Emily about to begin school. The innocence and imagination of childhood are recreated in this story of her extended family (including Indiana Senator Charles M. Kimbrough), of the birth of her baby brother, and of her growing understanding of the world. In *The Innocents from Indiana* (1950) the eleven-year-old Emily moves from Muncie to Chicago and learns to love the big city in a series of adventures that includes playing catch unawares with Douglas Fairbanks and driving around and around the block in an electric car that cannot be stopped because its clutch is stuck. In *Now and Then* (1972) K. goes back, through her twins' childhood experiences, to more of her own. These delightful, low-key books, reminiscent of James Thurber, should be included among adolescent reading selections, for they reproduce the puzzlement and triumph of a child growing into herself.

K.'s writing has a simplicity and directness that immediately attracts. Her own naive pleasure at what she has seen, heard, and experienced is communicated directly to the reader. Of course, such simplicity dates the travel books; they could hardly be written in these days of jet travel, inflation, and mass education. It is for this reason that K. is an important mid–20th-c. writer, for she manages to reproduce the wonderment of which the American, particularly the sophisticated American matron, is no longer capable.

In addition to a sharp sense of the times, K.'s books present a great deal of information that, even if much of it is dated, provides the sort of rich historical background which is only now being noted in the writings of such regionalists as Jewett and Chopin. K.'s readers can hardly help but experience an otherwise unrecapturable past. Each book ends before we want it to and dances around the edges of our memories. It is little wonder that *Our Hearts Were Young and Gay* remains in print, and beloved, to this day.

WORKS: *Our Hearts Were Young and Gay* (1942). *We Followed Our Hearts to Hollywood* (1943). *How Dear to My Heart* (1944). *The Innocents from Indiana* (1950). *Through Charley's Door* (1952). *Forty Plus and Fancy Free* (1954). *So Near and Yet So Far* (1955). *Water, Water Everywhere* (1956). *And a Right Good Crew* (1958). *Pleasure by the Busload* (1961). *Forever Old, Forever New* (1964). *Floating Island* (1968). *Now and Then* (1972). *Time Enough* (1974). *Better Than Oceans* (1976).

BIBLIOGRAPHY: For articles in reference works, see: *CA*, 17–20 (1976). *CB* (March 1944). *Indiana Authors and Their Books, 1917–1966*, Ed. D. E. Thompson, 1974.

Other references: *Atlantic* (Dec. 1942). *NYTBR* (22 Nov. 1942). *SatR* (11 Dec. 1943).

LORALEE MacPIKE

Caroline Matilda Stansbury Kirkland

B. 11 Jan. 1801, New York City; d. 6 April 1864, New York City
Wrote under: Mrs. Mary Clavers, Caroline M. Stansbury Kirkland,
Aminadab Peering
D. of Samuel and Eliza Alexander Stansbury; m. William Kirkland, 1828

K., an eldest child, came from a literary family (her mother was a writer and her great-grandfather was a Tory poet during the American Revolution). In the Quaker school of her aunt Lydia Mott she received an unusually good education for a girl born at the beginning of the 19th c. After her marriage to Kirkland the couple settled in Geneva, New York, where they established a school. In 1835, they crossed overland to Detroit, an already thriving "metropolis" on the edge of the frontier to direct the newly established Detroit female seminary. The land fever and get-rich schemes that were circulating through Detroit engaged their imagination, and two years later they located sixty miles west, in the tiny hamlet of Pinckney.

The pioneering experience was the impetus for K.'s writing career. *A New Home—Who'll Follow?* (1839), written by K. under the pseudonym "Mrs. Mary Clavers, an Actual Settler," gives her slightly fictionalized account of the early years of a new community on the frontier. Loosely constructed of character sketches, brief essays on events unique to frontier life, tales, and a few mild adventures, the book covers the development of the town from the log cabin to the community. Though K. claims that nothing very adventurous happens, the life she describes is, in fact, eventful and arduous. In her second book, *Forest Life* (1842), the device of a tour of Michigan allows K. to comment on the developing institutions of the frontier, to generalize on events, and to describe the natural terrain and the process of the transformation of the diverse aspects of pioneer life into a less precarious existence. Integrating her impressions, K. comments on the scene in retrospect and with accumulated insight.

K. returned to the East in 1843, where her husband would have better professional opportunities and their four children (Joseph Kirkland, the eldest son, later became a well-known novelist) could get proper schooling. After her husband's death in 1846, K. immediately took up his responsibilities at the *Christian Inquirer*, operated her school for girls, reviewed for Duyckinck's *Literary World*, and shortly thereafter undertook the editorship of the *Union Magazine of Literature and Art*. In its earliest days under K.'s leadership the *Union* was considered one of the best family magazines of its kind.

A New Home—Who'll Follow? brought immediate popularity; *Forest Life* followed to enthusiastic reviews. Poe thought *Western Clearings* (1845), a collection of sketches that move toward the short-story form, the best of all. Though best known for this western writing, K. also completed a travel book, a biography of Washington, a novel, and three collections of essays. But the work of the last twenty years of her life remains unexplored and unevaluated.

Though never identified with the women's rights movement, K.'s introduction to Reid's *A Plea for Women* (1845) appeared three years before the first women's rights convention at Seneca Falls. K. advocated equal legal and political rights, and was especially bitter on the problem of women's financial dependence. She was also deeply concerned about the slavery issue and, by 1856, after completing her Washington biography, wrote a friend, "I am terribly low-spirited about public affairs. I see nothing but civil war and disunion before us." Though a pacifist, she supported and worked for the Union.

In the early 1850s, her short stories and essays were brought out as gift-book collections: *The Evening Book* (1852); *A Book for the Home Circle* (1853); and *Autumn Hours* (1854). The major topic in each was the correction and improvement of American manners and morals, which she managed to urge with sophisticated, disarming simplicity quite different from the saccharine and somber utilitarianism that characterized most literature on the same topics. In one essay, "Literary Women," a spirited defense of women authors, K. with tongue in cheek suggests that shopkeepers not sell pens to women who write, and that women should be excluded from school—at least till they are over forty.

At a time when popular literature consisted of moralizing essays on self-improvement and sentimental tales, K., in contrast, expressed herself clearly, concisely, and humorously. Her themes, settings, characters, and moral vision were a realist's. Her range of female characters gives a more complete picture of the nature and condition of women than can be derived from the work of the first-ranking American authors of the period. K. wrote, "It has been thought necessary to dress up and render conspicuous a certain class of events, while another class, perhaps far more efficient in producing the real features of the age, are unnoticed and forgotten." K., with her realist's perspectives, makes a significant contribution to our own times.

WORKS: *A New Home—Who'll Follow? or, Glimpses of Western Life* (1839). *Forest Life* (1842). *Principles of Morality* by J. Dymond (edited by Kirkland, 1847). *Western Clearings* (1845). *Spenser and the Faery Queen* (edited by Kirkland, 1847). *Holidays Abroad* (1849). *The Book of Home Beauty* (1852). *The Evening Book* (1852). *Garden Walks with the Poets* (1852). *A Book for the Home Circle; or, Familiar Thoughts on Various Topics, Literary, Moral, and Social* (1853). *The Helping Hand* (1853). *Autumn Hours* (1854). *Memoirs of Washington* (1857). *The School-Girl's Garland* (1864). *Patriotic Eloquence* (1866).

BIBLIOGRAPHY: Dondore, D. A., *The Prairie and the Making of Middle America: Four Centuries of Description* (1926). Keyes, L. C., "Caroline Matilda Kirkland: A Pioneer in American Realism" (Ph.D. diss., Harvard Univ., 1935). Osborne, W. S., *Caroline Matilda Kirkland* (1972). Poe, E. A., "The Literati of New York City," *Godey's Lady's Book* (August 1846). Riordan, D. G., "The Concept of Simplicity in the Works of Mrs. Caroline Matilda Kirkland" (Ph.D. diss., Univ. of North Carolina, 1973). Roberts, A. J., "The Letters of Caroline Matilda Kirkland" (Ph.D. diss., Univ. of Wisconsin, 1976).

For articles in reference works, see: *AA. CAL. DAB*, V, 2. *NAW* (article by L. C. Keyes). *NCAB*, 5.

Other references: *MichH* (Sept. 1956; March 1958; Dec. 1961).

AUDREY ROBERTS

Sarah Kemble Knight

B. *19 April 1666, Boston, Massachusetts; d. 25 Sept. 1727, New London, Connecticut*
D. *of Thomas and Elizabeth Trerice Kemble; m. Richard Knight, 1689*

When K. was born, her family had already been in New England for a generation. Her husband was by some accounts a shipmaster, though a recent study suggests that he may have been the Richard Knight listed in two records as a publican. Upon her father's death, K. inherited a house on Moon Street, where she maintained a large household, which included her mother, her daughter, and several lodgers, some of whom may have been relatives.

K. herself was active in the copying and witnessing of legal documents and in the settling of estates. She kept a shop in the Moon Street house and is said to have run a writing school, though this has not been verified.

In the fall and winter of 1704–05, in order to settle an estate for one of the relatives in her household, K. traveled on horseback from Boston to New York and back. She was the first woman to accomplish such a feat, securing guides and stopping at various post-houses, inns, and, occasionally, homes in the towns she passed through.

There remains no further record of Richard Knight after 1706. In 1713, when K.'s daughter married, K. sold the Boston house and moved to Norwich and New London, Connecticut. There she speculated in Indian lands, ran several farms, and kept a house of entertainment.

During the journey from Boston to New York, K. kept notes which upon her return she fashioned into a journal. At that time overland travel between the colonies was difficult; there were no main roads, and a traveler had to secure local guides to get from one town or posting place to another. The colonies were separate in government and customs; there were as yet no newspapers; it was only through letters or travelers' tales that colonists learned about events and customs elsewhere. K.'s racy narrative describes the difficulties of travel, the inconveniences of inns, and the people she met, ranging from the governor of Connecticut, with whom she supped, to the poor family who allowed her refuge in their drafty hut. Her perceptive, sharp wit spares no one, not even herself. The narrative is a series of episodes pulled together by the vitality and strength of character of its author.

Brief as it is, and though it remained in manuscript until 1825, the journal is a landmark in our literature for several reasons. Along with the journal of Samuel Sewall, it represents the lay view as opposed to that of the ministers, who until this time dominated American letters. As K.'s account rushes along, she displays several of the types of humor and characters that were to develop as typically American. The pompous judge making a fool of himself, the laconic master of understatement, the country "bumpkin" who later may be seen as Yankee Doodle, and a succession of other tobacco-chewing yokels. Her use of generic names for characters, such as "Bumpkin Simpers," "Joan Tawdry," and "Gaffer," perhaps based on a reading of *Pilgrim's Progress*, presages the use of stereotyped characters in the newspapers soon to be started in England

and America. In one passage where K. is riding at night, she imagines the towers of towns and palaces, displaying a longing for Europe which recurs in much of American literature through Henry James and later expatriates, and her descriptions of the terrors of night resemble the Gothic effects later used by Irving.

Her journal indicates throughout that its author was well-versed in the popular literature of the day. Its prose is interlaced with poems in a variety of current styles; in one poem she uses the kind of couplets in vogue in England but not in America at the time. Altogether her journal represents an early movement toward the satire and other forms that were used throughout the 18th c. and presents an unusual and vivid series of pictures of the ordinary and extraordinary people of New England.

WORKS: The Journals of Madam Knight, and Rev. Mr. Buckingham (1825). *The Private Journal of a Journey from Boston to New York in the Year 1704 Kept by Madam Knight* (1865).

BIBLIOGRAPHY: Freiberg, M., Introduction to *The Journal of Madam Knight* (1972). Stanford, A., "Images of Women in Early American Literature," in *What Manner of Woman*, Ed. M. Springer (1977). Winship, G. P., Introduction to *The Journal of Madam Knight* (1920, 1935).

For articles in reference works, see: *AA. DAB*, V, 2. *NAW* (article by M. Freiberg).

Other references: *Bostonian Society Publications* 9 (1912). *CLAJ* (March 1964; Dec. 1966). *PBSA* (First quarter, 1964).

ANN STANFORD

Martha Joanna Reade Nash Lamb

B. *12 Aug. 1826, Plainfield, Massachusetts; d. 2 Jan. 1893, New York City*
Wrote under: Aunt Mattie, Mrs. Martha J. Lamb
D. of Arvin and Lucinda Vinton Nash; m. Charles A. Lamb, 1852

L. began her career as a writer of children's stories and a romantic novel. It was, however, as a historian of the city of New York and as an editor

(1883–93) of the *Magazine of American History* that she did her most significant work.

L.'s major publication is her *History of the City of New York*, the first volume appearing in 1877, the second in 1880. The two comprise the history of New York from the era of Hudson's discovery to the inauguration of Washington. After L.'s death, Constance Cary Harrison contributed a brief supplementary volume to the history, *Externals of Modern New York* (1896).

L.'s perspective in the *History of the City of New York* is that of the narrative historian, and she concentrates particularly on political developments. In the Dutch era, she traces with acuity the internal conflicts, giving special stress to the role of Peter Stuyvesant. She discusses with sympathetic insight the efforts of the British to amalgamate peacefully the two communities in the colony of New York. In the 18th-c. history, L. particularly stresses the growing conflict with the British and the city's role in the Revolution and the new nation.

L. also gives some attention to the social history of New York, noting particularly the roles of the emerging major families and their interlocking interests. On the other hand, she does not attempt to deal in any depth with the city's economic development.

L.'s *The Homes of America* (1879) is an account of historic homes, primarily of political leaders, from the early 17th to the mid-19th centuries. For the 19th c., she included residences of artists and writers. The work was not a history of American architecture but rather a descriptive account, including biographical sketches and a number of brief family histories.

As editor of the *Magazine of American History*, L. contributed some fifty signed and many unsigned articles. Her *Wall Street in History* (1883) consists of material that first appeared in three issues (May–July 1883). The book is a lively, well-researched account of three stages of the history of the street: the early Dutch and English developments; its 18th-c. role as "seat of fashion, aristocracy and state government"; and its 19th-c. role as financial center. L.'s account is descriptive rather than analytical, and she deals in very general and positive terms with Wall Street's financial role.

L. also wrote fiction. Her novel *Spicy* (1873) is a romantic mystery, with the recent Chicago fire giving dramatic climax to the work. She also wrote several children's stories, generally moralistic, and edited such publications as *The Christmas Basket* (1882), a collection of poetry.

It was as a narrative historian that L. was most successful. She handled with clarity and balance the broad developments of public life. She had a keen eye for character, and she wrote with a dramatic flair of such events as the Zenger trial. Her style is somewhat stilted at times, but she wrote with ease. Though somewhat discursive and occasionally pre-occupied with minute detail, on the whole she developed forcefully and with balanced judgment the major political themes.

L. was a thorough if untrained researcher with a great interest in pri-mary sources. She utilized manuscript collections, public records, private letters, and personal interviews. Accordingly, her historical work has depth and solidity. She wrote primarily for an educated general public. In her *History of New York* she best achieved her goal of combining sound historical scholarship with popular appeal.

WORKS: *Laughing Kittie and Purring Kittie, with Other Little Folks at Robinwood* (1868). *The Playschool Stories for Little Folks* (1869). *Aunt Mattie's Library* (1870). *Drifting Goodward* (1870). *Fun and Profit* (1870). *Spicy* (1873). *History of the City of New York: Its Origin, Rise, and Progress* (2 vols., 1877, 1880). *The Homes of America* (1879). *The Christmas Owl: A Budget of Entertainment* (edited by Lamb, 1881). *The Christmas Basket: Holiday Entertainment* (edited by Lamb, 1882). *Snow and Sunshine: A Story for Boys and Girls* (1882). *Wall Street in History* (1883). *A Guide·for Strangers to General Grant's Tomb in Riverside Park* (1886). *Our Country Fifty Years Ago: Some Incidents in Connection with Lafayette's Visit* (1887). *The Washington Inauguration* (1889).

BIBLIOGRAPHY: Lyman, S. E., *Lady Historian: Martha Joanna Lamb* (1969).
For articles in reference works, see: *AA. AW. DAB*, V, 2. *NAW* (article by R. H. Robinson). *NCAB*, 1.
Other references: *Godey's Lady's Book* (Nov. 1887). *NYT* (3 Jan. 1893).

INZER BYERS

Rose Wilder Lane

B. 5 Dec. 1886, De Smet, South Dakota; d. 30 Oct. 1968, Danbury, Connecticut
D. of Almanzo and Laura Ingalls Wilder; m. Gillette Lane, 1909

Unconventional from the first, L. left her parents' Mansfield, Missouri, home to work as a telegraph operator for Western Union. She married a land speculator whose ne'er-do-well behavior soon forced L. to fend for herself as the first woman real-estate agent in California. She was a reporter for the San Francisco *Bulletin* from 1914 to 1918. Written during this period, and indicative of her admiration for American heroes, are *Henry Ford's Own Story* (1917) and *The Making of Herbert Hoover* (1920), both panegyrics to men she considered archetypally American in their resourcefulness and individualism. After formally divorcing her husband, L. worked for the American Red Cross during World War I, primarily in Russia, Turkey, and Albania. *The Peaks of Shala* (1923) is a travelogue of her adventures in Albania.

In the 1920s, her articles and short stories filled the most popular magazines and journals. In 1922, she received the second-place O. Henry best short story of the year award for "Innocence." "Yarbwoman" was included in O'Brien's *The Best Short Stories of 1927*, and her "Old Maid" was singled out for O. Henry honors again in 1933. L. became one of the highest-paid writers in the U.S. "Innocence" and "Yarbwoman" are both set among poor whites of the South. Ironically, L.'s two prize-winning stories have an atypically eerie air. The dark forces are eventually shown to be those cruel and ignorant aspects of human nature that come from within man himself, especially as he is limited by moribund social structures.

Her Ozark novels, *Hill Billy* (1925) and *Cindy* (1928), were followed by her pioneer novels, *Let the Hurricane Roar* (1933) and *Free Land* (1938). In *Let the Hurricane Roar* two young pioneers struggle with the most intolerable conditions of the Dakota frontier, finding at last a sort of sad strength in themselves, even after their most cherished illusions are gone. The novel celebrates the capacity of the individual pioneer. *Free Land* takes a sardonic view of the governmental scheme to settle the frontier by the free grant of land. L.'s portrait of foolish expectations is satirical, but tempered by sympathy for the real sufferings of the naive settlers.

In *Old Home Town* (1935), a collection of stories about women in a midwestern town, L. dissects small-town life. Convention, intolerance, and gossip force the various women characters into unhappy marriages, into shame at being old maids of twenty-six, and even into suicide and murder. In the most overtly feminist story, "Immoral Woman," the lovely and talented Mrs. Sims is unjustly driven from the town by her clod of a husband and by the townspeople, who are held in thrall by the meanness of their accepted mores. She becomes a liberated woman and an internationally famous designer.

Give Me Liberty (1936) began L.'s overtly political career, and her belletristic efforts correspondingly diminished. In *The Discovery of*

Freedom (1943), she maintains that the progress of human civilization is towards "individualistic libertarianism" (with emphasis on private ownership) and individual freedom from coercion by collective society. Her adamant refusal to support New Deal programs such as social security and her opposition to taxation led her into increasingly conservative political company.

L. was editor of the National Economic Council's *Review of Books* from 1945 to 1950, but after some of her more bitter political disputes, she retreated from the public arena, concerning herself with domestic arts, local politics, and behind-the-scenes encouragement of individualistic libertarianism. In 1965, *Woman's Day* magazine called L. out of retirement to serve as their war correspondent in Vietnam. She died suddenly of a heart attack just before a projected trip abroad in 1968.

L. was a woman of varied adventures and several careers, but the greatest proportion of her prolific literary production centered around intensely American life. She wrote in praise of the American capitalist and of the pioneer woman of the American West. In many ways her style is simple, but delightful in its factual detail and portraiture of life from a primarily feminine point of view.

L.'s thought and work resist traditional labels. Brilliant, adventurous, and self-sufficient, she was very opposed to the socialistic idealism that has been historically connected with revolutionaries of her type in America. She saw governmental authority and small-town propriety as abstractions that had no right to control the actual pragmatic course of real people's lives. This fierce elevation of the actual is the bedrock theme of her literary celebration of the quintessential American spirit.

WORKS: *Art Smith's Story* (1915). *Henry Ford's Own Story* (1917). *Diverging Roads* (1919). *White Shadows in the South Seas* (1919). *The Making of Herbert Hoover* (1920). *The Dancers of Shamahka* (1923). *The Peaks of Shala* (1923). *He Was a Man* (1925). *Hill Billy* (1925). *Cindy* (1928). *Let the Hurricane Roar* (1933). *Old Home Town* (1935). *Give Me Liberty* (1936). *Free Land* (1938). *The Discovery of Freedom* (1943). *Woman's Day Book of American Needlework* (1963). *The Lady and the Tycoon* (1973).

BIBLIOGRAPHY: MacBride, R., ed., *The Lady and the Tycoon: Letters of Rose Wilder Lane and Jasper Crane* (1973). MacBride, R., *Rose Wilder Lane: Her Story* (1977). Weaver, H., *Mainspring, Based on the Discovery of Freedom* (1947).

For articles in reference works, see: *20thCA. 20thCAS.*

Other references: *NewR* (24 April 1944).

L. W. KOENGETER

Susanne Katherina Knauth Langer

B. 20 Dec. 1895, New York City
Writes under: Susanne K. Langer
D. of Antonio and Else Uhlich Knauth; m. William L. Langer, 1921

L. received her B.A., M.A., and Ph.D. degrees all from Radcliffe College. She studied for a year (1921–22) at the University of Vienna. L. served as a tutor in philosophy at her alma mater from 1927 to 1942 and taught at the University of Delaware in 1943 and at Columbia University from 1945 to 1950. She was professor of philosophy at Connecticut College for Women from 1954 to 1962. She has been the recipient of numerous research grants and honorary degrees.

L. has two sons. She was divorced in 1942. She now lives in Olde Lyme, Connecticut.

In her first major work, *The Practice of Philosophy* (1930), L. introduces many of the themes that engage her later thinking. Intended as an introduction to philosophy, the book defines philosophy as the search for the logical connections among meanings and contrasts it with science, which seeks the empirical connections among facts. The study of symbolic logic, the logic of relations, is therefore an indispensable preliminary to the study of the more engrossing problems of metaphysics, ethics, and aesthetics.

In *An Introduction to Symbolic Logic* (1937), L. sets out at length the system whose value she had proposed in *The Practice of Philosophy*.

Philosophy in a New Key: A Study in the Symbols of Reason, Rite, and Art (1942) is the explicit exposition of the theory of symbolism which had only been indicated in her two earlier works. The "new key" is the focus upon symbol-using as the essence of such diverse enterprises as mathematics, science, psychology, and art. L. does not claim to have been the first to strike this new key, but only to have recognized it and to have shown how some of the chief questions of philosophy have been transposed into it.

In *Feeling and Form: A Theory of Art Developed from Philosophy in a New Key* (1953), L. applies the theory of art proposed in the earlier book to the various major art forms. The arts are alike in that they all create forms symbolic of human feeling; they differ in that each creates a different "primary illusion."

All of the essays in *Philosophical Sketches* (1962) are preliminary studies for a complete philosophy of mind, which is attempted in *Mind: An Essay on Human Feeling* (1967, 1972). Her purpose here is to understand "the nature and origin of the veritable gulf that divides human from animal mentality, in a perfectly continuous course of development of life on earth that has no breaks." She develops the thesis that the departure of human from animal mentality "is a vast and special evolution of feeling in the hominid stock," a development so great that it adds up to a qualitative difference that sets human nature apart from the rest of the animal kingdom.

The fault she finds in most previous theories of mind is that they borrow their images from physics, and such images are inadequate to the richness of mental phenomena. L., in contrast, turns to works of art, which, as "images of the forms of feeling," can more adequately reveal the psychic life.

L.'s own works exhibit what she finds in the course of evolution: a process of growth in which there is no break in continuity from the beginning to the present and yet in which there is considerable development and enrichment. Her writings are from the earliest characterized by an exceptional sensitivity to both art and the dynamisms of the subjective life; she has combined with this sensitivity a familiarity with a broad range of scientific research.

L. has acknowledged the influence on her ideas of such diverse thinkers as Alfred North Whitehead, Bertrand Russell, Ludwig Wittgenstein, Sigmund Freud, and Ernst Cassirer; however, she is an original thinker whose insights have transformed what she has received from others. She has continued to present her insights within the framework of an overall empiricist philosophy, but even those who question this framework find much to value in her work. L.'s sensitivity to the life of feeling and her refusal to consign art (and myth, and ritual) to a place of less importance than that held by the discursive enterprises assure her a place of lasting influence among philosophers, art theorists, and the lay public.

WORKS: *The Cruise of the Little Dipper, and Other Fairy Tales* (1923; rev. ed., 1963). *The Practice of Philosophy* (1930). *An Introduction to Symbolic Logic* (1937; rev. eds., 1953, 1967). *Philosophy in a New Key: A Study in the Symbolism of Reason, Rite, and Art* (1942; rev. eds., 1951, 1957).

Language and Myth by E. Cassirer (translated by Langer, 1946). *Structure, Method, and Meaning: Essays in Honor of Henry M. Sheffer* (edited by Langer, with P. Henle and H. M. Kallen, 1951). *Feeling and Form: A Theory of Art Developed from Philosophy in a New Key* (1953). *Problems of Art: Ten Philosophical Lectures* (1957). *Reflections on Art: A Source Book of Writings by Artists, Critics, and Philosophers* (edited by Langer, 1958). *Philosophical Sketches* (1962). *Mind: An Essay on Human Feeling* (2 vols.; 1967, 1972).

BIBLIOGRAPHY: Liddy, R. M., *Art and Feeling: An Analysis and Critique of the Philosophy of Art of Susanne Katherina Langer* (1970).

For articles in reference works, see: *CA*, 41–44 (1974). *CB* (Nov. 1963). *20thCAS*.

Other references: *BJA* 8 (Oct. 1968). *Gregorianum* 53 (1972). *JAAC* (14, 1955–56; 27, 1968; 28, 1970; 29, 1970; 30, 1972; 31, 1972). *Personalist* 46 (1965). *Process Studies* 4 (Fall 1974). *Review of Metaphysics* (7, 1954; 16, 1962–63; 23, 1970).

HELENE DWYER POLAND

Lucy Larcom

B. *5 March 1824, Beverly, Massachusetts; d. 17 April 1893, Boston, Massachusetts*
D. *of Benjamin and Lois Barrett Larcom*

L. grew up in the seaport town of Beverly. Her father was a retired shipmaster; her mother raised a family of ten children, of which L. was next to the youngest. The events and experiences of her early childhood are vividly described in her autobiography, *A New England Girlhood, Outlined from Memory* (1889).

This work remains one of our most important authentic descriptions of the daily experience of a young working woman in the 19th c. Remarkably unsentimental, L. captures the sights and sounds of a bustling port town and relates the reactions of a growing girl to her social environment.

When L. was nine years old, her father died; having no other means of support, her mother moved the family to the mill town of Lowell, Massachusetts, where even the children could earn enough to contribute to the family income. L.'s mother ran a boardinghouse for the factory girls, and L. herself went to work in the mills at the age of eleven, as a "bobbin girl," changing the bobbins on the spinning frames. The hours of work were from 5 A.M. to 7 P.M.

L. and her sister Emeline initiated a series of biweekly journals to which they and other women in their boardinghouse contributed creative pieces. L.'s own contributions were mainly poetical, following a bent she had developed in early childhood. By 1840 creative works of the mill women were being published in two literary magazines, the *Lowell Offering* and the *Operatives' Magazine*. In 1842 these merged as the *Lowell Offering*, edited by Harriet Farley and Harriot Curtiss. It continued until 1847 and at its height had a subscription list of four thousand. L. contributed regularly to this journal, which is now recognized as a unique literary expression of working-class women.

At age sixteen L. was transferred to the position of bookkeeper in the Lawrence Mills. There she had more time to study and to write. In 1846 L. moved with her sister Emeline's family to Illinois, where she graduated in 1852 from the Monticello Female Seminary in Alton. She then returned to the East and in 1854 began teaching at the Wheaton Seminary in Norton, Massachusettts. That year she published her first book, *Similitudes from the Ocean and the Prairie*, a series of prose parables, which she later dismissed as an immature work.

During this period she published poetry in newspapers and in the *Atlantic Monthly*. In 1862 she resigned her teaching position and in 1865 became, along with Gail Hamilton (Mary Abigail Dodge) and J. T. Trowbridge, an editor of *Our Young Folks*, a leading juvenile magazine. In 1868 she was named sole editor. L. never married, mainly because she wished to remain independent enough to pursue her career as a writer.

Her first collection of verse, *Poems* (1868), was reissued in 1885 in the popular "household edition." L.'s most important poetical work was *An Idyl of Work* (1875), a long poem in blank verse, which dealt with the Lowell factory women she had known in the 1840s.

L. edited several anthologies with her friend John Greenleaf Whittier. These included *Child Life* (1871), *Child Life in Prose* (1873), and *Songs of Three Centuries* (1875). These collections were all published under Whittier's name, but it is clear that she had the major hand in their creation from the fact that he split the royalties with her. In the preface to *Child Life in Prose*, Whittier acknowledges that L. did most of the work. Works by both L. and Whittier were included in these collections. She also herself compiled several popular books of collected poems.

L.'s reputation today rests not so much on the popular verse which brought her fame in her own day, but rather on the straightforward, unsentimental picture of her life and times she has given us in her prose works.

WORKS: *Similitudes from the Ocean and the Prairie* (1854). *Lottie's Thought-Book* (1858). *Ships in the Mist, and Other Stories* (1860). *Leila among the Mountains* (attributed to Larcom, 1861). *Breathings of a Better Life* (1866). *Poems* (1868). *Child Life* (edited by Larcom, with J. G. Whittier, 1871). *Child Life in Prose* (edited by Larcom, with J. G. Whittier, 1873). *Childhood Songs* (1875). *An Idyl of Work* (1875). *Songs of Three Centuries* (edited by Larcom, with J. G. Whittier, 1875). *Roadside Poems for Summer Travellers* (compiled by Larcom, 1876). *Hillside and Seaside in Poetry: A Companion to 'Roadside Poems'* (compiled by Larcom, 1877). *Snow Bloom, and Other Poems* (ca. 1880–82). *Wild Roses of Cape Ann, and Other Poems* (1881). *Wheaton Seminary: A Centennial Sketch* (1885). *The Cross and the Grail* (1887). *A New England Girlhood, Outlined from Memory* (1889). *Easter Gleams: Poems* (1890). *As It Is in Heaven* (1891). *At the Beautiful Gate, and Other Songs of Faith* (1892). *The Unseen Friend* (1892). *Lucy Larcom: Life, Letters, and Diary* (Ed. D. D. Addison, 1894). *Beckonings from Every Day: A Calendar of Thought* (1895). *Letters of Lucy Larcom to the Whittiers* (Ed. G. F. Shepard, 1930).

The papers of Lucy Larcom are at the Essex Institute, James Duncan Phillips Library, Salem, Massachusetts.

BIBLIOGRAPHY: Eisler, B., *The Lowell Offering* (1971). Robinson, H. H., *Loom and Spindle; or, Life among the Mill Girls* (1898). Ward, S. H., ed., *The Rushlight, Special Number in Memory of L. L.* (1894). Westbrook, P. D., *Acres of Flint, Writers of Rural New England 1870–1900* (1951).

For articles in reference works, see: *AA. AW. DAB*, V, 2. *FPA. NCAB*, 1. *NAW* (article by D. Baldwin).

Other references: *Women's Studies* I (1973).

JOSEPHINE DONOVAN

Elizabeth Wormeley Latimer

B. 26 July 1822, London, England; d. 4 Jan. 1904, Baltimore, Maryland
Wrote under: Elizabeth W. Latimer, Elizabeth Wormeley
D. of Ralph Randolph and Caroline Preble Wormeley; m. Randolph Brandt
Latimer, 1856

L.'s family roots were planted in three soils: her father, although raised in England and a rear admiral in the British Navy, was of old-landed Virginia stock; her mother was the daughter of an East-India merchant of Boston. In her youth, L. lived in London, Paris, Boston, Newport, and Virginia. In London and Paris she attended the funeral of William IV and the reburial of Napoleon, saw Queen Victoria in coronation regalia, met William M. Thackeray, and attended Louis Philippe's balls. In Boston, in 1842, she met George Ticknor, William H. Prescott, and Julia Ward Howe, who encouraged her to write. Her first publication was a translation of a Mexican poem for the appendix of Prescott's *History of the Conquest of Mexico*.

In 1848, after witnessing the revolution in Paris and Chartist demonstrations in London, the Wormeley family moved back to New England. L. published several novels before marrying and moving to Maryland. She then spent twenty years rearing children and, during the Civil War, caring for wounded soldiers. Although her eyes were weak, she read assiduously and, during the last thirty years of her life, she published prolifically: novels, magazine articles, translations from French and Italian, and popular European histories that went through many editions.

L.'s best works are her histories, anecdotal in style. As a compiler and editor, she read copiously from magazines, newspapers, books, and private papers, then presented her information in lively, compact, confident prose. She did not claim to be a historian, but stated in her prefaces that she concentrated on the historical figures who interested her. She was fascinated by the adventures of royalty, explorers, and military people. Occasionally she inserted information from her family's experiences. In *France in the Nineteenth Century* (1892), for example, she wrote from personal observation, and in *Europe in Africa in the Nineteenth Century* (1898), L. mentioned some personal letters she had received from Liberians in 1854. In all the histories, one senses her desire to keep abreast of events in the world and, at the century's end, to sum up historic achievements.

Some of her novels are quite bad. *Salvage* (1880), for example, is largely a diatribe against easy divorce and in favor of long-suffering, dutiful love, especially of a wife towards her husband. The plot is wholly predictable, and the characters are flat.

Our Cousin Veronica (1855) is probably L.'s best novel. Its vividness of action and description derives from L.'s own experience in England and Virginia. At the novel's end, the female narrator marries a slave owner only after a serious discussion of abolition. He opposes freeing his slaves outright, for they would be harassed in their own state and unprotected if they moved north. Quoting Wilberforce, she impresses her husband with the responsibility they have as masters, not just for their slaves' physical needs, but for their souls. Husband and wife both hope for a general emancipation and in the meantime free and aid those of their slaves who are willing to emigrate to Liberia.

In her novels, L. is strongest when she is closest to historical anecdote. Her histories are valuable for the interest she generates in people and for her amassing of historic information often inaccessible to others.

WORKS: *Forest Hill: A Tale of Social Life in 1830–31* (1846). *Amabel: A Family History* (1853). *Our Cousin Veronica; or, Scenes and Adventures over the Blue Ridge* (1855). *Madame Gosselin* by L. Ulbach (translated by Latimer, 1878). *Recollections of Ralph Randolph Wormeley, Rear Admiral, R.N.; Written Down by His Three Daughters* (with A. R. W. Curtis, 1879). *Salvage* (1880). *My Wife and My Wife's Sister* (1881). *Princess Amelie: A Fragment of Autobiography* (1883). *Familiar Talks on Some of Shakespeare's Comedies* (1886). *The Steel Hammer: A Novel* by L. Ulbach (translated by Latimer, 1888). *For Fifteen Years: A Sequel to The Steel Hammer* by L. Ulbach (translated by Latimer, 1888). *History of the People of Israel* by E. Renan (translated by Latimer, with J. H. Allen, 1888–96). *A Chain of Errors* (1890). *Nanon* by G. Sand (translated by Latimer, 1890). *France in the Nineteenth Century, 1830–1890* (1892). *Russia and Turkey in the Nineteenth Century* (1893). *England in the Nineteenth Century* (1894). *My Scrap-book of the French Revolution* (edited by Latimer, 1894). *Italy in the Nineteenth Century and the Making of Austro-Hungary and Germany* (1896). *Spain in the Nineteenth Century* (1897). *Europe in Africa in the Nineteenth Century* (1898). *Judea from Cyrus to Titus, 537 B.C.–70 A.D.* (1899). *The Last Years of the Nineteenth Century* (1900). *The Italian Republics* by J. C. L. de Sismondi (translated by Latimer, 1901). *The Love Letters of Victor Hugo, 1820–1822* (translated by Latimer, 1901). *Men and Cities of Italy* (1901). *The Prince Incognito* (1902). *Talks of Napoleon at St. Helena with Gen. Baron Gourgaud, Together with the Journal Kept by Gourgaud on Their Journey from Waterloo to St. Helena* by G. Gourgaud (translated by Latimer, 1903).

BIBLIOGRAPHY: Hayden, H. E., *Virginia Genealogies* (1891). Logan, M. S., *The Part Taken by Women in American History* (1912). Preble, G. H., *Genealogical Sketch of the First Three Generations of Prebles in America* (1868).

For articles in reference works, see: *AA. AW. A Critical Dictionary of English Literature and British and American Authors*, S. A. Alibone (1872). *A Dictionary of American Authors*, Ed. O. F. Adams (1897). *DAB*, VI. *Index to Women of the World, from Ancient to Modern Times: Biographies and Portraits*, Ed. N. D. Ireland (1970). *NCAB*, 9.

Other references: Baltimore *American* (3, 4, 7 Jan. 1904). Baltimore *Sun* (4, 5 Jan. 1904). *Dial* (1 Feb. 1904). *Harper's* (Feb. 1856). London *Athenaeum* (1853). London *Literary Gazette* (1846). New England *Historical and Genealogical Register* (Oct. 1868). *NYT* (5 Jan. 1904). *Putnam's* (Feb. 1856).

KAREN B. STEELE

Emma Lazarus

B. *22 July 1849, New York City; d. 19 Nov. 1887, New York City*
D. *of Moses and Esther Nathan Lazarus*

L. was privately educated and revealed an early gift for poetry and languages. Although the family was part of the cultivated and fashionable New York society—her father was a wealthy industrialist—L. had little contact with literary groups until her twenties, when she met Ralph Waldo Emerson, who served as a sometime literary mentor. Trips to Europe brought her into contact with English writers and thinkers.

L.'s *Poems and Translations* (1867), published when she was just eighteen, contains translations of Hugo, Dumas, Schiller, and Heine, as well as original poems dealing with conventionally romantic subjects. The title poem in *Admetus, and Other Poems* (1871), dedicated to Emerson, retells in blank verse the myth of Alcestis, whose strength and courage saved her husband from death. In L.'s version, the heroic willingness of Alcestis to sacrifice herself as the substitute the Fates had demanded becomes the crucial incident, and the portrait is a significant advance in the depiction of women in romantic poetry. In another poem, "Epochs," L. personifies work as a woman. The maturity of L.'s thinking is reflected in "Heroes," which stresses the problems of the aftermath of war, rather than the presumed glory of the battlefield.

L.'s studies led her to an interest in Goethe; the novel *Alide* (1874) is based on an incident in his life. Turgenev praised the work, which considers the artist's quandary in choosing between ordinary life and the demands of his art.

Poems and Translations of Heinrich Heine (1881) is L.'s major achievement as a translator; in many instances her rendition is the definitive English version still in use today. Although translations of Heine's poems were among her earliest works, this volume contains for the first time Heine's poems on specifically Jewish subjects, on which L. worked in the 1870s. Particularly effective is her translation of the ironic "Donna Clara," in which the insouciant charm of the ballad form clashes with the mock revenge against the rabid anti-Semite.

The pogroms in Russia and the mass immigration of refugees to the U.S. mobilized L.'s energetic support of her people. *Songs of a Semite* (1882) was issued in an inexpensive edition so that it might reach as wide an audience as possible. Along with ballads, sonnets, and translations of Hebrew poets, it contains one of her finest works, *The Dance to Death*. In this verse drama L. tells the tragic events of a pogrom in the 14th c., and portrays a stirring affirmation of the life and spirit of the persecuted people: "Even as we die in honor, from our death / Shall bloom a myriad of heroic lives, / Brave through our bright example, virtuous / Lest our great memory fall in disrepute."

L. also relied on prose to explain the position of the Jewish people. While only a few selections are available in book form, these essays represent one of L.'s greatest accomplishments, explaining in sharp, incisive fashion the attainments of the Jewish people, their heroics and their contributions to the contemporary world, and—even at this early date—calling for the formation of a Jewish state.

L.'s essays on other topics are equally valuable, although they, too, are buried in the periodicals of the day. Her strong humanitarian spirit led her to readings in socialism, and a visit to William Morris's workshops in England is described in warm, affectionate terms. An essay on Longfellow, while pointing out the flaws in his work, calls for a specifically American literature, rather than one dependent on the English tradition.

The last few years of L.'s short life were wracked by cancer; she nonetheless produced *By the Waters of Babylon* (1887), a series of prose poems using the long, sweeping line reminiscent of Walt Whitman and full of prophetic fire.

L.'s fame today rests largely on the sonnet "The New Colossus," which was written to raise money for a base for the Statue of Liberty, and which, as James Russell Lowell said, gave it its spiritual basis. But consideration of her entire literary output leads to a more far-reaching appreciation. From a shy, sensitive girl writing on romantic topics in a stilted diction, she became a mature artist, an impassioned supporter of her people, of the downtrodden of all nations, and of her own country and its literary accomplishments.

WORKS: *Poems and Translations* (1867). *Admetus, and Other Poems* (1871). *Alide* (1874). *The Spagnoletto: a Drama in Verse* (1876). *Poems and Translations of Heinrich Heine* (1881). *Songs of a Semite* (1882). *By the Waters of Babylon* (1887). *The Poems of Emma Lazarus* (2 vols., 1889). *The Letters of Emma Lazarus, 1868–1885* (Ed. M. U. Schappes, 1949). *Emma Lazarus: Selections from Her Poetry and Prose* (Ed. M. U. Schappes, 3rd ed., 1967).

BIBLIOGRAPHY: Baym, M. I., *A Neglected Translator of Italian Poetry: Emma Lazarus* (1956). Harap, L., *The Image of the Jew in American Literature* (1974). Lazarus, J., Introduction to *The Poems of Emma Lazarus* (1889). Merriam, E., *Emma Lazarus* (1956). Rusk, R., *Letters of Emma Lazarus in the Columbia University Library* (1939).

For articles in reference works, see: *AA. AW. DAB*, IV, 1. *NAW* (article by S. J. Hurwitz). *NCAB*, 3.

Other references: *Poet Lore* (1893). *Publications of the American Jewish Historical Society* (Sept. 1952; June 1956).

CAROL B. SCHOEN

Ursula K. LeGuin

B. 21 Oct. 1929, Berkeley, California
D. of Alfred L. and Theodora K. Kroeber; m. Charles A. LeGuin, 1953

L. grew up in a stimulating environment; her father was an anthropologist and her mother, a writer. She studied at Radcliffe College and Columbia University. During a Fulbright year in France (1953) she married a historian. L. lives with him in Portland, Oregon; they have three children. L. is a member of Phi Beta Kappa and Science Fiction Writers of America.

L.'s first science-fiction novels were *Rocannon's World* (1966), *Planet of Exile* (1966), and *City of Illusions* (1967). They show an interest in anthropology and even in e.s.p., rather than in technology, which places them in the "New Wave" of science fiction. At the same time, their magical, romantic tone suggests a hint of "Sword and Sorcery."

These novels were followed by L.'s most unified work, the Earthsea trilogy, in which basic human problems are discussed in fairy-tale terms, complete with wizards and dragons. In *A Wizard of Earthsea* (1968), which won the Boston *Globe* Horn Book Award for excellence, she stresses the importance of coming to grips with the evil in one's own personality. In *The Tombs of Atuan* (1971), she shows a girl coming to trust a man whom she had seen as an intruder in her feminine world. And in *The Farthest Shore* (1972), which won the National Book Award for Children's Literature, she presents the fact that life is meaningless if one refuses to face the reality of death. But the relation of form to content is not that of the sugar helping the medicine go down: they are the same thing.

L. describes herself at times as a Taoist. This means that she feels that wholeness is reached through a dynamic balance of opposites. This philosophy is expressed most directly in *The Left Hand of Darkness* (1969), which won the Hugo and Nebula awards. In this novel the imaginary planet Gethen is peopled by "androgynes," who have a biologically regulated, almost guilt-free sex life and do not, as yet, wage war. L.'s aim is to show what it means to be simply human, working one's way through conflicts that are not based on sex roles. It is interesting to see that we are still left with love and faith, disappointment and betrayal, face saving, incest, religion, politics, and the weather.

Many of L.'s novels and short stories have won Hugo and Nebula awards. "The Word for World Is Forest" (1972), combines insight into dream states with a scathing satire on American involvement in Vietnam. *The Dispossessed* (1974) shows a physicist from an anarchist moon colony who is obliged to go to the capitalist mother planet in order to be able to continue his research. Finally he returns to his own society in the hopes of leading it back to its original free principles. *The New Atlantis* (1975), in contrast, depicts a repressive, bureaucratic U.S., which is destroyed by a visionary cataclysm out of Edgar Cayce. L. calls the stories in *The Wind's Twelve Quarters* (1975) "psychomyths."

Some of her most recent publications have been much closer to mainstream literature. *Orsinian Tales* (1976), a collection of stories about an imaginary East European country, is quite realistic. *Very Far Away from Anywhere Else* (1976), a novella for young adults, describes without any fantasy the pressures brought to bear on sensitive young Americans to force them into conformity.

On the whole, L. has shown a preference for science fiction and fantasy over the techniques of the mainstream novel. She has great faith in the creative imagination and wants it to be free; science fiction and fantasy give her the scope for this. Probably it is because she allows so much free play to the imagination that she is able to be concerned with moral issues without appearing moralistic and to discuss politics without being forced into other people's molds. Liberty, in short, is her watchword.

WORKS: Planet of Exile (1966). *Rocannon's World* (1966). *City of Illusions* (1967). *A Wizard of Earthsea* (1968). *The Left Hand of Darkness* (1969). *The Tombs of Atuan* (1971). *The Lathe of Heaven* (1971). *The Farthest Shore* (1972). *From Elfland to Poughkeepsie* (1973). *The Dispossessed* (1974). *Dreams Must Explain Themselves* (1975). *The New Atlantis* (1975). *Wild Angels* (1975). *The Wind's Twelve Quarters* (1975). *Orsinian Tales* (1976). *Very Far Away from Anywhere Else* (1976). *The Water Is Wide* (1976). *The Word for World Is Forest* (1976). *Leese Webster* (1979). *Malafrena* (1979). *The Language of the Night* (1979). *The Beginning Place* (1980). *Hard Words, and Other Poems* (1981).

BIBLIOGRAPHY: Bucknall, B., *Ursula K. LeGuin* (1981). LeGuin, U., "Is Gender Necessary?" in *Aurora, beyond Equality*, Eds. V. N. McIntyre and S. J. Anderson (1976). Scholes, R., "The Good Witch of the West," in *Structural Fabulation: An Essay on Fiction of the Future* (1975). Scholes, R., and E. S. Rabkin, "The Left Hand of Darkness," in *Science Fiction: History, Science, Vision* (1977). Slusser, G. E., *The Farthest Shores of Ursula LeGuin* (1976).

For articles in reference works, see: *CA*, 21–22 (1969).

Other references: *Extrapolation* (Dec. 1976). *Foundation* (July 1973). *QJLC* (April 1975). *RQ* (Feb. 1972). *SFS* (1, 1974; 2, 1975; 4, 1977).

BARBARA J. BUCKNALL

Madeleine L'Engle

B. 29 Nov. 1918, New York City
D. of Charles Wadsworth and Madeleine Barnett Camp; m. Hugh
Franklin, 1946

The only child of a foreign correspondent, playwright, and critic (her father) and a pianist (her mother), L. led a lonely, isolated city life until she was twelve, occupying her time with writing, drawing, and playing the piano. When her family moved to Europe, L. was put in an austere and strict English boarding school in Switzerland, where she learned to withdraw into the world of the imagination for solitude. After graduating from Smith College with honors, she published some magazine articles and then returned to New York City to work in the theater, taking the family name of L'Engle. After her marriage to an actor, L. gave up her stage career permanently for writing. Now parents (of three children) and grandparents, the Franklins live in an apartment in New York City in the winter and spend their summers in Connecticut at their two-hundred-year-old farmhouse.

L.'s earlier works, intended for adults, feature adolescent girls and grew out of her life as a child in New York City, in boarding schools, and later in the theater. Some of these early novels were rewritten for young people in the 1960s. Sensitive and perceptive, these books are important in showing the development of the author's style and philosophy.

The highly praised, family-centered fantasy *A Wrinkle in Time* (1962) was rejected by several publishers because it was so unusual for a children's book. It combines comedy and deep seriousness for exciting reading even though it suffers from a lack of unity and an overload of ideas. Adolescent Meg Murry "tesseracts"—takes a wrinkle in time—to go into space to rescue her scientist father from It, a disembodied brain. *A Wrinkle in Time* won the Newbery Medal. The complex and highly philosophical *A Wind in the Door* (1973) repeats the theme of the power of love with Meg rescuing her brother Charles Wallace. Although the highly imaginative and innovative *Wrinkle* has received the most critical acclaim, three later books about the conflict of good and bad (*The Arm* of the Starfish, 1965; *The Young Unicorns*, 1968; and *Dragons in the Waters*, 1976) are less didactic and contrived.

The witty verse-drama, *The Journey with Jonah* (1967), a retelling of the biblical story, stands out among the versatile L.'s other writings, as does her 1969 collection of intense, personal lyrics reflecting her experience and observation of life. Her autobiographical works for adults, *A Circle of Quiet* (1972), *The Summer of the Great-Grandmother* (1974), and *The Irrational Season* (1977), are not only thought-provoking and compelling as literature, they are essential for an understanding of her motivations and objectives as a writer.

Recurring themes in L.'s work are the conflict between good and evil and the problem of distinguishing one from the other, the nature of God, the dangers of conformity, and the necessity for giving love. A bold writer who dares to strike out in new directions and to challenge her readers, she obviously takes young people very seriously and regards them as being as worthy of intellectual stimulation as adults. In spite of her over-concern with ideas and her at-times uncontrolled virtuosity, L.'s ability to tell a good story has earned her a number of awards. She is regarded as one of today's outstanding writers for children and young people.

WORKS: *18 Washington Square* (1945). *The Small Rain* (1945). *Ilsa* (1946). *And Both Were Young* (1949). *Camilla Dickinson* (1951). *A Winter's Love* (1957). *Meet the Austins* (1960). *A Wrinkle in Time* (1962). *The Moon by Night* (1963). *The Twenty-four Days before Christmas* (1964). *The Arm of the Starfish* (1965). *Camilla* (1965). *The Love Letters* (1966). *The Journey with Jonah* (1967). *Prelude* (1968). *The Young Unicorns* (1968). *Dance in the Desert* (1969). *Lines Scribbled on an Envelope, and Other Poems* (1969). *The Other Side of the Sun* (1971). *A Circle of Quiet* (1972). *A Wind in the Door* (1973). *Everyday Prayers* (1974). *Prayers for Sunday* (1974). *The Summer of the Great-Grandmother* (1974). *Dragons in the Waters* (1976). *The Irrational Season* (1977). *A Swiftly Tilting Planet* (1978).

BIBLIOGRAPHY: Townsend, J. R., *A Sense of Story* (1971).

For articles in reference works, see: *CA*, 1–4 (1967). *More Books by More People*, L. B. Hopkins (1974). *More Junior Authors*, Ed. M. Fuller (1963). *Newbery and Caldecott Medal Books, 1956–1965*, Ed. L. Kingman (1965). *Something about the Author*, Ed. A. Commire (1971).

Other references: *Language Arts* 54 (1977).

ALETHEA K. HELBIG

Miriam Florence Folline Leslie

B. 5 June 1836, New Orleans, Louisiana; d. 18 Sept. 1914
Wrote under: Frank Leslie, Miriam Florence Folline Leslie, Miriam F. Squier
D. of Charles Follin and Susan Danforth; m. David Charles Peacock, 1854;
  m. Ephraim George Squier, 1856; m. Frank Leslie, 1873; m. William C.
  Kingsbury Wilde, 1891

L. changed her name, birth date, and the details of her parentage to suit her altered mood or circumstance. Although they probably never married, L.'s parents lived together as man and wife, and Susan used the Follin name. L. was educated at home by her father. The intellectual skills she honed at this time were matched by her seductive skills. Her first marriage, a shotgun marriage to a jeweler's assistant, was annulled after two years. L. then began a stage career, traveling with actress Lola Montez as her sister Minnie.

L. gave up acting in 1857 to marry Squier, an amateur archeologist. With him, she published a Spanish newspaper, *Noticias de Neuva York.* Through him, she met Frank Leslie, whom she married after divorcing Squier. Head of a successful publishing house, Leslie made L. the editor of his *Lady's Magazine.* L. also worked on *Frank Leslie's Chimney Corner* and *Frank Leslie's Lady's Journal,* and some said she was the power behind the Leslie throne. Financial mismanagement and the publisher's 1880 death nearly destroyed the business, but L. was a good manager and editor with sound news judgment and the ability to gauge the public's interests. Her decision to reduce the number of Leslie magazines and to concentrate on *Frank Leslie's Popular Monthly* displayed sound business sense.

L. also had a flair for personal publicity. She changed her name to Frank Leslie and lived extravagantly. Her every move made news. Her marriage to the brother of Oscar Wilde, sixteen years her junior, ended when she divorced him in 1893.

Tired of romance and work, L. sailed for Europe, leaving her publishing house in control of a syndicate. The group mismanaged the business, and L. was called home in 1898. Again she changed the Leslie fortunes;

and again she changed her name, to the Baroness de Bazus, after doubtful Huguenot ancestors. L. sold her business in 1903 for a half-million dollars. When she died, L. left nearly one million dollars to Carrie Chapman Catt, the suffrage leader, to mount the successful campaign for woman suffrage.

During the course of her colorful career, L. produced not only newspapers, but also newpaper columns and several books. She even wrote a play. *The Froth of Society*, L.'s translation of Dumas's *Demi-Monde*, opened in 1893 to terrible reviews. L.'s was the third adaptation of the work to be presented on the New York stage, and she had taken considerable liberties with the original play.

L.'s books of opinion and advice—*Rents in Our Robes* (1888), *Are Men Gay Deceivers?* (1893), and *A Social Mirage* (1899)—deal with essentially female interests: love, beauty, marriage, and sex. Dress is discussed extensively, L. believing that "fashion is not society—it is its genius."

The triumvirate of beauty, love, and fashion that L. said should motivate other women as it had motivated her is most evident in *Beautiful Woman of Twelve Epochs* (1890). This lavishly illustrated book begins with a picture of L. It describes, in flowery language, such generic females as the druidess, the Puritan maiden, and the Saxon maid, admiring them more for how they looked and who they loved than for what they did.

Written from the point of view of a grande dame, *California: A Pleasure Trip from Gotham to the Golden Gate* (1877) betrays intellectual snobbery and racial and regional elitism. The book, however, does present some graphic sketches of the West in 1877, and it excels in its portraiture, providing the reader with insights about Mormon women, American Indians, frontiersmen, Chinese immigrants, and especially about L. herself.

Rents in Our Robes warns women not to compete overzealously with men, not to become masculine, and *California* constantly alludes to the "feeble female mind." This attitude seems like a contradiction from the one woman of her time to run, and to run successfully, a major publishing house.

WORKS: *Travels in Central America* by A. Morelet (translated by Leslie, 1871). *California: A Pleasure Trip from Gotham to the Golden Gate* (1877). *Rents in Our Robes* (1888). *Beautiful Women of Twelve Epochs* (1890). *Are Men Gay Deceivers?* (1893). *A Social Mirage* (1899).

BIBLIOGRAPHY: Bird, C., *Enterprising Women* (1976). Ross, I., *Charmers and Cranks* (1965). Stern, M., *Purple Passage: The Life of Mrs. Frank Leslie* (1971).

For articles in reference works, see: *AA. DAB*, VI. 1. *NAW* (article by M. B. Stern). *NCAB*, 25.

Other references: Nevada *Daily Territorial Enterprise* (14 July 1878).

LYNNE MASEL-WALTERS

Meridel Le Sueur

B. 22 Feb. 1900, Murray, Iowa
D. of Marian Lucy Wharton Le Sueur and Winston Wharton

L.'s life and work are rooted in midwestern culture; she has often been referred to as the "Voice of the Prairie." Her mother was a militant feminist; her stepfather, Arthur Le Sueur, was a socialist lawyer. L.'s life-long association with artists of the radical left, Wobblies, Marxists, and prairie populists provides the rich backdrop for over fifty prolific years of prose, poetry, journalism, history, and philosophical writing.

L.'s social writing began during her teen-age years. In 1927, her short story, "Afternoon," was published in the *Dial* literary journal. During the 1930s, L. was a prominent figure on the "literary left"—writing and advocating a revolutionary aesthetic based on change in form, style, and content. L.'s work appeared in such varied journals and publications as the *Daily Worker, Partisan Review, New Masses, American Mercury, Pagany, Scribner's,* and the *Anvil.*

Salute to Spring (1940), a collection of L.'s short stories, reflects her deep commitment to the political struggles of the Depression, and the effects of the period's social trauma, especially on women, poor workers, and farmers in the Midwest. Included in the collection is perhaps her finest short story, "Annunciation." Celebrating the creative force, L. shares the intense feelings of an expectant mother as she meditates on her pregnancy and the impending birth. Speaking to the unknown child within her, the woman seeks to explain the world into which the child will be born. Rich in organic and transcendental imagery, "Annunciation" is representative of both the subject matter and style for which L. would become known. L. always sought to create outside the narrative form. "Annunciation" demonstrates her early success in creating a literary "moment" or reflection that stylistically integrates prose and poetry.

North Star Country (1945) is a lyrical history of the northern Midwest. Rich in the language of the common man and woman, the book is a unique document for the folklorist. Early criticism rejected the book's rich oral data base, but contemporary historians have looked more appreciatively on the original oral and written material.

The McCarthy era was particularly harsh on L. Her literary outlet continued through such radical journals as *Masses and Mainstream*, but she was excluded from a wider audience through an informal blacklist. She turned to writing children's stories, primarily historical treatments of American cultural myths and heroes: Johnny Appleseed, Davey Crockett, Abraham Lincoln, and Nancy Hanks Lincoln. She also wrote a delightful cross-cultural book for children about an Indian and a white boy, *Sparrow Hawk* (1950).

In addition to the reissuing of many of her works, L. published two new collections in the 1970s. One, *Rites of Ancient Ripening* (1975), is a collection of poetry which reflects her militant feminism, and in which she articulates her Indian philosophy. In *Rites*, the mature writer emerges, integrating rhythms and imagery of the rich plurality of American culture.

The Girl, a novel written in 1939, was not published until 1978. Here L. sensitively and brilliantly portrays the "girl" in all of us. *The Girl* has a unique and powerful style. The rhythm of a woman's culture is shown in patterns rather than through narrative development. The girl is not a heroine so much as a counterpoint to the world through which she moves.

L.'s journals (over 125 volumes) are yet to be published. They contain L.'s original contribution to American political philosophy. Students of indigenous American Marxist-Anarchism, American Indian philosophies, radical feminism, and the aesthetics of the left will find the journals a rich mine for future inquiry.

WORKS: *Annunciation* (1935). *Worker Writers* (193?). *Salute to Spring* (1940). *North Star Country* (1945). *Little Brother of the Wilderness: The Story of Johnny Appleseed* (1947). *Nancy Hanks of Wilderness Road* (1949). *Sparrow Hawk* (1950). *Chanticleer of Wilderness Road: A Story of Davey Crockett* (1951). *The River Road: A Story of Abraham Lincoln* (1954). *Crusaders* (1955). *Corn Village* (1970). *Conquistadors* (1973). *The Mound Builders* (1974). *Rites of Ancient Ripening* (Ed. M. E. Shaw, 1975). *Harvest: Collected Stories* (1977). *Song for My Time* (1977). *The Girl* (1978). *Women on the Bread Lines* (1978). *Ripening: Selected Work, 1927–1980* (1982).

BIBLIOGRAPHY: Halpert, S., and R. Johns, eds., *A Return to Pagany 1929–32* (1969). Hart, H., ed., *American Writers' Congress* (1935). Yount, N. J.,

" 'America: Song We Sang without Knowing—' Meridel Le Sueur's America" (Ph.D. diss., Univ. of Minnesota, 1978).

For articles in reference works, see: *CA*, 49–52 (1975). *Minnesota Writers,* Ed. C. N. Richards (ca. 1961). *More Junior Authors*, Ed. M. Fuller (1963).

Other references: Minnesota *Daily* (19 Nov. 1973). Minnesota *Leader* (10 Feb. 1975). *Moons and Lion Tailes* 11 (1976). *MS* (Aug. 1975). *North Country Anvil* (Feb.–March 1974; June–July 1977). *Sentinel* (28 Nov. 1954).

NEALA YOUNT SCHLEUNING

Denise Levertov

B. *24 Oct. 1923, Essex, England*
D. *of Paul Philip and Beatrice Spooner-Jones Levertoff; m. Mitchell*
  Goodman, 1947

L. grew up in Ilford, Essex, England. The younger of two daughters of a Welsh mother and Russian Jewish father, who became a Church of England clergyman, L. was educated chiefly at home by her mother, the BBC Schools Programs, and private tutors for French, art, and piano. She became a nurse in World War II, married writer Mitchell Goodman in 1947 (she had one son and was later divorced), emigrated to the U.S. in 1948, and was naturalized a U.S. citizen in 1955. L. has taught at several American universities. She is currently professor of English at Tufts University and has also served as poetry editor of the *Nation*. L. has long been a political activist, especially against the Vietnam War, and has given antiwar readings and helped in student demonstrations from Maryland and Massachusetts to California. Her distinctions and awards are many.

L.'s eleven major books of poetry, published between 1946 and 1975, show consistency of theme, tone, and technical control, with only moderate changes in emphasis caused by increasing maturity and increasing concern with social justice. Her mood is intense, ranging from tenderness to ebullience or outrage. Her subject matter is feminine without being feminist, and ranges from the smallest sensory or personal detail of domestic life to international social and military atrocities, especially those which involve children.

Many of the poems concern the creative process. L.'s technique is determined by the strongly emotional impulses which generate her poems. She writes in the rhythms of speech, often excited, impulsive speech, and in open forms which often reflect physical movement. L. writes with great attention to accurate sensory detail, is very sparing in her use of prose connective tissue, and uses metaphor and allusion moderately. She employs a significant amount of direct, emotionally charged statement, which tends to make the meanings of her poems more linear than multilevel, more explicit than mysterious. At her most successful, the poem is a single swift stab of experience which implies felt idea; at her least successful (most often in the political poems), she becomes sentimental and expository.

L.'s movement from the first poems to the most recent seems to be toward a larger proportion of ideological poems in a reflective or angry mood and a smaller proportion of poems expressing joy in terms of physical sensation. More typical of her earlier poems are "One A.M.," "The Curve," and "Jacob's Ladder." More typical of her later poems are "Conversation in Moscow," "Bus," and "The Distance."

L.'s prose analyses of her own creative process (many of them collected in *The Poet in the World*, 1973) consistently explain what her poems demonstrate: a reverence for and cultivation of the initial subconscious emotional impulse and a rhythm dependent on "the cadence of the thinking-feeling process." Though L. has often been classified with Charles Olson and the Projectivist or Black Mountain poets, she partly rejects that classification because she has "never fully gone along with Charles Olson's idea of the use of the breath."

L. also favors a "semiconscious" creation of metaphor from literal details and a use of diction and reference which achieves "a fairly constant balance between the aesthetic and humane needs" of the writer and her readers, that is, a style neither "elitist" nor "popular." In other words, L. believes that "a poem *is* a sonic, sensuous event and not a statement or a string of ideas." Her best poems are such events, as is "The Curve," from *Relearning the Alphabet* (1970), in which L. describes a literal walk along a railroad track: "Along the tracks / counting / always the right foot awarded / the tie to step on / the left stumbling all the time in cinders . . ." By means of sequence, selection of detail, and rhythm, she makes the experience represent not only the faith-doubt and hope-surprise inherent in taking such a walk, but in discovering even wider universal meanings or creating a poem as well.

WORKS: *The Double Image* (1946). *Here and Now* (1957). *5 Poems* (1958).

Overland to the Islands (1958). *With Eyes at the Back of Our Heads* (1959). *The Jacob's Ladder* (1961). *City Psalm* (1964). *O Taste and See* (1964). *Poems Concerning the Castle* (1966). *Out of the War Shadow: An Anthology of Current Poetry* (edited by Levertov, 1967). *The Cold Spring, and Other Poems* (1968). *In Praise of Krishna: Songs from the Bengali* (translated and edited by Levertov, with E. C. Dimock, Jr., 1968). *In the Night: A Story* (1968). *A Marigold from North Vietnam* (1968). *The Sorrow Dance* (1968). *Three Poems* (1968). *A Tree Telling of Orpheus* (1968). *Embroideries* (1969). *Selected Poems of Guillevic* (translated by Levertov, 1969). *A New Year's Garland for My Students, MIT 1969–70* (1970). *Relearning the Alphabet* (1970). *Summer Poems 1969* (1970). *To Stay Alive* (1971). *Footprints* (1972). *The Poet in the World* (1973). *The Freeing of the Dust* (1975). *Modulations for Solo Voice* (1977). *Light up the Cave* (1981). *Pig Dreams: Scenes from the Life of Sylvia* (1981). *A Wanderer's Dream* (1981).

BIBLIOGRAPHY: Mersmann, J., *Out of the Vietnam Vortex* (1974). Wilson, R. A., *A Bibliography of D. L.* (1967).

For articles in reference works, see: *CA*, 1–4 (1967). *Contemporary Poets*, Ed. R. Murphie (1970). *Contemporary Poets*, Eds. J. Vinson and D. L. Kirkpatrick (1975). *WA*.

Other references: *CentR* 17 (1973). *DAI* 36 (1975). *Descant: The Texas Christian University Literary Journal* 19 (1974). *HudR* 27 (1974). *MQ* 16 (1975).

ALBERTA TURNER

Estelle Anna Robinson Lewis

B. April 1824, Baltimore, Maryland; d. 24 Nov. 1880, London, England
Wrote under: Estelle Anna Lewis, Estelle Anna Blanche Lewis,
  Estelle Anna Robinson Lewis, Stella
D. of John N. Robinson; m. Sylvanus D. Lewis, 1841

L. was the daughter of a wealthy, cultivated, and influential Cuban of English and Spanish parentage, who died in her childhood. She attended Emma Hart Willard's Female Seminary, where she studied "masculine" subjects including law. After leaving school in 1841, she continued a regimen of independent study in classical and modern languages, comparative literature, and history. She published her first poem at fourteen; married, at seventeen, a counsellor at law, of Brooklyn; and published a first book of poems, in 1844, at twenty. Sharing an enthusiasm for the work of Edgar Allan Poe with whom the husband began a friendship in 1845, the Lewises are remembered in accounts of the Poe circle. As Poe pointed out—however ironically in view of his own goaded imagination —the predominant trait of L.'s disposition was "a certain romantic sensibility, bordering upon melancholy, or even gloom."

Divorced in 1858, L. traveled in Europe, read at the Vatican Library and the Bibliothèque Imperiäle, and lived for the last decades of her life in London, where she took a house in Bedford Square and studied frequently at the British Museum. Having published occasional translations of Virgil, articles on travel and American art, stories and a play, as well as additional poetry, she then wrote her most ambitious work, a dramatization in verse of Sappho's life. Appearing in 1868, it was widely reviewed in England, the U.S., and France, translated into modern Greek, and staged in Athens. In the complexity of characterization, L. anticipates the Sappho later revealed by scholarly research as a woman with primitive passions, unappeasable longing, frailties of ego, and an imperious will, but L.'s awareness of the poet's keen intelligence, charms, and genius is not matched by the pedestrian verse.

L. is usually mentioned in Poe biographies as a scribbling woman given to immense sentimentality, but she is rather an expert in the histrionics of passion. The title of the first poems, *Records of the Heart* (1844), could serve for all of L.'s major work; the convulsive emotions and fickle vows of love resulting in "frightful wrecks of mutual ill" for both men and women are her most persistent themes. Although she relies on the exhausted conventions, language and meters of romantic poetry in her period, she has nevertheless a disciplined energy for her criticisms of life from a woman's point of view. She is a formidable scribbler.

L.'s imagination is perhaps at its best in "Laone," a history of adolescent conflict. The poem depicts the harsh consequences of a relationship between two young people who have been inseparable for five years. The boy develops sexually and emotionally much earlier than the shy girl he has protected since their childhood as a promise to her dying father. Neither youth is censured for the disparity in needs or the failure to perceive them until it is too late. A century before Robert Frost's comparable poem, "The Subverted Flower," for instance, L. confronts the subject with more equanimity than either Frost or a mere sentimentalist, in spite of the fact that she writes in the cadences, images, and metaphors of an age when natural expression was inhibited by scrupulous nicety or plain prudery.

The ambitions of L., it has been said, "were underwritten by her husband and Poe." While she benefited from their aid, she also received early commendation by poets as different as William Cullen Bryant and Lamartine. *Records of the Heart* was, moreover, in an eleventh edition, and *Sappho*, in a sixth edition at the time of her death. The rapid decline in L.'s reputation can be accounted for not only by the derivative manner of the verse but also by radical changes in taste.

WORKS: *Records of the Heart* (1844). *Child of the Sea, and Other Poems* (1848). *Myths of the Minstrel* (1852). *Poems by Estelle Anna Lewis* (1857). *Sappho: A Tragedy in Five Acts* (1868). *The King's Stratagem; or, The Pearl of Poland* (1869). *Minna Monte* (1872).

BIBLIOGRAPHY: Poe, E. A., *Complete Works of Poe XIII* (Ed. J. A. Harrison, 1902). Poe, E. A., *The Literati* (1850).
For articles in reference works, see: *AA. CAL. FPA. LSL. NCAB,* 10.
Other references: *The Athenaeum* (4 Dec. 1880). *SLM* (Sept. 1848).

ELIZABETH PHILLIPS

Janet Lewis

B. 17 Aug. 1899, Chicago, Illinois
D. of Edwin Herbert and Elizabeth Taylor Lewis; m. Yvor Winters, 1926

L. received a Bachelor of Philosophy degree from the University of Chicago. She then worked for a time at the American Consulate in Paris and, in Chicago, as a proofreader for *Redbook* and as a teacher. L. married the poet and critic Yvor Winters. They settled in Los Altos, California, and had two children. Winters died in 1968. She has taught at Stanford and at other universities and has received several awards.

L.'s first novel, *The Invasion* (1932), established her talent for historical fiction. It is an account of the Johnston family, whose American ancestry began shortly after the Revolution, when John Johnston, an Irishman, settled with an Ojibway Indian wife in northern Michigan. The effects of the gradual invasion by white settlers of Indian lands are background to the family history.

Two subsequent novels take their sources from historical accounts of trials L. first encountered in the 19th-c. *Famous Cases of Circumstantial Evidence*. In *The Trial of Sören Qvist* (1947), set in 17th-c. Denmark, Qvist is framed for murder, convicted, and executed. In *The Wife of Martin Guerre* (1941), the setting is 16th-c. France. This is a classic novella that tells the story of Bertrande de Rols, the child bride of Martin Guerre. When Bertrande's husband presumably returns from war, after long absence, her growing conviction that the returning soldier is an impostor leads to a climactic trial that became a famous case in French jurisprudence. By focusing upon Bertrande, a devout young woman tormented by her love for two men, L. transforms a legal record into a moving domestic tragedy. In 1958, L. wrote a libretto based on her novel.

In her most ambitious novel, *The Ghost of Monsieur Scarron* (1959), L. again deals with French history, during the reign of Louis XIV. Here two plots and two worlds interweave. The first plot concerns the discovery at the Court of Versailles of a libelous pamphlet against the King and the effort of the King's authorities to find the man responsible. The second plot deals with the life of a devout and simple Parisian bookbinder, Jean Larcher. When Larcher is convicted, upon circumstantial evidence, of the crime against the King, the two plots merge, and the story becomes one of a wife's infidelity and an ensuing tragedy of betrayal and revenge.

The mark of L.'s fiction is craftsmanship, evident in the precision of her style, her command of historical detail, and her rigorous control of her narratives. Her approach to history is essentially dramatic; history provides her with the plots and settings of tragedy. Her interest is not in great historical personages, but in forgotten, everyday lives where, as with high tragedy, evil motives and passions may also elude human justice and destroy the innocent as well as the guilty.

L.'s poetry is composed of short lyrics, usually in traditional forms, meticulously executed. In contrast to the darker themes of her fiction, L.'s poetry is strongly affirmative. Her subjects—unfashionable in contemporary poetry—center in the contentments of domestic life. Although limited in range, these are not poems of complacency. Many are shaded by the one inevitable grief, the death of loved ones. A more inclusive theme is the spiritual discipline necessary to "combine despair and joy / Into a stable whole," as she writes in "Morning Devotion." For L. this means a moral commitment to constancy, an adherence to rationally chosen, enduring values. The failure of such commitment, and its consequences, is the subject of one of her most moving poems,

"Helen Grown Old," in which Helen of Troy epitomizes a life "ruled by passion," the threat of which, in assessing her own experience, L. is aware. In "The Candle Flame," she acknowledges in her nature the variability that might turn loyalty into "a flickering vagrancy" that leaves "nothing certain." One of her finest love poems, "Old Love," is a tribute to an enduring marriage in which love eventually becomes "Love that is rooted deep, / Quiet as friendship seeming, / Secure as quiet sleep." The ultimate wisdom, L. implies in "White Oak," is to achieve a stability subject only to death. The human analogy for the metaphoric white oak, "Forever stirring in the air yet not / Forsaking this one spot," is that of living experience rooted in permanent values.

Although L. has an excellent reputation among a select audience—mainly writers and poets themselves—she has not had the critical recognition merited by the quality of her work. Perhaps this is because she has never been a follower of fashion, and, in poetry, her production has been relatively small.

WORKS: *Indians in the Woods* (1922). *Adventures of Ollie Ostrich* (1923). *The Wheel in Midsummer* (1927). *The Invasion* (1932). *The Wife of Martin Guerre* (1941; libretto, 1958). *Against a Darkening Sky* (1943). *Goodbye Son, and Other Stories* (1946). *The Trial of Sören Qvist* (1947). *Poems, 1924–1944* (1950). *The Ghost of Monsieur Scarron* (1959). *Keiko's Bubble* (1961). *The Last of the Mohicans* (libretto by Lewis, 1977). *The Birthday of the Infanta* (libretto by Lewis, 1977).

BIBLIOGRAPHY: For articles in reference works, see: *20thCAS*.

MARGARET PETERSON

Laura Jean Libbey

B. 22 March 1862, Brooklyn, New York; d. 25 Oct. 1925, New York City
D. of Thomas H. and Elizabeth Nelson Libbey; m. Van Mater Stilwell, 1898

L. was one of this country's most prolific writers of fiction, publishing some eighty volumes in her thirty-year career as a popular novelist. Her fiction provided a formula for female escape literature which persists even into the present. Yet despite her productivity and popularity, L.'s current reputation is negligible and her biography obscure. Most of L.'s novels were printed serially in newspapers, magazines, and the weekly "story papers," and then reprinted in cheap paperbound editions. Few libraries kept these inexpensive copies of her once best-selling books.

The obscurity of her biography is partly owing to L.'s own sense that her private life was not the public's business. We do know that she lived most of her life in Brooklyn, although as an adult she traveled continually in order to promote her books. On most of these journeys, the author was accompanied by her mother, a strict, domineering woman who governed L.'s life and forbade her daughter to marry. L. disobeyed this command only after her mother's death in 1898. True to the heroines in her fiction, the popular novelist gave up her career upon marriage to a respectable husband. Only after nearly a decade of retirement could she be coaxed to work again.

L. was a leading practitioner of the so-called working-girl novel. These books about young, female proletarian protagonists netted the author over fifty thousand dollars a year, hardly a working-class income by any standard. All of the novels preached the same simple and not very original message: A young girl who remains virtuous (i.e., virginal) can ultimately expect to secure not only a husband and happiness, but a fortune too.

Not one of the novels can be singled out from the L. canon since each, invariably, tells the same story, shares the same plot, preaches the same moral, and portrays the same heroes, heroines, villains, and villainesses. The books all include compulsory scenes depicting the harshness of city life, thus echoing a standard theme in much popular fiction of the last decade of the 19th c. Named little Leafy, pretty Guelda, or poor Faynie, the heroine attempts to make her way alone in the cruel city. After having been cast out of her idyllic rural home, often by a wicked stepmother or selfish foster parent, she finds she now must support herself and frequently must support indigent siblings as well. In a backhanded and almost ludicrously sentimentalized fashion, this formulaic plot attests to a changing pattern in the American labor force after the Civil War, when women were finding employment in increasing numbers, frequently in low-paying factory jobs.

But L.'s novels do not focus much on the actual working conditions endured by the female protagonists. Instead, the heroine's energies are devoted to fending off often hostile masculine attentions. Only after a series of victimizations is the heroine finally rescued by the hero, a character both virtuous and prosperous. Their marriage presages happiness ever after and an end to both the threat of assault and the daily grind of a factory job. Although men are always the aggressors in these novels and the heroine's moral character is never even questioned, it is interesting to note that the heroine alone is responsible for maintaining her virtue.

The message of L.'s novels is a conservative one, and certainly one that ran counter to ideas endorsed by a growing number of feminists in late-19th-c. America; but the credo she preached is of interest to the social historian. What Horatio Alger did for American working-class men, L. did for female readers. Alger's heroes worked hard, took advantage of every opportunity, and, against all odds, realized the American dream. L.'s heroines worked hard too. But the 19th-c. business world held few opportunities for women. So real success for L.'s heroines came through successful marriage. L.'s socially conservative fables, however we might object to them, spoke to millions of working-class women who needed a fantasy of their own to take them away from the real grime of the sweatshops, the bookbinderies, and the cotton mills.

WORKS: This is a representative list of Libbey's novels, many of which are not even listed in the Library of Congress catalogues: *A Fatal Wooing* (1883). *All for Love of a Fair Face; or, A Broken Betrothal* (1885). *Madolin Rivers; or, The Little Beauty of Red Oak Seminary: A Love Story* (1885). *A Forbidden Marriage; or, In Love with a Handsome Spendthrift* (1888). *Miss Middleton's Lover; or, Parted on Their Bridal Tour* (1888). *Leonie Locke: The Romance of a Beautiful New York Working Girl* (1889). *Willful Gaynell; or, The Little Beauty of the Passaic Cotton Mills* (1890). *Little Leafy, the Cloakmaker's Beautiful Daughter: A Romantic Story of a Lovely Working Girl in the City of New York* (1891). *A Master Workman's Oath; or, Coralie the Unfortunate: A Love Story Portraying the Life, Romance, and Strange Fate of a Beautiful New York Working Girl* (1892). *Only a Mechanic's Daughter: A Charming Story of Love and Passion* (1892). *Parted at the Altar* (1893). *A Handsome Engineer's Flirtation; or, How He Won the Hearts of Girls* (190?). *Was She Sweetheart or Wife* (190?). *Wooden Wives: Is It a Story for Philandering Husbands?* (1923).

BIBLIOGRAPHY: Davidson, C. N., and A. E. Davidson, "Carrie's Sisters: The Popular Prototypes for Dreiser's Heroine," *MFS* (Autumn 1977). Noel, M., *Villains Galore: The Heyday of the Popular Story Weekly* (1954). Papashvily, H. W., *All the Happy Endings* (1956).

For articles in reference works, see: *NAW* (article by S. G. Walcutt). *NCAB*, 19.

Other references: *American Mercury* (Sept. 1931). *Historical Society of Michigan Chronicle* (4th quarter 1975).

CATHY N. DAVIDSON

Anne Morrow Lindbergh

B. 22 June 1906, Englewood, New Jersey
D. of Dwight and Elizabeth Cutter Morrow; m. Charles A. Lindbergh, 1929

Born into a family devoted to books and scholarship, L. learned to value education, self-discipline, and personal ambition from an early age. She acquired a sense of history firsthand from traveling with her parents throughout Europe. L. received a B.A. (1928) from Smith College, where she also earned recognition as a writer. With her marriage, the publicity engulfing Lindbergh extended to L., shattering the privacy she had treasured.

After her marriage L. learned to fly and operate radio, studied dead reckoning and celestial navigation, and became the first woman in America to obtain a glider-pilot's license. Between 1931 and 1933 L. assisted her husband in charting the international air routes later used for commercial air travel. For her work as copilot and radio operator in flights exceeding forty thousand miles over five continents, the National Geographic Society awarded her the Hubbard Gold Medal in 1934.

In the midst of these achievements the public curiosity haunting the Lindberghs reached frenzied levels with the kidnapping and murder of their twenty-month-old son in 1932. The tragedy and the prolonged investigation terminated with the conviction of Bruno Richard Hauptman. In December 1935, for protection and privacy, the Lindberghs left the U.S. for England, and later France; when World War II descended on Europe in 1939, the Lindberghs returned to the U.S. Since her husband's death in 1974, L. has continued to occupy the family home in Darien, Connecticut, while maintaining a residence on the Hawaiian island of Maui. Although her duties as celebrity and mother of a large family have drawn heavily on her energy, L. has never abandoned her writing career, producing both fiction and nonfiction throughout her life.

In *Gift from the Sea* (1955), originally conceived as a series of autobiographical essays, L. presents a microcosm of modern American womanhood as contemplated by a solitary figure in retreat at a seashore. With attention to the effects of marriage on woman's struggle for self-identity, L. traces the stages of marriage from the early self-contained relationship between man and woman, through the middle years weighed down with responsibilities, and finally to the mature marriage characterized by a newly acquired sense of freedom.

With the abandoned argonauta, one of several seashells used to symbolize the different stages of marriage, L. offers her view of the ideal relationship: "the meeting of two whole fully developed people as persons." Recognizing that the many demands of marriage hinder woman's growth, L. advocates as a counterbalance to these demands periods of solitude devoted to creativity. If practiced, such creativity would yield self-knowledge. Having reaffirmed her faith in the power of solitude, L. leaves the seashore, strengthened by her reflections, especially by her awareness of the dynamic nature of life. With her customary modesty, L. acknowledges that her answer to woman's predicament is not definitive, except in her assertion that the desire for self-identity will persist. Moreover, she admits new problems will appear just as certainly as the ebb and flow of the sea continues. With this, her most significant work, L. reveals not only her poetic sensitivity but her insight into the nature of womanhood as well.

L.'s single collection of poetry, *The Unicorn, and Other Poems* (1956), presents the spiritual odyssey of an individual pursuing personal freedom. Throughout the poems, L. identifies the demons obstructing this pursuit, all the while attempting to destroy them. Irregular lyric forms appropriately capture her meandering reflections, just as images drawn from winter effectively support passages dealing with spiritual isolation in contrast to the aerial images signaling hope and joy.

L. returns to the theme of marriage in her novel *Dearly Beloved* (1962). Writing in the tradition of the experimental novel, L. eschews simple narration in favor of the stream-of-consciousness technique as a means of revealing certain basic truths about marriage. Organized around the single event of a family wedding in a structure reminiscent of Virginia Woolf's *Mrs. Dalloway*, the novel examines the different attitudes towards marriage held by the wedding guests.

L.'s literary themes have their genesis in the five volumes of her letters and diaries. From these pages there emerges the figure of a sensitive individual with a penchant for writing, whose circumstances in life have plunged her into the maelstrom of public activity. The anxiety resulting from these conflicting forces and her determination to assert spiritual independence spill over into L.'s writing, making it all of one piece.

L.'s artistic forte lies in her ability to shape her themes into impressive forms. Since her themes are open-ended, her forms are appropriately organic: the lyric, the stream-of-consciousness novel, the familiar essay. L. manages aesthetic distance by objectifying nature. Seashells, barren trees, the sky, birds, and mountains are favorite images conveying her vision. L.'s astute handling of diverse forms and her instinct for selecting the near-perfect image have contributed to her reputation as a significant modern writer.

WORKS: *North to the Orient* (1935). *Listen! The Wind* (1938). *The Wave of the Future* (1940). *The Steep Ascent* (1944). *Gift from the Sea* (1955). *The Unicorn, and Other Poems: 1935–1955* (1956). *Dearly Beloved: A Theme and Variations* (1962). *Earth Shine* (1966). *Bring Me a Unicorn: Diaries and Letters of Anne Morrow Lindbergh, 1922–1928* (1971). *Hour of Gold, Hour of Lead* (1973). *Locked Rooms and Open Doors: Diaries and Letters of Anne Morrow Lindbergh, 1933–1935* (1974). *The Flower and the Nettle: Diaries and Letters, 1936–1939* (1976). *War Within and Without: Diaries and Letters, 1939–1944* (1980).

BIBLIOGRAPHY: For articles in reference works, see: *CA*, 17–20 (1976). *CB* (Nov. 1940; June 1976). *NCAB*, F. *20thCA*. *20thCAS*.

Other references: *America* (28 Feb. 1968). *NYT* (10 June 1962). *NYTBR* (20 March 1955; 27 Feb. 1972). *SR* (2 April 1955; 12 Jan. 1957).

ELSIE F. MAYER

Sara Jane Clarke Lippincott

B. *23 Sept. 1823, Pompey, New York; d. 20 April 1904, New Rochelle, New York*
Wrote under: *Sara J. Clarke, Grace Greenwood, Mrs. L. K. Lippincott*
D. of *Thaddeus and Deborah Baker Clarke; m. Leander K. Lippincott, 1853*

The youngest daughter among eleven children of a physician and a great-granddaughter of Jonathan Edwards, L. spent her childhood near Syracuse, New York, and attended school for eight years in Rochester, New York. When she was nineteen, she moved with her family to New Brighton, Pennsylvania.

L.'s first poems appeared in Rochester papers, and in 1844 her verse was published in N. P. Willis's *New Mirror*. Soon she wrote prose and informal letters for the *Mirror* and *Home Journal* under the pseudonym "Grace Greenwood." Later she worked as a journalist and correspondent for *Godey's Lady's Book, Graham's, Sartain's,* the *Saturday Evening Post,* the abolitionist *National Era,* the *New York Times,* and the New York *Tribune.* Throughout her career, because of her Puritan heritage or her own staunch sense of right, L. spoke out strongly for such causes as abolition, woman suffrage, prison reform, and Colorado's right to statehood and against capital punishment.

Her marriage was unhappy. She and Lippincott were coeditors of the early and highly popular juvenile magazine *The Little Pilgrim* (1853–75), but in 1876 Lippincott fled the country and disappeared after being indicted for embezzlement connected with his job at the Department of the Interior.

Greenwood Leaves (1850), L.'s first bestseller, epitomizes mid-19th-c. taste. It combines saccharine and sentimental tales and sketches ("Sly Peeps into the Heart Feminine," "A Spring Flower Faded") with a series of lively informal letters and parodies of Poe, Melville, Longfellow, and other authors. The letters, though often prolix and gushing, give promise of the journalism that would later be L.'s forte.

Haps and Mishaps of a Tour in Europe (1854) was another Greenwood bestseller and was still being reprinted in the 1890s. A lively and often humorous account of her journey alone to England, Scotland, Ireland, France, Germany, and Italy, it records visits to literary and historical sites, prisons, almshouses, and lunatic asylums and meetings with literary, artistic, and political lions. *Haps and Mishaps* mixes sentiment and gush, American chauvinism, and some of the dry Yankee wit later to be fully developed in Twain's *The Innocents Abroad.* As in the first and second series of *Greenwood Leaves,* the most interesting parts are the segments of straight reporting, especially L.'s impressions of people.

Merrie England (1855), like *Bonnie Scotland* (1861) and other juvenile works, first appeared in *The Little Pilgrim.* Linked with sites she visited on her first trip to Europe are "tales" or "historical sketches." Most of the history presented is highly suspect by modern standards and often seems comic in its invention and moralizing: "But the neighbors all shook their heads wisely, and said, 'Mrs. Shakespeare is spoiling that boy; he'll never make the man his father is.' I am sorry to say that, as he grew out of boyhood, the young poet fell into rather wild ways."

Much of L.'s best writing is in accounts of her travels in Europe during the 1870s and 1880s written for the *Independent,* after she stopped gushing. Her power and charm continued in letters from Washington, D.C., written through the 1890s and even into the 20th c.

Once-popular books by "Grace Greenwood" have now been largely forgotten, while the works of contemporaries she far outsold in her lifetime (e.g., Thoreau and Melville) have become American classics. L.'s poetry, sentimental tales and sketches, and children's books merit obscurity, but her strong-minded, firsthand reporting still deserves and rewards attention.

WORKS: *Greenwood Leaves* (1850). *History of My Pets* (1851). *Poems* (1851). *Greenwood Leaves, Second Series* (1852). *Recollections of My Childhood, and Other Stories* (1852). *Haps and Mishaps of a Tour in Europe* (1854). *Merrie England* (1855). *A Forest Tragedy* (1856). *Old Wonder-Eyes* (1857). *Stories and Legends of Travel and History* (1857). *Stories from Famous Ballads* (1859). *Bonnie Scotland* (1861). *Nelly, the Gypsy Girl* (1863). *Records of Five Years* (1867). *Stories and Sights of France and Italy* (1867). *Stories of Many Lands* (1867). *New Life in New Lands* (1873). *Heads and Tails: Studies and Stories of My Pets* (1874). *Emma Abbott, Prima Donna* (1878). *Treasures from Fairy Land* (with R. W. Raymond, 1879). *Queen Victoria: Her Girlhood and Womanhood* (1883). *Some of My Pets* (1884). *Stories for Home-Folks, Young and Old* (1884). *Stories and Sketches* (1892).

BIBLIOGRAPHY: Pattee, F. L., *The Feminine Fifties* (1940). Thorp, M. F., *Female Persuasion* (1949).

For articles in reference works, see: *AA. The American Female Poets*, Ed. C. May (1854). *American Literary Manuscripts*, Ed. J. A. Robbins. *AW. CAL. DAB*, VI, 1. *Eminent Women of the Age*, Eds. J. Parton et al. (1869). *FPA. The Female Prose Writers of America*, Ed. J. S. Hart (1857). *HWS. NAW* (article by B. Welter). *NCAB*, 4. *Woman's Record*, Ed. S. J. Hale (1853).

Other references: *AL* (Jan. 1938). *Atlantic* (June 1859; Sept. 1859). *NYT* (21 April 1904).

SUSAN SUTTON SMITH

Jane Erminia Starkweather Locke

B. 25 April 1805, Worthington, Massachusetts; d. 8 March 1859, Ashburnham, Massachusetts
Wrote under: Jane E. Locke
D. of Charles and Deborah Brown Starkweather; m. John Goodwin Locke, 1829

A deacon's daughter, L. reflects in her work the religious and patriotic idealism nurtured in her childhood home. Her uncle Ezra was a Massachusetts state senator and a member of the Constitutional Convention of 1820, as was L.'s father-in-law, John Locke. She was the youngest of ten children.

L. followed her husband to New York shortly after their marriage. The first of their seven children was born there; three of the children were to die in early childhood, and only one, Grace LeBaron Upham, was to survive to adulthood. The family settled in Lowell (1833) and in Boston (1849). While Locke pursued a career in business and government service, L. cared for the children and pursued her own literary interests.

L.'s first collection of poetry is *Miscellaneous Poems* (1842). In the preface, the author tells us that the poems were written "for the most part . . . to relieve the soul of what would cumber it unuttered. . . ." The poems range in subject from reminiscences of her childhood home to expressions of love and concern for husband and children, and beyond this family circle to acknowledgments of the genial accomplishments of others—mostly contemporaries.

One important aspect of L.'s poetry is the evidence of sincere personal concerns and beliefs pertaining to women. A poem entitled "To an Infant," dated 11 August 1837, commemorates the birth of her first daughter. However, rather than greet the child in cheerful language, L. bemoans the estate which the child inherits: the wearisome toil of woman's daily existence. Despite this pessimistic, recurrent theme, in other poems L. stresses in stronger, more positive language another aspect of woman's existence: motherhood.

Two of the most notable examples of this latter theme can be found in the poems "Mount Holyoke Seminary" and "A Poem Adapted to the Times." In the former, L. compares the glories of the school in Northampton to those of the Propylaea at Athens and says, "To learning's inner temple here / Pass *mothers* of the race. . . ." That L. believes generations of educated women will produce generations of enlightened men, implicit here, is explicit in the latter poem, which also reflects her sympathy with the abolitionist movement: "An influence benign she will exert . . . In childhood hearts, that, hence, *man's* common acts / Will be but deeds of charity and love, / And the forged bands of the dark slave fall off, Spontaneous and uninvoked."

L.'s firm, patriotic vision is set forth in a forty-six-page poem entitled *Boston: A Poem* (1846), dedicated "to the names of Appleton and Lawrence. . . ." In it, L. honors scientists, educators, and working men and women, as well as industrialists, all of whom, she believes, contributed to the economic and academic well-being of the "Athens of America."

In *Rachel; or, The Little Mourner* (1844) L. touches with astute sensitivity the problematic situation of the Christian who must try to reconcile joyful belief in eternal life with very real sorrow and pain at the earthly parting.

The Recalled, in Voices of the Past, and Poems of the Ideal (1854), is a collection of poetry that reflects the more mature mind at work. Rather than a random selection of poetry gathered almost at whim, L. arranges this volume in four sections. "Voices of the Past" commemorates public occasions, historic events, and the achievements of prominent personages and includes "Requiem for Edgar A. Poe," whom L. knew. The poems in "Passages from Life" are autobiographical, but L. is more selective than in *Miscellaneous Poems*. Love filtered through Christian belief is reflected in personal poems such as "One Thousandth Imitation of an Old Song," written for her husband, and "Proverbs," written to her son.

Throughout all of her work, L. alludes to the "ideal," which is also the subject of the third section, "Poems of the Ideal." "The Sisters of Avon," her most philosophical offering, suggests at least an acquaintance with Hermetic philosophy. The final section, a tribute to Daniel Webster consistent with L.'s political sympathies, was first published separately as *Daniel Webster: A Rhymed Eulogy* (1854).

Between 1850 and 1854, L. worked as a newspaper correspondent for the Boston *Journal* and the *Daily Atlas*.

In the same period, she also worked for the James Monroe Publishing Company, writing prefaces for the English publications which they reproduced in this country. L.'s writing, prose and poetry, is lucid and straightforward. Her poetry is representative of the popular poetry of the 19th c. in general, and of the varied interests of its women in particular.

WORKS: *Miscellaneous Poems* (1842). *Rachael; or, The Little Mourner* (1844). *Boston: A Poem* (1846). *The Recalled, in Voices of the Past, and Poems of the Ideal* (1854). *Daniel Webster: A Rhymed Eulogy* (1854). *Nothing Ever Happens* (1938).

BIBLIOGRAPHY: Baldwin, J. S., *Memories and Traditions* (1909). Locke, J. G., *Book of the Lockes* (1853). Starkweather, C. L., *A Brief Genealogical History of Robert Starkweather of Roxbury and Ipswich* (1904). Upham, G. L., *Contributions of the Old Residents' Historical Association, Lowell, Mass.* (1891).
For articles in reference works, see: *CAL.*
Other references: *Lowell Historical Society* (1940).

ROSALIE TUTELA RYAN

Mary Simmerson Cunningham Logan

B. *15 Aug. 1838, Petersburgh, Boone County, Missouri; d. 22 Feb. 1923, Washington, D.C.*
Wrote under: Mrs. J. A. Logan
D. *of Captain John M. and Elizabeth H. La Fontaine Cunningham; m. John Alexander Logan, 1855*

L. was born to parents of Irish-French ancestry. L.'s maternal grandfather, La Fontaine, owned many slaves and large tracts of land in Missouri, and her paternal grandfather was a slave owner in Tennessee. Shortly after her birth, L.'s parents moved to southern Illinois, where her father became registrar of the land office as well as an army officer.

L., the oldest of thirteen children, had little formal education except that provided by itinerant teachers. When L. was fifteen, she studied for a year at St. Vincent's Academy near Morganfield, Kentucky. After graduation, L. returned home to marry a friend of her father's. L. wrote in the preface of her autobiography, "To tell my own story is to tell that of my own famous husband, General John A. Logan. Our marriage was a real partnership for thirty-one happy years."

L. traveled with her husband and assisted him by drawing up the forms for indictments and helping draft briefs. When Logan ran for Congress, L. was by his side throughout the political campaign.

After the Civil War, both General Logan and L. were concerned about the welfare of returning veterans. They were enthusiastic participants in the development of the Grand Army of the Republic (GAR). L. was also closely associated with the women's auxiliary of the GAR: the Women's Relief Corps. The Logans were responsible for the establishment of Memorial Day as a national holiday. In 1868, L. noted that the graves of Confederate soldiers in a cemetery in Richmond, Virginia, were marked by small Confederate flags and flowers. As a Senator, Logan effected passage of legislation to perpetuate Memorial Day as a national holiday.

After the death of Logan, L. was forced to earn a living for herself and her two children. *The Home Magazine* was started especially for her to edit and was successful for seven years. However, L.'s political influence and good works were continued. President Harrison appointed her to the board of the Lady Managers of the Chicago World's Columbian Exposition. In 1919, four years before her death, L. received the Belgian medal of Queen Elizabeth for work during the First World War.

L.'s first book was *The Home Manual* (1889), which bore a direct relationship to L.'s magazine. A compendium of etiquette, nostrums, recipes, stories, and games, its focus was self-improvement and self-help. In one chapter, "Society Small Talk," L. writes, "It is true that the newcomer into society often discovers that his or her greatest difficulty lies in finding just the right thing to say at the right time."

Thirty Years in Washington (1901) and *Reminiscences of a Soldier's Wife* (1913) manifest L.'s pride in the city of Washington and in being the wife of a famous general and statesman. *Thirty Years* is composed of a series of vignettes that describe the many agencies and offices of the national government. L.'s descriptions of her privileged access to behind-the-scenes workings of the government make this work an interesting source of information. That there are inaccuracies in the work does not detract from the general interest provided by rich details and L.'s general enthusiasm.

This same enthusiasm is apparent throughout L.'s best work, the autobiographical *Reminiscences*. L.'s eyewitness narration of the Lincoln-Douglas debates, her husband's political campaigns, and battle scenes of the Civil War provide a moving, personal view of those well-known events.

Using the resources of the Library of Congress from 1902 to 1909, L. and her daughter, Mary Logan Tucker, prepared a compendium of biographies of American women. *The Part Taken by Women in American History* (1912) contains two thousand biographical sketches varying in length and organized under rubrics such as Aboriginal Women, Pioneers, Women of the Revolution, Suffragists, etc. Like many other compendiums of the time, effusive encomiums based on scant factual material abound. However, this work is valuable for its great number of biographies of worthy women.

Throughout her life, L. was accorded equal praise with her husband. However, she lived thirty-seven years longer than he, and forged a career of her own as an editor and writer. L.'s works, especially the autobiography, exhibit her enthusiastic appreciation of the historic times through which she lived.

WORKS: *The Home Manual* (prepared by Logan, 1889). *Thirty Years in Washington* (1901; reissued, with two additional chapters, as *Our National Government*, 1908). *The Part Taken by Women in American History* (1912). *Reminiscences of a Soldier's Wife* (1913).

The Logan family papers are in The Library of Congress.

BIBLIOGRAPHY: Busbey, K. G., "Concerning the Author, Mrs. John. A. Logan," in *The Part Taken by Women in American History* (1912).

For articles in reference works, see: *AW. NCAB*, 4. *NAW* (article by L. M. Young).

Other references: *American Historical Review* (Oct. 1902). *Independent* (14 June 1919). *NYT* (23 Feb. 1923).

DOROTHEA MOSLEY THOMPSON

Olive Logan

B. 22 April 1839, Elmira, New York; d. 27 April 1909, Banstead, England
Wrote under: Chroniqueuse, Olive Logan, Mrs. Wirt Sikes
D. of Cornelius Logan and Eliza Akeley; m. Henry A. DeLille, 1857;
m. William Wirt Sikes, 1871; m. James O'Neill, 1892

L., the daughter of a theatrical couple, made her stage debut as a child and continued acting in New York City and on tour throughout the U.S. until about 1868. Her career was interrupted in the mid-fifties for eight years during her first marriage. It was not for love of the theater that L. returned briefly to the stage in her own play, *Eveleen*, in 1864. The economic necessity brought on by her divorce from DeLille forced her resumption of one career, acting, that she always despised and one, writing, that she enjoyed. She had also by this time begun to make a name for herself as a feminist lecturer. The exact date of her retirement is uncertain, but she seems to have entirely abandoned acting by 1868, continuing her connection with the theater as playwright only. Three plays, *Surf* (1870), *Newport* (1879)—both mild satires of high society—and *Armadale* (1866), a dramatization of Wilkie Collins's novel, were produced for the stage but not published. Her second marriage in 1872 to Willaim Wirt Sikes lasted until his death in 1883. Her third husband, O'Neill, was twenty years her junior. L.'s literary productivity was particularly intense during those years when she was not being supported by a husband. The poverty and insanity which haunted her for most of her adult life became acute in old age and she died at the age of seventy in an English home for the insane.

L.'s literary career began with lectures, articles, and a lengthy record of "politics, art, fashion, and anecdote" in the Paris of 1862. *Photographs of Paris Life* (1862) was first published under the pseudonym Chroniqueuse. *Chateau Frissac: Home Scenes in France* (1865), L.'s first novel, attacked the evils in the French marriage of convenience. In the melodramatic style, love is temporarily thwarted by inadequate dowries, family disapproval, and arranged alliances. Another short novel followed in 1867; *John Morris' Money* is the story of a family of modest means who take in a widowed aunt, entertain her with four tales of the triumph of romantic love over greed, and finally, at the old woman's death, un-expectedly inherit her secret fortune.

In *Apropos of Women and the Theater* (1869), L. expounded upon a theme which often occupied her: the immorality of Lydia Thompson's "British Blondes," the lavish 1866 production of *The Black Crook*, both of which featured dancers in flesh-colored tights, and the subsequent seminudity which gave respectable actresses bad names. L.'s most impressive and longest work appeared in 1870 under the title *Before the Footlights and Behind the Scenes* and in 1871 as *The Mimic World*. This is one of the most informative but disorganized and often biased accounts of backstage life from the legitimate stage to the circus. It includes biographical sketches and anecdotes, arguments for treating actors with respect, and attacks on stage nudity and the third tier.

Also published in 1870, "The Good Mr. Bagglethorpe," is a cinderella story about a poor, orphaned young actress appearing in "moral dramas" who is seen and loved by the well-heeled, Willie Gentry. To make the union between the two possible, she must be taken from the stage and educated for two years.

L. continued her interest in writing nonfiction with *Get Thee Behind Me, Satan: A Home-born Book of Home-Truths* (1872), a celebration of marriage and the home under attack by free love and loveless "mercantile" marriages. L. also warns women of the dangers in believing that marriage is the only existence that awaits them and in allowing themselves to be treated as commodities. Portraits of several types of unhappy women underscore her thesis: one woman whose family is excessively eager to see her married, one considered only as a beautiful object, and one who is neglected by her husband.

They Met By Chance: A Society Novel (1873), L.'s last major work of published fiction, describes the life of the wealthy aristocrat in 19th-c. New York: the vacation spots, the entertainments, the matchmaking, and the petty games. As in her other novels of high society, much hangs on disguise, mistaken reports of a character's death, coincidence, and intrigue.

L.'s strengths lie, not in her imagination and creativity, but in her observations of attitudes and details which help to characterize the 19th-c. life and mind.

WORKS: *Photographs of Paris Life* (1862). *Chateau Frissac: Home Scenes in France* (1865). *John Morris' Money* (1867). *Apropos of Women and the Theater* (1869). *Before the Footlights and Behind the Scenes* (1870; reprinted as *The Mimic World*, 1871). *Get Thee Behind Me, Satan: A Home-born*

Book of Home-Truths (1872). *They Met By Chance: A Society Novel* (1873). *The American Abroad* (1882).

BIBLIOGRAPHY: Brown, T. A., *History of the American Stage* (1903). Ireland, J. N., *Records of the New York Stage* (1866–67). Ludlow, N., *Dramatic Life as I Found It* (1913). Winter, W., *The Wallet of Time* (1913).

For articles in reference works, see: *AA. DAB*, VI, 1. *NAW* (article by A. E. Johnson). *NCAB* 6.

CLAUDIA D. JOHNSON

Anita Loos

B. 26 April 1893, Sissons, California; d. 18 Aug. 1981, New York City
D. of Richard Beers and Minnie Ellen Loos; m. Frank Pallma, Jr., 1915;
   m. John Emerson, 1919

When L. was four, her family moved from Sissons (now Mount Shasta), California, to San Francisco's Barbary Coast, where her ne'er-do-well father engaged in a series of journalistic and theatrical schemes. L. became a child actress and the family's chief mainstay for many years. After a period in Los Angeles, where her father managed an early movie house, the family settled in San Diego. By this time a youthful correspondent for the New York *Morning Telegraph*, L. hit upon the idea of writing movie scenarios for the Biograph Company. *The New York Hat* (1912) was her first filmed scenario, and by 1915 she had sold D. W. Griffith over one hundred scripts.

Eager to leave her family behind, L. married in 1915. After one night she deserted her young husband and set out for Hollywood where Biograph quickly offered her a contract. (The marriage was later annulled.) It was L. who wrote the title cards for Griffith's epic, *Intolerance* (1916). Her wisecracking verbal humor seemed ill-suited to the silent screen, however, until the chance success of an early Douglas Fairbanks film proved that audiences were willing to read comic subtitles. For the next few years, L. worked closely with Fairbanks, with Constance Talmadge, and with the suave director John Emerson, whom she married in 1919. In collaboration with Emerson she wrote two books about the motion picture industry, *How to Write Photoplays* (1920) and *Breaking into the Movies* (1921), along with several Broadway plays.

Living in New York, L. became a friend of H. L. Mencken. As a spoof of his taste for dim-witted blondes, she wrote a comic diary which first appeared in *Harper's Bazaar* in 1925. *Gentlemen Prefer Blondes* (1925), featuring the irrepressible Lorelei Lee, was a runaway international success, gaining L. such celebrated admirers as Winston Churchill, George Santayana, Mussolini, and James Joyce.

As one of the first women who dared hike her hemlines and bob her hair, L. came to epitomize the flappers of the 1920s. But despite her earning power, she was not in all respects an independent modern woman. As a self-described pushover for rogues, she remained loyal to her husband even while he dated other women and tried to take credit for L.'s own achievements. When she returned to Hollywood as a highly-paid screenwriter under Irving Thalberg at MGM, she protected Emerson's fragile ego by finding him a sinecure at the studio. Seemingly proud of her financial ineptitude, she turned her entire income over to "Mr. E.", who put everything into his own name in a move that could have left her penniless upon his death. Emerson was ultimately diagnosed as a manic-depressive, and spent the last eighteen years of his life in a sanitarium. In her autobiographical *Kiss Hollywood Good-By* (1974), L. chronicles her strictly platonic relationships with several attractive men, among them "the love of her life," the gambler and con man Wilson Mizner.

L.'s Broadway successes include several musical versions of *Gentlemen Prefer Blondes*, two romantic comedies adapted from the works of Colette, and *Happy Birthday* (1947), written for her good friend Helen Hayes. Hayes, who had recently starred as Queen Victoria and Harriet Beecher Stowe, was "fed up with being noble," and L. obliged with a comic portrait of a drab librarian who blossoms in a barroom. With Hayes she has published *Twice Over Lightly* (1972), an exuberant tour of New York City, her adopted home.

In three play versions, a sequel, and such later works as *A Mouse Is Born* (1951), L. tried to repeat her triumph with *Gentlemen Prefer Blondes*, but she never again so artfully captured Lorelei's blend of innocence and avarice, nor her highly original gift of gab. Though L.'s later novels seem sadly dated, her gossipy Hollywood memoirs, *A Girl Like I* (1972) and *Kiss Hollywood Good-By*, are delightful souvenirs of a bygone age.

WORKS: *How to Write Photoplays* (with J. Emerson, 1920). *Breaking into the Movies* (with J. Emerson, 1921). *The Whole Town's Talking* (with J. Emerson, 1925). *Gentlemen Prefer Blondes* (1925; dramatized by Loos, with J. Emerson, 1926). *But—Gentlemen Marry Brunettes* (1928). *Happy Birthday*

(1947). *A Mouse Is Born* (1951). *Gigi* (dramatization of the story by Colette, 1951; revised, 1956). *Chéri* (dramatization of the novel by Colette, 1959). *No Mother to Guide Her* (1961). *A Girl Like I* (1966). *The King's Mare* (1967). *Twice Over Lightly: New York Then and Now* (with H. Hayes; 1972). *Kiss Hollywood Good-By* (1974). *Cast of Thousands* (1977).

BIBLIOGRAPHY: For articles in reference works, see: *CA*, 21–22 (1969). *CB* (Feb. 1974). *20thCA*. *20thCAS*.

Other references: *Atlantic* (Oct. 1966). *Film Comment* (Winter 1970–71). *NewR* (10 Aug. 1974). *NY* (28 Dec. 1946). *NYT* (27 Dec. 1925). *NYTBR* (18 Aug. 1974). *SatR* (24 Sept. 1966).

BEVERLY GRAY BIENSTOCK

Harriet Mulford Stone Lothrop

B. *22 June 1844, New Haven, Connecticut; d. 2 Aug. 1924, Concord, Massachusetts*
Wrote under: Margaret Sidney
D. *of Sidney Mason and Harriet Mulford Stone; m. David Lothrop, 1881*

L. grew up in a religious New England family whose ancestors included the Reverend Thomas Hooker and several distinguished colonial governors. L.'s father was a respected architect, and it was in deference to his disapproval of women writers that L. adopted the pen name of "Margaret Sidney." The disciplined atmosphere of learning and religion that pervaded L.'s childhood days is reflected in the tight moral tone dominating her many works.

In 1878, L. contributed a short story entitled "Polly Pepper's Chicken Pie" to *Wide Awake*, a children's magazine. Reader response was enthusiastic, and the editor requested that L. provide the magazine with twelve more installments. L. hesitated, unsure of her ability; but she succeeded in completing the requested chapters. They were later compiled into the best-selling children's book, *Five Little Peppers and How They Grew* (1881).

L. followed this first success with *Five Little Peppers Midway* (1890) and then proceeded to write ten more Pepper volumes, ending with *Our Davie Pepper* in 1916. The Pepper series traces the development of five energetic children from their early childhood days in the country, through their adolescent education in the big city, and on to the decisions of their adult lives. Although all the Pepper volumes were greeted with enthusiastic reviews, L.'s first volume remained the most popular, selling over two million copies by the time of her death.

Five Little Peppers and How They Grew opens in a little brown house in the country where five children and their recently widowed mother are struggling to survive through a bitter winter. L., herself from a well-to-do family, always wanted to live in a little brown house, and the picture she presents of impoverished country life is extremely romanticized. Despite their many misfortunes, the Peppers are never downcast and they meet all adversity with an amazing fortitude. They are intent on being good Christians, never giving in to petty emotions such as jealousy or conceit.

This moral tone does not get in the way of the narrative, however. The Pepper adventure is energetic and amusing, filled with mischief and practical joking. L. has a deep-rooted understanding of children and she provides the action as well as the repetition that her audience demands. Her language, although overworked, is effective and sincere. L. claimed that the Peppers lived independently in her imagination for years before she ever wrote about them, and this philosophy gives her narratives a natural fluidity.

In 1881, at the age of thirty-seven, L. married a Boston publisher of children's books, and they moved to Concord, Massachusetts. Here, L. gave birth to her only child, Margaret, and Lothrop bought the historic house, The Wayside, as a surprise for his wife. The Wayside had been the childhood residence of Louisa May Alcott, whose work L.'s so closely resembles. In Massachusetts, L. continued working on the Pepper narratives, as well as writing historical novels such as *A Little Maid of Concord Town* (1898) and *The Judges' Cave* (1900). L. had a strong interest in history and was a careful researcher, but she never succeeded in bringing life to these historical novels. Primarily written for an adult audience, they lack the spark and energy of the Pepper novels, while retaining their didactic overtones.

L. was always active in community life. She combined her interest in history with her interest in children by founding the national society of Children of the American Revolution. She belonged to innumerable clubs—women's, writers', and historical—but showed little interest in the woman suffrage movement. Shortly before her death at the age of eighty, she was still going strong, working on an article about Edgar Allan Poe.

WORKS: *Five Little Peppers and How They Grew* (1881). *So As By Fire* (1881). *The Pettibone Name* (1882). *Hester, and Other New England Stories* (1886). *The Minute Man* (1886). *A New Departure for Girls* (1886). *Dilly and the Captain* (1887). *How Tom and Dorothy Made and Kept a Christian House* (1888). *Five Little Peppers Midway* (1890). *Rob: A Story for Boys* (1891). *Five Little Peppers Grown Up* (1892). *Old Concord, Her Highways and Byways* (1893). *Whittier with the Children* (1893). *The Old Town Pump* (1895). *The Gingham Bag* (1896). *Phronsie Pepper* (1897). *A Little Maid of Concord Town* (1898). *The Stories Polly Pepper Told* (1899). *An Adirondack Cabin* (1900). *The Adventures of Joel Pepper* (1900). *The Judges' Cave* (1900). *Five Little Peppers Abroad* (1902). *Ben Pepper* (1903). *Sally, Mrs. Tubbs* (1903). *Five Little Peppers and Their Friends* (1904). *The Five Little Peppers at School* (1907). *Five Little Peppers in the Little Brown House* (1907). *A Little Maid from Boston Town* (1910). *Our Davie Pepper* (1916).

BIBLIOGRAPHY: Lothrop, M., *The Wayside: Home of Authors* (1940). Swayne, J. L., *The Story of Concord* (1906).

For articles in reference works, see: *AA. AW. DAB*, VI, 1. *NAW* (article by E. F. Hoxie). *NCAB*, 8.

Other References: *Book News Monthly* (Feb. 1910). *Boston Transcript* (4 Aug. 1924). *PW* (9 Aug. 1924).

CHRISTIANE BIRD

Amy Lowell

B. 9 Feb. 1874, Brookline, Massachusetts; d. 12 May 1925, Brookline, Massachusetts
D. of Augustus and Katherine Bigelow Lawrence Lowell

L., a descendant of a clan of cultivated New England intellectuals, was raised in a family of devout Episcopalians on a ten-acre estate (Sevenels); the stately brownstone mansion, with its high mansard roof and extravagant gardens, became her home on the death of her parents. Her life of opulence was reinforced by a full staff of servants and her secretary-companion, Ada Russell. L. disapproved of wasting time and money on frivolities, however, claiming she was "an old-fashioned Puritan," who "let each day pass, well ordered in its usefulness."

Following several years of solitary apprenticeship in the atmosphere of the seven-thousand-book–lined library at Sevenels, she became a student of verse, and finally, in 1902, settled into the serious business of being a poet. The image of the social *grand dame* was not easily overcome; however, L. was determined that she be recognized as a hardworking, serious poet. At the time her first serious poem, "Fixed Idea," appeared in *The Atlantic Monthly* (Aug. 1910) her recognition consisted of the admiration accorded the sister of an eminent astronomer and the president of Harvard.

Despite the uncharitable opinions of some of her relatives, the portly, liberated woman, who resembled the director of a girls' school in her mannish coat, stiff collar, and pince-nez, knew what she was about. For more than thirteen years, L. was an ardent and indefatigable campaigner for poetry, and her prominence in both social and literary circles, coupled with her histrionic presence, gave her easy access to poetry societies, publishing offices, and public platforms. As a self-appointed prophet, she felt her mission was to reconstruct the taste of the American public, whom she felt had little comprehension of contemporary poetry.

It was not until her meeting with the Imagists in London in 1913 that L. began to gain some recognition. Despite controversy with writers such as Ford Maddox Ford and Ezra Pound over the reconstructed version of Imagism she imported to America, L. successfully published three Imagist anthologies and continued unwavering in her determination to create a climate conducive to the creation of American poetry.

Together with her poetry, L. published two volumes of critical essays, *Six French Poets* (1915) and *Tendencies in Modern American Poetry* (1917), and numerous reviews, some of which reflected critical misjudgments particularly in the case of Pound, Eliot, and Marianne Moore.

Following the publication of her first volume of poems, *A Dome of Many-Colored Glass* (1912), highly conventional in subject and style, L. was more experimental, studiously noting in each of her prefaces the development of her own poetics, her experimentation with unrhymed cadence, fluctuating rhythm, and most notably "polyphonic verse," a flexible verse form which she first used in *Sword Blades and Poppy Seeds* (1914), and later in *Can Grande's Castle* (1918). Generally, L. was successful when she was on native ground; her lack of success is reflected in departures, such as her "oriental poems."

Occasionally a memorable poem ("Meeting-House Hill," "Patterns," "Lilacs") appears among the six hundred and fifty preserved in published volumes, but L. will not be memorialized for her poetry. She had unlimited faith in her own capacity and a shared concern with other poets for the enterprise of poetry; and until her death she was a tireless and dedicated impresario of modern poetry.

WORKS: *A Dome of Many-Colored Glass* (1912). *Sword Blades and Poppy Seeds* (1914). *Six French Poets* (1915). *Some Imagist Poets: An Annual Anthology* (1915–17). *Men, Women, and Ghosts* (1916). *Tendencies in Modern American Poetry* (1917). *Can Grande's Castle* (1918). *Pictures of the Floating World* (1919). *Fir-Flower Tablets* (translated by Lowell, with F. Ayscough, 1920). *Legends* (1921). *A Critical Fable* (1922). *John Keats* (1925). *What's O'Clock* (1925). *Eastwind* (1926). *Ballads for Sale* (1927). *Selected Poems* (1928). *Poetry and Poets* (1930). *Correspondence of a Friendship* (with F. Ayscough, 1946). *Complete Poetical Works of Amy Lowell* (Ed. L. Untemeyer, 1955).

BIBLIOGRAPHY: Damon, S. F., *Amy Lowell: A Chronicle, with Extracts from Her Correspondence* (1935). Gould, J., *Amy: The World of Amy Lowell and the Imagist Movement* (1963). Healey, C., "Amy Lowell Visits London," *NEQ* (Sept. 1970). Healey, C., "Some Imagist Essays: Amy Lowell," *NEQ* (March 1970). Ruihley, G. R., *The Thorn of a Rose: Amy Lowell Reconsidered* (1963). Scott, W. T., *Exiles and Fabrications* (1961).

For articles in reference works, see: *DAB*, VI, 1. *NAW* (article by W. Berthoff). *NCAB*, 19. *20thCA. 20thCAS.*

Other references: *JML* 5 (1963). *TQ* 6 (1964).

CLAIRE HEALEY

Mina Loy

B. 27 Dec. 1882, London, England; d. 25 Sept. 1966, Aspen, Colorado
D. of Sigmund and Julia Brian Lowy; m. Stephen Haweis, 1903; m. Arthur Cravan (Fabian Avenarius Lloyd), 1918

L. has always been considered an American modernist poet. Her modernist education began at seventeen with the study of painting in Munich, London, and Paris. She was elected to the Autumn Salon in 1906 and then left Paris for Florence. There she met the Futurists and incorporated their revolutionary theories of painting and literature into her early poetry. Her poems began appearing in the American little magazines in 1914, and she joined the New York avant-garde in 1916. L. shared the Americans' commitment to the rejuvenation of word and image and their search for new poetic forms, derived from modern painting, to depict the movement of consciousness. At the forefront of poetic experiment, L. earned notoriety for her structural innovations and her sexual subject matter. After 1925 she was largely forgotten, partly because she lacked the discipline to develop her early breakthroughs, and also because she gave much of her creative energy to painting.

L. was married twice: in 1903 to Stephen Haweis, an English painter; in 1918 to Dadaist Arthur Cravan. Of her four children, one died in infancy, one in adolescence. She lived in Paris from 1923 to 1936 and in New York from 1936 to 1954; she spent the remainder of her life with her daughters in Aspen, Colorado.

In her poetry, L. explores the self, "a covered entrance to infinity." Her main symbol is the eye; her enduring theme the necessity of persistent, self- and world-defining vision in a chaotic and indifferent universe. In poems written from 1914 to 1917, she analyzes a female self deformed by social mores that limit women to the roles of wife and mistress and make her success in the marriage market dependent on virginity and sexual ignorance. Educated on romantic love stories, the Italian matrons of "At the Door of the House" (1917) and "The Effectual Marriage" (1917) are soon disillusioned with marriage. The semiautobiographical *Anglo-Mongrels and the Rose* (first half, *Little Review*, 1923–24; second half, *Contact Collection of Contemporary Writers*, 1925) details the English version of the domestic drama. "Parturition" (1914) uses irregular typography to convey woman's physical pain and spiritual quest during childbirth. Her central work is the *Love Songs* (Poems I–IV, *Others*, 1915), or *Songs to Joannes* (Poems I–XXXIV, *Others*, 1917), thirty-four poems on the failure of romantic love, using irregular typography and a collage structure. Proto-surrealist images link sexuality and the psyche, and narrative blurs as the speaker is accosted by fragments of love that introduce her to a meaningless universe. L. retreats from nihilism in "Human Cylinders" (1917), "The Black Virginity" (1918), and "The Dead" (1920), where, recognizing the impossibility of attaining absolute answers to the cosmic mystery, she shifts her emphasis to the *act* of vision.

Lunar Baedeker (1923) contains early poems (thirteen *Love Songs* from 1914 and 1915) and new poems. The theme of the unique vision of the artist, who alone shapes chaos into divine Form, dominates the newer poems. L.'s heritage here is Art for Art's Sake as it developed through Baudelaire, Parnassianism, Laforgue, and the English 1890s. "Apology of Genius" (1922) stresses the artist's alienation from philistine society, the supremacy of art, and the importance of artistic craftsmanship. Other poems draw upon this heritage to defend abstract art. The title poem and "Crab-Angel" satirize the dishonest artist who abandons vision and treats art as a circus for self-display.

Lunar Baedeker reflects the development of L.'s imagery. Early poems alternate abstraction and image to depict the movement of consciousness between intellect and intuition. Later poems are series of vivid images, unified by the interplay of sounds (L.'s trademark), that unite abstraction and image in flashes of vision.

Lunar Baedeker & Time-Tables (1958) retraces former ground and includes a few later poems. In poems written during the 1940s and 1950s L. elaborates a minor early subject, the clownish bum who, as "in Hot Cross Bum," sidesteps vision to pursue false Nirvanas. His companions are other denizens of the metropolis who fabricate illusions in order to escape reality.

Since 1944 L. has been rediscovered by poets and critics who find in her, as in Gertrude Stein, Ezra Pound, and William Carlos Williams, elements of modernist poetry that feed the present. An innovative structuring of consciousness, honesty of subject, and deployment of radiant words and images are qualities that made L. a seminal modernist and connect her to the present.

WORKS: *Auto-Facial Constructions* (1919). *Psycho-Democracy* (1920). *Lunar Baedeker* (1923). *Lunar Baedeker & Time-Tables: Selected Poems of Mina Loy* (1958).

BIBLIOGRAPHY: Burke, G. G., in *Americans in Paris, 1920–1939* (Dictionary of Literary Biography, 1980). Burke, G. G., in *Women's Studies* (1980). Fields, K., "The Rhetoric of Artifice—Ezra Pound, T. S. Eliot, Wallace Stevens, Walter Conrad Arensberg, Donald Evans, Mina Loy, and Yvor Winters" (Ph.D. diss., 1967). Kouidis, V. M., *Mina Loy: American Modernist Poet* (1980). Kouidis, V. M., "Rediscovering Our Sources: An Introduction to the Poetry of Mina Loy," *Boundary 2* (Spring 1980).

For articles in reference works, see: *CB* (Oct. 1950).

Other references: *Circle* (1944). *ConL* (Spring-summer 1961). *Dial* (June 1926). *Little Review* (March 1918). *Nation* (May 1961). New York *Evening Sun* (13 Feb. 1917). *SoR* (July 1967).

VIRGINIA M. KOUIDIS

Clare Boothe Luce

B. 10 April 1903, New York City
Writes under: Clare Boothe, Clare Boothe Brokaw, Clare Boothe Luce
D. of William F. and Ann Clare Snyder Boothe; m. George Tuttle Brokaw,
1923; m. Henry R. Luce, 1935

L. has been a playwright, journalist, politician, diplomat, and feminist.
She planned a theatrical career, attending Clare Tree Major's School of
the Theater, but her direction was changed by a brief stint for the
woman suffrage movement and her marriage to George Brokaw in 1923.
Six years later when her marriage ended, she turned to journalism, serving in editorial posts for *Vogue* and then *Vanity Fair*. In 1931 she resigned, determined to write plays, and shortly thereafter married Henry
Luce, then president of Time Inc.

This second marriage did not interrupt her career. She wrote four
plays for Broadway, then devoted herself to journalism and politics. She
traveled and wrote for *Life*, campaigned for Wendell Willkie and later
for Eisenhower, served two terms as U.S. Congresswoman from Connecticut in the 1940s, and competed for a Republican senatorial nomina-
tion in the early 1950s. She lost the last race, but Eisenhower appointed
her Ambassador to Italy.

During these years, L. wrote and lectured, not only on politics but
also on Catholicism, to which she was converted in mid-life. After the
death of Henry Luce, she retired to Hawaii, where she still writes and
lectures on such diverse subjects as the women's movement, the Catholic
stance on abortion, and conservative Republicanism.

As a writer, L.'s most significant body of work is her plays. The first,
Abide with Me (1935), is a somber melodrama about a sadistic husband
who is finally shot by the faithful family servant. It ran for only thirty-six
performances. Fame came with *The Women* (1936), a vitriolic comedy
about wealthy ladies of leisure. The play centers on the struggles of a devoted wife to regain her husband while living amidst a jungle of catty
women nourished on gossip and the misfortunes of their acquaintances.
The play was filmed twice, in 1939 and 1956, and was revived on Broadway in 1973. In the light of the women's liberation movement of the
1960s and 70s, however, the play comes across as false and unworthy.

L. made Broadway again with *Kiss the Boys Good-Bye* (1938), a frivolous comedy about the much-ballyhooed Hollywood search for an unknown actress to play Scarlett O'Hara, which ran for 286 performances. L.'s last play, *Margin for Error*, a satiric melodrama with an anti-Nazi plot, was produced in 1939. All of her plays, except the first, were later filmed.

A review of L.'s journalistic writings reveals her personal development. Her first piece, *Stuffed Shirts* (1931), is a brittle series of sketches lampooning various New York characters, such as the newly rich dowager, the divorcee, and the Wall Street ladies' man. Later L.'s interests became more international. *Europe in the Spring* (1940) is a lively account of her European travels at the time of the great German offensive. After her seven years in politics, she wrote a series of articles for *McCall's* magazine (1947) describing her religious conversion. In 1952 she edited a volume of essays by American and British authors called *Saints for Now*. *Ladies' Home Journal* printed the essay "Growing Old Beautifully" in 1973.

Despite the more mellow works of her later years, L. is remembered best as a playwright with a heavy hand for sensationalism and sentimentality—two qualities with great appeal for audiences of the 1930s. Her plays are infused with social snobbery and a brisk but vituperative wit with which she characterized the wealthy, sophisticated class. It is a great irony that the hostile, unflattering portraits of her own sex, in plays such as *The Women* and *Kiss the Boys Good-Bye*, should overshadow the more constructive efforts of this feminist.

WORKS: *Stuffed Shirts* (1931). *Abide with Me* (1935). *The Women* (1936; film versions: *The Women*, 1939; *The Opposite Sex*, 1956). *Kiss the Boys Good-Bye* (1938; film version, 1941). *Margin for Error* (1940; film version, 1943). *Europe in the Spring* (1940). *Saints for Now* (edited by Luce, 1952).

BIBLIOGRAPHY: Betts, A. P., *Women in Congress* (1945). Gray, J., "Dream of Unfair Women," in *On Second Thought* (1946). Mersand, J., *American Drama 1930–1940* (1941).

For articles in reference works, see: *CA*, 45–48 (1974). *Catholic Authors: Contemporary Biographical Sketches, 1930–1947*, Ed. M. Hoehn (1952). *NCAB*, F. 20thCA. 20thCAS.

Other references: *NewR* (11 May 1953). *Newsweek* (26 Nov. 1973). *Woman's Home Companion* (Nov. 1955; Dec. 1955; Jan. 1956).

LUCINA P. GABBARD

Mabel Ganson Dodge Luhan

B. 26 Feb. 1879, Buffalo, New York; d. 13 Aug. 1962, Taos, New Mexico
Wrote under: Mabel Dodge, Mabel Dodge Luhan
D. of Charles and Sarah Ganson; m. Karl Evans, 1900; m. Edwin Dodge,
1905 (?); m. Maurice Sterne, 1917; m. Antonio Luhan, 1923

The only child of upper-class parents, L. had an economically and so-cially secure, but emotionally starved, childhood. Tended by nursemaids and kept at a distance by an ineffectual father and a strong-willed, so-cialite mother, L. felt like an orphan who spent her life in search of a community in which she could be "at home."

L. devoted her life to overcoming her anomie by directing her energies to the discovery and creation of her identity. She identified her-self with an enormous variety of aesthetic and political causes; con-structed model communities she hoped would define her role and purpose in modern society; collected famous artists and activists whose careers she tried to shape and who, in turn, she hoped would give shape and meaning to her life; spent twenty years in psychoanalysis while dabbling in a number of mind-cure philosophies; and left twenty-four volumes of autobiographical materials that bear witness to the multiple ways in which she sought self-definition.

Although financially independent and sexually liberated, L. was crip-pled by her belief in woman's cultural subservience. Believing women capable of only "secondary" forms of creativity, she played the role of Muse to men of genius, attempting to achieve an identity by inspiring their creativity. At the same time, she wished to create in her own right, so her relationships with men often turned destructive and self-destruc-tive. She was married four times; only in her last marriage to a full-blooded Pueblo Indian did she achieve any sense of fulfillment. Among the Pueblos, she found a culture in which individual, social, and religious values were integrated by a unifying mythos that was organically re-lated to a land in which she finally felt at home.

L. became a leading symbol of modernism, in fact and fiction. As a spokeswoman for the avant-garde, L. was a published poet, book re-viewer, essayist, biographer, and social critic. Her prose styles and sub-ject matter were a melting pot of Americana, ranging from the banality of the Dorothea Dix–type columns she wrote for the Hearst papers to superbly evocative descriptive prose on life in the Southwest.

L.'s major contribution to American literature is her book *Winter in Taos* (1935). While she sought for years to find writers (D. H. Lawrence and Robinson Jeffers were the two most famous) to publicize her southwestern paradise, she wrote its finest testament herself. *Winter in Taos* is a first-rank contribution to American regional literature, a work of intense lyrical beauty and metaphoric power that achieves a richly sustained integration of her emotional life with the landscape surrounding her.

L.'s discovery of the Indians as potential saviors for a declining white civilization led to the writing of her best-known works, *Intimate Memories* (4 vols., 1933–37). Begun in 1924 as part of an ongoing process of psychotherapy, L. presented her fragmented personality as a metaphor for a world she wished would die and be reborn, as she felt she had, through the grace offered by a prewestern tribal culture. Although L. was not a feminist, her self-portrait reveals the destructiveness of the feminine mystique of which she was both perpetrator and victim.

L.'s memoirs are a significant contribution to social, intellectual, and feminist history. In spite of her sometimes unreliable and self-serving observations, she is an insightful eyewitness to childrearing in Victorian America, the fin de siècle world of American expatriates in Europe, the major revolutionary movements of pre–World War I America, and the fascination of postwar intellectuals with "primitives."

WORKS: *Lorenzo in Taos* (1932). *Intimate Memories* (Vol. 1, *Background*, 1933; Vol. 2, *European Experiences*, 1935; Vol. 3, *Movers and Shakers*, 1936; Vol. 4, *Edge of the Taos Desert*, 1937). *Winter in Taos* (1935). *Taos and Its Artists* (1947).

BIBLIOGRAPHY: Crunden, R., *From Self to Society, 1919–1941* (1972). Hahn, E., *Mabel* (1978). Lasch, C., *The New Radicalism in America (1889–1963)* (1967). Rudnick, L. P., "The Unexpurgated Self: A Critical Biography of Mabel Dodge Luhan" (Ph.D. diss., Brown Univ., 1977).

For articles in reference works, see: *20thCA. 20thCAS.*

LOIS P. RUDNICK

Grace Lumpkin

B. 1903 (?), Milledgeville, Georgia

Raised and educated largely in South Carolina, L. later taught school in Georgia and worked as a home demonstration agent for the government, thereby coming into contact with the poverty of many southern farm families. Her sympathy for the poor was expanded by living and working among North Carolina mountain people and watching their migration to the cotton mills. She became a staunch anticapitalist and ardent supporter of industrial unionism.

L. went to New York when she was twenty-five and began to write short stories, becoming involved in liberal and radical politics. Her first story was published in *The New Masses,* and during the 1930s, like many young writers, she became a fellow traveler. During this period she wrote two proletarian novels, both about the southern poor. *A Sign for Cain* (1935) was the subject of a 1953 inquiry by the Senate Permanent Investigating Sub-Committee, at which L. testified that she had been forced to write communist propaganda into that novel, under threat of having her career "broken" by communist book reviewers. L., who lives now in Columbia, South Carolina, is said to be working at present on a new novel, *God and a Garden.*

L.'s first and best novel, *To Make My Bread* (1932), traces the movement of poor southern tenant farmers and sharecroppers from their rural homes to newly industrialized mill towns. It is a compassionate novel that uses the author's intimate knowledge of these people to explore the cultural shock and the disillusion that they encountered in the transition. While in the southern mountains, these people had endured a stable kind of poverty, ameliorated by the natural beauty of their surroundings, the intoxicating rituals of their fundamentalist religion, and the closeness of family and community ties. In the cotton mills, their large families became a burden, especially for the women who were needed as wage earners; their religion became a tool of the bosses who exploited and distorted its ideals of submissiveness; and the natural beauty was replaced by dreary industrial ugliness. L.'s heroine, Bonnie McClure, like many of the other women, is pushed, almost reluctantly, out of her traditional feminine role as childbearer by the economic exigencies of her life: sooner than watch children starve to death she will become a union organizer and strike leader. L.'s sympathies for factory women are strong, but she tends ultimately to see the resolution of their problems in a socialist transformation of society, despite the fact that their sufferings are markedly different in nature from those of their husbands and brothers.

In her second novel, *A Sign for Cain*, L. again attempts to demonstrate that the interests of all the poor are best served by communism, this time by exploring the potential power of a political alliance between black and white sharecroppers in the South. This novel has, as a kind of antiheroine, a rebellious bourgeois woman, Caroline Gault, who, modern and assertive in her sexual morality, is nevertheless condemned for trying to substitute a reactionary code of individualism for collective action. This novel proposes even more directly than the first that women should not seek sexual justice outside the framework of a socialist redistribution of society's resources.

L.'s third novel, *The Wedding* (1939) makes a movement away from political tendentiousness in favor of a rather sympathetic examination of a southern middle-class family in a state of personal crisis. Her last published work, *Full Circle* (1962), is a novel that has enhanced neither her political nor her literary reputation, dealing as it does with what one critic has called the overcultivated soil of international communist conspiracy.

It is in the first two novels that L. makes her most significant contribution to the literature of feminism. Both provide early examples of the continuing dialectical debate between the adherents of solidarity with other movements of oppressed groups and those who believe that no economic or social equality can ever exist without a prior radical revision of the relationships between men and women.

WORKS: *To Make My Bread* (1932; dramatization, *Let Freedom Ring* by A. Bein, 1936). *A Sign for Cain* (1935). *The Wedding* (1939). *Full Circle* (1962).

BIBLIOGRAPHY: Rideout, W. B., *The Radical Novel in the United States, 1900–1954: Some Interrelations of Literature and Society* (1956).

For articles in reference works, see: *20thCA. 20thCAS.*

Other references: *Books* (27 Oct. 1935). *Nation* (19 Oct. 1932). *NewR* (7 Dec. 1932; 23 Oct. 1935). *NYT* (26 Feb. 1939). *SatR* (9 Nov. 1935).

SYLVIA COOK

Alma Lutz

B. 2 March 1890, Jamestown, North Dakota; d. 31 Aug. 1973, Berlin, New York
D. of George and Matilda Bauer Lutz

L. was a free-lance writer, a journalist, and a contributing editor of *Equal Rights*, the official journal of the National Women's Party. She achieved her literary prominence primarily as the biographer of 19th-c. women leaders.

L.'s first work was *Emma Willard: Daughter of Democracy* (1929). For this narrative biography of the early 19th-c. educator, L. focuses particularly on Willard's early pioneering investigatory work to prove women's intellectual capacity and on Willard's achievements through her Troy, New York, school. L. later published a revised edition of this book entitled *Emma Willard, Pioneer Educator of American Women* (1964). This second version gives a tightened, more sharply honed study of Willard's mature thought and practice. L. portrays with sympathetic insight the consistency of Willard's views in the midst of changing circumstance.

In 1940 L. turned to the women's rights movement, publishing *Created Equal: A Biography of Elizabeth Cady Stanton*. L. gives relatively little attention to the formative experiences of Stanton's early life or even to her early career. She centers instead on the post-1860 years of Stanton's life, when she could devote nearly full-time attention to the women's rights cause as publicist, lecturer, and brilliant formulator of policy statements. L. places particular stress on Stanton as a "torchbearer for women," underscoring Stanton's broad-ranging concerns, the clarity of her perspective, and her role as pioneer anticipator of issues.

L. further extended the Stanton story by collaborating with Elizabeth's daughter, Harriot Stanton Blatch in Blatch's memoirs, *Challenging Years* (1940). The memoirs themselves deal largely with the women's-rights efforts of the late 19th and early 20th centuries.

In the work about Stanton, L. reveals a keen appreciation of the importance of the Stanton-Anthony collaboration. In 1959 Lutz published a significant biographical study of that second figure, *Susan B. Anthony: Rebel, Crusader, Humanitarian*. L. thoughtfully appraises the complementary nature of the two women's work and also traces with careful precision the separate line of Anthony's thought and action. She underscores the crucial importance of Anthony's organizing ability and the unflagging involvement which made her eventually the symbol of the woman-suffrage movement.

L.'s final work on 19th-c. women leaders was *Crusade for Freedom* (1968), a study of women's roles in the antislavery campaigns. In this collective biography L. evaluates the work of such varied personalities as the early antislavery writer, Elizabeth Chandler; the educator, Prudence Crandle; and the lecturer-writers, the Grimké sisters. She underscores the significance of the interwoven strands of antislavery efforts and the emerging women's-rights movement. L. sees this same interweaving of concerns reemerging as an important theme of the 1960s.

L. was essentially a narrative biographer, concerned primarily with the broad public record of 19th-c. women leaders. She developed a strong, dramatic style of writing and became a vivid portrayer of reform personalities. Though concerned with the ideas of the women's movement, L. focused primarily on the efforts to translate ideas into reality. She gave relatively little attention to intellectual history itself or to critical appraisal of the broad social context within which the women functioned. She excelled in the presentation of the individual personality and the detailed accounts of women's campaigns, rather than in analytical background studies.

L.'s studies of Willard and of Stanton in particular were pioneering works. The Stanton work was the first significant appraisal of that leader since the general *History of Woman Suffrage*. The Anthony biography and the study of antislavery women presented more familiar material and drew more on well-known sources. The works provided dramatic restatements of these women's roles.

L. wrote perceptively, lucidly, and with fervor about the 19th-c. struggles for women's rights. She had a strong, appreciative sense of what had been achieved, but also a personal concern for the unfinished tasks. In the years between the first and second women's movements, L. kept before the general public the sharply lit images of forceful women leaders of the past.

WORKS: *Emma Willard: Daughter of Democracy* (1929; rev. ed., *Emma Willard, Pioneer Educator of American Women*, 1964). *Mary Baker Eddy Historical House, Swampscott, Massachusetts: The Birthplace of Christian Science* (1935). *Challenging Years: The Memoirs of Harriot Stanton Blatch* (with H. S. Blatch, 1940). *Created Equal: A Biography of Elizabeth Cady Stanton, 1815-1902* (1940). *Mary Baker Eddy Historical House, Rumney Village, New Hampshire: The Rumney Years* (1940). *With Love, Jane: Letters of American*

Women on the War Fronts (1945). *Susan B. Anthony: Rebel, Crusader, Humanitarian* (1959). *Crusade for Freedom: Women of the Antislavery Movement* (1968).

BIBLIOGRAPHY: For articles in reference works, see: *CA*, 45–48 (1974); *Permanent Series* (1975).

Other references: *AHR* (July 1959; Dec. 1968). *NewR* (29 July 1940). *NEQ* (Dec. 1959). *NYT* (9 June 1919; 1 Sept. 1973). *SatR* (7 March 1959).

INZER BYERS

Grace Livingston Hill Lutz

B. 15 April 1865, Wellsville, New York; d. 23 Feb. 1947, Swarthmore,
Pennsylvania
Wrote under: Grace Livingston Hill, Grace Livingston Hill-Lutz, Grace
Livingston, Marcia Macdonald
D. of Charles Montgomery and Marcia Macdonald Livingston; m. Frank Hill,
1892; m. Flavius J. Lutz, 1916

L.'s mother published four romances under the name of Mrs. C. M. Livingston, but devoted herself primarily to being a preacher's wife. Apparently in order to honor her mother as an individual, L. published three novels under her mother's given name, Marcia Macdonald. L.'s father, a Presbyterian minister, also did some writing, exclusively on theological topics. His influence is reflected in L.'s establishment and direction of a mission Sunday school in Swarthmore. Perhaps the strongest of all family influences was that of L.'s aunt, Isabella Macdonald ("Pansy") Alden, an author who not only encouraged L. to write but persuaded her own publisher to print the youngster's first effort, *The Esseltynes; or, Alphonso and Marguerite*.

L.'s first husband, also a Presbyterian minister, died after seven years of marriage. L. was forced to publish enough to support herself and her two daughters. She began with Sunday-school lessons in a column syndicated by ten local newspapers, but soon turned to fiction. By 1904 she was successful enough to build herself a comfortable home in Swarthmore. L.'s second marriage was unhappy and soon led to separation, although L. remained adamant in her opposition to divorce. She was active as a writer until the end of her life, her final novel being completed by her daughter Ruth for posthumous publication.

L. worked in a wide range of genres, specializing in the adventure story and contemporary romance but also including fantasy (her first novel, *A Chautauqua Idyll*, 1887), nonfiction (*The War Romance of the Salvation Army*, 1919), historical romance (*Marcia Schuyler*, 1908), and mystery (*The Mystery of Mary*, 1912). She wrote 107 books, which sold over three million copies during her lifetime.

L. was especially successful at writing fast-paced adventures featuring intelligent and resourceful heroines. A good example is *The Red Signal* (1919), set during World War I. When the German truck farm where young Hilda Lessing works turns out to be swarming with German spy activity, Hilda shows herself to be both brave and lucky as she saves the U.S. from a major disaster and wins a presidential medal. She also wins the reward reserved for all of L.'s finest heroines—marriage with a handsome and affluent young man. Although the historical perspective is simplistic—World War I is explained as the result of Germany's "forgetting God"—and although the plot turns on some very unlikely coincidences, the narrative is compelling enough to have thrilled many a reader.

L.'s most popular books were contemporary romances, such as *Matched Pearls* (1933), *Beauty for Ashes* (1935), and *April Gold* (1936). The most widely read of all, *The Witness* (1917), brought her thousands of letters of gratitude. In it as in most of her books, L. utilizes one-dimensional characterization in which Christian believers are sincere, brave, and altruistic while unbelievers are selfish and corrupt. Paul Courtland is the typical L. hero: rich, handsome, popular, athletic, a Phi Beta Kappa man. A rich girl, who parallels the biblical "scarlet woman" by attempting to seduce Paul away from his faith, possesses a "nasty little chin" with "a Satanic point." She is contrasted with a poor orphan girl who, because of her modesty and integrity, wins the prize of marriage to the hero. L. manifests a lively sense of social justice by having Paul refuse a lucrative management position in a company that exploits its factory workers in unsafe conditions. The novel's theme is the actual presence of Christ in any life devoted to human concern and justice. As one character puts it, "It's heaven or hell, both now and hereafter."

L. knew how to wring human emotion and enlist current events to enliven her novels while she was making fairly overt attempts to convert her readers to Christ. For instance, a 1944 novel, *Time of the Singing of Birds*, features an attractive officer who returns wounded from World

War II. When he eventually marries the most deserving of his Christian girlfriends, an observer comments, "Heavens! If I thought I could have a marriage like that it would be worth-while trying to be a Christian."

Improbable coincidence, avoidance of moral ambiguity, unconscious sexism, and almost exclusive use of stock characters work together to keep L.'s fiction lightweight. But her fast-paced upbeat style has refreshed and relaxed many people. And there can be little doubt that L. provided a shining ideal for younger readers by featuring so many heroines of unshakable standards and determined, triumphant integrity.

WORKS: *A Chautauqua Idyll* (1887). *A Little Servant* (1890). *The Parkerstown Delegate* (1892). *Katharine's Yesterday, and Other Christian Endeavor Stories* (1895). *In the Way* (1897). *Lone Point; a Summer Outing* (1898). *A Daily Rate* (1900). *The Angel of His Presence* (1902). *An Unwilling Guest* (1902). *According to the Pattern* (1903). *The Story of a Whim* (1903). *Because of Stephen* (1904). *The Girl from Montana* (1908). *Marcia Schuyler* (1908). *Phoebe Deane* (1909). *Dawn of the Morning* (1910). *Aunt Crete's Emancipation* (1911). *The Mystery of Mary* (1912). *The Best Man* (1914). *The Man of the Desert* (1914). *Miranda* (1915). *The Finding of Jasper Holt* (1916). *A Voice in the Wilderness* (1916). *The Witness* (1917). *The Enchanted Barn* (1918). *The Red Signal* (1919). *The Search* (1919). *The War Romance of the Salvation Army* (with E. Booth, 1919). *Cloudy Jewel* (1920). *Exit Betty* (1920). *The Tryst* (1921). *The City of Fire* (1922). *The Big Blue Soldier* (1923). *Tomorrow About This Time* (1923). *Re-Creations* (1924). *Ariel Custer* (1925). *Not Under the Law* (1925). *Coming through the Rye* (1926). *A New Name* (1926). *The Honor Girl* (1927). *Job's Niece* (1927). *The White Flower* (1927). *Blue Ruin* (1928). *Crimson Roses* (1928). *Found Treasure* (1928). *Duskin* (1929). *An Interrupted Night* by I. M. Alden (introduction by Lutz, 1929). *Out of the Storm* (1929). *The Prodigal Girl* (1929). *The Gold Shoe* (1930). *Ladybird* (1930). *The White Lady* (1930). *The Chance of a Lifetime* (1931). *Kerry* (1931). *Memories of Yesterday* by I. M. Alden (edited by Lutz, 1931). *Silver Wings* (1931). *Beggarman* (1932). *The Challengers* (1932). *Happiness Hill* (1932). *Her Wedding Garment* (1932). *The House across the Hedge* (1932). *The Story of the Lost Star* (1932). *The Beloved Stranger* (1933). *Matched Pearls* (1933). *The Ransom* (1933). *Amorelle* (1934). *The Christmas Bride* (1934). *Rainbow Cottage* (1934). *Beauty for Ashes* (1935). *The Strange Proposal* (1935). *White Orchids* (1935). *April Gold* (1936). *Mystery Flowers* (1936). *The Substitute Guest* (1936). *Brentwood* (1937). *Daphne Deane* (1937). *Sunrise* (1937). *The Best Birthday* (1938). *The Divided Battle* (1938). *Dwelling* (1938). *Homing* (1938). *The Lost Message* (1938). *Maria* (1938). *Marigold* (1938). *The Minister's Son* (1938). *Patricia* (1939). *The Seventh Hour* (1939). *Stranger within the Gates* (1939). *Head of the House* (1940). *Partners* (1940). *Rose Galbraith* (1940). *Astra* (1941). *By Way of the Silverthorns* (1941). *In Tune with Wedding Bells* (1941). *Crimson Mountain* (1942). *The Girl of the Woods* (1942). *The Street of the City* (1942). *The Sound of the Trumpet* (1943). *The Spice Box* (1943).

Through These Fires (1943). *More than Conquerer* (1944). *Time of the Singing of Birds* (1944). *All through the Night* (1945). *A Girl to Come Home To* (1945). *Bright Arrows* (1946). *Where Two Ways Met* (1947). *Mary Arden* (completed by R. L. Hill, 1948).

BIBLIOGRAPHY: Karr, J., *Grace Livingston Hill: Her Story and Her Writings* (1948).

For articles in reference works, see: *DAB*, Suppl. 4. *NAW* (article on Grace Livingston Hill by P. S. Boyer). *Reader's Encyclopedia of American Literature*, Ed. M. J. Herzberg (1962). *20thCA. 20thCAS.*

Other references: *Book News Monthly* (Oct. 1915).

VIRGINIA RAMEY MOLLENKOTT

Helen Merrell Lynd

B. 1896, La Grange, Illinois; d. 30 Jan. 1982, Warren, Ohio
D. of Edward Tracy and Mabel Waite Merrell; m. Robert S. Lynd, 1921

Raised as a Congregationalist, L. shifted her religious orientation while at Wellesley College (B.A. 1919) to an explanation of the world based on Hegelian dialectics. She earned an M.A. (1922) and a Ph.D. (1944) in history from Columbia University; her teaching career centered around Sarah Lawrence College, where she taught from 1929 to 1964. L. shared with her husband a rich, full life as wife, mother of their two children, and professional colleague.

Middletown: A Study in Contemporary American Culture (1929) and the companion volume, *Middletown in Transition: A Study in Cultural Conflicts* (1935), written by L. and her husband, are well-documented studies outstanding in their comprehensiveness, accuracy, and interpretation of community life in the U.S. In 1924 and 1925, the Lynds and their research staff lived in the Middletown community and collected information from a variety of sources, as anthropologists study primitive tribes. The study is organized by an analysis of the major activities for community survival: getting a living, making a home, training the young, and engaging in religious practices and community activities. Although ending their first study on a cautious note recognizing the problems resulting from rapid social change, the prosperity and optimism of the community is evident.

The Lynds returned to Middletown during the Depression. Earning a living, staying healthy, and in general surviving the effects of financial collapse make life in 1935 starkly different from what it was in 1925. The ability of the city to recover and retain optimism is still striking though. Class privileges and strain are more apparent in the later study, yet a sense of worker solidarity is lacking. Radical social change did not occur as a result of radical changes in economics. Rather, the community adhered to "the American way," hoping for a better future.

These remarkable community studies provide a systematic view of an American city in times of stability and change. They also set a high standard of sociological expertise making them landmark studies of community development.

In *Field Work in College Education* (1945), L. studies student-teacher interaction and the application of social-science principles in everyday life. *England in the Eighteen-Eighties: Toward a Social Basis for Freedom* (1945) is a sweeping and powerful study, beautifully written, of the interaction between ideas, material changes, and social movements during a period of social ferment. In *On Shame and the Search for Identity* (1958), L. analyzed more contemporary problems arising from the relationship between the individual and society. The 1965 collection, *Toward Discovery*, serves as a brief overview of L.'s writings.

L.'s interests and skills cover a wide range of topics and disciplines. Always dedicated to the holistic approach to human behavior, her work reflects her standards of excellence and consistent probing for new insights into the human experience.

WORKS: *Middletown: A Study in Contemporary American Culture* (1929). *Middletown in Transition: A Study in Cultural Conflicts* (1935). *Field Work in College Education* (1945). *England in the Eighteen-Eighties: Toward a Social Basis for Freedom* (1945). *On Shame and the Search for Identity* (1958). *Toward Discovery* (Ed. B. J. Loewenberg, 1965).

BIBLIOGRAPHY: Loewenberg, B. J., Introduction to *Toward Discovery* (1965).
For articles in reference works, see: *20thCA. 20thCAS.*

MARY JO DEEGAN

Mary Margaret McBride

B. *16 Nov. 1899, Paris, Missouri; d. 7 April 1976, West Shokan, New York*
D. *of Thomas Walker and Elizabeth Craig McBride*

M., the daughter of a modestly successful farming couple, always knew she would be a journalist. Two relatives whose interest had permanent influence on M. were her maternal grandfather, a Baptist minister, who schooled her in bible readings, and her paternal grandfather, a scholar, who gave her an appreciation of Greek and Latin poetry. The first woman in her family to aspire to a career, she attended the University of Missouri, graduating in two and a half years, and financing her education by working on the Columbus *Times*. Successive feature-writing positions on the Cleveland *Press* and the New York *Mail* catapulted her to a syndicated column, a woman's-page editorship, and extensive magazine freelance work.

A second and third career for M. emerged from the Depression years when periodicals ceased publication or could no longer pay her prices. She turned to producing books and to conducting a daily program on radio (and ultimately on television), earmarking each media venture with her special vitality, her wide-ranging interests, her candor, and her respect for facts.

Though, on the one hand, M.'s work was characterized by deep-seated religious and moral convictions, plus sincere and un-self-conscious sentimentality, she was at the same time a tough and searching reporter. And though she struggled against and never conquered deep feelings of guilt and insecurity, she numbered among her close friends heads of state and celebrities in diverse fields in the U.S. and abroad. Testaments to her personal popularity and magnetism were the quarter of a million letters she received annually from listeners and a party on her tenth anniversary in radio, held at Madison Square Garden and attended by 125,000 "Mary Margaret" fans.

M.'s newspaper assignments were, for the most part, self-selected. She managed, whether the story involved a parade, a political convention, or a luncheon, to make the reader feel like a ringside spectator by introducing particulars of texture, smell, and other detail. Her acute sensory awareness coupled with searching curiosity and a zealot's concern for the truth contributed to M.'s being one of the most sought-after and highest-paid journalists in the country.

When the magazine market suffered reverses in the late 1920s, M. completed four travel books with coauthor and journalist, Helen Josephy. Though the books sold well because European travel was becoming popular, they have little value today except as social documents. Their pre-occupation with where celebrities dined, resided, and shopped, made these books highly palatable to middle America and were a harbinger of M.'s modus operandi and subsequent success in radio and television.

Several other volumes are autobiographical, nonintellectual, nonliter-ary, but highly readable. *A Long Way from Missouri* (1959) and its sequel, *Out of the Air* (1960), recount with modesty and pride the events of M.'s life. Both books are replete with names and anecdotes, her successes and her setbacks, all treated honestly and with the utmost simplicity.

Her shift in media to radio, and later to television, made no difference in the persona of M., though, for contractual reasons, she assumed initially the "radio name" of Martha Deane. The same buoyancy, frank-ness, and cozy confidentiality prevailed. Her selection of guests, books, professions, and hobbies were examined like feature stories, utilizing, for the first time, newspaper techniques in radio presentation. To the extent that material was written, she prepared it herself, including the commercials. Products were always personally pretested for acceptability before she agreed to their sponsorship. *Printer's Ink*, authoritative bible of the marketing world, commenting on the slavish acceptance of her listeners, described the response to her program and her merchandising prowess as "the most outstanding example of reliance upon the word of a human being in the commercial field."

With the death in 1954 of her friend and manager, Stella Karn, M. gave up her own program and restricted herself to guest appearances. Six years later she moved permanently to a refurbished barn in West Shokan, New York. Her own assessment of her career was characteris-tically candid and self-effacing: "I've enjoyed my life and don't regret any of it. But I can see that, taken altogether it is faintly, sometimes even blatantly ridiculous. I wanted to be a great writer, and now I never shall be."

WORKS: *Jazz: A Story of Paul Whiteman* (with P. Whiteman, 1926). *Charm* (with A. Williams, 1927). *Paris Is a Woman's Town* (with H. Josephy, 1929). *The Story of Dwight Morrow* (1930). *London Is a Man's Town* (with H. Josephy, 1931). *New York Is Everybody's Town* (with H. Josephy, 1931). *Beer and Skittles: A Friendly Modern Guide to Germany* (1932). *Here's Martha Deane* (1936). *How Dear to My Heart* (1940). *America for Me* (1941). *Tune in for Elizabeth* (1945). *How to be a Successful Advertising Woman* (edited by McBride, 1948). *Harvest of American Cooking* (1957). *Encyclopedia of Cooking* (1959). *A Long Way from Missouri* (1959). *Out of the Air* (1960). *The Giving Up of Mary Elizabeth* (1968).

BIBLIOGRAPHY: For articles in reference works, see: *CB* (1954; June 1976). *Ladies of the Press*, I. Ross (1974). *Successful Women*, I. Taves (1943). *Whatever Became of . . . ?*, R. Lamparski (1970).

Other references: *American Mercury* (Jan. 1949). *Life* (4 Dec. 1944). *NY* (19 Dec. 1942). *NYT* (8 April 1976). *SatR* (1 March 1947). *Scribner's* (March 1931).

ANNE S. BITTKER

Mary Therese McCarthy

B. *21 June 1912, Seattle, Washington*
D. *of Roy Winfield and Theresa Preston McCarthy; m. Harold Johnsrud, 1933; m. Edmund Wilson, 1938; m. Bowden Broadwater, 1946; m. James Raymond West, 1961*

M. graduated from Vassar in 1933 and then settled in New York City, where she began her writing career. M.'s early book reviews appeared in *The New Republic* and *The Nation*, and in 1937 she became drama editor of the *Partisan Review*. She quickly attracted the attention of the literary establishment, which she often sharply attacked.

Known primarily as a novelist, M. is a very fine expository writer, who covers a wide range of subjects, from theories of the novel to travel observations to art history. Many of her essays are on political subjects. Her prose is graceful and precise, showing the influence of her classical education. M. dislikes slang and often uses Latinate diction as well as long, balanced structures, but her writing is generally informal. M.'s sentences are often barbed, sometimes given to startling generalizations; but she is usually concrete, meticulous, and reasonable.

M. began writing fiction at the suggestion of her second husband, the critic Edmund Wilson, and published her first story in 1939. She was long admired by a small readership, but *The Group* (1963) was an enormous bestseller and vastly enlarged her public. The novel recreates an era as it follows the lives of eight Vassar girls of the class of 1933 during the seven years after their graduation. It details their experiences with sex, psychiatry, domesticity, and politics; a description of one character's defloration is both funny and shockingly graphic. The book has a unique third-person point of view: The narrative "voice" is that of the Group, sometimes in chorus, sometimes individually. The girls are comic characters by M.'s definition—ineducable, unchanging, and therefore immortal.

M. is an extremely personal writer whose uses of her acquaintances in fiction are often unflattering. *The Oasis* (1949), a prize-winning *conte philosophique* about a utopian experiment, is a case in point; Philip Rahv and Dwight Macdonald were the "originals" of two satiric portraits which expose the dishonesty and pretentiousness of liberals whose high ideals and rhetoric offer no immunity against human frailty. M. is no gentler with herself than with her friends. Some readers have mistaken "Artists in Uniform" for fiction, probably because of the uncomplimentary light it casts upon the author, but it is fact. So, M. says, are two of the short stories about Margaret Sargent, heroine of M.'s first novel, *The Company She Keeps* (1942), which is actually a collection of stories unified by Margaret's quest for self. Other characters based to some extent on M. include Kay (*The Group*), Martha Sinnott (*A Charmed Life*, 1955), and Rosamund Brown (*Birds of America*, 1971). These characters are self-consciously "superior" but at times self-doubting, and relentlessly honest with themselves, believing that if action is sometimes compromised, thought should never be. Although liberal intellectuals, they believe in ritual and ceremony and abhor the common, the cheap, and the ugly.

These characteristics are discernible in the child described in *Memories of a Catholic Girlhood* (1957), M.'s autobiography. A collection of memoirs brought together with an introduction and epilogues, the book derives its unity chiefly from the character of the young Mary and from its themes of education, Catholicism, Jewishness, the quest for superiority, and the difficulty of doing the right thing for the right reason.

In *The Groves of Academe* (1952), Henry Mulcahy, a physically and morally repulsive man, fights his dismissal from a "progressive" college by falsely confessing to membership in the Communist Party, thereby cynically enlisting the support of faculty liberals. The novel moves with relentless logic from Mulcahy's letter of dismissal to the resignation of Hoar, blackmailed by the triumphant Mulcahy. In conforming to liberal conventions, Hoar and the faculty override their own good sense and powers of observation.

Yet even when not self-deceived, the liberal in M.'s fiction finds moral integrity difficult to achieve. In *Birds of America*, Peter Levi, a nineteen-year-old egalitarian and literary kinsman of Candide, sees that the things he most loves—nature, tradition, art—are threatened by the advance of the thing he believes in most—equality; yet the evils of injustice and poverty persist undiminished. In *Cannibals and Missionaries* (1979) a committee of liberals en route to Iran to investigate the Shah's regime and a tour group of American art collectors are hijacked by an international terrorist group and held in Holland while the collectors are exchanged for their priceless paintings and a farmhouse is turned into an unlikely gallery. Liberals and paintings are then offered in exchange for Holland's withdrawal from NATO and severing of relations with Israel. The novel's moral center is a senator who comes to the recognition that terrorism is a "kid brother" of minority electoral politics; both are equally ineffectual against the inertia of facts. The outcome is grim, but the mode is comic; people and their institutions are impervious to these events, and at the end, the Reverend Mr. Frank Barber, among others, has survived to go on counting his blessings.

M.'s ear is true, and her fiction is rich with the sounds of authentic voices, heightened but not distorted. If her characters are often ridiculous, she tolerates their absurdities even as she exposes them, although she is merciless with self-professed intellectuals who exempt themselves from responsibility to facts. Her most malevolent characters—Henry Mulcahy and Norine Schmittlapp (*The Group*)—thrive in personal and moral squalor with no foothold in truth.

As social critic and moralist, M. has consistently and scrupulously sought truth. Neither hopeful nor sentimental, M.'s messages often fall on unwelcoming ears. Like most satiric writers, she sometimes writes about the topical. But her range is wide, her eye and ear are keen, and her literary commitment is to the durable and universal facts of human life candidly and often caustically recorded.

WORKS: *The Company She Keeps* (1942). *The Oasis* (1949). *Cast a Cold Eye* (1950). *The Groves of Academe* (1952). *A Charmed Life* (1955). *Sights and Spectacles: 1937–1956* (1956). *Venice Observed* (1956). *Memories of a*

Catholic Girlhood (1957). *The Stones of Florence* (1959). *On the Contrary: Articles of Belief, 1946–1961* (1961). *The Group* (1963). *Mary McCarthy's Theatre Chronicles, 1937–1962* (1963). *Vietnam* (1967). *Hanoi* (1968). *The Writing on the Wall, and Other Literary Essays* (1970). *Birds of America* (1971). *Medina* (1972). *The Mask of State: Watergate Portraits* (1974). *The Seventeenth Degree: How It Went, Vietnam, Hanoi, Medina, Sons of the Morning* (1974). *Cannibals and Missionaries* (1979).

BIBLIOGRAPHY: Auchincloss, L., *Pioneers and Caretakers: A Study of Nine American Women Writers* (1965). Goldman, S., *Mary McCarthy: A Bibliography* (1968). Grumbach, D., *The Company She Kept* (1967). Hardwick, E., *A View of My Own: Essays in Literature and Society* (1963). McKenzie, B., *Mary McCarthy* (1966). Mailer, N., *Cannibals and Christians* (1966). Stock, I., *Mary McCarthy* (University of Minnesota Pamphlets on American Writers, No. 72, 1968).

For articles in reference works, see: *CA*, 5–8 (1969). *20thCAS*.

Other references: *Columbia University Forum* 6 (1973). *Esquire* (July 1962). *JAmS* 9 (1975). *Paris Review* (Winter-Spring 1962).

WILLENE S. HARDY

Helen McCloy

B. *6 June 1904, New York City*
Writes under: *Helen Clarkson, H. C. McCloy, Helen McCloy*
D. of *William Conrad and Helen Worrell Clarkson McCloy;* m. *David Dresser, 1946*

M.'s father was managing editor of the New York *Evening Sun;* her mother wrote short stories under her maiden name. A Quaker, M. studied at the Brooklyn Friends School in New York. At fourteen, she published a literary essay in the Boston *Transcript;* at fifteen, she published verse in the *New York Times.* M. lived in France for eight years, studying at the Sorbonne in 1923 and 1924. M. was Paris correspondent for the Universal News Service (1927–31) and the monthly art magazine *International Studio* (1930–31). She also was London correspondent for the Sunday *New York Times* art section and wrote political sketches for the London *Morning Post* and the *Daily Mail.*

M. returned to the U.S. in 1931 and spent several years writing magazine articles and short stories. In 1938, she published her first mystery novel, *Dance of Death*. She has one daughter. She was divorced in 1961 from her husband, who writes mysteries under the name Brett Halliday.

M. has been rather prolific, writing twenty-eight novels of detection and suspense, many short stories, and newspaper and magazine articles. She won Ellery Queen Mystery Magazine awards for the short stories "Through a Glass, Darkly" (reprinted in *The Singing Diamonds*, 1965) and "Chinoiserie" (reprinted in *20 Great Tales of Murder*, 1951), and the Edgar Award from the Mystery Writers of America for the best mystery criticism. M. was the first woman president of the Mystery Writers of America.

Dance of Death features her detective, Dr. Basil Willing, a psychiatrist and an expert in forensic medicine; he appears in many of what are considered her strongest novels. The social satire in such novels as *Cue for Murder* (1942) and *Two-Thirds of a Ghost* (1956), as well as the fine presentation of New York society in *Alias Basil Willing* (1951) and *Unfinished Crime* (1954), suggests, as Erik Routley has indicated, that M. is one of those mystery writers in whom "there is a good deal of straight novel-writing." Anthony Boucher believes that M. "has always resembled the best British writers of the Sayers-Blake-Allingham school in her ability to combine a warm novel of likeable people with a flawless deductive plot."

M.'s choice of a psychiatrist-detective as hero reveals her interest in psychology, especially in its more paranormal manifestations, as is evident in *Through a Glass, Darkly* (1949), *Who's Calling?* (1942), and *The Slayer and the Slain* (1957). Her interest in the fragile structure upon which an individual's personality is based is shown in *The Changling Conspiracy* (1976), which deals with political kidnapping and brainwashing. This and other recent novels reflect M.'s interest in contemporary affairs; *The Goblin Market* (1943) and *Panic* (1944), which were written during World War II and deal with problems created by the war, suggest that this interest is not new.

In general, critics have preferred M.'s novels of detection to the novels of suspense or terror. M. herself believes that the current popularity of detective stories is related to "some lack in the accepted literary diet." The "moral understanding of common minds which results in sympathy for common lives" and the themes "that mean so much to the common man—love and death"—are missing from modern novels. In her best works, M.'s success in providing interesting characters and themes is matched with her ability in plotting.

WORKS: Dance of Death (1938). *The Man in the Moonlight* (1940). *The Deadly Truth* (1941). *Cue for Murder* (1942). *Who's Calling?* (1942). *Do Not Disturb* (1943). *The Goblin Market* (1943). *Panic* (1944). *The One That Got Away* (1945). *She Walks Alone* (1948). *Through a Glass, Darkly* (1949). *Alias Basil Willing* (1951). *20 Great Tales of Murder* (edited by McCloy, with B. Halliday, 1951). *Unfinished Crime* (1954). *The Long Body* (1955). *Two-Thirds of a Ghost* (1956). *The Slayer and the Slain* (1957). *The Last Day* (1959). *Before I Die* (1963). *The Singing Diamonds* (1965). *The Further Side of Fear* (1967). *Mister Splitfoot* (1968). *A Question of Time* (1971). *A Change of Heart* (1973). *The Sleepwalker* (1974). *Minotaur Country* (1975). *The Changling Conspiracy* (1976). *The Imposter* (1977). *The Smoking Mirror* (1979). *Burn This* (1980).

The papers of Helen McCloy are at the Boston University Library, Boston, Massachusetts.

BIBLIOGRAPHY: Routley, E., *The Puritan Pleasures of the Detective Story* (1972).

For articles in reference works, see: *CA*, 25-28 (1971). *A Catalogue of Crime*, J. Barzun and W. H. Taylor (1971). *Encyclopedia of Mystery and Detection*, Eds. C. Steinbrunner and O. Penzler (1976). *WA*.

Other references: *NYHTB* (28 Nov. 1943; 7 Oct. 1956)*. NYT* (27 Feb. 1938; 11 Oct. 1942; 18 June 1950).

DIANA BEN-MERRE

Anne O'Hare McCormick

B. 16 May 1880, Wakefield, England; d. 29 May 1954, New York City
Wrote under: Anne O'Hare, Anne O'Hare McCormick
D. of Thomas and Teresa Beatrice O'Hare; m. Francis J. McCormick, 1910

As an infant M. was brought from England to Columbus, Ohio, by her American-born parents. Intellectually influenced by her Catholic mother, a poet and woman's-page editor, M. was educated in private schools in Ohio, graduating from the College of St. Mary of the Springs. Following in her mother's footsteps, she published children's feature articles and soon became an associate editor for her mother's employer, Cleveland's weekly *Catholic Universe Bulletin*.

After her marriage to an engineer and importer, M. resigned her editorship and traveled with her husband on his European business trips. She wrote several impressionistic articles about European countries in the aftermath of World War I for the *New York Times Magazine*.

In 1921, her dispatches from Europe, serious assessments of the rise of fascism in Italy and of the role of Benito Mussolini (a figure then dismissed as a "posturing lout" by most journalists) impressed *Times* managing editor Carr V. Van Anda. He hired her as a foreign correspondent in 1922. She was the first woman hired as a regular contributor to the *Times* editorial page (1936) and the second woman to receive a Pulitzer Prize for journalism (in 1937, for her European correspondence).

Through the early 1950s she lectured in major U.S. cities, made radio broadcasts, and wrote "Abroad," a column based on reportage in Europe, Asia, and Africa. She also published editorials commenting on the American political scene.

The Hammer and the Scythe: Communist Russia Enters the Second Decade (1928) is based on articles M. originally wrote for the *Times* while traveling in Russia in the 1920s. M. reports her impressions of the Russian people, their conditions, and the clash of new and old. *The Hammer and the Scythe* is among the best of the books written by American journalists visiting Russia in the 1920s, but *The World at Home* (1956), one of two collections of M.'s *Times* columns posthumously edited by her personal friend, Marion Sheehan, better withstands the passage of time. Like other writers in the 1930s, M. "rediscovered America" in the pieces included in *The World at Home*. Her generalizations about the nation are convincing, particularly when examined together with the essays on Franklin Roosevelt. She connects small details that blend into larger patterns of the nation's character and dramatizes "that curious community . . . between the mind of the President and the mind of the people."

M. considered herself above all else a newspaperwoman. Aside from her book on Russia, she preferred to write "on top of the news while people were listening." Her reporting of foreign and domestic events was clear, incisive, and authoritative. It embodied her commitment to moral absolutes and professional standards of reporting. The body of correspondence (especially, warnings about fascism's rise in Europe), achievements as an influential political columnist, and eighteen years of service on the editorial board of America's most prestigious newspaper, secure M. an important place in the ranks of American journalists.

WORKS: *The Hammer and the Scythe: Communist Russia Enters the Second Decade* (1928). *The World at Home: Selections from the Writings of Anne O'Hare McCormick* (Ed. M. T. Sheehan, 1956). *Vatican Journal: 1921–1954* (Ed. M. T. Sheehan, 1957).

BIBLIOGRAPHY: Filene, P. G., *Americans and the Soviet Experiment: 1917–1933* (1967). Hohenberg, J., *Foreign Correspondence: The Great Reporters and Their Times* (1964). Marzolf, M., *Up from the Footnote: A History of Women Journalists* (1977). Talese, G., *The Kingdom and the Power* (1966).

For articles in reference works, see: *Catholic Authors: Contemporary Biographical Sketches, 1930–1947*, Ed. M. Hoehn (1952). *Ohio Authors and Their Books*, Ed. W. Coyle (1962). *20thCA. 20thCAS.*

Other references: *CathW* (Oct. 1954). *NYT* (30 May 1954). *SatR* (19 June 1954).

JENNIFER L. TEBBE

Carson Smith McCullers

B. 19 Feb. 1919, Columbus, Georgia; d. 29 Sept. 1967, Nyack, New York
Wrote under: Carson McCullers, Lula Carson Smith
D. of Lamar and Marguerite Waters Smith; m. Reeves McCullers, 1937; divorced 1940; remarried McCullers, 1945

M.'s childhood was remarkable more for imaginative activity than for external events. She knew firsthand the monotony and dreary heat of a small southern town, which later provided settings for her novels. Her family was very supportive of her artistic talents, which gave early promise in both writing and music.

In 1935, M. went to New York City to study music. She lost her tuition money to the Julliard School of Music, however, and took part-time jobs while studying writing at Columbia University. She married a young army corporal, whom she divorced in 1940 but remarried five years later.

Her health, always delicate, deteriorated steadily from a tragic series of paralyzing strokes, breast cancer, and pneumonia. Yet she received visitors, traveled, and worked at her writing while half paralyzed until a final stroke killed her when she was about fifty.

M. received immediate acclaim with her remarkable first novel, *The Heart Is a Lonely Hunter* (1940), written when she was twenty-two. She became one of the most controversial writers in America and had many prominent friends, including Tennessee Williams, W. H. Auden, Louis MacNiece, and Richard Wright.

With *The Heart Is a Lonely Hunter*, M. established the themes that concerned her in all subsequent writings: the spiritual isolation of the individual and the individual's attempt to transcend that loneliness through love. The action centers on a deaf-mute, John Singer, to whom an odd assortment of characters turn as to a being especially wise and benevolent. The adolescent Mick speaks to him passionately of music, although Singer has never heard music. Dr. Copeland, a black physician, confides desperately his dreams for educating his race. Jake Blount, an ineffectual agitator, rants about the workers' revolution. Biff Brannon, quiet observer of men, is fascinated by Singer because of his effect on all the others. But Singer loves another mute: an indolent, retarded Greek named Antonapoulos, who can never respond in kind to the outpourings of communication from Singer's expressive hands. Thus, each man creates a god fashioned after his own need—but such gods fail. When Antonapoulos dies in a mental hospital, Singer commits suicide. His death signals the fading of a dream for each of those who revered him. This novel, like many of M.'s works, is highly symbolic yet rich in concrete detail. A number of allegorical meanings have been suggested for the story, of which M.'s own, concerning fascism, seems least appropriate.

Reflections in a Golden Eye (1941) is technically more polished and controlled than the first novel but more grotesque in character and event. In the static, ingrown environment of a southern army post, Captain Penderton, a latent homosexual, is impotent with his beautiful wife, Leonora, but infatuated with their neighbor, Major Langdon, who is her lover. The catalyst is Private Williams, an inarticulate young man with an affinity for nature and horses, especially Leonora's high-spirited stallion, Firebird. Captain Penderton both loves and hates Private Williams with a repressed sado-masochism reminiscent of D. H. Lawrence's "The Prussian officer." Williams glimpses the naked Leonora through an open door, and thereafter he creeps into the Penderton house at night and crouches reverently beside Leonora's bed simply to watch her sleep. Captain Penderton discovers him there and shoots him. The influence of Freud is unmistakable in this novel; M. was one of the first American writers to deal openly with homosexual impulses. The approach is consistently objective and nonjudgmental, as though reflected in the disinterested eye of nature.

M.'s novella *The Ballad of the Sad Café* (1951) achieves more successfully the mode of archetypal myth she approached in *Reflections in a Golden Eye*. It combines realistic detail with the legendary quality of folk ballad, in a tale of love at once melancholy and sardonically humorous. Surely no more incongruous pair exists in literature than the manlike, independent, cross-eyed Miss Amelia and her self-centered little hunchback, Cousin Lyman. Singlehandedly running an excellent distillery and the only general store, Miss Amelia is the leading citizen of a tiny backwoods community. The townsfolk, like a stupid and malicious Greek chorus, have no recreation but observing her colorful career. Miss Amelia once married a local bad boy but quickly threw him out when he tried to augment their partnership with sexual attentions. The humiliated lover made threats, turned to crime, and landed in the penitentiary. Now, a pathetic, homeless dwarf who claims kinship to Miss Amelia straggles into town. Contrary to all expectations, she takes in the stranger and builds her life around him. She opens a café, which becomes the social hub of the community, and the misshapen Cousin Lyman becomes a strutting little prince in her modest castle. Eventually, however, her despised husband returns from prison. Ironically, the dwarf becomes enamored with Macy, who uses him to harass Miss Amelia. The competition culminates in a public fistfight between Miss Amelia and Macy. Miss Amelia is actually winning when the dwarf leaps savagely upon her back and turns her victory into physical and emotional defeat. The two men vandalize her café and distillery and then get out of town. Miss Amelia becomes a recluse, and the town seems to share in her emotional death. There is nothing to do there now but listen to the melancholy singing of the chain gang.

M. hardly surpassed the skill and originality of *The Ballad of the Sad Café*, but many people prefer her mood piece, *The Member of the Wedding* (1946). It is certainly the most autobiographical of M.'s novels, and may seem closer to everyday experience, although the view of life as painful and frustrating is consistent with her more bizarre creations. The story concerns a motherless adolescent girl's abortive attempt to outgrow her childhood and create a platonic bond of love with a dimly understood adult world. Frankie Addams wants to find the "we" of "me" and thus escape the prison of selfhood; she decides to go away with her brother and his bride at their forthcoming marriage. This preposterous dream is born of endless conversations in the kitchen with Berenice, the black maid who is her only adult companion, and her seven-year-old cousin, John Henry, who represents the relatively untroubled childhood she wishes to discard. The little boy dies unexpectedly at the end of the novel, suggesting not only that childhood passes but that even children are not exempt from tragedy. Frankie, of course, is denied her dream of the perfect threesome on the honeymoon. She does not die of this traumatic rejection, but something rare and fragile is broken. M. converted this novel into an award-winning play, which ran for 501 performances in New York.

M.'s other works include a number of significant short stories ("A Tree, A Rock, A Cloud," sometimes compared in theme to "The Rime of the Ancient Mariner," was chosen for *O. Henry Memorial Prize Stories of 1942*); some poetry for children; another, less successful play (*The Square Root of Wonderful*, 1958, with fifty-five performances on Broadway); and one other novel, written in the veritable shadow of death. *Clock without Hands* (1961) concerns a man who faces death from leukemia.

In the foreword to *The Square Root of Wonderful*, M. wrote: "I suppose a writer writes out of some inward compulsion to transform his own experiences (much of it unconscious) into the universal and symbolical. . . . Certainly I have always felt alone." She admired, and to some extent emulated, some of the very greatest writers: Tolstoy, Dostoevsky, and Flaubert. M.'s works do not have the psychological insight or concentrated impact of the European masters, but they still cherished Christian redemption as the answer to human failure, which M. cannot do. For her, there is only human love to pit against the indifferent universe—and that love is tragically flawed.

WORKS: The Heart Is a Lonely Hunter (1940; film version, 1968). *Reflections in a Golden Eye* (1941; film version, 1967). *The Member of the Wedding* (1946; dramatization, 1951; film version, 1952). *The Ballad of the Sad Café* (1951; dramatization by E. Albee, 1963). *The Square Root of Wonderful* (1958). *Clock without Hands* (1961). *Sweet As a Pickle and Clean As a Pig: Poems* (1964). *The Mortgaged Heart* (Ed. M. G. Smith, 1971).

BIBLIOGRAPHY: Carr, V. S., *The Lonely Hunter, a Biography of Carson McCullers* (1975). Eisinger, C. E., *Fiction of the Forties* (1963). Evans, O., *The Ballad of Carson McCullers* (1966). Schorer, M., in *The Creative Present*, Eds. N. Balakian and C. Simmons (1963).

For articles in reference works, see: *American Writers*, Ed. L. Unger (1972). *CA*, 5–8 (1969); 25–28 (1971). *Contemporary American Novelists*, M. Felheim (1964). *20thCA. 20thCAS.*

Other references: *CE* (Oct. 1951). *GaR* (12, 1958; Summer 1963). *Jahrbuch fur Amerikastudien* 8 (1963). *Kenyon Review* (Winter 1947). *SAQ* 56 (1957). *WSCL* (1, 1960; Feb. 1962).

KATHERINE SNIPES

Betty Bard MacDonald

B. 26 March 1908, Boulder, Colorado; d. 7 Feb. 1958, Seattle, Washington
Wrote under: Betty MacDonald
D. of Darsie and Elsie Sanderson Bard; m. Robert Eugene Heskett, 1927;
  m. Donald Chauncey MacDonald, 1942

The second of five children, M. lived in Mexico, Idaho, and Montana before her mining-engineer father transferred the family to Seattle. After his death, the children were raised by M.'s mother and paternal grandmother. In 1927, M. abandoned art studies at the University of Washington to marry an insurance salesman, who brought her to a chicken ranch on the Olympic Peninsula. They separated in 1931, eventually divorcing in 1935. M. remained with her two daughters in her mother's home, holding a variety of jobs until her second marriage.

In 1943, at her sister Mary's urging, M. took a day from work to prepare a book outline for a visiting publisher's representative. That book became *The Egg and I* (1945), and her writing career was launched.

M. lived with her husband on Vashon Island, Puget Sound, until they purchased a California ranch in 1955. Stricken with cancer in 1957, she returned to Seattle for treatment and died at the age of forty-nine.

M.'s major books are autobiographical and are written in high humor. *The Egg and I*, her witty account of life on a primitive chicken ranch, achieved immediate popularity; one million copies were sold in the first year of publication. In 1947, Universal International released the movie, starring Fred MacMurray and Claudette Colbert and featuring Marjorie Main and Percy Kilbride as Ma and Pa Kettle.

Much of M.'s charm as author-character lies in her zealous determination to do the right thing. Nevertheless, her homemade bread is a disaster and her autopsies of spraddled chick carcasses futile ("Cause of death: Eggzema"). Amid the humor, M. probes the loneliness of the farm wife, discovering in a fair exhibit of knotted gunnysacks a pathetic symbol of what isolation can do to a woman. Behind her parade of outlandish characters, she offers carefully muted evidence of her crumbling marriage.

The Plague and I (1948) details M.'s battle against tuberculosis at age thirty. Confined in a sanatorium, she sketches other inmates with an artist's precision, barely touching on her own fears. *Anybody Can Do Anything* (1950) encompasses her years as a career woman during the Depression, and *Onions in the Stew* (1955) depicts family life on Vashon Island.

A born humorist with a fine sense of timing, M. knows how to tell a story. Her observations are succinct ("piddocks are clams with some sort of neurosis that makes them afraid to face life"), her caricatures barbed ("a small sharp-cornered woman with a puff of short gray hair like a gone-to-seed dandelion"), and her language friendly and pleasantly earthy. Less generally recognized is her affinity to nature. In M.'s almost lyric descriptions of mountains in the mist, damp green rain forests, and the earth itself, the eye of the art student never deserts her.

M.'s humor is frequently self-deprecatory. Actually quite competent, M. creates an impression of hopeless ineptness, at the same time praising courageous women like her mother and sister. Her ambivalence toward housework and domesticity is striking. She genuinely loves children and displays a gregarious nature, yet one senses in her writing a barely repressed undercurrent of frustration, almost anger, at the subordinate role that wife and mother must play in society.

Critically dismissed as a "regional" and "popular" writer, M. still projects an easy warmth and familiarity that draw her reader close. Though her popularity has waned since the 1950s, M.'s work is worthy of rediscovery; her comments are as pungent, her characters as delightful as ever.

WORKS: *The Egg and I* (1945; film version, 1947). *Mrs. Piggle-Wiggle* (1947). *The Plague and I* (1948). *Mrs. Piggle-Wiggle's Magic* (1949). *Anybody Can Do Anything* (1950). *Nancy and Plum* (1952). *Mrs. Piggle-Wiggle's Farm* (1954). *Onions in the Stew* (1955). *Hello, Mrs. Piggle-Wiggle* (1957). *Who, Me? The Autobiography of Betty MacDonald* (1959).

BIBLIOGRAPHY: Spacks, P. M., *The Female Imagination* (1975).
Other references: *NYT* (8 Feb. 1958). *SatR* (14 May 1955). Tacoma *News Tribune* (28 Aug. 1977).

JOANNE McCARTHY

Jessica Nelson North MacDonald

B. 7 Sept. 1894, Madison, Wisconsin
Writes under: Jessica Nelson North
D. of David Willard and Elizabeth Nelson North; m. R. I. MacDonald, 1921

Early in life M. showed signs of the literary potential that would bring her recognition as poet, novelist, critic, and editor. A precocious child, she memorized and recited poetry from the time she could speak. By the age of five, she read the newspaper and composed rhymes. In her youth M. competed successfully with other young poets, including Edna St. Vincent Millay, in the contests conducted by Mary Mapes Dodge, editor of *St. Nicholas Magazine.*

M. discovered *Poetry Magazine* while a student at Lawrence College, from which she was graduated in 1917. When M. moved to Chicago in 1920, she began to contribute poems to *Poetry;* through the next few decades, she placed poems in such magazines as the *Dial,* the *Forge, Atlantic Monthly,* the *London Mercury, the Double-Dealer, Nation, The New Yorker, Voices,* the *Lyric,* and the *Saturday Evening Post.* In 1927 she was awarded the Reed Poetry prize.

M.'s best poetry is finely crafted, and even the weakest shows inventiveness. Her first volume, *A Prayer Rug* (1923), while evincing control of traditional techniques and forms, reveals modernist influences. As Elizabeth Tietjens pointed out, M. creates images with the best of her peers, but knows that "a single image is not enough to make a poem." M. treats a wide range of everyday topics, and a number of the poems shed light on the complexity of woman's role in society. Her calm ironic voice registers clearly in such poems as "Hunger Inn," "The Marionette," and "The Sleeper."

The poems in *The Long Leash* (1928) demonstrate M.'s growth as a poet. The volume exhibits what Horace Gregory calls her "technique of restraint." The selections focus on the power of the creative woman to capture and examine intensely dramatic male-female relationships. The title poem, considered one of her best, treats the confidence with which reciprocated love enables the creative woman to face life's realities and fulfill her artistic potential. "A Sumerian Cycle" and "Hibernalia" illustrate the breathless emotion M. is capable of producing through understatement. M. succeeds best in the longer poems, where she develops and multiplies dramatic scenes.

M.'s artistic control and keen sensibility appear again in *Dinner Party* (1942), although this volume seems to lack the modernity of her other poetry of that period. As late as 1982, she was at work on a fourth volume of poetry.

Although M. is primarily a poet, she has also produced two successful novels: *Arden Acres* (1935) and *Morning in the Land* (1941). *Arden Acres* draws upon her observations of life in a suburban area outside Chicago during the Depression years. The narrator depicts the lives of the Chapin family, plagued by poverty and shocked by the father's murder. Although the emotional impact of the novel is effective, its real strength lies in the characterization of women from three generations —Gram, Loretta, and Joan—each of whom demonstrates unusual resilience and aptitude for survival.

Morning in the Land, based on the recollections of M.'s father, is a fictional account of an English immigrant family in Wisconsin between 1840 and 1861, when the son is about to leave for service in the Civil War. The novel centers on the frontier achievements of the protagonist, Dick Wentworth, but it also calls attention to the difficulties both Indian and white women endured within the male-oriented social structure.

Throughout the period in which her prose and poetry were being published, M. also gained a reputation as editor and critic. She began by editing the Chicago Art Institute *Bulletin* under the direction of Robert Harshe. Learning on the job, M. prepared catalogues for exhibits and published many articles describing various holdings of the institute. In 1927, she moved to *Poetry*, where over the next twenty years, under the tutelage of Harriet Monroe, she helped make *Poetry* a showcase for the best young American and British authors. M. filled various editorial posts and, in later years, served as a member of the advisory committee. During this period she wrote twenty-one articles and fifty book reviews. Her contributions ranged from caustically critical pieces such as "The Wrong-Headed Poets," "The Hungry Generations," and "Quality in Madness," to the gently appreciative tribute commemorating the death of Harriet Monroe. In her criticism, as in her poetry, M. displays a sharp eye for honesty of emotion and perfection of form.

WORKS: *A Prayer Rug* (1923). *The Long Leash* (1928). *Arden Acres* (1935). *Morning in the Land* (1941). *Dinner Party* (1942). *Paintings: An Introduction to Art* (with C. J. Bulliet, 1934). *History of Alpha Delta Pi* (1929).

LUCY M. FREIBERT

Katherine Sherwood Bonner McDowell

B. 26 Feb. 1849, Holly Springs, Mississippi; d. 22 July 1883, Holly Springs, Mississippi
Given name: Catherine Sherwood Bonner
Wrote under: Sherwood Bonner
D. of Charles and Mary Wilson Bonner; m. Edward McDowell, 1871

As a young teenager, M. experienced the harsh realities of the Civil War, when Union troops occupied Holly Springs and even her family home. M. also suffered personal losses during the war years, with the deaths of her youngest sister in 1863 and her mother in 1865. In 1871, M. married another native of Holly Springs; their only child was born in 1872. The McDowells separated in 1873; finally, M. established residence in Illinois and obtained a divorce in 1881.

In 1873, M. moved to Boston to pursue a career in writing; there Nahum Capen, who had published her first story in 1864, recommended her to Henry W. Longfellow, with whom she worked and established a close friendship. During 1876, M. sent from Europe a number of travel articles for the Memphis *Avalanche* and the Boston *Times*. Her only novel, *Like Unto Like*, was published in 1878.

M. returned to Holly Springs in the fall of 1878 and nursed her father and brother through fatal illnesses with yellow fever. In 1881, as her writing career was gaining momentum, M. learned that she had breast cancer. Until her death, she continued to write and to prepare her short stories, which had appeared in such magazines as *Lippincott's*, *Harper's Weekly*, and *Youth's Companion*, for publication in two volumes, *Dialect Tales* (1883) and *Suwanee River Tales* (1884).

M.'s Gran'Mammy tales present a distinctive element of southern life; M. creates one of the finest literary portraits of the black mammy, who sustained and taught the members of her white family. "Gran'Mammy's Last Gifts" (1875) may well be the first example of black dialect published in a northern magazine. The most successful story of the group is "Coming Home to Roost" (1884), in which M. perceptively treats slave superstition. The child narrator has a significant role in the story's action, for her chance remark causes Aunt Beckey to believe she has been bewitched. The story is humorous, yet suspense builds as Beckey weakens spiritually and physically. She is cured by the brash young medical student, Henry, who is able to deal with the "trickery" on Beckey's level. M.'s detailed and accurate descriptions are effective, as is the realistic attitude of the rest of the white family, who can view Henry's actions only as a "fraud."

A study of M.'s fiction does not reveal any sustained development from purely regional to more sophisticated realistic works. Even though she began writing as a teenager, M. wrote for too short a period of time to develop her talents fully. *Like Unto Like* was reviewed favorably, but M. is appreciated today chiefly for her short stories, especially for her realistic use of dialects—lower-class midwestern, southern mountain, and black—and her humor. Many readers also enjoy her characterizations and plots. She is important as a forerunner of later southern women writers like Flannery O'Connor and Eudora Welty.

WORKS: Like Unto Like (1878). *Dialect Tales* (1883). *Suwanee River Tales* (1884). *Gran'Mammy* (1927).

BIBLIOGRAPHY: Frank, W. L., *Sherwood Bonner* (1976). McAlexander, H. H., *The Prodigal Daughter: A Biography of Sherwood Bonner* (1981).

For articles in reference works, see: *AA. DAB*, VI, 2. *NAW* (article by L. J. Budd).

Other references: *ALR* (Winter 1972). *MissQ* (Winter 1963–64). *NMW* (Spring 1968; Spring 1969).

MARTHA E. COOK

Phyllis McGinley

B. 21 March 1905, Ontario, Oregon; d. 22 Feb. 1978, New York City
D. of Daniel and Julia McGinley; m. Charles L. Hayden, 1937

Beginning her career as a teacher in New Rochelle, New York, M. wrote poetry in her spare time. Her success in publishing it in magazines enabled her to give up teaching. To keep going, M. held various other positions, including poetry editor for *Town and Country* and copywriter for an advertising agency. According to an interview in *Newsweek*, she started writing in the style of Swinburne, but switched to light verse when she found out that that was what *The New Yorker* wanted from her.

Faithful to the eastern seaboard, although brought up in Colorado and Utah, she hymned New York to begin with and then, when she moved to Westchester County, the suburbs. In a volume of essays, *The Province of the Heart* (1959), she speaks out in favor of the Easterner and praises the village in which she lives for the way the neighbors love one another. A suburban housewife and mother was what she was and what she was happy to be.

Her first volume of verse, *On the Contrary*, was published in 1934. It contains mainly occasional verse—light comments on contemporary events. It was followed by *One More Manhattan* (1937), in which M. developed more of the tone we associate with her—light, astringent, and witty. There are times when M. comes close to Emily Dickinson, but she deliberately avoids total seriousness. *A Pocketful of Wry* (1940) contains a fair amount of political comment. In *Husbands Are Difficult; or, The Book of Oliver Ames* (1941), M. pokes fun at her husband, but her mockery is very mild and loving. In *Stones from a Glass House* (1946), she comments on the war but refuses to hate. *The Love Letters of Phyllis McGinley* (1954) shows her improving and maturing, and won several awards.

M. won the Pulitzer Prize in 1961 for her volume of collected poetry, *Times Three* (1960), which was prefaced by W. H. Auden. The collection starts with the poems of the 1950s and works backward through the 1940s and 1930s. Some of the most charming poems are about saints and reformers, bearing testimony to her religious convictions as a Catholic but also to her moderation and warmhearted reasonableness. In a second volume of essays, *Sixpence in Her Shoe* (1964), M. writes of the trials and rewards of a wife and mother, a state which she accounted woman's most honorable profession.

A Wreath of Christmas Legends (1967) and *Saint-Watching* (1969) show her more deeply entrenched in the Catholic faith. In *Saint-Watching*, M. deliberately brings out the human side of the saints, whom she treats as people endowed with a special form of genius; it is a delight to read and can be described without irony as heartwarming. M. also wrote a number of children's books, but these do not have the distinction of her writing for adults.

Staunchly traditional, M. believed in lifelong vows and in the special vocation of women to motherhood. She also believed in the reality of sin, but was sure it could be forgiven. For her, manners were morals. Her lightness of touch was always backed by an acute intelligence and the feeling that she had found her proper place. She was probably a happy woman.

WORKS: *Mary's Garden* (1927). *On the Contrary* (1934). *One More Manhattan* (1937). *A Pocketful of Wry* (1940). *Husbands Are Difficult; or, The Book of Oliver Ames* (1941). *The Horse Who Lived Upstairs* (1944). *The Plain Princess* (1945). *Stones from a Glass House* (1946). *All Around the Town* (1948). *A Name for Kitty* (1948). *The Most Wonderful Doll in the World* (1950). *Blunderbus* (1951). *The Horse Who Had His Picture in the Paper* (1951). *A Short Walk from the Station* (1951). *The Make-Believe Twins* (1953). *The Love Letters of Phyllis McGinley* (1954). *The Year without a Santa Claus* (1957). *Merry Christmas, Happy New Year* (1958). *Lucy McLockett* (1959). *The Province of the Heart* (1959). *Sugar and Spice: The ABC of Being a Girl* (1960). *Times Three: Selected Verse from Three Decades with Seventy New Poems* (1960). *Mince Pie and Mistletoe* (1961). *The B Book* (1962). *Boys Are Awful* (1962). *A Girl and Her Room* (1963). *How Mrs. Santa Claus Saved Christmas* (1963). *Sixpence in Her Shoe* (1964). *Wonderful Time* (1966). *A Wreath of Christmas Legends* (1967). *Wonders and Surprises* (1968). *Saint-Watching* (1969). *Confessions of a Reluctant Optimist* (1973).

BIBLIOGRAPHY: Auden, W. H., Foreword to *Times Three* by P. McGinley (1960).

For articles in reference works, see: *CB* (Nov. 1961). *20thCAS*.

Other references: *Commonweal* (9 Dec. 1960). *Newsweek* (26 Sept. 1960). *SatR* (10 Dec. 1960).

BARBARA J. BUCKNALL

Sister Madeleva

B. 24 May 1877, Cumberland, Wisconsin; d. 25 July 1964, Boston, Massachusetts
Given name: Mary Evaline Wolff
D. of August and Lucy Arntz Wolff

The daughter of a German-born harness maker and a former teacher, M. grew up in a mill town in rural Wisconsin. After a year at the University of Wisconsin, M. transferred to St. Mary's College at Notre Dame, Indiana, from which she graduated in 1909. She received an M.A. from the University of Notre Dame and a Ph.D. in English from the University of California. By 1908, she had joined the Congregation of the Holy Cross which conducts St. Mary's, taking the name Sister Mary Madeleva, and her entire life was devoted to educating women. From 1934 to 1961, M. served as president of St. Mary's; during this time she was responsible for the founding of the first American Catholic graduate school of theology for the laity. From 1942–48 she was president of the Catholic Poetry Society of America.

Her prose works include essays and addresses on education as well as literary criticism. M.'s best-known study is "Chaucer's Nuns" (1925), in which she interprets details of the portrait of the prioress in the prologue to the Canterbury Tales by observing her in the context of religious life.

With the publication of Knights Errant, and Other Poems (1923), M. became the first of the modern "nun-poets"—a peculiarly American phenomenon.

Most of M.'s poems are short lyrics, usually under twenty lines. M.'s only leisure, she explained, came in recuperating from illnesses; other moments were snatched between tasks, in walking from building to building, or during nights of insomnia.

Only occasionally do her poems focus on secular themes: her visits to Oxford and the Holy Land, glimpses of nature, or literary interests. "Marginalium," for example, protests the death of the Lady of Shalott. The great bulk of M.'s work deals with religious experience.

M.'s religious poetry is always personal and devotional, never didactic or public. By dealing with her own experience, M. avoids the pious and the platitudinous. Her verse abounds in nature imagery of an amiable sort. "My Windows," from *Penelope, and Other Poems* (1927), describes two "wonder-windows": One lets in "tranquillity and noon . . . magic and the moon"; the other looks on a garden with "a sudden rose, / A poppy's flame. . . ." It is through these windows that the poet sees God. Here as always M.'s theme is constant love and serene beauty; images of horror or despair are absent.

Even the tone of religious longing is usually carefully modulated. In "Petals and Wings," from *Four Girls, and Other Poems* (1941), field flowers—"Silent, at peace, and beautiful"—are contrasted with "wild, unlettered birds, / Song-silver things." The poet's question as to whether "petalled peace" or "wilding flight / Into the sun" is ultimately preferable remains unanswered, except in the hidden mind of God.

The mystical "The King's Secret" (in *Penelope*), generally recognized as M.'s best poem, is unlike almost all her other work. In this poem, her longest, M. abandons her usual reticence and in explicitly erotic language, inspired by and even echoing the Song of Songs, speaks ecstatically of union with "this King Who is God and your Lover." Some critics, presumably not recognizing the biblical precedent, were critical of this breach of nunly decorum, and the poem was not included in *Selected Poems* (1939). In her later published work M. returned to the ascetic restraint of her first volume.

WORKS: *Knights Errant, and Other Poems* (1923). *Chaucer's Nuns, and Other Essays* (1925). *Pearl—A Study in Spiritual Dryness* (1925). *Penelope, and Other Poems* (1927). *A Question of Lovers, and Other Poems* (1935). *The Happy Christmas Wind, and Other Poems* (1936). *Christmas Eve, and Other Poems* (1938). *Gates, and Other Poems* (1938). *Selected Poems* (1939). *Four Girls, and Other Poems* (1941). *Addressed to Youth* (1944). *A Song of Bedlam Inn, and Other Poems* (1946). *Collected Poems* (1947). *A Lost Language, and Other Essays on Chaucer* (1951). *American Twelfth Night, and Other Poems* (1955). *The Four Last Things* (1959). *My First Seventy Years* (1959). *Conversations with Cassandra* (1961). *A Child Asks for a Star* (1964).

BIBLIOGRAPHY: For articles in reference works, see: *CB* (1942; 1964). *NCAB*, 51. *20thCA*. *20thCAS*.

Other references: *America* (57, 1937; 58, 1938). *Catholic Library World* (12, 1940). *Commonweal* (63, 1956). *Spirit* (6, 1939; 15, 1948). *Thought* (23, 1948).

ARLENE ANDERSON SWIDLER

Theresa Serber Malkiel

B. *1 May 1874, Bar, Russia; d. 17 Nov. 1949, New York City*
M. *Leon A. Malkiel, 1900*

M. emigrated to the U.S. with her family in 1891. Her political activity began when she became a member of the Russian Workingmen's Club. In 1892, she helped organize the Woman's Infant Cloak Maker's Union, was elected its first president, and served as its delegate to the Knights of Labor. In 1893, she joined the Socialist Labor Party and was a delegate to the first convention of the Socialist Trade and Labor Alliance in New York City. M. split from the Socialist Labor Party in 1899 and joined the Socialist Party, in which she continued to be active for many years. M.'s interest in the relationship between feminism and socialism became central to her political work in 1907 when she helped organize the Women's Progressive Society of Yonkers, New York. When a vacancy occurred in the National Woman's Committee, she was elected a member by the national committee of the Socialist Party.

In addition to extensive labor-union organizing throughout the northeast and midwest, M. was an ardent champion of "women's issues." She wrote of the coming "free woman," whose goals could be realized only within the framework of a socialist future. Similarly, M. disagreed with party members who claimed that feminism detracted from the class struggle; to M., the woman question was an important key to the emancipation of all humanity. Throughout her career, M. wrote extensively in such party-affiliated journals as *Socialist Woman, Progressive Woman,* and *Coming Nation* and such periodicals as New York *Call,* Chicago *Daily Socialist,* and *Daily Forward* (New York). She also edited a woman's column in the *Jewish Daily News* (New York).

Both *Woman of Yesterday and Today* (1915) and *Woman and Freedom* (1915) vigorously argue the implicit relationship and politically necessary connection between feminist and socialist goals. Both works establish the historical connections between the women's rights movement and the entrance of women into the wage-earning labor force. In

Woman of Yesterday and Today, M. writes a brief history of the changing economic status of American women since the revolutionary war, focusing on how working conditions and experiences create a new self-definition for women and a concomitant desire for expanded rights. In *Woman and Freedom*, M. links this new consciousness with the history of political advancement of all working people. M. also underscores the double oppression of the working woman: "Under the present system the working man has only one master—his employer, the workingwoman must bow to the will of husband as well." Both pamphlets stress the importance of a direct and personal involvement in political activity on the part of American women: "She who would be free must herself strike the blow."

In *Diary of a Shirtwaist Striker* (1910), a fictionalized account of the New York shirtwaist maker's strike, M. dramatizes both the obstacles faced and the triumphs attained through direct and personal political activism. Written from the point of view of a native-born American woman who works not for survival but for extra money, the novel depicts the heroine's conversion, first to the immediate goals of the strike and eventually to the wider goals of the Socialist Party. It provides an excellent introduction to many of the problems that were central to the unionization of women during the early years of the 20th c.: the tensions between native and immigrant workers, the hostility of male trade unions, the class bias of the Women's Trade Union League, and the questions about "woman's place" raised by parents and lovers when their daughters and fiancées were on picket lines. M.'s main focus is on the self-respect, comradeship, and capabilities that develop among young women as a result of their strike experiences. Her heroine becomes a vividly portrayed mouthpiece for M.'s vision of the woman of the future, a woman for whom the goals of feminism and socialism have become inseparable.

The resurgence of attention paid to the connection between issues of sex and class has generated a new interest in M.'s writings. Her tireless investigation of the relationship between a woman's personal and political self-definition will strike many readers as surprisingly modern. *Diary of a Shirtwaist Striker* should prove of invaluable interest to any reader interested in questions about the relationship between social movements and literary representation.

WORKS: *Diary of a Shirtwaist Striker* (1910). *Woman and Freedom* (1915). *Woman of Yesterday and Today* (1915).

BIBLIOGRAPHY: Blake, F., *The Strike in the American Novel* (1972). Buhle, M. J., "Feminism and Socialism in the United States, 1820–1920" (Ph.D. diss., Univ. of Wisconsin, 1974). Dancis, B., "Socialism and Women in the United States, 1900–1917," in *Socialist Revolution* (1976). Hill, V., "Strategy and Breadth: The Socialist-Feminist in American Fiction" (Ph.D. diss., SUNY at Buffalo, 1979). Maglin, N., "Rebel Women Writers, 1894–1925" (Ph.D. diss., Union Graduate School, 1975).
Other references: *Progressive Woman* (May 1909).

VICKI LYNN HILL

Catherine Marshall

B. 27 Sept. 1914, Johnson City, Tennessee; d. March 1983
D. of John Ambrose and Leonora Whitaker Wood; m. Peter Marshall, 1936;
m. Leonard Earle LeSourd, 1959

M.'s father was a pastor of a Presbyterian church in Canton, Mississippi, and later in Keyser, West Virginia. M. earned a B.A. in history from Agnes Scott College. Her first husband was already a well-known pastor in Atlanta when they were married. In 1937, they moved to the New York Avenue Church in Washington, D.C., and in 1946 Peter became chaplain of the U.S. Senate. After her husband's death in 1949, M. became an editor and writer in order to support herself and her son. Her second husband was editor of *Guideposts*, an inspirational magazine that has published many of M.'s shorter articles. M. was woman's editor of the *Christian Herald* from 1958 to 1960, when she became a roving editor for *Guideposts*.

In 1953, M. was named "Woman of the Year" in the field of literature by the Women's National Press Club. She is a member of Phi Beta Kappa, has served Agnes Scott College as a trustee, and has received honorary doctorates from Cedar Crest College and Taylor University.

M.'s first independent work was editing a few of Marshall's sermons and prayers, which were published as *Mr. Jones, Meet the Master* (1949). *Mr. Jones* stayed on the nonfiction best-seller list for almost a year and led to the contract for her most important work, *A Man Called Peter* (1951), a bestseller for many years.

A Man Called Peter has been categorized as "a biography, an auto-biography-biography, a fairy story with a sad ending, a Horatio Alger novel, a how-to book on successful marriage, and a straight-from-the-shoulder devotional on God." Whatever its genre, this book sold over four million copies during its first twenty years and is still selling well. With M. assisting in production, it was made into a successful movie (1955), and it has been translated into Dutch, printed in a large-print edition, and recorded for the blind.

This "autobiography-biography" is, of course, the story of Peter Marshall, the Scotsman who grew up in poverty, emigrated to America, and became one of the most widely admired preachers of the 20th c. The prose is clear, concise, concrete; and the book is saved from excessive sentiment by its simple sincerity, honesty, and forthrightness.

M.'s novel, *Christy* (1967), features a protagonist whose fortitude grows from her faith, much as Marshall's does in *A Man Called Peter*. Based on the experiences of the author's mother, *Christy* is the story of a nineteen-year-old woman who, in 1912, leaves her comfortable home to spend a year teaching in the Smoky Mountains of Tennessee. The clear style and obvious sincerity that mark all of M.'s works enable this long novel to maintain its charm, even though it sometimes moves very slowly.

M. has also written or edited fourteen other book-length works, including several children's books, and many articles for popular and religious magazines. Her latest publication, *The Helper* (1978), is a series of forty devotionals about the Holy Spirit, which M. says "has been written out of my own spiritual need to speak to those who share my longing for thirst-quenching quaffs of the Living Water." Probably everything M. has ever published could be prefaced by those words.

WORKS: *The Mystery of the Ages* (with P. Marshall, 1944). *Mr. Jones, Meet the Master: Sermons and Prayers of Peter Marshall, D.D.* (edited by Marshall, 1949; rev. ed., 1950). *A Man Called Peter: The Story of Peter Marshall* (1951; film version, 1955). *Let's Keep Christmas* by P. Marshall (introduction by Marshall, 1953). *God Loves You: Our Family's Favorite Stories and Prayers* (with P. Marshall, 1953; rev. ed., 1967). *The Prayers of Peter Marshall* (edited by Marshall, 1954). *Friends with God: Stories and Prayers of the Marshall Family* (1956). *The Heart of Peter Marshall's Faith: Two Inspirational Messages from "Mr. Jones, Meet the Master"* (introduction by Marshall, 1956). *To Live Again* (1957). *The First Easter* (by P. Marshall, edited and introduction by Marshall, 1959). *John Doe, Disciple: Sermons for the Young in Spirit* (by P. Marshall, edited and introduction by Marshall, 1963). *Beyond Ourselves* (1966). *Christy* (1967). *Claiming God's Promises:*

Selections from "Guideposts" by Catherine Marshall and Others (1973). *Something More: In Search of a Deeper Faith* (1974). *Adventures in Prayer* (1975). *The Helper* (with P. Marshall, 1978). *My Personal Prayer Diary* (with E. LeSourd, 1979). *Meeting God at Every Turn* (1980).

BIBLIOGRAPHY: Davis, E. L., *Fathers of America: Our Heritage of Faith* (1958). Hosier, H. K., *Profiles: People Who Are Helping to Change the World* (1977).

For articles in reference works, see: *CA* (1976). *Something about the Author*, Ed. A. Commire (1971).

Other references: *Newsweek* (4 April 1956). *PW* (18 Oct. 1971). *SatR* (10 April 1954).

PEGGY SKAGGS

Paule Marshall

B. 9 April 1929, Brooklyn, New York
D. of Samuel and Ada Burke; m. Kenneth E. Marshall, 1957; m. Nourry Menard, 1970

A first-generation American born of Barbadian parents, M. spent her childhood in Brooklyn. At the age of nine, she visited the native land of her parents and discovered for herself the quality of life peculiar to that tropical island. After writing a series of poems reflecting her impressions, M. began a long period of reading. She graduated Phi Beta Kappa from Brooklyn College (1953) and attended Hunter College (1955) for postgraduate study.

M. has worked in libraries and, as a staff writer for *Our World* magazine, has traveled on assignment to Brazil and the West Indies. She has lectured at several colleges and universities within the U.S. and abroad and has contributed short stories and articles to various magazines and anthologies. M. has been the recipient of several awards and grants.

In her first novel, *Brown Girl, Brownstones* (1959), M. explores the coming of age of Selina Boyce and the struggle for survival of a black immigrant family and community. Divided into four sections, the novel functions on several imaginative levels and devotes some attention to the ramifications of power as experienced by the dawning political consciousness of a small black community.

M.'s consistent use of imagery and symbolism, and her concise, rhythmic, and passionate style dramatically define and technically underscore themes of rebirth and self-definition. The end result is a picture of a world not blurred by racial bitterness, but sharply focused in its unabashed honesty and deliberate confrontation of Western cultural values.

Her language is strikingly beautiful and powerfully effective, capturing the essence of black language as a weapon of survival and revealing how spoken communication can itself be a form of art. M. adopts and adapts the West Indian dialect, fusing it with biblical and literary allusions to create a language that compels imaginative associations and entertains with the sheer delight of sound.

Soul Clap Hands and Sing (1961), a collection of short stories, borrows its title from Yeats's "Sailing to Byzantium." Thematic connections are obvious as we read the accounts of four men of different national origins experiencing the inevitable decline of age.

Caught up in the Western credo of amassing wealth and prestige, the characters have developed a hardened exterior impervious to meaningful human relationships. When the submerged need for love and acceptance emerges, they can only respond by reaching out to the young. That itself remains a selfish motivation, and the implications of their wasted lives are recognized too late. Unable to translate harsh reality into lyrical song, their dying moments sound the notes of lamentation and doom, as Marcia Keiz observes in *Negro American Literature Forum*.

The Chosen Place, the Timeless People (1969) is a massive epic novel recapitulating and expanding upon themes developed in earlier works. The main story line concerns a small group of Americans who travel to the Caribbean island of Bournehills. Sponsored by a philanthropic foundation, they intend to design a project to assist an "underdeveloped" but curiously unified people. Juxtapositions and correspondences give the novel its texture, but the cohesive element is achieved through the paradoxical characterization of the native woman Merle Kinbona. With her, we explore the political, sociological, and psychological dimensions of power not only as it influences racial and sexual roles, but also as it shapes cultural patterns and assumptions.

Never sacrificing art to propaganda, M. sustains full human portraiture within a racially turgid atmosphere and concludes with the vision of a world not solely defined by territorial boundaries or even by cultural distinctions.

M. has exceptional talent born of solid scholarship and careful craftsmanship. By choosing to depict West Indian-American culture, M. makes a valuable contribution toward helping contemporary society understand the multidimensional aspects of the black experience.

WORKS: *Brown Girl, Brownstones* (1959; dramatization by CBS Television Workshop, 1960). *Soul Clap Hands and Sing* (1961). *The Chosen Place, the Timeless People* (1969).

BIBLIOGRAPHY: For articles in reference works, see: *Black American Writers Past and Present*, T. Rush, C. Myers, and E. Arata (1975). *Contemporary Novelists*, Ed. J. Vinson (1976).

Other references: *CLAJ* 16 (1972). *Encore American and Worldwide News* (23 June 1975). *Journal of Black Studies* 1 (1970). *Negro American Literature Forum* 9 (1975). Trinidad *Guardian* (12 Sept. 1962).

DOROTHY L. DENNISTON

Margaret Mead

B. *16 Dec. 1901, Philadelphia, Pennsylvania; d. 15 Nov. 1978, New York City*
D. *of Edward Sherwood and Emily Fogg Mead; m. Luther Cressman, 1923;*
  m. Reo Fortune, 1928; m. Gregory Bateson, 1935

M. was the eldest of five children. Her father was a professor at the Wharton School of Finance and Commerce. She was educated informally at home by her grandmother until high school. After a disappointing year at DePauw University, M. transferred to Barnard College, where she studied anthropology under Franz Boas and Ruth Benedict (B.A. 1923). Her Ph.D. is from Columbia University (1929). M. held almost forty positions, including professor of anthropology at Columbia. She was the recipient of many honorary degrees and some thirty-five awards. M. was married three times and was the mother of one daughter.

M.'s long and productive career as an author-anthropologist blossomed with the publication of her first and most popular book, *Coming of Age in Samoa* (1928). It has since been translated into seven languages and has reappeared in seven editions. The book is based on M.'s first fieldwork, undertaken at the age of twenty-three, in which she set out to discover whether the problems that trouble American adolescents are due to the biological nature of adolescence or to culturally learned attitudes. Her study of the individual within a culture was unique. M. vividly describes the basic character of Samoan life and how attitudes and behavior are shaped from birth to maturity. The results of her nine months of work showed that much of individual behavior is culturally learned. Stripped of the technical jargon of anthropology, M.'s clear presentations of life in Samoa and her answers to a fascinating anthropological question have reached a wide and enthusiastic audience.

Sex and Temperament in Three Primitive Societies (1935), which has been translated into twelve languages, was the outcome of fieldwork in three villages in New Guinea. When going into the field in 1931, M.'s original intentions were to study the cultural conditioning of the personalities of the two sexes. After working for two years in three different villages, M. discovered that her findings revealed more about differences in human temperament than about gender. Among the Mountain Arapesh, both men and women are gentle and maternal; among the Mundugumor, both sexes are fierce and virile; and among the Tchambuli, the roles of men and women are reversed from our traditional roles. Thus, gender is only one of the ways in which a society can group its social attitude toward temperament.

In 1949, M. wrote *Male and Female: A Study of the Sexes in a Changing World*. It is based on fourteen years of fieldwork in seven different societies, and was written at a time when traditional roles of male and female were undergoing scrutiny in our society. M. discusses ways in which physical similarities and differences are the basis on which we learn about our own sex and our relationship to the other sex. M. includes a discussion of how societies develop myths to answer the questions about differences between men and women, and about how children grow up to be a member of one or the other group. In the final section M. brings her knowledge back to America and discusses ways in which we can make improvements in our society.

Culture and Commitment: A Study of the Generation Gap, written in 1970 and revised extensively in 1978, is written in the belief that if we know and understand enough, our knowledge will breed optimistic and constructive thinking. M. feels that we are experiencing an irreversible evolutionary change brought about by modern technology, population explosion, and destruction of the natural environment, and that it is a change of which, for the first time in human history, we have a full awareness.

M.'s autobiography, *Blackberry Winter: My Earlier Years* (1972), is perhaps her most interesting book, providing the reader with some insight into the person behind the prolific and influential personality. In the first and third sections, M. writes about her family life, first from her early point of view as a granddaughter and then from her later view as a grandmother. The middle section is devoted to her field experiences.

M.'s contributions as an anthropologist have been unparalleled. She taught us about the behavior of other human beings—human beings like ourselves in everything but their culture—and in so doing gave us a better understanding of ourselves within a broad perspective. M. applied the results of her studies in primitive cultures to the questions of the day in our rapidly changing world. With the insight and knowledge she gained as a granddaughter and a grandmother, M. was able to span the gaps between the generations to which she spoke. As a person who watched children from isolated primitive societies grow up into a modern world, M. gained and shared a knowledge of cultural change and continuity. M. was a person who made her home the entire world and who communicated what she learned in such a felicitous, direct, and vivid style that people everywhere have benefited from her insights.

WORKS: *Coming of Age in Samoa: A Psychological Study of Primitive Youth for Western Civilization* (1928). *An Inquiry into the Question of Cultural Stability in Polynesia* (1928). *Growing Up in New Guinea: A Comparative Study of Primitive Education* (1930). *Social Organization of Manu'a* (1930). *The Changing Culture of an Indian Tribe* (1932). *Kinship in the Admiralty Islands* (1934). *Sex and Temperament in Three Primitive Societies* (1935). *Cooperation and Competition among Primitive Peoples* (edited by Mead, 1937). *The Mountain Arapesh* (Vol. 1, *An Importing Culture*, 1938; Vol. 2, *Supernaturalism*, 1940; Vol. 3, *Socio-Economic Life*, 1947; Vol. 4, *Diary of Events in Alitoa*, 1947; Vol. 5, *The Record of Unabelin with Rorschach Analysis*, 1949). *From the South Seas: Studies in Adolescence and Sex in Primitive Societies* (1939). *And Keep Your Powder Dry: An Anthropologist Looks at America* (1942). *Balinese Character: A Photographic Analysis* (with G. Bateson, 1942). *Male and Female: A Study of the Sexes in a Changing World* (1949). *Growth and Culture: A Photographic Study of Balinese Childhood* (with F. C. MacGregor, 1951). *The School in American Culture* (1951). *Soviet Attitudes toward Authority* (1951). *Cultural Patterns and Technical Change: A Manual Prepared by the World Federation for Mental Health* (edited by Mead, 1953). *Primitive Heritage: An Anthropological Anthology* (edited by Mead, with N. Calas, 1953). *The Study of Culture at a Distance* (edited by Mead, with R. Metraux, 1953). *Themes in French Culture: A Preface to a Study of French Community* (with R. Metraux, 1954). *Childhood in Contemporary Cultures* (edited by Mead, with M. Wolfenstein, 1955). *New Lives for Old: Cultural Transformation—Manus, 1928–1953* (1956). *An Anthropologist at Work: Writings of Ruth Benedict* (1959). *People and Places* (1959). *The Golden Age of American Anthropology* (edited by Mead, with R. L. Bunzel, 1960). *Anthropology, a Human Science: Selected Papers 1939–1960* (1964). *Continuities in Cultural Evolution* (1964). *American Women* (edited by Mead, with F. B. Kaplan, 1965). *Anthropologists and What They Do* (1965). *Family* (with K. Heyman, 1965). *The Wagon and the Star: A Study of American Community Initiative* (with M. Brown, 1966). *Science and the Concept of Race* (edited by Mead, with T. Dobzhansky, E. Tobach, and R. E. Light, 1968). *The Small Conference: An Innovation in Communication* (with P. Byers, 1968). *Culture and Commitment: A Study of the Generation Gap* (1970; rev. ed., 1978). *A Way of Seeing* (edited by Mead, with R. Metraux, 1970). *A Rap on Race* (with J. Baldwin, 1971). *Blackberry Winter: My Earlier Years* (1972). *To Love or to Perish: The Technological Crisis and the Churches* (edited by Mead et al., 1972). *Twentieth Century Faith: Hope and Survival* (1972). *Ruth Benedict: A Biography* (1974). *World Enough: Rethinking the Future* (with K. Heyman, 1975). *The Atmosphere: Endangered and Endangering* (edited by Mead, with W. W. Kellogg, 1977). *Letters from the Field, 1925–1975* (1977). *Aspects of the Present* (with R. Metraux, 1980).

BIBLIOGRAPHY: Cottler, J., and H. Jaffe, in *More Heroes of Civilization* (1969). Gordan, J., ed., *Margaret Mead: The Complete Bibliography 1925–1975* (1976). Moss, A., *Shaping a New World: Margaret Mead* (1963). Rossi, A. S., *The Feminist Papers from Adams to de Beauvoir* (1973). Stoddard, H., in *Famous American Women* (1970). Yost, E., in *American Women of Science* (1955).

For articles in reference works, see: *Britannica Yearbook of Science and the Future* (1971). *NCAB*, 1. *20thCA*. *20thCAS*.

Other references: *Louisiana Academy of Sciences Proceedings* 31 (1968). *New York Magazine* (13 Aug. 1973). *NY* 97 (1961). *NYTMag* (26 April 1970). *SatR* 4 (1977). *Science* 184 (1974). *Science Year: The World Book Science Annual* (1968).

MIRIAM KAHN

Cornelia Lynde Meigs

B. 6 Dec. 1884, Rock Island, Illinois; d. 10 Sept. 1973, Hartford County, Maryland
Wrote under: Adair Aldon, Cornelia Meigs
D. of Montgomery and Grace Lynde Meigs

The strong sense of family tradition that pervades much of M.'s writing for young people comes naturally from her own appreciation of kinship and its values. A descendant of Commodore John Rogers of Revolutionary fame, M. grew up in a close-knit family on the Mississippi, where her father was a government engineer.

Graduating from Bryn Mawr College in 1907, M. taught in Davenport, Iowa (1912–1913), where she began "to tell stories to the younger children . . . finding quickly just what sort they liked and what they would have none of." M.'s first book of short stories, *The Kingdom of the Winding Road* (1915), resulted from this experience. Novels, two plays (*The Steadfast Princess* won the Drama League prize in 1915), and four pseudonymous adventure stories followed during the next two decades.

From 1932 to 1950 M. taught English at Bryn Mawr. M.'s work as a literary scholar culminated in her editing and contributing to the landmark book *A Critical History of Children's Literature* (1953; rev. ed., 1969). Ann Pellowski refers to it as "a definitive survey of the literature," and Frances Sayers says that M.'s section "The Roots of the Past" has the "storyteller's narrative pace, the novelist's eye for endearing detail, and the scholar's control of historic perspective."

These talents are evident in most of the fiction, history, and biography that M. wrote. Her historical romances, beginning with *Master Simon's Garden* (1916), are compelling narratives. This first novel is suitable for an adolescent audience and traces the vicissitudes and final triumph of puritan Master Simon's family and garden ("a symbol of tolerance and understanding" according to Constantine Georgiou) through several generations. The sense of continuity of family ideals is strong, and the many characters are clearly individualized.

Invincible Louisa: The Story of the Author of Little Women (1933) won the Newbery Medal in 1934. "A thoroughly readable and satisfactory life," Bertha Miller called this labor of scholarship and love. In her acceptance paper for the prize, M. stated that she read Alcott's letters and journals "over and over again through my growing years" and in times of difficulty for "the stimulation of courage" they brought. Her biography carries this same "stimulation of courage," as does her last major work, *Jane Addams: Pioneer for Social Justice* (1970), another excellent biography of a strong woman.

M.'s young heroines, although brave and sensible, often play a comparatively passive role, but of the two real-life models that M. chose for her biographies, each, like Alcott, "gallantly went her own way and won her own triumph." M.'s talents seem fully realized only in her biographies. However, her books, of whatever type, have, as Bertha Miller notes, "given expression to America's best in thought, feeling and action."

WORKS: *The Kingdom of the Winding Road* (1915). *Master Simon's Garden* (1916). *The Steadfast Princess* (1916). *The Island of Appledore* (1917).

The Pirate of Jasper Peak (1918). *The Pool of Stars* (1919). *At the Sign of the Heroes* (1920). *The Windy Hill* (1921). *Helga and the White Peacock* (1922). *The Hill of Adventure* (1922). *The New Moon: The Story of Dick Martin's Courage, His Silver Sixpence, and His Friends in the New World* (1924). *Rain on the Roof* (1925). *As the Crow Flies* (1927). *The Trade Wind* (1927). *Clearing Weather* (1928). *The Wonderful Locomotive* (1928). *The Crooked Apple Tree* (1929). *The Willow Whistle* (1931). *Swift Rivers* (1932). *Invincible Louisa: The Story of the Author of Little Women* (1933). *Wind in the Chimney* (1934). *The Covered Bridge* (1936). *Young Americans: How History Looked to Them While It Was in the Making* (1936). *Railroad West* (1937). *The Scarlet Oak* (1938). *Call of the Mountain* (1940). *Mother Makes Christmas* (1940). *Vanished Island* (1941). *Mounted Messenger* (1943). *The Two Arrows* (1949). *The Violent Men: A Study of Human Relations in the First American Congress* (1949). *The Dutch Colt* (1952). *A Critical History of Children's Literature: A Survey of Children's Books in English from Earliest Times to the Present* (edited by Meigs, 1953; rev. ed., 1969). *Fair Wind to Virginia* (1955). *What Makes a College? A History of Bryn Mawr* (1956). *Wild Geese Flying* (1957). *Saint John's Church, Havre de Grace, Md. 1809–1959* (1959). *Mystery at the Red House* (1961). *The Great Design: Men and Events in the United Nations from 1945 to 1963* (1964). *Glimpses of Louisa: A Centennial Sampling of the Best Short Stories* (edited by Meigs, 1968). *Jane Addams: Pioneer for Social Justice* (1970). *Louisa M. Alcott and the American Family Story* (1971).

BIBLIOGRAPHY: Georgiou, C., *Children and Their Literature* (1969). Pellowski, A., *The World of Children's Literature* (1968).

For articles in reference works, see: *CA*, 9–12 (1974); 45–48 (1974). *Junior Book of Authors*, Eds. S. J. Kunitz and H. Haycraft (1934; 1951). *Newbery Medal Books, 1922–1955*, Eds. B. M. Miller and E. W. Field (1955).

Other references: *Horn Book* (Sept. 1944). *LJ* (July 1934). *PW* (30 June 1934; 25 April 1936).

CELIA CATLETT ANDERSON

Marguerite Merington

B. ca. 1860, Stoke Newington, England; d. 19 May 1951, New York City
D. of Richard Whiskin Crawford Merington

Although born in England, M. spent most of her life in America after her father emigrated because of business interests. M. was teaching Greek at the Normal College in New York City when she wrote her most famous work, *Captain Lettarblair*, for the prominent actor E. H. Sothern.

The play was produced by Daniel Frohman at the Lyceum Theatre in 1891 and revived during the next two seasons.

Captain Lettarblair Litton of the Irish Fusilliers has been scrimping to pay off a debt to clear the name of his wronged, deceased father. He hopes to marry Fanny Hadden. So strongly does she desire a proposal from him that she contrives to send him a large sum of money as though it came from his estate. However, in order to do so, she must press for payment of an old debt owed to her estate, not realizing that the debtor is Lettarblair himself.

The captain is forced to sell all his possessions, including his mare, and to renounce hope of marrying Fanny. The check that Fanny sends him is stolen from the mail pouch by the villainous Merivale, a rival for Fanny's hand, who leads her to believe that Lettarblair has squandered the money. By such complications is the flimsy plot sustained until the lovers are united in act 3. It is further buoyed up by moments of farcical business, such as the scene in which Lettarblair negotiates a sale through the window of his quarters while his valet tries to hold the door against the collection agent, or the scene in which Fanny is stranded in Lettarblair's room with her skirt caught in the door and the knob fallen off out of reach.

The popularity of *Captain Lettarblair* may be attributed to the performance of Sothern. To the modern reader, the play is belabored and contrived, but it won critical acclaim from the *New York Times*: "Miss M. has a knack of devising pictures which is a valuable theatrical gift, and she writes dialogue with great facility. Some of the Hibernicisms of the hero are delightful." In 1906, it was published in an elaborate book edition with numerous photographs from the production.

Love Finds the Way (1898) was M.'s last professionally produced play and the one M. considered her best. Thereafter, M. turned to writing mostly fairy-tale plays for young children and literary adaptations and historical dramas for high-school students. M.'s sincere dedication to these audiences is evident in her article "The Theatre for Everybody" in *The World's Work* (December 1910): "I regard the stage, rightly employed, as part of a broad general training. To language it is invaluable —and what trade is there, what calling, in which language is not a tool? . . . The theatre was part of the national life of the Greeks in their civilization's heyday—and there are matters in which we have yet to outstrip the wisdom of the Greeks."

Although M.'s children's plays now seem dated, they were popular in their time. *Snow White* (1905), written for the dramatic department of the Hebrew Educational Alliance, drew hundreds of children to each Sunday matinee.

In addition to M.'s several collections of fairy-tale plays and plays for holidays, one collection of particular interest is her *Picture Plays* (1911). These are very short one-act plays based upon famous paintings: *The Last Sitting* (da Vinci's "Mona Lisa"), *A Salon Carré Fantasy* (Titian's "Man with the Glove"), *His Mother's Face* (Watteau's "Une Fête champêtre"), and so forth. *Scribner's* magazine published many of M.'s sonnets, which, she later told an interviewer, one editor liked to call "Meringtonʼs 57 Varieties of Love, Life, and Death."

M. had met Elizabeth Bacon Custer, the widow of General George A. Custer, in 1894. They became close friends, and when Mrs. Custer died, M. was her literary executor. M.'s only major nondramatic work was an edition of the letters of General Custer and his wife, published in 1950. At the time of M.'s death, she was working on a book of recollections of the pianist Paderewski.

The success of M.'s fifty-nine-year career as a writer may be attributed to the dedication and sincerity of purpose by which she labored at her craft.

WORKS: *Captain Lettarblair* (1891). *Oh, Belinda* (1892). *Goodbye* (1893). *An Everyday Man* (1895). *Daphne; or, The Pipes of Arcadia* (1896). *Bonnie Prince Charlie* (1897). *Love Finds the Way* (1898). *Old Orchard* (1900). *The Gibson Play* (1901). *Cranford* (1905). *The Lady in the Adjoining Room* (1905). *Snow White* (1905). *The Turn of the Tide* (1905). *Scarlet of the Mounted* (1906). *The Vicar of Wakefield* (1909). *Holiday Plays* (1910). *Picture Plays* (1911). *The Elopers* (1913). *Festival Plays* (1913). *More Fairy-Tale Plays* (1917). *A Dish o' Tea Delayed* (1937). *Booth Episodes* (1944). *The Custer Story: The Life and Intimate Letters of General George A. Custer and His Wife Elizabeth* (1950).

Ten undated plays in typewritten manuscripts are at the New York Public Library.

BIBLIOGRAPHY: NYT (23 Oct. 1891; 21 May 1951). NYTBR (12 Feb. 1950). *Theatre Magazine* 6 (Oct. 1906).

FELICIA HARDISON LONDRÉ

Elizabeth Avery Meriwether

B. 19 Jan. 1824, Bolivar, Tennessee; d. ?1917, Memphis, Tennessee
Wrote under: George Edmunds, Elizabeth Avery Meriwether
D. of Nathan and Rebecca Avery; m. Minor Meriwether, 1850

In her autobiography, M. reveals little about her childhood other than to note that her family moved from Bolivar to Memphis when she was eleven. It is obvious, however, that M. was well educated, for after the death of her parents, she became a teacher. When the Civil War began, her husband, a civil engineer, joined the army, leaving M. in Memphis. The city was occupied by the Union army in 1862, and after several unpleasant encounters with Northern generals, M. decided to seek refuge in Alabama.

While in Tuscaloosa, M. resumed her childhood pastime of writing. She won a competition sponsored by the Selma *Daily Mississippian* offering $500 for the best story dealing with the war. "The Refugee" is based partly on her own experiences traveling through Alabama and Tennessee. Encouraged by this success, M. wrote "The Yankee Spy," which the newspaper planned to publish as a book. However, when the Confederacy fell, these plans were abandoned.

After the war, M. combined writing with an interest in social reform. In 1872, she edited and published a weekly newspaper, *The Tablet*, which lasted for a year. A strong believer in woman suffrage, M. "cast a vote" in the Memphis elections of 1872 and began a correspondence with leading feminists. In 1881, M. joined Elizabeth Cady Stanton and Susan B. Anthony on a speaking tour of New England. There she met Henry George and became a supporter of his "single tax" theory of economics.

M.'s first novel, *The Master of Red Leaf*, was published in 1872. It is basically a description of life on a southern plantation before the Civil War and a justification of secession. Her other works include novels, a play, and several works of popular history. M.'s autobiography, *Recollections of 92 Years*, was published the year before her death.

In many ways, M. can be considered a "professional Confederate." Not only do most of her works deal with the antebellum South, but unlike other postwar southern authors, M. refused to acknowledge that slavery had been a moral or social evil. M.'s fiction is replete with stereotyped black characters—happy, carefree, childlike, and unable to govern themselves without the discipline of slavery.

However, with the end of slavery, M. saw her ordered world turned upside down. "Life in the South," M. wrote, "became one long nightmare; then a miracle happened—for surely the way the South escaped from that frightful nightmare was little short of miraculous." The "miracle" was the Ku Klux Klan. M. writes about the Klan with an insider's knowledge and sympathy, for her husband was a member. She witnessed its night raids, terrorism, and destruction of black property, claiming that the corruption of the carpetbaggers and the insolence of "uppity" blacks justified any actions by disfranchised whites. M. concludes: "No doubt many abuses were committed by the Ku Klux. In large bodies of men some unwise ones, some mean ones will inevitably be found. But considered as a whole the work of the Ku Klux was done in a patriotic spirit for patriotic purposes, and I rejoice to see . . . that History is beginning to do justice to that wonderful secret movement. At the time it was misunderstood; in the North it was reviled. But in truth it accomplished a noble and necessary work in the only way in which that work was then possible."

Despite M.'s obvious prejudices, her works are enjoyable. She had a knack for telling a good story and making her characters real. M.'s descriptions of poor white hill people are charming and convey the spirit of these people.

WORKS: *The Master of Red Leaf* (1872). *The Ku Klux Klan; or, The Carpet-bagger in New Orleans* (1877). *English Tyranny and Irish Suffering* (1881). *Black and White: A Novel* (1883). *The Devil's Dances: A Play* (1886). *The Sowing of Swords* (1910). *Recollections of 92 Years* (1916).

BIBLIOGRAPHY: Horn, S. F., *Invisible Empire: The Story of the Ku Klux Klan* (1939). Patton, J. W., *Unionism and Reconstruction in Tennessee, 1860–1869* (1934).

JANET E. KAUFMAN

Annie Nathan Meyer

B. 19 Feb. 1867, New York City; d. 23 Sept. 1951, New York City
D. of Robert Weeks and Annie Florance Nathan; m. Alfred Meyer, 1887

Born in New York City, the youngest of four children, M. proudly claimed her heritage in a prominent Jewish family that dated to the revolutionary era. After the 1875 stock-market crash, her family moved to the Midwest, where M. lived until just before her mother's death in 1878, when the three youngest children were sent to New York to live with M.'s grandfather. Later M. lived with her father until her marriage; she spent the rest of her life in New York City.

In 1885 she secretly studied for and passed the entrance examinations for Columbia University's collegiate course for women. At that time women were not allowed to attend Columbia's classes but could be admitted to the collegiate course for women and allowed to study independently for the same examinations taken by men. When her father learned of her activities, he warned, "You'll never marry" because "men hate intelligent wives." Undaunted by his criticism, she decided "to forego all chances of winning a husband." This potential sacrifice, described in her autobiography, *It's Been Fun* (1951), and in her account of the founding of Barnard College, *Barnard Beginnings* (1935), proved unnecessary. She described her husband, Dr. Meyer, as sympathetic to her literary ambitions.

Although M. felt continuation of the Columbia course no longer necessary for her literary ambitions, she did begin campaigning for a women's college affiliate of Columbia that would allow women the full advantages of a collegiate education comparable to that available to Columbia's male students. As an incorporator and trustee of Barnard College, M. continued throughout her life to support the college she had helped found in 1889.

M. also pursued her own literary career, writing novels, plays, and short stories; articles on education, art, and feminism; and frequent letters to the editors of various publications. Her stories and articles appeared in such periodicals as *Bookman, Critic, Harper's Bazaar, North American Review, Putnam's,* and *Century.*

Many of M.'s works deal with the special problems resulting from women's search for new roles in the late 19th and early 20th centuries. After expressing her concern for the improvement of education for women in the late 1880s, she turned to the special problems of the women who entered the professions in *Woman's Work in America* (1891), a collection of essays by prominent women, such as Mary Putnam Jacobi, Frances Willard, and Clara Barton.

In 1892 M. anonymously published *Helen Brent, M.D.*, a novel about the special problems of a woman doctor. The heroine refuses to surrender her career to marriage and insists that she has as much right to ask a man to give up his ambition as he does to demand such a sacrifice from her. Until she can find a man willing to accept a wife who will continue her career, she will forgo marriage. Of all of M.'s works, this one stirred the most controversy among reviewers.

Several of M.'s plays also addressed complexities faced by the new woman. M. did not, however, maintain any consistent prowoman philosophy. In *The Dominant Sex* (1911), she satirizes the club woman who ignores her own child while she campaigns for child-protection legislation. This play also satirizes the tendency of some women to assume that they are the superior sex. Eventually chastened by the knowledge that her husband represents the dominant sex, the club woman gives up her club work and returns to her proper role at home.

The Dominant Sex dramatizes the strong antisuffrage views M. presented in "Woman's Assumption of Sex Superiority" (*North American Review*, Jan. 1904), which rejects both the ideas that women could combine marriage and career and that women represent a morally superior group. Although M. claimed in her autobiography that *Helen Brent, M.D.* and *The Advertising of Kate*—a play about the "delicate adjustment of the claims of sex to the work of the business woman," written in 1914 and produced on Broadway in 1922—were ahead of their times, other works seem very dated in their opposition to the new woman.

Among her approximately twenty-six plays, several addressed other social issues. In *The New Way*, a comedy directed by Jessie Bonstelle at the Longacre Theatre in New York in 1923, M. treated humorously the complexities of marriage and divorce. Her more serious *Black Souls* (1932), directed by James Light in 1932 at the Provincetown Playhouse in New York and including members of Zora Neale Hurston's choral group, dealt with the horrors of the lynching of blacks and the hypocrisy of white attitudes toward blacks.

In addition to numerous published works, M.'s unpublished manuscripts and correspondence reveal both her wide-ranging social interests and her occasionally contradictory convictions about the issues of her day.

WORKS: *Woman's Work in America* (1891). *Helen Brent, M.D.* (1892). *My Park Book* (1898). *Robert Annys, Poor Priest* (1901). *The Dominant Sex: A Play in Three Acts* (1911). *The Dreamer: A Play in Three Acts* (1912). *P's and Q's: A Play in One Act* (1921). *The New Way: A Comedy in Three Acts* (1925). *Black Souls: A Play in Six Scenes* (1932). *Barnard Beginnings* (1935). *It's Been Fun: An Autobiography* (1951).

The papers of Annie Nathan Meyer are at the American Jewish Archives, Cincinnati, Ohio.

BIBLIOGRAPHY: Askowith, D., *Three Outstanding Women: Mary Fels, Rebekah Kohut, and Annie Nathan Meyer* (1941).

For articles in reference works, see: *AW*.

Other references: *Harper's Bazaar* (4 June 1892). *NY* (23 Oct. 1943; 30 Oct. 1943). *NYT* (2 April 1911; 9 May 1922; 31 March 1932; 24 Sept. 1951; 25 Sept. 1951).

JEAN CARWILE MASTELLER

Josephine Miles

B. *11 June 1911, Chicago, Illinois*
D. *of Reginald Odber and Josephine Lackner Miles*

M. is descended from an English business family which came to America on the Mayflower. M.'s mother studied history and education with John Dewey and Colonel Parker at the University of Chicago.

M. attended grammar and high school in Los Angeles and graduated Phi Beta Kappa from the University of California at Los Angeles in 1932. She took graduate degrees from the University of California at Berkeley and joined the Berkeley faculty in 1940. She retired, university professor emerita, in 1978.

M. began writing poems at age eight. In high school, she gained a strong foundation in Latin and Greek poetry, followed in college by rigorous training in literary history. During early graduate study, M. developed her compelling interests in poetic language and form. The metaphysical poets and Yeats led her own early verse in a direction counter to that of a number of her contemporaries. Later, the writing of Neruda and Rilke offered in subject and approach modern alternatives to the more oblique expression of the metaphysical poets. The contemporary poets she has regarded most highly include Eberhart, Rukeyser, Levertov, Dickey, Stafford, Nathan, and Ammons. Those characteristics M. identifies as important in their verse—incisiveness, factualness, simplicity, power, and lyricism—are evident in her own finest poems. M. has received distinguished awards for her poetry and for her literary scholarship.

M.'s approach to what she calls "verse composition" is often determined by "the idea of speech . . . people talking . . . as the material from which poetry is made." In an early poem, "Speaker," the voice admits: "My talking heart talked less of what it knew / Than what it saw." What is known in many of M.'s poems is conveyed obliquely by what is observed in commonplace landscapes. Long a city resident, M. includes in these landscapes the repeated sights of urban life. In "Entry," the quantifiable city where "the small matter is put down already / To depreciation" is contrasted with the country, a place of hints and expectation.

M.'s poetry has not received the critical attention it deserves. It is difficult to generalize about M.'s writing except to note its condensation, craft, unexpected juxtaposition of images, pleasure in "the space and active interplay of talk," and—in recent volumes—willingness to employ more irregular form and an increasingly more direct political and ethical stance. Negative criticism of her work has centered on a miscellaneous quality of a number of the poems, as well as a control which has seemed to some to force a too moderate, reasonable, and civil response. However, longer poems, such as "Two Kinds of Trouble (for Michelangelo)," "Ten Dreamers in a Motel," and "Views from Gettysburg," show M. capable of sustaining and varying form.

M.'s doctoral dissertation, "Wordsworth and the Vocabulary of Emotion," was published in 1942. In this systematic study, M. establishes a historical and quantitative approach to criticism based on a method which she later refined and applied to other poets and eras and to prose style as well. By "counting the number of previously established names of emotion and standard signs of emotion in every poem, group, and in the complete poetical works" of a poet, the literary scholar could, M. demonstrates, formulate a more scientific, evidential basis for analyzing the relationship of thought and feeling in an era and the specific vocabulary a poet considered "poetic." In *Style and Proportion* (1966), by tabulating numerous British and American writers' use of adjectives, nouns, verbs, and connectives, M. recognizes "three styles distinguishable on the basis of structural choice: the predicative, the connective-subordinate, and the adjectival." At times reluctant to acknowledge the prior necessity of such tabulation, some scholars have praised M.'s aesthetic criticism and insight into the social nature of language at the expense of appreciation of the scientific method she employed in describing English poetry from the 16th c. to the present.

WORKS: *Lines at Intersection* (1939). *Poems on Several Occasions* (1941). *Pathetic Fallacy in the Nineteenth Century* (1942). *Wordsworth and the Vocabulary of Emotion* (1942). *Local Measures* (1946). *The Vocabulary of Poetry: Three Studies* (1946). *Criticism: The Foundations of Modern Literary Judgment* (edited by Miles, with M. Schorer and G. McKenzie, 1948; rev. ed., 1958). *The Continuity of English Poetry from the 1540's to the 1940's* (1951). *Prefabrications* (1955). *Eras and Modes in English Poetry* (1957; rev. ed., 1964). *The Poem: A Critical Anthology* (edited by Miles, 1959; rev. and abridged ed., *The Ways of the Poem*, 1969; rev. ed., 1973). *Poems, 1930–1960* (1960). *Renaissance, Eighteenth-Century, and Modern Language in English Poetry: A Tabular View* (1960). *Classic Essays in English* (edited by Miles, 1961; rev. ed., 1965). *Ralph Waldo Emerson* (1964). *Civil Poems* (1966). *Style and Proportion* (1966). *Kinds of Affection* (1967). *Fields of Learning* (1968). *Poetry and Change: Donne, Milton, Wordsworth, and the Equilibrium of the Present* (1974). *To All Appearances: New and Selected Poems* (1974). *Coming to Terms* (1980).

BIBLIOGRAPHY: Bogan, L., in *A Poet's Alphabet* (1970). Dickey, J., in *Babel to Byzantium* (1968). Smith, L., in *Rereadings*, Ed. G. Kuzma (1978).

For articles in reference works, see: *CA*, 1–4 (1967). *Contemporary Poets*, Ed. R. Murphie (1970). *Contemporary Poets*, Eds. J. Vinson and D. L. Kirkpatrick (1975). *20thCAS*.

Other references: *PrS* (Winter 1958–9). *TLS* (25 April 1975).

THEODORA R. GRAHAM

Margaret Millar

B. 5 Feb. 1915, Kitchener, Ontario, Canada
D. of William and Lavinia Ferrier Sturm; m. Kenneth Millar, 1938

M. studied at the University of Toronto; her early interests were classics, archeology, music, and psychiatry. M.'s husband writes mysteries under the name Ross Macdonald. M. is a former president of the Mystery Writers of America and widely known as an environmentalist. *The Birds and the Beasts Were There* (1967) recounts the difficulties and the pleasures of a major current interest, bird watching.

Primarily known as a mystery writer, M. created two series detectives. Dr. Paul Prye, psychiatrist and witty amateur sleuth, appears in *The Invisible Worm* (1941) and *The Weak-Eyed Bat* (1942), which details Prye's search for a killer and his courtship of clever, brash Nora Shane. Their wedding, in *The Devil Loves Me* (1942), is complicated by a murder and allows for the introduction of the second continuing character, Detective-Inspector Sands.

Sands, unprepossessing but perceptive and humane, is more typical of M.'s characters and appears in two other novels. *Wall of Eyes* (1943) uses an important M. device—characters who are not what or who they seem. The relationship between the Heath sisters, pliant Alice and blind, shrill Kelsey, asks who is prey and who is predator. *The Iron Gates* (1945) finds Sands investigating the disappearance of Lucille Morrow, one of M.'s most successfully complex characters. The novel also features another important M. motif, dream imagery, and a key theme, the evil power of love.

Fire Will Freeze (1944) and *Rose's Last Summer* (1952) are comedy-mysteries. *Fire* provides amusing characters, a measure of terror, and a clever surprise ending. All the early novels employ the "closed circle of suspects" technique.

Psychotic personalities are the focus of *The Cannibal Heart* (1949) and *Beast in View* (cited as best mystery of 1955 by the Mystery Writers of America). In *The Cannibal Heart*, the relative innocence of young Jessie Banner and adolescent Luisa Roma contrasts with the corruption of Janet Wakefield as she attempts to compensate for disappointment in marriage and motherhood. *Beast in View* is the study of Helen Clarvoe, rejected and repressed as a child and dangerous as a woman. Hurtful family impact is a central theme, and the novel employs yet another pattern, the outsider drawn into a turmoil of family entanglements.

Perhaps M.'s best novels are *Vanish in an Instant* (1952) and *The Fiend* (1964). The former compares the relationship between Virginia Barkley, accused of a murder, and her overprotective mother with that between Earl Loftus, who confesses to the killing, and his alcoholic mother. *The Fiend*, compassionate and unsentimental, probes the interactions within and between five families as Charlie Gowen, former child molester, struggles against his interest in little Jessie Brant. The characterizations are vivid, and M. uses a variation of the mother-child theme here, as a childless woman interferes with another's daughter.

The Listening Walls (1959) compares the self-protective instincts of a Mexican hotel maid with those of a pampered California matron. *Beyond This Point Are Monsters* (1970) and *Ask for Me Tomorrow* (1976) have fine Southern California settings, and in each M. provides sensitive examinations of the position of Mexican-Americans within that culture.

How Like an Angel (1962) interweaves two plots—a disappearing husband and the fate of the True Believers, a strange religious cult. The Believers' impact on the elderly Sister Blessing and teenaged Sister Karma are of especial interest, as is the portrait of Charlotte Keating, the seemingly controlled, competent, independent physician of *Do Evil in Return* (1950). The detectives in these novels, Quinn and Easter, are imperfect but decent men doing their best to cope with murder and with love.

Experiment in Springtime (1947), *Wives and Lovers* (1954), and *A Stranger in My Grave* (1960) treat failed marriages. In each, recognition of failure and termination of the marriage symbolize growth toward maturity for at least one partner. *Experiment in Springtime* contrasts the "second youth" of Martha Pearson and Steve Ferris, reunited lovers, with the realistic adolescence of Laura Shaw, who also loves Steve. *A Stranger in My Grave* effectively combines gothic overtones with a search for self-definition as Stevens Pinata discovers factual reasons for Daisy Harker's nightmares.

M. is considered a novelist of skill and power, especially noted for her effective imagery and excellent characterizations.

WORKS: *The Invisible Worm* (1941). *The Weak-Eyed Bat* (1942). *The Devil Loves Me* (1942). *Wall of Eyes* (1943). *Fire Will Freeze* (1944). *The*

Iron Gates (1945). *Experiment in Springtime* (1947). *It's All in the Family* (1948). *The Cannibal Heart* (1949). *Do Evil in Return* (1950). *Rose's Last Summer* (1952). *Vanish in an Instant* (1952). *Wives and Lovers* (1954). *Beast in View* (1955). *An Air That Kills* (1957). *The Listening Walls* (1959). *A Stranger in My Grave* (1960). *How Like an Angel* (1962). *The Fiend* (1964). *The Birds and the Beasts Were There* (1967). *Beyond This Point Are Monsters* (1970). *Ask for Me Tomorrow* (1976). *The Murder of Miranda* (1979). *Mermaid* (1982).

BIBLIOGRAPHY: For articles in reference works, see: *CA*, 13–16 (1975). *Encyclopedia of Mystery and Detection*, Eds. C. Steinbrunner and O. Penzler (1976). *WA*.

Other references: *The Armchair Detective* (Jan. 1970). *NYT* (13 Oct. 1976). *NYTBR* (30 May 1954; 21 June 1964).

JANE S. BAKERMAN

Edna St. Vincent Millay

B. 22 Feb. 1892, Rockland, Maine; d. 19 Oct. 1950, Steepletop, New York
Wrote under: Nancy Boyd, Edna St. Vincent Millay
D. of Henry and Cora Buzzelle Millay; m. Eugen Boissevain, 1923

M. was the oldest of three daughters. Her father, a schoolteacher and school superintendent, left the household when M. was seven. Her mother supported the family by working as a practical nurse. She also did her utmost to encourage all three girls to develop their creative talents.

M. first received recognition as a poet when her long poem "Renascence" was selected in 1912 for inclusion in *The Lyric Year*. However, "Renascence" narrowly missed receiving one of the three prizes awarded for the best poems in the volume. Publication of the anthology brought forth a storm of protest. Readers maintained that M.'s youthful statement of despair, rebirth, and affirmation was the strongest in the book.

M.'s success brought her to the attention of Caroline Dow, who made it possible for the poet to attend Vassar College. In 1917, soon after graduation, M. moved to Greenwich Village, where she quickly became a legend.

Several images of M. during this period emerge: the serious artist living on limited funds; the bohemian, careless of health and propriety; the passionate woman involved in brief, intoxicating love affairs. During her

Village years, M. published *Renascence, and Other Poems* (1917) and *A Few Figs from Thistles* (1920). The latter, with its famous "candle" quatrain (beginning "My candle burns at both ends; / It shall not last the night") and flippant love poems, captured the imaginations of the "emancipated" youth of the early 1920s. At the same time, M. finished the poems that would appear in *Second April* (1921), and wrote and directed a pacifist verse play, *Aria da Capo* (1920).

In 1922, M. received the Pulitzer Prize for *The Ballad of the Harp-Weaver*, an expanded edition of *Figs* with eight new sonnets. The following year, she married a Dutch businessman. Boissevain's first wife had been Inez Milholland, the famous suffragist, who died in 1916. M., who had admired Milholland at college, dedicated to her a sonnet honoring the women's rights movement.

Eventually, Boissevain gave up his coffee business to manage M.'s highly successful poetry-reading tours, and to superintend Steepletop, their farm in upstate New York. Their marriage lasted twenty-seven years, until Boissevain's death in 1949. During these years, M. produced several books of poems—*The Buck in the Snow* (1928), *Fatal Interview* (1931), *Wine from These Grapes* (1934)—that are more subdued and more contemplative in tone than her earlier work.

In 1927, M. became active in the movement to save Sacco and Vanzetti. She signed petitions, demonstrated, and, in a futile interview, tried to persuade the governor of Massachusetts to grant clemency. Her involvement in this case is reflected in several poems, most notably "Justice Denied in Massachusetts."

Growing increasingly concerned about the spread of fascism throughout Europe and the start of World War II, M. renounced her former pacifism in the late 1930s. In a series of political poems, she argued for American military preparedness and aid to France and England. Unfortunately, these poems are quite poor, relying on jangling rhythms and trite language. Collected in *Make Bright the Arrows* (1940), they drew a barrage of adverse criticism.

M. is particularly interesting because, at a time when modern poetry was abandoning traditional forms, she chose to write ballads, lyrics, and sonnets. Though M.'s later work is somewhat more experimental, she usually stayed within familiar structures, adapting them to her own use. M.'s strongest poems work precisely because of the balance maintained between the emotional intensity of her subjects and the disciplined craftmanship of her forms. As Floyd Dell said, "She learned the molds first, into which she poured her emotions while hot."

Many of her first poems ("Renascence," "God's World") reveal innocence and youthful exuberance. In "Recuerdo," the young lovers, after riding "back and forth all night on the ferry," impulsively give bags of fruit and "all our money but our subway fares" to an old woman newspaper seller. Other early verses, however, exhibit a mocking, skeptical attitude toward life and love. In many of the poems from *A Few Figs from Thistles*, M. creates a bold, unconventional woman persona who is frankly attracted to men and who initiates and terminates love affairs at will. In *Sonnet xi*, for instance, she tells her lover: "I shall forget you presently, my dear, / So make the most of this, your little day." The poem ends with the forthright statement: "Whether or not we find what we are seeking / Is idle, biologically speaking." In another poem, the persona glories in being a "wicked girl" and declares: "if I can't be sorry, why, / I might as well be glad."

A more serious note appears in *Second April* (1921). The skepticism remains, but the lightness is gone. In "Spring," M. states that "Life in itself / Is nothing" and compares the month of April to "an idiot, babbling and strewing flowers." The love poems in this book are somber. *Sonnet xix*, for example, begins: "And you as well must die, beloved dust / And all your beauty stand you in no stead."

Throughout all of M.'s poetry runs the message that life is short and love ephemeral. Human relationships, however sweet, cannot last. The theme of death constantly recurs. The early "Passer Mortuus Est" begins "Death devours all lovely things" and the late "Epitaph for the Race of Man" mourns, "Earth, unhappy planet, born to die."

M. has been criticized for writing only of herself and her love affairs, but many of her poems reflect wider concerns. However, her love poems, far from being sentimental effusions, are central to her vision of life's brevity and impermanence.

The recipient of much acclaim in the 1920s, M. is less popular today. Feminist readers tend to dismiss her work as old-fashioned and conventional. This is unfortunate because M., though no structural innovator, is in many ways close to the feminist-oriented poets of the 1970s. Certainly M.'s use of highly personal material; her fresh, forthright language; and her creation of strong female personae anticipate modern women's poetry. M.'s finest poems, moreover, ensure her position as an important American woman poet.

WORKS: *Renascence, and Other Poems* (1917). *Aria da Capo* (1920). *A Few Figs from Thistles* (1920). *The Lamp and the Bell* (1921). *Second April* (1921). *Two Slatterns and a King* (1921). *The Harp-Weaver, and Other Poems* (1923).

Distressing Dialogues (1924). *The King's Henchman* (1927). *The Buck in the Snow* (1928). *Poems Selected for Young People* (1929). *Fatal Interview* (1931). *The Princess Marries the Page* (1932). *Wine from These Grapes* (1934). *Flowers of Evil* by Baudelaire (translated by Millay, with George Dillon, 1936). *Conversation at Midnight* (1937). *Huntsman, What Quarry?* (1939). *Make Bright the Arrows* (1940). *Collected Sonnets* (1941). *Invocation to the Muses* (1941). *The Murder of Lidice* (1942). *Collected Lyrics* (1943). *Poem and Prayer for an Invading Army* (1944). *Mine the Harvest* (1954). *Collected Poems* (1956).

BIBLIOGRAPHY: Atkins, E., *Edna St. Vincent Millay and Her Times* (1936). Bogan, L., *Achievements in American Poetry* (1951). Cheney, A., *Millay in the Village* (1975). Dash, J., *A Life of One's Own* (1973). Dell, F., *Homecoming: An Autobiography* (1933). Gould, J., *The Poet and Her Book* (1969). Gray, J., *Edna St. Vincent Millay* (Univ. of Minnesota Pamphlets on American Writers, 1967). Gurko, M., *Restless Spirit* (1962). Sheean, V., *The Indigo Bunting* (1951). Wilson, E., *I Thought of Daisy* (1929). Wilson, E., in *The Shores of Light* (1952).

For articles in reference works, see: *NAW* (article by J. M. Brinnin). *NCAB*, B.

ENID DAME

Kate Millett

B. 14 Sept. 1934, St. Paul, Minnesota
D. of James and Helen Feely Millet; m. Fumio Yoshimura, 1965

The second of three daughters, M. attended parochial schools in St. Paul. Her father, a contractor, abandoned the family when M. was fourteen. Her mother took a job selling insurance, and the girls helped support the family. M. was graduated from the University of Minnesota, magna cum laude and Phi Beta Kappa, in 1956. She studied literature for two years at St. Hilda's College, Oxford, and earned first honors.

M. taught briefly at the Women's College of the University of North Carolina, but later resigned her post and went to New York to paint and sculpt. In 1961, M. moved to Japan, where she taught English and sculpted.

On returning to New York in 1963, M. exhibited "pop furniture," such as chairs with human legs. She joined the civil rights and peace movements, and in 1966 became one of the first members of the National Organization for Woman (NOW). Her first book, *Token Learning* (1967), was a pamphlet for NOW, challenging the validity of the curricula at women's colleges.

In 1968, M. was hired to teach at Barnard College, and began work on a Ph.D. in English and comparative literature at Columbia. M.'s activism in the causes of women's liberation and student rights led to her being relieved of her teaching post in December of her first year. However, a speech M. delivered to a women's group at Cornell became the germ of her doctoral thesis.

M.'s thesis may be considered the first major literary criticism of the new wave of feminism. She sets forth the postulate that the oppression of women is essentially political, and then discredits religious, literary, philosophical, and "scentific" constructs erected by male supremacists to justify their advantage. A second section documents the feminist revolution and male chauvinist counterrevolution in the history of ideas, and the third section exposes the phallic supremacism of three modern male literary idols: D. H. Lawrence, Henry Miller, and Norman Mailer. Finally, M. sets up Jean Genet, the French homosexual writer, as master social critic who reverses every status hierarchy in western culture, including that of masculine and feminine.

In March 1970, M. was awarded the doctoral degree with distinction, and in August her thesis was published by Doubleday. It sold 80,000 copies in the first six months of publication. *Sexual Politics* offered the public a major new concept, and many reviewers merely used the title as a springboard for their personal tirades against feminism. The media both praised and lambasted the book and its author, seizing upon them as a reification of "women's lib."

The Prostitution Papers began as a chapter for Vivian Gornick's *Woman in a Sexist Society* (1971). M. edited oral narratives from two prostitutes and a feminist lawyer, and added an essay of her own arguing that prostitution is only one salient example of the ways in which femaleness has been reduced to a commodity. M. called the chapter "a quartet for four voices," and had the four statements printed side by side in columns; but when the chapter was published separately as a book, the experimental layout was abandoned. The 1976 edition includes M.'s firsthand account of the 1975 French prostitutes' revolt.

M.'s experience with spoken language led her to make the film *Three Lives*, and inspired her fourth book. Frankly confessional, *Flying* (1974) was M.'s response to the enforced two-dimensionality of being created as a media feminist and showed M.'s need to bring together disparate private and public selves. M. had originally planned to write a scholarly treatise in defense of homosexuality, but wrote instead a supremely vulnerable book about her own sexuality, her work, her feelings, her friends, and the movement. Using the writing of the book itself as a framework, M. intercuts scenes from other periods of her life, giving the effect of a sculptural assemblage.

Sita (1977) resembles *Flying* stylistically, but it is focused on a narrower theme. M. takes the reader on a *tour de force* of a dissolving romance between herself and an older woman. Again, M. makes sculpture out of confession. She repeatedly reconstructs her theme, each time from a slightly different perspective, building up the paradigm of emotional attitudes toward a single set of facts. More tightly controlled than *Flying*, *Sita* conveys a relentless progressive present that both encompasses and reshapes history.

M.'s capacity for obsession drives her art. For ten years, she sculpted almost nothing but cages, her response to a newsmagazine article about the murder of a sixteen-year-old girl by her female guardian and a group of kids. *The Basement: Meditations on a Human Sacrifice* (1979) is a cage of words. M. verbalizes the bars of the cage—her subjects' poverty, their isolation from societal restraints, their rationalizations and guilts and enjoyment of petty drama—and fills the cage with monologues representing the interior voices of torturer and victim. There is a constant sliding back and forth between M.'s ideas and voice and those of her characters, as the author performs the ritual of becoming them, the self-abasement of taking on their impoverished language and brutal experience. Much of the tension of the book results from M.'s continual refusal to permit herself to explain the deed cleanly away.

A pacifist and international feminist activist, M.'s politics are frequently denigrated and her works sometimes harshly reviewed in the major press. Nevertheless, her influence is pervasive, and a generation of feminist writers has taken her for its model. She has set a standard for powerful feminist criticism, and provoked reevaluation of confessional and journal writing as artistic literary forms.

WORKS: *Token Learning* (1967). *Sexual Politics* (1970). *The Prostitution Papers* (1971; rev. ed., 1976). *Flying* (1974). *Sita* (1977). *The Basement: Meditations on a Human Sacrifice* (1979). *Going to Iran* (1981).

BIBLIOGRAPHY: Chrysalis (1977; 1978). *Harper's* (1970). *Ms.* (1974).

FRIEDA L. WERDEN

Jessica Mitford

B. 11 Sept. 1917, Batsford Mansion, Gloucestershire, England
D. of David and Sydney Bowles Mitford; m. Esmond Romilly, 1936;
  m. Robert E. Truehaft, 1943

M. is the daughter of the second baron of Redesdale. Her eccentric siblings include Nancy, the biographer, Diana, the wife of fascist Oswald Mosley, and Unity, disciple of Hitler. After receiving a private education at home, M. ran away with her second cousin, Esmond Romilly, in 1936 to assist the Loyalist cause in Spain. They worked briefly as journalists before returning to England, where M. was a market researcher for an advertising agency. M. and her husband emigrated to the U.S. in 1939, where each took odd jobs while traveling along the eastern seaboard.

M. worked in Washington, D.C., for two years in the Office of Price Administration after Romilly was killed in action during World War II. She married a lawyer in 1943, and became a naturalized U.S. citizen in 1944. After moving to Oakland, California, M. worked as executive secretary for the Civil Rights Congress, where she pressed for the investigation into charges of police brutality. In 1973, M. was appointed distinguished visiting professor in sociology at San Jose State College, where she taught a class on "The American Way" and a seminar on muckracking.

M.'s first book, *Lifeitselfmanship*, was privately published in 1956. Her autobiography, *Daughters and Rebels* (1960), hilariously recounts her childhood and marriage to Romilly.

M.'s first investigative study, *The American Way of Death* (1963), exposed the greed and commercialism of the funeral industry. Relying on extensive research and quotations from the industry's own publications, M. satirically deflated the pretentious hypocrisy of such establishments as Forest Lawn Memorial-Park. Although the book was viciously denounced by the industry, it was used as the basis for a television documentary.

M.'s second investigative study, *The Trial of Dr. Spock, William Sloane Coffin, Jr., Michael Ferber, Mitchell Goodman, and Marcus Raskin* (1969), concluded with the observation that conspiracy laws threatened personal and civil rights: "Does not the cherished concept of due process of law, the foundation of our system of jurisprudence, become merely an elaborate sham to mask what is in reality a convenient device to silence opponents of governmental policies?"

M. next attacked the Famous Writers School in a lengthy article entitled "Let Us Now Appraise Famous Writers" (*Atlantic*, July 1970). M. charged the Westport, Connecticut, school with deception in advertising and criticized writers who allowed the school to use their names.

Kind and Usual Punishment: The Prison Business (1973) exposes the atrocities of the penal system. In a chapter entitled "Clockwork Orange," M. listed the techniques used in prisons to modify behavior and reform "antisocial personalities," including chemotherapy, aversion therapy, neurosurgery, and drugs. M. points out that prisons have become the "happy hunting ground for the researcher." M. condemns lengthy and indeterminate sentences, the parole system, and the use of prisoners in psychological and physiological research, while supporting the idea of a prisoners' union. M. concludes that prisons are "inherently unjust and inhumane," institutions that demean all people in society.

M. published the sequel to her autobiography *Daughters and Rebels* in 1977. *A Fine Old Conflict* traces M.'s involvement with the Communist Party in America. As M. puts it, being fiercely anti-Fascist and antiracist, the Communist Party seemed to her the only practical outlet for her political and social beliefs. Recreating the ambience of the "witch-hunting" 1950s, M. recalls such activities as her trip to Mississippi in 1951 to appeal the conviction of a black rapist and her efforts to raise money for the party by organizing chicken dinners. After defecting from the party after twenty years, M. describes it as "an embattled, proscribed (and, to me, occasionally comical) organization." The appendix reprints her previously unavailable spoof of party jargon, *Lifeitselfmanship*.

In addition to her book-length studies, M. has published extensively in *Life*, *Esquire*, *The Nation*, and the San Francisco *Chronicle*. A staunch supporter of civil liberties, M. has often been accused of communist sympathies and "un-American" activities. All M.'s writings, however, reveal a satirical perspective on the fraud and corruption of organizations that victimize and exploit human beings.

WORKS: *Lifeitselfmanship* (privately published, 1956). *Daughters and Rebels* (1960; published in England as *Hons and Rebels*). *The American Way of Death* (1963). *The Trial of Dr. Spock, William Sloane Coffin, Jr., Michael Ferber, Mitchell Goodman, and Marcus Raskin* (1969). *Kind and Usual Pun-*

ishment: The Prison Business (1973). *A Fine Old Conflict* (1977). *Poison Penmanship: The Gentle Art of Muckracking* (1979).

BIBLIOGRAPHY: For articles in reference works, see: *CA* (1967). *CB* (1974).

DIANE LONG HOEVELER

Penina Moise

B. 23 April 1797, Charleston, South Carolina; d. 13 Sept. 1880, Charleston, South Carolina
D. of Abraham and Sarah Moise

M. was the sixth of nine children of parents who had fled to Charleston during the slave insurrections in Santo Domingo. The death of M.'s father forced M. to abandon formal education and help support the family by needlework, but she nevertheless continued to study and write, publishing poems and stories in newspapers and periodicals. Devoutly religious, M. served as superintendent of the religious school of Beth Elohim beginning in 1842. After the Civil War, although ill and nearly blind, M. founded a school for girls and conducted literary salons.

Fancy's Sketch Book (1833) was probably the first published book to which a Jewish woman appended her full name. Primarily a volume of verse, it includes light satires, epigrams, lyrics, and occasional poems commemorating prominent events. Conventional themes of love, death, and nature predominate, but in many instances they are distinguished by charming poignancy, delicate wit, and clever word play. For example, in "The Disconcerted Concert" M. uses the double meaning of musical terms to describe a quarrel among the instruments.

Serious themes are not neglected, and the book reveals a wide range of interests and knowledge, including Greek mythology, the Bible, Shakespeare, music, art, and history. Women are generally presented in terms of love or motherhood, but in one instance M. writes movingly of the women who donated their wedding rings to support Koscivszko's efforts to liberate Poland.

Hymns Written for the Use of Congregation Beth Elohim, first published in 1842 and enlarged in three subsequent editions, is primarily the work of M. The art of hymn writing, which requires decided meter with little variation, simple language that conveys an immediate sense of emotion, and above all sincere devoutness, brought out M.'s talents to the fullest—her hymns are still included in modern hymnals. In writing the lyrics, M. often added images that echoed many parts of the service, and her dramatic images greatly enhance the effectiveness of the prayer.

Although the bulk of M.'s writings still lies buried in the numerous newspapers and periodicals to which she contributed, a selection of her poems and hymns was collected in *Secular and Religious Works of Penina Moise* (1911). Some of the verses from the earlier volumes were included, but the collection is notable for works on specifically Jewish subjects and a number of previously uncollected poems dealing with political and social issues. The refusal by the British House of Lords to grant constitutional rights to Jews became for M. "that dark deformity from Freedom's code," and when the Jews of Damascus were being persecuted, she reproached the rest of the world that could "the suppliants scorn / From whose inspired relics revelation was born."

Limited by poverty, by social tradition, by illness, and by blindness, M. nevertheless produced a substantial body of poems and hymns. Much of M.'s work reveals an excessive concern for the poetic diction and conventions of her time, but several of her satiric pieces can still delight readers. M.'s poems on serious subjects reveal an unusual awareness of social and moral problems. Her hymns, expressing a deep, sincere faith in God's mercy, continue to evoke a solemn piety. All contemporary accounts of M. emphasize her cheerfulness, good humor, and wit, despite the hardships under which she lived. The mark of suffering which found no voice in her poetry was expressed only in the lines M. wrote for her epitaph: "Lay no flowers on my grave. They are for those who live in the sun, and I have always lived in the shadow."

WORKS: *Fancy's Sketch Book* (1833). *Hymns Written for the Use of Congregation Beth Elohim* (1842). *Secular and Religious Works of Penina Moise* (1911).

BIBLIOGRAPHY: Elzas, B. A., *The Jews of South Carolina* (1905). Moise, H., *The Moise Family of South Carolina* (1961). Reznikoff, C., and U. Z. Engleman, *The Jews of Charleston* (1950).

For articles in reference works, see: *AA. DAB*, VI, 2. *NAW* (article by C. Reznikoff).

Other references: *American Jew's Annual* (1885–86). *American Jewish Yearbook* (1905–06). *Critic* (28 Dec. 1889). *Southern Jewish Historical Society* (1978).

CAROL B. SCHOEN

Harriet Monroe

B. 23 Dec. 1860, Chicago, Illinois; d. 26 Sept. 1936, Arequipa, Peru
D. of Henry Stantan and Martha Mitchell Monroe

Poet, editor, and journalist, M. was an influential force in the publication of modern poetry in the U.S. and an important figure in the Chicago Renaissance. Both her parents had moved to the growing city shortly before their marriage in 1855: her father, who became a prominent lawyer, from western New York and her mother from Ohio. Decidedly more erudite and socially ambitious than his beautiful but uneducated wife, Monroe inspired in his daughter a keen interest in literature, painting, music, and the theater; and much of her early education was acquired from reading in his substantial library.

The tensions in her parents' marriage, increased after 1871 by her father's business reverses, contributed along with frail health to M.'s reserved, nervous character as a girl. At the Georgetown Visitation Convent in Washington, D.C. (1877–79), she outgrew her former reticence, forming lifelong friendships with several affluent classmates and discovering the satisfactions of an independent, critical mind. She also blossomed into an aspiring poet.

During the 1880s involvement in the Fortnightly, a literary women's club, and publication of occasional art and drama reviews provided M. entrée into the world of Chicago's writers and journalists, among them Margaret Sullivan and Eugene Field, who became her friends and sponsors. While she had several opportunities to marry, she chose not to.

M. spent the winter of 1888–89 with her sister Lucy in New York as an art, drama, and music correspondent for the Chicago *Tribune*. At E. C. Stedman's Sunday evenings, she tasted the culture of the New York art and literary scene, meeting such luminaries as W. D. Howells and Joseph Pulitzer. Yet, despite her growing knowledge of contemporary art and theater, she considered journalism always second to her poetry and worked during her free time that winter on the verse play *Valeria*.

On her return to Chicago she was commissioned by a group of businessmen to write a cantata for the dedication ceremony of Louis Sullivan's new Auditorium in 1889. After a visit to London and northern

France in 1890, she established herself as a free-lance art and music reviewer and, from 1909 to 1914, worked as art critic for the *Tribune*. Her most public success as a poet came in 1892: the performance of her "Columbian Ode," a long poem composed (with music for lyric passages by G. W. Chadwick) for the World's Columbian Exposition in Chicago. *Valeria, and Other Poems* appeared in a private edition in 1891 and a memoir of her brother-in-law, the Chicago architect John Wellborn Root, in 1896.

M. traveled extensively in the U.S., Europe, and Asia. On her return from a P.E.N. congress in Buenos Aires in 1936, she traveled to Peru intending to view the Inca ruins at Machu Picchu. During a stop at Arequipa, however, she died and was buried in the Andean village.

Although M.'s poetry never gained the wide audience and critical notice she hoped for, she continued thoughout her life to write occasional verse, competent but largely conventional in sentiment and language. Among her more interesting poems are short lyrics about the deserts and mountains of the American southwest; longer descriptions of foreign locations she visited—among them, Constantinople, Peking, the Parthenon; and a few ironic observations of modern society like "The Hotel."

M.'s most distinguished and lasting achievement was the founding of *Poetry: A Magazine of Verse* in October 1912 and editing the monthly for twenty-four years. In June 1911, at the suggestion of her friend H. C. Chatfield-Taylor, M., then fifty-one, began the arduous task of soliciting subscriptions of fifty dollars a year for five years from 100 Chicago business leaders and professionals to establish a magazine "which shall give the poets a chance to be heard." To develop a public "interested in poetry as art" became her persistent aim.

The circular and personal letter she sent to many poets, established and unknown, discovered through ardent research—and through Elkin Mathews's fortuitous presentation to her in London in 1910 of two of Ezra Pound's early books—drew favorable response to her ambitious venture. It also stimulated a flow of letters from Pound, who became the magazine's unpaid foreign correspondent with the second issue. Along with Alice Corbin Henderson, her associate editor, Pound influenced M. to include in *Poetry*'s early years the writing of Yeats, Lawrence, Frost, William Carlos Williams, his own work, and in 1915, Eliot's "The Love Song of J. Alfred Prufrock."

Ellen Williams locates the great years of *Poetry* in 1914 and 1915, when M. opened the publication to controversy over Imagism, experimental verse, and the poet's relation to his audience. In general, M.'s preference for democratic and more accessible American poetry led her to espouse Lindsay, Masters, and many lesser poets. But the contribution she made, despite criticism and financial difficulties, in gaining recognition for poets in the U.S., in articulating modern standards in opposition to those of the powerful established outlets, and in calling attention to new writing and ideas in editorials and reviews was invaluable.

WORKS: *Valeria, and Other Poems* (1891). *The Columbian Ode* (1893). *John Wellborn Root: A Study of His Life and Work* (1896). *The Dance of the Seasons* (1911). *You and I* (1914). *The New Poetry: An Anthology* (edited by Monroe, with A. C. Henderson, 1917; rev. ed., 1932). *The Difference, and Other Poems* (1924). *Poets and Their Art* (1926). *A Book of Poems for Every Mood* (edited by Monroe, with M. D. Zabel, 1933). *Chosen Poems: A Selection from My Books of Verse* (1935). *A Poet's Life: Seventy Years in a Changing World* (1938).

Manuscripts, diaries, letters, and personal papers are located in the Harriet Monroe Collection, University of Chicago Library.

BIBLIOGRAPHY: Cahill, D. J., *Harriet Monroe* (1973). Duffey, B., *The Chicago Renaissance in American Letters* (1956). Hoffman, F. J., et al., *The Little Magazine* (1947). Redle, K. G., "Amy Lowell and Harriet Monroe: Their Correspondence" (Ph.D. diss., Northwestern Univ., 1968). Williams, E., *Harriet Monroe and the Poetry Renaissance: The First Ten Years of Poetry, 1912–22* (1977).

For articles in reference works, see: *DAB*, Suppl. 2; *NAW* (article by M. D. Zabel); *20thCA*.

Other references: *JML* 5 (1976). *Illinois Quarterly* 37 (1975). *Poetry* (Jan. 1961).

THEODORA R. GRAHAM

Marianne Craig Moore

B. 15 Nov. 1887, Kirkwood, Missouri; d. 5 Feb. 1972, New York City
Wrote under: Marianne Moore
D. of John Milton and Mary Warner Moore

M. was raised by her mother and grandfather, a Presbyterian minister. M. was seven when her grandfather died, and her mother moved the two children to Carlisle, Pennsylvania. She became an English teacher in the Metzger Institute, where M. was educated before entering Bryn Mawr college (B.A. 1909). In college M. specialized in biology and histology, but also submitted poetry to the campus literary magazine.

For four years after graduating from the Carlisle Commercial College in 1910, M. taught stenography, typing, and bookkeeping at the U.S. Indian School in Carlisle.

M.'s publishing career began in 1915 when the *Egoist*, a London journal dedicated to the new Imagist movement in poetry, accepted "To the Soul of Progress," a short satire on war. The same year, *Poetry* published M. for the first time in a U.S. magazine of general circulation.

In Greenwich Village, where M. lived with her mother, she became part of a literary group that included poets William Carlos Williams, Wallace Stevens, and Alfred Krembourg. *Poems* (1921) was published without M.'s knowledge by her admirers in England. M. added several poems, including the long *Marriage* (issued first as a pamphlet in 1923), before the collection was published in the U.S. as *Observations* (1924). It won the $2,000 Dial Award for "distinguished service to American letters," and M. was asked to become acting editor of the *Dial*, where she worked from 1926 until the magazine ceased publication in 1929. Thereafter, her vocation was solely poetry and writing.

M. was the recipient of many honorary degrees and awards, including the Bollingen and Pulitzer prizes for her *Collected Poems* (1951). In 1955, M. was elected to the American Academy of Arts and Letters.

Observations shows clearly M.'s celebrated innovations in prosody, formal structuring of verse, and poetic vision of animals and of man. In "The Fish," M.'s sharp powers of close observation enable M. to render vividly the world of the ocean. That poem also reveals M.'s intense interest in design and pattern, indicated by the distinctive forms of typography, and her new emphasis on the whole stanza as a formal unit, rather than on the line. In the first few lines of "Poetry," M. tells us that she, too, dislikes poetry, but that by reading it, one may discover "the genuine." This poem includes M.'s famous description of poetry as seeing real toads in imaginary gardens.

In his introduction to M.'s *Selected Poems* (1935), T. S. Eliot linked her with the Imagist poets, yet pointed out unique characteristics of her work. He acknowledges her as the greatest master of *light* rhyme, admiring her intricate forms and patterns. Eliot recognizes M.'s work as being part of a small number of durable poems from our time.

In "The Mind Is an Enchanted Thing" (from *Nevertheless*, 1944), M.

argues, through her own intricate form of syllabics, that contemplation of art has the power to transform spiritual dejection into spiritual joy. The most emotional of all M.'s poems is "In Distrust of Merits." It has been called the best poem to come out of World War II; the theme is the tragedy of war, and the poem reflects M.'s profound hope that contagion, so effective in sickness, may also become effective in creating trust.

M.'s major scholarly work, on which she spent nine years, is a translation of the fables of La Fontaine (1954). The fables are all slyly satirical and entertaining in their striking wisdom and new typographical forms. M.'s criticism, collected in *Predilections* (1955), is eclectic; her topics include Louise Bogan, D. H. Lawrence, Sir Francis Bacon, Ezra Pound, Henry James, and Anna Pavlova. She also wrote a play, *The Absentee: A Comedy in Four Acts* (1962), based on the 1812 Irish novel by Maria Edgeworth. M.'s most popular book, *A Marianne Moore Reader* (1961), includes selections from her best prose and poems.

M.'s main literary contribution is the development of the artful flexibility of direct language in poems. She is remembered as a genius of invention in poetry, for humane wit and intellectual energy, and as a loved and gracious literary artist.

WORKS: *Poems* (1921). *Marriage* (1923). *Observations* (1924). *Selected Poems* (1935). *The Pangolin, and Other Verse* (1936). *What Are Years* (1941). *Nevertheless* (1944). *Rock Crystal, a Christmas Tale* by A. Stifter (translated by Moore, with E. Mayer, 1945). *A Face* (1949). *Collected Poems* (1951). *The Fables of La Fontaine* (translated by Moore, 1954). *Gedichte* (1954). *Predilections* (1955). *Like a Bulwark* (1956). *Idiosyncrasy & Technique: Two Lectures* (1958). *Letters from and to the Ford Motor Company* (1958). *O to Be a Dragon* (1959). *A Marianne Moore Reader* (1961). *The Absentee: A Comedy in Four Acts* (1962). *Puss in Boots, the Sleeping Beauty, and Cinderella* by Charles Perrault (translated by Moore, 1963). *The Arctic Ox* (1964). *Poetry and Criticism* (1965). *Tell Me, Tell Me; Granite, Steel, and Other Topics* (1966). *The Complete Poems of Marianne Moore* (1967). *The Accented Syllable* (1969).

BIBLIOGRAPHY: Abbott, C. S., *Marianne Moore: A Descriptive Bibliography* (1977). Engel, B. F., *Marianne Moore* (1964). Garrigue, J., *Marianne Moore* (University of Minnesota Pamphlets on American Writers, No. 50, 1965). Hadas, P. W., *Marianne Moore: Poet of Affection* (1977). Hall, D., *Marianne Moore: The Cage and the Animal* (1970). Jennings, E., in *American Poetry*, Ed. I. Ehrenpreis (1965). Nitchie, G. W., *Marianne Moore: An Introduction to the Poetry* (1969). Sheehy, E. P., and K. A. Lohf, *The Achievement of Marianne Moore: A Bibliography, 1907–1957* (1958). Stapleton, L., *Marianne Moore: The Poet's Advance* (1978). Thérèse, Sister Mary, *Marianne Moore:*

A Critical Essay (1969). Tomlinson, C., ed., *Marianne Moore: A Collection of Critical Essays* (1969). Watts, E. S., *The Poetry of American Women from 1632 to 1945* (1977).

For articles in reference works, see: *CA*, 33 (1973) *CB* (Dec. 1952; April 1968). *20thCA. 20thCAS.*

Other references: *CE* (Feb. 1953). *Harper's* (May 1977). *Quarterly Review of Literature* (4, 1948; 16, 1969).

ROBIN JOHNSON

Sarah Parsons Moorhead

M. lived during the tumultuous Great Awakening, the religious revival of the 1740s which shook New England. M.'s one slender published work, *To the Reverend James Davenport on His Departure from Boston by Way of a Dream* (1742), is an extended poetic comment on the controversy that occurred in Boston over Davenport's theological opinions and religious practices.

Davenport, deeply affected by the religious zeal of the 1740s, deserted his congregation of Southold, Long Island, and began itinerant preaching. He attacked the piety and sincerity of local ministers, creating internal dissension in many congregations. M. comments sharply on his behavior and admonishes backsliding and bickering Bostonians. Her public criticism of the clergy is significant because it was published contemporaneously with the events discussed in the poem. That is, a woman writer had been accepted as a critic of current events as early as 1742.

Stylistically, M. mimics the poetical taste of the day. Paradoxically, although her subject is religious, M. speaks with the voice of a distressed sentimental lover. M. also employs the technique of a dream vision. She interjects a femine feeling through florid description, creating an elaborate tapestry quality. Perhaps M. recognized that using such sugared language would make her severe criticism acceptable to the public. Her style and subject matter thus appear as a strange but well-presented mixture of the religious and the secular, the pious and the sentimental.

M.'s criticism, perhaps influenced by Charles Chauncy, the conservative minister of the First Church of Boston, focuses on the extremist elements of the Great Awakening and on a prevalent religious hypocrisy. She also discusses free grace. Dealing with a major problem among the Puritans—the difficulty of differentiating between moral action and faith—M. depicts the good-deeds churchgoers, who salve their conscience while actually remaining "immers'd in the black Gulph of sin, / . . . Pleas'd with the fancy'd Freedom of their Will." She believed that salvation can be secured only through the gift of free grace.

The poem also emphasizes the breakdown of morale in the Congregationalist churches—a result of continued quarreling over theological differences, notably among the ministers. M. admonishes the New England churches to remain united against external opposition if they are to survive. She restates this notion in a short poetic postscript published with the longer Davenport verse.

M.'s two poems have historical importance as well as poetic merit. They indicate a general easing of social and religious restraints among New England's Puritans, which allowed women a wider range of subjects and an emergent, if limited, public voice in the New England colonies.

WORKS: *To the Reverend James Davenport on His Departure from Boston by Way of a Dream: With a Line to the Scoffers at Religion Who Make an Ill Improvement of His Naming Out Our Worthy Ministers* (1742).

BIBLIOGRAPHY: Benedict, A., *A History and Genealogy of the Davenport Family* (1851).

JACQUELINE HORNSTEIN

Lillian Mortimer

D. 18 Dec. 1946, Petersburg, Michigan
Wrote under: Lillian Mortimer, Naillil Remitrom
M. J. L. Veronee

M.'s date of birth is unknown, but she was acting in her own plays by 1895. M. began producing her plays and achieved her greatest success with *No Mother to Guide Her* (1905). For a number of years, M. played the comic soubrette Bunco in that melodrama. M. evidently had a repertoire of *lazzi* to use whenever her stage directions indicated "funny business," and she must have been able to put across lines such as this: "Christopher Columbus! Burglars! I thought dere was somethin' crooked about dat guy. De oder one didn't want to do it. Hully gee—what'll I do? Guess I'll have to take my trusty and go after dem. Dey're comin' back." *No Mother to Guide Her* was revived in 1933 for thirteen performances with a cast of fifteen midgets.

The popularity of *No Mother to Guide Her* can scarcely be comprehended by the reader of the published text. The dialogue is little more than a framework on which to hang innumerable bits of comic business, scuffles, pratfalls, abductions, faintings, fisticuffs, knife fights, and revolver shots. The stage directions at the ends of the acts illustrate the genre: At the end of act 2, "they fight. Livingstone gets the better of the knife fight—stabs Jake and throws him off. Livingstone starts for Jake again with knife, to give him another thrust, and as he does so, Bunco enters from R., shoots him; he staggers. During all this action there is a terrible storm raging."

In 1915, M. left the popular-priced melodrama theater circuit to become a headliner in vaudeville. In an interview about her plans for the future, M. said, "I shall write again—when I get time . . . I've got enough scenarios to keep me busy for the next year if I should make plays of all the plots that I have in mind; but I'm always waiting for a little 'leisure,' and then along comes a new contract, and I jump to the road again." Although M. remained on the Keith Circuit for twenty years, she found leisure time during the 1920s to write three to five full-length "comedy-dramas" each year. Most were published for use by amateur theater groups.

In these plays, M. frequently used ethnic characters for the secondary roles—Irish, German, and Jewish "types," country folk, and blacks. In *Mammy's Lil' Wild Rose* (1924), M. specified that Mammy be "made up with minstrel black (not mulatto) and mammy wig." *Headstrong Joan* (1927) includes a courtship between the lovable middle-aged Irish maid Honora and Abie, a "typical Jewish peddler," who wears a paper collar and his derby pulled down to make his ears stand out. This subplot spoofs the long-running Broadway hit *Abie's Irish Rose*. The various dialects M. used provide a counterpoint to the bright, slangy speech of the lively young couples.

The plot formula that M. found most useful set up a confrontation between two young couples. The more attractive pair is virtuous and romantically idealized. The other two, motivated by greed or jealousy, create obstacles for the innocent lovers. But the lovers are so young and appealing that the plotters finally repent and accept the ethics and values that will enable them to live happily ever after.

The photograph of M. in the New York *Dramatic Mirror* (12 May 1915) is of a self-assured middle-aged woman, flamboyantly dressed. She stands with hand on hip and chin tilted back, archly gazing from heavy-lidded eyes. It is hardly the image one would expect of the author of more than forty moral dramas that reaffirm the values of girlish innocence and of decency and noble self-abnegation for young men.

WORKS: *No Mother to Guide Her* (1905). *A Man's Broken Promise* (1906). *The City Feller* (1922). *Little Miss Jack* (1922). *The Path Across the Hill* (1923). *The Road to the City* (1923). *Yimmie Yonson's Yob* (1923). *Mammy's Lil' Wild Rose* (1924). *That's One on Bill* (1924). *An Adopted Cinderella* (1926). *The Bride Breezes In* (1926). *Mary's Castle in the Air* (1926). *Nancy Anna Brown's Folks* (1926). *Ruling the Roost* (1926). *Headstrong Joan* (1927). *He's My Pal* (1927). *Nora, Wake Up!* (1927). *The Winding Road* (1927). *His Irish Dream Girl* (1928). *Love's Magic* (1928). *Paying the Fiddler* (1928). *Two Brides* (1928). *The Open Window* (192–?, by Naillil Remitrom, pseud.). *Manhattan Honeymoon* (1929). *The Gate to Happiness* (1930). *The Wild-Oats Boy* (1930). *Jimmy, Be Careful!* (1931). *Mother in the Shadow* (1936).

BIBLIOGRAPHY: Leverton, G. H., ed., *America's Lost Plays* (Vol. 8, 1940). Mantle, B., ed., *The Best Plays of 1933–34* (1934).

Other references: New York *Dramatic Mirror* (12 May 1915). *NYT* (26 Dec. 1933; 20 Dec. 1946).

FELICIA HARDISON LONDRÉ

Martha Morton

B. 10 Oct. 1865, New York City; d. 18 Feb. 1925, New York City
M. Hermann Conheim

M.'s family included two playwrights and several novelists and journalists. Her mother encouraged M. to write poems and short stories, some of which were published in magazines. Since the stories were mostly in dialogue, M. was persuaded to try writing a play. Unable to interest any managers in her first effort, *Hélène*, she mounted it at her own expense, for one performance, in 1888. The *New York Times* called it "a lugubrious and ill-made though not wholly ineffective drama," but actress Clara Morris revived it in 1889 for a two-year run that returned fifty thousand dollars to the novice playwright.

M.'s second produced play, *The Merchant*, won the New York *World* Play Contest. M. described the prejudice she had to face while directing a rehearsal: "The men shook their heads. They said the drama was going to the dogs. Then they crept in through the stage door and watched that 'green girl' direct the rehearsal and one of them came up to me and said, 'Are you going to make a business out of this?' . . . I looked him straight in the eyes and answered fervently, 'God help me, I must!' Then he put out a friendly hand, crushed my fingers into splinters and gave me the comforting assurance that a woman would have to do twice the work of a man to get one-half the credit."

Because women were barred from membership in the American Dramatists' Club, M. organized the Society of Dramatic Authors. Thirty women constituted its charter membership, but male playwrights were also invited to join. In 1907, the older group proposed consolidation, and the result was the Society of American Dramatists and Composers.

By 1910, M. was called "America's pioneer woman playwright," "the first successful woman playwright," and "the dean of women playwrights." She wrote about thirty-five forgotten plays, fourteen of which were professionally produced in New York City between 1888 and 1911.

M.'s most successful plays were written for the popular comedian William H. Crane: *Brother John* (1893), *His Wife's Father* (1895), *A Fool of Fortune* (1896), and *The Senator Keeps House* (1911). These were considered "good and clean, not too subtle and not too obvious." M.'s favorite subjects were marital adjustments, ups and downs in the business world, and the foibles of high society. *A Bachelor's Romance* (1896) showed members of the frivolous social élite redeemed by exposure to rural life. M.'s plays pleased audiences despite the critics' continual readiness to point out their hackneyed qualities.

M. traveled widely in Europe, and was well read in French and German literature. Her most ambitious work was an adaptation of Leopold Kampf's *On the Eve* (1909), about revolutionary unrest in Russia. For the part of the heroine, M. sent for German actress Hedwig Reicher, who made a personal triumph of her first English-speaking role. Of that character, M. said: "Woman is the tragic element in the social body. . . . The chief woman figure in *On the Eve* symbolizes the woman of today, the universal woman seeking her work and finding it." Critics called this play "a collection of antiquated theatrical effects," but M.'s professionalism afforded her a degree of prestige attained by few other women playwrights.

WORKS: *Hélène* (1888). *The Triumph of Love: The Merchant* (1891). *Geoffrey Middleton* (1892). *Brother John* (1893). *His Wife's Father* (1895, produced in London as *The Sleeping Partner*, 1897). *A Bachelor's Romance* (1896). *A Fool of Fortune* (1896). *The Diplomat* (1902). *Her Lord and Master* (1902). *A Four Leaf Clover* (1905). *The Truth Tellers* (1905). *The Movers* (1907). *On the Eve* (1909). *The Senator Keeps House* (1911).

BIBLIOGRAPHY: *Bookman* (Aug. 1909). *Green Book Magazine* (May 1912). *Theatre Magazine* (10, 1909; 18, 1913). *World To-Day* (July 1908).

FELICIA HARDISON LONDRÉ

Sarah Wentworth Apthorp Morton

B. *Aug. 1759, Boston, Massachusetts; d. 14 May 1846, Quincy, Massachusetts*
Wrote under: Constantia, Sarah Wentworth Apthorp Morton, Philenia
D. of James and Sarah Wentworth Apthorp; m. Perez Morton, 1781

M. was the scion of two influential, wealthy early New England families. She had a thorough education, evidenced in the literary quality of her verses. When the revolution started, M.'s family was accused of Tory loyalties, but she expressed strong patriot sentiments in her post-revolutionary verse. In 1781, M. married a Harvard graduate, a patriot lawyer during the revolution and a prominent figure in state government in the Republic's early years. During their early married life, M. and her husband headed Boston's socialites and remained leading figures in Massachusetts' social and political life. Five of their six children lived to maturity, but all died before M.

In 1788, Perez had an affair with M.'s sister Frances, ending in her sister's suicide. This affair appeared fictively in the first American novel, *The Power of Sympathy; or, The Triumph of Nature* (1789), by William Mill Brown.

M. and her husband led the fight for repeal of Massachusetts's antitheater laws in 1793, subscribing to Boston's first theater. M. supported the earliest American abolitionist groups. In later life she was a patron to young writers.

M.'s subject matter is wide-ranging. Her earliest poems are sentimental plaints or elegies filled with neoclassic devices. Her post-1800 works are mainly occasional poems. Themes throughout focus primarily on moral and political issues.

In much of her work, M. speaks through a languishing, affected female persona, whose sentimental sufferings are suffused with the soft glow of flowery diction. M.'s interest in sentimental neoclassicism also appears in "Ode to Mrs. Warren," a notable example of one early American female poet praising another. In her concern for female attitudes and behavior, M. was a "Sappho," the woman's poet.

However, M. was also an "American" poet, for she wrote verse about the new nation's ideological issues. Her best works in this vein demonstrate a well-developed social and moral conscience, independent thought, and notable poetic scope.

M.'s poem "Beacon Hill" (*Columbian Centinal*, 4 Dec. 1790), written in neat neoclassic couplets, celebrates the sacred, solemn events which transpired on Boston Hill during the revolution. With revisions and enlargements, this poem reappeared as *Beacon Hill: A Local Poem, Historic and Descriptive, Book I* (1797). Here M. tries to revitalize and mythologize the revolutionary era. The poem's introductory section reviews early events: Warren's death, Bunker Hill, Washington's camp at Cambridge. The central section discusses the "natural, moral, and political history" of the colonies. Book One closes with a shepherd-soldier figure defending "his hereditary farm," while the prophetic Columbian muse bears the message of "Equal Freedom" around the earth. Although thoroughly nationalistic in this work, M. also presents a critique of southern slavery.

M.'s "sister" poems, *Ouâbi; or, The Virtues of Nature: An Indian Tale in Four Cantos* (1790) and *The Virtues of Society: A Tale Founded on Fact* (1799), show further interest in moral and social issues. They exemplify her mixed vision of the sentimental-domestic and historical-heroic. *Ouâbi*, perhaps the first American "Indian" poem, discusses a contemporary problem: the survival of simple American virtues beset by luxury and sophistication. *The Virtues of Society*, a spin-off of the failed epic *Beacon Hill*, is a romantic tale based on an incident in the American Revolution.

My Mind and Its Thoughts, in Sketches, Fragments, and Essays (1823) is M.'s only work to appear under her real name. It consists of numerous aphorisms, short essays, and poems—some previously published and rewritten, others new to print. Her "Apology" explains that she made the collection to ease her distress (her son had recently died). The book is a curious mixture of the public and private, the patriotic and sentimental, summarizing M.'s life's interests.

M. was quite popular in the 1790s, but she outlived the vogue for her neoclassical style and post-revolution themes. Her last book was praised nostalgically, not for innate achievement. Her reputation as a poet died with her.

WORKS: *Ouâbi; or, The Virtues of Nature: An Indian Tale in Four Cantos* (1970). *Beacon Hill: A Local Poem, Historic and Descriptive, Book I* (1797). *The Virtues of Society: A Tale Founded on Fact* (1799). *My Mind and Its Thoughts, in Sketches, Fragments, and Essays* (1823).

BIBLIOGRAPHY: Evans, C., *American Bibliography* (1912). Field, V. B., *Constantia: A Study of the Life and Works of Judith Sargent Murray* (1931). Otis, W. B., *American Verse, 1625–1807: A History* (1909). Pearce, R. H., *The Savages of America* (rev. ed., 1953). Pendleton, E., and Milton Ellis, *Philenia: Life and Works of Sarah Wentworth Morton* (1931). Watts, E. S., *The Poetry of American Women from 1632 to 1943* (1977).

For articles in reference works, see: *AA. CAL. DAB*, VII, 1. *NAW* (article by O. E. Winslow).

JACQUELINE HORNSTEIN

Lucretia Coffin Mott

B. 3 Jan. 1793, Nantucket Island, Massachusetts; d. 11 Nov. 1880, Roadside, Pennsylvania
D. of Thomas and Anna Folger Coffin; m. James Mott, 1811

Born to a hearty, seafaring Quaker family, M. was sent to a Friends' school in New York, where she subsequently served as an assistant teacher. There she met her husband, with whom she had six children. M. was designated a minister of the Society of Friends in 1821. During the Great Separation of the Society in 1827, she allied herself with the liberal Hicksite faction. Within the next decade she became a vocal abolitionist who helped found the Philadelphia Female Anti-Slavery Society. Within the abolitionist movement, M. backed the radical faction of William Lloyd Garrison, which urged immediate emancipation of the slaves.

The diary in which M. recorded her experiences at the 1840 World's Anti-Slavery Convention in London, where, because of her sex, she was denied recognition as a delegate of the U.S., has been edited by Frederick B. Tolles (*Slavery and "The Woman Question,"* 1952). M. describes the political wrangling among abolitionists and Quakers, her meeting with English female reformers, her conversations with Elizabeth Cady Stanton, and her travels throughout the British Isles. M.'s friendship with Stanton, begun at the convention, resulted in a decision to call the first women's rights convention in 1848 at Seneca Falls, New York.

A preacher and reformer, M.'s literary corpus consists almost entirely of recorded sermons and discourses. Her appeal to reason and moral principle, powerful delivery, and personal presence gave M.'s words great impact. Her preaching was shot through with the liberal religious belief that practical righteousness was more important than theological speculation. In *A Sermon to the Medical Students* (1849), M. laid out her self-proclaimed heretical view that true religion is not mysterious, but is based on the universal and self-evident conviction that the kingdom of God is within. Humanity is not depraved, and does not need to be brought to righteousness by the atonement of Christ. The work of the present age is to reveal the nobility, and hence the divinity, of humanity through works of reform.

In response to a lecture by Richard Henry Dana, M. delivered her logical and powerful *Discourse on Woman* (1849), in which she shows that the present position of woman is neither her natural nor original one. Her equality with man is established by God, but she is everywhere in subjection to man. Woman's natural ability is illustrated historically in the lives of great women, but society promotes her inferiority. Woman, like the slave, has no liberty. She is subject to laws she does not make, excluded from a pulpit that disciplines her, and bound by a marriage contract that degrades her. She asks for no favors, but for the right to be acknowledged as a moral, responsible being.

In *A Sermon at Yardleyville* (1858), M. affirms the divinity of human instincts and claims that the attempt to create greater equality among people is characteristic of the work of the real Christian. In *A Sermon at Bristol* (1860), she urges Christians to be nonconformists like Jesus, and women to reject sectarianism, which sets limits on the divinity within them. M. maintains in *Discourse at the Friends' Meeting, N.Y.* (1866) that human progress is really moral progress and that skepticism and critical thinking are religious duties.

"Truth for authority, rather than authority for truth" was M.'s central concern. In her preaching and speaking M. attempted to uncover truth. Through her personal involvement in a myriad of reform movements she tried to live truth and help realize it in her own time. In her home, where M. offered hospitality to hundreds of fellow reformers and society's most oppressed, she helped sustain truth and those who sought it.

WORKS: *Discourse on Woman* (1849). *A Sermon to the Medical Students* (1849). *A Sermon at Yardleyville* (1858). *A Sermon at Bristol* (1860). *Discourse at the Friends' Meeting, N.Y.* (1866). *Discourse at the Second Unitarian Church, Brooklyn* (1867). *Sermon on the Religious Aspects of the Age* (1869). *Life and Letters of James and Lucretia Mott* (Ed. A. D. Hallowell, 1884). *Slavery and "The Woman Questions": Lucretia Mott's Diary of her Visit to Great Britain to Attend the World's Anti-Slavery Convention of 1840* (Ed. F. B. Tolles, 1952). *Lucretia Mott: Complete Sermons and Speeches* (Ed. D. Greene, 1980).

The letters of Lucretia Mott are in the Friends Historical Library, Swarthmore College, and the Sophia Smith Collection, Smith College Library.

BIBLIOGRAPHY: Bacon, M., *Valiant Friend: The Life of Lucretia Mott* (1980). Cromwell, O., *Lucretia Mott* (1958).

For articles in reference works, see: *AW. DAB*, VI, 1. *HWS*, 1. *NAW* (article by F. B. Tolles). *NCAB*, 2.

Other references: *American Scholar* (Spring 1951). *Bulletin of the Historical Society of Montgomery County, Pa.* (April 1948).

DANA GREENE

Louise Chandler Moulton

B. *10 April 1835, Pomfret, Connecticut; d. 10 Aug. 1908, Boston, Massachusetts*
Wrote under: Ellen Louise Chandler, Louisa Chandler, A Lady, Ellen Louise,
  Louise Chandler Moulton
D. *of Lucius Lemuel and Louisa Rebecca Clark Chandler; m. William Upham*
  Moulton, 1855

M. was born on a farm outside a town settled by her Puritan ancestors. Her parents were wealthy, conscientious Calvinists. M.'s childhood was solitary and circumscribed, but reasonably happy. Precocious, M. published her first verses at fifteen. When she entered Emma Willard's Female Seminary in Troy, New York, fellow students knew her as "Ellen Louise," editor of *The Book of the Boudoir* (1853) and author of *This, That, and the Other*, a collection of sentimental stories and sketches which appeared in 1854 and sold 20,000 copies.

Soon after M.'s graduation in 1855, she married the editor and publisher of *The True Flag*, a Boston literary journal. Members of the city's literary society, the Moultons entertained Whittier, Longfellow, Holmes, and Emerson. In 1870, M. became the Boston literary correspondent for the New York *Tribune*. She began contributing stories to magazines such as *Harper's, Galaxy*, and *Scribner's;* her poem "May-Flowers" achieved great popularity after appearing in the *Atlantic*. Other works during this period include *June Clifford* (1855), a novel; *Some Women's Hearts* (1874), short stories; and *Bed-Time Stories* (1873), the first in a series of children's books.

After an initial trip to Europe in 1876, M. divided her life between the two continents. Her overwhelming success in London literary society began in 1877 with a letter of introduction to Lord Houghton (Richard Monckton Milnes) from "the Byron of Oregon," Joaquin Miller. From this time, M. was firmly established in European artistic circles.

Although she had published an earlier volume of poetry in America, *Swallow-Flights* (1877) brought M. her first wave of extravagant praise. Professor William Minto compared her to Sir Philip Sidney; other critics mentioned the lyric poets of the 16th and 17th centuries. *In the Garden of Dreams* (1890) and *At the Wind's Will* (1899) confirmed her reputation. Critics rated her love poetry close to Mrs. Browning's and considered her sonnets second only to Christina Rossetti's. During these years, M. also brought out two delightful volumes of Irvingesque travel sketches and a book of social advice culled from her newspaper column in *Our Continent*.

Certainly any assessment of M.'s achievements must cite her "genius for friendship." Her correspondence, now in the Library of Congress, fills fifty-two volumes; its index is a virtual directory of late Victorian authors. M.'s library, bequeathed to the Boston Public Library, comprised nine hundred books, many of them rare editions and autographed presentation copies. However, M.'s greatest legacy stemmed from her critical astuteness and sympathy. As a European literary correspondent for the Boston *Sunday Herald* and the New York *Independent* during the

1880s and 1890s, M. gained recognition in the U.S. for the Pre-Raphaelites, Décadents, and French Symbolist poets.

Like many late Victorians, M. wrote in traditional forms such as the sonnet, the French ballade, triolet, and rondel. She was known for her polished metrics, sensuous imagery, and meticulous workmanship. While critics appreciated her spontaneity, rarely do her emotions burst their poetic form; poise is all. However, M.'s meditations on love and approaching death hint at deep feeling below the restrained surface.

Upon her death, M.'s reputation reached its crest. According to Whiting, she "had left a place in American letters unfilled and that no successor is in evidence will hardly be disputed." M. lamented half-seriously that she seemed to have only two themes: love and death. But, as her biographer Lilian Whiting commented, these are surely two of the very greatest. As a poet, her contribution was small, but worth noting. As a critic and literary publicist, she played a valuable role in American letters. As a woman, her social success and "feminine" artistry reveal a great deal about late Victorian expectations.

WORKS: *The Waverly Garland: A Present for All Seasons* (edited by Moulton, 1853). *The Book of the Boudoir; or, A Momento of Friendship* (edited by Moulton, 1853). *This, That, and the Other* (1854). *June Clifford: A Tale* (1855). *My Third Book* (1859). *Evaline, Madelon, and Other Poems* (1861). *Bed-Time Stories* (1873). *Some Women's Hearts* (1874). *More Bed-Time Stories* (1875). *Jessie's Neighbor, and Other Stories* (1877). *Swallow-Flights* (American title, *Poems*, 1877). *New Bed-Time Stories* (1880). *Random Rambles* (1881). *Poems* (1882). *Firelight Stories* (1883). *Garden Secrets* by Philip Bourke Marston (edited, with biographical sketch, by Moulton, 1887). *Ourselves and Our Neighbors* (1887). *Education for the Girls* (1888). *Miss Eyre from Boston* (1889). *A Ghost at His Fireside* (1890). *In the Garden of Dreams* (1890). *Stories Told at Twilight* (1890). *A Last Harvest* by Philip Bourke Marston (edited, with biographical sketch by Moulton, 1891). *Collected Poems of Philip Bourke Marston* (edited by Moulton, 1892). *Arthur O'Shaughnessy, His Life and His Work* (1894). *In Childhood's Country* (1896). *Lazy Tours in Spain and Elsewhere* (1896). *Against Wind and Tide* (1899). *At the Wind's Will* (1899). *Four of Them* (1899). *The American University Course (State Registered): Second Month Conduct of Life* (1900). *Jessie's Neighbor* (1900). *Her Baby Brother* (1901). *Introduction to the Value of Love and Its Compiler Frederick Lawrence Knowles* (1906). *Poems and Sonnets of Louise Chandler Moulton* (Ed. H. P. Spofford, 1908).

The papers of Louise Chandler Moulton are at the Library of Congress and the American Antiquarian Society.

BIBLIOGRAPHY: Howe, J. W., *Representative Women of New England* (1904). Spofford, H. P., *A Little Book of Friends* (1916). Spofford, H. P., *Our Famous Women* (1884). Whiting, L., *Louis Chandler Moulton, Poet and*

Friend (1910). Winslow, H. M., *Literary Boston of Today* (1902).

For articles in reference works, see: *AW. CAL. DAB*, VII, 1. *Female Prose Writers of America* (1857). *NAW* (article by L. M. Young). *NCAB*, 3.

Other references: Boston *Transcript* (12 Aug. 1908). *Poet-Lore* (Winter 1908).

SARAH WAY SHERMAN

Mary Noailles Murfree

B. 24 Jan. 1850, Murfreesboro, Tennessee; d. 31 July 1922, Murfreesboro, Tennessee
Wrote under: Charles Egbert Craddock, R. Emmet Dembury
D. of William Law and Fanny Dickinson Murfree

Born at the family plantation, M. was the daughter of a lawyer and author and a mother whose love of music greatly influenced the family. Illness at the age of four left M. with permanent lameness.

In 1855, M. spent the first of fifteen summers at Beersheba Springs in the Cumberland Mountains, which she fictionalized as New Helvetia Springs. Soon the family moved to Nashville, where M. and her sister Fanny were educated at the Nashville Female Academy. After the Civil War, which the Murfrees spent in Nashville, M. continued her education at Chegary Institute in Philadelphia, a French finishing school.

M.'s writing career began in earnest with the publication of "The Dancin' Party at Harrison's Cove" in the *Atlantic Monthly* (May 1878) under the pseudonym Charles Egbert Craddock. M.'s mountain fiction was very well received; by 1885, when *The Prophet of the Great Smoky Mountains* was being serialized, her popularity had led to increased speculation about the author's identity, and the sensation following its revelation gained M. invaluable publicity.

Although the modern reader may find M.'s decorous mountain fiction more romantic than realistic, and may be bored by the lack of individualization in her characters, contemporary readers were fascinated by the minute detail, often gleaned through research, with which M. portrayed people and their activities. The dominant feature of M.'s earlier work is the mountains themselves. The juxtaposition of florid prose with dialect is probably its weakest trait.

In spite of M.'s desire for realism, her characters tend to be stereotypes. Most of the young "mountain-flower" girls, such as Cynthia Ware in "Drifting Down Lost Creek" and Clarsie Giles in "The 'Harnt' That Walks Chilhowee," are almost indistinguishable. " 'Harnt,' " probably M.'s best-known work, is notable for its theme of the superiority of mountain life.

M.'s greatest achievement is her first volume of stories, *In the Tennessee Mountains* (1884), with its emphasis on the picturesque details of regional life. M.'s stories appealed to the awareness of sectional differences which had been heightened by the Civil War, as the popularity of this volume indicates.

Except for M.'s first novel, *Where the Battle Was Fought* (1884), based on personal experiences during the Civil War, M.'s work through the late 1890s focuses on mountain places and themes. When the popularity of local-color writing waned, M. turned to historical subjects in undistinguished novels such as *The Story of Old Fort Loudon* (1899) and *The Amulet* (1906). By 1910, M.'s public appeal had diminished to the point that Houghton-Mifflin rejected a proffered novel and collection of stories.

M. has been favorably compared to local colorists such as Bret Harte, Sarah Orne Jewett, and fellow southerner George Washington Cable. Her reputation is based on her mountain stories and novels; the body of her work is flawed by M.'s tendency to repeat characters and plots. However, *In the Tennessee Mountains* remains an important contribution to regional literature in the late 19th c.

SELECTED WORKS: *In the Tennessee Mountains* (1884). *Where the Battle Was Fought* (1884). *The Prophet of the Great Smoky Mountains* (1885). *In the "Stranger People's" Country* (1891). *The Mystery of Witch-Face Mountain, and Other Stories* (1895). *The Phantoms of the Foot-Bridge, and Other Stories* (1895). *The Story of Old Fort Loudon* (1899). *A Spectre of Power* (1903). *The Amulet* (1906). *The Fair Mississippian* (1908). *The Raid of the Guerilla, and Other Stories* (1912). *The Story of Duciehurst* (1914).

BIBLIOGRAPHY: Cary, R., *Mary Noailles Murfree* (1967). Parks, E. W., *Charles Egbert Craddock (Mary Noailles Murfree)* (1941). Wright, N., Introduction to *In the Tennessee Mountains* (1970).

For articles in reference works, see: *AW. CAL. DAB*, VII; 1. *NAW* (article by E. W. Parks).

Other references: *ALR* (Autumn 1974). *Appalachian Journal* (Winter 1976). *MissQ* (Spring 1978).

MARTHA E. COOK

Judith Sargent Murray

B. 1 May 1751, Gloucester, Massachusetts; d. 6 July 1820, Natchez, Mississippi
Wrote under: Constantia, Honoria, Honoria-Martesia, Judith Sargent,
  Judith Stevens
D. of Winthrop and Judith Saunders Sargent; m. John Stevens, 1769;
  m. John Murray, 1788

M. was the oldest child of a well-to-do merchant who was active during the Revolution on the colonists' side. M. was better educated than most women of her time, because her father permitted her to study with a brother who was preparing for Harvard. She spent most of her life in Gloucester, where she was married twice: to a sea captain and, two years after his death, to Murray, founder of the American Universalist Church. Two children were born of the second marriage, a son who died shortly after birth and a daughter who survived her mother. Financial difficulties marked the final years of both marriages.

In 1798, M. collected many of her writings into a three-volume work called *The Gleaner*. These volumes include one series of essays that appeared originally from 1792 to 1794 in the *Massachusetts Magazine*, additional essays previously unpublished, and two plays—*Virtue Triumphant* and *The Traveller Returned*, produced with little success at the Federal Street Theatre in Boston. There remain uncollected a number of essays and poems published in periodicals and a catechism for children, which was published as a book under the name of Judith Stevens. In addition, M. edited Murray's letters and autobiography.

M. is best known for her periodical essay series, "The Gleaner." These essays purport to be written by Mr. Vigilius, a well-off, philanthropic man of reason and sensibility who has adopted the pen name of the Gleaner to write about moral, religious, political and family matters. M. reveals her liberal religious views, federalism, cultural nationalism, concern for the special problems of bringing up daughters, and commitment to education, about which she had modern views. Much of the interest, however, centers less on discussions of general issues than on the Gleaner's accounts of his family. Because the story of his daughter is so fully developed, this series has been referred to as a novel of sensibility. In a subplot there is, in contrast with traditions of 18th-c. sensibility, an unusually realistic cameo view of women's experience.

M. is also known for her feminist statement "On the Equality of the Sexes," which she claimed to have written in 1779, before Wollstonecraft's *Vindication of the Rights of Woman* appeared, although it was not published until 1790 in the *Massachusetts Magazine*. Concerned here with arguing the intellectual equality of women, M. went on in the later Gleaner essays to elaborate her defense of women's abilities.

M.'s essay series has attracted some scholarly attention in the past, and her plays, which combine American settings and sentiments with traditions of the Restoration stage, read surprisingly well and are of historic interest. Recently, her essays have attracted attention because of M.'s feminist defense of women's intellectual potential and her insistence on the importance of education and economic independence for women. M.'s work reflects an acceptance of the literary and intellectual traditions of her time and the strength of mind to reject tradition when she believed it incorrect or unfair.

WORKS: *Some Deductions from the System Promulgated* (1782). *The Gleaner* (3 vols., 1798). *Letters and Sketches of Sermons*, by John Murray (3 vols., edited by Murray, 1812–13). *Records of the Life of the Rev. John Murray, Written by Himself, with a Continuation by Mrs. Judith Sargent Murray* (edited by Murray, 1816).

BIBLIOGRAPHY: Benson, M. S., *Women in Eighteenth Century America* (1935). Field, V. B., *Constantia: A Study of the Life and Works of Judith Sargent Murray* (1933). Hanson, E. R., *Our Women Workers* (1882).

For articles in reference works, see: *DAB*, VII, 1. *NAW* (article by J. W. James).

Other references: *AL* 12 (1940). *AQ* 28 (1976). *EAL* (9, 1975; 11, 1976–77). *SP* 24 (1927).

PHYLLIS FRANKLIN

Pauli Murray

B. 20 Nov. 1910, Baltimore, Maryland
D. of William Henry and Agnes Georgianna Fitzgerald Murray

Orphaned at the age of three, M. was raised by her mother's sister, an elementary school teacher in a small black school. M. attended her aunt's classes and learned to read and write at an early age.

M. received a B.A. from Hunter College in New York. In 1938, she applied to the graduate school of the University of North Carolina but was denied admission to the white institution. During this period, M. wrote prose and poetry under the guidance of Stephen Vincent Benét. M. suspended her literary work to serve as special field secretary for the Workers Defense League. After Benét's death in 1943 she resumed her efforts to write the epic poem which he had urged her to write about blacks in America. She finished the first version of "Dark Testament" during the Harlem riot of 1943.

In 1944, M. was graduated with honors from Howard University Law School in Washington, D.C. As a woman, she was denied admission to Harvard Law School in 1944 and 1946, but received an M.A. in 1945 from the University of California Law School at Berkeley and a Ph.D. from Yale in 1965. From 1948 to 1960, she was in private practice in New York. In 1960 and 1961, M. was senior lecturer on constitutional and administrative law at the Ghana School of Law. While in Accra, she joined Leslie Rubin in the writing of *The Constitution and Government of Ghana* (1961). M. has practiced law, taught law and political science, and served on numerous national committees.

Dark Testament, and Other Poems (1970) includes poems originally published in several magazines. The longest and best is "Dark Testament." Part 1 of "Dark Testament" questions the possibility of hope but ends on a note of determination, saying ". . . let the dream linger on." M. contends that universal brotherhood must be the goal of humanity. Part 2 contains poems dealing with specific historical events: a Detroit riot, the lynching of Mack Parker, and the death of Franklin Roosevelt. The third part focuses upon the universal human predicament and has no racial emphasis. Neither has the fourth part, which takes images from nature for poems dealing with love, friendship, death, and loneliness.

Proud Shoes: The Story of an American Family (1956) is the story of M.'s ancestors. Asserting that "true emancipation lies in the acceptance of the whole past, in deriving strength from all my roots, in facing up to the degradation as well as the dignity of my ancestors," M. traces the family back to great-grandparents who were slaves. But the major portion of *Proud Shoes* is devoted to her greatest source of pride, her grandfather, who taught M. that she ought to cherish "courage, honor, and discipline."

Though she knew her parents only briefly during early childhood, M. found great sources of pride in her mother's family. *Proud Shoes* does more than account for the pride that has made M. such a successful black woman. It analyzes miscegenation as a social phenomenon and examines its bearing on race relations. It attacks stereotypes of the black family as broken and matriarchal. Thus, it is a valuable social document as well as an interesting biography of an American family.

Though M. has chosen to make her social contribution primarily though service rather than literature, her small oeuvre is significant. Her legal writing establishes her as a scholar, *Proud Shoes* proves her a capable biographer, and *Dark Testament* reveals a talented poet whose lines combine the skills of both biographer and lawyer—precision of language and vision—with the compression of poetic forms to achieve powerful effects.

WORKS: *All for Mr. Davis* (with M. Kempton, 1942). *States Law on Race and Color* (1950). *Proud Shoes: The Story of an American Family* (1956). *The Constitution and Government of Ghana* (with L. Rubin, 1961). *Dark Testament, and Other Poems* (1970).

BIBLIOGRAPHY: Diamonstein, B., *Open Secrets* (1972).
For articles in reference works, see: *Black American Writers Past and Present*, T. G. Rush, C. F. Myers, and E. S. Arata (Vol. 2, 1975).
Other references: *Afro-American* (20 Jan. 1968).

GWENDOLYN THOMAS

Alice Ruth Moore Dunbar Nelson

B. *19 July 1875, New Orleans, Louisiana; d. 18 Sept. 1935, Philadelphia, Pennsylvania*
Wrote under: *Alice Dunbar, Alice Dunbar-Nelson, Alice Ruth Moore*
D. *of Joseph and Patricia Wright Moore; m. Paul Laurence Dunbar, 1889; m. Robert John Nelson, 1916*

The younger of two daughters of middle-class working parents, N. attended public schools and Straight College, New Orleans. After graduation, she began to teach and to submit poetry to the Boston *Monthly Review*.

One of these poems and the accompanying photograph of N. attracted Dunbar, then a young poet. He wrote N., conversationally raising literary issues, and enclosed a copy of his "Phyllis." This began a friendship that led to marriage.

N. separated from Dunbar after a quarrel in 1902, and returned to teaching—she had taught kindergarten at Victoria Earle Matthews's White Rose Mission in New York—becoming head of the English Department at Howard High School in Wilmington, Delaware. She retained this position for eighteen years until she was fired for defying an order to abstain from political activity.

During World War I, N. became involved in organizing black women on behalf of the U.S. Council of National Defense. N. was the first black woman to serve on Delaware's Republican State Committee.

N. became associate editor of the *Wilmington Advocate*, a weekly newspaper published by her second husband and dedicated to the achievement of equal rights for blacks. She also wrote a weekly column for the Washington, D.C., *Eagle* and contributed occasional pieces to the *American Methodist Episcopal Church Review*. Her later years were devoted to social work, especially with delinquent black girls, and to the cause of world peace.

N.'s reply to Dunbar's first letter to her set forth her views on the literary use of "the Negro problem:" "I haven't much liking for those writers that wedge the Negro problem and social equality and long dissertations on the Negro in general into their stories. It is too much like a quinine pill in jelly. . . . Somehow when I start a story I always think of my folk characters as simple human beings, not of types of a race or an idea, and I seem to be on more friendly terms with them." N.'s letter also mentioned the forthcoming publication of her first book, *Violets, and Other Tales* (1895). In accord with her philosophy, the book presents "simple human beings" caught in universal dilemmas such as poverty and love betrayed.

While many of the twelve poems and seventeen tales and sketches in *Violets, and Other Tales* are romantic and slight, they give evidence of a fresh, lively style. Noteworthy in this collection for their sprightliness and originality are the humorous "In Unconsciousness," a mock-epic inspired by a tooth extraction, and "The Woman," a lively meditation on the independent woman. This piece decries "this wholesale marrying of girls in their teens, this rushing into an unknown plane of life to avoid work," and reassures readers that an independent, intelligent woman, a lawyer or doctor, does not lose her ability to love when she gains a vocation.

During the period of her marriage to Dunbar, N. published her second collection, *The Goodness of St. Rocque, and Other Stories* (1899), fourteen local-color stories of New Orleans life. These are crisply written sketches, portraying struggling, heroic characters trapped in difficulties. Most have a surprise twist at their conclusions.

While teaching at Howard High School, N. edited two collections of poems and prose for oratory students, *Masterpieces of Negro Eloquence* (1914) and *The Dunbar Speaker and Entertainer* (1920). Included in the latter are several pieces by N., many of them (such as the one-act play *Mine Eyes Have Seen*) expressing conventional patriotic sentiments and racial pride. The short lyric "I Sit and Sew," while sharing the conventional patriotism of the others, is also a statement of a woman chafing at the limited range of appropriate female activity; it has an intensity, freshness, and power which the other pieces lack.

N. was a pioneer in the black short-story tradition. Her second volume shows an increase in power, which promised further development, had she continued to write in this genre. Instead, N., an energetic woman of diversified talents, devoted her later life to journalism and political and social activism.

WORKS: *Violets, and Other Tales* (1895). *The Goodness of St. Rocque, and Other Stories* (1899). *Masterpieces of Negro Eloquence* (edited by Nelson, 1914). *The Dunbar Speaker and Entertainer* (edited by Nelson, 1920).

BIBLIOGRAPHY: Bernikow, L. *The World Split Open: Four Centuries of Women Poets in England and America* (1974). Brawley, B., *Paul Laurence Dunbar* (1936). Brown, H. Q., *Homespun Heroines, and Other Women of Distinction* (1926). Kerlin, R. T., *Negro Poets and Their Poems* (1935). Loggins, V., *The Negro Author* (1931). Martin, J., ed., *A Singer in the Dawn* (1975). Whiteman, M., *A Century of Fiction by American Negroes, 1853–1952: A Descriptive Bibliography* (1955).

For articles in reference works, see: *NAW* (article by N. A. Ford).

Other references: *Delaware History* 17 (Fall–Winter 1976).

KAREN F. STEIN

Eliza Jane Poitevent Nicholson

B. 11 March 1848, Pearlington, Mississippi; d. 15 Feb. 1896, New Orleans,
* Louisiana*
Wrote under: Pearl Rivers
D. of Captain William James and Mary Amelia Russ Poitevent;
* m. Alva Morris Holbrook, 1872; m. George Nicholson, 1878*

N. was raised by an aunt near the Louisiana-Mississippi border. She entertained herself by roaming the piney woods along the Pearl River, developing in her youth an affectionate regard for nature.

In 1867, N. began submitting the poems she had been writing since age fourteen to newspapers and magazines. Her first published poem appeared in the New Orleans literary sheet *The South* in 1868. Soon poems by "Pearl Rivers" appeared in the New York *Home Journal*, the New York *Ledger*, and the New Orleans *Times* and *Daily Picayune*.

In 1868, N. met A. M. Holbrook, owner and editor of the *Daily Picayune*. He offered her a job as literary editor for $25 a week. Over the strenuous objections of her family, N. accepted, becoming New Orleans' first female journalist. Her lively prose and intelligent selections markedly improved the paper's literary section. In 1872, she married Holbrook, divorced and forty years her senior. (His angry ex-wife returned from New York a month after the wedding and proceeded to attack N. with a pistol and a bottle of rum. The subsequent trial was covered in scandalous detail by the *Daily Picayune*.)

When Holbrook died, four years later, N. assumed ownership and management of the *Picayune*, which was eighty thousand dollars in debt. At twenty-seven, she thus became the first woman ever to own and operate a metropolitan daily paper. With the assistance of a loyal staff, including the part owner and business manager, George Nicholson, whom she married in 1878, N. transformed the *Picayune* into a profitable paper and the first general-interest daily in the South. N.'s most significant innovations were directed at women. She introduced a society column, personal notes, fashion news, home and medical advice columns, children's pages, and plentiful illustrations. N. also employed talented writers, including several women. N.'s own poetry and prose also appeared, including columns of her personal and imaginative commentary. In 1884, N. became president of the Women's National Press Association and was the first honorary member of the New York Women's Press Club.

In N.'s only volume of poetry, *Lyrics* (1873), the theme is almost without exception nature and seasonal change. N.'s rhymed quatrains are characterized by personifications of the months and seasons and by fairylike perspectives of plants and animals. Occasionally, she writes of feminine heartbreak. Technically pedestrian, N.'s poems reveal a delight in nature and an eye for authentic detail. To N., poetry was a "gift of song," intended to cheer and please her audience.

Two later poems, "Hagar" and "Leah," published first in *Cosmopolitan* in 1893 and 1894, suggest a richer dimension of N.'s talent. Long dramatic poems in blank verse, they are uneven but vivid and insightful evocations of their heroines' bitterness and jealousy as overlooked women. "Hagar" is the stronger of the two poems, with an effective use of meter and imagery.

Although her early pastoral poetry is slight, N.'s later poems reflect an ability to dramatize emotion effectively. But it is N.'s journalistic ability that distinguishes her. Her columns are filled with a sure, lively prose, whose mark was entertaining dialogue and reflective commentary. Her paper stands as a model of innovative and responsible publishing. A remarkable and sensitive woman, N. is said to have possessed little confidence in her abilities. Nevertheless, her strong sense of duty and courage often substituted for self-confidence and forged the means by which her creativity and discriminating intelligence were expressed.

WORKS: *Lyrics* (1873). *Four Poems by Pearl Rivers* (1900). *Two Poems by Pearl Rivers* (1900?).

The papers of Eliza Jane Poitevent Nicholson are at the Howard-Tilton Library, Tulane University, New Orleans, Louisiana.

BIBLIOGRAPHY: Dabney, T. E., *One Hundred Great Years* (1944). DeMenil, A. N., *The Literature of the Louisiana Territory* (1904). Farr, E. S., *Pearl Rivers* (1951). Gill, H. M., *The South in Prose and Poetry* (1916). Harrison, J. H., *Pearl Rivers, Publisher of the Picayune* (1932). Holdith, W. K., "The Singing Heart: A Study of the Life and Work of Peark Rivers," *SoQ* 22 (Winter 1982). Mount, M., *Some Notables of New Orleans* (1896). Ross, I., *Ladies of the Press* (1936).

For articles in reference works, see: *DAB*, VII, 1. *Dictionary of American Authors*, Ed. O. F. Adams (1904). *Living Female Writers of the South*, Ed. M. T. Tardy (1872). *The Living Writers of the South*, J. W. Davidson (1869). *NAW* (article by W. Wiegand). *NCAB*, 1.

Other references: *Louisiana Historical Society* (Oct. 1923). New Orleans *Daily Picayune* (16 Feb. 1896). New Orleans *Times-Democrat* (16 Feb. 1896). *Teachers' Outlook* (Feb. 1901).

BARBARA C. EWELL

Marjorie Hope Nicolson

B. 18 Feb. 1894, Yonkers, New York; d. 9 March 1981, White Plains, New York
D. of Charles Butler and Lissie Hope Morris Nicolson

The daughter of a newspaper editor, N. spent most of her adult life in an academic environment, studying at Michigan, Yale, and Johns Hopkins, and teaching at Minnesota, Goucher, Smith, Columbia, and Claremont. She was a member of the Institute for Advanced Studies at Princeton from 1963 to 1968, and now resides in White Plains, New York.

N. earned many honors during her long and distinguished career and blazed many new trails for academic women. As the first woman president of the United Chapters of Phi Beta Kappa (1940), she explained that most academic women had not been able to distinguish themselves because it was hard to be "both scholars and ladies," in that women scholars "have no wives to look after social contacts and to perform the drudgery for them." She was the first woman to be elected president of the Modern Language Association, the first woman to receive Yale's John Addison Porter Prize for original work, and the first woman to hold a full professorship on Columbia University's graduate faculty.

N. was fascinated with the impact on the literary imagination made by science and philosophy, especially in the 17th and 18th centuries. As early as 1935, N.'s lifelong interest surfaced in a study of *The Microscope and English Imagination*, in which she describes how the invention of the microscope had stimulated both serious and satiric themes in literature, even influencing the remarkable technique of Swift's *Gulliver's Travels*.

Several of her best volumes focus on the way scientific advances alter aesthetic judgments and hence modify literary treatments. For instance, *A World in the Moon* (1937) describes the changing attitudes toward the moon brought about by the telescope; *Mountain Gloom and*

Mountain Glory (1959) describes humanity's shift from abhorrence of mountains as reflecting sin's disruption to attraction to mountains as symbols of the infinite; and *Breaking of the Circle* (1950) describes the dislocating insecurity caused by the Copernican Revolution as reflected in the works of John Donne and his contemporaries. Although this latter was her most influential book, it also caused considerable scholarly controversy because many argued that N. had overestimated the importance of scientific theory to people who were accustomed to finding their security not in science but in religion. *Newton Demands the Muse* (1946), a study of how Newtonian optics affected 18th-c. poets, merited the Rose Mary Crawshay Prize of the British Academy.

It is not surprising that a woman so interested in science and literature should turn her attention to John Milton, who was similarly attracted to the advanced scientific thought of his day. Accordingly, Nicolson edited a volume of Milton's major poems and published *A Reader's Guide to Milton* (1963), which has proved popular on many campuses.

This Long Disease, My Life: Alexander Pope and the Sciences (1968), written with G. S. Rousseau, after N.'s retirement, includes a detailed medical history of the poet, a study of five medical themes or episodes in his work, an extensive section on Pope and astronomy, and a concluding section on Pope's interest in the other sciences of his day, especially geology.

In addition to her books, N. was a frequent contributor to periodicals. She edited *American Scholar* from 1940 to 1944 and served on the editorial board of the *Journal of the History of Ideas* for many years. Her work is never academic in the "dry-as-dust" sense; it pulsates with the fascination, wry wit, and human involvement she feels toward her subject. It is N.'s flair for making her point memorably that ensures her a continuing influence among lovers of literature.

WORKS: The Art of Deception (1926). *Conway Letters* (1930). *The Microscope and English Imagination* (1935). *A World in the Moon* (1937). *Newton Demands the Muse* (1946). *Voyages to the Moon* (1948). *Breaking of the Circle* (1950; rev. ed., 1960). *Science and Imagination* (1956). *Mountain Gloom and Mountain Glory* (1959). *Milton: Major Poems* (edited by Nicolson, 1962). *A Reader's Guide to Milton* (1963). *Pepys' Diary and the New Science* (1965). *This Long Disease, My Life: Alexander Pope and the Sciences* (with G. S. Rousseau, 1968).

BIBLIOGRAPHY: CA (1964). CB (1940).

VIRGINIA RAMEY MOLLENKOTT

Josephina Niggli

B. 13 July 1910, Monterrey, Mexico
D. of Frederick Ferdinand and Goldie Morgan Niggli

N.'s father, of Swiss and Alsatian ancestry, left Texas in 1893 to manage a cement plant in the village of Hidalgo, Mexico; her mother was a concert violinist from Virginia. In 1913 and in 1925, when revolutions broke out in Mexico, the family fled to San Antonio, Texas, where N. had her only formal schooling. She graduated from Main Avenue High School in 1925 and from Incarnate Word College in 1931.

N. studied playwriting at the University of North Carolina, a center for the development of regional and folk drama. She wrote a three-act play, *Singing Valley*, for her thesis, and received her M.A. degree in drama in 1937. N.'s work with Professor Frederick H. Koch's Carolina Playmakers was a major influence on her writing. Koch himself edited an anthology of her work, *Mexican Folk Plays*, in 1938. Since then, N. has lived in North Carolina, except for sojourns with Bristol University and the Bristol Old Vic in England and with the Abbey Theatre in Dublin. N. has taught English and radio scriptwriting at the University of North Carolina, and she established a drama department at Western Carolina University in Cullowhee.

N.'s one-act plays of Mexican folk life have long been favorites of discerning high-school drama groups. These plays enliven a small cast and simple scenic requirements with abundant stage action, sound effects, and opportunities for characterization. N.'s special skill is her ability to blend closely observed local color and customs with universally understood emotions and humor. Although written in the 1930s, her plays have not become dated.

In *This Bull Ate Nutmeg* (1937), N. drew upon her childhood memories of a one-man sideshow attraction and of mock bullfights. The play includes folk music, a romantic rivalry, and a climactic backyard bullfight, underscored by the cheers and laughter of village spectators.

This is Villa! (1939) is a portrait of the murderous Pancho Villa. N. created an incident that reveals his sentimental and childlike side as well as his cruelty. Despite momentary lapses into swashbuckling melodrama, the play, like all N.'s dramatic and narrative fiction, has a convincing documentary quality.

N.'s most frequently performed play is *Sunday Costs Five Pesos* (1939). In her book *New Pointers on Playwriting* (1945), N. commented: "My *Sunday Costs Five Pesos* has made me more money than a best-selling novel, primarily because it is presented again and again in contests."

N.'s first narrative fiction work, *Mexican Village* (1945), a collection of ten stories of daily life in the village of Hidalgo, using recurrent characters, was uniformly praised by critics. *Step Down, Elder Brother* (1947) is set among the aristocracy in Monterrey. N. again studied the impact of social and historical change in Mexico in *Farewell, Mama Carlotta* (1950) and *Miracle for Mexico* (1964). If her writing is occasionally criticized as "excessively romantic," that is also its strength, for it ensnares the reader with the devices of good storytelling and vividly conveys N.'s warm affection for the people of northern Mexico.

WORKS: *Mexican Silhouettes* (1931). *Tooth or Shave* (1936). *Singing Valley* (1937). *This Bull Ate Nutmeg* (1937). *Mexican Folk Plays* (1938). *Sunday Costs Five Pesos* (1939). *This is Villa!* (1939). *Miracle at Blaise* (1944). *Mexican Village* (1945). *New Pointers on Playwriting* (1945). *Pointers on Radio Writing* (1946). *Step Down, Elder Brother* (1947). *Farewell, Mama Carlotta* (1950). *Miracle for Mexico* (1964).

BIBLIOGRAPHY: Spearman, W., *The Carolina Playmakers: The First Fifty Years* (1970).

For articles in reference works, see: *American Novelists of Today*, H. R. Warfel (1951). *CB* (1949). *National Playwrights Directory*, Ed. P. J. Kaye (1977).

Other references: *NYT* (21 Jan. 1939).

FELICIA HARDISON LONDRÉ

Anaïs Nin

B. 21 Feb. 1903, Paris, France; d. 14 Jan. 1977, Los Angeles, California
D. of Joaquin and Rosa Culmell Nin; m. Hugh P. Guiler, 1923

N. was the eldest of three children of a Spanish composer and concert pianist and a French-Danish mother. N. began keeping a diary after her father's desertion. N.'s departure with her mother and brothers for New York, her return to Paris, and her home in Louveciennes in the outskirts of Paris were all delineated. Purposely omitted was her marriage to Guiler, a bank and financial consultant who was also known as the engraver and filmmaker Ian Hugo.

D. H. Lawrence: An Unprofessional Study (1932) marked N.'s entrée into "creative criticism." N. was an enemy of naturalism, realism, positivism, and rationalism, which she felt distorted reality; what was of import for her was the catalytic effect of Lawrence's work on the reader's senses and imagination. To know Lawrence, she maintained, was to take a fantastic voyage: to "flow" forward with his characters and situations, to follow their feelings as manifested in impulses and gestures.

N.'s feelings of timidity and inadequacy became so disruptive that in 1932 she consulted the psychiatrist René Allendy, who encouraged her to begin *The House of Incest* (1936). "It is the seed of all my work," N. wrote, "the poem from which the novels were born." Affinities with Lawrence, Joyce, Woolf, and the surrealists were evident in her reliance upon dream sequences and in her use of stream-of-consciousness style.

Dr. Otto Rank's attitude to the problem of creativity was more to N.'s liking, and she became his patient in 1933. When he moved his offices to New York in 1934, he invited N. to practice as a lay analyst. Although successful, N. understood that her mission in life was artistic and not therapeutic. She returned to France, where she lived until the outbreak of World War II. Her friends included Miller, Artaud, Brancusi, Supervielle, Orloff, Durrell, Breton, Dali, Barnes, Young, Varèse, Varda, and many more.

In New York, artistic and financial setbacks encouraged N. to print her own works: *Winter of Artifice* (1939) and *Under a Glass Bell* (1947). To probe her heroine's dream world in *Winter of Artifice*, N. chose the anti-novel technique, with its pastiches, repetitions, omissions, and ellipses, instead of the structured characters and plot of the psychological novel.

Cities of the Interior (1959), a "continuous novel," includes six short works: *Ladders to Fire* (1946), *Children of the Albatross* (1947), *The Four-Chambered Heart* (1950), *A Spy in the House of Love* (1954), *Solar Barque* (1958), and *Seduction of the Minotaur* (1961). Labeled "space fiction," *Cities of the Interior* is centered in the unconscious, upon clusters of visual configurations. In this inner space, characters confront, respond, act, and react to each other like multiple satellites. N.'s deepening psychological acumen and intuitive faculties, her heightened powers of observation are brought into play in the recording of minute vibrations in nuanced and counterpuntal relationships.

The Diary of Anaïs Nin (7 vols., 1966–78) is a "woman's journey of self-discovery," which Henry Miller placed "beside the revelations of St. Augustine, Petronius, Abélard, Rousseau, Proust." The *Diary* is a historical document in that it reports and deals with events chronologically. It is of psychological import because it analyzes inner scapes (dreams, reveries, motivations) and a variety of approaches to the unconscious; it is of aesthetic significance because it introduces readers to the world of the novelist, poet, musician, painter, and the artistic trends of the day: cubism, realism, surrealism, op, pop, and minimal art.

It was with her *Diary* that N. won an international reputation. She was called upon to lecture throughout North America at universities, poetry centers, and clubs. N. synthesized and elaborated her earlier statements of her artistic credo—*Realism and Reality* (1946)—in *The Novel of the Future* (1968), in which she endorses the dictum of C. G. Jung: "Proceed from the Dream Outward."

N.'s writings express an inner need; truth shaped and fashioned into an art form. Thought, feeling, and dream are captured in metaphors, images, and alliterations, which are interwoven in complex designs. The techniques of free association and reverie enable her to penetrate the inner being, evoke a mood, and arouse sensations in an impressionistic and pointilliste manner. N.'s work offers readers perpetual transmutations of matter and spirit. Hers is a very personal, authentic, and innovative talent, unique in her time.

WORKS: *D. H. Lawrence: An Unprofessional Study* (1932). *The House of Incest* (1936). *Winter of Artifice* (1939). *Under a Glass Bell* (1944). *Ladders to Fire* (1946). *Realism and Reality* (1946). *Children of the Albatross* (1947). *On Writing* (1947). *The Four-Chambered Heart* (1950). *A Spy in the House of Love* (1954). *Solar Barque* (1958). *Cities of the Interior* (1959). *Seduction of the Minotaur* (1961). *Collages* (1964). *The Diary of Anaïs Nin* (7 vols., 1966–78). *The Novel of the Future* (1968). *A Woman Speaks: The Lectures, Seminars, and Interviews of Anaïs Nin* (1975). *In Favor of the Sensitive Man, and Other Essays* (1976). *Delta of Venus: Erotica* (1977). *Waste of Timelessness, and Other Early Stories* (1977). *Linotte: 1914–1920* (1978). *The Early Diary of Anaïs Nin: 1920–1923* (1982).

BIBLIOGRAPHY: Evans, O., *Anaïs Nin* (1968). Franklin, V. B., and D. Schneider, *Anaïs Nin: An Introduction* (1979). Harms, V., ed., *Celebration with Anaïs Nin* (1973). Hinz, J. E., *The Mirror and the Garden* (1971). Hinz, J. E., *The World of Anaïs Nin* (1978). Knapp, B. L., *Anaïs Nin* (1979). Spencer, S., *Collage of Dreams* (1977).

BETTINA L. KNAPP

Kathleen Thompson Norris

B. 16 July 1880, San Francisco, California; d. 18 Jan. 1966, San Francisco, California
Wrote under: Jane Ireland, Kathleen Norris
D. of James Alden and Josephine E. Moroney Thompson; m. Charles Gilman Norris, 1909

The second of six children, N. grew up in rural Mill Valley, where her father, a San Francisco bank manager, commuted daily by ferry. In 1899, both parents died within a month, leaving the children to shift for themselves. N. worked as clerk, bookkeeper, librarian, and newspaper reporter to help support the family. While covering a skating party, she met her future husband, a writer. She followed him to New York City when he became arts editor for the *American* magazine.

N. published fiction in the New York *Telegram*, winning fifty dollars for the best story of the week. Her husband encouraged N. to send out others, and the *Atlantic* accepted "The Tide-Marsh" and "What Happened to Alanna" in 1910. N. began *Mother* (1911) for another story contest, but it grew too long; it was enlarged to become a popular novel.

For the next half century, despite crippling arthritis, N. wrote ninety books, numerous stories and magazine serials, a newspaper column, and a radio soap opera. A pacifist, she campaigned vigorously against capital punishment and foreign involvement.

Much of N.'s writing is rooted in her own life and California background. Typical is *Little Ships* (1921), centering on a large nouveau-riche Irish-Catholic family and its less fortunate relatives, including a fine old peasant grandmother. Although the book is marred by sentimentality and prejudice, N. creates deft characterization and effective dramatic tension in her family scenes.

Certain People of Importance (1922) is considered N.'s most ambitious work. In this impressive family chronicle spanning more than a century, descendants of Forty-niner Reuben Crabtree invent a "first family" history not in the least based on fact. Scandals and intrigues worthy of any soap opera are plentiful, yet no one lifts an eyebrow. Although N. denies a "knowledge of those dark forces which fascinate modern writers," the novel's true subject seems to be human greed, hypocrisy, and deceit.

One of the book's strengths is its precise attention to forgotten detail —fashions, furnishings, eating habits, and amusements. N. writes sympathetically of independent young women who chafe under the restrictions of parents or brother. She also offers a grim reminder of the risks of pregnancy, childbirth, and poverty. This, N.'s most realistic book, was not well received.

Through a Glass Darkly (1957) is noteworthy only because its first half depicts a Utopia where war does not exist, the government feeds anyone who needs it, and people take care of each other. Those who die on earth "arrive" in Foxcrossing to live happily. But the protagonist, who longs to "go back" to our world to help suffering children, loses her life trying to rescue hurricane victims and is reincarnated in the book's second half. The story moves disappointingly into N.'s familiar formula of a working girl's struggle to survive. The Utopian world is forgotten.

N. also published two sometimes conflicting autobiographies, *Noon* (1925) and *Family Gathering* (1959). Many of her books remain in print, but most of these are frothy romances with pink-and-gold heroines and contrived endings. These characters seem suspended in an eternal 1910, regardless of the real year. N.'s best writing shows more depth: family warmth, sincerity, and pettiness; condemnation of the self-centered rich; and vivid accounts of early California. She portrays men and women of another generation, almost another world, meeting life however they can—with love, with humor, with desperation.

WORKS: *Mother* (1911). *The Rich Mrs. Burgoyne* (1912). *Poor, Dear Margaret Kirby* (1913). *Saturday's Child* (1914). *The Treasure* (1914). *The Story of Julia Page* (1915). *The Heart of Rachael* (1916). *Martie, the Unconquered* (1917). *Undertow* (1917). *Josselyn's Wife* (1918). *Sisters* (1919). *Harriet and the Piper* (1920). *The Beloved Woman* (1921). *Little Ships* (1921). *Certain People of Importance* (1922). *Lucretia Lombard* (1922). *Butterfly* (1923). *Uneducating Mary* (1923). *The Callahans and the Murphys* (1924). *Rose of the World* (1924). *Noon* (1925). *The Black Flemings* (also published as *Gabrielle*, 1926). *Hildegarde* (1926). *The Kelly Kid* (1926). *Barberry Bush* (1927). *The Fun of Being a Mother* (1927). *My Best Girl* (1927). *The Sea Gull* (1927). *Beauty and the Beast* (1928). *The Foolish Virgin* (1928). *Home* (1928). *What Price Peace?* (1928). *Mother and Son* (1929). *Red Silence* (1929). *Storm House* (1929). *Beauty in Letters* (1930). *The Lucky Lawrences* (1930). *Margaret Yorke* (1930). *Passion Flower* (1930). *Belle-Mère* (1931). *Hands Full of Living: Talks with American Women* (1931). *The Love of Julie Borel* (1931). *My San Francisco* (1932). *Second-Hand Wife* (1932). *Treehaven* (1932). *Younger Sister* (1932). *The Angel in the House* (1933). *My California* (1933). *Walls of Gold* (1933). *Wife for Sale* (1933). *Maiden Voyage* (1934). *Manhattan Love Song* (1934). *Three Men and Diana* (1934). *Victoria: A Play* (1934). *Beauty's Daughter* (1935). *Shining Windows* (1935). *Woman in Love* (1935). *The American Flaggs* (1936). *Secret Marriage* (1936). *Bread into Roses* (1937). *You Can't Have Everything* (1937). *Baker's Dozen* (1938). *Heartbroken Melody* (1938). *Lost Sunrise* (1939). *Mystery House* (1939). *The Runaway* (1939). *The Secret of the Marshbanks* (1940). *The World Is like That* (1940). *These I Like Best* (1941). *The Venables* (1941). *An Apple for Eve* (1942). *Come Back to Me, Beloved* (1942). *Dina Cashman* (1942). *One Nation Indivisible* (1942). *Star-Spangled Christmas* (1942). *Corner of Heaven* (1943). *Love Calls the Tune* (1944). *Burned Fingers* (1945). *Motionless Shadows* (1945). *Mink Coat* (1946). *Over at the Crowleys'* (1946). *The Secrets of Hillyard House* (1947). *High Holiday* (1949). *Morning Light* (1950). *Shadow Marriage* (1952). *The Best of Kathleen Norris* (1955). *Miss Harriet Townshend* (1955). *Through a Glass Darkly* (1957). *Family Gathering* (1959).

BIBLIOGRAPHY: Kilmer, J., *Literature in the Making: By Some of Its Makers* (1917). Woollcott, A., *While Rome Burns* (1934).

For articles in reference works, see: *Catholic Authors: Contemporary Biographical Sketches 1930–1947*, Ed. M. Hoehn (1948). *20thCA. 20thCAS.*

Other references: *Bookman* (Sept. 1922). *NR* (11 Oct. 1922). *NYT* (19 Jan. 1966). *NYTBR* (6 Feb. 1955).

JOANNE McCARTHY

Joyce Carol Oates

B. 16 June 1938, Lockport, New York
D. of Frederick J. and Caroline Bush Oates; m. Raymond J. Smith, 1961

One of three children, O. was born into an Irish-Catholic working-class family in a rural area near Millerport, New York, the "Eden County" country of many of her stories and novels. O., who attended a one-room schoolhouse, graduated Syracuse University, phi beta kappa, in 1960 with a B.A. in English, and earned an M.A. from the University of Wisconsin in 1961.

O. taught English for six years at the University of Detroit. She was in Detroit during the race riots, an event she documents in *them* (1969). Winner of many awards, O. has been elected to the National Academy and Institute of Arts and Letters.

From 1967 to 1977, O. and her husband taught literature at the University of Windsor, Ontario. They now live in Princeton, where they publish *Ontario Review* and run the Ontario Review Press and where O. is writer-in-residence at Princeton University.

In O.'s fiction, the individual is always viewed in the perspective of the larger world. O.'s protagonists strain to escape the world in which they live, but they do not succeed, except in madness or death. As O. drives her characters into a recognition of the boundaries of the real, the ideal is collapsed into the actual, the hope for freedom is converted into a hope for initiation, and the isolated self is confronted with its otherness.

With Shuddering Fall (1964) begins with idealized, romantic characters—a godlike, paternal figure, Herz; his virginal, religious daughter, Karen; and the violent rebel, Shar. The novel relates the story of Karen's initiation, which is effected not by a complete submission to an authoritarian order represented by her father, but by a rejection of the rootless freedom represented by Shar.

A Garden of Earthly Delights (1967), *Expensive People* (1968), and *them* constitute a trilogy exploring rural, suburban, and urban America. *A Garden of Earthly Delights* focuses on the condition of alienation, a condition O. views as rooted in the circumstances of American history and intensified by the American ideals of autonomy and self-sufficiency.

As in *them* and in *Wonderland* (1971), the Depression dislodges the characters from their paternal roots. Clara, the daughter of a migrant laborer who was forced from his land, maniacally and successfully plots to marry a man for his money and land to bequeath to her son a name that wields power. Ironically, rather than accept the world his mother has usurped for him, her son is possessed by a sense of alienation so intense that he finally commits suicide.

Matricide is the solution that Richard, child-hero of *Expensive People* (1968), finds for his mother's narcissistic assertion of freedom that denies him love and recognition. O. portrays affluent suburbia as an antithetical "paradise" into which one is admitted by virtue of greed; the dominant metaphor of the novel is gluttony, which stands not only for excessive material acquisition but for an inflated sense of self that leads to a denial of the world.

Although O. has not overtly associated herself with the women's movement, *Do With Me What You Will* (1973) attests to her sympathy with its cause. Elena, the novel's heroine, who tries to avoid reality by an almost psychotic passivity, finally reenters time and history when she leaves her husband and escapes with a lover. For O., the mask of passivity is as narcissistic as the mask of megalomania: The world must be confronted, not avoided or overcome.

O.'s later fiction demonstrates her increasing interest in the novel as an aesthetic object. In these works, form *is* theme. The monistic absolutists who populate the world of *The Assassins: A Book of Hours* (1975) are revealed through their streams of consciousness. Each consciousness is isolated from the others in a separate section of the novel, just as each character is isolated from the living totality of being by virtue of a stubborn adherence to a personal version of reality. A character's refusal to accommodate to the pluralistic universe is a surrender to Thanatos, an "assassination" of reality.

In *Bellefleur* (1980), a best-selling novel, O. employs the gothic to create a haunting fictional world perched between the fantastic and the real. Indeed, O. has woven a shimmering tapestry made of odd and contradictory threads: A hermaphrodite birth, a vulture who devours an infant, a dwarf with "powers," and a vampire are harmoniously woven into a history of the powerful Bellefleur family whose significance is not only historical but sociological, psychological, and mythic.

O. is a much anthologized short-story writer. A favorite of anthologists is the haunting "Where Are You Going, Where Have You Been" from *The Wheel of Love* (1970). It concerns an encounter between

Arnold Friend, a demon-lover figure, and the adolescent Connie. The same volume contains the powerful "The Region of Ice," the film version of which won an Academy Award in 1977.

All of O.'s fiction affirms that humanity is located in a universe that it cannot avoid, transcend, or control, and from which there is no separation or redemption. She is a writer obsessed with reconciling an age convinced that the isolated self is the final authority of reality and value to experiential plurality and human reciprocity, to time, history, and the manifest world.

Although O.'s fiction has received a good deal of critical attention, much of it intelligent and probing, some critics have tended to catalogue the novels' violent events, ignoring the careful structure of the works and the moral vision that informs them.

WORKS: *By the North Gate* (1963). *With Shuddering Fall* (1964). *Upon the Sweeping Flood* (1966). *A Garden of Earthly Delights* (1967). *Expensive People* (1968). *Women in Love, and Other Poems* (1968). *them* (1969). *Anonymous Sins, and Other Poems* (1969). *The Wheel of Love, and Other Stories* (1970). *Love and Its Derangements, and Other Poems* (1970). *Wonderland* (1971). *Marriages and Infidelities* (1972). *The Edge of Impossibility: Tragic Forms in Literature* (1972). *Do With Me What You Will* (1973). *Angel Fire* (1973). *Dreaming America* (1973). *The Goddess and Other Women* (1974). *The Hungry Ghosts: Seven Allusive Comedies* (1974). *Where Are You Going, Where Have You Been?: Stories of Young America* (1974). *New Heaven, New Earth: The Visionary Experience in Literature* (1974). *The Assassins: A Book of Hours* (1975). *The Poisoned Kiss, and Other Stories* (1975). *The Seduction, and Other Stories* (1975). *The Fabulous Beasts* (1975). *Childwold* (1976). *The Triumph of the Spider Monkey: The First Person Confession of the Maniac Bobby Gotteson, as Told to Joyce Carol Oates* (1976). *Crossing the Border: Fifteen Tales* (1977). *Son of the Morning* (1978). *All the Good People I've Left Behind* (1978). *Women Whose Lives Are Food, Men Whose Lives Are Money* (1978). *Unholy Loves* (1979). *Bellefleur* (1980). *Angel Light* (1981).

BIBLIOGRAPHY: Bellamy, J. D., ed., *The New Fiction: Interviews with Innovative American Writers* (1974). Creighton, J. V., *Joyce Carol Oates* (1979). Friedman, E. G., *Joyce Carol Oates* (1980). Friedman, E. G., "The Journey from the 'I' to the 'Eye': Joyce Carol Oates' *Wonderland*," in *Studies in American Fiction* (1980). Wagner, L. W., ed., *Critical Essays on Joyce Carol Oates* (1979). Waller, G. F., *Dreaming America: Obsession and Transcendence in the Fiction of Joyce Carol Oates* (1978).

Other references: *AL* (43, 1971; 49, 1977). *Commonweal* (5 Dec. 1969). *Critique* 15 (1973). *NYTBR* (28 Sept. 1969). *Paris Review* 74 (1978). *Soundings* 58 (1975). *Spirit* 39 (1972). *Studies in the Novel* 7 (1975).

ELLEN G. FRIEDMAN

Flannery O'Connor

B. 25 March 1925, Savannah, Georgia; d. 3 Aug. 1964, Milledgeville, Georgia
Given name: Mary Flannery O'Connor
D. of Edward Flannery and Regina Cline O'Connor

O. was the only child of parents whose Georgia manners and Catholic background influenced her deeply. She began writing at an early age and after graduation from Georgia State College for Women in 1945 attended the Writers' Workshop at the University of Iowa (M.F.A. 1947). "The Geranium" was accepted by *Accent* in 1946. Publication of other stories followed, and O.'s first novel, *Wise Blood*, triggered by the stories from the Iowa thesis, appeared in 1952.

Described by O. as "a comic novel," *Wise Blood* is the story of Haze Motes, a religious fanatic in an electric blue suit who preaches that "there was no Fall because there was nothing to fall from and no Redemption because there was no Fall and no Judgment because there wasn't the first two. Nothing matters but that Jesus was a liar." In his insistence that "there's only one truth and that is that there's no truth," Motes ricochets from a pseudo-blind prophet and his libidinous daughter, to the company of the moronic Enoch Emery, the one with "wise blood," to a final resting place with a rapacious landlady who plots to marry him. In his desperate quest for meaning, Motes mutilates himself with broken glass in his shoes, blinds himself with lye, and finally dies in a squad car on the way back to the landlady's bed. His physical humiliations and self-flagellations are enacted without hope of redemption; at the end of the novel, he has become a new and distorted Christ who can offer no salvation, even to himself.

Although the book was received with mixed reviews and an uneasy feeling that the cast of characters was too grotesque even for a public used to Faulkner's southern Gothics, the critics were aware that a new talent had indeed appeared. But in 1950, O. had learned that she, like her father, had lupus. She moved back to Milledgeville to a farm where she could raise herds of peacocks and have time to write. She received a *Kenyon Review* Fellowship in 1953, and published her first book of short stories, *A Good Man Is Hard to Find*, in 1955.

The title story of this book is described by O. as "the story of a family of six which, on its way driving to Florida, gets wiped out by an escaped convict who calls himself the Misfit." The Misfit is another Haze Motes, who also equates himself with Jesus and who realizes he is damned if Jesus did what He is said to have done and doomed to an absurd life in which there is "no pleasure but meanness" if Jesus didn't.

Motes and the Misfit, as well as a myriad of O.'s protagonists, are psychic cripples with what Hawthorne called "ice in the blood." They have become consumed with an image of Christ, and hence have lost all human feelings. O. commented in a 1960 lecture that "while the South is hardly Christ-centered, it is most certainly Christ-haunted."

The character in "Good Country People" who is preoccupied with religion in order to deny it is a one-legged spinster Ph.D., O.'s most obvious caricature. The lumpish young maid entices a young Bible salesman into a loft with plans to seduce him and instead has her wooden leg stolen by him. The Bible salesman, Manley Pointer, is thus one of the conmen who appear in O.'s fiction with as much regularity as her mad prophets. In "The Life You Save May Be Your Own," the con man, who steals an old woman's car by marrying her daughter, is named Tom T. Shiftlet—or possibly Aaron Sparks or George Speeds—since the identity of these opportunists shifts with equal regularity.

This lack of a secure identity for the characters is also apparent in O.'s use of the double. In countless stories, the protagonist is not only a distorted double for Christ but also has another character who is his own double. In some cases the double can even be an animal, generally a pig, but in "The Displaced Person," the double of the displaced person/Christ figure is a peacock. This story also demonstrates O.'s most skillful use of dramatic irony, and the reader anticipates helplessly as the survivor of a Nazi concentration camp becomes an obsession to the Georgia locals and is finally crushed, literally beneath a tractor, by another collection of good country people.

In 1959, O. received a Ford Foundation grant for creative writing, and in 1960 her second novel, *The Violent Bear It Away*, appeared. The fanatics are back, and this book contains three: old Tarwater, a mad prophet; young Tarwater, his grandson with an obsession to rid himself of Jesus by baptizing his idiot second cousin, Bishop; and his atheist uncle Rayber, who is equally obsessed by preventing the baptism. The violent clashes between the Tarwaters and Rayber become a struggle for young Tarwater's soul, and Rayber loses when the boy drowns Bishop and flees. Young Tarwater tries, with the desperation of a Motes, to convince himself that all old Tarwater had told him was false. But as he flees the murder of Bishop, he is picked up, drugged, and seduced by a man in a lavender car—which the old man had warned him was possible. The book ends as Tarwater gives in to his terrible destiny of prophecy, becoming as mad as his grandfather.

The title story of *Everything That Rises Must Converge* (1965) has as its central conflict the struggle between children and their parents, most often the mother, that appears in some of O.'s best work. The best story in the collection, "Revelation," shows O.'s child-parent conflict at its finest. This story presents another of the maimed and ugly daughters, this time characterized by ferocious acne, and another of those good country people, Mrs. Turpin, so complacent about their own virtue that they become almost evil in their selfishness. In the final story, "Parker's Back," the last story O. wrote before she died, the ubiquitous reversed Christ appears as a tattoo on Parker's back.

In 1972, *The Complete Stories* appeared and received the National Book Award. This book included all the previously published stories as well as those from O.'s Iowa thesis never before published.

The Habit of Being (1979), O.'s selected letters, presents a composite portrait of a writer who constantly emphasized this necessity of seeing. When one newspaper put her in the "realistic school," O. wrote to reject that label, insisting, "I am interested in making up a good case for distortion, as I am coming to believe it is the only way to make people see." The letters, edited by her longtime friend Sally Fitzgerald, offer brilliant glimpses of O.'s personality while they provide invaluable insights into her methods and fiction.

To call O.'s stories of death and destruction comic seems a contradiction in terms, but as she says blithely in the introduction to *Wise Blood*, "all comic novels that are any good must be about matters of life and death." O. will simply not allow identification with a single character, even when that character is so blatantly O. herself. With her sharp cartoonist's eye, O. has etched the outlines of her characters in stone, and they stonily resist all empathy. O. consistently utilizes the dramatic point of view in which she presents her characters as though on a stage, and the reader is never allowed to see the innermost thoughts of the character's head—or heart.

This lack of heart thus becomes central to O.'s themes, and the single-minded self-centeredness of the characters who are concerned only with their own salvation makes those characters essentially grotesque. As O. said: "whenever I'm asked why Southern writers particularly have a penchant for writing about freaks, I say it is because we are still able to recognize one." In creating her gallery of freaks, O. has eschewed not only the heroic but the normal.

The fact that her comic characters must suffer mentally and physically gives O.'s fiction overtones of tragedy, and it is perhaps significant that O. read *Oedipus Rex* just before completing the blinding episode in *Wise Blood*. Yet in the final analysis, O.'s work is more comic than tragicomic. Her comedy is not merely that of technique, but of vision; ultimately, the fiction becomes positive despite all its horrors and doubts. There is basically a maturation in the stories, an essential growing up in which the dreadful children do learn from their equally dreadful mothers and perhaps become equipped to cope and accept a moment of grace. In the southern ability to recognize a freak, there is the implicit idea of what a whole man must be, and ultimately this Swiftian view of man as capable of reforming—once his freakishness and his grotesqueness are revealed to him—breaks through the clouds of O.'s bleak fiction to show the pale light of hope.

WORKS: Wise Blood (1952). *A Good Man Is Hard to Find* (1955). *The Violent Bear It Away* (1960). *Everything That Rises Must Converge* (1965). *Mystery and Manners* (Ed. S. and R. Fitzgerald, 1969). *The Complete Stories* (1972). *The Habit of Being* (Ed. by S. Fitzgerald, 1979).

BIBLIOGRAPHY: Drake, R., *Flannery O'Connor* (1966). Driskell, L. V., and J. Brittain, *The Eternal Crossroads* (1971). Eggenschwiter, D., *The Christian Humanism of Flannery O'Connor* (1972). Feeley, K., *Flannery O'Connor* (1972). Friedman, M. J., and L. A. Lawson, eds., *The Added Dimension* (1966). Golden, R. E., *Flannery O'Connor and Caroline Gordon: A Reference Guide* (1977). Hendin, J., *The World of Flannery O'Connor* (1970). Hyman, S. E., *Flannery O'Connor* (1966). Martin, C. W., *The True Country* (1969). May, J. R., *The Pruning Word* (1976). McFarland, D. T., *Flannery O'Connor* (1976). Muller, G. H., *Nightmares and Visions* (1972). Reiter, R. E., ed., *Flannery O'Connor* (1968). Walters, D., *Flannery O'Connor* (1973).

Other references: *Bulletin of Bibliography* (1967). *Critique* (Fall 1958). *Esprit* (Winter 1964). *Flannery O'Connor Bulletin.*

PAT CARR

Lillian O'Donnell

B. *15 March 1926, Trieste, Italy*
D. *of Zoltan D. and Maria Busutti Udvardy; m. J. Leonard O'Donnell, 1954*

O. is a New Yorker; she grew up in the city, where she attended parochial and public schools, pursued a career in the theater, married, and continues to live in the city. With a minor role in *Pal Joey*, O. became involved in Broadway productions as an actress and dancer. Later, she appeared in television productions, and then moved on to direct summer stock, becoming one of the first women managers. After her marriage, O. left the theater and decided to try writing novels.

O.'s early mystery stories reflect a gothic dimension in exotic settings, country-estate motifs, and genteel characters. *Death Schuss* (1963), for example, takes place in Canada at the height of the ski season amid the luxurious environs of an heiress's home. This unlucky young lady becomes the victim in this murder puzzle which is fraught with romantic entanglements and glamour. These early works are too filled with cliches to be unique.

The turning point in O.'s literary career occurred when she cast off the trappings of the mystery cum gothic style and moved into the real world of the police thriller to create Norah Mulcahaney of the New York City Police Department as her serial heroine. Norah Mulcahaney is a credible character. O. gives her heroine ethnic roots and a strong moral fiber. Norah is also appropriately attractive: tall and slim, with long dark tresses. Norah makes her first appearance in *The Phone Calls* (1972); she is just learning the ropes in the department when she is assigned to the case of a psychopathic killer who preys on women. In *Don't Wear Your Wedding Ring* (1973), Detective Mulcahaney becomes more self-assured; this time she is in pursuit of a female prostitution ring. "The chase" as well as the nature of the crime lives up to the tradition of the thriller as Norah eludes a murderous gang. Her relationship with Sgt. Joe Capretto develops in this case; the reader perceives a match is in the making. (Ultimately Norah marries Joe, but she neither retires nor loses her individuality; they do not become a "crime team.")

The crimes which O. chooses for her heroine are usually crimes against women, such as rape (*Dial 577 R-A-P-E*, 1974). Norah Mulcahaney meets all challenges with conviction—she is a feminist who is concerned with the plight of other women (other policewomen in *No Business Being a Cop*, 1978).

O. learned about the inner workings of the police world through observation and careful research. Amid growing concern for the victims of crime, O. chose another dimension to investigate and a different kind of heroine. Mici Anhalt, an investigator for the New York City Victim/Witness Project, makes her debut in *Aftershock* (1977). A combination social worker and detective, she often experiences personal danger. She too is attractive; though a liberated thirtyish female, she has the youthfulness and enthusiasm of a teenager.

In both *Aftershock* and *Falling Star* (1979), Mici does her sleuthing by assignment and under less than optimum conditions. She experiences on-the-job harassment and departmental jealousies, not to mention the perils of attack from malevolent assailants. But, like Norah Mulcahaney, she endures, proving that a resilient female can make her own way in a tough world.

O.'s novels have achieved success not because her characters are profound or unusual, or because her plots are mind-boggling or aesthetically interesting. Hard-core realism, neither sweetened by gingery femininity nor leavened by blood or brutality, is O.'s metier. Her unadorned literary style is honest and appropriate to the street crimes she depicts.

WORKS: *Death on the Grass* (1959). *Death Blanks the Screen* (1960). *Death Schuss* (1963). *Murder Under the Sun* (1964). *Death of a Player* (1964). *The Babes in the Woods* (1965). *The Sleeping Beauty Murders* (1967). *The Tachi Tree* (1968). *The Face of the Crime* (1968). *Dive into Darkness* (1971). *The Phone Calls* (1972). *Don't Wear Your Wedding Ring* (1973). *Dial 577 R-A-P-E* (1974). *The Baby Merchants* (1975). *Leisure Dying* (1976). *Aftershock* (1977). *No Business Being a Cop* (1978). *Falling Star* (1979). *Wicked Designs* (1980).

BIBLIOGRAPHY: Booklist (15 July 1977). *KR* (1 July 1979). *LJ* (Aug 1973). *Ms.* (Oct. 1974). *NYTBR* (8 Aug. 1976). *SatR* (29 Jan. 1972).

PATRICIA D. MAIDA

Cora Miranda Baggerly Older

B. 1875, Clyde, New York; d. 26 Sept. 1968, Los Gatos, California
Wrote under: Mrs. Fremont Older
D. of Peter and Margaret Baggerly; m. Fremont Older, 1893

O. was a Syracuse University student on vacation when she met and married her journalist husband, who was soon fighting both corporations and labor as editor of the San Francisco *Bulletin* and later of the *Call.* In her early married years, O. wrote reviews, society news, and celebrity interviews for her husband's paper. Her first novels were fictionalized versions of muckraking journalism. When the family moved to a ranch in the Santa Clara foothills in 1915, O. took charge of managing the property and its staff of paroled convicts.

O. wrote in three distinct genres. O.'s early novels were social melodramas that reflected current events. In *The Socialist and the Prince* (1903), Paul Stryne whips up resentment of cheap Chinese labor into a string of workingmen's clubs, a paramilitary organization, and an enormous political influence, but ultimately loses all for a beautiful, self-willed society girl who flirts with socialism. *The Giants* (1905) plays off the free children of the West against the railroad-monopoly capital of the East. *Esther Damon* (1911) is mildly utopian. The hero, a Civil War veteran reduced to alcoholism through wartime pain and postwar bitterness, reforms and begins a cooperative community. His protegée wins her way back to a place in society after she has been ruined by her parents' excessive Methodism and has had an illegitimate child.

During this period, O. also wrote magazine articles on social questions, including a long account of the San Francisco graft prosecutions for *McClure's.* Her novels were, for the most part, condemned as too sensational, stark, and evident of purpose. Turning away from fiction, O. wrote plays (none of which have been published), and in the 1930s "authorized" and highly laudatory biographies of William Randolph Hearst (who was her husband's employer) and his father George.

O.'s last works took up the matter of California in a more sophisticated fashion. *Savages and Saints* (1936), a novel, two collections of short stories, and a book about San Francisco combine carefully researched history with fictionalized versions of the lives and legends of Hispanic and Anglo pioneers.

O.'s style was not far removed from that of the dime novel. She wrote a spare, journalistic prose, with short simple sentences and abrupt paragraphs; she aroused emotion with predictable confrontations, duels, and love scenes played out on cliffs beside the sea during a thunderstorm. Yet although she shared the western naturalist's admiration for the successful—even brutal—man, she also wrote about women who took action instead of simply being acted upon. Flirtatious, dependent, clinging women are assigned to the villainous role; happy women generally earn a place of their own before marrying. Many of the stories in *California Missions and their Romances* (1938) and *Love Stories of Old California* (1940) tell of women who endured enormous hardship to keep the flames of religion and civilization alive in an unwelcoming land.

WORKS: The Socialist and the Prince (1903). *The Giants* (1905). *Esther Damon* (1911). *George Hearst, California Pioneer* (with F. Older, 1933). *Savages and Saints* (1936). *William Randolph Hearst, American* (1936). *California Missions and their Romances* (1938). *Love Stories of Old California* (1940). *San Francisco: Magic City* (1961).

The diary of Cora Miranda Baggerly Older is in the Bancroft Library, Berkeley, California.

BIBLIOGRAPHY: Older, F., *My Own Story* (1926).

Other references: *Bancroftiana* 59 (1974). *NYT* (29 Sept. 1965). *Time* (27 April 1936).

SALLY MITCHELL

Rose Cecil O'Neill

B. 25 June 1874, Wilkes-Barre, Pennsylvania; d. 6 April 1944, Springfield,
Missouri
Wrote under: Rose O'Neill, Rose Cecil O'Neill, Mrs. H. L. Wilson
D. of William Patrick and Alice Asenath Cecelia Smith O'Neill;
m. Gray Latham, 1896; m. Harry Leon Wilson, 1902

O. was educated in parochial schools in Omaha, Nebraska. Her professional career began at thirteen, when she won a children's drawing contest sponsored by the Omaha World-Herald, which then engaged her to do a weekly cartoon series. O. later moved to New York City, where her work found a ready market. At nineteen, she was a nationally known illustrator and later was also a regular contributor of stories and poems to women's magazines. In 1896, she married Gray Latham, whom she divorced in 1901. The next year she married Wilson, the novelist and playwright; that marriage ended in 1907.

O. is best remembered for the Kewpies, sentimentalized "little cupids" whose illustrated adventures in verse appeared first in the 1909 Christmas issue of the Ladies' Home Journal and later in other magazines and in several books. In 1913, O. patented the design, and Kewpie dolls and other Kewpie-decorated articles earned a fortune in royalties.

The first of four novels, The Loves of Edwy (1904), shows O.'s characteristic charm, humor, and tenderness; it reveals much about her own childhood and youth in a large, needy family. The Lady in the White Veil (1909) is a farcical mystery story in which a stolen Titian portrait is repeatedly recovered and lost anew. In spite of prodigious energy and O.'s unremitting mirth, it soon becomes tedious. Garda (1929) presents a fantasy world both beautiful and bizarre. Garda and her twin brother, Narcissus, symbolize a single mystical being represented as body and soul, the one joyously sensual, the other sensitive and suffering. They are in conflict over and ultimately reconciled by a common passion. The Goblin Woman (1930) is unsuccessful in attempting to combine a theme of sin and redemption with a milieu of contemporary sophistication.

The Master-Mistress (1922) is a collection of poems, varying in quality from excellent to trivial, on many moods and aspects of natural and supernatural love. Like all O.'s works, it is illustrated by the author.

In spite of substantial critical appreciation, none of the works for adults had a second edition. Their conspicuous merits were overwhelmed by excesses of whimsy and sentimentality. O.'s Irish forebears were given both credit and blame for qualities in her writing described as "Celtic." A modern reader will find much wit, originality, and beauty of language and atmosphere in O.'s works.

WORKS: *The Loves of Edwy* (1904). *The Lady in the White Veil* (1909). *The Kewpies and Dotty Darling* (1912). *The Kewpies: Their Book: Verse and Pictures* (1913). *Kewpie Kutouts* (1914). *The Master-Mistress* (1922). *The Kewpies and the Runaway Baby* (1928). *Garda* (1929). *The Goblin Woman* (1930).

BIBLIOGRAPHY: Brooks, V. W., *Days of the Phoenix* (1957). Kummer, G., *Harry Leon Wilson* (1963). McCanse, R. A., *Titans and Kewpies: The Life and Art of Rose O'Neill* (1968). Wood, C., *Poets of America* (1925).

Other references: *Independent* (15 Sept. 1904). *International Studio* (March 1922). *NY* (24 Nov. 1934).

EVELYN S. CUTLER

Sarah Osborn

B. 22 Feb. 1714, London, England; d. 2 Aug. 1796, Newport, Rhode Island
Wrote under: Sarah Osborn
D. of Benjamin and Susanna Haggar; m. Samuel Wheaton, 1731;
  m. Henry Osborn, 1742

O. emigrated to America with her family in 1722. They first settled in Boston, Massachusetts, and later moved to Newport, Rhode Island, where O. spent the remainder of her life. In Newport, O. met and married a seaman, who was lost at sea in November 1733. O. cared for their child alone, sometimes through great hardships, until she remarried.

O. was admitted to the Congregationalist church in Newport in 1737, an event of great significance to a Puritan in the early part of the 18th c. O.'s spiritual autobiography, *The Nature, Certainty, and Evidence of True Christianity* (1755), was evidently written in retrospect over a ten-year period from 1743 to 1753. It was originally couched in terms of a letter from one friend to another "in great Concern of Soul." This fifteen-page work reappeared in later editions and reprints in 1793, and apparently was expanded by or with the help of her minister, Samuel Hopkins, as *Memoirs of the Life of Mrs. Sarah Osborn* (1799). The *Life* was meant as an example of piety for a younger generation.

O.'s work is characterized by foreshadowings of the sentimental, moralistic fiction of the late 18th and early 19th centuries. The work is replete with tear-stained emotion and signs of O.'s sensibility. O.'s moments of doubt are linked to hysterics and excessive agitation. She relates that she could neither eat nor sleep for a week after Satan had suggested to her that the state of her soul was hopeless. Typically, O. weeps when asking her minister for church admittance, a change from the austere intellectualizing of earlier spiritual autobiographies by New England women.

O.'s writing evidences a notable stylistic as well as contextual change from earlier spiritual autobiographies. In her conscious attempt to tell a life story, O. increases the cast of characters to include not only the self, the savior, and the devil, but also. family, friends, ministers, and various incidental personages. She includes a variety of incidents and events to carry the story forward. Thus, while the narrative still focuses on her saving experience, it is broadened to contain plot, action, and dialogue. There is even an echo of the English novel of sentiment.

O. shows an ambitious desire to create a lengthy, complex story. As such, her memoirs have importance. Although the content often appears unexceptional or repetitive to the modern reader, it stands out as an early attempt by a woman writer to use available, socially acceptable materials to fabricate a readable and entertaining story.

WORKS: *The Nature, Certainty, and Evidence of True Christianity* (1755). *Memoirs of the Life of Mrs. Sarah Osborn* (Ed. S. Hopkins, 1799).

JACQUELINE HORNSTEIN

Frances Sargent Locke Osgood

B. 18 June 1811, Boston, Massachusetts; d. 12 May 1850, New York City
Wrote under: Ellen, Florence, Kate Carol, Frances Sargent Osgood
D. of Joseph and Mary Ingersoll Foster Locke; m. Samuel Stillman Osgood,
1835

O. was the daughter of a Boston merchant. She was educated primarily at home. O.'s parents encouraged her to write, and she also benefited especially from the influence of a half-sister, Anna Maria Foster Wells, and an older brother, Andrew Aitchison Locke, both of whom became writers. O. began publishing verse at the age of fourteen in the first American children's monthly, *Juvenile Miscellany*.

O. lived in England (1835–40) with her husband, an artist; her success there in turn commended her to readers at home. She was estranged from her husband in 1844, but they were reconciled, even though there was much gossip about her literary "romance" with Edgar Allan Poe.

The major subject of O.'s poetry and prose sketches is the relationship between men and women. Love—passionate, spiritual, seductive, secret, instant, eternal, consummated, holy, pious, true, false, forbidden, self-denying, transforming, transcendent, destructive—receives such a variety of expression that it cloys the appetite.

Although O. is adept in the traditional forms—songs, sonnets, ballads, rhymed narratives, and dramatic blank verse—her meters often lack the force or tension of the inevitable line; her rhymes are conventional, so that blank verse is her best measure. She frequently runs symbol and abstraction together. The poems are customarily straightforward; emotions are often stated directly.

More interesting are her verses about children. Several of the poems describe O.'s own daughters: one of them sleeping with "beautiful abandonment" on a downy carpet; Fanny smiling for the first time; May trying to lift the sun's rays, or inquisitively playing with a watch. The best of these poems is "A Sketch," which describes two little, careless girls—their straw bonnets flung among the leaves—as, silent with delight, they make garlands for one another, and think of nothing but their own sweet play.

It is also in poems about children and their fate that O. reveals a view of life she rarely allowed herself to express. In "The Daughter of

Herodias," O. imagines Salomé, a light and blooming child, without trouble or care, suddenly bewildered and terror-struck as her revengeful mother snares her in an unspeakable woe. The change in Salomé's character is dramatically realized: "Now, reckless, in her grief she goes / A woman stern and wild." Chilled with fear, the once thoughtless girl curses her fatal grace.

During a period of literary nationalism, as well as an age of sentiment, O. was the most popular and most admired of American women poets. There is little of excruciating or evil design in O.'s work; she wished "to live in blessed illusion." As a writer, she idealizes almost every image and sentiment that engages her attention. But O. deserves the appreciation she enjoyed for her verses about children.

WORKS: *Philosophical Enigmas* (183?). *A Wreath of Wild Flowers from New England* (1838, reissued as *Poems*, 1846). *The Casket of Fate* (1839). *Flower Gift* (1840, reissued as *The Poetry of Flowers and the Flowers of Poetry*, 1841, reissued again as *The Floral Offering*, 1847). *The Rose: Sketches in Verse* (1842). *The Snow-drop* (1842?). *Puss in Boots, and the Marquis of Carabas* (1844). *The Flower Alphabet in Gold and Colors* (1845). *The Cries of New York* (1846). *A Letter About Lions* (1849). *Poems* (1849, reissued as *Osgood's Poetical Works*, 1880).

BIBLIOGRAPHY: Hewitt, M. E., ed., *The Memorial: Written by Friends of the Late Mrs. Osgood* (1851). Griswold, R. W., ed., *The Literati* by E. A. Poe (1850). Mabbott, T. O., *Collected Works of Edgar Allan Poe, Poems I* (1969). Moss, S. P., *Poe's Literary Battles* (1963). Quinn, A. H., *Edgar Allan Poe: A Critical Biography* (1941).

For articles in reference works, see: *American Female Poets*, C. May (1848). *FPA. NAW* (article by J. G. Varnet). *The Poets and Poetry of America*, Ed. R. W. Griswold (1847).

Other references: *Godey's* (March 1846; Sept. 1846). *Graham's* (Jan. 1843). *Southern Literary Messenger* (Aug. 1849).

ELIZABETH PHILLIPS

Sarah Margaret Fuller Ossoli

B. 23 May 1810, Cambridgeport, Massachusetts; d. 19 July 1850, off Fire Island, New York
Wrote under: Margaret Fuller, S. M. Fuller, S. Margaret Fuller, J.
D. of Timothy and Margaret Crane Fuller; m. Giovanni Angelo, Marchese d'Ossoli, 1850

O.'s father was a lawyer and politician; her mother bore nine children, seven of whom survived infancy. Having hoped for a son, Fuller gave his oldest child a masculine education. Pushed by her father's ambitions and by her own growing sense that she could achieve greatness, O. read Horace, Ovid, and Virgil in the original at seven and continued reading widely in her father's library until she first attended school at fourteen. Two unhappy years at school in Groton, Massachusetts, made clear the social problems caused by what she herself considered her lack of a normal childhood. Back in Cambridge, she studied French, German, Italian, Greek, and philosophy, and made friends with future Transcendentalists Frederick Henry Hedge and James Freeman Clarke. In 1833, O.'s father retired from public life and moved his family to a farm at Groton, forty miles from Boston. For two years, O. took care of the house and of her younger brothers and sisters while teaching four of the children five to eight hours a day. She also continued her ambitious "self-culture," reading widely in history, literature, philosophy, and religion.

When O.'s father died in 1835, she became breadwinner and head of the family. She taught at Bronson Alcott's school in Boston (1836–37) and the Greene Street School in Providence, Rhode Island (1837–39). In 1839, she moved her family to Jamaica Plain and began her "Conversations" in Boston and Cambridge, which continued until 1844. From July 1840 until July 1842, at the urging of Emerson and other Transcendentalist friends, she edited the *Dial*.

In 1843, O. accompanied James and Sarah Clarke on a trip to Illinois and Michigan. In December 1844, she went to New York City as a correspondent for Horace Greeley's *Daily-Tribune*. In part because of an unfortunate romantic involvement with James Nathan, O. sailed in

August 1846 for Europe and subsequently traveled in England, Scotland, and France, still acting as a *Tribune* correspondent. In Rome, in 1847, she met her future husband, the Marchese d'Ossoli. Her son Angelo was born in September 1848. Ossoli supported the Roman Republic, and the family stayed in Rome throughout the French siege. O. directed a hospital and cared for the wounded. After the Republic fell, the family went to Florence and then sailed for America. All three were drowned when their ship broke up in a storm off Fire Island.

O. began writing with translations of Eckermann's *Conversations with Goethe* (1839) and the *Correspondence of Fräulein Günderode and Bettina von Arnim* (1842); some unhappy attempts at fiction; and rhapsodic, sentimental verse of little merit. Her first successful and original work, *Summer on the Lakes* (1844), used the frame of her western visit with the Clarkes for a mixture of realistic reporting, autobiography, historical and philosophical musings, and literary criticism. The result resembles Thoreau's later *A Week on the Concord and Merrimack Rivers* (1849).

Using a journal she had kept on the trip, O. provides fresh and perceptive comments on places and people from Chicago and the prairie settlements of Illinois to Milwaukee and Mackinaw. Whatever is rhapsodic or overly Romantic in her approach to the West usually succumbs before her own observations and her commonsense good will. O. admires the spirit of the new land, even as she recognizes the cruelty with which the native American has been forced from his country.

Papers on Literature and Art (1846) collected O.'s critical pieces, but the only other book she wrote was *Woman in the Nineteenth Century* (1845), a revision and amplification of her July 1843 *Dial* article, "The Great Lawsuit—Man *versus* Men; Woman *versus* Women." O.'s Transcendental tract endorses above all the idea that the powers of each individual should be developed through his or her apprehension of an ideal. Her insistence on the godlike possibilities of *all* humans differs little from the same radical idealism in the writings of Emerson and Thoreau, but O. emphasizes that the fullest possible development of man will not come without the fullest possible development of woman.

O. says that women must not wait for help from men, continuing their old, bad habits of dependence, but must help themselves; self-reliance and independence are the best ways of aiding themselves and their sisters. The capacity for economic independence is prerequisite to moral and mental freedom, and the freedom to choose celibacy over a degrading or unequal and merely convenient marriage is essential. Late in her book she makes her famous statement that women should be able to do anything for which their individual powers and talents fit them —"let them be sea-captains if they will."

The myths that have grown up around O.'s brief life and her relatively small oeuvre make her contributions difficult to assess. Some contemporary and many later critics have maintained that the genius she displayed in conversation, whether natural or guided, never became fully evident in her writings: "Ultimately she should be remembered for what she was rather than what she did" (Blanchard). The *Dial* has always been seen as central to the 'Transcendentalist movement; some contend that the magazine reflects O. more than it does "the generality of Transcendentalist thought" (Rosenthal). O.'s writings for the *Dial* and the *Tribune* gave her a chance to introduce European culture to America, to promote American literature, and to diffuse her social ideals while contrasting them with harsh reality. With Poe she must be considered America's first major literary critic, but her reporting gives evidence of a livelier, more supple prose that might have matured given time. Undoubtedly, she contributed much to American Romanticism and the feminist movement.

WORKS: Conversations with Goethe by J. P. Eckermann (translated by Ossoli, 1839). *Correspondence of Fraulein Günderode and Bettina von Arnim* (translated by Ossoli, 1842). *Summer on the Lakes* (1844). *Woman in the Nineteenth Century* (1845). *Papers on Literature and Art* (2 vols., 1846). *Memoirs of Margaret Fuller Ossoli* (Eds. R. W. Emerson, W. H. Channing, and J. F. Clarke; 2 vols., 1852). *At Home and Abroad* (Ed. A. B. Fuller, 1856). *Art, Literature, and the Drama* (Ed. A. B. Fuller, 1860). *Life Without and Life Within* (ed. A. B. Fuller, 1860). *Margaret and her Friends* (Ed. C. W. H. Dall, 1895). *Love-Letters of Margaret Fuller, 1845–1846* (1903). *The Writings of Margaret Fuller* (Ed. M. Wade, 1941).

The papers of Margaret Fuller, Marchesa d'Ossoli, are at the Boston Public Library and the Houghton Library, Harvard.

BIBLIOGRAPHY: Blanchard, P., *Margaret Fuller: From Transcendentalism to Romanticism* (1978). Boller, P. F., *American Transcendentalism 1830–1860: An Intellectual Inquiry* (1974). Brown, A. W., *Margaret Fuller* (1964). Buell, L., *Literary Transcendentalism: Style and Vision in the American Renaissance* (1973). Cooke, G. W., *An Historical and Bibliographical Introduction to Accompany the Dial* (2 vols., 1961). Deiss, J. J., *The Roman Years of Margaret Fuller* (1969). Durning, R. E., *Margaret Fuller, Citizen of the World* (1969). Emerson, R. W., *The Journals and Miscellaneous Notebooks of Ralph Waldo Emerson* (Eds. W. H. Gilman et al.; 14 vols. to date, 1960–   ). Hawthorne, N., *The American Notebooks* (Ed. C. M. Simpson, 1972). Miller P., *The American Transcendentalists* (1957). Miller, P., *The*

Transendentalists (1950). Myerson, J., *Margaret Fuller: A Descriptive Bibliography* (1978). Myerson, J., *Margaret Fuller: A Secondary Bibliography* (1977). Rosenthal, B., in *ELN* 8 (Sept. 1970). Stern, M. B., *The Life of Margaret Fuller* (1942). Swift, L., *Brook Farm* (1900). Thoreau, H. D., *The Correspondence of Henry David Thoreau* (Eds. W. Harding and C. Bode, 1958). Wade, M., *Margaret Fuller: Whetstone of Genius* (1940). Wilson, E., *Margaret Fuller: Bluestocking, Romantic, Revolutionary* (1977).

For articles in reference works, see: *AA. The Female Prose Writers of America*, Ed. J. S. Hart (1855). *NAW* (article by W. Berthoff).

Other references: *SAQ* 72 (Autumn 1973).

SUSAN SUTTON SMITH

Mary White Ovington

B. 11 April 1865, Brooklyn, New York; d. 15 July 1951, Newton, Massachusetts
D. of Theodore Tweedy and Louise Vetcham Ovington

The daughter of a well-to-do New York family, O. was raised by abolitionists and radicals. O.'s education at Radcliffe College (1891–93) was followed by two years in society, after which O. worked as registrar at the Pratt Institute, and then opened the Greenpoint Settlement of the Pratt Institute Neighborhood Association, where she served as headworker from 1895 to 1903.

O.'s fifty years of work in the cause of full equality for black Americans began with *Half a Man: The Status of the Negro in New York* (1911). Begun by O. while she was a Greenwich House fellow in 1904–05, the interviews and research in New York and in the South continued for seven years. Meanwhile, O. had also convinced Henry Phipps to build The Tuskegee in New York City as an experiment in model housing for blacks; had caused a national sensation as the central white female participant in the 1908 interracial Cosmopolitan Club dinner at Peck's Restaurant; had cofounded the Lincoln Settlement for Negroes with Verina Morton-Jones, a black physician; and had been the leading figure in the founding of the National Association for the Advancement of Colored People (NAACP) in 1909.

Work with the NAACP was to consume O.'s energies for the rest of her life. O. was dubbed "Fighting Saint," "Saint Mary," and "Mother of the New Emancipation" by people in and out of that organization. Able to get along with almost everyone, O. was described by co-workers as sensitive, modest, shy, retiring, but fearless and unshakable wherever she encountered injustice, poverty, or exploitation.

O.'s major writing can be grouped into sociological study, children's books, fiction, drama, and biography/autobiography. *Half a Man* is a highly readable and insightful sociological study of what was in 1911 a nearly invisible minority populace. It gives a thorough picture of the differences between white and black women's roles early in the 20th c., and provides a rare early depiction of the peculiar burdens and strengths of the American black woman.

O. wrote two books and helped edit another to fill the gap she perceived in literature for black children. *Hazel* (1913), a novel for girls, was dramatized and performed at the YWCA in Brooklyn in 1916. *Zeke: A School Boy at Tolliver* (1931), was written for boys. With Myron Thomas Pritchard, O. compiled *The Upward Path: A Reader for Colored Children* (1920), an excellent collection of stories and poems by black writers.

Notable in O.'s fiction is a short story, "The White Brute," printed in *The Masses* in 1915 and also in her autobiography. Based on actual incident, the story seeks to realistically reverse the image of the "black brute" so often touted in the South as excuse for lynching. Dialogue and description are effectively done. *The Shadow* (1920) combines O.'s interests in race problems and the labor movement.

Of O.'s two plays, *The Awakening* (1923) and *Phillis Wheatley* (1932), the latter, shorter play remains the less dated. *The Awakening* is primarily a propaganda piece for the NAACP. *Phillis Wheatley* is based on letters of the 18th-c. black poet to her friend Obour Tanner, and on the biographical notes prefacing editions of Wheatley's poems.

O.'s other two long books, *Portraits in Color* (1927) and *The Walls Came Tumbling Down* (1947), show again the clear, appealing writing style evident in *Half a Man*. *Portraits in Color* depicts the life and work of twenty black men and women. *The Walls Came Tumbling Down* is O.'s autobiography, concentrating not so much on the inward person as on O.'s political activities. It provides an excellent personalized picture of the early days of the NAACP and the people, black and white, who helped push down walls of discrimination and exploitation.

WORKS: *Half a Man: The Status of the Negro in New York* (1911). *Hazel* (1913). *The Shadow* (1920). *The Upward Path: A Reader for Colored Children* (edited by Ovington, with M. T. Pritchard, 1920). *The Awakening: A Play* (1923). *Portraits in Color* (1927). *Zeke: A School Boy at Tolliver* (1931). *Phillis Wheatley: A Play* (1932). *The Walls Came Tumbling Down* (1947).

Most of the papers of Mary White Ovington are in the NAACP papers, Library of Congress Manuscript Division.

BIBLIOGRAPHY: Archer, L., *Black Images in the American Theatre: NAACP Protest Campaigns—Stage, Screen, Radio, and Television* (1973). Hughes, L., *Fight for Freedom: The Story of the NAACP* (1962). Kellogg, C. F., Introduction to *Half a Man* by Ovington (1969). Kellogg, C. F., *NAACP: A History of the National Organization for the Advancement of Colored People* (1967). Ross, B. J., *J. E. Spingarn and the Rise of the NAACP, 1911–1939* (1972).

CAROLYN WEDIN SYLVANDER

Mary Alicia Owen

B. 29 Dec. 1858, St. Joseph, Missouri; d. 5 Jan. 1935, St. Joseph, Missouri
Wrote under: Mary Alicia Owen, Julia Scott
D. of James Alfred and Agnes Jeannette Cargill Owen

The daughter of a midwestern lawyer and financial writer, O. was educated in private schools and at Vassar College. She began her career by submitting verses, reviews, and travel sketches to a weekly newspaper in St. Joseph; eventually she became its literary editor. Under the pseudonym "Julia Scott," O. published short stories in *Peterson's Magazine*, *Overland Monthly*, *Century*, and *Frank Leslie's Illustrated Newspaper*. However, O.'s most important work stemmed from her lifelong study of folklore.

O.'s native Missouri sheltered four groups that deeply influenced each other: the native Musquakie (Sacs) Indians, the French and English settlers, and the transplanted African slaves. Raised among these disparate peoples, O. began collecting folklore, customs, and mythology. In 1888, she announced her findings on the voodoo magic practiced by ex-slaves; in 1891, she presented a paper on the Missouri-Negro tradition before the

International Folk-Lore Congress in London. In 1893, with the encouragement of folklorist Charles Godfrey Leland, O. published *VooDoo Tales*.

O. cast this book in a form similar to Joel Chandler Harris's *Uncle Remus:* Five old slave women gather around the cabin fire to share their tales with little "Tow Head," the plantation owner's daughter. "Big Angie" carries her eagle-bone whistle with her missal, her "saint's toe on her bosom and the fetish known as a 'luck-ball' under her right arm." Rendered in dialect appropriate to each speaker, the exploits of Woodpeckeh, Ole Rabbit, and Blue Jay have the flavor of true oral tradition. Although the form of *VooDoo Tales* suffers from the effort to combine serious research with literary entertainment, O.'s materials are compelling and accurate and the plots, language, and imagery are fresh.

O. describes gypsy tribes in *The Daughter of Alouette* (1896). The Musquakie Indians, who granted O. tribal membership in 1892, are described in a paper presented before the British Association at Toronto in 1897. O. later expanded this paper into a monograph, published by the English Folk-Lore Society in 1904. Accompanying the text is a catalogue of O.'s extensive collection of Musquakie artifacts.

Folk-Lore of the Musquakie Indians (1904) is a formal anthropological description of the tribe during a critical "clash of cultures." After carefully surveying their myths and yearly festivals, O. introduces the catalogue of her collection. Although she rejects the merely picturesque or aesthetically pleasing artifact in favor of the sacred or ceremonial, O. also recognizes that "to the wild man surrounded by civilization and making a stand against it, everything that pertains to his free and savage past has become a ceremonial object."

Among O.'s other works are *The Sacred Council Hills* (1909), a "folk-lore drama" portraying the Indian's plight, and *Home Life of Squaws*, of which no extant copy has been located.

O.'s writing, like the cultures it described, was influenced by many different traditions: regional humor, pastoral romanticism, the reform spirit, and the pioneering research of other folklorists. Although *VooDoo Tales* retains considerable charm, O.'s books are most interesting for their eclectic blend of literature and science. In an age when specialization was less narrow, O. synthesized several elements of late-19th-c. thought. A member of numerous scientific societies, she based her work on professional, firsthand observations; her conclusions were guided by deep respect for the people of the Mississippi Valley and their ways of life.

WORKS: *VooDoo Tales, as Told among the Negroes of the Southwest, Collected from Original Sources by Mary Alicia Owen* (1893; English title, *Old Rabbit, the Voodoo, and Other Sorcerors*; reissued as *Ole Rabbit's Plantation Stories*, 1898). *The Daughter of Alouette* (1896). *Oracles and Witches* (1902). *Folk-Lore of the Musquakie Indians of North America* (1904). *The Sacred Council Hills: A Folk-Lore Drama* (1909). *Home Life of Squaws* (n.d.). *Messiah Beliefs of the American Indians* (n.d.). *Rain Gods of the American Indians* (n.d.).

BIBLIOGRAPHY: Dorsen, R. M., *The British Folklorists* (1968). Hartland, E. S., Preface to *Folk-Lore of the Musquakie Indians* by M. A. Owen (1904). Leland, C. G., Preface to *VooDoo Tales* by M. A. Owen (1893).
    For articles in reference works see: *AW. Dictionary of American Authors Deceased before 1950*, Ed. W. S. Wallace (1951). *NCAB*, 13.

SARAH WAY SHERMAN

Rochelle Owens

B. *2 April 1936, Brooklyn, New York*
D. *of Maxwell Bass and Molly Adler Bass; m. George Economou, 1962*

The daughter of a postal inspector, O. graduated from Lafayette High School and then attended the Herbert Berghof Studio. O. then moved to Greenwich Village and held numerous clerical positions; while on the job, she wrote poetry. O. also attended the New School and traveled extensively.

In 1967, O. received wide critical attention for her play *Futz* (1962; revised version, 1968), which established her career as a playwright. The same year, *Futz* received an Obie committee citation as one of the distinguished new plays of 1966–67. In 1973, *The Karl Marx Play* was nominated for an Obie. In addition to her theater pieces, O. is the author of six books of poetry. ·

Futz opened at the Tyrone Guthrie Workshop, Minnesota Theatre Company, in 1965. It is a violent and controversial tragicomedy, dealing with a simple farmer, Cy Futz, who is emotionally and sexually in love with his pig Amanda. He lives with her in domestic bliss until "the world" invades their privacy.

Majorie Satz, a promiscuous townswoman, seduces Futz and participates in his lovemaking with Amanda. Later, shamed by her actions, she denounces him to the town. Oscar Loop and Ann Fox inadvertently discover Futz and Amanda cavorting together. Oscar becomes mad, beats Ann to death, and blames his violence on what he has seen. The community rises up against Futz. The sheriff places him in protective custody, but Futz cannot escape his fate. Ned Satz enters Futz's cell and stabs him to death.

The emotional center is Futz's relationship to Amanda. Futz is an instinctual being, and his affection for his sow is contrasted to the brutal and bitter relationships among the other characters. Futz says, "I like Amanda because she is good," and, ironically, Futz is the only character in the piece to display a sensitive and deep emotional life. Thus, Futz's murder at the end tragically symbolizes the destructive force of society's rigid, puritanical, and repressive codes. *Futz* is characterized by O.'s crude and passionately intense poetry. She employs words for their alliterative and associative impact, and her images are surreal and shocking.

By working outside the conventions of stage realism, O. underlines the idea that *Futz* is a modern morality fable. Above all, the inventiveness of her story and the raw power of her language make *Futz* an arresting and vibrant theater composition.

In *Homo* (1968), O. explores the unconscious sexual, racial, and economic fantasies of men and women. Each scene depicts a master/slave relationship in which one individual or group is manipulated, threatened, and humiliated by another. This dream, O. suggests, is the root of people's primordial drives.

In *The Karl Marx Play* (1974), the characters do not relate to each other through the story and dialogue but through the subject and theme. At each moment and in each segment the same images and ideas recur. Thus, the piece is "a play with music whose story is told as much by its imagery and tonal 'meanings' as it is by its plot."

O. focuses on Marx's painful physical debilities, his financial dependence on Engels, his rejection of his Jewish heritage, his lust for his wife, and his emotional need to complete his writings. Through this technique, therefore, we do not see the journey of Marx through his life, but the critical threads which constitute the fabric of his existence in the mid-1850s.

O.'s aim in this piece is to create "a theatrical experiencing of the extreme humanness of Karl Marx." She sacrifices a complex portrait of Marx to a theatrical concept. Thus, despite the play's verbal and musical richness, the text lacks the immediacy and power of O.'s other works.

All O.'s plays are characterized by a fluid and free use of language and time. She is a poet of the stage. Her dramatic imagination and verbal creativity mark O. as a notable modern writer.

WORKS: *Not Be Essence That Cannot Be* (1961). *Futz* (1962; revised version, *Futz and What Came After*, 1968). *Homo* (1968). *Salt and Core* (1968). *I Am the Babe of Joseph Stalin's Daughter* (1971). *Spontaneous Combustion: Eight New American Plays* (edited by Owens, 1972). *Poems from Joe's Garage* (1973). *The Joe 82 Creation Poems* (1974). *The Karl Marx Play, and Others* (1974). *The Widow and the Colonel* (1977). *The Joe Chronicles/Part 2* (1977).

BIBLIOGRAPHY: Brustein, R., *The Third Theatre* (1969). Kerr, W., *God on the Gymnasium Floor* (1969). Novick, J., *Beyond Broadway* (1968). Poggi, J., *Theatre in America: The Impact of Economic Forces, 1870–1967* (1968).

For articles in reference works, see: *Contemporary Dramatists*, Ed. J. Vinson (1977). *Notable Names in the American Theatre*, Ed. R. D. McGill (1976).

TINA MARGOLIS

Dorothy Myra Page

B. ca. 1899, Newport News, Virginia
Given name: Dorothy Gary
Wrote under: Dorothy Page Gary, Dorothy Markey, Dorothy Myra Page, Myra Page
D. of Benjamin Roscoe and Willie Alberta Barham Gray; m. John Markey

P.'s interest in writing was explicitly tied to her sense of art as social commentary. Her earliest memories are of accompanying her doctor father in his carriage as he made rounds. It was here that P. first recognized the severe extremes of class and race that characterized her town. When she was told that her brother, not she, would be encouraged to pursue a career in medicine, her sense of social inequity deepened. Writing became her vehicle for social investigation and self-expression.

P. published her first poem at age nine in the Richmond *Times* and wrote fiction throughout high school. In 1918, she graduated from Westhampton College in Richmond, where she edited the yearbook and won an award for her short story, "Schuman's Why." After an unsatisfying year teaching literature and history in a local junior high school, P. went to Columbia University. She received her Master's degree in political science, writing a thesis on yellow journalism. During the months in New York City, P. also became familiar with the goals of the trade union movement and revolutionary socialism.

P. returned to Virginia as an industrial secretary for the YWCA. Her job was to organize women working in department stores and silk mills into cultural and educational clubs to prepare them for unionization, but P. became disenchanted with the conservative attitude of the local YWCA leadership. She began to work with the Amalgamated Clothingmakers Union in Philadelphia, St. Louis, and Chicago. Her writing, primarily as a journalist covering labor issues, continued sporadically during this period.

In the late 1920s, P. received a teaching fellowship at the University of Minnesota. While in Minnesota she worked with the Minnesota Federation of Labor and the Farmers' Labor Party and married another graduate student. P. earned her Ph.D. in 1928, majoring in sociology and minoring in economics and psychology. Her dissertation was published as *Southern Cotton Mills and Labor* in 1929. Although she taught briefly at Wheaton College, most of P.'s time was given to her political work and her writing. She was a contributor to *Nation, New Masses, New Pioneer,* and *Labor Age* and a member of the Revolutionary Writers' Federation.

Gathering Storm (1932) is a fictional dramatization of several of the most significant events in the history of the American labor movement. The novel begins with an aging woman telling her spirited granddaughter about how the North Carolina hill people originally came to work in the cotton mills, and then traces the various characters through their involvement in and impressions of the 1910 shirtwaist makers' strike in New York City, the Russian Revolution, the political repression that accompanied patriotic zeal after World War I, the political debate between the Socialist Party and the IWW, the Chicago meatpackers' strike, and the formulation of an American Communist Party. The novel culminates with the cotton mill workers' strike in Gastonia, North Carolina, in 1929. Although heavily didactic, *Gathering Storm* is interesting because of P.'s attempts to make the problems of both women and black workers central to her discussion of the events and their possible resolution.

In the early 1930s, P. went to Europe to study and write about teachers' unions, and went from there to the Soviet Union. In the Soviet Union P. worked as a journalist and lived in a thriving artists' community. *Soviet Main Street* (1933) describes the changes which occur in Poldolsk, a small factory town outside of Moscow, as the residents adjust to the new life made possible by the revolution. *Moscow Yankee* (1935), a fictionalization of P.'s impressions of life in postrevolutionary Russia, is especially memorable for its portrayal of the personal dimensions of the conversion to Communism, most significantly the evolution of sexual relationships in a changing political climate.

With Sun in Our Blood (1950) is a fictionalized biography of Dolly Hawkins, the daughter, wife, and mother of coal miners in the Cumberland Mountains of Tennessee. P.'s admirable blend of local-color realism, lyrical, often ballad-like descriptions, and astute social commentary make the novel one of lasting significance.

Blacklisted during the repressive literary and political climate of the 1950s, P. adopted her husband's name when she could not get work published under her own. As Dorothy Markey, she wrote two biographies of American scientists for adolescent readers: *The Little Giant of Schenectady* (1956), a biography of Charles Steinmetz, and *Explorer of Sound* (1964), a biography of Michael Pupin.

P. is currently working on the first two volumes of her fictionalized autobiography, *Soundings* and *Midstream*. She writes in her preface to *Soundings*: "A man's reach must exceed his grasp, what then about a woman's?"

WORKS: *Southern Cotton Mills and Labor* (1929). *Gathering Storm: A Story of the Black Belt* (1932). *Soviet Main Street* (1933). *Moscow Yankee* (1935). *It Happened on May First* (1940). "The March on Chumley Hollow," *100 Non-Royalty Plays* (Ed. W. Konzlenko, 1941). *With Sun in Our Blood* (1950; reprinted as *Daughter of the Hills: A Woman's Part in the Coal Miners' Struggle*, 1977). *The Little Giant of Schenectady* (1956). *Explorer of Sound* (1964).

BIBLIOGRAPHY: Blake, F., *The Strike in the American Novel* (1972). Hill, V., "Strategy and Breadth: The Socialist-Feminist in American Fiction" (Diss., SUNY at Buffalo, 1979). Rideout, W., *The Radical Novel in the United States, 1900–1954* (1956).

Other references: *In These Times* (May 1978). *Mountain Heritage* (May 1978). *Social Research* (1971). *Westchester Gannet* (23 Jan. 1978).

VICKI LYNN HILL

Phoebe Worrall Palmer

B. 18 Dec. 1807, New York City; d. 2 Nov. 1874, New York City
D. of Henry and Dorothea Wade Worrall; m. Walter Clark Palmer, 1827

Author and evangelist of the "Holiness" movement, P. was the fourth of ten children of an American Methodist mother and an English father. In 1827, P. married a doctor and fellow Methodist. Both were lifelong New Yorkers. The Palmers had six children, only three of whom survived infancy.

In the 1840s, P. distributed tracts in the slums and regularly visited the Tombs, the legendary New York prison. For eleven years she was corresponding secretary of the New York Female Assistance Society for the Relief and Religious Instruction of the Sick Poor. P.'s most lasting contribution was the founding of the Five Points Mission in 1850 in the city's worst slum. Supported by the Methodist Ladies' Home Missionary Society, it was the forerunner of later settlement houses.

P.'s sister Sarah Worrall Lankford (1806–1896, who became the second wife of Walter Palmer in 1876) experienced "entire sanctification" in 1835. Though the experience was one testified to by many early Methodists in response to John Wesley's teachings on Christian perfection, it had not been stressed by American Methodists. In August 1835, Sarah founded the Tuesday Meeting for the Promotion of Holiness, which met in the home the Palmers and Lankfords shared. This weekly meeting for prayer, Scripture reading, and testimony, which continued for more than sixty years, was widely copied and became the catalyst for the "Holiness" or "Lay" revival of 1857–58, which eventually led to the formation of such holiness denominations as the Church of the Nazarene and such Pentecostal groups as the Assemblies of God.

P. testified to the same experience in 1837. Her writing and speaking, as well as her leadership in the Tuesday Meeting, soon made P. the more prominent sister. For six months each year "Dr. and Mrs. Phoebe Palmer" spoke in churches and camp meetings throughout the eastern U.S. and Canada. In 1859, they took the revival to the British Isles. Magazine reports on this trip were published as a book, Four Years in the Old World, in 1865.

P. was also a frequent contributor to the *Guide to Christian Perfection*, founded in Boston in 1839. Rechristened the *Guide to Holiness* in 1843, it was merged with the *Beauty of Holiness* when the Palmers purchased both in 1864. P. became editor, a post she held until her death. P.'s series of articles, "Fragments from My Portfolio," were collected as *Faith and Its Effects* in 1849.

Revivalist Charles G. Finney and his colleague at Oberlin College, President Asa Mahan, began in 1836 and 1837 to develop what came to be known as "Oberlin Perfectionism." Finney had transformed the old Puritan notion of religious conversion as an agonizing process contingent on divine election into a simple decision of human free will, an act, and an event.

P. transformed Wesley's idea of perfection as a lifelong process into an act and an experience. In response to a Presbyterian elder's question as to whether "there is not a *shorter way* of getting into the way of holiness?" P. replied in the *Christian Advocate and Journal*, "THERE IS A SHORTER WAY!" Her articles became her most famous work, *The Way of Holiness* (1843). P. begins with the premise that "God requires *present* holiness." Using Finney's logic that God would not command something people cannot do, P. declares that a person must consecrate all to God. (For eighty descriptions of this by ministers who have experienced it, see P.'s *Pioneer Experiences*, 1868.) Using rather dubious biblical exegesis, P. termed this "laying all upon the altar." She declared that the altar was Christ and that "whatever *touched* the altar became holy, virtually the *Lord's property, sanctified to His use.*" Since God has declared this to be true, any person who consecrates everything to God can simply claim sanctification and testify to it publicly, whether or not he or she receives any inner confirmation from the Holy Spirit (as Wesley taught) or has any emotional experience. A person simply claims holiness on the basis of faith in God's promise.

P.'s other significant work was *Promise of the Father* (1859), in which she argued from Scripture, church history, and biographical example for the right of women to preach. Although P. never considered herself a "woman's rights" advocate or sought ordination for her own ministry, she strongly supported the right, and even Christian duty, of women to publicly testify to their religious experience and to become full-time preachers if they felt that to be God's call.

P.'s understanding of holiness, despite her very controversial "altar terminology," transformed the notion from one of process to one of experience. The movement P. helped give birth to left a lasting impact on American religious culture. P.'s defense of women's ministry was the first of many in the holiness-Pentecostal tradition, which led such churches to ordain women more than fifty years before "mainline" Protestantism.

WORKS: *The Way of Holiness* (1843). *Faith and Its Effects* (1849). *Present to My Christian Friend on Entire Devotion to God* (1853). *The Useful Disciple; or, A Narrative of Mrs. Mary Gardner* (1853). *Incidental Illustrations of the Economy of Salvation* (1855). *Promise of the Father* (1859). *Four Years in the Old World* (1865). *Pioneer Experiences* (1868). *A Mother's Gift* (1875).

BIBLIOGRAPHY: Wheatley, R., *The Life and Letters of Mrs. Phoebe Palmer* (1876). Hughes, G., *The Beloved Physician, Walter C. Palmer, M.D.* (1884). Hughes, G., *Fragrant Memories of the Tuesday Meeting* (1886). Roche, J., *The Life of Mrs. Sarah A. Lankford Palmer* (1898). Peters, J. L., *Christian Perfection and American Methodism* (1956). Smith, T., *Revivalism and Social Reform in Mid-Nineteenth Century America* (1957). Dayton, D. W., *Discovering an Evangelical Heritage* (1976).

For articles in reference works, see: *NAW* (article by W. J. McCutcheon).

NANCY A. HARDESTY

Helen Waite Papashvily

B. 19 Dec. 1906, Stockton, California
Writes under: Helen Papashvily, Helen Waite Papashvily
D. of Herbert and Isabella Findlay Lochhead Waite; m. George Papashvily, 1933

P. was educated in public schools and at the University of California at Berkeley. She graduated in 1929, and then opened a bookstore. The next year she met her husband, an immigrant from Kobiankari in Soviet Georgia who had come to the U.S. in 1923. About the same time P. began her writing career with a variety of short pieces.

In 1933, the Papashvilys moved to New York City, where P. collected books for private libraries and wrote short stories, works for children, and articles. In 1935, they bought the Ertoba Farm in Bucks County, Pennsylvania, where P. still lives.

It was P.'s idea to set down her husband's accounts of his involved and colorful twenty-year Americanization. *Anything Can Happen* (1945) quickly sold 600,000 copies, was translated into fifteen languages, and was made into a film.

Anything Can Happen looks back to a period early in this century, just before the National Origins Act (1924) cut off the large wave of immigration from southern and eastern Europe. The book, told from a personal perspective, constitutes a "psychological case-study in the adjustment of the alien" (H. Fields). P. approaches the immigrant's quest for food, shelter, and matrimony with wit, enthusiasm, honesty, and gracious old-world manners. His story presents a version of the old theme of innocence encountering experience—with not all the innocence on the immigrant's side.

Part of the book's popularity originally stemmed from its optimistic portrayal of life in America, its tone being one of philosophic acceptance rather than rebellion against injustices. Consequently, the book lends credence to the vision of America as a melting pot. Its appeal, however, is also attributable to its vivid, charming, and often poetic use of language. This can be credited in part to P., who set out to capture the rhythm and flavor of her husband's English rather than his exact speech.

The Papashvilys' five joint works constitute total and perfect collaboration. Papashvily supplied the material; his wife, seeing its potential, transformed it from verbal anecdotes into written words. (Papashvily, coming from a rural, oral tradition, and involved in tactile rather than verbal pursuits, eventually learned to read English, but never to write it.) Moreover, as an American married to an immigrant, P. sensed how best to present her husband's material to an American audience. Perhaps because the collaboration was so successful, the extent of P.'s contribution to it is often glossed over.

Of the Papashvilys' other works the most important is *Yes and No Stories* (1946), one of the few books to render the folklore of Georgia, a country inaccessible both geographically and linguistically, into a language other than Russian. Because Georgian history involves recurrent invasions that resulted in the grafting of diverse ethnic cultures upon native materials, the tales, "though circumscribed in their locale, merge with the main stream of Indo-European folk matter" (H. Wedeck).

P.'s most important independent effort, *All the Happy Endings* (1956), was the first book to study in detail the enormous quantities of popular 19th-c. American fiction written by, for, and about women; to discuss its authors individually; and to assess the relationship of their work to feminism. Treating domestic fiction as a social and psychological phenomenon, P. concluded that while the suffragists of the period waged outright rebellion, the novelists engaged in surreptitious warfare "to destroy their common enemy, man." As Nancy Cott notes, P. thus found "the roots of feminism, in a shrewdly adapted form, in domesticity itself."

WORKS: *Anything Can Happen* (with G. Papashvily, 1945; film version, 1952). *Yes and No Stories: A Book of Georgian Folk Tales* (with G. Papashvily, 1946). *Thanks to Noah* (with G. Papashvily, 1951). *Dogs and People* (with G. Papashvily, 1954). *All the Happy Endings: A Study of the Domestic Novel in America, the Women Who Wrote It, the Women Who Read It, in the Nineteenth Century* (1956, 1972). *Louisa May Alcott* (1965). *Russian Cooking* (with G. Papashvily and the editors of Time-Life Books, 1969). *Home, and Home Again* (with G. Papashvily, 1973). *George Papashvily: Sculptor, A Retrospective Catalogue* (1979).

BIBLIOGRAPHY: Cott, N., *Bonds of Womanhood* (1977). Fields, H., in *Saturday Review* (13 Jan. 1945). Wedeck, H., in *NYTBR* (1 Dec. 1946).
Other references: *Christian Science Monitor* (22 Oct. 1956; 4 Nov. 1965; 17 Oct. 1973). *New Republic* (15 Jan. 1945). *NYHTB* (5 April 1951; 21 Oct. 1956). *NYT* (21 Nov. 1954). *NYTBR* (31 Dec. 1944; 21 Oct. 1956). San Francisco *Chronicle* (8 Nov. 1946). *SatR* (9 Nov. 1946; 10 Nov. 1956).

JANET SHARISTANIAN

Dorothy Rothschild Parker

B. 22 Aug. 1893, West End, New Jersey; d. 7 June 1967, New York City
Wrote under: "Constant Reader," Dorothy Parker, Dorothy Rothschild
D. of Henry and Eliza A. Marston Rothschild; m. Edwin Pond Parker, 1917;
  m. Alan Campbell, 1933

P. was the only daughter of a Jewish father and a Scottish mother who died while P. was still an infant. After a very restricted youth and adolescence, P. entered the publishing world in a minor editorial position at *Vogue* in 1916. A year later, she became drama critic for *Vanity Fair* and married Parker, whose name she retained even after their divorce in 1928.

P. became the acknowledged leader of the (Hotel) "Algonquin Round Table," surrounded by such notables as Edna Ferber, Robert Benchley, and Alexander Woollcott. She left *Vanity Fair* in 1926, after her first volume of poetry, *Enough Rope*, became a bestseller.

The opening poems of *Enough Rope* are composed of love lamentations and reiterate the desire for death in a dismal, often dirgelike tone. However, the tender lovers and passive victims soon give way to the carefree adventuress and the jaundiced "flapper." The poems are characterized by regular lines of alternating rhyme and lapidary verse. Romance is often countered by a satiric thrust: "All of my days are gray with yearning. / (Nevertheless, a girl needs fun.)"

Sunset Gun (1928) achieves a solidarity through alternating voices of melancholy and seriousness. The cavalier tone often reveals the comic dimensions of sorrow, but various poems, such as those concerning Mary's pain at the loss of Jesus, touch on the universal nature of tragedy. *Death and Taxes* (1931) emphasizes the artistic integrity of the poetry by moving even further into the realm of the dramatic monologue. The usual caustic verse alternates with statements by various historical and literary figures. The contemplative verse shows a fine mastery of mood and tone and a manipulation of public myths, which places P. far above the level of light entertainer. Poems from all three volumes were collected in *Not So Deep as a Well* (1936).

In 1927, P. began writing stories and a book-review column signed "Constant Reader" for *The New Yorker*. P. wrote for many popular magazines, but her most sustained critical endeavor was the "Constant Reader" column. Like her play reviews of the same period, the forty-six pieces are characterized by an easy conversational tone that seems to effortlessly interweave epigrams, puns, and personal anecdotes. Notwithstanding the subjective mode of approach, sound literary commentary and insightful critical evaluations distinguish most of P.'s work.

P. published stories in *Laments for the Living* (1930) and *After Such Pleasures* and collected them in *Here Lies* (1939). The stories reveal her as a master of cutting, ironic fiction.

"Big Blond," won the O. Henry Prize for 1930. Hazel Morse works hard at being a "good sport." However, when near thirty, she marries Herbie and delights in being able to relax and give in to her moods. Unfortunately, he tires of her and leaves. The need to be a "good sport" again prevails. Hazel is provided for by a succession of men, but always in a mist of alcohol, depressed and longing for peace. The four-part presentation traces the progressive disintegration from contentment through despair over a number of years with an admirable unity of effect. The analogy made between the nonintrospective, passive victim and a "beaten driven, stumbling" horse struggling "to get a footing" is the heart of the narrative and is all the more vivid for the stark rendering of the background details.

"A Telephone Call" (1930) provides a striking example of P.'s proficiency in the modified stream-of-consciousness technique. As a woman futilely awaits a promised telephone call, the shifting phases of desperation and pain are revealed through a superb rhetorical display that encompasses rushing prayers, meandering introspections, and angry threats.

"Clothe the Naked" (1939) concerns Big Lannie, a stoic black laundress whose only surviving daughter dies in childbirth leaving her with a blind grandson. The distanced narrative tone imparts a sense of sustained suffering throughout.

Although P.'s reputation has suffered a sharp decline, the literary merit of her short stories and much of her poetry can scarcely be contested. The perennial concerns of alienation and loss of love are treated with an irony that only barely masks the sense of deep tragedy beneath. The economy of language, flawless dialogue, and sharp eye for detail that characterize the short stories is directly attributable to P.'s poetic sense. The crystalline, concise sentences set the tone and sum up the characters as aptly as the measured, polished verse.

WORKS: *Enough Rope* (1926). *Sunset Gun* (1928). *Laments for the Living* (1930). *Death and Taxes* (1931). *After Such Pleasures* (1933). *Not So Deep as a Well* (1936). *Here Lies* (1939). *Dorothy Parker* (1944).

BIBLIOGRAPHY: Keats, J., *You Might As Well Live: The Life and Times of Dorothy Parker* (1972). Wilson E., *Classics and Commercials* (1950).

Other references: *EJ* 23 (1934). *Esquire* 70 (1968). *Horizon* 4 (1962). *Paris Review* 13 (1956). *Poetry* (30, 1927; 33, 1928; 39, 1931). *Rendezvous* 3 (1968). *Revue de Paris* 54 (1947).

FRANCINE SHAPIRO PUK

Elsie Worthington Clews Parsons

B. 27 Nov. 1875, New York City; d. 19 Dec. 1971, New York City
Wrote under: John Main
D. of Henry and Lucy Madison Clews; m. Herbert Parsons, 1900

P. was the daughter of wealthy and socially prominent parents. She was educated in New York City, receiving from Columbia University a B.A. in 1896, M.A. in 1897, and Ph.D. in 1899. In 1900, she married a New York attorney who became a Congressman and a leader in the Republican Party. The marriage lasted until his death in 1925 and seems to have been unusual in the degree of autonomy P. achieved within it. There were six children born of this marriage, four of whom survived P.

Primarily a researcher and writer, P. taught only briefly, from 1899 to 1905 at Barnard College and then at the New School for Social Research in 1919. But her professional achievements were well recognized: She presided over the American Folklore Society (1918), the American Ethnological Association (1923–25), and the American Anthropological Association (1940–41); she was also associate editor of the *Journal of American Folklore* (1910–1941) and vice-president of the New York Academy of Sciences (1936).

P.'s career may be divided into two periods, the first beginning in 1899 when she undertook speculative work in sociology, committed to the belief that individuals have the right to self-development, and that civilized society must allow for and benefit from such development. Occasionally, P.'s objective observations of her own society made readers uncomfortable. For example, a college textbook titled *The Family* (1906) attracted unusual attention because it was directed at both students and "intelligent mothers" of daughters, and discussed not only the family but also the inequities of the double standard and the advantages of trial marriage.

P.'s next five books also dealt with social oppression, but from a broader perspective. *The Old-fashioned Woman* (1913) is a book written with wit and quiet irony. Here P. reviews attitudes and customs relating to women in so-called primitive societies and in her own society so that the limitations of her society are revealed as being painfully like the limitations of primitive societies. In *Social Freedom* (1915) P. explores the negative effects of such social categorization by age and sex on the development of individual personality. In *Social Rule* (1916) she argues that social categories are used as a way of controlling such groups as women, children, employees, and "backward peoples." Of special interest in this book is P.'s view of the ideal role of feminism.

The second stage of P.'s career began about 1915, when she became interested in the anthropological approach of Franz Boas. P. did not abandon her commitment to self-development, but turned from speculating about the way society functioned to collecting ethnographic data that could indicate how a specific culture functioned. After 1915, P. undertook at least one field trip a year to study various groups, though her chief work was done with American and West Indian blacks and with Indians of the southwest Pueblos. On occasion, she returned to her earlier speculations and her interest in feminist-related issues when she wrote journal articles.

Boas and other anthropologists cite two works of this period as having special significance—*Pueblo Indian Religion* (1939) and *Mitla: Town of the Souls, and Other Zapoteco-speaking Pueblos of Oaxaca, Mexico* (1936)—but these books are aimed at the specialist reader.

Vital to any assessment of P. is a consideration of her character, which was marked by an uncompromising commitment to her work and to living in accordance with her beliefs. She was, Boas wrote: "intolerant towards [herself], tolerant towards others, disdainful of selfish pettiness and truthful in thought and action." So strong was her personality that Robert Herrick, a novelist of the period, used it as the basis for several characterizations in *Wanderings* (1925), *Chimes* (1926), and *The End of Desire* (1932).

Since P.'s death, her work has attracted little general attention, though at the time of her death the value of her work and the significance of her support of the American Folklore Society and of the field work of other anthropologists were acknowledged by many.

WORKS: Educational Legislation and Administration of the Colonial Governments (1899). *The Family* (1906). *The Old-fashioned Woman* (1913). *Religious Chastity* (1913). *Fear and Conventionality* (1914). *Social Freedom: A Study of the Conflicts between Social Classifications and Personality* (1915). *Social Rule: A Study of the Will to Power* (1916). *Notes on Zuñi* (1917). *Folk-tales of Andros Island, Bahamas* (1918). *Notes on Ceremonialism at Laguna* (1920). *Winter and Summer Dance Series in Zuñi in 1918* (1922). *Folk-lore from the Cape Verde Islands* (1923). *Folk-lore of the Sea Islands, South Carolina* (1923). *Laguna Genealogies* (1923). *The Scalp Ceremonial of*

Zuñi (1924). *The Pueblo of Jemez* (1925). *Tewa Tales* (1926). *Kiowa Tales* (1929). *The Social Organization of the Tewa of New Mexico* (1929). *Isleta, New Mexico* (1932). *Folk-lore of the Antilles, French and English* (1933). *Hopi and Zuñi Ceremonialism* (1933). *Mitla: Town of the Souls, and Other Zapoteco-speaking Pueblos of Oaxaca, Mexico* (1936). *Taos Pueblo* (1936). *Pueblo Indian Religion* (2 vols, 1939). *Taos Tales* (1940). *Notes on the Caddo* (1941). *Pequche, Canton of Otavelo, Province of Imbabura Ecuador: A Study of Andean Indians* (1945).

BIBLIOGRAPHY: Boas, F., in *The Scientific Monthly* 54 (May 1942).

Other references: *American Anthropologist* 45 (1943). *Journal of American Folk-lore* 56 (1943). *Proceedings of the American Philosophical Society* 94 (1950).

PHYLLIS FRANKLIN

Louella Oettinger Parsons

B. 6 Aug. 1893, Freeport, Illinois; d. 9 Dec. 1972, Beverly Hills, California
D. of Joshua and Helen Wilcox Oettinger; m. John Parsons, 1910;
m. Dr. Harry Martin, 1931

As a youngster, P. showed an interest in writing and had her first story published in the Freeport *Journal-Standard* before she reached high-school age. While in high school, P. acquired her first newspaper job, working as the dramatic editor and assistant to the city editor on the Dixon, Illinois, *Morning Star*. P. received most of her journalism education through such practical experiences.

In 1910, P. married a real-estate agent. The couple soon moved to Burlington, Iowa, where P. became frustrated and bored. After the birth of a daughter in 1911, P. left with the child to visit an uncle in Montana. From then on, P. and her husband drifted apart.

After the death of her husband in 1914, P. took her daughter to Chicago and worked as a reporter for the *Tribune*. P. soon became involved in the movie business and took a job with the Essanay Company reading scripts and writing scenarios.

P. was later able to convince the Chicago *Record-Herald* to run a series of her articles on how to write for the movies. These articles were well received, and P. realized that if people were interested in a behind-the-scenes look at films, they would also be interested in a more surface view—a look at the movie stars.

In 1918, P. moved with her daughter to New York City. She became the movie critic for the *Morning Telegraph*, where she remained until 1924. During her five years with the *Telegraph*, P. was made editor of the motion picture section and was presented with an all-female staff nicknamed the "Persian Garden of Cats."

P. started writing for the Hearst papers in 1924. In 1925, P. discovered that she had tuberculosis; she spent a year (on full salary) resting. After she recovered from the illness, Hearst sent P. to California, and she wrote her stories from Hollywood. At this time P.'s column became syndicated.

In 1931, P.'s work expanded to the broadcast field when she was hired by the Sunkist Orange Company to do a thirteen-week radio show. She began a second radio show in 1934, on which she interviewed movie stars. For four years, "Hollywood Hotel" was one of the leading radio programs.

Throughout the 1940s, P. continued to write her column, which was by then widely syndicated. Even at the age of sixty-four, P. was still doing a weekly radio show, writing her column, covering hard news events, writing stories for *Photoplay* and *Modern Screen*, and reviewing movies for *Cosmopolitan*. She retired in 1964.

Besides writing columns and doing radio shows, P. was also the author of three books. The first, *How to Write for the Movies*, was published in 1915 and used as a text in early film classes at Ohio State University. With the advent of the "talkie," however, the book became dated.

The Gay Illiterate (1944) is a delightful account of P.'s life until 1939. P.'s entertaining style of writing makes the book a pleasure to read even today.

Tell It to Louella (1961) is an account of some of P.'s more memorable celebrity interviews. Her quick and often acerbic wit provides greater insight into P.'s life and personality than into the personalities of the stars she covered.

P. was the first widely read gossip columnist in the U.S. She once wrote that she would "do almost anything" in order to get a scoop. Her columns were largely devoted to interviews with the most popular movie stars and reports on weddings, divorces, and births; she was most proud of "scooping" the divorces of famous stars. P. maintained a colorful reputation throughout her career.

WORKS: *How to Write for the Movies* (1915). *The Gay Illiterate* (1944). *Tell It to Louella* (1961).

BIBLIOGRAPHY: Eells, G., *Hedda and Louella* (1972).
    For articles in reference works, see: *CA* 37 (1973). *CB* (1940).

SANDRA CARLIN GUIN

Sara Payson Willis Parton

B. *9 July 1811, Portland, Maine; d. 10 Oct. 1872, New York City*
Wrote under: Olivia Branch, Fanny Fern
D. *of Nathaniel and Hannah Parker Willis; m. Charles Eldredge, 1837;*
    m. Samuel Farrington, 1849; m. James Parton, 1856

P. preferred her talented mother to her harsh, narrowly religious father; she believed that her mother would have distinguished herself in literature had she not had such a large family. P. said her pen name, "Fanny Fern," was inspired by happy childhood memories of her mother picking sweet fern leaves.

When P. was a small child, her family moved to Boston, where her father established a religious newspaper. P. attended Boston schools and Catharine Beecher's famous seminary in Hartford, Connecticut, at the time when Harriet Beecher was a student teacher. Despite a lack of studiousness, P. wrote witty essays at the Beecher school and on her return to Boston contributed to her father's new publication, *Youth's Companion.*

In 1844, P.'s mother died, and in the next two years she lost the older of her three daughters and her first husband, a bank cashier. P. was reduced to relative poverty, with only grudging support from her father and in-laws. She tried marriage to a Boston merchant, but he soon left her. Although P. attempted to forget her second marriage, never directly referring to it, she later used Farrington as a model for one of her characters. In *Rose Clark* (1856), a "hypocrite" and "gross sensualist" tricks a reluctant widow into marriage and then slanders her and leaves her penniless.

When P. failed in her attempts to earn a living teaching and sewing, she appealed unsuccessfully to her brother, a successful poet and editor in New York, for help in launching a literary career. P. began to write short sketches, and by 1851 she was placing her work in small Boston magazines. Her magazine pieces were so popular that in 1853 J. C. Derby published a collection of them as *Fern Leaves from Fanny's Portfolio*. P. continued the next year with a second series and a juvenile, *Little Ferns for Fanny's Little Friends*. The three books sold an astonishing 180,000 copies in America and England, and P. was suddenly rich and famous.

Based very closely upon P.'s own experience, *Ruth Hall* (1855) recounts the struggles of a widow to support herself and her children. Ruth Hall finds few opportunities open to women and is treated shabbily by her relatives, who can tolerate neither a passive dependent nor the successful and assertive writer Ruth finally becomes. *Ruth Hall* caused a sensation in the literary world. P. had apparently thought herself protected by her pseudonym and neglected to disguise the characters, who were obviously based on P.'s relatives. P.'s true identity was discovered and the family quarrel aired in public.

Ruth Hall was admired by Hawthorne, and attacked by the critics for the same reasons he praised it—its lack of restraint and "female delicacy"; one critic referred to it as "Ruthless Hall." Soon after the publication of *Ruth Hall*, the anonymous *Life and Beauties of Fanny Fern* appeared, satirizing P. as a spendthrift, adventuress, and ingrate to her family.

In the meantime, P. moved to New York City and was engaged by Robert Bonner, publisher of the New York *Ledger*, to write a weekly column for the then outlandish sum of $100 a week. For the next twenty years, P. wrote weekly for the *Ledger*, never missing a column. P. lived a relatively quiet life with her third husband, James Parton, a well-known biographer eleven years her junior.

After *Ruth Hall*, P. wrote only one more novel, *Rose Clark* (1856), but her talent was not for fiction, and after *Rose Clark* she stuck with the form she was best at—the informal essay, sometimes lightly fictionalized but always short. She published several collections of these from her *Ledger* columns.

Because her early work is best known, P. has been mistakenly classified as a sentimentalist. However, P.'s writing changed and developed significantly after her initial success. In the first series of *Fern Leaves* there are two parts: the first, which comprises about three quarters of the book, is indeed lachrymose, but the remaining quarter consists of humorous and satirical pieces. In the second series of *Fern Leaves* the proportion is exactly reversed.

In *Folly as It Flies* (1859), P. adopted a new voice, which she would maintain for the rest of her career. Her sentimentality and heavy-handed satire give way to relaxed, humorous philosophizing. She abandons the artificiality and straining for effect of her earlier pieces, and writes more naturally and spontaneously. While P.'s staple continued to be everyday domestic topics, like child care and the annoying habits of husbands, she became conscious of social conditions in New York City and began to depict poverty, prostitution, exploitation of workers, and prison life.

P. also became more direct and outspoken in her championship of women. Women's estate and the relationship between the sexes had always been P.'s major subject, but in her early fiction she protested injustice to women by portraying them as passive victims of male brutality. By the end of the 1850s, P. came to support the women's rights movement and encourage her readers to seek suffrage, better education, and wider fields of endeavor.

WORKS: *Fern Leaves from Fanny's Portfolio* (English title, *Shadows and Sunbeams;* 1st series, 1853; 2nd series, 1854). *Little Ferns for Fanny's Little Friends* (1854). *Ruth Hall* (1855). *Rose Clark* (1856). *Fresh Leaves* (1857). *Play-Day· Book* (1857). *Folly as It Flies* (1859). *A New Story Book for Children* (1864). *Ginger-Snaps* (1870). *Caper-Sauce* (1872). *Fanny Fern: A Memorial Volume* (Ed. J. Parton, 1873).

BIBLIOGRAPHY: Adams, F. B., *Fanny Fern* (1966). Derby, J. C., *Fifty Years Among Authors, Books and Publishers* (1884). *The Life and Beauties of Fanny Fern* (1855).

For articles in reference works, see: *NAW* (article by E. B. Schlesinger).

Other references: *AL* (Nov. 1957). *Biblion* (Spring 1969). *Colophon* (Sept. 1939). *NY Historical Society Quarterly* (Oct. 1954). *WS* 1 (1972).

BARBARA A. WHITE

Elia Wilkinson Peattie

B. 1862, Kalamazoo, Michigan; d. 12 July 1935, Wellington, Vermont
Wrote under: Elia W. Peattie, Sade Iverson
Given name: Elia Wilkinson
M. Robert Burns Peattie, 1883

P.'s family moved from Michigan to Chicago shortly after the 1871 fire. They built a comfortable house, in which P. and her husband later raised their own children.

In 1884, P. became the first "girl reporter" on the Chicago *Tribune*. After ten years in Omaha, where P. wrote pot-boiler histories and her best stories while her husband managed the *World-Herald*, P. returned to Chicago in 1898, when she bore their third son. A daughter died in childhood; all three sons survived their parents, two becoming writers who married writers.

From 1901 to 1917, P. was Chicago *Tribune* literary critic, while also publishing prolifically. Invitations to the Peatties' Sunday afternoon gatherings represented acceptance into the Chicago literary establishment.

P. left Chicago in 1917, when her husband joined the *New York Times*. They retired to Tryon, North Carolina, in 1920, where P. remained after his death in 1930.

Many of P.'s publications were primarily commercial ventures. *The Story of America* (1889) has neither original interpretation nor careful writing to recommend it, yet P. published several editions and adaptations. Similarly commercial were the two poetry anthologies that the *Tribune*'s influential literary critic edited in 1903.

P.'s other historical works reflect her involvement in Chicago's cultural "uplift" movement. Her early historical romances and romanticized histories promoted the cultural establishment's fascination with knighthood's European flowering. P.'s one-act costume pageant of women's changing status from mythological to modern times, *Times and Manners* (1918), was written specifically for a Chicago Woman's Club production.

P.'s involvement with club theatricals also inspired several fine one-act plays late in her career. The title piece of *The Wander Weed* (1923) is probably her best, dealing with a Blue Ridge mountain girl's encounter with a sphinxlike old woman who breaks silence to convince Lu Constant of the need to accept the pains and joys of ongoing family relationships.

Family settings and themes are the common denominators for P.'s girls' books. *Azalea* (1912) is representative; its young heroine forsakes nomadic circus adventures for the everyday continuities and domestic affections of small-town family life. Such small-town virtues also win out over artistic ambition and urban wealth in *Lotta Embury's Career* (1915) and *Sarah Brewster's Relatives* (1916).

The best of P.'s early magazine short stories, collected in *A Mountain Woman* (1896), call domestic sentimentality into question. In "Jim Lancy's Waterloo," newly married Annie Lancy confronts the hard facts of premature aging and madness among neighboring Nebraska wives and of infant death in her own home. Generally, the *Mountain Woman* stories embody a conviction that city and frontier pose irreconcilable cultures, engendering psychic disorientation for intercultural migrants.

Similarly critical of domestic sentimentality are P.'s two adult novels. An implicitly erotic relationship between father and daughter informs the violent action of *The Judge* (1890), while *The Precipice* (1914) exposes patriarchal tyranny and neighborly hypocrisy underlying small-town family life. Nonetheless, Kate Barrington's search for independence in *The Precipice* is undercut by her friends' dramatizations of feminine limitations and the joys of motherhood. Kate's own social-work activities—modeled on those of Julia Lathrop, first head of the U.S. Children's Bureau—remain in the novel's background. The organizing marriage-versus-career theme ultimately resolves itself ambiguously in Kate's decision to relinquish "prideful" independence for marital commitment, yet to subordinate "womanly" fulfillment to civic duty by living in Washington, D.C., apart from her husband.

A few of P.'s short stories and one-act plays are fully realized literary works, and *The Precipice* is fascinating in its treatment of feminist issues. However, P.'s career was ultimately compromised by easy commercial productions and thematic contradictions. As a critic and romancer, she upheld derivative genteel standards of "noble" thoughts and "classic" forms. Yet her best fictions and plays are realistic, and "The Milliner" (1914), a pseudonymous free verse poem for *The Little Review*, met with deserved acclaim.

WORKS: The Story of America (1889; rev. eds., 1892, 1896; reprinted as *America in Peace and War*, 1898). *A Journey through Wonderland* (1890). *The Judge* (1890). *With Scrip and Staff* (1891). *The American Peasant* (with T. Tibbles, 1892). *A Mountain Woman* (1896). *Our Chosen Land* (1896). *The Pictorial Story of America* (1896). *Pippins and Cheese* (1897). *The Love of a Calaban: A Romantic Opera* (1898; adapted by E. Freer as *Massimillano*, 1925). *The Shape of Fear, and Other Ghostly Stories* (1898). *Ickery Ann, and Other Boys and Girls* (1899). *The Beleaguered Forest* (1901). *How Jacques Came into the Forest of Arden* (1901). *Castle, Knight, and Troubador* (1903). *The Edges of Things* (1903). *Poems You Ought to Know* (edited by Peattie, 1903). *To Comfort You* (edited by Peattie, 1903). *Edda and the Oak* (1911). *Azalea* (1912). *Annie Laurie and Azalea* (1913). *Azalea at Sunset Gap* (1914). *The Precipice* (1914). *The Angel with a Broom* (1915). *Azalea's Silver Web* (1915). *Lotta Embury's Career* (1915). *Sarah Brewster's Relatives* (1916). *The Newcomers* (1917). *Painted Windows* (1918). *Times and Manners* (1918). *The Wander Weed, and Seven Other Little Theater Plays* (1923). *The Great Delusion* (1932). *The Book of the Fine Arts Building* (n.d.).

BIBLIOGRAPHY: Atlantic 83 (1899). *Bookman* (April 1914; Jan. 1916). Boston *Transcript* (18 Feb. 1914). *NYT* (24 Dec. 1916).

SIDNEY H. BREMER

Julia Mood Peterkin

B. 31 Oct. 1880, Laurens County, South Carolina; d. 10 Aug. 1961,
 Fort Motte, South Carolina
D. of Julius Andrew and Alma Archer Mood; m. William Peterkin, 1903

The youngest of four children, P. spent several years with her grandparents in rural South Carolina after her mother's early death. Later, she lived in Sumter, South Carolina, with her father. After receiving her B.A. and M.A. degrees from Converse College, Spartanburg, South Carolina, P. taught at Fort Motte, a small, isolated community. She married the owner of Lang Syne plantation there. There were few whites and many blacks on the two-thousand-acre plantation. Because of her husband's ill health, P. took over most of the responsibilities of running Lang Syne until her son William was able to assume the actual management.

P. began writing in her early forties, and her work was centered around Fort Motte and Murrell's Inlet, a coastal village in South Carolina where she had a summer home.

Plantation stories were a popular genre from antebellum days until well into the 20th c., and it is one of P.'s contributions that she brought to this genre a sense of realism and dignity in her portrayal of the lives of black characters. In most of her work there is no stereotyped or affected local color, a common characteristic of plantation stories. P. also broke out of the southern pattern of sentimentality.

P.'s first works, which appeared in many magazines in the early 1920s, may be divided generally into two groups: Gullah-dialect sketches and more conventionally structured short stories. The former are usually dramatic monologues in the words of coastal South Carolina blacks, but the dialect at times becomes obtrusive. The larger group, in which P. departs from extended use of dialect but maintains the rhythm and syntax of the speech, are stark, powerful portrayals of the lives of these isolated people. The stories in *Green Thursday* (1924) continue in this vein, but there is more description of the land and the natural cycles, which always play an integral part in the lives of her characters. The stories may be read almost as a novel, centering on Killdee and his family.

Black April (1927), P.'s first novel, incorporates some of the incidents of the stories. The book is episodic rather than tightly plotted. It gives a convincing picture of the daily lives of the characters and a strong sense of community.

In *Scarlet Sister Mary* (1928), P.'s Pulitzer Prize–winning novel, P. creates a fully conceived heroine of modern fiction. Mary reveals a strong affirmation of life as she steers between the restrictive mores of the community and her sense of freedom and selfhood. Mary's guiding principle is, "Everybody has a selfness that makes the root of his life and being." Like many of Eudora Welty's women characters, Mary, intelligent but uneducated, frequently articulates her emotions through metaphorical identifications with the natural world.

Bright Skin (1932) is a sensitive portrayal of the developing relationship of a boy and girl as they mature.

Roll, Jordan Roll (1933) is P.'s commentary on photographs of blacks at Lang Syne. In this book, P. loses her artistic objectivity and becomes somewhat nostalgic. Interestingly, Doris Ullman's photographs capture much of the dignity and realism that is portrayed in P.'s fiction. In *A Plantation Christmas* (1934), P. seems overwhelmed by a sense of the past, and although there are fine descriptions, the total effect is local color for its own sake, nostalgic and sentimental. These two books are weakened by the presence of a white narrator; in P.'s best works, all the characters are black and events are viewed entirely through their eyes.

Though P. lived and wrote in isolation from the literary world, she was helped and encouraged by many literary figures who praised her economy of style, detachment, and compassion. P.'s characters live in an isolated but believable society in which folk beliefs and folk wisdom aid them in the struggle between personal responsibility and fate. Their lives reveal the drama and dignity of the ordinary events of life.

WORKS: *Green Thursday* (1924). *Black April* (1927). *Scarlet Sister Mary* (1928). *Bright Skin* (1932). *Roll, Jordan Roll* (with D. Ulmann, 1933). *A Plantation Christmas* (1934). *The Collected Short Stories of Julia Peterkin* (Ed. F. Durham, 1970).

BIBLIOGRAPHY: Clark, E., *Innocence Abroad* (1931). Davidson, D., in *The Spyglass: Views and Reviews, 1924–1930*, Ed. J. Fain (1963). Durham, F., Introduction to *The Collected Short Stories of Julia Peterkin* (1970). Landers, T. H., *Julia Peterkin* (1976).
Other references: *NYHT* (17 Jan. 1933).

ANNE NEWMAN

Ann Lane Petry

B. *12 Oct. 1908, Old Saybrook, Connecticut*
Writes under: Ann Petry
D. *of Peter Clark and Bertha James Lane; m. George D. Petry, 1938*

P. was born into a poor black family of Old Saybrook, Connecticut, a predominantly white New England community. Her father was the local druggist. After receiving her Ph.G. in 1931 from the University of Connecticut, P. returned home to work as a pharmacist in the family drugstores from 1931 to 1938. In 1938, she married Petry (they have one daughter) and moved to New York City, becoming an advertising salesperson and writer for the *Amsterdam News* (1938–41), and then reporter and woman's-page editor for the rival *People's Voice* of Harlem (1941–44). P. was also a member of the American Negro Theater and wrote children's plays.

P. studied creative writing at Columbia University from 1944 to 1946 and published her first short stories in *The Crisis* and *Phylon*. In addition to writing, P. has lectured at Berkeley, Miami University, and Suffolk University, and was a visiting professor of English at the University of Hawaii (1974–75).

After P. had served her literary apprenticeship as a journalist, she began to publish short stories. "Like a Winding Sheet" was reprinted in *Foley's Best American Short Stories of 1946*, and another story led to a Houghton Mifflin Literary Fellowship, under which P. completed her first novel, *The Street* (1946). *The Street* is a naturalistic novel usually associated with the Wright school of protest fiction. The protagonist, Lutie Johnson, imbued with the American success ethic of Benjamin Franklin, is defeated in her attempts to improve her life by the detrimental influences of Harlem. Critics see the novel as gripping yet simplistic.

Country Place (1947) is an "assimilationist" novel set in the small town of Lennox, Connecticut. The major characters are white, and are enmeshed in a plot and setting reminiscent of a cross between *Winesburg, Ohio* and *Peyton Place*, as an apocalyptic autumn storm brings out the true natures of the townspeople. *Country Place* is considered P.'s most successful novel in scope and use of symbol and metaphor to parallel action and evoke character. The plot is unified and the prose clear and powerful.

The Narrows (1953) demonstrates a return to the theme of race. The plot revolves around the classic love conflict between heroic black man and rich white woman. Link Williams, the protagonist, is a fine portrayal of a young black man, an orphan and possessor of a college degree who has chosen to tend bar in the hub of the Narrows, the black section of Monmouth, Connecticut, rather than become a member of the black bourgeoisie. *The Narrows* is simultaneously sophisticated and melodramatic, as brilliantly conceived characters outshine a standard plot.

The rest of P.'s opus consists of four juvenile books and a collection of short stories, *Miss Muriel, and Other Stories* (1971). "In Darkness and Confusion" concerns a poor black couple's way of coping with their son's mistreatment in a segregated army by participating in looting and property damage during the Harlem riot of August 1943. The well-wrought title story is semiautobiographical, told from the perspective of a twelve-year-old black girl. Set in the drugstore of a New England town, the story treats the loss of innocence that comes with a growing awareness of maturity.

P.'s fiction is of a fine quality. Her stories succeed better than her novels, although the novels certainly belong in the mainstream of American naturalism and realism. P.'s work has not yet received thorough treatment by literary critics.

WORKS: *The Street* (1947). *Country Place* (1947). *The Drugstore Cat* (1949). *The Narrows* (1953). *Harriet Tubman* (1955). *Tituba of Salem Village* (1964). *Legends of the Saints* (1970). *Miss Muriel, and Other Stories* (1971).

BIBLIOGRAPHY: Bone, R. A., *The Negro Novel in America* (1958; rev. ed., 1965). Royster, B. H., "The Ironic Vision of Four Black Women Novelists: A Study of the Novels of Jessie Fauset, Nella Larsen, Zora Neale Hurston, and Ann Petry" (Ph.D. diss., Emory Univ., 1975).

For articles in reference works, see: *CB* (March 1946). *Great Black Americans*, Eds. B. Richardson and W. A. Fahey (1976). *Twentieth Century Children's Writers*, Ed. D. L. Kirkpatrick (1978).

Other references: *Crisis* 53 (1946). *Crit* (Spring 1974). *NEQ* 47 (1974). *NYHT* (16 Aug. 1953). *Opportunity* 24 (1946). *SBL* (Fall 1975).

ANN RAYSON

Almira Hart Lincoln Phelps

B. *15 July 1793, Berlin, Connecticut; d. 15 July 1884, Baltimore, Maryland*
D. *of Samuel and Lydia Hensdale Hart; m. Samuel Lincoln, 1817;*
m. John Phelps, 1832

P. and her elder sister, Emma Hart Willard, shared a love for study, an aptitude for teaching, and a desire to improve the intellectual status of women. Close association with the pioneering Troy, New York, Female Seminary has made Emma more celebrated than her equally productive but more eclectic sister. P.'s early schooling was in Berlin, and she later studied at Middlebury and Pittsfield, Massachusetts.

After teaching for several years, P. married a Federalist editor. Left a widow with two small daughters in 1823, she returned to teaching and to writing to earn a family income. After joining Emma at the Troy Female Seminary, she studied science with Amos Eaton, a professor of natural science at nearby Rensselaer Institute. In 1832, P. remarried. She continued to write, and in 1838 her husband urged her to accept the principalship of a promising new seminary in West Chester, Pennsylvania. After brief administrations in Pennsylvania and at the Rahway,

New Jersey, Female Institute, P. headed the Patapsco Female Institute in Ellicott's Mills, Maryland, from 1841 to 1855.

An imaginative and successful educator, P. was also a prolific writer. Her first textbook, *Familiar Lectures on Botany* (1829), was her most original and useful. Botany was a popular subject, and P.'s text provided a middle ground between the conversational style of many books written for young ladies and the formal presentation of scientific principles designed for advanced students. Traditional in its reliance on the Linnean artificial classification system, the book provides diagrams and suggestions for study designed to engage the student's participation in learning; appendixes provide all necessary reference material, including a description of genera and species, a dictionary of terms, and a common-name index. Frequently revised and used widely in academies for boys and girls, the volume went through twenty-eight editions (275,000 copies) by 1872. There were eighteen editions of an abridged version, *Botany for Beginners* (1833). Moral observations, literary references, and history were combined with sound science in a text designed to develop specific skills while integrating student learning. The success of the botanical text led P. to write books on chemistry, natural philosophy, and geology; but these were more derivative in content and less popular. *Familiar Lectures on Chemistry*, for example, used similar teaching techniques, but a reliance on household examples circumscribed its audience, and borrowed material caused the book to lack cohesion.

Most of P.'s writing was intended to educate and elevate young women. P.'s stories were in the popular, melodramatic, and didactic mode of antebellum novels. *Caroline Westerley; or, The Young Traveler from Ohio* (1833) presents a series of letters from an older sister to a younger; it is a guide through the New England landscape, an educational commentary on topics from plant life to housing styles, and a moral analysis of people encountered. Sarah Josepha Hale's review found this story "a charming picture of a young girl, engaged in improvement, and finding happiness. . . ." P.'s two other novels held more drama but similar purposes. Both *Ida Norman; or, Trials and Their Uses* (1848) and *The Blue Ribbon Society; or, The School Girls' Rebellion* (1879) were presented chapter by chapter for evening discussion at Patapsco Institute and were later published.

As educator and writer, P. could not resist contemporary discussion about the purpose and nature of education for young women, whether in public addresses, journal articles, or books. Although a domestic feminist, P. did not advocate a curriculum to develop household skills, but stressed classical subjects as well as the sciences. Her *Lectures to Young Ladies* (1833) stressed the need to study widely and to discipline the mind. Discussions of morality became more common in later editions. *The Female Student* (1836) emphasized the value of study but also stressed the need for a good diet, proper exercise, and proper clothing. This volume, like *Lectures*, was published as part of the School Library series, under the sanction of the Massachusetts School Board. P. moved with the vanguard of women educational reformers of the mid–19th c.

After the Civil War, P. retired from teaching but continued to write for national journals. Some of her essays explored the fine arts. P. also dedicated her energy to opposing the woman suffrage movement, although she continued to advocate educational equality for women. P.'s ideas and leadership, so significant to her own generation, were often disregarded or even dismissed by the suffragists and co-educational reformers of the late 19th c. Herself the model of the self-determination she taught, P. helped establish the possibility for women's public and political roles.

WORKS: *Familiar Lectures on Botany* (1829). *Address on the Subject of Female Education in Greece and the General Extension of Christian Intercourse among Females* (1831). *The Child's Geology* (1832). *Botany for Beginners* (1833). *Caroline Westerley; or, The Young Traveler from Ohio* (1833). *Lectures to Young Ladies* (1833). *Chemistry for Beginners* (1834). *The Female Student; or, Lectures to Young Ladies on Female Education* (1836; republished as *The Fireside Friend*, 1840). *Familiar Lectures on Natural Philosophy* (1837). *Lectures in Chemistry for the Use of Schools, Families, and Private Students* (1838). *Natural Philosophy for Beginners* (1838). *Ida Norman; or, Trials and Their Uses* (1848). *Christian Households* (1858). *Hours with My Pupils* (1859; republished as *The Educator*, 1868). *Foreign Correspondence in Relation to the Rebellion in the United States* (1863). *Our Country, in Its Relations to the Past, Present, and Future* (edited by Phelps, 1864). *Reviews and Essays on Art, Literature, and Science* (1873). *Women's Duties and Rights, the Woman's Congress: An Address to the Women of America* (1876). *The Blue Ribbon Society; or, The School Girls' Rebellion* (1879).

BIBLIOGRAPHY: Bolzau, E. L., *Almira Hart Lincoln Phelps: Her Life and Work* (1936). Lutz, A., *Emma Willard: Daughter of Democracy* (1929). Woody, T., *A History of Women's Education in the United States* (2 vols., 1929).

For articles in reference works, see: *DAB*, VII, 2. *NAW* (article by F. Rudolph). *NCAB*, 11.

SALLY GREGORY KOHLSTEDT

Elizabeth Stuart Phelps

B. 13 Aug. 1815, Andover, Massachusetts; d. 29 Nov. 1852, Andover, Massachusetts
Wrote under: E. S. Phelps, H. Trusta
D. of Moses and Abigail Clark Stuart; m. Austin Phelps, 1842

P.'s mother was a long-term invalid and her father a clergyman and professor of Greek and Hebrew literature at Andover Theological Seminary. At age ten, P. began to compose tales to amuse family and servants.

P. was educated at Abbot Academy in Andover. At age sixteen, she went to live in Boston with the Reverend Jacob Abbott, author of the juvenile Rollo series, and attended the Mount Vernon School. P.'s first publications—brief articles written over the name "H. Trusta," an anagram of "Stuart"—appeared in a religious magazine edited by Abbott. According to P.'s husband, P.'s early literary ambition was to gain her father's approval. By 1834, P. was beginning to suffer from a "cerebral disease" characterized by headache, partial blindness, and temporary paralysis. When P. began to write, her health improved, although she was never again "for any long time" without symptoms of disease.

P.'s daughter, who became a successful author writing under her mother's name, was born in 1844. P.'s father died in January 1852. She herself followed within eleven months, never fully recovering from the birth in August of her second son.

P. wrote newspaper and magazine articles as well as children's books, the latter published anonymously and later not identifiable even by P. After her marriage, P. kept a "Family Journal" as well as journals of her children's lives. She reviewed contemporary books and continued to write for children as well as older readers. From the late 1840s until her death in 1852, P. wrote five juvenile books, two collections of short fiction, and two novels.

P.'s husband located one of the strong motivations for P.'s juvenile writing in her childhood sleeplessness from a deep fear of death. Finding in children's Sunday-school literature an association of "early piety with the necessity of an early death," P. wished to provide a counter to such association in the depiction of "religious principle as it is in *life*." From 1851 to 1853, P.'s four "Kitty Brown" books appeared. In *Little Kitty*

Brown and Her Bible Verses (1851), anecdotes demonstrate to a juvenile reader the behavioral correlates of various biblical dicta. These highly didactic tales present numerous realistic details from everyday living. *Little Mary; or, Talks and Tales for Children* (1854) was probably written for P.'s own children.

All of P.'s short writings point clear morals, but they demonstrate a literary advance over P.'s juvenilia, first by leaving morals implied and second by achieving greater realism from increased attention to the documentation of daily life. *The Angel over the Right Shoulder* (1852), one of P.'s best works, describes the daily round of duties expected of a mother, develops the mother's deep concern for the future of her daughter, and reveals the conflict existing between these expectations and a woman's need to "cultivate her own mind and heart." P.'s two posthumously published collections consider a range of topics. *The Tell-Tale* (1853) includes six sketches concerning marital relationships, and one each about the relationships between father and daughter and between older women and younger women, as well as a satiric view of celebrating July 4th.

P.'s two anonymous novels sold well. *The Sunny Side; or, The Country Minister's Wife* (1851) received international recognition and by P.'s death claimed 300,000 to 500,000 readers. *A Peep at "Number Five"; or, A Chapter in the Life of a City Pastor* (1852), a partially autobiographical fiction and P.s favorite, sold 20,000 copies in less than one year. *The Sunny Side* first brought to P. renown as an author. The book follows Emily Edwards from wedding through marriage and motherhood to funeral, detailing her domestic and familial trials and triumphs. Undoubtedly the popularity of this book comes from its sympathetic and realistic presentation of a woman's daily life. *A Peep at "Number Five"* delineates the burdened life of Lucy Holbrook, who for the six years of the novel must meet parishioners' expectations at the expense of her own needs, but who nonetheless is relieved that her husband declines a call to a more prestigious position in favor of their remaining within the city parish. In both novels, P. presents a detailed view of a 19th-c. minister's household as seen through the eyes of his wife, and thus demonstrates the wife's excessive burdens and need for relief.

In her best work, P. depended little upon imaginative fabrication and largely upon meticulous observation. Along with her Andover neighbor Harriet Beecher Stowe, P. must be counted among the earliest depicters of the New England scene. She wrote at the beginning of the transition of American women's writing from domestic sentimentality to regional realism.

WORKS: *Little Kitty Brown and Her Bible Verses* (1851). *The Sunny Side; or, The Country Minister's Wife* (1851). *The Angel over the Right Shoulder* (1852). *Kitty Brown and Her City Cousins* (1852). *Kitty Brown and Her Little School* (1852). *A Peep at "Number Five"; or, A Chapter in the Life of a City Pastor* (1852). *Kitty Brown Beginning to Think* (1853). *The Last Leaf from Sunny Side* (1853). *The Tell-Tale; or, Home Secrets Told by Old Travellers* (1853). *Little Mary; or, Talks and Tales for Children* (1854).

BIBLIOGRAPHY: Hart, J. D., *The Popular Book* (1950). Kessler, C. F., "'The Woman's Hour': Life and Novels of Elizabeth Stuart Phelps, 1844–1911" (Ph.D. diss., Univ. of Pennsylvania, 1977). McKeen, P., and P. McKeen, *Annals of Fifty Years: A History of Abbot Academy* (1880). Phelps, A., "Memorial of the Author" in *The Last Leaf from Sunny Side* (1853). Robbins, S. S., *Old Andover Days: Memories of a Puritan Childhood* (1909). Ward, E. S. P., *Austin Phelps: A Memoir* (1891). Ward, E. S. P., *Chapters from a Life* (1896).

For articles in reference works, see: *AA. CAL. DAB*, X, 1. *NAW* (article by O. E. Winslow). *NCAB*, 9.

Other references: *Frontiers: A Journal of Women Studies* (1976; 1980).

CAROL FARLEY KESSLER

Josephine Lyons Scott Pinckney

B. 25 Jan. 1895, Charleston, South Carolina; d. 4 Oct. 1957, New York City
Wrote under: Josephine Pinckney
D. of Thomas and Camilla Scott Pinckney

P.'s Charleston heritage is evident in most of her writing. During the 1920s, she was active in the Poetry Society of South Carolina, which she helped to found; she was also one of its leading poets. Some of P.'s work was published in *Poetry* before she gathered it together in *Sea-Drinking Cities* (1927).

P.'s poetry skillfully evokes scenes and moods of the Carolina Low Country; at times, however, it tends to be artificial and contrived. Realizing her limitations, P. soon turned to writing prose fiction. During the 1930s, P. published short stories in some of the better literary magazines.

Hilton Head (1941) is a fictionalized account of the life of Henry Woodward, one of the first English settlers of South Carolina. P.'s research into Woodward's life and into the Indian and Spanish, as well as early English, settlements of the period was painstaking. The prose style is at times marred by P.'s background as a poet of the imagist school, producing descriptions with the quality of stiff brocade. The major flaw is P.'s failure to dramatize the complex actions she presents. The novel's best passages are those which describe landscapes and personal interactions.

P. realized her inability to dramatize action, and in *Three O'Clock Dinner* (1945) she found a genuine fictional mode in the novel of manners, especially the manners of Charleston. A Literary Guild selection, this was the most popular of P.'s works and perhaps her best. Set in early 20th-c. Charleston, the story is of the inroads made by the daughter of a German immigrant family into one of the bastions of Charleston aristocracy, the Redcliff family. Although the girl fails to breech the family bulwark, she does shake and weaken its foundations. P.'s skillful description of Charleston manners displays both the charms and shortcomings of her characters, and she retains the ability to capture the scenery and moods of her native city.

Charleston is also the setting for *Great Mischief* (1948), but here it is the Charleston of the late 19th c. In addition to her careful research on the period, P. explores the superstitions of the time and includes a historically accurate account of 19th-c. witchcraft. These elements are woven together so skillfully that the line between fantasy and reality is blurred not only for the characters but also for the readers. The night of the witches' sabbath coincides with the great Charleston earthquake of 1886 so that both the main character and the reader are left to wonder if the witching was real or merely a dream.

In *My Son and Foe* (1952), P. abandons the Charleston setting to study the interactions of her characters in the crucible of a small, remote Caribbean island—interactions of love and jealousy, good and evil.

P. returned to a Charleston setting with *Splendid in Ashes* (1958). She chronicles the feelings of a generation of Charlestonians about the life and times of Augustus Grimshawe, recently deceased. Grimshawe's career and personality, as well as the personalities of those with whom he came into contact, are revealed as the characters react to the news of his death. P. ties the past to the present with a skillful combination of reminiscence and flashback.

P.'s first two books are the works of a literary novice. With her third book, P. found herself and became not only a writer with popular appeal but also a skillful delineator of the manners of the rigid Charlestonian society she knew so well. In her best novels, P. reveals the Charlestonian mind with wit and ironic humor.

WORKS: *Sea-Drinking Cities* (1927). *Hilton Head* (1941). *Three O'Clock Dinner* (1945). *Great Mischief* (1948). *My Son and Foe* (1952). *Splendid in Ashes* (1958).

BIBLIOGRAPHY: Davidson, D., *The Spyglass: Views and Reviews* (1963).
For articles in reference works, see: *American Novelists of Today*, H. R. Warfel (1951). *20thCAS*.
Other references: *NYHTBR* (20 Jan. 1952). *NYTBR* (23 Sept. 1945; 21 March 1948; 4 May 1958).

HARRIETTE CUTTINO BUCHANAN

Sylvia Plath

B. 27 Oct. 1932, Boston, Massachusetts; d. 11 Feb. 1963, London, England
Wrote under: Victoria Lucas, Sandra Peters, Sylvia Plath
D. of Otto Emil and Aurelia Schober Plath; m. Ted Hughes, 1956

P.'s father emigrated from the Polish corridor and became a biologist at Boston University; her mother, also a German immigrant, taught high-school English. P. was instilled with an achievement ethic which fueled her precocious talent for writing and drawing.

The facts of P.'s biography directly inform her writing, especially her idyllic yet menaced childhood by the sea, which ended abruptly with her father's death when P. was eight. His death, its dramatic circumstances, and the ensuing move inland to Wellesley affected P. profoundly. Writing poetry became "a new way of being happy." Sea, father, and childhood became a haunting amalgam of loss.

P.'s legend as superachiever began early. By the time she won a scholarship to Smith (1950), P. had drawings, poems, and stories in national publications, including *Seventeen*. Maintaining her momentum at Smith with school honors and steady publication, she won *Mademoiselle*'s College Fiction Contest, was named Guest Editor ("the literary woman's 'Miss America' "), and in June 1953 was initiated to "Mad"-ison Avenue.

Exhausted, demoralized, and at odds with her hard-won image as the all-American girl, P. had a mental breakdown and attempted suicide. After psychiatric treatment she returned to Smith, graduating summa cum laude (1955), again winning top awards and also a Fulbright to Cambridge for graduate work.

During her two years at Cambridge, P. married Hughes, a poet. Returning to Smith as English professor, she found the conflict between teaching and writing untenable. After another year attending Robert Lowell's poetry seminar and Yaddo, P. made her life in England, immersing herself in writing, Devon country life, and motherhood.

Worn down by competing pressures of motherhood and muse, chronic ill health, a cold winter, a failed marriage, and recurrent depression, P. gassed herself at the age of thirty-one.

In her apprentice work, P. submerges her specific concerns about identity, creation, death, and muse beneath detached, synthetic, allusive pieces on nature and art. P.'s early poems attest to her control, not only over form but over the emotion it contains. Her middle poems are best represented by *The Colossus* (1960), which spans her college, breakdown, scholar, and marriage phases of development. Painstakingly wrought, word by well-chosen word, the clenched poems elicit admiration for their mature technical virtuosity, and criticism (shared by P.) for their elaborate "checks and courtesies," "maddening docility," and "deflections."

Three Women: A Monologue for Three Voices (1962) is a transitional, formative work. Always obsessed by, and ambivalent about, female creativity, P. now presents her Darwinian value system: the mother is victor, for *she* produces, while the Girl and the Secretary are "empty," "restless and useless," creating "corpses." The three voices represent P.'s consciousness of her role conflict as artist, wife, and mother. The radio-play format opens up her style. After this, her poetry is dramatic rather than narrative or expository, written "all of one piece," to be read aloud; its imperfect cadences, careless-seeming rhymes, and impression of spontaneity and free association underlie P.'s new aesthetics, which demand of the poems that they be "possessed . . . as by the rhythms of their own breathing."

The poems in *Ariel* (1965), *Crossing the Water* (1971), and *Winter Trees* (1971) are the culmination of themes and images of P.'s previous works. They are different only in degree—"extremist" in their profound disillusionment in her idealized marriage and the "years of doubleness, smiles, and compromise." P. releases her long-suppressed rage and is, at the same time, disconcertingly gleeful and triumphant, gaily macabre, and erotically murderous. Vitality, not iambics, produces the rhythm, and the half, slanted rhymes sound like a drunk's.

While the poems appear autobiographical and private in imagery (the "toe" of "Daddy," one of P.'s best-known poems, refers to her father's amputated foot) and bare of artifice, years of practice with form and poetics underlie these outbursts, and the literal concrete metaphors universalize the meaning.

P.'s fiction contains the same preoccupation with her own experience, but it never loosens control as in her breakthrough poetry and hence never assumes the poetry's powerful voice. It was written throughout P.'s career, largely for the commercial market. Yet in these manufactured stories, with their studied moralistic formulas, P. gives candid expression to her own anxieties. In "The Fifty-ninth Bear," she projects a wife's canny hostility to her husband. "Den of Lions" reveals the Plathian voice at its best, where the persona is "game," wryly humorous, and self-deprecating about her traumas.

The engaging narrator of "Den of Lions" turns up again in *The Bell Jar* (1963), P.'s autobiographical novel about her mental breakdown. Again, disillusionment fuels the criticism P. now levels about growing up female in middle-class America. P.'s approach is satiric; the world's injustice is more absurd than evil. The heroine's summer on "Mad" Avenue is an initiation ritual into "the real world," which turns out to be a disillusioning joke. P.'s refusal to moralize and her naive insistence on the private nature of her vision effectively result in a moving book with tragic and universal overtones.

Her earnest effort to conform as woman and artist led to P.'s breakdown. As P. herself disengages the gagging mask of pleasing, pleased normalcy, her literature devolves from its disguised interest in landscapes and events to the subject of raw, terrifying self released from the pretense of objectivity: "Peel off the napkin / O my enemy. / Do I terrify?" ("Lady Lazarus"). Accompanying the unmasking of the subject is the conversion of duty-bound literary behavior to the exuberant anarchies of a released prisoner of style.

WORKS: *The Colossus* (1960). *A Winter Ship* (1960). *American Poetry Now* (edited by Plath, 1961). *The Bell Jar* (1963; film version, 1979). *Ariel* (1965). *Uncollected Poems* (1965). *Three Women: A Monologue for Three Voices* (1968; BBC television broadcast, 1962). *Crossing the Water* (1971). *Crystal Gazer* (1971). *Fiesta Melons* (1971). *Lyonesse* (1971). *Winter Trees* (1971). *Pursuit* (introduction by T. Hughes, 1973). *Letters Home: Correspondence 1950–1963* (edited by A. S. Plath, 1975). *The Bed Book* (1976). *Johnny*

Panic and the Bible of Dreams, and Other Prose Writings (edited by T. Hughes, 1978). *The Collected Poems* (Ed. T. Hughes, 1981).

The Sylvia Plath collection is at the Lilly Library, Bloomington, Indiana.

BIBLIOGRAPHY: Aird, E., *Sylvia Plath: Her Life and Work* (1973). Alvarez, A., *The Savage God* (1971). Butscher, E., *Sylvia Plath: Method and Madness* (1976). Butscher, E., ed., *Sylvia Plath, The Woman and Her Work* (1977). Gilbert, S. M., in *Shakespeare's Sisters*, Eds. Sandra M. Gilbert and Susan Gubar (1979). Howard, R., in *Alone With America: Essays on the Art of Poetry in the United Statest Since 1950* (1969). Kroll, J., *Chapters in a Mythology: The Poetry of Sylvia Plath* (1976). Lane, G., and M. Stevens, *Sylvia Plath: A Bibliography* (1978). Newman, C., ed., *The Art of Sylvia Plath: A Symposium* (1970). Rosenthal, M. C., "Confessional Poets" in *The New Poetry* (1975). Steiner, G., *Language and Silence* (1969).

For articles in reference works, see: Crowell's *Handbook of Contemporary American Poetry*, Ed. Karl Malkoff (1973). *WA*.

Other references: *London Magazine* (Feb. 1962). *Mademoiselle* (July 1975). *Ms.* (October 1975). *Southern Review* (Summer 1973).

BARBARA ANTONINA CLARKE MOSSBERG

Eleanor Hodgman Porter

B. 1868, Littleton, New Hampshire; d. 23 May 1920
Wrote under: Eleanor Stewart
D. of Francis H. and Llewella Woolson Hodgman; m. John Lyman Porter, 1892

When P. died, the headline of her brief obituary in *The New York Times* read simply: "Author of *Pollyanna* dies." P. had written four volumes of short stories and fourteen novels, but it was the phenomenal success of *Pollyanna* that had made her famous.

P. dropped out of high school to lead a more robust outdoor life. Later she studied music at the New England Conservatory in Boston, going on to make public appearances as a singer and traveling with church choirs. In 1892, P. married a businessman. Switching her profession from music to writing, P. began to submit stories to magazines, at first with little success, but finally with the publication of her novel *Cross Currents* (1907) the tide began to turn. P. wrote a sequel in 1908 called *The Turn of the Tide*. An even more significant turning point was reached in 1913, when *Pollyanna* appeared, an event described by one commentator as "only less influential than the World War."

Pollyanna, that incredibly cheerful champion of the Glad Game, who could find in even the grimmest situation something to be glad about (if you break a leg, "be glad 'twasn't two"), stirred the hearts and hopes of people of all ages all over the world. After selling a million copies in this country, the book appeared in editions in France, Germany, Holland, Poland, Czechoslovakia, Norway, Sweden, Switzerland, Scotland, and Japan.

Critics sang *Pollyanna*'s praises: "It is a wholesome, charming book, moral but not preachy," said the popular *Literary Digest*. The *Bookman* earnestly agreed: "If the *Pollyanna* books are read with the sympathetic comprehension they deserve, many a child's life will be made happier. . . ." With this end in view, Glad Clubs sprang up everywhere—and not just for children. One branch, "The Pollyanna Glad Kids," was started by inmates of a penitentiary. Mary Pickford paid the then astronomical fee of $115,112 for the silent screen rights for *Pollyanna*.

Although P. won instant celebrity, she was not thereby admitted to the ranks of serious authors. A growing number of readers irked by the sentimental and simplistic outlook would join in Aunt Polly's exasperated demand that Pollyanna "stop using that everlasting word. . . . It's 'glad'—'glad'—'glad'—from morning till night until I think I shall go wild." In a recent survey of girl's fiction, the authors dismiss Pollyanna as hopelessly "puerile" and "intellectually debilitating," her "imbecile cheerfulness" issuing from stupidity and an infuriating tactlessness, especially when she tells a chronic invalid to be glad other folks aren't like her—"all sick, you know"; or when she tells the elderly gardener, bent with arthritis, to be glad he doesn't have to stoop so far to do his weeding.

Some critics claim that P.'s later writing was not as relentlessly cheerful as her earlier works, but evidence provided by the posthumously published *Hustler Joe, and Other Stories* (1970) indicates otherwise. In each of the stories a downbeat plot works itself miraculously into an upbeat ending. Hustler Joe, for instance, who shoots his father in the opening chapter, discovers in the closing chapter that the bullet didn't kill him after all.

When accused of being overly optimistic, P. was quoted as saying, "I have never believed that we ought to deny discomfort and pain and evil. I have merely thought that it is far better to greet the unknown with a cheer." That she did, and—despite her critics—there are readers of Pollyanna even today who are still cheering.

WORKS: *Cross Currents* (1907). *The Turn of the Tide* (1908). *Miss Billy* (1911). *The Story of Marco* (1911). *Miss Billy's Decision* (1912). *Pollyanna* (1913). *Miss Billy Married* (1914). *Pollyanna Grows Up* (1915). *Just David* (1916). *The Road of Understanding* (1917). *Oh Money! Money!* (1918). *Dawn* (1919). *May-Marie* (1919). *Sister Sue* (1921). *The Tie that Binds: Tales of Love and Marriage* (1924). *Across the Years* (1924). *Money, Love, and Kate* (1924). *The Tangled Threads* (1924). *Hustler Joe, and Other Stories* (1970).

BIBLIOGRAPHY: Cadogan, M., and P, Craig, *You're a Brick, Angela! A New Look at Girls' Fiction from 1839–1975* (1976). Overton, G., *The Women Who Make Our Novels* (1918).

For articles in reference works, see: *20thCA.*

Other references: *Bookman* (60, 1914; 61, 1915; 63, 1916). *Good House-keeping* (July 1947). *PW* (19 July 1941). *Woman's Home Companion* (April 1920).

JACQUELINE BERKE

Katherine Anne Porter

B. 15 May 1890, Indian Creek, Texas; d. 18 Sept. 1980, Silver Spring, Maryland
D. of Harrison Boone and Mary Alice Jones Porter; m. ?, 1906; m. Eugene
  Dove Pressly, 1933; m. Albert Russel Erskine, Jr., 1938

P. was the fourth of five children, a descendant of pioneers. Her mother died as a young woman, and P. was raised by her father and paternal grandmother.

Although P. is generally acknowledged to be a master stylist, she rarely earned her living directly through her writing. Instead, she supported herself through a variety of related activities: as a reporter, writer of screenplays in Hollywood, translator, hack writer, and most often, as a lecturer, writer-in-residence, and guest speaker. She received a number of honorary degrees and an impressive range of prestigious literary awards, including Guggenheim fellowships in 1931 and 1938, Fulbright and Ford Foundation grants in the 1950s, an O. Henry Award in 1962, and the Pulitzer Prize in 1966 for her *Collected Stories* (1965).

P. traveled extensively, living often in Europe and Mexico; was married three times; and involved herself in political events. Yet these activities are only peripherally reflected in her stories. P. makes a clear distinction between *adventure*, something you do to find an "illusion of being more alive than ordinarily," and *experience*, which is "what really happens to you in the long run; the truth that finally overtakes you." The latter is the subject of P.'s prose. She delights in revealing through microcosmic events truths about human nature.

"The Downward Path to Wisdom" (*The Leaning Tower, and Other Stories*, 1944) is a pivotal story in understanding the etiology of disillusionment in P.'s work. The protagonist, a child named Stephen, is shuffled from adult to adult in an awkward and futile attempt to keep him unaware of his parents' quarreling. P. emphasizes Stephen's genuineness by continually alluding to his sensual awareness of being warm, bare, embraced, sticky, scrubbed roughly, etc. In contrast, P. shows us, through the overheard dialogue of the parents, that they experience him simply as a reminder of their growing antipathy. She deftly controls the emergence of Stephen's final decision to set himself emotionally apart from these people who "love" him by juxtaposing the child's motives with the adults' harsh judgments of him. Stephen's final rejection of them seems healthy, yet P. manages to convey that the act of rejection forecasts Stephen's own inability to love as an adult.

Some of P.'s best stories reflect the deterioration of relationships, especially of marriages, which are corrupted by the bitterness and anger accompanying dependence. P. has said that one's spouse is a "necessary enemy," for whom we cannot help but feel both love and hate because we resent our need for him or her. P. characterizes one such marriage in "Rope" (*Flowering Judas, and Other Stories*, 1930). The husband and wife quarrel over his purchase of some unneeded rope, and their discussion evolves into a destructive verbal battle about the entire relationship and their disappointments in one another.

P.'s portraits of relationships ring true because she has a perfect eye for the tiny, telling domestic detail. Time and again, a single incident conveys the character of an entire relationship. In "Noon Wine" (*Pale Horse, Pale Rider*, 1939), Mr. Thompson affectionately yet cruelly pinches his wife Ellie, and we are introduced to those notions about himself, his intense, masculine pride, that will make Mr. Thompson capable of killing a man later in the story. "Noon Wine" is a study of sources of violence and self-betrayal in essentially good people.

The disappointments that grow between people are evident in both men and women in P.'s stories, but perhaps because her own awareness is based so firmly in feminine realities, P. is especially effective in depicting the limitations in relationships as women experience them, or rather, the limiting relationships that she saw as the only ones allowed to women. In stories based around the experiences of Miranda (the character who seems most similar to P.), Miranda's grandmother (based on P.'s grandmother), and others, P. implies that for a woman the rejection of close and demanding relationships is virtually the only means of finding autonomy.

For all of P.'s thoughtful characters, life involves introspection, disappointment, and moral dilemmas. If her characters (like her married couples) stay in their oppressive relationships, resentment eats away at them. If they break free, they are terribly alone. It is not surprising that P. projects onto her primitive characters—such as the eponymous Mexican Indian in the story "María Concepción" (*Flowering Judas*) and the Spanish dancers in *Ship of Fools* (1962)—the very strengths which she believes introspective people cannot achieve: a passionate, unselfconscious, unquestioning spontaneity that carries with it no moral complications.

Ship of Fools, P.'s long-awaited novel, appeared in 1962. P. was deeply shaken by the two world wars and by world events that for decades threatened the human race with catastrophe. She tells us that much of her energy in those years was given to an attempt "to grasp the meaning of those threats, to trace them to their sources and to understand the logic of this majestic and terrible failure of the life of man in the Western world." P.'s allegorical novel became an exploration into the possible sources of human evil and particularly into the states of mind which could account for such horrors as the Holocaust.

The story takes place on a German freighter-passenger ship traveling from Veracruz, Mexico, to Bremerhaven, Germany, in late summer of 1931, with a passenger list representing various nationalities. To the degree that the characters become stereotypes for particular countries, the novel seems a failure, for its ironies are heavy-handed and the notes of prophecy seem contrived, written as they were long after World War II. But on the level of individual human encounters, P.'s portrayals are meticulous, vivid, and often engrossing. In depicting a range of individuals preoccupied with their narrow personal concerns, she shows acute perception of how we tend to blind ourselves to external realities and become culpable in evil events.

Ultimately, the pleasures we find in reading P.'s stories prove to be subtle ones: the frequent perfection of her choice of words and details and commentary on a character's behavior; the telling scenes; the recognitions about human nature; the ironic narrative; and P.'s understanding of the pleasures of childhood (always being crushed by somber adult realities), of the stories we tell ourselves to make our lives make sense, of the self-delusions, self-betrayals, and ultimate isolation of each of us. Her perceptions are acute, and her prose is often superb. P. severely limited the number of stories she would allow to be published, yet her choices seem to have been wise ones, for they offer us a surprisingly consistent vitality in their revelation of human truths.

WORKS: *Outline of Mexican Popular Arts and Crafts* (1922). *Flowering Judas, and Other Stories* (1930; republished with added stories, 1935). *Katherine Anne Porter's French Song Book* (1933). *Hacienda: A Story of Mexico* (1934). *Noon Wine* (1937). *Pale Horse, Pale Rider: Three Short Novels* (1939). *The Itching Parrot* (1942). *The Leaning Tower, and Other Stories* (1944). *The Old Order: Stories of the South* (1944). *The Days Before* (1952). *A Defense of Circe* (1955). *Holiday* (1962). *Ship of Fools* (1962). *The Collected Stories of Katherine Anne Porter* (1965). *A Christmas Story* (1967). *The Collected Essays and Occasional Writings of Katherine Anne Porter* (1970).

BIBLIOGRAPHY: Auchincloss, L., *Pioneers and Caretakers: A Study of Nine American Women Writers* (1965). Emmons, W. S., *Katherine Anne Porter: The Regional Stories* (1967). Hardy, J. E., *Katherine Anne Porter* (1973). Hartley, L., and G. Core, eds., *Katherine Anne Porter: A Critical Symposium* (1969). Hendrick, G., *Katherine Anne Porter* (1965). Kiernan, R. F., *Katherine Anne Porter and Carson McCullers: A Reference Guide* (1976). Krishnamurthi, M. G., *Katherine Anne Porter: A Study* (1971). Liberman, M. M., *Katherine Anne Porter's Fiction* (1971). Mooney, H. J., Jr., *The Fiction and Criticism of Katherine Anne Porter* (1962). Nance, W. L., *Katherine Anne Porter and the Art of Rejection* (1964). Waldrip, L., and S. A. Bauer, eds., *A Bibliography of the Works of Katherine Anne Porter, and A Bibliography of the Criticism of the Works of Katherine Anne Porter* (1969). Wescott, G., "Katherine Anne Porter, Personally," *Images of Truth: Remembrances and Criticism* (1962). West, R. B., Jr., *Katherine Anne Porter* (1963).

GAIL MORTIMER

Rose Porter

B. 6 Dec. 1845, New York City; d. 10 Sept. 1906, New Haven, Connecticut
D. of David and Rose Anne Hardy Porter

The author or editor of more than seventy books on religious themes, P. was descended from New England clergymen. Her father was a prosperous businessman and her mother an upper-class Englishwoman. P. attended a New York City private school and spent time in England. After her parents' deaths, she became a semiinvalid and lived alone in New Haven.

Besides her fifteen novels and her volumes of religious essays, P. produced devotional exercises; anthologies of consolatory verse, such as *Hope Songs* (1885) and *Comfort for the Mothers of Angels* (1881); prayer books for the sick, such as *In the Shadow of His Hand* (1892); and collections of texts from literature and scripture arranged on calendars or diaries. P. also edited selections from many poets.

Her first success was *Summer Driftwood for the Winter Fire* (1870). Presented as the diary of a nineteen-year-old girl, the book records a summer's travel, during which she falls in love and her lover dies. But most of the pages are occupied by the girl's meditations about Ruskin, heaven, her dead mother, and the beauties of nature. At the end, she is consoled in her single life because she has found work helping orphans.

Most of P.'s novels are similar: calm, retrospective, meditative, and told without suspense or emotional tension. P. seldom created a villain or even a character with whom the hero or heroine might have serious conflict. When she did attempt novels with more plot, P. used the conventions of sentimental melodrama.

In *Foundations; or, Castles in the Air* (1871), Alfred Merwin leaves his widowed mother in the country and goes off to be a city merchant's clerk. He falls into temptation—stays home from church, goes to "places of amusement" (unspecified), and gambles—and the farm is mortgaged to pay his debts. Ultimately, his mother's faith saves him; he prospers, gives to charity, returns to church, and marries his childhood sweetheart. The action is omitted; we do not see his debauchery or even his confession to his mother, but are told about both much later.

The masochistic elements of victory through suffering are most clearly visible in *Uplands and Lowlands* (1872). After an idealized relationship with his mother, orphaned Paul Foster goes to Rome and paints a magnificent holy picture. Because he will do no crass commercial work, he starves to death. His genius, of course, is recognized as soon as he has died.

The devotional books make P.'s basically conservative theology explicit. Her God is not human and domesticated but other and unfathomable. P. emphasizes faith rather than works. Most importantly, she extols weakness and submission and suffering, which subdue the individual will and open the mind to God, and which are also particularly suitable for women. In *Life's Everydayness* (1893), P. praises the daily annoyances and petty discouragements of the household because they enable one constantly to deny self and to exercise passivity and renunciation. Sympathy is woman's special vocation; many days may be well spent doing nothing but attending to the interests of others. P. also finds it important to fight discontent; a woman should daily count her blessings and be happy with the people and circumstances around her.

P.'s writing gave theological support to a conception of woman as domestic, virtuous, passive, weak, devoted to the trivial, inculcating morality by example, enforcing obedience by suffering, and utterly unfit for any sphere beyond house walls. Reviewers praised P.'s novels for their purity; they were often included in series for young readers; and, to judge from the sheer number of titles, they must have had a fairly steady sale.

SELECTED WORKS: *Summer Driftwood for the Winter Fire* (1870). *Foundations; or, Castles in the Air* (1871). *Uplands and Lowlands* (1872). *The Winter Fire* (1874). *The Years That Are Told* (1875). *Christmas Evergreens* (1876). *A Song and a Sigh* (1877). *In the Mist* (1879). *Charity, Sweet Charity* (1880). *Comfort for the Mothers of Angels* (1881). *Our Saints: A Family Story* (1881). *The Story of a Flower* (1883). *Foregleams of Immortality* (1884). *Honoria; or, The Gospel of a Life* (1885). *Hope Songs* (1885). *A Modern Saint Christopher* (1887). *Driftings from Mid-Ocean* (1889). *Looking toward Sunrise* (1890). *Open Windows, a Heart-to-Heart Diary* (1890). *Saint Martin's Summer; or, The Romance of the Cliff* (1891). *Women's Thoughts for Women: A Calendar* (1891). *In the Shadow of His Hand* (1892). *Life's Everydayness: Papers for Women* (1893). *My Son's Wife* (1895). *One of the Sweet Old Chapters* (1896). *The Pilgrim's Staff* (1897). *A Daughter of Israel* (1899). *The Everlasting Harmony* (1900).

BIBLIOGRAPHY: For articles in reference works, see: *NCAB*, 10. *A Woman of the Century*, Eds. F. Willard and M. Livermore (1893).

Other references: *Harper's* (Sept. 1870; June 1871). *NYT* (11 July 1870).

SALLY MITCHELL

Sarah Porter

P. lived during the late 18th c. and probably the early 19th c. She was probably a resident of Plymouth, Massachusetts, and a member of either a Congregationalist or a Presbyterian church.

P.'s slender volume of published poetry, *The Royal Penitent, in Three Parts, to Which Is Added David's Lamentation over Saul and Jonathan* (1791), contains work of such quality and interest that it seems probable that she produced other works. This work reveals ambition and talent in its three hundred and fifty-two lines, which deal with David's guilt and repentance for his seduction of Bathsheba and betrayal of her husband, his loyal general, Uriah. P.'s handling of this subject includes not only religious but also political and social themes relevant to contemporary interests of late-18th-c. Americans. The structure and content indicate at least a passing familiarity with Dryden's *Absalom and Achitophel* and the American poet Timothy Dwight's epic, *The Conquest of Canaan*.

P.'s poem presents two major themes: the workings of divine providence and the necessity for morality in government. The poem particularly emphasizes the concept that a country is only as good (moral) as its leaders. A decadent ruling class subverts national morals. P.'s was not a very veiled criticism of the contemporary political situation in the U.S. in the decade after the revolutionary war. During those years, a major complaint of those who remained staunch republicans was that the government and the nation as a whole were being subverted from the high ideals of the revolutionary era. This "subversion" was a result of an influx of new wealth, followed by a vulgar taste for luxury. P. shows this type of moral decay through the example of King David as he remembers his humble beginnings, his rise to power, and his subsequent immoral behavior, the result of his lust for material possessions. Thus, David's downfall becomes a warning for P.'s compatriots about their politics.

P.'s poetic ambitions appear also in her choice of style and form. She exhibits a thorough understanding of neoclassical poetic techniques and evidently possessed the training and ability to employ them with success.

P. produced a heroic poem in which characters of great personal and historical stature act against a background of national events as the supernatural and natural worlds mingle. The narrative alternates between descriptive passages and dialogue, producing an effective variety.

Published along with the successful *Royal Penitent* is a short work, a paraphrase of David's lament for Saul and Jonathan (2 Samuel 1:17). Taking full advantage of the substance of her biblical model, P. uses the elegy to convey both religious and political themes. Using the Puritan concept of America as the new Israel, P. draws an implied analogy between the dead Hebrew heroes and the dead American revolutionary heroes, stressing the recurrent theme of late-18th-c. American literature—the necessity for national political unity in the face of anarchic and external incursions.

P. made important contributions to the broadening thematic materials in the poetry of American women. She enlarged the scope of women's poetry to encompass current political and ideological interests through the device of the contemporaneously popular heroic verse form.

WORKS: *The Royal Penitent, in Three Parts, to Which is Added David's Lamentation over Saul and Jonathan* (1791).

JACQUELINE HORNSTEIN

Emily Price Post

B. 3 Oct. 1873, Baltimore, Maryland; d. 25 Sept. 1960, New York City
Wrote under: Emily Post
D. of Bruce and Josephine Lee Price; m. Edwin Post, 1892

P. was a member of New York society, raised in the well-educated and proper atmosphere of Tuxedo Park. Her early career was prescribed by the conventions of upper-class leisure and manners: governesses, trips to Europe, private schooling, and debutante balls. After being divorced and then forced by economic stress to explore and expand upon her native talents, P. began her public life with interior decoration schemes. She wrote travelogues and a series of light novels of manners about Americans vacationing in Europe and associating with the Continental gentry.

P. soon expanded her scope and wrote about American standards of manners, mores, and taste in manuals of etiquette and home decor.

The original dean of modern American decorum, P. was the first in a line of inventive women writers of handbooks on etiquette and manners. She remains a key figure in setting the tone for civil behavior in a rapidly changing world of styles, relationships, and attitudes—a kaleidoscopic social scene of shifting patterns in class, money, taste, and mobility, intensified by the departure from 19th- and early 20th-c. "laws" of social procedure, which had long been relied on as fixed and permanent. The need for more relaxed and flexible standards of behavior suited to the millions of upwardly mobile Americans after World War I made P.'s *Etiquette: The Blue Book of Social Usage* (1922) an immediate and long-lived success.

P.'s name quickly became a household word for "proper" manners, even if in a new key. Ironically, the conventions of formality and civility now associated so firmly with her were heartily opposed in all P.'s analysis and advice, her most famous aphorism being, "Nothing is less important than which fork you use."

P.'s *Blue Book* was the most popular and influential book of etiquette by a woman of social standing since Mary Sherwood's *Manners and Social Usages* (1884). P.'s easy readability and practical approach to the myriad problems of interpersonal relations posed by the unfamiliar contexts of changing times have made the *Blue Book* a perennial best-seller. In recent years, more progressive works by younger writers have supplanted the *Blue Book*, but P.'s emphasis on the spirit rather than the letter of the law of manners has made the *Blue Book* adaptable to change, assuring it a lasting place as a reference statement in the field. For example, in the 1940s, a supplementary edition was devised to deal with the special circumstances of wartime.

The book's success led to a newspaper column and a radio broadcast series, as well as many requests for P.'s endorsement of food, drink, and household products. The formulations P. established for diplomatic protocol were adopted by Washington offices as a uniform code, and *The Personality of a House* (1930), used as a text in courses about taste and decoration, is further evidence of her strong feeling for atmosphere and the quality of life. This feel for style informs such other works as *Children Are People* (1940).

To P., it was obvious that simplicity and grace are the fundamental precepts of manners, and that there is an urgent need to state this principle in detail, dramatizing its application in every conceivable setting and circumstance. Her writing ushered in a new era, which thought about etiquette not as a fixed system of gestures and words but as an ever-changing rule of thumb, based on a much more open, democratic, and classless view of society with an active sense of mobility and impermanence. P.'s interpretation of etiquette as a "science of living" sets the terms of discussion later taken up and developed in the contemporary scene by a core of women social arbiters including Jean Kerr, Peg Bracken, Amy Vanderbilt, Abigail Van Buren, and Ann Landers.

WORKS: *The Flight of a Moth* (1904). *Purple and Fine Linen* (1906). *Woven in the Tapestry* (1908). *The Title Market* (1909). *The Eagle's Feather* (1910). *By Motor to the Golden Gate* (1915). *Etiquette: The Blue Book of Social Usage* (1922; rev. ed., 1955). *Parade* (1925). *How to Behave Though a Debutante* (1928). *The Personality of a House* (1930; rev. ed., 1948). *Children Are People* (1940). *Emily Post Institute Cook Book* (with E. M. Post, Jr., 1949). *Motor Manners* (1950).

BIBLIOGRAPHY: For articles in reference works, see: *CB* (1941).
    Other references: *AH* (April 1977). *NYT* (27 Sept. 1960).
                                                MARGARET J. KING

Mary Traill Spence Lowell Putnam

B. 3 Dec. 1810, Boston, Massachusetts; d. 1898, Boston, Massachusetts
Wrote under: M. L. P., Mary Lowell Putnam
D. of Charles and Harriet Brackett Spence Lowell; m. Samuel R. Putnam

P.'s mother imbued her Christian rectitude and love of learning in her children. Her father, a minister at West Church in Boston, was descended from Judge John Lowell, who was a member of the Continental Congress and a district and circuit court judge. Judge Lowell's benevolence toward black people, the family's proud New England heritage, and a fervent Christian faith are all reflected in P.'s work.

P. is noted for translating Fredrika Bremer's play, *The Bondmaid*, from Swedish (1844). Her fluency in French, coupled with her voracious reading, allowed P. to take on the editor of the *North American Review*, Francis Bowen, who had sharply criticized Kossuth and the Magyars after their revolution. In two essays in the *Christian Examiner* P. shreds Bowen's articles, taking them line by line and proving their inaccuracy and bad logic.

P.'s four chief works, all published anonymously and centered on the issue of slavery, are told from the vantage point of Edward Colvil, a New England farmer-poet transplanted to the South. *Record of an Obscure Man* (1861) and *Fifteen Days: An Extract from Edward Colvil's Journal* (1866) are filled with exposition and speculation about black history and alternatives to slavery. *Tragedy of Errors* (1862) and *Tragedy of Success* (1862), both plays, embody some of P.'s theories about the beauty of black music, the eloquence of black preaching, and black people's special capacity for loyalty and revenge.

Record of an Obscure Man is narrated by a friend of Colvil's who listened to Colvil's discussion of African history and theories about slavery and, after Colvil's death, arranged for publication of his two verse plays, *Tragedy of Errors* and its sequel, *Tragedy of Success*. Written "in the dramatic form, but not intended for the stage," the plays form the core of P.'s series.

Their plot is overly complicated. The intrigue of a jilted mulatto woman, Dorcas, catapults a young white woman, Hecate, into slavery. She has a child by her plantation owner, Stanley, switches her baby with that of his wife, and watches her illegitimate daughter, Helen, grow up as a generous, highly intelligent, free woman who endears herself with the slaves and longs to accomplish some great work but feels hampered by a weak-spirited husband. After the baby-switching comes to light, Helen takes her place as a slave, but escapes with her son when her husband tells her that he wants to keep her as his mistress. Just as he sees the light (encouraged by proof that Helen is white), Helen is captured and dies in jail from loss of hope (but not faith).

In contrast to P.'s very readable prose, the verse in the plays is only occasionally strong; but a few of the scenes have convincing dialogues: in one, Dorcas successfully confronts her remorseful accomplice, a slave trader, by skillfully reminding him of his self-doubts and mixed motivations. In another, Helen powerfully decries the severe limitations of woman's freedom to her sister-in-law Alice: "Restrained and cramped / In all her outward acts, she cannot know / The joys of self-possession,

—man's great bliss; / She only claims those of renunciation." Despite her limits, however, woman is "man's second conscience," and must speak "the word God printed on her soul."

Fifteen Days is the most unified work in the series. The journal starts on Good Friday, 1844, and describes Colvil's meeting with a charismatic figure, Harry Dudley, a young visiting botanist from Massachusetts who tries to buy a slave so that he can free him. *Fifteen Days* balances the joy of deepening friendship between Colvil and Dudley against the sense of looming tragedy. Colvil seems excessively anxious to live up to Dudley's expectation, but his anxiety is interestingly confirmed when Dudley is killed at the end, ironically by a good friend who was also the slave's former owner.

The central victims in P.'s tragic series are all young, perceptive, and white, but her exposition of African history shows a sensitivity to the intelligence and culture of black people. P.'s writings on Hungary show her capable of imagining herself in other people's shoes. Although her characters are scarce on flesh and blood, their sensibility is frequently compelling.

WORKS: The Bondmaid by Fredrika Bremer (translated by Putnam, 1844). *The North American Review on Hungary* (reprinted from the *Christian Examiner*, Nov. 1850; March 1851). *Record of an Obscure Man* (1861). *Tragedy of Errors* (1862). *Tragedy of Success* (1862). *[Memorial of William] Lowell Putnam* (1863). *Fifteen Days: An Extract from Edward Colvil's Journal* (1866). *Guépin of Nantes: A French Republican* (1874). *Memoir of Rev. Charles Lowell, D.D.* (1885).

BIBLIOGRAPHY: Adelman, J., *Famous Women* (1926). Dorland, W. A. N., *The Sum of Feminine Achievement* (1917). *Homes of American Authors* (1857).

For articles in reference works, see: *American Authors, 1795–1895: A Bibliography*, Ed. P. K. Foley (1897). *American Fiction, 1851–1875*, Ed. L. H. Wright (1965). *A Critical Dictionary of English Literature and British and American Authors*, Ed. S. A. Allibone (1872). *A Dictionary of American Authors*, Ed. O. F. Adams (1897). *DAB* (article on James Russell Lowell) VI, 1. *Index to Women of the World, from Ancient to Modern Times: Biographies and Portraits*, Ed. N. O. Ireland (1970). *Women's Record*, Ed. S. J. Hale (1870).

Other references: *North American Review* (Jan. 1862; April 1862).

KAREN B. STEELE

Ayn Rand

B. 2 Feb. 1905, St. Petersburg, Russia; d. 6 March 1982, New York City
M. Frank O'Connor, 1929

R.'s early life of relative comfort was abruptly terminated when the family business was nationalized after the Russian Revolution. An excellent student whose far-ranging interests included mathematics, literature, philosophy, and engineering, R. graduated from the University of Leningrad with a degree in history. Not able to adjust to the Communist regime, she accepted an invitation to visit relatives in New York in 1926.

R. went to Hollywood to write screen scenarios and was given a job as an extra by Cecil B. de Mille. Though de Mille rejected her first five scenarios as too romantic, unrealistic, and improbable, R. did eventually work as a screenwriter.

We, the Living (1936) received a lukewarm critical reception. The themes are the sanctity of human life and the evil of collectivism in Russia. Written at the same time, *The Night of January 16th* (1936) is an effective dramatic piece. The play's originality derives from the gimmick of allowing each night's audience to serve as the jury in a murder trial.

The Fountainhead (1943) established R. as a popular writer and is considered her best work. The world of contemporary architecture serves as the backdrop for this battle between the forces of individualism and collectivisim, between creativity and derivativeness.

The plot follows protagonist Howard Roark's career from the day he is expelled from architectural school, through his difficulties in establishing a career, to his professional and personal victory and vindication. The book ends with the triumph of the virtuous and the creative. The heavy moralizing has drawn negative reactions from some commentators.

The philosophies set forth in *The Fountainhead* were amplified in *Atlas Shrugged* (1957), the fullest novelistic treatment of R.'s theories. *Atlas Shrugged* established R. as an intellectual cult figure. A novel which can be read to satisfy many different tastes, it has been categorized by various critics as a mystery story, science fiction, a philosophical diatribe, a female fantasy novel, and a justification of capitalism.

The protagonist, Dagny Taggart, whose attempts to run a transcontinental railroad are complicated by networks of bureaus, councils, and committees that strangle productive initiatives, fights a losing battle against a group that wants to "stop the motor of the world" in order to rebuild a society of free enterprise, devoid of government controls. She inadvertently finds a projection of this society, Galt's Gulch, a utopia in a hidden valley in Colorado. Galt's Gulch was born as a reaction against the collectivist maxim, "From each according to his ability, to each according to his need"; its motto is "I swear by my life and my love of it that I will never live for the sake of another man nor ask another man to live for mine."

R. is also known as a philosopher. All of her publications since *Atlas Shrugged* have been nonfiction. During the 1960s she was a popular campus lecturer. In conjunction with *The Objectivist*, a newsletter published to explain R.'s philosophy, courses in Objectivism were taught by the Nathaniel Branden Institute.

R.'s novels, though popular, have received little serious consideration as works of literature; she is something of a cultural phenomenon. Though R.'s politics are anathema to most feminists, her commitment to self-actualization both as a philosopher and as creator of one of the most positive female protagonists in American literature (Dagny Taggart) suggests that perhaps her works need to be reevaluated by women.

WORKS: *We, the Living* (1936). *The Night of January 16th* (1936). *Anthem* (1938; rev. ed., 1946). *The Fountainhead* (1943; film version, 1949). *Atlas Shrugged* (1957). *For the New Intellectual: The Philosophy of Ayn Rand* (1961). *The Virtue of Selfishness* (1964). *Capitalism: The Unknown Ideal* (1966). *The Romantic Manifesto* (1969). *The New Left: The Anti-Industrial Revolution* (1971). *Introduction to Objectivist Epistemology* (1979). Newsletters: *The Objectivist Newsletter* (1962–65). *The Objectivist* (1966–71). *The Ayn Rand Letter* (1971–76).

BIBLIOGRAPHY: Branden, N., and B. Branden, *Who is Ayn Rand?* (1962). Ellis, A., *Is Objectivism a Religion?* (1968). O'Neill, W., *With Charity toward None* (1971).

Other references: *Commonweal* (8 Nov. 1957). *NY* (26 Oct. 1957). *College English* (Feb. 1978). *NYTBR* (16 May 1943). *Playboy* (March 1964). *SatR* (12 Oct. 1957).

MIMI R. GLADSTEIN

Marjorie Kinnan Rawlings

B. 8 Aug. 1896, Washington, D.C.; d. 14 Dec. 1953, Crescent Beach, Florida
D. of Arthur F. and Ida May Traphagen Kinnan; m. Charles A. Rawlings,
1919; m. Norton Sanford Baskin, 1941

Daughter of a U.S. patent examiner, R. graduated Phi Beta Kappa from the University of Wisconsin in 1918 with a major in English. R. wrote for the Louisville *Courier-Journal* and the Rochester *Journal-American* from 1920 to 1928. Needing solitude, she bought an orange grove in Hawthorn, Florida, near Cross Creek, where she farmed and wrote from 1928 to 1947. R. traveled in England, Alaska, and Bimini. Her marriage to a journalist ended in divorce (1933). R.'s second husband was a hotel owner in St. Augustine. Sued for libel, R. left Florida to buy a New York farm.

R.'s earliest published story was "Cracker Chidlings" (1930) in *Scribner's*. Her humorous sketches about local figures contained accounts of a squirrel feast at a church picnic, domestic squabbling, and an explanation of "Cracker" as the whip-cracking country cattle driver. In 1931, *Scribner's* published "Jacob's Ladder," a sensitive odyssey of a young Cracker pair through storm-ridden piney woods and scrub. These were R.'s continuing subjects: the human bond to the earth, and the Florida Crackers with their folklore, language, and struggles.

South Moon Under (1933) received critical acclaim. Three generations of a Cracker family subsist in the Florida scrub. Old Lantry, an irascible loner and moonshiner, moves his family into obscurity to elude the law for murdering a Prohibition official. He gives up moonshining and tries to farm. His grandson, Lant Jacklin, forced to early manhood by his father's death, labors at farming and trapping. Hardships finally compel Lant to moonshine. Betrayed, he repeats his grandfather's crime and kills a man, condemning himself to a life of restless fear and flight. The moon of the title symbolizes the powerful necessity laid upon all creatures, men and animals, forcing them to act against their will. Moon lore abounds. Deer feed in the moonlight. "South moon under" meant that the moon was directly under the earth, unseen, and yet "it reached through the earth" with a "power to move the owls and rabbits," and drive a man to kill. Despite R.'s descriptions of the earth's beauty, these dark lunar forces, the treachery of kin, the legacy of family violence, and the intractability of the wilderness, convey her somber vision of the human lot.

Golden Apples (1935) describes an uneasy idyll between a frail ignorant Cracker girl and a callous, hard-drinking young English planter who comes to the fertile hummock to reclaim his father's homestead. R. deals more frankly than elsewhere with sexuality: Desire seems to rise up out of the steamy Florida undergrowth. But the man's real view of the land is that it is a "damn rotten crawling place," and when the girl he seduces looks "all eyes and belly" as she wordlessly kneels to clean his boots, he looks at her with repugnance. The girl dies in premature labor. A strange reconciliation takes place between her brother and her lover, as they join together to plant an orange grove.

The Yearling (1938) won the 1939 Pulitzer Prize for fiction. R.'s editor, Maxwell Perkins, liked her hunt and river scenes, and urged her to do a boy's book. *The Yearling*'s theme is the passage from childhood to manhood for fourteen-year-old Jody Baxter. The plot is based on Jody's adopting a baby fawn when its mother is slain. After thirteen months, the fawn is no longer a baby but a yearling that destroys the family's crops and whose wild nature cannot be subdued. Jody is at first unable to obey his father's directive to kill the yearling, which has become a part of himself, but is forced to do so when his mother's faulty aim wounds the creature. His grief drives him from home to a river journey, and he wishes for the death of his gentle father, who, it seems, has betrayed him. Jody's homecoming shows him ready to put a child's happiness behind him and embrace the lonely hardships of manhood.

R. creates a Floridian earthly paradise. With all its loveliness, however, this wilderness reveals to the growing boy many signs of nature's cruelty. This sacrifice of the wild creature is a gesture implying that to attain maturity a man must quell his own rapturous, irresponsible, animal nature. Biblical echoes reinforce the end of innocence.

When the Whippoorwill (1940) collects R.'s best magazine stories. Noteworthy is "Gal Young Un," about a gaunt gray woman married for her wealth by a flashing opportunist. Several stories introduce R.'s fine comic narrator, Quincey Dover, "a woman with a tongue sharp enough to slice soft bacon." Others treat of moonshining, alligator hunting, and family life.

In 1942, R. published *Cross Creek*, chronicling her years in this chosen spot. R. describes the farmhouse, the tall old orange trees, the coral honeysuckle twisting on the wire fence. She gathers materials that will feed her fiction: scenes, animals, anecdotes, personalities. Her portraits of the neighbors whose lives she shared, notably of black women, are both humorous and painful, revealing R.'s sure grasp on human realities. In "Hyacinth Drift," two women, R. and a friend, navigate several hundred miles of river in an eighteen-foot boat. Beset with cares, R. had momentarily "lost touch with the Creek"; this is a journey of renewal that enables R. once again to long for home. "Because I had known intimately a river, the earth pulsed under me." *Cross Creek* ranks as a classic of the American pastoral scene.

Although she was admired as a regional writer, R.'s ambivalence about this designation led her to approach new subjects. She believed that a "great" writer could write anywhere, and she broke from Cross Creek. R.'s last novel, *The Sojourner* (1953), about a Hudson Valley farm after the Civil War, lacks the power of her earlier work.

R. belongs to the tradition of Thoreau and Whitman. Nature for R. is cruel as well as beneficent, and she accepts the savagery as part of the cycle of living and dying. R.'s witty revelation of regional character and language places her in the mainstream of writers from Mark Twain on. R.'s typical fictional perspective is that of a male, usually naive, forced to acknowledge the sinister side of a seductive pastoral world.

WORKS: *South Moon Under* (1933). *Golden Apples* (1935). *The Yearling* (1938; film version, 1945). *When the Whippoorwill* (1941). *Cross Creek* (1942). *The Sojourner* (1953). *The Secret River* (1955).

BIBLIOGRAPHY: Bellman, S., *Marjorie Kinnan Rawlings* (1974). Berg, A. S., *Max Perkins, Editor of Genius* (1978). Bigelow, G. E., *Frontier Eden: The Literary Career of Marjorie Kinnan Rawlings* (1966). Bigham, J. S., Introduction to *The Marjorie Rawlings Reader* (1956).

Other references: *Collier's* 116 (29 Sept. 1945). *EJ* 64 (1975). *Family Circle* (7 May 1943). *NYT* Sunday Travel Section (27 Jan. 1980). *SLJ* 9 (1977).

MARCELLE THIÉBAUX

Lizette Woodworth Reese

B. 9 Jan. 1856, Waverly, Maryland; d. 17 Dec. 1935, Baltimore, Maryland
D. of David and Louisa Reese

R.'s life as a child and young woman in Waverly, a suburban village of Baltimore, provided the material for most of her writing, both poetry and prose. In R.'s poems and reminiscences, Waverly becomes the symbol for a time and a value system more stable than those of the present. R. not only grew up in Waverly but began her long teaching career in the local parish school. Her first poem, "The Deserted House," appeared in the *Southern Magazine* in June 1874. From that time until her death, R. continued to write lyric poetry that was of fairly consistent quality.

R.'s first volume of poetry, *A Branch of May* (1887), was privately printed through subscriptions from friends. This volume of thirty-three poems was sent to several of the leading critics of the day, all of whom received it favorably. R.'s reputation grew with *A Handful of Lavendar* (1891), which was published by a national publisher.

The subject matter and style of R.'s poetry remained constant through her subsequent volumes. Her subjects are the eternal truths of life and death—joy and sorrow, expressed in images drawn from her childhood experiences in the Maryland countryside and readings in English literature. Her best poems make arrestingly fresh use of images from ordinary experience. R.'s central images are of village and orchard. The orchard becomes a primary image, for, as R. says, "although not so open as the lane, or so secret as the wood, it keeps the free heart of the one, and somewhat of the privileged quiet of the other."

R. was generally praised for the freshness of her images in a time when most lyric poetry was marked by the tired conventions of excessive and archaic expression. Her forte was the short lyric, but she was also an accomplished sonneteer. Her best-known poem was the sonnet "Tears," which first appeared in *Scribner's* magazine in 1899 and was repeatedly anthologized. The poem presents a series of arresting metaphors about the futility of grieving over the fugitive cares of life.

Although primarily a lyric poet, R. published one successful long narrative poem, *Little Henrietta* (1927), and was at the time of her death working on another, which was published posthumously as *The Old*

House in the Country (1936). *Little Henrietta* probes the grief and eventual reconciliation over the death of a young child, and *The Old House* is an attempt to unify the diverse recollections of childhood memories.

Childhood memories form the substance of two volumes of autobiographical reminiscence, *A Victorian Village* (1929) and *The York Road* (1931). These prose works poetically present the recollections and associations brought to R.'s mind by people, places, and events from her childhood and young adulthood. At the time of her death, R. was reworking these experiences into an autobiographical novel, published posthumously as *Worleys* (1936).

R. is neglected today, although she was one of the finest poets writing during the last decade of the 19th c. and the first decade of the 20th. She is a transition figure between the stylized conventions of the Victorian poets and the free form and subject matter of the moderns. At its best, R.'s poetry is characterized by a striking intensity and freshness of image.

WORKS: *A Branch of May* (1887). *A Handful of Lavendar* (1891). *A Quiet Road* (1896). *A Wayside Lute* (1909). *Spicewood* (1920). *Wild Cherry* (1923). *The Selected Poems* (1926). *Little Henrietta* (1927). *A Victorian Village* (1929). *White April, and Other Poems* (1930). *The York Road* (1931). *Pastures, and Other Poems* (1933). *The Old House in the Country* (1936). *Worleys* (1936).

BIBLIOGRAPHY: Gregory, H., and M. Zaturenska, *A History of American Poetry, 1900–1940* (1946). Klein, L. R. M., "Lizette Woodworth Reese" (Ph.D. diss., Univ. of Pennsylvania, 1943). Rittenhouse, J. B., in *The Younger American Poets* (1906).

Other references: *Personalist* 31 (1900). *SAQ* (April 1930; Jan. 1957). *SUS* 8 (1969).

HARRIETTE CUTTINO BUCHANAN

Agnes Repplier

B. 1 April 1855, Philadelphia, Pennsylvania; d. 16 Dec. 1950, Philadelphia, Pennsylvania
D. of John George and Agnes Mathias Repplier

R. did not learn to read until she was almost ten. Her formal education was limited to two years at the Convent of the Sacred Heart and three terms at Miss Irwin's School in Philadelphia. Both schools dismissed her because of independent behavior, so that R. was entirely self-educated after the age of sixteen. Her intensive reading was augmented by numerous trips (the first in 1890) and long periods of residence in Europe.

Urged by her mother, R. began publishing at sixteen to increase the family's income when her father's fortune collapsed, and throughout her life she loyally supported her family. R.'s first writings were stories and sketches for Philadelphia newspapers. After publishing "In Arcady" in *Catholic World* (1881), the editor urged R. to write essays, since she knew a great deal about books and not much about life. This set the direction of R.'s career, for she made the familiar essay distinctively her own form—witty, graceful, and richly textured with allusions from her vast reading.

In 1886, R. was accepted by the American literary establishment. "Children, Past and Present" appeared in the *Atlantic Monthly*. Here she continued to publish frequently—ninety essays in all, the last in 1940. A highly disciplined writer, R. was determined from the start that her work would have permanence. In 1888, R. arranged the first of many collections, *Books and Men*, which included the first seven essays from *Atlantic Monthly*. Similar volumes appeared throughout the years. R. was a popular public lecturer, noted for her sharp perceptions, lively manner, and witty expression.

A plain child and woman with an incisive mind and quick wit, R. never married. She thought the feminist cause a just one and opposed any kind of discrimination. She had, however, no use for reformers in any area because of their excessive claims and simplistic and sentimental solutions. "Woman Enthroned" presents her case, as do "The Strayed Prohibitionist" and "Consolations of the Conservative." For R., happiness was fleeting and lay in "the development of individual tastes and acquire-ments."

The urbane stance is typical of R. However, before U.S. involvement in World War I, R. argued passionately for several years against neu-trality, collaborating with Dr. J. W. White on a pamphlet, *Germany and Democracy* (1914), and writing many essays, collected in *Counter-Currents* (1916).

A lifelong and devout Roman Catholic, R. wrote from a strong ethical code that provided a firm base for her relentlessly skeptical view of hu-man performance. R.'s specifically Catholic writings are among her most successful and include a merry autobiography, *In Our Convent Days* (1905), and three distinguished biographies of American religious lead-ers: *Père Marquette* (1929), *Mère Marie of the Ursulines* (1931), and *Junipero Serra* (1933).

Addressing herself to a wide range of literary subjects and social change for more than half a century, R. was usually provocative but rarely inelegant in her commentary. Her familiar essays provide a dis-tinctive and pleasing alternative to the prevailing realism of American literature. Perhaps R.'s most characteristic mode is epitomized by two collections separated by half her writing career, *A Happy Half-Century* (1908) and *In Pursuit of Laughter* (1936). R.'s range is broad, but her audience was always a select and patrician one.

WORKS: Books and Men (1888). *Points of View* (1889). *A Book of Famous Verse* (edited by Repplier, 1892). *Essays in Miniature* (1892). *Essays in Idleness* (1893). *In the Dozy Hours, and Other Papers* (1894). *Varia* (1897). *Philadelphia: The Place and the People* (1898). *The Fireside Sphinx* (1901). *Compromises* (1904). *In Our Convent Days* (1905). *A Happy Half-Century* (1908). *Americans and Others* (1912). *The Cat, being a Record of the En-dearments and Invectives Lavished by Many Writers* (1912). *Germany and Democracy, the Real Issue* (with J. W. White, 1914). *Counter-Currents* (1916). *J. William White, M. D.: A Biography* (1919). *Points of Friction* (1920). *Under Dispute* (1924). *Père Marquette* (1929). *Mère Marie of the Ursulines* (1931). *Times and Tendencies* (1931). *To Think of Tea!* (1932). *Junipero Serra* (1933). *Agnes Irwin* (1934). *In Pursuit of Laughter* (1936). *Eight Decades* (1937).

BIBLIOGRAPHY: Repplier, E., *Agnes Repplier: A Memoir by Her Niece* (1957). Stokes, G. S., *Agnes Repplier: Lady of Letters* (1949).

For articles in reference works, see: *Catholic Authors: Contemporary Biographical Sketches, 1930–1947*, Ed. M. Hoehn (1948). *DAB*, Suppl. 4. *NAW* (article by G. S. Stokes). *NCAB*, 9.

Other references: *Nation* (29 Nov. 1933). *NYHTB* (13 Jan. 1929; 29 Nov. 1931). *SatR* (23 Dec. 1933). *YR* (March 1937).

VELMA BOURGEOIS RICHMOND

Alice Caldwell Hegan Rice

B. 11 Jan. 1870, Shelbyville, Kentucky; d. 10 Feb. 1942, Louisville, Kentucky
Wrote under: Alice Caldwell Hegan, Alice Hegan Rice
D. of Samuel Watson and Sallie Caldwell Hegan; m. Cale Young Rice, 1902

R. was born and raised in Kentucky, the setting for most of her fiction. She married Rice shortly after the publication of her first book. They traveled widely in Asia and Europe, associating with many of the most prominent literary figures of the 20th c. Their permanent home was Louisville. Though Rice was primarily a poet and R. a writer of fiction, they worked closely together, publishing short stories by each of them in three collections (*Turn About Tales*, 1920; *Winners and Losers*, 1925; and *Passionate Follies*, 1936). R. also published an autobiography (*The Inky Way*, 1940) and two collections of religious meditations (*My Pillow Book*, 1937, and *Happiness Road*, completed by her husband in 1942).

R.'s best works are set among Kentucky's poor, particularly the urban poor whom she came to know as a volunteer settlement worker. *Mrs. Wiggs of the Cabbage Patch* (1901), inspired by a real person and a slum area in Louisville, is noteworthy both for its fidelity to the facts of the lives of poor urban whites and for the gentle humor with which it depicts their characters. These are the "deserving poor," honest and willing to work. Mrs. Wiggs, a widow with five children, is poor and illiterate but wise and proud; she straightens out the personal lives of the wealthy young woman and man who, in turn, give her surviving children a chance to make something of themselves. The novel's humor comes from its use of dialect, from Mrs. Wiggs's malapropisms, and from the children's pranks and mishaps. *Lovey Mary* (1903) is a sequel about an orphan girl who flees the orphanage and is taken in by Mrs. Wiggs and her friends. Both novels are trite and sentimental in plot, but their restraint and gently comic tone keep them from becoming mawkish.

Four other novels center on poor but meritorious characters trying to make their way in a hostile world. *Sandy* (1905), loosely based on the experiences of the magazine editor S. S. McClure, tells of a Scottish waif finally lucky enough to be taken in by a wealthy Kentuckian. Also dealing with an adolescent boy is *Our Ernie* (1939), whose title character quits school at fourteen to support his loving but feckless family.

He rises in the business world, becoming entangled with the daughter of his employer, but in a reversal of the Horatio Alger motif, frees himself from her while retaining his position. A rather melodramatic subplot concerns German spies. R.'s dedication describes it as "a happy book about funny people," a valid description for most of her novels.

Mr. Pete & Co. (1933) tells of a middle-aged derelict who returns home to Louisville when he inherits a riverfront tenement. The unaccustomed responsibility for the building and its inhabitants regenerates him, and by novel's end he has instigated an urban-renewal project and transformed the lives of his tenants.

R.'s most ambitious attempt to depict urban poverty and inspire reform is *Calvary Alley* (1917), which recounts the life of Nance Molloy, at eleven a mistress of gang-fighting techniques, later a reform-school inmate, and then a factory worker. Through much of the novel her prime goal is to escape the slum, but she matures and through hard work and good luck becomes a nurse in a clinic serving her people. R. was disappointed that this book was generally received as another comic novel rather than as the serious indictment of slum conditions she intended.

Most of R.'s other novels concern family situations, the central characters bearing responsibility for unworldly and eccentric relatives. Particularly interesting is *The Buffer* (1929), which centers on Cynthia Freer, an aspiring writer who is strong and self-sacrificing but has a sense of humor. At the novel's conventional happy ending, she seems to be ready to subordinate her literary ambitions to marriage—but she takes the manuscript of her novel with her.

R.'s novels are readable and amusing, though lacking in roundness of characterization or thematic depth. Compared to the works of her naturalistic contemporaries, who used many similar materials, R.'s treatments seem shallowly optimistic. She had few pretensions, however, always considering her husband's serious poetry more important than her own light fiction. But his work is largely forgotten today, while at least one of her characters, Mrs. Wiggs, still lives.

WORKS: *Mrs. Wiggs of the Cabbage Patch* (1901; film version, 1934). *Lovey Mary* (1903). *Sandy* (1905). *Captain June* (1907). *Mr. Opp* (1909). *A Romance of Billy-Goat Hill* (1912). *The Honorable Percival* (1914). *Calvary Alley* (1917). *Miss Mink's Soldier, and Other Stories* (1918). *Turn About Tales* (with C. Y. Rice, 1920). *Quinn* (1921). *Winners and Losers* (with C. Y. Rice, 1925). *The Buffer: A Novel* (1929). *Mr. Pete & Co.* (1933). *The Lark Legacy* (1935). *Passionate Follies: Alternate Tales* (with C. Y. Rice, 1936). *My Pillow Book* (1937). *Our Ernie* (1939). *The Inky Way* (1940). *Happiness Road* (1942).

BIBLIOGRAPHY: Overton, G., *The Women Who Make Our Novels* (1919). Other references: *Book News Monthly* (Oct. 1909). *Boston Transcript* (31 Oct. 1917; 14 Sept. 1921; 23 Sept. 1933). *NYHTB* (10 Nov. 1940).

MARY JEAN DeMARR

Adrienne Cecile Rich

B. 16 May 1929, Baltimore, Maryland
D. of Arnold and Helen Rich; m. Alfred H. Conrad, 1953

R. was brought up in a southern, Jewish household which she has described as "white and middle-class . . . full of books, with a father who encouraged me to read and write." From her father's library R. read such writers as Rosetti, Swinburne, Tennyson, Keats, Blake, Arnold, Carlyle, and Pater, and as a child she was already writing poetry. Neither she nor her younger sister was sent to school until fourth grade: Dr. Rich, a professor of medicine, and Helen Rich, a trained composer and pianist, believed that they could educate their own children in a more enlightened, albeit unorthodox, way. In fact, most of the responsibility fell to the mother; she carried out the practical task of teaching them all their lessons, including music.

R.'s later education was conventional, and she graduated from Radcliffe in 1951. From 1953 to 1966, she lived in Cambridge, Massachusetts, with her three sons and her husband. These were years of personal and political growth and crisis for R. Her teaching career reflected her political commitment as she became involved in the SEEK and Open Admissions Programs of City College in New York City, where she took up residence after 1966. Her husband died tragically in 1970. R. continued teaching in the New York area until 1979, when she gave up her professorship at Rutgers University and settled in western Massachusetts with "the woman who shares my life."

W. H. Auden chose *A Change of World* (1951) for the Yale Younger Poets Award. Although Auden's tone in the preface has been criticized as condescending, he focused immediately on R.'s careful handling of form and clarity of thought: "The poems a reader will encounter in this book are neatly and modestly dressed, speak quietly but do not mumble, respect their elders but are not cowed by them, and do not tell fibs: that for a first volume is a good deal." Indeed, critic after critic has noted R.'s stylistic control and elegance as the hallmark of her early achievement.

This restrained style was to continue through the 1950s and be perfected in her second volume, *The Diamond Cutters* (1955). In a review of that volume, Randall Jarrell called her an "enchanting poet," an "endearing and delightful poet." But in the early 1960s, R. startled her critical audience with a shift to more political and feminist themes and an increasingly experimental style. Of her early experience, she has said, "In those years formalism was part of the strategy—like asbestos gloves, it allowed me to handle materials I couldn't pick up bare-handed . . . In the late Fifties I was able to write, for the first time, directly about experiencing myself as a woman."

R. wrote the title poem of *Snapshots of a Daughter-in-Law* (1963) "in a longer and looser mode than I'd ever trusted myself with before. It was an extraordinary relief to write that poem." This and other poems here, composed of irregular stanzas, are about madness, anger, waste, and failure in women's lives. "A Marriage in the 'Sixties," "End of an Era," "Novella," and "Readings of History" explore the self in relation to society, intimacy, war, violence, and pacifism.

In the 1970s, R.'s poetry revealed an urgent and driving tone that was expressive of her militant feminism. Critics worried that politics and ideology were undermining the poetry, but R. made no such distinction between politics and poetry. *Diving into the Wreck* (1973) is an attempt to start from the bottom, speaking of matters as yet unspoken in words as yet undefined. There are disturbing poems of pain, anger, and violence. Yet coexistent with this anger is a deep sorrow over our vulnerabilities and our frustrated ideals.

In *The Dream of a Common Language* (1978), R. begins to rebuild and to document the difficult process of re-vision. Expanding on an earlier method, she draws some of her material from historical figures: Marie Curie, Clara Westhoff (who married the poet Rainer Maria Rilke), and Elvira Shatayev (the leader of a women's mountain-climbing team). But her primary concern seems to be to provide mythic structures that will confirm and nourish the vital hopes and experiences of women. Thus in her latest phase R. has not abandoned form and restraint; rather she is searching for a new poetics defined by and for women.

R.'s concern with myth has also appeared in her prose. *Of Woman Born: Motherhood as Experience and Institution* (1976) is a carefully documented attempt to demystify motherhood as a patriarchal institution. She has also published widely on poetry, feminism, and lesbianism.

Among contemporary poets, R. is regarded highly. The integrity of her craft and the timeliness of her themes have earned her not only an academic audience but also a popular one. Above all her voice is directed towards other women, sharing her perceptions and partaking of a common experience.

WORKS: *A Change of World* (1951). *The Diamond Cutters* (1955). *Snapshots of a Daughter-in-Law* (1963). *Necessities of Life* (1966). *Selected Poems* (1967). *Leaflets* (1969). *The Will to Change* (1971). *Diving into the Wreck* (1973). *Poems: Selected and New* (1975). *Twenty-One Love Poems* (1975). *Of Woman Born: Motherhood as Experience and Institution* (1976). *The Dream of A Common Language: Poems 1974–1977* (1978). *On Lies, Secrets, and Silence: Selected Prose, 1966–1978* (1979). *A Wild Patience Has Taken Me This Far: Poems, 1978–1981* (1981).

BIBLIOGRAPHY: Gelpi, B. C., and A. Gelpi, *Adrienne Rich's Poetry: The Texts of the Poems, the Poet on Her Work, Reviews and Criticism* (1975). Juhasz, S., *Naked and Fiery Forms: Modern American Poetry by Women* (1976). Karp, S. H., "Beginning Here: A Reading of Adrienne Rich's *The Dream of a Common Language* as Feminist Manifesto and Myth," in *The Proceedings of the Second CUNY English Forum* (1981).

Other references: *Anonymous* 2 (1975). *Hollins Critic* (Oct. 1974). *The Island* 1 (May 1966). *Ms.* (July 1973). *Newsweek* (24 Dec. 1973). *NYT* (3 Feb. 1980). *The Ohio Review* 13 (1971). *Parnassus* (2, 1973; 4, 1975). *Poetry* 109 (Jan. 1967). *Salmagundi* 22–23 (1973). *SatR* (22 April 1972). *Southwest Review* 60 (Autumn 1975).

SHEEMA HAMDANI KARP

Lola Ridge

B. 12 Dec. 1873, Dublin, Ireland; d. 19 May 1941, Brooklyn, New York
Given name: Rose Emily Ridge
Wrote under: Lola, L. R. Ridge, Lola Ridge
D. of Joseph Henry and Emma Reilly Ridge; m. Peter Webster, 1895; m.
  David Lawson, 1919

R. lived with her mother in Australia and New Zealand as a child. R.'s early interests included art and music, and when her marriage to the manager of a New Zealand gold mine proved unhappy, she moved to Sydney to study painting under Julian Ashton. R. later regretted having destroyed poems she wrote during this period, but a collection of her work has recently been discovered at the Mitchell Library in Sydney.

R. emigrated to San Francisco in 1907, and moved to New York City in 1908. She supported herself as a writer of fiction and poetry for popular magazines. She also served as one of the first organizers of Ferrer Association Modern School.

The Ghetto (1918), written during a five-year absence from New York City, was hailed as a book that seemed destined for greatness. Revolutionary in spirit and written in free verse, the title poem dwells on life among the Jewish immigrants of New York's Lower East Side and illustrates themes that recur throughout R.'s work—the moral courage of ordinary men and women, the paramount importance of liberty in human lives, and faith in the possibilities that America holds.

After the success of *The Ghetto*, R. edited a number of issues of *Others* and served as the American editor of *Broom*. She also toured the Midwest, speaking on subjects such as "Individualism and American Poetry" and "Woman and the Creative Will."

Sun-Up (1920) contains both personal and public poems. The title poem draws heavily on the author's own childhood. Technically, its flashing pictures resemble those of the Imagists; psychologically, it shares ground with the experiments of James Joyce. The public poems "Sons of Belial" and "Reveille" demonstrate R.'s sympathy with an exploited working class and affirm her function as a poet "[blowing] upon [their] hearts / kindling the slow fire."

Red Flag (1927) also includes poems saluting those who have fallen in the cause of freedom. "Red Flag" focuses on Russia and figures in the Russian revolution, and "Under the Sun" commemorates martyrs of other struggles. Most of the poems in this volume, however, are poems about natural and spiritual beauty and imagistic portraits of R.'s contemporaries.

R.'s last two books are characterized by an increasingly stylized language and growing mysticism. *Firehead* (1929), R.'s response to the executions of Sacco and Vanzetti in 1927, retells the story of the Crucifixion. The nine sections view the Crucifixion from a variety of points of view, including those of Judas, the two Marys, and Jesus himself; the Christ of the poem is viewed as "one who had proclaimed men equal—aye / Even unto slaves and women . . . / And babbled of some communal bright heaven." During her lifetime, *Firehead* was widely acclaimed as R.'s masterpiece.

On a visit to Yaddo in 1930, R. outlined a poem cycle, "Lightwheel," which was to occupy the greatest portion of her creative energies in her last years. "Lightwheel" was to include *Firehead* and five other books treating ancient Babylon, Florence during the Renaissance, Mexico at the time of Cortez and Montezuma, France during the Revolution, and Manhattan after World War I. R. traveled to the Near East (1931–32) and to Mexico (1935–37) to research her epic work, but the cycle remained unfinished at her death.

R.'s theory of history also shapes a sonnet sequence called "Via Ignis," the central poem in *Dance of Fire* (1935). But despite the poem's large theme—that we are at a crucial stage in history, but "may come forth, for a period, into a time of light"—its language is essentially private.

Though plagued by illness during much of her life, R. is remembered for her charisma. Her work attests to the continuous if not special concern that American women poets have had with social issues.

WORKS: *The Ghetto* (1918). *Sun-Up* (1920). *Red Flag* (1927). *Firehead* (1929). *Dance of Fire* (1935).

BIBLIOGRAPHY: Gregory, H., and M. Zaturenska, *A History of Modern Poetry: 1900–1940* (1946). Perkins, D., *A History of Modern Poetry: From the 1890s to the High Modernist Mode* (1976). Untermeyer, L., *The New Era in American Poetry* (1919).

For articles in reference works, see: *Living Authors: A Book of Biographies*, Ed. S. J. Kunitz (1931). *NAW* (article by A. Guttmann).

Other references: *SatR* (31 May 1941).

ELAINE SPROAT

Mary Roberts Rinehart

B. 12 Aug. 1876, Allegheny, Pennsylvania; d. 22 Sept. 1958, New York City
D. of Thomas Beveridge and Cornelia Gilleland Roberts; m. Dr. Stanley
Marshall Rinehart, 1896

R. began her career in 1903, publishing short stories in magazines like *All-Story* and *Munsey's*. In three or four weeks in 1905, R. wrote *The Man in Lower 10* for serialization in *All-Story*, and she followed that the next year with *The Circular Staircase*. When Bobbs-Merrill published the *Circular Staircase* in 1908, R.'s long period of success began. These mysteries fleshed out the novel of deduction with fuller if somewhat stereotyped characters, a second, romantic plot line, a good deal of Gothic atmosphere, and frequently comic elements.

R. essentially stopped writing mystery novels after 1914, returning to the form in 1930 with *The Door*, her first novel to be published by her sons' new publishing house, Farrar and Rinehart. In the next twenty-three years, R. published eleven full-length mysteries in which she exploited fully the "buried story"—a sequence of events never narrated in the novel and emerging only as "outcroppings," places at which material about the past of the characters supplies clues to the solution of the mystery. R.'s "buried stories" most often center on errors of passion leading to sexual alliances across class lines and leading inexorably to crime some years later.

The villains in R.'s mysteries are frequently lower-class women who have ensnared richer, more aristocratic men. The heroines most often are unmarried young women with little money but of good family, who serve as the center of the romantic plot as well as the focus of the murder story. R.'s intention in establishing the young female narrator was to link her mystery plot as closely as possible with her romantic plot; however, the use of this central character type has had the effect of placing her work, erroneously, in the class of Gothics.

Although R. is remembered today as a writer of mysteries, she was more popular in her own time for her serious novels. Beginning with *The Street of Seven Stars* (1914) and *"K"* (1915), R. produced romances with some attention to contemporary problems. This emphasis became stronger with World War I; R. depicted life near the western front in *The Amazing Interlude* (1918) and sabotage and attempted insurrection on the home front in *Dangerous Days* (1919) and *A Poor Wise Man* (1920). Both critical and popular success eluded R. in her most serious attempt at fiction, *This Strange Adventure* (1929), a dark look at the life of a fairly typical married woman. R. recouped in 1931 with her fine autobiography, *My Story*.

R.'s humor was not restricted to isolated episodes in mystery novels. With the creation in 1910 of Letitia Carberry, "Tish," R. produced a character who would remain a staple of *The Saturday Evening Post* and a favorite of American readers for nearly thirty years. Tish is an undaunted spinster of about fifty who with her two companions travels America and Europe, resolving lovers' problems, rounding up bandits and kidnappers, once capturing an entire German company, and maintaining throughout her own slightly askew brand of absolute moral rectitude.

R. also achieved considerable success in the theater. In collaboration with Avery Hopwood, she wrote *Seven Days* (1909), with nearly four hundred performances, and *The Bat* (1920), with 878 performances and six road companies. *The Bat*, with close affinities to *The Circular Staircase*, mixes murder, romance, and comedy.

From 1910 to 1940, R. was America's most successful popular writer. Eleven of R.'s novels were among the ten top bestsellers of the year they were published, and in the 1930s mass-circulation magazines paid as much as $65,000 to serialize her novels. From its infancy the movie industry sought her work, and later radio and television used her material. Today, R.'s serious novels are dated by her cautious attitude toward popular morality; she was careful to offend neither editors nor audience. R.'s mystery novels have fared better with time, continuing to sell well in reissue. *The Circular Staircase* has achieved the status of a classic in the genre.

WORKS: *The Circular Staircase* (1908). *The Man in Lower 10* (1909). *When a Man Marries* (1909). *The Window at the White Cat* (1910). *The Amazing Adventures of Letitia Carberry* (1911). *Where There's a Will* (1912). *The Case of Jennie Brice* (1913). *The After House* (1914). *The Street of Seven Stars* (1914). *"K"* (1915). *Kings, Queens, and Pawns* (1915). *Through Glacier Park* (1916). *Tish* (1916). *The Altar of Freedom* (1917). *Bab: A Sub-Deb* (1917). *Long Live the King* (1917). *The Amazing Interlude* (1918). *Tenting Tonight* (1918). *Twenty Three and a Half Hours Leave* (1918). *Dangerous Days* (1919). *Love Stories* (1919). *Affinities* (1920). *Isn't That Just Like a Man? Well! You Know How Women Are!* (with I. S. Cobb, 1920). *A Poor Wise Man* (1920). *The Truce of God* (1920). *The Breaking Point* (1921). *More Tish* (1921). *Sight Unseen and the Confession* (1921). *The Out Trail* (1922). *Temperamental People* (1924). *The Red Lamp* (1925). *Nomad's Land* (1926). *Tish Plays the Game* (1926). *Two Flights Up* (1926). *Lost Ecstasy* (1927). *The Trumpet Sounds* (1927). *The Romantics* (1929). *This Strange Adventure* (1929). *The Door* (1930). *Mary Roberts Rinehart's Mystery Book* (1930). *The Book of Tish* (1931). *Mary Roberts Rinehart's Romance Book* (1931). *My Story* (1931; rev. ed., 1948). *Miss Pinkerton* (1932). *The Album* (1933). *The Crime Book* (1933). *The State Versus Elinor Norton* (1933). *Mr. Cohen Takes a Walk* (1934). *The Doctor* (1936). *Married People* (1937). *Tish Marches On* (1937). *The Wall* (1938). *Writing Is Work* (1939). *The Great Mistake* (1940). *Familiar Faces* (1941). *Haunted Lady* (1942). *Alibi for Isabel, and Other Stories* (1944). *The Yellow Room* (1945). *A Light in the Window* (1948). *Episode of the Wandering Knife* (1950). *The Swimming Pool* (1952). *The Frightened Wife, and Other Mur-*

der Stories (1953). *The Best of Tish* (1955). *The Mary Roberts Rinehart Crime Book* (1957).

BIBLIOGRAPHY: Cohn, J., *Improbable Fiction: The Life of Mary Roberts Rinehart* (1980). Disney, D. C., and M. Mackaye, *Mary Roberts Rinehart* (1948). Doran, G. H., in *Chronicles of Barrabas* (1935). Overton, G., et al., *Mary Roberts Rinehart: A Sketch of the Woman and Her Work* (1921?). Overton, G., in *When Winter Came to Main Street* (1922).

Other references: *American Magazine* (Oct. 1917). Boston *Evening Transcript* (12 June 1926). *Good Housekeeping* (April 1917). *Life* (25 Feb. 1946). *Writer* (Nov. 1932).

JAN COHN

Anna Cora Mowatt Ritchie

B. 5 March 1819, Bordeaux, France; d. 21 July 1870, Twickenham, England
Wrote under: Helen Berkeley, Henry C. Browning, Cora, Isabel, Charles A.
Lee, M. D., Anna Cora Mowatt, Anna Ritchie
D. of Samuel Gouvernour and Eliza Lewis Ogden; m. James Mowatt, 1834;
m. William Fouchee Ritchie, 1854

The ninth of fourteen children, R. was descended from old colonial families. Her early years were spent in France, but when she was seven the family moved to New York, where R. was educated in private girls' schools. Although "Lily," as she was called, was not outstanding at her studies, she was considered precocious by her family because of her ability to write and act in home theatricals.

At fifteen she eloped with Mowatt, a wealthy young lawyer, and moved to Melrose, his estate on Long Island. Here she wrote *Pelayo* (1836), a romantic poem in six cantos "founded strictly upon historical facts." R.'s preface to this poem reveals an extensive acquaintance with literature. It was not well received, however, and R. retaliated with *Reviewers Reviewed* (1837), a satiric essay on criticism.

An attack of tuberculosis, her constant enemy, led R. to visit Europe in 1838. Ironically, as her health improved that of her husband began to fail. Nonetheless, they returned to the U.S. and celebrated his "cure" with a ball at which R.'s blank verse melodrama in five acts, *Gulzara; or, The Persian Slave*, was presented with R. in the title role. The play attracted much favorable attention from critics when it was published in the *New World* in 1841.

Her husband's fragile health and the loss of his fortune led R. to give public poetry readings. When she became too ill to perform, she began to write articles for *Godey's Lady's Book, Graham's Magazine, The Democratic Review,* and other magazines. Under the pseudonym "Henry C. Browning," she wrote a life of Goethe, and as "Charles A. Lee, M.D." compiled *Management of the Sickroom* (1844). In 1842, R. won a hundred-dollar prize from *New World* for her novel *The Fortune Hunter* (1842). R.'s play *Fashion* (1845) had an unprecedented three-week run, and was long a favorite of audiences in England and America. The money she earned not only supported her and James, but three orphans she had taken into her childless home.

Even more profitable than writing was R.'s career as an actress. Starting as a star, she remained one for eight years of touring the U.S. and Great Britain.

After Mowatt's death in 1851, R. returned to New York. Again she turned to writing to supplement her income, and her lively *Autobiography of an Actress* (1854) was an immediate success.

In 1854, R. married a prominent Virginian and editor of *The Richmond Enquirer*. In 1861 R. left her husband because of irreconcilable political and personal differences. She went to Florence, where she supported herself by writing novels and sketches. In 1865, R. visited England, became too ill to travel back to Italy, and took a small house in Twickenham, where she died five years later.

Fashion (1845), R.'s most important work, is a bright, witty satire of 19th-c. New York society. The basic plot line is a standard love story with melodramatic elements; but the sharp comedy has kept its freshness. The play reveals a remarkable sense of theater and a grasp of dramaturgy rare in a first effort. The action moves rapidly, the plot turns are cleverly planned, and the climax satisfies the comedic expectations. The first American social comedy, *Fashion* was successfully revived in 1924 and again in 1959.

R.'s early novels, *The Fortune Hunter* (1842) and *Evelyn* (1845), are also contemporary views of New York life; R. draws upon her own experience as a member of upper-class society, giving these works more substance than is usual in such tales. She paints the evils of money marriages and juxtaposes them with marriages based on honesty in values and actions.

Most of R.'s later stories make use of her theatrical experiences in setting and characters; both background and types are recognizable and timeless. Her plots are traditional romantic love stories, and her characters are often embodiments of the sentimentality so prevalent in that time. They are seasoned, however, with humor and a Dickensian awareness of the ridiculous.

R.'s reliance upon action precludes the development of profound characters, but her use of detailed description removes them from the stock types in most popular novels of the time. She also differs from her contemporaries in her treatment of women, for she places a high value on independence. Dependent females in her stories invariably fall victim to circumstances or villains, whereas the heroines not only think for themselves but are usually self-supporting. R. believed women should be wives and mothers, but she contemplated, and in some cases endorsed, the single life. A unique author, combining a European elegance with an American admiration for practical labor, she is, in the truest sense, the first transatlantic writer.

WORKS: *Pelayo; or, The Cavern of Covadongo* (1836). *Reviewers Reviewed* (1837). *The Fortune Hunter* (1842). *Evelyn; or, A Heart Unmasked* (1845). *Fashion; or, Life in New York* (1845). *Armand; or, The Peer and the Peasant* (1847). *The Autobiography of an Actress* (1854). *Mimic Life* (1856). *Twin Roses* (1858). *Fairy Fingers* (1865). *The Mute Singer* (1866). *The Clergyman's Wife, and Other Selections* (1867). *Italian Life and Legends* (1870).

BIBLIOGRAPHY: Barnes, E. W., *The Lady of Fashion* (1954). Bernard, B., *Tallis's Drawing Room Table Book* (1851). Blesi, M., *The Life and Letters of Anna Cora Mowatt* (1938). Harland, Mr., "Recollections of a Christian Actress," in *Our Continent* (1882). Howitt, M., "Memoirs of Anna Cora Mowatt," in *Howitt's Journal* (1848). McCarthy, I., *Anna Cora Mowatt and Her American Audience* (1952).

HELENE KOON

Elizabeth Madox Roberts

B. 30 Oct. 1881, Perryville, Kentucky; d. 13 March 1941, Orlando, Florida
D. of Simpson and Mary Elizabeth Brent Roberts

About 1884, R. moved with her family to Springfield, Kentucky, the town which would become the center of her stories and novels. As a child, R. listened to her father's storytelling. An equally important influence on R. as a child were family legends, including the tale of a great-grandmother who had come to Kentucky by the Wilderness Road.

R. attended a private academy in Springfield and later graduated from high school in nearby Covington, Kentucky. In 1900, she entered the State College of Kentucky but withdrew from school, probably because of ill health and financial problems. In 1917, R. registered at the University of Chicago—a college freshman at the age of thirty-six. R. wrote poetry while at Chicago and took part in a group—including such talented friends as Yvor Winters and Glenway Westcott—which met frequently to discuss one another's work. R. graduated in 1921 with honors in English.

In 1922, R. returned to Springfield, where she was to spend most of her life and devoted herself to writing, even after she learned in 1936 that she had Hodgkin's disease.

The quality of R.'s work is uneven. Few people would claim greatness for *Jingling in the Wind* (1928), an allegorical novel of the courtship of two rainmakers, or *He Sent Forth a Raven* (1935), a highly artificial and contrived novel, but other novels are more successful.

The Time of Man (1926) chronicles the life of Ellen Chesser, a poor white girl who is a descendant of Kentucky pioneers. Ellen is fourteen at the opening of the novel. R. portrays Ellen's early love affair, her marriage to Jasper Kent, and the hardships she suffers as wife and mother. The real strengths of the novel lie in R.'s use of Ellen's consciousness as we see her transcend the bleakness of her life and in the poetic quality of the narrative.

My Heart and My Flesh (1927) traces Theodosia Bell's initial rejection and ultimate acceptance of life. Theodosia, with a good family, wealth, and pride, loses her lover, her friends, her home, and her health. She is driven to suicide, but at last reaffirms her love for life.

The power of the self to transcend external forces is the controlling thesis of *The Great Meadow* (1930), set during the revolutionary-war period in Virginia and Kentucky. R.'s central characters are Berkeleian idealists whose lives appear as spiritual dramas deriving their substance from the mind of God. The protagonist, Diony Hall, chooses to leave the order and safety of her family's farm to enter the wilderness of the frontier. The most notable element of the novel is the mental or spiritual ordering Diony exerts over the chaos of her life and her surroundings.

R. wrote poetry throughout her life—her first important volume, *Under the Tree* (1922), was poetry—and, although her output in verse is slim in comparison with her prose, she wrote several first-rate poems, including "Love in the Harvest" and "Sonnet of Jack." R. also published two volumes of short stories—*The Haunted Mirror* (1932) and *Not by Strange Gods* (1941)—but they are less successful than her novels.

R. deserves further study and analysis. A fine prose writer whose experiments in stream-of-consciousness narration and feminine characterization seem far ahead of her time, she is of especial interest today for her penetrating analysis of the female consciousness.

WORKS: *In the Great Steep's Garden* (1915). *Under the Tree* (1922). *The Time of Man* (1926). *My Heart and My Flesh* (1927). *Jingling in the Wind* (1928). *The Great Meadow* (1930). *A Buried Treasure* (1931). *The Haunted Mirror* (1932). *He Sent Forth a Raven* (1935). *Black Is My Truelove's Hair* (1938). *Song in the Meadow* (1940). *Not by Strange Gods* (1941).

BIBLIOGRAPHY: Auchincloss, L., *Pioneers and Caretakers: A Study of Nine Women Writers* (1965). Campbell, H. M., and R. Foster, *Elizabeth Madox Roberts: American Novelist* (1956). McDowell, F. P. W., *Elizabeth Madox Roberts* (1963). Rovit, E. H., *Herald to Chaos: The Novels of Elizabeth Madox Roberts* (1960).

Other references: *Kentucky Historical Society Review* (April 1966). SatR (2 March 1963).

ANNE ROWE

Jane Roberts

B. 8 May 1929, Albany, New York
D. of Delmar and Marie Burdo Roberts; m. Robert F. Butts, Jr., 1954

R. dedicated herself early to writing, beginning with poetry in her teens and later writing fiction. Nothing in R.'s life, however, foreshadowed the development of her mediumistic abilities or the messages from Seth—"an energy personality essence no longer focused in physical reality"—which form the backbone of her literary production.

R.'s first novel, *Bundu*, was published in 1958 and her second, *The Rebellers*, in 1963. In September 1963, R. had her first psychic experience, during which she wrote almost automatically while simultaneously feeling the conditions about which she was writing. Shortly after this event, R. and her painter husband began research for *How to Develop Your ESP Power* (1966), using a Ouija board. In 1963, Seth introduced himself via the Ouija board and soon afterward R. started speaking as Seth's voice. Since then, more than one thousand similar sessions have taken place, providing the material for R.'s five Seth-dictated books and for seven books associated with the Seth communications. Virtually all the Seth dictations have been recorded in shorthand by Butts. Butts is also author of the running commentary which provides background and framework for the Seth-dictated material in the Seth books.

The cosmology voiced through R. by Seth is vastly different from the usual "spirit messages." Seth depicts a monist creation of which this universe is only a small fraction. Everything has consciousness. God is "All That Is" and, as a whole and in all Its parts, is constantly evolving.

As well as being parts of All That Is, humans are also parts of entities greater than themselves; humans have free will nonetheless. They have existed before birth as individuals and, after death, will continue to do so. The Seth teachings emphasize the power and potential of the individual human. "You create your own reality" is a basic tenet of his message.

Since Seth's advent, R. has not limited herself to material dictated by him. R.'s books depicting her own experiences in attempting to understand and apply Seth's philosophy add a poignantly personal dimension to the Seth communications. R. has also written two fast-paced novels about Oversoul 7, which embody and vivify Seth's teachings. A more recent development in R.'s career is her work on the "after-death journal." Two of these have been published, one received from the painter Paul Cézanne, and the other from the psychologist William James (*The Afterdeath Journal of an American Philosopher*, 1978).

The Seth teachings are complex, intellectually demanding, and not for everyone. Readers of like mind will find R.'s Seth books uniquely challenging, expanding, and—if fortune smiles—deeply satisfying.

WORKS: *Bundu* (1958). *The Rebellers* (1963). *How to Develop Your ESP Power* (1966; reissued as, *The Coming Of Seth*, 1976). *The Seth Material* (1970). *Seth Speaks: The Eternal Validity of the Soul* (1972). *The Education of Oversoul 7* (1973). *The Nature of Personal Reality: A Seth Book* (1974). *Adventures in Consciousness: An Introduction to Aspect Psychology* (1975). *Dialogues of the Soul and Mortal Self in Time* (1975). *Psychic Politics* (1976). *The Unknown Reality: Volume One of a Seth Book* (1977). *The World View of Paul Cézanne* (1977). *The Afterdeath Journal of an American Philosopher* (1978). *The Unknown Reality: Volume Two of a Seth Book* (1979). *The Further Education of Oversoul 7* (1979). *Emir's Education in the Proper Use of Magical Powers; The Nature of the Psyche: Its Human Expression: A Seth Book* (1979). *The Individual and the Nature of Mass Events: A Seth Book* (1981). *The God of Jane: A Psychic Manifesto* (1981). *If We Live Again; or, Public Magic and Private Love* (1982).

BIBLIOGRAPHY: Andreae, C., *Seances and Spiritualists* (1974). Bentov, I., *Stalking the Wild Pendulum* (1977).

Other references: *New Realities* 1 (1977). *VV* (9 Oct. 1978; 16 Oct. 1978).

LUCY MENGER

Harriet Jane Hanson Robinson

B. 8 Feb. 1825, Boston, Massachusetts; d. 22 Dec. 1911, Malden, Massachusetts
Wrote under: Harriet J. Hanson, Harriet H. Robinson, Mrs. W. S. Robinson
D. of William and Harriet Browne Hanson; m. William Stevens Robinson,
1848

R.'s father, a carpenter, died in 1831, and her mother took her four children to Lowell, where she managed a factory boardinghouse. R. began working as a bobbin-doffer at ten. After working a fourteen-hour day, she went to evening schools until she was able to attend Lowell

High School for two years. At fifteen her regular formal education ceased. She tended a spinning frame and then became a "drawing-in girl"—one of the most skilled jobs in the mill. Taking private lessons in German, drawing, and dancing, R. read widely and began publishing poetry in newspapers, annuals, and *The Lowell Offering*.

One of her verses caught the attention of William Stevens Robinson, assistant editor .of the *Lowell Courier;* after a two-year courtship, in which R. was torn between love and literary ambition, they were married. W. S. Robinson published *The Lowell American,* one of the first free-soil papers, from 1849 to 1854. R. joined him in his support of abolition and worked as editorial assistant while becoming the mother of four children. (Her elder girl became the second woman admitted to the bar in Massachusetts.) After the Civil War, R. and her husband worked for woman suffrage until his death in 1876. R. became the Massachusetts leader of Susan B. Anthony's National Woman Suffrage Association and a strong organizer and supporter of women's clubs.

All of R.'s books were published after her husband's death. Her first is *"Warrington" Pen-Portraits* (1877), which combines her memoir of her husband with a collection of his works. (The title refers to the name under which his militant abolitionist writings had been published.) It gives valuable pictures of abolitionist circles of the 1850s and of two eras in Concord, Massachusetts, where W. S. Robinson grew up and the couple lived from 1854 to 1857. "Among his schoolmates were John and Henry D. Thoreau; 'David Henry,' as he was then called. Of the elder, John, Mr. Robinson was very fond. He was a genial and pleasant youth, and much more popular with his schoolmates than his more celebrated brother. Mr. Robinson had a high opinion of his talents and said that he was then quite as promising as Henry D." *Pen-Portraits* also records impressions of John Thoreau, Sr., as "the most silent of men, particularly in the presence of his wife and gifted son," and of Cynthia Dunbar Thoreau as "one of the most graphic talkers imaginable, [who] held her listeners dumb."

In *The New Pandora* (1889), a verse drama, R. writes, "A woman should no more obey a man / Than should a man a woman. . . . My mate's no more my slave than I am hers;" and "Sex cannot limit the immortal mind. / We are ourselves, with individual souls, / Still struggling onward toward the infinite." Her pleas for equality of the sexes and the equal representation of women in councils of state, however, bog down in archaic verbs and verb forms and poetic diction.

Loom and Spindle (1898), R.'s most important work, adds personal history, anecdotes, and detail to the account she already had given in *Early Factory Labor in New England* (1883) of life in the cotton mills and corporation boardinghouses. *Loom and Spindle* provides analyses of the social hierarchy of Lowell and unforgettable vignettes, such as that of backwoods Yankee farm girls arriving to work in the city. R. also provides a full account of *The Lowell Offering* and biographical sketches of its chief contributors, carried through to 1898 whenever possible. R. admits that her account of "the life of every-day working-girls" may omit a darker side of their existence, but says, "I give the side I knew best—the bright side!"

R.'s play may be only a relic of feminist propaganda, but her lucid first-person accounts of Lowell life in the 1830s and 40s, of *The Lowell Offering*, and of Concord will always be valuable to literary and social historians as well as enjoyable reading.

WORKS: *"Warrington" Pen-Portraits* (edited by Robinson, 1877). *Massachusetts in the Woman Suffrage Movement* (1881). *Early Factory Labor in New England* (1883). *Captain Mary Miller* (1887). *The New Pandora* (1889). *Loom and Spindle; or, Life among the Early Mill Girls* (1898).

BIBLIOGRAPHY: Eisler, B., ed., *The Lowell Offering: Writings by New England Mill Women* (1977). Foner, P. S., *The Factory Girls* (1977). Josephson, H. G., *The Golden Threads: New England's Mill Girls and Magnates* (1949). Merk, L., "Massachusetts and the Woman-Suffrage Movement" (Ph.D. diss., Radcliffe College, 1961). Rothman, E., "Harriet Hanson Robinson: A Search for Satisfaction in the Nineteenth Century Woman Suffrage Movement" (Ph.D. diss., Radcliffe College, 1973).

For articles in reference works, see: *American Literary Manuscripts*, Ed. J. A. Robbins (1977). *NAW* (article by G. Blodgett).

SUSAN SUTTON SMITH

Anna Katharine Green Rohlfs

B. 11 Nov. 1846, Brooklyn, New York; d. 11 April 1935, Buffalo, New York
Wrote under: Anna Katharine Green
D. of James Wilson and Catherine A. Whitney Green; m. Charles Rohlfs, 1884

R. was the youngest child of a lawyer father and a mother who died when R. was three. R. received a B.A. from the Ripley Female Seminary in Poultney, Vermont, and began publishing poetry in *Scribner's, Lippincott's,* and other journals.

Although not the first American detective novel, *The Leavenworth Case* (1878) has been our most famous early mystery. Because of the decided success of *The Leavenworth Case,* R. gradually turned away from poetry writing. Only two of her forty books are not mysteries: a volume of verse, *The Defense of the Bride, and Other Poems* (1882), and a verse drama, *Risifi's Daughter* (1887).

In 1884, R. married a tragedian turned furniture designer. They made their home in Buffalo, New York. Over the next eight years, R. produced three children and eight books. The last two decades of the century were her most fertile writing years. She produced twenty-two published volumes between 1880 and 1900—for an ever-widening audience.

R.'s popularity grew with each new published thriller. She soon became the grande dame of the American mystery novel. R.'s international fame made her an effective lobbyist for international copyright.

The Leavenworth Case was, for many years, considered both the first American detective novel and the first detective novel by a woman, although it is neither. It is, however, a well-plotted, vastly entertaining murder puzzle of a type now classic. The rich Mr. Leavenworth is found murdered in his locked study. The suspects include his servants, employees, and two nieces. The sleuth is Ebenezer Gryce—a kind, rheumatic man and G.'s most frequently used detective. *The Leavenworth Case* was very popular. The Pennsylvania legislature even debated its authorship, consensus being that "the story was manifestly beyond a woman's powers."

Miss Hurd: An Enigma (1894) is a powerful mystery-melodrama in which the woman is the mystery to be solved. Vashti Hurd had wanted a "broad, free life." Instead, she was forced to marry the rich Mr. Murdoch. The murder puzzle that eventually develops is a subplot to the greater problem of Vashti's hatred for her husband and her need for freedom. Contemporary male critics found Miss Hurd an unsympathetic character. But feminist readers will find Vashti both sympathetic and heroic. Despite its rather sensational plot elements, the novel transcends its identity as a mystery novel and becomes a women's novel.

That Affair Next Door (1897) introduces R.'s prototype spinster sleuth, Miss Amelia Butterworth. A sharp, independent woman, Miss Butterworth works both with and against the police, as personified by the now-elderly Mr. Gryce. Amelia's own, rather satirical, narration makes the book a delight. It is also one of R.'s most challenging mysteries. Miss Butterworth would make two more appearances: a starring role in *Lost Man's Lane* (1898) and a cameo appearance in *The Circular Study* (1900).

The Golden Slipper, and Other Problems for Violet Strange (1915) is a short-story collection featuring a professional woman detective. Violet Strange is worthy of respect both as an investigator specializing in women's "problems" and for her motivation in becoming an investigator—to support a dearly loved but disinherited older sister.

R. brought detective fiction to a more "cultured" reading public. She frankly and proudly wrote for a popular audience, but her books were published in hardbound editions by respected houses. No longer was the American mystery relegated to dime-novel status. Prime ministers, presidents, and honored writers were avowed fans.

R.'s long and prolific career spanned from the infancy of the genre to its "golden age." But changing tastes within this fast-growing fiction formula dealt harshly with R. at the end of her career. Soon her poetic touches, her fondness for melodrama, her Victorian verbiage, were judged worthless by the jaundiced eye of the interwar reading public. The genre became rigidly formularized, lean, and cynical. By the 1940s, R.'s work was forgotten, or remembered only to ridicule.

R. is worthy of reexamination, both as a female forerunner in a largely female genre and as a writer with a real respect for women. R.'s female characters are strong, brave, and resolute against evil and largely male violence. There is a recurrent theme of sisterhood in R.'s works among women who pool their energies for survival. R. gave us some of the first female sleuths, both amateur and professional. Unlike many 20th-c. mystery writers who think of women only as victims or secondary characters, R. portrayed women as characters of primary importance who refused to be victimized.

WORKS: The Leavenworth Case (1878). *A Strange Disappearance* (1880). *The Sword of Damocles* (1881). *The Defense of the Bride, and Other Poems* (1882). *Hand and Ring* (1883). *X.Y.Z.* (1883). *The Mill Mystery* (1886). *Risifi's Daughter* (1887). *7 to 12: A Detective Story* (1887). *Behind Closed Doors* (1888). *The Forsaken Inn* (1890). *A Matter of Millions* (1890). *The Old Stone House* (1891). *Cynthia Wakeham's Money* (1892). *Marked 'Personal'* (1893). *Miss Hurd: An Enigma* (1894). *The Doctor, His Wife, and the Clock* (1895). *Dr. Izard* (1895). *That Affair Next Door* (1897). *Lost Man's Lane* (1898). *Agatha Webb* (1899). *The Circular Study* (1900). *A Difficult Problem* (1900). *One of My Sons* (1901). *Three Women and a Mystery* (1902). *The Filigree Ball* (1903). *The Amethyst Box* (1905). *The House in the Mist* (1905). *The Millionaire Baby* (1905). *The Woman in the Alcove* (1906). *The Chief Legatee* (1906). *The Mayor's Wife* (1907). *The House of Whispering Pines* (1910). *Three Thousand Dollars* (1910). *Initials Only* (1911). *Dark Hollow* (1914). *The Golden Slipper, and Other Problems for Violet Strange* (1915). *To the Minute / Scarlet and Black* (1916). *The Mystery of the Hasty Arrow* (1917). *The Step on the Stair* (1923).

BIBLIOGRAPHY: Harkins, E. F., and C. H. L. Johnson, *Little Pilgrimages among the Women Who Have Written Famous Books* (1901). Overton, G., *The Women Who Make Our Novels* (1928).

Other references: *Bookman* 70 (1929). *Reading and Collecting* 2 (1938). *The Writer* 2 (1888).

KATHLEEN L. MAIO

Constance Mayfield Rourke

B. *14 Nov. 1885, Cleveland, Ohio; d. 23 March 1941, Grand Rapids, Michigan*
D. *of Henry Button and Constance E. Davis Rourke*

R. was an only child; her father was a lawyer, her mother a kindergarten teacher. R. moved to Grand Rapids, Michigan, at age seven when her father died. Her close relationship with her mother, who passed on to R. an appreciation for painting and handicrafts, probably encouraged R.'s later concern for native American folk arts. In addition, R.'s professional interest in the details of ordinary life may have been a midwestern inheritance. This regard for the near-at-hand was never mere provincialism, however; for R. understood, as have all the best mid-western writers and critics, the profound relationship between local details and national myth, between particular experience and its more universal implications.

R. attended Vassar College (B.A. 1907); her primary interests were aesthetics and literary criticism. From 1908 to 1910, R. was a researcher at the Bibliothèque Nationale in Paris and the British Museum in London. She became an English instructor at Vassar in 1910, but in 1915 resigned from Vassar to live with her mother in Grand Rapids, and to do free-lance research and writing on American history and culture.

R. is best known for her advocacy of a native American culture, her use of popular culture and other "living research" sources and methods, and her popular, highly readable prose style. R. argued from a social and anthropological view of history against a belief that the quality of American society made it difficult for "culture" to live and prosper in the U.S. She saw a significant relationship between low and high cultures, and believed that America had a robust cultural tradition wherein unique native arts grew and flourished. R. proposed that American culture, woven from a great number of low- and high-culture strands, was more unified and vigorous than some scholars had believed.

Implicit in R.'s work, especially in *American Humor: A Study of the American Character* (1931), is the belief that American culture need not be judged against European models. Rather, it has its own characteristics, resulting from the particular conditions of the national history that produced it. The first part of *American Humor* recreates the rich climate in which this culture arose. R. traveled widely and used personal interviews, oral history, and popular culture documents as well as traditional historical materials to present a vivid picture of the rise of American humor. She saw this humor as an essential element in the definition of American character and culture. The second part of the book analyzes mainstream- or high-culture American writers in relationship to their antecedents in native American humor.

In *American Humor*, R. demonstrates a remarkable harmony between style and thematic approach. She writes in a lively, unacademic prose, often using fictional narration and the present tense, which makes history come alive and which celebrates ordinary American experiences and the common man.

Although *American Humor* and *The Roots of American Culture* (1942) include the most explicit statements of R.'s ideas, *Charles Sheeler: Artist in the American Tradition* (1938) is also a convincing application of R.'s theories about the interrelations between the popular American cultural experience and the mainstream art it produces. Similarly, *Troupers of the Gold Coast; or, the Rise of Lotta Crabtree* (1928) exemplifies R.'s approach. This is the lively biography of two women: Mary Ann Crabtree and her actress-comedienne daughter, Lotta. Like all of R.'s social histories, it provides a myriad of everyday details from America's past. Lotta Crabtree's story is not only the chronicle of an important life, but the vital dramatization of San Francisco in the later days of the gold rush, and of the popular theater and American humor on the Gold Coast.

Critics have attacked R. for overstating her case on behalf of American culture and the interdependence of popular and so-called "high" arts; however, R.'s reputation has been sustained not only by later studies that support her views, but by the increased use of R.'s popular-culture research methods and by the continuing influence of her readable, scholarly books.

WORKS: *Trumpets of Jubilee* (1927). *Troupers of the Gold Coast; or, The Rise of Lotta Crabtree* (1928). *American Humor: A Study of the American Character* (1931). *Davy Crockett* (1934). *Audubon* (1936). *Charles Sheeler: Artist in the American Tradition* (1938). *The Roots of American Culture* (Ed. V. W. Brooks, 1942).

BIBLIOGRAPHY: Brooks, V. W., Preface to *The Roots of American Culture* (1942). Hyman, S. E., *The Armed Vision* (1948). Rubin, J. S., *Constance Rourke and American Culture* (1980).

For articles in reference works, see: *CB* (May 1941). *Contemporary American Authors*, F. B. Millett (1940). *DAB*, Suppl. 3. *NAW* (article by K. S. Lynn). *NCAB*, 32.

Other references: *Nation* (17 Sept. 1938; 24 Oct. 1942). *NewR* (31 Aug. 1942). *WF* (April 1967).

NANCY POGEL

Susanna Haswell Rowson

B. 1762, Portsmouth, England; d. 2 March 1824, Boston, Massachusetts
Wrote under: Mrs. Rowson, Susannah Rowson, Susannah Haswell
D. of William and Susanna Musgrave Haswell; m. William Rowson, 1786

The English-born R. was raised in America after 1868. By age twelve, she was considered remarkably well-read in the Classics. Due to her father's Tory allegiances, R.'s family was "interned" during the Revolutionary War but finally allowed to return in poverty to England. R. worked as a governess until 1786, the year she published her first novel, *Victoria*, and married a hardware merchant and musician.

When her husband's business failed, R. assumèd the role of primary economic provider. During the five-year theatrical career which brought her back to America in 1792, she demonstrated considerable versatility as an actress, dancer, dramatist, and popular-song writer. She spent the next twenty-five years in the Boston area successfully running one of the first schools to offer girls an education above the elementary level. R. also wrote more than a dozen plays and novels, several books of poetry, a collection of tales, and several textbooks. She was contributing editor to the *Boston Weekly Magazine* for several years and also wrote for other magazines. In addition, the childless R. managed a household consisting of her husband's younger sister and his illegitimate son, her own niece, and an adopted daughter.

R.'s fame in literary history rests on her highly successful novel *Charlotte Temple: A Tale of Truth* (1791), a sentimental story about an English schoolgirl seduced by a British officer. He abandons her in America, where she dies after the birth of a daughter. Despite its wooden characters, this popular classic's appeal probably lies in its sensational portrayal of the dangerous power of the sexual impulse. For an early American novel, it displays a surprising unity of purpose and protest, albeit indirect, against the dependent status of women and the disloyalty of women to other women.

Although the didactic sentimentality of Richardson and Fanny Burney permeates her novels, R. could be considered an incipient realist in her use of colloquial dialogue, homely detail, and her own and others' experiences. R. claimed that her two seduction novels, *Victoria* and *Charlotte Temple*, were taken from "Real Life," and it has been suggested that

R. drew upon her frustrations with her own marriage in the moving descriptions of Charlotte's responses to her unfaithful lover. Certainly, *Rebecca; or, The Fille de Chambre* (1792), her second best novel, is semi-autobiographical in its presentation of the shipwreck and poverty faced by the friendless but virtuous heroine, as is *Sarah; or, The Exemplary Wife* (1813), a novel about the struggles of a woman who, like herself, raises her husband's illegitimate son. In the frontispiece to *Mentoria; or, The Young Ladies Friend* (1791), a collection of essays and moral tales on similar themes, R. advises, "From my experiences, *dearly* bought, / Blush not, my Anna, to be taught."

R.'s contributions as an early American dramatist and feminist writer have been largely ignored. Her only extant play, *Slaves in Algiers; or, A Struggle for Freedom* (produced in 1794), which was inspired by the crisis of Americans held hostage by Barbary pirates, dramatizes the escape of freedom-loving American women from the submissive harem of the Dey of Algiers. Several scenes satirize the macho postures of male captors and a would-be rescuer, and in a clever epilogue, R. imagines the women in the audience approving the good sense of her women's rights theme. Unlike most of her contemporary dramatists, R. evidently exploited American materials also in her lost plays.

Feminist themes are also present in R.'s otherwise undistinguished poetry. In "The Choice"—written more than a hundred years before Virginia Woolf's *A Room of Ones Own*—R. asks for "a competent estate, / . . . About five hundred pounds a year" and that "One little room should sacred be / To study, solitude, and me." Although "Rights of Woman" argues that women should have domestic rights only, R.'s domestic woman is an active, productive, and assertive person who refuses the passive role of sex object. Her collected poems also include patriotic odes, naval songs, and nature lyrics.

R.'s contributions to early American literature need to be reassessed. Not only did she write America's first bestseller, but she was a significant early American dramatist who should rank with the best of that period. In addition, her entire canon deserves to be reexamined for its early development of feminist themes in American literature.

WORKS: *Victoria* (1786). *The Inquisitor; or, Invisible Rambler* (1788). *A Trip to Parnassus; or, The Judgment of Apollo on Dramatic Authors and Performers: A Poem* (1788). *Mary; or, The Test of Honor* (1789). *Charlotte Temple: A Tale of Truth* (1791). *Mentoria; or, The Young Ladies Friend* (1791). *Rebecca; or, The Fille de Chambre* (1792). *Slaves in Algiers; or, A Struggle for Freedom* (1794). *Trials of the Human Heart* (1795). *Reuben and Rachel; or, Tales of Old Times* (1798). *Miscellaneous Poems* (1804). *Sarah; or,*

The Exemplary Wife (1813). *Biblical Dialogues between a Father and his Family: Comprising Sacred History from the Creation to the Death of our Savior* . . . (1822). *Lucy Temple; or, The Three Orphans: A Sequel to Charlotte Temple* (1828).

BIBLIOGRAPHY: Kirk, C. M., and R. Kirk, Introduction to *Charlotte Temple* (1964). Loshe, L. D., *The Early American Novel* (1907). Mates, J., *The American Musical Stage before 1800* (1962). Nason, E. A., *A Memoir of Mrs. Susanna Rowson* (1870). Quinn, A. H., *A History of American Drama: From the Beginnings to the Civil War* (1943). Rourke, C., *The Roots of American Culture* (1942).

For articles in reference works, see: *AA. DAB*, XVI. *NAW* (article by R. D. Birdsall). *NCAB*, 9.

KATHLEEN L. NICHOLS

Anne Newport Royall

B. 11 June 1769, near Baltimore, Maryland; d. 1 Oct. 1854, Washington, D.C.
D. of William and Mary Newport; m. William Royall, 1797

R. began her long and colorful life in Maryland, but moved with her family to Westmoreland County, Pennsylvania, when she was three. The family lived in a rude cabin where William Newport taught his daughter to read and write. Newport, a Tory in those prerevolutionary days, died a few years later, and Mary Newport remarried. After the death of her second husband, she and R. moved to Sweet Springs, now in West Virginia. A planter, Major William Royall, took them in and gave Mary domestic work. R., then eighteen years old, had access to the gentleman's ample library and to his tutelage. Ten years later Anne married her benefactor and mentor, who was then in his mid-fifties. When he died in 1812, he left Anne wealthy, and she began to travel.

If a nephew had not broken Royall's will, charging R. with forgery and "barbarous treatment" of her husband, the world probably would not have heard of this strong-minded woman. Because she was without income, R. turned to writing as a livelihood. *Sketches of History: Life and Manners in the United States by a Traveller* (1826) is the product of R.'s trip from Alabama to New England in 1823, containing sketches of well-known and unknown people, descriptions of landscape and cities, and personal reflections. R.'s blend of documentary material with gossipy tidbits fulfills the promise of the book's subtitle. Although R.'s books have limited literary value, they contribute to our knowledge of the social history of America.

In spring 1824, R. arrived in the District of Columbia, a sprawling community that would eventually become her home. Her first activity there was to lobby Congress for a commutation-of-pay resolution that would give her an income from her husband's military service in the Revolutionary War. R., in near-rags, solicited political, literary, and financial support from whomever she could interview, including Secretary of State John Quincy Adams. During the next seven years, R. continued to crusade, travel, write, and interview influential people.

When age forced R. to stop traveling in 1831, she settled in Washington, where she founded and printed, in her kitchen, a weekly newspaper, *Paul Pry*. R. served not only as editor and printer but also as reporter, writer, and solicitor of subscriptions. For years R. had been attacking anti-Masons and fundamentalists, and she continued her propaganda against them in *Paul Pry*. One of her best-known conflicts with the "Holy Willies," as she called evangelicals, resulted in her conviction as a "common scold." R. was fined ten dollars.

Deciding that *Paul Pry* sounded too much like a gossip sheet, R. changed the name to *The Huntress* in 1836. In the prospectus for the new paper, R. vowed to "expose corruption, hypocrisy and usurpation, without favor or affection." Among the causes R. championed were states' rights on the issue of slavery, justice for the American Indian, separation of church and state, tolerance for foreigners and Roman Catholics, and abolition of the United States Bank monopoly. She interspersed editorials and diatribes against Congress with gossip and with stories and poems written by others. R.'s crusading journalism continued in *The Huntress* for eighteen years.

WORKS: *Sketches of History: Life and Manners in the United States by a Traveller* (1826). *The Tennessean: A Novel Founded on Facts* (1827). *The Black Book: A Continuation of Travels in the United States* (3 vols., 1828–29). *Mrs. Royall's Pennsylvania* (2 vols., 1829). *Mrs Royall's Southern Tour* (3 vols., 1830–31). *Letters from Alabama* (1830).

BIBLIOGRAPHY: Dodd, D., and B. Williams, " 'A Common Scold': Anne Royall," *American History Illustrated* 10 (1976). Griffith, L., Introduction to *Letters from Alabama, 1817–22* (1969). Jackson, G. S., *Uncommon Scold: The Story of Anne Royall* (1937). James, B. R., *Anne Royall's U.S.A.* (1972). Porter, S. H., *The Life and Times of Anne Royall* (1909).

LYNDA W. BROWN

Muriel Rukeyser

B. 15 Dec. 1913, New York City; d. 12 Feb. 1980, New York City
D. of Lawrence B. and Myra Lyons Rukeyser

R. was educated at the Fieldston schools, Vassar College, and Columbia University. She was vice-president of the House of Photography, New York (1946–60), taught at Sarah Lawrence College (1946, 1956–60), and later served as a member of the Board of Directors of the Teachers-Writers Collaborative in New York, a member of the National Institute of Arts and Letters, and president of PEN.

R. wrote and published a play, TV scripts, a novel, juveniles, biographies, criticism, translations, and fourteen volumes of poetry. R.'s poems have been translated into European and Asian languages, and her readings from *Waterlily Fire* (1962) have been recorded for the Library of Congress. R.'s first book of poems, *Theory of Flight* (1935), won the Yale Series of Younger Poets competition in 1935.

From R.'s poems we can study much that has happened in modernist and postmodernist poetry in the last fifty years—from distance to confession, social protest, and feminism; from Yeats and Eliot to Ginsberg, Bly, and Levertov.

R.'s personality is manifest in the exuberant, hyperbolic, and generally optimistic tone that dominates her work. R. insists on experiencing and feeling *everything*, private or social, from the smallest physical sensation to transcendence of the physical. She treats sex, a cockroach, social injustice, and mystical self-dissolution with equal exuberance; *being* is its own excuse.

The result is that R.'s poetry, but not the individual poems, is multidimensional. Some poems are almost pure sensation ("Stroking Songs"); some are explanation ("Written on a Plane"); some are vituperation ("Despisals"); and some are pure fun ("From a Play: Publisher's Song"). Both her personal and artistic credos are expressed in the poem "Whatever."

For each mood or concept, R. selects or creates a perfectly suitable form. She is skillful enough so that her forms embody rather than contain their meanings: "Afterwards" is a poem that reaches into the unconscious for a "deep-image" ("We are the antlers of that white animal") expressed in breath rhythm. "Flying There: Hanoi" uses the incremental repetition and the rhythm of nursery rhyme to rededicate a poet. "Two Years" uses three terse stream-of-consciousness lines to express the dislocation of grief. "Rational Man" is a list of man's tortures of his kind in the rhythm of a dirge, ending in a prayer.

R.'s temperament and talent are best suited for writing the Dionysian sort of poems written by Bly and Levertov at their best—sensation, the concrete and physical, in ecstasy, rage, or prayer. R. weakens when she philosophizes and explains, and she frequently explains more than is necessary.

For a poet whose published volumes of poetry spanned more than forty years, R.'s range and energy were remarkable. Her changes were toward greater variety and flexibility and personal involvement.

WORKS: *Theory of Flight* (1935). *Mediterranean* (1938). *U.S. 1* (1938). *A Turning Wind: Poems* (1939). *The Soul and Body of John Brown* (1940). *Wake Island* (1942). *Willard Gibbs* (1942). *Beast in View* (1944). *The Children's Orchard* (1947). *The Green Wave* (1948). *Elegies* (1949). *The Life of Poetry* (1949). *Orpheus* (1949). *Selected Poems* (1951). *Come Back Paul* (1955). *One Life* (1957). *Body of Waking* (1958). *I Go Out* (1961). *Waterlily Fire: Poems 1932–1962* (1962). *Selected Poems of Octavio Paz* (translated by Rukeyser, 1963). *Sun Stone* by O. Paz (translated by Rukeyser, 1963). *The Orgy* (1966). *Bubbles* (1967). *The Outer Banks* (1967). *Selected Poems of Gunnar Ekelöf* (translated by Rukeyser, with L. Sjöberg, 1967). *Three Poems by Gunnar Ekelöf* (translated by Rukeyser, 1967). *Poetry and Unverifiable Fact: The Clark Lectures* (1968). *The Speed of Darkness* (1968). *Mayes* (1970). *Twenty-nine Poems* (1970). *The Traces of Thomas Hariot* (1971). *Breaking Open* (1973). *Brecht's Uncle Eddie's Moustache* (translated by Rukeyser, 1974). *The Gates* (1976). *The Collected Poems of Muriel Rukeyser* (1978). *More Night* (1981).

BIBLIOGRAPHY: Jarrell, R., *Poetry and the Age* (1953). Kertesz, L., *The Poetic Vision of Muriel Rukeyser* (1979). Rexroth, K., *American Poetry in the Twentieth Century* (1971).

For articles in reference works, see: *Contemporary Poets*, Eds. J. Venison and D. L. Kirkpatrick (1975).

Other references: *Carolina Quarterly* (Spring 1974). *Christian Century* (21 May 1980). *LJ* (1 Oct. 1976). *Ms.* (April 1974). *Nation* (19 March 1977; 8 March 1980). *NR* (24 Nov. 1973). *NYTBR* (25 Sept. 1977). *Poetry* (Oct. 1974).

ALBERTA TURNER

Adela Rogers St. Johns

B. *20 May 1894, California*
D. *of Earl and Harriet Greene Rogers; m. William Ivan St. Johns, 1914; m. (?),*
1930s

The diversity of S.'s reporting may well have been anticipated by her unusually sophisticated childhood. She was the daughter of a renowned criminal lawyer and a displaced Southern Belle—a woman S. has described as having been extremely unhappy and violently cruel. Her parents' tumultuous relationship proved a daily trial, and their marriage, divorce, and remarriage frequently placed her with relatives or at boarding schools in various parts of California. She charts her father's career and his tremendous influence on her in *Final Verdict* (1962). In 1913, when she was eighteen, he introduced her to William Randolph Hearst, and until 1918 she worked for the Hearst papers in San Francisco and Los Angeles.

During these early years, S. also began writing for Hollywood. In order to work at home when her children were young, she wrote and collaborated on several scripts. She became "Mother Confessor to the Stars" for *Photoplay Magazine* and later wrote biographies of movie stars for a Hearst series called "Love, Laughter, and Tears" (a title she would use for her memoirs of this period).

S.'s journalism began setting precedents in the 1920s when she became the country's first woman sports writer. But it was in the 1930s, while an International News Service reporter, that she created her best stories. Among them is her Depression series on the plight of unemployed women. These articles are largely based on personal experiences. Despite the artificiality of the premise—S. set out to look for a job with only a dime in her pocket—they dramatize the misery of these women and expose the uncharitableness of several charitable institutions.

S.'s fiction shares with her journalism a heavily emotive style (she was known as a "Sob Sister") and topical subject matter and background. She writes about Prohibition and WWII, and sometimes bases her plot on a publicized crime or incident. She can write engagingly, but the predominant concerns of her fiction can be traced to a few fixed themes. One of these themes, that of the "modern woman," is treated with some depth in her autobiography, *The Honeycomb* (1969), but in her fiction it appears as a much less complex phenomenon. It is often merely a decorative element in stories that are largely examples of women's escape fiction.

Several of her novels are romances set in Hollywood or in "high society." Women protagonists may, in fact, possess the characteristics of modern women—they may be important executives (*Field of Honor*, 1938) or women who freely engage in affairs (*The Single Standard*, 1928)—but as one critic put it, they are ultimately unconventional heroines too faithful to the conventions of their type. Characterizations are superficial and limited in depth and originality by the author's moralizing. Nonetheless, S.'s novels and more than two hundred short stories appealed to a large readership. She published in all the leading fiction and women's magazines of her time. This commercial success was in all likelihood the motivation for her 1956 book, *How to Write a Story and Sell It.*

Unlike some of the characters in her fiction, the people she describes and the persona she reveals in her autobiographies are vivid, authentic, and moving. Her memoirs ramble sentimentally, but they are candid and provide lively insights into political and cultural history. S. discusses her professional progress as well as such traumas as the death of a child, divorce and custody trials, and her alcoholism; her personal philosophy emerges as the distillation of family values, religious faith, and her self-consciousness as a modern woman.

This consciousness, however, has little to do with any overt alliance with feminist issues. In her opinion, a "single standard" for men and women will remain unattainable so long as women are mothers. S. approaches her ideal of modern woman through speculation on the moral integrity women should maintain in the flux of modern society. She sees this ideal most inspiringly realized in such admirable individuals as Eleanor Roosevelt and Anne Morrow Lindbergh.

In recent years, S.'s writing has explored her deepening religious faith and her belief in the afterlife. *First Step up toward Heaven* (1959), is the account of the founder of Forest Lawn Cemetery; *Tell No Man* (1966) is a novel of a religious conversion, and her latest book, *No Goodbyes: My Search Into Life Beyond Death* (1981), relates her communications with her deceased son.

S. is one of this century's most famous women journalists. In 1970, she was awarded the Medal of Freedom by President Richard Nixon, her former newspaper boy in Whittier, California.

WORKS: *A Free Soul* (1924). *The Skyrocket* (1925). *The Single Standard* (1928). *Field of Honor* (1938). *The Root of All Evil* (1940). *Never Again, and Other Stories* (1949). *Affirmative Prayer in Action* (1955). *How to Write a Story and Sell It* (1956). *First Step up toward Heaven: Hubert Eaton and Forest Lawn* (1959). *Final Verdict* (1962). *Tell No Man* (1966). *The Honeycomb* (1969). *Love, Laughter, and Tears: My Hollywood Story* (1978). *No Goodbyes: My Search into Life Beyond Death* (1981).

BIBLIOGRAPHY: *Collier's* (24 Jan. 1924). *Foremost Women in Communications* (1970). *Newsweek* (27 June 1936). *NYTBR* (7 June 1925; 28 Aug. 1927) 3 June 1928; 7 Aug. 1938; 12 June 1949; 10 April 1966).

ELINOR SCHULL

Lucy Maynard Salmon

B. 27 July 1853, Fulton, New York; d. 14 Feb. 1927, Poughkeepsie, New York
D. of George and Maria Clara Maynard Salmon

S.'s father was a staunch Presbyterian and a Republican with abolitionist sentiments. Her mother was head of the Fulton Female Seminary from 1836 until her marriage to George Salmon. With this strong heritage of female education, it is not surprising that S. received an excellent education for a woman of her day and age. She attended grammar school in Oswego, New York, and the coeducational Falley Seminary, formerly the Fulton Female Seminary.

S. was one of only fifty women at the University of Michigan. Under the tutorship of Charles Kendall Adams, she majored in history and graduated with a B.A. degree in 1876. She received her M.A. degree in 1883, after several years as assistant principal and principal of a high school in MacGregor, Iowa. While teaching at the Indiana State Normal School, S. published her first significant historical work, *Education in Michigan during the Territorial Period* (1885). After further graduate study in American history at Bryn Mawr College, S. accepted a position as the first professor of history at Vassar College in 1887. Except for a time spent studying in Europe (1898–1900), she remained at Vassar the rest of her professional career.

S. became a recognized leader within the Vassar College community. She believed the student should be the principal agent in her own education (S. taught her history courses in a seminar format, with emphasis placed on student research) and that the heart of any college is its library. She also anticipated future trends in historical research and methodology when she encouraged the development of a collection of periodical literature at the Vassar college library. Her personal contribution to the periodical collection was the guide *The Justice Collection of Material Relating to the Periodical Press in the Vassar College Library* (1925).

S. was a charter member of the American Historical Association. From 1896 to 1899, she served as a member of the association's "Committee of Seven," whose report *The Study of History in Schools* (1915), formed the guide for teaching history in secondary schools for generations. In addition to her professional activities, S. was an active supporter of woman suffrage and an advocate of world peace.

As a scholar, S.'s work followed no developmental pattern until her later years. Her most important early work is the volume *History of the Appointing Power of the President* (1886), which investigates the creation of the appointing power of the president by the Constitutional Convention, its precedents in English law, and the experience of the states under the Articles of Confederation. While this work is dated, and while S.'s hopes for a future when presidents would again make appointments based on merit, as they had during the Federalist era, were certainly not borne out by history, it is still a significant historical work for anyone interested in presidential use and abuse of power.

Domestic Service (1897) and *Progress in the Household* (1906) document S.'s increasing interest in what are considered today to be nontraditional subjects and methods of writing history. *Domestic Service* is based on a survey conducted in 1889 and 1890. It presents an analysis of household employment within a historical perspective, beginning with a discussion of domestic service in colonial America. S. suggests that there should be specialization of the work of domestic servants—paralleling the division of labor in other fields—and that servants be compensated fairly for their work, through higher wages and profit-sharing plans.

Progress in the Household is, in essence, a supplement to *Domestic Service*, as the essays outline "recent progress in the study of domestic service." These books are dated, and the institutions and problems described by S. are for the most part nonexistent today. Still, they present the modern reader with a picture of domestic life and service in the years before the technological revolution of the 20th c. and express the issues of concern to American women at that time.

S.'s departure from the then-current traditional school of history, which emphasized study of the political institutions of America, led to the writing of her most important historical works, *The Newspaper and the Historian* and *The Newspaper and Authority*, both published in 1923.

The Newspaper and the Historian discusses the advantages and limitations of newspapers and other periodicals as sources in the writing of history. S. points out how the periodical press reveals the personality of its time or environment. The companion volume, *The Newspaper and Authority*, is international in scope and investigates the press with reference to its external government controls.

Just three months prior to her death, S. completed *Why Is History Rewritten?* (1929). "History must be continually rewritten because there is always a new history. To the end of time, as far as the human mind can see, history will need to be rewritten and in that very fact the historian finds one of its greatest interests." S. was a pioneer in liberating the study of history from the narrow confines of a political perspective and introducing historians to a new range of sources for historical study.

WORKS: *Education in Michigan during the Territorial Period* (1885). *History of the Appointing Power of the President* (1886). *Domestic Service* (1897; rev. ed., 1901). *History in the German Gymnasia* (1898). *Progress in the Household* (1906). *Some Principles in the Teaching of History* (1908). *Patronage in the Public Schools* (1908). *History in the Back Yard* (1913). *The Dutch West India Company on the Hudson* (1915). *"Is This Vassar College?"* (1915). *Main Street* (1915). *What Is Modern History?* (1917). *The Newspaper and the Historian* (1923). *The Newspaper and Authority* (1923). *The Justice Collection of Material Relating to the Periodical Press in the Vassar College Library* (1925). *Why Is History Rewritten?* (1929). *Historical Material* (1933).

BIBLIOGRAPHY: Brown, L. F., *Apostle of Democracy: The Life of Lucy Maynard Salmon* (1943).

For articles in reference works, see; *DAB*, VIII, 2. *NAW* (article by V. Barbour).

PAULA A. TRECKEL

Mari Sandoz

B. 1896, Sheridan County, Nebraska; d. 10 March 1966, New York City
Wrote under: Marie S. Macumber, Mari Sandoz
D. of Jules Ami and Mary Elizabeth Fehr Sandoz

S. grew up in northwest Nebraska, in a frontier area at the edge of Indian country. Despite little formal education and much opposition from her father to a literary career, S.'s life was dedicated to writing. In both fiction and nonfiction she depicted the difficulties of frontier life and its violence, the harsh beauty of the country, the changes that have come to the area as Indians have been pushed aside and whites have imposed their way of life, the effects of political and social corruption upon the lives of the people, and the relations between ranchers, farmers, and Indians.

S.'s first published book was *Old Jules* (1935), a biography of her father; three years of research and two years of writing went into it. The book's subject is a vigorous frontiersman, opinionated and cruel as well as creative and foresighted; S.'s mixture of fear and admiration for him are ably conveyed. In his story S. epitomized the recent history of her part of the West.

Five other works later joined *Old Jules* as parts of the Great Plains series. *Crazy Horse* (1942) is a biography of the Oglala chief, stories of whom S. had heard in her girlhood from old traders, frontiersmen, and Indians; *Cheyenne Autumn* (1953) tells of an epic flight of the northern Cheyenne Indians. *The Buffalo Hunters* (1954), *The Cattlemen* (1958), and *The Beaver Men* (1964) study aspects of the economic history of the West, evoking people, landscape, and events and showing their interactions through several hundred years. Two projected volumes were never written; one, the introduction to the series, would have dealt with stone-age people, the other with the impact of oil upon the history of the region. S. considered this series the contribution upon which her reputation would rest. As history the books are flawed by lack of documentation and by fuzzy handling of dates and chronology; as evocative recreations of their time and place they are unsurpassed.

S.'s fiction uses similar materials. Of her novels, only *Capital City* (1939) is set in the present. One of many antifascist novels of the period, it analyzes a thinly disguised Nebraska and is flawed by its lack of a clear central character and focus.

The four novels set in the past are firmly rooted in historical fact. *Slogum House* (1937), the story of a woman who ruthlessly uses her family to build an empire, vividly depicts frontier violence. Murders, prostitution, and the castration of a man she perceives as an enemy are incidents in the growth of the central character's power. *The Tom-Walker* (1947) follows three generations of war veterans (of the Civil War, World War I, and World War II) from their return home, wounded in body and spirit, through their disillusioning attempts to adjust to a corrupt society. *Miss Morissa* (1955), the story of a young woman doctor who makes a life for herself on the frontier, is dedicated to three actual women doctors of the period. *Son of the Gamblin' Man* (1960) is a fictionalized biography of the painter Robert Henri, son of a frontier gambler and community builder. Through her imaginative recreation of the complicated relationship between father and son, S. mirrored the development of a section of Nebraska.

In her late years, S. received many honors, both as novelist and as historian. Her brutally realistic depictions of frontier violence and lawlessness and her penetrating analyses of western history give her a secure place among those who have tried to understand that region both as it actually was and as a mythic force in the American consciousness.

WORKS: Old Jules (1935). *Slogum House* (1937). *Capital City* (1939). *Crazy Horse, the Strange Man of the Oglalas: A Biography* (1942). *The Tom-Walker* (1947). *Cheyenne Autumn* (1953). *The Buffalo Hunters: The Story of the Hide Men* (1954). *Winter Thunder* (1954). *Miss Morissa: Doctor of the Gold Trail* (1955). *The Horsecatcher* (1957). *The Cattlemen: From the Rio Grande across the Far Marias* (1958). *Hostiles and Friendlies: Selected Short Writings* (1959). *Son of the Gamblin' Man: The Youth of an Artist* (1960). *Love Song to the Plains* (1961). *These Were the Sioux* (1961). *The Far Looker* (1962). *The Story Catcher* (1963). *The Beaver Men: Spearheads of Empire* (1964). *Old Jules Country: A Selection from Old Jules and Thirty Years of Writing since the Book Was Published* (1965). *The Old Jules Home Region* (1965). *The Battle of the Little Bighorn* (1966). *Sandhill Sundays, and Other Recollections* (1966). *The Christmas of the Phonograph Records: A Recollection* (1966).

BIBLIOGRAPHY: *American West* 2 (Spring 1965). PrS (40, 1966; 41, 1967; 42, 1968; 45, 1971).

MARY JEAN DeMARR

Margaret Sanger

B. 14 Sept. 1879, Corning, New York; d. 6 Sept. 1966, Tucson, Arizona
D. of Michael and Anne Purcell Higgins; m. William Sanger, 1902;
m. J. N. H. Slee, 1922

S.'s mother died, leaving eleven children, when S. was seventeen. Profoundly affected by her mother's death, S. would later refer to women like her as "breeders," and would dedicate *Women and the New Race* (1920) to her.

S. trained as a nurse, married Sanger, an architect, had three children, and lived in suburban Hastings-on-Hudson for ten years. After the destruction of their new home (an event which S. was later to see as symbolic), the Sangers moved to New York City and became involved in socialist and union activities. This activity and her earlier experiences led to S.'s feminist writings. The Sangers' 1913 trip to Europe spelled the end of their eleven-year marriage. After visiting Glasgow to research an article on the benefits of municipal ownership for women and children, S. went to France where she discovered that, in contrast to Scotland and America, contraceptive information was available and poverty was limited. After some time of "inactive, incoherent brooding," S. returned to America, with her three children but without her husband.

On her return S. took up the cause of woman suffrage, linking it loosely to birth control. In 1914, she founded the journal *The Woman Rebel*, written by women and for women. Contributors included Voltairine De Cleyre and Emma Goldman. The first issue was an unfocused burst of rage, with a rather sharp statement of feminist community and less concern for birth control than for emancipation. Although *The Woman Rebel* never included much birth-control information, sending any through the mail was illegal, so S. was arrested and forced to flee to Canada and Europe until the charges were dropped.

In 1916, S. opened the first birth-control clinic in America in the Brownsville section of Brooklyn. She also established the *Birth Control Review*, a publication greatly superior to *The Woman Rebel*. S.'s feminist rage had become sharply focused on the problem of birth control. *Birth Control Review* continued until 1928.

S.'s greatest successes came with her association with America's health professionals in achieving the legalization and availability of birth control. With physicians, social workers, and technicians to staff it, she opened the Clinical Research Bureau. When the police raided the clinic in 1929 and seized the confidential physicians' records, the medical profession defended its right to dispense birth-control information. In 1936, a U.S. District Court upheld that right, which had been denied previously by the Comstock Law. In 1932, S. had rallied individuals across the nation to join the National Committee on Federal Legislation for Birth Control, and in 1937—one year after the court decision—the American Medical Association publicly endorsed birth control, bringing American physicians and their prestige to the side of S.'s cause. The National Birth Control League and S.'s clinics were combined in 1942 to form the Planned Parenthood Association of America.

S.'s many publications consistently express her view that women are victim and need to "free themselves from involuntary motherhood." Concerned mainly for working-class women, S. believed that they were victimized by their husbands, their doctors, and their priests. They suffered from the sexual appetites and insensitivity of the first, from the passivity of the second, and from the doctrine of the third. S. writes in *Woman and the New Race* (1920): "Women are determined to decide for themselves whether they shall become mothers, under what conditions and when. This is the fundamental revolt. . . . It is for woman the key to the temple of liberty."

In *Happiness in Marriage* (1926), S. claims that men are the sexual aggressors, while women are sexually passive. Female sexuality, she maintains, has not been expressed; if it were, it could become a creative force; and birth control is the means by which it could be released.

Even after her marriage to Slee, a wealthy industrialist, S. continued to address the problems of working-class women. *Motherhood in Bondage* (1928) is based on five thousand of the two hundred and fifty thousand letters she claimed to have received in response to *The New Woman*. The letters are arranged in chapters entitled "Girl Mothers," "The Problem of Poverty," "The Trap of Maternity," "The Struggle of the Unfit," and "The Sins of the Fathers."

To S., the birth-control movement meant not only prevention of unwanted babies and abortions but, more importantly, the rational control of the individual woman's body and spirit, synthesized into female sexuality, as well as the subsequent lessening of war and of suffering. Her numerous publications, starting from the premise that women had always been the victims of men and society, are devoted to changing that role.

WORKS: *What Every Girl Should Know* (1913). *Family Limitation* (1914). *What Every Mother Should Know* (1914). *Dutch Methods of Birth Control* (1915). *Woman and the New Race* (1920). *Appeals from American Mothers* (1921). *Sayings of Others on Birth Control* (1921). *The Pivot of Civilization* (1922). *Happiness in Marriage* (1926). *Problems of Overpopulation* (1926). *Religious and Ethical Aspects of Birth Control* (1926). *What Every Boy and Girl Should Know* (1927). *Motherhood in Bondage* (1928). *My Fight for Birth Control* (1931). *Woman of the Future* (1934). *Margaret Sanger: An Autobiography* (1938).

BIBLIOGRAPHY: Dash, J., *A Life on One's Own: Three Gifted Women and the Men They Married* (1973). Douglas, E. T., *Margaret Sanger: Pioneer of the Future* (1970). Kennedy, D., *Birth Control in America: The Career of Margaret Sanger* (1970).

JULIANN E. FLEENOR

May Sarton

B. 3 May 1912, Wondelgem, Belgium
Given name: Eléanore Marie Sarton
D. of George and Mabel Elwes Sarton

S. is an only child. Her father was a noted historian of science; her mother, an artist and designer. S. became a naturalized U.S. citizen in 1924. She originally planned a career in the theater and served a valuable apprenticeship in Eva LeGallienne's Civic Repertory Theater. She founded and was director at the Apprentice Theatre (New School for Social Research) and was director of the Associated Actors Theatre in Hartford, Connecticut. From her mid-twenties, however, S. has devoted herself to the craft of writing.

S.'s autobiographical writings achieve a clear, candid, conversational tone and are significant explorations of the life of the mind and of the writer at work. It is S.'s belief that genuinely valid autobiography must move beyond reportage of event or even feeling and extend into an examination of motive, impulse, thought, and belief; and her journals are enriched by miniature informal essays which provide these explorations.

I Knew a Phoenix (1959) closely traces S.'s early life. In *Plant Dreaming Deep* (1968), S. uses her renovation of an old house in Nelson, New

Hampshire, as an effective metaphor for the establishment of roots and nourishment of the spirit. *Journal of a Solitude* (1973) deals frankly with the pain, frustration, and rage of the human experience. *A World of Light* (1976) is a series of fascinating character sketches of S.'s friends and relatives. In *The House by the Sea* (1977), S.'s home in York, Maine, is a symbol of the joys of productive solitude. S.'s recuperation from a mastectomy becomes the symbol for overcoming emotional deprivation and despondancy caused by harsh reviews in *Recovering* (1980), one of her most effective journals.

S.'s poetry often discusses the balance growing from difficult human choices. Her tenet that "form is freedom" accounts for the frequent employment of traditional poetic forms, although she also works in free verse. S. believes that the "white heat" of inspiration fuses the poet's critical and emotional selves to trigger artistically productive revision. "Prayer before Work," from *Inner Landscape* (1939), is an evocation of such inspiration.

In both poetry and fiction, S. treats the social and political questions of the day. "Night Watch," from *A Grain of Mustard Seed* (1971), compares human sickness and social ills. *Faithful Are the Wounds* (1955) fictionalizes the political witch hunts of the 1950s with force, wisdom, and understanding. *Crucial Conversations* (1975) includes comments about the Watergate scandal.

Mrs. Stevens Hears the Mermaids Singing (1965) is the story of an elderly, successful writer who reviews her life and work during an important interview and in preparation for helping a young friend at odds with himself and his sexuality. Frank, direct, powerful, this novel ranks among S.'s best work and is an example of why S. is often hailed as a spokesperson for women writers.

Death is a topic S. treats in all the genres she employs, and the tonal and philosophical span is generous, ranging from the contemplative comments of *The House by the Sea* through the furious protest of Caroline Spencer, the protagonist of *As We Are Now* (1973), who transforms her death into an indictment of society's attitudes toward the aged and the infirm. Brief, spare, blunt, the splendid characterizations of *As We Are Now* elevate it far above most protest fiction.

One of S.'s constant and most compelling themes is friendship, as in *The Birth of a Grandfather* (1957), in which the terminal illness of a close friend engenders a middle-aged man's reconsideration of himself and his values, and *Kinds of Love* (1970), a character study of two lifelong women friends.

The Small Room (1961) compares and contrasts Lucy Winter's growth as a teacher with her developing ability to function as an independent person. Her many committed colleagues serve as Lucy's mentors as she seeks to understand not only herself but also a brilliant student who has broken under the demands of personal pride and faculty pressure. Honest, compassionate, discerning, *The Small Room* is a major novel, its treatment of the student-teacher relationship singularly effective.

Steadily productive, unusually successful in her explorations of both isolation and union, S. is a serious writer who has won great popularity, with significant achievements in three major genres.

WORKS: *Encounter in April* (1937). *The Single Hound* (1938). *Inner Landscape* (1939). *The Bridge of Years* (1946). *The Underground River: A Play in Three Acts* (1947). *The Lion and the Rose* (1948). *Leaves of the Tree* (1950). *Shadow of a Man* (1950). *A Shower of Summer Days* (1952). *The Land of Silence* (1953). *Faithful Are the Wounds* (1955). *The Birth of a Grandfather* (1957). *The Fur Person* (1957). *In Memorium* (1957). *The Writing of a Poem* (1957). *In Time Like Air* (1958). *I Knew a Phoenix* (1959). *Cloud, Stone, Sun, Vine* (1961). *The Small Room* (1961). *The Design of a Novel* (1963). *Joanna and Ulysses* (1963). *Mrs. Stevens Hears the Mermaids Singing* (1965). *Miss Pickthorn and Mr. Hare* (1966). *A Private Mythology* (1966). *As Does New Hampshire* (1967). *Plant Dreaming Deep* (1968). *The Poet and the Donkey* (1969). *Kinds of Love* (1970). *A Grain of Mustard Seed* (1971). *A Durable Fire* (1972). *As We Are Now* (1973). *Journal of a Solitude* (1973). *Collected Poems (1930–1973)* (1974). *Punch's Secret* (1974). *Crucial Conversations* (1975). *The Leopard Land: Alice and Haniel Long's Santa Fé* (1976). *A Walk through the Woods* (1976). *A World of Light* (1976). *The House by the Sea* (1977). *A Reckoning* (1978). *Selected Poems* (Eds. S. Hilsinger and L. Byrnes, 1978). *Halfway to Silence* (1980). *Recovering* (1980). *Writings on Writing* (1981).

BIBLIOGRAPHY: Anderson, D. H., in *Images of Women in Fiction*, Ed. S. K. Cornillon (1972). Bakerman, J. S., "May Sarton's *The Small Room*: A Comparison and an Analysis," *Chrysallis* 1 (Summer 1975). Blouin, L. P., *May Sarton: A Bibliography* (1978). Sibley, A., *May Sarton* (1972).

Other references: *Hollins Critic* (June 1974). *NewR* (8 June 1974). *PW* (24 June 1974).

JANE S. BAKERMAN

Alma Sioux Scarberry

B. 24 June 1899, Carter County, Kentucky
Writes under: Beatrice Fairfax, Annie Laurie, Alma Sioux Scarberry
D. of George Washington and Caledonia Lee Patrick Scarberry; m. Theodore
  A. Klein, 1930

S. is the daughter of a Kentucky fundamentalist minister. Her early home life was difficult; her father, a stern disciplinarian, remarried several times, and S. often had to support herself as a child. She began to write prose and poetry at an early age, and writing always seemed natural to her.

After working her way through a semester at New Bethlehem Business College in Pennsylvania, S. moved in 1917 to New York City, selling varnish to pay her way. S. first found a sales job in a Brooklyn department store, but soon enlisted in the Navy, serving a year as one of the first Yeomanettes. S. took a position with King Features in 1920, first writing daily love columns under the names Beatrice Fairfax and Annie Laurie, but soon writing under her own byline for the New York *American, Graphic*, and *Mirror*. She won fame for her feature articles and daring publicity stunts. S. also appeared on Broadway in Irving Berlin's Music Box Revue (1922–23) and in the Shubert revival of *The Mikado* (1924).

In 1926, S. moved to Pittsburgh to write a daily column and features for the Pittsburgh *Sun Telegraph*. On her editor's dare, she wrote her first novel. The tremendous popularity of *Make Up* (1931) won her a contract as columnist and serial writer with Central Press in 1928. After her marriage, S. moved to Chicago, where her first radio drama, *The Girl Reporter*, was purchased and produced by NBC. In 1930, she began to write for the Bell Syndicate and North American Newspaper Alliance. The next fourteen years would see all twenty-one of her romances published serially; only twelve were republished in book form. S.'s son was born in 1930.

In 1940, S. took a publicity job with Columbia Broadcasting System in Hollywood, soon moving to head the writing department of the Mutual Don Lee Network to write radio dramas and general continuity. From 1944 to 1946, S. directed the Radio Bureau of the National War Fund in New York. The years after 1946 were productive; she wrote features, columns, and songs for films. *The Doofer Family*, a serial fantasy for children which was inspired by songs and jokes she enjoyed with her young son and is S.'s own favorite, appeared through General Features (1955–56).

During the Korean War, S. was a soldier show technician for the U.S. Army, stationed at Fort Chaffee, Arkansas. S. worked as public relations director for Columbus Plastics in Columbus, Ohio, from 1959 until 1965, when she moved to Austin, Texas. Since 1965, she has handled public relations for good causes and has contributed columns to magazines and newspapers. S. is currently featured in a local radio talk show and writes and stars in television commercials.

S.'s romances are readable, with interesting characters, rapidly developed action, and lively dialogue. The serials reflect the author's experiences and views. Like Janet James of *Make Up* and Rosalie March of *Dimpled Racketeer* (1931), S.'s heroines are often attractive and talented country girls who come to the city naive but eager to get ahead. But like singer Elanda Lee of *High Hat* (1930), determined to get a break in radio, or dancer Jan Keats of *Rainbow over Broadway* (1936), determined to become a Broadway star, S.'s heroines are characterized by independence, hard work, and a refusal to compromise values and expectations. After finding independence and success, they can make room in their lives for love, happiness, and a home with a reliable, honest, and sensitive man. All offer readers the vicarious experience of the best of both a brilliant career and a loving family. Each novel climaxes with the happy marriage of hero and heroine, a marriage that resolves all subplots.

For S., writing has always meant the use of a particular kind of talent for profit. Inspiration usually begins with characters. When these are fully developed, a plot forms around them. From the plot outline, the writing comes quickly. As S. puts it: "Writing takes three things. It requires an active creative imagination which leads to a pattern, a formula. And it requires a market. Without a market, a writer really has no purpose." The great popularity of S.'s serial fiction indicates her success and understanding in creating for the market of her choice.

WORKS: *The Flat Tire* (1930). *High Hat: A Radio Romance* (1930). *Dimpled Racketeer* (1931). *Make Up: A Romance of the Footlights* (1931). *Flighty: A Romance of Gypsy O'Malley—A Girl Who Lived Down Her Family* (1932). *Puppy Love: A Hollywood Romance* (1933). *Penthouse Love* (1934). *Too Wise to Marry* (1935). *Rainbow Over Broadway* (1936). *Too Many Beaus* (1936). *Thou Shalt Not Love* (1937). *The Lady Proposes* (1941).

KATHERINE STAPLES

Dorothy Scarborough

B. 27 Jan. 1878, Mount Carmel, Texas; d. 7 Nov. 1935, New York City
D. of John B. and Mary Adelaide Ellison Scarborough

S. came from a prosperous southern background—both grandfathers owned large plantations, and her father was a lawyer and judge. S. received her B.A. (1896) and M.A. (1898) from Baylor University, where she taught from 1905 to 1914. She did advanced graduate work at the University of Chicago, Oxford University, and Columbia University (Ph.D. 1917). She joined the faculty of Columbia, specializing in teaching short-story writing.

S.'s doctoral dissertation, *The Supernatural in Modern English Fiction* (1917), is an important scholarly work. She establishes the Gothic romance and French, Italian, German, and Russian works as primary influences on the use of the supernatural in modern literature. She discusses the supernatural by categories: modern ghosts, the devil, folktales, and supernatural science. S. concludes that the war was the cause for the contemporary interest in the supernatural and that American writers are essentially responsible for combining humor and the supernatural.

S. contributed book reviews, sometimes covering more than twenty works in a single review, to publications such as the New York *Sun*, *The Bookman*, and *The Dial*. She attacks writers who use fiction as a vehicle for propaganda or didacticism. Unfortunately, as many reviewers have noted, this criticism is applicable to her own novels and short stories. S. is praised for her realistic presentation, but condemned for her editorializing.

Many of S.'s novels use the Texas farmlands as setting. The plots revolve around romance, but love is frequently hampered by the problems facing the tenant farmer, the economics of the cotton industry, the threat of drought, flood, and the boll weevil. The depiction of natural forces in *The Wind* (1925) has been compared with that of Conrad (*Times Literary Supplement*, 5 Nov. 1925); the 1928 film, starring Lillian Gish, was, however, criticized for excessive use of nature imagery.

Impatient Griselda (1927) is one novel not flawed by propagandizing. Again the setting is a small Texas town with its typical inhabitants: the minister and his wife and children, the doctor, the do-gooder, the busybody, the Negro cook. S. contrasts two types of women: the seductress

(Lilith) and the wife (Irene). The novel opens with the death of one Lilith as she gives birth to a second. Irene marries Lilith's widower (Guinn the minister) and raises the stepdaughter Lilith and her own four children, but feels she never replaces either Lilith in her husband's heart. The book closes with the death of the second Lilith as she gives birth to a third-generation Lilith. Irene sees the cycle continuing as her own daughter must stand in for another Lilith. The types remain unreconciled.

S. did important research in collecting folk songs and ballads; her interest dated back to her early teaching career in Texas. In *On the Trail of Negro Folk-Songs* (1925) and *A Song Catcher in Southern Mountains* (sponsored by "Project 41" at Columbia University and published posthumously in 1937), S. discusses origins, influences, instruments, and variations and provides melodies for many songs. (Ola Lee Gulledge collected and transcribed the music in the first book.) *On the Trail of Negro Folk-Songs* includes a chapter on the blues based primarily on a visit with W. C. Handy. S. uses these songs extensively in her novels and the autobiographical *From a Southern Porch* (1919).

Humor pervades S.'s writings; she employs informal language, coins words, and puns. A modern reader may be annoyed by S.'s facile stereotyping of races (she shows blacks as a happy people singing while they toil in field or kitchen) or amused by her genteel treatment of passion and illegitimate birth, but her novels are entertaining. A scholar may be frustrated by the lack of scholarly apparatus in *The Supernatural in Modern English Fiction*, but S. has made significant contributions to scholarship with her dissertation and folk-song collecting.

WORKS: *Fugitive Verses* (1912). *The Supernatural in Modern English Fiction* (1917). *From a Southern Porch* (1919). *Famous Modern Ghost Stories* (edited by Scarborough, 1921). *Humorous Ghost Stories* (edited by Scarborough, 1921). *In the Land of Cotton* (1923). *On the Trail of Negro Folk-Songs* (with O. L. Gulledge, 1925). *The Wind* (1925; film version, 1928). *Impatient Griselda* (1927). *Can't Get a Red Bird* (1929). *The Stretch-berry Smile* (1932). *The Story of Cotton* (1933). *Selected Short Stories of Today* (edited by Scarborough, 1935). *A Song Catcher in Southern Mountains: American Folk-Songs of British Ancestry* (1937).

BIBLIOGRAPHY: Overton, G., *The Women Who Make Our Novels* (1928). For articles in reference works, see: *DAB*, Suppl. 1. *20thCA*.

Other references: *Bookman 50* (Jan. 1920). *PW* (16 Nov. 1935). *NYT* (8 Nov. 1935). *NYTBR* (11 Nov. 1917; 14 Aug. 1927; 27 Oct. 1929; 14 Feb. 1932; 11 April 1937). *TLS* (15 Nov. 1917; 5 Nov. 1925; 20 Nov. 1937).

NANCY G. ANDERSON

Evelyn Scott

B. 17 Jan. 1893, Clarksville, Tennessee; d. 1963, New York City
Given Name: Elsie Dunn
Wrote under: Evelyn Scott, E. Souza
D. of Seely and Thomas Dunn; common law marriage, Frederick Creighton
Wellman (Cyril Kay Scott), 1919; m. John Metcalf, 1928

Although S.'s family no longer held the moneyed position it enjoyed before the Civil War. S. was trained the values of the southern aristocratic tradition. At fifteen, she rejected the role of the southern woman and became an ardent feminist. The Dunn family moved to New Orleans when S. was eighteen. She enrolled in Sophie Newcomb College, but never finished her studies there; instead, she educated herself.

In 1913, S. ran away to Brazil with the dean of the School of Tropical Medicine of Tulane University. They changed their names to Evelyn and Cyril Kay Scott. One son was born of this union in Brazil.

The Scotts returned from Brazil in 1920, lived in Greenwich Village and Cape Cod, and separated in Bermuda. In 1928, S. married British novelist John Metcalf.

Escapade (1923) is an account of S.'s six-year exile with her lover in Brazil. It is written in a subjectively impressionistic style, controlled by a conception: the entanglement of life and death in a conflict between the lush tropical growth soaring above villages of earthy natives and S.'s deathlike isolation. By selecting images that express feelings and actions, S. balances emotionalism with understanding, and avoids immersion in subjectivity. S. endured hunger, squalor, severe illness, and a fearful pregnancy. Each episode or carefully composed moment is imbued with S.'s belief that only in the presence of death do we discover life.

Background in Tennessee (1937) is an autobiographical history in which S. discusses the sociological, economic, religious, and cultural growth of the South, integrating her own experiences and judgments. S. believed the slow growth of culture in the South was due to the short span of time between the Revolution and the Civil War; most of the important men of the South were orators and politicians, not artists.

S. wrote several triologies of novels. *The Narrow House* (1921), *Narcissus* (1922), and *The Golden Door* (1925) are about three generations of a family attempting to hold on to their self-made ideals and hollow beliefs. *Migrations* (1927), *The Wave* (1929), and *A Calendar of Sin* (1932) cover American history from 1850 to 1918. In *The Wave*, set during the Civil War, S. combined over one hundred episodes in a deliberately structured mosaic, illustrating the conflict of individuals with society and with themselves. S. equated the perversion of war with the perversion of love lying in the heart of each individual.

The range of S.'s other publications is broad. *Precipitations* (1920), her first book, is of imagist poetry. *The Winter Alone* (1930) contains poetry more varied in subject and techniques. *Love*, a play, was performed by the Provincetown Players in 1930. S. wrote a mystery, *Blue Rum* (1930), under the name E. Souza, and three juvenile books: *In the Endless Sands* (1925), *Witch Perkins* (1928), and *Billy, the Maverick* (1934).

S. possessed the rare combination of emotional intuition and an artistic genius for style and technique. She was a fervent intellectual, sensitive but analytical. She had no strict philosophy, but she consistently strove in her life and work for freedom from every limitation. S. believed in authorial intrusion and wrote all her fiction from an omniscient point of view, a technique which gave her the freedom she desired. S.'s major works can be read and studied simultaneously on psychological, philosophical, and artistic levels.

WORKS: *Precipitations* (1920). *The Narrow House* (1921). *Narcissus* (1922). *Escapade* (1923). *The Golden Door* (1925). *In The Endless Sands* (1925). *Ideals* (1927). *Migrations* (1927). *Witch Perkins* (1928). *The Wave* (1929). *Blue Rum* (1930). *The Winter Alone* (1930). *A Calendar of Sin* (1932). *Eva Gay* (1933). *Breathe upon These Slain* (1934). *Billy, the Maverick* (1934). *Bread and a Sword* (1937). *Background in Tennessee* (1937). *Shadow of a Hawk* (1941).
The papers of Evelyn Scott and two unfinished novels are in the possession of Robert L. Welker.

BIBLIOGRAPHY: Scott, C. K., *Life Is Too Short* (1943). Welker, R. L., "Liebestod with a Southern Accent," *Reality and Myth* (1964).
For articles in reference works, see: *America Now*, Ed. H. E. Stearns (1938). *Living Authors*, Ed. D. Tante (1935).

PEGGY BACH

Catharine Maria Sedgwick

B. 28 Dec. 1789, Stockbridge, Massachusetts; d. 31 July 1867, West Roxbury, Massachusetts
Wrote under: Miss Sedgwick
D. of Theodore and Pamela Dwight Sedgwick

S.'s father was from a family of New England farmers and tavern keepers. He served in both houses of Congress and as Massachusetts Supreme Court chief justice. Her mother belonged to one of the wealthiest colonial families. Because she was sickly, her seven surviving children were raised by a black servant, Elizabeth Freeman, whom they called "Mumbet."

Education was an important part of the Sedgwicks' daily life. All the children were required to read Hume, Butler, Shakespeare, and Cervantes. S. attended the local grammar school at Stockbridge and was sent to Mrs. Bell's School in Albany and Payne's Finishing School in Boston. S. later commented that the greatest influence on our characters is our childhood home.

Shortly before her father's death in 1813 he unexpectedly confided his liberal religious beliefs to a close friend, the Unitarian minister William Ellery Channing. At this time, S. began to express in her journals and letters her own disapproval of Calvinism, the predominant religion of her Berkshire community. Several years later she joined the Unitarian church in New York. Her brothers Theodore and Henry, both noted lawyers and advocates of social reform, also joined the Unitarian church, but other of her relatives objected to S.'s conversion. An aunt told S., "Come and see me as often as you can, dear, for you know, after this world, we shall never meet again."

In 1822, S. began to write a small pamphlet protesting religious intolerance. This work evolved into a full-length novel entitled *A New England Tale*, which was published anonymously that year. The book is set in the New England countryside, and includes characters who speak in the local dialects. It is the story of a virtuous orphan girl, Jane Elton, who is reduced to extreme poverty. The heroine is mistreated by ostensibly pious relatives until she marries a Quaker gentleman and lives happily ever after. The book exposes the hypocrisy of certain church officials, and includes subplots concerning corrupt lawyers, dueling, and gambling. It was an immediate success. At that time, most books read in the U.S. were British imports or American imitations of British works. *A New England Tale* was recognized as one of the first novels to include authentic American settings, situations, and characters. It was soon a bestseller on both sides of the Atlantic.

With the publication of her second novel, *Redwood* (1824), S. became as popular as her contemporaries Cooper and Irving. *Redwood* was translated into German, Swedish, Italian, and French. The novel is about the marriage of a Southern gentleman to the daughter of a Vermont farmer. It also has a subplot involving the Shaker sect and a charter study of a strong, outspoken New England spinster.

With her third novel, *Hope Leslie* (1827), S. became the most famous American woman writer of her day. S.'s own mother had nearly been a victim in an Indian raid, and one of the family ancestors had married an Indian. The book contains lengthy discussions of Mohawk customs and colonial history. It is the story of three American women: Faith Leslie, who is captured by Indians, marries into the tribe, and adopts its way of life; her sister Hope, who is pursued by a villainous English admiral until his ship sinks in Boston harbor; and Madawisca, an Indian woman who saves Hope's fiancé when Mohawks attack him, and loses her arm in the process. *Hope Leslie* was hailed by critics as an American masterpiece.

S.'s next novel, *Clarence* (1830), discusses fashionable New York society. *The Linwoods* (1835) is a historical romance set during the Revolutionary War. S.'s last novel, *Married or Single?* (1857) was designed, in her words, "to lessen the stigma placed on the term 'old maid.' "

S., who never married, divided her time among the Sedgwick family homes in Stockbridge, Lenox, and New York City. She also toured Europe. Her tea parties were attended by Cooper, Hawthorne, Bryant, Emerson, and Melville. S. kept a journal for most of her life; it describes her spiritual quest, her travels, and her daily activities. She was an active social reformer: she founded the Society for the Aid and Relief of Poor Women and organized the first free school in New York, primarily for Irish immigrant children.

During the second half of her career, S. became famous as the author of didactic stories intended for children and working-class people. She hoped to convince her readers of the importance of education, democracy, and a close-knit family life. She believed that in America social mobility was largely determined by manners. Her most famous didactic novels were the trilogy consisting of *Home* (1835), *The Poor Rich Man and the Rich Poor Man* (1836), and *Live and Let Live* (1837). These books went through fifteen, sixteen, and twelve editions respectively.

S. lived to the age of seventy-eight and was buried next to her nurse Mumbet in Stockbridge. Her contemporary Hawthorne called S. "our most truthful novelist." Her finely crafted writing is more direct than the embellished style of most novels of her time. She was one of the creators of the American literary tradition, and one of the first American novelists to achieve international popularity.

WORKS: *A New England Tale* (1822). *Redwood* (1824). *Hope Leslie* (1827). *Clarence* (1830). *Home* (1835). *The Linwoods* (1835). *The Poor Rich Man and the Rich Poor Man* (1836). *Live and Let Live* (1837). *Letters from Abroad to Kindred at Home* (1841). *The Boy of Mount Rhigi* (1848). *Married or Single?* (1857). *Memoir of Joseph Curtis* (1858).

BIBLIOGRAPHY: Dewey, M., ed., *The Life and Letters of Catharine Maria Sedgwick* (1871). Foster, E. H., *Catharine Maria Sedwick* (1971).
For articles in reference works, see: *NAW* (article by R. E. Welch, Jr.).

JANE GILES

Anya Seton

B. 1916, New York City
Writes under: Anya Seton
D. of Ernest Thompson and Grace Gallatin Seton; m. Hamilton Chase, 1934 (?)

S.'s father was a nature writer; her mother was a feminist, explorer, and writer. S. was educated in England, France, and the U.S. She is married and the mother of two children. She has written thirteen novels, all historical, although her preferred term is "biographical." The variety of periods depicted is remarkable, but the settings are generally either British or American. All tell exciting stories, usually from the point of view of a female protagonist.

The heroines of the fictionalized biographies are related in some way to men who made history. *My Theodosia* (1941), S.'s first novel and the story of Aaron Burr's only child, dramatizes an obsessive, almost unnatural relationship between father and daughter. *Katherine* (1954) sympathetically recreates the life of Katherine Swynford, mistress and then wife of

John of Gaunt and sister-in-law of Geoffrey Chaucer. *The Winthrop Woman* (1958) centers on Elizabeth Fones Winthrop, niece and daughter-in-law of Jonathan Winthrop, a settler with him of the Massachusetts Bay Colony but a rebel against harsh Puritan rule. *Devil Water* (1962) studies Jenny Radcliffe, daughter of an English Jacobite nobleman who was executed for his participation in the rebellions of 1715 and 1745; her conversion to participation in his cause and her life in England and in Virginia are recreated.

Among the novels not centered on actual events is S.'s best-known work, *Dragonwyck* (1944). Set among Dutch patroons on the Hudson River in the mid-19th c., it contains an effective portrait of a Gothic villain and a heroine who is his innocent accomplice, for her passion and ambition have unconsciously helped cause his crimes. *The Turquoise* (1946), set in late 19th-c. New Mexico and New York, shows its destitute heroine's rise to the top of New York society, inadvertently causing a catastrophe. Her repentance and later life of contrition are movingly depicted. *The Hearth and the Eagle* (1948), set in 19th- and 20th-c. Marblehead, with a flashback to the 17th c., contains another strong heroine whose passionate and impulsive behavior leads her to a series of disappointments, then to ultimate acceptance of values she had earlier rejected.

In recent years, S.'s interest in the occult has led her to the theme of reincarnation. In *Green Darkness* (1972), contemporary characters redress evils that occurred in 1552–1559. *Smouldering Fires* (1975), a mixture of popular psychology and the occult, depicts an ungainly high-school girl who must, through hypnosis, relive the anguish of her Acadian ancestress in order to exorcise it and become a normal young woman.

The Mistletoe and the Sword (1955), set in Roman Britain, tells of the relationship between a Celtic girl and a Roman soldier, their initial enmity gradually being transformed to love. *Avalon* (1965), which moves through the British and Norse worlds of the late 10th c., follows the relationship of a Cornish girl and a French-English prince, whose lives are intertwined but who are always at cross-purposes. These two novels are unusual for S. in that male and female protagonists are balanced against each other, both angles of vision being used about equally.

Foxfire (1950) is the only one of S.'s novels that is not clearly historical. It is set in Arizona in the 1930s and combines the common western myth of the fabulous lost mine with the motif of a Shangri-la.

S.'s female protagonists are passionate and ambitious. In their youthful romantic idealism, they often rush into relationships that are doomed to disaster. The novels generally end with the heroines recognizing their responsibility for their fates and either doing penance or making a new beginning. In the process, they become "strong to endure." The historical backgrounds are based on thorough research. In her afterword to *Avalon*, S. stated her goal as being the attempt "to tell an accurate story, and to illuminate a shadowy corner of the past." That goal she has succeeded in accomplishing in many of her novels.

WORKS: *My Theodosia* (1941). *Dragonwyck* (1944; film version, 1946). *The Turquoise* (1946). *The Hearth and the Eagle* (1948). *Foxfire* (1950; film version, 1954). *Katherine* (1954). *The Mistletoe and the Sword: A Story of Roman Britain* (1955). *The Winthrop Woman* (1958). *Washington Irving* (1960). *Devil Water* (1962). *Avalon* (1965). *Green Darkness* (1972). *Smouldering Fires* (1975).

BIBLIOGRAPHY: *NY* (6 Feb. 1946). *NYTBR* (16 March 1941; 16 Feb. 1958; 21 Nov. 1965). *SatR* (9 Oct. 1954; 15 Feb. 1958; 3 March 1962).

MARY JEAN DeMARR

Anne Sexton

B. 2 Nov. 1928, Newton, Massachusetts; d. 4 Oct. 1974, Weston, Massachusetts
D. of Ralph and Mary Staples Harvey; m. Alfred M. Sexton II, 1948

Although her childhood included winters with her beloved great-aunt at the spacious family residence in Weston, Massachusetts, as well as happy seaside summers in Maine, S. was a demanding, rebellious child who felt rejected by her upper middle-class parents. Her impulsive marriage in 1948 to Alfred Sexton weathered many years of crises before it ended in divorce in 1973. S.'s sudden bouts of suicidal depression, which for several years necessitated separating her from her two small daughters, continued throughout her life, as did her psychiatric care in and out of mental hospitals. All of these problematic relationships form the basis of much of her poetry.

Discovering her poetic interests at age twenty-eight, this attractive housewife from the suburbs of Boston began studying under mentors such as Robert Lowell. S. taught at Boston University from 1970 until she took her life at the age of forty-five.

In *To Bedlam and Part Way Back* (1960), S. probed the intensely personal terrain of madness, guilt, and loss. As she undertakes her poetic journey from madness to partial sanity, her most frequent voice is that of the helpless, dependent child searching into the past for the lost parents and the disinherited self. Her two most famous *Bedlam* poems, "You, Doctor Martin" and "Ringing the Bells," capture the helpless childishness of mental patients who are "like bees caught in the wrong hive."

While many readers objected to her subject matter, the raw power of the *Bedlam* poetry quickly established S. as a new and significant "confessional" poet.

In the Pulitzer Prize–winning *Live or Die* (1966), religious parallels tend to universalize the dilemma of the "mad" persona. Thus, in "For the Year of the Insane," S. tries to overcome the passivity which keeps her "locked in the wrong house" but fumbling for a fragmented prayer to Mary, the "tender physician" who could heal the spiritual sickness of the "unbeliever." A new voice of awareness and self-irony is also heard. In one of her best poems, "Flee on Your Donkey," S. realizes that her madness has lost its "innocence." All the years of "dredging" dreams, "like an old woman with arthritic fingers, / carefully straining the water out," have only brought her back to the same "scene of the disordered senses," the "sad hotel" or mental institution from which she urges herself to flee. This book ends on an affirmative note: "I say *Live, Live* because of the sun, / the dream, the excitable gift."

Probably most notable are her poems on womanhood. In "Those Times . . .," S. remembers childhood humiliations and how she "hid in the closet" waiting "among shoes / I was sure to outgrow" while she "planned my growth and my womanhood." The joyous lyric "Little Girl, My Stringbean, My Lovely Woman" is addressed to her daughter who is about to discover that "women are born twice." The frustrations of being female are the focus of poems like "One for My Dame," "Man and Wife," and "Menstruation at Forty," frustrations which, in "Consorting with Angels," culminate in S.'s weariness with the "gender of things"—her own and that of the "men who sat at my table, / circled around the bowl I offered up."

S.'s interest in the religious drama of self led to an only moderately successful psychodrama, the one-act play *Mercy Street* (produced at the American Place Theatre, New York City, 1969) as well as several experimental short stories. More successful was Conrad Susa's free-form operatic adaptation of *Transformations* (1971), S.'s colloquially rendered poetic fairy tales, which was produced by the Minneapolis Opera Company in 1973 and televised in 1978. These experiments foreshadow some of the characteristics of S.'s later poetry: the looser poetic-prose line, the bold image, and the informal interpretations of mythic characters and situations.

Although S.'s poetry has sometimes been labeled bathetic or hysterical, the startling force of the hyperbolic image is her forte. In her best poetry,

S. explores the intensely personal but also universal conflict between the creative and self-destructive selves, a schizophrenic drama controlled by formal metrical patterns and casually placed rhymes. The elegaic voice searches for the lost, original self that has been tainted with experience and repressed in shame.

Although the frankness of her approach and the rather limited range of her autobiographical themes will continue to alienate some readers, S. has attained a significant ranking among contemporary confessional poets.

WORKS: *To Bedlam and Part Way Back* (1960). *All My Pretty Ones* (1962). *Eggs of Things* (with M. Kumin, 1963). *More Eggs of Things* (with M. Kumin, 1964). *Live or Die* (1966). *Selected Poems* (1967). *Poems* (with D. Livingston and T. Kinsella, 1968). *Love Poems* (1969). *Transformations* (1971). *Joey and the Birthday Present* (with M. Kumin, 1971). *The Book of Folly* (1972). *O Ye Tongues* (1973). *The Death Notebooks* (1974). *The Awful Rowing toward God* (1975). *The Wizard's Tears* (with M. Kumin, 1975). *45 Mercy Street* (Ed. L. G. Sexton, 1976). *Anne Sexton: A Self-Portrait in Letters* (Ed. L. G. Sexton, 1977).

BIBLIOGRAPHY: Fields, B., in *Poets in Progress: Critical Prefaces to Thirteen Modern American Poets*, Ed. E. Hungerford (1967). Fields, B., in *American Poets in 1976*, Ed. W. Heyen (1976). Lacey, P. A., *The Inner War: Forms and Themes in Recent American Poetry* (1976). McClatchy, J. D., ed., *Anne Sexton: The Artist and Her Critics* (1978). Mills, Jr., R. J., *Contemporary American Poetry* (1966). Nicholas, K. L., "The Hungry Beast Rowing Toward God: Anne Sexton's Later Religious Poetry," *NMAL*3 (Summer 1979). Northouse, C., and Walsh, R. P., *Sylvia Plath and Anne Sexton: A Reference Guide* (1974). Phillips, R., *The Confessional Poets* (1973). Rizza, P., "Another Side of This Life: Women as Poets," in *American Poetry Since 1960: Some Critical Perspectives*, Ed. R. Shaw (1973). Rosenthal, M. L., *The New Poets: American and British Poetry Since World War II* (1967).

Other references: *CentR* 19 (Spring 1975).

KATHLEEN L. NICHOLS

Mary Elizabeth Wilson Sherwood

B. 27 Oct. 1826, Keene, New Hampshire; d. 12 Sept. 1903, New York City
D. of James and Mary Lord Richardson Wilson; m. John Sherwood, 1851

S. was the oldest of seven children of a distinguished family of Scotch-Irish origin. She attended a fashionable private school for girls in Boston, where the training focused on good manners, not academic studies. S. became part of Washington social life as a hostess during her father's term in Congress (1847-50). Upon her mother's death in 1884 S. also assumed the duties of family management.

After her marriage to a New York lawyer, S. settled in Manhattan. She had four sons. Robert Sherwood, the playwright, was a grandson.

S. first began to sponsor literary events in a fund-raising effort for the restoration of Mount Vernon. By the 1870s, the Sherwood residence had become an establishment in New York literary and philanthropic circles. S. served as president of the Causeries, a literary gathering of distinguished New York women and was a member of several benevolent societies.

The drain on the family resources induced by entertaining persuaded S. to turn her efforts toward writing professionally. She had already published short stories and occasional verse in New York and Boston magazines. *A Transplanted Rose* (1882), her second novel, about the acceptance of a western girl into New York society, and a later, similar novel, *Sweet-Brier* (1889), were well-received. S. also published a volume of poetry and two autobiographical books, *An Epistle to Posterity* (1897) and *Here & There & Everywhere* (1898). Her style is lively, idiomatic, and touched with humor. S.'s most notable works, however, are in the field of etiquette. S.'s experience in Washington and Europe, where she traveled extensively, gave her great familiarity with a variety of styles of manners. Her articles on manners appeared in *Atlantic, Scribner's, Harper's, Appleton's Journal,* and *Frank Leslie's Weekly. Manners and Social Usages* (1884) was the most successful of S.'s books.

S. wrote popular manuals of style treating such standard topics as table manners and the art of conversation. Like later 20th-c. philosophers of social convention such as Emily Post, Amy Vanderbilt, and Peg Bracken, S.

pointed to kindness and regard for others as the universal law of manners. S. was, however, keenly aware of class differences. She was frank and firm in advocating the leadership of society by a class possessing talent and money. This was largely in reaction to the "upstarts" of the lower orders who were coming into sudden fortunes and social prominence.

S.'s several books on etiquette are addressed to a *status quo* of domestic women in the roles of wives and mothers—ladies of leisure and some means, whose main duties were, in S.'s belief, to temper the uncivilized tendencies of men and to serve as exemplars of congenial and decorous interpersonal relations. Like those social arbiters following her, S. sees women as the directors and managers of social setting and action.

Although S. can be criticized for not using her talents for more serious ends, and although her assessment of the role of good manners and the position of women in society was conservative, she should be remembered as the author of the most influential etiquette book of her time.

WORKS: *The Sarcasm of Destiny; or, Nina's Experience* (1878). *Amenities of Home* (1881). *A Transplanted Rose* (1882). *Etiquette* (1884). *Home Amusements* (1884). *Manners and Social Usages* (1884). *Royal Girls and Royal Courts* (1887). *Sweet-Brier* (1889). *The Art of Entertaining* (1892). *Poems by M.E.W.S.* (1892). *An Epistle to Posterity: Being Rambling Recollections of Many Years of My Life* (1897). *Here & There & Everywhere: Reminiscences* (1898).

BIBLIOGRAPHY: For articles in reference works, see: *AW. NAW* (article by B. A. Weller).
Other references: *NYT* (15 Sept. 1903).

MARGARET J. KING

Lydia Howard Huntley Sigourney

B. *1 Sept. 1791, Norwich, Connecticut; d. 10 June 1865, Hartford, Connecticut*
D. *of Ezekiel and Zerviah Wentworth Huntley*

S. was christened "Lydia Howard," in memory of her father's deceased first wife. As a child, she was favored by the widow of Dr. Daniel Lathrop, who employed S.'s father as a gardener. Mme. Lathrop made a pet of the clever, bookish girl, read with her and nurtured her sentimental tastes. After Mme. Lathrop's death in 1806, S. became acquainted with Lathrop's relatives, the Wadsworths of Hartford, and with their assistance, she and a friend—Nancy Maria Hyde—opened a school in Hartford in 1814. In 1815 Daniel Wadsworth helped her publish her first volume of poetry, *Moral Pieces*. In the following year, S. published her first elegiac volume, a tribute to her former colleague, Nancy Maria Hyde.

In 1819, S. gave up teaching to marry Charles Sigourney, a widower with three young children. Five children were born to her, of whom two survived infancy. When her husband's hardware business began to fail in the 1820s, S. turned to writing as a source of income and quickly became successful. A book of her poems was published by Samuel Goodrich ("Peter Parley") in 1827. By 1830, according to her biographer Gordon Haight, more than twenty periodicals were regularly accepting her occasional verse.

S. was early labelled "the American Hemans," a reference to her English counterpart, Mrs. Felicia Hemans, a popular writer of elegiac verse. S.'s work was indeed derivative and, like Heman's, unstintingly sentimental. Best known as a contributor to the "graveyard school" of popular verse, her "tributes," sometimes written at the request of unknown admirers, combine stilted rhetoric, conventional Christian consolation, and commonplace references to the condition or character of the deceased. Collections of her verse catalogue occasions on which the mourning note may be sounded. In one such volume, "The Anniversary of the Death of An Aged Friend" is followed by other verses lamenting deaths—"The Faithful Editor," "The Babe Who Loved Music," "The Good Son," "A Sunday

School Scholar," and "The Original Proprietor of Mount Auburn" (a well-known rural cemetary near Boston). Despite the individualized titles, the verses are almost interchangeable evocations of genteel religiosity and the postures of decorous sorrow. Such collections, prettily printed and illustrated, were republished throughout S.'s lifetime. Their popularity reflects conventional attitudes toward death, the quality of popular piety, and the widespread admiration for cultured refinement in Victorian America.

Always a popular writer, S. was never respected by contemporary literati. Edgar Allan Poe condemned her imitation of Hemans and her "gemmy," or over-colored, diction. (S. described her home, for example, as a "domain . . . beloved by flowers" where life "in its varied forms, biped and quadrupedal, leaped and luxuriated among us.") Bayard Taylor in *Diversions of the Echo Club* (1876) parodied her verse "to see whether a respectable jingle of words, expressing ordinary and highly proper feelings, can be so imitated as to be recognized." The best known parody of S.'s style and its imitators is Mark Twain's "Ode to Stephen Dowling Bots, Dec'd" in *The Adventures of Huckleberry Finn* (1884). However meagre its merits, S.'s verse is an important index of an era in American taste, and she herself was hailed by Taylor as "good old Mother Sigourney" who had once been "almost our only woman-poet." John Greenleaf Whittier, in a memorial verse of 1887, also noted that "She sang alone, ere womanhood had known / The gift of song which fills the air today."

WORKS: *Moral Pieces* (1815). *The Writings of Nancy Maria Hyde* (1816). *The Square Table* (1819). *Traits of the Aborigines of America* (1822). *Sketch of Connecticut Forty Years Since* (1824). *Poems* (1827). *Female Biography* (1829). *Biography of Pious Persons* (1832). *Evening Readings in History* (1833). *The Farmer and Soldier* (1833). *How to Be Happy* (1833). *The Intemperate* (1833). *Letters to Young Ladies* (1833). *Memoir of Phebe P. Hammond* (1833). *Report of the Hartford Female Beneficient Society* (1833). *Poems* (1834). *Poetry for Children* (1834). *Sketches* (1834). *Tales and Essays for Children* (1835). *Memoir of Margaret and Henrietta Flower* (1835). *Zinzendorff, and Other Poems* (1835). *History of Marcus Aurelius* (1936). *Olive Buds* (1836). *Poems for Children* (1836). *History of the Condition of Women* (1837). *The Girl's Reading-Book* ... (1838). *Letters to Mothers* (1838). *The Boy's Reading-book* . . . (1839). *The Religious Souvenir for 1839* (1839). *Memoir of Mrs. Mary Ann Hooker* (1840). *The Religous Souvenir for 1840* (1840). *Letters to Young Ladies* (1841). *Pocahontas, and Other Poems* (1841). *Poems, Religious and Elegiac* (1841). *Pleasant Memories of Pleasant Lands* (1842). *The Pictorial Reader* . . . (1844). *The Lovely Sisters* (1845). *Poetry for Seamen* (1845). *Scenes in My Native Land* (1845). *Myrtis, with Other Etchings and Sketchings* (1846). *The Voice of Flowers* (1846). *The Weeping Willow* (1847). *Water-drops* (1848). *The Young Ladies Offering* (with others, 1848). *Illustrated Poems* ... (1849) *Poems for the Sea* (1850). *Whisper to a Bride* (1850). *Letters to My Pupils* (1851). *Examples of Life and Death* (1852). *Margaret and Henrietta* (1852). *Olive Leaves* (1852). *Voices of Home* (1852). *The Faded Hope* (1853). *Memoir of Mrs. Harriet Newell Cook* (1853). *Past Meridian* (1854). *The Western Home, and Other Poems* (1854). *Sayings of the Little Ones, and Poems for their Mothers* (1855). *Examples from the Eighteenth and Nineteenth Centuries* (1857). *Lucy Howard's Journal* (1858). *The Daily Counsellor* (1859). *Gleanings* (1860). *The Man of Uz, and Other Poems* (1862). *Selections from Various Sources* (1863). *Sayings of Little Ones* (1864). *Letters of Life* (1866). *The Transplanted Daisy: Memoir of Frances Racilla Hackley* (n.d.).

BIBLIOGRAPHY: Haight, G. S., *Mrs. Sigourney: The Sweet Singer of Hartford* (1930).

JANE BENARDETE

Bertha Muzzy Sinclair

B. *15 Nov. 1871, Cleveland, Minnesota; d. 23 July 1940, Los Angeles, California*
Wrote under: B. M. Bower
D. of Washington and Eunice A. Miner Muzzy; m. Clayton J. Bower, 1890;
m. Bertrand W. Sinclair, 1906; m. Robert Ellsworth Cowan

S. moved to Montana as a youngster, where she gained expertise in ranching and acquaintance with cowboys, which she would later use in her novels. S. lived in the West most of her life. She was married three times and was the mother of four children.

S. wrote nearly sixty Westerns from 1904 to 1940. Her use of initials as a pseudonym led many to assume that her works were written by a man. In this guise she was probably the first woman, and certainly the most prolific, to write in the genre of the "formula" Western.

Chip of the Flying U (1904) furnishes the basic plot for S.'s writing and introduces characters for later works. "The Happy Family," the cowboys of the Flying U Ranch, appear in several subsequent novels and furnish prototypes for others. Chip is the first of many young heroes predictably tall, handsome, taciturn, and, by modern standards, remarkably naive about his emotions. Della, the heroine, is petite and dimpled, and has the tiny hands and feet so admired in the 19th c. Their love affair suffers many vicissitudes before it reaches its foregone conclusion, with intimations that they will live happily ever after. Later books sometimes offer more violence and villainy, but in most of the novels the happy outcome is predictable.

S.'s detailed descriptions of ranch life in the early 20th c. make her books attractive. The habits—down to the typical gestures—of the cowboys are well depicted, from the back-hand twist the practiced roper uses to catch a calf to the apparently eternal preoccupation of all cowboys with their cigarettes. The men's affection for their horses is an inevitable part of the Western, but, in addition, the actions of horses often affect the stories, with scenes in which the individual characteristics of horses play a major role. Dialogue especially reflects both the western setting and the period in which S. wrote. When a man declares his love it is apt to be in terms of a card game: "It's my deal . . . do you want to know what's trump?"

Characterization of males is, on the whole, weak, with one hero almost indistinguishable from another and supporting characters flat. S.'s women, on the other hand, are often accomplished and independent, indicating S.'s interest in unconventional roles for women. She introduces two women doctors in *Chip of the Flying U*, for example, in which the heroine is not only a doctor, she is also a crack shot and brave in the face of danger. Housewifely skills assume little importance in other books as well. In *The Five Furies of Leaning Ladder* (1935), five orphan girls run their ranch in the face of many obstacles; the one sister who is domestic is relegated to a minor role.

The suffering young mother in *Cabin Fever* (1918), whose little boy has been kidnapped, is much more interesting than the male hero in this mining story. The heroine of *The Heritage of the Sioux* (1916) is an Indian. She travels a long distance alone to find the man she loves. Later, when she learns the man she promised to marry has betrayed her friends, she kills herself.

S.'s books read like early Western scenarios, and with good reason. The uncluttered scenery and rapid uncomplicated actions of her characters lend themselves easily to film. Several of S.'s novels were made into movies. Some books, written in the 1910s, in the early days of the film industry, portray the cowboys forming their own film company and making Westerns in New Mexico.

S. brought a fairy-tale West to life for her readers. In spite of the realism of her descriptions of western life and specific details of ranch scenes, S.'s description of the larger scene is vague and ephemeral. The background, no matter what state is named, is simlpy "the West," and her books are typical formula Westerns. There are many weaknesses in S.'s writing; nevertheless, her stories are fun—warm and full of humor.

WORKS: *Chip of the Flying U* (1904). *The Lure of the Dim Trails* (1907). *Her Prairie Knight* (1908). *The Lonesome Trail* (1909). *The Long Shadow* (1909). *The Happy Family* (1910). *The Range Dwellers* (1910). *Good Indian* (1912). *Lonesome Land* (1912). *The Gringos* (1913). *The Uphill Climb* (1913). *Flying U Ranch* (1914). *The Ranch at the Wolverine* (1914). *Flying U's Last Stand* (1915). *Jean of the Lazy A* (1915). *The Heritage of the Sioux* (1916). *The Phantom Herd* (1916). *The Lookout Man* (1917). *Starr of the Desert* (1917). *Cabin Fever* (1918). *Skyrider* (1918). *The Thunder Bird* (1919). *The Quirt* (1920). *Rim o' the World* (1920). *Casey Ryan* (1921). *Cow Country* (1921). *Trail of the White Mule* (1922). *The Parowan Bonanza* (1923). *The Voice of Johnnywater* (1923). *The Bellehelen Mine* (1924). *Desert Brew* (1924). *Black Thunder* (1925). *Meadowlark Basin* (1925). *Van Patten* (1926). *White Wolves* (1926). *The Adam Chasers* (1927). *Points West* (1928). *The Swallowfork Bulls* (1928). *Rodeo* (1929). *Fool's Goal* (1930). *Tiger Eye* (1930). *Dark Horse* (1931). *The Long Loop* (1931). *Laughing Water* (1932). *Rocking Arrow* (1932). *Open Land* (1933). *Trails Meet* (1933). *The Flying U Strikes* (1934). *The Haunted Hills* (1934). *The Dry Ridge Gang* (1935). *The Five Furies of Leaning Ladder* (1935). *Trouble Rides the Wind* (1935). *The North Wind Do Blow* (1936). *Shadow Mountain* (1936). *Pirates of the Range* (1937). *Starry Night* (1938). *The Wind Blows West* (1938). *The Singing Hill* (1939). *The Man on Horseback* (1940). *The Spirit of the Range* (1940). *Sweet Grass* (1940). *The Family Failing* (1941).

BIBLIOGRAPHY: For articles in reference works, see *20thCA*.
Other references: *NYHT* (24 July 1940). *NYT* (24 July 1940).

HELEN STAUFFER

Cornelia Otis Skinner

B. *30 May 1901, Chicago, Illinois; d. 9 July 1979, New York City*
D. *of Otis and Maud Durbin Skinner; m. Alden S. Blodget, 1928*

S. was the only child born to a theatrical couple. Her mother retired from the stage shortly after S. was born, but her father went on to gain national prominence as an actor and matinee idol. Skinner spent much of his time on tour, but the family's desire for a stable and respectable home life led them to settle in Bryn Mawr, Pennsylvania, where S. grew up.

Tall and lanky, S. thought of herself as an ugly duckling. The autobiographical *Family Circle* (1948) underscores the embarrassing contrast between her mother's effortless charm and S.'s adolescent gawkiness. Nevertheless, from an early age S. gravitated toward the theater. After two years at Bryn Mawr, where she proved herself hopelessly unmathematical, S. departed for Paris. There she attended lectures at the Sorbonne while also receiving classical theater training from Jacques Copeau and Émile Dehelly of the Comédie Francaise. S.'s father paved her way onto the Broadway stage by providing a small role for her in his own production of the Spanish novel *Blood and Sand*.

While undertaking small roles in a number of productions, S. wrote a play for her father. Called *Captain Fury*, it opened in December, 1925. Soon S. was using her writing talents for her own benefit, creating lively theatrical monologues, which she performed in the United States and London. The monologues grew into a series of historical costume dramas, with S. herself playing all the roles.

From a sentimental novel of the day, *Edna His Wife*, S. developed a monodrama in which she portrayed three generations of women. This ambitious work toured the country in 1938, generating great public enthusiasm, although the New York critics were less kind. She was much better received by them in the title role of Shaw's *Candida* and in other full-fledged productions.

S. also contributed light verse and humorous essays to *The New Yorker, Harper's Bazaar, Ladies' Home Journal*, and other magazines. The witty depiction of human social foibles is her particular specialty, and her sketches often turn on comic self-deprecation. S. married in 1928 and has one son, and she often wrote of domestic matters. Her satirical treatment of her own ineptness as wife, mother, and social animal is good-natured enough so that readers can identify easily with her tales of woe. Her essays have been collected into a number of genuinely funny volumes, among them *Tiny Garments* (1932), *That's Me All Over* (1948), and *Bottoms Up!* (1955).

S.'s most famous volume is *Our Hearts Were Young and Gay* (1942), an uproarious account of a youthful trip abroad in the company of a schoolmate, Emily Kimbrough. The book details how these two naive young ladies spent the night in a brothel, came down with childhood diseases at inopportune moments, and otherwise found themselves in hot water. It captured the public fancy, and a million copies were sold. Inevitably there was soon a motion picture version (1944), and in 1948 Jean Kerr adapted the book into a popular play. Through all of this, S. did not neglect her own stage career. With Samuel Albert Taylor she wrote a successful Broadway comedy, *The Pleasure of His Company* (1959), and herself played one of the key supporting roles to general acclaim. Her one-woman shows also continued.

S.'s skills as a biographer were first displayed in *Family Circle* (1948), which is as much about her parents as herself. Her major work on Sarah Bernhardt, *Madame Sarah* (1967), was well received, less for its scholarship than for the vivid and affectionate portrait it draws.

S.'s reputation today rests on the grace with which she moved in several directions at once. Both a master of the comic sketch and a serious researcher into theater history, she brought to her writing projects an effortless quality that tends to obscure her very real talent.

WORKS: *Tiny Garments* (1932). *Excuse It, Please!* (1936). *Dithers and Jitters* (1938). *Soap Behind the Ears* (1941). *Our Hearts Were Young and Gay* (with E. Kimbrough, 1942). *Popcorn* (1943). *Family Circle* (1948). *That's Me All Over* (1948). *Nuts in May* (1950). *Bottoms Up!* (1955). *The Ape in Me* (1959). *The Pleasure of His Company* (with S. A. Taylor, 1959). *Elegant Wits and Grand Horizontals* (1962). *Madame Sarah* (1967). *Life with Lindsay & Crouse* (1976).

BIBLIOGRAPHY: *The New Yorker* (21 Nov. 1942). *NYT* (5 Sept. 1948; 10 July 1979). *NYTBR* (8 Jan. 1967). *SatR* (19 Nov. 1938; 14 Nov. 1942; 11 Sept. 1948). *TLS* (27 April 1967).

BEVERLY GRAY BIENSTOCK

Tess Slesinger

B. 16 July 1905, New York City; d. 21 Feb. 1945, Los Angeles, California
D. of Anthony and Augusta Singer Slesinger; m. Herbert Solow, 1928;
m. Frank Davis, 1936

S. could be said to have had everything but time: well-to-do parents who sacrificed in order to give her the best education at the Ethical Culture

Society School in New York, Swarthmore College, and Columbia University; immediate and continued success when she started to write; a happy marriage and children. But her works show that this success was not achieved without pain. Through her first husband she became part of a left-wing circle important in publishing, and she was able to publish her first short-story at age twenty-three; but S. found radical theorizing and intellectualizing insufficient to give meaning to life and divorced Herbert Solow. In 1935, S. went to Hollywood to begin a new career as a script writer.

After working on the screenplay for Pearl Buck's *The Good Earth* (produced in 1937), S. began a collaboration with Frank Davis which led to many successful scripts. She was able to combine a happy marriage to Davis and having two children with full professional activity until her untimely death of cancer at 39. Just a week after her death, *A Tree Grows in Brooklyn*, for which she and her husband had written the script, opened in New York. S. was politically active in helping to make the Screen Writers Guild a viable union and in many other human rights causes.

Received by contemporaries as a realistic portrayal of the "lost generation," *The Unpossessed* (1934) reveals S.'s profound understanding of her own time. The central character Margaret Flinders attempts to please her egotistical husband, even undergoing an abortion in order to "free" him; S. lets us see her act as a violation of her own being in exchange for his pretentious and selfish ambition. S. reveals his attempts to find meaning through endless discussions with other intellectuals, without any commitment to action, as typical of the futilities of the 1930s. Her skillful use of stream-of-consciousness establishes a light tone while revealing her persona's despair; the reader identifies with her because her problems are questions, her attempts to solve them are processes, not authoritative answers. The final chapter, "Missis Flinders," also published as a short story, is a masterpiece of ironic understatement affirming both the pain and the power to endure of her character.

The title of S.'s 1935 collecton of short stories *Time: The Present* is ironic in that its very contemporary concerns are timeless. S. touches on the emptiness of middle-class life, disillusionment with the American dream, the ruthlessness of the struggle to survive brought on by the Depression, the hypocrisy of whites toward blacks, the ambiguities for women of their relationships to their adulterous husbands and to their mothers, the problems of the artist attempting to reduce the felt hugeness of experience into effective form. Her story on this last theme, "A Day in the Life of a Writer," shows S.'s mastery of form and her typical ironic tone. Following the mental ramblings of a male writer trying to overcome a writing-block, she shows his "life in the day"—his self-loathing for not being able to repeat the success of his first book, his childish projection of his failure onto his "deaf-mute" typewriter and his wife. The reader understands both his ambivalence toward writing as a prison and the anger of his wife, who supports him.

S.'s stories about women show particular acuity. "On Being Told that Her Second Husband has Taken his First Lover" focuses on the continuance of the double-bind for women even with the sexual revolution. A wife who did not originate adultery feels she must accept her husband's announced infidelity as his right to freedom but cannot perceive her right to respond in kind as viable. Her only recourse is to accept his decision, with wit and anguish; rejecting him will only be a repetition of the end of her first marriage. "Mother to Dinner" explores the dilemma of a young wife caught between her husband's demands for her entire devotion and her mother's need for emotional support. The character sees no way out. (S., in divorcing her first husband, refused such a commitment and devoted herself to her writing.)

S.'s works show not only promise but accomplishment; her short stories and her film scripts will long outlive her. Although her works have been republished, twenty of her stories remain uncollected. Excerpts from recently discovered notes for another novel, focusing on the real workers of Hollywood, confirm her importance as one who saw through the pretensions and complexities of her own time to basic human issues.

WORKS: *The Unpossessed* (1934). *Time: The Present* (1935; reprinted as *On Being Told That Her Second Husband Has Taken His First Lover, and Other Stories,* 1971). Screenplays produced: *The Good Earth* (1937). *The Bride Wore Red* (1937). *Dance, Girl, Dance* (with F. Davis, 1940). *Remember the Day* (with F. Davis, 1941). *Are Husbands Necessary?* (with F. Davis, 1942). *A Tree Grows in Brooklyn* (with F. Davis, 1945).

BIBLIOGRAPHY: Sharistanian, Janet, in *MQR* (Summer 1979).
For articles in reference works, see *20thCA. 20thCAS.*
Other references: *AR* (Spring 1977). *Jewish Social Studies* (Summer 1976). *NYT* (20 May 1934). *Prospects* (1981). *WLB* (Dec. 1934).

MARY ANNE FERGUSON

Agnes Smedley

B. *1892, Missouri; d. 6 May 1950, London, England*
D. *of Charles and Sarah Ralls Smedley; m. Ernest Brundin, 1912*

S.'s life began in the drab rural poverty of northwestern Missouri. She grew to maturity in the squalor of Colorado mining towns, where her father, an uneducated, hard-drinking, defiant man, had hoped to find his fortune and where her mother took in laundry and died of overwork when S. was sixteen.

Determination to avoid her mother's fate led S. to leave home, work at odd jobs throughout the Southwest, and supplement her grade school education with a year at Tempe Normal School in Arizona. A brief "egalitarian" marriage ended in divorce.

Around 1917, S. began a decade of deep involvement, in New York and Berlin, with the efforts of Indian nationalists to free India from British rule. At the same time she wrote in support of socialist and feminist causes, established birth control clinics, and studied Asian history and Marxism. A relationship during the 1920s with exiled revolutionary leader Virendranath Chattopadhyaya drove S. to a nervous breakdown; she wrote her autobiographical novel *Daughter of Earth* (1929) in an attempt to reorient her life.

S. went to China in 1928 and dedicated the rest of her life to the Chinese revolutionary cause. She developed friendships with Communist leaders, traveled with the Red Army as it fought Chiang Kai-Shek's Kuomintang and later the Japanese, and worked unstintingly to secure medical treatment for the wounded. S. wrote prolifically, producing three books during the 1930s and a profusion of articles for European, American, and Asian periodicals.

Ill health forced S. to return to the U.S. in 1941, and in 1943 she published her widely acclaimed *Battle Hymn of China*. Although she had never joined the Communist Party, the forces of McCarthyism hounded S. out of the country in the late 1940s. She died in London enroute to the new People's Republic of China.

Daughter of Earth, S.'s only novel, tells of a working-class woman who develops a feminist and a class consciousness as she pits her determination to be a free person against the traps society lays for women and the poor.

Marie Rogers, the narrator of this first-person account, attains and pre-
serves her independence—the book's plot is taken from S.'s own life right
up to the moment of its writing—but the emotional cost is high. Marie
must cope with the persistent guilt, confusion, and pain of a woman who
refuses to fit into expected roles.

S.'s novel differs from standard proletarian fiction in its outspoken feminism and its emphasis on the psychological. Although it is not reliable autobiography, especially in the concluding sections, the book suffers artistically from its close identification with the still-unfolding events of S.'s
own life. But what this startlingly up-to-date novel lacks in balance and
perspective it makes up for in emotional power.

Chinese Destinies: Sketches of Present-Day China (1933), the first of
S.'s five books about China in upheaval, is a collage of articles, stories, and
impressions; it communicates a vivid sense of the corruption and utter
wretchedness of life in the old China and the revolutionary fervor of
those who hoped to build the new. S. focuses on individual lives, often
women's lives; the tales are well told and the effect is moving. *China's Red
Army Marches* (1934) follows a similar but less kaleidoscopic format, its
sketches relating loosely to the Red Army's historic progress as it widens
and secures its territory in inland China. In *China Fights Back: An American Woman with the Eighth Route Army* (1938), S. becomes an active
participant in her story, using her journal entries to give the Western
world a rare inside account of what life was like in the Red Army as it
battled the Japanese invaders. S.'s zeal and haste sometimes lead to simplistic characterizations and inelegant style, but at their best these books display stirring narrative power.

In *Battle Hymn of China*, history, autobiography, war reporting, and
story telling intermingle, as S. tries to tell wartime America all she had experienced and learned during her twenty-two years in China. This most
comprehensive of S.'s China books is also S.'s comprehensive autobiography. Like all her books, this one is strongly partisan, but its very fervor
helps promote an understanding of modern Chinese history by capturing
and communicating that spirit which made revolution possible.

The Great Road: The Life and Times of Chu Teh, S.'s enthusiastic biography of the peasant who became commander-in-chief of the Red
Army—and S.'s personal friend—was begun in the 1930s and published
posthumously in 1956. Despite stylistic inadequacies, the book is strong in
its depiction of rural Chinese society and its detailed look at life and politics within the Red Army.

S. saw herself as an interpreter of the Chinese revolution to the West.

Her vivid and sensitive observations from the center of one of the century's great dramas constitute her most important professional achievement. But S. also saw herself as a woman who, as she once wrote, refused to "live the life of a cabbage."

WORKS: *Daughter of Earth* (1929). *Chinese Destinies: Sketches of Present-Day China* (1933). *China's Red Army Marches* (1934). *China Fights Back: An American Woman with the Eighth Route Army* (1938). *Battle Hymn of China* (1943). *The Great Road: The Life and Times of Chu Teh* (1956). *Portraits of Chinese Women in Revolution* (Eds. J. MacKinnon and S. MacKinnon, 1976).

BIBLIOGRAPHY: Howe, F., Afterword to *Portraits of Chinese Women in Revolution* (1976). Huberman, L., and P. M. Sweezy, Publisher's Foreword to *The Great Road: The Life and Times of Chu Teh* by A. Smedley (1956). Lauter, P., Afterword to *Daughter of Earth* by A. Smedley (1973). Lovett, R. M., Preface to *China's Red Army Marches* (1934). MacKinnon, J., and S. MacKinnon, Introduction to *Portraits of Chinese Women in Revolution* (1976 by A. Smedley; a shorter version of this introduction is in *Bulletin of Concerned Asian Scholars*, Jan.–March 1975).

For articles in reference works, see: *CB* (1944, 1950). *DAB*, Suppl. 4 (article by K. E. Shewmaker). *NAW* (article by R. Gottesman). *20thCA*. *20thCAS*.

Other references: *Chinese Literature* (Oct. 1980). *Monthly Review* (April 1978). *Nation* (19 Feb. 1949). *NewR* (29 May 1950; 14 Dec. 1974). *New Statesman and Nation* (20 May 1950). *NYT* (9 May 1950; 6 April 1978). *Survey* (Autumn 1974).

PEGGY STINSON

Betty Wehner Smith

B. 15 Dec. 1896, Brooklyn, New York; d. 17 Jan. 1972, Shelton, Connecticut
Wrote under: Betty Smith
D. of John C. and Katherine Hummel Wehner; m. George Smith (1924?);
* m. Joseph Jones, 1943; m. Robert Finch, 1957*

Born and raised in the Williamsburg section of Brooklyn, S. attended public schools until the age of fourteen when, having completed eighth grade, she began working at a series of factory and clerical jobs. An avid reader as a young girl, she also wrote poems and acted in amateur productions at the Williamsburg YMCA. Moving to the Midwest, she met and married George Smith, a law student at the University of Michigan. There her two daughters were born. She audited literature and writing classes at the university and, although not a regular student, had two plays published in a collection of undergraduate work and won an Avery Hopwood prize.

From 1930 to 1934 S. studied with George Pierce Baker and others at the Yale Drama School. S.'s first two marriages ended in divorce. After the first divorce, S. accepted a Rockefeller fellowship in playwriting at the University of North Carolina; she remained in Chapel Hill, writing, occasionally lecturing at the university, and playing small roles in local productions. Her third husband, Robert Finch, a writer with whom she had collaborated on several plays, died about a year and a half after their marriage.

A dramatist by inclination, S. wrote over seventy plays and edited several collections and texts for drama classes. Most of her plays were not published and none received critical acclaim or even major professional performances. Typical of her plays meant for youth groups or schools are *The Boy, Abe* and *First Sorrows*, both about the young Abe Lincoln and the death of his mother. Other one-act plays range in tone from burlesque to sentimentality and in setting from a mid-19th-c. rural political rally (*Freedom's Bird*, written with Robert Finch) to the sidewalk in front of an illegal abortionist's office on a late depression era Christmas Eve (*So Gracious Is the Time*).

Though she preferred drama, S. won fame through her fiction. Drawing upon her own memories and those of her mother, she expanded an earlier work, "Francie Nolan," into *A Tree Grows in Brooklyn* (1943), her most successful novel. It sold millions of copies and was made into a movie and a Broadway musical. Whereas the plot and much of the writing can be criticized for excessive sentimentality, the strength of this highly autobiographical novel lies in the richness of detail with which S. recreates a young girl's childhood and adolescence in the slums of early-20th-c. Brooklyn, including both the pains of a poverty-stricken childhood and the good times. The characters are vivid and three-dimensional; even the minor characters come alive as recognizable types.

S.'s next novel, *Tomorrow Will Be Better* (1948) is set against the same background as her first, but reviewers were not impressed with this effort; they found the dialogue authentic but the book as a whole less spontaneous and more self-conscious than *A Tree Grows in Brooklyn*. In *Maggie-Now* (1958), the character types are similar to those in *A Tree Grows in Brooklyn*—charming, irresponsible men and their long-suffering, hard-working wives and daughters—but this novel too lacks the depth of the earlier one. In her fourth novel, *Joy in the Morning* (1963), S. shifted the locale from Brooklyn to a midwestern college campus. In some ways, this book is a sequel to the first novel, as the heroine, a Brooklyn girl with only a grade school education, marries a law student, audits literature and writing classes, and has her work published in a student collection.

S. obviously drew heavily upon her own experiences for the material for her novels. Her accurate ear for dialogue (a legacy of her dramatic training) is a strength in all of them. But the wealth of detail in *A Tree Grows in Brooklyn* may have exhausted her memories. Each of the succeeding books was less rich in characterization and atmosphere. Her greatest weakness, however, was her inability to shape her novels into realistic and meaningful form; thus they tend to be overly sentimental and to end mechanically or without resolution.

WORKS: (including the novels and a selection of the plays) *Folk Stuff* (1935). *His Last Skirmish* (1937). *Naked Angel* (1937). *Popecastle Inn* (1937). *Saints Get Together* (1937). *Plays for Schools and Little Theaters: A Descriptive List* (edited by Smith, with R. Finch and F. H. Koch, 1937). *Trees of His Father* (1937). *Vine Leaves* (1937). *The Professor Roars* (1938). *Western Night* (1938). *Darkness at the Window* (1938). *Murder in the Snow* (1938). *Silver Rope* (1938). *Youth Takes Over; or, When a Man's Sixteen* (1939). *Lawyer Lincoln* (1939). *Mannequins' Maid* (1939). *They Released Barabbas* (1939). *A Night in the Country* (1939). *Near Closing Time* (1939). *Package for Ponsonby* (1939). *Western Ghost Town* (1939). *Bayou Harlequinade* (1940). *Fun After Supper* (1940). *Heroes Just Happen* (1940). *Room for a King* (1940). *Summer Comes to the Diamond O* (1940). *To Jenny with Love* (1941). *25 Non-Royalty One-Act Plays for All-Girl Casts* (edited by Smith, 1942). *A Tree Grows in Brooklyn* (1943, dramatization by Smith, with G. Abbott, 1951; film version by Tess Slessinger and F. Davis, 1943). *20 Prize-Winning Non-Royalty One-Act Plays* (edited by Smith, 1943). *The Boy, Abe* (1944) *Tomorrow Will Be Better* (English title: *Streets of Little Promise*, 1948). *Young Lincoln* (1951). *Maggie-Now* (1958). *A Treasury of Non-Royalty One-Act Plays* (edited by Smith et al., 1958). *Durham Station* (1961). *Joy in the Morning* (1963).

BIBLIOGRAPHY: For articles in reference works, see: *CA*, *5–8* (1969). *CB* (1943, 1972). *20thCAS*.

ELAINE K. GINSBERG

Eliza Roxey Snow Smith

B. 21 Jan. 1804, Becket, Massachusetts; d. 5 Dec. 1886, Salt Lake City, Utah
D. of Oliver and Rosetta Leonora Pettibone Snow; m. Joseph Smith, 1842;
  m. Brigham Young, 1847

When S., the second of seven children, was very young, her parents migrated to Ohio, where her father successfully took up farming. S. received the most liberal education allowed a young woman at the time, attending the local schools of Ravenna, Ohio, and a grammar school taught by a Presbyterian minister. In her early teens, S. began writing poetry. Her first efforts were published in local newspapers and journals under pennames. These verses are typical of her day—sentimental, religious, and didactic.

In the 1820s, S., with her parents, joined the Reformed Baptist or "Campbellite" church, and she began a devoted study of the Bible. S. converted to the Church of Jesus Christ of the Latter Day Saints early in 1835, and that year left her family's home for the Mormon stronghold of Kirtland, Ohio, where she lodged with the Prophet Joseph Smith and his family. In 1838, S. followed Smith and his flock first to Missouri and then to Illinois, where S. began her rise to prominence in the Mormon church. S. probably became the Prophet's fourth or fifth wife when she secretly wed him in 1842.

After the murder of Smith and the dispersal of the followers, S. was among the first pioneering companies to reach the valley of the Great Salt Lake. During the course of the journey west, she kept a diary (published in *The Improvement Era*, 1943-44), and wrote patriotic, religious, and eulogistic poetry. Her poetry served as an inspiration to trail-weary Mormons, and encouraged them to continue on their way to the promised land: "Altho' in woods and tents we dwell / Shout, shout O Camp of Israel. / No Christian males on earth can bind / Our thoughts, or steal our peace of mind." On this trip westward, S., along with several of Smith's widows, was married to Brigham Young.

S. became the most beloved and powerful woman in Utah, as she increased her involvement with charitable, spiritual, and educational projects. In addition to publicly defending polygamy, S. was an ardent feminist. As head of the Women's Suffrage Society, she worked to dispel the myth that Mormon women lived lives subject to their husband's wills. She worked hard to ensure Utah's women the right to political franchise and won success in 1870.

S. continued to write poetry, hymns, and religious essays, published in several Utah journals, as well as practical educational texts while living in Utah. Her first volume of poetry, incorporating many of the poems she had written while on the trail from Illinois, was published in 1856, and a second volume was published in 1877. S. compiled a number of hymnals for the church, containing some of her own hymns, the most popular of which was "O My Father, Thou that Dwellest." She contributed an account of the "assassination" of Smith and his brother and several poems to Lucy Smith's *Biographical Sketches of Joseph Smith* (1853). With her brother Lorenzo Snow, the fifth president of the Mormon church, S. wrote *The Correspondence of Palestine Tourists* (1875), the record of their missionary trip to the Middle East. S. was reticent to write of her own experiences, but she did write an autobiographical sketch, which was published in the *Relief Society Magazine* (1944). S.'s best-known work, and an excellent source for historians interested in the foundations of the Mormon religion, is *The Biography and Family Record of Lorenzo Snow* (1884).

Married in turn to the two most important figures in the history of the Mormon church, S. made a name for herself through her own involvement in church affairs and education, and she pointed with pride to Utah women's right to vote and active participation in church affairs as evidence of Mormon women's freedom and equality. In addition, S. wrote poems and songs for the church; she provided the young Mormon church with its chief hymns.

WORKS: The Story of Jesus (1845). *Poems, Religious, Historical, and Political* (2 vols., 1856 and 1877). *The Correspondence of Palestine Tourists* (1875). *Bible Questions and Answers for Children* (1883). *Biography and Family Record of Lorenzo Snow* (1884). *Recitations for the Primary Associations* (edited by Smith, 1887). *Hymns and Songs: Selected from Various Authors for the Primary Associations of the Children of Zion* (edited by Smith, 1888). *Recitations for the Primary Associations in Poetry, Dialogues, and Prose* (edited by Smith, 1891).

A copy of Eliza Roxey Snow Smith's 1847 diary and her autobiographical sketch are in the Bancroft Library, University of California.

BIBLIOGRAPHY: Brodie, F. M., *No Man Knows My History: The Life of Joseph Smith, the Mormon Prophet* (1971). Crocherson, A. J., *Representative Women of Deseret* (1884). Gates, Susa Young, and L. D. Widstoe, *Women of the Mormon Church* (1926). Hill, D., *Joseph Smith: The First Mormon* (1977). Tullidge, E., *The Women of Mormondom* (1877).

For articles in reference works, see: *DAB*, IX, 1. *NAW* (article by M. S. De Pillis).

PAULA A. TRECKEL

Elizabeth Oakes Prince Smith

B. *12 Aug. 1806, North Yarmouth, Maine; d. 15 Nov. 1893, Hollywood, North Carolina*
Wrote under: E., Ernest Helfenstein, Elizabeth Oakes Smith, Oakes Smith, Mrs. Seba Smith
D. of David and Sophia Blanchard Prince; m. Seba Smith, 1823

As a child, S. lived in the country near the south coast of Maine, where she spent much time even after her family moved to Portland when she was eight. At the age of sixteen, S. married Seba Smith, an editor and publisher and the author of the popular Major Jack Downing stories. S.'s first poems and sketches appeared anonymously in his newspapers. In Portland, S. had five sons; one died as a young child.

After a series of financial reverses, the Smiths moved to New York in 1837 and took their places in that city's literary circles. S. contributed to the support of her family through her writing. Her stories, sketches, and poems appeared in the *Ladies' Companion, Godey's Lady's Book, Graham's Magazine,* and other popular monthlies of the day, in addition to her husband's various periodical publications. She contributed to thirty-six gift books (sentimental annual publications) between 1836 and 1856, editing some of them with her husband and some of them on her own.

From about the midpoint of her life, the "busy devil" with which S. professed to be afflicted directed her into intense reform activity. She was an active participant in the women's rights conventions of 1848, 1851, 1852, and 1878. In 1851, as an advocate of the working woman, S., with Lucretia Mott, sponsored a tailoring cooperative that employed women in Philadelphia. Under the auspices of the YMCA, she was a social worker in New York City. In 1868, she became a charter member of New York's first women's club; she served as its vice-president in 1869. In 1877, after a lifetime of religious searching and questioning, S. became the minister of an independent congregation in Canastota, New York.

S.'s early writings draw heavily on her immediate environment and include Indian myths and legends, Down East characters, and stories of Maine. These early writings also include sketches of women whose lives were far outside her experience, such as Charlotte Corday and Mme. de Staël, which reappear in later writings and in her lectures on the Lyceum circuit.

S. won popular and critical acclaim for "The Sinless Child," a long narrative poem which first appeared in the *Southern Literary Messenger*, to which she was a frequent contributor. In the poem, the unworldly heroine is released from a corrupt world through death. Its publication as the title piece in a collection of her poems in 1843 established S.'s reputation.

S.'s first novel, *Riches without Wings*, was published in 1838. Its themes and values are conventional: the superiority of natural beauty, temperance in all things, modesty, cleanliness. Worldly riches are not to be pursued at the expense of spiritual purity, but wealth and recognition do reward hard work and honesty. Her dialogues and asides to her readers are intended to instruct, and in these, along with the dominant themes, S. occasionally disparages convention, as when the leading female character asserts the value of passion in women as well as in men, and again when she refuses to wear the prescribed mourning dress on the death of a relative.

In her later work, S. continued to use the conventional themes of her first novel. A strong strain of mysticism, present in most of her writing, becomes more marked in the later writing. Patriotism and progress are typical themes. The evils of cities, the romantic theme of the superiority of the natural, or country life, is the major theme in *The Newsboy* (1854), a novel credited with influencing social reform in New York.

S.'s beliefs that women had the right to develop fully as individuals and that the current constraints of the marriage relation inhibited their development, were articulated in a series of essays in the New York *Tribune*, published as a monograph in 1851, under the title *Woman and Her Needs* (reprinted in 1974).

As a writer, S. was spurred always by financial necessity. Her work is remarkable for variety, volume, and inventiveness; it ranges from sonnets to very informal travel sketches and reminiscences, from children's stories to tragic drama. Though in general her characters have the conventional virtues and vices and her intensely romantic themes were chosen to appeal to a wide audience, S.'s fiction, poetry, and essays expose the occasional "burr under the saddle" that placed her among contemporary reformers and made her a significant contributor to the popular literature of the middle third of the 19th c.

WORKS: Riches without Wings (1838). *The Western Captive* (1842). *The Sinless Child, and Other Poems* (1843). *The Dandelion, The Rose-bud and The Moss Cup* (1845). *The Lover's Gift* (1848). *The Salamander* (1848). *The Roman Tribute* (1850). *The Good Child's Book* (1851). *Woman and Her Needs* (1851). *Hints on Dress and Beauty* (1852). *Shadowland* (1853). *Old New York* (1853). *The Sanctity of Marriage* (1853). *Bertha and Lily* (1854).

Black Hollow (1864). *The Newsboy* (1854). *Bald Eagle* (1867). *The Sagamore of Saco* (1868). *Selections from the Autobiography of Elizabeth Oakes Smith* (Ed. M. A. Wyman, 1924).

The New York Public Library has a collection of Elizabeth Oakes Smith's unpublished papers, including the manuscript of her autobiography.

BIBLIOGRAPHY: Wyman, M. A., *Two American Pioneers: Seba Smith and Elizabeth Oakes Smith* (1927).

For articles in reference works, see *Appleton's Annual Cyclopedia* (1893). *CAL. DAB, IX, 1. FPA, NAW* (article by A. F. Tyler).

Other references: *Broadway Journal* (23 Aug. 1845). *Graham's* (June 1843; Sept. 1853; April 1856). *North American Review* (Oct. 1854).

VIVIAN H. SHORTREED

Hannah Whitall Smith

B. 7 Feb. 1832, Philadelphia, Pennsylvania; d. 1 May 1911, Iffley, England
Wrote under: H.W.S.
D. of John Mickle and Mary Whitall; m. Robert Pearsall Smith, 1851

After a happy childhood in her Quaker home, S. married in 1851 and had four children.

S. departed early from strict Quaker ways, which seemed to her too rigid, to set out on a spiritual pilgrimage. Eventually, she began to preach, alongside her husband. The Smiths preached the "Higher Life" in America, in England, and on the Continent, being particularly active around 1873. Because S.'s husband was suspected of preaching false doctrine and also of improper conduct with female admirers, they returned to the U.S., but they settled permanently in England in 1886.

S.'s preaching was nonsectarian and the influences on her thought were various. After her marriage, S. came under the influence of the Plymouth Brethren, the Baptists, and the Methodists. But she had inherited from her father an attachment to the works of the 17th-c. French quietist Mme Guyon. S. also treated as a guide Mme Guyon's friend Fénelon, whose *Spiritual Letters* she quoted with approval.

Because S. was open to religious enlightenment from any source, she worked out for herself a safeguard against fanaticism, which she offers to her readers in *The Christian's Secret of a Happy Life* (1875). Her message is that God's guidance comes to us in four ways: "through the Scriptures, through providential circumstances, through the convictions of our own higher judgment, and through the inward impressions of the Holy Spirit on our minds." In early editions S. also included a chapter warning against taking emotional states as proof of the baptism of the Holy Spirit.

Both *The Christian's Secret of a Happy Life* and *The God of All Comfort* (1906) are still religious bestsellers today. They owe their appeal to the clarity, simplicity, and directness with which S. expresses her complete trust in God. Of at least equal interest, but out of print, is S.'s spiritual autobiography, *The Unselfishness of God, and How I Discovered It* (1903).

In the end, S. found that she had returned to a basic Quaker principle: that God has power to save us from sin, not only in a legalistic sense but also in a practical way, by preserving us from it and giving us constant guidance. Because of this interest in the practical applications of Christian teaching, S. was also active in the temperance and woman suffrage movements.

S. believed in will power as the chief condition for total trust in God. Her orthodoxy may have been suspect at one time, but her outlook suits the modern Christian.

WORKS: *The Record of a Happy Life: Being Memorials of Franklin Whitall Smith* (1873). *The Christian's Secret of a Happy Life* (1875). *John M. Whitall: The Story of his Life* (1879). *Every-Day Religion* (1893). *The Science of Motherhood* (1894). *The Unselfishness of God, and How I Discovered It* (1903). *The God of All Comfort* (1906). *Religious Fanaticism* (Ed. R. Strachey, 1928). *Philadelphia Quaker: Letters of Hannah Whitall Smith* (Ed. L. P. Smith, 1950).

BIBLIOGRAPHY: Pearsall, C. E., H. M. Pearsall, and H. L. Neall, *History and Genealogy of the Pearsall Family* (1928). Smith, L. P., *Unforgotten Years* (1939). Smith, R. M., *The Burlington Smiths* (1877). Strachey, R., *A Quaker Grandmother: Hannah Whitall Smith* (1914).

For articles in reference works, see: *DAB*, IX, 1. *NAW* (article by E. C. Kaylor, Jr.).

BARBARA J. BUCKNALL

Lillian Smith

B. 12 Dec. 1897, Jasper, Florida; d. 28 Sept. 1966, Atlanta, Georgia
D. of Calvin and Anne Simpson Smith

S. was the seventh of nine children. She tasted the "strange fruit" of racial segregation early in her childhood, when her well-to-do, genteel Methodist parents took in an apparently white orphan found living with a black family. The Smiths welcomed the girl until they learned she was part black. Then the children were hastily separated, leaving S. in conflict over the paradox of a culture that teaches hospitality, democracy, and Christian charity at the same time that it violently denies the humanity of blacks.

S.'s traditional southern upbringing led her to value literature, art, and music and to want to be socially useful. Her education (at Piedmont College and Baltimore's Peabody Conservatory of Music) was repeatedly interrupted by declining family fortunes, which had forced the Smiths to move to their summer home in Clayton, Georgia, in 1915. S. joined the Student Nursing Corps in WWI and, after the Armistice, taught for a year in an isolated mountain school in Georgia. She spent three years teaching music at a Methodist mission school in Huchow, China, and then returned to help run Laurel Falls Camp for Girls, the exclusive summer camp her father founded at their Georgia home, and to act as secretary to her brother Austin, the city manager of Fort Pierce, Florida. In 1928, she attended Columbia University's Teachers College, adding to her already considerable knowledge of child development and Freudian psychology. After her father died in 1930, S. assumed heavy family responsibilities, including the care of her invalid mother. And, in the next five years, she wrote five novels, never published and all lost in a 1944 house fire.

Along with her lifelong companion, Paula Snelling, another young, liberal southern intellectual hired to help run the camp, S. founded *Pseudopodia*, a little magazine heavily influenced by the editors' Freudian persuassion and their antisegregationist political and social views. At first, the magazine concentrated on reviewing works by and about blacks and took a literary stand against, among other things, Margaret Mitchell's *Gone with the Wind* and the Agrarians. It was renamed twice—as the *North American Review* (1937–42) and *South Today* (1942–44)—as the editors broadened their liberal crusade against the consequences of caste in the South and in other countries and as it became a forum also for S.'s fervent views on sexuality and childrearing.

Strange Fruit (1944), S.'s first published novel, sold over three million copies and was translated into sixteen languages. It was banned from the bookstores and libraries of Boston and from the bookstores of Detroit; Eleanor Roosevelt intervened to remove the Post Office ban. Much of the uproar stemmed from the realistic language and the ironic treatment of miscegenation, sexuality, and abortion. Set in racially segregated Maxwell, Georgia, in the years following WWI, the plot traces from its youthful beginning the secret interracial love affair of Tracy Deen—a war veteran, son of the town's respected white doctor and his aristocratic wife—and Nonnie Anderson—a black college graduate who can only find a job as a maid in Maxwell.

As in Theodore Dreiser's *American Tragedy* and Richard Wright's *Native Son*, S.'s fictional world is deterministic. Characters breaking a taboo in this segregated society must suffer violence. Tracy Deen is murdered by the brother of his pregnant lover. A mob lynches the black servant Deen had paid to marry Nonnie so that he could marry as his mother and the town expect him to. S. handles the stream-of-consciousness technique well, aptly combining it with the sensational plot and subject matter to create a strongly moving, finely detailed picture of the tragedy of racism for both black and white southerners.

The furor over *Strange Fruit* created the national publishing and speaking outlet S. needed to wage her campaign against racism. She published a second novel, *One Hour* (1959), and five nonfiction books that preach racial justice and denounce any person or organization that did not seem as liberal as she. Each book contains eloquent stories about her personal life and the lives of those she encountered on her travels through the South and abroad. Her ability to recreate atmosphere through physical detail allows her to carry out the psychological, social, and political analysis that is her purpose.

S. also wrote a column for the Chicago *Defender* and articles and book reviews for such widely read magazines as *New Republic*, *Saturday Review*, *Redbook*, the *Nation*, and *McCall's*.

S.'s contribution to the cause of racial justice in the U.S. won her the reputation as the most liberal white advocate of civil rights in the South in the 1940s. In the 1950s and 1960s, despite recurrent battles with lung cancer, S. continued to fight against the evils of segregation by championing the nonviolent movement of Rev. Martin Luther King, Jr.

Her conviction was deep and sincere, but her view of literature and art was limited by the intensity of her belief in the perfectability of mankind. She took daring stands against segregation, but the impact of her writing is diminished by her moralizing. S. is justifiably recognized as a minor literary figure and a major social reformer.

WORKS: *Strange Fruit* (1944). *Killer of the Dream* (1949). *The Journey* (1954). *Now Is the Time* (1955). *One Hour* (1959). *Memory of a Large Christmas* (1962). *Our Faces, Our Words* (1964). *From the Mountain* (writings from *South Today*, Eds. H. White and R. S. Suggs, Jr., 1972). *The Winner Names the Age* (Ed. M. Cliff, 1978).

BIBLIOGRAPHY: Blackwell, L., and F. Clay, *Lillian Smith* (1971). Sosna, M., *In Search of the Silent South* (1977).
    For articles in reference works, see: *CB* (1944).

SUZANNE ALLEN

Margaret Bayard Smith

B. *20 Feb. 1778, near Philadelphia, Pennsylvania; d. 7 June, 1844, Washington, D.C.*
D. *of John Bubenheim and Margaret Hodge Bayard; m. Samuel Howard Smith, 1800*

S. married the editor of the Jeffersonian newspaper the *National Intelligencer* and brought with her to Washington in 1800 a lively curiosity, a warm understanding of human relationships, and an openness to experience.

During her early life in Washington, S. wrote privately, chiefly letters and notebooks. Her public career as a writer began in the 1820s. She published two novels based on Washington life, *A Winter in Washington* (1824) and *What is Gentility?* (1828). She also wrote short stories, essays, and verse for such publications as *Godey's Lady's Book*, the *National Intelligencer*, and the *Southern Literary Messenger*. In addition, S. wrote several biographical accounts for James Herring and John B. Longacre's *National Portrait Gallery of Distinguished Americans*.

S.'s reputation as a writer rests primarily on the collection of her letters and notebook entries edited by Gaillard Hunt in 1906 and published under the title *The First Forty Years of Washington Society*. This miscellany revealed S. as a person of wit, insight, and affection and as a discerning observer of the society of her time.

S.'s Jeffersonian sympathies are evident in her work, but her circle of friends far transcended party lines. She found the transition from Jeffersonian republicanism to Jacksonian democracy a difficult one. Though flexible by nature, S. belonged to an earlier age of gentility and ordered society. Her writing about the pre-Jacksonian period combined the personal world and public political concern; in the latter period, her focus was more on the private side of Washington life.

S. was a novelist whose primary concern was the changing ways and values of society. *A Winter in Washington* had its elements of suspense and mystery, including an abducted child and a murder. But the central theme of this book and of *What is Gentility?* is the clash of moral values and cultural ways. S. saw the Jeffersonian era as a kind of republican golden age, and she sought to convey the values of that period to a later generation.

S. portrayed the political scene as women saw it—as outsiders. For her novels, she drew on some of the sketches of real-life events she had recorded previously in her notebooks as historical memoirs.

On the whole, S. held traditional views about women and their role in society. In *A Winter in Washington* she did voice, through Mrs. Mortimer, perhaps the most original and nonconformist of her female characters, some of the discontent experienced by women of the day. An incipient feminist, Mrs. Mortimer thinks it folly for women to talk of government when they are "slaves to all" or "mill horses" or "captive birds." But S. herself affirmed the theory of separate spheres and home as the "place of highest duties . . . and most enduring pleasures."

As a novelist S. is on soundest ground in depicting the social and political world of which she had been a part. S.'s private papers have proved a storehouse of information about that society. As a letter writer, S. has charm and liveliness. She clearly enjoyed people, and her portraits of the personalities of her age are drawn with an affectionate yet keen-eyed view. It is both the quality of the person S. is and the perceptive insight she brings to bear on her society that give her work its vitality and durability.

WORKS: *A Winter in Washington; or, Memoirs of the Seymour Family* (1824). *What Is Gentility?* (1828). *The First Forty Years of Washington Society* (Ed. by G. Hunt, 1906).

BIBLIOGRAPHY: Green, C. M. *Washington: Village and Capital, 1800–1878* (1962). van der Linden, F., *The Turning Point: Jefferson's Battle for the Presidency* (1962).

For articles in reference works, see: *NAW* (article by L. Mayo).

INZER BYERS

Susan Sontag

B. 16 Jan. 1933, New York City
m. Philip Rieff, 1950

Raised in Arizona and California, S. studied at the University of California at Berkeley and the University of Chicago, from which she received her B.A. when she was only eighteen, a year after marrying sociologist Philip Rieff. Her M.A. and Ph.D. in philosophy are from Harvard University. In the late 1950s, she divorced her husband and settled with her son (born in 1952) in New York City. She spends a good portion of each year in Europe. Through the mid-1960s she taught English and philosophy at several American colleges and universities. She began publishing fiction, critical essays, and reviews when she was twenty-eight. She is also a writer and director as well as a critic of films. The provocative *Duet for Cannibals* (1969) and *Brother Carl* (1971) were both made in Sweden; *Promised Lands* (1974) is a documentary about Israel.

S. is one of our most influential cultural critics. *Against Interpretation, and Other Essays* (1966) is a brilliant expression of the modernist sensibility. Despite the title, she does interpret, making accessible the most striking experiments in avant-garde film and criticism. From her treatment of new-wave critics to her famous "Notes on Camp," she is always provocative and original, so much so that one critic observed: "Perhaps what makes *Against Interpretation* valuable and exciting is not so much its erudition, which is considerable . . . as its passionate irresponsibility, its determined outrageousness."

In *Styles of Radical Will* (1969), S. again investigates the difficulties of confronting new artistic modes. Part of her appeal lies in her ability to move from the world of high culture to low—from Karl Marx to Harpo Marx, for instance. She flirts with the demonic, the underside of human experience. Her "dark and complex vision of sexuality" is not to feminists' taste, but it is worth paying some attention to what she has to say about our impulses towards violence and destruction. Elsewhere, as in "The Third World of Women" (*Partisan Review*, 1973), she shows that she can be a brilliant spokeswoman for feminism.

Politically, S. takes the part of adversary, as in the autobiographical *Trip to Hanoi* (1968). She sees art as something that expands consciousness; thus, in *Styles of Radical Will*, her views on politics and art are related, "for it is sensibility that nourishes our capacity for moral choice."

As a novelist, S. has never been autobiographical. The heroes of her full-length works are male. *The Benefactor* (1963) is about a European man who looks back on his sixty-plus years and on such surrealistic adventures as selling his mistress to an Arab merchant. Despite the brilliance of isolated perceptions, the work as a whole lacks the passionate conviction of those writers (Djuna Barnes, Dostoevsky, Nietzsche) who influenced it. To many readers, the work requires an interpreter to give it meaning.

In *Death Kit* (1967), S. wittily combines mythical, religious, and philosophical elements within the structure of a who-done-it that makes use of the journey-to-hell theme. Despite the high praise of some critics, such as Granville Hicks, most readers are more excited by S.'s criticism than her fiction.

The reader of the short-story collection *I, etcetera* (1978) has a greater sense of the intimate self with all its pain and longing, than is usual in her fiction.

In *Illness as Metaphor* (1977), S. describes "not what it is really like to emigrate to the kingdom of the ill and live there [a theme that would have had autobiographical relevence], but the punitive or sentimental fantasies concocted about that situation: not real geography, but stereotypes of national character." She applies a moralist's scorn to the use of tuberculosis and cancer as metaphor.

Yet S.'s own metaphoric power is freely employed in equally dubious contexts, as when, in *On Photography* (1979), she labels those who take or view photographs as junkies, rapists, and murderers. In some ways, the aesthetic position here is the antithesis of that in *Against Interpretation* and *Styles of Radical Will*: art, at least the art of the photographer, is now an amoral force rather than one which enlivens sensibilities and consciousness. "By getting us used to what, formerly, we could not bear to see or hear, because it was too shocking, painful, or embarrassing, art changes morals. . . ."—for the worse, it is implied.

Like the camera, to which she is addicted at the same time that she bewails it, S. always brings to the reader a new awareness of the world.

WORKS: *The Benefactor* (1963). *Against Interpretation, and Other Essays* (1966). *Death Kit* (1967). *Trip to Hanoi* (1968). *Styles of Radical Will* (1969). *Duet for Cannibals* (1970). *Brother Carl* (1974). *On Photography* (1977). *I, Etcetera* (1978). *Illness as Metaphor* (1978). *Under the Sign of Saturn* (1980).

ELAINE HOFFMAN BARUCH

Emma Dorothy Eliza Nevitte Southworth

B. 26 Dec. 1819, Washington, D.C.; d. 30 June 1899, Washington, D.C.
Wrote under: Mrs. E.D.E.N. Southworth
D. of Charles LeCompte and Susanna Wailes Nevitte; m. Frederick H.
  Southworth, 1840

S. and her sister were educated in Washington, D.C., at the school run by her step-father, Joshua Henshaw, whom her mother had married after the death of Captain Nevitte. S. taught school in Washington after her graduation. Deserted by her husband within a few years of their marriage, S. was left with two young children to support. Despite ill health, which plagued her for many years, she returned to teaching in Washington and began to write.

S.'s first publication was a short story, "The Irish Refugee," which appeared in the Baltimore *Saturday Visitor.* This was followed by other short stories. Her first novel, *Retribution* (1849), was serialized in 1847 in the columns of the Washington *National Era,* which published most of her early stories. It is reported that S. never knew how long her serials would be; she would continue on week after week, with characters presumed dead sometimes reappearing. When the serial had reached a certain length, the book publisher would bring out as one volume the work written so far and later publish the rest as a sequel. Many of her works were reprinted in other countries and translated into several languages.

S. produced about three novels per year throughout most of the rest of her life and even at that rate could hardly satisfy the demands of her readers, so popular were her works. *The Hidden Hand* (1888), first published serially in the New York *Ledger,* is said to have been the most popular work that paper ever printed. In book form it sold almost two million copies; it was also transformed into several dramatic versions, one of which starred John Wilkes Booth. *Ishmael* (1876) and *Self-Raised* (1876) sold over two million copies each. Others tried to capitalize on S.'s popularity by writing under names such as S. A. Southworth, Ella Southworth, or Emma S. Southworth; her publishers insisted however that the only genuine novels were those signed with the famous initials E.D.E.N.

A typical theme in S.'s novels is the "rags and riches" romance, exemplified in *The Curse of Clifton* (1853). Clifton, heir to an ancestral fortune, loves a humble mountain girl. Clifton's "curse" is his step-mother—one of S.'s more malignant villains, who in her most furious soliloquies echoes the most evil moments of Lady Macbeth. Some criticis consider *The Hidden Hand* S.'s best work. The heroine, Capitola, is a multi-faceted character, though she is portrayed as thoroughly good. The plot has a great deal of variety, with pranks, outlaws, and much mystery. The villain, Colonel LeNoir, is a model of the type; he grinds his teeth in impotent rage and vows revenge for afronts both real and imagined. S. considered *Self-Made* her best work. It was originally published in 1876 in two parts, the first called *Ishmael; or, In the Depths* and the second *Self-Raised; or, Out of the Depths*. This novel has an interesting rags-to-riches theme, a degenerate villain, and a highborn young woman who refuses to marry the hero, Ishmael, because of his low birth but who is justly punished for her pride. It also has a fine touch of humor and well-handled descriptions of setting and costume.

Villains in S.'s novels are thoroughly evil, heroes and heroines thoroughly pure. The situations in which they are brought together are the familiar fare of most novels written originally in serialized form: sudden catastrophic illnesses, bankruptcies, murders or other calamitous deaths, ancestral secrets revealed, hidden passions unleashed. A voracious reader herself, S. perhaps unconsciously echoes in her work such 19th-c. authors as Scott, Dickens, and Cooper. Some of her favorite settings—wild mountain roads and fearful chasms—are reminiscent of the novels of the Brontës. Finally, however, the enormous popularity of S.'s novels seems to be attributable to the simple black and white morality of her tales, her fine melodramatic touch, and her innate storytelling ability.

WORKS: *Retribution* (1849). *The Deserted Wife* (1850). *The Mother-in-Law* (1851). *Shannondale* (1851). *The Discarded Daughter* (1852). *The Curse of Clifton* (1853). *Old Neighborhoods and New Settlements* (1853). *The Lost Heiress* (1854). *India: The Pearl of Pearl River* (1855). *The Missing Bride* (1855). *Vivia; or, The Secret of Power* (1857). *Virginia and Magdalene* (1858). *The Lady of the Isle* (1859). *The Haunted Homestead* (1860). *The Gipsy's Prophecy* (1861). *Hickory Hall* (1861). *The Broken Engagement* (1862). *Love's Labor Won* (1862). *The Fatal Marriage* (1863). *The Bridal Eve* (1864). *Allworth Abbey* (1865). *The Bride of Llewellyn* (1866). *The Fortune Seeker* (1866). *The Coral Lady* (1867). *The Widow's Son* (1867). *Fair Play* (1868). *The Bride's Fate* (1869). *The Changed Brides* (1869). *The Family Doom* (1869). *How He Won Her* (1869). *The Prince of Darkness* (1869). *The Christmas Guest: A Collection of Stories* (1870). *The Maiden Widow* (1870). *Cruel as the Grave* (1871). *Tried for Her Life* (1871). *The Artist's Love*

(1872). *The Lost Heir of Linlithgow* (1872). *A Noble Lord* (1872). *A Beautiful Fiend* (1873). *Victor's Triumph* (1874). *The Mystery of Dark Hollow* (1875). *The Spectre Lover* (1875). *Ishmael; or, In the Depths* (1876). *Self-Raised or, Out of the Depths* (1876). *The Fatal Secret* (1877). *The Red Hill Tragedy* (1877). *The Phantom Wedding* (1878). *Sybil Brotherton: A Novel* (1879). *The Hidden Hand* (1888). *A Leap in the Dark* (1889). *Nearest and Dearest* (1889). *Unknown* (1889). *For Woman's Love* (1890). *The Lost Lady of Lone* (1890). *Broken Pledges* (1891). *David Lindsay* (1891). *Gloria: A Novel* (1891). *Lillith* (1891). *The Unloved Wife* (1891). *"Em": A Novel* (1892). *Em's Husband: A Novel* (1892). *Brandon Coyle's Wife* (1893). *Only a Girl's Heart* (1893). *A Skeleton in the Closet* (1893). *Gertrude Haddon* (1894). *The Rejected Bride* (1894).

BIBLIOGRAPHY: Boyle, R. L., *Mrs. E.D.E.N. Southworth, Novelist* (1939). Hart, J. D., *The Popular Book* (1950). Mott, F. L., *Golden Multitudes* (1947). Pattee, F. L., *The Feminine Fifties* (1940).
For articles in reference works, see: *AW. DAB*, IX, 1.

ELAINE K. GINSBERG

Elizabeth Spencer

B. 19 July 1921, Carrollton, Mississippi
D. of James Luther and Mary James McCain Spencer; m. John Rusher, 1956

A native of Mississippi and the progeny of a family whose ancestors had lived in Carroll County, Mississippi, since the 1830s, S. spent her childhood in the kind of rural South that she depicts with topographic precision in several of her novels. S. studied English at Belhaven College in Jackson, Mississippi, (B.A. 1942) and Vanderbilt University (M.A. 1943). S. taught for two years, first in Mississippi and then in Tennessee, resigning from teaching to work as a reporter for the Nashville *Tennessean*. In 1946, S. abandoned the craft of the journalist for that of the novelist, and her first novel, *Fire in the Morning*, was published two years later. Recipient of a Guggenheim Fellowship in 1953, S. traveled to Italy, the scene of two later novels, *The Light in the Piazza* (1960) and *Knights and Dragons* (1965). She has served as writer-in-residence at several colleges and universities in the U.S. and Canada.

Fire in the Morning, published with the encouragement of the Fugitive poet Donald Davidson, reveals S.'s first-hand knowledge of the intricate workings of a small Southern town—its layers of intrigue and the complexities of relationships that span several generations. With the Southerner's sense of local story as possessing the power of myth, S. delineates the history and works out the fate of two antagonistic families in Tarsus, Mississippi, in a fashion that recalls the conflicts in various "houses" of Greek drama. The movement of the novel is predicated on a young man's gradual discovery of the interwoven affairs of love, fraud, and violence which underlie one family's dominance of the town. In the process of uncovering the private histories which link together the inhabitants of Tarsus, he comes to terms with the town, his own family, and himself in relationship to what had seemed an inexplicable past.

In *Fire in the Morning*, S. suggests that there are sociological differences between the regions of Delta and hill country in Mississippi. In *This Crooked Way* (1952), these regions provide symbolic points of reference for charting Amos Dudley's odyssey from poverty to riches and from damnation to salvation. Convinced as a consequence of a religious experience that God will support him in his opportunistic endeavors, Dudley leaves the Yocona hills, striding into the Delta in Colonel Sutpen fashion to wrest a plantation out of the overgrown land. His success, however, leaves destruction in its wake; and it is not until he brings the remnants of his hill-country family to the Delta to share his affluence that he finds a measure of peace and is able to reconcile himself with his past.

S.'s third novel, *The Voice at the Back Door* (1956), which treats of politics and the cost of equal justice for blacks and whites in a Southern town, is the last to deal with the Mississippi South. She returns in *The Snare* (1972) to a southern locale; but in this novel it is to the New Orleans atmosphere of the French Quarter, where her heroine becomes involved in the city's underworld of jazz musicians.

In 1960, with the publication of *The Light in the Piazza*, S. shifts locales, delineating in this novella the crisis of conscience of an American woman who decides to allow her beautiful but mentally retarded daughter to marry her young Italian suitor. S. treats such a dilemma, which might otherwise be too ponderous, with grace and charm; and her evocation of the Florentine atmosphere and its impact upon the Americans makes the city a powerful force in the story.

In *Knights and Dragons*, S. again utilizes the Italian scene; but in her recounting of an American divorcee's love involvement there, Rome and Venice are only backdrops for a story dealing essentially with Americans.

She expands both the concern of failing marriages and the setting in *No Place for an Angel* (1967), a novel which focuses upon the complexities of a pair of marital relationships against backgrounds as diverse as Texas, Washington, New York, Rome, and Sicily.

S.'s seven novels, moving as they do from the fixed geography and traditions of the South to an international scene, demonstrate the scope of a writer who may have begun under the shadow of the mythic South but whose vision is not regionally limited. She explores in several contexts and with considerable artistry the individual as an outsider to the environment, whether that environment be the Mississippi Delta or the Italian city.

WORKS: Fire in the Morning (1948). *This Crooked Way* (1952). *The Voice at the Back Door* (1956). *The Light in the Piazza* (1960; film version, 1962). *Knights and Dragons* (1965). *No Place for an Angel* (1967). *Ship Island, and Other Stories* (1968) *The Snare* (1972). *The Stories of Elizabeth Spencer* (1981).

BIBLIOGRAPHY: Bradbury, J. M., *Renaissance in the South: A Critical History of Literature, 1920–1960* (1963). Burger, N. K., in *South Atlantic Quarterly* 63 (Summer 1964). Pugh, D. G., in *The Fifties: Fiction, Poetry, Drama*, Ed. W. C. French (1970). Sullivan, W., "The Continuing Renascence: Southern Fiction in the Fifties," *South: Modern Southern Literature in its Cultural Setting*, Eds. L. D. Rubin, Jr., and R. D. Jacobs (1961).

GUIN A. NANCE

Harriet Elizabeth Prescott Spofford

B. 3 April 1835, Calais, Maine; d. 14 Aug. 1921, Deer Island, Massachusetts
Wrote under: Harriet Prescott, Harriet Prescott Spofford
D. of Joseph Newmarch and Sarah Jane Bridges Prescott; m. Richard Smith Spofford, 1865

S. was born into a distinguished New England family that had suffered economic reversals since the War of 1812. S. spent most of her early years in a household of women, including her mother and four Prescott aunts, while her father sought his fortune in the West. In 1849, she settled with her mother in Newburyport, Massachusetts, where she attended Putnam Free School, finishing her education later at the Pinkerton Academy in Derry, New Hampshire. In 1856, when her father returned an invalid and her mother soon was stricken, Harriet became the support of the family. She turned to writing, one of the few lucrative careers open to women in her day. This early work, published anonymously in Boston family story-papers in the 1850s, remains uncollected and unacknowledged. Quantity was demanded rather than quality, as each piece earned S. between two dollars and fifty cents and five dollars. Only with the publication of her short story "In a Cellar," in the young *Atlantic Monthly* (February 1859) did her career really begin.

S.'s marriage to Spofford, a Newburyport lawyer, was long and successful, although their only child died as an infant in 1867. They lived briefly in Washington (*Old Washington*, 1906, is based on S.'s memories); traveled abroad twice; and finally settled on Deer Island, a five-acre island in the Merrimac River near Newburyport. The scenery, legends, and people of her New England home supplied much of the material for S.'s writing, especially her poetry. In "June on the Merrimac," John Greenleaf Whittier called attention to the setting in which "Deer Island's mistress sings." S. lived on Deer Island for the rest of her life, often visited by and visiting a circle of women writers in Boston that included Sarah Orne Jewett, Elizabeth Stuart Phelps Ward, and Julia Ward Howe.

From the 1860s until her death, S. was one of the most widely published of American authors. Many stories, essays, and poems appeared in *Harper's Bazar, Atlantic Monthly*, the *Knickerbocker*, the *Cosmopolitan*, and in juvenile magazines such as *Youth's Companion*.

Two strengths save S. from being dismissed as merely a popular-magazine contributor producing only "romantically frothy tales." The first, for which she is alternately highly praised and condemned, is her vivid and often graphic description. In *Sir Rohan's Ghost: A Romance* (1860), for instance, her description of a wine cellar was so convincing and memorable that connoisseurs sent her tributes of wine for years afterward. In a century when woman's sphere was domestic, S. utilized her special knowledge to make textures, jewelry, even furniture definitive of character. In *Art Decoration Applied to Furniture* (1878), S. observed that furniture is "emblazoned, as one might say, with the customs of a people and the manners of a time." Her ability to capture character through setting and inanimate objects is nowhere more stunning than in the title story of *The Amber Gods* (1863), where the two women, Yone and Lu, are defined by the jewels they wear ("This amber's just the thing for me, such a great noon creature!") and the materials that suit them ("I never let Lu wear the point at all; she'd be ridiculous in it,—so flimsy and open and unreserved; that's for me.").

S.'s second strength is that although she too divides her women into opposites reminiscent of the fragile blondes and passionate brunettes who represent saint and sinner for most romantics—and only too accurately represent the roles in which contemporary women were cast—S. reveals the woman within the role. If she takes sides, her vibrant heart urges her to admire the passionate Yones over the dutiful Lus; but Lu, too, is always loved. In "Desert Sands," for instance, the submissive wife Eos has artistic talent that is recognized immediately and appreciated by the seductive Vespasia, and her cousin Alain berates her husband for suppressing it: "This aptitude, this power, this whatever you choose to call it, genius or inspiration, for which you refuse her utterance, this has produced a spiritual asphyxia."

Beginning her career in the 1850s, S. found herself caught between the dying school of romanticism and the newly-vociferous advocates of realism. Her discerning eye and ability to capture the character of her New England neighbors in dialect and description earned the praise of W. D. Howells and the young Henry James, but they were both bothered by her romantic lushness and discouraged her from "fine writing." Although her realistic talent would culminate in her last collection, *The Elder's People* (1920), it could at best earn her recognition as a strong minor writer scarcely comparable to Mary E. Wilkins Freeman. It is in her romantic tendencies that the uniqueness of S.'s writing can be found, even though in response to the fickle changes in popular taste and literary approach, she often either abandoned (always reluctantly) or failed to develop and control the poetic promise of her early romantic work.

WORKS: *Sir Rohan's Ghost: A Romance* (1860). *The Amber Gods, and Other Stories* (1863). *Azarian: An Episode* (1864). *New England Legends* (1871). *The Thief in the Night* (1872). *Art Decoration Applied to Furniture* (1878). *The Servant Girl Question* (1881). *Hester Stanley at St. Marks* (1882). *The Marquis of Carabas* (1882). *Poems* (1882). *Ballads about Authors* (1887). *House and Hearth* (1891). *A Lost Jewel* (1891). *A Scarlet Poppy, and Other Stories* (1894). *A Master Spirit* (1896). *In Titian's Garden, and Other Poems* (1897). *An Inheritance* (1897). *Stepping-Stones to Happiness* (1897). *Hester Stanley's Friends* (1898). *Priscilla's Love-Story* (1898). *The Maid He Married* (1899). *Old Madame, and Other Tragedies* (1900). *The Children of the Valley* (1901). *The Great Procession, and other Verses for and about Children* (1902). *That Betty* (1903). *Four Days of God* (1905). *Old Washington* (1906). *The Fairy Changeling: A Flower and Fairy Play* (1911). *The Making of a Fortune: A Romance* (1911). *The King's Easter* (1912). *A Little Book of Friends* (1916). *The Elder's People* (1920).

BIBLIOGRAPHY: Cooke, Rose Terry, *Our Famous Women* (1883). Halbeisen, E. K., *Harriet Prescott Spofford* (1935). Hopkins, A. A., *Waifs, and Their Authors* (1879). *The Development of the American Short Story* (1923). Pattee, F. L., *A History of American Literature since 1870* (1915). Ward, Elizabeth Stuart Phelps, "Stories that Stay," *The Century Magazine*, N.S. 59 (Nov. 1910). Richardson, C. F., *American Literature (1607–1885)* (1902).

For articles in reference works, see: *NCAB*, IV.

Other references: *Bookman* 62 (Nov. 1925).

THELMA J. SHINN

Elizabeth Cady Stanton

B. 12 Nov. 1815, Johnstown, New York; d. 26 Oct. 1902, New York City
D. of Daniel and Margaret Livingston Cady; m. Henry Brewster Stanton, 1840

S. was the fourth of six children. Her father was a lawyer, politician, and judge. Listening to his clients and reading his law books, she learned at an early age of the injustices women suffer. When the family's only son died in 1826, she resolved to take his place. She was tutored in Greek by her Presbyterian minister and later studied Latin and mathematics at the Johnstown Academy. She graduated from Emma Willard's Troy Female Seminary in 1832.

A strong advocate of the reforms of the day—temperance, abolition, and women's rights—she had the word "obey" omitted from the ceremony at her marriage to Stanton, an antislavery lecturer. On their honeymoon, the couple attended a world anti-slavery convention in London, where S. met Lucretia Mott, a delegate the convention refused to seat because she was a woman. After the European tour, they settled in Johnstown, where the first of their seven children was born in 1842. They moved to Boston shortly thereafter and, in 1847, to Seneca Falls, New York. S. and Lucretia Mott organized the first convention for women's rights there in 1848. S. was commissioned to draft the Declaration of Principles, in which she included a most controversial resolution demanding suffrage.

S. met Susan B. Anthony in 1851, and the two formed a very fruitful collaborative friendship which spanned the next half century. S. was the writer and speaker whenever possible; Anthony the strategist, organizer, and intrepid traveler. In the years after the Civil War there were increasing divisions in the women's movement, due partly to differing assessments of priorities. S. campaigned against the Fourteenth and Fifteenth Amendments because they did not extend rights to women. This alienated many reformers who argued that "this is the Negro's hour." In 1868, S. and Anthony published a magazine, *Revolution*, financed by erratic entrepeneur George Francis Train, in which they included his controversial views on economics and labor unions as well as their own radical views on marriage and divorce. In 1869, S. and Anthony formed the National Woman Suffrage Association, which S. led as president for twenty-one years. Other reformers, generally more conservative, formed the American Woman Suffrage Association. When the two suffrage associations merged in 1890, she served as president for two years.

In order to finance her children's education, S. spent many years delivering lectures, on subjects such as the education of women and divorce, for the New York Lyceum Bureau. Throughout a half-century career, she wrote many letters and articles, not only on suffrage but on a wide range of social and political questions affecting women, for feminist and general newspapers. In addition to numerous tracts and pamphlets reprinting her speeches and articles, she published three major works.

With Anthony, she edited the first three volumes of the monumental *History of Woman's Suffrage* (1881–86), covering the years from 1848 to 1885. Admittedly one-sided, their history contains a rich store of speeches, summarized debates, letters, and evaluations of the early women's rights conventions, both national and state.

S.'s most controversial work is *The Woman's Bible* (2 vols., 1895–1898). Her unorthodox views had been known for years, through essays like "The Effect of Woman Suffrage on Questions of Morals and Religion," included in pamphlets such as *The Christian Church and Women* (1881) and *Bible and Church Degrade Women* (1885). She believed that "whatever the Bible may be made to do in Hebrew or Greek, in plain English it does not exalt and dignify woman." Although she invited a panel of women scholars to assist her, most declined. The bulk of the brief notes on each book are S.'s, and the results are eclectic and sketchy. Despite an appeal from Anthony for tolerance of differing opinions, the 1896 national convention of the National American Woman Suffrage Association passed a resolution dissociating the organization from the work.

S.'s autobiography, *Eighty Years and More* (1898), contains the candid and delightful reminiscences of a woman who, at eighty-three, was still trying to expand the frontiers for her sisters.

WORKS: *History of Woman Suffrage* (with S. B. Anthony, Vols. 1–3, 1881–86). *The Woman's Bible* (2 Vols., 1895–98). *Eighty Years and More* (1898). *Elizabeth Cady Stanton as Revealed in her Letters, Diary, and Reminiscences* (Eds. T. Stanton and H. S. Blatch, 2 vols., 1922).

BIBLIOGRAPHY: Blatch, H. S., and A. Lutz, *Challenging Years: The Memoirs of Harriot Stanton Blatch* (1940). Lutz, A., *Created Equal* (1940), Lutz, A., *Susan B. Anthony: Rebel, Crusader, Humanitarian* (1959).

NANCY A. HARDESTY

Gertrude Stein

B. 13 Feb. 1874, Allegheny, Pennsylvania; d. 27 July 1946, Neuilly-sur-Seine, France
D. of Daniel and Amelia Keyser Stein

S., the youngest of seven children, spent her early years in Europe, before her intense, restless, argumentative father settled his family in Oakland, California. Both her parents died while she was an adolescent. Her principal companion until she was well into her thirties was her brother Leo, a brilliant but erratic lifelong student of the arts.

She studied at Radcliffe College (1893–97), with William James, and then studied neurology at Johns Hopkins Medical School, where she completed two satisfactory years before becoming undisciplined in her work. She did not receive her degree.

In 1903, S. joined Leo in Paris at 27, rue de Fleurus, the site of her now legendary salon, and under his guidance she began to collect modern art. She and Alice B. Toklas established the love relationship that would endure for the remainder of their lives in 1907. Two years later, Toklas moved to the rue de Fleurus, where she remained with S. after the brother and sister formally separated in 1913.

Except for a visit to America (1934–35), S. spent the rest of her life in Europe. She and Toklas did war-relief work during WWI. During the 1930s, S.'s reputation grew, especially with the extensive promotion of

The Autobiography of Alice B. Toklas (1933). With Toklas, she spent much of WWII in the French countryside, where their fellow villagers protected them as Jews during the Nazi occupation.

The range of her work is great, and her innovations in style make strict classifications difficult and misleading. She wrote poems, plays, novels, autobiography, theory, and criticism; and, in addition, she created new kinds of works, such as the "portraits."

Her first full-length work charts the dynamics of a lesbian love triangle. *Q. E. D.* was written in 1903 and published posthumously in 1950 as *Things as They Are*. Adele, the principal character, is modeled in S.'s own image, and the plot is patterned after her thwarted love affair at medical school. The novel is largely realistic, with an established set of characters and a sequential plot line. S. is most concerned with the revelation of character through plot and believes character determines events. In this respect, she differs from contemporary naturalistic and realistic writers and their concern with the effects of deterministic forces external to the individual.

Written between 1903 and 1911 but not published until 1925, *The Making of Americans; or, The History of a Family's Progress* is S.'s most voluminous and possibly most accomplished prose work. Her original intention was to write a history of every American "who ever can or is or was or will be living," but her goal changed in the course of writing the novel. It begins in the realistic mode, with attention to delineation of time, place, and character, but swiftly becomes an autobiographical record in which she meditates on partially transformed aspects of her past and the movement of her consciousness at the moment of composition. S. seeks to express the "bottom nature"—that rhythmic movement of consciousness that is what one essentially is, that makes up one's identity. As a consequence, the work becomes increasingly abstract, for narrative is abandoned and associative patterning determines the ordering of word and phrase and sentence.

Three Lives (1909) contains three stories of lower-class women. The heroines of "The Good Anna" and "The Gentle Lena" are lightly sketched, flat characters. "Melanctha," the most accomplished work of *Three Lives*, represents a great change and advance in S.'s style. Ostensibly, "Melanctha" concerns the relationship between a young mulatto woman and a black doctor; the fairly sympathetic portrayal of black characters is remarkable for the time. The work also concerns the same love triangle S. had written of earlier. Now the focus is on Jeff Campbell, who shares the cerebral, bourgeois quality of S.'s alter ego Adele in *Q. E. D.*; Melanctha, a vibrant, sensual woman corresponds to Adele's beloved. S. later contended that the detailed and complex characterization was the result of writing in the spirit of a Cézanne portrait, for she accords substantial attention to each aspect of her characters' composition. She was praised for using sentence forms that reflect her characters' mode of dealing with reality. For example, compound declarative sentences, replete with participial modifiers, represent Jeff Campbell's habitual recoiling from experience into endless rumination.

During the years from 1908 to 1913, S. wrote one- to three-page prose "portraits" of her friends and acquaintances. The portraits were published in a variety of places: Alfred Stieglitz published "Picasso" and "Matisse" in *Camera Work* (1912); many were included in *Portraits and Prayers* (1934). In far shorter works than "Melanctha," S. continues her study of how sentence forms can express character.

The portraits are helpful in charting the increasing abstraction of S.'s style, the change from the minimal narrative and direct characterization of *Three Lives* to the hermetic style of *Tender Buttons* (1914). Instead of portraying the character of others, in the latter she meditates on her own individual mode of perceiving and reacting to experience. Virtually without referents and narrative, *Tender Buttons* is unified by a single consciousness.

S.'s early plays, some of which are included in *Geography and Plays* (1922), use conventional dramatic elements in an idiosyncratic way to call attention to their mere conventionality. "Counting Her Dresses," for example, contains numerous "parts" and "acts" randomly assigned; most have one line, only one has three. Yet the subject is fairly accessible: the eccentricities, frailties, and vanities of women who identify with their outward appearance.

Composition as Explanation (1926) builds on the substance of talks S. addressed to the literary societies of Oxford and Cambridge universities. By "composition" she means both the world as a set of phenomena perceived in any moment of time and the expression of this perception in a work of art. The artist creates an impression of what is seen in her time, but because her realization is far more sensitive and acute than that of others, her work is termed ugly by contemporaries. The greater the masterpiece, the more surely it will be judged ugly. Only in the future will the validity and beauty of such a work be established.

Operas and Plays (1932) contains works spanning the years 1913 to 1931, including S.'s best-known opera, "Four Saints in Three Acts" (1927), for which Virgil Thomson composed the music. It deals with the condition of being a saint—of being constant in faith, of sustaining internal balance, of knowing one's identity clearly and truly.

The Autobiography of Alice B. Toklas is S.'s most popular work and also her most stylistically accessible. By writing as if she were Toklas, she distances herself from her material and creates her own legend, and she takes advantage of a certain latitude with the truth allowed by the semi-fictional mode that results from her innovative use of narrative voice. It remains unclear to what degree Toklas herself contributed to the work's composition and editing. S. recounts with sympathy and wit Toklas's life in San Francisco and arrival in Paris in 1907, relates her own early years (not necessarily accurately), and then treats the women's lives in Paris.

Lectures in America (1935) is S.'s theoretical explanation and justification of her work. It is fairly straightforward, highly egocentric, and thoroughly charming. Her assessment of her place in the history of literature must be looked at in the light of her intense sense of self-importance, but the lectures are significant because in them she sets up the critical framework (relating her writing to the goals of cubist painters) that is the most frequent means of explaining her innovative style. *The Geographical History of America; or, The Relation of Human Nature to the Human Mind* (1936) is S.'s formal treatise on the nature and operation of consciousness.

In *Paris France* (1940), S. attempts to justify remaining in France despite the specter of war. For her, politics is irrelevant; she retreats into the security of a harmoniously composed and ordered everyday life and asserts its viability against imminent physical danger. "I cannot write too much upon how necessary it is to be completely conservative that is particularly traditional to be free."

Of particular interest in *Wars I Have Seen* (1945) is S.'s almost exclusive focus on domestic affairs and her acceptance of the Vichy regime. Her placid attitude may be the result of her age—she was then seventy—her consistently conservative political views, and her lifelong need to bring events within the spectrum of her personal philosophy, often at the expense of the truth.

S.'s forty-three-year career was as prolific as it was long. It is however, her lot to be remembered primarily for her support and encouragement of other artists, and neglected for her own accomplishments as a writer. Undoubtedly, S.'s patronage of abstract painters encouraged and supported Picasso, Matisse, and others in their work. Her friendship with and close reading of such writers as Ernest Hemingway and Sherwood Anderson clearly affected the direction of their writing. Her own work was read by American and European writers, and the simplicity and purity of her language was well appreciated by a number of them. S.'s salon was a site of intellectual ferment at a time when Americans and Europeans were forging an artistic community in Paris. Still, S. was accomplished as a writer herself, and it is time that increased critical attention is paid her and the measure of her innovative work made.

S.'s work rests firmly on autobiographical features and on her attempt to find a stylistic equivalent for her philosophy of perception. Her first writings are fairly traditional in form, but swiftly convention gives way to innovation. All of her works are difficult if the reader demands conventional stylistic devices, because S. employs them only to ask: what purpose do they serve? what limits do they place on expression and comprehension? When she innovates in style, it is to sharpen her own scrutiny of language: its sounds, its meanings, its sequence. Hence, her writing is essentially metalinguistic, for the subject of her work is the work itself.

WORKS: *Three Lives* (1909). *Tender Buttons* (1914). *Geography and Plays* (1922). *The Making of Americans* (1925). *Composition as Explanation* (1926). *Useful Knowledge* (1928). *Lucy Church Amiably* (1930). *Operas and Plays* (1932). *The Autobiography of Alice B. Toklas* (1933). *Matisse, Picasso, and Gertrude Stein, with Two Shorter Stories* (1933). *Four Saints in Three Acts* (1934). *Portraits and Prayers* (1934). *Lectures in America* (1935). *Narration* (1935). *The Geographical History of America* (1936). *Everybody's Autobiography* (1937). *Picasso* (1938). *The World Is Round* (1939). *Paris, France* (1940). *What Are Masterpieces?* (1940). *Ida: A Novel* (1941). *Wars I Have Seen* (1945). *Brewsie and Willie* (1946). *Four in America* (1947). *Blood on the Dining Room Floor* (1948). *The Gertrude Stein Reader and Three Plays* (1948). *Last Operas and Plays* (1949). *Things as They Are* (1950). *The Unpublished Works of Gertrude Stein* (8 vols., 1951–58). *Gertrude Stein: Writings and Lectures, 1909–1945* (1967). *Gertrude Stein on Picasso* (Ed. E. Burns, 1970). *Fernhurst, Q. E. D., and Other Early Writings* (1971). *Sherwood Anderson/Gertrude Stein: Correspondence and Personal Essays* (1972). *A Book Concluding with As a Wife Has a Cow: A Love Story* (1973). *Reflections on the Atomic Bomb* (1973). *How Writing Is Done* (1974). *In Savoy; or, "Yes" Is for Yes for a Very Young Man* (1977; produced, 1949).

BIBLIOGRAPHY: Bridgman, R., *Gertrude Stein in Pieces* (1970). Brinnin, J. M., *The Third Rose: Gertrude Stein and Her World* (1959). Gallup, D., ed., *The Flowers of Friendship: Letters Written to Gertrude Stein* (1953). Gass, W. H., *The World within the Word* (1978). Hobhouse, J., *Everybody Who Was Anybody: A Biography of Gertrude Stein* (1975). Hoffman, F., *Gertrude Stein* (Univ. of Minnesota Pamphlets on American Writers, 1961). Hoffman, M., *The Development of Abstractionism in the Writings of Gertrude Stein* (1965). Hoffman, M., *Gertrude Stein* (1976). Katz, L., "The First Making of *The Making of Americans*: A Study Based on Gertrude Stein's Notebooks and Early Versions of Her Novel (1902–1908)" (Ph.D. diss., Columbia Univ., 1963). Kawin, B., *Telling It Again and Again* (1972). Klaich, D., *Woman +*

Woman: Attitudes towards Lesbianism (1974). Mellow, J. R., *Charmed Circle: Gertrude Stein & Company* (1974). Miller, R., *Gertrude Stein: Form and Intelligibility* (1949). Reid, B. L., *Art by Subtraction* (1958). Sprigge, E., *Gertrude Stein: Her Life and Work* (1957). Stein, L., *Journey into the Self* (1950). Stewart, A., *Gertrude Stein and the Present* (1950). Sutherland, D., *Gertrude Stein: A Biography of Her Work* (1951). Thomson, V., "A Very Difficult Author," in *NYRB* (8 April 1971). Thomson, V., *Virgil Thomson* (1966). Toklas, A. B., *Staying on Alone: Letters of Alice B. Toklas* (1973). Toklas, A. B., *What Is Remembered* (1963). Wilson, E., *Axel's Castle* (1931). Wilson, E., *The Shores of Light* (1952).

Other references: *AL* 45 (1973). *Ascent* 18 (Autumn 1958).

JANIS TOWNSEND

Elizabeth Gertrude Levin Stern

B. 14 Feb. 1889, Skedel, Poland; d. 9 Jan. 1954, Philadelphia, Pennsylvania
Wrote under: Eleanor Morton, Leah Morton, E. G. Stern, Elizabeth Stern,
* Elizabeth Gertrude Stern*
D. of Aaron and Sarah Leah Rubenstein Levin; m. Leon Thomas Stern, ca. 1911

The infant S. emigrated with her parents in 1890 from Poland to Pittsburgh, where she was raised and educated, graduating from the University of Pittsburgh in 1910. After a year at the New York School of Philanthropy, she married penologist Leon Stern, and began a career that successfully combined marriage and motherhood with social work and writing. S. was a night school principal in New York and Galveston, supervised welfare work for Wanamaker's in Philadelphia, and directed two New York settlement houses. A journalist from 1914 to 1937, S. included features in the *New York Times* and a regular column in the Philadelphia *Inquirer* among her accomplishments. In the 1940s she wrote, lectured, and was active in many Quaker and philanthropic organizations. She died at sixty-four after a long illness.

S.'s best works are fictionalized autobiographies that focus on her movement from Polish-Jewish ghetto to American mainstream. Theodore Roosevelt introduced S.'s first book, *My Mother and I* (1917), which poignantly describes how education loosens bonds between an immigrant mother and her daughter. While the young protagonist is proud of her achieved status as middle-class housewife, she regrets her mother's alienation from the world maternal self-sacrifice helped her reach. In *I Am a Women—and a Jew* (1926), S. explores the confrontation between a rebellious daughter and her rabbi-father, with the mother as mediator. The first-person narrator's rejection of both orthodox Judaism and feminine domesticity is complicated by a lingering sense of responsibility to both traditions, and inability to escape anti-Semitism and sexism.

S. also used her work experience as raw material for fiction. With her husband, she wrote *A Friend at Court* (1923), the "casebook" of an idealized female probation officer. The work is marred by a predictable romantic subplot and panegyrics on probation as a social panacea. The middle-aged social worker in *When Love Comes to Woman* (1929) provides no such pat answers to women involved in unconventional living arrangements; S.'s ideal is a dual-career marriage promising lifelong friendship. Her telling comparisons between the sexual experimentation of the "new women" of the 1920s and the seriousness of the suffragists of her youth offer insights into important and still-contemporary issues.

Family relationships are central to S.'s other novels. In *A Marriage Was Made* (1928), a mother's domination of her daughter thwarts the girl's promising career by making her too passive to express emotion in her music or life. The mother-daughter theme is also important in *Gambler's Wife* (1931), which traces a strong but self-sacrificing woman from her youth in the Arkansas hills, through her elopement with a drifter who repeatedly abandons her, to her last years with her grown, but immature, children.

Later in life, S. moved from fiction to essay and biography. A collection of her newspaper columns, *Not All Laughter* (1937), reveals her consuming interest in relationships, and her version of woman's true role: the thinking wife, the comrade. S. wrote biographies of a businesswoman (*Memories: The Life of Margaret McAvoy Smith*, 1943) and a Quaker inventor (*Josiah White: Prince of Pioneers*, 1946). In her last book, *The Women behind Gandhi* (1953), S. concentrates on Gandhi's wife and his Indian and European female disciples, highlighting the women's rights phase of his movement for India's full liberation.

In her works, S. accurately accounts the costs and benefits of both the Americanization process and the application of feminist principles to life.

Her books may appear dated by their romanticism and frequent concentration upon battles considered long won (particularly on the right of married women to work), but S.'s emphasis upon the sacrifices involved in family relationships complicated by cultural change is of continuing interest, and her perspective as a daughter of immigrants makes her insights especially important.

WORKS: *My Mother and I* (1917). *A Friend at Court* (with L. T. Stern, 1923). *I Am a Women—and a Jew* (1926). *This Ecstasy* (1927). *A Marriage Was Made* (1928). *When Love Comes to Woman* (1929). *Gambler's Wife* (1931). *Not All Laughter: A Mirror to Our Times* (1937). *Memories: The Life of Margaret McAvoy Scott* (1943). *Josiah White: Prince of Pioneers* (1947). *The Women behind Gandhi* (1953).

BIBLIOGRAPHY: Baum, C., P. Hyman, and S. Michel, *The Jewish Woman in America* (1976).

For articles in reference works, see: *NCAB*, 39.

Other references: *Bookman* (Aug. 1917). *NYT* (8 July 1917; 24 April 1929; 19 Feb. 1928; 12 April 1931; 10 Jan. 1954). *SatR* (18 Dec. 1926; 7 Sept. 1929; 8 Aug. 1953). *Survey* (15 Oct. 1923; Feb. 1947).

HELEN M. BANNAN

Annis Boudinot Stockton

B. *1 July 1736, Darby, Pennsylvania; d. 6 Feb. 1801, Burlington County, New Jersey*
Wrote under: "Emelia" (sometimes spelled "Amelia")
D. of Elias and Catherine Williams Boudinot; m. Richard Stockton, ca. 1755

Although few records of S.'s childhood remain, her extant manuscripts and Stockton family histories leave a considerable body of material for reconstructing her adult life. Born to a tradesman of French Huguenot descent, S. apparently received a more substantial education than was common for girls of her time. Her first poems were written before her marriage to Stockton, a well-known New Jersey lawyer, landowner, and future signer of the Declaration of Independence. Some of these poems celebrate their courtship: " . . . I find on earth no charms for me / But what's connected with the thought of thee!" After her marriage, S. moved to the Stockton estate near Princeton, naming her home "Morven," after the imaginary land of Ossian's (James Macpherson's) Fingal. The romance of that title and the elaborately stylish gardens S. cultivated at Morven reflect the impulses of much of her verse: pastoral, sentimental, and imitative of popular British modes.

The quiet life at Morven was interrupted by the Revolutionary War. Because both S. and her husband were committed patriots, Morven was occupied by the British under Cornwallis during the Battle of Princeton in December, 1776. The estate was sacked; plate and papers (including some of Stockton's early poems) were stolen. And although the family had been evacuated, Richard Stockton was taken prisoner soon after their escape. Washington's quick recapture of Princeton allowed S. and her children to return to their ruined home. Richard Stockton was released later in 1777, but ill treatment in prison probably hastened his death in 1781. S.'s watch by her husband's deathbed occasioned two of her most moving elegies: "But vain is prophesy when death's approach, / Thro' years of pain, has sap'd a dearer life, / And makes me, coward like, myself reproach, / That e're I knew the tender name of wife." S. continued to live at Morven until the marriage of her eldest son, at which time she left the estate to him and moved to the home of her youngest daughter, Abigail Field of Burlington County, where she died in 1801.

Much of S.'s life had been occupied with the raising of her six children and the managing of a sizeable household. But however demanding those responsibilities became, she continued to make time for her verse. Richard Stockton encouraged her work, and S.'s audience gradually expanded beyond the family circle. She exchanged verses, for example, with Philadelphia poet Elizabeth Graeme Fergusson. Noting the support she found in her "sister" poet, S. addressed Fergusson directly in "To Laura" (Fergusson's pseudonym): "Permit a sister muse to soar / To heights she never try'd before, / And then look up to thee. . . ." Additionally, S. became a close friend of Esther Burr, who preserved two of S.'s poems in her journal. She wrote a number of odes to George Washington, many of them warmly acknowledged in his letters to her. Such encouragement from family and friends may have suggested to S. the possibility of an even wider audience: her first known publication, "To the Honorable Colonel Peter Schuyler," appeared in the *New-York Mercury* for 9 January, 1758, and in the *New American Magazine* for January, 1758. Although other Philadelphia, New York, and New Jersey periodicals printed S.'s verse from time to time, most of her work remained in manuscript.

Throughout her life, S. continued to work in the couplets and alternately rhymed quatrains of Pope, Young, Thomson, and Gray. Using these models, she developed themes of courtship, marriage, nature, friendship, patriotism, old age, and grief. But even as she imitated conventional forms, S. worried about the propriety of her activities: she confided to her brother Elias in a letter dated 1 May, 1789, about one of her odes to Washington, that "if you think it will only add one sprig to the wreath the country twines to bind the brows of my hero, I will run the risk of being sneered at by those who criticize female productions of all kinds." Fearful for her reputation, yet wishing recognition for her work, S. faced a dilemma common to colonial women poets. The number of her publications and the size of her extant manuscript collection may indicate that the desire to write finally outweighed her fear of impropriety.

WORKS: Poems by Stockton were published in the *New-York Mercury*, the *New American Magazine*, the *Pennsylvania Magazine*, the *Columbian Magazine*, and the *New Jersey Gazette*. Some poems are appended to the Reverend Samuel Stanhope Smith's *Funeral Sermon on the Death of the Hon. Richard Stockton . . .* (1781). Manuscripts are in Princeton University Library, Historical Society of Pennsylvania, and Library of Congress, and several poems from this collection were reprinted in *PULC* (Nov. 1944; Nov. 1945).

BIBLIOGRAPHY: Bill, A., *A House Called Morven* (1954). Cowell, P., *Women Poets in Pre-Revolutionary America, 1650–1775* (1981). Ellet, E., *Women of the American Revolution* (1850). Glenn T., *Some Colonial Houses and Those Who Lived in Them* (1899). Green H. C., and M. W. Green, *Pioneer Mothers in America* (1912). Stockton, J., *A History of the Stockton Family* (1881). Stockton, T. C., *The Stocktons of New Jersey, and Other Stocktons* (1911).

PATTIE COWELL

Harriet Elizabeth Beecher Stowe

B. *14 June 1811, Litchfield, Connecticut; d. 1 July 1896, Hartford, Connecticut*
Wrote under: Christopher Crowfield, Harriet Beecher Stowe
D. of Lyman and Roxana Beecher; m. Calvin Stowe, 1836

S. was the daughter, sister, wife, and mother of New England Calvinist clergymen. Instead of speaking from the pulpit as a man could do, she used her pen to offer moral guidance on contemporary issues. She began writing as a child and first published (primarily contributions to gift books) while teaching at the school of her sister, the famous educator Catharine Beecher, in Cincinnati.

Her husband, a theology professor, did not earn much to support their family as they moved from Ohio to Maine, to Massachusetts, and to Connecticut, where S. had been raised. She bore seven children. In the early years of her marriage, she occasionally wrote short stories and sketches, and the income provided some relief from her domestic drudgery. Her commitment to writing increased after a collection of stories, *The Mayflower*, was published in 1843.

Her first novel, *Uncle Tom's Cabin* (1852) became one of the most popular novels of the century, and it gave her widespread recognition in the U.S. and Great Britain. S. wrote ten novels, short stories for children and adults, travel sketches of Europe and Florida, religious poems, biographies of Civil War heroes, a book on Lady and Lord Byron's marriage (which is critical of Byron), and numerous articles on homemaking and other subjects. Throughout her life, S. wrote quickly and prolifically under the pressure of meeting the financial needs of her husband and children, even long after they had become adults. Many lesser works were published under the name Christopher Crowfield.

Like her sister Catharine, she contributed to the 19th-c. cult of domesticity and gospel of womanhood. S. rejected the intellectual formula for salvation propagated by the overly speculative male clergy of New England and substituted a belief in the function of women as spiritual redeemers of husbands and sons necessarily involved in worldly struggles. As one of her characters explains, "I believe it is woman who holds faith in the world. I'd rather have my wife's . . . opinion of the meaning of a text of Scripture than all the doctors of divinity."

Literary romanticism, such as that of Byron, Scott, Burns, and Goethe, provides a framework for her glorification of women who trust their hearts more than their minds and favor nature over urban environments. Her novels are simple, romantic, and sentimental. The plots are formulas, involving the redemptive power of love, and usually culminate in both marriage and salvation of the soul. The heroine frequently saves the hero through the purity of her sentiment. S.'s novels are often set in the colonial era, which she believed to be wholesomely moral in contrast to 19th-c. urban decadence.

Her best-known novel, *Uncle Tom's Cabin*, did much to stir northern indignation against slavery. It has been suggested by various biographers that there were personal motivations behind S.'s response to slavery. She herself explained that "much that is in that book . . . had its root in the awful scenes and bitter sorrows of that summer" of 1847, when her infant son died in a cholera epidemic. She learned what a slave mother felt when her child is taken from her, and she also identified with black women because of her own heavy domestic duties, her never ending labors to take care of her children on a meager income and with a melancholy husband.

The slavery novels are significant in the development of S.'s belief in women as saviors. Uncle Tom is portrayed as motherly, submissive, feminine; Little Eva's death saves onlookers moved by her angelic innocence; Rachel, the Quaker mother, is a model of piety. A mature woman, however, is not yet central. She wrote two additional books to show the disastrous effect of slavery on the family—*The Key to Uncle Tom's Cabin* (1853) and *Dred: A Tale of the Great Dismal Swamp* (1856)—and then turned to her major theme of women as agents of salvation.

In *The Minister's Wooing* (1859), the heroine, Mary Scudder, is described as a "pure priestess of a domestic temple" who had a "strange power" to inspire boys. Mary lives in the late 18th c.; Agnes of *Agnes of Sorrento* (1862) lives in 15th-c. Italy, but is also a divinity to the nobleman she married. Mara, in *The Pearl of Orr's Island* (1862) is yet another fairy princess, angel, and saint, whose pious death brings salvation to Moses, the young man who loves her. Tina, in *Oldtown Folks* (1869), is "one of the species of womankind that used to be sought out as priestesses to the Delphic Oracle."

Lillie, in *Pink and White Tyranny* (1871), is an exception to S.'s archetypal heroine, although her husband is a "romantic adorer of womanhood." She illustrates the power of the environment: Lillie's beauty causes her to be shallow and spoiled by men. Only her suffering during illness and her husband's compassion save her soul at the end of the story.

S.'s last novel, *Poganuc People* (1878), is semiautobiographical. The heroine, Dolly, reflects S.'s struggle with the conversion requirements established by New England theology, which she could not meet. Like S., Dolly turns to the Episcopal church, which granted membership to any sincere believer. Dolly is another soul-saver; S. describes her as "exhorting with a degree of fervor and fluency in reciting texts of Scriptures."

S.'s novels aroused great feeling against slavery and popularized the notion of woman's place as guardian angel of the home. She said that she wrote her books so that children as well as adults could read them. Perhaps it is for this reason that they are cast in repetitious formulas of angelic heroines, absurd male clergy tangled in the inconsistencies of their theological systems, and well-meaning sons and husbands dependent on mothers and wives for spiritual inspiration. Her readers found in her books what they read sentimental fiction for; they were titillated by scenes of her characters' struggles, such as the passionate death of the young, virginal heroine—most famous being Little Eva's death in *Uncle Tom's Cabin*.

She does not often develop her characters beyond the obvious typologies, but the reader identifies with their problems nevertheless, perhaps because S. did herself. She was not a complex or sophisticated writer, but she mirrored and evoked common beliefs and concerns of her era: the desire to sanctify woman and the family to provide solutions, first, to the problem of slavery and, then, to the corruption of industrial urban life.

WORKS: An Elementary Geography (1835). *The Mayflower; or, Sketches of Scenes and Characters of the Descendants of the Pilgrims* (1843; rev. ed., 1855; English title, *Let Every Man Mind His Own Business*). *The Two Altars* (1852). *Uncle Tom's Cabin* (2 vols. 1852). *The Key to Uncle Tom's Cabin* (1853). *Uncle Tom's Emancipation* (1853). *Sunny Memories of Foreign Lands* (2 vols., 1854). *Dred: A Tale of the Dismal Swamp* (2 vols., 1856; reissued as *Nina Gordon*, 1866). *My Expectation* (1858). *My Strength* (1858). *Our Charlie and What to Do with Him* (1858). *Strong Consolation* (1858). *Things that Cannot Be Shaken* (1858). *A Word to the Sorrowful* (1858). *The Minister's Wooing* (1859). *Agnes of Sorrento* (1862). *The Pearl of Orr's Island* (1862). *House and Home Papers* (1865). *Little Foxes* (1865). *Stories about Our Boys* (1865). *Religious Poems* (1867). *Daisy's First Winter, and Other Stories* (1867). *Queer Little People* (1867). *The Chimney Corner* (1868). *Men of Our Times* (1868). *The American Woman's Home* (with C. E. Beecher, 1869). *Oldtown Folks* (1969). *Lady Byron Vindicated* (1870). *Little Pussy Willow* (1870). *My Wife and I* (1871). *Pink and White Tyranny* (1871). *Sam Lawson's Old Town Fireside Stories* (1872). *Palmetto Leaves* (1873). *Women in Sacred*

History (1873; reissued as *Bible Heroines*, 1878). *Deacon Pitkin's Farm* (English, 1875; similar American collection, *Betty's Bright Idea, and Other Tales*, 1876). *We and Our Neighbors* (1875). *Footsteps of the Master* (1876). *Poganuc People* (1878). *A Dog's Mission; or, The Story of Old Avery House, and Other Stories* (1881). *Nellie's Heroics* (1888). *Our Famous Women* (1884). *The Collected Works of Harriet Beecher Stowe* (16 vols., 1896).

BIBLIOGRAPHY: Adams, J., *Harriet Beecher Stowe* (1963). Ashton, J. W., *Harriet Beecher Stowe: A Reference Guide* (1977). Cross, B., ed., *Autobiography of Lyman Beecher* (2 vols., 1961). Crozier, A., *The Novels of Harriet Beecher Stowe* (1969). Fields, Annie Adams, *Life and Letters of Harriet Beecher Stowe* (1897). Foster, C. H., *The Rungless Ladder* (1954). Gerson, N. B., *Harriet Beecher Stowe: A Biography* (1976). Gilbertson, C., *Harriet Beecher Stowe* (1937). Johnston, J., *Runaway to Heaven* (1963). Kimball, G., *The Religious Ideas of Harriet Beecher Stowe: Her Gospel of Womanhood* (1982). McCray, F. T., *The Life-Work of the Author of Uncle Tom's Cabin* (1889). Stowe, C. E., and L. Stowe, *Harriet Beecher Stowe: The Story of Her Life* (1911). Stowe, L., *Saints, Sinners, and Beechers* (1934). Wagenknecht, E., *Harriet Beecher Stowe: The Known and the Unknown* (1965). Wilson, F., *Crusader in Crinoline* (1941).

GAYLE KIMBALL

Gene Stratton-Porter

B. 17 Aug. 1863, Wabash City, Indiana; d. 6 Dec. 1924, Los Angeles, California
D. of Mark and Mary Shellabarger Stratton; m. Charles Dorwin Porter, 1886

S. was the youngest of twelve children. She married in 1886; there was one daughter. From early childhood, S. spent most of her time outdoors with her father and brothers and was fascinated by plants and birds. From her father, S. learned her first lessons as a naturalist.

Few authors claim to write so directly from life. S. stressed that she based fictional characters on her beloved family and admired friends, insisting that true-to-life portraits need not focus on undesirable human traits. Similarly, the three areas in which she lived—the Wabash River Basin, the Limberlost Swamp in northeastern Indiana, and Southern California—figure importantly in her work.

Although S. was enormously popular and successful at several types of imaginative writing (magazine articles, short stories, poetry, and novels), she considered herself primarily a naturalist. In natural history as in fiction, S. relied wholly on her own observations, devoting enormous energy and facing considerable danger to achieve veracity. Largely self-educated, S. also trained herself as an expert photographer and polished her drawing skills to illustrate the nature books. Although critics have questioned the accuracy of some of her observations, S. had total confidence in her field work as in her personal experience.

S.'s aim was to teach love of nature, God, and one's fellow man, and these themes regulate all her fiction. An equally important motif is familial heritage and relationships. Often a mystery about the family's background lends tension. Another powerful pattern is the consistent strength and capability of the females. Although these characters believe that their first obligation is to run a perfect home and to nurture husband and children, they are also frequently committed to a life work of their own. They are able, productive citizens, usually equal partners in their marriages, who value the money earned for the independence it represents.

S.'s enduring popular reputation is based largely on her novels. *Freckles* (1904), the story of a maimed orphan who works his way to fame, position, and wealth through honesty, bravery, and tremendous effort, is a prime example of the pluck-makes-luck school of American fiction. The sequel, *A Girl of the Limberlost* (1909), portrays Elnora Comstock, born in the Limberlost and dedicated to studying and earning her way out of it and to resolving a severely damaged relationship with her mother. Some of the values the Limberlost youngsters share—the desires for urban life, fine clothing, wealth, and social position—have been sharply criticized, but for S., these were the logical rewards of ability and extremely hard work. These two novels celebrate the swamp's danger as well as its beauty and are surprisingly little concerned with conservation; S. depicts the area as a natural prey to progress.

Other novels clearly reflect S.'s lifelong commitment to conservationism, and their protagonists value money in part as a means of serving humanity. David Langston in *The Harvester* (1911) and Linda Strong in *Her Father's Daughter* (1921) earn their livings from the flora, but they also make deliberate efforts to harvest wisely and to save threatened species.

Though accused of preoccupation with happy endings and the sunny side of life, S. intended thoughtful examination of serious human problems. *At the Foot of the Rainbow* (1907) and the long narrative poem,

Euphorbia (*Good Housekeeping*, Jan.–Mar. 1923) treat serious marital discord, and *The Magic Garden* (1927) explores problems faced by children of divorced parents. In *Michael O'Halloran* (1915), S. examines the work ethic as spiritual salvation for both Mickey, a slum child, and Nellie Minturn, a woman whose inherited wealth has barred her from genuine love. Mahala, of *The White Flag* (1923), struggles for self-definition as well as purity. Always, the S. formula prevails: central love stories embellished by nature lore, a pattern devised deliberately to make nature study and moral guidance palatable and salable.

More than twenty films were based on the novels, and S. organized her own company, Gene Stratton-Porter Productions, to protect the moralistic tone of her work. The movies she produced were popular but not landmark productions.

Perhaps the most widely read female American author of her day, S. is generally considered somewhat limited in her world view, but she is an author of power, invention, and strong narrative ability.

WORKS: *The Song of the Cardinal* (1903). *Freckles* (1904). *At the Foot of the Rainbow* (1907). *What I Have Done with Birds* (1907). *Birds of the Bible* (1909). *A Girl of the Limberlost* (1909). *Music of the Wild* (1910). *After the Flood* (1911). *The Harvester* (1911). *Moths of the Limberlost* (1912). *Laddie* (1913). *Birds of the Limberlost* (1914). *Michael O'Halloran* (1915). *Morning Face* (1916). *Friends in Feathers* (1917). *A Daughter of the Land* (1918). *Homing With the Birds* (1919). *Her Father's Daughter* (1921). *The Firebird* (1922). *Jesus of the Emerald* (1923). *The White Flag* (1923). *Wings* (1923). *The Keeper of the Bees* (1925). *Tales You Won't Believe* (1925). *Let Us Highly Resolve* (1927). *The Magic Garden* (1927).

BIBLIOGRAPHY: Bakerman, J. S., "Gene Stratton-Porter: What Price the Limberlost?" *The Old Northwest* 3 (June 1977). MacLean, D. G., *Gene Stratton-Porter: A Bibliography and Collector's Guide* (1976). Meehan, J. P., *The Lady of the Limberlost: The Life and Letters of Gene Stratton-Porter* (1928). Overton, G., *American Night's Entertainment* (1923). Richards, B., *Gene Stratton-Porter* (1980). S. F. E. [E. F. Saxton], *Gene Stratton-Porter: A Little Story of the Life and Works and Ideals of "The Bird Woman"* (1915).

Other references: *Harper's* (Oct. 1947). *Smithsonian* 7 (April 1976).

JANE S. BAKERMAN

Anna Louise Strong

B. 14 Nov. 1885, Friend, Nebraska; d. 29 March 1970, Peking, China
Wrote under: "Anise," Anna Louise Strong
D. of Sydney and Ruth Tracy Strong; m. Joel Shubin, 1932

S. descended from Puritan families who arrived in New England in 1630. Her father was a Congregational minister; her mother an important figure in the church's missionary organizations. S. completed secondary schooling by the age of fourteen, studied languages in Germany and Switzerland, and obtained her bachelor's degree at Oberlin. Her first writing, poetry and stories, was published in *Youth's Companion* during her teens.

After college, S. took her first journalism position as an associate editor and writer for a fundamentalist weekly, the *Advance*, where she was overworked and fired by the publisher as soon as she had increased circulation. "As for their exploitation of myself, I was only eager to do more work for the salary than anyone else could do; this seemed the road to advancement." Partially to save face, she enrolled in a philosophy program at the University of Chicago. At the age of twenty-three, S. defended her doctoral thesis on the psychology of prayer before the combined theology and philosophy faculties and became the youngest student ever awarded such a degree at the university.

For several years, S. worked in urban social-reform projects, including organizing child-welfare exhibits in cities across America. She began to combine political activism and journalism after rejoining her father in Seattle, Washington, in 1915. S. was elected to the Seattle School Board, but was recalled in 1918 because of her activism in antiwar groups and her reportage (under the pseudonym "Anise") for the Seattle *Daily Call* and the Seattle *Union Record*, both socialist newspapers. Her first major article was a rather detached, "impartial" account of the Everett Massacre (New York *Evening Post*, 4 Feb. 1919). As events led to the Seattle General Strike of 1919, S. became their major chronicler. After the strike, she analyzed what happened and the lessons to be learned in a pamphlet, *The Seattle General Strike* (1918). Roger Sale, a historian of Seattle history, considers the chapter on the strike in S.'s autobiography, *I Change Worlds: The Remaking of an American* (1935), as the "best single work on Seattle in one of its most critical periods."

In 1921, S. did publicity work on the famine in Poland and Russia for the American Friends Service Committee, and she reported on the famine in both countries for the International News Service. From Moscow she wrote in defense of the Bolsheviks' new government and made several trips to the U.S. to lecture and raise money for projects aimed at promoting friendship between the two nations. In 1930, S. founded the *Moscow News*, an English-language newspaper for foreigners in Russia. Despite working as hard as she once did for the *Advance*, S.'s ultimate inability to reconcile her American view of the proper style and philosophy of reporting with the perspectives of the Russian staff, caused her to leave the newspaper. Eventually concluding that she would always remain an "outsider," S. ceased to dream of "becoming a creator in chaos. . . . I would organize no more. . . . I could always write." For the next forty-five years, S. reluctantly embraced a life of "roving to revolutions and writing about them for the American press."

In addition to her coverage of Russia from the 1920s through the 1940s, S. reported on the course of revolutionary change in Mexico, the civil war in Spain, the advance of the Red Army against the Germans in Poland— her only novel, *Wild River* (1943), is a celebration of the courage shown by Russians during the German invasion—and, most regularly, on the revolution in China. S.'s most famous single piece of reportage is "The Thought of Mao Tse-Tung" (*Amerasia*, June 1947), an article she based on an interview with the leader at the Chinese Revolutionary Army's headquarters in Yenan in 1946. Mao's first use of the phrase "paper tiger" is found here. Perhaps the most widely read of S.'s writing among intellectuals, academics, and government officials is *Letter from China*, a monthly newsletter which she published from 1962 until January 1969. During this period, it represented one of the few reliable sources of information about life in China and the position of the Chinese leadership on their rift with the Soviet Union.

Besides her China reportage, S.'s best works are her only book on the U.S., *My Native Land* (1940), and her autobiography, *I Change Worlds*. The first belongs to the genre of documentary reportage in which American intellectuals sought to "discover America." Her account is moving, filled with human interest stories, and governed by a simple—although not reductive—vision of the world. S. condemns the failures of the American capitalist system; yet, she does not entirely deny the past, but rather affirms a kind of populist democracy.

Most of S.'s journalism is flawed by a consistent naiveté, a disinterest in explaining theory, and an overabsorption in portraying personality and action. The best of her work, however, is informative and meaningful "for the great middlewestern masses," because of S.'s well-constructed images, dialogue, and use of the human-interest story.

WORKS: *The Psychology of Prayer* (1909). *Child Welfare Exhibits: Types and Preparation* (1915). *The Seattle General Strike* (1918). *The First Time in History: Two Years of Russia's New Life* (1924). *Children of Revolution* (1925). *China's Millions* (1928). *Red Star in Samarkand* (1929). *The Soviets Conquer Wheat* (1931). *The Road to the Grey Pamir* (1931). *I Change Worlds: The Remaking of an American* (1935). *The Soviet World* (1936). *My Native Land* (1940). *The Soviets Expected It* (1941). *Wild River* (1943). *The Chinese Conquer China* (1949). *Cash and Violence in Laos and Vietnam* (1962). *Letters From China, Nos. 1–10* (1963). *Letters From China, Nos. 21–30* (1966).

The papers of Anna Louise Strong are at the University of Washington, Seattle.

BIBLIOGRAPHY: Chen, P., *China Called Me* (1979). Friedham, R. L., *The Seattle General Strike* (1967). Milton, D., and N. Dall, *The Wind Will Not Survive* (1976). Nies, J., *Seven Women: Portraits from the American Radical Tradition* (1977). Ogle, S. F., "Anna Louise Strong: Seattle Years" (M.A. Thesis, Seattle Univ., 1973). Ogle, S. F., in *Notable American Women: The Modern Period*, Eds. B. Sicherman and C. H. Green (1980). Pringle, R. W., "Anna Louise Strong: Propagandist of Communism" (Ph.D. diss., Univ. of Virginia, 1972). Sale, R., *Seattle: Past to Present* (1976).

Other references: *Eastern Horizon* (1970). *NewR* (25 April 1970). *Newsweek* (13 April 1970). *NYT* (30 March 1970). *Survey* (Oct. 1964).

JENNIFER L. TEBBE

Mary Alsop Sture-Vasa

B. *10 July 1885, Cape May Point, New Jersey; d. 15 Oct. 1980, Chevy Chase, Maryland*
Given name: *Mary O'Hara Alsop*
Wrote under: *Mary O'Hara*
D. *of Reese Fell and Mary Lee Spring Alsop; m. Kent Kane Parrott, 1905; m. Helge Sture-Vasa, 1922*

S. was privately educated, with the emphasis on languages and music. She traveled widely during her youth in the eastern U.S., and she also lived in California and Wyoming, locales important to her career as popular novelist, screen writer, and composer. For example, *The Catch Colt* (1964), a musical drama, blends all these influences. S. was married twice and had two children.

In *Wyoming Summer* (1963), a fictionalized autobiography, S. defines a story as "a reflection of life plus beginning and end (life seems not to have either) and a meaning." She applied her definition to ranch life as recorded in her journals to create this book and her best-known works, the Flicka series. Like the straight autobiographical works, *Novel-in-the-Making* (1954) and *A Musical in the Making* (1966), *Wyoming Summer* conveys a clear sense of the artist, writer, and composer at work. Episodic but smooth, highly personal but detached, it includes poignant comments about women and their careers and is embedded with tiny, insightful essays about adversity, loneliness, religion, creativity, happiness, and love.

Now regarded as young people's classics, the very popular series *My Friend Flicka* (1941), *Thunderhead* (1943), and *Green Grass of Wyoming* (1946) shares these themes and reflects S.'s knowledge and love of animals. These novels trace the maturation of Ken McLaughlin and his development of a line of horses destined to realize his family's dreams. In the first novel, Ken's struggle to master the filly is clearly the symbol for his efforts to discipline himself. The parallelism continues in the next two books, where Ken's development is symbolized by the difficulty of training Flicka's colt, Thunderhead, a promising but wild stallion. Ken learns to differentiate between absolute freedom and freely exercised responsibility, between dream and reality, and is thus prepared for his role as young man and young lover. The characterization is well wrought, persuasive, and sound.

Thunderhead and *Green Grass of Wyoming* are more intricately plotted than *My Friend Flicka* and more appealing to adults, for in each an important subplot explores the sometimes strained marriage (complicated by possessiveness, financial worries, and parenthood) of Rob and Nell McLaughlin. Nell's portrait is particularly strong in its presentation of the tensions engendered by traditional women's roles. Defining herself only as Rob's wife, the mother of Ken and Howard, Nell learns to subordinate herself to her husband in *Thunderhead*. In *Green Grass of Wyoming*, she finds herself at a stage of life she has always desired—she has at last borne a daughter, has taught her sons to be self-reliant young men, and has helped her husband achieve some financial security. But Nell is unprepared for this new era, and it precipitates a physical and emotional breakdown. Her resolution of these difficulties remains traditional and is honestly depicted; she does not alter her self-definition, but she does learn to invest herself in herself as well as in others. Beautifully rendered natural settings and details of ranch life underscore the realism of all three works.

Christian faith is a major theme in S.'s work. *Let Us Say Grace* (1930) explains the Trinity in a fable framing a parable. The parable compares the function of the monetary system to the relationships within the Trinity. In the Flicka series, Nell's musings and her talks with her sons often concern religion. *The Son of Adam Wyngate* (1952), a less well-received novel, portrays a clergyman whose faith is tested when he confronts his wife's adultery.

S. is considered a talented, careful writer who reveals a genuine understanding of human nature and a fine ability to project into animal "mentality" without anthropomorphizing.

WORKS: *Let Us Say Grace* (1930). *My Friend Flicka* (1941; film version, 1943). *Thunderhead* (1943; film version, 1945). *Green Grass of Wyoming* (1946; film version, 1948). *The Son of Adam Wyngate* (1952). *Novel-in-the-Making* (1954). *Wyoming Summer* (1963). *The Catch Colt* (1964). *A Musical in the Making* (1966).

BIBLIOGRAPHY: Witham, W. T., *The Adolescent in the American Novel, 1921–1960* (1964).

Other references: *NYTBR* (24 Aug. 1941; 27 Oct. 1946). *SatR* (1 Nov. 1941; 17 May 1952).

JANE S. BAKERMAN

Ruth Suckow

B. 6 Aug. 1892, Hawarden, Iowa; d. 23 Jan. 1960, Claremont, California
D. of William John and Anna Mary Kluckhohn Suckow; m. Ferner Nuhn, 1929

The second daughter of a Congregational minister, S. grew up in Iowa. A moving and useful account of her childhood, which examines many of the materials used in novels and stories, is "A Memoir," published in *Some Others and Myself* (1952). She was educated in Iowa schools, Grinnell College, the Curry School of Expression in Boston, and the University of Denver (B.A. 1917; M.A. 1918—her thesis dealt with woman novelists). Learning the apiary business, she later supplemented her earnings by beekeeping. In 1929, she married Ferner Nuhn, another Iowa writer. Arthritis eventually necessitating a dry climate, she spent her last years in Southern California.

A regional realist, S. created fiction that is remarkably even in quality and consistent in theme and tone, although her stories treat a wider variety of character types than are fully portrayed in the novels; they also tend to end less hopefully. Her almost invariable setting is rural Iowa. Early reviewers praised her knowledge of her characters and her skill in description; often they also accused her of stressing the unpleasant side of Iowa life and of the indiscriminate piling up of detail. In mid-career, she was praised for her realism and for the warmth now seen in her work. Critics found the late novels nostalgic and less pessimistic than the early works. But today they seem very much of a piece: all show disappointed lives but end on a positive note. What changed was not S.'s view of her world but the critical expectations of her.

Country People (1924) tells the story of August Kaetterhenry, dour son of German immigrants. Years of toil, leading finally to prosperity, leave him unable to enjoy the results of his labor. After his death, however, his wife discovers an unsuspected independence in herself and lives more happily than before. This novel seems static, as it is presented almost entirely through narration; dialogue and dramatized action are lacking.

The next four novels, *The Odyssey of a Nice Girl* (1925), *The Bonney Family* (1928), *Cora* (1929), and *The Kramer Girls* (1930), make effective use of dramatized scenes and of accurately rendered and functional dialogue. All are concerned with family relationships, but most particularly with women. Their fully and sympathetically drawn characters are ordinary people about whom S. makes us care.

The Odyssey of a Nice Girl and *Cora* follow the lives of two Iowa girls from childhood into adulthood. In the first, Marjorie is a middle-class girl; while "nice," she is also shallow. Her marriage strikes many readers as an unsatisfactory, conventional ending to a pointless "odyssey." Cora is from working-class backgrounds; her success in a career and her failed marriage leave her facing the future with courage; although not happy, she is strong and would not change her life. The experiences of both women are so presented as to be typical for their time and place.

The Bonney Family and *The Kramer Girls* deal with families. The Bonney family consists of parents, two sons, and two daughters; in the novel, the initially happy family is followed to its eventual breakup. The final focus is on Sarah, the oldest daughter, as she sets out on a new career. In *The Kramer Girls*, the central family group is three sisters, the two eldest sacrificing themselves to give the youngest a chance. All three lead narrow lives, but the youngest, after years of struggle, eventually reaches a balance, content in her marriage and in her job. The depictions of the mannish Georgie and feminine Annie, the two older sisters, breathe new life into the stereotype of the "old maid."

The Folks (1934), S.'s most ambitious novel, shows a natural progression from earlier themes and techniques. Fred Ferguson, his wife Annie, and their children are all developed fully and believably. Each of the children is given a section of the novel, while the opening and closing sections focus on their parents. All four children ultimately disappoint the parents: Carl, the most apparently successful, is trapped in an unhappy marriage, and Bunny marries a young woman whom his parents can neither approve nor understand. Dorothy, conventionally pretty and popular, makes an apparently ideal marriage; her section, set near the center of the novel, describes her wedding as a perfect moment against which everything else is measured. Margaret's section, the longest, follows her from college, through a Bohemian period in New York City, into an obsessive affair with a married man. The novel's structure is thematic rather than chronological, presenting some key events from several viewpoints. Margaret is the most complex of the characters; the depiction of her rebellion against middle-class midwestern standards is well handled.

Only two more novels followed. They continue S.'s earlier themes but are more heavily symbolic, abstract, and moralistic. *New Hope* (1942) is a parable of the American experience. The town of New Hope is presented in the first optimism of its early years. But the settlers bring their old sins with them, and S. makes it clear that New Hope will never become more than a village. The novel centers around two families, those of a businessman and a minister. The minister's arrival and departure several years later give the novel its form; events are seen through the perspective of the little son of the businessman. A central theme is the loss of innocence. Like *The Folks*, *New Hope* is organized thematically, though without any complication of chronology or point of view.

The John Wood Case (1959) studies the effects on family, church, and community of the revelation that a trusted small-town business and church leader is an embezzler. The town's hypocrisy is revealed, but some characters behave well under the pressure. The novel ends hopefully, as the culprit's son is shown courageously facing the future.

While never considered a major writer, S. has always been deservedly respected for her contributions to regional realism, her sensitive characterizations of Iowa women and men, and her honest, unflinching studies of decent people meeting the disappointments of their lives with dignity. Her fiction is always carefully crafted; to read her work is to be carried to rural Iowa as it was not long ago.

WORKS: Country People (1924). *The Odyssey of a Nice Girl* (1925). *Iowa Interiors* (1926). *The Bonney Family* (1928). *Cora* (1929). *The Kramer Girls* (1930). *Children and Older People* (1931). *The Folks* (1934). *Carry-Over* (1936). *New Hope* (1942). *Some Others and Myself* (1952). *The John Wood Case* (1959).

BIBLIOGRAPHY: Kissane, L. M., *Ruth Suckow* (1969). McAlpin, S., "Enlightening the Commonplace: The Work of Sarah Orne Jewett, Willa Cather, and Ruth Suckow" (Ph.D. diss., Univ. of Pennsylvania, 1971). Omreanin, M. S., *Ruth Suckow: A Critical Study of Her Fiction* (1972). Stewart, M. O., "A Critical Study of Ruth Suckow's Fiction" (Ph.D. diss., Univ. of Illinois, 1960).

Other references: *Bl* 13 (Nov. 1970). *Palimpsest* 35 (Feb. 1954).

MARY JEAN DeMARR

May Swenson

B. 28 May 1919, Logan, Utah
D. of Dan Arthur and Anna Margaret Hellberg Swenson

One of a large family, S. grew up and was educated near the State University in Logan, where her father was professor of mechanical engineering. After graduation, S. worked as a reporter on the Salt Lake City *Deseret News* and then moved to New York where she held various jobs, becoming an editor for New Directions in 1959. In 1966 she resigned to devote full time to her writing, with interludes as poet-in-residence at several American and Canadian universities. S. has received numerous honors for her poetry, including Guggenheim and Rockefeller Fellowships, the Shelley Memorial Award, and an Award in Literature from the National Institute of Arts and Letters. In 1970 she was elected to membership in the Institute.

Though S. has done translations from the work of the Swedish poet Tomas Tranströmer and has written a play and some prose, she is best known as a poet. Her first book, *Another Animal* (1954), indicated the directions and methods much of her later work would follow; it demonstrates the qualities of freshness, vitality, and keen and often unusual observations of natural phenomena and a magical balancing of surface and interior meanings. Often the balancing takes the form of metaphor as in the equation between landscape and the human body in "Sketch for a Landscape." In this book she begins, too, the riddling pattern often followed later of refusing to name lest naming interfere with the observer's truly identifying the object.

S.'s second book, *A Cage of Spines* (1958), a solid volume both in length and quality, continues the pressure upon the things of this world, turning them into emblems of other, deeper structures. For example, in "Promontory Moment," the poet evolves from the image of a yellow pencil tilted in sand like the mast of a ship, the whole relationship of the works of man, nature, the sea, and sun where "little and vast are the same to that big eye / that sees no shadow." But S.'s cosmic images are rarely solemn, so interspersed are they with vivid accounting of the immediate world. Depth and wit come together in this book described by Richard Wilbur as "happy throughout in both senses of the word."

To Mix with Time: New and Selected Poems (1963) reproduces most of the poems of her first two volumes, along with an entire new collection. Some of the poems came as a response to France, Italy, and Spain, which S. visited in 1960 and 1961 with an Amy Lowell Travelling Scholarship. Of particular interest is "Death Invited," in which S. combines an awareness of the ongoingness of death with the ritual of the bullfight.

Half Sun Half Sleep (1967) continues the search for "the clarities of Being" through the landscapes of city, country, and the sea. She continues also her experiments with unusual typography suited to the material of the poem which has marked her work from the beginning.

All the poems in *Iconographs* (1970) are in such shapes. It is important to notice, however, that S. has never sacrificed the sense of the poem to its iconography; the shapes are imposed upon the poems after composition. *Iconographs* marks too a further expression of passion in such poems as "Feel Me," "A Trellis for R.," "Wednesday at the Waldorf," and "The Year of the Double Spring." Here S. releases some of the intense feeling that remained as a strong undercurrent in many of the earlier poems.

New & Selected Things Taking Place (1978) marks a return to more conventional typography while the poet carries on her exact, often witty, exploration of the world, together with more somber remembrances of family and aging. Here is a complete collection of new poems, with a large selection from the earlier books as well.

Besides her six volumes of original verse, S. has published three books for young readers. Most of the poems in the first two of these, *Poems to Solve* (1966) and *More Poems to Solve* (1971), have been chosen from her already published work.

S. has carried the perception of visual detail farther than any other contemporary poet, and probably none so successfully joins freshness of vision with serious undercurrents of ideas. Moreover, she is aware of the textural connotations of sound, consistently using them to enhance meaning. Wit, too, enlivens poem after poem in the metaphysical sense, being a play between intellect and object in a serious sleight of hand. As Richard Howard has said, "her attention is to the quality of being itself in order to encounter, to espouse form as it *becomes* what it is." S.'s poetry is unique in such encounter and well deserves the high praise it has from the beginning received.

WORKS: *Another Animal* (1954). *A Cage of Spines* (1958). *To Mix with Time: New and Selected Poems* (1963). *Poems to Solve* (1966). *Half Sun Half Sleep: New Poems* (1967). *Iconographs: Poems* (1970). *More Poems to Solve* (1971). *Windows and Stones: Selected Poems* by Tomas Tranströmer (translated by Swenson, 1972). *The Guess & Spell Coloring Book* (1976). *New & Selected Things Taking Place* (1978).

BIBLIOGRAPHY: Stanford, Ann, "The Art of Perceiving," *SoR* (Winter 1969).

Other references: *American Poetry Review* (March–April 1978). *Nation* (10 Aug. 1963; 28 Feb. 1972). *NYTBR* (7 May 1971). *Poetry* (Nov. 1971; Feb. 1979). *PrS* (Winter 1960; Spring 1968). *TriQ* (7 Fall 1966).

ANN STANFORD

Jane Grey Cannon Swisshelm

B. 6 Dec. 1815, Pittsburgh, Pennsylvania; d. 22 July 1884, Sewickley, Pennsylvania
Wrote under: Jennie Deans, J. G. S., Jane Grey Swisshelm
D. of Thomas and Mary Scott Cannon; m. James Swisshelm, 1836

When S. was seven, her father died of tuberculosis. Her mother, who had previously lost four children to the disease, disregarded the doctor's prescription when S. showed symptoms, treating her with fresh air, fresh food, and exercise. S. recovered, and at the age of fourteen was teaching in the public school in Wilkinsburg, Pennsylvania. S. joined the church of her Scotch Covenanter parents at the age of fifteen, after a period of torment. The church provided her with a sense of purpose and a source of conflict throughout her life. In 1836, she married James Swisshelm, entering upon a marriage that was stormy and intermittent.

A short stay in Louisville, Kentucky, where her husband went into business, provided S. with material for her later writing against slavery. She started a school for blacks, but gave it up when threats were made to burn her house. From 1840 on, S.'s articles attacking capital punishment, advocating woman suffrage and the right of women to hold property, and urging the abolition of slavery appeared, at first anonymously, in newspapers in and around Pittsburgh. She contributed stories and poems as well. When Pittsburgh was left without an abolitionist paper in 1847, S. resolved to edit one herself. S. delighted in the criticism she drew as a woman editor with pronounced political views. She continued to write for the Pittsburgh *Saturday Visiter* after it merged with Robert Riddle's *Journal* in 1852. Her zeal for reform included advocacy of the "water-cure treatment," advice on woman's health, dress, reading, and education.

An opponent of the Mexican War, S. went to Washington, D.C., in 1850 to observe the debate over disposition of Mexican territory acquired through the War. At that time Horace Greeley engaged her as a Washington correspondent to the New York *Tribune*. The first woman to have such a regular assignment, she sought and secured a seat in the Congressional reporters' gallery.

In 1857, S. severed her connection with the *Family Journal and Visiter*, left her husband, and took her small daughter to northern Minnesota. There she agreed to revive and edit a defunct Democratic newspaper, which had as a major purpose attracting immigration to Minnesota. Her agreement with its proprietor included, however, the right to express her own views. The St. Cloud *Visiter* readily offended one of the leading political powers in the territory, and in March, 1858, three men broke into her office and destroyed her press. S. first discovered she had an aptitude for public speaking at a meeting to raise funds to procure a new press, and for some years afterward made a lecture tour each year. As she traveled, she sent vivid letters to the St. Cloud *Democrat*, the weekly which had emerged under her editorship in July, 1858, when, in order to avoid a libel suit, she had promised never again to use the *Visiter* as a political organ.

In 1863, following a revolt by the Sioux Indians, S. went on a lecture tour through the East to arouse opinion in favor of sterner treatment of the Indians. At this time, she characterized the Washington scene as "treason, treason, treason all around about—paid treason—official treason." She served as a nurse in military hospitals around Washington, while waiting to begin her duties as a clerk in the War Department. Her letters continued, castigating all whose conduct she disapproved: public officials, the Sanitary Commission, women who knit in the office.

Her last journalistic venture, the *Reconstructionist* (1865), was a radical newspaper, outspoken in its criticism of Andrew Johnson. Johnson responded by dismissing her from her post in the War Department, and without this source of income, she could not continue publication of the *Reconstructionist*.

S.'s autobiography, *Half a Century* (1880), is unquestionably flawed by her biases. In addition, it was reconstructed from memory, as she had systematically destroyed letters and diaries during her unhappy marriage. It is, nevertheless, an important first-hand account of events of her time, as well as of her struggle as a woman. The last third of the book contains her picture of her experiences nursing the sick and wounded during the Civil War, putting to use her powers of keen observation, willingness to sacrifice herself, her sense of humor, her strong will, and her personal warmth.

A journalist who espoused many reform causes, S. was best known as an abolitionist. Her unrestrained style often provoked violent response, physical as well as verbal. Her writing is simple and direct, distinguished by dramatic narrative, graphic description, and vivid characterization. Although S. is noted and remembered for her ruthlessness, invective, and sarcasm, her brilliant style is equally effective in describing men and women she admired, and in conveying her warmth and her sense of pride in places and events which, to her, meant progress.

WORKS: *Letters to Country Girls* (1853). *True Stories about Pets* (1879). *Half a Century* (1880). *Crusader and Feminist: The Letters of Jane Grey Swisshelm, 1858–1865* (Ed. A. J. Larsen, 1934).

Files of the St. Cloud *Visiter* and the St. Cloud *Democrat* and a partial file of the Pittsburgh *Saturday Visiter* are in the Minnesota Historical Society. A file of the Pittsburgh *Saturday Visiter* and a few issues of the *Reconstructionist* are in the Carnegie Library in Pittsburgh.

BIBLIOGRAPHY: McCarthy, A., in *Women of Minnesota*, Ed. B. Stuhler and G. Kreuter (1977). Thorp, M. F. *Female Persuasion* (1949).

For articles in reference works, see *DAB* IX, 2. *NAW* (article by A. F. Tyler).

Other references: *Abraham Lincoln Quarterly* 6 (Dec. 1950). *American Historical Review* 37 (July 1932). *Minnesota History* 32 (March 1951). *Mississippi Valley Historical Review* 7 (Dec. 1920). *NYT* (23 July 1884). *Western Pennsylvania Historical Magazine* 4 (July 1921).

VIVIAN H. SHORTREED

Gladys Bagg Taber

B. 2 April, 1899, Colorado Springs, Colorado; d. 11 March 1980, Hyannis,
Massachusetts
D. of Rufus Mather and Grace Raybold Bagg; m. Frank Albion Taber, 1922

T. was born in the West, grew up in the Midwest, and lived her adult life in Virginia, New York, and New England. She graduated from Wellesley in 1920; took an M.A. at Lawrence College, Appleton, Wisconsin, in 1921; and did graduate work at Columbia University. In 1922, she married a professor of music at Randolph-Macon College in Virginia, who lost his hearing and had to leave his profession. T. had one daughter.

T.'s early work includes a play and a book of poems, but most of it is popular romance, sometimes serialized in magazines such as the *Ladies' Home Journal*. Her fiction is light and uplifting; her heroines usually find true love despite an unsympathetic father or class differences. In later novels, her heroines are long-suffering middle-aged housewives. T.'s fiction shows a remarkable concentration on her own life, with the same themes and characters appearing again and again, and, as often happens with popular writers about whom the public is very curious, she became increasingly open about her own life when she turned completely to nonfiction after publishing her last novel, a barely disguised autobiography, in 1957.

T.'s father is a perennial character in her books, fiction or autobiography. She wrote one book about him, *Especially Father* (1949), and portrays him in detail again in *Harvest of Yesterdays* (1976). He is harshly dealt with in her fiction, where he is the tyrant who keeps his daughter from marrying the man she loves, but in T.'s nonfiction she tries to sympathize with him. Nevertheless, T. always portrays him as a hyperactive domestic tyrant with the social responsibility of a sand flea. T.'s literary treatment of her father is an interesting case history in the making of capital from one of life's burdens.

T.'s fiction is not the work which gained her the loyal fans that she has attracted over the years; rather, her magazine columns and the books she made from them are the cornerstone of her success. From November 1937 to December 1957, her column, Diary of Domesticity, ran in the country's leading women's magazine, the *Ladies' Home Journal*, where S. was also assistant editor (1946–58). Then for ten more years the column continued, in *Everywoman's Family Circle*, the supermarket magazine, as Butternut Wisdom. These columns, and the books she made from them, chronicle the life of T. and her family at Stillmeadow, a farmhouse built in 1690, near Southbury, Connecticut. The first Stillmeadow book, *Harvest at Stillmeadow*, was published in 1940. There is a lot of repitition in the Stillmeadow books, which are organized seasonally, but these are the most popular mid-20th-c. examples by a woman of the subgenre of semiautobiographical books about country life.

Sharing Stillmeadow with T. and her daughter is Jill (Eleanor Mayer), T.'s beloved "life-long friend," and her two children. Jill was widowed in 1943. T.'s husband is seldom mentioned; he died in 1964. Throughout the series, the reader follows the changes that come to the lives of T. and Jill as their children grow up and they struggle with the usual problems of country life. Jill is portrayed by T. as the stereotyped demon gardener. Her death in 1960 was acknowledged in T.'s columns and became the subject of a book on coping with grief, *Another Path* (1963). T. characterizes herself, like the usual middle-aged heroines in her later novels, as timid and incompetent in mechanical things, unable to use the telephone or the vacuum cleaner.

Like other women who write for the popular audience, T. portrays herself as much more of an average housewife than she could have been. In *Mrs. Daffodil* (1957), an autobiographical novel in which the heroine is a columnist who lives in an old house in New England, an interviewer asks Mrs. Daffodil why she is so successful as a writer. "I think it's because I am not a special person at all. . . . I am just any woman with a house and a family and dogs and a garden. So if I put down what I feel, others feel the same way. I've often wished I were a literary writer, like Virginia Woolf, but I'm just the common garden variety." Such is indeed the nature of popular appeal; the readers want to read what they already think.

WORKS: *Lady of the Moon* (1928). *Lyonesse* (1929). *Late Climbs the Sun* (1934). *Tomorrow May Be Fair* (1935). *The Evergreen Tree* (1937). *Long Tails and Short* (1938). *A Star to Steer By* (1938). *This is For Always* (1938). *Harvest at Stillmeadow* (1940). *Nurse in Blue* (1943). *The Heart Has April Too* (1944). *Give Us This Day* (1944). *Give Me the Stars* (1945). *Especially Spaniels* (1945). *The Family on Maple Street* (1946). *Stillmeadow Kitchen* (1947). *The Book of Stillmeadow* (1948). *Especially Father* (1949). *Stillmeadow Seasons* (1950). *When Dogs Meet People* (1952). *Stillmeadow and Sugarbridge* (with B. Webster, 1953). *Stillmeadow Daybook* (1955). *Mrs. Daffodil* (1957). *What Cooks at Stillmeadow* (1958). *Spring Harvest* (1959). *Stillmeadow Sampler* (1959). *Stillmeadow Road* (1962). *Another Path* (1963). *Stillmeadow Cookbook* (1965). *Stillmeadow Calendar* (1967). *Especially Dogs* (1968). *Stillmeadow Album* (1969). *Amber: A Very Personal Cat* (1970). *My*

Own Cape Cod (1971). *My Own Cook Book* (1972). *Country Chronicle* (1974). *Harvest of Yesterdays* (1976). *Conversations with Amber* (1978). *Still Cove Journal* (1981).

BIBLIOGRAPHY: *Ladies' Home Journal* (Oct. 1946). *NYT* (9 Oct. 1955). *WLB* (April 1952).

BEVERLY SEATON

Genevieve Taggard

B. 28 Nov. 1894, Waitsburg, Washington; d. 8 Nov. 1948, New York City
D. of James Nelson and Alta Gale Arnold Taggard; m. Robert Wolf, 1921;
  m. Kenneth Durant, 1935

T. was the eldest child of schoolteacher-missionaries, whose Scots-Irish pioneer ancestors had migrated to Washington from Vermont. Feeling alienated from the spiritual and cultural sterility of eastern Washington, T.'s devout parents moved the family to Hawaii when she was two. Except for two traumatic returns to Washington necessary for her father's health, T. lived eighteen years in what she later idealized as innocent, exotic poverty.

The contrast between Hawaii, where caste, race, and wealth seemed irrelevant, and Waitsburg's small-town prejudice and rude materialism, focused T.'s moral vision. Her social conscience was a logical extension of her parents' preachings, but their faith as fundamentalist Disciples of Christ allowed only biblical reading; Keats and Ruskin were illicit pleasures. Defiantly, T. embarked upon her writing career at age twelve.

By the time she graduated from the University of California at Berkeley (1920), T. was both poet and socialist. Nationally published, T. was offered work in New York by Max Eastman at the *Liberator*. She took a leading role in the literary and social developments of the 1920s and 1930s, working first for B. W. Huebsch's avant-garde *Freeman* and helping found and edit the *Measure*, a lyric poetry journal. T. taught at several colleges, traveled in Europe and Russia, raised a daughter, and was active in humanitarian and proletarian causes. Her two husbands were also radical writers. T. retired in 1946 in Vermont; she died in 1948 of the effects of hypertension.

Known primarily to scholars for her biography of Emily Dickinson (1930), a passionate, bold interpretation of the father-daughter relationship and Dickinson's psychology, T. received wide recognition throughout her career as a literary activist and poet, who was published and reviewed in journals ranging from *The New Yorker* to *New Masses*.

Her first book of poetry, *For Eager Lovers* (1922), established her unique idiom as a metaphysical Marxist, a lyric intellectual who incorporates Hawaiian exotica into poems about revolution and a woman's experience in love. Even such Marxist visions of doomed decadence as "Twentieth Century Slave-Gang" eschew rhetoric and combine modern directness ("the ants are hurried") with extraordinary images: oaks bend knotted knees in labor, a pond is wrinkled with velvet oil, wasps carry spider-spoil to where crude honey hangs in mud.

While this volume commemorates a first year of marriage, and T. occasionally speaks as an "eager lover," she insists on the necessary independence—even defiance—of soul, voice, whole being, especially in the potentially compromising love relationship. Her resolute quest for freedom (personal, artistic, social, and political) is the dominant theme of T.'s poetry; here the tone is "caged arrogance" as the voice celebrates its emancipation.

In *Collected Poems, 1918–1938*, T. juxtaposes early and late poems to show their essential continuity, that love of beauty and hatred of oppression are not contradictory. T. brings her modernist and ideological rebellion against romanticism to the lives of "mothers, housewives, old women" to capture with compassion, "the kitchens they knew, sinks, suds, stew-pots, and pennies . . . / Dull hurry and worry, clatter, wet hands and backache."

In *Slow Music* (1946), T. is still working to support her lifelong conviction that the desire to be socially relevant and the belief that art obeys its own laws must coexist.

Charges that her poetry lacks a "unified sensibility" point to what makes T.'s poetry unusual: the lifelong synthesis of her experience and vision as sister, daughter, mother, wife, lover, professor, activist, and poet, whose words were heard on records and on the radio, sung at Carnegie Hall to music of Copland and Schuman, and read in Moscow and in bean fields. T. lived paradox as naturally as she wrote metaphysical verse. The synthesis of mangoes, metaphor, and Marx makes T.'s poetry complex. But her passion for precision makes abstract idea and mood arresting and accessible: T. renders psychological and social states through metaphors of the physical world.

WORKS: For Eager Lovers (1922). *Hawaiian Hilltop* (1923). *Continent's End* (edited by Taggard, with G. Sterling and J. Rorty, 1925). *May Days* (edited by Taggard, 1925). *Words for the Chisel* (1926). *The Unspoken, and Other Poems* by Anne Brenner (edited by Taggard, 1927). *Travelling Standing Still* (1928). *Circumference: Varieties of Metaphysical Verse, 1459–1928* (1929). *The Life and Mind of Emily Dickinson* (1930). *Remembering Vaughan in New England* (1933). *Ten Introductions* (with Dudley Fitts, 1934). *Not Mine to Finish* (1934). *Calling Western Union* (1936). *Collected Poems, 1918–1938* (1938). *Long View* (1942). *Falcon* (1942). *A Part of Vermont* (1945). *Slow Music* (1946). *Origin Hawaii* (1947).

BIBLIOGRAPHY: Aaron, D., *Writers on the Left* (1961). Lins, K. L., "An Interpretive Study of Selected Poetry by Genevieve Taggard" (M.A. thesis, Univ. of Hawaii, 1956). Mossberg, B.A., and C. L. Mossberg, *Genevieve Taggard* (Western Writers Series, forthcoming). Peck, D. R., "Development of an American Marxist Literary Criticism: The Monthly New Masses" (Ph.D. diss., Temple University, 1968). Wilson, E., "A Poet of the Pacific," in *The Shores of Light* (1952).

For articles in reference works, see: *DAB*, Suppl. 4. *NAW* (article by B. Rauch). *The Oxford Companion to American Literature*, James D. Hart (1965). *20th CA*.

Other references: *Masses and Mainstream* (Jan. 1949). *Ms.* (1979). *Nation* (19 Jan. 1927). *New Masses* (Jan. 1927). *Poetry* (Dec. 1934; May 1936; Feb. 1947). *SatR* (7 Nov. 1936; 14 Dec. 1946). *Scholastic* (17 May 1938). *Time* (22 Nov. 1948). *WLB* (Jan. 1930).

BARBARA ANTONINA CLARKE MOSSBERG

Ida Minerva Tarbell

B. 5 Nov. 1857, Erie County, Pennsylvania; d. 6 Jan. 1944, Bridgeport, Connecticut
D. of Franklin Sumner and Esther Ann McCullough Tarbell

T. grew up in what was then the heartland of America's oil region. As a child, T. evinced considerable intellectual curiosity and independence, which her parents (both former teachers) encouraged. The Tarbell family was closely knit and espoused the typical virtues of the early American Dream: hard work, honesty, thrift, and moral good. To the end of her life, T. tended to judge all character (of person or corporation) on the basis of its adherence to what she called "the fair and open path." It was this high moral sense that animated her best writing.

An adolescent struggle to reconcile the Holy Writ with scientific fact (T. found a solution in theories of evolution) led T. to study biology at Allegheny College, as the sole female in a freshman class of forty. After graduating in 1880, T. took an onerous and poorly paid teaching position with a Poland, Ohio, seminary (like her college, not far from her family home). In 1882, she returned home and soon became a staff member of the *Chautauquan*, a monthly magazine connected with the Chautauqua movement and its home studies program. Beginning as an editorial secretary, T. advanced, during her eight-year employment on the magazine, to writer and annotator.

At the age of thirty, T. decided she was "dying of respectability" and gave vent to her need for adventure by quitting her job and going to Paris to write a biography of a French revolutionary, *Madame Roland: A Biographical Study* (1896).

Despite her own (and others') assessment of her ability as "not a writer but a dead scholar," T. supported herself in France by writing for American magazines. In this manner she was noticed by S. S. McClure, publisher of the fledgling *McClure's* magazine. Her contribution on Napoleon, in 1894, boosted the magazine's popularity and T.'s reputation as a journalist of note. From 1894 until 1906, T. was a writer for *McClure's*; from 1906 to 1915, for *American Magazine*. In this twenty-one-year period as a staff writer, T. produced the works which support her journalistic reputation. Almost all resulted from assignments for articles, which later were published separately as books; they are either biographies (not critical or analytical but thoroughly researched) or studies of complex issues (such as the oil corporations or tariffs), which T. could explain in concepts and language understandable to the average person. These studies, however, are not purely objective analyses but reflect the attitudes and values of her background. T. was one of the investigative journalists popular in the early 20th-c. who were given the name "muckrakers" by Theodore Roosevelt.

Like many others, T. was profoundly affected by WWI and its alteration of traditional beliefs; this is reflected in her focus, from 1911 until the 1920s, on war and peace and resultant social problems. Her writings after WWI are fewer; in these years, T. was more active as lecturer or delegate to various national and international conferences. She herself considered her postwar writings "musty"; it seems probable that she no longer was able to write from the fierce certainties of youth and that the concerns of the reading public had been altered substantially by the war.

Perhaps T.'s best writing from the later years of her life is her autobiography, *All in the Day's Work* (1939), written when she was eighty-two. She relates that at fourteen, she had prayed never to be married; as a college student, she avoided "entangling alliances." The phrase (hers) is telling; throughout her autobiography, T. repeatedly notes her need for independence and freedom—freedom from marriage and from groups, especially the suffragists or other women's groups.

T. was not a feminist; indeed, she opposed the woman suffrage movement because she felt the suffragists belittled women's contributions to society. As her autobiography, her study of Mme Roland, and her two treatises on "womanhood"—*The Business of Being a Woman* (1912) and *Ways of Woman* (1915), reveal, T. answered "the woman question" with the cliché that the hand that rocks the cradle rules the world. The home, which T. felt to be a sufficient and necessary sphere in which women could operate, was to T. the most vital unit in a healthy society. Thus she approved patriarchial practices by big business (such as Henry Ford's workers communities) and she herself flourished under the direction of patriarchal males.

T. deserves recognition, however, for her pioneering role in journalism and especially for her classic study of the oil industry, *The History of the Standard Oil Company*, a two-volume work first published in 1904. H. H. Rogers, a Standard Oil executive, guided T. through selected corporate documents during her two-year research effort, but she consulted other sources, as the massive documentation reveals. The *History* does not by any means whitewash Standard Oil; T. frankly regards the corporation as guilty of "commercial sin." But she is equally honest in recognizing the genius of John D. Rockefeller: he early understood that control of the oil industry depended on control of the transportation of that oil. While he embodied the industry and verve she had been taught to admire, he created the corporate entity she recognized as death to the individual businessman—a clear negation of the American dream. *The History of the Standard Oil Company* is a landmark in both business and journalism because it represents Standard Oil's first serious attempt at public relations and because it was in the vanguard of serious investigative reporting by American periodicals.

WORKS: *A Short Life of Napoleon Bonaparte* (1895). *Early Life of Abraham Lincoln* (1896). *Madame Roland: A Biographical Study* (1896). *The Life of Abraham Lincoln* (2 vols., 1900). *Napoleon's Addresses* (1902). *The History of the Standard Oil Company* (2 vols., 1904; re-issued in one volume, 1963; abridged, by David Chalmers, 1966). *He Knew Lincoln* (1907). *Father Abraham* (1909). *Selections from the Letters, Speeches, and State Papers of*

Abraham Lincoln (1911). *The Tariff in Our Times* (1911). *The Business of Being a Woman* (1912). *Ways of Woman* (1915). *New Ideals in Business: An Account of Their Practice and Their Effects upon Men and Profits* (1916). *The Rising of the Tide: The Story of Sabinsport* (1919). *In Lincoln's Chair* (1920). *Boy Scout's Life of Lincoln* (1922). *He Knew Lincoln, and Other Billy Brown Stories* (1922). *Peacemakers, Blessed and Otherwise: Observations, Reflections, and Irritations at an International Conference* (1922). *In the Footsteps of the Lincolns* (1922). *Life of Elbert H. Gary: The Story of Steel* (1925). *A Life of Napoleon Bonaparte* (1927). *A Reporter for Lincoln: Story of Henry E. Wing, Soldier and Newspaper Man* (1927). *Owen D. Young: A New Type of Industrial Leader* (1932). *The Nationalizing of Business, 1878–1898* (Vol. 9, A History of American Life series, 1936). *Women at Work: A Tour Among Careers* (1939). *All in the Day's Work: An Autobiography* (1939).

T.'s papers are in the collections of the Reis Library of Allegheny College and the Sophia Smith Collection at Smith College.

BIBLIOGRAPHY: Chalmers, D., *The Social and Political Ideas of the Muckrakers* (1964). Filer, L., *Crusaders for American Liberalism* (1939). Fleming, A., *Ida Tarbell: First of the Muckrakers* (1971). Hamilton, V., "The Gentlewoman and the Robber Baron," *American Heritage* 21 (April 1970). Marzolf, M. *Up from the Footnote* (1977). Tomkins, M., *Ida M. Tarbell* (1974).

SALLY BRETT

Phoebe Atwood Taylor

B. 18 May 1909, Boston, Massachusetts; d. 8 Jan. 1976, Boston, Massachusetts
Wrote under: Phoebe Atwood Taylor, Alice Tilton
D. of John D. and Josephine Atwood Taylor; m. Grantley Walden Taylor

T.'s parents were both natives of Cape Cod; her father was a physician. T. graduated from Barnard College in 1930. She published her first detective novel in 1931 and published up to three detective novels a year every year afterwards for almost twenty years. She wrote between midnight and 3:00 A.M., "after housekeeping all day," "beginning three weeks before the deadline for the novel to be delivered to her New York publishers." (Her Leonidas Witherall novels include heartfelt depictions of the harried popular author, besieged by telegrams from his publisher, struggling to meet his deadlines.) T. married a prominent Boston surgeon of the same surname and lived in Newton Highlands and then in Weston, suburbs of Boston, always keeping a summer home at Wellfleet on Cape Cod. She died of a heart attack.

T.'s first book, *The Cape Cod Mystery* (1931), features her most famous detective, Asa Alden (Asey) Mayo. A "man of all work" to the wealthy Porter family, he is a "fine and bleak" Cape Cod native who chews tobacco and must be sixty but could be anything from thirty-five to seventy. Using what he calls "common sense," he extricates a Porter scion suspected by incompetent local officials of murdering a popular novelist and identifies the actual killer—the three-hundred-pound widow of a Boston minister who bashed the writer with an advance copy of his latest book, a sensational account of her husband's life.

By the last of the Cape Cod mysteries, *Diplomatic Corpse* (1951), the hero's character has evolved and, like many of his fellow series detectives, he has become a superman. "Tall, lean, salty Asey Mayo" has changed from chewing tobacco, as in the first two books, to smoking a pipe, and from being the Porters' handyman to being Chairman of the Board of Porter Motors. In intervening novels he has been revealed as a more and more expert marksman, knife-thrower, hand-to-hand fighter, driver, sailor, and cook.

The charm of the Cape Cod novels lies not only in Asey's role as the wryly humorous Yankee, but also in their settings. T.'s eye for detail and lively sense of place combine with many glimpses of the daily life of the times, and now increase the historical interest and fun of her novels.

Leonidas Xenophon Witherall, hero of the mysteries T. wrote under the pen name of Alice Tilton, solves crimes that take place in a recognizable prewar and wartime Boston and its suburbs. He is a master, then headmaster and owner of Meredith's Academy, a private boys' school. His escapades are even crazier and more convoluted, if possible, than Asey Mayo's. *The Hollow Chest* (1941) concerns a samurai sword as murder weapon, an antique horse car, a Lady Baltimore cake, a papier-maché lion's head, and the manuscript of a treatise on the "eleventh-century vowel shift," and requires a massive suspension of disbelief.

Many of T.'s works are notable for their brisk, even breathless, pace. Both detectives encounter problems and solve them within a day or two, and their chases—by car, on foot, by plane, by motorboat, or via antique horsecar—often make their adventures tests of physical stamina and agility as well as mental ability. This pace and T.'s zany plots rife with eccentric characters and odd props often make her mysteries seem the literary equivalents of the classic screwball film comedies of the 1930s.

T.'s mystery comedies also incorporate many elements of the classic detective story. Asey has a trio of Dr. Watsons and a Lestrade. T. includes one case of young love per story: the ingénue is never guilty, nor is the young man who falls in love with her. Like many British detective stories of the same era, T.'s works are touched with xenophobia, racism, and anti-Semitism. Some of this narrowness is of the "Napoleon was a great man and a great general, but he was an off-Islander" variety and goes with T.'s regional-comedy territory.

T.'s mystery-farces will never appeal to those who want realism in their criminal fiction, but they have withstood the passage of time at least as well as those of her Golden Age sisters, Agatha Christie and Ngaio Marsh. T.'s characters, settings, and historical interest still provide excellent entertainment, and explain why the novels have been reissued in the 1960s and again in the 1980s.

WORKS: *The Cape Cod Mystery* (1931). *Death Lights a Candle* (1932). *The Mystery of the Cape Cod Players* (1933). *The Mystery of the Cape Cod Tavern* (1934). *Sandbar Sinister* (1934). *Deathblow Hill* (1935). *The Tinkling Symbol* (1935). *The Crimson Patch* (1936). *Out of Order* (1936). *Beginning with a Bash* (1937). *Figure Away* (1937). *Octagon House* (1937). *The Annulet of Gilt* (1938). *Banbury Bog* (1938). *The Cut Direct* (1938). *Cold Steal* (1939). *Spring Harrowing* (1939). *The Criminal C.O.D.* (1940). *The Deadly Sunshade* (1940). *The Left Leg* (1940). *The Hollow Chest* (1941). *The Perennial Boarder* (1941). *The Six Iron Spiders* (1942). *Three Plots for Asey Mayo* (1942). *File for Record* (1943). *Going, Going, Gone* (1943). *Dead Ernest* (1944). *Proof of the Pudding* (1945). *The Asey Mayo Trio* (1946). *Punch with Care* (1946). *The Iron Clew* (1947). *Diplomatic Corpse* (1951).

T.'s manuscripts are collected in the Mugar Memorial Library, Boston University.

BIBLIOGRAPHY: Haycraft, H., *Murder for Pleasure* (1941).

For articles in reference works, see: *A Catalogue of Crime*, Barzun, J., and W. H. Taylor, eds. (1971). *Encyclopedia of Mystery and Detection*, Steinbrunner, C., and O. Penzler, eds., (1976). *20th CA. 20th CAS. Twentieth-Century Crime and Mystery Writers*, Reilly, J. M., ed. (article by M. H. Becker, 1980).

Other references: *Barnard Alumnae Monthly* (Oct. 1932; March 1936). *NYT* (12 Jan. 1976). Washington *Post* (17 Jan. 1976).

SUSAN SUTTON SMITH

Sara Teasdale

B. 8 Aug. 1884, St. Louis, Missouri; d. 29 Jan. 1933, New York City
Given name: Sarah Trevor Teasdale
D. of John Warren and Mary Elizabeth Willard Teasdale;
  m. Ernst B. Filsinger, 1914

The youngest of four children, T. was born into comfortable circumstances provided by her father, a prominent businessman, and her independently wealthy mother. Because of her nervous temperament, she was educated at home until she was nine. After attending Mary Institute (founded by T. S. Eliot's grandfather) for a year, she completed her education at Hosmer Hall, a school designed to prepare young women for college. She was already writing poetry, and she received much encouragement from her teachers; she also read Heine and Sappho, who, along with Christina Rossetti, were the greatest influences on her own work.

Following graduation in 1902, T., together with several of her friends, published a manuscript magazine, *The Potter's Wheel,* in which many of her early poems appeared. Her first professional publication came in May, 1907, when her dramatic monologue "Guenevere" appeared in *Reedy's Mirror.* The poem attracted much attention, as did *Sonnets to Duse, and Other Poems* published that same autumn, though the book was not a financial success.

T. literally sacrificed herself to poetry, and therein lay her tragedy. Frail and high-strung, she lived perforce a disciplined life which brought both unhappiness and loneliness, for she was innately an outgoing person, capable of great emotional depth. Her line, "O, beauty, are you not enough? Why am I crying after love?" reveals her constant ambivalence. She experienced two major romantic involvements, one with the poet Vachel Lindsay, and the other with Ernst Filsinger, a St. Louis businessman whom she married in December, 1914. But the demands of poetry brought about a gradual estrangement, and the marriage was dissolved in 1929, by T.'s decision. After courageously enduring four years of rapidly deteriorating health and acute depression, exacerbated by the fear that she might become a helpless invalid, she took an overdose of barbiturates, and died in 1933.

At first glance, T.'s poetry appears to be simple, but its simplicity is deceptive. Although it does not lend itself to involved critical exegesis, its highly connotative language can imply deeply felt emotion which evokes an equal response. T. treads a fine line between revelation and reticence. *Sonnets to Duse* and *Helen of Troy, and Other Poems* (1911) reveal her experimentation to find her own poetic voice, and successive volumes demonstrate her constant striving to speak from her own experience, honestly and without sentimentality. Her constant theme is love, its joys, and, as her own life grew more difficult, its tragedies. The source of her imagery is invariably nature, which serves equally well for moments of exaltation—"I am the pool of gold / Where sunset burns and dies / You are my deepening skies, / Give me your stars to hold,"—or, as in her posthumous volume *Strange Victory* (1933), for moments of deepest pain: "Nothing but darkness enters this room, / Nothing but darkness and the winter night, / Yet on this bed once years ago a light / Silvered the sheets with an unearthly bloom; / It was the planet Venus in the west / Casting a square of brightness on this bed, / And in that light your dark and lovely head / Lay for a while and seemed to be at rest." Here the controlled objectivity of the language deepens the sense of anguish and desolation; the words must be read for implication and nuance, as well as for obvious meaning. In T.'s poetry, every word is important.

Though deprecated by critics of the post-*Wasteland* generation, T. continues to be read and admired. One reason for her popularity doubtless derives from her ability to write about bitter experience without bitterness, and to laugh wisely, especially at herself. But even more important is a sense of that inner courage and integrity, which compelled her to write in her own way, uninfluenced by the work of her contemporaries: "Let the dead know, but not the living see— / The dead who loved me will not suffer, knowing / It is all one, the coming or the going— / If I have kept the last essential me. / If that is safe, then I am safe indeed. . . ." She recognized that her way inevitably incurred suffering. Even at her moments of deepest despair, however, T. exercises a control born of a conscious choice, and the ultimate effect of her poetry is one of confident affirmation: "If this be the last time / The melody flies upward / With its rush of sparks in flight, / Let me go up with it in fire and laughter. . . ."

WORKS: *Sonnets to Duse, and Other Poems* (1907). *Helen of Troy, and Other Poems* (1911). *Rivers to the Sea* (1915). *The Answering Voice: Love Lyrics by Women* (edited by Teasdale, 1917). *Love Songs* (1917). *Flame and Shadow* (1920). *Rainbow Gold* (edited by Teasdale, 1922). *Dark of the Moon* (1926). *Stars To-Night* (1930). *Strange Victory* (1933). *Collected Poems* (1937).

BIBLIOGRAPHY: Brenner, R., *Poets of Our Time* (1946). Carpenter, M. H.,

Sara Teasdale: A Biography (1960). Sprague, R., *Imaginary Gardens: A Study of Five American Poets* (1969). Untermeyer, L., *The New Era in American Poetry* (1919).

ROSEMARY SPRAGUE

Tabitha Gilman Tenney

B. 7 April 1762, Exeter, New Hampshire; d. 2 May 1837, Exeter,
  New Hampshire
Wrote under: Tabitha Tenney
D. of Samuel and Lydia Robinson Giddinge Gilman; m. Samuel Tenney, 1788

T. was descended from early pioneers in New Hampshire who had raised themselves to prominent social positions in the town of Exeter. She was the oldest of the seven children, and probably remained at home with her mother to help raise her younger siblings after the death of her father. T. was somewhat older than was typical for her time and social class when she married. The couple had no children. Her husband, who served as a physician in the Revolutionary army, later directed his attention chiefly to politics and scientific inquiry.

Although T. was described as an "accomplished lady," it is unlikely that her formal schooling differed greatly from that of other respectable 18th-c. American women, or from that form of "female education" which she satirizes in her novel, *Female Quixotism: Exhibited in the Romantic Opinions and Extravagant Adventures of Dorcasina Sheldon* (1801). Her education, like Dorcasina's, would have provided her with a command of the fine points of fashion and household management, some acquaintance with the classics, and a fuller knowledge of contemporary novels. While married, T. produced two books which largely derived from her reading. After her husband's death in 1816, she spent the remainder of her life concentrating on her needlework, which was renowned for its intricacy.

T.'s first publication was *The Pleasing Instructor* (1799), an anthology of classical literature addressed to young women. It was intended to "inform the mind, correct the manners, or to regulate the conduct" while at the same time blending, in best classical fashion, "instruction with rational amusement."

T. dedicated *Female Quixotism* "to all Columbian Young Ladies, who Read Novels and Romances." But unlike most novels so dedicated, T.'s book satirizes both sentimentality and sentimental fiction in general. *Female Quixotism* is roughly modeled on Charlotte Ramsay Lennox's *The Female Quixote; or, The Adventures of Arabella* (1752), but T. alters the pattern of her model to emphasize a different message. In the earlier book, the main character is basically innocent but is corrupted by the ideals of the sentimental fiction she reads. T., however, portrays a character who rationalizes her foolishness by blaming it on the novels that she has read.

This change gives *Female Quixotism* an effective focus. Dorcasina, who is an adolescent when we first see her, remains frozen in the kind of prolonged adolescence that sentimental fiction requires. She is intelligent, occasionally witty, but entirely blind to the increasing disparity between her own life and the sentimental life she envisions for herself. Dorcasina early rejects a sensible suitor, Lysander, because his letter proposing marriage fails to use words like "angel" or "goddess." Ironically, Lysander is as close as Dorcasina ever comes to making the sentimental match she aspires to.

Over the years, Dorcasina is duped by, and deceives herself about, men who seek to humiliate her or gain her fortune. Finally, the malicious ridicule of Seymour, a most despicable character who intends to marry the toothless, white-haired Dorcasina and then have her committed to a mental institution so that he can enjoy her fortune unhindered by her company, leads Dorcasina to recognize the folly of her life and warn her young readers "to avoid the rock on which I have been wrecked."

The novel is a satire, but it is written with a sensitivity to its main character seldom encountered in satire. As silly as Dorcasina's version of reality is, it is in many ways preferable to the world she faces. Most of the men she meets are singularly cruel, spiteful, misogynistic creatures, and, on this level, T.'s novel covertly warns women that they must be particularly cautious in a world where they have little place and little power. T.'s satire is also effectively double-edged in another sense. While she criticizes the women who get their education from fiction, she equally criticizes a social system that denies women any real education.

F. L. Pattee once described *Female Quixotism* as the most popular novel written in America before *Uncle Tom's Cabin*. This is not the case, but T.'s novel did run through at least six separate editions between the time of its publication and 1841. However, no current edition of the novel is available. Ironically, *Female Quixotism* fell into obscurity by the middle of the last century, while novels it satirized, such as Susanna Rowson's

Charlotte Temple (1791), continued to be popular into our own century, and even now are available in modern editions.

WORKS: *The Pleasing Instructor* (1799). *Female Quixotism: Exhibited in the Romantic Opinions and Extravagant Adventures of Dorcasina Sheldon* (1801).

BIBLIOGRAPHY: Bell, C.H., *History of the Town of Exeter* (1888). Brown H. R., *The Sentimental Novel in America, 1789–1860* (1940). Gilman, A., *The Gilman Family* (1869). Loshe, L. D., *The Early American Novel, 1789–1830* (1907). Petter, H., *The Early American Novel* (1971). Tenney, M. J., *The Tenney Family; or, The Descendants of Thomas Tenney of Rowley, Massachusetts, 1638–1890* (1891).

For articles in reference works, see: *CAL. NAW* (article by O. E. Wilson).

CATHY N. DAVIDSON

Mary Virginia Hawes Terhune

B. *21 Dec. 1830, Dennisville, Virginia; d. 3 June 1922, New York City*
Wrote under : Marion Harland
D. *of Samuel Pierce and Judith Anna Smith Hawes; m. Edward Payson Terhune, 1856*

T. was tutored at home and began contributing regularly to Richmond papers at fourteen. She wrote a version of her first published novel at sixteen and had published two very successful novels when she married a Presbyterian minister at twenty-six. She continued to write while she successively moved with her husband to Newark, New Jersey; Springfield, Massachusetts; and Brooklyn, New York. He assisted her in her work, providing "the first reading and only revision of her MSS., before they are given into the hands of the printer." She bore six children, three of whom survived childhood. Christine Terhune Herrick and Virginia Terhune Van de Water followed their mother as writers on domestic matters, and Albert Payson Terhune became "the collie's Balzac," an enormously popular author of dog stories.

Alone (1854), the first of T.'s many novels and her most popular, follows the trials of Ida Ross, who must live "alone" at fifteen after the death of her widowed mother, "a being more than human—scarcely less than divine." The first scene of the book depicts Ida throwing herself upon her mother's coffin as it is lowered into the grave. She must leave her plantation home and live in Richmond with a cynical, worldly guardian who has raised his daughter to be as cold-hearted as himself. For a time, under their influence, Ida becomes almost misanthropic, but she blossoms again when she meets the loving and merry Dana family. She finds and loses and finds again her true love, the Reverend Morton Lacy, and they are happily married at the novel's end. *Alone* depicts life in Richmond and a prewar plantation—slaves are all happy, devoted family "servants." In a closing scene Ida strikes the book's keynote: "A woman is so lonely without a home and friends! They are to us—I do not say to you [men]— necessaries of life."

Many of T.'s twenty-five novels and three collections of short stories have the same antebellum southern background and sentimental message: women can and should be educated and able to support themselves, but their truest position is dependence and their proper sphere the home.

T.'s most famous book on household affairs, *Common Sense in the Household: A Manual of Practical Housewifery* (1871), became a best seller and was translated into French, German, and Arabic. She advocates learning by doing, attention to the presentation of food and a varied menu, and she deprecates the "vulgar prejudice against labor-saving machines." Here, the housewife can consult a thirteen-page essay on how to handle her servants; she can find out how to clean and cook a catfish or restore luster and crispness to black alpaca and bombazine. The style is informal, the advice practical.

T.'s twenty-five books of advice are by no means confined to the culinary and domestic. *Eve's Daughters; or, Common Sense for Maid, Wife, and Mother* (1892) covers all facets of the growing girl's physical, mental, and moral health, including the way in which a mother should educate her daughter about sex: "Get some good familiar treatise upon Botany,—I know of none better than Gray's 'How Plants Grow,'—and read with her of the beautiful laws of fructification and reproduction."

Eve's Daughters also counsels women through marriage and motherhood to menopause—the "climacteric"—and a postmenopausal "Indian Summer." In the chapter "Shall Baby Be?" T. voices her convictions on the sin of childlessness; she believed that American mothers had a duty to bear "troops" of boys and girls to withstand the invasion of "massed filth" —"Irish cottiers and German boors, and loose and criminal fugitives from everywhere."

T.'s ideas on woman's role seem as dated today as her methods for healing cuts, but her cookbooks and domestic advice profoundly influenced Americans for half a century.

WORKS: *Alone* (1854). *The Hidden Path* (1855). *Nemesis* (1860). *Miriam* (1862). *Husks* (1863). *Moss-Side: Husbands and Homes* (1865). *Colonel Floyd's Wards* (1866). *Sunnybank* (1866). *The Christmas Holly* (1867). *Phemie's Temptation* (1869). *Ruby's Husband* (1869). *At Last* (1870). *Common Sense in the Household: A Manual of Practical Housewifery* (1871). *The Empty Heart: "For Better, for Worse"* (1871). *True as Steel* (1872). *Jessamine* (1873). *From My Youth Up* (1874). *Breakfast, Luncheon, and Tea* (1875). *My Little Love* (1876). *The Dinner Year-Book* (1878). *Loiterings in Pleasant Paths* (1880). *Our Daughters: What Shall We Do with Them?* (1880). *Handicapped* (1881). *The Cottage Kitchen* (1883). *Judith: A Chronicle of Old Virginia* (1883). *Cookery for Beginners* (1884). *Common Sense in the Nursery* (1885). *Country Living for City People* (1887). *Not Pretty, but Precious* (1887). *Our Baby's First and Second Years* (1887). *A Gallant Fight* (1888). *House and Home* (1889). *Stepping-Stones* (with Virginia F. Townsend and Louise Chandler Moulton, 1890). *With the Best Intentions* (1890). *Eve's Daughters* (1892). *His Great Self* (1892). *The Story of Mary Washington* (1892). *Mr. Wayt's Wife's Sister* (1894). *The Premium Cook Book* (1894). *The Royal Road* (1894). *Home of the Bible* (1895). *Talks upon Practical Subjects* (1895). *Under the Flag of the Orient* (1895). *The Art of Cooking by Gas* (1896). *The National Cook Book* (with Christine Terhune Herrick, 1896). *The Secret of a Happy Home* (1896). *An Old-Field School-Girl* (1897). *Ruth Bergen's Limitations* (1897). *Some Colonial Homesteads and Their Stories* (1897). *The Comfort of Cooking and Heating by Gas* (1898). *Where Ghosts Walk* (1898). *Charlotte Brontë at Home* (1899). *Cooking Hints* (1899). *Home Topics* (1899). *More Colonial Homesteads and Their Stories* (1899). *William Cowper* (1899). *Dr. Dale* (with Albert Payson Terhune, 1900). *Hannah More* (1900). *John Knox* (1900). *In Our County: Stories of Old Virginia Life* (1901). *Marion Harland's Complete Cook Book* (1903). *Everyday Etiquette* (with Virginia Van de Water, 1905). *When Grandmamma Was Fourteen* (1905). *The Distractions of Martha* (1906). *Marion Harland's Cook Book of Tried and Tested Recipes* (1907). *The Housekeeper's Week* (1908). *Ideal Home Life* (with Margaret E. Sangster et al., 1910). *Marion Harland's Autobiography* (1910). *The Story of Canning and Recipes* (1910). *Home Making* (1911). *The Helping Hand Cook Book* (1912). *Should Protestant Ministers Marry?* (1913). *Looking Westward* (1914). *A Long Lane* (1915). *The Carringtons. of High Hill* (1919). *Two Ways of Keeping a Wife* (n.d.).

BIBLIOGRAPHY: Baym, N., *Woman's Fiction: A Guide to Novels by and about Women in America, 1820–1870* (1978). Griswold, W. M., *A Descriptive List of Novels and Tales, Dealing with the History of North America* (1895). Halsey, F. W., *Women Authors of Our Day in Their Homes* (1903). Pattee, F. L., *The Feminine Fifties* (1940).

For articles in reference works, see: *AA. The Living Female Writers of the*

South, Ed. I. Raymond (1872). *The Living Writers of the South,* Ed. J. W. Davidson (1869). *NAW* (article by M. Cross). *Southland Writers,* Ed. I. Raymond (1870). *Women of the South Distinguished in Literature,* Ed. M. Forrest (1861).

Other references: *Harper's* (Nov. 1882). *NYT* (4 June 1922).

SUSAN SUTTON SMITH

Celia Laighton Thaxter

B. *29 June 1835, Portsmouth, New Hampshire; d. 26 Aug. 1894, Appledore Island, Isles of Shoals, Maine*
D. *of Thomas B. and Eliza Rymes Laighton; m. Levi Lincoln Thaxter, 1851*

Raised on a lighthouse island in the Isles of Shoals ten miles off the New Hampshire coast, T. grew up within the sound and sight of the sea and early learned to appreciate its beauty and its cruelty. This dual awareness became a major theme in her poetry, which established her literary reputation at a relatively young age.

T.'s father became the lighthouse keeper when she was four years old. T., her father, mother, and two brothers were the sole human inhabitants of the island for many years. In 1841, the family moved to another of the islands, Smutty-Nose, where they began receiving paying summer guests. As this proved a successful venture, Thomas Laighton in 1847 began building a resort hotel on Appledore Island, the largest of the Shoals island group. This he completed the following year with the help of Levi Lincoln Thaxter, a young Harvard graduate.

The Appledore House opened the following year and became a major summer resort attracting artists and writers including Hawthorne, Thoreau, Emerson, Whittier, Lowell, Mark Twain, Charlotte Cushman, Ole Bull, Lucy Larcom, Sarah Orne Jewett, Annie Adams Fields, and Childe Hassam. Hassam completed a series of remarkable paintings of the islands, including some of T. in her garden (1892), which are now in the Smithsonian. Many of these artists were attracted by T. as well as by the scenery, and she established a kind of literary salon on the islands beginning in the 1860s.

Levi Thaxter had become T.'s tutor in her early teens, and in 1851 they married. The couple had three sons. The marriage was not successful, as T. pined for her island home when, off and on in the 1850s, they lived on the mainland, in several Massachusetts towns. Levi, on the other hand, began to resent her literary success. By the end of the 1860s, T. and her husband lived essentially separate lives, although they never divorced. She remained on Appledore with her mother and her oldest son Karl, who was retarded.

The death of her mother in 1877 was a severe shock to T., precipitating a religious crisis wherein she attempted to communicate through seances with her mother. This endeavor may have inspired a similar experience described fictionally by Sarah Orne Jewett in her spiritualistic story, "The Foreigner" (1900). Although a religious skeptic in her early years, T. did turn to spiritualism, theosophy, and Eastern religions in her later years.

T. was an extraordinarily accomplished water-colorist; this is an overlooked aspect of her considerable talent. Her prose publications, *Among the Isles of Shoals* (1873) and *An Island Garden* (1894), also remain as gems of descriptive prose.

T.'s first poem, significantly entitled "Land-Locked," appeared in the *Atlantic Monthly* in March 1861. She continued to publish poems in the major literary journals of her day, namely *Scribner's*, *Harper's*, the *Independent*, the *Century*, and the *Atlantic*. She also published juvenile material in *Our Young Folks* and *St. Nicholas Magazine*. The first collection of T.'s poetry, *Poems*, appeared in 1871. Many subsequent revised editions were printed.

Most of T.'s poetry deals with nature, not the benign nature of the Romantics, but a harsh, indifferent ocean. Several poems deal with actual shipwrecks that occurred on the Isles of Shoals while she was there. In "The Wreck of the Pocohantas," T. asks: "Do purposeless thy children meet/Such bitter death? How was it best/These hearts should cease to beat?" She returns often in her poetry to this basic theological question. T.'s tones is sometimes bitter and despairing, and occasionally somewhat cynical about traditional religious explanations. At times her austere, harsh imagery anticipates that of 20th-c. poets such as Anne Sexton and Sylvia Plath. Probably some of T.'s bitterness, like theirs, stemmed from the frustrations she encountered trying to play the many and conflicting roles of wife, mother, and artist. These conflicts are apparent in T.'s letters, published in 1895.

WORKS: *Poems* (1871). *Among the Isles of Shoals* (1873). *Drift-Weed* (1878). *Poems for Children* (1884). *The Cruise of the Mystery* (1886). *Idyls and Pastorals* (1886). *My Lighthouse, and Other Poems* (1890). *An Island*

Garden (1894). *Stories and Poems for Children* (1895). *The Letters of Celia Thaxter* (Eds. Annie Adams Fields and Ruth Lamb, 1895). *The Heavenly Guest, and Other Unpublished Writings* (Ed. O. Laighton, 1935).

BIBLIOGRAPHY: Faxon, S., et al., *A Stern and Lovely Scene: A Visual History of the Isles of Shoals* (1978). Hawthorne, Nathaniel, *The American Note-books* (1881). Laighton, O., *Ninety Years at the Isles of Shoals* (1930). Spofford, Harriet Prescott, *A Little Book of Friends* (1916). Thaxter, R., *Sandpiper: The Life and Letters of Celia Thaxter* (1962). Westbrook, P. D., *Acres of Flint, Writers of Rural New England 1870–1900* (1951).

JOSEPHINE DONOVAN

Dorothy Thompson

B. 9 July 1894, Lancaster, New York; d. 30 Jan. 1961, Lisbon, Portugal
D. of Peter and Margaret Grierson Thompson; m. Josef Bard, 1923; m. Sinclair Lewis, 1928; m. Maxim Kopf, 1943

T. was the daughter of an English clergyman who married an American woman and settled in upper New York State. Left motherless when she was still a child, T. turned early to history, literature, and languages for pleasure as well as study. She attended the Lewis Institute in Chicago, and received the B.A. degree from Syracuse University in 1914.

T. began her writing career as a publicist for woman suffrage groups and the Red Cross. This work took her abroad, where she secured free-lance writing assignments and made influential friends among the overseas press corps. Within a few years she had become a regular correspondent for the Philadelphia *Public Ledger* and the New York *Evening Post*. Later, she became a bureau chief in Berlin.

T. was fluent in German and thoroughly at ease with German culture and politics—which was perhaps why she was among the first, and among the most perceptive and persistent, critics of Nazism. Her enduring reputation rests chiefly on the worldwide recognition and respect she won as the plain-speaking reporter who, through her widely syndicated New York *Herald Tribune* column On the Record, alerted the English-speaking world to the brutality and menace of the Hitler regime.

Although she broke with the *Herald Tribune* over her support for President Franklin Roosevelt in 1940 (she had originally favored the paper's candidate, Wendell Willkie), T. continued writing until virtually the end of her life. In addition to her newspaper column, she contributed a monthly article to the *Ladies' Home Journal* and did regular radio broadcasts. A series of wartime talks sent by short wave to Germany was published under the title *Listen, Hans* (1942). *Let the Record Speak* (1939) was culled from her political columns. *The Courage to be Happy* (1957), drawn from T.'s *Journal* pieces and dealing mainly with personal and social topics, reflects the rigorous, work-centered ethic of her Methodist childhood.

By the 1940s, T. was one of the most widely read columnists in the country, and the press of travel and speaking engagements made her writing of necessity a collaborative effort with researchers and editorial aides. Critics should look to her early work for the full flavor of her journalistic style. In *The New Russia* (1928), for example, she combines cogent political analysis with vivid personal detail to give a memorable picture of the Soviet Union after ten years of Communist rule. T. compares the pioneering work of the Soviet experiment to the development of the American frontier. She is, however, astute and clear-sighted in her recognition of the ways in which classical communist ideals have been jettisoned for practical political purposes.

Perhaps T.'s greatest gift as a journalist was her ability to maintain an enthusiastic receptivity to her subject while tempering enthusiasm with objective judgment. T. was considered a highly opinionated writer, but in general, her opinions represent moral convictions which the reader can easily detect and allow for. In *I Saw Hitler* (1932) T.'s scorn for the subject of her interview is everywhere apparent, yet personal antipathy does not lead her to underestimate the leadership potential of the Nazi dictator.

One of T.'s biographers suggests that she felt keenly her failure to produce a body of writing that would transcend the topical. In particular, she seems to have wanted to write her own autobiography, and she made several efforts, which she abandoned as unsatisfactory. T. seems to have been a writer with greater powers than her subjects called forth.

WORKS: *Depths of Prosperity* (with P. Bottome, 1925). *The New Russia* (1928). *I Saw Hitler* (1932). *Refugees* (1938). *Political Guide* (1938). *Let the Record Speak* (1939). *Listen, Hans* (1942). *The Courage to be Happy* (1957).

BIBLIOGRAPHY: Sheean, V., *Dorothy and Red* (1963). Sanders, M., *Dorothy Thompson: A Legend in Her Time* (1973).

Other references: *Atlantic* (July 1945). *CB* (1940). *Colliers* (June 1945). *Newsweek* (20 Oct. 1944). NY (20 April 1940; 27 April 1940).

ANN PRINGLE ELIASBERG

Mabel Loomis Todd

B. *10 Nov. 1856, Cambridge, Massachusetts; d. 14 Oct. 1932, Hog Island, Muscongus, Maine*
D. *of Eben Jenks and Mary Alden Wilder Loomis; m. David Todd, 1879*

T., an only child, was a descendant of Priscilla and John Alden of Plymouth Colony. T.'s father, astronomer at the U.S. Naval Observatory, poet, and naturalist, was a friend of Asa Gray, Henry David Thoreau, and Walt Whitman. Educated at private schools in Cambridge and Georgetown, D.C., T. later studied at the New England Conservatory of Music. She married an astronomer, and their one child was born in 1880. They moved to Amherst College in 1881, when her husband became director of the observatory and a member of the faculty. Upon his retirement in 1917, they made their winter home in Coconut Grove, Florida, where T. fostered the movement to establish the Everglades National Park; her Maine island, where they had a summer house, became a National Audubon Society wildlife sanctuary.

T., who was responsible for the publication of the first volumes of Emily Dickinson's poetry, undertook the editorial work at a time when no one else would. The Todds had been initially well-received, when they moved to Amherst, by Susan Gilbert Dickinson and her husband Austin, treasurer of the College and the poet's brother. A liaison developed between T. and Austin in the fall of 1882 and continued until his death in 1895. Although the men remained friends, animosity between the wives extended to family imbroglios over T.'s legitimate claims as the editor, at the request of the poet's family, of Dickinson's verse and selected letters.

The editing was a formidable job. Dickinson's handwriting was idiosyncratic; her grammar and punctuation were not always conventional. There were tentative words, alternate lines, or different versions of the same poem between which to choose. The labor required a sure grasp of the poet's intentions, but also anticipation of readers' resistance to an original and imaginatively daring language. T. enlisted the help of her husband, of Austin, and of the reluctant T. W. Higginson, editor of the *Atlantic*, with whom Dickinson had begun correspondence as early as 1862. A modest selection, *Poems by Emily Dickinson*, appeared in 1890, with a preface by Higginson, who assisted in securing a publisher and launching the book. "You," he told T., "did the hardest part of the work."

T. is less well known for the books she wrote. She first published *Footprints* (1883), which in retrospect seems fictionalized autobiography. The story of a quiet, lonely man—a forty-year-old physician for whom life's mysteries are cold and bleak—ends as he comes to know a spirited young woman who shares his sense of the autumnal beauty of the New England seacoast and they glimpse a promise of joy together. Lyrical descriptions of an austere landscape with its granite cliffs, wild flowers, and expanse of sky and ocean suggest emotions that are not overtly described in the narrative.

T. wrote *Total Eclipses of the Sun* (1894), the first volume in the Columbian Knowledge series, edited by her husband. She traces the separation of modern scientific astronomy from the inaccurate poetic views characterized by mysticism, superstition, and terror of the past. Authoritative without being pedantic, T. writes a muted poetry describing an eclipse she witnessed with her husband in Japan during 1887. "A startling nearness to the gigantic forces of nature," she concludes, "seems to have been established," and personalities, hates, jealousies, even mundane hopes "grow very small and very far away."

T. also collaborated with her husband in other scientific writing. She published informal essays, reviews of new books, three serialized novels, and a sonnet sequence. T. wrote two travel books. *Corona and Coronet* (1898) is a leisurely account of a yacht trip to Japan to view the total eclipse of the sun in 1896. *Tripoli the Mysterious* (1912) describes Libya's ancient desert city, its changeless etiquette, sand-blown ruins, architecture, crafts, trades, and the people T. met on two "eclipse trips" in 1900 and 1905. In the tour de force, *A Cycle of Sunsets* (1910), she observes changes of light, hues, tones, and atmosphere at the end of every day throughout a year as attentively as an artist like J. M. W. Turner studies sky and land. Sixty of her paintings are in the Hunt Institute for Botanical Documents, Carnegie-Mellon University.

T.'s judgments are apt to be aesthetic rather than conventionally moral; her condescension toward "village" insularity is tempered if not tolerant. Her tensions are disciplined, her feelings cultivated. Graceful in manner, she values decorum appropriate to occasions and is sensitive to the nuances of the moment. Human presences rarely dominate the scenes or subjects to which T. responds with subtlety, composure, and intelligent interest.

WORKS: *Footprints* (1883). *Poems by Emily Dickinson* (edited by Todd, with T. W. Higginson; First Series, 1890; Second Series, 1891). *Letters of*

Emily Dickinson (edited by Todd, 1894; enlarged edition, 1931). *Total Eclipses of the Sun* (Columbian Knowledge Series No. 1, 1894). *A Cycle of Sonnets* (1896). *Poems by Emily Dickinson* (edited by Todd; Third Series, 1896). *Corona and Coronet* (1898). *Steele's Popular Astronomy* (edited by Todd, with D. P. Todd, 1899). *A Cycle of Sunsets* (1910). *Tripoli the Mysterious* (1912). *Bolts of Melody: New Poems of Emily Dickinson* (edited by Todd, with Millicent Todd Bingham, 1945). *The Thoreau Family Two Generations Ago* (Thoreau Society Booklet No. 13, 1958).

BIBLIOGRAPHY: Bingham, Millicent Todd, *Ancestor's Brocades* (1945). Blake, C. R., and C. F. Wells, eds., *The Recognition of Emily Dickinson* (1967). Sewall, R. B., *The Life of Emily Dickinson* (1974).
    For articles in reference works, see: *NAW* (article by D. Higgins).
                                                                    ELIZABETH PHILLIPS

Amélie Rives Troubetzkoy

B. 23 Aug. 1863, Richmond, Virginia; d. 16 June 1945, Charlottesville, Virginia
Wrote under: Amélie Rives
D. of Alfred and Sarah Macmurdo Rives; m. John Chanler, 1888; m. Pierre Troubetzkoy, 1896

Both of T.'s parents were of prominent Virginia families. Her father was a colonel of engineers on Robert E. Lee's staff. Soon after her birth, T. and her mother were moved to Castle Hill, the home of her father's parents, a gracious colonial estate in the foothills of the Blue Ridge not far from Charlottesville. Her grandparents took a great interest in T.'s education, and she developed sophisticated tastes in the rich cultural milieu of Castle Hill. It became a center of security for her throughout her active life and provided the setting for a number of her novels.

By all accounts, T. was a beautiful and dynamic woman; and many of her heroines are reflections of herself in their vivacity, intelligence, sensitivity—and their luxuriant blond hair. She traveled widely and maintained contacts with many outstanding English and American authors of her time. Her first marriage proved incompatible and ended, amicably, in divorce in 1895. Her second marriage, to Prince Pierre Troubetzkoy, a young portrait painter who had given up his wealth and position in Russia, was long and happy.

T.'s long writing career spanned several American literary movements and several trends in American reading tastes. Frequently, the fiction that appealed most strongly to the public was not her strongest work. T.'s first published story, "A Brother to Dragons" (*Atlantic*, March 1886), is a romantic, sentimental tale written in Elizabethan diction. Weak novels that appealed to the public primarily for their exotic settings or melodramatic situations are interspersed throughout her career; still, the strength and development of T.'s talents can be seen.

In *Virginia of Virginia* (1888), we can see the beginning of the strong T. heroine. Most critics praised its realism and dialogue while pointing out that it is an uneven work. It was the novel *The Quick or the Dead?* (1888) that caused a public furor. The heroine is a young widow. Her debating whether to remarry shocked propriety; most shocking were the scenes of sensuality, especially the implications that they were instigated by Barbara herself. But the novel is more than a deliberately sensational one; it is a sincere portrayal of the painful self-questioning that Barbara undergoes as she considers the conflict between what she sees as her duty and feels as her need for fulfillment. Tinged with sentimentality and flowery diction, it is not consistently realistic; but in many ways *The Quick or the Dead?* is a more open, honest statement of the sexuality of women than the major realists of the period allowed.

The Quick or the Dead? became a bestseller as a result of its notoriety. In its sequel, *Barbara Dering* (1893), Barbara continues to show a conflict between her true nature and her expected role. In both novels, T. uses nature imagery to reveal this conflict.

Another strong heroine is Phoebe, the protagonist of *World's End* (1914), a novel that won high critical praise and had large sales. Phoebe, like earlier heroines, is a young woman of feeling and intellect; but she is less perfect and more realistic and develops more as a character than her predecessors. In this novel, for the first time, the heroine is matched by a fully developed, strong male character. T.'s later works move more and more to sympathetic, less stereotyped male characters, possibly because of her years of happy marriage with Pierre. In *World's End*, the conflict is resolved in the sense that the heroine comes to some self-knowledge; but, as is usual in T.'s novels, there is no totally happy ending.

Shadows of Flame (1915)—reflecting her own experience with drug addiction—*The Queerness of Celia* (1926), and her last novel, *Firedamp* (1930), are all among T.'s best works, but do not quite equal the achievement of *World's End*.

In addition to her novels, T. wrote drama and poetry throughout her career. She published several plays written in blank verse and a long narrative poem, *Seléné* (1905), which shows a skillful handling of sustained verse, with many fine sensuous passages.

During and after WWI, T. wrote a series of plays which had successful Broadway runs, including *Allegiance*, *The Fear Market* (of which a movie version was made), and an adaptation of Mark Twain's *The Prince and the Pauper*. *Love-in-a-Mist* (1927) was an effective comedy of manners, and her only commercially successful play to be published after its Broadway run. Her last play, *The Young Elizabeth* (1938), shows her admiration for the young queen who is torn between love and duty; Elizabeth becomes a true T. heroine.

T. has been called a realist, a fine local colorist, and an important social historian; she has also been called a semierotic, a sensationalist, a romantic who revels in morbid scenes and hysterical passions. Both strengths and weaknesses can be found in her work. T. did not always use her many talents to their best artistic effect; her active life and spontaneity may have led her away from careful revision. But the vitality and sincerity of much of her work remain fresh and significant for modern readers.

WORKS: *A Brother to Dragons, and Other Old-Time Tales* (1888). *Herod and Mariamne* (1888). *The Quick or the Dead?* (1888). *Virginia of Virginia* (1888). *The Witness of the Sun* (1889). *According to Saint John* (1891). *Athelwold* (1893). *Barbara Dering* (1893). *Tanis, the Sang-Digger* (1893). *A Damsel Errant* (1898). *Seléné* (1905). *Augustine, the Man* (1906). *The Golden Rose: The Romance of a Strange Soul* (1908). *Trix and Over-the-Moon* (1909). *Pan's Mountain* (1910). *Hidden House* (1912). *World's-End* (1914). *Shadows of Flames* (1915). *The Ghost Garden* (1918). *As the Wind Blew* (1920). *The Sea-Woman's Cloak and November Eve* (1923). *The Queerness of Celia* (1926). *Love-in-a-Mist* (1927). *Firedamp* (1930).

BIBLIOGRAPHY: Clark, E., *Innocence Abroad* (1931). Longest, G., *Three Virginia Writers: Mary Johnston, Thomas Nelson Page, and Amélie Rives Troubetzkoy: A Reference Guide* (1978). Manly, L., *Southern Literature from 1579–1895* (1895). Meade, J., *I Live in Virginia* (1935). Painter, F., *Poets of Virginia* (1907). Taylor, W., *Amélie Rives (Princess Troubetzkoy)* (1973).

For articles in reference works, see: *LSL*, 10 (article by R. Duke).

Other references: *Lippincott's* (Sept. 1888). *Mississippi Quarterly* (Spring 1968). *Virginia Cavalcade* (Spring 1963).

ANNE NEWMAN

Barbara Tuchman

B. 30 Jan. 1912, New York City
Writes under: Barbara Tuchman, Barbara Wertheim
D. of Maurice and Alma Morgenthau Wertheim; m. Lester Reginald
  Tuchman, 1940

T.'s grandfather was Henry Morgenthau, Sr., the businessman and diplomat; her uncle was Henry Morgenthau, Jr., Roosevelt's secretary of the Treasury; and her father was an international banker and owner of the *Nation*. T. was educated at Radcliffe College. Her first job, with the Institute of Pacific Relations, took her to Tokyo in 1935. One of her earliest works is an essay on the Japanese character published in the prestigious *Foreign Affairs* when she was only twenty-three. T.'s work as a journalist during the next seven years, reporting from the war in Spain and writing in London for the magazine *The War in Spain*, led to the publication in England of her first book, *The Lost British Policy: Britain and Spain Since 1700* (1938).

T. is the mother of three daughters. She is now divorced.

Bible and Sword: England and Palestine from the Bronze Age to Balfour (1956) argues that the support for the Jewish homeland in Palestine had a double root: on the one hand, imperial strategy in a part of the world vital to the defense of Suez, India, and the oil fields of the Mideast; and, on the other hand, the attitude toward what Thomas Huxley called the "national epic of Britain," the Bible.

The Zimmerman Telegram (1958) is a work of history that aroused both professional respect and popular notice. It tells the story, only partly known until then, of efforts made by German Foreign Minister Arthur Zimmerman, before America's entrance into WWI, to bring about an alliance with Mexico in return for territorial concessions in the U.S. *The Zimmerman Telegram* is an artful narrative offering both the excitement of action and the color of personalities.

The Guns of August (1962), which brought T. a Pulitzer prize, applied a similar technique to a broader and more significant moment in WWI. Beginning with the description of the funeral of Edward VII, T. sketches the familial and political ties of Germany, England, and France and makes clear the interrelatedness of their world on the eve of its dissolution. It is typical of the T. style in its mix of detail and long view, character and event. She aims at an account of the way things happen rather than seeking the underlying causes or attempting to convert events into arguments for historical theory.

Nevertheless, in her next book, *The Proud Tower* (1966), T. describes her interest in writing about the decade before WWI as coming in part from a desire to understand the war. Although the individual chapters—for example, on the Dreyfus case—are beautifully done, it is not easy to see how these particular parts of a social history support a coherent conception of the origins of the war. T. admits to a certain arbitrariness in her choice of chapter subjects.

In *Stilwell and the American Experience in China, 1911–45* (1970), the career of General Joseph W. Stilwell becomes the central focus of an examination of the relationship of America and China. T. sees Stilwell as quintessentially American and his career in China as a "prism of the times," representing America's greatest effort in Asia as well as the "tragic limits" of America's experience there. T. believes that the efficiency and aggressiveness Stilwell brought were like the Christianity and democracy he also represented—all foreign to Chinese society and not assimilable. T.'s conceptual framework is equal to the complex narrative and able to raise it to a higher order of historical writing.

While the response of professional historians to *Stilwell and the American Experience in China* was very positive, *A Distant Mirror* (1975) has been the most criticized of any of T.'s books. However, it has received the same enthusiastic greeting from the layman eager to read well-shaped narrative about an unfamiliar period. T. regards the 14th c. as a period like our own, "a distraught age whose rules were breaking down under the pressure of adverse and violent events." Her original plan to follow the effects of the bubonic plague was changed to allow her to explore the marriage alliances and treaties that made up medieval diplomacy and to examine the code of chivalry. Whatever professional questions have been raised about the book's overarching concept, its sense of time and place are as brilliant as in any of T.'s works.

Practicing History (1981) is a collection of essays in which T. discusses the techniques and role of the historian. She also comments on some crucial events of her own day: the Six Day War, Watergate, and Vietnam.

WORKS: *The Lost British Policy: Britain and Spain since 1700* (1938). *Bible and Sword: England and Palestine from the Bronze Age to Balfour* (1956). *The Zimmerman Telegram* (1958). *The Guns of August* (1962). *The Proud Tower: A Portrait of the World Before the War, 1890–1914* (1966). *Stilwell and the American Experience in China, 1911–45* (1970). *Notes from China* (1972). *A Distant Mirror* (1975). *Practicing History* (1981).

BIBLIOGRAPHY: *Nation* (26 April 1971). *NYT* (19 Oct. 1958). *NYTBR* (28 June 1962; 3 Feb. 1968; 28 Sept. 1978).

LOIS HUGHSON

Jane Turell

B. 25 Feb. 1708, Boston, Massachusetts; d. 26 March 1735, Medford, Massachusetts
D. of Benjamin and Jane Colman; m. Ebenezer Turell, 1726

T.'s father was minister of the innovative Brattle Street Church and an influential figure in Boston's cultural and religious life. Like the fathers of other notable 18th-c. New England women, Colman carefully attended to his daughter's education, so that by the time T. was four she had amassed amounts of knowledge remarked upon by her father's peers. She began writing poetry under her father's guidance when she was about eleven years old. Throughout her life, Colman remained her mentor in spiritual and literary matters, partly through a lively, intimate exchange of letters and poems.

T.'s husband, a Congregationalist minister, had a pastorate in Medford, Massachusetts, where the couple settled. Of their four children, three died in infancy; one survived to age six, dying eighteen months after his mother. T. suffered from bouts of illness and depression for many years and died at age twenty-seven.

T. wrote poetry and prose throughout her adolescent years, and her poetic ambitions were not diminished by domestic duties and pregnancies. Her reading ranged from divinity to history, medicine, public debates, and poetry. After her death, her husband wrote a short biography, interspersed with selections from her works, to illustrate her talent and piety. He wished her life and work to serve as examples for young New England women. First published in Medford in 1735 as *Reliquiae Turellae et Lachrymae Paternal*, the slim volume contains correspondence, diary extracts, short religious essays, and verse—the only extant samples of T.'s writing. Unfortunately, because he published her work to illustrate her piety, her husband excluded material, such as her humorous verse, that he judged unsuitable.

It is probable that, even before her death, T.'s works circulated in manuscript form among her friends and acquaintances, as was customary in 18th-c. New England. She achieved enough contemporary fame as a writer to warrant a second edition of the biography, published in 1741 as *Memoirs of the Life and Death of the Pious and Ingenious Mrs. Jane Turell.*

Like many of her female contemporaries, T. had no wish to compete with male writers or to be published; she wrote privately, discussing personal events and religious ideas. She read widely in the neoclassic English poets and copied their style, adapting it to her religious subjects. Even her eulogies of other writers find their meaning in religious themes. She praises the English moralist poet Elizabeth Singer because Singer attacked evil: "A Woman's Pen Strikes the curs'd Serpents Head, / And lays the Monster gasping, if not dead."

T.'s neoclassicism is evident in a poetic enticement to her father to pass the hot summer months in Medford. "An Invitation into the Country in Imitation of *Horace*" is exactly what the title indicates. She compares harsh city life to the joys of innocent country living, transforming her small New England village and rural domicile into a model Arcadia. She lures her father with pastoral descriptions of "soft Shades" and "balmy Sweets / of Medford's flow'ring Vales, and green Retreats" and an occasional New England touch: "Yet what is neat and wholsom . … Curds and Cream just turn'd."

She again mixed the neoclassic, religious, and personal in what is perhaps her most moving work, a lament for her dead children, written during her last pregnancy. She recollects the pains of childbirth in vivid tropes, but ends the poem with a reaffirmation of faith in Christ, as she pledges her next child to God's service.

The major portion of T.'s verse consists of skillful paraphrases of psalms and canticles, which reveal her understanding of Puritan ideas and historiography. For example, she transforms Psalm 137 to dramatize the Puritan's experiences in the New World, changing a Babylonian landscape into American wilderness.

Most of T.'s prose pieces are simple meditations on religious subjects, often expressing doubts and fears over the state of her soul. In letters to her father, she repeatedly sought comfort from anxiety. Often, in more serene moments, she wrote short, essaylike letters to her younger sister, guiding her towards a life of virtue and pietry and advising her to abandon the frivolities of youth. Her prose works are thoughfully serious, although undisinguished in style and content.

Since only fragments of T.'s work are available, a thorough assessment remains impossible. Clearly, she imitated her father's style and ideas, and she followed the prescriptions of early-18th-c. poetics. Religious themes are ever present, and abstractions and personifications are common in her poetry. Much of her later verse indicates a potential never realized.

WORKS: *Reliquiae Turellae et Lachrymae Paternal* (Ed. E .Turell, 1735; reissued as *Memoirs of the Life and Death of the Pious and Ingenious Mrs. Jane Turell . . . Collected Chiefly from Her Own Manuscripts*, 1741).

BIBLIOGRAPHY: Brooks, C., *History of the Town of Medford* (1855). Evans, C., *American Bibliography* (1912).
For articles in reference works, see: *NAW* (article by O. E. Winslow).
JACQUELINE HORNSTEIN

Agnes Sligh Turnbull

B. *14 Oct. 1888, New Alexandria, Pennsylvania; d. 31 Jan. 1982, Livingston, New Jersey*
D. *of Alexander Halliday and Lucinda Hannah McConnell Sligh; m. James Turnbull, 1918*

Of Scots Presbyterian background, T. grew up in western Pennsylvania and was graduated from Indiana (Pennsylvania) State College in 1910. She then attended the University of Chicago for one year. She was married in 1918 and has one daughter.

T.'s fiction is varied and uneven. She began with a number of sentimental and undistinguished narratives about actual and imagined Biblical women. Scattered throughout her career are a few children's books: *Elijah the Fishbite* (1940), *Jed, the Shepherd's Dog* (1957), *George* (1965), and *The White Lark* (1968).

Her best fiction deals with Scottish settlers in the coal country of western Pennsylvania. Major concerns are the difficult lives of pioneer women and the effect upon them of their strict Presbyterianism. Her attitude toward that faith is ambivalent. While she dramatizes the psychological damage done by adherence to the Calvinistic doctrine of predestination and portrays Episcopalianism as gentler (see especially *The Rolling Years*, 1936, and *The Bishop's Mantle*, 1947), she also shows the comfort and sense of community given by the faith. In some books (notably *The Gown of Glory*, 1952, and *The Nightingale*, 1960) set in the early years of this century, she writes nostalgically of small-town life centered around the local Presbyterian church. Her women are strong and self-reliant, but they also are traditionally home and family centered.

Two of T.'s finest novels are set on the Pennsylvania frontier during the Revolutionary War. Vividly depicting the joys and hardships of the frontier, *The Day Must Dawn* (1942) tells of a gently bred pioneer woman who schemes to have her daughter go east to an easier life. The novel climaxes with an Indian raid, based on an actual incident, and ends with her dying acceptance of the fact that her daughter will marry a frontiersman and go west to still wilder country, postponing the dream for another generation.

The King's Orchard (1963), set in the same period and using some of the same historical material, is a fictionalized biography of James O'Hara, who came to this country shortly before the Revolution, traveled west to Indiana, became Washington's quartermaster during the war, and was prominent in the early history of Pittsburgh. Many other historical personages, of minor as well as major importance, figure in its pages. It effectively contrasts settled Philadelphia, rough young Pittsburgh, and the wilderness that would become Indiana and Illinois.

For other novels T. turned to the late 19th and early 20th centuries. The most ambitious of these, *The Rolling Years*, studies three generations of Scots Presbyterian women in western Pennsylvania. Sarah McDowell bears twelve children (of whom five survive) to her dour Calvinistic husband; her bitterness about her repeated, difficult confinements is effectively shown. Her last child, Jeannie, has an easier and yet more restricted life. A gay and loving girl, she marries a minister and moves to town. As a young widow, she rears her daughter, Constance, with the help of her spinster sisters, who are also strikingly portrayed. Engaged to a Presbyterian divinity student, Constance faces her crisis when he denies some of the tenets of their faith. Thus the novel dramatizes the gradual weakening of the strict Calvinism of the Scottish immigrants as their life grows increasingly easy.

Remember the End (1938) tells of Alex MacTay, a poetic young Scotsman who comes to Pennsylvania in 1890. Suppressing his aesthetic interests, he rises to great wealth and power, but at the cost of deeply wounding his wife and alienating his only son. Sympathetically portrayed, he typifies the strengths and weaknesses of the great tycoons of the period, such as his own model, Andrew Carnegie.

Much of T.'s fiction tends toward the sentimental and some of her novels seem written to inculcate an easy and conventional morality. In addition, her novels tend to use trite plot devices. But at her best, in the novels studying her Scottish background in western Pennsylvania, she has created moving and believable pictures of women's joys and sufferings.

WORKS: *Far above Rubies* (1926). *The Wife of Pontius Pilate: A Story of the Heart of Procla* (1928). *In the Garden: A Story of the First Easter* (1929). *The Four Marys* (1932). *The Colt that Carried a King* (1933). *Old Home Town* (1933). *This Spring of Love* (1934). *The Rolling Years* (1936). *Remember the End* (1938). *Elijah the Fishbite* (1940). *Dear Me: Leaves from the Diary of Agnes Sligh Turnbull* (1941). *The Day Must Dawn* (1942). *Once to Shout* (1943). *The Bishop's Mantle* (1947). *The Gown of Glory* (1952). *The Golden Journey* (1955). *Jed, the Shepherd's Dog* (1957). *Out of My Heart* (1958). *The Nightingale: A Romance* (1960). *The King's Orchard* (1963). *Little Christmas* (1964). *George* (1965). *The Wedding Bargain* (1966). *The White Lark* (1968). *Many a Green Isle* (1968). *Whistle and I'll Come to You: An Idyll* (1970). *The Flowering* (1972). *The Richlands* (1974). *The Winds of Love* (1977).

BIBLIOGRAPHY: *NYHTB* (26 Oct. 1947). *NYTBR* (9 Feb. 1936; 27 Nov. 1938; 25 Oct. 1942; 26 Oct. 1947; 16 March 1952). *SatR* (17 Oct. 1942; 19 Nov. 1955).

MARY JEAN DeMARR

Anne Tyler

B. 25 Oct. 1941, Minneapolis, Minnesota
D. of Lloyd Parry and Phyllis Mahon Tyler; m. Taghi Mohammad Modaressi, 1963

T. was raised in North Carolina. She graduated from Duke University with a major in Russian (1961) and pursued graduate work at Columbia (1962). She served as Russian bibliographer at Duke University Library and as assistant to the librarian at McGill University Law Library, Montreal. In 1963, T. married a child psychiatrist, and they now live in Baltimore with their two daughters.

T. has been prolific: she has written eight novels in sixteen years and numerous short stories, which appear in diverse magazines from *McCalls* to *The New Yorker*.

T. introduces most of the major characteristics of her novels in her first, *If Morning Ever Comes* (1964). Plots involve the complexities of family life and are geographically bound to small towns in North Carolina or to withering row houses or more fashionable Roland Park in Baltimore. The title of each novel appears in the text and focuses on a major theme. Humor, often bittersweet, is important. Characterization is T.'s greatest strength, especially of old people who are presented with compassion and of invincible and usually eccentric women. T. uses diction and grammar that establish characters' backgrounds and imagery that reflects characters' problems and traits: "Pieces of Emerson were lodged with Elizabeth like shrapnel." She has established herself, particularly with her last four novels, as a writer of unquestioned talent.

Jeremy Pauling, of *Celestial Navigation* (1974), is a sensitive and shy artist who lives in his own mind and who finds forays into the real world puzzling and, finally, destructive. The chapters centering on him employ a narrative voice, but the six chapters devoted to four women in Jeremy's life all use first-person voices. Ironically, Jeremy experiences his greatest happiness and creativity after his mother's death (an event his sisters thought would devastate his life) and after Mary and their children depart, leaving only a note on the refrigerator door. Both Jeremy—"Wasn't that what life was all about: steadfast endurance?"—and Mary—"I don't know which takes more courage: surviving a lifelong endurance test because you once made a promise or breaking free, disrupting your whole world"—embody the trait that T. insists on for most of her characters: endurance.

Searching for Caleb (1975) juxtaposes the comic and the serious, chronicling three generations of a Baltimore family of Roland Park. Family strife climaxes when the first cousins, Justine and Duncan, marry each other. These two set out on adventures best symbolized by the Mayflower truck that moves their rosewood chests and crystal from Roland Park and by the orange U-Haul van that, much later, moves only their books and clothes to a circus's winter trailer park. Like *Celestial Navigation*, this novel brings characters into Chekhovian scenes where people talk to unlistening ears, Daniel and Caleb Peck, T.'s most endearing old people; Justine, Daniel's fortune-telling, nomad-like granddaughter; other Pecks; and eccentric strangers make up this comic novel, which details man's foibles, charms, mores, weaknesses, and flaws.

In *Earthly Possessions* (1977), Charlotte Emory gives a minute account of being kidnapped in a Maryland bank and abducted to Florida. In alternate chapters she tells the history of her own life (a struggle to dispossess herself of encumbering possessions) and the histories of the peculiar and unhappy families of her mother and husband. Richly humorous, this novel epitomizes in Charlotte a woman T. frequently portrays—a woman denied the autonomous existence she craves. No shrill feminist cries rise from T.'s fiction, but an existential longing for freedom does.

Eccentric characters are prominent in T.'s work; they settle into a private world, unconcerned with the day-to-day activities that dominate the lives of others. *Morgan's Passing* (1980), her most recent novel, presents a highly eccentric character, Morgan Gower, in fascinating detail. The reader, however, is left somewhat at a loss, never completely sure of the character or of his personae.

A skillful writer, T. treats serious and often tragic themes without sacrificing the comic. Her prose, as some critics charge, is not stylistically daring, and her concerns are not with depressed minorities or with mythic ghosts. Instead, she writes truly about the lives of middle-class Americans, and her characters dwell, as John Updike has said, "where poetry and adventure form as easily as dew."

WORKS: *If Morning Ever Comes* (1964). *The Tin Can Tree* (1965). *A Slipping-Down Life* (1970). *The Clock Winder* (1972). *Celestial Navigation* (1974). *Searching for Caleb* (1975). *Earthly Possessions* (1977). *Morgan's Passing* (1980). *Dinner at the Homesick Restaurant* (1982).

BIBLIOGRAPHY: *Atlantic* (March 1976). *NY* (29 March 1976; 6 June 1977). *NYTBR* (15 July 1965). *SoR* 14 (Jan. 1978).

ELIZABETH EVANS

Dorothy Uhnak

B. 1931, Bronx, New York

For fourteen years, U. served as a member of the New York City Transit Police, achieving the rank of detective first class. She is married and the mother of one daughter.

Her first book, *Policewoman* (1964) is a partially fictionalized account of the transformation of the narrator (who shares U.'s name and background) from applicant to fullfledged, working member of the New York City Police Department. No attempt is made to gloss over the frustrations engendered by tedious procedures, the reluctance of citizens to testify against offenders, the use of influence to free criminals justly apprehended, or the hardening process through which a beginning officer must pass. In contrast, however, the excitement of the work and the sense of service rendered and assignments well done is also dramatized, making *Policewoman* a strong, compelling first book.

U. then introduced a cast of continuing characters who appear in a series of three novels. The protagonist, Detective Christie Choriopoulos Opara, works for the district attorney's Special Investigations Squad. The problems common to working mothers—Opara is a young widow whose husband, also a policeman, was killed while on duty—and the presence of Opara's family, which serves as a support group, both contribute to the realism of the series. The developing personal and professional relationships between Opara and her boss, Casey Reardon, one of fiction's best realized "tough cops," provide subplots throughout the trilogy. Other members of the squad lend depth, color, comic relief, and effective detail.

The plot of *The Bait* (1968) springs from an arrest Opara unwillingly makes while on her way to the culmination of a seemingly more important undercover assignment. U.'s development of the background and motivation of the murderer enhances the suspense and offsets the book's dependence on coincidence. The organization and the machinations of the Secret Nation, a black religio-political gang, form the subplot of *The Witness* (1969); seen through the eyes of initiate Eddie Campion, the scenes involving the Nation are especially powerful. Elena Vargas of *The Ledger* (1970) is one of U.'s most vibrant and complex characters, and her attitudes and history are fully explored. Vargas and Opara engage in a long, absorbing battle of wills which contributes enormously to the book's success.

Law and Order (1973) is not a crime novel but rather the panoramic saga of a family of New York policemen, their connections, their work, their sense of self and place. The central character, Brian O'Malley, is a study of an essentially decent man struggling to master himself, his work, and the necessarily shady world into which that work takes him.

Sergeant Joe Peters, the officer investigating the murder of two little boys, is the protagonist and narrator of *The Investigation* (1977). Both the police and public opinion point to Kitty Keeler, the children's mother, as the killer, and Peter solves a double mystery to achieve the book's climax. Much of the tension springs from the contradictory and intense appraisals other characters make of the accused. She is believed by some to be nearly saintly in her generosity, warmth, and kindness; believed by others to be a sensual, self-indulgent, fiendish woman. Kitty Keeler's real motivations and personality are the plot's true mystery. *The Investigation* is U.'s best novel to date.

False Witness (1981) portrays two women who have achieved success in professions dominated by men. Sanderalee Dawson, model, television personality, and political activist, is the victim of rape and attempted murder; Lynne Jacobi, a bureau chief in the New York City District Attorney's Office, investigates the crime, forcing the two women into an uneasy alliance. The extreme violence of the attack on Sanderalee underscores the brutality of the struggles for power and control the protagonists experience professionally. *False Witness* is a superior novel whose characterizations are expecially strong.

Remarkably well able to convey tellingly the ambiences of home, squad room, and mean streets, U. is a good writer noted for her mastery of realistic detail in plot, setting, and characterization.

WORKS: *Policewoman* (1964). *The Bait* (1968). *The Witness* (1969). *The Ledger* (1970). *Law and Order* (1973). *The Investigation* (1977). *False Witness* (1981).

BIBLIOGRAPHY: *Best Sellers* (1 Feb. 1964). *Mystery Fancier* (Jan. 1978). *Newsweek* (13 April 1973).

JANE S. BAKERMAN

Frances Jane Crosby Van Alstyne

B. *24 March 1820; Putnam County, New York; d. 12 Feb. 1915, Bridgeport, Connecticut*
Wrote under: *Fanny Crosby, etc.*
D. *of John and Mercy Crosby; m. Alexander Van Alstyne, 1858*

At the age of six weeks, V. was permanently blinded as a result of an eye infection treated by hot poultices that destroyed the optic nerves. This trauma was compounded when her father died before she was one year old, but as an eight-year-old she wrote the lines: "O what a happy soul am I! / Although I cannot see, / I am resolved that in this world / Contented I will be!" V. spent her childhood studying the Bible and developing the powers of her memory. In fact, she later told friends that she had memorized the first five books of the Bible, the Psalms, and most of the New Testament.

At the age of fifteen, V. enrolled in the New York Institution for the Blind, where she remained as a student for the next eight years. Here she developed her poetic talents by reciting topical poems for visitors, such as Jenny Lind and Henry Clay. She also recited on fund-raising tours for the institution from 1842 to 1844. One of her favorites on such occasions began: "Contented, happy, though a sightless band, / Dear friends, this evening we before you stand." After graduating at the age of twenty-three, V. stayed at the institution and taught a number of subjects for the next fifteen years.

V.'s first volume of poetry, *The Blind Girl, and Other Poems* (1844), was published when she was twenty-four. Ironically, the preface states that "any pecuniary advantage" to the authoress will be appreciated since she is in "declining health." V. died at the age of ninety-five. The volume concentrates on the extremely morbid subjects so popular at the time. Typical poems are "My Mother's Grave," "Ida, the Broken-Hearted," and "On the Death of a Child."

In her next volume of poetry, *Monterey, and Other Poems* (1851), V. again appeals to her readers' sympathy: she states that her health is "sadly impaired," while she hopes her "declining years" will be supported by the sale of this volume. The contents are even more maudlin, including "The Dying Daughter," "Let Me Die on the Prairie," "Weep Not for the Dead," "The Stranger's Grave," and "Reflections of a Murderer."

A Wreath of Columbia's Flowers (1858) is a collection of short fiction. Although V. claims that her writings are "natural and true to life," this volume contains the story "Annie Herbert," about a girl who hears flowers talking to her.

Her final volume of poetry, *Bells at Evening, and other Verse* (1897), includes a biographical sketch by Robert Lowry. V. considered *Bells at Evening* her finest poetic effort. It contains such secular poems as "A Tribute to Cincinnati" and other patriotic fare. The final section includes some sixty-five of her most famous hymns.

Hymn writing was V.'s major claim to fame. She began writing popular songs with the composer George F. Root in 1851, and the two collaborated on about fifty songs, including "Rosalie, the Prairie Flower," which earned three thousand dollars in royalties. In 1864, V. began writing hymns with William B. Bradbury, generally considered the father of Sunday-school music in America. Over her long career, she wrote around eight thousand hymns. Not even she could remember the exact figure, since so many were published under her more than two hundred pseudonyms. Her most successful hymns include "Rescue the Perishing" and "Safe in the Arms of Jesus," used by Dwight L. Moody and Ira D. Sankey in their missionary work and by Frances E. Willard in her temperance work.

V.'s final literary efforts were two versions of her autobiography, *Fannie Crosby's Life-Story* (1903) and the more detailed volume, *Memories of Eighty Years* (1906). In the latter volume she gives one paragraph to her marriage to another blind teacher at the institution. The two moved to Brooklyn, where V. continued to write hymns and her husband worked as a music teacher until his death in 1902. One suspects, from V.'s autobiographical volumes, that beneath her saccharine surface she was a shrewd businesswoman who prospered by presenting to the public the popular sentiments they wanted to hear.

WORKS: *The Blind Girl, and Other Poems* (1844). *Monterey, and Other Poems* (1851). *A Wreath of Columbia's Flowers* (1858). *Bells at Evening, and Other Verses* (1897). *Ode to the Memory of Captain John Underhill* (1902). *Fanny Crosby's Life-Story* (1903). *Memories of Eighty Years* (1906).

BIBLIOGRAPHY: Van Alstyne, F. C., *Fanny Crosby's Life-Story* (1903). Van Alstyne, F. C., *Memories of Eighty Years* (1906).

For articles in reference works, see: *NAW* (article by C. E. Rinehart).

DIANE LONG HOEVELER

Marie Van Vorst

B. 23 Nov. 1867, New York City; d. 16 Dec. 1936, Florence, Italy
D. of Hooper Cumming and Josephine Treat Van Vorst;
m. Count Gaetano Gaiati, 1916

V. was the daughter of a financially prosperous and socially prominent family, and she was educated by private tutors; but most of her best-known writings are animated by a conscious dedication to social reform. She most likely inherited this commitment to reform from her father who, during his tenure on the New York City Superior Court, was involved in an investigation of urban corruption which contributed to the demise of the Tweed Ring.

V. began writing short stories, poems, and nofiction essays for periodical publication during the late 1890s. Shortly after the death of her brother, John, she and her sister-in-law, Bessie, moved to France where they both served as correspondents for American journals. With only occasional visits to the U.S., primarily to gather research material for her writing, V. lived in various European cities until her death in 1928. Although she wrote for many American, French, and British periodicals, her association with *Harper's* was the most sustained and significant. One of her most important assignments for *Harper's* was a cultural series, "Rivers of the World" (1906–09), which included information gathered at the Seine, Tiber, and Nile.

V. began writing before her sister-in-law, but it was their collaboration on a novel and, particularly, on an exposé of women factory workers that initially brought the work of both women public attention. After the two ceased actively writing together, Bessie remained V.'s most constant friend, critic, and consultant.

V. and Bessie returned to the U.S., assumed aliases, and worked in factories to gather information for *The Woman Who Toils* (1903). As "Bell Ballard," V. worked in a shoe factory in Lynn, Massachusetts, and in cotton mills in South Carolina. Describing herself as a "mirror, expositor and mouthpiece" for working women, she was more sympathetic to her co-workers than Bessie. Although she never identified herself with these women, she was more understanding in her estimation of their values. Where Bessie criticized the women for their frivolity, V. saw in it an incipient rebellion against the deadening limitations of their lives. Similarly, she was more hopeful of reforms coming within the industrial workplace rather than by removing the women from the mills. Although sharply critical of "the abnormality, the abortion known as Anarchy, Socialism," she championed the cause of labor unions: "Organize labor, therefore, so well that the work-woman who obtains her task may be able to continue it and keep her health and self-respect."

V.'s experiences in the cotton mills provided her with enough information to write a fictionalized account of the situation in one of her better novels, *Amanda of the Mill* (1905). She presents both the history of how the hill people came to work in the mills and the world they found there, primarily through two characters—the somewhat idealized, but none the less interesting heroine, Amanda Henchley, and the man she loves, Henry

Euston, a drunkard whose reformation is effected through the dual inspirations of Amanda and reform-oriented labor organizing. The novel is memorable for its accurate and concerned reporting of industrial issues.

In *Amanda of the Mill*, V. leads her characters through a series of crises that seemingly could be resolved only through economic revolution. She avoids this conclusion through a propitious natural disaster, which clears the way for a new era without requiring confrontation with the problems the narrative so carefully raises. Although a tendency to equivocate also occurs in the later novels—in which dilemmas posed by marital incompatibility and illicit sexual passion predominate, and spouses conveniently die before virtue is endangered—these books are entertaining and occasionally of more lasting interest.

The most significant of the later novels is *Mary Moreland* (1915), the story of a stenographer in love with and loved by her employer, a married Wall Street financier. In *Mary Moreland*, V. writes her most sophisticated discussion of the moral issues surrounding marital dissatisfaction and infidelity and creates her most complex and admirable heroine. Mary, a self-supporting suffragist dedicated to her career while searching for a passionate love that is neither compromising nor limiting, is a memorable fictional portrait of a young American woman seeking her identity in a world of shifting social and sexual values.

Although V.'s fiction fails to fulfill the promise engendered by her vivid moral and economic observations, the novels, especially *Amanda of the Mills* and *Mary Moreland*, deserve some renewal of critical interest. Perhaps because of her continued inability to solve the problems she raises without resorting to catastrophe and coincidence, V.'s writings provide a remarkable record of the turmoil of a society in transition. Although she never abandoned the traditional codes of behavior, she raised penetrating questions about their viability.

WORKS: *Bagsby's Daughter* (with B. Van Vorst, 1901). *Philip Longstreth* (1902). *The Woman Who Toils* (with B. Van Vorst, 1903). *Poems* (1903). *Amanda of the Mill* (1905). *Miss Desmond* (1905). *The Sin of George Warrener* (1906). *The Sentimental Adventures of Jimmy Bulstrode* (1908). *In Ambush* (1909). *First Love* (1910). *The Girl from His Town* (1910). *The Broken Bell* (1912). *His Love Story* (1913). *Big Tremaine* (1914). *Mary Moreland* (1915). *War Letters of an American Woman* (1916). *War Poems* (1916). *Fairfax and His Bride* (1920). *Tradition* (1921). *The Queen of Karmania* (1922). *Sunrise* (1924). *Goodnight Ladies!* (1931). *The Gardenia* (1933).

BIBLIOGRAPHY: Blake, F., *The Strike in the American Novel* (1972). Filler, L., *The Muckrakers* (1976). Hill, Vicki Lynn, "Strategy and Breadth: The Socialist-Feminist in American Fiction" (Ph.D. diss., State Univ. of New York at

Buffalo, 1979). Maglin, N., "Rebel Women Writers, 1894–1925" (Ph.D. diss., Union Graduate School, 1975). Rose, L., "A Descriptive Catalogue of Economic and Politico-Economic Fiction in the United States, 1902–1909" (Ph.D. diss., Univ. of Chicago, 1936). Taylor, W., *The Economic Novel in America* (1942).

For articles in reference works, see: *NAW* (article by L. Filler).

Other references: *Athenaeum* (18 April 1908). *Bookman* (May 1902; April 1903; June 1905; Jan. 1910). *Critic* (Jan. 1902; Oct. 1903). *Dial* (1 Sept. 1906). *Overland* (May 1903). *SatR* (18 August 1906).

VICKI LYNN HILL

Frances Fuller Victor

B. 23 May 1826, Rome, New York; d. 14 Nov. 1902, Portland, Oregon
Wrote under: Frances Barritt, Dorothy D., Florence Fane, Frances Fuller,
Frances Fuller Victor
D. of Adonijah and Lucy A. Williams Fuller; m. Jackson Barritt, 1853;
m. Henry Clay Victor, 1862

V. was the eldest of five daughters, descended from an old colonial family. V. and her sister Metta, with whom she wrote poetry, received their schooling at a young-ladies seminary in Wooster, Ohio. At the age of nine she wrote verses on her slate and directed her fellow students in plays she had written. The publication of her verses in the Cleveland *Herald* in 1840 marked the beginning of a long writing career.

V.'s turbulent private life frequently interrupted her prolific writing career. When her father died in 1850, she stopped writing poetry and returned home to live with her family, who by then had moved to St. Clair, Michigan. Her first marriage broke up after a period of homesteading in Omaha, but V. didn't obtain a divorce until March, 1862, two months before she married her sister's brother-in-law, Henry Clay Victor, a navy engineer. V. and her husband moved to the West Coast, but his position in the navy often took him away for long periods of sea duty. Left alone, V. embarked on a successful career as a historian, and continued it after her husband was drowned in 1875 in the wreck of the *Pacific*.

As teenagers, V. and her sister Metta together wrote poetry and published it locally and, eventually, in the New York *Home Journal.* In 1848, they moved to New York, and in 1851 they published *Poems of Sentiment and Imagination,* a collection of descriptive and highly melodramatic poetry. The remainder of their poetry was written and published separately. After V. moved west in 1862, she wrote numerous poems of a more descriptive quality for western magazines.

In 1848, V. published her first melodramatic romance, *Anizetta, the Guajira; or, The Creole of Cuba.* She abandoned this genre when she discovered she had more talent as a realistic dime novelist. For her brother-in-law's editions of Beadle's Dime Novels, V. wrote *East and West; or, The Beauty of Willard's Mill* (1862) and *The Land Claim: A Tale of the Upper Missouri* (1862), both realistically treating Nebraska farm life, especially the hardships faced by women. Her short stories, published in the western magazines, reflect this same concern for the hard lot of frontier women; the regional writing of Bret Harte was a major influence on these realistic short stories.

V.'s work as a satirist and crusader began when she moved to the West Coast in the 1860s. As Florence Fane, she took satiric pokes at all levels of society in regular contributions to the San Francisco *Bulletin* and the *Golden Era.* Her brief crusade as a temperance supporter resulted in one temperance tract, *The Women's War with Whiskey* (1874). She also served as a columnist for the *Call-Bulletin* under the name of Dorothy D.

The thirty years V. spent as a historian and folklorist proved the most successful aspect of her writing career. She discovered history was her forte in 1864 when she began studying local Oregon history. She interviewed many western pioneers and researched family papers and archives. *The River of the West* (1870), based on an interview with Joseph Meek, is his first-person account of life as a Rocky Mountain trapper. V. acknowledges in her introduction her debt to Washington Irving's *Astoria* (1836) and *Captain Bonneville* (1837), which reveal a romantic attachment to historical places.

V.'s second attempt at this new genre, *All Over Oregon and Washington* (1872) contains less folklore than *The River of the West.* The book covers the discovery, early history, natural features, resources, and business and social conditions of these two states. V.'s response to rapid social and economic change is nostalgic. She emphasizes her disappointment at the close of the frontier, but points with pride to the cultural developments of the Northwest Coast.

V.'s major historical endeavor was her contribution to Hubert Howe Bancroft's voluminous *History of the Pacific States* (1890); she contributed to all but two of the twenty-eight volumes. V. joined the staff as a chief assistant and its only woman in 1878, three years after the death of her husband. By this time, she had accumulated a wealth of journalistic, literary, and historic experience. As a member of Bancroft's staff, she prepared all of the two-volume history of Oregon, Washington, Idaho, and Montana and was the major writer and researcher for the history of Utah. She also wrote over half of the two California volumes and researched *Northwest Coast* and *California Inter Pocula*. The series is written in textbook style, but V.'s volumes, like her other historical works, exhibit a sensitive response to the aesthetics of the land and a nostalgia for the past.

V.'s historical accounts reflect a keen understanding of the economic and social elements of a slowly diminishing frontier; these works also reveal a seemingly contradictory perception of the West as a land of hardships and cherished memories. Her main contribution to American letters rests with these history and travel books and their blend of fact and romance. Her realistic dime novels and short stories, her sentimental and descriptive poetry, and her satiric and crusading pieces, however, also earn a place for her in American letters.

WORKS: *Anizetta the Guajira; or, The Creole of Cuba* (1848). *Poems of Sentiment and Imagination* (with M. F. Victor, 1851). *The Land Claim: A Tale of the Upper Missouri* (1862). *East and West; or, The Beauty of Willard's Mill* (1862). *Border Law; or, The Land Claim* (1862). *The River of the West* (1870). *All Over Oregon and Washington* (1872; revised edition, *Atlantis Arisen*, 1891). *The Women's War with Whiskey* (1874). *The New Penelope, and Other Stories and Poems* (1877). *Eleven Years in the Rocky Mountains* (1879). *History of the Pacific States* (with H. Bancroft et al., 1884–90). *The Early Indian Wars of Oregon* (1894). *Poems* (1900). *Letters to Matthew P. Deady, F. G. Young, and Others, 1866–1902* (1902).

BIBLIOGRAPHY: Caughey, J. W., *Hubert Howe Bancroft: Historian of the West* (1946). Morris, W. A. "Historian of the Northwest: A Woman Who Loved Oregon," *In Memoriam: Frances Fuller Victor; Born May 23, 1826; Died November 14, 1902* (1902). Morris, W. A., "The Origin and Authorship of the Bancroft Pacific States Publications," *Oregon Historical Society Quarterly* 5 (1903).

For articles in reference works, see: *AW. NAW* (article by F. Walker).

DONNA CASELLA KERN

Metta Victoria Fuller Victor

B. 2 March 1831, Erie, Pennsylvania; d. 26 June 1885, Hohokus, New Jersey
Wrote under: George E. Booram, Corinne Cushman, Eleanor Lee Edwards,
   Metta Fuller, Walter T. Gray, Louis LeGrand(?), Rose Kennedy, Mrs. Mark
   Peabody, Seeley Regester, the Singing Sybil, Mrs. Henry J. Thomas, Metta
   Victor
D. of Adonijah (Adanigh?) and Lucy Williams Fuller; m. Dr. Morse, 1850(?);
   m. Orville J. Victor, 1856

Five years younger than her sister Frances, V. was eight years old when the family moved to Wooster Village, Ohio. Soon thereafter, she began her writing career. By the age of thirteen she was publishing in journals and papers. By fifteen, she had published *The Last Days of Tul: A Romance of the Lost Cities of Yucatan* (1846). That same year V. began publishing as "The Singing Sybil" in Willis and Morris' *New York Home Journal.* Her poetry was much praised, but after producing one joint poetry volume with her sister, she turned her greatest energies to the writing of stories and novels.

V.'s early novels are often moralistic as well as melodramatic and focus on a particular social ill. One example, *The Senator's Son* (1853; sometimes called *Parke Madison*), is a temperance novel. It was also V.'s first bestseller, running to ten editions in the U.S., and selling some thirty thousand copies in pirated British editions.

There is some evidence (see Johansen) that, by 1851, while living in Michigan, V. was married to a Dr. Morse. Nothing is known about this marriage, which does not appear in records for St. Clair, Washtenaw, or Oakland County, Michigan. Her first marriage is even more mysterious than that of her sister to Jackson Barritt. It is known that in 1856 V. married Orville J. Victor, a young journalist who would soon become one of the architects of the Beadle Dime Novel empire. Besides untold poems, stories, articles, manuals, and novels, V. produced nine children. She was still an active writer when she died, at age fifty-four, of cancer.

Not surprisingly, V. was one of Beadle's prime resources. She edited their journal, the *Home,* and was the author of manuals and cookbooks as well as fiction. She produced more than twenty books for Beadle. Dime Novel Number Four was V.'s *Alice Wilde* (1860). Her most popular Beadle novel was *Maum Guinea and Her Plantation Children,* first published in 1861. This impassioned story of slave life is said to have been praised by both President Lincoln and Henry Ward Beecher. It sold some one hundred thousand copies in the U.S. and was also reprinted widely in Britain.

Although V. is perhaps best known for sensationalist sermons on issues like temperance and slavery, her most important contribution is probably her landmark work in the American detective novel. Under the pseudonym Seeley Regester, V. produced *The Dead Letter*. First published by Beadle in 1866 (but believed to have been originally published two years earlier), *The Dead Letter* is one of the first detective novels. It antedates, by at least twelve years, Anna Katharine Green (Rohlf's) *The Leavenworth Case*, which was long believed to be the first American detective novel.

Still a highly readable tale of treachery, true love, and murder, *The Dead Letter* features a professional gentleman sleuth named Mr. Burton. Besides the help of the young hero, Redfield, Burton also relies on the considerable talents of his young daughter, a psychic. V. produced a second novel as Seeley Regester, *The Figure Eight; or, The Mystery of Meredith Place* (later called *A Woman's Hand*) in 1869. Other novels by V. during this period, although not pure detective puzzles, certainly feature violent crimes and their detection. One example, *Too True: A Story of Today* (1868), was published under V.'s real name and features a good deal of detection by a woman artist.

V. deserves recognition as one of the earliest creators of the detective novel and as a writer with facility in any formula of popular fiction. She wrote romance, pioneer adventure, detective, sensation, and social issue novels. Late in her career she also created a comic realm populated by bad boys, bashful men, and prosperous pork merchants. During the heyday of the American dime novel and serial V. was in great demand. At one point in the 1870s, V. received twenty-five thousand dollars for exclusive story rights from the *New York Weekly*.

V. could easily be labeled a hack writer. But she was also a writer of undeniable skill whose inventiveness anticipated the needs of her reading public. Sensational thrillers like *The Dead Letter* opened new frontiers in popular fiction and have the power to entertain even a modern reader.

WORKS: *The Last Days of Tul* (1846). *Poems of Sentiment and Imagination* (with F. F. Victor, 1851). *Fresh Leaves from Western Woods* (1852). *The Senator's Son* (1853). *Fashionable Dissipation* (1854). *Mormon Wives* (1856). *The Arctic Queen* (1858). *Miss Slimmen's Window* (1859). *The Dime Cook Book* (1859). *The Dime Recipe Book* (1859). *Alice Wilde: The Raftsman's*

Daughter (1860). *The Backwood's Bride* (1860). *Myrtle: The Child of the Prairie* (1860). *Uncle Ezekiel and his Exploits on Two Continents* (1861). *Maum Guinea and Her Plantation Children* (1861). *The Emerald Necklace* (1861). *The Unionist's Daughter* (1862). *The Gold Hunters* (1863). *Jo Daviess' Client* (1863). *Laughing Eyes* (1868). *The Country Cousin* (1864). *The Two Hunters* (1865). *The Housewife's Manual* (1865). *The Dead Letter* (1866). *Who Was He?* (1866). *Too True: A Story of Today* (1868). *The Betrayed Bride* (1869). *The Figure Eight* (1869). *Black Eyes and Blue* (1876). *Passing the Portal* (1876). *Brave Barbara* (1877). *The Hunted Bride* (1877). *Guilty or Not Guilty* (1878). *The Locked Heart* (1879). *A Wild Girl* (1879). *A Bad Boy's Diary* (1880). *The Black Riddle* (1880). *Madcap: The Little Quakeress* (1880). *The Mysterious Guardian* (1880). *Pretty and Proud* (1880). *Pursued to the Altar* (1880). *The Blunders of a Bashful Man* (1881). *At His Mercy* (1881). *Miss Slimmen's Boarding House* (1882). *A Woman's Sorrow* (1882). *The Bad Boy Abroad* (1883). *Morley Beeches* (1883). *Naughty Girl's Diary* (1883). *Abijah Beanpole in New York* (1884). *Mrs. Rasher's Curtain Lectures* (1884). *The Bad Boy at Home* (1885). *A Good Boy's Diary* (1885). *The Brown Princess* (1888). *The Phantom Wife* (1888). *Born to Betray* (1890). *The Gay Captain* (1891). *Who Owned the Jewels?* (1891). *The Georgie Papers* (1897).

BIBLIOGRAPHY: Johannsen, A., *The House of Beadle and Adams*, Vol. 2 (1950).

Other references: *Cosmopolitan Art Journal* (March 1857).

KATHLEEN L. MAIO

Mary Heaton Vorse

B. 9 Oct. 1874, New York City; d. 14 June 1966, Provincetown, Massachusetts
D. of Hiram and Ellen Cordelia Blackman Heaton; m. Albert White Vorse, 1898; m. Joe O'Brien, 1912; m. Robert Minor, 1920

V. was born to an old New England family. As a child, she spent her summers in the college town of Amherst, Massachusetts, and her winters in New York City and Europe. Although seemingly cosmopolitan, V. wrote, in later life, about how the sheltered academic atmosphere of her youth enabled her to acquire a dedication to intellectual speculation, but left her isolated from the industrial and economic changes that characterized late 19th-c. America.

V. was married three times and had three children. After the death of her first husband, V. supported herself through her writing.

V.'s earliest published writings were short sketches, which appeared in diverse periodicals including *Criterion, Critic, Woman's Home Companion*, and *Atlantic Monthly*. Both *The Very Little Person* (1911) and *The Prestons* (1918) include short fiction excerpted from these early publications. V. drew on the experiences of her first years of marriage to Albert Vorse in her first novel, *The Breaking-in of a Yachtsman's Wife* (1908). *The Autobiography of an Elderly Woman* (1911), an anecdotal and entertaining narrative, is told from the point of view of a woman her mother's age who resents the circumscriptions youth imposes on the aged.

In 1906, V. moved to Greenwich Village, where she and her husband founded the A Club, an experimental cooperative living arrangement frequented by Mark Twain, Theodore Dreiser, Mother Jones, Maxim Gorky, and others. Primarily a collection of liberal reformers who flirted with varieties of socialism, the participants in the A Club were devoted to a thoughtful and stimulating analysis of American society. V. wrote favorably about her experiences in the club. Still, she affectionately satirizes the Greenwich Village lifestyle in the novel *I've Come to Stay* (1915). The heroine, Camilla Deerfield, justifies the excesses and absurdities of the village residents as a necessary and long overdue response to their Calvinist heritage: "We are the flaming shadows cast by unfulfilled joys which died unborn in our parents' souls. We come of people who lived in the ordinary hypocrisies so long that some of us cast away even the decencies in our endaevor not to be hypocritical."

From 1906 through the mid-1940s, V. spent a portion of each year in Provincetown, Massachusetts, as did other members of the Greenwich Village radical intelligentsia. It was here that V., prompted by a series of articles on infant education she had researched in Italy for *Woman's Home Companion*, organized a Montessori school. More importantly, here V. was among the founding members of the experimental theater group, the Provincetown Players, that staged Eugene O'Neill's earliest plays.

In *A Footnote to Folly* (1935), an autobiographical account of the years 1912 to 1922, V. identified the 1912 Lawrence, Massachusetts, textile strike as the single most significant event in her political and literary development. She described how her experiences at Lawrence led both her and Joe O'Brien, the labor reporter who became her second husband, to active identification with the problems and struggles of the American working class. Henceforth, V. was to write the bulk of her work in explicitly politicized terms.

This dedication is reflected in the prolific writing of her major phase. For more than thirty years she was a tireless reporter of current events on labor and battle fronts throughout the U.S., Europe, and the Soviet Union. Most of this writing is ephemeral; it appeared in Hearst newspapers, *Harper's* the *Nation, New Republic, Advance, World Tomorrow, Outlook,* and the *Masses* (which she edited) and was never collected. As a war correspondent during WWI, V. covered the 1915 International Congress of Women in Amsterdam and the International Woman Suffrage Convention in Budapest. Her journalism was enhanced by personal involvement with the Red Cross, the American Relief Association, and the Committee for Public Information; her coverage of the war, like that of labor disputes, often focused on the ignored victims—women and children.

With the exception of *The Ninth Man* (1918), a novel set in 12th-c. Italy, all of V.'s book-length publications spring from her experiences as a radical journalist. They vary from compilations recording her coverage of actual events, such as *Men and Steel* (1920) and *Labor's New Millions* (1938), to fictionalized accounts of actual strikes, such as *Passaic* (1926) and *Strike* (1930), and novels springing from her impressions of a world in turmoil, such as *Second Cabin* (1928), based on an ocean voyage from inflation-ravaged postwar Germany to the U.S., after a visit to "optimistic" postrevolutionary Russia.

For the contemporary reader, unfamiliar with the events V. so passionately described throughout her lengthy career, the best introduction to her writing and sensibilities probably will be found in either *A Footnote to Folly*—in which she effectively describes the relationship between personal identity and political commitment and growth—and *Of Time and the Town* (1942). The latter deals with her years in Provincetown; the legends and traditions of the fishing village provide a background for her history of the Provincetown Players and cultural attitudes during the first half of the 20th c. Both books reflect the perspective V. acknowledges in *A Footnote to Folly*: "Indeed, my book is the record of a woman who in early life got angry because many children lived miserably and died needlessly."

WORKS: *The Breaking-in of a Yachtsman's Wife* (1908). *The Whole Family* (with others, 1908). *The Very Little Person* (1911). *The Autobiography of an Elderly Woman* (1911). *The Heart's Company* (1913). *I've Come to Stay* (1915). *The Ninth Man* (1918). *The Prestons* (1918). *Growing Up* (1920). *Men and Steel* (1920). *Fraycar's Fist* (1923). *Wreckage* (1924). *Passaic* (1926). *Second Cabin* (1928). *Strike* (1930). *A Footnote to Folly* (1935). *Labor's New*

Millions (1938). *Of Time and the Town: A Provincetown Chronicle* (1942). *Here Are the People* (1943).

The Mary Heaton Vorse Collection is in the Archives of Labor History and Urban Affairs, Wayne State University, Detroit, Michigan.

BIBLIOGRAPHY: Aaron, D., *Writers on the Left* (1961). Blake, F., *The Strike in the American Novel* (1972). Hill, Vicki Lynn, "Strategy and Breadth: The Socialist-Feminist in American Fiction" (Ph.D. diss., SUNY at Buffalo, 1979). Overton, G., *The Women Who Make Our Novels* (1918). Rideout, W., *The Radical Novel in the United States, 1900–1954* (1956). Sochen, J., *The New Woman in Greenwich Village, 1910–1920* (1972). Sochen, J., *Movers and Shakers* (1973). "The Reminiscences of Mary Heaton Vorse" (transcript of interviews conducted for the Oral History Research Office of Columbia University, 1957).

For articles in reference works, see: *American Women*, Ed. D. Howes (1939). *20th CA*.

Other references: *Nation* (4 June 1908; 15 Jan. 1936). *NewR.* (13 July 1942). *Time* (23 Dec. 1935).

VICKI LYNN HILL

Margaret Walker

B. 7 July 1915, Birmingham, Alabama
D. of Sigismund and Marion Walker; m. M. Alexander, 1943

W.'s middle-class parents were both university graduates; her father was a Methodist minister, and her mother a musicologist and third-generation educator. W. graduated from Gilbert Academy (1930) and studied at Northwestern University (B.A. 1935) and the University of Iowa (M.A. 1940; Ph.D. 1965).

After working on the federal government's Writers Project in Chicago and as a newspaper and magazine editor, she began teaching. Since 1949, W. has been a professor of English at Jackson State College, Mississippi. She is director of the Institute for the Study of History, Life, and Culture of Black People and has organized black culture and writers' conferences, notably the Phillis Wheatley Poetry Festival (in November 1973), at which twenty blackwomen poets read. W. has four children.

W. began writing poetry at the age of twelve. She is the first of her race to receive the Yale Younger Poets Award for her first volume of poetry, *For My People* (1942), and other awards have followed. Her work is widely published in periodicals.

For My People is an early indication of W.'s poetic talent. She experiments with traditional and modern poetic forms. There are ten occasional poems, written in unmistakably black poetic rhythms; ten ballads with superimposed jazz rhythms or blues metrics; and six sonnets, the most traditional of her poetry in substance and structure. The volume begins at a dramatic, intense pitch, continues in a relaxed tone, and ends in contemplative modulation.

In *Prophets for a New Day* (1970), W. limits her subject to the often fatal struggle to secure human rights—chiefly for blacks. Substance clearly dominates form, whether sonnet or ballad.

W. dedicates *October Journey* (1973), a volume of ten poems, to two of her greatest influences: her father and Langston Hughes, her "friend and mentor." Her verse is at its most melodramatic here. The first poem, "October Journey," establishes the volume's tone: "A music sings within my flesh / I feel the pulse within my throat." The final piece, "A Litany from the Dark People," is a skillful, rhythmic composition.

Jubilee (1966), W.'s gripping novel, spans several genres: Civil War epic, historical fiction, and the slave narrative. It is the story of Vyre, daughter of a slave and her master. She experiences simultaneously the rite of passage to womanhood and the change from slavery to freedom. W. frees her epic from the traditional male-oriented sense of the heroic, structuring her novel around Vyre, her maternal great-grandmother. Vyre's first husband, a free and literate Negro, functions only in a supportive role to underscore Vyre's heroism. W.'s poetic style is evident in *Jubilee*'s rhythmic prose and biblical overtones.

In all her poetry, W. reveals an emotional depth as lyrical and spiritual as her personal convictions about her identity and her Protestantism. But despite her political polemics and deep racial sensitivities, W. always maintains a reasonably critical objectivity.

WORKS: *For My People* (1942). *Jubilee* (1966). *Prophets for a New Day* (1970). *How I Wrote Jubilee* (1972). *October Journey* (1973). *A Poetic Equation: Conversations with Nikki Giovani* (1974).

BIBLIOGRAPHY: Untemeyer, L., in *Yale Review* (1943).

For articles in reference works, see: *CB* (Nov. 1943). *Ebony Success Library* 1 (1973).

Other references: *Black World* (Dec. 1971).

ADRIANNE BAYTOP

Elizabeth Stuart Phelps Ward

B. 3 Aug. 1844, Boston, Massachusetts; d. 28 Jan. 1911, Newton, Massachusetts
Given name: Mary Gray Phelps
Wrote under: Mary Adams, E. S. Phelps, Elizabeth Stuart Phelps
D. of Austin and Elizabeth Stuart Phelps; m. Herbert Dickinson Ward, 1888

W. was the oldest child and only daughter of the popular author, Elizabeth Stuart Phelps. Her father was professor of sacred rhetoric at Andover Theological Seminary in Massachusetts. She identified strongly with her mother, who wrote of frustration with the role of a minister's dutiful wife. At some point after her death when W. was eight, W. adopted her mother's name. She attended Abbot Academy and Mrs. Edwards' School for Young Ladies, both in Andover.

By 1868, W. had written eleven undistinguished Sunday-school works and her first story to receive literary recognition, "The Tenth of January" (*Atlantic*, 1868), conceived under the influence of Rebecca Harding Davis. During the next two decades, W. found strong support from many other women writers, such as Lucy Larcom, Mary Bucklin Claflin, Annie Adams Fields, Harriet Prescott Spofford, and Harriet Beecher Stowe.

In the late 1870s and early 1880s, W.'s "boon companion" was Dr. Mary Briggs Harris, a physician in Andover. W.'s female characters during this period were innovatively independent. But with the deaths of her brother [Moses] Stuart Phelps and Dr. Harris in the mid-1880s, the ever-declining health of her father, and her own increasing invalidism, W.'s desire for male companionship increased, and her female characters showed decreased self-confidence. Letters suggest that W. hoped for literary companionship from the much younger man she married in 1888. Although the couple continued to summer together in Gloucester, Massachusetts, after 1900 she and her husband spent their winters apart.

W.'s career as a writer was established with the immediate and international popularity of *The Gates Ajar* (1868). As commonly interpreted, it offers the consolation of a heavenly afterlife to those bereaved by Civil War deaths. This, however, was the first of a series of books presenting W.'s major theme of women's right to self-fulfillment. *The Gates Ajar* shows the quality of female support required for women to gain fulfillment; *Beyond the Gates* (1883), the social and cultural institutions needed; and *The Gates Between* (1887), the behavior required of husbands and fathers. In 1901, W. recast the last book as a play—*Within the Gates*, which was never produced—strengthening the wife-mother role. The Gates series suggests that if earthly society—including a misguided clerical establishment—could not meet the rightful demands of women and the poor, then surely a heavenly society must exist as compensation for such earthly deprivation. These books antedate the outpouring of Utopian literature that followed Edward Bellamy's *Looking Backward* (1888).

From 1869 until her marriage in 1888, W. actively supported women's rights. In the early 1870s, she wrote feminist articles, published in *The Independent* and reprinted in the *Woman's Journal*. They dealt with the sexual double standard, women's economic and emotional independence, the sources of women's ill health, the "true woman" stereotype, and the problems of women in traditional marriages. She also used these themes in fiction for youth and adults. Early fictional examples include *Hedged In* (1870), about the social constraints placed on an unwed mother, and *A Silent Partner* (1871), dealing with men's prejudice against making a woman a business partner. Both novels emphasize women's not men's reliable support for women and women's persistent innovation of social structures designed to meet, rather than frustrate, people's basic needs.

In *The Story of Avis* (1877), W. tackled an imaginative reworking of her mother's life and fiction as well as of her own life. It is her most interesting work and contains her favorite heroine. W. shows that marriage has a devastating effect on a woman's artistic potential: Avis is expected to be dedicated only to her husband and children. *The Story of Avis* was praised by such literati as James T. Fields, Henry Wadsworth Longfellow, and John Greenleaf Whittier. But it aroused indignation in others. In 1879 and 1881, W.'s father opposed her support for women by publishing two essays decrying woman suffrage. They were later collected in *My Portfolio* (1882).

Two humorous books draw on W.'s experience as owner of a summer seaside cottage in Gloucester. *An Old Maid's Paradise* (1879), a series of sketches, shows women enjoying typically masculine pleasures, unhampered by male protection. *Burglars in Paradise* (1886), a spoof of detective fiction, reveals men's protection of women to be a mere charade and suggests that the most insidious burglar of all is the suitor.

W.'s only male protagonists appear in works written during her courtship and marriage. After her father's death in 1890, W. memorialized him in *Austin Phelps: A Memoir* (1891), then based her favorite hero, Emanuel Baynard of *A Singular Life* (1895), on her father's youthful ideals.

W. also supported antivivisection legislation, a cause that two novels connect with social wrongs against women: the vivisectors are men experimenting callously on dogs and women alike in *Trixy* (1904) and *Though Life Us Do Part* (1908).

W.'s autobiography, *Chapters from a Life* (1896), is as tantalizing for what it omits as it is useful for its revelations. In addition to some twenty-five novels, she wrote poetry and short stories for the leading magazines of her day. The poetry is mediocre, but some of the stories are outstanding. They are collected in five volumes.

Although W.'s work frequently lacks aesthetic merit, its importance lies in her ability to translate the psychological and sociological realities of her own life into literary figures. She was pulled in opposite directions by a woman's movement urging the self-fulfillment for which her mother yearned and a conservative Calvinist tradition adovacting the "feudal views" of women her father held.

WORKS: *Mercy Gliddon's Work* (1865). *Up Hill; or, Life in the Factory* (1865). Gypsy series (1866–67). *The Gates Ajar* (1868). *Men, Women and Ghosts* (1869). *Hedged In* (1870). *The Trotty Book* (1870). *The Silent Partner* (1871). *Trotty's Wedding Tour and Story-book* (1873). *What to Wear?* (1873). *Poetic Studies* (1875). *The Story of Avis* (1877). *My Cousin and I* (1879). *An Old Maid's Paradise* (1879). *Sealed Orders* (1879). *Friends: A Duet* (1881). *Doctor Zay* (1882). *Beyond the Gates* (1883). *Songs of the Silent World, and Other Poems* (1885). *Burglars in Paradise* (1886). *The Gates Between* (1887). *The Struggle for Immortality* (1889). *Austin Phelps: A Memoir* (1891). *Fourteen to One* (1891). *Donald Marcy* (1893). *A Singular Life* (1895). *Chapters from a Life* (1896). *The Story of Jesus Christ: An Interpretation* (1897). *The Successors of Mary the First* (1901). *Within the Gates* (1901). *Avery* (1902). *Confessions of a Wife* (1902). *Trixy* (1904). *The Man in the Case* (1906). *Walled In: A Novel* (1907). *Though Life Us Do Part* (1908). *The Oath of Allegiance, and Other Stories* (1909). *A Chariot of Fire* (1910). *The Empty House, and Other Stories* (1910). *Comrades* (1911).

BIBLIOGRAPHY: Bennett, M. A., *Elizabeth Stuart Phelps* (1939). Coultrap-McQuin, S. M., "Elizabeth Stuart Phelps: The Cultural Context of a Nineteenth-Century Professional Writer" (Ph.D. diss., Univ. of Iowa, 1979). Douglas, A., *The Feminization of American Culture* (1976). Hart, J. D., *The Popular Book* (1950). Kelly, L. D., "'Oh the Poor Women'—A Study of the Works of Elizabeth Stuart Phelps" (Ph.D. diss., Univ. of North Carolina, 1979). Kessler, C. F., *Elizabeth Stuart Phelps* (1982). Phelps, A., *My Portfolio* (1882). Smith, H. S., ed., *The Gates Ajar* by E. S. P. Ward (1964). Stewart, G. B., *A New Mythos* (1979). Welter, B., *Dimity Convictions: The American Woman in the Nineteenth Century* (1976).

For article in reference works, see: *AW. DAB*, X, 1. *NAW* (article by B. K. Hofstadter).

Other references: *AQ* 29 (1977). *Frontiers: A Journal of Women Studies* 5 (Fall 1980). *MR* 13 (1972). *PMLA* 91 (1976). *Regionalism and the Female Imagination* 3 (Fall 1977). *Women's Studies* 6 (1978).

CAROL FARLEY KESSLER

Susan Bogert Warner

B. 11 July 1819, New York City; d. 17 March 1885, Highland Falls, New York
Wrote under: Susan B. Warner, Elizabeth Wetherall
D. of Henry Whiting and Anna Bartlett Warner

W.'s family was prosperous during her childhood, but the depression of 1837 saw the collapse of their fortunes. Thereafter, W. and her sister Anna were responsible for the support of themselves, their father (their mother had died young), and a paternal aunt. Their father had purchased Constitution Island, in the Hudson River opposite West Point, as a summer retreat, but the family was forced to make it their permanent home. The sisters cooked, gardened, chopped wood, and fished.

At her aunt's suggestion, and because of a great need for money, W. wrote *The Wide, Wide World* (1850), which went through many editions in many languages. She and her sister were among the century's most prolific writers, but their earnings were small, partly due to literary piracy.

A sensitive, rather morbid personality distinguished W. from her younger sister socially, but hers was the greater talent. Although poverty and hard work narrowed her world, she managed to travel some, meeting Emerson and other New England literary figures in Boston. She spent almost every winter in New York, where she knew such writers as Alice and Phoebe Cary.

The Wide, Wide World, which had been rejected by several publishers, was a literary phenomenon. Its basic appeal is to girls and women. After her mother dies, Ellen Montgomery must live with other relatives —first an old-maid aunt who runs her own farm and then a worldly Scottish family who claim her for a time. Ellen finds that they try her Christian patience—and they disapprove of her priggish ways. No matter what the issue, Ellen expresses herself by bursting into tears. (Biographers say that W. was apt to cry frequently herself.) However sentimental this novel appears today, W.'s ability to tell a story and to involve the reader in the lives of her characters is superior.

W.'s second novel, *Queechy* (1852), almost as popular as her first, tells how, after the death of her grandfather and the business failure of her uncle, young Fleda Ringgan helps support her family by selling flowers and garden produce. Throughout the novels of both sisers, young women in financial difficulties are commonplace; they are often furnished with a father, uncle,or guardian who cannot function once his money is gone. The autobiographical element is obvious. While the sisters preserved a pious respect for their father (who lived unttil 1875), their books reveal their annoyance with such helpless characters. In *Queechy* even the resourceful heroine feels faint if she must answer the door or eat with the hired girl, but the late novel *Nobody* (1882) shows a family of sisters who do their own work and thrive on it. Presumably, as the years passed, W. became more accustomed to her status in life.

By herself and in collaboration with Anna, she wrote many children's books. Most of them are highly didactic and were popular in the Sunday-school libraries of the time. Although both sisters were evangelical Presbyterians—they disapproved of the theater, but not of *all* novels—W.'s books are centered on accepting and serving Christ, with little interest in doctrinal or controversial themes.

Most of her adult novels are what she called "true stories" (she didn't like the word "novel"). The books usually have a good Christian heroine (or hero) who overcomes poverty and becomes successful. Meals of bread and molasses are to be found in these books, but generous meals are much more common.

In *Diana* (1877), W. attributes her fascination with writing about food to her intimate knowledge of is preparation. "Sympathy and affection and tender ministry are wrought into the very pie crust, and glow in the brown loaves as they come out of the oven; and are specially seen in the shortcake for tea and the favourite dish at dinner and the unexpected dumpling." W. had a gift for describing the material things of life; a reading of her novels will give the modern reader a close look into 19th-c. American kitchen cupboards, desk drawers, and clothes closets.

Interest today in W.'s books is mainly historical. She is one of the best of the "damned mob of scribbling women" of her time, however, and deserves serious consideration from literary scholars.

WORKS: (The following is a list of Susan Bogert Warner's more important works. A complete bibliography is included in *They Wrote for a Living,* compiled by D. H. Sanderson, 1976). *The Wide, Wide World* (1850). *Queechy* (1852). *The Law and the Testimony* (1853). *The Hills of the Shatemuc* (1856). *The Old Helmet* (1863). *Melbourne House* (1864). *Daisy* (1868). *Walks from Eden* (1870). *The House in Town* (1872). *A Story of Small Beginnings* (1872). *Willow Brook* (1874). Say and Do Series (1875). *Bread and Oranges* (1877). *Diana* (1877). *Pine Needles* (1877). *The Broken Wall of Jerusalem and the Rebuilding of Them* (1878). *The Flag of Truce* (1878). *The Kingdom of Judah* (1878). *My Desire* (1879). *The End of the Coil* (1880). *Nobody* (1882). *The Letter of Credit* (1882). *Stephen, M.D.* (1883). *A Red Wallflower* (1884). *Daisy Plains* (1885).

BIBLIOGRAPHY: Sanderson, D. H., *They Wrote for a Living* (1976). Stokes, O. E., *Letters and Memoirs of Susan and Anna Bartlett Warner* (1925). Warner, Anna, *Susan Warner* (1909).
Other references: *N. Y. History* 40 (April 1959).

BEVERLY SEATON

Mercy Otis Warren

B. 25 Sept. 1728, Barnstable, Massachusetts; d. 19 Oct. 1814, Plymouth, Massachusetts
D. of James and Mary Allyne Otis; m. James Warren, 1754

W. was the third of thirteen children. Her father, a staunch Whig, was a district judge whose life revolved around politics. Although women were customarily denied formal education, her father permitted W., his eldest daughter, to be tutored with her brothers by their paternal uncle, Rev. Jonathan Russell. Russell encouraged her to take lessons in all fields except Greek and Latin, so her elder brother James, an exceptionally brilliant young man, instructed her in these languages. Theirs was an unusually close relationship. He introduced her to Locke's *Essay on Government*, which became the foundation of the political theory they shared. Her writing shows the influence of Raleigh, Pope, Dryden, Milton, Shakespeare, and Molière, but she learned the art of writing from her study of her uncle's sermons.

W.'s husband, like her brother James, was a Harvard graduate. In this cultured and politically astute man she found a husband she loved and respected, who returned her feelings, and they enjoyed a long and happy life together. She bore five sons to him between 1757 and 1766, all of whom survived to adulthood. Warren took much pride in his wife's intelligence and literary talents. He not only brought stimulating guests like John and Samuel Adams regularly into their home but he himself gave her companionship and stability.

During the early years of marriage, W. served her literary apprenticeship, writing verse on every subject considered proper for poetry. She also wrote many letters. Perhaps her favorite correspondent was Abigail Adams, but she exchanged letters with many distinguished people on both sides of the Atlantic.

During the 1770s, W. became active in politics, along with her husband, father, and brother. "Be it known unto Britain even American daughters are politicians and patriots," she wrote. She began writing political satires in the form of plays. None of them has plot or women characters. They are not stage-worthy pieces, but they were not intended to be. They accomplished their task, firing their readers' imaginations and urging them to turn the depicted events into reality and punish the easily recognized villains.

The Adulateur (1772), published anonymously in two installments in the *Massachusetts Spy*, presents "Rapatio, the Bashaw [ruler] of Servia whose principal mission in life is to crush the ardent love of liberty in Servia's freeborn sons," who clearly is the colony's Governor Thomas Hutchinson. The classical names of her characters do not obscure their identities: for example, Brutus is James Otis, Jr., champion of the patriots. The "play" was so well received that the names W. had given the characters were widely and gleefully used in the community.

Her second play, *The Defeat* (1773), published by the *Boston Gazette*, continued Rapatio (Hutchinson) as arch villain. It pictures Rapatio planning to charge the improvements he has made on his house to the public taxes. Together with his self-incriminating letters then being circulated among the patriots, it brought about Hutchinson's disgrace and recall.

The Group (1775), the most popular of W.'s political satires, appeared in pamphlet form only two weeks before the clash of "Minutemen" and British soldiers at Lexington. John Adams himself arranged its printing and, years later, personally verified that W. was its author. Almost pure propaganda, the play has only villains, the Tory leaders who are the group of the play's title. Chief is Brigadier Hate-All, really the American-born Tory Timothy Ruggles, a longtime enemy of the Otis family. Other characters include Hum Humbug, Esq.; Crusty Crowbar, Esq.; Dupe; and Scrblerius Fribble.

After the collapse of the Confederation, W. wrote *Observations on the New Constitution, and on the Federal Conventions* (1788), under the pen name "A Columbian Patriot," opposing the Constitution as it was originally proposed. She was an anti-Federalist who believed, as she said, in "a union of the states on the free principles of the late Confederation." The pen name caused some confusion, and the author's identity was in dispute until 1930.

History of the Rise, Progress, and Termination of the American Revolution, Interspersed with Biographical and Moral Observations (1805) was published in three volumes nearly seventeen years after W. finished it. By that time, other histories of the Revolution had appeared. However, hers is the only contemporary history told from a Republican point of view. Much of its value lies in the fact that more than ten percent of the work is devoted to character analyses of the people she knew. John Adams broke off their long friendship over her analysis of him, but a number of years later a mutual friend brought them together again. Her history did not enjoy the success she had expected or that it deserved; yet it has endured, and her reputation survives principally upon its merits.

W. was given a chance—rare for a woman—to use her talents, and she made the most of them. Although she was much respected in her own time, her reputation has dimmed somewhat, perhaps because so much of her writing was published in pamphlets and newspapers, perhaps because so much of it is topical, and perhaps because so much of it reflects the classical pretensions of the time. Her history of the Revolution, however, is viewed by modern scholars as having enduring value, as being, according to M. Curti, "a realistic history of the struggle for independence."

WORKS: *The Adulateur: A Tragedy* (1772). *The Defeat: A Play* (1773). *The Group: A Farce* (1775). *Observations on the New Constitution, and on the Federal Conventions* (1788). *Poems, Dramatic, and Miscellaneous* (1790). *History of the Rise, Progress, and Termination of the American Revolution, Interspersed with Biographical and Moral Observations* (3 vols., 1805).

BIBLIOGRAPHY: Anthony, K., *First Lady of the Revolution: The Life of Mercy Otis Warren* (1958). Brown, A., *Mercy Warren* (1896). Fritz, J., *Cast for a Revolution: Some Friends and Enemies 1728–1814* (1972). Smith, W., *History as Argument: Three Patriot Historians of the American Revolution* (1966).

Other references: *New England Magazine* (April 1903). PMHS 64 (March 1931). WMQ (July 1953).

BILLIE W. ETHERIDGE

Jean Webster

B. 24 July 1876, Fredonia, New York; d. 11 June 1916, New York City
Given name: Alice Jane Chandler Webster
D. of Charles Luther and Annie Moffett Webster; m. Glenn Ford McKinney,
1915

W. was a grandniece of Mark Twain; her father was Twain's partner in has ill-fated publishing ventures. She attended the Lady Jane Grey School in Binghamton, New York, and was graduated from Vassar College in 1901. She was a frequent contributor to college publications and literary editor of the yearbook. W.'s friend and roomate at Vassar, Adelaide Crapsey, was probably the inspiration for Patty in her books *When Patty Went to College* (1903) and *Just Patty* (1911). W. became a freelance writer, lived in Greenwich Village, and traveled extensively, touring the world in 1906–07. After her marriage in 1915 to a lawyer, she and her husband lived in New York City and the Berkshires. She died a day after the birth of her only child, a daughter.

When Patty Went to College collects sketches W. began writing while still at Vassar. It depicts the escapades of Patty Wyatt and Priscilla Pond, seniors in a turn-of-the-century women's college where the students surreptitiously brew afternoon tea and evening cocoa on alcohol stoves in their rooms, receive gentleman callers in the parlor after a maid has carried up cards, dine in evening dress, evade obligatory chapel, and study Greek and ethics. A sequel, *Just Patty*, concerns the innocent adventures of Patty and Priscilla as seniors at a high-church boarding school.

The epistolary novel *Daddy-Long-Legs* (1912) presents a modern Cinderella, Jerusha Abbot ("Judy"), who leaves her life-long home in a depressing orphanage to attend a women's college. She must report her progress to her nameless benefactor, whom she christens "Daddy-long-legs" and whom she marries four years later. W.'s dramatization became highly successful on Broadway, starring Ruth Chatterton, and has since appeared in several film versions, including a silent version with Mary Pickford. A 1915 reviewer criticized the drama on the ground that "the chief object of the play" was to provide "sentimentalism sentimentally interpreted, turnip smothered in sugar offered as an apple of life." The novel, however, largely avoids sentimentalism, and the brisk irreverence and piquancy of its humor have made it a perennial favorite with both adults and children.

Dear Enemy (1914), an epistolary sequel to *Daddy-Long-Legs*, follows Judy's college friend Sallie McBride as she arrives to reform the old-fashioned orphanage from which Judy had escaped and stays to fall in love with its dour Scotch doctor. Once again, a potentially sentimental story is saved from stickiness by the practical point of view and the lively prose of its narrator.

Both *Daddy-Long-Legs* and *Dear Enemy* have remained constantly in print for almost seventy years. Their strong stories and charming characters, together with W.'s real interest in reforms in the care of dependent children, will secure them an audience for many years to come.

WORKS: *When Patty Went to College* (1903). *The Wheat Princess* (1905). *Jerry, Junior* (1907). *The Four Pools Mystery* (1908). *Much Ado about Peter* (1909). *Just Patty* (1911). *Daddy-Long-Legs* (1912; dramatization by Webster, 1914). *Asa* (1914). *Dear Enemy* (1914).

The papers of Jean Webster are collected in the Lockwood Library of Vassar College. An authorized biography is being written by Alan Simpson and Mary McQueen Simpson.

BIBLIOGRAPHY: For articles in reference works, see: *Junior Book of Authors*, Eds. S. J. Kunitz and H. Haycraft (1951). *NAW* (article by R. Salisbury, 1971). *20thCA*.

Other references: *NewR* (13 March 1915). *NYT* (9 Nov. 1914; 13 Dec. 1914; 12 June 1916). *Vassar Quarterly* (Nov. 1916).

SUSAN SUTTON SMITH

Carolyn Wells

B. *18 June 1869, Rahway, New Jersey; d. 26 March 1942, New York City*
Wrote under: Carolyn Wells, Rowland Wright
D. *of William E. and Anna Wells; m. Hadwin Houghton, 1918*

A precocious child, W. hated formal schooling and refused to attend college. Scarlet fever, suffered at the age of six, caused her to become hard of hearing. Reared in New Jersey, she made her home in New York City after her marriage. She loved puzzles, bridge, chess, charades, and detective stories (her discovery of a mystery by Anna Katharine Green was pivotal, inspiring her both to read voraciously and to write voluminously in that genre). Her literary career began almost by accident, with the contribution of jingles to humorous periodicals. She considered 1902 an important date in her career: by then she had written eight books and had begun composing juveniles; after that date she consistently published at least three or four books annually. From 1909 on she wrote mysteries, and she claimed in an autobiographical work (*The Rest of My Life*, 1937) to have written 170 books, including seventy detective stories—"so far." Her other main literary activity was as an anthologist, but she was also an important collector and bibliographer of the works of Walt Whitman. Her parody of Sinclair Lewis' *Main Street* (*Ptomaine Street*, 1921), in which Carol Kennicott becomes Warble Petticoat, is funny and full of witty puns. Sometimes it misses its mark because both locale and social class are changed, but it wickedly refashions a number of episodes from the original.

W.'s juveniles are intended for young girls; different series are aimed at different age groups. Marjorie is in her early teens, for example, and is presented as a child, sometimes mischievous though generally a model little girl (in *Marjorie's Vacation*, 1907, and five other novels through 1912). Patty, on the other hand, is in her later teens, and the final books in her series lead to her marriage (in *Patty Fairfield*, 1901, and sixteen other novels through 1919). In the middle are "two little women", who are fifteen when their series begins (see *Two Little Women*, 1915, and two other novels through 1917). All these novels are seriously dated by their intense concern for the social conventions of the early 20th c. For example, Patty's main problems and decisions grow from situations in which she has (either apparently or actually) been led to behave in an unconventional manner (such as going out without a chaperone).

Although also clearly limited by its time and place, W.'s detective fiction holds up somewhat better. She claimed the title of "Dean of American Mystery Writers" and was widely considered an authority. *The Technique of the Mystery Story* (1913; rev. ed. 1929), heavily larded with quotations of both primary and secondary materials, is a thorough survey of the field, written for aspiring authors. Unfortunately, W.'s own style is undistinguished; dialogue and dialect are often clumsily handled. Characterization is flat, characters often being hard to distinguish from each other. Her women are often irritatingly coy, shallowly coquettish ingenues—whom the reader is clearly expected to find charming—and she made it a rule that a woman could never be the murderer (though women were sometimes the victims in her stories). Although male figures are more varied, heroes and detectives are consistently well educated and wealthy. Plotting, however, is inventive, and W. made interesting use of such conventional types as the "locked room" mystery.

W. created a number of detectives, the best known and most frequently used (in sixty-one novels) being Fleming Stone, a professional detective who is a cultivated gentleman, moving easily in the elevated social circles in which W.'s mysteries occur. He was her first creation (*The Clue*, 1909), and she continued to use him until the end of her career (*Who Killed Caldwell?*, 1942). Similar to Stone in characterization and methods of detection is Kenneth Carlisle, but he is distinguished by being a former screen star and matinee idol (in *Sleeping Dogs*, 1929, and two other novels). More interesting is the team of Pennington ("Penny") Wise and Zizi (in *The Man Who Fell Through the Earth*, 1919, and five other novels). His approach to detection is rational while hers is intuitive; both are fallible, although Zizi is more often right. She is presented as a mysterious young sprite of a girl who seems to have no background or past. W.'s other detectives are Lorimer Lane (in *More Lives Than One*, 1923, and another novel) and Alan Ford (in *Faulkner's Folly*, 1917, and two other novels). W.'s sleuths often work wonders of detection, but they occasionally err and thus illustrate her distaste, often expressed, for the "omniscient detective."

Once well known and highly respected, W.'s works now languish unread. She was too prolific, wrote too easily and rapidly, reflected her age too uncritically, and restricted herself too narrowly to popular genres and formulas. Her importance thus is largely historical, and is most clearly found in her practice of the detective novel.

SELECTED WORKS: *At the Sign of the Sphinx* (1896). *The Jingle Book* (1899). *Patty Fairfield* (1901). *A Nonsense Anthology* (edited by Wells, 1902). *A Parody Anthology* (editied by Wells, 1904). *The Rubaiyat of a Motor Car* (1906). *A Whimsey Anthology* (edited by Wells, 1906). *Fluffy Ruffles* (1907). *Marjorie's Vacation* (1907). *The Clue* (1909). *A Chain of Evidence* (1912). *The Techniques of the Mystery Story* (1913; rev. ed., 1929). *Two Little Women* (1915). *Faulkner's Folly* (1917). *Vicky Van* (1918). *The Man Who Fell through the Earth* (1919). *The Book of Humorous Verse* (edited by Wells, 1920). *Ptomaine Street: The Tale of Warble Petticoat* (1921). *More Lives than One* (1923). *The Fleming Stone Omnibus* (1932). *The Rest of My Life* (1937). *Murder Will In* (1942). *Who Killed Caldwell?* (1942).

BIBLIOGRAPHY: For articles in reference works, see: *Encyclopedia of Mystery and Detection*, Eds. C. Steinbrunner and O. Penzler (1976). *NCAB*, 13. Other references: *NYT* (27 March 1942). *NYTBR* (4 Dec. 1937).

MARY JEAN DeMARR

Emmeline Blanche Woodward Wells

B. 29 Feb. 1828, Petersham, Massachusetts; d. 25 April 1921, Salt Lake City, Utah
Wrote under: Amethyst, "Aunt Em," Blanche Beechwood, E.B.W., Emmeline B. Wells
D. of David and Deiadama Hare Woodward; m. James Harvey Harris, 1843; m. Newell K. Whitney, 1845; m. Daniel H. Wells, 1852

W. converted to Mormonism when she was fourteen, married James Harris at fifteen, and moved the following year to Nauvoo, Illinois, then the Mormon headquarters. Deserted by Harris, W. married Whitney and joined the exodus of Mormons to Salt Lake City. After Whitney's death in 1850 she married Wells. Five daughters were born of W.'s last two marriages.

An ardent suffragist and women's rights advocate, W. was a member of numerous national and state woman-suffrage and other (especially literary) organizations. As president of the Utah Woman's Suffrage Association, she successfully lobbied for the inclusion of woman suffrage in Utah's constitution in 1895. In 1910, at age eighty-two, W. was appointed general president of the Mormon woman's Relief Society, serving until three weeks before her death in 1921. The *Woman's Exponent*, a Mormon woman's journal that W. edited from 1877 to 1914, gave her an influential voice in women's affairs. She used its editorial page to promote equal rights for women, and also to defend the Mormon practice of plural marriage.

W.'s only collection of poetry, *Musings and Memories*, (1896), is aptly named. The poems are reflective and personal, most of them a sentimental backward look at a past both pleasant and painful. "A Glance Backward" illustrates the portentous mood pervading much of her retrospective verse. The festive celebration in honor of two young lovers who "plighted their troth" is underscored by ominous intimations. Shadows of a fire creep "like spectres," trees stand "phantom-like," and laughter echoes "in a hollow sound." The lovers are doomed, yet choose to shun the "potent sway of dread" and exchange their vows in "fond expectancy." W. subtly sustains the fateful mood, which she delicately balances on a thin narrative thread that gives the piece its unity.

As a poet, W. fits comfortably under Hawthorne's rubric of "scribbling women." While much of her poetry has definite merit, it occasionally demonstrates the stilted manner and excessive sentiment typical of the period. Poetry, she said, was "a history of the heart." She wrote for a receptive local audience appreciative of her style; a second edition of her poems was published in 1915. W. did not use poetry as a medium for polemics, reserving her feminist arguments for the editorial page. She left a collection of diaries spanning nearly half a century. A prominent figure in the Mormon female hierarchy, she wrote perceptively and intelligently, if not always disinterestedly, of events in Mormon history, especially during the critical period of 1876 to 1896. She is often frustratingly elusive in her references to personal affairs but remarkably informative in her observations of the effect on women of a changing Mormon society.

It is as a journalist that W. is most noted. The majority of her editorials for the *Woman's Exponent* responded to the "woman question" of her century, her rhetoric often echoing the polemics of other feminists. In them she exercised both logic and analysis, sometimes interlacing her premises with poetic imagery. Other editorials dealt with local issues, particularly those centering on the religious and political tensions polarizing Utah and the rest of the nation. Writing initially as a contributor to the *Exponent* under the name of Blanche Beechwood, W. dropped the pseudonym soon after becoming editor. She created another literary identity, however, "Aunt Em," who wrote eighty-seven articles and stories incorporating traditional Victorian values and sentiments. W., the editor, and "Aunt Em," the contributor, symbolize the different views of woman battling for women's allegiance and formed the double dimension of W.'s literary personality.

W. was a woman of her time, her literary products felicitously harmonizing with its concerns and values. While her poetry was addressed to another audience, her editorials are relevant to the contemporary woman's movement. One of the most influential of 19th-c. Mormon women, W. made a literary impact both substantial and effective.

WORKS: *Memorial of the Mormon Women of Utah to the President and Congress of the United States, April 6, 1886* (1886). *Charities and Philanthropies: Women's Work in Utah* (1893). *Songs and Flowers of the Wasatch* (edited by Wells, 1893). *Musing and Memories* (1896).

BIBLIOGRAPHY: Anderson, R., "Emmeline B. Wells: Her Life and Thought" (M.A. thesis, Utah State Univ., 1975). Burgess-Olson, V., *Sister*

Saints (1978). Crocheron, A. J., *Representative Women of Deseret* (1884). Gates, S. Y., *History of the Young Ladies Mutual Improvement Association, 1869–1910* (1911). Madsen, C. C., " 'Remember the Women of Zion': A Study of the Editorial Content of the *Woman's Exponent,* a Mormon Woman's Journal" (M.A. thesis, Univ. of Utah, 1977). Whitney, O.F., *History of Utah,* vol. 4 (1904).

For articles in reference works, see: *Latter-day Saint Biographical Encyclopedia.* Ed. A. Jenson (1914). *NAW* (article by M. DePillis).

Other references: *Improvement Era* (June 1921). *NYT* (27 April 1921). *Relief Society Magazine* (Feb. 1915; Feb. 1916). *Sunset* (May 1916). *Utah Historical Quarterly* (Fall 1974). *Young Woman's Journal* (April 1908).

CAROL CORNWALL MADSEN

Eudora Welty

B. 13 April 1909, Jackson, Mississippi
D. of Mary Chestina Andrews and Christian Webb Welty

Although she is thoroughly southern, W.'s family came from Ohio (her father's home) and West Virginia (her mother's home, which figures prominently in *The Optimist's Daughter*). W.'s childhood in Jackson was in a household of readers and in a town not yet industrialized, where schools and parks and grocery stores were all within walking distance of her home. W. attended Mississippi State College for Women from 1925 to 1927, received her B.A. in 1929 from the University of Wisconsin, and spent 1930 to 1931 at Columbia University, studying advertising. With jobs scarce in Depression days, and with her father's death in 1931, W. returned to Jackson where she has continued to live. Various jobs with local newspapers, Jackson radio station WJDX, and the Works Progress Authority (WPA) occupied her in the mid 1930s; but all the while she was writing, and her first story, "Death of a Traveling Salesman," appeared in *Manuscript* (May–June 1936).

W. possesses the coveted honors America awards its writers: the National Medal for Literature, the American Academy of Arts and Letters Howells Medal, the National Institute of Arts and Letters Gold Medal for the Novel, the Presidential Medal of Freedom, and numerous honorary degrees.

Predictably, it was not easy to convince an editor to publish a collection of W.'s short stories before a novel appeared, but Doubleday, Doran did bring out *A Curtain of Green, and Other Stories* in 1941. The volume, distinguished in having an introduction by Katherine Anne Porter, brought W. critical acclaim, and readers still find that it contains many favorite stories—"Petrified Man," "Why I Live at the P.O.," "Keela, the Outcast Indian Maiden." These stories establish W.'s voice in portraying lower-middle-class characters with convincing dialogue, in her lyrical descriptive power, and in her sense of place.

Reviewers generally were puzzled by *The Wide Net, and Other Stories* (1943), finding the stories (except "Livvie") radically different and less accessible than those in the first collection. "First Love," "A Still Moment," and "The Wide Net" show W.'s ability to use historical background, explore the mystery of human relationships, and incorporate levels of myth.

W.'s third collection, *The Golden Apples* (1949), presents seven interrelated stories based on three generations of families in Morgana, Mississippi, whose lives intertwine publicly and privately. It is a work that draws heavily on myth to give added dimension to the lives and deeds of characters whose daily activities are of great interest. The MacLain, Morrison, Stark, Rainey, and Carmichael families undergo the many experiences of life and the reader is drawn into the generations of this fictional world.

The Collected Stories of Eudora Welty (1980), containing work published from 1936 to 1966, confirms that W. is among the great practitioners of the short story. It includes stories from the four earlier collections and two previously uncollected stories, excluding only five published stories. By the inclusion of *The Golden Apples*, her own favorite, W. denies that this volume should be classified as a novel, as many critics have argued. Anne Tyler has noted that the early stories are left unrevised, although W. has privately made changes by hand on her own printed copies. Recently, W. has commented on her first published story, "Death of a Traveling Salesman." She sees some weaknesses in it, but declares her respect for it because it still presents a challenge to writer and reader.

W.'s first novel, *The Robber Bridegroom* (1942), is a short work that integrates stories of the Old Natchez Trace and remnants of Grimms' fairy tales and American frontier humor to relate the story of Clement Musgrove, his fair daughter Rosamond, and Jamie Lockhart, her "robber bridegroom." As W. has pointed out, this work is not a *historical* historical novel and many critics see it as "an examination of the theme of disenchantment in the pursuit of a pastoral, and fundamentally American,

Eden." *Delta Wedding* (1946), W.'s first full-length novel, had its origin in a short story, "The Delta Cousins." The novel is set in 1923, a year chosen for its relative calm so that domestic concerns in the Fairchild household might take precedence over outside involvements in a narrative that presents a southern demiparadise on the verge of social change. W.'s comic masterpiece, *The Ponder Heart* (1954), has enjoyed success as a short novel and as a Broadway play (adapted by Joseph Fields and Jerome Chodorov) in which the antics of Uncle Daniel and Bonnie Dee Peacock, Miss Teacake Magee, Mr. Truex Bodkin, the Peacock clan, and the populace of Clay, Mississippi, combine with the firm narrative voice of Edna Earle Ponder to form a work of boundless humor.

Two more novels appeared much later. After a virtual silence of fifteen years, W. published *Losing Battles* in 1970. A work of brilliant parts, *Losing Battles* is a long novel and has not pleased all readers; its diffusion and loose structure, however, are for many compensated by its comic richness —its eccentric characters, amusing situations, and details of places, names, and objects. Telescoped into a day and a half, the novel presents the community of Banner, Mississippi, during the Depression, with kin and neighboring connections joined by choice or chance at the Beecham family reunion. It is an expression of W.'s persistent emphasis on the mystery surrounding human relationships and on the redeeming power of love.

For *The Optimist's Daughter* (1972) W. won the Pulitzer Prize, an award many thought she should have received already. This novel presents both lower-middle-class characters and the upper-middle-class citizens of Mount Salus, Mississippi. The second marriage of Judge Clinton McKelva to Wanda Fay Chisom evokes consternation in the town gossips, forces the Judge's daughter Laurel McKelva Hand to reassess her life, and in the end leaves her able to give up the ties of the past and to live in the present.

The spirit of celebration, of lived life, is of singular importance in much of W.'s fiction. While there are always serious matters at the heart of her fiction, it is also true that the comic spirit is a significant force, not merely entertaining but also conveying thoughtful commentary. Standard comic devices are found: disingenuous characters (Leota in "Petrified Man"), eccentric characters (Aunt Cleo in *Losing Battles*), and homely figures of speech. In "Why I Live at the P.O.," Sister valiantly cooks away, trying "to stretch two chickens over five people and a completely unexpected child into the bargain without one moment's notice." Comedy of situation, comic one-liners, and ironic juxtapositions—used by W. in a variety of stories—confirm the presence of the comic spirit at the base of W.'s fiction. She writes, in the essay "The Radiance of Jane Austen," that comedy "is social and positive, and exacting. Its methods, its boundaries, its *point*, all belong to the familiar." For W., the comic spirit is true and natural.

The recent publication of *The Collected Stories* has given critics the opportunity to reassess three decades of W.'s work. Reviewers were particularly impressed with the range of W.'s work. Indeed, Walter Clemons found her "an experimental writer with access to the demonic. . . . She is bigger and stranger than we have supposed." If some of W.'s prose has occasionally been described as deformed, if she has sometimes been charged with presenting an imprecise landscape and using vague language, most of her fiction challenges our reading power, speaks to our hearts, and convinces us that her world of fiction embodies the best and truest of human experience.

WORKS: *A Curtain of Green, and Other Stories* (1941). *The Robber Bridegroom* (1942). *The Wide Net, and Other Stories* (1943). *Delta Wedding* (1946). *The Golden Apples* (1949). *The Ponder Heart* (1954). *The Bride of Innisfallen* (1955). *The Shoe Bird* (1964). *Losing Battles* (1970). *One Time, One Place: Mississippi in the Depression. A Snapshot Album* (1971). *The Optimist's Daughter* (1972). *The Eye of the Story* (1978). *The Collected Stories of Eudora Welty* (1980).

The manuscripts and papers of Eudora Welty are in the Department of Archives and History, Jackson, Mississippi, and at the University of Texas at Austin.

BIBLIOGRAPHY: Appel, A., Jr., *Eudora Welty* (1965). Bryant, J. A., Jr., *Eudora Welty* (1968). Desmond, J. F., ed., *A Still Moment: Essays on the Art of Eudora Welty* (1978). Dollarhide, L., and A. Abadie, eds., *Eudora Welty: A Form of Thanks* (1979). Howard, Z., *The Rhetoric of Eudora Welty's Short Stories* (1973). Isaacs, N., *Eudora Welty* (1968). Kreyling, M., *The Achievement of Eudora Welty* (1980). Manz-Kunz, M., *Eudora Welty: Aspects of Reality in Her Short Fiction* (1971). Prenshaw, P., ed., *Eudora Welty: Critical Essays* (1979). Vande Kieft, R., *Eudora Welty* (1962).

Other references: *Delta Review* (Nov. 1977). *Eudora Welty Newsletter* (Toledo, Ohio). *Mississippi Quarterly* 26 (1973). *Shenandoah* 20 (1969).

ELIZABETH EVANS

Jessamyn West

B. *18 July 1902, near Butlerville, Indiana*
D. *of Eldo Roy and Grace Anna Milhous West; m. Harry Maxwell McPherson,*
1923

The eldest of four children, W. was reared in Yorba Linda, California. She began writing—novels, short stories, essays, autobiography, articles, reviews—after a severe case of tuberculosis halted her formal education while she was in graduate school. W. is married, and she has adopted an Irish girl.

The female maturation process is a frequent pattern in W.'s fiction, which treats girls' social, emotional, and familial joys and difficulties evenhandedly and well. A central problem for the young protagonists is often the mother-daughter relationship: mothers, uneasy with their own rigidly controlled sensuality, teach their daughters to fear sexuality; furthermore, they often insist that the elder daughters help to curb sexual impulses in their younger sisters.

In *The Witch Diggers* (1951) and *South of the Angels* (1960), the maturation stories are embedded in a cluster of subplots. Here, the healthy acceptance of sexuality is the symbol of genuine maturity and the ability to love. The locales, eras, and atmospheres of both books are beautifully wrought. Despite some problems with structure, these novels succeed through the power of the maturation device, and the portraits of the sisters Cate and Em Conboy in the first are splendid.

Leafy Rivers (1967) and *The Massacre at Fall Creek* (1975), both set on the Indiana frontier, provide variations of the female maturation pattern. In W.'s most traditional maturation novel, Leafy comes to terms with her flawed marriage by undergoing the usual *Bildungsroman* journey, presented in flashbacks. The story of the first whites to be executed for murdering Indians is the subject of *The Massacre at Fall Creek*, told largely through the perceptions of Hannah Cape, who learns to accept her own limitations as well as those of her lover. Clearly, this novel compares Hannah's maturation with the coming of age of the frontier; the device is compelling and works well. These books present large casts of characters portrayed with W.'s usual sound insight.

One of W.'s most successful forms is the collection of a series of inter-related short stories into books having the impact of novels. *Cress Dela-hanty* (1953), set in the California of W.'s youth, is the sunniest of the female maturation pieces, the portrait of a gifted girl who learns to value herself and her abilities. *The Friendly Persuasio*n (1945) and *Except for Me and Thee* (1969) draw upon the Quaker family background and Indiana locale of W.'s mother's memories, which provided W. with "the look of the land, the temper of the people, the manner of speech." Probably the best known of her books, these "Quaker stories," depicting the deepening relationship and developing family of Jess and Eliza Birdwell, avoid sentimentality through splendid use of humor. *The Friendly Persuasion* was made into a successful movie in 1956; *To See the Dream* (1957) is W.'s account of her work on the film.

Central to all W.'s work is her basic theme: genuine love is acceptance; the lover may not approve of all the traits and habits of the loved one, but to demand alteration as the price of love is unfair. This theme is stated most overtly in the autobiographical *The Woman Said Yes* (1976), which celebrates Grace West's influence upon her daughters. The emphasis is on Grace's life-enhancing qualities, and W. attributes both her own recovery from tuberculosis and her sister Carmen's capacity to defeat cancer (by choosing suicide) to strength learned from their mother.

A Matter of Time (1966), which is W.'s best novel, also deals with a mother's influence and love, but here redemptive understanding occurs late. As Tassie nurses Blix, her younger sister, through terminal illness, the middle-aged women discuss their mother's use of Tassie to control Blix's behavior. This exploitation has severely damaged the women and their relationship, but they now validate their sisterly love by acceptance of themselves and one another. The maturation story appears in flashbacks, its strength completely overshadowing any moral question arising from the fact that Tassie helps Blix commit suicide. This decision is presented as a final affirmation of Blix's humanity and her will.

In *The Life I Really Lived* (1979), Orpha Chase, successful novelist, attempts to put her experiences into perspective. She recounts the central events of her Kentucky girlhood and of her later life in California and Hawaii. Each step of the real journey as well as the maturation journey is illuminated by Orpha's analysis of the people—parents, husbands, daughter, lover, friends—who influenced and formed her. As in *A Matter of Time*, the impact of a sibling is especially important. Serious and sometimes grim, *The Life I Really Lived* is less successful than *A Matter of Time* and sometimes recalls *The Massacre at Fall Creek*, for it reflects W.'s clear grasp of the danger, difficulty, and complexity as well as the joys and triumphs of the life of her protagonist, who stands for the women whose lives bridged the gap between the frontier and "civilization."

Considered an able, serious craftsperson, W. is noted for her detailed, accurate settings and the careful development of motivation which makes fine characterization a dominant quality in her sound work.

WORKS: *The Friendly Persuasion* (1945; film version, 1956). *A Mirror for the Sky* (1948). *The Witch Diggers* (1951). *The Reading Public* (1952). *Cress Delahanty* (1953). *Love, Death, and the Ladies' Drill Team* (1955). *To See the Dream* (1957). *Love Is Not What You Think* (1959). *South of the Angels* (1960). *The Quaker Reader* (1962). *A Matter of Time* (1966). *The Chilekings* (1967). *Leafy Rivers* (1967). *Except For Me and Thee* (1969). *Crimson Ramblers of the World, Farewell* (1970). *Hide and Seek* (1973). *The Secret Look* (1974). *The Massacre at Fall Creek* (1975). *Violence* (pamphlet, 1976). *The Woman Said Yes* (1976). *The Life I Really Lived* (1979). *Double Discovery: A Journey* (1980).

BIBLIOGRAPHY: Shivers, A. S., *Jessamyn West* (1972).

Other references: *EJ* (Sept. 1957). *Expl* (Dec. 1964). *Indiana Magazine of History* (Dec. 1971). *Nation* (30 March 1957). *NYTBR* (14 Jan. 1951). *SatR* (24 Oct. 1970). *Writers Digest* (May 1967; Jan. 1976).

JANE S. BAKERMAN

Mae West

B. *17 Aug. 1893, Brooklyn, New York; d. 22 Nov. 1980, Los Angeles, California*
D. *of John and Mathilda Doegler West*

W.'s description of her childhood (in the early chapters of her autobiography, *Goodness Had Nothing to Do with It*, 1959) illustrates the qualities that were to become her caricature: She learned early that "two and two are four, and five will get you ten if you know how to work it." She began her performing career at age seven. When, as a young actress and singer, she was criticized for "wriggling" on stage during performances, she realized that it was the "force of an extraordinary sex-personality that made quite harmless lines and mannerisms seem suggestive." Her one marriage was annulled; she had no children.

W. was producer, author, and star of *SEX* (1927). At first, the title scared away both booking agents and theatergoers. Ultimately, however, the play was a success, firmly casting the stylistic idiom in which W., actress, author, and woman, would be known: the tough, street-smart, unashamedly sexual "dame"—no man's fool—whose unrelenting self-promotion is exceeded only by her vanity.

She believed that *The Drag* (1928), in which she did not appear, was a serious approach to a modern social problem, but her sensitivity to the issue of homosexuality is relative to her time. She writes that the homosexual's "abnormal tendencies (have) brought disaster to his family, friends, and himself"; and her message is that "an understanding of the problems of all homosexuals by society could avert such social tragedies."

SEX and *The Drag* ran simultaneously—*SEX* in New York City (for forty-one weeks, before, thanks to efforts by the Society for the Suppression of Vice, W. was arrested and jailed for a short time) and *The Drag* in Paterson, New Jersey. The district attorney in New York had *The Drag* closed and the entire cast arrested after only two performances.

Diamond Lil (1932) was written specifically to attract the female audience her earlier plays had failed to draw. Later filmed (as *She Done Him Wrong*, 1933) and even turned into a novel (1932), it features perhaps the most famous W. character in a "grand Bowery folk play." One critic wrote an appropriately picturesque summation: "It's worth swimming to Brooklyn to see her descend those dance hall stairs, to be present while she lolls in a golden bed reading the *Police Gazette*, murders her girlfriend, wrecks the Salvation Army, and sings as much of 'Frankie and Johnny' as the mean old law allows."

The novel follows the footsteps and idiom of Diamond Lil. The narrative is liberally dosed with "kinda," "an'," and their counterparts in diction. Women are "skirts," policemen are "dicks," and they are all vividly drawn types. It is lively and reasonably well written, given the genre.

In *The Constant Sinner* (originally titled *Babe Gordon*, 1930), a novel, the siren Babe "starts low and ends up high"—reversing everything mothers tell their daughters about the fate of bad girls. Babe is celebrated by the author, in part, for knowing her own mind and keeping the control of her body up to no one but herself. Again, W. deals with subjects (such as interracial sex) socially unmentionable in the U.S. of the 1930s; yet she does it all within the confines of her public's expectations of the W. caricature.

Pleasure Man (1975), W.'s novelization of *The Drag*, is about a bisexual Broadway headliner, Rodney Terrill, "whose wild sex-affairs with women," W. declares, "led to unexpected but well-deserved difficulties."

Again, street talk prevails, but in the novel the prose is often laced with attempts at more eloquent diction—mixed usage with mixed results.

Beginning in 1932, W. appeared in many films. She wrote (or cowrote —as with her plays and novels, her collaborative debts are often unclear) at least six of these. Films such as *She Done Him Wrong, I'm No Angel* (1933), and *My Little Chickadee* (1939)—the last of which was written with her costar, W. C. Fields—are considered comedy classics.

Her novel, stage, and film personae are one and the same, often a mirror of W. herself: the woman who will not conform, in her words, to the "old-fashioned limits" men have "set on a woman's freedom of action." Unfortunately, W.'s sex-personality became legitmate for the American public only as she became more and more a caricature of herself. Her public self was laundered into a distant cousin, twice-removed, from W. the woman, thereby making her frank yet refreshing sexuality laughable and comic, but legitimate.

An extension of American pulp literature, W.'s fiction receives little attention. She is well known, however, as the queen of the reverse-sexist one-liners: Hatcheck Girl: "Goodness, what lovely diamonds!" W.: "Goodness had nothing to do with it, dearie." Her contributions to American culture are immeasurable, yet—perhaps because her outrageous persona commands so much attention—her written work is virtually unrecognized. She was not only the performer but the author of plays and films in which she appeared, and she deserves to be acknowledged as a creative and successful comic playwright.

WORKS: Babe Gordon (1930, reissued as *The Constant Sinner*, 1931). *She Done Him Wrong* (alternate title, *Diamond Lil*, 1932). *Goodness Had Nothing to Do with It* (1959). *The Wit and Wisdom of Mae West* (Ed. J. Weintraub, 1967). *Pleasure Man* (1975).

DEBORAH H. HOLDSTEIN

Edith Newbold Jones Wharton

B. 24 Jan. 1862, New York City; d. 11 Aug. 1937, St. Brice-sous-Forêt, France
Wrote under: Edith Jones, Edith Wharton
D. of George and Lucretia Rhinelander Jones; m. Edward Wharton, 1885

W. was born into the very wealthy and extremely traditional society of "old New York." She had her debut in 1879 and seemed to be well on her way to realizing her ambition—to be, like her mother, the best-dressed woman in New York. Her marriage to a socially prominent Bostonian, however, was not a success; they both suffered nervous breakdowns. After her husband's prolonged bouts with mental illness and his numerous and public infidelities, the Whartons were divorced in 1913.

By this time, partly as a cure for her own illness, she had seriously turned her energies toward writing. She had already established her permanent residence in France; had had an affair that continued intermittently from 1907 to 1910 and was to have a profound effect on her artistic life; had cemented her close friendship with Henry James; and had come to depend on the international lawyer Walter Berry as her most dependable literary advisor and closest personal friend.

During WWI, she organized such an extensive refugee program, helping literally thousands of people, that in 1916 the French government awarded her the Legion of Honor. W. returned to the U.S. only once, for a few days in 1923 to receive an honorary doctorate from Yale. Her last years were spent in a continuous literary and social activity at Pavillon Colombe, her large 18th-c. home near Paris.

W. began writing as early as 1873. She published poetry, short stories, a book on interior decoration, and a novel. All of these works were critically acclaimed, but W. was not recognized as an important writer until the appearance of *The House of Mirth* in 1905.

The House of Mirth (the title comes from *Ecclesiastes*) is set in New York's aristocratic society of the first years of the 20th c. It is an outstanding novel of manners focusing on the excruciating social fall and personal rise of its complex, appealing, and somewhat pathetic heroine, Lily Bart. Lily, orphaned as a young woman and now living with her wealthy aunt, has been raised by her mother to abhor the dingy and sordid in life, and is determined to find a husband to keep her in luxury. She is attracted to Lawrence Selden, but he lacks the money she desires. Yet neither is she willing to marry merely for money; "what she craved, and really felt herself entitled to, was a situation in which the noblest attitude should also be the easiest." In the fall of both heroine and hero, we see W.'s attacks on the moral failures of "old New York" and the *nouveaux riches* invading it, and on any society which trains its women to be decorative objects, subject to breakage.

W. followed her 1905 triumph with three years of tremendous productivity, but little artistic success. She published a novella, a full-length novel, a travel book, and two volumes of short stories. Although a few stories in *Tales of Men and Ghosts* (1910) show her brilliance, she did not regain her artistic strength until 1911, with her novella *Ethan Frome*.

In this book, W. left the familiar territory of Fifth Avenue and Europe and went north to the harsh environment and psychological realities of impoverished rural Massachusetts. The narrator is told the story of the young Ethan Frome, twenty-five years earlier. Out of loneliness he marries a sickly wife, Zeena. Her young cousin, Mattie Silver, is hired to help with the chores, and as Mattie and Ethan fall in love, Zeena protests by firing Mattie. During Ethan's trip with Mattie to the train that will take her away, they plan a dual suicide run on a sled, only to have the suicide misfire, sparing them both for a lifetime of crippled endurance. When the narrator encounters Ethan at fifty-two, he is still maimed and prematurely aged by hardship. Zeena is caring for him and the once lovely, now ugly, querulous, and paralyzed Mattie. This tale of unremitting isolation, loneliness, intellectual starvation, and mental despair is among W.'s very best.

W. followed this bleak story with her most Jamesian, and some say her most autobiographical novel, *The Reef* (1912). This tale of the courtship of Mrs. Leath and her old admirer George Darrow and of the subsequent trials caused by Darrow's previous brief affair with a governess is a problem to readers and critics alike. The James circle loved it. More recently, however, Louis Auchincloss has written: "it is a quiet, controlled, beautiful novel, but its theme has always struck me as faintly ridiculous."

In her text on aesthetics, *The Writing of Fiction* (1925), W. acknowledges her debt to James. *The Reef* is proof positive of direct literary influence, but W. did better when she avoided James's subtle, speculative, indirect style. The narrative line in her best works—*The House of Mirth*, *Ethan Frome*, *The Custom of the Country* (1913), and *The Age of Innocence* (1920)—is more direct than his, her sense of life more despondent.

"I want to get a general view of the whole problem of American marriages," says Mrs. Fairford in W.'s next novel, *The Custom of the Country*. She is promptly told that the main problem is "that the average American looks down on his wife . . .*"; it is the "custom of the country" for the American man to keep his wife totally ignorant of "the real business of life." In this story of Undine Spragg, W. returns to New York of the turn of the century, and caustically satirizes its burgeoning aristocracy of wealth and its values, especially those pertaining to marriage. Armed with beauty, money, and confidence, Undine leaves the security of Apex City (W. displays her prejudice against the Midwest) and assails New York, directing her energies at the only market open to women, the marriage mart. Undine's rise in society is as rapid as Lily Bart's fall, for Undine is not troubled by morality.

The Age of Innocence is W.'s retrospective self-confrontation with the world of her childhood. She is deadly in her attack on this world which dreaded scandal worse than disease, which kept its women encased in invincible innocence. But W. also saw the social order as the domain of life's most important values: decency, honesty, moral commitment. To defy the social ethic was to threaten the very fabric of a moral universe. Archer opts for a stable society and the dullness of May, but he does so at what was most probably great personal loss. Yet the alternative would also extract a great price, one that most of us, says W., lack the strength to pay.

W.'s later works, the eight novels and novellas that follow *The Age of Innocence*, are not as strong as her previous fiction. Indeed, her next, *The Glimpses of the Moon* (1922) is generally considered her worst book. *Hudson River Bracketed* (1929) and *The Gods Arrive* (1932), companion novels, are valuable because the central character, Vance Weston, is W.'s self-portrait of an artist who voices the aesthetic theories she had earlier presented in *The Writing of Fiction*, but as fiction these two books are negligible. Some attribute the falling-off to haste, others to diminished powers. The latter theory is weak, for her unfinished last novel, *The Buccaneers* (1938), shows a return to her old powers. Whatever the reason for these last failures, the novels evidence what Irving Howe has called a "hardening of the moral arteries," a somewhat mean-spirited dismissal of a younger generation she could not understand.

W.'s themes are eclectic, and perhaps as hard to categorize as their author, who has variously been called a novelist of manners, a psychological realist, and a naturalist. She wrote out of her conviction that the true drama of life takes place within the soul. Old New York provided a manageable backdrop for these dramas, and early in her career its flaws were the object of her detached irony. Over the years, as she remarks in *A Backward Glance* (1934), she mellowed enough to grant that New York society, in its three hundred years of "consecrated living up to long-established standards of honour and conduct, of education and manners," has contributed enough to the "moral wealth of our country" to justify itself. Despite this mellowing, her vision throughout the novels remains dark. Her juvenilia is especially morbid, and although she later tempers this pessimism, human beings always remain inadequate and seem consistently to fail each other. Men especially fare poorly, disappointing their women less out of malice than inertia and insensitivity.

W. has been criticized for so often limiting herself to a small social range and narrow historic span—from the 1870s to the 1920s—but even her detractors admit that she depicts her own sphere with consummate skill. Contemporary reviewers of her work repeatedly admired her "perfect plots" or her "graceful, felicitous language." Like her life, her style is formal, and at its best it is terse, caustic, epigrammatic, with sparse use of dialogue and little first-person narration (*Ethan Frome* is the only novel told in the first person). W. has also been criticized for her aloof tone. She was painfully shy, a person who covered her insecurity with what could be an imposing frigidity supported by an undeviating sense of her own social class; but this aloofness can become, in her writing, acid satire motivated by a truly humanistic empathy with the victims of the society she attacks.

The new scholarship resulting from the opening of the Yale University collection of W.'s papers in 1968 is reversing much of the impression of her as haughty, snobbish, and limited, as we see the humanity beneath the glacial reserve bred into her class. So too has the new interest in women's writing led to a broader understanding and more perceptive critical account of her fiction. With increasing admiration, critics and readers alike continue to recognize the consummate craft and sensitivity with which she takes us on an intimate visit into the drawing rooms of society and the mind.

WORKS: *Verses* (1878). *The Decoration of Houses* (1897). *The Greater Inclination* (1897). *The Touchstone* (1900). *Crucial Instances* (1901). *The Joy of Living*, by H. Suderman (translated by Wharton 1902). *Valley of Decision* (1902). *Sanctuary* (1903). *The Descent of Man, and Other Stories* (1904). *Italian Villas, and Their Gardens* (1904). *The House of Mirth* (1905). *Italian Backgrounds* (1905). *Fruit of the Tree* (1907). *Madame de Treyms* (1907). *The Hermit and the Wild Woman, and Other Stories* (1908). *A Motor Flight through France* (1908). *Artemis to Actaeon, and other Verses* (1909). *Tales of Men and Ghosts* (1910). *Ethan Frome* (1911). *The Reef* (1912). *The Custom of the Country* (1913). *Fighting France, from Dunkerque to Belfort* (1915).

The Book of the Homeless (1916). *Xingu, and Other Stories* (1916). *Summer* (1917). *The Marne* (1918). *French Ways and Their Meaning* (1919). *The Age of Innocence* (1920). *In Morocco* (1920). *The Glimpses of the Moon* (1922). *A Son at the Front* (1923). *Old New York* (1924). *The Mother's Recompense* (1925). *The Writing of Fiction* (1925). *Here and Beyond* (1926). *Twelve Poems* (1926). *Twilight Sleep* (1927). *The Children* (1928). *Hudson River Bracketed* (1929)). *Certain People* (1930). *The Gods Arrive* (1932). *Human Nature* (1933). *A Backward Glance* (1934). *The World Over* (1936). *Ghosts* (1937). *The Buccaneers* (1938). *Eternal Passion in English Poetry* (1939). *The Collected Short Stories of Edith Wharton* (2 vols., Ed. R. W. B. Lewis, 1968).

BIBLIOGRAPHY: Auchincloss, L., *Edith Wharton* (1961). Bell, M., *Edith Wharton and Henry James: The Story of Their Friendship* (1965). Howe, I., ed., *Edith Wharton: A Collection of Critical Essays* (1962). Lawson, R. H., *Edith Wharton* (1977). Lewis, R. W. B., *Edith Wharton: A Biography* (1975). Lubbock, P., *Portrait of Edith Wharton* (1947). Lyde, M., *Edith Wharton: Convention and Morality in the Work of a Novelist* (1959). Maxwell, D. E. S., *American Fiction: The Intellectual Background* (1963). McDowell, M., *Edith Wharton* (1976). Nevius, B., *Edith Wharton: A Study of Her Fiction* (1953). Springer, M., *Edith Wharton and Kate Chopin: A Reference Guide* (1976). Tuttleton, J., *The Novel of Manners in America* (1972). Walton, G., *Edith Wharton: A Critical Interpretation* (1970). Wolff, C. G., *A Feast of Words: The Triumph of Edith Wharton* (1977). Ammons, E., *Edith Wharton's Argument with America* (1980).

MARLENE SPRINGER

Phillis Wheatley

B. *1753 (?), Senegal, Africa; d. 5 Dec. 1784, Boston, Massachusetts*
M. *John Peters, 1778*

Facts about W.'s birth are unknown. The speculation of biographers that she was seven years old in 1760, when she was sold as a slave in Boston, is based on the condition of her teeth at the time. Susannah Wheatley, the wife of a prosperous Boston tailor, bought the frail, asthmatic child. It is inferred from her later recollection of a sunrise ritual and familiarity with Arabic script that her African background was that of a Senegalese Moslem.

W.'s nurturing with the Wheatley's two eighteen-year-old twins was remarkably pleasant and unique to the period. Struck by her sharp intellect, the Wheatleys, contrary to the law and the accepted morality of the times, immediately began to teach her to read and write. In sixteen months, W. was reading the Bible, and at the age of twelve, she began to learn Latin and read the classics of English literature.

Greatly influenced by Pope, W. began poetry at thirteen. After she started publishing at seventeen, she received the attention of Boston society and was invited to social gatherings. Whether to advance their social status or to further W.'s career, the Wheatleys greatly supported her success among the Boston elite. Her fame soon spread from Boston to New York, Philadelphia, and England. She became a freedwoman in 1772. In 1773, the Wheatleys financed her trip to England, where—on a visit cut short by Mrs. Wheatley's illness—W. was presented to London society. In 1776, W. was warmly received by General Washington, with whom she had corresponded and to whom she had addressed a forty-two-line poem, published in the *Pennsylvania Magazine*, edited by Thomas Paine (April 1776).

By 1778, the Wheatleys were either dead or had moved to England; W. fended for herself as a poet and seamstress. After marrying Peters, she moved to Wilmington, Massachusetts, and lived in poverty for the rest of her life. According to the Massachusetts Historical Society record, when Peters was jailed for debts, W. experienced drudgery for the first time in her life, working in a boarding house for blacks in Boston. She bore three children. Two had died by 1783; the third died a few hours after her own death in 1784.

Poems on Various Subjects, Religious and Moral was first published in England in 1773; the first American edition did not follow until 1784. It includes thirty-nine poems of varying merit, some published earlier in magazines. Most of the poems are occasional; some are elegies. "Niobe in Distress for Her Children Slain by Apollo" and "Goliath of Gath," both long poems, reveal the two all-encompassing passions in W.'s life, for the Bible and the classics. The first, along with short poems such as "An Hymn to Morning" and "An Hymn to Evening," exhibits her characteristic classical allusions and use of heroic couplets. A very few poems, such as her odes to Washington and Major General Charles Lee reflect her response to the war.

W. has been criticized for not being concerned enough with her own background and the problems of her race. Only two poems, "On Being Brought from Africa" and "To S. M., a Young African Painter, on Seeing

His Works," deal with African subjects. There are clear references to Africa in only another nine poems. Richard Wright suggests that W.'s lack of racial protest must be explained by her acceptance in Boston society. It may well be that what we consider weaknesses in the collection of her poetry are the results of the temper of contemporary New England and the literary tastes of W.'s time.

W. was celebrated by her contemporaries as a child prodigy and poet and regarded as a skillful letter writer and entertaining literary conversationalist. Her poetry is impersonal, with a self-effacement that subordinates her racial and sexual identities to her identities as Christian and poet. She retains, however, the distinction of being the first famous black woman poet.

WORKS: Poems on Various Subjects, Religious and Moral (1773; American edition, 1784). *Letters of Phillis Wheatley, the Negro-Slave Poet of Boston* (Ed. C. Deane, 1864).

BIBLIOGRAPHY: Hughes, L., *Famous American Negroes* (1954). Mason, J., Introduction to *The Poems of Phyllis Wheatley* (1966). Odell, M. M., *Memoir and Poems of Phillis Wheatley* (1834). Richmond, M. A., *Bid the Vassal Soar: Interpretive Essays on the Life and Poetry of Phillis Wheatley and George Moses Horton* (1974). Robinson, W. H., *Phillis Wheatley in the Black American Beginnings* (1975).

ADRIANNE BAYTOP

Frances Miriam Berry Whitcher

B. 1 Nov. 1813 (?), Whitesboro, New York; d. 4 Jan. 1852, Whitesboro, New York
Wrote under: Aunt Maguire, Frank, Widow Bedott, Widow Spriggins
D. of Lewis Berry and Elizabeth Wells; m. Benjamin Whitcher, 1847

The eleventh of fifteen children, W. was the daughter of a prominent Whitesboro innkeeper. Deemed a precocious child, she was educated both at home and at a local academy. In spite of close family ties, she recalled having a lonely childhood because of her keen sense of the ridiculous; the neighbors sternly disapproved of her cariacutures of them. As a young woman, however, she participated in many community activities.

In her mid-thirties, W. married an Episcopal minister and moved with him to his new pastorate in Elmira, New York. Although her marriage was happy, her life in Elmira apparently was not. In 1848, her husband resigned his pastorate and returned to Whitesboro, where she gave birth to her only child, Alice Miriam. W. died of tuberculosis at the age of thirty-nine.

W.'s first humorous sketches (published posthumously as *The Widow Spriggins*, 1867), written to entertain a literary society, are burlesques of a popular English sentimental novel, *Children of the Abbey* (1798), by Regina Maria Roche. The sketches ridicule both sentimental fiction and women who attempt to imitate literary heroines; W.'s persona, Permilly Ruggles Spriggins, is an uncouth sentimentalist who models her language and her every action on Roche's Amanda.

W.'s most famous series of sketches, written at the request of Joseph Neal of the *Saturday Gazette* (1846–47), are dramatic monologues presented entirely in the malapropian vernacular language of the Widow Bedott, who is a parody of a small-town gossip. The sketches are laced with references to contemporary fads, such as phrenology lectures and literary-society meetings.

Bedott devotes considerable energy to a search for a second husband. The first widower she shamelessly pursues seems about to propose, but instead asks for permission to court her daughter. Her second major effort succeeds when she encourages the rumor that she is a woman of means; she succeeds in marrying the Reverend Sniffles, who is as pompous as Bedott is conniving.

After W.'s move to Elmira, she began a third series of sketches for the widely popular *Godey's Lady's Book* (1847–49). Her new persona, Aunt Maguire, is more compassionate than her fictive sister Bedott and speaks a more colloquial language. Inspired by her own observations and experiences as a minister's wife, W. satirizes the residents of small towns for their uncharitable conduct and genteel pretensions.

In one sketch, "The Donation Party," W. satirizes the custom whereby parishioners augment their minister's meager salary by giving him "donations" of substantial commodities. In her story, the minister's guests bring only trifling gifts, break the wife's heirloom china, eat more food than they contribute, and exhibit crude and socially reprehensible behavior. At the end, the fictive minister resigns, declaring that one more donation party would ruin him financially.

W.'s most controversial Aunt Maguire sketches focus on a fictional sewing society that was created ostensibly for charitable purposes, but whose participants turn the meetings into malicious gossip sessions. The series ends when Aunt Maguire travels to a neighboring village where the inhabitants mistakenly believe it is their sewing society that served as the model for the story in *Godey's* and their minister's wife who is the offending author.

Although W.'s responsibility for the sketches had been a closely guarded secret, rumors persisted that the author lived in Elmira. So realistic and biting were the sketches that when Benjamin Whitcher confirmed that his wife was indeed "Aunt Maguire," he was threatened with a law suit and ultimately forced to resign his Elmira pastorate. Not since Frances Trollope's *Domestic Manners of the Americans* (1832) had readers been so stung by a woman's social satire. W. responded by abandoning humorous writing.

Following the tradition of writers such as Seba Smith (who created Jack Downing), W. used first-person vernacular humor as a medium for social criticism. She was unique in humorously depicting small-town life from a woman's perspective, and she thus became one of America's first significant woman humorists. Her work was widely popular in the 19th-c., and modern readers will find much to admire and enjoy in W.'s humor.

WORKS: *The Widow Bedott Papers* (1856; containing also the Aunt Maguire sketches). *The Widow Spriggins, Mary Elmer, and Other Sketches* (1867).

BIBLIOGRAPHY: Curry, J. A., "Woman as Subjects and Writers of Nineteenth-Century American Humor" (Ph.D. diss., Univ. of Michigan, 1975). Derby, J. C., *Fifty Years among Authors, Books, and Publishers* (1884). Hart, J. D., *The Popular Book: A History of America's Literary Taste* (1961). Morris, Linda A. Finton, "Women Vernacular Humorists in Nineteenth-Century America: Ann Stephens, Frances Whitcher, and Marietta Holley" (Ph.D. diss., Univ. of California, Berkeley, 1978). Neal, A., Introduction to *The Widow Bedott Papers* (1856). Whitcher, Mrs. M. L. Ward, Introduction to *The Widow Spriggins, Mary Elmer, and Other Sketches* (1867).

For articles in references works, see: *NAW* (article by M. L. Langworthy).

Other references: *Godey's* (July 1853: Aug. 1853). *New York History* (1974).

LINDA A. MORRIS

Elizabeth White

B. ca. 1637; d. 1699
M. 1657

W. was born in New England, possibly in or near Boston, around 1637, and married in 1657; she had at least one child. There are apparently no extant records of her life, except for these sketchy details which she put into the one published work, her spiritual autobiography.

The Experience of God's Gracious Dealing with Mrs. Elizabeth White, published as a short pamphlet in 1741, is a notable example of early American women's spiritual autobiography. It contains imaginative and personally revealing details about the psychic life of a Puritan woman in 17th-c. New England. This work was discovered after her death in W.'s "closet," a small room used for private meditation and writing. Although it was probably circulated among friends and relatives for many years, as was the practice, it was not published until four decades after W.'s death, during a period of religious revival in New England; her confession would have evoked for its readers an earlier, much admired pious period.

The lack of polish and sophistication in W.'s autobiography is made up for by spontaneity and vividness as she reveals the internal landscape of the darkest recesses of her soul in an attempt to express her redemptive experience. Three experiences of deepest despair about her soul's destiny occurred, concurrently with her marriage, the birth of her first child, and the weaning of this infant. A month before her marriage, she relates, her father desired her to take communion; but she suddenly had grave doubts about her preparedness for taking part in the sacrament. Similarly, she experienced a crisis three days after delivering her first child; she was tempted by the devil with a vision of the Trinity, but escaped Satan's clutches through the suckling of her infant and finally through sleep in which she dreamt of her assured place in heaven, a place secured for her after death in childbirth. A third great trial coincided with weaning, and relates directly to W.'s stated feelings of guilt for the affection she lavished on her first born. Tempted to believe that the Bible is not God's word, she was uplifted by Christ, and the darkness about her soul dispelled.

Although she felt renewed after this final experience, moments of doubt continued to plague her. But she felt secure enough in her salvation and regeneration to commit to writing her account of repentance and trust in Christ. In talking about the trials and religious doubt in the period of early womanhood, W. reveals the deep-seated conflicts and uncertainties felt by a Puritan woman when facing the responsibilities and struggles of marriage and motherhood. As a Puritan, she views these external events only as markers by which she identifies moments of acute spiritual awareness. For the modern reader, the conjunction of W.'s internal and external experiences provides thought-provoking clues to the psychic life of Puritan women.

WORKS: *The Experiences of God's Gracious Dealing with Mrs. Elizabeth White* (1741).

BIBLIOGRAPHY: Shea, D., *Spiritual Autobiography in Early America* (1968).

JACQUELINE HORNSTEIN

Ellen Gould Harmon White

B. 26 Nov. 1827, Gorham, Maine; d. 16 July 1915, St. Helena, California
Wrote under: Ellen G. White
D. of Robert and Eunice Harmon; m. James White, 1846

The daughter of a hatter, W. had only a third-grade education. Although baptized in the Methodist church, by the age of seventeen she was enthusiastically involved with the activities of William Miller—an itinerant preacher who believed the Second Coming of Christ, and the end of the world, would occur during the fall of 1844. In that year, W. had the first of a series of over two thousand visions, which revealed to her why Miller's prediction failed and what God intended her to accomplish.

W. married a fellow "Millerite," and together they spread the message of the coming of Christ to the New England area. She had four children; the first died at sixteen and the last in infancy, but the other two boys became active in the church their mother helped found.

The Whites moved to Battle Creek, Michigan, in 1855, and W., prompted by her visions, preached and wrote on the significance of the imminent (if unknown) coming of Christ, the validity of biblical prophecies, fundamental Christianity, and the divine desire for observing the Sabbath not on Sunday but on the seventh day of the week, Saturday. The Seventh Day Adventist church was eventually established on those principles in 1863. When her husband died in 1888, W. increased her writing and speaking activities, campaigning for Adventist Christianity, health reform, and temperance. As many as twenty thousand people gathered to hear her orations against alcohol. Her travels included two years touring Europe and ten years as a missionary to Australia. In 1902, W. moved the Adventist headquarters from Battle Creek to a suburb of Washington, D.C., and she settled in California. She died at the age of eighty-seven from complications following a hip fracture.

It has been estimated that W. wrote over one hundred and five thousand pages of published and unpublished materials. She maintained that, because of her poor health and lack of education, only God's visions enabled her to produce this literary corpus. Much of her writing was done late at night or in the early morning when domestic tasks were completed.

The foundation of the Seventh Day Adventist church rests on the belief that the Bible reveals the ultimate truth concerning the nature of God, the origin and purpose of human life, and the future of the world. Divine inspiration was not sufficient to convince most 19th-c. Americans that Adventist doctrine was the ultimate truth; W. wanted to show the continuity of biblical prophecy and the course of historical events. Five books, the Conflict of Ages series, are devoted to tracing the history of the battle between God and Satan as predicted in the Old and New Testaments. Four books tell the biblical story from Genesis to the Pauline epistles. *The Great Controversy* (1888), although actually written first, continues the story into the European and American historical settings. W. used the history of Western civilization to underline certain central themes in Adventist belief: the reality of Satan, the evil of Roman Catholicism, and the redemptive quality of William Miller's proclamation.

Much of W.'s writings were composed during a period of general social reform in the U.S. Women's rights, prison reform, the settlement-house movement, and prohibition were important issues at grassroot and national levels. Such late 19th-c. reforms were a part of the "social gospel movement," which emphasized the role of Christianity as a force for social change, rather than as a promoter of the status quo. W. fueled this movement with her tracts on health, education, temperance, and diet; and she encouraged her followers to adopt a life-style encompassing many of the contemporary reforms.

According to W., God intends humans to lead a simple life: pure air, deep breathing, regular sleeping and eating habits, and good sanitation promote moral as well as physical well being; tobacco, coffee, alcohol, meat, and sugar are all detrimental to the body, soul, and mind. Her views on dress reform echo some of the earlier sentiments of Amelia Bloomer and Elizabeth Cady Stanton. In *The Ministry of Healing* (1905), she condemns the restrictive and overly decorative style of contemporary dress: "Every article of dress should fit easily, obstructing neither the circulation of the blood nor a free, full, natural respiration. Everything should be so loose that when the arms are raised, the clothing will be correspondingly lifted."

Educational reform also figures prominately in W.'s writings. Education must include not only the Biblical and historical basis of Adventism but also a foundation in physiology, diet, health, and medicine. Traditional secular education should be limited to basic English, arithmetic, and history ("from the Divine point of view"). She sought to purge from Adventist education "pagan" languages and literature, modern literature by immoral authors, frivolous fiction writers, non-Christian science, biblical criticism, spiritualism, and anarchy. Seventh Day. Adventist education included girls as well as boys and even encouraged some fluidity in sex-role education: "Boys as well as girls should gain a knowledge of household duties. . . . it is a training that need not make any boy less manly; it will make him happier and more useful."

W.'s writings on practical reforms have antecedents in the work of earlier reformers, but she was able to institutionalize them in the doctrine of the Seventh Day Adventist church. She remains a unique woman in the history of American religions, for her writings act as a foundation not only for a growing religious organization but for that religion's extensive system of schools, hospitals, and sanatoriums.

WORKS: *Sketches from the Life of Christ and the Experience of the Christian Church* (1882). *The Great Controversy Between Christ and Satan During the Christian Dispensation* (1888). *Christian Temperance* (1890). *Gospel Workers; Instructions for the Minister and the Missionary* (1892). *Steps to Christ* (1892). *The Story of Patriarchs and Prophets; the Conflict of the Ages Illustrated by the Lives of Holy Men of Old* (1890). *Christ Our Savior* (1895). *The Desire of Ages* (1898). *Christ's Object Lessons* (1900). *Testimonies for the Church* (1901). *Education* (1903). *The Ministry of Healing* (1905). *The Acts of the Apostles in the Proclamation of the Gospel of Jesus Christ* (1911). *Counsel to Teachers, Parents and Students Regarding Christian Education* (1913). *Life Sketches of Ellen G. White, Being a Narrative of her Experience to 1881 as Written By Herself* (1915). *The Captivity and Restoration of Israel; the Conflict of Ages Illustrated in the Lives of Prophets and Kings* (1917). *Christian Experience and Teachings of Ellen G. White*, vol. 1 (1922). *Counsels on Health and Instruction to Medical Missionary Workers* (1923). *Spiritual and Subject Index to the Writings of Mrs. Ellen G. White* (1926). *Principles of True Science* (1929). *Message to Young People* (1930). *Medical Ministry* (1932). *An Appeal for Self-Supporting Laborers* (1933). *A Call to Medical Evangelism* (1933). *Selections from the "Testimonies"* (1936). *Counsels on Sabbath School Work* (1938). *The Sanctified Life* (1937). *Counsels on Diet and Food* (1938). *Counsels to Editors* (1939). *Counsels on Stewardship* (1940).

BIBLIOGRAPHY: Noorbergen, R., *Ellen G. White: Prophet of Destiny* (1972). Numbers, R., *Prophetess of Health: A Study of Ellen G. White* (1976). Spalding, A. W., *There Shines a Light* (1976). White, A., *Ellen G. White: Messenger to the Remnant* (1969).

For articles in reference works, see: *Comprehensive Index to the Writings of Ellen G. White* (3 vols., 1962–63). *NAW* (article by C. C. Goen).

M. COLLEEN McDANNELL

Rhoda Elizabeth Waterman White

Wrote under: Uncle Ben of Rouses Point, N.Y. Uncle Ben, Rhoda E. White
D. of Thomas G. and (?) Whitney Waterman; m. James W. White

No biographical data on W. appears in the standard 19th-c. sources; however, some general information about her background can be abstracted from *Memoir and Letters of Jenny C. White Del Bal* (1868), a book she wrote following her daughter's death. W. was the oldest daughter of General Waterman, a New York state lawyer who married the eldest daughter of General Joshua Whitney, founder of Binghamton, New York. Her parents were socially prominent Episcopalians. She married a member of an explemplary Irish Catholic family. W. converted to Catholicism in 1837, and the Catholic religion was one of the major influences in her life.

Her husband, a wealthy lawyer, became a judge of the Superior Court of New York City. She traveled in fashionable New York society, vacationed at Newport and Saratoga, and enjoyed the privileges of the rich, but her life was not idle. She studied throughout her marriage and received private lessons in all subjects from the best teachers. The mother of eight children, including six daughters, she tutored her family at their home, "Castle Comfort."

The title page of *Jane Arlington; or, The Defrauded Heiress: A Tale of Lake Champlain* (1853) lists *The "Buccaneer" of Lake Champlain* as an earlier work of Uncle Ben. Any prior publications, however, have been lost. *Jane Arlington*, a short novel, is the story of a "young lady perfect and accomplished in every aspect" who, after she is orphaned, is deceived by her kindly step-father's villainous brother into leaving home and finding employment in the frontierlike Lake Champlain region. The plot is predictable; Jane receives both charity and cruelty from employers and others she encounters, but her moral fortitude and personal goodness enable her to survive and regain her rightful inheritance. W. does make use of the unprincipled scoundrel, but her premise is that villainy, or virtue, is frequently disguised and unanticipated. As a corollary, W. exposes class pretensions and distinctions as inadequate measures of individual merit. In developing her theme of false class consciousness, she reveals a keen comic talent that emerges most fully in the caricatures of Mrs. Prim and her family.

W. extends her humorous portrayal of human foibles in *Portraits of My Married Friends; or, A Peep into Hymen's Kingdom* (1858), a series of six sketches narrated by a wry old bachelor, Uncle Ben, who terms his married acquaintances "more fortunate" than he, but who mainly tells of the problems of marital discord and unhappy matches. Most of the portraits, whether comic or tragic, are slight, melodramatic treatments, but the most effective integrate character and theme with moral vision and social consciousness. One of these, "Jerome and Susan Daly," idealizes the love between a village couple and their children, while at the same time it contrasts childrearing practices in the village with those in the city, depicts Scotch and Irish servant girls in the homes of the rich, and proposes "cultivated hearts" as a means of leveling class distinctions. Another effective portrait, "Kate Kearney," combines social realism—including graphic descriptions of tenement life and the plight of abused wives—with a strong story line.

W.'s main concern in *Mary Staunton; or, The Pupils of Marvel Hall* (1860), the most fully realized of her fiction, is the detrimental effects of poor training and environment on young girls, even if their natures are gentle, loving, and sensitive. The novel is an exposé of a fashionable boarding school in New York City, whose pupils acquire little meaningful education and only superficial training in social amenities. Mary is an unlikely heroine; mean, vengeful, and "coarse," she has been neglected by Mrs. Marvel, who is satirized for her false values. Deprived throughout her childhood of affection as well as of religious and moral instruction, she receives a chance for a different life when her long-absent father returns from India and attempts to repair the damage done to his motherless daugher. Although the novel is weakened by W.'s penchant for exaggerating virtues and faults, it is for the most part refreshingly frank and unsentimental.

Two ideas dominate W.'s fiction—Catholicism and education. Her recurrent theme is that children, regardless of their socio-economic status, develop best when they are instilled with faith and love. Her style is at times stilted and melodramatic, and she uses dialogue excessively in forwarding plots. Nevertheless, W. captures voices accurately, particularly immigrant brogues and regional dialects, and she is skillful in rendering realistic scenes of both lower- and upper-class life. Her treatment of New York tenement dwellers and their living conditions, though neither extensive nor primary, is a forerunner of the work of Stephen Crane and Jacob Riis. All of W.'s writing stems from a sense of ethical and social responsibility, but her view of conventional situations is generally from an unexpected angle. Her humorous perspective raises even her most commonplace subjects from the level of cliché and stereotype.

WORKS: *Jane Arlington; or, The Defrauded Heiress: A Tale of Lake Champlain* (1853). *Portraits of My Married Friends: or, A Peep Into Hymen's Kingdom* (1858). *Mary Staunton; or, The Pupils of Marvel Hall* (1860). *Memoir and Letters of Jenny C. White Del Bal* (1868). *From Infancy to Womanhood: A Book of Instructions for Young Mothers* (1881). *What Will the World Say? An American Tale of Real Life* (1885).

THADIOUS M. DAVIS

Lilian Whiting

B. 3 Oct. 1847, Olcott, New York; d. 30 April 1942, Boston, Massachusetts
D. of Lorenzo Dow and Lucretia Calista Clement Whiting

W. was an only daughter and the eldest of three children. While she was still very young, her parents moved to a farm near Tiskilwa, Illinois, where both parents served as principals of the local school. W., however, was educated privately and at home, where she became acquainted early with literary classics. With the assistance of her mother, her father became editor of the Bureau County *Republican*, published in Princeton, Illinois. A leader in the Grange movement and a fighter against the expansion of the railroads and for the expansion of waterways, he served as both representative and senator in the state legislature and assisted in framing the state constitution.

W.'s writing career started when her articles were accepted by the local newspaper, of which she later became editor. In 1876, she went to St. Louis as a journalist and soon became associated with the idealist Philosophic Club. In 1879, she went to work for the Cincinnati *Commercial*, after it published two papers W. had written on Margaret Fuller. The following year, she moved to Boston to become the art editor—and later literary editor—of the Boston *Traveler*.

In 1890, she became editor-in-chief of the Boston *Budget*, to which she also contributed literary reviews (among them, favorable commentary on Emily Dickinson's poems) and a column, "Beau Monde," credited with helping to break down the artistic parochialism of contemporary Boston.

In Boston, W. was a member of a circle that included James Russell Lowell, Lucy Stone, Mary Livermore, Frances Willard, Oliver Wendell Holmes, and many others active in the intellectual life of the time. She visited Bronson Alcott's School of Philosophy and attended Thomas Wentworth Higginson's Round Table. She went to Europe for the first time in 1895 (to do research for the first of several biographies, *A Study of Elizabeth Barrett Browning*, 1899) and thereafter made eighteen pilgrimages abroad. While there, she became the friend of artists such as Auguste Rodin, Harriet Hosmer, and Rosa Bonheur and the theosophist

Annie Besant. Benjamin O. Flower, editor of the *Arena*, said of her that she "knew more men and women of letters than any other woman in America."

So widespread was W.'s reputation as a writer and critic and as a spiritual influence that in 1897 a Lilian Whiting Club was formed in New Orleans with the aim of inspiring its members in matters relating to the arts and sciences.

W.'s spiritualist leanings had deep roots: her father was a descendent of Cotton Mather and her mother of a long line of New England Episcopalian ministers. She wrote ten inspirational books and became one of the most popular of New Thought writers. (William James called New Thought the "religion of healthy-mindedness.") Liberal in her acceptance of a variety of religious sects—in *Life Transfigured* (1910), she discusses spiritualism, theosophy, Christian Science, the Vedantic philosophy, psychotherapy, and Bahai, all as means of salvation—her philosophy is optimistic. She believed in the primacy of the spiritual world and referred to death merely as "change"; she viewed the time she lived in as the "dawn of a new perfection." The death of the journalist Kate Field, a close friend, led W. to write *After Her Death: The Story of a Summer* (1897), which she considered her best work. It spells out her belief in communication between the living and the dead. The essays, such as "Success as a Fine Art," collected in the World Beautiful series (three volumes, 1894–96, which ran to fourteen editions) are typical of W.'s approach to living.

Boston Days: The City of Beautiful Ideals (1902) was the first of her eight books dealing with places she visited in North America, Europe, and Africa. The chatty tone of her accounts of popular landmarks and works of art as well as the liberal sprinkling of names of her famous acquaintances no doubt were the chief sources of the popularity of her travel writing.

W.'s third-person autobiography, *The Golden Road* (1918), is effusive rather than factual. She published one volume of poetry, *From Dreamland Sent* (1895). The poems are largely personal in subject and traditional in form and tone.

W. is of interest to those studying popular taste rather than excellence and originality in the literary arts. It is worth noting, however, that she achieved fame and success as a professional among professionals and moved freely in an international society of artists in a way few women of her time were privileged to do.

WORKS: *The World Beautiful* (3 vols., 1894–96). *After Her Death: The Story of a Summer* (1897). *Kate Field: A Record* (1899). *A Study of the Life and Poetry of Elizabeth Barrett Browning* (1899). *The Victory of the Will* (edited by Whiting, 1899). *The Spiritual Significance; Or, Death As An Event in Life* (1900). *The World Beautiful in Books* (1901). *Boston Days: The City of Beautiful Ideals* (1902). *The Life Radiant* (1903). *The Florence of Landor* (1905). *The Joy That No Man Taketh From You* (1905). *The Outlook Beautiful* (1905). *From Dream to Vision of Life* (1906). *Italy, the Magic Land* (1907). *Paris, the Beautiful* (1908). *The Land of Enchantment* (1909). *Life Transfigured* (1910). *Louise Chandler Moulton: Poet and Friend* (1910). *The Brownings: Their Life and Art* (1911). *Athens, the Violet-Crowned* (1913). *The Lure of London* (1914). *Women Who Have Ennobled Life* (1915). *The Adventure Beautiful* (1917). *Canada, the Spellbinder* (1917). *The Golden Road* (1918). *Katherine Tingley* (1919). *They Who Understand* (1919).

BIBLIOGRAPHY: Flower, B. O., *Progressive Men, Women, and Movements in the Past Twenty-Five Years* (1914). Gardner, W. E., *Memorial* (1942).

For articles in reference works, see: *AW. NCAB* IX.

Other references: *Arena* (April 1899). Boston *Globe* (1 May 1942). Boston *Herald* (1 May 1942). *NYT* (1 May 1942).

VIRGINIA R. TERRIS

Sarah Helen Power Whitman

B. *19 Jan. 1803, Providence, Rhode Island; d. 27 June 1878, Providence, Rhode Island*
Wrote under: Helen, Sarah Helen Whitman
D. of Nicholas and Anna Marsh Power; m. John Winslow Whitman, 1828

Both W.'s parents were from old Rhode Island families. Her father was absent from home for many years when, after being captured at sea by the British in 1813, he chose to continue his seafaring career until 1832. W. was educated, for brief periods, at private schools in Providence and at a Quaker school in Jamaica, Long Island, where she lived with an aunt. Although a taste for poetry and novels was thought pernicious, she preferred them to lessons and read the classics and French and German literature in the library of another aunt, in Providence. She lived in Boston with her husband, an attorney, editor, and writer, but returned to Providence after his death in 1833. She traveled in Europe in 1857.

W.'s first published poem was "Retrospection," signed "Helen" (*American Ladies Magazine*, 1829). The editor, Sarah Josepha Hale, encouraged further contributions. W. wrote scholarly essays on Goethe, Shelley, and Emerson and served as a correspondent for the New York *Tribune* and the Providence *Journal.*

W. was an advocate of educational reforms, divorce, the prevention of cruelty to animals, the liberal ethics of Fourier, women's rights, and universal suffrage. Opposing the materialism of the Protestant churches, she subscribed to the intellectual and spiritual idealism of the Transcendentalists. She was also noted for her belief in prenatal influences and occult and psychic phenomena.

A woman of unusual intelligence and charm, W. knew many prominent people, but today she is best known as a friend of Edgar Allan Poe. Following their first meeting on 2 September 1848, exchanges of poems, and a romantic correspondence, they were engaged to be married by the end of the year, but the engagement was broken at the time the banns were to be published. After Poe's death in 1849, W. cherished his memory and worked to exonerate the maligned author when, in many circles, it was not considered respectable to have been associated with him. She searched for and located materials and, lent valuable items in her possession, and as the Poe controversy became international, she answered all inquiries about him.

W.'s one volume of verse, *Hours of Life, and Other Poems* (1853) is more carefully composed than the work of most women who were her contemporaries, but it is too genteel and restrained to be of moment by comparison with rougher, more original writers. The subjects are typical for the period: dreams and memories of love, the reality of death, visions of paradise, and the comforts of serene religious faith. Her voice is subdued or languorous; her eyes are sensitive to light and color; her heart is tender. Sixteen poems are the record of her love for Poe; they constitute a structure of illusions for reconciling the "orient phantasies," the experience of mundane and rather ugly stresses, the shame and guilt, the grief, and what she calls the "silent eyes of destiny." The reconciliation freed her for the most radical writing of her career, *Edgar Poe and His Critics* (1860).

Having witnessed a decade of what she calls "remorseless violation" to the memory of Poe, W. wished her vindication of him to be impersonal and authoritative. She refrains from discussing her troubled romance with Poe but does take advantage of having known him, of long familiarity with what he wrote, and a scrupulous reading of all that had been written about him. She draws legitimately on the recollections of others who knew him and her own trenchant knowledge of literature and familiarity with the national scene.

Finally, taking into account Poe's mental desolation and periodic insanity, W. views his "unappeased and restless soul" in relation to an era when a prevailing skepticism and "divine dissatisfaction everywhere present" showed that the age was moving feverishly through processes of transition and development, "yet gave no idea of where they were leading us." Poe was, for W., one of the men of "electric temperament and prophetic genius" who anticipate those latent ideas about to unfold themselves to humanity. Nothing would have been gained, she observes, had he been another Wordsworth or Longfellow.

W. was a woman of courage, independent mind, tact, and dignity—and one of the most impressive of American literary critics of the 19th c.

WORKS: *Hours of Life, and Other Poems* (1853). *Edgar Poe and His Critics* (1860). *The Life and Poems of Edgar Allan Poe*, by E. Didier (introduction by Whitman, 1877).

BIBLIOGRAPHY: Harrison, J. A., ed., *The Last Letters of Edgar Allan Poe to Sarah Helen Whitman* (1909). Miller, J. C., *Building Poe Biography* (1977). Miller, J. C., *Poe's Helen Remembers* (1979). Osgood, F. S., *Poems* (1849). Ostrom, J. W., ed., *The Letters of Edgar Allan Poe* (1966). Robertson, J. W., *Edgar A. Poe: A Psychopathic Study* (1923). Ticknor, Caroline, *Poe's Helen* (1916).

For articles in reference works, see: *American Female Poets*, Ed. C. May (1849). *NAW* (article by J. G. Varner).

ELIZABETH PHILLIPS

Phyllis Ayame Whitney

B. 9 Sept. 1903, Yokohama, Japan
Writes under: Phyllis A. Whitney
D. of Charles Joseph and Lillian Mandeville Whitney; m. Lovell F. Jahnke, 1950

Born of American parents, W. first came to the U.S. at the age of fifteen, after living in Japan, China, and the Philippines. She was graduated from high school in Chicago. She married a business man in 1950 and has one daughter. She lives in Staten Island, New York, and northern New Jersey.

W. has written more than fifty novels, which she divides into three groups: novels for young people, mysteries for young people, and adult novels. Almost all of the last are gothic romances. During her long career, she has reviewed books for newspapers and has taught courses, lectured, and written widely on the business and craft of writing fiction. Two novels, *Mystery of the Haunted Pool* (1960) and *Mystery of the Hidden Hand* (1963) have received Edgars from the Mystery Writers of America.

The novels for young people (all except one from the years between 1941 and 1949) appeal to young girls rather than boys. Many of them carry girls' names in the title: *A Place for Ann* (1941), *A Star for Ginny* (1942), *A Window for Julie* (1943), *Linda's Homecoming* (1950), *Nobody Likes Trina* (1972). Many of these didactic novels have been favorably reviewed by educators and librarians, and W.'s success in this field has made her an authority. She has published two text books, *Writing Juvenile Fiction* (1947; rev. ed., 1960) and *Writing Juvenile Stories and Novels* (1976).

Her mysteries for young people can be easily recognized because, with the exception of *The Vanishing Scarecrow* (1971), each of them has a title beginning with "mystery" or "secret." These too are primarily written for girls, although the adventure aspect is strong. They are all characterized by vivid backgrounds.

W.'s early life abroad provided exotic background material for many of her novels. In recent years, she has made each of her many trips serve a double purpose: she uses the background material gathered for one juvenile novel and one adult gothic romance. Thus a trip to the Virgin Islands produced both *Secret of the Spotted Shell* (1967) and *Columbella* (1966). She has set novels in Turkey, Norway, Japan, Greece, South Africa, and a wide variety of places in the U.S.

W.'s first adult novel was *Red is for Murder* (1943), a straightforward mystery novel set in a department store. She did not return to adult fiction until some time later; the next adult book, *The Quicksilver Pool* (1955), is a historical novel set on Staten Island during the Civil War draft riots. Although there is a domestic mystery, the most important aspect of the plot is a love story, a pattern she also uses in a number of novels in the late 1950s and early 1960s.

After the successful contemporary romantic adventures *Seven Tears for Apollo* (1963) and *Black Amber* (1964), W. only once, in *Sea Jade* (1964), uses a historical setting for her novels. The mystery element becomes a more important part of the plot than it had been before.

W.'s preoccupation with women and their identities in these novels is often very sophisticated. (She has written that she relies on Karen Horney for psychological insight about women.) In novels such as *Columbella*, *Silverhill* (1967), *Lost Island* (1970), *Listen for the Whisperer* (1972), *The Turquoise Mask* (1974), and *The Golden Unicorn* (1976), she is increasingly concerned with relationships between mothers and daughters and with questions of feminine identity as they relate to the past—with the problems of women trying both to come to terms with and transcend their family background. In recent years, most of her heroines are seeking their own identities through returning to their ancestral home or through a reconciliation with another woman in the family. The solution of the mystery provides both a conclusion for the plot and an answer to the significant questions asked by the heroine of her past.

Although each of these books ends with clear answers, the process of finding them is arduous and uncompromising. The mystery genre imposes limits on the ambiguity W. can allow in the resolution, but it does not keep her from an honest and rigorous development of the issues. Her women make mistakes: they marry the wrong man, they misjudge character, one of them has an illegitimate child. But they are allowed the opportunity to see what they have done and to change it and themselves. Many authors write gothic romances; very few write them with the sophistication and wisdom of W.

WORKS: *A Place for Ann* (1941). *A Star for Ginny* (1942). *A Window for Julie* (1943). *Red Is for Murder* (1943; alternate title, *The Red Carnelian*). *The Silver Inkwell* (1945). *Willow Hill* (1947). *Writing Juvenile Fiction* (1947; rev. ed., 1960). *Ever After* (1948). *Mystery of the Gulls* (1949). *Linda's Homecoming* (1950). *Island of the Dark Woods* (1951; alternate title, *Mystery of the Strange Traveler*). *Love Me, Love Me Not* (1952). *Step to the Music* (1953). *A Long Time Coming* (1954). *Mystery of the Black Diamonds* (1954). *Mystery of the Isle of Skye* (1955). *The Quicksilver Pool* (1955). *The Fire and the Gold* (1956). *The Highest Dream* (1956). *The Trembling Hills* (1956). *Mystery of the Green Cat* (1957). *Skye Cameron* (1957). *The Moonflower* (1958). *Secret of the Samurai Sword* (1958). *Creole Holiday* (1959). *Mystery of the Haunted Pool* (1960). *Thunder Heights* (1960). *Secret of the Tiger's Eye* (1961). *Blue Fire* (1961). *Mystery of the Golden Horn* (1962). *Window of the Square* (1962). *Mystery of the Hidden Hand* (1963). *Seven Tears for Apollo* (1963). *Black Amber* (1964). *Sea Jade* (1964). *Secret of the Emerald Star* (1964). *Mystery of the Angry Idol* (1965). *Columbella* (1966). *Secret of the Spotted Shell* (1967). *Silverhill* (1967). *Hunter's Green* (1968). *Secret of Goblin Glen* (1968). *Mystery of the Crimson Ghost* (1969). *Secret of the Missing Footprints* (1969). *The Winter People* (1969). *Lost Island* (1970). *The Vanishing Scarecrow* (1971). *Listen for the Whisperer* (1972). *Nobody Likes Trina* (1972). *Mystery of the Scowling Boy* (1973). *Snowfire* (1973). *The Turquoise Mask* (1974). *Secret of the Haunted Mesa* (1975). *Spindrift* (1975). *The Golden Unicorn* (1976). *Writing Juvenile Stories and Novels* (1976). *Secret of the Stone Face* (1977). *The Stone Bull* (1977). *The Glass Flame* (1978). *Domino* (1979). *Poinciana* (1980). *Vermillion* (1981).

BIBLOGRAPHY: CA 1–4 (1967). *NYTBR* (2 July 1967). *Time* (12 April 1971). *Writer* (Feb. 1960; Feb. 1967).

KAY MUSSELL

Kate Douglas Smith Wiggin

B. 28 Sept. 1856, Philadelphia, Pennsylvania; d. 24 Aug. 1923, Harrow-on-Hill, England
Wrote under: Mrs. Riggs, Kate Douglas Wiggin
D. of Robert and Helen Dyer Smith; m. Samuel Wiggin, 1881; m. George Riggs, 1895

W. was born to a prosperous Philadelphia lawyer and his wife, a native of Maine. Her childhood was spent in the village of Hollis, Maine, after the death of her father and her mother's remarriage. She was educated at home and then at various schools in New England. In the mid-1870s, she moved with her family to California, where they came on hard times.

W. became interested in the new kindergarten movement and took a course under Emma Marwedel in Los Angeles, and then opened the Silver Street Kindergarten in a slum in San Francisco, the first free kindergarten in California. For a number of years, she was a national leader in the kindergarten movement, and she began her own training school in San Francisco in 1880. To raise money for the free-kindergarten movement, W. published privately two short sentimental novels, *The Story of Patsy* (1883) and *The Bird's Christmas Carol* (1887).

Her first husband, a lawyer, died in 1889. W. had given up kindergarten work in 1884, and she began writing full-time after the successful commercial publication of *The Birds' Christmas Carol* in 1889. She returned to the East Coast and lived in New York City and Hollis, giving readings from her works and traveling to Europe. Her second husband was a businessman. Among her New York circle were William Dean Howells, Mary E. Wilkins Freeman, and Carolyn Wells. W. suffered periodically from nervous exhaustion; the opening chapters of *Rebecca of Sunnybrook Farm* (1903) were written in a sanatorium.

The Birds' Christmas Carol became a seasonal classic, published in multiple editions in various languages. In this edifying tale, Carol Bird, a wealthy but sick ten-year-old, gives a Christmas dinner for the children of a poor family in the neighborhood, the Ruggles. Although the heroine dies after the children leave on Christmas night, the book's popularity did not rest on sentiment alone; the portrayal of the Ruggles family is realistic and humorous.

Two children's novels set in California, *A Summer in a Canon* (1889) and *Polly Oliver's Problem* (1893), are not very good, and the same may be said of a series of travel novels, most of which have Penelope Hamilton as the heroine. W. is best known for stories set in Maine, and these are undoubtedly her best work.

Timothy's Quest (1890) and some early short stories have Maine backgrounds, but W. only began to concentrate on regional material after the success of *Rebecca of Sunnybrook Farm*. Today this is considered a children's book, but it was first a best-selling adult novel. Set in a village similar to Hollis, in the Saco River valley, the story is a classic orphan story without the orphan: Rebecca, the daughter of a poor widow, is sent to live with two maiden aunts in order to be "made." In traditional fashion, she wins their hearts, even that of the stern Aunt Miranda. A spirited child, Rebecca accomplishes many things in the course of the story, including the saving of her family fortunes. She graduates from boarding school in a cheesecloth dress, but her time at school has been a success—she is class president. Rebecca's character and the local color of her background are both appealing. This story did not end with a marriage, but with only the hint of an attachment. There was no sequel, only a volume of "missing chapters," or stories about Rebecca set in the time of the first novel: *The New Chronicles of Rebecca* (1907).

Mother Carey's Chickens (1911) is another of W.'s popular New England novels. A more saccharine story than *Rebecca of Sunnybrook Farm*, it tells how the Carey family, under the leadership of young Nancy, manages to survive economically after the death of their father. Other Maine stories with good regional description are another Christmas story, *The Old Peabody Pew* (1907), and *Susanna and Sue* (1909), which features a Shaker colony. *The Story of Waitstill Baxter* (1913) shows more mature character development than the average W. novel. Set in the early 19th c., this novel of Saco-valley life features an historical figure, the traveling evangelist Jacob Cochrane, and describes the disruption he brings to a family.

W.'s autobiography, *My Garden of Memory* (1923), is a charming and valuable document, revealing its author as a woman of spirit and sense. Several of her novels were filmed more than once. These movies mirror the popular modern conception of W. as a silly sentiment a list, but her novels, slight as they are, belie that reputation. She was a chronicler of the romance of real life, not a romanticist. And while there is sentimentality in her earlier works, her major novels are free of it. Most of her heroines —Rebecca, Nancy Carey, Polly Oliver, Waitstill Baxter—are active, intelligent young women, unlike the Little Eva stereotype, Carol Bird. W.

argued for wholesomeness, not hypocrisy, in fiction, and her point of view was that of a sophisticated professional writer, not that of a sheltered matron. She was a popular writer who expressed what her contemporaries themselves thought of as "real life."

WORKS: The Story of Patsy (1883). *The Birds' Christmas Carol* (1889). *A Summer in a Canon* (1889). *Timothy's Quest* (1890; film versions, 1922 and 1936). *Polly Oliver's Problem* (1893). *A Cathedral Courtship and Penelope's English Experiences* (1893). *The Village Watch-tower* (1895). *Marm Lisa* (1896). *Penelope's Progress* (1898). *Penelope's Irish Experiences* (1901). *Diary of a Goose Girl* (1902). *Rebecca of Sunnybrook Farm* (1903; film versions, 1917, 1932, 1938). *Rose o' the River* (1905). *New Chronicles of Rebecca* (1907). *The Old Peabody Pew* (1907). *Susanna and Sue* (1909). *Mother Carey's Chickens* (1911; film versions, 1938 and, as *Summer Magic*, 1963). *The Story of Waitstill Baxter* (1913). *Penelope's Postscripts* (1915). *The Romance of a Christmas Card* (1916). *Ladies in Waiting* (1919). *My Garden of Memory* (1923). *Creeping Jenny, and Other New England Stories* (1924). Fifteen books, some collection of stories and some about kindergartens, written with her sister, Nora Archibald Smith.

BIBLIOGRAPHY: Benner, H., *Kate Douglas Wiggin's Country of Childhood* (1956). Smith, N., *Kate Douglas Wiggin as Her Sister Knew Her* (1925).

Other references: *Bookman* (32, 1910; 59, 1924). *Lamp* 29 (1905). London *Bookman* 38 (1910). *NEQ* 41 (June 1968).

BEVERLY SEATON

Ella Wheeler Wilcox

B. 5 Nov. 1850, Johnstown Center, Wisconsin; d. 30 Oct. 1919, Short Beach, Connecticut
Wrote under: Ella Wheeler, Ella Wheeler Wilcox
D. of Marcus Hartwell and Sarah Pratt Wheeler; m. Robert Marius Wilcox, 1884

W. was the youngest of four children born to a music teacher turned farmer and a mother who had strong literary ambitions. She claimed that her mother's extensive reading of Shakespeare, Scott, and Byron was a prenatal influence that shaped her entire career. Her mother helped her to find time to read and write rather than work on the bleak Wisconsin farm.

W. was influenced early by the romantic melodramas of Ouida, Mary J. Holmes, May Agnes Fleming, and Mrs. Southworth. At the age of ten she wrote a "novel" in ten chapters, printing it in her childish hand on scraps of paper and binding it in paper torn from the kitchen wall. The New York *Mercury* published an essay when she was fifteen. In 1867, she enrolled at the University of Wisconsin, where, however, she remained only a short time. She begged her family to be allowed to remain at home and write.

By the time she was eighteen, she was earning a substantial salary, which aided her impoverished family. People from Madison, Milwaukee, and Chicago began to seek out the little country girl with the "inspired pen," and she in turn was delighted to visit their city homes. By 1880, the "Milwaukee School of Poetry" was at its height with W. as its shining light; the poets were all well known throughout the West, and some had even gained recognition in the East.

Maurine (1876), a narrative poem, introduces two types of women W. often wrote about: Helen, a weak and passive person who bears a daughter and soon dies, and Maurine, an aggressive and highly intelligent artist who eventually marries an American poet-intellectual. Maurine travels to Europe, where her paintings are favorably received. Helen and Maurine reappear in more complex form as Mabel and Ruth, two of the characters in *Three Women* (1897).

When W. attempted to publish *Poems of Passion* (1883), a collection of poems that had appeared previously in various periodicals, the book was rejected because of the "immorality" of several poems, and its author became the subject of unpleasant notoriety. When a Chicago publisher brought out the book, however, it was an immediate success, and W.'s reputation was made. In this work, she brought into her love poetry the element of sin. By 1888, she was a leader in what was called the "Erotic School," a group of writers who rebelled against the stricter rules of conventionality. By 1900, a whole feminine school of rather daring verse on the subject of the emotions followed W.'s lead.

The symbolism of sexual passion is depicted throughout her poems as a tiger who is "a splendid creature," as in "Three and One" (*Poems of Pleasure*, 1888); sex for W. is "all the tiger in my blood." In "At Eleusis," motherhood is praised and welcomed, a common theme of her poetry.

W. wrote editorials and essays for the New York *Journal* and the Chicago *American* as well as contributing to *Cosmopolitan* and other magazines. In 1901, she was commissioned by the New York *American* to write a poem on the death of Queen Victoria and was sent to London, where she was presented at the court of St. James. During WWI, she toured the army camps in France, reciting her poems and counseling young soldiers on their problems.

Throughout her life, W. enjoyed great popularity, and she took her work most seriously. In defending her poetry against critics, she maintained that "heart, not art" is most important in poetry and pointed out that her poems comforted millions of weary and unhappy people.

WORKS: *Drops of Water* (1872). *Shells* (1873). *Maurine* (1876). *Poems of Passion* (1883). *The Birth of the Opal* (1886). *Mal Moulee: A Novel* (1886). *Perdita, and Other Stories* (1886). *Poems of Pleasure* (1888). *The Adventures of Miss Volney* (1888). *A Double Life* (1891). *How Salvatore Won* (1891). *The Beautiful Land of Nod* (1892). *An Erring Woman's Love* (1892). *A Budget of Christmas Tales* (1895). *An Ambitious Man* (1896). *Custer and Other Poems* (1896). *Men, Women, and Emotions* (1896). *Three Women* (1897). *Poems of Power* (1901). *The Heart of the New Thought* (1902). *Kingdom of Love* (1902). *Sweet Danger* (1902). *Around the Year* (1904). *Poems of Love* (1905). *A Woman of the World* (1905). *Mizpah* (1906). *New Thought Pastels* (1906). *Poems of Sentiment* (1906). *New Thought Common Sense and What Life Means to Me* (1908). *Song of Liberty* (1908). *Poems of Progress* (1909). *Sailing Sunny Seas* (1909). *The New Hawaiian Girl* (1910). *Yesterdays* (1910). *The Englishman, and Other Poems* (1912). *Gems* (1912). *Picked Poems* (1912). *The Art of Being Alive* (1914). *Cameos* (1914). *Lest We Forget* (1914). *Poems of Problems* (1914). *World Voices* (1916). *The Worlds and I* (1918). *Poems* (1918). *Sonnets of Sorrow and Triumph* (1918). *Collected Poems* (1924).

BIBLIOGRAPHY: Ballou, J., *Period Piece: Ella Wheeler Wilcox and Her Time* (1940). Brown, N., *Critical Confessions* (1899). Town, C. H., *Adventures in Editing* (1926). Watts, E. S., *The Poetry of American Women, 1632–1945* (1977). Wheeler, M. P., *Evolution of Ella Wheeler Wilcox and Other Wheelers* (1921). Wilcox, E. W., "Literary Confessions of a Western Poetess," in *Lippincott's* (May 1886). Wilcox, E. W., "My Autobiography," in *Cosmopolitan* (Aug. 1901).

For articles in reference works, see: *AA. NAW* (article by J. T. Baird, Jr.).

Other references: *American Mercury* (Aug. 1934). *Bookman* (Jan. 1920). *Cosmopolitan* (Nov. 1888). *Harper's* (March 1952). *Literary Digest* (22 Nov. 1919). London *Times* (31 Oct. 1919). *NYT* (31 Oct. 1919). *Poetry and Drama* 1 (March 1913).

ANNE R. GROBEN

Laura Ingalls Wilder

B. 7 Feb. 1867, Pepin County, Wisconsin; d. 10 Feb. 1957, Mansfield, Missouri
D. of Charles and Caroline Quiner Ingalls; m. Almanzo Wilder, 1885

Born in a cabin in the Wisconsin woods, W. is perhaps America's best-known female pioneer. While her books do not follow the pattern of her early life exactly, they are very close. Her parents moved their family many times, searching for a better life for W. and her three sisters. After living in Missouri, Kansas, Iowa, and Minnesota, they settled in De Smet, South Dakota, where W. met and married her husband. After a difficult early married life, in which one daughter, was born and a baby son died, the W.'s bought a farm near Mansfield, Missouri, where they lived the rest of their lives.

At Rocky Ridge Farm, W. raised chickens and made butter, helped her husband build their home, and began to write articles for various rural papers and a column, As a Farm Woman Thinks, for the Missouri *Ruralist*. She stopped writing for the papers in 1924, but her daughter, Rose Wilder Lane, a writer herself, encouraged her to write about her early life. So, in 1930 at the age of sixty-three, W. began to write the Little House books.

The seven autobiographical volumes published during W.'s lifetime cover the years from about age four to her marriage and reflect the changing point of view of the maturing heroine. *Little House in the Big Woods* (1932) describes life in a log cabin in the forest, as seen by a young child. This volume features stories about Pa's adventures in the woods, a jolly Christmas, and a maple sugaring dance. *Little House on the Prairie* (1935) takes the Ingalls family across the Mississippi into Indian lands, where they create a homestead but are forced by the government to leave. Minnesota is the scene of *On the Banks of Plum Creek* (1937) where Laura goes to school and first encounters Nellie Oleson, a tiresome brat who appears in later books as well. The Ingalls life in Minnesota is dominated by the plague of grasshoppers.

By the Shores of Silver Lake (1939) takes the family to South Dakota, where they live at a railroad camp, then spend the winter in the surveyor's house so they will be on hand when the town is established. *The Long*

Winter (1940) describes the severe winter of 1881, which the Ingalls spend in a house in De Smet. The book ends with the arrival of the train (snowbound since fall) and the celebration of Christmas in May. *Little Town on the Prairie* (1941) gives scenes of Laura's life as a teenager in town. At the end of the book, she is given a certificate to teach school, although she is only fifteen. The final volume, *These Happy Golden Years* (1943), tells of her teaching and her courtship with Almanzo W. They are married at the end of the volume. One other volume of the Little House books, *Farmer Boy* (1933), does not deal with her own life but with her husband's boyhood on a large farm near Malone, New York.

The other three books published under her name are all posthumous. *The First Four Years* (1971) covers the early, difficult years of her marriage, ending with the death of her baby boy and the burning of their home. *On the Way Home* (1962) is a journal she kept during their trip to Missouri and the beginning of their life at Rocky Ridge Farm. *West from Home* (1974) is a group of letters written to her husband from San Francisco when visiting Rose there in 1915.

The only major award won by W. was a special award given at the Newbery-Caldecott dinner in 1954, but her Little House books are among the most popular children's classics. The Children's Library Association set up the Laura Ingalls Wilder Award, of which she was the first recipient, to be given every five years. A popular television series has been based on her work, although the scripts depart a good deal from the themes and spirit of the original books, giving more emphasis to exciting and unusual events. Many of the places W. lived have memorials of some sort, and Rocky Ridge Farm is now a museum.

The Little House books' description of everyday life in pioneer times appeals to both children and adults. As children's fiction, their greatest achievement is the ease and grace with which W. speaks to children. She never patronizes, yet she retains a suitable perspective. Laura and her sisters are not glamorized; Laura is adventurous, but in contrast to children in other books about pioneer life, she performs no heroic deeds. Of course, these novels are cosmetic reality, for only a few of the harsher aspects of pioneer life are depicted, as a study of those parts of W.'s life left out of the story reveals. No doubt the romance of pioneer life, aided by the appeal of a series, is no small part of the success of the Little House books, but the heart of W.'s achievement is the literary artistry with which she uses a simple, declarative style and shapes her narrative around ordinary events.

WORKS: *Little House in the Big Woods* (1932). *Farmer Boy* (1933). *Little House on the Prairie* (1935). *On the Banks of Plum Creek* (1937). *By the Shores of Silver Lake* (1939). *The Long Winter* (1940). *Little Town on the Prairie* (1941). *These Happy Golden Years* (1943). *On the Way Home* (1962). *The First Four Years* (1971). *West from Home* (1974).

BIBLIOGRAPHY: Erisman, F., in *Studies in Medieval, Renaissance, and American Literature: A Festschrift*, Ed. B. Colquitt (1971). Zochert, D., *Laura* (1976).

Other references: *Atlantic* (Feb. 1975). *Children's Literature: The Great Excluded* 4 (1975). *Horn Book* (Sept. 1943; Dec. 1954; Oct. 1965).

BEVERLY SEATON

Emma Hart Willard

B. *23 Feb. 1787, Berlin, Connecticut; d. 15 April 1870, Troy, New York*
D. *of Samuel and Lydia Hinsdale Hart; m. John Willard, 1809; m. Christopher Yates, 1838*

W. was the sixteenth of her father's seventeen children, the ninth born to his second wife. Books were the center of life on the Hart family farm. Captain Hart had served in the Revolution, and in addition to Chaucer, Milton, and Shakespeare, the family savored stories of Washington and Lafayette.

W. attended the Berlin Academy (where within two years she was teaching younger children), but she was extensively self-taught. She took advantage of the medical books of her husband—a fifty-year-old physician and politician who had four children from two previous marriages—and the books of his nephew—a student at Middlebury College who lived in their home in Vermont. W. had been preceptress of a school in Middlebury before her marriage, and in 1814—to aid family finances—she opened the Middlebury Female Seminary, where she began to introduce "higher subjects," such as mathematics, history, and languages, in addition to the "ornamental" subjects usually deemed proper for women.

W. realized that private means were too limited to provide suitable housing, adequate libraries, and the necessary apparatus for quality education. She presented New York governor DeWitt Clinton with her *Plan for Improving Female Education* (1819), published at her own expense and sent to prominent men throughout the country. It received enthusiastic response from all quarters, but the legislature voted no funds. In 1821, however, the Troy, New York, Common Council voted to raise four thousand dollars for female education. Five years before the first public high schools for girls opened in New York (and closed shortly thereafter) and sixteen years before Mary Lyon founded the Mount Holyoke Female Seminary, W. was offering women a serious course of study equivalent to the best men's high schools and sometimes superior to their college work.

She was supported in her work by her husband (until his death in 1825), her sister, Almira Hart Lincoln Phelps, and later by her one son and his wife. Her brief second marriage (to a man who turned out to be a gambler and fortune hunter) was not successful, but W. had had the foresight to draw up an unusual prenuptial financial agreement that protected her property, income, and school.

The work that established W.'s reputation is her *Plan for Improving Female Education*. Incisive as any lawyer's brief, it argues that the current system of privately financed education was inadequate because most proprietors saw schools only as money-making ventures and because many schools, particularly girls' schools, had no entrance requirements, few regulations, and a shallow curriculum. She declares that education "should seek to bring its subjects to the perfection of their moral, intellectual, and physical nature, in order that they may be of the greatest possible use to themselves and others" and concludes by noting that since women give society its moral tone, the country would benefit from quality female education. In 1833, W. expanded these ideas in a series of lectures published as *The Advancement of Female Education* to promote a female seminary in Greece.

Even while running the seminary herself, W. found time to write several textbooks, which made her financially independent. The first is *A System of Universal Geography* (1822), written with William Channing Woodbridge. Older texts had been written as if London were the center of the world and emphasized rote learning. W. encourages students to study and draw maps and to use a globe. She describes the climate, customs, and history of different countries.

W. is best known for her history texts. *Republic of America* (1828) begins with a chronological table dividing American history into ten epochs and concludes with the "political scriptures" she learned as a child. Lafayette endorsed her account of the Revolution, and Daniel Webster wrote, "I keep it near me as book of reference, accurate in facts and dates." It was popular for both the student and the general reader.

Her Episcopal faith gave the books a popular moral tone. *A System of Universal History in Perspective* (1837) details the "virtues which exalt nations and the vices which destroy them." In 1844, she published *Temple of Time*, the first in a series of books in which she charted world history as a multi-storied temple, in which each floor is held up by groups of ten pillars on which are engraved the names of the principal sovereigns of each century. Each floor contains various groupings of nations and the roof displays the names of heroes. Although these books may appear stilted and moralistic today, they were hailed as educationally innovative, making history exciting in their time.

W. never participated in women's rights activities, but she opposed Almira's Anti-Woman Suffrage Society. She wrote to Celia Burr Burleigh in support of her career as a feminist lecturer: "After all, you have only entered now upon a work that I took up more than half a century ago—pleading the cause of my sex. I did it in my way, you are doing it in yours, and as I have reason to believe that God blessed me in my efforts, I pray that he will bless you in yours."

WORKS: *An Address to the Public, Particularly to the Members of the Legislature of New York, Proposing a Plan for Improving Female Education* (1819). *Universal Peace, to Be Introduced by a Confederacy of Nations Meeting at Jerusalem* (1820; rev. ed., 1864). *A System of Universal Geography on the Principles of Comparison and Classification* (1822; alternate title, *Ancient Geography*). *Geography for Beginners; or, The Instructor's Assistant* (1826). *Republic of America; or, History of the United States* (1828). *Advancement of Female Education* (1833). *Journal and Letters from France and Great Britain* (1833). *A System of Universal History in Perspective, Accompanied by an Atlas, Exhibiting Chronology in a Picture of Nations and Progressive Geography in a Series of Maps* (1937). *Temple of Time; or, Chronographer of Universal History* (1844). *Chronographer of Ancient History* (1846). *Chronographer of English History* (1846). *Historic Guide to the Temple of Time* (1846). *A Treatise on the Motive Powers which Produce the Circulation of the Blood* (1846). *Respiration and Its Effects, Particularly as Respects Asiatic Cholera* (1849). *Last Leaves of American History* (1849 enlarged ed., *Late American History: Containing a Full Account of the Courage, Conduct, and Success of John C. Fremont,* 1856). *Astronomy; or, Astronomical Geography* (1853). *Morals for the Young; or, Good Principles Instilling Wisdom* (1857). *Appeal to South Carolina* (1860). *Via Media* (1862).

BIBLIOGRAPHY: Lord, J., *The Life of Emma Willard* (1873). Lutz, A., *Emma Willard: Daughter of Democracy* (1929; rev. ed., *Emma Willard: Pioneer Educator of American Women,* 1964). Woody, T., *A History of Women's Education in the U.S.* (1929).

For articles in reference works, see: *NAW* (article by F. Rudolph).

NANCY A. HARDESTY

Frances Elizabeth Caroline Willard

B. 28 Sept. 1839, Churchville, New York; d. 17 Feb. 1898, New York City
Wrote under: Frances E. Willard
D. of Josiah Flint and Mary Thompson Hill Willard

In 1840, W.'s family moved from New York to Oberlin, Ohio, where both parents attended classes at the then-young college. In 1846, they moved further west, to a homestead on the Wisconsin frontier. W. had very little formal education before college. After graduating from North Western Female College in 1859, she taught in local schools and at female seminaries and colleges and then spent two years traveling in Europe, Russia, and the Near East, meeting expenses by writing weekly articles for Illinois papers.

She was president of Evanston College for Women from 1871 to 1873, when it was absorbed by Northwestern University. She then became dean of women and professor of English and Art. Her career as an educator ended with her resignation in 1874, probably due to conflicts with the university's president, who happened to be W.'s ex-fiancé.

That same summer, W. was asked to lead the Chicago Women's Christian Temperance Union (W.C.T.U.). In October, she became secretary of the state organization, and one month later, at the Cleveland convention that founded the national W.C.T.U., she was chosen as corresponding secretary. She was elected national president in 1879 and remained in that position until her death in 1898, leading for over two decades the largest organization of American women in the 19th c.

From 1876 to 1879, she was head of the publications committee, and she used the W.C.T.U. journal, Our Union, to promote her own views on the necessity of linking the temperance cause with other political issues, particularly woman suffrage. She lectured widely across the country and became a nationally known figure.

The W.C.T.U. advocated not temperance but prohibition. W. was herself responsible for their slogan, "For God, Home, and Native Land," and regularly rang that theme in pamphlets such as Home Protection Manual (1879). This was to some extent a means to retain the support of a basically middle-class and conservative movement for the aims of the more radical W., but it is also a reflection of the fact that alcoholism was not only an individual problem, but a threat to women and children who, in the 19th c., had little protection against the financial and physical exploitation of drunken husbands. In the 1890s, she became interested in socialism and argued that poverty is the cause of intemperance. Long before this country's experiment with prohibition she came to believe that education, not prohibition, is the solution of the problem of alcohol abuse. After her death, however, the W.C.T.U. limited its attention to prohibition and abstinence.

With Mary A. Livermore, W. edited *A Woman of the Century* (1893), the most important 19th-c. biographical reference work on American women. In their preface, the editors draw attention to the "vast array of woman's achievements here chronicled, in hundreds of new vocations and avocations." The articles are laudatory, but also concise and factual.

Nineteen Beautiful Years (1864), W.'s first book, is a brief account of the life of her sister, who died in 1861. It is certainly sentimental, but considerably less so than the flowery preface by John Greenleaf Whittier to the second edition (1885). Her sentimentality is particularly evident in *What Frances Willard Said* (1905), a collection of aphorisms and brief exhortations such as the following appeal for woman suffrage: "by the hours of patient watching over beds where helpless children lay, . . . I charge you, give mothers power to protect, along life's treacherous highway, those whom they have so loved." In fact, W. developed a clear and fairly simple style in which, as in her organizational work, appeals to the ideals of piety, domesticity, and patriotism—although still unpleasant to the modern reader—are connected with a usually well-reasoned argument about the needs of women.

In *Glimpses of Fifty Years* (1889), W.'s sentimental tendencies are used to good effect in the autobiography of a feminist who did not mean to undervalue the "household arts or household saints": "All that I plead for is freedom for girls as well as boys, in the exercise of their special gifts and preferences of brain and hand." For personal and political reasons, W. did not choose to dissociate herself from the sentimental or the domestic modes in either her writing or her organizational work.

WORKS: *Nineteen Beautiful Years; or, Sketches of a Girl's Life* (1864; rev. ed., 1885). *Hints and Helps in Our Temperance Work* (1875). *History of the Women's National Christian Temperance Union* (1876). *Home Protection Manual: Containing an Argument for the Temperance Ballot for Woman and How to Obtain It as a Means of Home Protection* (1879). *Woman and Temperance; or, The Work and Workers of the Women's Christian Temperance Union* (1883). *How to Win: A Book for Girls* (1886). *Woman in the Pulpit*

(1888). *Glimpses of Fifty Years: The Autobiography of an American Woman* (1889). *The Year's Bright Chain: Quotations for the Writings of Frances E. Willard* (1889). *A Classic Town: The Story of Evanston by "an Old Timer"* (1891). *A Woman of the Century; Fourteen Hundred-Seventy Biographical Sketches Accompanied by Portraits of Leading American Women in All Walks of Life* (1893; rev. ed., *American Woman*, 1897). *A Great Mother: Sketches of Madam Willard* (with M. B. Norton, 1894). *Do Everything: A Handbook for the World's White Ribboners* (1895?). *A Wheel within a Wheel: How I Learned to Ride the Bicycle, with Some Reflections by the Way* (1895). *Occupations for Women* (with H. M. Winslow and S. J. White, 1897). *What Frances Willard Said* (Ed. A. A. Gordon, 1905).

BIBLIOGRAPHY: Earhart, Mary, *Frances Willard: From Prayers to Politics* (1944). Strachey, R., *Frances Willard: Her Life and Work* (1912).

For articles in reference works, see: *DAB*, X, 2. *NAW* (article by Mary Earhart Dillon). *NCAB*, 1.

LANGDON FAUST

Catharine Read Arnold Williams

B. *31 Dec. 1787, Providence, Rhode Island; d. 11 Oct. 1872,*
Providence, Rhode Island
D. *of Alfred and Amey Read Arnold; m. Horatio N. Williams, 1824*

W.'s father was a sea captain. Because her mother died when she was a child, W. was raised and educated by two religious aunts. She did not marry until her mid-thirties, after which she and her husband moved to western New York. Two years later, W. returned to Providence with her infant daughter, Amey, and secured a divorce, although she continued to call herself "Mrs. Williams." W. opened a school, but soon abandoned teaching for health reasons. It was then that she turned to writing.

W.'s first book, *Original Poems on Various Subjects* (1828), sold by subscription, contains some poems that had been published previously. Her next book, *Religion at Home* (1829), was quite successful and went through several editions. During the next two decades, W. wrote histories, biographies, and fiction. About 1849, she moved to Brooklyn, New York, to care for an aged aunt. When her aunt died, she returned to Rhode Island, but never to writing.

In theme and choice of subject, W. always expressed patriotic, republican sentiments. *Tales, National and Revolutionary* (2 vols., 1830–35) and *Biography of Revolutionary Heroes* (1839) reflect her belief in American democracy and her desire to encourage good citizenship. In W.'s opinion, both men and women need to know about and emulate the heroism of Americans in defense of liberty; both need to understand the political and judicial systems. She praises the virtues of patience, industry and self-control, not the display of wealth and aristocratic style, as the marks of a good citizen.

Religion is also a major theme in her works. According to W., dignified and sincere religious expression, not showy religious fervor, was appropriate in the new nation. In *Fall River* (1833), for example, W. argues that the religious display at camp meetings and revivals threatens people's morality, health, and self-control; genuine religion, accordingly, is practiced at home and expressed in the heart. Good manners and useful accomplishments blossom from pure religious sentiment.

There are admirable characters of both sexes in W.'s works. In *Religion at Home, Aristocracy, or, The Holbey Family*, (1832) and other works, "true women" and admirable men are intelligent, sincerely pious, and courageous; they have good natures and even tempers. The men are distinguished from the women principally by their responsibilities and occupations. Honor and admiration characterize men's relationships with their wives; therefore, husbands frequently ask their wives, opinions on public matters. W. is critical of aristocratic pretentions in both sexes, but evil doing is mostly a male trait. When a reader pointed out to W. that her worst characters are male, she responded in the preface to the second volume of *Tales, National and Revolutionary* that she only told stories as they were told to her.

W. insists on the truth and high moral purpose of all her works. To prove that her stories are based on fact, she inserts written "proof" into the text, alluding to her personal acquaintance with the characters, explains where her information was gathered, or gives an historical account of the events behind her story. Sometimes this documentation becomes pedantic, as in *The Neutral French* (1841), but the attention W. gives to historical truth is still impressive. To emphasize the moral of a story, W. sometimes embellishes the facts, as she admits in *Tales, National and Revolutionary*, but she insists she never distorts them. Through her historical fiction, W. warns her readers against errors in personal habits and governmental practices.

W. described her own life as quiet; she said she excluded herself from gaiety not only to have time to earn a living, but also out of a sense of propriety. Prefatory remarks in *Aristocracy; or, The Holbey Family* and elsewhere indicate that W. was somewhat self-conscious about being a *woman* writer on political, legal, and historical topics, yet she never hid the fact of her sex from her readers. In recognition of her talents in those areas, W. was elected to several state historical societies.

For contemporary readers, it is not W.'s moralistic fiction, but her histories that are most interesting. *Fall River* is a fascinating study of ministerial corruption, female textile workers, and legal abuses in the early Republic. *The Neutral French* is a gold mine of carefully collected information on the Acadians. *Tales, National and Revolutionary* and *Biography of Revolutionary Heroes* contain much information about Americans in Revolutionary times. One can't help but regret that this intelligent woman stopped publishing books some twenty-five years before her death.

WORKS: *Original Poems, on Various Subjects* (1828). *Religion at Home: A Story Founded on Facts* (1829). *Tales, National and Revolutionary* (2 vols., 1830–35). *Aristocracy; or, The Holbey Family: A National Tale* (1832). *Fall River: An Authentic Narrative* (1833). *Biography of Revolutionary Heroes, Containing the Life of Brigadier General William Barton, and also of Captain Stephen Olney* (1839). *The Neutral French; or, The Exiles of Nova Scotia* (1841). *Annals of the Aristocracy, Being a Series of Anecdotes of Some of the Princpal Families of Rhode Island* (2 vols., 1843–45). *Rhode Island Tales* (Ed. H. R. Palmer, 1928; including 5 stories by Williams).

BIBLIOGRAPHY: Rider, S. S., *Biographical Memoirs of Three Rhode Island Authors* (Rhode Island Tracts, no. 11, 1880).

For articles in reference works, see: *DAB*.

Other references: Providence *Daily Journal* (14 Oct. 1872).

SUSAN COULTRAP-McQUIN

Helen Maria Winslow

B. *13 April 1851, Westfield, Vermont; d. 27 March 1938*
Wrote under: *Aunt Philury, Helen M. Winslow*
D. *of Don Avery and Mary Salome Newton Winslow*

Educated at the Westfield Vermont Academy, the Vermont Normal School, and the New England Conservatory of Music, W. began her literary career writing pastoral poems and short fiction for such children's periodicals as *Youth's Companion*, *Wide Awake*, and *Cottage Hearth*. Although she continued to write poetry and children's fiction sporadically throughout her life, she is best remembered not for these "Aunt Philury Papers," but for her newspaper and club work

Early in W.'s career as a journalist, after the death of her parents, she lived in the Boston area with her three sisters. During the 1880s, she wrote for numerous Boston papers, including the *Beacon*, the *Transcript*, the *Advisor*, and the *Saturday Evening Gazette*. Her first novel, *A Bohemian Chapter* (1886), the story of a struggling woman artist, was serialized in the *Beacon*. Her journalistic experiences led her to help form the New England Woman's Press Association (which she served as first treasurer) and the Boston Author's Club (which she served as secretary); she was also vice-president of the Women's Press League.

W.'s most sustained activity resulted from her involvement with the General Federation of Woman's Clubs. In the early 1890s, she was assistant editor of the *Woman's Cycle*, the federation's first official journal, and editor and publisher of its second journal, The *Club Woman*. She also edited the *Delineator's* "Woman's Club" department for thirteen years and was founder and editor of the "Woman's Club Column" in the Boston *Transcript*. From 1898 through 1930, W. annually published the official *Woman's Club Register*. In addition to her direct affiliation with the club movement and its numerous publications, W. wrote numerous articles celebrating club women and their work in journals such as the *Arena*, the *Critic*, and the *Atlantic Monthly*. The most significant of these articles was her extensive history of American woman's clubs, "The Story of the Woman's Club Movement," (*New England Magazine*, June and October 1908).

Among the more interesting of W.'s generally forgotten novels is *Salome Shepard, Reformer* (1893), an indictment of industrial working conditions with suggestions for reform. Salome, a young society woman, awakens to a sense of social responsibility after discovering the unsafe working and intolerable living conditions in the mills she has inherited from her father. Almost single-handedly, Salome initiates a series of reforms, including a model dormitory for the women workers, a social hall for the families of workers, and profit sharing.

W. partly duplicates this plot in *The President of Quex* (1906). In this novel, written in response to Agnes Surbridge's strident denunciation of club women in "The Evolution of a Club Woman—A Story of Ambition Realized" (*Delineator*, 1904), W.'s heroine, the president of a woman's club concerned with municipal reform, becomes aware of abusive child-labor conditions in her factories. Again, the women, this time through their club work, initiate and effect the necessary reforms, with no sacrifice to their home lives.

A Woman for Mayor (1909) is W.'s most effective dramatization of the political sensibilities and capabilities of middle-class women. Written in support of the "municipal-housekeeping" concept of social reform, moderate women's rights, and the Progressive-era concept of expanded social services in local government, the novel relates the story of a young woman who is elected mayor on a platform dedicated to the eradication of political graft and corruption.

Despite both her own achievements and those of her many heroines, W. showed a lifelong ambivalence about the public role of women. In each of her novels, the heroine, after ably demonstrating her superiority, retires willingly to marriage; she claims that marriage will not bring an end to her public activism, although her primary forcus will necessarily be on her home life. In no novel, however, does W. present her heroine after marriage. It is unclear whether this seeming ambivalence results from W.'s desire to defend club women and meet the demands of a literary public in search of the happy ending or from an uncertainty about her own life-style—as her article "Confessions of a Newspaperwoman" (*Atlantic*, February 1905) might suggest. Whatever the reason, W.'s fiction provides useful material for any reader interested in the ongoing debate about the public and private roles of women.

WORKS: *A Bohemian Chapter* (1886). *Salome Shepard, Reformer* (1893). *Mexico Picturesque* (with M. R. Wright, 1897). *Occupations for Women* (with F. Willard, 1898). *Concerning Cats* (1900). *Concerning Polly* (1902). *Little Journeys in Literature* (1902). *Literary Boston of Today* (1903). *Confessions of a Club Woman* (1904). *The Woman of Tomorrow* (1905). *The President of Quex* (1906). *The Pleasuring of Susan Smith* (1908). *Spinster Farm* (1908). *A Woman for Mayor* (1909). *The Road to a Loving Heart* (1926). *Keeping Young Gracefully* (1928).

BIBLIOGRAPHY: Blair, K., "The Clubwoman as Feminist: The Woman's Culture Club Movement in the United States, 1868–1914" (Ph.D. diss., State Univ. of New York at Buffalo, 1976). Blake, F., *The Strike in the American Novel* (1972). Hill, Vicki Lynn, "Strategy and Breadth: The Socialist-Feminist in American Fiction" (Ph.D. diss., State Univ. of New York at Buffalo, 1979). Taylor, W., *The Economic Novel in America* (1942).

For articles in reference works, see: *American Women*, Ed. Howes (1939). *NCAB*, B. *National Cyclopaedia of American Biography* (1927).

Other references: *Atlantic* (Dec. 1894). *Godey's* (Nov. 1893). *Independent* (26 Nov. 1893). *Literary World* (17 June 1893). *Picayune* (7 May 1893).

VICKI LYNN HILL

Sally Sayward Barrell Wood

B. 1 Oct. 1759, York, Maine; d. 6 Jan. 1855, Kennebunk, Maine
Wrote under: Sally Keating
D. of Nathaniel and Sarah Sayward Barrell; m. Richard Keating, 1778; m. Abiel
  Wood, 1804

The first of eleven children, W. was born into a colonial New England family while her father was serving with General James Wolfe, British leader of the attack on Quebec. Her mother was the daughter of Judge Jonathan Sayward, with whom W. lived until she was eighteen. During the American Revolution, Judge Sayward was a Loyalist, and much of his conservatism·is evident in W.'s work.

Her first husband was a clerk in her grandfather's office. The Judge gave them a house as a wedding present, and they settled into the cultivated social life that had surrounded her childhood. Two daughters and a son were born before Keating died suddenly in 1783. W. turned to writing, not from any pressing financial need, but because it "soothed many *melancholy*, and sweetened many *bitter* hours." Her work was well received, and she gained a considerable literary reputation.

She stopped writing when she married General Abiel Wood, in 1804. "Madam Wood," as she was then known, took up writing again, after his death in 1811.

Following in the path of such early American novelists as Sarah Wentworth Morton, Susannah H. Rowson, and Hannah Webster Foster, W. occupies an important niche in the development of American fiction, although her work does not mark a radical break from the traditions imported from England. In accordance with her 18th-c. upbringing, she was serious, moralistic, and sentimental. Her stories generally follow a Cinderella pattern centering on a virtuous young woman who either is, or is reputed to be, a poor orphan but who after severe trial is rewarded with a wealthy marriage. Virtue, for W., is more than chastity; it is linked to intelligence and education with a strong infusion of patience and submission. Her heroines redeem, reform, or blunt the evil of the world by the example of their behavior, and if they are passive in suffering vicissitudes, they are strong in the face of vice.

Julia and the Illuminated Baron (1800) is perhaps her best-known work. Certainly it is the most complex, and Julia's progress from nameless orphan to respectably pedigreed wife and mother involves a set of characters (all related by blood) in a series of Gothic adventures. The baron of the title is a member of the Illuminati, a secret society that shocked W.; she presents him as an atheist, anarchist, and mystic who announces proudly, "I am to myself a God, and to myself accountable. . . . if anyone stands in my way, I put him out of it, with as little concern as I would kick a dog." The setting is France, but the characters are clearly recognizable as Americans in their actions and values.

Amelia; or, The Influence of Virtue (1802) states her most constant theme. The gentle heroine, married to a rake, prefers death to divorce and meekly bears the taunts of her husband's mistress and rears his illegitimate children without complaint. She is rewarded in the end with a repentant husband, adoring children, and a respectable position in society. As in all her works, W. does not plumb psychological depths, and the solution is simplistic, but the action is rapid, and her gift for creating melodramatic moments holds the reader's attention.

Ferdinand and Elmira (1804) is an adventure tale, again with intertwined lives of a single family, in a Russian setting that gives an exotic flavor to a moral tale. As it opens, Elmira is a captive in a mysterious castle, and the explanation of this circumstance leads to another mystery. This pattern (of one mystery following the solution of another) is consistent throughout, and the resultant suspense is the primary means of moving the action forward. The ending resolves all, pairs the heroine and hero, rewards the good, and permits the villains an extravagant repentance. W.'s focus is on the morality of the simple life as opposed to the corruption of courts; and, despite her Loyalist grandfather, the tale is clearly antiroyalist in tone.

W. is one of the first writers to embody distinctly American ideals. She does not admire aristocratic idleness; indeed, one of her heroes is praised for his ambition to go into trade, and her young lovers rarely end with titles of nobility. She reflects strongly the responsibilities of freedom so uppermost in the consciousness of the young nation. Typical of her time in sentimental morality and her view of woman's place in society, her work nevertheless reveals an inquiring and imaginative mind searching for new horizons.

WORKS: *Julia and the Illuminated Baron* (1800). *Dorval; or, The Speculator* (1801). *Amelia; or, The Influence of Virtue* (1802). *Ferdinand and Elmira* (1804). *Tales of the Night* (1827).

BIBLIOGRAPHY Goold, W., in *Collections and Proceedings of the Maine Historical Society* (1890). Dunnack, H. E. *The Maine Book* (1920). Sayward, C. A. *The Sayward Family* (1890). Spencer, W. D. *Maine Immortals* (1932).

HELENE KOON

Sarah Chauncey Woolsey

B. 29 Jan. 1835, Cleveland, Ohio; d. 9 April 1905, Newport, Rhode Island
Wrote under: Susan Coolidge
D. of John Mumford and Jane Woolsey

W. spent her formative years in a lively household, amusing her three younger sisters, brother, and cousin with games and stories. She was first educated in Cleveland private schools, then sent to a boarding school in Hanover, New Hampshire, nicknamed "The Nunnery." From 1855 to 1870, W. lived with her parents in New Haven, Connecticut, where her uncle Theodore Dwight Woolsey was president of Yale. During the Civil War, she spent one summer working with her friend Helen Hunt Jackson in the New Haven Government Hospital and ten months serving as an assistant superintendent at the Lowell General Hospital, Portsmouth Grove, Rhode Island.

After her father's death in 1870, W. moved to Newport, Rhode Island, a residence interrupted only by journeys to Europe, California, and Colorado and, in her later years, by summers in the Catskills. In 1871, her career as children's author began with the publication of *The New Year's Bargain*. The Katy series (1872–91) brought her fame. She also wrote poetry and magazine articles, served for a time as children's book reviewer for the *Literary World*, and worked as reader and editor for her publishers, Roberts Brothers.

Although *The New Year's Bargain* employs fantasy reminiscent of Andersen in a story of two German children who trick the months into telling them stories, *What Katy Did* (1872) establishes W. as a writer of realistic juvenile fiction, similar to Louisa Alcott in her gift of depicting real American girls in an appealing family setting. Katy Carr, an impulsive, boisterous, and ever-well-intentioned girl who leads her younger sisters and brothers into scrapes, finally matures through suffering and the acceptance of responsibility. Her adventures continue in *What Katy Did at School* (1873) when Katy and her sister Clover become students at a New England boarding school and meet the irrepressible Rose Red, beloved by more than one generation of schoolgirl readers in America and England.

Katy travels to Europe and finds romance in *What Katy Did Next* (1886), where W. uses the travelogue, a popular formula in children's literature of the period, to carry a rather pedestrian plot. The Katy series concludes with *Clover* (1888) and *In the High Valley* (1891), as the six Carrs grow up and marry. The charm of the final books lies less in the portraits of the young people than in the Colorado setting, which W. remembered so vividly from her trips to visit Helen Hunt Jackson.

W.'s other juvenile novels also feature plucky girls in realistic settings, but none of the heroines has Katy's imagination and vitality.

Among the notable collections of W.'s short stories are *Mischief's Thanksgiving* (1874), *Nine Little Goslings* (1875), *Cross Patch* (1881), *A Round Dozen* (1883), and *Just Sixteen* (1889). These volumes illustrate her capacity for invention and her range—stories for children and for adolescents, tales of realism and of fantasy. *Nine Little Goslings* and *Cross Patch* cleverly translate Mother Goose stories into tales peopled with real children in contemporary settings.

Although W. hoped to achieve distinction as a poet, her three volumes of verse for adults, *Verses* (1880), *A Few More Verses* (1889), and *Last Verses* (1906), reveal little more than careful workmanship, a sober acceptance of suffering and death, and a certain flair for the narrative poem.

A talented and versatile writer of children's fiction, W. was once almost as popular as Louisa Alcott in both England and America. Today she is still remembered for her stories of the incomparable Katy Carr.

WORKS: *The New Year's Bargain* (1871). *What Katy Did* (1872). *What Katy Did at School* (1873). *Mischief's Thanksgiving, and Other Stories* (1874). *Nine Little Goslings* (1875). *For Summer Afternoons* (1876). *Autobiography and Correspondence of Mrs. Delany* (edited by Woolsey, 1879). *Eyebright* (1879). *The Diary and Letters of Frances Burney, Madame D'Arblay* (edited by Woolsey, 1880). *A Guernsey Lily; or, How the Feud Was Healed* (1880). *Verses* (1880). *Cross Patch, and Other Stories* (1881). *My Household Pets* by T. Gautier (translated by Woolsey, 1882). *A Round Dozen* (1883). *A Little Country Girl* (1885). *One Day in a Baby's Life* by M. Arnaud (translated by Woolsey, 1886). *What Katy Did Next* (1886). *A Short History of the City of Philadelphia from Its Foundation to the Present Time* (1887). *Clover* (1888). *A Few More Verses* (1889). *Just Sixteen* (1889). *The Day's Message* (1890). *In the High Valley* (1891). *Letters of Jane Austen* (edited by Woolsey, 1892). *Rhymes and Ballads for Boys and Girls* (1892). *The Barberry Bush* (1893).

Not Quite Eighteen (1894). *An Old Convent School in Paris, and Other Papers* (1895). *Curly Locks* (1899). *A Little Knight of Labor* (1899). *Little Tommy Tucker* (1900). *Two Girls* (1900). *Little Bo-Peep* (1901). *Uncle and Aunt* (1901). *The Rule of Three* (1904). *Last Verses* (1906). *A Sheaf of Stories* (1906).

BIBLIOGRAPHY: Banning, E., *Helen Hunt Jackson* (1973). Darling, R. L., *The Rise of Children's Book Reviewing in America, 1865–1881* (1968). Kilgour, R. L., *Messrs. Roberts Brothers, Publishers* (1952). Meigs, C., *A Critical History of Children's Literature* (rev. ed., 1969).

For articles in reference works, see: *NAW* (article by F. C. Darling).

Other references: *Horn Book* 35 (1959).

PHYLLIS MOE

Constance Fenimore Woolson

B. 5 March 1840, Claremont, New Hampshire; d. 24 Jan. 1894, Venice, Italy
Wrote under: Anne March, Constance Fenimore Woolson
D. of Charles Jarvis and Hannah Cooper Pomeroy Woolson

W. was the sixth of nine children. She was the grand-niece of James Fenimore Cooper. After the death of three older sisters from scarlet fever, W. moved at a very early age with her family to Cleveland. She attended school there until enrolling in Madame Chegary's school in New York City, from which she graduated in 1858. Her childhood summers were spent at the family cottage at Mackinac Island, later to become the setting for a number of her short stories. After her father's death in 1869, she travelled extensively in the South with her mother. Upon her death in 1879, W. and her sister, Clare Benedict, traveled in Europe, where W. spent the remainder of her life. She died in Venice after falling or leaping from her bedroom window. Whether her death was the result of delirium from influenza or of depression has never been determined. At the time of her death she had achieved a moderate degree of recognition as a writer; today her works are virtually unknown.

W.'s first book, *The Old Stone House*, a book for children, was published in 1872 under the pseudonym of Anne March. Of more importance, however, is the collection *Castle Nowhere: Lake-Country Sketches*

(1875), which contains nine stories fashioned from her observations of Mackinac Island. *Castle Nowhere* has been compared favorably with Sarah Orne Jewett's *Deephaven* (1877) and Mary Noailles Murfree's *In the Tennessee Mountains* (1884).

Of even better quality is her second volume of short stories, *Rodman the Keeper: Southern Sketches* (1880), which sympathetically treats the Reconstruction period. One of the most skillfully written pieces in this collection, "Old Gardiston," depicts the downfall of an ancient southern family, and concludes with the burning of their mansion before it can be possessed by a northern businessman and his wife.

Anne (1882) was published as a novel shortly after its serialization in *Harper's*. Set in various places, including Mackinac Island, Pennsylvania, and West Virginia, the novel tells the story of Anne Douglas in a somewhat melodramatic plot including a love affair and a murder trial. In the 1880s *Anne* was a popular novel; today it is a forgotten work which deserves renewed attention.

For the Major (1883), set in Far Edgerly, a mountain village in western North Carolina, is a tale of Sara Carroll's return home from a long journey and her discovery that her father, Major Carroll, has become senile and that her stepmother is laboring to shield both the Major and the townspeople from this knowledge. W.'s story provides an excellent blend of comic treatment of the inhabitants of Far Edgerly and a noble portrait of the declining Major and his compassionate wife. It is considered one of W.'s finest works.

East Angels (1886), set in Florida, was also a popular work at the time of its publication. W. brings together a group of wealthy northerners and impoverished southern aristocrats in this postwar novel of reconciliation.

In her novel *Jupiter Lights* (1889), W. incorporates Georgia, the Lake Country, and Italy as settings. Although the plot is contrived and the action melodramatic, the work has been noted for its advances in the psychological complexity of the characters, especially the heroine, Eve Bruce.

W.'s final novel, *Horace Chase* (1894), set in Asheville, North Carolina, after the war, chronicles the marriage of Horace Chase, self-made millionaire, and Ruth Franklin, his headstrong young wife. Ruth becomes infatuated with a young man of her own age, but is forgiven by her husband who says at the close of the novel, "I don't know that I have been so perfect myself, that I have any right to judge you." In a letter to Henry Mills Alden, W. notes that the essence of the novel lies in that last sentence and concludes, "Do you think it is impossible? I do not."

Two volumes of Italian stories, *The Front Yard, and Other Italian Stories* (1895) and *Dorothy, and Other Italian Stories* (1896), as well as a volume of travel sketches, *Mentone, Cairo, and Corfu* (1896) were published after W.'s death. The Italian stories include some of her best work, such as "The Front Yard," the story of Prudence Wilkin, a New England woman who accompanies her wealthy cousin to Italy. Prudence marries an Italian waiter who dies after their first year of marriage leaving her a house inhabited by eight children and other assorted relatives whom Prudence supports until her death sixteen years later.

A minor writer who produced a number of fine stories, W. is to be noted as a pioneer both in local-color writing and in her depiction of a number of female characters—such as Ruth Franklin of *Horace Chase* or Margaret Harold of *East Angels*—which anticipates female characterization of 20th-c. literature.

WORKS: *The Old Stone House* (1872). *Castle Nowhere: Lake-Country Sketches* (1875). *Rodman the Keeper: Southern Sketches* (1880). *Anne* (1882). *For the Major* (1883). *East Angels* (1886). *Jupiter Lights* (1889). *Horace Chase* (1894). *The Front Yard, and Other Italian Stories* (1895). *Dorothy, and Other Italian Stories* (1896). *Mentone, Cairo, and Corfu* (1896).

BIBLIOGRAPHY: Benedict, C., ed., *Five Generations (1785–1923)* (3 vols., 1929–30). James, H., *Partial Portraits* (1888). Kern, J., *Constance Fenimore Woolson: Literary Pioneer* (1934). Moore, R., *Constance F. Woolson* (1963).

Other references: *SAQ* (38, April 1938; 39, June 1940). *Miss Q* 29 (Fall 1976).

ANNE ROWE

Katharine Prescott Wormeley

B. *14 Jan. 1830, Ipswich, England; d. 4 Aug. 1908, Jackson, New Hampshire*
D. *of Ralph and Caroline Wormeley*

W. was descended, on her mother's side of the family, from Boston merchants and, on her father's, from a long line of Virginians. The family lived in England for many years, settling in the U.S. after her father's death in 1852.

At the beginning of the Civil War, W. threw herself into volunteer work. She formed the local chapter of the Woman's Union in Newport, Rhode Island, and headed it until 1862. She also obtained a contract from the federal government to manufacture clothing for the troops, thus giving employment to otherwise destitute soldiers' wives. In April, 1862, W.

began working for the U.S. Sanitary Commission, a private volunteer organization, as a matron on a hospital ship. Later that year, she became "lady superintendent" of Lowell General Hospital in Portsmouth Grove, Rhode Island. Her health, however, gave out after a year, and she returned home to Newport.

After the war, W. continued her charitable work. She helped found the Newport Charity Organization Society in 1874 and served it in various capacities for the next fifteen years. She also established an industrial school for girls that offered classes in cooking, sewing, and domestic management.

Besides charity work, W.'s passion was for literature. Fluent in French, she translated many of the works of Balzac, Molière, Daudet, and Saint-Simon. In 1892, she published *A Memoir of Honoré de Balzac*.

In *The Other Side of War* (1889), W. describes her function on the hospital ship *Daniel Webster*: "Our duty is to be very much that of a housekeeper. We attend to the beds, the linen, the clothing of the patients; we have a pantry and store-room, and are required to do all the cooking for the sick, and see that it is properly distributed according to the surgeons' orders; we are also to have a general superintendence over the condition of the wards and over the nurses, who are all men." W. and her companions were on duty almost constantly; when they could relax, space and privacy were limited.

When W. was loaned temporarily to the Medical Department of the Army, she discovered conditions that were, incredibly, worse than what she had already seen. Accustomed to abundant supplies of food, bandages, and medications, she found the Army lacked adequate stores of all three. Because of that, many men died whom, W. believes, the Sanitary Commission might have saved. The commission's example finally shamed the government into reorganizing its medical department in July 1862. Then, W. claims with pride, the commission could resume its original functions, "inspecting the condition of the camps and regiments, and continuing on a large scale its supply business."

The Other Side of War is an appropriate title for W.'s work. As she notes, it is far too easy, both for her contemporaries and modern historians, to get caught up in the romance and glory of war without fully acknowledging the human suffering which invariably accompanies it. She and the countless other women, who worked in the hospitals of the Civil War, in both the North and South, remind us of its true horror.

WORKS: *The United States Sanitary Commission: A Sketch of Its Purpose and Work* (1863). *The Other Side of War* (1889). *A Memoir of Honoré de Balzac* (1892).

BIBLIOGRAPHY: Brockett, L. P., and M. C. Vaughn, Woman's Work in the Civil War (1867). Massey, M. E., Bonnet Brigades (1966). Maxwell, W. O., Lincoln's Fifth Wheel (1956).

JANET E. KAUFMAN

Mabel Osgood Wright

B. 26 Jan. 1859, New York City; d. 16 July 1934, Fairfield, Connecticut
Wrote under: Barbara, Mabel Osgood Wright
D. of Samuel and Ellen Murdock Osgood; m. James Osborne Wright, 1884

W.'s father was a Unitarian minister who late in life became an Episcopalian; the Osgood family lived in a large house in lower Manhattan when there were still cows pastured nearby. Educated at home and at a private school, W. was a keen amateur naturalist from her youth, enjoying long summer vacations at the family summer home.

With her husband, a dealer in rare books and art (whom she referred to as "Evan" in her semi-autobiographical Barbara books) she lived in Fairfield, Connecticut. She apparently had no children.

W. was the first president of the Audubon Society of Connecticut and a member of the American Ornithologists' Union and the Connecticut Society of Colonial Dames—a much more exclusive organization than the Daughters of the American Revolution, which she ridiculed in The Woman Errant (1904).

W.'s first published books were about nature. Three—The Friendship of Nature (1894), Birdcraft (1895), and Flowers and Ferns in Their Haunts (1901)—were written for adults, but most are for children. As was common in 19th-c. children's nature books, W. taught about nature in story form, creating fictional children to lead the little readers through their lessons. Tommy-Anne and the Three Hearts (1896) and its sequel, Wabeno the Magician (1899), tell of a young tomboy who discovers the "Magic Spectacles" that combine truth with imagination. Wearing her spectacles she can converse with the grass, flowers, insects, squirrels, and even her dog, Waddles.

Among W.'s most popular works are the semiautobiographical Barbara books, particularly the first, *The Garden of a Commuter's Wife* (1901), which introduces her alter ego, Barbara, who lives in the country with her husband and shares her life with many eccentric friends. W. calls this book and *The Garden, You, and I* (1906) "pages from Barbara's Garden Book"; three other Barbara books bear designations intended to reveal other aspects of Barbara's life. *People of the Whirlpool* (1903) is "from the Experience Book," *Princess Flower-Hat* (1910) is "from the Perplexity Book," and *A Woman Errant* is "from the Wonder Book." W. blends fanciful fiction with social comment, showing that she was an interested observer of the changes taking place in New York society—particularly among her own class of people. Servants provide comic relief.

A Woman Errant is the most serious book of the series. It is a melodramatic statement of W.'s belief that woman lives for and through man. According to W., women who leave their proper sphere for a career become bisexual. She shows a woman doctor who causes her own son's death because of her lack of the right kind of ability. W.'s attack on career women is not atypical of popular writers, even the professional women writers.

W.'s novels, set in the same area as her Barbara stories, are all romances, and in most of them she focuses on marriage as the most important part of life. In her last, *Eudora's Men* (1931), she underlines the importance of men to women by tracing a family from the beginning of the Civil War down to the present, when one of the youngest generation, a woman doctor, almost ruins the life of her husband by her "unnatural" concept of marriage.

In her autobiography, *My New York* (1926), she writes of her life up to the death of her beloved father and her engagement, focusing entirely on the city. It is a beautifully written picture of life in lower Manhattan in the 1860s and 1870s, giving her gift for observation and social comment its best exercize; it memorializes old New York, which had all but vanished when she wrote the book.

While W. is historically an important figure in popular nature writing, she did not make a successful transition to fiction as did Gene Stratton-Porter. But her autobiography is a charming, nostalgic book written without the bitterness she showed in other books when writing of the changes in society.

WORKS: *The Friendship of Nature* (1894). *Birdcraft* (1895). *Tommy-Anne and the Three Hearts* (1896). *Citizen Bird* (1897). *Four-footed Americans and Their Kin* (1898). *Wabeno the Magician* (1899). *The Dream Fox Story Book* (1900). *Flowers and Ferns in Their Haunts* (1901). *The Garden of a Commuter's Wife* (1901). *Dogtown* (1902). *Aunt Jimmy's Will* (1903). *People of the*

Whirlpool (1903). *The Woman Errant* (1904). *At the Sign of the Fox* (1905). *The Garden, You, and I* (1906). *Gray Lady and the Birds* (1907). *The Open Window* (1908). *Poppea of the Post-office* (1909). *Princess Flower Hat* (1910). *The Love that Lives* (1911). *The Stranger at the Gate* (1913). *My New York* (1926). *Captains of the Watch of Life and Death* (1927). *Eudora's Men* (1931).

BIBLIOGRAPHY: *NAW* (article by R. H. Welker). *NYT* (18 July 1934).

BEVERLY SEATON

Edith Franklin Wyatt

B. 14 Sept. 1873, Tomah, Wisconsin; d. Oct. 1958, Chicago, Illinois
D. of Franklin and Marian La Grange Wyatt

A self-designated "middle-class American," W. spent her earliest years in midwestern towns where her father was a railroad and mining engineer. Settled in a modest, neighborly Chicago home in the 1880s, she and her two younger sisters shared wide-ranging interests with their mother, who was later a privately published poet. W. attended Bryn Mawr from 1892 to 1894 and taught at a local girls' school for five years.

W.'s first publication, "Three Stories of Contemporary Chicago" (1900), caught the attention of William Dean Howells, who publicly praised her early fiction and remained an admiring friend. While teaching at Hull House and participating in The Little Room, Chicago's preeminent salon, she produced most of her fiction during this decade.

After her *McClure's* report on the 1909 Cherry Mine fire, W. was in great demand during the 1910s as a social commentator and Progressive activist, promoting the causes of working-class women, child laborers, victims of the Eastland pleasure-boat disaster, and suffragists. A founding Board member of *Poetry*, her concurrent literary work included a report on working-women's budgets, a documentary play, poems, and literary criticism. Socially conscientious but temperamentally retiring, W. lived with her mother and maintained a few close friendships with people who shared her commitments.

Her creative talent seems to have exhausted itself in 1923, when she published her second novel after a year as assistant editor for *McClure's*.

Her remaining work was mostly retrospective; she memoralized deceased colleagues and Chicago's past and also collected her earlier short stories.

The stories first published in *Every One His Own Way* (1901) demonstrate W.'s attention to the everyday strengths and distinctive mannerisms of urban ethnic types as well as her exposure of genteel intolerance. Recurring characters and neighborhood settings link together stories ranging from tragedy to satire. "A Matter of Taste" is representative: it recounts a literary critic's disdain for the participative, popular musical tastes of a German-American couple, while embodying W.'s own characteristic perspective in the clear-sighted observations of the critic's sister.

A similar dichotomy between conventionality and wholesomeness informs W.'s first novel, *True Love* (1903). Snobbish Norman Hubbard —whose "sepulchral" Chicago home traps visitors in vacuous conversation —engages himself to an equally convention-bound woman, until they can no longer stand each other's narrowness. A second romance between unpretentious Chicagoan Emily Marsh, whose simple family home welcomes friends to billiards and cards, and an equally ordinary country man, leads to marriage.

W. believed that heterogeneous Americans share primarily the experience of migration: "Movement through a variety of country" is, she declares, the unifying theme of the poems in *The Wind in the Corn* (1917). "To a River God" exemplifies her poetry's dynamic attention to geography; unity-in-diversity theme; and ritualistic, chanting rhythms, which occasionally disintegrate into sing-song. Most admired were W.'s urban poems; "November in the City" and "City Equinoctial" epitomize her unconventional portrayal of natural cycles in city as well as country scenes.

Original observation and social perspective mark W.'s literary criticism and social commentary. A well-chosen selection in *Great Companions* (1917) demonstrates her concerns with national literary culture, writers' attitudes toward women, and autobiographies of working people. "The Dislike of Human Interest" clarifies the political basis for her objections to standardized literary stereotypes.

Invisible Gods (1923) tries to combine W.'s fictional talents with her political commitments in a sociological novel about three generations of a Chicago family. But an uncharacteristically loose, episodic structure and wordy prose undercut her uncompromising vision and talent for characterization.

W. combined a pluralistic appreciation of common people and regional integrity with original observation and satiric humor in her fiction, poetry, literary criticism, and social commentaries. Her early fiction and essays represent her best work, as fine as that of Howells and undeservedly ignored by literary historians and critics.

WORKS: Every One His Own Way (1901). *True Love: A Comedy of the Affections* (1903). *The Whole Family* (with W. D. Howells, H. James, et al., 1907). *Making Both Ends Meet* (with S. A. Clark, 1911). *Great Companions* (1917). *The Wind in the Corn, and Other Poems* (1917). *The Invisible Gods* (1923). *Art and the Worth While* (with R. M. Lovett, Z. Gale, et al., 1929). *The Satyr's Children* (1939). *Two Fairy Tales: The Pursuit of Happiness and The Air Castle* (n.d.).

The Edith Franklin Wyatt Manuscripts at the Newberry Library, Chicago, Illinois, include a box of correspondance and three boxes of published and unpublished works.

BIBLIOGRAPHY: Boston *Transcript* (22 Dec. 1917). *Harper's* (Oct. 1901). New York *Tribune* (11 March 1923). *North American Review* (May 1903; March 1917). *Poetry* (Jan. 1918).

SIDNEY H. BREMER

Elinor Hoyt Wylie

B. 7 Sept. 1885, Somerville, New Jersey; d. 16 Dec. 1928, New York City
Wrote under: Elinor Wylie
D. of Henry Martyn and Anne McMichael Hoyt; m. Philip Hichborn, 1905; m.
Horace Wylie, 1916; m. William Rose Benét, 1923

W., the eldest of five children born into a socially and politically prominent family, grew up and attended private schools in Philadelphia and Washington, D.C. Her elopement in 1910, with a married Washington lawyer, Horace Wylie, and abandonment of her husband and son became a highly publicized scandal. To escape the notoriety, the couple lived for a few years in England as Mr. and Mrs. Horace Waring. There she published—privately and anonymously—her first book of poetry, *Incidental Numbers* (1912). The pair returned to the U.S. before WWI, living first in Boston, then in Augusta, Georgia, and Washington, D.C.

In Washington, W. became friendly with the writers William Rose Benét, Edmund Wilson, and John Dos Passos, who encouraged her to take her writing seriously. After separating from Wylie in 1921, she moved to New York and captivated the literary world with her beauty, elegance, conversation, and acid wit. She married Benét in 1923.

During the eight years from 1921 until her death, W. served as a contributing editor of the *New Republic* and wrote short stories, literary criticism, four volumes of poetry, and four novels. Two of the latter derive from her great interest in the Romantic movement, especially in the poet Shelley. *The Orphan Angel* (1926) is a fantasy of Shelley searching across the expanding American West for a mysterious and beautiful woman. *Mr. Hodge and Mr. Hazard* (1928) recounts the decline of Romanticism in the tale of "the last Romantic poet" confronting the bourgeois world of the Victorians. Much careful scholarship went into the backgrounds of these novels.

W.'s talent is notable, but problematic. A tension between opposing impulses often led her to miss her mark; but when these tensions were confronted and developed, her work achieved its full potential in powerful poems of heightened irony. W.'s technical facility and taste for elegance produced in her novels and some of her verse a polished surface with little sustaining depth. No doubt aware of this, she called her first full-length novel, *Jennifer Lorn* (1923), "a sedate extravaganza." One critic described it as "a dish of curds and cream flavoured with saffron." The book's heroine is such a delicacy herself—elaborately confected, a visual delight, but entirely unsubstantial. One focus of the novel's rather mild satire is society's vision of women as decorative objects.

The Venetian Glass Nephew (1925) concerns itself with the conflicting claims of art and nature, but thematic development is submerged to elegant sensual richness. Rosalba Berni undergoes the painful transformation into glass in order to become a suitable bride for the manufactured Virginio. One of the characters notes: "The result, although miraculous, is somewhat inhuman. I have known fathers who submitted their daughters to the ordeal, husbands who forced it upon their wives."

In her best poetry, W. dealt more pointedly with the conflicts that claimed her attention: the problem of the feeling self smoldering beneath its decorative surface. Statements of this theme appear in "Sleeping Beauty," "Sanctuary," "Where, O Where?" "The Lie," and "Full Moon." In the last poem, the speaker, dressed elegantly in "silk and miniver," cries: "There I walked, and there I raged; / The spiritual savage caged. . . ." Images of falsehood—masks, disguises, and costumes—convey the tension between beautiful exterior and turbulent interior, between felt passion and enforced restraint.

Carl Van Vechten called *Jennifer Lorn* "the only successfully sustained satire in English with which I am acquainted." Praise for her other works was equally adulatory. Recent criticism has been scanty and less favorable. The inclusion of W. in recently published anthologies of women poets indicates a reawakening of appreciation; it is time for her to receive a full-scale literary reappraisal.

WORKS: *Incidental Numbers* (1912). *Nets to Catch the Wind* (1921). *Black Armour* (1923). *Jennifer Lorn* (1923). *The Venetian Glass Nephew* (1925). *The Orphan Angel* (1926). *Angels and Earthly Creatures* (1928). *Mr. Hodge and Mr. Hazard* (1928). *Trivial Breath* (1928). *Collected Poems of Elinor Wylie* (1932). *Collected Prose of Elinor Wylie* (1933). *Last Poems of Elinor Wylie* (1943).

BIBLIOGRAPHY: Colum, M., *Life and the Dream* (1947). Gray, T. A., *Elinor Wylie* (1969). Gregory, H., and M. Zaturenska, *A History of American Poetry, 1900–1940* (1942). Hoyt, N., *Elinor Wylie: The Portrait of an Unknown Lady* (1935). Kazin, A., *On Native Grounds* (1942). Olson, S., *Elinor Wylie: A Life Apart* (1979). Van Doren, C., *Three Worlds* (1936). Van Vechten, C., Introduction to *Jennifer Lorn* (1923). West, R., *Ending in Earnest* (1931). Wilson, E., *The Shores of Light* (1952).

Other references: *The Dial* (June 1923). *ES* 20 (Dec. 1938). *NewR* (5 Dec. 1923; 6 Feb. 1929; 7 Sept. 1932). *PMLA* (1941). *VQR* (July 1930).

KAREN F. STEIN

Anzia Yezierska

B. ca. 1880, Plinsk, Russian Poland; d. 21 Nov. 1970, Ontario, California
D. of Baruch and Pearl Yezierska; m. Jacob Gordon, 1910;
    m. Arnold Levitas, 1911

Y. was born into the poverty and orthodoxy of an East European *shtetl*. When her large family came to the Lower East Side of New York in the 1890s, her father clung to his life of full-time Talmudic study and the wife and children supported the family.

Y. had little opportunity for formal education; she worked in sweatshops and laundries and learned what she could from night-school English classes and borrowed books. A scholarship enabled her to attend a training program for domestic science teachers, and from 1905 to 1913 she taught cooking in an elementary school. Her determination to rise from the dirt and drudgery of poverty to "make from herself a person" led to an early break with her family, the failure of two brief marriages, and the surrender of her daughter to the father's care.

A meeting with John Dewey, then dean at Columbia Teachers College, led to a romantic involvement that Y. wrote about repeatedly, in disguised form, in her later fiction. Dewey wrote a number of poems to Y. during the years 1917 and 1918; two of these recently unearthed poems appear in Y.'s books of 1932 and 1950, attributed only to the Dewey-figures "Henry Scott" and "John Morrow."

Y. published her first short story in 1915; in the next decade her stories appeared in respected magazines. Edward J. O'Brien praised "The Fat of the Land" as the best short story of 1919. When Hollywood bought the film rights to the short-story collection *Hungry Hearts* (1920) and also hired Y. as a salaried writer, the impoverished immigrant became overnight a wealthy celebrity.

But Y. could not write in materialistic Hollywood. She wrote productively in New York for a few more years, but by the time she lost her money in the Depression, she had also lost her creative inspiration. She joined the Work Projects Administration (WPA) Writers Project in the 1930s; published an autobiography in 1950 and then a few stories about old age; and was poor and forgotten long before her death in 1970.

In *Hungry Hearts* (1920), ten stories of Lower East Side life, Y.'s immigrant characters struggle with the disillusioning America of poverty and exploitation while they search for the "real" America of their ideals. The stories, like all of her fiction, are realistic, passionate, occasionally autobiographical, sometimes formless and overwrought; their effusive language suggests the style and intonation of an immigrant speaker. Women are the chief protagonists—women whose bodies are tied to sweatshop or household drudgery but whose spirits hunger for love, beauty, and some measure of independence, self-expression, and dignity.

In *Salome of the Tenements* (1922), her first novel, she exhibits more passion than craftsmanship. It explores the attraction between two of Y.'s stock character types: the "Russian Jewess," idealistic and emotional, and the rational, aloof, "born American" male. Sonya Vrunsky, poor girl of the ghetto, marries wealthy John Manning. But Sonya is not happy; she renounces her marriage and seeks to build an independent life based on her own talents.

Y. prefaces the short-story collection *Children of Loneliness* (1923) with a revealing essay, "Mostly about Myself," in which she discusses her tortured efforts to write. *Bread Givers* (1925) is an autobiographical novel about a dominating, unbending Talmudic scholar and his daughter's struggle to break free of subservient roles and to forge for herself an independent, fulfilling life. It is worth rediscovering.

Arrogant Beggar (1927) mixes social criticism with sentimentality for an effect that is at once trite and moving. Adele Lindner is from a poor neighborhood on New York's East Side; her gratitude to the Hellman Home for Working Girls turns to disgust with the patronizing attitudes and policies of her rich benefactors. She denounces the home and finds true charity and a satisfying life among her own people.

All I Could Never Be (1932), Y.'s last and not very successful novel, is at least a useful companion to her autobiography, *Red Ribbon on a White Horse* (1950). The latter is semifictional and unreliable, but the book is interesting for its discussion of the bureaucratic absurdities of the WPA and for its account of Y.'s painful attempts to come to terms with herself, her values, and her immigrant Jewish heritage, and to find some real happiness and peace.

Y. was not a master of style, plot development, or characterization, but the intensity of feeling and aspiration evident in her narratives often transcends the stylistic imperfections. Her work deserves consideration as one of the few chronicles of the immigrant experience from a woman's viewpoint and as an early attempt in American fiction to present the struggles of women against family, religious injunctions, and social and economic obstacles to create for themselves an independent identity.

WORKS: *Hungry Hearts* (1920; film version, 1922). *Salome of the Tenements* (1922, film version, 1925). *Children of Loneliness* (1923). *Bread Givers* (1925). *Arrogant Beggar* (1927). *All I Could Never Be* (1932). *Red Ribbon on a White Horse* (1950). *The Open Cage: An Anzia Yezierska Collection* (1979).

BIBLIOGRAPHY: Auden, W. H., Introduction to *Red Ribbon on a White Horse* by A. Yezierska (1950). Baum, C., P. Hyman, and S. Michel, *The Jewish Woman in America* (1975). Boydston, J., Introduction to *The Poems of John Dewey* (1977). Harris, A. K., Introduction to *Bread Givers* by A. Yezierska (1975). Harris, A. K., Introduction to *The Open Cage* by A. Yezierska (1979). Henriksen, L. L., Afterward to *The Open Cage* by A. Yezierska (1979). Sullivan, R. M., "Anzia Yezierska: An American Writer" (Ph.D. diss., Univ. of California, Berkeley, 1975).

For articles in reference works, see: *20thCA. 20thCAS.*

Other references: *Bookman* (Nov. 1923). *MELUS* (1980). *NYT* (23 Nov. 1970; 6 April 1978; 27 April 1978; 24 Feb. 1980). *Studies in American Jewish Literature* 1 (Winter 1975).

PEGGY STINSON

BIBLIOGRAPHY: Hopkins, L. B., *Books Are by People* (1969). Williams, P., in *Mademoiselle* (Jan. 1973). Wintle, J., and E. Fisher, *The Pied Pipers: Interviews with the Influential Creators of Children's Literature* (1974). Zolotow, C., "The Revolution in Children's Books," in *Prism* (Dec. 1974).

For articles in reference works, see: *Children's Literature Review*, Vol. 2, Ed. C. Riley (1976). *Something about the Author*, Ed. A. Commire (1971).

Other references: Houston *Post* (10 April 1976). New Orleans *Times-Picayune* (30 April 1974). New York *Daily News* (18 May 1971). Palo Alto *Times* (20 Sept. 1976). *PW* (10 June 1976).

EDYTHE M. McGOVERN

Leane Zugsmith

B. Jan. 1903, Louisville, Kentucky
Writes under: Leane Zugsmith, Mrs. Carl Randau
D. of Albert and Gertrude Zugsmith; m. Carl Randau, 1940

Z. spent most of her childhood in Atlantic City, New Jersey. Her formal education consisted of a year each at Goucher College, the University of Pennsylvania, and Columbia University. She has lived in New York since 1924, except for a year in Europe and some months in Hollywood, where she worked as a screen writer for Goldwyn studio. She has also worked as a copy editor for pulp magazines like *Detective Stories* and *Western Story Magazine* and written advertising copy. In the early 1940s, after marrying a newspaperman, she was a special feature writer on the staff of the New York newspaper *P.M.*

Her first novel, *All Victories Are Alike* (1929) is the story of a newspaper columnist's loss of ideals. *Goodbye and Tomorrow* (1931), which Z. said is "shamelessly derivative of Virginia Woolf," is about a romantic spinster who becomes a patron of artists. *Never Enough* (1932) is a panorama of American life during the 1920s. *The Reckoning* (1934) tells the story of a New York slum boy.

A Time to Remember (1936) is concerned with labor troubles and unionization in a New York department store. Its heroine, Aline Weinman, a Dreiseresque, middle-class, Jewish employee of the store, goes out on strike. She pays the price of painful separation from her family for her political ideals because her father, who has lost his job, would disapprove if he knew Aline's politics.

The Summer Soldier (1938) is about a small group of men and women, mostly northerners, who travel by train to a southern county to hold a hearing on the abuse of black workers. Their mission, however, is not successful. The novel is a slick character sketch of different political types.

Home Is Where You Hang Your Childhood (1937) is a collection of short stories. "Room in the World" describes the desperation unemployment causes in a young family. The title story, about a very young high school girl's movement from childish innocence to experience, uses one of Z.'s favorite themes. *Hard Times with Easy Payments* (1941) is another collection of short stories, all from *P.M.*

With her husband, Z. wrote *The Setting Sun of Japan* (1942) about the Randaus' flying trip through the Far East for *PM*; a mystery story, *Visitor* (1944); and "Year of Wrath," a novel serialized in *Collier's* in 1942. Stories by Z. appeared infrequently until 1949 in *Good Housekeeping*, *The New Yorker*, and *Collier's*.

In the early 1940s, Z. was considered one of the most promising young left-wing novelists. She said her greatest influences were Albert Maltz and Irwin Shaw in the short story and Josephine Herbst in the novel. All of her six novels are political, and her political themes gained considerable sophistication and some cynicism during the decade of her productivity (1929–38). Her sympathetic treatment of Jewish characters is of interest to the history of Jewish-American writers because her Jewish characters solve the problem of assimilation by becoming socialists. Z. belongs with those Jewish writers of the 1930s who attempted to transform ethnic background into meaningful politics. Her work became dated and of historical interest after WWII and the anti-Soviet backlash of the 1950s.

WORKS: *All Victories Are Alike* (1929). *Goodbye and Tomorrow* (1931). *Never Enough* (1932). *The Reckoning* (1934). *A Time to Remember* (1936). *Home Is Where You Hang Your Childhood, and other stories* (1937). *The Summer Soldier* (1938). *Hard Times with Easy Payments* (1941). *The Setting Sun of Japan* (with C. Randau, 1942). *The Visitor* (with C. Randau, 1944).

BIBLIOGRAPHY: Eisinger, C. E., in *Proletarian Writers of the Thirties*, Ed. D. Madden (1968). Smith, B., Introduction to *The Democratic Spirit: A Collection of American Writings from the Earliest Times to the Present Day* (1941).

For articles in reference works, see: *Contemporary American Authors*, Ed. B. Millett (1944). *20thCA*. *The Universal Jewish Encyclopedia*, Ed. I. Landman (1943-48).

CAROLE ZONIS YEE

INDEX

Names and page numbers in bold face refer to subject articles

Abbott, Edith, 72, 73
Abel, Annie Heloise, 3–4
abolition. *See also* slavery
   activists for, 109–10, 111, 113–14, 228–29, 278–
     79, 295–96, 518–19, 712–13, 740–41
   southern, 278–79, 280
   in drama, 612–13
   in fiction, 395, 612–13, 724–26
   history of, 444, 639
   in poetry, 109
   religious arguments for, 278–79, 280
   split within movement for, 278–79
actresses
   film, 814–15
   stage, 269–70, 426, 512, 549, 684–85, 813–15
Adams, Abigail Smith, 5–6, 799
Adams, Hannah, 7–8
Adams, Harriet Stratemeyer, 9–10
Adams, John, 5–6, 799, 800
   and M. O. Warren, 799, 800
Adams, Léonie Fuller, critical comment by, 57
Adams, Mary. *See* Ward, Elizabeth Stuart Phelps
Addams, Jane, 11–13, 39, 244, 483
advertising, women in, 213, 317
advice. *See also* etiquette
   books, 205, 263, 404, 757–58
   columns, 243, 263–64, 289, 664
aesthetics, philosophy of, 389–90, 703, 817–18
Afro-American studies. *See* black studies
Aiken, Conrad, and Bradstreet, 69
Akins, Zoë, 13–15
Alcott, Louisa May, 15–18, 111, 431, 483, 858,
   859
Alden, Isabella MacDonald, 445
Aldington, Richard, and H. Doolittle, 176
Aldon, Adair. *See* Meigs, Cornelia Lynde
Aldrich, Bess Streeter, 18–19
Aldrich, Mildred, 20–21
A.L.F. *See* Henry, Alice
Allen, Samantha. *See* Holley, Marietta
Allen, Sarah A. *See* Hopkins, Pauline Elizabeth
Allingham, Margery, 192
A.M. *See* Alcott, Louisa May
American Academy of Arts and Letters. *See also*
   National Institute of Arts and Letters
   awards received from, 238, 360
   grants received from, 76

members of, 509, 542
American Association of University Women, 72
American history. *See* United States history
American literature
   development in, 104, 125, 153, 301, 383, 555,
     594, 646, 647, 672
   the "left" in, 405
   literary criticism in (*see* literary criticism)
   naturalism in, 153
   the novel in, 646
   poetry in (*see* poetry)
   realism in, 104, 124, 302, 351, 405
   the short story in, 124–25, 467, 468
American Woman Suffrage Association, 713
   founders of, 323
Ames, Mary E. Clemmer, 21–23
Amethyst. *See* Wells, Emmeline Blanche
   Woodward
Anderson, Sherwood, and G. Stein, 717
Andrews, Eliza Frances, 23–24
Andrews, Jane, 25–26
anthologists, 392, 475, 667, 691, 695, 803
   of poetry, 584
   of short stories, 117, 562
Anthony, Susan Brownell, critical comment by,
   319
anthropology, 44–46, 478–81, 563–64, 577–78. *See*
   also cultural studies
   scholars in, 478–81, 577–78
anti-Semitism
   in drama, 397
   in fiction, 219, 317
antislavery movement. *See* abolition
antiwar literature. *See under* world peace
Appleton, Victor, II. *See* Adams, Harriet
   Stratemeyer
Arendt, Hannah, 26–28
Armstrong, Charlotte, 28–29
Arnow, Harriette Louisa Simpson, 30–31
artists, 760, 764. *See also:* illustrators; photogra-
   phers
art, philosophy of, 389–90
Asmodeus. *See* Atherton, Gertrude Franklin
   Horn
Atherton, Gertrude Franklin Horn, 32–34
Auchincloss, Louis, critical comment by, 817
Auden, W. H., critical comment by, 625–26

Aunt Em. *See* Wells, Emmeline Blanche
    Woodward
Aunt Fanny. *See* Gage, Frances Dana Barker
Aunt Maguire, *See* Whitcher, Frances Miriam
    Berry
Aunt Pilbury. *See* Winslow, Helen Maria
Australian-American writers, 627–29
aviators, 416

Bagley, Sarah G., 200
Baldwin, Faith. *See* Cuthrell, Faith Baldwin
Barbara. *See* Wright, Mabel Osgood
Barnard, A. M. *See* Alcott, Louisa May
Barnes, Djuna, 34–35
Barnes, Margaret Ayer, 36–37, 198
Barnett, Ida B. Wells, 38–39
Barrell, Sarah Sayward. *See* Wood, Sally Sayward
    Barrell
Barton, May Hollis. *See* Adams, Harriet
    Stratemeyer
Beard, Mary Ritter, 40–41
Beecher, Catharine Esther, 42–44, 278, 724
Benedict, Ruth Fulton, 44–46, 479
Benét, Stephen Vincent, and P. Murray, 689
Benson, Sally, 46–47
Berkley, Helen. *See* Ritchie, Anna Cora Ogden
    Mowatt
Bernard, Delores. *See* Ridge, Lola
Bernhardt, Sarah, 685
Betts, Doris, 48–49
Bible, the
    in poetry, 147, 149
    stories of, retold, 402
    studies of, 827
    and women, 713
Bierce, Ambrose, and Coolbrith, 126
Bildungsroman, the, 294, 350, 733, 811. *See also*
    under women in fiction
biography, the, techniques of, 61, 717
    and the autobiography, 661
birth control, advocates of, 185, 659–61
Bishop, Elizabeth, 49–51
black Americans, 208–9, 490, 527, 528. *See also:*
    black American writers; black fiction;
    black literature; civil rights
    and the black consciousness, 77–78
    folklore of, 563, 564
    as freed slaves, 321
    music of, 667
    photographic commentary on, 587
    in white fiction, 587
    and the woman's experience, 77, 128–29, 352–
        53, 477, 562
black American writers
    Barbadian, 477–79
    feminist, 128–29, 295–97
        18th-c., 820–22
        19th-c., 38–39, 128–29, 295–97, 690–91
        20th-c., 77–78, 208–9, 273–75, 291–92, 320–
            22, 331–32, 352–53, 527–30, 588–90, 791–
            92

black fiction, 77, 123, 208–9, 296–97, 321–22,
    477–79, 588–90
    folklore in, 331–32
    tradition in, 530
        thematic, 208–9, 589
    women in, 77, 78, 322, 477, 792, 811
black literature. *See also:* black fiction; black
        studies
    drama in, 291–92
    and the Harlem Renaissance, 208, 352, 353
    magazines of, 38, 208, 274, 291, 321, 322
    newspapers of, 599
    poetry in, 76–78, 208, 296, 352–53, 527, 791–
        92, 821–22
    black studies, 274–75, 321, 561–63
Blaine, James G., and A. Dodge, 173, 174
Blake, Lillie Devereux, 52–53
Blanchard, P., critical comment by, 560
blank verse, 392, 532, 767
    drama (*see* verse drama)
Bloomer, Amelia Jenks, 54–56
Bly, Nellie. *See* Cochrane, Elizabeth
Boas, Franz, critical comment by, 578
Bogan, Louise, 56–58
Bolton, Ann, critical comment by, 63
Bonner, Sherwood. *See* McDowell, Katherine
    Sherwood Bonner
book editors, 105, 228
    of anthologies (*see* anthologists)
    history, 866
    in-house, 423, 737, 875
    of letters, 5, 486, 547
    poetry, 534, 763
    of reference works, 850 (*see also under:* black
        studies; women's studies)
book publishers, 875
book reviewers. *See under* literary criticism
Boothe, Clare. *See* Luce, Clare Boothe
Boucher, Anthony, critical comment by, 456
Bowen, Catherine Drinker, 60–62
Bower, B. M. *See* Sinclair, Bertha Muzzy
Bowers, Bathsheba, 62–63
Bowles, Jane Auer, 64–65
Boyd, Nancy. *See* Millay, Edna St. Vincent
Boyle, Kay, 66–67
Bradstreet, Anne Dudley, 68–69
Branch, Anna Hempstead, 70–71
Branch, Olivia. *See* Parton, Sara Payson Willis
Brawne, Fanny, 224, 225
Breckinridge, Sophonisba Preston, 72–74
Breuer, Bessie, 74–76
British-American writers, 68–69, 85–86, 369–70,
    407–8, 434–36, 502–3
Broadway, plays produced on, 81, 224–25, 236–
    37, 291–92, 304–5, 371–72, 428–29, 437–
    38, 490, 685, 691, 767, 801
Brook Farm, 161
Brooks, Gwendolyn, 76–78
Brooks, Maria Gowen, 78–80
Brooks, Van Wyck, critical comment by, 124
Brown, Alice, 80–83

Bryant, William Cullen, and E. A. R. Lewis, 411
Buck, Pearl Sydenstricker, 83–85
Burke, Fielding. *See* Dargan, Olive Tilford
Burleigh, Celia Burr, 848
Burnett, Frances Eliza Hodgson, 85–87
Burns, Lucy, 333
Burr, Esther Edwards, 87–89
Butler, Frances Anne. *See* Kemble

Calhoun, Lucy Monroe. *See* Monroe, Lucy
Campbell, Helen Stuart, 89–91
Canadian-American writers, 364–66, 494–95
Canfield, Dorothy. *See* Fisher, Dorothea Frances Canfield
Carey, Alice. *See* Cary, Alice
Carrighar, Sally, 92–93
Carrington, Elaine Sterne, 94–96
Carson, Rachel Louise, 96–98
Cary, Alice, 21, 22, 98–99, 796
Cary, Phoebe, 98, 796
Cather, Willa, 14, 100–103, 349, 350
Catherwood, Mary Hartwell, 103–5
Catholic fiction, 272, 374, 545–47
Catholic literature, 457. *See also* Catholic fiction
    autobiography in, 622
    biography in, 622
    conversion narratives in, 154, 374
    journalism in, 374
    and socialism, 155
Catholics, 272, 281–82, 374, 457, 545–48, 621–22, 829–31
    influence of, as reflected in writings (*see*: Catholic fiction; Catholic literature)
Catt, Carrie Lane Chapman, 106–7, 297, 404
Caulkins, Frances Manwaring, 107–8
censorship of literature, 700
Chandler, Elizabeth Margaret, 109–10
Chandler, Louise. *See* Moulton, Louise Chandler
Channing, William E., and Follen, 228, 229
charity workers. *See* social workers
Cheney, Ednah Dow Littlehale, 110–12
Chenoweth, Alice. *See* Gardener, Helen Hamilton
Child, Lydia Maria Francis, 112–15
child development
    in primitive cultures, 480, 481
children's drama, 214, 402, 485–86, 691
    and children's theater, 256
children's fiction, 111–12, 161–62, 229, 286–87, 347, 358, 482–83, 582, 589, 840. *See also*: children's magazines; young adult literature
    animal stories in, 876
    classics adapted for, 204
    classics in, 86, 175, 216–17, 430–31
    fairy tales in, 228, 485–86
    family stories in, 228, 401, 402, 875–76
    folklore adaptations for, 189
    historical, 215
    of inanimate objects, 228–29
    for interracial understanding, 25–26
    for minority children, 562

moralistic, 228, 334, 336, 357, 358, 385, 399, 419, 593–94, 671, 797
nature stories, 253–54, 864
of other lands and peoples, 25–26, 189, 367–68, 406
pioneer, 844–45
regional, 90, 214–15, 217, 840
religious, 216–17, 228–29, 402, 593–94
series, 9–10, 16–17, 216–17, 286–87, 356–57, 367–68, 430–31, 665, 844–45, 858–59
Sunday-school. *See* Sunday-school movement, the
on women, 162, 356–57
children's literature, 419, 762. *See also*: children's drama; children's fiction; children's poetry; young adult literature
    awards received in, 399, 845 (*see also* Newbery awards)
    biographies in, 59–60, 81, 205, 483
    history of, 483
    on history, 7, 108, 483
    the realistic trend in, 875–76
    religious education in, 107, 525
    suitability for, 259
    technique in, 228–29
children's magazines, 113, 175, 228, 238, 257–58, 286, 392, 419, 430, 556, 760
    for black children, 208
children's poetry, 214, 229, 238–39, 402, 738
Chopin, Kate O'Flaherty, 115–17
Christian Science, founder of church of, 193–94
Christie, Agatha, 192
Chubbuck, Emily. *See* Judson, Emily Chubbuck
civil liberties, campaigns for, 502–3. *See also*: civil rights; women's rights
civil rights, 38–39, 122–23, 208, 274, 561, 562, 712, 792. *See also*: abolition; black Americans
    for black education, 77, 296
    for black suffrage, 39
    against lynching, 38–39, 77, 490
    movement, of the 1960's, 77, 291, 502–3
    southern activists for, 699–700
Civil War, the
    and the Confederacy
      life in, 23–24, 424–25, 468, 487–88
      social history of, sources for, 23
    diaries and journals of, 23
    fictional treatment of, 153, 524, 669, 792
    and Native Americans, 3–4
    nurses in, 16, 202, 740, 741, 858, 863
Clark, Eleanor, 117–18
Clarke, James Freeman, and Ossoli, 558
Clarkson, Helen. *See* McCloy, Helen
Clavers, Mrs. Mary. *See* Kirkland, Caroline Matilda Stansbury
Clemens, Samuel
    and Coolbrith, 126
    critical comment by, 680
    and M. M. Dodge, 175
    and Keller, 362

Clemmer, Mary. *See* Ames, Mary E. Clemmer
Clemons, Walter, critical comment by, 810
Cochrane, Elizabeth, 118–20
Colette, 223
comedies, 750–751
    films as, 815
    novels of manners as, 266–67, 286
    plays as, 14, 224, 236, 256, 257, 371–72, 438
    tragi-, 548
Commager, Henry Steele, critical comment by, 102
communism. *See also* socialism
    American hysteria against, 303, 406, 662, 688
    analysis of, 762
    and the Communist Party
        fellow travelers of, 441, 688–89
        members of, 226, 503
    and feminism, 689
    in fiction, 568–69, 614–15
composers, 273–74, 732–33
Comstock, Anna Botsford, 120–22
Comstock, John Henry, and A. Comstock, 120, 121
confessional literature, 500–1, 675–76
Congregationalists, 124, 200, 554, 730, 734, 770–72
    morale among, 512
Constantia. *See* Murray, Judith Sargent
conversion literature, 8, 327–28, 438
    fiction in, 272, 446–47, 653
    personal accounts in, 154, 374
Cook, Fannie, 122–24
Cook, George Cram, and Glaspell, 268, 269
Cooke, Rose Terry, 124–26
cookery, 757, 758, 874
Coolbrith, Ina Donna, 126–27
Coolidge, Susan. *See* Woolsey, Sarah Chauncey
Cooper, Anna Julia Haywood, 128–29
Cornelia. *See* Hale, Sarah Josepha Buell
Cott, Nancy, critical comment by, 574
Cousin Kate. *See* McIntosh, Maria Jane
Crabtree, Mary Ann, 645
Craddock, Charles Egbert. *See* Murfree, Mary Noailles
Craighead, Jean C. *See* George, Jean Craighead
Crapsey, Adelaide, 130–31
Crocker, Hannah Mather, 132–33
Croly, Jane Cunningham, 134–36
Crosby, Fannie. *See* Van Alstyne, Frances Jane Crosby
cultural studies. *See also*: anthropology; sociology, studies in
    African, 361
    Afro-American, 274
    American, 480, 644–45, 703, 704 (*see also* Native American culture)
    Asian, 360–61
        Chinese, 284, 689
        Japanese, 45, 361
    European, 222–23
    Jewish (*see* Jewish culture)

popular, 222–23, 284, 360–61
    of primitive societies, 479–81
    travel books as (*see under* travel books)
cultures, foreign. *See also* cultural studies
    in children's literature (*see under* children's literature)
    in newspaper correspondence, 419–20, 507, 559, 560
    as portrayed in drama, 535
    as portrayed in fiction, 83–84, 284, 360–61, 478, 536
    series on, 781
    in travel books (*see* travel books)
Cummins, Maria Susanna, 136–38
Curtiss, Harriot, 392
Cushman, Corinne. *See* Victor, Metta Victoria Fuller
Custer, Elizabeth Bacon, 138–39, 486
Custer, George Armstrong, and E. B. Custer, 138–39
Cuthrell, Faith Baldwin, 140–43

Dall, Caroline Wells Healey, 143–44
dancers, 157–59
Dargan, Olive Tilford, 145–47
Davidson, Lucretia Maria, 147–48, 148, 149
Davidson, Margaret Miller, 148–49
Davis, Mary Evelyn Moore, 150–52
Davis, Paulina Kellogg Wright, 143
Davis, Rebecca Harding, 152–54, 793
Davis, Sylvester. *See* Babb, Sanora
Day, Dorothy, 154–55
Deane, Martha. *See* McBride, Mary Margaret
Deans, Jennie. *See* Swisshelm, Jane Grey Cannon
de Cleyre, Voltairine, 659
Deland, Margaret Wade Campbell, 156–57
Dell, Floyd, critical comment by, 497
De Mille, Agnes, 157–59
Denslow, Grace, 282
Depression literature
    fiction in, 345, 685, 809
        Marxist, 145–46
    journalistic, 652
Deutsch, Babette, 159–60
Dewey, John, and Yezierska, 871
diaries and journals, 369–70, 383–84, 417, 519, 538, 701, 702
    of the Civil War era (*see under* Civil War)
    of early America, 88–89
    of frontier life, 559, 845
    religious, 88–89
    of travels, 383–84
Diaz, Abby Morton, 161–63
Dickinson, Emily, 163–66, 745, 763
didactic fiction, 594, 696, 786–87. *See also under* children's fiction
Didion, Joan, 166–68
dime novel, the, 552, 784, 785, 786–87
Dinsmore, Herman, critical comment by, 307
diplomatic history, 361, 769
Disney, Doris Miles, 168–70

Dix, Dorothy. *See* Gilmer, Elizabeth Meriwether
Dixon, Franklin W. *See* Adams, Harriet
    Stratemeyer
Dock, Lavinia Lloyd, 170–72
Dodge, Mabel. *See* Lunan, Mabel Ganson
    Dodge
Dodge, Mary Abigail, 173–74, 392
Dodge, Mary Mapes, 174–75, 465
domestic literature, 257–59, 424, 583
    advice in (*see* advice)
    in history, 655–56
    humorous, 258–59, 341, 371–72
    magazine column, 742–43
    novels in, 162, 179–80, 229, 306
Doolittle, Hilda, 176–78
Dorr, Julia Caroline Ripley, 178–80
Dorr, Rheta Childe, 180–82
Dow, Caroline, 496
drama
    critical studies in, 293, 574
    innovations in, 256, 268, 270, 566, 647
    reviews of (*see*: magazine columns; newspaper
        columns)
    technique in, 304–5, 716
dramatic adaptations
    by women, of others' works, 14, 224, 244–45,
        255, 404, 426, 510, 515, 684, 767
    of women's work, 237, 462, 685, 705, 801, 809
dramatic poetry, 151. *See also* verse drama
    and the monologue, 70, 752, 823
DuBois, Shirley Graham. *See* Graham, Shirley
DuBois, W. E. B.
    critical comment by, 322
    and Fauset, 208
    and S. Graham, 274
Dunbar, Alice. *See* Nelson, Alice Ruth Moore
    Dunbar
Duniway, Abigail Scott, 182–84
Durant, Mrs. Kenneth. *See* Taggard, Genevieve
Dykeman, Wilma, 184–86

Earle, Alice Morse, 186–88
Eastman, Elaine Goodale, 188–90
Eberhart, Mignon Good, 190–92
E. B. W. *See* Wells, Emmeline Blanche Woodward
ecology literature, 96–97
economics. *See also* financial analysts
    history of, 40
Eddy, Mary Baker Glover, 193–94
editors. *See*: book editors; magazine editors and
    publishers; newspaper editors and
    publishers
education. *See specific areas of education*
    for blacks, 111, 296
    and curriculum, 827–28, 873, 874
    day-care centers for, 261
    of infants, 789
    internationalism in, 25
    kindergarten, 188–89, 839
    methods in, 873, 874
    for Native Americans, 188–89

reform, 25, 59, 72–73, 111, 827–28
sociology of, 449
textbooks in (*see* textbooks)
for women (*see* education for women)
education for women, 500, 591–92, 846–47
    advocates of higher, 42, 55, 143–44, 288, 290,
        489–90
    schools for, 42, 489, 504, 846–47, 863
    studies on, 59
    textbooks for, 591, 847
educators, 24, 128–29, 299, 529, 590–92, 846–47,
        849
    and administrators, 24, 471, 849
    in Asia, 699
    of Native Americans, 188–89
    university faculty as, 44, 121, 491, 625, 666,
        849
        in education, 654
        in English, 407, 483, 535, 542, 791, 849
        in foreign languages, 24
        in history, 448, 654
        in literature, 24, 130, 533
        in natural science, 120–21
        in philosophy, 389
Edwards, Eleanor Lee. *See* Victor, Metta Victoria
    Fuller
Egan, Lesley. *See* Linington, Elizabeth
Eliot, Alice C. *See* Jewett, Sarah Orne
Eliot, T. S., critical comment by, 34, 509
Ellen Louise. *See* Moulton, Louise Chandler
Ellet, Elizabeth Fries Lummis, 195–96
Ellis, Anne, 196–98
Emerson, Ralph Waldo
    and Alcott, 16
    critical comment by, 336, 396
    and Ossoli, 558
emigré writers. *See specific nationalities*
Emilia. *See* Stockton, Annis Boudinot
Episcopalians, 130, 180, 432, 823
    influence of, as reflected in writings, 156, 726,
        848
epistolary novel, the, 801
essayists, 117, 166–67, 247, 248, 324, 621–22, 647,
        703–4
ethnic literature, 867. *See also* ethnology
    black (*see*: black fiction; black literature)
    Jewish, 720, 871–72
ethnology. *See also*: anthropology; cultural
        studies; folklore
etiquette, classics in, 609–11, 678
expatriates, 176–78, 714–18
    in fiction, 34–35
    justification for, 717

Fairbank, Janet Ayer, 198–200
Fairfield, Flora. *See* Alcott, Louisa May
family saga, the, 198–99, 374, 411, 540, 616, 668,
        735–36, 773, 775, 777, 808, 867
Fane, Florence. *See* Victor, Frances Fuller
fantasy fiction, 553
Farley, Harriet, 200–202, 392

Farnham, Eliza Woodson Burhans, 202–4
Farquharson, Martha. *See* Finley, Martha
Farrar, Eliza Ware Rotch, 204–6
Faugeres, Margaretta V. Bleecker, 206–7
Fauset, Jessie Redmon, 208–10
feminist fiction. *See also* women in fiction
   humorous, 318–19
   Marxist, 146, 679
   mystery, 641–42
   19th-c., 53, 115–16, 247–48, 318–19
   20th-c., 36–37, 74–76, 146, 210–11, 333–34,
     387, 406, 679
feminist literature, 11–12, 180–82, 241, 248, 263–
   64, 345–46, 559, 659–60, 703, 805–6. *See*
   also under: woman suffrage; woman's
   experience; women's rights; women's
   studies
   18th-c., 526
   fiction in (*see* feminist fiction)
   literary criticism in, 500, 501, 573–74
   magazines of, 54–55, 805, 806
   newspapers of, 54–55, 183
   poetry in (*see* feminist poetry)
   on religion, 193
   on sexuality, 241, 263, 794
   on socialism, 473–74
   superiority theory in, 202, 203, 323–24
feminist movement. *See*: woman suffrage;
   women's liberation movement; women's
   rights
feminist poetry. *See also* women in poetry
   contemporary, 406, 626–27
   18th-c., 647
   late 19th-c., 260
   likenesses to, 498
   militant, 406
feminists. *See also under* woman suffrage
   contemporary, 241, 405–6, 499–501, 626–27
   criticism of, 167
   discussion group of, 180–81 (*see also* women's
     clubs)
   18th-c., 647
   literature of (*see*: feminist literature; women;
     women's studies)
   19th-c.
     early, 54–55, 113–14, 278–79, 280–81, 519,
       559–60
     late, 59–60, 143–44, 173–74, 247–48, 260–62,
       296, 323–24, 793–95, 805–6, 849–50
     split among, 241
   20th-c., early, 87–88, 143–44, 180–81, 247–48,
     260–62, 473–74, 659–60, 793–95, 805–6
Ferber, Edna, 210–12
Fern, Fanny. *See* Parton, Sara Payson Willis
Field, Kate, 212–14, 833
Field, Peter, *See* Hobson, Laura Keane Zametkin
Field, Rachel Lyman, 214–16
Fields, Annie Adams, 281, 349
Fields, James T., critical comment by, 794
Fillebrown, Charlotte A. *See* Jerauld, Charlotte
   Ann Fillebrown

film adaptations, 237, 317, 329, 544, 573, 601,
   631, 666, 686, 729, 801, 812, 840
   of biographies, 476
   for children, 86, 356–57
   of comedies, 438, 463, 685
   as documentaries, 96
   as musicals, 47, 691
   of mysteries, 312
   of plays, 94, 437–38, 767, 814
   of westerns, 682
film critics, 580
film industry, the
   experience in, 428–29, 579–80
   gossip about, 580
   screenwriters for, 428–29, 500, 614, 652, 686,
     687, 733, 815
Finley, Martha, 216–18
Fisher, Dorothea Frances Canfield, 218–20
Fiske, Sarah Symmes, 221–22
Fitzgerald, Sally, 547
Flanner, Janet, 222–24
Fleeta. *See* Hamilton, Kate Waterman
Flexner, Abraham, critical comment by, 224
Flexner, Anne Crawford, 224–25
Florence. *See* Osgood, Frances Sargent Locke
Flynn, Elizabeth Gurley, 225–27
folklore
   American, 189, 331–32, 406, 616, 784
   black American, 331–32, 563–64
   for children, 189
   fictional use of, 332, 564, 573, 616 (*see also*
     under regional fiction)
   Native American, 189
   Russian, 573
Follen, Eliza Lee Cabot, 228–30
Foote, Mary Hallock, 230–32
Forbes, Esther, 232–34
Ford, Ford Madox, critical comment by, 271
foreign correspondents. *See under* journalists
Forrester, Fanny. *See* Judson, Emily Chubbuck
Foster, Hannah Webster, 234–35, 856
founders, 515, 531–32, 671, 688, 862–63
   of churches, 193–94, 380–81, 570, 827–28
   of magazines (*see under* magazine editors and
     publishers)
   of the NAACP, 38
   of NOW, 241
   of schools (*see* schools, founders of)
   of settlement houses, 11–12, 561
   of suffrage organizations (*see under* woman
     suffrage)
   of temperance organizations (*see under*
     temperance movement)
   of theater companies, 268, 661, 789
   of women's clubs (*see under* women's clubs)
Frank. *See* Whitcher, Frances Miriam Berry
Franken, Rose, 236–38
Freeman, Mary Eleanor Wilkins, 238–40
freethinkers, 246
Freud, Sigmund, and Doolittle, 176
Friedan, Betty, 240–42

frontier life
  accounts of, 138–39, 197, 231, 380–81, 559,
    657–58, 844–45
  in fiction, 18–19, 93, 100–101, 104, 182–83,
    231, 269–70, 387, 388, 585, 657–58, 772–
    73, 784, 844–45
  histories of, 195, 784–85
Fulbright grant, recipients of, 599, 602
Fuller, Frances. See Victor, Frances Fuller
Fuller, Margaret. See Ossoli, Sarah Margaret
  Fuller
Fuller, Metta Victoria. See Victor, Metta Victoria
  Fuller

Gage, Frances Dana Barker, 242–44
Gale, Zona, 244–45
Gardener, Helen Hamilton, 246–48
gardening books. See under nature study
Garland, Hamlin, and Catherwood, 104
Garrigue, Jean, 248–50
Garrison, William Lloyd, 296
Gary, Dorothy Page. See Page, Dorothy
  Myra
gay liberation movement, the. See under
  homosexuality
Gellhorn, Martha, 250–52
Genêt. See Flanner, Janet
George, Jean Craighead, 253–55
Gerstenberg, Alice, 255–57
Gilman, Caroline Howard, 257–59
Gilman, Charlotte Perkins Stetson, 89, 244, 260–
  62, 364
Gilmer, Elizabeth Meriwether, 262–64
Gish, Lillian, 666
Glasgow, Ellen Anderson Gholson, 264–68
Glaspell, Susan, 268–70
Godey, Louis, and S. J. B. Hale, 289
Goldman, Emma, 659
Goodale, Elaine. See Eastman, Elaine Goodale
Gordon, Caroline, 271–73
Gothic fiction
  romance, 301–2, 549, 837
  southern, 545–48
Gottschalk, Laura Riding. See Jackson, Laura
  Riding
Graham, Shirley, 273–75
Grant, Margaret. See Franken, Rose
Grau, Shirley Ann, 275–77
Graves, Robert, and L. R. Jackson, 338, 339
Gray, Walter T. See Victor, Metta Victoria Fuller
Greeley, Horace, and Ossoli, 558
Green, Anna Katherine Rohlfs. See Rohlfs, Anna
  Katherine Green
Greenwood, Grace. See Lippincott. Sara Jane
  Clarke
Gregory, Horace, critical comment by, 465
Grimké, Angelina Emily, 278–79, 280
Grimké, Sarah Moore, 279, 280–81
Guggenheim Fellowship, recipients of, 48, 66, 96,
  117, 271, 293, 308, 602, 707, 737
Guiney, Louise Imogen, 81, 281–83

Hahn, Emily, 283–85
Hale, Edward Everett, 286
Hale, Lucretia Peabody, 285–87
Hale, Sarah Josepha Buell, 288–90, 591
Hale, Susan, 285
Hamilton, Gail. See Dodge, Mary Abigail
Hammett, Dashiell, and Hellman, 303–4
handicapped writers, 362–63, 355–57, 778–80,
  802–4
Hansberry, Lorraine, 291–93
Hanson, Harriet J. See Robinson, Harriet Jane
  Hanson
Hardwick, Elizabeth, 293–95
Harland, Marion. See Terhune, Mary Virginia Hawes
Harlem renaissance. See black literature
Harper, Frances Ellen Watkins, 295–97
Harper, Ida Husted, 297–99
Harris, Bernice Kelly, 299–301
Harris, Mary Briggs, 793
Harris, Miriam Coles, 301–3
Harris, Mrs. Sidney S. See Harris, Miriam Coles
Harrison, Constance Cary, 385
Harte, Bret, and Coolbrith, 126
Hartwell, Mary. See Catherwood, Mary Hartwell
Hawthorne, Nathaniel, critical comment by, 137,
  582, 672
Hay, Elzey. See Andrews, Eliza Frances
Hay, Timothy. See Brown, Margaret Wise
Hayes, Helen, 429
H. D. See Doolittle, Hilda
Hegan, Alice Caldwell. See Rice, Alice Caldwell
  Hegan
Helen. See Whitman, Sarah Helen Power
Helfenstein, Ernest. See Smith, Elizabeth Oakes
  Prince
Hellman, Lillian, 303–5
Hemingway, Ernest
  and Gellhorn, 251
  and Stein, 717
Hemingway, Martha. See Gellhorn, Martha
Henderson, Alice Corbin, 507
Hentz, Caroline Lee Whiting, 306–7
Herbst, Josephine, 366
Herrick, Christine Terhune, 756
H. H. See Jackson, Helen Maria Fiske Hunt
Hicks, Granville, critical comment by, 239, 704
Higgins, Marguerite, 307–9
Higginson, Ella Rhoads, 310–11
Higginson, Thomas Wentworth, 336
  and Dickinson, 763
Highet, Helen MacInnes, 312–13
Highsmith, Patricia, 314–16
Hill, Grace Livingston. See Lutz, Grace
  Livingston Hill
historians
  diplomatic, 769
  of U.S. history, 3–4, 7–8, 384–86, 644–45, 654–
    56, 657–58, 783–85
historical fiction, 215, 233–34, 351, 394–95, 411–
  12, 431, 524, 613, 669, 672–74, 792, 851–
  53. See also regional fiction

historical fiction (*continued*)
  about abolition (*see under* abolition)
  biographical, 182–83, 412, 596
  for children (*see under* children's fiction)
  about the Civil War (*see under* Civil War)
  about frontier life (*see under* frontier life)
  about the Reconstruction era, 296–97, 861
  about the Revolutionary War, 70, 326, 405–6,
    517, 773, 852–53
  romance, 103–4, 483, 671, 836
  about the world wars, 251–52, 312, 598, 652
historical poetry, 517
history. *See also:* historians; local history; U.S.
    history; *specific subject areas of history*
  awards received in, 233
  for children (*see under* children's literature)
  diplomatic, 361–62, 769
  European, 394–95
  fictional (*see* historical fiction)
  of the Middle Ages, 769
  of the Middle East, 768
  popular, 394–95, 584
  and research, 654–56
  scholars of (*see* historians)
  textbooks, 847
  world, 848
  of World War I, 768, 769
Hobson, Laura Keane Zametkin, 316–17
Holden, Roger. *See* Guiney, Louise Imogen
Holley, Marietta, 318–20
Holme, Saxe. *See* Jackson, Helen Maria Fiske
    Hunt
homosexuality
  in drama, 814
  in fiction, 715
  and lesbianism, 627, 715
    confessional literature of, 500–501
Hope, Laura Lee. *See* Adams, Harriet Stratemeyer
Hopkins, Pauline Elizabeth, 320–22
hostesses
  literary-salon, 98, 352, 504, 584, 717
  society, 516, 677
House Un-American Activities Committee, the
    (McCarthyism)
  blacklisting by, 688
  in fiction, 662
Howard, Richard, critical comment by, 739
Howe, Irving, critical comment by, 818
Howe, Julia Ward, 322–25, 394, 710
  critical comment by, 112
Howells, William Dean
  critical comment by, 260, 711
  and Jewett, 351
  and Wyatt, 866
Howes, Barbara, 325–27
Hughes, Langston, and Walker, 792
Hull House, 11–12, 72
Hume, Sophia, 327–28
humorous literature, 630, 684–85, 794, 808–10,
    823–24. *See also* comedies
  domestic, 341–42, 463–64

feminist, 318–19
purpose of, 808, 809–10
the study of, 644
Hunt, Helen. *See* Jackson, Helen Maria Fiske
    Hunt
Huntley, Lydia Howard. *See* Sigourney, Lydia
    Howard Huntley
Hurst, Fannie, 329–30, 331
Hurston, Zora Neale, 331–33
H. W. S. *See* Smith, Hannah Whitall
Hyde, Nancy Maria, 679
Hyman, Stanley, and S. Jackson, 340
hymn writers, 504–5, 694, 779–80

illustrators, 120, 230–32, 360, 553, 728
Imagist poetry, 177–78, 249–50, 679, 753
  and the Imagist movement, 176–78, 507
  and the Imagists' influence, 51, 130, 131, 159,
    249–50, 509
immigrant experience, the, 573, 720, 721
  in fiction, 366–68, 871, 872
  sociological studies on, 72–73
Indians, American. *See* Native Americans
industrialization. *See* labor, industrial
investigative literature
  journalism, 747, 748 (*see also under* muckraking
    literature)
  studies, 502–3
Iola. *See* Barnett, Ida B. Wells
Ione. *See* Hewitt, Mary Elizabeth Moore
Irish-American writers, 627–29
Irving, Washington, critical comment by, 149
Irwin, Inez Haynes, 333–35
Isabel. *See* Ritchie, Anna Cora Ogden Mowatt
Iverson, Sade. *See* Peattie, Elia Wilkinson

Jackson, Andrew, and Hentz, 306
Jackson, Helen Maria Fiske Hunt, 335–37, 858
Jackson, Laura Riding, 338–40
Jackson, Shirley, 340–42
Jacobi, Mary Putnam, 342–44
James, Henry
  critical comment by, 711
  and Wharton, 816
Janeway, Elizabeth, 344–46
Jarrell, Randall, critical comment by, 626
Jerauld, Charlotte Ann Fillebrown, 347–48
Jewett, Sarah Orne, 349–52, 710, 769, 861
Jewish-American writers, 240–41, 303–5, 316–17,
    338–39, 396–98, 489–91, 504–5, 714–18,
    719–21, 877–78
  East-European, 423–25, 870–72
Jewish culture, 397, 505, 878
  and anti-Semitism (*see* anti-Semitism)
  ethnic literature of, 720, 871–72
  history of, 8
Johnson, Georgia Douglas Camp, 352–53
Johnson, Josephine Winslow, 354–56
Johnston, Annie Fellows, 356–58
Jones, Edith. *See* Wharton, Edith Newbold Jones
Josephy, Helen, 451

Josiah Allen's Wife. *See* Holley, Marietta
journalists. *See also entries beginning* magazine
    and newspaper
  broadcast, 450, 762
  exposé, 119, 153
  foreign correspondent, 66, 181, 251, 284, 308,
    455, 458, 731, 761, 768, 790
    19th-c., 119, 558, 560, 781
  investigative, 263, 747, 748
  muckraking, 180–82, 246–48, 747
  political, 21–22, 154, 222–23, 225–27, 405, 458,
    730–31, 740, 741, 761–62, 768, 790
journals. *See* diaries and journals
Judson, Emily Chubbuck, 358–60
June, Jennie. *See* Croly, Jane Cunningham

Kaufman, George S., and Ferber, 210
Keating, Sally. *See* Wood, Sally Sayward Barrell
Keemle, Mary Katherine. *See* Field, Kate
Keene, Carolyn. *See* Adams, Harriet Stratemeyer
Keith, Agnes Newton, 360–62
Keiz, Marcia, critical comment by, 478
Keller, Helen Adams, 362–64
Kelley, Edith Summers, 364–66
Kelly, Bernice. *See* Harris, Bernice Kelly
Kelly, Myra, 366–68
Kemble, Frances Anne, 369–71
Kemble, Miss Fanny. *See* Kemble, Frances Anne
Kennedy, Rose. *See* Victor, Metta Victoria Fuller
Kerr, Jean Collins, 371–73
Keyes, Frances Parkinson Wheeler, 373–75
Kilmer, Aline Murray, 376–77
Kilmer, Joyce, and Kilmer, 376
Kimbrough, Emily, 377–79
Kipling, Rudyard, and M. M. Dodge, 175
Kirkland, Caroline Matilda Stansbury, 380–82
Knight, Sarah Kemble, 382–84
Knowles, Sarah. *See* Bolton, Sarah Knowles
Kuhns, Dorothy. *See* Heyward, Dorothy Hartzell
    Kuhns

labor, industrial, 11. *See also*: labor, industrial,
    and women; labor reform
  child, 391–92
  history, 226
  magazines of, 200–201, 392
  and unionization (*see* unionization)
labor, industrial, and women
  factory, 200–201, 391–92, 639–40, 781–82
  in fiction, 414–15, 474
  history of, 473–74
  reform in, 90–91, 161, 162, 171–72, 781–82
  sociology of, 181
  and unionization, 161, 474, 568, 781–82
labor reform, 59, 226, 789–90. *See also* unioniza-
    tion
  for women, 90–91, 161–62, 781
Lafayette, Marquis de, critical comment by, 847
La Flesche, Suzette "Bright Eyes," 336
Lamb, Martha Joanna Reade Nash, 384–86
Lane, Rose Wilder, 386–88, 844

Langdon, Mary. *See* Pike, Mary Hayden Green
Langer, Susanne Katherina Knauth, 389–91
Langstaff, Josephine. *See* Herschberger, Ruth
Lankford, Sarah Worrall, 570
Larcom, Lucy, 391–93
Larkin, Maia. *See* Wojciechowska, Maia
Larrimore, Lida. *See* Turner, Lida Larrimore
Latern, M. H. *See* Hazlett, Helen
Lathrop, Julia, 585
Latimer, Elizabeth Wormeley, 394–96
Lawson, Delores. *See* Ridge, Lola
lawyers, 527, 528
Lazarus, Emma, 396–98
lecturers, 54–55, 106, 183, 295–96, 673, 716, 717,
    740
  and literary readings, 632–33
Lee, Marion. *See* Comstock, Anna Botsford
Lee, Pattie. *See* Cary, Alice
LeGuin, Ursula K., 398–400
L'Engle, Madeleine, 401–2
Lennox, Charlotte Ramsay, 755
Leslie, Frank. *See* Leslie, Miriam Florence Folline
Leslie, Miriam Florence Folline, 403–5
Le Sueur, Meridel, 405–7
letters, collected, 5–6, 278–79, 280–81, 283, 417,
    419, 547, 701–2, 760
  editors of, 486, 547
  18th-c., 5–6
Levertov, Denise, 407–9
Lewis, Estelle Anna Robinson, 409–11
Lewis, Janet, 411–13
Lewis, Sarah Anna. *See* Lewis, Estelle Anna
    Robinson
Lewis, Sinclair, 364
L. H. *See* Hooper, Lucy
Libbey, Laura Jean, 413–15
Lin, Frank. *See* Atherton, Gertrude Franklin
    Horn
Lindbergh, Anne Morrow, 416–18
Lindsay, Vachel, and Teasdale, 752
Lippincott, Sara Jane Clarke, 418–20
Lisagor, Peter, and M. Higgins, 309
literary clubs, 506, 677, 759
literary criticism, 160, 282, 293, 471, 521–22, 533–
    34, 537, 666, 667, 867
  in book reviews, 56–57, 575, 584, 666, 699, 700
  on drama, 20, 293, 452, 574
  feminist, 53, 500, 501, 573
  first major American, 559, 560
  on poetry, 56–57, 160, 338–39, 433, 466, 492
  satire on, 632
  scholars in (*see* literary scholars)
literary prizes and awards, recipients of, 399, 509.
    See also: *under* children's literature;
    National Book Award; Pulitzer Prize in
    Letters
  for criticism, 293
  for drama, 291, 565, 691
  fellowships and grants as, 76–77, 398, 546, 589,
    598, 602, 737 (*see also* Guggenheim
    Fellowship)

literary prizes and awards (*continued*)
  for fiction, 31, 84, 118, 238, 807 (*see also* O.
    Henry Memorial Prize Stories)
  mystery, 191, 314, 456, 837
  science fiction, 399
  for nonfiction, 97, 534
  for poetry, 50, 465, 509, 625, 650, 737, 738,
    791–92
literary salons, hostesses of, 504, 584, 759
literary scholars, 533–34, 835–36
literature. *See*: American literature; literary
    criticism; literary history
Livingston, Mrs. C. M. *See* Lutz, Grace
    Livingston Hill
L. M. A. *See* Alcott, Louisa May
local color, fiction of. *See*: regional fiction;
    regional literature
local history. *See also* regional literature
  of Appalachia, 31, 184–85
  fiction based on (*see* regional fiction)
  of the midwest, 405–6
  of New England, 7–8, 107–8
    sources for, 640
  of New York City, 385–86
  of the northwest, 784–85
  of the south, 668 (*see also* Civil War, the)
  of the southwest, 53
  of the west, 657–58, 784, 785
    sources for, 197–98, 202–3, 210, 211, 231
Locke, Jane Erminia Starkweather, 421–23
Logan, Mary Simmerson Cunningham, 423–25
Logan, Olive, 426–28
Lola. *See* Ridge, Lola
Longfellow, Henry Wadsworth
  critical comment by, 794
  and McDowell, 467
Loos, Anita, 428–30
Lothrop, Harriet Mulford Stone, 430–32
love poetry
  contemporary, 249–50, 413
  early 20th-c., 498
  19th-c., 164, 521–22, 556
Lowell, Amy, 432–34
Lowell, James Russell, critical comment by, 398
Loy, Mina, 434–36
Lucas, Victoria. *See* Plath, Sylvia
Luce, Clare Boothe, 437–38
Luhan, Mabel Ganson Dodge, 439–40
Lumpkin, Grace, 441–42
Lundy, Benjamin, and Chandler, 109
Lutz, Alma, 443–45
Lutz, Grace Livingston Hill, 445–48
Lynd, Helen Merrell, 448–49
lyric poetry
  contemporary, 412–13, 471
  drama, 145
  early 20th-c., 282, 471, 619
  19th-c., 619

McBride, Mary Margaret, 450–52
McCarthy, Joseph. *See* House Un-American
    Activities Committee
McCarthy, Mary Therese, 452–55
McCloy, Helen, 455–57
McCormick, Anne O'Hare, 457–59
McCullers, Carson Smith, 459–62
MacDonald, Betty Bard, 463–64
MacDonald, Golden. *See* Brown, Margaret Wise
MacDonald, Jessica Nelson North, 465–67
MacDonald, Marcia. *See* Lutz, Grace Livingston
    Hill
McDowell, Katherine Sherwood Bonner, 467–68
McGinley, Phyllis, 469–70
MacInnes, Helen. *See* Highet, Helen MacInnes
McKinney, Alice Jean Chandler Webster. *See*
    Webster, Jean
McKinnon, Edna Rankin, 185
Macumber, Marie S. *See* Sandoz, Mari
Madeleva, Sister, 471–72
magazine columns, 241, 761. *See also* newspaper
    columns
  correspondence, 66, 200–201, 222, 223, 284
  drama review, 574
  literary, 575
  political, 373
  woman's, 289, 297–98, 742–43
magazine editors and publishers, 20, 100, 646,
    699, 786
  art, 466
  black, 38, 208, 274, 321, 322
  children's, 175, 208, 228, 392
  feminist, 54
  history, 385
  literary, 18, 176, 293, 321, 466, 507–8, 509,
    542, 560, 744
  political, 155, 789
  professional, 171, 577
  religious, 155, 475, 571
  scholarly, 534
  women's, 288–90, 377–78, 403, 742, 805–6,
    854
    factory, 200–201, 392
    policy of, 289
  women's movement, 54–55, 180, 261, 444,
    659, 713
magazines. *See: under* magazine editors and
    publishers; *specific subject areas*
Main, John. *See* Parsons, Elsie Worthington
    Clews
Malkiel, Theresa Serber, 473–75
Mann, Horace, and J. Andrews, 25
manners
  comedies of, 266, 286, 515
  novels of, 266–67, 286, 596–97, 610–11, 702,
    816–20
  poetry of, 492
Marah. *See* Jackson, Helen Maria Fiske Hunt
March, Anne. *See* Woolson, Constance
    Fenimore
Markey, Dorothy. *See* Page, Dorothy Myra
Marsh, Ngaio, 192
Marshall, Catherine, 475–77

Marshall, Paule, 477–79
Matisse, Henri, and Stein, 717
maturation novels. *See: Bildungsroman; under*
    women in fiction
M. C. A. *See* Ames, Mary E. Clemmer
Mead, Margaret, 479–82
medicine. *See also*: nurses; psychiatrists;
    psychology
    doctors of (*see* physicians)
    and women, 144, 343
    medieval studies, 769
Meigs, Cornelia Lynde, 482–84
melodramas, 512–13, 632
Meloney, Franken. *See* Franken, Rose
Meloney, William Brown, and Franken, 236
Mencken, H. L., and Loos, 429
Merington, Marguerite, 484–86
Meriwether, Elizabeth Avery, 487–88
metaphysics
    and poetry, 218, 491–92, 745
    in religion, 193–94
Methodists, 762, 791
    leadership of, 570–572
M. E. W. S. *See* Sherwood, Mary Elizabeth
    Wilson
Meyer, Annie Nathan, 489–91
Miles, Josephine, 491–93
Milholland, Inez, 497
Millar, Margaret, 494–96
Millay, Edna St. Vincent, 465, 496–99
Miller, Bertha, critical comment by, 483
Miller, Elizabeth Smith, 54
Miller, Henry, critical comment by, 538
Miller, Joaquin, and Coolbrith, 126
Miller, Olive Thorne. *See* Miller, Harriet Mann
Millett, Kate, 499–501
Minerva. *See* Smith, Eliza Roxey Snow
ministers, 328, 695, 697–98, 826
missionaries
    biographies of, 359
    Seventh Day Adventist, 827
Mitford, Jessica, 502–4
M. L. P. *See* Putnam, Mary Traill Spence Lowell
Moise, Penina, 504–5
Monroe, Harriet, 466, 506–8
Moore, Alice Ruth. *See* Nelson, Alice Ruth
    Moore Dunbar
Moore, Marianne Craig, 497, 498, 508–11
Moore, Mollie E. *See* Davis, Mary Evelyn
    Moore
Moorhead, Sarah Parsons, 511–12
Morgan, Carrie Blake, 310
Morgan, Claire. *See* Highsmith, Patricia
Morison, Samuel Eliot, critical comment by, 69
Mormons, 693–94, 805–6
    in fiction, 319
    history of, 806
        sources for, 694
    journals of, 805, 806
    and polygamy, 319, 693, 805
Mortimer, Lillian, 512–14

Morton, Eleanor. *See* Stern, Elizabeth Gertrude
    Levin
Morton, Lea. *See* Stern, Elizabeth Gertrude
    Levin
Morton, Martha, 514–16
Morton, Sarah Wentworth Apthorp, 516–18
Morton-Jones, Verina, 561
motion-picture industry. *See* film industry
Mott, Lucretia Coffin, 518–20, 695, 712
Moulton, Louise Chandler, 520–23
Mowatt, Anna Cora. *See* Ritchie, Anna Cora
    Ogden Mowatt
muckraking literature
    fictional, 551
    journalistic, 119, 181–82, 247, 747
Murfree, Mary Noailles, 523–24, 861
Murray, Aline. *See* Kilmer, Aline Murray
Murray, Judith Sargent, 525–26
Murray, Pauli, 526–28
musical, the
    adaptation of women's works, 210, 233, 429,
        691
    and music drama, 273, 733
musicians, 273–74, 733
mystery drama, 631
mystery fiction, 777–78, 836, 838
    classics of, 631, 641
    comedies in, 494, 553, 750–51
    feminist, 641–42, 837–38
    genre, development of, 642, 787
    Gothic, 549, 836, 837
    psychological, 169, 314–15, 340–41, 456, 837–
        38
    romantic, 191–92, 385, 630
    series, 168–69, 494, 549–50, 750, 777, 803–4
    and the spy novel, 312–13
    technique in, 28, 158–59, 191, 494–95, 630,
        803
Mystery Writers of America, 456
    awards given by, 314, 456, 837
mysticism
    in fiction, 696
    in poetry, 628
myth
    in fiction, 79–80, 460, 808
    in poetry, 177–78, 626
    and womanhood, 177–78, 626–27

NAACP. *See* National Association for the
    Advancement of Colored People
Narcissa. *See* Smith, Eliza Roxey Snow
narrative poetry, 619–20, 696, 767, 842, 859
National American Woman Suffrage Associa-
    tion, 52–53, 297. *See also*: American
    Woman Suffrage Association; National
    Woman Suffrage Association
    officer of, 72, 713
National Association for the Advancement of
    Colored People (NAACP), 208, 562
    advisers to, 123
    founders of, 38, 561

National Book Award
  for Arts and Letters, 118, 303
  for Children's Literature, 399
  for Nonfiction, 96, 97
  for Poetry, 50
  for the Short Story, 547
National Institute of Arts and Letters, 76. *See also* American Academy of Arts and Letters
  awards given by, 117, 737, 807
  members of, 156, 238, 542, 650, 737
National Organization of Women (NOW), 241, 499–500
National Woman's Party, 333
National Woman's Christian Temperance Union. *See* Woman's Christian Temperance Union
National Woman Suffrage Association, 183, 639, 713
Native American culture
  for children's reading, 189
  folklore in, 189, 564
  studies on, 44, 564, 578
Native Americans. *See also* Native American culture
  abuse of, 336
  assimilation of, 189
  education for, 188–89
  in fiction, 336–37, 671
  history of, 3–4, 657
    sources for, 138–39
  rights of, 336–37
  women, 681
natural history. *See also*: anthropology; natural science
  educators in, 120–22
  studies in, 96–97, 120–22
natural science, 764
  of biology, 96–97, 284, 873–74
  scholars of, 96–97
naturalism in fiction, 354, 589, 590
nature poetry, 164–65, 326, 760
  religious, 471–72
nature study, 92–93, 864
  on birds, 494
  for children, 253–54
  in fiction, 102, 350, 617, 618, 728
  teachers in, 120–22
Nelson, Alice Ruth Moore Dunbar, 528–30
Newbery award medals, 214, 233, 254, 401, 483
New Criticism, 271, 272
newspaper columns, 458, 582, 610, 700, 719, 720, 784, 877. *See also*: magazine columns; newspaper correspondents
  advice (*see under* advice)
  gossip, 580
  political, 226–27, 761–62
  reviews, 832
    book, 584
    drama, 20

syndicated, 134, 263, 308, 450, 580, 581
  women's, 134, 243, 263, 297–98, 311, 473, 844
newspaper correspondents, 21, 652, 835
  cultural, 506, 558–59, 560
  foreign, 119, 181–82, 308–9, 455, 458, 599, 560, 761, 768
  literary, 521–22
  political, 21–22, 458, 740–41, 761–62
  travel, 213
newspaper editors and publishers, 213, 243, 531, 649, 832
  of arts section, 832
  of drama section, 579–80
  feminist, 54–55, 182–83
  labor, 155
  of literary section, 531, 832
  political, 740
  religious, 59, 115
  of women's section, 109, 450
newspaper reporters, 74, 119, 253, 263, 308, 450–51, 457–58, 579–80, 652, 719, 730–31. *See also* newspaper correspondents
Nicholson, Eliza Jane Poitevent, 531–33
Nicolson, Marjorie Hope, 533–34
Niggli, Josephina, 535–36
Nin, Anaïs, 537–39
  critical comment by, 35
"No Name Author" series novels, 336
Nobel Prize
  for Literature, 84
  for Peace, 11
Nordstrom, Ursula, 875
Norris, Kathleen Thompson, 539–41
North, Jessica N. *See* MacDonald, Jessica Nelson North
novel, the. *See also specific types of novels*
  development of early American (*see under* American literature)
  techniques of writing, 168–69, 234–35, 453, 537–38, 543, 669, 715–16, 809
novel of manners, the. *See under* manners
NOW. *See* National Organization of Women
nursing, 170–72, 659
  history of, 171, 172
  in the Civil War, 16, 202, 740–41, 858, 863

Oates, Joyce Carol, 542–44
O'Brien, Edward J., critical comment by, 871
Occidente, Maria del. *See* Brooks, Maria Gowen
O'Connor, Flannery, 468, **545–48**
O'Donnell, Lillian, 549–50
O'Hara, Mary. *See* Sture-Vasa, Mary Alsop
O. Henry Memorial Prize Stories, 47, 66, 333, 387
Older, Cora Miranda Baggerly, 551–52
Older, Mrs. Fremont. *See* Older, Cora Miranda Baggerly
one-act plays, 81, 214, 245, 255–56, 269, 486, 584–85, 675, 691
O'Neill, Eugene

and Day, 154
and Glaspell, 268
O'Neill, Rose Cecil, 553–54
opera, 675
by women, 273, 716
organizations, professional. *See also under*
women's associations
in history, 233, 655
literary, 515, 533, 568, 650
in music, 515
organizations, special interest and cause. *See*
also: organizations, professional;
women's associations
academic, 533
civil liberties, 660
civil rights, 38–39, 123, 208, 274, 561, 562
Ku Klux Klan, 488
nature, 864
for refugees, 816
for unionization, 226
ornithology. *See under* nature study
Osborn, Sarah, 554–55
Osgood, Frances Sargent Locke, 556–57
Ossoli, Sarah Margaret Fuller, 558–61
Ovington, Mary White, 561–63
Owen, Mary Alicia, 563–65
Owens, Rochelle, 565–67

Packard, Clarissa. *See* Gilman, Caroline
Howard
pacifism. *See* world peace
Page, Dorothy Myra, 567–69
Palmer, Phoebe Worrall, 570–72
Papashvily, George, 572, 573
Papashvily, Helen Waite, 572–74
Parker, Dorothy Rothschild, 574–76
Parsons, Elsie Worthington Clews, 577–79
Parsons, Louella Oettinger, 579–81
Parton, Sara Payson Willis, 581–83
patriotic literature, 219, 852
poetry in, 207, 517
Pattee, F. L., critical comment by, 755
Paul, Alice, 333
Peabody, Mrs. Mark. *See* Victor, Metta Victoria
Fuller
peace efforts. *See* world peace
Pearson, Norman Holmes, critical comment by,
178
Peattie, Elia Wilkinson, 584–86
Peering, Aminadab. *See* Kirkland, Caroline
Matilda Stansbury
Pellowski, Ann, critical comment by, 483
Percy, Mabel. *See* Hatch, Mary R. Platt
Perkins, Maxwell, and Rawlings, 617
Peterkin, Julia Mood, 586–88
Peters, Phillis. *See* Wheatley, Phillis
Petry, Ann Lane, 588–90
pharmacists, 588
Phelps, Almira Hart Lincoln, 590–92
Phelps, Elizabeth Stuart, 593–95, 793

Phelps, Elizabeth Stuart (daughter). *See* Ward,
Elizabeth Stuart Phelps
Philenia. *See* Morton, Sarah Wentworth
Apthorp
philosophers, 26–27, 389–90, 614–15
philosophy
of aesthetics, 389–90, 703–4, 817, 818
humanistic, 45
of human nature, 390
Indian, 406
of Objectivism, 615
of perception, 716, 718
political, 26–27 (*see also under* socialism)
religious, 246, 247–48 (*see also* religious
literature)
Transcendental, 559, 560, 835
physicians, 342–44
in fiction, 490
Picasso, Pablo, and Stein, 716, 717
Pilbury, Aunt. *See* Winslow, Helen Maria
Pinckney, Josephine Lyons Scott, 595–97
Plath, Sylvia, 597–600
Pocahontas. *See* Smith, Eliza Roxey Snow
Poe, Edgar Allan
critical comment by, 148, 381, 410, 411, 556,
680
and Whitman, 835, 836
poetry
criticism of (*see under* literary criticism)
development
of black American, 352–53
of modern American, 160, 338–39, 508,
620, 650, 842
Imagistic (*see* Imagist poetry)
19th-c., characteristics of, 679–80
readings, 296, 633
studies on, 131, 160, 408
technique in, 77, 130–31, 165, 338–39, 492,
509, 650–51, 662, 737, 739
P. O. L. *See* Guiney, Louise Imogen
political figures
communist (*see* communism)
contemporary activist, 155, 789–90 (*see also*
under feminists)
18th-c., 799
government officeholders as, 185
in party politics, 198, 225, 226, 333, 473, 503
persecution of, 154, 225–27, 303, 406, 688
socialist (*see* socialism)
in women's movements (*see*: feminists; *under*
woman suffrage)
political literature. *See also*: communism
conservative, 337–38
18th-c., 799–800
fiction in, 66–67, 145, 146, 199, 265–66, 405–
6, 702, 878
on foreign politics, 284, 688–89, 731, 761–62,
768
journalistic (*see under* journalists)
on party politics, 333, 740

political literature (*continued*)
  and philosophy, 26–27, 406
  poetry in, 77, 407–8, 497, 608, 628, 745
  on war, 768
  and women (*see under*: feminist literature;
    woman suffrage)
Porter, Eleanor Hodgman, 600–602
Porter, Gene Stratton. *See* Stratton-Porter, Gene
Porter, Katherine Anne, 602–5
  critical comment by, 564–65
Porter, Rose, 606–7
Porter, Sarah, 608–9
Post, Emily Price, 609–11
Pound, Ezra
  and H. Doolittle, 176, 178
  and H. Monroe, 507
Presbyterians, 156, 654, 756, 797
  influence of, in fiction, 772–73
  Sunday-school fiction of, 216–17
Prescott, Harriett. *See* Spofford, Harriett
    Elizabeth Prescott
prison reformers, 202
  and penal systems studies, 503
prizes and awards, recipients of, 146, 533. *See
    also*: Fulbright grant; Guggenheim
    Fellowship; literary prizes and awards
  in film, 317
  government, 653, 807, 816
  in history, 233
  medical, 343
  in natural science, 97
  for peace efforts, 11
  women's, 122, 475
prohibition. *See* temperance movement, the
"proletarian" fiction. *See* socialist-realism
prosody. *See* poetry
protest literature. *See* social criticism
psychics, 637–38. *See also* spiritualism
psychological drama, 256, 257
psychological fiction, 345, 538. *See also under*
    women in fiction
  in mystery/crime novels, 169, 314–15, 340–41,
    456
psychology. *See also* psychiatrists; psychothera-
    pists
  and anthropology, 45
  in fiction (*see*: psychological fiction; *under*
    women in fiction)
  poetic treatment of, 674–76
  and psychobiographies, 176, 440, 538
  and therapy, 440, 538
  of women, 538
psychotherapists, 537
public relations, careers in, 665
publishers. *See*: book publishers; magazine
    editors and publishers; newspaper editors
    and publishers
Pulitzer Prize in Letters
  for Drama, 14, 245, 269
  for Fiction, 276, 602
  for General Nonfiction, 768
  for History, 233
  for the Novel, 36, 84, 100, 210, 267, 354, 587,
    617
  for Poetry, 50, 76, 77, 469, 497, 509, 675
Puritanism. *See also*: Congregationalists;
    Presbyterians
  and Calvinism, 125, 520
  diaries and letters of, 5–6, 88–89, 771
  in fiction, 125
  and the Great Awakening, 107, 511–12
  histories of, 186–87
  in poetry, 68–69, 164–65, 511–12, 771–72
  spiritual autobiographies of, 825–26
Putnam, Mary. *See* Jacobi, Mary Putnam
Putnam, Mary Traill Spence Lowell, 611–13

Quakers. *See* Society of Friends
Quinn, H. *See* Aldrich, Mildred

racism. *See also* civil rights
  in drama, 291–92
  in fiction, 219, 700
  and interracial understanding, 185, 700
    awards for attempts to promote, 185
    fiction promoting, 25–26, 321–22, 700
radio programs, 610, 762
  hostesses of, 450, 451, 580
  plays for, 631, 664
  production of, 664
  serials, 94–95, 237
Rand, Ayn, 614–15
Randau, Mrs. Carl. *See* Zugsmith, Leane
Rank, Otto, and Nin, 537
Rawlings, Marjorie Kinnan, 616–18
Ray, John. *See* Carrington, Elaine Stern
realism in American fiction, 104–5, 125, 302,
    351, 646, 711, 715, 735–36, 784, 785
  critical, 104
  psychological, 302
  socialist-, 104, 354, 688–89
Redfield, Martin. *See* Brown, Alice
Reese, Lizette Woodworth, 619–20
refugee relief workers, 816
Regester, Seeley. *See* Victor, Metta Victoria
    Fuller
regional fiction
  Appalachian, 30–31, 184–85, 365, 523–24
  eastern, 772–74, 861
  midwestern, 104, 210–11, 269–70, 564, 735–36
    frontier, 18–19, 93, 100, 101, 104, 387
    urban, 867
  New England, 81, 82, 124, 214–15, 239, 288,
    350, 351, 670–71, 710–11, 750, 840
  northwestern frontier, 182–83
  southern, 145–46, 265–67, 271–72, 276–77,
    300, 459–62, 468, 530, 545–48, 595–97,
    616–18, 635–36, 707–9, 808–9, 861
    antebellum, 257, 307, 487, 757
    black, 123, 296, 331–32
    Creole, 115, 116, 150–51, 211
    plantation, 586–87, 757

of poor whites, 441–42, 623–24
of primitives, 276
southwestern, 101, 150–51, 211, 666
western, 310–11, 365, 681–83
frontier, 231, 551–52, 657–58
regional literature. *See also*: local history;
    regional fiction
Appalachian, 184–86
drama in, 93, 239, 300
frontier (*see* frontier life)
midwest, 99, 380–81
New England, 258
poetry in, 219, 311, 595, 710
southern
    domestic, 258
    pro-Ku Klux Klan, 488
southwestern, 150–51
western, 197–98, 202–3, 463–64
Reid, Christian. *See* Tiernan, Frances Christine
    Fisher
religious affiliations. *See also* Puritanism
African Methodist Episcopalian, 208
Baptist (*see* Baptists)
Catholic (*see* Catholics)
Christian Scientist, 193–94
Congregationalist (*see* Congregationalists)
Disciples of Christ, 744
Episcopalian (*see* Episcopalians)
Jewish (*see* Jewish-American writers)
Methodist (*see* Methodists)
Moravian Brotherhood, 176
Mormon (*see* Mormons)
and New Thought, 833
Presbyterian (*see* Presbyterians)
Quaker (*see* Society of Friends)
Scotch Covenanters, 740
Seventh Day Adventists, 827–28
Unitarian (*see* Unitarians)
religious educators, 107, 826–28
religious fiction, 84, 101–2, 734. *See also*:
    conversion literature; Sunday-school
    movement
biblical, 402, 609
Catholic (*see* Catholic fiction)
for children (*see under* children's fiction)
Episcopalian, 156
Presbyterian, 216–17, 772–73
Puritan, 124–25
Unitarian, 229, 670
religious literature, 697–98, 833, 851–52. *See*
    also: Catholic literature; conversion
    literature; Puritanism; religious fiction;
    religious poetry; Society of Friends
autobiographical, 63, 476, 825–26
biblical studies in, 827
biographical, 476, 694
Christian Science, 193–94
diaries in (*see under* diaries and journals)
drama in, 716
evangelical, 327–28
history in, 7–8

inspirational, 141, 475, 476
and literary criticism, 471
magazines of, 155, 475, 571
meditations in, 606, 623
on Mormons (*see* Mormons)
newspapers of, 59, 581
on philosophy, 246, 247–48
psychic, 637–38
revivalist, 570–71
sermons in, 519–20
Seventh Day Adventist, 826–28
theology in, 42–43, 53
on women (*see under* woman's experience)
religious movements
the Great Awakening, 64–65, 511–12
and the Holiness-Pentecostal tradition, 570–72
and Transcendental philosophy, 558–60, 835
religious poetry
autobiographic, 148–49
on biblical themes, 69, 149, 608–9
contemporary, 471–72
18th-c., 511–512, 608–9, 771, 772, 821
hymns as, 504–5, 694, 779–80
late 19th- to early 20th-c., 282–83
mystic, 472
19th-c., 98–99, 147, 149, 164–65
17th-c., 68–69
Religious Society of Friends. *See* Society of
    Friends
Remitrom, Naillil. *See* Mortimer, Lillian
Repplier, Agnes, 621–22
Rhoads, Ella. *See* Higginson, Ella Rhoads
Rice, Alice Caldwell Hegan, 224, **623–25**
Rice, Cale Young, 623, 624
Rich, Adrienne Cecile, 625–27
    critical comment by, 57
Rich, Barbara. *See* Jackson, Laura Riding
Ridge, Lola, 627–29
Riding, Laura. *See* Jackson, Laura Riding
Riggs, Mrs. *See* Wiggin, Kate Douglas Smith
Rinehart, Mary Roberts, 629–32
Rip Van Winkle. *See* Jackson, Helen Maria
    Fiske Hunt
Ritchie, Anna Cora Mowatt, 632–34
Rivers, Pearl. *See* Nicholson, Eliza Jane
    Poitevent
Rives, Amélie. *See* Troubetskoy, Amélie Rives
Roberts, Elizabeth Madox, 635–36
Roberts, Jane, 637–38
Robinson, Harriet Jane Hanson, 638–40
Robinson, William Stevens, and Robinson, 192
Rogers, Adela. *See* St. Johns, Adela Rogers
Rohlfs, Anna Katharine Green, 641–43
romance fiction
contemporary, 653, 742, 836–38
18th-c., 857
Gothic (*see* Gothic fiction)
historical (*see under* historical fiction)
late 19th-c. to early 20th-c., 85–86, 121–22,
    321–22, 414–15, 710–11, 766, 767, 784
mystery in, 374, 385

romance fiction (*continued*)
  19th-c., 113, 385, 426, 671, 705–6, 725–26
  religious, 446–47
  20th-c., 94–95, 374, 446–47, 630–31, 664
Roosevelt, Theodore
  critical comment by, 161
  and M. Kelly, 368
Rourke, Constance Mayfield, 643–45
Rousseau, G. S., 534
Routley, Erik, critical comment by, 456
Rowson, Susanna Haswell, 646–48, 856
Royall, Anne Newport, 648–49
Rubin, Leslie, 527
Rukeyser, Muriel, 650–51
rural fiction, 300, 354, 617–18, 695. *See also*
  regional fiction
Russian-American writers, 473–74, 614–15

Sacco and Vanzetti, poetic response to, 497, 628
Sagas. *See* family saga, the
St. Johns, Adela Rogers, 652–54
Salmon, Lucy Maynard, 654–56
Sandoz, Mari, 657–58
Sanger, Margaret, 659–61
Sappho, 410, 411
Sarton, May, 661–63
satire. *See* social satire
Sayers, Dorothy L., 192
Sayers, Frances, critical comment by, 483
Scarberry, Alma Sioux, 664–65
Scarborough, Dorothy, 666–67
schools, founders of, 671, 679
  kindergartens, 839
  for women, 42, 489, 504, 863
  for writing, 140
science fiction, 398–400
  for children, 399
  the "New Wave" in, 399
Scott, Evelyn, 366, 668–69
Scott, Julia. *See* Owen, Mary Alicia
screenwriters, 236, 237, 652, 686, 687, 733, 815
sculptors, 499, 501
Seaman, Elizabeth Cochrane. *See* Cochrane,
  Elizabeth
Sedges, John. *See* Buck, Pearl Sydenstricker
Sedgwick, Catharine Maria, 148, **670–72**
sentimental literature
  fiction, 53, 296, 337, 646–47 (*see also* romance
    fiction)
  poetry, 517
series fiction, 237, 665, 865
  children's (*see under* children's fiction)
  mystery, 169, 494–95, 549, 777, 804
Seton, Anya, 672–74
settlement houses
  affiliations with, 70, 89
  founders of, 11–12, 561
Sexton, Anne, 674–76
Shannon, Dell. *See* Linington, Elizabeth
Sheehan, Marion, 458
Sheldon, Ann. *See* Adams, Harriet Stratemeyer

Sherwood, Mary Elizabeth Wilson, 677–78
short story, the
  development of, 125
  technique in, 603, 716
Shuler, Nettie Rogers, 106
Sidney, Margaret. *See* Lothrop, Harriet Mulford
  Stone
Sigourney, Lydia Howard Huntley, 58, **679–81**
Sinclair, Bertha Muzzy, 681–83
Sinclair, Upton, and E. S. Kelley, 364
Singing Sybil, The. *See* Victor, Metta Victoria
  Fuller
Singleton, Anne. *See* Benedict, Ruth Fulton
Skinner, Cornelia Otis, 378, **683–85**
slavery. *See also*: abolition; slaves
  in fiction, 289, 307, 487, 725, 792
  and the Native American, 3
  in poetry, 109, 296
  pro-, 258, 487–88
slaves
  owners of, 23
  writers who were born, 128–29, 820
  writers who were children of, 38–39
Slesinger, Tess, 685–87
Smedley, Agnes, 688–90
Smith, Betty Wehner, 690–92
Smith, Eliza Roxey Snow, 693–94
Smith, Elizabeth Oakes Prince, 695–97
Smith, Hannah Whitall, 697–98
Smith, Josephine Donna. *See* Coolbrith, Ina
  Donna
Smith, Lillian, 699–701
Smith, Lula Carson. *See* McCullers, Carson
  Smith
Smith, Margaret Bayard, 701–2
Smith, Mrs. Seba. *See* Smith, Elizabeth Oakes
  Prince
Smith, Seba, 824
Snow, Eliza Roxey. *See* Smith, Eliza Roxey Snow
soap opera, the, for radio, 94–95
social criticism, 502–3, 551, 703, 704, 717, 731.
    See also: social reformers; social satire
  in fiction, 145–46, 315, 365–66, 441–42, 453–
    54, 542–43, 551, 589, 662, 817–18, 819,
    830–31, 871–72
  in literary criticism, 294–95
  in poetry, 207, 628–29
social history. *See also*: folklore; sociology
  American, 40–41, 205, 644–45
    Appalachian, 31, 184–85
    black (*see under* black Americans)
    Jewish (*see under* Jewish culture)
    Native (*see under*: Native American culture;
      Native Americans)
  of New York, 385, 865, 871–72
  of the south, 23–24
  sources of, 23–24, 73, 639–40, 649, 871
  European, 205
  of woman suffrage, 299
socialism. *See also* communism
  anti-, 387–88

in communes, 364–65
and feminism, 473–74
fiction of, 146, 474, 568, 877–78
newspapers of, 154, 155, 226
poetry of, 745
political activists in, 154–55, 170–72, 225–27,
  473–74, 568, 688, 730–31, 744–45, 789–90
and religion, 155, 473, 474
and unionization (see unionization)
socialist-realism, 104, 354–55, 688–89
social protest. See: social criticism; *specific
  subject areas of protest and reform*
social reformers, 11–13, 70–73, 90–91, 519–20,
  730, 740–41, 866. See also: civil liberties,
  campaigns for; social criticism; social
  workers
in birth control, 185, 659–60, 688
for black Americans (see civil rights)
in education, 25, 59
in labor (see labor reform, unionization)
for Native Americans, 188–89, 336–37
prison, 202
in religion (see religious movements)
in sex education, 171
for temperance (see temperance movement,
  the)
for women (see: woman suffrage; women's
  liberation movement; women's rights)
social satire, 633–34, 784, 823–24
development of, 383–84
in drama, 256, 426
feminist, 426
in fiction, 338, 453, 456, 755, 818, 830–31
in poetry, 260
social welfare. See social workers
social workers, 11–13, 72–73, 695, 719, 730
with black Americans, 529, 561–62
in charities, 154–55, 865
education for, 72–73
fictional treatment of, 720
with the handicapped, 363
Society of Friends (Quakers), 365, 719, 812
and the Great Separation, 518
members of, 109, 204, 222, 230, 327, 697–98
ministers of, 62–63
reform among, 328
sociology, studies in. See also: anthropology;
  cultural studies
of black Americans, 562
of the family, 577
of industry, 11
of penal systems, 503
scholars of, 577
urban, 11–12
of women, 562, 577–78
sonnets
contemporary, 792
19th-c., 347, 522, 619
20th-c., early, 71, 145, 486, 497, 503, 629, 753
Sontag, Susan, 703–4
Southey, Robert, critical comment by, 147

**Southworth, Emma Dorothy Eliza Nevitte, 705–
7**
Spencer, Elizabeth, 707–9
spiritual autobiographies, 221–22, 554–55, 825–
26
spiritualism, 653, 760, 833. *See also* psychics
**Spofford, Harriet Elizabeth Prescott, 283, 709–
12**
Squier, Miriam. *See* Leslie, Miriam Florence
  Folline
**Stanton, Elizabeth Cady, 53, 54, 298, 299, 443,
  444, 487, 519, 712–14**
critical comment by, 247
Stedman, Edmund Clarence
and J. C. R. Dorr, 179
and H. Monroe, 506
Stein, Gertrude, 714–19
Stella. *See* Lewis, Estelle Anna Robinson
Stephens, Margaret Dean. *See* Aldrich, Bess
  Streeter
Stern, Elizabeth Gertrude Levin, 719–21
Sterne, Elaine. *See* Carrington, Elaine Sterne
Stevens, Wallace, critical comment by, 102
Stewart, Eleanor. *See* Porter, Eleanor Hodgman
Stockton, Annis Boudinot, 721–23
Stoddard, George, critical comment by, 127
Stokeley, James, and Dykeman, 184, 185
Stokely, Wilma Dykeman. *See* Dykeman, Wilma
**Stowe, Harriet Beecher, 42, 58, 260, 286, 306,
  307, 581, 594, 724–27, 793**
Stratton-Porter, Gene, 727–29
Strong, Anna Louise, 730–32
Sture-Vasa, Mary Alsop, 732–34
Suckow, Ruth, 366, 734–37
suffrage
for black Americans, 39
for women (see woman suffrage)
Sullivan, Anne, 362, 363
Summers, Edith. *See* Kelley, Edith Summers
Sunday-school movement, the, fiction of, 216–
  17, 228, 593–94, 793, 797
suspense fiction. *See* mystery fiction
Sweet, Sarah O. *See* Jewett, Sarah Orne
Swenson, May, 737–39
Swisshelm, Jane Grey Cannon, 739–41
Sylvia. *See* Smith, Anna Young

Taber, Gladys Bagg, 742–44
Taggard, Genevieve, 744–46
Tarbell, Ida Minerva, 746–49
Tate, Allen, 271
Tate, Caroline. *See* Gordon, Caroline
Taylor, Bayard, critical comment by, 680
Taylor, Phoebe Atwood, 749–51
Teasdale, Sara, 752–54
television programs, 292, 314
adaptations of women's work for, 631, 845
situation comedies for, 372
temperance movement, the
activists in, 54–55, 58, 243, 784, 849–50
in fiction, 243, 319, 652, 786

Tenney, Tabitha Gilman, **754–56**
Terhune, Albert Payson, 756
Terhune, Mary Virginia Hawes, 756–59
Terry, Rose. *See* Cooke, Rose Terry
textbooks, 219, 646
   in cookery, 874
   in history, 40–41
   in the sciences
      natural, 24, 591, 847, 873–74
      sociological, 577
   in writing, 580
Thaxter, Celia Laighton, 759–61
theater. *See also* actresses
   children's, 256
   directors, 549, 661
   experience, 426, 646, 691, 813
      fictionalized, 633–34
   experimental, 268, 789
   founders of groups in, 268, 661
   and the little-theater movement, 256–57
theology. *See under* religious literature
Thomas, Caroline. *See* Dorr, Julia Caroline
   Ripley
Thomas, Mrs. Henry J. *See* Victor, Metta
   Victoria Fuller
Thompson, Dorothy, 761–62
Thomson, Virgil, and Stein, 716
Thorndyke, Helen Louise. *See* Adams, Harriet
   Stratemeyer
Tietjens, Elizabeth, critical comment by, 18
Todd, Mabel Loomis, 763–65
tragedy
   blank-verse, 207
   and comedy, 548
   historical fiction as, 412
Transcendentalism, 15, 110, 162, 558–60, 835
   and Brook Farm, 161
translators, 219, 737, 873–74
   from the French, 396, 510, 863
   from the German, 397, 559
travel books
   African, 764, 833
   on the Americas, 833
   Asian, 387, 764
   for children, 419
   as cultural studies, 184–85, 263, 404
   diaries as, 383–84
   and early American means of travel, 383–84
   European, 117–18, 179, 213, 378–79, 419,
      832–33
   guidebooks, 378
   journalistic, 213, 419
   personal impressions in, 117–18, 258–59, 419,
      648–49, 862
   as social documents, 451
   in the U.S., regional, 184–85, 336, 383–84,
      404, 648–49, 833
Tremaine, Paul. *See* Johnson, Georgia Douglas
   Camp
Troubetzkoy, Amélie Rives, 765–67

Trusta, H. *See* Phelps, Elizabeth Stuart
Truth, Sojourner, 243
Tuchman, Barbara, 768–70
Turell, Jane, 770–72
Turnbull, Agnes Sligh, 772–74
Twain, Mark. *See* Clemens, Samuel
Tyler, Ann, 774–76
   critical comment by, 808

Uhnak, Dorothy, 776–78
Ullman, Doris, 487
Umsted, Lillie Devereux. *See* Blake, Lillie
   Devereux
Uncle Ben. *See* White, Rhoda Elizabeth
   Waterman
unionization, 781
   fictional treatment of, 123, 474, 781–82, 790,
      877
   organizers for, 226, 473, 686
   for women, 72, 161, 474, 568, 781
Unitarians, 134, 228, 257, 670
United States history, 584, 748. *See also*: Civil
   War, the; local history; Native Americans;
   specific subject areas of history
   of the cavalry, sources for, 138–39
   colonial, 7–8, 186–87
      sources for, 5–6, 671 (*see also* Puritanism)
   cultural, 643–45
   domestic, 186–87, 195–96, 385, 655
      sources for, 257–59, 797
   economic, 40
   fictionalized (*see* historical fiction)
   from a foreign viewpoint, sources for, 369–70
   magazines of, 385
   of pioneers (*see* frontier life)
   of presidential social circles, 196
   of the Reconstruction era, 4
   of the Revolutionary War, 40, 385, 800
      sources for, 722, 852–53
   social (*see under* social history)
   of travel, sources for, 258–59, 383–84
   in the Vietnam War (*see* Vietnam War)
   women in (*see* women's studies)
   in the world wars (*see* World War I *and* II)
United States presidents, 5–6, 161, 368, 722,
   799, 800, 821
   social circles of, 196
   wives of, 5–6, 700, 799
Untermeyer, Louis, and J. Untermeyer, 131
Updegraff, Alan, and Kelley, 364
Updike, John, critical comment by, 776
utopian communities, 161, 162
utopian fiction, 540, 794

Valentine, Jo. *See* Armstrong, Charlotte
Van Alstyne, Frances Jane Crosby, 778–80
Van Buren, Abigail, 611
Van de Water, Virginia Terhune, 756
Van Vorst, Marie, 780–83
Vechten, Carl Van, critical comment by, 869–70

verse drama, 70, 207, 397, 410–11, 632–33, 639, 641
Victor, Frances Fuller, 783–85
Victor, Metta Victoria Fuller, 783, 784, **786–88**
Victorian literature, characteristics of, 21–22, 521–22
Vietnam War, the
  activists against, 407
  history of, 309
  war correspondents of, 251, 308–9
Vorse, Mary Heaton, 788–91

Walker, Margaret, 791–92
war correspondents, 181–82, 251, 308, 768
  in the Korean War, 308
  in Vietnam, 251, 309
  in World War I, 181, 182, 790
  in World War II, 251–52
Ward, Elizabeth Stuart Phelps, 710, **793–96**
Warner, Susan Bogert, 796–98
Warren, Mercy Otis, 5, **798–800**
Watergate scandal, the, 662
Watkins, Frances Ellen. *See* Harper, Frances Ellen Watkins
WCTU. *See* Woman's Christian Temperance Union
Webster, Daniel, critical comment by, 847
Webster, Jean, 801–2
Weeks, Helen C. *See* Campbell, Helen Stuart
Weld, Angelina Grimké. *See* Grimké, Angelina Emily
Wells, Anna Maria Foster, 556
Wells, Carolyn, 802–4
Wells, Emmeline Blanche Woodward, 805–7
Wells, Ida B. *See* Barnett, Ida B. Wells
Welty, Eudora, 468, **807–10**
Wertheim, Barbara. *See* Tuchman, Barbara Wertheim
West, Jessamyn, 811–13
West, Mae, 813–15
western novels, 316, 681–83
Wetherall, Elizabeth. *See* Warner, Susan Bogert
Wharton, Edith Newbold Jones, 14, **816–20**
Wheatley, Phillis, 820–22
Wheaton, Campbell. *See* Campbell, Helen Stuart
Whitcher, Frances Miriam Berry, 822–24
White, Elizabeth, 825–26
White, Ellen Gould Harmon, 826–29
White, Rhoda Elizabeth Waterman, 829–31
Whiting, Lilian, 832–34
  critical comment by, 522
Whitman, Sarah Helen Power, 834–36
Whitney, Phyllis Ayame, 836–38
Whittier, John Greenleaf
  critical comment by, 98, 680, 794
  and Larcom, 839
  and F. Willard, 850
W. H. S. *See* Smith, Hannah Whitall
Wiggin, Kate Douglas Smith, 839–41

Widow Bedott. *See* Whitcher, Frances Miriam Berry
Widow Spriggins. *See* Whitcher, Frances Miriam Berry
Wilbur, Richard, critical comment by, 738
Wilcox, Ella Wheeler, 841–43
Wilder, Laura Ingalls, 844–46
Wilkins, Mary E. *See* Freeman, Mary Eleanor Wilkins
Willard, Emma Hart, 443, 590, **846–48**
Willard, Frances Elizabeth Caroline, 319, **849–51**
Williams, Catharine Read Arnold, 851–53
Williams, Ellen, 507
Williams, Paul, critical comment by, 876
Wilson, Mrs. H. L. *See* O'Neill, Rose Cecil
Winslow, Helen Maria, 853–55
Winters, Yvor, and J. Lewis, 411
Winthrop, Margaret, 187
wives of presidents, *See under* United States presidents
Wolf, Mrs. Robert. *See* Taggard, Genevieve
Wolff, Mary Evaline. *See* Madeleva, Sister
woman, superiority of, theory, 289–90, 850
woman suffrage
  activists for
    early, 52–53, 161, 171, 183, 243, 323, 487, 693, 712–14, 740, 850
    20th-c., 39, 105–6, 180–82, 198, 297–99, 333, 639, 659, 761, 805–6
  anti-, 490, 592, 748
  children's literature for, 162
  in England, 333
  in fiction, 199
  founders of organizations for, 323, 333, 712–14
  histories of, 298, 333, 713
  journalism for, 297–99
  lecturers for, 105–6, 183, 712–14
  and the 19th Amendment, 105–6
  periodicals of, 180, 713
  in poetry, 639
  political strategies for, 105–6, 248
  radical wing of movement for, 333
  theological arguments for, 53
Woman's Christian Temperance Union, 849–50. *See also* temperance movement
woman's columns. *See under:* magazine columns; newspaper columns
woman's experience. *See also:* feminist literature; women in drama; women in fiction; women in poetry; women's rights; women's studies
  Appalachian, 184, 185
  black (*see under* black Americans)
  frontier (*see* frontier life)
  in health matters, 144, 171–72, 343
  in history, 113, 132–33, 187, 584
  lesbian, 500–501, 627
  in marriage, 416–17, 426–27, 577, 696

woman's experience (*continued*)
  as a moral force, 42, 171–72, 289–90, 653, 850
  with motherhood, 626–27
  and myth, 345–46
  with oppression, 280–81, 361, 500, 659, 660
  in prison, 227
  psychology of, 538
  in religion, 41–42, 53, 261–62, 693, 694, 713
  and the search for identity, 538
  with sexual exploitation, 241, 500, 660
  with social status, 577–78, 580, 584
women in drama
  dependence of, 14
  emancipation of, 515
  and marriage, 490
  and the "new woman," 269, 489–90
  search of, for identity, 15, 515
  sexuality of, 814, 815
  unflattering portraits of, 437, 438, 716
women in fiction, 191–92, 318–19, 339, 348,
      405–6
  aging, 789
  as artist, 261, 265
  black (*see under* black fiction)
  frontier, 185, 269–70, 387, 388, 585, 658, 772–
      73, 774, 784
  independence of, 64–65, 115–16, 211, 269–70,
      334, 473–74, 549, 552, 634, 642, 665, 682,
      728, 766, 778, 797, 814–15, 854–55, 872
  and lesbianism, 715
  and marriage, 24, 417, 817–18
    vs. a career, 141, 317, 350, 490, 585, 865
    vs. spinsterhood, 671, 735–36
    status in, 247, 794
  failed, 755, 816–17
  maturation of, 244–45, 293–94, 350, 477, 635–
      36, 663, 673–74, 733, 735, 811–12
  morality of, conventional, 330, 334, 414
  and motherhood, 405
  and the "new woman," 32, 75, 247
  relationships of
    with men, 167, 686, 687
    with other women, 64–65, 167, 345, 350,
      646, 666–67, 710–11, 720, 777–78, 793–
      94, 811–12, 837–38
  roles of
    conflict of, 37, 146, 302, 365
    conventional, 53, 152, 594, 702, 726, 733,
      757, 855, 865
  search of, for identity, 538, 776, 782, 838
  sexuality of, 766, 811
  southern, 146, 266–67, 331–32, 441–42, 757
  superiority of, 170–71, 206, 724–25, 726, 856
  survival of, 441–42
  victimization of, 167–68, 261, 575–76, 583
    and passivity, 543, 575–76, 583
  working, 140–41, 171, 201, 414–15, 473–74,
      781–82
women in poetry, 504, 842
  common experience of, 57, 352–53, 626, 674–
      75, 676, 745

creative, 465–66
and marriage, 98–99, 435
and motherhood, 98–99, 421–22, 435, 469,
    470
mythic structures for, 626
roles of
  conflict of, 598
  conventional, 288, 435
sacrifices of, 396
suffering of, 99, 421, 422
women's associations. *See also* women's clubs
  colonial, 864
  feminist, 241, 499–500
  for peace, 11, 72
  professional, 230, 532, 854
  for unionization, 220, 474
  woman suffrage, 52–53, 72, 183, 297, 323,
      333, 639, 693, 713
women's clubs, 72, 161, 695, 854–55. *See also*
      women's associations
  federation of, 854
  histories of, 135, 854
  leaders in, 98, 134, 135, 323, 639
  literary, 306, 506, 677
  satirized, in fiction, 490
  Sorosis, 98, 134, 135
  university, 72
women's columns. *See under:* magazine
      columns; newspaper columns
Women's International League for Peace and
      Freedom, 11, 72
women's liberation movement, 346. *See also:*
      feminists; women's rights
  history of, 241, 500
  split within, 241
women's magazines. *See under* magazine editors
      and publishers
women's rights. *See also:* woman suffrage;
      women's liberation movement
  advocates of
    colonial, 6
    early 19th-c., 113, 132–33, 278–79, 280–81,
      381, 519, 583, 693–94, 695–96, 740–41
    late 19th- to early 20th-c., 135, 143–44, 173,
      261–62, 323–24, 793–95, 805, 806
  anti-, 290
  to birth control (*see* birth control)
  for black women, 128–29, 278, 296
  conventions for, 695, 712
  in domestic matters, 135
  for dress reform, 54
  for economic equality, 143–44, 173, 260–61,
      381, 526, 559, 794
  to education (*see* education for women)
  fiction of (*see under* women in fiction)
  history of movement for, 443–44
  for intellectual recognition, 281, 526, 559–60
  lecturers for, 54–55, 183, 323–24
  legislation for, 52–53, 73, 106
  periodicals for, 54–55, 183, 261
  in the professions, 571–72

religious arguments for, 280–81, 519
working (*see* labor, industrial, and women)
women's studies
  on women artists, 284
  as biographical sketches, collections of, 59,
    289, 339, 425, 444, 720, 850
  in literature, 284, 573–74
  pioneering works in, 40–41, 195
  on professional women, 73, 171, 490
  on the roles of women in history, 40–41, 59,
    73, 113, 195
  on woman suffrage (*see under* woman
    suffrage)
  on women's rights (*see under* women's rights)
Women's Trade Union League, 72, 474
Wood, Sally Sayward Barrell, 856–58
Woodward, Blanche. *See* Wells, Emmeline
    Blanche Woodward
Woolsey, Sarah Chauncey, 858–60
Woolson, Constance Fenimore, 860–62
world peace
  activists for, 11, 106, 407, 848
  and the Nobel Peace Prize, 11
World War I, 20–21, 747
  activity in, 387, 424, 816, 843
  advocates of U.S. involvement in, 81, 622
  histories of, 768, 769
  nursing in, 699
  peace efforts during (*see* world peace)
  war correspondents of, 181, 182, 790

World War II
  activity in, 360–61, 717
  in fiction, 251–52, 312, 604, 652
  in poetry, 510
  war correspondents of, 251–52
Wormeley, Elizabeth. *See* Latimer, Elizabeth
    Wormeley
Wormeley, Katharine Prescott, 862–64
Wright, Mabel Osgood, 864–66
Wright, Richard, critical comment by, 822
Wright, Rowland. *See* Wells, Carolyn
Wyatt, Edith Franklin, 866–68
Wylie, Elinor Hoyt, 868–70

Yezierska, Anzia, 870–72
Youmans, Eliza Ann, 873–74
Young, Brigham, wives of, 693, 694
Young, Eliza Roxey Snow Smith. *See* Smith,
    Eliza Roxey Snow
Young, Maigret. *See* Moore, Marianne Craig
young adult literature
  on adolescent problems, 254, 399–400
  biographies in, 274, 378–79, 569
  dramas in, 485–86
  historical, 483
  novels in, 254, 399–400, 401, 483, 585, 601,
    606–7, 617, 733, 803, 836–37

Zolotow, Charlotte Shapiro, 875–77
Zugsmith, Leane, 877–78